Magnum Opus or the Great Work

Of the Ancient and Accepted Scottish Rite of Freemasonry

Albert Pike

KESSINGER
PUBLISHING

We publish thousands of books on
Freemasonry, Metaphysics and Philosophy.

Visit our website to view our extensive catalog list:

http://www.kessinger.net

Albert Pike

The greatest and most maligned Freemason that ever lived.

Albert Pike's

MAGNUM OPUS or "Great Work"

One of the rarest and most important books ever published on the Ancient and Accepted (Scottish) Rite of Freemasonry is now available as a first ever facsimile reprint.

In 1855 the Supreme Council 33°, Ancient and Accepted (Scottish) Rite, Southern Masonic Jurisdiction, U.S.A. appointed a committee to revise the fragmentary rituals in their possession. This task was completed two years later when, in 1857, Albert Pike single-handedly published the so-called *Magnum Opus* or *"Great Work,"* being his first revision of the complete rituals of the Scottish Rite. Only 100 copies were printed—less than thirty are said to survive. Pike's ritualistic revisions were so impressive he was made an active member of the Supreme Council and became the most revered Sovereign Grand Commander in the history of the Rite.

Thanks to the generous loan of a copy from a European antiquarian, this special reprint makes available to the serious student the complete authentic rituals which served as the foundation of the Scottish Rite's philosophy.

This invaluable work is not to be confused with either the various ritualistic "exposures" of anti-Masons, or the rituals currently used by either American Scottish Rite. The *Magnum Opus* contains Albert Pike's complete, original text of the Scottish Rite degrees.

Some of Pike's rituals were used by other Supreme Councils as a foundation for their own practices; while more recently the Supreme Council 33°, Southern Masonic Jurisdiction, U.S.A. has appointed a committee to revise the current Pike rituals. The *Magnum Opus* allows researchers to trace the divergence to discover shifts in Masonic symbolism.

An invaluable reference aid and research tool, the scarcity and cost of an original copy placed it beyond the reach of almost all Masonic bibliophiles. This affordable facsimile reprint places Masonic knowledge where it belongs—in the hands of those seeking Light.

To Our Masonic Brethren

To alleviate the possibility of unnecessary concern caused by the publication of this rare work, Kessinger Publishing Company wishes to make known the following:

1. The rituals in the Magnum Opus are not those currently used by the Supreme Council 33°.

2. The publication of old Masonic Rituals was encouraged by Albert Pike who sold reprints through the Supreme Council (See James D. Carter, *History of the Supreme Council 33 °1861 - 1891* [Washington, DC: Supreme Council, 1967], Vol. 2, page 176).

3. The Publication of old Masonic Rituals is currently practiced by the Masonic Grand College of Rites, U.S.A. as well as by members of Quatuor Coronati Lodge (London, England).

4. We, as Masons, are bound by obligation to spread true Masonic Light and knowledge to the less informed.

Kessinger Publishing Company believes that the publication of this work will fulfill a genuine need as a research tool for serious students of the Scottish Rite.

INTRODUCTION

(Excerpted in part from Ray Baker Harris and James D. Carter, History of the Supreme Council, 33d Degree [Washington: Roberts Pub. Co., 1964] 1:244-257)

"In his last Allocution as Grand Commander [1890] Albert Pike remarked, 'I never heard of the Scottish Rite until 1853.'[1] On March 20, 1853, [Albert G.] Mackey [Secretary of the Supreme Council], communicated the degrees from 4th to the 32nd to Albert Pike at Charleston. But he did more than confer the degrees. He urged Pike to study the rituals in detail at his leisure, and that he participate actively in the work of the Rite.

"I found all [old rituals] at Charleston when I received the degrees. I took most of them home with me the year afterwards, and had the rest sent to me, and copied the whole of them, from beginning to end, in a book now in the archives of the Supreme Council.[2]

"It was another five years before Albert Pike became an active member of the Supreme Council, but Mackey kept in touch with him during this time, constantly encouraging his interest in the Rite and planning to enlist his active participation. Ten days after conferring the degrees, Mackey notified Pike of his appointment as Deputy Inspector General in Arkansas.[3] At this time a Deputy Inspector General did not have to be of the 33rd Degree....

"Mackey had doubtless, in loaning all of the rituals to Pike, invited the latter's suggestions as to revisions and improvements. He also took steps to formalize this, as will be seen in his letter to [Claude P.] Samory, dated March 21, 1855:

"At an extraordinary meeting of this Supreme Council held at Charleston on the 8th instant, the following resolution was adopted:

Resolved, that the M∴P∴ Grand Commander be requested to appoint a committee of five brethren, none of whom shall be less than a Sublime Prince of the Royal Secret, who shall be empowered to prepare new copies of our ritual from the 4th to the 32nd degree inclusive, and to bring them to that state of perfection originally intended by the founders of the Rite; and the said rituals to be submitted to this Supreme Council for approbation and adoption.

Whereupon, the following Illustrious Brethren were appointed, the Grand Commander being placed on the committee at the special request of the Council.

[Committee]

Albert G. Mackey, 33°	of Charleston, S.C.
John H. Honour, 33°	of Charleston, S.C.
W.S. Rockwell, 33°	of Milledgeville, Georgia
C. Samory, 33°	of New Orleans, Louisiana
Albert Pike, 32°	of Little Rock, Arkansas

"From all indications, the 'preparation of new copies' was in the hands of Albert Pike. He was then in New Orleans, and may have conferred with Samory in this work, but neither of them ever mentioned such collaboration in their numerous letters written in this period.

"Writing of this work in later years, Albert Pike commented:

"I found it almost equivalent, as to the degrees I selected, to making something out of nothing...I first endeavored to find in the degree...a leading idea, and then to carry that out, and give the degree as high a character as I could.[4]

"In returning some of the degrees to Mackey [as chairman of the committee] Pike wrote from Little Rock:

"I have retained all the signs, words, etc., and generally the substantial parts of the obligations...I have completed the 21°, 22°, 23°, 24°, 25°, 26°, 27°, 28°, 29°, and 30°. An abstract will explain what I have done with each. If I touch any other of the degrees, which is doubtful, I may take up and spiritualize the 32° to harmonize with what I have done in the 30°.[5]

"The revision of the rituals by Pike is not to be confused with the far more extensive revisions which he undertook as Grand Commander, and the printing of the rituals in separate volumes for the Lodge, Chapter, Council, and Consistory degrees....

"Albert Pike had not only completed his first revision of the rituals from the 4th to the 32nd, but had 100 copies printed at his own expense. On March 31, 1857, from Washington, he forwarded a copy to Mackey at Charleston, writing:

"I send you by this evening's express a copy of the revised ritual. I had five copies bound in [Russian leather], one of which I send you, and French [Benjamin B. French, Washington, D.C.] has insisted on having one; and one I let Sam Ward of New Orleans have.
I hope you will at you earliest leisure examine the book carefully and thoroughly. Everything in it has been carefully and well considered, and I have tried to adopt the crude materials of the old rituals, as skillfully as I could, to the great, general,

connected purpose of the work. It forms <u>now</u>, one coherent system, and I am sure will, if adopted, give astonishing impetis to the movement of the Scottish Rite.

I hope, also, that after you have read it all over carefully, you will <u>at once</u> bring it before the Supreme Council, and get them to act upon it....

"No doubt Mackey was profoundly impressed by the revision. He wrote at once to acknowledge it, and described the volume as Pike's <u>Magnum Opus</u> [Great Work]. If it had been his desire to enlist Albert Pike in the active leadership of the Rite, this first revision of the ritual must have confirmed his belief in the wisdom of his decision many times over. Considering the condition in which the degree copies had been for so long, this full version, and clearly presented in print for the first time, represented a tremendous asset to the Supreme Council and Rite.

"On the other hand, the unexpected arrival of the completed work in printed form placed Mackey in somewhat of a dilemma. Pike had undertaken the task at Mackey's urging. Mackey had arranged for a committee on ritual revision to be appointed, of which he was name Chairman, and the Grand Commander a member, and Albert Pike was the only member of the Committee not an Active Member. The Supreme Council had very little money, and there is no record that the Supreme Council authorized the printing; nor that it, or even the committee, was aware that Pike had completed his revision. Except for his correspondence with Mackey in 1854, there is no evidence that he collaborated with other members of the committee, even Samory at New Orleans. Characteristically, he had proceeded to do what Mackey had asked him to do, carrying it through himself to the completed printed work. However pleased Mackey was with the results, persuading the Council to adopt it and reimburse Pike for the printing expense probably, under the circumstances, presented Mackey with some embarrassment.

"A month later Pike wrote to Mackey from New Orleans as follows:

"Write to me at Little Rock, and do not fail to get the Supreme Council's decision on the <u>Magnum Opus</u> as you are pleased to call it. It is far from perfect; but it is an improvement, I know. It is at least due to me from the Supreme Council as I have bestowed two years work on it, and paid $1200. to print it, that they should read it. I don't think it will do any of them any harm, or be time wasted...

"With only one copy of the revision at Charleston for examination by the members was another possible reason for the delay in formal adoption; but after four months Pike still had received no word from Mackey, and wrote again from

Arkansas:

"I have been a long and in vain looking to receive a letter from you, but none has come, until hope deferred has made the heart sick.... I shall be in Little Rock in August where a letter from you in reply to this one will find me.

I had hoped by this time to have heard that you had read consecutively and understood the plan, order and arrangement, of what you are pleased to call my Magnum Opus; and to have received your frank and candid opinion as to its merits. I knew that you would not give, and I should not wish you to give, any other than such an opinion. In one sense it was a 'great' work -- for it was a great labor, costing many months of toil. I would fain hope it may be of use; and I know it is an improvement on what we had before; though I am, of course, equally conscious that it is very very far from perfect, and that it needs pruning and correcting. No one head was competent to make such a work what it ought to be. In another respect it was somewhat of a work. It cost me to print it, $1,200. and $500 more to purchase books to use in compiling it. Naturally I should be glad to have part of the $1,200, reimbursed; and I do most earnestly hope that the Supreme Council may think it worthy of adoption.

I conferred the eleven degrees of the Lodge of Perfection, according to it, in full form, in Little Rock, on the most intelligent Masons we have and they were delighted with the work....

"No later correspondence on this subject has survived, and perhaps there was none. Early in the following year Pike was made an Active Member, which could not have occurred if there had been any opposition even on the part of a single member. Then, or at some other time the subject was no doubt discussed in person between Mackey and Pike, and probably with other members of the Council. Pike's revisions of the ritual were to continue for many years, and into many subsequent printings. From a note made on his letter to Mackey of March 31, 1857, dated May 8, 1885, Pike states that the Council did not, and could not, reimburse him for the cost of the first printing of 1857. However, there is no evidence that throughout the next thirty years the Council made any effort to do otherwise than leave ritual revisions and printings entirely in Albert Pike's hands." (end of excerpts)

Henry Wilson Coil remarked in his Masonic Encyclopedia that the degrees Pike received (by "communication," not "conferral") were similar to those found in the Rev. David Bernard's anti-Masonic exposure Light on Masonry (Utica: William Williams, 1829). This is far from certain. Bernard's book contains ritualistic matter in three forms: (1) complete rituals, (2) fragmentary rituals, and (3) ritualistic catechisms. Fortunately, the complete, original degrees which served as the foundation of the American

4

Scottish Rite are still in existence. This collection of degrees (it was unknown to Pike[6]) is called the <u>Francken Ms.</u> of 1783, and is housed in the archives of the Supreme Council 33°, A.A.S.R., Northern Masonic Jurisdiction, U.S.A.[7] While some of the Francken degrees agree almost verbatim with Bernard, others differ substantially.[8]

Although it is often assumed that the rituals of the Northern Jurisdiction were inferior to Pike's, or that they were the fragmentary Bernard versions, this viewpoint is erroneous.[9] It is true that the Northern Jurisdiction later adopted some of Pike's work, but its ritualists were as competent if more traditional than Pike.

Pike's reconstruction of the Scottish Rite degrees was more drastic than he intimated. Although he remarked that his revision "retained <u>all</u> the signs, words, etc." of the various degrees, this was not the case. Many of the "significant words" were muddled beyond recognition in 1853, and Pike sought to discover their etymolgical roots and restore the original words.

In some cases however, Pike completely changed pass-words without explanation. The thirteenth (Royal Arch) degree provides a notable example. In this degree, Pike listed the following pass-words and attributions for the nine arches:

1st Arch:	Athom:.....Egyptian:
2d "	Amun:......Egyptian:
3d "	Bel:.......Phoenician:
4th "	Alhim:.....Hebrew:
5th "	Adonai:....Hebrew:
6th "	Aum:.......Indian:
7th "	Assur:.....Assyrian:
8th "	San:.......Assyrian:
9th "	Yav:.......Assyrian:

These pass-words are unique to the <u>Magnum Opus</u> and were eliminated in subsequent revisions (Compare Pike's <u>Book of the Words</u> p. 117).[10] It will also be noticed that throughout the <u>Magnum Opus</u> the Hebrew alphabet, rather than Samaritan, is employed. No one has yet satisfied the question as to why Pike made the switch in later revisions.[11]

The <u>Magnum Opus</u> also includes material familiar to Pike enthusiasts. Substantial portions of the "lectures" were later incorporated in <u>Morals and Dogma</u>, which serves as his commentary on the current degrees.

This first reprint of Pike's extremely scarce work -- less than thirty of the original are said to survive -- will not only provide information on early versions of the A.A.S.R. degrees, but also on Pike's growing understanding of Masonic symbolism.

ENDNOTES

1. Official Bulletin, X, 420.

2. Albert Pike, "Beauties of Cerneauism," No. 6, p. 7.

3. Official Bulletin, X, 420.

4. Official Bulletin, VII, 356.

5. Albert Pike to Albert G. Mackey, September 13, 1855.

6. Pike sought in vain to explain the words "Salix, Nonis, Tengu" which occur in the thirty-second degree. In the Magnum Opus he presents one "solution," (pp. XXXII...7 - XXXII...8) while his later revision -- in current use -- omits the explanation. He also sought unsuccessfully to explain these same words in his 1880 work, Readings XXXII. The solution appears in the twenty-fifth degree of the Francken Ms., "The Royal Secret, or knights of St Andrews, and the Faithful guardians of the Sacred Treasure." The "words" are formed from the initials of a French phrase, "Soutenons apresent L Invincible Xerxes, Nous offres Notres Incomparable Sacre Tresor, Et nous gagnerons, Victorieusement" ("Let us now offer to the invincible Xerxes our sacred incomparable treasure, and we shall succeed victoriously").

7. There are, actually, three Francken manuscripts, dated 1771, 1783 and ca. 1786. See Ars Quatuor Coronatorum 89:208-210; 97:200-202. The 1783 version seems to be the most complete.

8. A comparison of Francken's (1783) and Bernard's (1829) "Kadosh" degrees reveals that the early Northern Jurisdiction ritualists, like Pike, also sought the etymological roots of "significant words." While the two degrees agree virtually verbatim, the Hebrew in Bernard's version is substantially more accurate.

9. See Irving E. Partridge, Jr., The Rituals of the Supreme Council 33d Degree for the Northern Masonic Jurisdiction U.S.A. (Lexington, Mass.: Supreme Council, 33°, 1976). Following Bernard's Light on Masonry, the first significant exposure of the rituals of the Northern Jurisdiction was George R. Crafts, ed., The Mysteries of Freemasonry (1852). Like other exposures of this era (Allyn's, Richardson's, etc.) much of Crafts' work was purloined from Bernard, but he introduces new material relating to the Ineffable Degrees of the Scottish Rite. The accuracy of Crafts' "new" material suggests that he had access to a "Secret Directory" (official ritual book) while preparing his exposition.

10. [Albert Pike] The Book of the Words [Sephar h'Debarim] (N.p., 1878: reprint ed., Kila, MT: Kessinger Publishing Co., 1992). This extremely valuable work is explanatory of the words in the rituals.

11.   A.C.F. Jackson notes in his <u>Rose Croix</u> [rev. ed] (London: Lewis Masonic, 1980, 1987), p. 232, that, "In the True and Perfect Master's degree in the <u>London French Ms</u>...there is a curious story, nowhere else mentioned, of the Sacred Word being turned into Samaritan characters...." In 1815 Fabre d'Olivet published his massive two-part French work, <u>The Hebraic Tongue Restored</u>, (english reprint ed., York Beach, Maine: Samuel Weiser, 1991), which includes a liberal use of the Samaritan alphabet. Pike, an avid reader of French Masonic, occult and religious works, may have been familiar with similar works.

THE SECRET WORK DECODED

Fourth Degree.
Secret Master.

THE SIGN: Place the {2} first fingers of the {r} hand on the lips.

ANSWER: Place the {2} first fingers of the {l} hand on the lips.

TOKEN: Begin with the {true grip} of a M∴M∴. The slip the {r} hand up the other's arm, taking hold of the elbow on the under side; and say -- one, {Zi} -- the other, {Zon}.

THE PASSWORD: The two syllables last foregoing.

SACRED WORDS: {Iao∴. Adonai∴. Jua∴.}

Fifth Degree.
Perfect Master.

1st SIGN: Of Admiration... Raise both {arms} and {eyes} towards Heaven; and then let the former fall crosswise on the {belly}; and drop the latter on the ground.

2d SIGN: Of recognition... Each advances his {r foot}, until the points meet, and the right {knees} come together. Then each places his {r hand} upon his {heart}.

TOKEN: Take each other with the {masters} grip; and at the same time each place the {l hand} behind the {r shoulder} of the other, and press it {4} times, with the {4} first fingers closed; saying, by syllables alternately, {ma∴.ha∴.ben∴.i∴.} Then clench the {4} fingers of the two {r} hands together, closing them, not interlaced, raising the {thumbs} and putting them together at the points, so as to form a triangle.

PASS-WORD: {Acacia}

SACRED WORD: {Jeva}

Sixth Degree.
Confidential Secretary.

Page VI...6

SIGN: Bring the {r hand} to the {l shoulder}, and then diagonally downwards to the {r hip}.

ANSWER: Cross the {2 hands}, with the {thumbs} extended, and raise them to the height of the {forehead}; the {thumbs} touching it: then bring them down rapidly to the {hilt} of the {sword}, raising the {eyes} to Heaven.

TOKEN: Take each other in the ordinary manner by the {r hand}: and turn the {hands} over {3} times; saying alternately, at the several turns: {Bereth:. Neder:. Shelemoth:.}

PASS-WORDS: {Joabert:. Zerbal:.}

SACRED WORD: {Jova:.} or {Ivah:.}

Seventh Degree.
Provost and Judge.

Page VII...5

SIGN: Place the {index} and {middle} fingers of the {r} hand, on the {r} side of the {nose}.

ANSWER: Place the {index} finger of the {r} hand on the {nose}; the {thumb} under the {chin}; thus forming a square.

TOKEN: Interlace the {little fingers} of the {r hand}, and tap each other mutually {7} times [by 3 3 1], with the {thumb}, in the {palm} of the {hand}.

PASS-WORD: {Tito:.}

SACRED WORD: {Shekinah:.} or, in French, {Jachinai:.}

OTHER WORDS: {Kivi:. Kum:. Stolkin:. Xinkuh:. Izrachiah:.}

Eighth Degree.
Intendant of the Buildings.

Page VIII...5

9

1st SIGN: of Surprise:... Place the {thumbs}, one on each {temple}; the {hands} extended in front of the {forehead}, and forming a square; as if to protect the {eyes} from the {light}. In this attitude, take two steps forward, and then {2} backward; and say: {Benkhurim:.}

2d SIGN: of Admiration:... In Answer to the first:... Interlace the fingers of the two hands in front of the {forehead}, and let them fall to a level with the {waist}; looking upward, and saying: {Achar:.}

3d SIGN: of Sorrow:... Each places his {r hand} on his {heart}, and his {l hand} on his {l hip}: then each balancing himself three times on his {knees}, one says {Hua:.} and the other, {Jah:.}

TOKEN: Each places his {r hand} on the {heart} of the other: then each with his right hand takes the other by the {r elbow} and puts his {l hand} on the {r shoulder} of the other. Then one says {Shekinah:.} and the other {Jeva:.}

PASSWORDS: {Ben-khurim:. Achar:.}

SACRED WORDS: {Hua:. Jah:. Shekinah:. Jeva:.}

Ninth Degree.
Knight Elu of Nine.

SIGN: Strike with the right hand, as if with a {dagger}, first at the {forehead}, and then at the {heart} of the other; saying {Nekum:.}

ANSWER: Pass the right hand over the {forehead}, as if to see if it is bloody; and then place it on the {heart}, and say {Nekah:.}

TOKEN: Close the {fingers of the r hand}, and present it to the other, with the {thumb} raised. He takes the {thumb} in his {r hand}, closing his own {fingers}, and raising his {thumb}. Thus there are {8 fingers} closed, and a {thumb} raised, representing the {9 elu:.}

PASS-WORDS: One says {Nekum:.} -- the other answers, {Joabert:.} -- Then the first says {Abiram:.} -- the other answers, {Akirop:.}

SACRED WORD: {Gebur-khil:.}

Tenth Degree.
Illustrious Elu of Fifteen.

Page X...7

SIGN: Make the motion of bringing a {poniard} up under the {chin}, {hilt} upwards, and strike perpendicularly {downward}, as if opening your {abdomen}.

ANSWER: Make the {apprentices} sign, with the {fingers} closed and the {thumb} raised.

TOKEN: Close the {fingers} and raise the {thumb} of the {r hand}: Then, with that {thumb} close to the {body} of the other, make a transverse motion as if cutting across his {abdomen}. He does the same to you. As you do it, you say {Zerbal:.} As he does it, he says {Al-khanan:.}

PASS-WORD: {Zerbal:.}

SACRED WORD: {Al-khanan:.}

Eleventh Degree.
Prince Ameth, or Sublime Elu of Twelve.

Page XI...6

SIGN: Cross the {arms} upon the {chest}, with the {fingers clenched} and {thumb} raised.

FIRST TOKEN: Each presents to the other the {thumb} of the {r hand}, with the {fingers closed}. One takes the {thumb} of the other; and they turn the {wrist 3} times -- saying alternately, as they do so, {Berith:. Neder:. Shelomith:.}

SECOND TOKEN: Take the {r hand} of a brother, and tap {3} times with your {thumb} on the {phalange} of the {middle finger}.

PASS-WORD: {Ameth:.}

SACRED WORD: {Adonai:.}

Twelfth Degree.
Grand Master Architect.

Page XII...7

SIGN: Lay the {right hand} in the middle of the {left}. Pause a moment; and then {close} the {fingers} of the {r hand}, and with the {thumb} seem to trace a plan or figure in the palm of the {left}; looking at the Gr:. Master, as if receiving directions from him.

TOKEN: {Interlace} the {fingers} of the {r hands}, and place his other {hand} on his {hip}.

PASS-WORD: {Rab-benin:.}

SACRED WORD: {Adonai:.}

Thirteenth Degree.
Royal Arch.

Page XIII...6

1st SIGN: Of Admiration:... {Raise both hands} towards Heaven; the {head} inclined to the left and the {r knee} on the ground.

2d SIGN: Of Adoration:... {Fall} upon both {knees}, bring the {l hand} down from the {l shoulder} to the {r hip}: and place, at the same time, the {l hand behind} the {back}.

TOKEN: Place your hands under the {arm pits} of the Brother, as if to help him to rise.

PASS-WORD: {Hamelek Kheblim:.}

1st Arch:..	{Athom:.}	....Egyptian:
2d "	{Amun:.}	.....Egyptian:
3d "	{Bel:.}	......Phoenician:
4th "	{Alhim:.}	....Hebrew:
5th "	{Adonai:.}	...Hebrew:
6th "	{Aum:.}	......Indian:
7th "	{Assur:.}	....Assyrian:
8th "	{San:.}	......Assyrian:
9th "	{Yav:.}	......Assyrian:

Fourteenth Degree.
Grand, Elect, Perfect and Sublime Mason.

Page XIV...9

1st SIGN: Bring the {r hand} quickly and {horizontally} from the left side of the {abdomen} to the right, as if cutting it open.

2d SIGN: Place the {open r hand} upon the {l cheek}, as if to protect it from the heat of the fire, holding the {r elbow} with the {left hand}. Then change, and put the {r hand} before the {r cheek}, holding the {l elbow} with the {r hand}.

        3d SIGN: Raise the {two hands}, {open} towards
Heaven, the head inclining backward and the {eyes
raised}: and then put the {2 first fingers} of the {r
hand} on the {lips}.

        1st TOKEN: Take each other by the right hand, and
{turn} the {hands over 3} times -- saying,
alternately.. {Berith:. Neder:. Shelomith:.}

        2d TOKEN: Begin with the {masters grip}. One
asks "{can you go further}." The other replies by
passing, first to the {middle} of the {fore arm}, and
then to the {elbow} of the other, {underneath}. The
other does the same. Then each puts his {left hand} on
the other's {r shoulder}, and advances his {right foot}
so as to pass it beyond the {left foot} of the other;
and they then {balance 3 times}.

Page XIV...10

        3d TOKEN: Each takes the other by the {1 elbow}
with his {r hand}, and puts his {1 hand behind} the
other's {back}; as if to {draw} him {close} to himself.

        COVERED WORDS: (1st. .. {Kheblim:.}
                        (2d. .. {Mahabeni:.}
                        (3d. .. {Adonai:.}

        PASS-WORDS: (1st. .. {Shibboleth:.}
                        (2d. .. {Al-khanan:.}
                        (3d. .. {Marah-maur-abrec:.}

        GRAND SACRED WORD: {Ihuh}

Page XIV...15

[Line 18]
        Ans:. The term of my Apprenticeship, and the {3}
Masters, {adonhiram joabert and stolkin}, who descended
into the earth, and bore thence to King Solomon the
Sacred Treasure, placed there before the Deluge by
Enoch the Patriarch.

[Line 30]

        Ans:. The age of a Master Mason: the {7 provosts
and judges}, and the {7} years occupied in {building
the temple}.

Page XIV...16

[Line 8]

        Ans:. {Mahaboneh} was substituted in its place,
after the death of Hiram Abi.

13

[Line 44]

  Ans:. {Gebur-khil:.}

[Line 48]

  Ans:. {Necum:.}, meaning vengeance, the signal agreed upon by the fugitives who had murdered our Gr:. Master, and the exclamation of the Chief Assassin when his retreat was discovered: {Joabert:. Abiram:.} and {Akirop:.}

Page XIV...17

[Line 37]

  Ans:. {Zerbal:.} and {Al-khanan:.}

[Line 43]

  Ans:. {Rab-benin:.} -- Chief of the Architects.

Page XIV...18

[Line 22]

  Ans:. {Gabaon:.}

[Line 31]

  4th SIGN: Bear upon the {toe} of the {l foot}, raising the heel. At the same time raise the {eyes and arms} towards Heaven. This is the sign of Admiration.

  5th SIGN: Of Distress... Interlace the fingers of your hands, and put them on the {top} of your {head}, {palms} upward.

  6th SIGN: Give the 4th Sign, each turning his back on the other. Then {look at each} other, over the {shoulder}.

  7th SIGN: {Clap} your {r hand} on your {heart}: raise the same {arm} towards {heaven}, and bringing it down, {strike} with it your {r hip}.

  8th SIGN: Place your {r hand} on your {mouth}, as if to pull out your {tongue}, and thence carry it quickly to your {heart}.

  9th SIGN: As if holding a {dagger}, {strike at} the Brother's {forehead}; then {clap} your {l hand} to your own {forehead}.

Page XIV...28

They do so; and place their {hands} on their {heads}, in the attitude of the 5th sign.

Fifteenth Degree.
Knights of the Sword, of the East, or of the Eagle.

Page XV...11

SIGN: Bring the {r hand} to the {l shoulder}, and thence with a {zigzag} motion to the {r hip}, imitating the waves of a river.

ANSWER: Place the {r hand} upon the {l hip}, and then bring it across the {body} to the {r hip}.

TOKEN: Take each other by the {left hand}, {fingers interlaced}, the {l arm} raised and extended, as if {forcing back} an enemy, and forcing a passage: and then place each the {point} of his {sword} against the other's {heart}. In this attitude, one says {Judah:.} and the other, {Benjamin:.}

PASS-WORDS: {Libertas:. Havaron-hamim:.}

GRAND WORDS: {Shalal:. Shalum:. Abi:.}

Sixteenth Degree.
Princes of Jerusalem.

Page XVI...8

SIGN: Advance boldly, with the {sword raised}, as if to engage in combat; the {l hand} on the {l hip}.

ANSWER: {Stretch out} the {arm} at the height of the {shoulder}, as if to commence the combat; the {r foot} forming a {square} with the {point} of the {left}.

TOKEN: {Tap} each other mutually with the {r thumb} on the {joint} of the {little finger} of the {r hand -- 5 taps} -- thus --, and {twice 2} At the same time place the {right feet} together at the {points}, forming a straight line; and let the {knees} touch each other. Then reciprocally place the {left hand} on the {shoulder} of the other, {opening} the {fingers}. One says {twenty}, and the other, {twenty-three}. Then form a square with the {left wrist} on the {right} -- let go the {hands}, bring the {point} of the {r foot} to the {l heel}, and salute each other by bowing.

PASS-WORD: {Tebet:.}

15

SACRED WORD: {Adar:.}

Seventeenth Degree.
Knight of the East and West.

Page XVII...11

SIGN: Look at your {right shoulder:.}

ANSWER: Look at the {left shoulder}: one says {Abaddon:.} the other {Yah-balin}.

FIRST TOKEN: Put the {left hand} in a brother's {right}: He {covers} yours with his {left}: Then look mutually at the {r shoulder}.

SECOND TOKEN: {Touch} with your {left hand} the {l shoulder} of the Brother; who answers by {touching} your {r shoulder} with his {l hand}.

SIGN TO ENTER THE LODGE: Put the {r hand} upon the {forehead}.

PASS-WORD: {Yah-balin:.}

COVERED WORD: {Abaddon:.}

Eighteenth Degree.
Knight, or Sovereign Prince of Rose Croix, of Heredon.

Page XVIII...11

{Repeat}, Sir Knight, {in the same order the initials} of the {four words} you have {repeated}.

Page XVIII...12

FIRST SIGN: Lift the eyes to Heaven; {interlace} at the same time the {fingers} of the {hands}, {raise} them to the {forehead}, turn the {palms} upwards, and let them {fall} upon the {belly}.

ANSWER: Raise the {r hand} as high as the {forehead}, the {thumb and fingers}, (except the {first finger}), {closed}: the meaning of which is, that there is but one God, Sovereign and Eternal.

SIGN OF DISTRESS: {Cross} the {legs}, the left {behind}. The answer is the same.

TOKEN: {Cross} the {hands} on the {breast}, left uppermost.

ANSWER: The same: after which the Brother who

16

demanded the sign, {crosses} his {hands} again, and
puts the left hand on the {right breast} of the other,
without {uncrossing} the {arms}: in which position the
pass-word is given.

PASS-WORD: {Emanuel:.}

GENERAL WORD: {Raph-adon:.}

SACRED WORD: {Inri:.}

Page XVIII...13

The Sovereign Master then raises the Candidate,
and gives him the grip, which is, each {puts} his
{right hand} on the other's {right shoulder}, and his
{l} on the other's {l shoulder}; and in that position
one {kisses} the other's {forehead}, and says
{Emanuel:.} and the other says {Pax Vobis:.}

Nineteenth Degree.
Grand Pontiff, or Sublime Scotch Mason.

Page XIX...7

SIGN: Raise the {right hand} to a {horizontal}
{position}, the {fingers} extended; and then drop the
{3 last fingers} perpendicularly.

TOKEN: Place reciprocally the {palm} of the {r
hand} on the {forehead} of the other.... The first
says {Hallelu-yah:.} The second, {Praise the Lord:.}
The first, {Amnu-al:.} The second, {may God assist
us:.} And both say, {amen:.}

PASS-WORD: {Amnu-al:.}

SACRED WORD: {Hallelu-yah:.}

Twentieth Degree.
Venerable Master of All Symbolic Lodges;
or Master ad Vitam.

Page XX...5

FIRST SIGN: Form four {squares}, thus: Place the
{right hand} on the {heart}, the {fingers together and
extended}, the {thumb} raised: thus making with the
{elbow} one {square}, and with the {thumb} one. Place
the {l hand} on the {lips}, making a similar {square}
with the {thumb}; and with the {heels} of the {two
feet} form a {square}.

SECOND SIGN: {Kneel} on both {knees}; and place

17

the {elbows} on the {ground}, leaning the head a little to the left.

THIRD SIGN: Cross the {two hands} on the {chest -- fingers together} and {extended -- thumbs erect} and {r hand} uppermost. The {elbows} and {thumb} thus form four {squares}: then place the {heels together} in a {square}.

TOKEN: Take each the {elbow} of the other with the {r hand} the {thumb} on the {outside}, and the fingers closed together on the {inside}: {press} the {elbow} thus {2 times} -- then {slip} the {hands} down as far as the {wrist}, as if to {give} each other the {grip}: then raise the {3 last fingers}, and {press} with the {index finger} the {wrist} of each other.

TOKEN UPON INTRODUCTION: Take each other by the right hand, with the {thumb} upon the {vein} of the {wrist}, and {slip} your {hand down} that of the other, to the {ends} of the {fingers}.

PASS-WORD: {Yakhsin:.}

ANSWER: {Stolkin:.}

2d PASS-WORD: {Yah-balin:.}

ANSWER: {Yakhsin:.}

3d PASS-WORD: {Zanabazare:.}

SACRED WORD: {Rashah-betsir-yah:.}

Twenty-First Degree.
Noachite; or Prussian Knight.

Page XXI...6

SIGN: Raise {both hands} with the {fingers extended}, the {thumbs} opposite the {ears}: and at the same time make {3 genuflections} with the {1 knee}.

PASS-WORD: {Phaleg:.} pronounced {3} times, slowly and in a melancholy tone.

SACRED WORD: {Shem:.}... {Kham:.}... {Yapeth:.}; given only thus:...

TOKEN: One brother takes the {forefinger} of a Brother between his own {thumb and forefinger}, and {presses} it; saying {Shem:.}: the other responds by like {pressure} of the {forefinger} of the first brother, saying {Kham:.} and the first again {presses}

18

the {forefinger} of the second, saying {Yapeth:.}

To enter a Chapter, a brother {holds up 3 fingers}. The Sentinel or Guardian does the same. The Brother then gives the sign, takes the {3 fingers} of the Sentinel or Guardian, and says -- {Frederic Barbarossa}. The other responds {3} times {Noakh:.} and the first says {3} times {Phaleg:.}

Twenty-Second Degree.
Knight of the Royal Axe, or Prince of Libanus.

Page XXII...5

SIGN: Raise {both hands} towards the {r shoulder}, the {thumbs and fingers separated} as much as possible, and let them fall upon the {left thigh}, as if {stroking} with an {axe}. It alludes to {felling} the {cedars} of Libanus.

ANSWER: Raise {both hands} to the {height} of the {forehead}, {fingers extended}, and let them {fall down} together, in front.

TOKEN: Take {mutually} each other's {hands, crossing} them, in sign of good faith.

PASS-WORDS: {Noah:. Betsel-al:. Yaphet:. Ahli-ab:. Tsiduni:. Libanus:.}

SACRED WORDS: {Al-shedi:. Ishuah:.}

Twenty-Third Degree.
Chief of the Tabernacle.

Page XXIII...6

SIGN: Advance the {1 foot} and with the right hand make a motion as if taking something from {the left}. It alludes to the manner in which the H:. Priest bore the Holy Oil to feed the Sacred fire, when he entered the Tabernacle to perform the sacrifices.

TOKEN: Mutually take the {1 elbow} of each other with the {r hand}, {arching the arms}, so as to form a kind of circle.

PASS-WORDS: One says {Auri-al:.} The other answers, {tabernacle of revealed truth:.}

SACRED WORD: {Yehouah:.}

Twenty-Fourth Degree.
Prince of the Tabernacle.

1st SIGN: of Recognition:... Raise the eyes to Heaven, and {cover them with} the {l hand}, {open}, as if to {protect} them from {intense light}. At the same time, place the {r hand} on the {l breast}, inclining the {head} towards the {l shoulder}: the {draw} the {r hand down diagonally} to the {r hip}.

2d. THE GRAND SIGN: Place both hands {upon} the {head}, with the {thumbs} and {forefingers extended}, and joining so as to form a triangle; the {points} of the {forefingers} above.

3d SIGN: of closing:... Make a similar triangle with the {forefingers}, the {arms} extended and the {thumbs} turned {downward}: the body being the base, the {arms}, {hands} and {forefingers} the sides, and the {meeting} of the {points} of the latter the apex, of the Triangle.

TOKEN: Mutually take each other's hands; the {r} with the {r} and the {l} with the {left}, {crossing} them -- and give the Pass-word.

PASS-WORD: {Derek-Yehuah:.} [Substitute for the latter word, {Adonai}]:...or, in English, {the journey of God}.

SACRED WORD: {Yekhapets Yehuah} [substitute {Adonai}]...or in English, {God wills it}.

Twenty-Fifth Degree.
Knight of the Brazen Serpent.

DUE-GUARD: {Incline} the {head}, and with the forefinger {point at} some object on the {ground}... or, {extend} the {r hand} and {arm} to a distance before you, looking forward, as if descrying some object afar off, and {pointing to it}.

1st SIGN: Place the {l wrist} in the {r hand}, forming a {cross}: they lay {both} on the {stomach} and {bow}.

2d SIGN: Place the {l hand} over the {heart},

inclining the {body} to the same side, as if you {felt} a {sharp pain} there.

3d SIGN: Make the {sign} of the {cross} on {yourself} as a {Catholic} does.

TOKEN: Place yourself upon the right of the person to be examined, and take his {l wrist} with your {l hand}.

ANSWER: He takes your {r wrist} with his {r hand}.

2d TOKEN: {Clench} the {fingers} of each other's {hands}, and put the {thumbs} against each other, so as to form a {triangle}.

PASS-WORD: {Khalati:.}

SACRED WORD: {Al-khanan:.}

Twenty-Sixth Degree.
Prince of Mercy or Scottish Trinitarian.

Page XXVI...13

1st SIGN: Of Entrance:... Place the {r hand} over the {eyes} as if to protect {them} from the {light} of the {sun}.

2d SIGN: Of the Trinity:... Form a {triangle} with the {2 thumbs} and {2 forefingers} -- and place them over the {stomach}, {united} at the {points}.

3d SIGN: Of Appeal:... {Cross} the {2 arms} over the {head} -- {palms upward} and the {hands open} -- and say {Li-Beni-Ameth:.} ["TO ME," (i.e. Help -- a moi!) "SONS OF THE TRUTH!"]

DUE-GUARD: {R hand} on the {r hip}.

TOKEN: Press {both hands} lightly on the {shoulder} of a brother, pronouncing at the same time the Pass-Word.

PASS-WORD: {Gomel:.}

SACRED WORD: {YHVH}

[Editor's note: The four hebrew letters comprising the "Sacred Word" are YOD, HEH, VAV and HEH, which form the "tetragrammaton" or "four lettered name" of the Hebrew God. They are commonly rendered "Yahweh" or "Jehovah," but Pike prefers "IHUH."]

21

Twenty-Seventh Degree.
Knight Commander of the Temple, or Teutonic Knight of the House of St. Mary of Jerusalem.

Page XXVII...5

SIGN: Of Recognition... Make the sign of the cross upon a brother's {forehead} with your {r thumb}, the {fingers closed}.

ANSWER: He {kisses} your {forehead}. This is done only in the Chapter. Elsewhere the answer is to place the two first fingers of the right hand {over} the {mouth} -- {closing} the {other fingers}, and turning the {palm outward}.

DUE-GUARD: In open Chapter, place the right hand upon the {round table}, and extend the {thumb} so as to form a {square}. When standing, place it in like manner on the {belly}.

TOKEN: Strike gently the {l shoulder} of a brother {3} times with the right hand.

ANSWER: He gently {squeezes} your {r hand 3 times}.

PASS-WORD: {Solomon:.}

GRAND WORD: {Inri:.} alternating the letters.

Twenty-Eighth Degree.
Knight of the Sun; or Knight Adept.

Page XXVIII...4

Th:. Ven:. My Brethren [placing his {r hand} on his {heart}], answer the sign! [He raises the {thumb} of that {hand}, so as to form a {square}. All the brethren {raise} the {r hand above} the {head}, the {forefinger} extended {upward}, and the other {fingers} and {thumb clenched}; and then drop the {arm} by the {side}.

Page XXVIII...8

SIGN: {Clap} the {r hand} on the {heart}, the {thumb} forming a {square}.

ANSWER: Raise the {forefinger} of the {r hand} above the {head}, perpendicularly, the {thumb} and {other fingers clenched}; to indicate that there is but one God and one true religion.

22

PASS-WORD: {Stibium:.}

ANSWER: {Alkebir:.}

SACRED WORD: {Adonai lal Aliun:.}

TOKEN: One says to the other; {give me your hands}: takes {them} in {his}, kisses his forehead, and says {alpha}. The other answers {omega}.

Twenty-Ninth Degree.
Grand Ecossais of St:. Andrew,
or Patriarch of the Crusades.

Page XXIX...1

...the initials of the words {Boaz:. Iakin:. Machbenach:. Nekhamah:.}

Pass-word in the Court of the Sultan...{Alborak:.}

Page XXIX...7

FIRST SIGN: Of the Earth:... {Bow} the {head} gently {forward} -- and {wipe} the {forehead} with the {back} of the {4 fingers} of the {r hand}.

FIRST TOKEN: Mutually and successively take, with the ends of the {thumb} and {forefinger} of the {r hand}, each the {1}st -- {2}d and {3}d {phalanges} of the {forefinger} of the {r hand} of the other; mutually spelling the word {Boaz:.}

SECOND SIGN: Of Water:... Place the {r hand} over the {heart}, and then extending the {arm} to the front at the height of the {breast}, let it gracefully {fall} to the {r side}, as if {saluting} one.

SECOND TOKEN: Mutually and successively take, with the {thumb} and {2}d {finger} of the {r hand}, each the {1}st -- {2}d and {3}d {phalanges} of the {2}d {finger} of the other; mutually spelling {Yakin:.}

THIRD SIGN: Of the Air:... Turn the {head} to the {left side}, looking upon the {floor}; raise the {two hands clasped} together, carry {them} to the {right}, and let {them} drop by the {sides}

Page XXIX...8

THIRD TOKEN: Take between the {tips} of the {thumb} and {3}d {finger}, mutually and successively, each the {tip} of the {3} {finger} of the other, one saying {Mach:.} and the other {Be:.} -- the the first takes in the same way the first {phalanx} of the same {finger}, and says {Nach:.}

FOURTH SIGN: Of Fire:... {Interlace} all the {fingers} and the {thumbs}, and cover the {eyes} with the {backs} of the {hands}, {palms} outwards.

RESPONSE: Stretch forth the {r hand} and {arm}, {palm} downwards, to the height of the {shoulder}, and directly to the {front}.

FIFTH SIGN: Of Admiration:... Raise the eyes towards Heaven, the hands {uplifted}, the right somewhat {higher} than the left, as the Catholic Priest does, when he says {Dominum Vobiscum}; the {heel} of the {l foot} being somewhat elevated, so that the left {knee} may form a {square} with the right.

SIXTH SIGN: Of the Sun:... Place the thumb of the right hand upon the {r eye}, raising the {forefinger} of the {same hand} so as to form a {square}, with a gesture as if you had some distant object in view, saying {Anirah Hashemesh:.}

SEVENTH (or GENERAL) SIGN: Form a St. Andrew's Cross upon {your breast}, with the {arms crossed} and {hands} upwards.

GENERAL TOKEN: Each takes successively, between the {tips} of the {thumb} and {forefinger} of the {r hand} the {first joint} of the {forefinger} of the {r hand} of the other; one saying {Ne:.} and the other {Kha:.} then each takes, successively, with the same, the {first joint} of the {little finger} of the other, and one says {Mah:.} and the other {Nekhamah:.}

PASS-WORDS: 1st {Phoreh-lak:.} Angel of the Earth.
2d {Talliud:.} Angel of the Water.
3d {Casmaran:.} Angel of Air.
4th {Auri-al:.} Angel of Fire.

SACRED WORD: {Nekhamah:.}

Thirtieth Degree.
Knight Kadosh.

Page XXX...5

[Then with the Gr:. Comm:. he pronounces the word {Tsedekah:.}]

[Repeats with the Gr:. Com:. {Shuh-Laban:.}]

Page XXX...6

24

[Repeats {Metuk:.}]

[Repeats {Amunah:.}]

[Repeats {Amel-Saghia:.}]

[Repeats {Sabel:.}]

[Repeats {Gemul-Binah-Tabunah:.}]

[The ladder has two supports or sides. The one on the right, as you ascend the steps is inscribed and called {aheb-aluh} ... The Love of God: and the one on the left, {aheb-kerobu} ... Love of our Neighbor.

{Tsedekah:.}...Truth, Justice, Righteousness.

{Shuh-Laban:.}...Pure or perfect Equity.

{Metuk:.}...Amiability.

{Amunah:.}...Good Faith.

{Amel-Saghia:.}...Much Labour or Exertion.

{Sabel:.}...Patience or Endurance.

{Gemul-Binah-Tabunah:.}...Elaboration; Prudence;
                                 Discrimination.

Pages XXX...18 through XXX...19

SIGN: Place the {r hand} upon the {heart} with the {fingers extended}, and then let it {fall} on the {r thigh} -- at the same time {bending} the {knee}. Then seize the {poniard} which is {suspended} from the {scarf}, and raise it to the height of the shoulder, as if to {strike} -- saying {Nekam Adonai:.}

ORDER: Sword in the left hand; the right on the {red cross} on the {breast:.}

TOKEN: The {points} of the {r feet} together, and {knee} against {knee}. Then one presents the {r hand clenched} with the {thumb raised}. The other encloses the {thumb} with his {four fingers}, his own {thumb elevated}, thus showing {eight fingers shut} and a {thumb} in sight. Then they unclose, and the same thing is done again, with a change of persons. Then unclosing, each {recoils} a {step}, with the left arm {raised} as if to {strike} -- in which attitude the first says {Nekhamah-Menukhim:.} and the other answers {Pheresh-Kol:.}

PASS-WORD: {Nek...} as above: another is {Habemah:.}

25

ANSWER: {Phe...} as above.

WORD OF ENTRANCE: {Nekam Adonai:.}

SACRED WORDS: {Ali-Al:.} and {Mi Kamuk Balim Ihuh:.}

Thirty-First Degree.
Grand Enquiring Commander.

Page XXXI...6

SIGN: {Cross} the {two hands} over the {navel} -- the {left} over the {right}.

ANSWER: {Cross them} over the {head} -- the {fingers} extended and {separated} and {palms} upward.

TOKEN: Place {foot} to {foot} and {knee} to {knee} -- take each other by the {left hand}, and with the {right} strike gently the {1 shoulder} of the other; one giving the pass-word, and the other the answer.

PASS-WORD: {Zoroaster:.}

ANSWER: {Alfred:.}

SACRED WORDS: One says {justice:.} The other answers {equity:.} And both say {so mote it be:.}

Thirty-Second Degree.
Sublime Prince of the Royal Secret.

Page XXXII...3

Th:. Ill:. {Salix:.}

1st Lt:. Com:. {Nonis:.}

2d Lt. Com:. {Tengu:.}

[All give the Sign, by laying the {r hand} one the {breast}, then holding it {perpendicularly up}, and letting it {fall} by the right {side}].

Page XXXII...6

SIGN: As already described.

TOKEN: The ordinary grasp in shaking hands, one passing his {little finger} as he does so, between the {third finger} of the other.

1st PASS-WORD: {Pala-Kol:.}

2d PASS-WORD: {Pharas-Kol:.}

ANSWER: {Nekam-Makah:.}

SACRED WORD: {Al-Schedi:.}

Page XXXII...7

...are an abbreviation of the words {Nekam:. Makah:.}, signifying Vengeance, and a blow or calamity.

Page XXXII...60

Th:. Ill:. {Salix:.}

1st Lt:. Com:. {Nonis:.}

2d Lt:. Com:. {Tengu:.}

Alphabetical Index of Significant Words

Abaddon [Covered word] 17° Knight of the East and West.

Abi [3d grand word] 15° Knights of the Sword, of the East, or of the Eagle.

Abiram [3d pass-word] 9° Knight Elu of Nine; Grand, Elect, Perfect and Sublime Mason.

Acacia [Pass-word] 5° Perfect Master.

Achar [2d pass-word] 8° Intendant of the Buildings.

Adar [Sacred word] 16° Princes of Jerusalem.

Adonai [2d sacred word] 4° Secret Master; [Sacred word] 11° Prince Ameth, or Sublime Elu of Twelve; [Sacred word] 12° Grand Master Architect; [5th arch word] 13° Royal Arch; [3d covered word] Grand, Elect, Perfect and Sublime Mason; Prince of the Tabernacle.

Adonai lal Aliun [Sacred word] 28° Knight of the Sun; or Knight Adept.

Adonhiram 14° Grand, Elect, Perfect and Sublime Mason.

Ahli-ab [4th pass-word] 22° Knight of the Royal Axe, or Prince of Libanus.

Akirop [4th pass-word] 9° Knight Elu of Nine; Grand, Elect, Perfect and Sublime Mason.

Alborak [Pass-word in the court of the Sultan] 29° Grand Ecossais of St. Andrew, or Patriarch of the Crusades.

Alfred [Answer to pass-word] 31° Grand Enquiring Commander.

Alhim [4th arch word] 13° Royal Arch.

Ali-Al [1st sacred word] 30° Knight Kadosh.

Alkebir [Answer to pass-word] 28° Knight of the Sun; or Knight Adept.

Al-khanan [Sacred word] 10° Illustrious Elu of Fifteen; [2d pass-word] 14° Grand, Elect, Perfect and Sublime Mason; [Sacred word] 25° Knight of the Brazen Serpent.

Alpha [1st word given with token] 28° Knight of the Sun; or Knight Adept.

Al-Schedi [Sacred word] 32° Sublime Prince of the Royal

Secret.

Al-Shedi [1st sacred word] 22° Knight of the Royal Axe, or Prince of Libanus.

Amel-Saghia [Name of 5th step] 30° Knight Kadosh.

Ameth [Pass-word] 11° Prince Ameth, or Sublime Elu of Twelve.

Amun [2d arch word] 13° Royal Arch.

Amunah [Name of 4th step] 30° Knight Kadosh.

Amnu-al [Pass-word] 19° Grand Pontiff, or Sublime Scotch Mason.

Anirah Hashemesh [6th sign word] 29° Grand Ecossais of St. Andrew, or Patriarch of the Crusades.

Assur [7th arch word] 13° Royal Arch.

Athom [1st arch word] 13° Royal Arch.

Aum [6th arch word] 13° Royal Arch.

Auri-al [1st pass-word] 23° Chief of the Tabernacle; [4th pass-word] 29° Grand Ecossais of St. Andrew, or Patriarch of the Crusades.

Bel [3d arch word] 13° Royal Arch.

Benjamin [2d word given with token] 15° Knights of the Sword, of the East, or of the Eagle.

Benkhurim; Ben-khurim [1st pass-word] 8° Intendant of the Buildings.

Bereth-Neder-Shelemoth [Token words] 6° Confidential Secretary.

Berith-Neder-Shelomith [1st token words] 11° Prince Ameth, or Sublime Elu of Twelve; [1st token words] 14° Grand, Elect, Perfect and Sublime Mason.

Betsel-al [2d pass-word] 22° Knight of the Royal Axe, or Prince of Libanus.

Boaz [1st token word] 29° Grand Ecossais of St. Andrew, or Patriarch of the Crusades.

Casmaran [3d pass-word] 29° Grand Ecossais of St. Andrew, or Patriarch of the Crusades.

Derek-Yehuah [Pass-word] 24° Prince of the Tabernacle

Dominum Vobiscum [Words associated with 5th sign, though not spoken] 29° Grand Ecossais of St. Andrew, or Patriarch of the Crusades.

Emanuel [Pass-word] 18° Knight, or Sovereign Prince of Rose Croix, or Heredon.

Equity [2d sacred word] 31° Grand Enquiring Commander.

Frederic Barbarossa [1st entrance word] 21° Noachite; or Prussian Knight.

Gabaon [Name of Ineffable Mason] 14° Grand, Elect, Perfect and Sublime Mason.

Gebur-khil [Sacred word] 9° Knight Elu of Nine; Grand, Elect, Perfect and Sublime Mason.

Gemul-Binah-Tabunah [Name of 7th step] 30° Knight Kadosh.

Gomel [Pass-word] 26° Prince of Mercy or Scottish Trintarian.

Habemah [2d pass-word] 30° Knight Kadosh.

Hallelu-yah [Sacred word] 19° Grand Pontiff, or Sublime Scotch Mason.

Hamelek Kheblim [Pass-word] 13° Royal Arch.

Havron-hamim [2d pass-word] Knights of the Sword, of the East, or of the Eagle.

Hua [1st sacred word] 8° Intendant of the Buildings.

Iakin; Yakin [2d token word] 29° Grand Ecossais of St. Andrew, or Patriarch of the Crusades.

Iao [1st sacred word] 4° Secret Master.

Ihuh [Grand sacred word] 14° Grand, Elect, Perfect and Sublime Mason.

Inri [Sacred word] 18° Knight, or Sovereign Prince of Rose Croix, of Heredon; [Grand word] 27° Knight Commander of the Temple, or Teutonic Knight of the House of St. Mary of Jerusalem.

Ishuah [2d sacred word] 22° Knight of the Royal Axe, or Prince of Libanus.

Ivah (or Jova) [Sacred word] 6° Confidential Secretary.

Izrachiah [5th "other" word] 7° Provost and Judge.

Jachinai (Shekinah) [Sacred Word] 7° Provost and Judge.

Jah [2d sacred word] 8° Intendant of the Buildings.

Jeva [Sacred word] Perfect Master; [4th sacred word] Intendant of the Buildings.

Jova (or Ivah) [Sacred word] 6° Confidential Secretary.

Joabert [1st pass word] 6° Confidential Secretary; [2d pass word] Knight Elu of Nine; Grand, Elect, Perfect and Sublime Mason.

Jua [3d sacred word] 4° Secret Master.

Judah [1st word given with token] 15° Knights of the Sword, of the East, or of the Eagle.

Justice [1st sacred word] 31° Grand Enquiring Commander.

Khalati [Pass-word] 25° Knight of the Brazen Serpent.

Kham [2d sacred word] 21° Noachite; or Prussian Knight.

Kheblim [1st covered word] 14° Grand, Elect, Perfect and Sublime Mason.

Kivi [1st "other" word] 7° Provost and Judge.

Kum [2d "other" word] 7° Provost and Judge.

Libanus [6th pass-word] 22° Knight of the Royal Axe, or Prince of Libanus.

Li-Beni-Ameth [3d sign words] 26° Prince of Mercy or Scottish Trintarian.

Libertas [1st pass-word] 15° Knights of the Sword, of the East, or of the Eagle.

Machbenach [3d token word] 29° Grand Ecossais of St. Andrew, or Patriarch of the Crusades.

Mahabeni [Token word] 5° Perfect Master; [2d covered word] Grand, Elect, Perfect and Sublime Mason.

Mahaboneh [Substitute Master's word] 14° Grand, Elect, Perfect and Sublime Mason.

Marah-maur-abrec [3d pass word] 14° Grand, Elect, Perfect and Sublime Mason.

Metuk [Name of 3d step] 30° Knight Kadosh.

Mi Kamuk Balim Ihuh [2d sacred word] 30° Knight Kadosh.

Necum [Pass-word of 9°] 14° Grand, Elect, Perfect and

Sublime Mason.

Nekah [Answer word] 9° Knight Elu of Nine.

Nekam Adonai [Word of entrance] 30° Knight Kadosh.

Nekam Makah [Answer to 2d pass-word] 32° Sublime Prince of the Royal Secret.

Nekhamah [Sacred word] 29° Grand Ecossais of St. Andrew, or Patriarch of the Crusades.

Nekhamah Menukhim [1st pass-word] 30° Knight Kadosh.

Nekum [1st pass-word] 9° Knight Elu of Nine.

Noah [1st pass-word] 22° Knight of the Royal Axe, or Prince of Libanus.

Noakh [2d entrance word] 21° Noachite; or Prussian Knight.

Omega [2d word given with token] 28° Knight of the Sun; or Knight Adept.

Pala-Kol [1st pass-word] 32° Sublime Prince of the Royal Secret.

Pax Vobis; Pax Vobiscum [2d word given with grip] 18° Knight, or Soverign Prince of Rose Croix, of Heredon.

Phaleg [3d entrance word] 21° Noachite; or Prussian Knight.

Pharash-Kol [2d pass-word] 32° Sublime Prince of the Royal Secret.

Pheresh-Kol [2d pass-word] 30° Knight Kadosh.

Phoreh-lak [1st pass-word] 29° Grand Ecossais of St. Andrew, or Patriarch of the Crusades.

Rab-benin [Pass-word] 12° Grand Master Architect; 14° Grand, Elect, Perfect and Sublime Mason.

Raph-adon [General word] 18° Knight, or Sovereign Prince of Rose Croix, of Heredon.

Rashah-betsir-yah [Sacred word] 20° Venerable Master of All Symbolic Lodges; or Master ad Vitam.

Sabel [Name of 6th step] 30° Knight Kadosh.

Salix Nonis Tengu 32° Sublime Prince of the Royal Secret.

San [8th arch word] 13° Royal Arch.

Shalal [1st Grand word] 15° Knights of the Sword, of the

East, or of the Eagle.

Shalal-Shalum-Abi [Grand words] 15° Knights of the Sword, of the East, or of the Eagle.

Shalum [2d grand word] 15° Knights of the Sword, of the East, or of the Eagle.

Shekinah (Jachinai) [Sacred word] 7° Provost and Judge; [3d sacred word] Intendant of the Buildings.

Shem [1st sacred word] 21° Noachite; or Prussian Knight.

Shuh-Laban [Name of 2d step] 30° Knight Kadosh.

Solomon [Pass-word] 27° Knight Commander of the Temple, or Teutonic Knight of the House of St. Mary of Jerusalem.

Stibium [Pass word] 28° Knight of the Sun; or Knight Adept.

Stolkin [3d "other" word] 8° Provost and Judge; 14° Grand, Elect, Perfect and Sublime Mason; [Answer to 1st pass-word] 20° Venerable Master of All Symbolic Lodges; or Master ad Vitam.

Talliud [2d pass-word] 29° Grand Ecossais of St. Andrew, or Patriarch of the Crusades.

Tebet [Pass-word] 16° Princes of Jerusalem.

Tito [Pass-word] 7° Provost and Judge.

Tsedekah [Name of 1st step] 30° Knight Kadosh.

Tsiduni [5th pass-word] 22° Knight of the Royal Axe, or Prince of Libanus.

Xinkuh [4th "other" word] 7° Provost and Judge.

Yah-balin [Pass-word] 17° Knight of the East and West; [2d pass-word] 20° Venerable Master of All Symbolic Lodges; or Master ad Vitam.

Yakhsin [1st pass-word] 20° Venerable Master of All Symbolic Lodges; or Master ad Vitam.

Yakin; Iakin [2d token word] 29° Grand Ecossais of St. Andrew, or Patriarch of the Crusades.

Yapeth [3d sacred word] 21° Noachite; or Prussian Knight; Knight of the Royal Axe, or Prince of Libanus.

Yav [9th arch word] 13° Royal Arch.

Yehouah [Sacred word] 23° Chief of the Tabernacle.

Yekhapets Yehuah [Sacred word] 24° Prince of the Tabernacle.

YHVH (or IHUH) [Sacred word] 26° Prince of Mercy or Scottish Trintarian.

Zanabazare [3d pass-word] 20° Venerable Master of All Symbolic Lodges; or Master ad Vitam.

Zerbal [2d pass-word] 6° Confidential Secretary; [Pass-word] 10° Illustrious Elu of Fifteen; 14° Grand, Elect, Perfect Sublime Mason.

Zi-zon [Pass-word] 4° Secret Master.

Zoroaster [Pass-word] 31° Grand Enquiring Commander.

Fourth Degree.

Secret Master.

THE LODGE, ITS DECORATIONS, FURNITURE, ETC.

The hangings are black, strewed with white tears. The Lodge represents the Sanctum Sanctorum; the East being separated from the body of the room by a railing running from one side to the other, with a gate in the middle.

Over the Master's seat hangs a circle, within which is an equilateral triangle, and in the centre of that a blazing star, in the centre of which is the Hebrew letter י.

The Lodge is lighted by eight lights, two by two, in the north, south, east, and west. Besides these principal lights, there may be as many others as may be desired.

The battery of this degree is ; —
The age of a Secret Master is : years.

OFFICERS, TITLES, DECORATIONS, ETC.

The Master represents King Solomon, and is styled *Thrice Puissant*. He sits in the east, wearing a black robe lined with ermine, with a sceptre in his hand. Before him is a triangular altar, on which is a crown, made of branches of laurel and olive.

There is but one Warden, who represents Adonhiram, is styled *Inspector*, and sits in the west.

No working-tools are used in the Lodge, for the reason that the labours on the temple were suspended after the death of our Grand Master Hiram Abi.

The Master wears a broad blue watered ribbon, from the right shoulder to the left hip, at the end of which hangs, as a jewel, an equilateral triangle of gold, with the letters ♀.·. ☉.·. ☿.·. upon it.

The Warden and all the Brothers wear a broad white ribbon edged with black, at the end of which hangs the jewel of the Degree, which is an ivory key, on the wards of which is the letter Z.·. in black.

The apron is white, edged with black : the gloves white, turned over with black at the wrists. The flap of the apron is blue, with an open eye embroidered on it in gold. The strings are of black ribbon. Two branches, one of laurel and the other of olive, cross each other in the middle of the apron, and at their crossing is the letter Z.·. embroidered in gold.

1

TO OPEN.

Th∴ P∴ Bro. Adonhiram, in our sorrow we must not forget the demands of duty. Are all present, Secret Masters? Let any who are not so, retire.

Insp∴ Th. Puissant, all present are Secret Masters.

Th∴ P∴ What is the first duty of a Secret Master, when the Lodge is about to open?

Insp∴ To see that the entrance to the Holy of Holies is duly guarded, that we may be secret and secure.

Th∴ P∴ Attend, my Brother, to that duty, through your proper officer, and cause the Tyler to be informed that I am about to open this Lodge of Secret Masters here, and direct him to tyle accordingly.

Insp∴ Bro. Jun. Deacon, see that the entrance to this holy place is duly guarded; and inform the Tyler that the Th∴ P∴ King is about to open a Lodge of Secret Masters in this place, and direct him to tyle accordingly.

[The Jun∴ Deacon goes to the door, opens it, informs the Tyler, closes it, raps on it [:] equal and then [.], which is answered by the Tyler, and then returns to his place and remains standing, and says]:

Jr∴ D∴ Ven∴ Inspector, we are well tyled, and the entrance to this Holy Place is well guarded.

Insp∴ How tyled and guarded, my Brother?

Jr∴ D∴ By a Secret Master at the entrance without, armed with a drawn sword.

Insp∴ His duty there?

Jr∴ D∴ To repel all intruders and cowans, and allow none to enter here who have not the Pass-word, nor until after your permission obtained.

Insp∴ It is well, my Brother. Th∴ P∴ King Solomon, we are well tyled, secret and secure.

Th∴ P∴ It is well, my Brother. Are you a Secret Master?

Insp∴ I have passed from the Square to the Compass. I have seen the Tomb of our Master Hiram Abi; and with my Brethren have shed tears thereon.

Qu∴ Where were you received a Secret Master?

Ans∴ Under the laurel and olive trees.

Qu∴ What were the lessons taught you in this degree?

Ans∴ Secrecy, Obedience, and Fidelity.

Th∴ P∴ Bro∴ Jun∴ Deacon, your place in this Lodge?

Jr∴ D∴ In the West, in front of the Ven∴ Warden, to his right.

Th∴ P∴ Your duty there?

Jr∴ D∴ To keep inviolably the secrets entrusted to me.

Th∴ P∴ Bro∴ Sen∴ Deacon, your place in the Lodge?

Sen∴ D∴ In the East, in front of the Th∴ P∴ Master, to his right.

Th∴ P∴ Your duty there?

Sen∴ D∴ To obey the laws of God, of the Order, and of the Th∴ P∴ Master.

Th∴ P∴ Ven∴ Bro∴ Adonhiram, your station in the Lodge?

Insp∴ In the West, Th∴ P∴; between the lights.

Th∴ P∴ Your duty there?

Insp∴ To be faithful unto death.

Th∴ P∴ The station of the Master of the Lodge?

Insp∴ In the East, in front of the Tomb of our deceased Master, the Worker in Metals, and Son of a widow of Tyre.

Th∴ P∴ His duties there?

Insp∴ To provide for the welfare of the Order, and to teach the Craftsmen their duties; remembering that though their Master, they are still his equals in the eye of God and of Masonry.

Th∴ P∴ I acknowledge the truth, and recognize the duty. My Brothers, the husband must labour to give his children bread, while their mother, the wife of his bosom, lies under his roof unburied, cold and still in her coffin; and the mother, while her tears still flow fast for her first born that lies dead before her.

The poor have no leisure to mourn: and Masons must not permit their sorrows to encroach upon the domain of their duties. Brother Adonhiram, what is your age?

Insp∴ The cube of [?].

Th∴ P∴ What is the hour?

Insp∴ The Dawn has chased away the Darkness, and the great Light is about to shine in our Lodge.

Th∴ P∴ Since the Dawn has chased away the Darkness, and the great Light is about to shine in our Lodge, give notice to the Brethren that I am about to open this Lodge of Secret Masters by the mysterious numbers.

Insp∴ Brethren in the North and South, the Dawn has chased away the Darkness, the great Light is about to shine, and the Th∴ P∴ is about to open this Lodge of Secret Masters, by the mysterious numbers. You will take due notice and govern yourselves accordingly.

[Then the Th∴ P∴ raps [:] [.]—the Inspector [:] [.]—and all the brethren the same, with their hands. Then the Th∴ P∴ gives the sign, and all the Brothers give the answer; and the Th∴ P∴ says]:

Th∴ P∴ I therefore declare this Lodge of Secret Masters duly opened; and I charge you all, my Brethren, to be secret, silent, obedient and faithful during our labours.

RECEPTION.

The Candidate appears in the preparation-room, in the clothing, and wearing the jewel of a Master Mason. The Master of Ceremonies goes to him and examines him thoroughly in the work of the three first degrees, [which is done now once for all, that it may never be necessary, in any subsequent degree, to examine a candidate in any work but that of the degree immediately preceding]. He then deprives him of his clothing and jewel of Master, and places a small silver square upon his forehead, securing it there by a bandage that covers his eyes. He also places a cord round his neck, and a light in his left hand, causes him to lay the two first fingers of his right hand upon his lips, and then leads him to the door of the Lodge, and raps [;] [.]. The Jun∴ Deacon opens the door and inquires

Jr∴ D∴ Who comes here? Who approaches this place of sadness and sorrow?

M∴ Cer∴ The Bro∴ Master of Ceremonies, with a Bro∴, who having been regularly initiated an entered Apprentice Mason, passed to the Degree of Fellow Craft, and been raised to the Degree of Master Mason, now desires to be admitted to the degree of Secret Master.

Jr∴ D∴ Is he duly and truly prepared to receive the degree he seeks?

M∴ Cer∴ He is.

Jr∴ D∴ Has he made suitable proficiency in the three first Degrees?

M∴ Cer∴ I have examined him carefully, and find him well instructed and proficient in the three degrees.

Gr∴ D∴ Is the Master's Lodge, to which he belongs, satisfied with his conduct and behaviour as a Mason, and content that he should advance?

M∴ Cer∴ It is.

Jr∴ D∴ Do you vouch to this Lodge for his zeal, his candour, and his constancy, and that he will be silent, obedient, and faithful?

M∴ Cer∴ I do, as for myself.

Jr∴ D∴ It is well. Let him wait a time in silence, until the Th∴ P∴ Master be informed of his request, and his will ascertained.

[The Jun∴ Deacon closes the door, and reports to the Th∴ P∴; the same questions being asked, and like answers returned as at the door.]

Th∴ P∴ It is well. Since the candidate comes endowed with these necessary qualifications, and duly vouched for, let him be admitted and received in due and ancient form.

[The door is opened, and the candidate enters, led by the M∴ of Cer∴, by the cord around his neck. The Sen∴ D∴ meets him, and says]:

Sen∴ D∴ My Brother, upon entering the Lodge in the several degrees of Entered Apprentice, Fellow-craft, and Master Mason, you were received in a particular manner in each, which was then explained. Upon your entrance into this Lodge of Secret Masters, I seal your lips with this seal of secrecy and discretion. [He presses a seal upon the candidate's lips, first removing his fingers from them, and then replacing them again.] Let this ceremony ever remind you that you cannot, in any emergency, divulge our secrets without violating your obligation as a Mason, and your honour as a man.

[The candidate is then conducted four times around the Lodge, while the following sentences are read aloud, the Warden and Master rapping as he passes them on each circuit [,], then [?], then [;] : and then [;,] :

1st Circuit. . . . I, the Lord thy God, did bring thee out of the land of Egypt, out of the house of bondage. Thou shalt worship no other gods, nor make any graven image, nor any likeness of anything in heaven or on earth, in the sea, or under the earth, whereunto to bow down and serve them.

. . . . Thou shalt not irreverently or unnecessarily pronounce my name יהוה; for if thou doest so, thou committest an offence which I will punish.

2d Circuit. . . . Turn ye not unto idols, nor make to yourselves molten gods, nor profane the name of יהוה your God, nor swear by His name falsely.

. . . . . If a man vow a vow unto the Lord, or swear an oath to bind his soul with a bond, he shall not break his word : he shall do according to all that proceedeth out of his mouth.

3d Circuit. . . . . When thou liftest up thine eyes unto heaven, and seest the sun and the moon and the stars, even all the armies of heaven, do not thou worship them, nor adore them, like the ancient nations.

. . . . . . Ye shall observe to do as the Lord your God hath commanded you. Ye shall not turn aside to the right hand or to the left. Ye shall walk in all the ways which the Lord your God hath commanded you, that ye may live, and that it may be well with you, and that your days may be prolonged in the land which ye possess.

4th Circuit. . . . . What does the Lord thy God require of thee but to fear Him, to walk in all His ways, to love Him, and to serve Him with all thy heart and with all thy soul? Love Him, walk in all His ways, and cleave unto Him.

[At the conclusion of the four circuits, the candidate is halted in front of the Warden, who asks] :
Insp∴ Who is this that journeys with you, Bro∴ M∴ of Cer∴, in bondage and in darkness?
M∴ Cer∴ A Master Mason, Bro∴ Adonhiram, who seeks the lost word.
Insp∴ Alas, my Brother, it hath not yet been found. What does the Brother desire?
M∴ Cer∴ To receive the degree of Secret Master.

[*A Voice in the extreme East says, gravely and slowly*] :

Voice : . . Wo unto those who aspire to that for which they are unfitted!

[*Another Voice in the North cries*] :

V∴ . . . . Wo unto those who assume a burthen which they cannot bear!

[*A Voice in the South cries*] :

V∴ . . . . Wo unto those who assume duties lightly, and afterwards neglect them!

Insp∴ You hear, my Brother. Masonry is duty, and its honours the reward of work, which is the performance of duty. Are you prepared to assume its duties?
Cand∴ I am.
Insp∴ Your labours may not be rewarded; for he who sows not often reaps. Are you prepared to perform those duties because they are duties, without regard to the reward, and satisfied with the approbation of your own conscience alone?
Cand∴ I am.
Insp∴ Repair, then, to our sacred altar, and there kneeling, not to us, but to the Great Architect of the Universe, enter into a covenant with us and an obligation to Him, ever to perform the duties of this degree.

[The candidate is led to the altar, and placed, standing, in front of it, facing the East: and the Th∴ P∴ says] :

Th∴ P∴ Who stands before the altar, under the sign of Secrecy?

M∴ Cer∴ A worthy Brother Master Mason, who has been duly examined, has made the four circuits, and answered suitably the questions of the worthy Inspector Adonhiram, and now stands here by his permission to receive the obligation of a Secret Master.

[*A Voice in the East says*] :

V∴ Duty is with us always, inflexible as Fate.

[*A Voice in the North says*] :

V∴ In health or sickness, in prosperity or in adversity, duty is with us always, exacting as Necessity.

[*A Voice in the South says*] :

V∴ It rises with us in the morning, and watches by our pillow at night. In the roar of the City, and in the loneliness of the Desert, Duty is with us always, imperative as Destiny.

Th∴ P∴ You hear, my Brother. Do you with all your heart agree that Duty is the one great law of Masonry, inflexible as Fate, exacting as Necessity, imperative as Destiny?

Cand∴ I do.

Th∴ P∴ What seek you in your journeying?

M∴ Cer∴ Truth, and the Lost Word.

Th∴ P∴ Like the light you bear, which yet you cannot see, Truth and the Lost Word, which are Light, are within the reach of every man that lives, would he but open his eyes and see. The broad highway of Duty, straight as an arrow, leads directly to them; but men seek shorter routes by by-paths, and lose themselves in the labyrinths of error. If you would find the True Light and the Lost Word, kneel at our Sacred Altar, and enter into a sincere covenant with us, and a firm obligation to the Gr∴ Arch∴ of the Universe, that you will faithfully keep the secrets, and perform the duties of this degree.

[The candidate kneels on both knees. His left hand, holding the light, is placed upon the Holy Bible and Compasses, and the two first fingers of his right upon his heart; in which position he assumes the following]

OBLIGATION.

I, A ... B ...., in the presence of the Gr∴ Arch∴ of the Universe, and of the Brethren now here assembled, do hereby and hereon most solemnly and sincerely covenant with them and bind and oblige myself by vow and oath to Him, that I will never reveal the secrets of this degree to any person in the world, who shall not be entitled at the time to receive them, and I having power and right to communicate them.

I furthermore promise and swear that I will hold allegiance to the Supreme Council of Sovereign Gr∴ Insp∴ Gen∴ of the 33d Degree, for the Southern Jurisdiction of the United States, so long as I continue to reside or be within its jurisdiction, and will pay due obedience to its Regulations, Laws and Edicts not subversive of the true Principles of Masonry nor contrary to the Ancient Land-marks; and that I will obey and abide by the by-laws, rules and regulations of the Lodge of Secret Masters and of Perfection to which I may belong, so long as I continue a member thereof.

I furthermore promise and swear, that Duty shall hereafter be the rule and guide of my conduct, inflexible as fate, exacting as necessity, and imperative as destiny.

I furthermore promise and swear, that wherever secrecy may be enjoined or required by the rules or interest of Masonry or of a brother, or by the order of a Lodge, Council, Chapter, or the Supreme Council, and I may as a good citizen, obedient to the laws of my country, lawfully and laudably be so, I will be silent and secret as the grave, as to all matters and things improper to be divulged.

I furthermore promise and swear that I will ever be obedient to Divine and all human constitutional and legal authority, secular, civil and masonic, and cheerfully comply with and carry out the lawful will and legal orders of my superiors.

I furthermore promise and swear that I will be faithful unto death to every trust reposed in me, to every obligation imposed on me, to every duty required to be performed, to God, my country, the Lodge, my family, my brother and my friend; nor ever fail country, Lodge, family, brother or friend in time of need, distress, danger or persecution.

All of which I do most sincerely covenant and solemnly promise and vow; and may God aid me to keep and perform the same!

[The cord is then taken from the candidate's neck, and the light from his left hand, and the two first fingers of his right hand replaced upon his lips. Then the Th∴ P∴ takes off the bandage from his eyes, and says to him]:

Th∴ P∴ My Brother, late in darkness, I restore you to Light, and set your feet in the path of Duty, which leads to that True Light of which this is but an emblem. Arise, my Brother! Let this Square, which lay upon your forehead, ever remind you to walk uprightly, and turn not aside into the inviting paths of error. Let it also remind you that you have now passed from the Square to the Compasses, as the Geometrician passes from the straight lines and angles by which he measures the surface of the earth, to the great curves and circles by which he calculates the movements of the Stars. Begin now to rise above the earth, and climb the Skies of Spiritual Knowledge; for there, and not upon the Earth, are Truth and the Lost Word to be found.

You see our Lodge clad in mourning, my Brother, and the Brethren wearing the emblems of grief, for the death of our Gr∴ Master Hiram Abi, and for the eclipse of Light and Truth, by the dark, frowning and baleful clouds of Darkness and Error. Grief for the loss of those we love is natural and proper. But we lament not only the death of a friend and a benefactor, of him who had elevated labour and set it by the side of Kings, and made worth and virtue equal to patents of nobility and hereditary rank; but also the loss of the True Word, of which we are deprived by his death, and which we have henceforth to seek for until it is recovered.

This Lodge represents that of the Princes of Israel, held immediately after the death of Hiram, and before his murderers were discovered; when Adonhiram, who had been over the levy and tribute, was made Warden and chief of the work in his place, and Azariah the Son of Nathan, [who had been over the seven officers, Azariah the Son of Zadok, Elihoreph, Ahiah, Jehoshaphat, Benaiah, Zadok, and Abiathar], was set over the Tribute in the place of Adonhiram; and in his place Jehoshaphat was set over the Seven Princes, and Jeroboam was made a Prince and Master to fill the vacancy so created.

And as Jeroboam was then made a Prince in Israel, and a Superintendent of the labours upon the Temple, so do I now receive and accept you, my Brother, as one of the Seven Secret Masters of this Lodge, that you may at once engage in the performance of the more exalted duties which your higher rank imposes upon you. Remember that the Princes of Masonry are those who best work and best agree; that no valuable result is to be attained in this world without exertion, and that you have yet many steps to ascend, before you reach the heights on which Truth sits enthroned, and discover The Lost Word, known to the ancient Patriarchs.

Remember that, as the Seven Princes of Israel were under their Chief, so you are subordinate to your Chiefs in Masonry; and still more to your Country; and most of all and above all, to God; and therefore prepare yourself to command, by learning to obey. Remember that life is short, and in it there is much to do, and Death approaches, and is nearer and nearer to us at every breath we draw; and therefore loiter not by the way-side, but press onward, up the slopes of the mountain, lest Death overtake you and his cold hand clutch you, before you reach its summit.

I crown you with this garland of laurel and olive; of laurel, emblem of victory and triumph, and sacred to Apollo, God of Light. Those who went to consult the Delphic Oracle wore garlands of it, as did the Roman Priests, on festivals. You march towards an Oracle greater than that at Delphi; that of Masonic Truth, which gives no equivocal answers, to mislead and deceive. You now commence the upward course that is to fit you to be Truth's Minister and Priest; and I crown you with the laurel, and with the olive, emblem of fruition, in hopeful expectation of your ultimate success and victory.

I also invest you with the apron, collar and gloves of this degree. Their colour, white, edged with black, is emblematical of the grief of our ancient brethren, on account of the Death of our Gr∴ M∴ H∴ A∴ and the loss of the Master's Word. It is also symbolical of the contest, in the universe of things, and in the soul of every man that lives, between LIGHT and DARKNESS, GOOD and EVIL, TRUTH and ERROR; a struggle which commenced with Time, and is typified in Masonry by the efforts and anxiety of the Candidate to attain the Light.

The Eye upon the blue flap of the apron is a symbol of the sun in the sky, eye of the universe, and to the Ancients an emblem and image of the Deity, the great Archetype of Light. "Light and darkness," said Zoroaster, "are the world's eternal ways." An Eye, the Egyptian hieroglyphic for the word IRI, [to perform religious ceremonies], was the second syllable of the name of Osiris, [OSH-IRI], the Sun deified, Personification of the Principle of Good.

I also present you with this key of ivory, the jewel of this Degree, and an emblem of SECRECY. The letter *Z*∴ upon the wards, is the initial of the Pass-word of the Degree.

The East of this Lodge represents THE HOLY OF HOLIES of the First Temple at Jerusalem, and the most Secret Mysteries of Masonry, from which you are now separated by a barrier at present impassable. But you bear the key; and some day it will be permitted you to unlock the gate, and pass the barrier. Passion, prejudice and error interpose many barriers between man and the Truth; but there are none that energy and perseverance, with honest intentions and pure motives, cannot surmount.

Receive now the signs, words and tokens of this degree.

THE SIGN... Place the ? first fingers of the ‡ hand on the lips.

ANSWER... Place the ? first fingers of the † hand on the lips.

TOKEN. . . Begin with the ♈‡♃☾♄♌‡♀♄ of a M∴ M∴ Then slip the ‡ hand up the other's arm, taking hold of the elbow on the under side; and say—one, ♍♀—the other, ♍☿♒.

THE PASSWORD: the two syllables last foregoing.

SACRED WORDS: ♀☉☿∴ ☉♊♒☉☿♀∴ ♂♃☉.

These three words are three names by which the Deity has been known: and their initials are engraved upon the Triangle, which is the jewel of the Master; and which, as well as that within the circle, suspended in the East, represents the Grand Architect of the Universe. The three sides of each are Wisdom, Power and Harmony; three Divine Attributes much spoken of by Masons:—WISDOM, which *conceived;* POWER, which *created;* and HARMONY [inaccurately styled Beauty], which *regulates* and *preserves*, the Universe. That Universe is symbolized by us, as it was by the Ancient Nations, by a circle. The Blazing Star represents the great Central Light, which so many nations have worshipped in the Sun, its representative: and the LETTER, surrounded by its splendors, is the Hebrew Initial of the name of the Great Archetype of Light, the true God, whom all Masons revere.

Listen now to the Lecture of this Degree.

LECTURE.

According to the Masonic Legend, Hiram, the Phœnician, son of a widow of the Tribe of Dan or Naphtali, by a man of Tyre, died before the Temple was completed. Sent by King Hiram to his friend and ally, Solomon, as a sensible and scientific man, skilful to work in gold, silver, brass, iron, stone and wood, in purple, blue, fine linen and crimson, and to grave any manner of graving, and to find out every device that could be put to him, he had been the principal architect of the Temple. His skill and his many virtues, caused him to be treated by both kings, it is said, as their equal. Considering the exclusiveness of the Jews, and their habit of utterly exterminating the petty Tribes which they conquered in Palestine, as well as the heavy penalties denounced against such of them as should marry women who worshipped strange Gods, it must needs excite some surprise to learn that King Solomon, even before building the temple, married a daughter of the King of Egypt, and formed an alliance with the King of Phœnicia, thus establishing the closest relations of amity between himself and the worshippers of Amun and Osiris, of the Elohim and Melkarth. Hiram Abi, reared at Tyre, no doubt followed the religion of his mother and of her country. Gebal, from which the Ghiblemites or stone-squarers came, was a Phœnician city. The subjects of Solomon and Hiram sailed together in the same vessels to Ophir and Tarshish, and planted colonies together on the coasts of Ireland and Spain, and perhaps of America.

The King of Tyre came into Palestine to see the cities that Solomon had given him, and addressed him as his brother. It is evident that there was some bond of union between them, and between the Jews and the Egyptians and Phœnicians, other than their religion; which must constantly have tended to make them hate each other.

So Moses married Tsi-PaRaH [daughter of the God Ra] the daughter of Jethro, a Pagan Priest of Midian; as Joseph had married ASNEI TH, [devoted to the Goddess Neith], daughter of PeT-HeR-PHRE, [belonging to the Gods Horus and Ra], a Priest of Heliopolis.

As Moses and Joseph could not thus have married, without having first been initiated into the Egyptian mysteries, so there can be no doubt that Solomon was required to receive such initiation, before he could intermarry with a daughter of the King of Egypt. These mysteries had also spread into Syria and Phœnicia, and were known of course to the king, his nobles and favorites; and teaching there as in Palestine the doctrine of one God, of whom all the host of Pagan Deities were but images and emblems, they united the Jewish to the Phœnician initiates in bonds of harmony and union that were not broken for many years.

By the death of Hiram Abi, the works upon the Temple were suspended, the craft overwhelmed with sorrow, and changes rendered necessary among the great officers of the realm. In what manner these needful changes were effected, you have already heard, and that your admission here is in imitation of that of Jeroboam (afterwards King of Israel), as one of the seven Princes of the Court of King Solomon.

We do not assert that this legend is true. We only know that it has come to us by tradition. At what time the legend of the death of Hiram took the place of the older legends in the mysteries of Persia, India, and Egypt, we have no information. Nor is it important for us to know. For masonry is a succession of allegories, the mere vehicles of great lessons in morality and philosophy. You will more fully appreciate its spirit, its object, its purposes, as you advance in the different degrees, which you will find to constitute a great, complete and harmonious system.

If you have been disappointed in the three first degrees; if it has seemed to you that the performance has not come up to the promise, and that the common-places which are uttered in them with such an air, the lessons in science and the arts, merely rudimentary, and known to every school-boy, the trite maxims of morality, and the trivial ceremonies are unworthy the serious attention of a grave and sensible man, occupied with the weighty cares of life, and to whom his time is valuable, remember that those ceremonies and lessons come to us from an age when the commonest learning was confined to a select few, when the most ordinary and fundamental principles of morality were new discoveries; and that the three first degrees stand in these latter days, like the columns of the old, roofless Druidic Temple, in their rude and primeval simplicity, mutilated also and corrupted by the action of time, and the additions and interpolations of illiterate ignorance. They are but the entrance to the great Masonic Temple, the mere pillars of the portico.

You have now taken the first step over its threshold, the first step towards the inmost sanctuary and heart of the Temple. You are in the path that leads up the slope of the Mountain of Truth; and it depends upon your Secrecy, Obedience and Fidelity, whether you will advance or remain stationary.

Imagine not that you will become a thorough Mason by learning what is commonly called the work, or merely by becoming familiar with our traditions. Masonry has a history and a literature. Its allegories and its traditions will teach you much; but much is to be sought elsewhere. The streams of learning that now flow broad and wide must be followed to their heads in the springs that well up in the far distant Past, and there you will find the meaning and the origin of Masonry.

A few trite lessons upon the rudiments of architecture, a few ordinary maxims of morality, a few unimportant and unsubstantiated traditions will no longer satisfy the earnest inquirer after Masonic Truth. Let him who is satisfied and content with them, remain where he is, and seek to ascend no higher. But let him who desires to understand the harmonious and beautiful proportions of Masonry, read, study, reflect, digest and discriminate. The true Mason is an ardent seeker after knowledge; and he knows that books are vessels which come down to us full-freighted with the intellectual riches of the past; and that in the lading of these Argosies is much that sheds light upon the history of Masonry, and proves its claims to be regarded as the great benefactor of mankind.

Knowledge is the most genuine and real of human treasures; for it is Light, as Ignorance is Darkness. It is the development of the human soul, and its acquisition the growth of the soul, which at the birth of man knows nothing, and therefore, in one sense, may be said to *be* nothing. It is the seed, which has in it the power to grow, to acquire, and by acquiring to be developed, as the seed is developed into the shoot, the plant, the tree. We need not pause at the common argument that by learning man excelleth man, in that wherein man excelleth beasts; that by learning man ascendeth to the Heavens and their motions, where in body he cannot come, and the like. Let us rather regard the dignity and excellency of knowledge and learning in that whereunto man's nature doth most aspire, which is immortality or continuance. For to this tendeth generation, and raising of Houses and Families; to this buildings, foundations and monuments; to this tendeth the desire of memory, fame and celebration, and in effect the strength of all other human desires. That our influences shall live after us, and be a living power when we are in the grave; and not merely that our names shall be remembered; but rather that our works shall be read, our acts spoken of, our names recollected and mentioned when we are dead, as evidences that those influences live and rule, sway and control the world or a portion of it,—this is the aspiration of the human soul. We see then how far the monuments of genius and learning are more durable than monuments of power or of the hands. For have not the verses of Homer continued twenty-five hundred years or more, without the loss of a syllable or letter, during which time infinite palaces, temples, castles, cities, have been decayed and demolished. It is not possible to have the true pictures or statues of Cyrus, Alexander, Cæsar, no, nor of the Kings or great personages of much later years; for the originals cannot last, and the copies cannot but lose of the life and truth. But the images of men's genius and knowledge remain in books, exempted from the wrong of time, and capable of perpetual renovation. Neither are they fitly to be called images, because they generate still, and cast their seeds in the minds of others, provoking and causing infinite actions and opinions in succeeding ages; so that if the invention of the ship was thought so noble, which carrieth riches and commodities from place to place, and consociateth the most remote regions in participation of their fruits, how much more are letters to be magnified, which, as ships, pass through the vast seas of time, and make ages so distant to participate of the wisdom, illumination and inventions, the one of the other.

To learn, to attain knowledge, to be wise, is a necessity for every truly noble soul; to teach, to communicate that knowledge, to share that wisdom with others, and not churlishly to lock up his exchequer, and place a sentinel at the door to drive away the needy, is equally an impulse of a noble nature and the worthiest work of man.

'There was a little city,' says the Preacher, the Son of David, 'and few men within it; and there came a great King against it and besieged it, and built great bulwarks against it. Now there was found in it a poor wise man, and he by his wisdom delivered the city; yet no man remembered that same poor man. Then said I, wisdom is better than strength: nevertheless the poor man's wisdom is despised, and his words are not heard.' If it should chance to you, my brother, to do mankind good service, and be rewarded with indifference and forgetfulness only, still be not discouraged, but remember the further advice of the wise King. 'In the morning sow the seed, and in the evening withhold not thy hand; for thou knowest not which shall prosper, this or that, or whether both shall be alike good.' Sow you the seed, whoever reaps. Learn, that you may be enabled to do good; and do so because it is right, finding in the act itself ample reward and recompense.

To attain the Truth, and to serve mankind, our country and our fellows. This is the noblest destiny of man, your object henceforward and forever. If you desire to ascend to that destiny, advance! If you have other and more ignoble objects, and are contented with a lower flight, halt here, return, and leave Masonry to fulfil her mission.

If you will advance, gird up your loins for the struggle; for the way is long and toilsome. Pleasure, all

2

smiles, will beckon to you on the one hand, and Indolence will invite you to sleep among the flowers, upon the other. Prepare, by Secrecy, Obedience and Fidelity, to resist the allurements of both.

Secrecy is indispensable in a Mason of whatever degree. It is the first and almost the only lesson taught to the Entered Apprentice. The obligations which we have each assumed towards every Mason that lives, requiring of us the performance of the most serious and onerous duties towards those personally unknown to us until they demand our aid,—duties that must be performed, even at the risk of life, or our solemn oaths be broken and violated and we be branded as false Mason and faithless man, teach us how profound a folly it would be to betray our Secrets to those who, bound to us by no tie of common obligation, might, by obtaining them, call on us in their extremity, when the urgency of the occasion should allow us no time for inquiry, and the peremptory mandate of our obligation compel us to do a brother's duty to a base impostor.

The Secrets of our brother, when communicated to us, must be sacred, if they be such as the law of our country warrants us to keep. We are required to keep none other, when the law that we are called on to obey is indeed a law, by having emanated from the only source of power, the People. Edicts which emanate from the mere arbitrary will of a despotic power, contrary to the law of God or the Great Law of Nature, destructive of the inherent rights of man, violative of the right of free thought, free speech, free conscience, it is lawful to rebel against and strive to abrogate.

For obedience to the Law does not mean submission to tyranny; nor that, by a profligate sacrifice of every noble feeling, we should offer to despotism the homage of adulation. As every new victim falls, we may lift our voice in still louder flattery. We may fall at the proud feet, we may beg, as a boon, the honour of kissing that bloody hand which has been lifted against the helpless. We may do more: we may bring the altar and the sacrifice, and implore the God not to ascend too soon to Heaven. This we may do, for this we have the sad remembrance that beings of a human form and soul have done. But this is all we can do. We can constrain our tongues to be false, our features to bend themselves to the semblance of that passionate adoration which we wish to express, our knees to fall prostrate; but our heart we cannot constrain. There virtue must still have a voice which is not to be drowned by hymns and acclamations; there the crimes which we laud as virtues, are crimes still, and he whom we have made a God, is the most contemptible of mankind; if, indeed, we do not feel, perhaps, that we are ourselves still more contemptible.

But that law which is the fair expression of the will and judgment of the people, is the enactment of the whole and of every individual. Consistent with the law of God and the great law of nature, consistent with pure and abstract right as tempered by necessity and the general interest, as contra-distinguished from the private interest of individuals, it is obligatory upon all, because it is the work of all, the will of all, the solemn judgment of all, from which there is no appeal.

In this degree, my brother, you are especially to learn the duty of obedience to that law. There is one true and original law, conformable to reason and to nature, diffused over all, invariable, eternal, which calls to the fulfilment of duty, and to abstinence from injustice, and calls with that irresistible voice which is felt in all its authority wherever it is heard. This law cannot be abrogated or diminished, or its sanctions affected, by any law of man. A whole senate, a whole people, cannot dispense from its paramount obligation. It requires no commentator to render it distinctly intelligible: nor is it one thing at Rome, another at Athens, one thing now, and another in the ages to come; but in all times and in all nations, it is, and has been, and will be, one and everlasting;—one as that God, its great Author and Promulgator, who is the Common Sovereign of all mankind, is Himself One. No man can disobey it without flying, as it were, from his own bosom, and repudiating his nature; and in this very act he will inflict on himself the severest of retributions, even though he escape what is regarded as punishment.

It is our duty to obey the laws of our country, and to be careful that prejudice or passion, fancy or affection, error and illusion, be not mistaken for conscience. Nothing is more usual than to pretend conscience in all the actions of man which are public and cannot be concealed. The disobedient refuse to submit to the laws, and they also in many cases pretend conscience, and so disobedience and rebellion are become conscience, in which there is neither knowledge nor revelation, nor truth nor charity, nor reason nor religion. Conscience is tied to laws. Right or sure conscience is right reason reduced to practice, and conducting moral actions, while perverse conscience is seated in the fancy or affections—a heap of irregular principles and irregular defects—

and is the same in conscience as deformity is in the body, or peevishness in the affections. It is not enough that the conscience be taught by nature; but it must be taught by God, conducted by reason, made operative by discourse, assisted by choice, instructed by laws and sober principles; and then it is right, and it may be sure. All the general measures of justice, are the laws of God, and therefore they constitute the general rules of government for the conscience; but necessity also hath a large voice in the arrangement of human affairs and the disposal of human relations, and the dispositions of human laws; and these general measures, like a great river into little streams, are deduced into little rivulets and particularities, by the laws and customs, by the sentences and agreements of men, and by the absolute despotism of necessity, that will not allow perfect and abstract justice and equity to be the sole rule of civil government in an imperfect world; and that must needs be law which is for the greatest good of the greatest number.

When thou vowest a vow unto God, defer not to pay it. It is better thou shouldest not vow than that thou shouldest vow and not pay. Be not rash with thy mouth, and let not thine heart be hasty to utter anything before God: for God is in Heaven, and thou art upon earth; therefore let thy words be few. Weigh well what it is you promise; but once the promise and pledge is given, remember that he who is false to his obligation will be false to his family, his friend, his country, and his God.

Fides servanda est. Faith plighted is ever to be kept, was a maxim and an axiom even among pagans. The virtuous Roman said, either let not that which seems expedient be base, or if it be base, let it not seem expedient. What is there which that so-called expediency can bring so valuable as that which it takes away, if it deprive you of the name of a good man and rob you of your integrity and honour? In all ages, he who violates his plighted word has been held unspeakably base. The word of a Mason, like the word of a knight in the times of chivalry, once given must be sacred; and the judgment of his brothers, upon him who violates his pledge, should be stern as the judgments of the Roman Censors against him who violated his oath. Good faith is revered among Masons as it was among the Romans, who placed its statue in the capitol, next to that of Jupiter Maximus Optimus; and we, like them, hold that calamity should always be chosen rather than baseness; and with the knights of old, that one should always die rather than be dishonored.

Be faithful, therefore, to the promises you make, to the pledges you give, and to the vows that you assume: since to break either is base and dishonorable.

Be faithful to your family, and perform all the duties of a good father, a good son, a good husband and a good brother.

Be faithful to your friends; for true friendship is of a nature not only to survive through all the vicissitudes of life, but to continue through an endless duration; not only to stand the shock of conflicting opinions, and the roar of a revolution that shakes the world, but to last when the heavens are no more, and to spring fresh from the universe.

Be faithful to your country, and prefer its dignity and honour to any degree of popularity and honour for yourself, consulting its interest rather than your own, and rather than the pleasure and gratification of the people, which is often at variance with their welfare.

Be faithful to Masonry, which is to be faithful to the best interests of mankind. Labour, by precept and example, to elevate the standard of Masonic character, to enlarge its sphere of influence, to popularize its teachings, and to make all men know it for the Great Apostle of Peace, Harmony, and Good-will on earth among men.

Masonry is useful to all men: to the learned, because it affords them the opportunity of exercising their talents upon subjects eminently worthy of their attention; to the illiterate, because it offers them important instruction; to the young, because it presents them with salutary precepts and good examples, and accustoms them to reflect on the proper mode of living; to the man of the world, whom it furnishes with noble and useful recreation; to the traveller, whom it enables to find friends and brothers in countries where else he would be isolated and solitary; to the worthy man in misfortune, to whom it gives assistance; to the afflicted, to whom it lavishes consolation; to the charitable man, whom it enables to do more good, by uniting with those who are charitable like himself; and to all who have a soul capable of appreciating its importance, and of enjoying the charms of a friendship founded on the same principles of religion, morality and philanthropy.

A Free-Mason therefore should be a man of honour and of conscience, preferring his duty to everything beside, even to his life; independent in his opinions, and of good morals; submissive to the laws, devoted to humanity, to his country, to his family; kind and indulgent to his brethren, friend of all virtuous men, and ready to assist his fellows by all the means in his power.

Thus will you be faithful to yourself, to your fellows and to God, and thus will you do honour to the name and rank of Secret Master; which, like other Masonic honours, degrades if it is not deserved.

TO CLOSE.

Th∴ P∴. Bro∴ Adonhiram, what is the hour?

Insp∴. Th∴ P∴., the close of day.

Th∴ P∴. Doth any work of charity or benevolence remain unperformed?

Insp∴: None that is within our power to do.

Th∴ P∴. Have we no brother who is sick, to be watched with and his wants supplied? Are there no widows unprovided for, no orphans to be maintained and educated?

Insp∴. None that are at our charge.

Th∴ P∴. What then remains for us to do?

Insp∴. To practice virtue, avoid vice, and remain in silence.

Th∴ P∴. Since nothing remains for us to do, but to practice virtue and avoid vice, let us remain in silence, that the will of God may be done and accomplished. Give notice, my brother, by the mysterious numbers, that I am about to close this Lodge of Secret Masters.

[The Inspector raps [; ,]—then the Th∴ P∴. [; ,]—and then all the Brothers [; ,] with their hands: then the Th∴ P∴. gives the sign of silence, and all the Brothers give the response, and the Th∴ P∴. says]:

Th∴ P∴. Brethren, this Lodge is closed.

FINIS.

Fifth Degree.

Perfect Master.

THE LODGE, ITS FURNITURE, DECORATIONS, ETC.

The hangings are green. In each corner of the room is a white column. The lodge is lighted by sixteen lights, four at each of the cardinal points. The altar is covered with a black cloth, strewed with white tears.

OFFICERS, CLOTHING, AND JEWELS.

The master is styled *Th∴ Honorable.* He represents *Adonhiram* the Son of Abda, who was at first in command of the workmen on Mount Lebanon, and after the death of Hiram was appointed Chief Architect of the Temple. He is seated in the East.

There is one Warden, who sits in the West, and represents *Zabud*, the Son of Nathan, who was Principal Officer, and the King's friend.

The apron is of white sheepskin, lined and bordered with green, and the flap green. In the middle of the apron are painted or embroidered three circles, with a cube in the centre, and in the centre of that the letters יה.

The Jewel is a compass open to sixty degrees, the points on the arc of a circle. It hangs from a wide green watered ribbon, which is worn from the right shoulder to the left hip.

The *battery* is   [;] [?]
The *age* of a Perfect Master is the square of [;] or [z].

TO OPEN.

[The *Th∴ Hon∴* gives one rap, and says] :

Th∴ Hon∴ My Brethren, I am about to open a Lodge of Perfect Masters in this place for the despatch of business. I will thank you to be clothed and assist me. The officers will repair to their appropriate stations. Bro∴ Zabud, are all present Perfect Masters?

[The Warden goes round and receives the Pass-word from all the Brothers, returns to his station, and reports] :

Ward∴ Th∴ Hon∴ all present prove themselves to be Perfect Masters.

Th∴ Hon∴ Bro∴ Jr∴ Deacon, what is the first care of a Lodge of Perfect Masters, when about to open?

Jun∴ D∴ To see that the Lodge is duly tyled.

Th∴ Hon∴ You will attend to that duty, and inform the Tyler that we are about to open this Lodge of Perfect Masters, and direct him to tyle accordingly.

[The Jun∴ Deacon goes out, returns, gives the battery at the door, it is responded to from without, and he returns to his place, and reports] :

Jun∴ D∴ Th∴ Hon∴ the Lodge is duly tyled.

Th∴ Hon∴ How tyled?

J∴ D∴ By a Perfect Master without the door, armed with a drawn sword.

Th∴ Hon∴ His duty there?

Jun∴ D∴ To guard the door, and see that none approach and enter, except such as are duly qualified, and have permission of the Th∴ Honorable Master.

Th∴ Hon∴ Thank you, my Brother. Bro∴ Zabud, are you a Perfect Master?

Ward∴ I have seen the three circles enclosing the cube, upon the crossed columns.

Th∴ Hon∴ Where were they?

Ward∴ Over the tomb where the body of our Gr∴ Master Hiram Abi was laid.

Th∴ Hon∴ What do the two columns represent?

Ward∴ The columns *Jachin* and *Boaz*, which I knew before I obtained the degree of Perfect Master.

Th∴ Hon∴ Why did King Solomon institute this degree?

Ward∴ To encourage the Brethren in their sorrow; and to cause them to venerate the memory of our Gr∴ Master Hiram Abi; as also to incite them to search for and discover his murderers, who were then unknown; but were presumed to be among the workmen; and the roll having been called, suspicion had fallen upon three in particular, who were missing.

Th∴ Hon∴ What does the Cubical Stone in the centre of the circle represent?

Ward∴ The finite Universe, the Work of God, of whom the three circles are the emblems.

Th∴ Hon∴ What do the three circles represent?

Ward∴ The WISDOM, POWER and BENEVOLENCE of God; the Great Trinity of his Attributes.

Th∴ Hon∴ Where were you received a Perfect Master?

Ward∴ At the Tomb of our deceased Grand Master, in a regular and full Lodge of Perfect Masters.

Th∴ Hon∴ How many compose a Lodge of Perfect Masters?

Ward∴ Nine or more.

Th∴ Hon∴ When composed of but nine, of whom does it consist?

Ward∴ The Th∴ Hon∴ *Master*, the Hon∴ *Warden*, the *Orator*, the *Treasurer* and *Secretary*, the *Sen∴* and *Jun∴ Deacons* and two *Brothers*.

Th∴ Hon∴ The Jun∴ Deacon's place in the Lodge?

Ward∴ In front, to the right, of the Warden in the West.

Th∴ Hon∴ Your duty there, Bro∴ Jun∴ Deacon?

Jun∴ D∴ To receive and execute the commands of the Hon∴ Warden, and to make known to the Lodge those who, being worthy, need, and *therefore* are entitled to its assistance.

Th∴ Hon∴ The Sen∴ Deacon's place in the Lodge?

Jun∴ D∴ In front, to the right, of the Th∴ Hon∴ Master.

Th∴ Hon∴ Your duty there, Bro∴ Sen∴ Deacon?

Sen∴ D∴ To receive and execute your commands, and to make known the claims of the widow and orphan.

Th∴ Hon∴ The Secretary's place in the Lodge.

Sen∴ D∴ In the South, Th∴ Hon∴

Th∴ Hon∴ Your duty there, Bro∴ Secretary?

Sec'y∴ To receive and record all applications for assistance and charity; to register the proceedings of the Lodge, proper to be written; and to receive all moneys and pay them over to the Treasurer.

Th∴ Hon∴ The Treasurer's place in the Lodge?

Sec∴ In the North, Th∴ Hon∴

Th∴ Hon∴ Your duty there, Bro∴ Treasurer?

Treas∴ To receive and account for the moneys and property of the Lodge; and to pay them out, upon proper authority, for purposes of charity or for the good of the Lodge.

Th∴ Hon∴ The Orator's Station in the Lodge?

Treas∴ On your right, Th∴ Hon∴

Th∴ Hon∴ Your duty there, Bro∴ Orator?

Orat∴ To deliver the Lecture of this degree to the Candidate; to celebrate the memory of our deceased Gr∴ Master; and to inculcate the practice of the virtues of beneficence, charity and liberality.

Th∴ Hon∴ The Hon∴ Warden's Station in the Lodge?

Orat∴ In the West, Th∴ Hon∴

Th∴ Hon∴ Your duty there, Bro∴ Zabud?

Ward∴ To honour the memory of all virtuous and zealous Masons; to aid you in the performance of your duties; and to exhibit in my conduct and conversation all the virtues of a Perfect Master.

Th∴ Hon∴ The duties of the Th∴ Hon∴ Master of the Lodge?

Ward∴ To preside over the work; to brighten the chain of friendship, expound the ancient traditions of the craft, dispense the charities of the Lodge, maintain its honor and respectability, and labour to advance the interests of Masonry.

Th∴ Hon∴ I acknowledge the duty. But man is weak and prone to error, and God alone can give him strength to perform his duties. Let us invoke His aid.

[All kneel, and the Th∴ Hon∴ reads the following

PRAYER.

:O Jehovah, our Lord, Grand Architect of the Universe, who hast created the Heavens, the earth, all living creatures and the Souls of Men; whose name excels all others on the earth, and Thy glory is above that of all others in the Heavens! When we consider thy Heavens, created by Thy Thought, the Stars and Worlds whose motion and harmony is ordained by Thee; and their infinity and our littleness; what is man that Thou art mindful of him, or the son of man that Thou concernest Thyself for his welfare? Thou art clothed with Honour and Majesty! Thou coverest Thyself with Light as with a garment, and stretchest out the Heavens like a curtain. Thou layest the beams of Thy Chambers on the Waters, and makest the clouds Thy Chariot, and walkest on the wings of the wind. Thou art the Lord, and there is none else. There is no God besides Thee. Thou formest the Light and createst Darkness. Thou makest Good and createst Evil. Thou the Lord dost all these things. And yet Thou dost regard and protect, as Thou didst frame and make, the smallest thing that lives; and watchest over the life and fortunes of the living but invisible atoms that float in the air, and by tens of thousands inhabit the water-drops, and toil in the sea to build up Continents. Therefore wilt Thou be kind and merciful to man, whom Thou hast made, and to whom Thou hast given a living Soul. Preside Thou over our Work! Increase harmony and disinterested friendship among us, and among all men! Increase everywhere, and spread abroad, the knowledge of the Ancient Truth! Incline us by our charities and the purity of our lives to imitate Thee at an infinite distance from Thee; and aid and strengthen us to perform all the duties which Thy Law and our obligations as men and Masons require of us! and to Thee be all Honour, Praise and Glory forever: Amen!

Th∴ Hon∴ Bro∴ Zabud, what is your age as a Mason?

Ward∴ The Square of [;], or [z]: perfection of the number of a Master Mason.

Th∴ Hon∴ What is the hour?

Ward∴ It is the first hour of the day.

Th∴ Hon∴ Since it is the first hour of the day, it is time to set the labourers at work. Give notice, therefore, that this Lodge of Perfect Masters is about to be opened and its labours resumed.

Ward.·. My brethren, the Lodge of Perfect Masters is now about to be opened, and the labours upon the Temple resumed. You will take due notice thereof, and govern yourselves accordingly.

Th.·. Hon.·. Together, my brethren.

[All give the sign of admiration. Then the warden raps [; ?]—the Th.·. Hon.·. the same; and then all the brethren the same with their hands; and the Th.·. Hon.·. says]:

Th.·. Hon.·. This Lodge of Perfect Masters is open.

RECEPTION.

The Preparation-Room is hung with black. There is a small table, covered with black, on which are a skull and cross-bones; and on one side of the Room is a coffin. On the Table are pens, ink and paper. The candidate is dressed in the clothing and jewel of a Secret Master; and received by the Master of Ceremonies; who first examines him in the words, signs and token of a Secret Master; and then asks him:

M. Cer.·. My Brother, what were the three principles inculcated at your admission to the degree of Secret Master?

[If the candidate is imperfect in the *work*, he may be instructed, in cases where he is otherwise a good mason and so known to be; but if he cannot reply to *this* question, "SECRECY, OBEDIENCE and FIDELITY," he should be immediately sent away; for if he have forgotten *that*, he is wholly unfit to advance. This rule is *inflexible; and never in any case to be disregarded*].

[When he answers properly, the M.·. of Cer.·. directs him to be seated at the Table, and handing him a printed paper, containing what is stated hereafter, says to him]:

M.·. Cer.·. Since you desire now to advance to the degree of Perfect Master, and are prepared to be in all proper respects secret, obedient and faithful, read this paper which I lay before you. Read it slowly and carefully, and reflect upon it well. Then, upon another paper, answer in writing the questions as they are numbered, and sign the obligation, and draw up and sign the instrument required:

THE PAPER.

"Neophyte, desiring to advance, be patient, thoughtful and deliberate!

"Read carefully and ponder well what follows; and answer truly and sincerely, remembering that the eye of Him who made you is upon you, and sees your thoughts and knows the Secrets of your Heart.

"If, after reading, you are not disposed to answer, you are free to retire.

"If you decide to answer, then approach the Temple with respect, with calmness, with a desire to learn, with the courage and presence of mind necessary to undergo the tests that may be required of you! Read now, and write; or depart!

"1° . . . Are you living in the commission of any crime against the laws of God or man, or any offence against those of propriety and decency, which you are conscious, if known, ought to, and would, prevent us from receiving you in this Degree?

"2° . . . Have you done any grave wrong to any person whatever, which remains unrepented of, and for which you have not made reparation to the utmost of your power?

"3° . . . You believe in a First Great Cause, Author and Preserver of the universe and of yourself. Therefore you have duties to perform towards Him. What are those duties?

"4° . . . All men, made by one God, are brothers. What are your duties towards your fellow-men?

"5° . . . Man, composed of a body and a soul, has duties of two kinds to perform towards himself. What are those duties?

" PERSONAL OBLIGATION.

" Conscious that the Eye of the Grand Architect of the Universe is upon me. I do promise to Him and to those who shall receive me here, that I will strenuously endeavor to perform the duties which I have now acknowledged do devolve upon me; and be governed by their dictates in the world and in the Lodge, as a good and faithful Mason; actuated by benevolence and fraternal feeling, and complying with all my obligations as a Mason, heretofore, now, or hereafter assumed; and I will never reveal or make known the mode of my admission into this degree, even if I should retire without completely receiving it. So help me God!

Signed at

The   day of   A. D. 18

" Write now your last will and testament; as if in five minutes you were about to engage in battle, leading the forlorn hope to storm a breach, with the almost absolute certainty of falling in the assault."

[When the Candidate has concluded, the M∴ Cer∴ takes the paper containing his responses and what he has written, and says to him]:

M∴ C∴ Remain here a time in patience, until what you have answered and written is submitted to the Th∴ Hon∴ and the Brethren, and their judgment had thereon; when I will return to you.

[The M∴ Cer∴ then enters the Lodge, leaving him alone. He hands the paper to the Master, who reads it to the Brethren. If he regards the answers as unsatisfactory, he so declares, and directs the Candidate shall be dismissed. If he considers them sufficient, he puts the question to the Brethren, thus]:

Th∴ Hon∴ Brethren, you have heard the responses, the obligation and the last will and testament of the candidate. Are you satisfied with them, and do you consent that he shall be admitted? Those of you who are so, will give the affirmative sign.

[It is given by raising the right arm perpendicularly above the head.]

Th∴ Hon∴ Those who are not satisfied or who do not consent, will give the negative sign.

[It is given by extending the right arm in front, hand open and palm outwards; as if repelling a person.]

Th∴ Hon∴ Bro∴ Zabud, do any answer in the negative?

[If there is any negative, the Candidate is dismissed. If none, the Th∴ Hon∴ says]:

Th∴ Hon∴ Bro∴ M∴ of Cer∴, the Brethren consent that the Candidate shall be admitted. The Secretary will file his responses, his obligation and his testament; and being properly prepared, he may be allowed to enter.

[The Master of Ceremonies goes out, and says to the Candidate]:

M∴ Cer∴ The Th∴ Honorable Master, the Warden and the Brethren are satisfied with your responses, your obligation and your testament. They are deposited in the Archives of the Lodge, for a testimony during all time. Our Lodge is now sorrowful and in mourning; for it is the anniversary of the final burial of our Gr∴ Master Hiram Abi; and while we mourn for him, we mourn also for that darkness and death of pain and evil and sorrow, into which man hath fallen, and of which his death is to us a most expressive symbol. Reflect upon their sad condition, and let feelings of pity and commiseration for sinful, suffering humanity fill your heart; and in that spirit prepare to receive this degree.

.[The M∴ of Cer∴ then divests him of his Masonic clothing, and puts on him a robe of white linen, and slippers upon his feet, and a green silk cord around his neck, and blindfolds him. Then, with the end of the cord in one hand and a drawn sword in the other, he leads him into the Lodge, and makes the Circuit thereof five times, while the Master and Warden read alternately as follows]:

M∴ . . . . 1st Circ∴ . . If ye will indeed obey my voice, and keep my covenant, then ye shall be a peculiar treasure unto me above all people: for all the Earth is mine: and ye shall be unto me a Kingdom of Priests, and an Holy Nation.

W∴ . . . 2d Circ∴ . . Ye shall do my judgments, and keep my ordinances, to walk therein: I am the

3

Lord your God: ye shall therefore keep my statutes and my judgments, which if a man do, he shall live in them.

Sanctify yourselves, and be holy, that ye may be my people; for I am holy.

M∴ 3d Circ∴ If ye walk in my statutes, and keep my commandments, and do them, then I will give you rain in due season, and the land shall yield her increase, and the trees of the field shall yield their fruit; and your threshing shall reach unto the vintage, and your vintage shall reach unto the sowing time, and ye shall eat your bread to the full, and dwell on your land safely: and I will give peace in the land, and ye shall lie down, and none shall make you afraid: and I will rid evil beasts out of the land; neither shall the sword go through your land: I will have respect unto you, and make you fruitful, and multiply you, and establish my covenant with you; and ye shall eat old store, and give away the old, because of the abundance of the new: and I will set my tabernacle among you, and be not angry with you, and will be with you and be your God, and ye shall be my people.

W∴ 4th Circ∴ Thou shalt love the Lord thy God with all thine heart, and with all thy soul, and with all thy might: and these words which I command thee this day shall be in thy heart; and thou shalt teach them diligently unto thy children, and shalt talk of them when thou sittest in thy house, and when thou walkest by the way, and when thou liest down, and when thou risest up: and thou shalt bind them for a sign upon thy hand, and they shall be as frontlets between thine eyes: and thou shalt write them upon the posts of thy house, and on thy gates.

Thou shalt fear the Lord thy God, and shalt serve him, and swear by his name.

M∴ 5th Circ∴ As a man chasteneth his Son, the Lord thy God chasteneth thee. Ye shall diligently keep his commandments, his testimonies and his statutes. Beware lest ye forget or tempt Him; but do that which is right and good in His sight, and fear him, and observe all his commandments.

[At the end of the 5th Circuit, the M∴ of Cer∴ and Candidate halt in front of the Warden, who asks]:

Ward∴ Whom bring you here with you, Bro∴ M∴ of Cer∴, in darkness and in bondage?

M∴ Cer∴ Bro∴ A . . . B . . . . a worthy Secret Master, who has thus far trodden the path that leads to light, and desires to press further onward, by being admitted to the degree of Perfect Master.

Ward∴ Is this he whose answers, obligation and testament have lately been deposited in our archives?

M∴ Cer∴ It is.

Ward∴ Does he know the lessons that are inculcated in this degree?

M∴ C∴ He does not; but having learned secrecy, obedience and fidelity, as a Secret Master, he has come here to learn the duties that we practise.

Ward∴ Pass on, then, to the East, and let him make known his desire to the Th∴ Hon∴ Master.

[They pass on to the East, and halt in front of the Th∴ Hon∴, who asks the same questions, receives the same answers, and says]:

Th∴ Hon∴ Is not this he, who, to become a Master Mason, represented our deceased Grand Master Hiram Abi?

M∴ Cer∴ It is.

Th∴ Hon∴ To day we keep in sorrow the anniversary of his funeral and final burial. Through the frowning gates of death lies the way to eternal life. Let him again assume the character of our Grand Master; and return to the state from which he arose to be a Master.

[The candidate is again conducted to the preparation room and placed in the coffin; which is then lifted up and carried into the lodge, and set in the middle of the room; when the following ceremonies take place]:

FUNERAL CEREMONIES.

The Th∴ Hon∴ gives one loud rap with his gavel, which is answered by the Warden; and says:

Th∴ Hon∴ All the world is a storm; and men rise up in their several generations, like bubbles descending from God and the dew of heaven, from a tear and a drop of rain, from Nature and Providence; and some of these instantly sink into the deluge of their first parent, and are hidden in a sheet of water, having had no other business in the world, but to be born, that they might be able to die; others float up and down two or three turns, and suddenly disappear, and give their place to others: and they that live longest upon the face of the waters, are in perpetual motion, restless and uneasy, and being crushed with the great drop of a cloud sink into the flat level of dead humanity.

All the succession of time, all the changes in nature, all the varieties of Light and Darkness, the thousand thousands of accidents in the world, and every contingency to every man, and to every creature, doth preach our funeral sermon; and calls us to look and see how Time ever digs the grave where we must lay our sins or our sorrows; and our mortal bodies moulder away and again become in atoms a portion of the great material world. Every revolution which the earth makes around the sun, divides between life and death; and death possesses both those portions by the next morrow; and we are dead to all those months which we have already lived, and we shall never live them over again; and still God makes little periods of our age.

Every day's necessity calls for a reparation of that portion which death fed on all night, when we lay in his lap, and slept in his outer chambers. While we think a thought, we die; and the clock strikes, and reckons on our portion of eternity. We form our words with the breath of our nostrils: we have the less to live upon for every word we speak.

Death reigns in all the portions of our time. The autumn with its fruits provides disorders for us; and the winter's cold turns them into sharp diseases; and the spring brings flowers to strew our hearse; and the summer gives green turf and brambles to bind upon our graves. Fevers and surfeit, cold and agues, are the four quarters of the year, and all minister to death; and you can go no whither, but you tread upon a dead man's bones.

Death meets us everywhere; and is procured by every instrument, and in all chances, and enters in at many doors; by violence and secret influence, by a heat or a cold, by the sharp tooth of an unregarded serpent, the shying of an unruly horse at the sudden flutter of a garment; by stumbling at a loose stone lying in the way, by the scratch of an envenomed lancet, by a little spark of fire upon a swift boat that of a dark night descends a deep broad river; all are the instruments of death, and overtake us with a sudden fate. And all this is the law and constitution of Nature, the unalterable event of Providence, and the decree of Heaven. The chains that confine us to this condition are strong as Destiny, and immutable as the eternal laws of God.

Death is the portion of every man and every woman; the heritage of worms and serpents, of rottenness and cold dishonour. This day is mine and yours; but we know not what shall be on the morrow; and every morning creeps out of a dark cloud, leaving behind it an ignorance and silence deep as midnight, and undiscerned as are the phantasms that make an infant smile; so that we cannot discern what comes hereafter.

Even our joys are troublesome; and the fear of losing them takes away the present pleasure. They are brief and fleeting as the remembrance of a traveller that stayeth but a night. They arise from vanity, and they dwell upon ice, and they converse with the wind, and they have the wings of a bird, and are serious but as the resolutions of a child, and end in vanity and forgetfulness. Man is ever restless and uneasy. He dwells upon the waters, and leans upon thorns, and lays his head upon a sharp stone.

The sadnesses of life help to sweeten the bitter cup of death. For let our life be never so long, if our strength were great as that of the Titans, and our sinews strong as the cordage at the foot of an oak, yet still the period shall be, that all this shall end in death, and the people shall talk of us awhile, good or bad, according as we deserve or as they please; and once it shall come to pass, that concerning every one of us, it shall be told in the neighbourhood that we are dead.

Such, my Brethren, are the uncertainty and vanity of Life. And if we could, from one of the battlements of Heaven espy how many men and women at this moment lie fainting and dying for want of bread; how many young men are hewn down by the sword of war; how many poor orphans are now weeping over the graves of their fathers, by whose life they were enabled to eat; if we could but hear how many mariners and passengers are at this moment in a storm, and shriek out because their keel dashes against a rock, or their foundering vessel far out at sea shudders as she sinks down into the ocean; how many people there are that weep with want, or are mad with oppression, or are desperate by too quick a sense of a constant infelicity; we should rejoice to be beyond the noise and participation of so many evils.

Let us therefore, my Brethren, imitate the example of our illustrious Gr∴ Master Hiram Abi ; and by a wise and virtuous life make the best preparation for a peaceable death. Let us remember that God gives us our time, not as Nature gives us rivers, but drop by drop, minute after minute, so that we never can have two minutes together; but He takes away one, when he gives us another. This should teach us to value our time ; since God so values it, and by this so small distribution of it, tells us it is the most precious thing we have. He that would die well and happily, must lead an upright life, under the conduct of prudence and observation; a life of warfare and sober counsels, labour and watchfulness. No one of us wants cause of tears and a daily sorrow. Let each of us consider in what he fails, and acknowledge his misery ; let us confess our sins and chastise them ; let us bear our crosses patiently and our persecutions nobly, and our repentances willingly and constantly ; let us pity the evils of all the world, and bear our share of the calamities of our brother; let us ever keep our house in order that we may be fit to die ; remembering that our errors and our offences are numerous and increasing, like the families of the northern people, or the genealogies of the first Patriarchs of the World ; and that the computations of a man's life are busy as the tables of sines and tangents, and intricate as the accounts of eastern merchants. Let us therefore keep constant account of our actions, and thus restrain the inundation of evils ; and as every night we must make our bed the memorial of our grave, so let our evening thoughts be an image of the judgment of Him who made us. Let us not covet many things greedily, nor snatch at high things ambitiously, nor despise our neighbour proudly, nor bear our crosses peevishly, nor our prosperity impotently and passionately, nor be prodigal of our precious time, nor tenacious and retentive of evil purposes.

My Brethren, we have been taught, as Masons, that we should implore the assistance of God, in every great and important undertaking. Let us ask His aid to enable us to live well and to die in peace, that our memories may be respected among men and Masons.

[The Brethren all kneel ; and the Th∴ Hon∴ recites the following]

PRAYER.

O Almighty and Eternal God, and Great Architect of the Universe ! there is no number of Thy days or of Thy mercies : Thou hast sent us into this world to serve Thee, and to live according to Thy laws ; but we wander far from Thee into the paths of error, and have planted thorns and sorrows round about our dwellings. Our life is but a span in length, and yet very tedious, because of the calamities that enclose us on every side ; the days of our pilgrimage are few and evil, our bodies frail, our passions violent and distempered, our understandings weak and our wills perverse. Look Thou upon us, oh our Father, in mercy and pity ! let not our weaknesses make us sin against Thee, nor our fear cause us to betray our duty, nor the calamities of this world vex us into impatience ! Let not temptation be too strong for us, nor our feet stray too far from the right path ! We adore Thy Majesty, and submit to Thy Prudence, and revere Thy justice, and trust like little children to Thine Infinite Mercies, when Thou dost please to deliver one among us out of the miseries of this world. Thy counsels are secret and Thy wisdom Infinite, and we do not presume to murmur at Thy Dispensations, nor repine at the sufferings with which Thou dost afflict us for our good. Give us patience, oh our Father, and resolution to live well, and firmness to resist evil, and faith and confidence in Thee and in Thy Wisdom and Benevolence ; and enable us so to live, that when we come to die, we may lie down in the grave like one who composes himself to sleep, and that we may be worthy to be afterwards remembered in the memories of men ! Amen !

All : .. So mote it be !

[Then the organ plays, and the Brothers sing the following lines] :

> Oh, weep not, mourn not o'er this bier !
> On such death none should look with fear ;
> He died as dies a brave, true man ;
> And with his death, true life began.

Coffin and grave we deck with care;
His body reverently we bear;
It is not dead; but rests in God;
Softly to sleep beneath the sod.

God breathed into this house of clay
The Spirit that hath passed away:
He gave the true courageous mind,
The noble heart, strong, calm and kind.

Our brave Grand Master, who preferred
Death to the utterance of a word;
Shall to the Mason ever be
The type of true fidelity.

[An alarm is now given at the door; and the Jun.·. Deacon says: "Th.·. Hon.·., the M.·. Ill.·. Kings, Solomon and Hiram, our Grand Masters, approach this sacred place, to unite with us in performing the last honours to our deceased Gr.·. Master, their lamented Brother."]

Th.·. Hon.·. [Rapping]: Arise, my Brethren, and receive our M.·. Ill.·. G.·. Masters in silence.

[Two brothers come forward, representing King Solomon and Hiram King of Tyre; and the former says]:

K.·. Sol.·. My Brethren, when we have received the last breath of our friend, and closed his eyes and composed his body for the grave, then seasonable is the counsel of the Son of Sirach: "Weep bitterly and make great moan, and use lamentation, as he is worthy; and that a day or two; lest thou be evil spoken of; and then comfort thyself for thy heaviness. But take no grief to heart, for there is no turning again; thou shalt not do him good, but hurt thyself." Solemn and appointed mournings are good expressions of our affection for the departed soul, and of his worth and our value of him; and it hath its praise in nature, and in manners, and in public customs. Something is to be given to custom, something to fame, to nature and to civilities, and to the honour of our deceased friends; for that man is esteemed to die miserable, for whom no friend or relative sheds a tear, or pays a solemn sigh.

When thou hast wept a while; compose the body to burial: which that it be done gravely, decently and charitably, we have the example of all nations to engage us, and of all ages of the world to warrant; so that it is against honesty, and public fame and reputation, not to do this office.

Place therefore on the coffin of our brother the square, the compass, the gavel and the rule; emblems of the virtues and authority of our Grand Master, Hiram Abi; and let him who wears the jewels of that distinguished and murdered Mason, remember henceforward and forever, that he can commit no graver offence against the laws of Masonry and honour, than to degrade them by any act which that illustrious martyr would scorn or be ashamed to do.

[The square, compass, gavel and rule are laid upon the coffin by four different brothers, each advancing separately and depositing one of them.]

K.·. Sol.·. Place now upon the coffin the apron, collar and jewel of a Perfect Master; and let him who shall hereafter wear them, be careful that he wear them worthily; lest Masonic justice pluck them from him if he disgrace them by sloth or baseness; as the spurs were in former times hacked from the heels of him who proved false gentleman and disloyal knight.

It is a great act of piety, and honorable, to inter our friends and relatives according to the proportions of their condition; and so to give evidence that we appreciate and desire to imitate their virtues. For so Jacob was buried with great solemnity, and Joseph's bones were carried unto Canaan, after they had been embalmed and kept four hundred years. Those that die should not be commended at a price, nor the measure of their legacy be the degree of their virtue; lest to want a monument should best preserve the memories of the great and good, while the succeeding ages should by their instances remember the changes of the world, and the dishonours of death, and the equality of the dead. The reward of the greatest virtue should be preserved like laurels and coronets, to incite and encourage to the noblest things.

Let us also right the causes of the dead, and assert their honour. For certainly it is the noblest thing in the world, to do an act of kindness to him whom we shall never see, and yet who hath deserved it of us ; and unless we do so, our charity is mercenary, and our friendships are mere merchandise ; but what we do to the dead, or to the living for their sakes, is gratitude, and virtue for virtue's sake, and the noblest portion of humanity. Let us do our duty to the dead, lest peradventure they should perceive our neglect, and be witnesses of our transient affections and forgetfulness.

It remains, my Brethren, that we who are alive should so live, and so perform our duties, and play our parts upon this stage of life, that we neither be surprised by death, nor leave our duties unperformed, nor our sins uncancelled, nor our persons unreconciled, nor God unappeased.

K∴ Sol∴ Bro∴ M∴ of Ceremonies, distribute to our brethren the mysterious branches, symbols of immortality.

[The M∴ of Cer∴ gives to each brother a branch of Acacia. Then K∴ Sol∴ says] :

K∴ Sol∴ Brothers Adonhiram and Zabud, invite the brethren in the North, South, East and West to assemble and aid us in depositing the body of our Gr∴ Master Hiram Abi in the tomb; and in performing our pious pilgrimage around it.

Ward∴ Brethren in the North, South, East and West, it is the desire of the Wise and Powerful King Solomon our Gr∴ Master that you assemble together and aid him and our Gr∴ Master the King of Tyre in depositing the body of our Gr∴ Master Hiram Abi in the Tomb, and performing our pious pilgrimage around it.

Th∴ Hon∴ Brethren in the East, it is the desire, &c.

[The Th∴ Hon∴ raps thrice ; and the Brethren all assemble and form in procession. The coffin is taken up, and borne three times around the Lodge, while the organ plays, and the following hymn is sung:

> The buried grain of wheat must die,
> Withered and worthless long must lie,
> Before its soft shoot seeks the air,
> Its new stalk the new grain can bear.
>
> Even so this body made of dust
> To earth we once again entrust;
> And painless it shall slumber here,
> Until the appointed Time appear.

[The coffin is then deposited in the monument, and the following verse is sung:

> Now it is hidden from our eyes,
> Till God shall bid it wake and rise;
> Who ne'er the creature will forget,
> On whom his image He hath set.

[Then the Th∴ Hon∴ gives three raps, and K∴ Sol∴ says:

K∴ Sol∴ Thus Masonry honours the memory of the virtuous and good. It mourns their loss, but consoles itself with the reflection that the Souls of the Great Dead are immortal, and that their influences live beyond the grave. Death is dreadful to the man whose all is extinguished with his life; but not to him whose glory and whose influences can never die.

These Honours, and the general regard of Posterity, and to follow their illustrious and excellent examples, are the fit rewards of those who have deserved well of their Order, their Country and the World. Not to gratify or please the dead, whose souls are lifted far above such honours, but to do that which it is eminently fit and becoming for ourselves to do, we perform these ceremonies.

A desire for our name to be perpetuated to after times, by monuments erected by public gratitude, in memory of noble deeds, is a worthy spring of action everywhere, and most of all in a Republic. Is an inducement to great deeds: and a monument to the memory of a great and good man is an Orator in bronze or marble, teaching glorious lessons to after generations; the silent but impressive evidence of his immortal influence; and itself exercising an influence not often inconsiderable upon men's actions, their country's welfare and the world's destiny. The record of noble actions and heroic devotion is more fitly written on the enduring marble or the pyramid of granite, than on the paper pages of a destructible book. The marble or the granite is itself a book, like those on which the Hierophants of Egypt cut in hieroglyphics the history of the Ancient Ages. Such monuments regard not alone those to whom they are erected. How noble an office do they not fulfil in making known to future ages that a People or Fraternity had loftiness of soul enough to appreciate, honour and glorify great deeds! They are the best evidence of the virtues of those who erect them; silent exhorters to lofty actions, perpetual Teachers of the finest lessons of virtue and patriotism!

It does not become any one to set little value on the general opinion of his own time, or on the final judgment of posterity. That the desire for fame and reputation is universal and instinctive, proves that it is laudable and proper; for it is a Force and Power: one of those Laws of God which He has been pleased to enact, as part of the great laws of Harmony and Attraction by which He rules the Universe.

But as that judgment and that opinion are not infallible; as the World and Posterity may condemn the good, the wise, the disinterested, and decree honours to the bad, the ignorant and the base; to gain that judgment of approval must not be the only or even the chief motive of a Mason's action. For Duty is the great Law that governs him; to be obeyed, no matter with what result; and his conscience the true judge, from whose judgment there is no appeal except to God.

If you would fain direct your regards on high, and aspire to an eternal happiness hereafter, you neither will regard the rumours of the vulgar, nor will you rest your hopes and your interest on human rewards. Virtue herself must attract you by her own charms to true glory. What others may say of you, as they will talk, so let themselves consider. For all that is so said is confined to the narrow limits of these regions that you see. None respecting any man was ever eternal. It is extinguished by the death of the individual, or perishes altogether in the oblivion of posterity.

The swan that wings her way to the lofty heights of heaven, inquires not whether the shadow of her wings falls on the sordid earth below. The monuments which we erect in human memories, are transient as the delicate tracery of frost-work woven from leaf to leaf, of a morning in the spring. Time, like a river, carries them all away with a rapid course; they swim above the stream for a while, but are quickly swallowed up and seen no more. The marbles that men rear to perpetuate their names, are consumed by time and silently moulder away, and proclaim their own mortality while they testify to ours. But the enjoyments of the immortal soul in that future existence promised us by God will be superior to decay, and endless in duration. They will be ever full, fresh and entire, like the stars and orbs above, which shine with the same undiminished lustre, and move with the same unwearied motion with which they did from the first date of their creation. Nay, the joys of heaven will abide when these lights of heaven will be put out, and when sun and moon and nature itself shall be discharged their stations, and be employed by Providence no more. The good Mason shall then appear in his full glory; and fixed in the Divine presence, enjoy one perpetual and everlasting day; a day commensurate to the unlimited Eternity of God Himself, the Great Sun of Righteousness, who is always rising, and never sets.

The world is filled with the voices of the dead. They speak, not from the public records of the great world, only, but from the private history of our own experience. They speak to us in a thousand remembrances, incidents, events, associations. They speak to us, not only from the silent graves, but from the throng of life. They are invisible, and yet life is filled with their presence. They are with us by the silent fireside, and in the secluded chamber; in the paths of society, and in the crowded assemblies of men. They speak to us from the lonely wayside; and from the venerable walls that echo to the steps of a multitude and to the voice of prayer. Go where we will, the dead are with us always. We live and converse with those who once lived and conversed with us. Their well-remembered voices mingle with the whispering breeze, with the sound of the falling leaf, with the songs and melodies of spring. The earth is filled with their shadowy train. Everywhere are leaves from the long scroll of time, borne on the breath of ages, invested with the attributes of universality and eternity ; a heritage, from family to family, among all the dwellings of the world.

The world is filled with the *labours* and *works* of the dead. Almost all its literature, the discoveries of science, the glories of art, the ever-enduring temples, the dwelling-places of generations, the comforts and improvements of life, the languages, the maxims, the opinions of the living, the very frame-work of Society, the institutions of nations, the fabrics of Empires,—all are the works of the dead ; and by them, they who are dead yet speak. The small Province of Life is little, compared with the vast Empire of Death. It is a moment in the centre of Eternity ; a point in the centre of Immensity ; a breath of existence amidst the ages and regions of the Everlasting. The dead live in our thoughts, in our blessings, and in our very life.

The world would be but an ordinary and indifferent place, if it contained nothing but the workmanship, the handicraft, the devices of living men. We love to see dwellings which speak to us of other things than earthly convenience or fleeting pleasure ; which speak to us the holy recollections of lives that were passed in them, and have passed away from them. We love to see temples, in which successive generations of men have prayed ; ruins, on whose mighty walls is inscribed the touching story of joy and sorrow, love, heroism, patience, which lived there, and there breathed their first hope and their last sigh, ages ago ; scenes which offer more to our eye than fair landscape and living stream ; telling us of inspired genius, glorious fortitude, martyred faith, that studied there, suffered there, died there. We would fain behold the Earth as more than mere soil and scenery : we would behold it, as written over with histories ; as a sublime page, on which are inscribed the lives of men and empires.

And now, my Brethren, in presence of this emblem of our sorrow and our regret ; under these funereal arches, dumb witnesses of our religious homage ; before these symbols of the nothingness of our own nature and the immensity of God, let every selfish and hateful thought be banished. Take now with me, my brethren, the oath of forgetfulness of all wrongs and injuries that may have been inflicted upon us. May Peace and Concord dwell evermore among us! May we and all Masons be no more divided by vain and empty disputes and quarrels! May we henceforward be inspired by an ardent devotion to the interests of our country, of Masonry and of mankind! And may we ever recollect, and be at all times governed and guided by, that precept which is the corner stone of Masonry, *do unto others whatever you would wish that they should do unto you.* My Brethren, join me in the solemn vow !

All. . . . WE DO SO VOW AND PROMISE.

K.·. Sol.·. Heaven hears and the angels record the vow. And now, my brethren, in token of our belief in the soul's immortality, and of that resurrection to a new life for which we all confidently hope, you will raise our brother from that coffin which represents the earthly prison that confines the soul, and all the impediments of sin and error that environ it here below ; and place him at the Holy Altar, that he may be there made a Perfect Master.

[The Master of Ceremonies, assisted by a sufficient number of brethren, raises the Candidate from the coffin, uncovers his eyes, and relieves him from the cord around his neck. He is then led to the Altar ; and directed to kneel on both knees, and place both hands on the Holy Bible, interlacing the fingers. An arch of steel is formed over him, and the points of three swords, held by three brothers, converging to one point are pressed against his bosom. In this position he repeats the following obligation] :

OBLIGATION.

I, A . . . . B . . . . in the presence of the Gr.·. Architect of the Universe and of this Right Worshipful Lodge of Perfect Masters, do hereby and hereon most solemnly and sincerely promise and vow, that I will never reveal or make known, intentionally or by indiscretion, any of the secrets of this degree of Perfect Master, to any person in the known world, except to one who may be legally authorized to receive, when I am legally authorized to communicate, them.

I furthermore promise and swear that I will at all times hereafter remember, and endeavour to practice, that which befits the character of a Perfect Master; and especially that I will be honest in my contracts, sincere in affirming, frank and straight-forward in bargaining, and faithful in performing, with all men; that I will pretend not what is false, nor cover what is true, nor lie either in a little thing or a great, neither in the substance nor in the circumstance, nor in word nor deed; but the measure of my affirmation or denial shall be the understanding of the person with whom I contract; and that I will religiously keep all my promises and covenants, though made to my disadvantage, and though afterward I perceive I might have done better; nor shall anything make me break my promise, unless to perform it be unlawful or impossible; or unless it have been unlawfully, or by force or fraud, obtained from me.

All of which I do most solemnly and sincerely promise and vow, binding myself under the penalty of being despised by all mankind while living, and after my death; and buried in an undistinguished grave, with none to shed a tear over me or to lament that I am dead; in case I wilfully violate this my solemn obligation of a Perfect Master.

[The Th.·. Hon.·. then raises the candidate, and says to him, relieving him of the white robe]:

Th.·. Hon.·. As you have been already relieved of the cord which was around your neck, symbol of the enthralment of vice and indulgence, so now I relieve you of this robe, symbol of your novitiate; which having passed, I do, by the authority in me vested, raise you to the rank and dignity of Perfect Master: and I do now invest you with this collar, apron and jewel; which, as they lay upon your heart when you represented our excellent and illustrious Gr.·. Master in his coffin, you will now and forever wear as the representative of him living; making him ever your model, and deeming yourself bound to strive to equal his virtues, as you wear his clothing and his jewel; that *your* memory may deserve such honours as have to day been rendered unto his.

Receive now the signs, token and words of a Perfect Master.

1st Sign . . . Of Admiration . . . Raise both ⊙‡♋♎ and ☾♄☾♎ towards Heaven; and then let the former fall crosswise on the ♏☾††♄ ; and drop the latter on the ground.

2d Sign . . . Of Recognition . . . Each advances his ‡♉☿ ☿♈, until the points meet, and the right ¶♒☾☾♎ come together. Then each places his ‡ & ⊙♒□ upon his &☾⊙‡♈.

Token: . . . Take each other with the ♋⊙♎♈☾‡♎ grip; and at the same time each place the †&⊙♒♊ behind the ‡♎&☿♑†♊☾‡ of the other, and press it ! times, with the ! first fingers closed; saying, by syllables alternately, ♋⊙.·.&⊙.·.♏☾♒.·.♀.·. Then clench the ! fingers of the two ‡ hands together, closing them, not interlaced, raising the ♈&♑♋♏♎ and putting them together at the points, so as to form a triangle.

Pass-Word: . . . . . ⊙♐⊙♐♀⊙.·.
Sacred Word: . . . ♁☾✱⊙.·.

The Candidate is then seated; and receives the following History and Lecture:

HISTORY AND LECTURE.

King Solomon, having learned that the body of Hiram had been found, and deposited in the Western part of the unfinished Temple, and being greatly rejoiced that the precious remains of his Brother the Artificer were found, immediately ordered Adonhiram, who was afterwards appointed Chief Architect and Inspector of the works in his stead, to prepare a funeral that should correspond with the eminent virtues of the deceased. And that the recollection of his sad fate might be more vividly remembered, and the general indignation against his murderers not be diminished, he directed that the stains made by his blood upon the floor of the Temple should not be washed out, until they should be apprehended and punished for their awful crime.

All the workmen upon the Temple, on Mount Libanus and in the quarries, were ordered to be present at the funeral ceremonies. In nine days Adonhiram completed a superb mausoleum to the memory of the Gr∴ Master, destined to receive his body; a tomb of white marble, surmounted by a triangular obelisk of the black marble of Egypt, upon which was a great urn of the same, pierced with a sword. On the urn was carved a branch of acacia, and on its base, in Hebrew, the letters מ∴ פ∴ [M. P∴] In this urn was to be deposited his heart, which had for that purpose been embalmed.

This monument was erected in the Western part of the Temple, rather to the North; marking the spot where the murderers first deposited the body, after they committed the great crime. It being determined not to perform the funeral ceremonies until the monument was completed, the body was embalmed, placed in a coffin, and kept in an apartment of the Temple where it had been the habit of the Gr∴ Masters to hold their Lodge-Meetings, and communicate the Mysteries of Masonry.

Three days after the monument was completed, the remains of the murdered Gr∴ Master were deposited there by King Solomon, assisted by Adonhiram the Son of Abda, Zabud the Son of Nathan, who was over his Household, and all his Nobles, Princes and Captains, and all the workmen, with Hiram, King of Tyre, who had come from his own country to be present at the imposing ceremony.

Annually afterwards, the anniversary of this funeral was religiously observed, and on each such occasion some Brother represented the deceased, and was thereafter called a Perfect Master; because he was thenceforward considered to be, in his character and conduct, a representative of Hiram Abi, whose place he had occupied in the coffin, and worn his clothing and his jewel.

And, still further to perpetuate the memory of the murder of Hiram Abi, a representation of his murder was thereafter substituted in the Master Mason's degree, in place of the ceremonies brought by Moses from Egypt, and of those practised in Phœnicia; all of them emblems of one great truth and leading idea, common to all the ancient nations, and hereafter to be at the proper time unfolded to you.

Our Grand Master Hiram Abi, my Brother, was an industrious and an honest man. What he was employed to do, he did diligently, and he did it well and faithfully. Industry and honesty are the virtues peculiarly inculcated in this degree. They are common and homely virtues, but not for that beneath our notice. The bees love not drones, nor Masons the idle and the lazy; for those who are so, are liable to become dissipated and vicious: and perfect honesty, which ought to be the common qualification of all, is more rarely met with than diamonds. To do earnestly and steadily, and to do faithfully and honestly, that which we have to do:—perhaps this wants but little, when looked at from every point of view, of including the whole body of the moral law: and these virtues belong to the character of a Perfect Master, even in their homeliest and commonest applications.

Idleness is the burial of a living man. For an idle person is so useless to any purposes of God and man, that he is like one that is dead, unconcerned in the changes and necessities of the world; and he only lives to spend his time, and eat the fruits of the earth. Like a vermin or a wolf, when his time comes, he dies and perishes, and in the mean time does no good. He neither ploughs nor carries burthens: all that he does is either unprofitable or mischievous.

It is a vast work that any man may do, if he never be idle: and it is a huge way that a man may go in virtue, if he never goes out of his way by a vicious habit or a great crime: and he that perpetually reads good books, if his parts be answerable, will have a huge stock of knowledge.

St. Ambrose, and from his example, St. Augustine, divided every day into eight *tertias* of employment: eight hours they spent in the necessities of nature and recreation; eight hours in charity, and doing assistance to others, despatching their businesses, reconciling their enmities, reproving their vices, correcting their errors, instructing their ignorances, transacting the affairs of their dioceses; and the other eight hours they spent in study and prayer.

We think, at the age of twenty, that life is much too long for that which we have to learn and do, and that there is an almost fabulous distance between our age and that of our Grandfather. But when at the age of sixty, if we are fortunate enough to reach it, or unfortunate enough, as the case may be, and as we have spent or wasted our time, we halt and look back along the way we have come, and cast up and try to balance our accounts with Time, we find that we have made Life much too short, and thrown away a huge portion of it. We then in our mind deduct from the sum total of our years the hours that we unnecessarily have spent in sleep; the waking hours each day, during which the surface of the mind's sluggish pool has not been stirred and ruffled by a single thought; (for the soul lives without thought far more than we suspect); the days that we have got rid of, to attain some real or fancied object that lay beyond, in the way between which and us stood irksomely the intervening days; and the hours mis-spent, and worse than wasted, in folly and dissipation; and we acknowledge with a sigh that we could have learned and done, in half a score of years well-spent, more than we *have* done in our forty years of manhood.

To learn, and to do! This is the soul's work here below. The soul grows as truly as an oak grows. As the tree takes the air, and the elements and particles that float in the air, the dew and rain, and the food that in the earth lies piled around its roots; and by its potent chemistry transmutes them into sap and fibre, into wood and leaf, and flower and fruit, and colouring and perfume; so the soul drinks in knowledge, and by a divine alchemy changes what it learns into its own substance, and developes itself from within outwardly, and grows, with an inherent Force and Power like that which lies hid in the grain of wheat.

The soul hath its senses, like the body, that may be cultivated, enlarged, refined, as itself grows in stature and proportion: and he who cannot appreciate a beautiful painting, or a noble poem, or a sweet harmony, or a heroic thought or a disinterested action, only lives upon the level of common-place, and need not pride himself upon that inferiority of the soul's senses, which is the inferiority and imperfect development of the soul itself.

To sleep little, and to study much; to say little, and to hear and think much; to learn, that we may be able to do; and then to do earnestly and vigorously, whatever duty, and the good of our fellows, our country and mankind require,—these are the duties of every one who would imitate our deceased Grand Master.

The duty of a Mason as an honest man is plain and easy. It requires of us honesty in contracts, sincerity in affirming, simplicity in bargaining, and faithfulness in performing. Lie not at all, neither in a little thing nor in a great, neither in the substance nor in the circumstance, neither in word nor deed: that is, pretend not what is false; cover not what is true; and let the measure of your affirmation or denial be the understanding of your contractor; for he that deceives the buyer or the seller by speaking what is true, in a sense not intended or understood by the other, is a liar and a thief. A Perfect Master must avoid that which deceives, equally with that which is false.

Let your prices be according to that measure of good and evil, which is established in the fame and common accounts of the wisest and most merciful men, skilled in that manufacture or commodity; and the gain such, which, without scandal, is allowed to persons in all the same circumstances.

In intercourse with others, do not do all which thou mayest lawfully do; but keep something within thy power; and, because there is a latitude of gain in buying and selling, take not thou the utmost penny that is lawful, or which thou thinkest so; for although it be lawful, yet it is not safe; and he that gains all that he can gain lawfully, this year, will possibly be tempted, next year, to gain something unlawfully.

Let no man, for his own poverty, become more oppressing and cruel in his bargain; but quietly, modestly, diligently and patiently recommend his estate to God, and follow its interest, and leave the success to Him.

Detain not the wages of the hireling; for every degree of detention of it beyond the time, is injustice and uncharitableness, and grinds his face till tears and blood come out: but pay him exactly according to covenant, or according to his needs.

Religiously keep all promises and covenants, though made to your disadvantage, though afterward you perceive you might have done better; and let not any precedent act of yours be altered by any after-accident. Let nothing make you break your promise, unless it be unlawful or impossible; that is, either out of your nature or out of your civil power, yourself being under the power of another; or that it be intolerably inconvenient to yourself, and of no advantage to another; or that you have leave expressed or reasonably presumed.

Let no man take wages or fees for a work, that he cannot do, or cannot with probability undertake; or in some sense profitably, and with ease, or with advantage manage. Let no man appropriate to his own use, what God, by a Special Mercy, or the Republic, hath made common; for that is against both Justice and Charity.

That any man should be the worse for us, and our direct act, and by our intention, is against the rule of equity, of justice and of charity. We then do not that to others, which we would have done to ourselves; for we grow richer upon the ruins of their fortune.

It is not honest to receive any thing from another without returning him an equivalent therefor. The gamester who wins the money of another is dishonest. There should be no such thing as bets and gaming among Masons: for no honest man should desire that for nothing which belongs to another. The merchant who sells an inferior article for a sound price, the speculator who makes the distresses and needs of others his exchequer are neither fair nor honest.

It should be the earnest desire of every Perfect Master so to live and deal and act, that when it comes to him to die, he may be able to say, and his conscience to adjudge, that no man on earth is poorer, because he is richer; that what he hath, he has honestly earned, and no man can go before God and claim that, by the rules of Equity administered in His Great Chancery, this house in which we die, this land we devise among our heirs, this money which enriches those who survive to bear our name, is his and not ours, and we in that Forum only his Trustees. For it is most certain that God is just, and will sternly enforce every such trust; and that to all whom we despoil, to all whom we defraud, to all from whom we take any thing whatever without fair consideration and equivalent, He will decree a full and adequate compensation.

Be careful then, my Brother, that thou receive no wages, here or elsewhere, that are not thy due. For if thou dost, thou wrongest some one, by taking that which in God's Chancery belongs to him;—and whether that which thou takest thus, be wealth, or rank, or influence or reputation.

TO CLOSE.

[The Th.˙. Hon.˙. gives one rap, and says]:

Th.˙. Hon.˙. Bro.˙. Zabud, what is the hour?

Ward.˙. Th.˙. Hon.˙. it is the 5th hour of the day.

Th.˙. Hon.˙. Then the hour of refreshment has arrived, and it is time to close the Lodge. Give notice to the Brethren that I am about to do so.

Ward.˙. Brethren, the Th.˙. Hon.˙. Master is about to close this Lodge of Perfect Masters, that you may rest from your labours and refresh yourselves. Arise, my Brethren, and assist him in doing so.

Th.˙. Hon.˙. Together, my Brethren.

[The Brethren all give the sign of admiration. Then the Master raps [; ?] the Warden the same, and all the Brothers the same with their hands; and the Master says]:

Th.˙. Hon.˙. This Lodge of Perfect Masters is closed.

FINIS.

Sixth Degree.

Confidential Secretary.

THE LODGE, ITS DECORATIONS, ETC.

The place in which this Lodge is held represents the Audience Chamber of King Solomon. It is hung with black, strewed with white tears; and lighted by 27 lights, in 3 candlesticks, each having 9 branches, placed on three sides of the Altar, in the middle of the room, as in the Master's Lodge.

Upon the Altar are two naked swords, crossed, and a roll of parchment.

OFFICERS, ETC.

The Master and Warden represent King Solomon, and Hiram, King of Tyre. They sit in the East, clothed in blue mantles, lined with ermine, each with a crown on his head and a sceptre in his hand.

There is but one other officer, the Captain of the Guards, styled Zerbal.

When there is a reception, the Master and Warden alone are in the room. The other brethren are all in an adjoining room, armed with swords, and representing King Solomon's Guards. Except during a reception, they sit in the Lodge, and the Captain of the Guards occupies the West.

CLOTHING AND JEWEL.

The apron is of a white sheepskin, lined and bordered with bright crimson. On the flap is painted or embroidered a triangle with equal sides. In the middle of the apron are the Hebrew letters הי [In]. Below this word, at the bottom of the apron, the letter ב [B]: in the upper right hand corner, the letter נ [N]: and in the upper left hand corner, the letter שׁ [Sn].

The jewel is a triple triangle: in the centre of each triangle whereof is engraved one of the foregoing letters. It is a plate of gold; and is worn suspended from a crimson collar.

The battery is [; ;].

The age is ‖ × ? . . . i. e. [, .] years.

TO OPEN.

K∴ S∴ Bro∴ Zerbal, we are about to open a Lodge of Confidential Secretaries in this place for the despatch of business. You will see that the approaches to the Audience Chamber are duly guarded.

[The Captain of the Guards goes out, returns, and reports]:

C∴ G∴ Thrice Ill∴, the Guards are at their posts, and the approaches are duly guarded.

K∴ S∴ Bro∴ Zerbal, you will assure yourself, by receiving the word, that all present are Confidential Secretaries.

[The Capt∴ of the G∴ goes round and receives the word from each; and returning to his place, reports]:

C∴ G∴ Th∴ Ill∴, all the Brothers present are in possession of the word, and prove themselves Confidential Secretaries.

K∴ S∴ Bro∴ Zerbal, are you a Confidential Secretary?

C∴ G∴ [Raising his eyes towards Heaven] Th∴ Ill∴, I am.

Qu∴ What led to your obtaining this degree?

Ans∴ My curiosity.

Qu∴ What risk did you incur thereby?

Ans∴ That of losing my life.

Qu∴ How did you escape?

Ans∴ I was found to have offended through my zeal for my Sovereign's welfare, and so was pardoned and even rewarded.

Qu∴ How many compose a Lodge of Confidential Secretaries?

Ans∴ Two, or more, Th∴ Ill∴.

Qu∴ When composed of two only, of whom does it consist?

Ans∴ Of the Th∴ Ill∴ Master and Warden, representing King Solomon and Hiram, King of Tyre.

Qu∴ Where do they sit in the Lodge?

Ans∴ In the East.

Qu∴ Their duty in the East?

Ans∴ To punish idle curiosity; to reward zeal and fidelity; and to settle and reconcile disputes and dissensions among the brethren.

K∴ Sol∴ Give notice then, my Brother, that it is the will of the Th∴ Ill∴ Warden and myself, that this Lodge of Confidential Secretaries be now opened, by the customary Proclamation.

C∴ G∴ [Giving 3 raps, and all the Brethren rising]: My brethren, it is the pleasure of the Th∴ Ill∴ Master and Warden that this Lodge of Confidential Secretaries be now opened. Let those who are here for idle curiosity only, depart from among us! Let all, by zeal and fidelity, merit honour and reward! Let disputes and dissensions cease, and friendship and brotherly love reign among us!

K∴ Sol∴ Together, my brethren.

[All kneel on the right knee, and place the two hands, crossed, upon the head, the thumbs against the forehead. All say in a low voice, ♂ ☿ *∴ ♂☿*☉∴ ♂☿*☉∴ and then rise, and draw their swords. The Th∴ Ill∴ and Warden then give the questioning sign, and all the brothers the answer. Then the Th∴ Ill∴ raps [:] and the Warden [;]: and the Th∴ Ill∴ declares the Lodge open.

RECEPTION.

The Captain of the Guards receives the candidate in the preparation room, and takes from him the ornaments and clothing of a Perfect Master, and any weapons which he may have about him.

The Warden then passes hastily through the preparation room, and without ceremony enters the Lodge, in which there is no one besides the Master. The Captain of the Guards then places the candidate near the door of the Lodge, which is left ajar, directing him to listen carefully to what passes within.

$K\therefore H\therefore$ [In a loud voice, and angrily :] My Brother, Adonhiram hath shown me the twenty cities in the land of Galilee. Are they those which thou hast given me?

$K\therefore S\therefore$ They are, my Brother.

$K\therefore H\therefore$ Then call me not brother, for they please me not, nor are they such as thou didst promise me. Thou hast not kept thy faith. My Servants did cut thee down as many trees out of Libanus as thou didst want, and conveyed them in rafts by sea to Joppa; cedars, and fir-trees and pine-trees from Libanus; providing timbers in abundance for the houses which thou didst desire to build; and I sent thee Hiram, my father, a wise and most skilful man, to devise ingeniously all the work needed for thy houses, who hath lost his life in thy service. There was peace between us, and we made a league together, notwithstanding that my Gods were not thine, because we were brothers in the Sacred Mysteries; and thou didst promise to give me twenty cities, for the services to be rendered thee.

$K\therefore Sol\therefore$ My brother, I have even done that which I promised. Thou hast the twenty cities, in the land of Galilee. How have I not kept my faith with thee?

$K\therefore H\therefore$ Solomon, God hath given thee wisdom and understanding exceeding much, and largeness of heart as the sand that is on the sea-shore. Thy wisdom surpasses that of all the men of the Orient and of all the Egyptians. Thou art wiser than all men: wiser than Ethan the Ezrahite, and Heman and Chalcol and Dorda, the sons of Mahol; and thy renown hath gone into all the nations round about. Thou hast spoken three thousand parables, and thy poems are a thousand and five. Thou hast treated about trees, from the cedar of Libanus, unto the hyssop that groweth out of the wall; of beasts, of birds, of reptiles and of fishes; and all nations, and the kings of all nations of the Earth have heard of thy wisdom, and have come to consult thee and hear thy wise words : and yet thou art not wise enough to know that cunning is not wisdom. He is not wise, because he is not honest, who doth not keep his word, in spirit, as well as in the letter. Are not all Perfect Masters taught to let the measure of their affirmation or denial be the understanding of their contractor?

$K\therefore Sol\therefore$ And how, my Brother, have I failed to keep my word to thee, in spirit, as well as in the letter? How hath the measure of my affirmation or denial *not* been your understanding of my promise?

$K\therefore H\therefore$ Thou didst promise me twenty cities. I looked not to receive so many ruined and dilapidated villages, surrounded by howling wildernesses; but twenty populous and flourishing places, cinctured by smiling fields and fruitful meadows. These cities which thou hast given me are Chabul, and shall be called so from this day henceforward; dirty, dilapidated and worthless; fit to entail expense, and yield no revenue. Retain them, therefore, and leave me with thy unperformed promise, and let the league between us cease.

$K\therefore S\therefore$ Be pacified, my Brother, and hear me patiently. It was my intention . . . .

$K\therefore H\therefore$ Ah! Some one listens. Since when are spies set at the door to note my words?

$K\therefore Sol\therefore$ Never. None listen. Thou art deceived by thy imagination.

[The Warden goes hastily to the door, throws it open, seizes the candidate, and drags him into the Lodge-room, and near to the Master; and says] :

$K\therefore H\therefore$ So, then, none listen! Behold the eaves-dropper, taken in the very act. Who is he?

$K\therefore Sol\therefore$ Alas! it is Zabud, the Son of Nathan, until now my faithful friend and servant!

$K\therefore H\therefore$ Then let him suffer the punishment that his baseness merits. [The Warden snatches a sword from the altar, and draws back his arm as if to thrust the candidate through. The Master seizes his arm, and says] :

$K\therefore Sol\therefore$ Pause, and reflect, my Brother! Jehovah hath said, "Thou shalt not take human life. Whoso sheddeth man's blood, by man shall his blood be shed: for in the image of God made he man. At the hand of every man's brother will I require the life of man." [He raps 3; and all the Brethren enter]. Dishonour not thyself, my Brother, by becoming the Executioner. Zabud shall be tried, and heard in his defence; and if condemned, he shall be duly punished. His offence is no less against me than thee, if he be guilty. Bro∴ Captain of the Guards, Zabud is your prisoner. Fetter him, and keep him safely until my further order.

[The candidate is hand-cuffed, and taken into the preparation room, all the Brethren also retiring. The door is left ajar; so that he can still hear what passes.]

$K\therefore Sol\therefore$ It was my intention, my Brother, to rebuild the twenty cities which I gave thee, and to settle husbandmen in the country round about, before I gave the territory into thy possession : but thou hast come to receive them sooner than I expected. What I intended, I will still do, and keep my promise in the spirit, as well as in the letter. Thou shalt receive the twenty cities, with fertile and cultivated country round about them. Such was the meaning of my promise, and such shall likewise be its performance. For good faith is the brightest jewel of a regal crown. I will break my word to no man, and least of all to thee, my Brother.

K∴ H∴ [Taking the Master by the right hand]: My brother, forgive me for my hasty words, and my unjust suspicions.

K∴ Sol∴ They are forgiven and forgotten. Forgiveness is a divine virtue; for every day God forgives us much, or He would not suffer us to live. Is there no one whom we can forgive, as God forgives our faults and errors?

K∴ H∴ Zabud?

K∴ Sol∴ Even so; for death would be too harsh a punishment for curiosity. [Raps 3.] Let the Prisoner be set before us.

[The candidate is led in, and placed in front of the Master and Warden. The Captain of the Guards stands by his side, and the other Brothers take their seats.]

K∴ Sol∴ Zabud, you have received many and frequent marks of my favour, and I believed you devoted to my service, and obedient to my wishes. You have been found acting the dishonourable part of an eaves-dropper, hateful from of old to all Masons. My Brother of Tyre, justly indignant, was about to inflict upon you exemplary punishment. I can scarcely believe that baseness and impertinent curiosity could have actuated you; and, at my intercession, he has consented to hear you in your defence, and to forgive you, if there be any thing that can excuse or explain your conduct.

C∴ G∴ Th∴ Ill∴ Kings Solomon and Hiram, it was not curiosity that led Zabud to listen. Seeing you, Th∴ Ill∴ King Hiram, whom he knew not personally, enter hastily and angrily into the audience chamber, and not knowing what evil purpose led you thither, he approached the door, that he might be ready to enter, and protect and defend his King, in case his assistance should become necessary. His zeal and attachment causing him to neglect the precautions which curiosity would have taken against discovery, (for he did not endeavour to conceal himself), he was seen, and supposed to be an eaves-dropper.

K∴ Sol∴ My Brother, of all my servants, Zabud has ever shown the warmest attachment for my person. I am satisfied that not curiosity, but what he deemed his duty, led him to the door. I will vouch for his discretion and his zeal; and I beg you to forgive him, and restore him to your royal favour.

K∴ H∴ My Brother, there is nothing to forgive. I honour him for his fidelity and attachment, and gladly receive him among the number of my friends. Alas! I need one, to fill the void caused by the sad death of my dear friend and Brother, Hiram Abi.

K∴ Sol∴ Let the memory of the dead friend cement more firmly the amity of the living. My Brother, if the cities in the land of Galilee suit thee not, choose wherever else thou wilt in my dominions, and whatsoever cities thou choosest shall be thine.

K∴ H∴ My Brother, thy friendship is of greater value than cities or even kingdoms. If I govern well and justly my present dominions, they are sufficiently extensive for my ambition. Even let thy people remain under thine own government and laws. Accept again the cities, as a token of my brotherly regard, and of the renewal of our league and firm alliance. And I give thee also an hundred and twenty talents of gold, from my treasury, toward the expenses of the House of the Lord, and thine own House, and to aid in building the walls of Jerusalem and thy other cities.

K∴ Sol∴ In what words, my Brother, can I thank thee for thy royal generosity? Doubt not that I will find some way in which to return thy kindness.

K∴ H∴ I am repaid already. Thy friendship over-pays me.

K∴ Sol∴ That friendship shall be perpetual; between thee and me, and between thy children and my children forever.

K∴ H∴ Let a new Treaty be drawn and sealed as a perpetual memorial to all generations of our people. Build thou a fleet in Asiongaber, by Ailath, on the shore of the Red Sea, in the land of Edom, and I will send my mariners in the fleet, sailors that have knowledge of the sea, with thy servants; and they shall sail to Ophir, the land of Gold, and to the Blessed and Sacred Island in the far Northern Seas, and to the unexplored lands in the great Western Ocean; and bring us much wealth, to rebuild our cities and make our dominions prosperous.

K∴ Sol∴ Even so let it be, my Brother.

K∴ H∴ Let then thy Secretary write the Treaty in Hebrew and Phœnician; and, sealed with our seals, let it be laid up in the archives of each kingdom.

K∴ Sol∴ Alas, my Brother, since the death of the good Hiram Abi, I have no Secretary; and I am at a loss with whom to fill his place.

K∴ H∴ Zabud has proven his zeal for your service, and his attachment for your person. Why may we not make him our Confidential Secretary?

K∴ Sol∴ He is competent and faithful, and I gladly accept the suggestion. Zabud, my friend, at the instance of the Th∴ Ill∴ King of Tyre, you are appointed our Confidential Secretary, in the place of our deceased Brother and Gr∴ Master, Hiram Abi. To you will be confided the knowledge of those important arrangements and transactions, growing out of our new Alliance. Do you feel that you can observe inviolable secrecy as to all matters so confided to you, and perform with fidelity the duties of the office which we offer you?

Cand∴ I do.

K∴ Sol∴ Are you willing to engage yourself thereto by a solemn and binding obligation?

Cand∴ I am.

K∴ Sol∴ Kneel then at the Altar; and placing both hands upon the Book of the Law and the Crossed Swords, repeat your names and say after me:

OBLIGATION.

I, A . . . . . B . . . . . in the presence of the Gr∴ Architect of the Universe, and appealing to Him to attest the sincerity of my intentions, do hereby and hereon most solemnly and sincerely promise and swear, that I will never reveal the secrets of this degree, or which may become known to me in my character of Confidential Secretary, to any person in the world, unless it be to one who shall be legally known to me to be duly authorized to receive the same.

I furthermore promise and swear that I will make the disinterestedness and generosity of the King of Tyre, as exhibited in this degree, my model and example during all my days; being better pleased to confer than to receive a favour; and never, if I can help it, allowing a day to pass without doing some liberal and generous action.

I furthermore promise and swear, that I will be ever zealous and faithful, in the service of Masonry, the Master, and my Brother.

I furthermore promise and swear that I will at all times endeavour to heal all dissensions and differences, settle all disputes, and reconcile all quarrels among my Brethren, upon terms honourable and just to every party concerned.

To all of which I do most sincerely promise and solemnly swear, under the penalty of being considered by all the world, by man and woman alike, as false Mason, faithless and forsworn brother, and unworthy man. So help me God! and keep me steadfast in the due performance of this my obligation!

K∴ S∴ Arise, my Brother. As our ancient Gr∴ Masters, Solomon, King of Israel, and Hiram, King of Tyre, after the death of our Gr∴ Master Hiram Abi, received in his place and stead as their confidential or intimate Secretary, Zabud, whom in this degree you have represented, as the Master and Warden represent the two Kings; so do I receive you a Confidential Secretary, and advance you to the Sixth Degree of the Ancient and Accepted Rite; devoting you to the service of Masonry, and of the Gr∴ Architect of the Universe. Again as in the 5th Degree, you assume the place of our lamented Gr∴ Master, and so become still more strongly bound to practice the virtues by which he was so eminently distinguished. The representation of his Tomb is still before you; the black hangings and the tears remind us of the affliction which overwhelmed our ancient brethren at his death. Let them recall to your mind his virtues and his excellencies, and incite you so to act that your memory may be honored among Masons.

Receive this sword, type of that zeal, that ardour and that firm and constant resolution, with which you are hereafter to war against error, vice, wrong and injustice, and defend the rights of men, and the cause of the oppressed against the oppressor.

I invest you with the collar of this degree. Let its colour ever remind you that you, like our deceased Gr.·. Master should be ever ready to shed your blood rather than dishonour yourself by revealing our secrets.

I invest you with the apron of this degree. Behold in its centre the initial letters of the mysterious name of Deity. The three other letters upon it are the initials of the Hebrew Words, ברית, [Brith]: נדר [Ndr]: שלמות [Shlmuth] : . . . meaning Covenant or Alliance: a vow, pledge or Promise; and Perfection, Completion or Recompense: . . The new *Alliance* and *Covenant* between the two Kings, our Ancient Grand Masters: the *Promise* made by Solomon to Hiram, which the latter imagined had been broken: and. the *Reward* or *Recompense* obtained by Zabud for his zeal for, and devotion to, the interests of his Sovereign.

They have also a profounder meaning to us as Masons: The Covenant made by the Deity with man; by the Creator with his erring creatures: His Promise of Mercy and Forgiveness: and that Recompense of Happiness which awaits those who emulate the virtues and follow the example of our illustrious Grand Master Hiram Abi. When you look upon it, remember the Covenants you have made at the altars of Masonry, with God and your brethren; the Vows which you have taken in the degrees of this Rite especially; and that an approving conscience is the best recompense of a Mason's labours here below.

I invest you also with the jewel of this Degree, the Triple Triangle, bearing upon it the same initials.

Receive now the signs, token and words of the Degree:

Sign: . . . Bring the ‡ & ☉ ♒ ♊ to the † ♎ & ☿ ƺ † ♊ ☾ ‡, and then diagonally downwards to the ‡ & ♀ §.

Answer: . . . Cross the ‡ & ☉ ♒ ♊ ♎, with the ♈ & ƺ ♋ ♏ ♎ extended, and raise them to the height of the ♑ ☿ ‡ ☾ & ☾ ☉ ♊; the ♈ & ƺ ♋ ♏ ♎ touching it: then bring them down rapidly to the & ♀ † ♈ of the ♎ ♃ ☿ ‡ ♊, raising the ☾ ♄ ☾ ♎ to Heaven.

Token: . . . Take each other in the ordinary manner by the ‡ & ☉ ♒ ♊: and turn the & ☉ ♒ ♊ ♎ over [;] times; saying alternately, at the several turns: ♏ ☾ ‡ ☾ ♈ &∴ ♒ ☾ ♊ ☾ ‡∴ ♎ & ☾ † ☾ ♋ ☿ ♈ &∴

Pass-words: . . . ♂ ☿ ☉ ♏ ☾ ‡ ♈∴ ♍ ☾ ‡ ♏ ☉ †∴

Sacred Word: . . . ♂ ☿ * ☉∴ or ♀ * ☉ &∴

Listen now to the lecture of this degree:

LECTURE.

The legend of this Degree needs little explanation. King Solomon, in pursuance of his promise made to his ally Hiram King of Tyre, gave to him, upon the completion of the Temple, twenty towns in the Province of Galilee. The latter King, coming to Jerusalem to aid in performing the last duties of friendship to his murdered friend Hiram Abi, called by him affectionately, "Hiram, my father," went to see the cities so assigned to him; and finding them almost depopulated, and fallen greatly into decay, the country around them uncultivated and sterile, and the inhabitants small in number, and rude and uncivilized in habits and manners; so that the Province, in that condition, would be rather a charge upon his Treasury than a source of revenue; he concluded that his ally, regardless of his Royal Honour and Masonic good faith, had kept his promise in the letter only, while breaking it in the spirit: while in truth it was the intention of King Solomon, before putting him in possession, to rebuild and adorn the cities, to place colonies in the country, and to change the waste and inhospitable desert into cultivated gardens, fields and meadows; thus making them worthy of his ally's acceptance, and faithfully complying with his own promise.

Arriving at Jerusalem, King Hiram went directly to the Palace of King Solomon, and without waiting to be announced, angrily passed through the Guards in the Court, and into the audience chamber, where he found King Solomon, and charged him with bad faith, and violation of his kingly promise.

Zabud, the devoted servant and favourite of King Solomon, seeing King Hiram thus enter, and not personally knowing him, and seeing also that he was excited and enraged, feared that he intended some violence, and approached the door of the audience chamber, to be ready to rush in and defend his Master, if there should be occasion. His zeal and devotion causing him to neglect the precaution which mere curiosity would have observed, he was seen by King Hiram, seized upon by him and dragged into the Hall, where he would have been at once slain by the enraged King, but for the interference of his own Sovereign.

The result we need not repeat to you, as you have represented Zabud throughout the entire scene, even to his pardon, and his appointment as Confidential Secretary of the two kings.

You are specially taught in this degree to be zealous and faithful; to be disinterested and benevolent; to act the peace-maker, in case of dissensions, disputes and quarrels among the brethren.

Duty is the moral magnetism which controls and guides the true Mason's course over the tumultuous seas of life. Whether the stars of honour, reputation and reward do or do not shine, in the light of day or in the darkness of the night of trouble and adversity, in calm or storm, that unerring magnet still shows him the true course to steer, and indicates with certainty where-away lies the Port, which not to reach involves ship-wreck and dishonour. He follows its silent bidding, as the mariner, when land is for many days not in sight, and the ocean without path or landmark spreads out all around him, follows the bidding of the needle, never doubting that it points truly to the North. To perform that duty, whether the performance be rewarded or unrewarded, is his sole care. And it doth not matter though of this performance there may be no witnesses; and though what he does will be forever unknown to all mankind.

A little consideration will teach us that Fame has other limits than mountains and oceans; and that he who places happiness in the frequent repetition of his name, may spend his life in propagating it, without any danger of weeping for new worlds, or necessity of passing the Atlantic sea.

If, therefore, he that imagines the world filled with his actions and praises, shall subduct from the number of his encomiasts, all those who are placed below the flight of fame, and who hear in the valleys of life no voice but that of necessity; all those who imagine themselves too important to regard him, and consider the mention of his name as a usurpation of their time; all who are too much or too little pleased with themselves to attend to anything external: all who are attracted by pleasure, or chained down by pain to unvaried ideas; all who are withheld from attending his triumph by different pursuits: and all who slumber in universal negligence; he will find his renown straitened by nearer bounds than the rocks of Caucasus; and perceive that no man can be venerable or formidable, but to a small part of his fellow-creatures. And therefore, that we may not languish in our endeavours after excellence, it is necessary that, as Africanus counsels his descend-ants, we raise our eyes to higher prospects, and contemplate our future and eternal state, without giving up our hearts to the praise of crowds, or fixing our hopes on such rewards as human power can bestow.

We are not born for ourselves alone; and our country claims her share, and our friends their share of us. As all that the earth produces is created for the use of man, so men are created for the sake of men, that they may mutually do good to one another. In this we ought to take nature for our guide, and throw into the public stock the offices of general utility, by a reciprocation of duties; sometimes by receiving, sometimes by giving, and sometimes to cement human society by arts, by industry, and by our resources.

Suffer others to be praised in thy presence, and entertain their good and glory with delight; but at no hand disparage them, or lessen the report, or make an objection; and think not the advancement of thy brother is a lessening of thy worth. Upbraid no man's weakness to him to discomfit him, neither report it to disparage him, neither delight to remember it to lessen him, or to set thyself above him; nor ever praise thyself or dispraise any man else, unless some sufficient worthy end do hallow it.

Remember that we usually disparage others upon slight grounds and little instances; and if a man be highly commended, we think him sufficiently lessened, if we can but charge one sin of folly or inferiority in his account. We should be more severe to ourselves, or less so to others, and consider that whatsoever good any one can think or say of us, we can tell him of many unworthy and foolish and perhaps worse actions of ours, any one of which, done by another, would be enough, we think, to destroy his reputation.

If we think the people wise and sagacious, and just and appreciative, when they praise and make idols of us, let us not call them unlearned and ignorant, and ill and stupid judges, when our neighbour is cried up by public fame and popular noises.

Every man hath in his own life sins enough, in his own mind trouble enough, in his own fortunes evils enough, and in performance of his offices failings more than enough, to entertain his own inquiry; so that curiosity after the affairs of others cannot be without envy and an ill-mind. The generous man will be solicitous and inquisitive into the beauty and order of a well-governed family, and after the virtues of an excellent person; but anything for which men keep locks and bars, or that blushes to see the light, or that is either shameful in manners or private in nature, this thing will not be his care and business.

It should be objection sufficient to exclude any man from the society of Masons, that he is not disinterested and generous, both in his acts, and in his opinions of men and his constructions of their conduct. He who is selfish and grasping, or censorious and ungenerous, will not long remain within the strict limits of honesty and truth; but will shortly commit injustice. He who loves himself too much, must needs love others too little; and he who is inclined to *harsh* judgment will not long delay to give *unjust* judgment; and afterwards, or not at all, hear the case.

The generous man is not careful to return no more than he receives; but prefers that the balances upon the leger of benefits shall be in his favour. He who hath received pay in full for all the benefits and favours that he has conferred, is like a spendthrift who has consumed his whole estate, and laments over an empty exchequer. He who requites my favours with ingratitude, adds to, instead of diminishing my wealth: and he who cannot return a favour is equally poor, whether that inability arise from poverty of spirit, sordidness of soul, or actual pecuniary poverty.

If he is wealthy who hath large sums invested, and the mass of whose fortune consists, in obligations that bind other men to pay him money; he is still more so, to whom many men owe large returns of kindnesses and favours. Beyond a moderate sum each year, the wealthy man merely invests his means; and that which he never uses is still, like favours unreturned and kindnesses unreciprocated, an actual and real portion of his fortune.

Covetousness teaches men to be cruel and crafty, industrious in evil, full of care and malice; it devours young heirs, and grinds the face of the poor, and undoes those who specially belong to God's protection, helpless, craftless and innocent people; it inquires into our parents' age, and longs for the death of our friends; it makes friendship an act of rapine, and changes a partner into a vulture, and a companion into a thief.

But generosity and a liberal spirit teach men to be human and genial, open-hearted, frank and sincere, earnest to do good, easy and contented, and well-wishers of all mankind. They protect the feeble against the strong, and the defenceless against rapacity and craft. They succour and comfort the poor, and are the guardians under God, of His innocent and helpless wards. They value friends more than riches or fame, and gratitude more than money or power. They are noblemen by God's patent, and their escutcheons and quarterings are to be found in Heaven's great book of Heraldry. Nor can any man any more be a Mason than he can be a gentleman, unless he is generous, liberal and disinterested.

> The rank is but the guinea's stamp,
> The man's the gold:

and true nobility of soul is as likely to be found in the heart that beats under homespun, the hunting-shirt and the mechanic's jacket, as in that which throbs under star or coronet.

To be liberal, but only of that which is our own; to be generous, but only when we have first been just; to give, when to give costs something in the way of deprivation of luxury or comfort, this is Masonry indeed.

He who is worldly, covetous, or sensual must change, before he can be a good Mason. If we are governed by inclination and not by duty; if we are unkind, severe, censorious or injurious, in the relations or intercourse of life; if we are unfaithful parents, or undutiful children; if we are severe masters or faithless servants; if we are treacherous friends, or bad neighbours, or bitter competitors, we are wandering at a great distance from true Masonic light.

Masons must be kind and affectionate, one to another. Coming to the same Lodge, kneeling at the same altar, they must feel that respect and kindness for each other, which their common relation and common approach to one God should inspire. There needs to be more of the spirit of the Ancient Fellowship among us; more tenderness for each other's faults, more zeal and solicitude for each other's improvement and good fortune.

Nothing should be allowed to interfere with that kindness and affection: neither the spirit of business, absorbing, eager and overreaching, ungenerous and hard in its dealings, keen and bitter in its competitions, low and sordid in its purposes; nor that of ambition, selfish, mercenary, restless, circumventing, living only in the opinion of others, envious of the good fortune of others, miserably vain of its own success, unjust, unscrupulous and slanderous.

He that does me a favour, hath bound me to make him a return of thankfulness. The obligation comes not by covenant; not by his own express intention, but by the nature of the thing; and is a duty springing up within the spirit of the obliged person, to whom it is more natural to love his friend, and to do good for good, than to return evil for evil; because a man may forgive an injury, but he must never forget a good turn. He that refuses to do good to them whom he is bound to love, or to love that which did him good, is unnatural and monstrous in his affections, and thinks all the world born to minister to him; with a greediness worse than that of the sea; which, although it receives all rivers into itself, yet it furnishes the clouds and springs with a return of all they need. Our duty to those who are our benefactors is, to esteem and love their persons, to make them proportionable returns of service, or duty, or profit, according as we can, or as they need, or as opportunity presents itself; and according to the greatnesses of their kindness.

The generous man cannot but regret to see dissensions and disputes among his brethren. It is the base and ungenerous only that delight in discord. It is the poorest occupation of humanity to labour to make men think worse of each other; and yet a multitude of men work assiduously, with tongue and pen, in that occupation alone. It is the duty of the Mason to strive to make man think better of his neighbour; to quiet, instead of aggravating difficulties; to bring together those who are severed and estranged; to save friends from becoming foes, and to persuade foes to become friends. To do this, he must needs control his own passions, and be not rash and hasty, nor swift to take offence, nor ready to be angered.

For anger is a professed enemy to counsel. It is a direct storm, in which no man can be heard to speak or call from without: for if you counsel gently, you are disregarded; if you urge it and be vehement, you provoke it more. It is neither manly nor ingenuous. It makes marriage to be a necessary and unavoidable trouble; friendships and societies and familiarities, to be intolerable. It multiplies the evils of drunkenness, and makes the levities of wine to run into madness. It makes innocent jesting to be the beginning of tragedies. It turns friendship into hatred; it makes a man lose himself, and his reason and his argument, in disputation. It turns the desires of knowledge into an itch of wrangling. It adds insolency to power. It turns justice into cruelty, and judgment into oppression. It changes discipline into tediousness and hatred of liberal institution. It makes a prosperous man to be envied, and the unfortunate to be unpitied.

See therefore, my Brother, that first controlling your own temper, and governing your own passions, you fit yourself to keep peace and harmony among other men, and especially the brethren. Above all, remember that Masonry is the realm of peace, and that among Masons there must be no dissension, but only that noble emulation, which can best work and best agree. Wherever there is strife and hatred among the brethren, there is no Masonry; for Masonry is Peace, and Brotherly Love and Concord.

Masonry is the great Peace Society of the world. Wherever it exists, it struggles to prevent international difficulties and disputes; and to bind Republics, Kingdoms and Empires together in one great band of peace and amity.

Who can sum up the horrors and woes accumulated in a single war? Masonry is not dazzled with all its pomp and circumstance, all its glitter and glory. War comes with its bloody hand into our very dwellings. It takes from ten thousand homes those who lived there in peace and comfort, held by the tender ties of family and kindred. It drags them away, to die untended, of fever or exposure, in infectious climes; or to be hacked, torn and mangled in the fierce fight; to fall on the gory field, to rise no more, or to be borne away, in awful agony, to noisome and horrid hospitals. The groans of the battle field are echoed in sighs of bereavement, from thousands of desolated hearths. Returning, the soldier brings worse sorrow to his home, by the infection which he has caught, of camp vices. The country is demoralized. The national mind is brought down, from the noble interchange of kind offices with another people, to wrath and revenge, and base pride, and the habit of measuring brute strength against brute strength, in battle. Treasures are expended, that would suffice to build ten thousand churches, hospitals and universities, or rib and tie together a continent with rails of iron. If that treasure were sunk in the sea, it would be calamity enough; but it is put to worse use; for it is expended in cutting into the veins and arteries of human life, until the earth is deluged with a sea of blood.

Such, my Brother, are the lessons of this Degree; and you have sworn to make them the rule, the law and the guide, of your life and conduct. If you do so, you will be fitted and entitled to advance in Masonry. If you do not, you have already gone too far.

TO CLOSE.

M∴ Bro∴ Zerbal, what is the hour?

C∴ G∴ Th∴ Ill∴, it is the 6th hour of the day.

M∴ If that be the hour, it is time to rest from our labours. Does any dispute remain unreconciled, or any enmity unappeased among the brethren?

C∴ G∴ None, Th∴ Ill∴, within my knowledge.

M∴ Doth any brother entertain ill-will against his brother; or hath any one unsettled quarrel with his Brother? If so, it must be settled before we part.

— — —

M∴ Doth any one complain of promise unperformed, or performed in letter only; or of any wrong or injury or injustice, by act or word? If so, let him now make it known, that the promise may be fulfilled, or the injury atoned for.

— — —

M∴ Even as they do now, so evermore may peace and harmony prevail amongst us! Give notice, Bro∴ Zerbal, that we are about to close this Lodge.

C∴ G∴ [Rapping 3 times, at which all the brethren rise]: Brethren, the Th∴ Ill∴ Master and Warden are about to close this Lodge. You will take due notice, and govern yourselves accordingly.

M∴ Together, my Brethren!

[All kneel, and the same ceremonies are performed as in opening; and the Master declares the Lodge closed.]

FINIS.

Seventh Degree.

Provost and Judge.

THE LODGE, ITS DECORATIONS, ETC.

The Lodge is hung with red, and lighted by 5 Great Lights, one in each corner, and one in the middle.

In the East is a canopy, painted to represent the sky, with stars shining. Under it is suspended a box of Ebony, ornamented with jewels, supposed to contain the records of the Tribunal of Provosts and Judges.

In the middle of the Lodge hangs an equilateral Triangle; in the centre of which is the Word יה; [In]: and under it hangs an equal balance.

OFFICERS, TITLES, ETC.

The Master is styled *Illustrious*, and sits in the East. He represents *Azarias*, Son of Nathan, the Chief Provost and Judge.

There are two Wardens, who represent *Elihoreph* and *Ahia*, the Scribes; and sit in the West.

The Recorder sits in the South and represents *Josaphat*, the Son of Ahilud.

There is also a Master of Ceremonies.

The Candidate represents *Zabud*, the Son of Nathan.

The Wardens are styled *Sen.·. and Jun.·. Inspectors.*

ORNAMENTS AND JEWELS.

The apron is white, edged with red. In the middle is a pocket, with a red and white rosette. On the flap is painted or embroidered a key.

The cordon is crimson, worn across the body. From it hangs the jewel: which is a Key of Gold.

The *battery* is ; ; ,

The *Age* of a Provost and Judge is £ × ? or , ! years.

TO OPEN.

Ill.·. M.·. Bro.·. Sen.·. Inspector, I am about to open this Lodge of Provosts and Judges. See that we are properly tyled.

Sen∴ Insp∴ Bro∴ Junior Inspector, the Ill∴ Master is about to open this Lodge. You will see that it is properly tyled, and inform the tyler that the Lodge is about to be opened.

[The J∴ W∴ goes out, returns, raps ; ; , — which is returned by the tyler; and reports:

Jun∴ Insp∴ Bro∴ Sen∴ Inspector, the Lodge is properly tyled.

Sen∴ Insp∴ Ill∴ Master, the Lodge is duly tyled, and we are secure from intrusion.

Ill∴ M∴ Bro∴ Sen∴ Inspector, are all present Provosts and Judges?

Ans∴ They are, Ill∴ Master.

Qu∴ Bro∴ Sen∴ Inspector, are you a Provost and Judge?

Ans∴ I dispense justice to all the workmen ; and administer the law, without prejudice or partiality.

Qu∴ Where were you made a Provost and Judge?

Ans∴ In the middle chamber.

Qu∴ What is the especial emblem of your rank?

Ans∴ An equal balance, symbol of justice, accuracy and impartiality.

Qu∴ Where is your Master stationed?

Ans∴ Everywhere.

Qu∴ Why?

Ans∴ To adjust the demands of the workmen, hear their complaints, and do justice to all.

Qu∴ What is your age?

Ans∴ Twice £ years—♊ ☿ ♄ ♍✝☾ the age of a Master Mason.

Qu∴ What is the hour?

Ans∴ The last hour of the night. The day cometh.

Ill∴ M∴ Give notice then that I am about to open this Lodge of Provosts and Judges, that the labours of the day may be recommenced.

Sen∴ Insp∴ Bro∴ Jun∴ Inspector, it is the pleasure of the Ill∴ Master that this Lodge of Provosts and Judges be now opened. Make known his will to the Brethren.

· *Jun∴ Insp∴* Brethren, it is the pleasure of the Ill∴ M∴ that this Lodge of Provosts and Judges be now opened. Take notice thereof, and prepare to recommence your labours.

[The Ill∴ M∴ raps ;—the Sen∴ W∴ ;—and the Jun∴ W.,—then all the Brethren rap ; ; , with their hands. The Master gives the sign, and all the others the answer; and the Master declares the Lodge open].

RECEPTION.

The Candidate, in the dress and with the jewel of a Confidential Secretary, is received in the ante-room by the Master of Ceremonies, who conducts him to the door of the Lodge, and gives the alarm ; ; , The door is opened, and the Junior Warden asks,

Jun∴ Insp∴ Who comes here?

_ *M∴ Cer∴* A Brother, who being a Perfect Master and Confidential Secretary, desires to obtain the degree of Provost and Judge.

Jun∴ Insp∴ How hath he fitted himself to receive this degree?

M∴ Cer∴ By being faithful, obedient and honest; by being zealous, ardent and devoted to Masonry and to his brethren ; by being generous and disinterested ; and by having aided to preserve peace and harmony among men.

Jun∴ Insp∴ For what purpose does he desire to advance further in Masonry?

M∴ Cer∴ That he may be the better qualified to do good, and live as becomes a Mason.

Jun∴ Insp∴ Since such is his object, let him wait until the Ill∴ M∴ is informed of his request.

[The Jun∴ W∴ closes the door, and reports to the Sen∴ W∴ and he in his turn to the Master ; the same questions being asked, in each case, and like answers returned as at the door.]

Ill∴ M∴ Let him enter, and be received upon the edge of the sword of justice.

[The door is opened, and the M∴ of Ceremonies leads in the candidate, and places him in front of the two Wardens]. ·

Ill∴ M∴. Let him who desires to advance in Masonry, first kneel, bending his knee and bowing his head to the God that made and that preserves him.

[The Candidate kneels and inclines his head, and the Sen∴ W∴ presses upon his neck the sharp edge of a naked sword, saying] :

Sen∴ Insp∴. In this degree you are received upon the edge of the sword of justice. You desire, as a Provost and Judge, to grasp its hilt. See that you do not, by violating the moral law, expose yourself to be smitten with its edge.

Ill∴ M∴. Arise.

[He rises, and is led 7 times around the Lodge. At the end of each of the first six circuits, he halts in front of the Ill∴ Master, and gives the signs of the preceding degrees, one at each circuit, commencing with that of E∴ A∴. During the circuits, the Ill∴ Master reads as follows] :

1st Circuit : . . . . Thou shalt provide out of all the People able men, such as fear God, men of Truth, and Haters of Injustice, and set them to judge the People at all Seasons. Hear the causes between your brethren, and judge righteously between man and man, and between the citizen and the stranger. Ye shall not respect persons in judgment ; but shall listen to the humble as well as to the great. Ye shall not fear the face of man ; for the judgment is God's.

2d Circuit : . . . . Thou shalt not follow a multitude to do evil ; neither shalt thou, floating on the popular current, speak in a cause in order to pervert judgment. Nor shalt thou as a judge lean towards the side of a poor man, because he is poor ; nor strain any point to give judgment in his favour.

3d Circuit : . . . . · See that ye judge not falsely, nor slay the innocent and the righteous : and take no gift : for a gift blindeth the wise, and perverteth the words of the righteous.

4th Circuit : . . . . Ye shall do no unrighteousness in judgment : ye shall not lean to the side of the poor, nor honour the person of the great ; but shall impartially judge your neighbour. Ye shall do no injustice in judgment, in mete-yard, in weight or in measure. Just balances, just weights and just measures shall ye have ; and no one shall cheat or over-reach another.

5th Circuit : . . . . Ye shall have one manner of law, as well for the stranger as for one of your own country. One ordinance shall be for you and the stranger who sojourneth with you ; the same ordinance forever in your generations : as ye are, so shall the stranger be before the Lord : one law and one custom shall be for you, and for the stranger that sojourneth with you.

6th. Love justice, you that are the judges of the earth : for he that speaketh unjust things cannot be hid ; neither shall the chastising judgment pass him by. Justice is perpetual and immortal. Oppress not the poor just man ; but spare the widow, and honour the ancient grey hairs of the aged. Let not your strength be the law of justice ; nor hold that which is feeble to be nothing worth.

7th Circuit : . . . . The just that is dead condemneth the wicked that are living. They shall live for evermore ; and their reward is with God, and the care of them with the Most High, to whom justice is as a breastplate, and true judgment as a helmet, and equity as an invincible shield ; and He will sternly judge those, who being ministers of His Kingdom, do not judge rightly, nor keep the law of justice, nor walk according to his will.

[The Candidate is then halted in front of the Ill∴ M∴ who says] :

Ill∴ M∴. Whom bring you hither, Bro∴ M∴ of Ceremonies ?

M∴ Cer∴. Bro∴ A . . . . B . . . . , a Perfect Master and Confidential Secretary, who desires to attain the Degree of Provost and Judge, and so become a Master in Israel.

Ill∴ M∴. He desires to assume a heavy burthen. Hath he a sufficient sense of the important duties and heavy responsibilities of the office ?

M∴ Cer∴. Ill∴ Master, he will answer for himself.

Ill∴ M∴. My Brother, are you aware that he who would assume the character of Provost and Judge, and in that character judge and decide between his Brethren, must be himself a just and upright man, impartial, cautious, merciful ; of pure morals and blameless life and conversation ; for that what judgment he measures

6

unto others, God will measure unto him; and that he must first of all give judgment against his own faults and vices?

Cand∴. I am.

Ill∴. M∴. Are you sensible that he who pardons or ignores his own errors and offences, and punishes the self-same errors and offences, or those that are of their kindred, in others, is a false judge and disloyal Mason?

Cand∴. I am.

Ill∴. M∴. Do you feel the grave responsibility of deciding between man and man, where incorrect decision is injustice; and the effects of indolence, of inattention, of hasty examination and rash conclusion, are as grave as those of corruption, or of decision purchased by bribes, or prompted by enmity or prejudice?

Cand∴. I do.

Ill∴. M∴. Do you feel that he who would assume the character of judge, is guilty of a serious offence, if he does not fully inform himself of the laws and jurisprudence which he is to be called on to construe, to apply, to administer and enforce?

Cand∴. I do.

Jun∴. Insp∴. Let the unjust judge tremble; for God will smite him with the sharp sword of his wrath!

Sen∴. Insp∴. Let the corrupt magistrate shake with terror; for Remorse and his accusing conscience shall hunt him like hounds, and pursue him far beyond the grave!

Orator : . . Let him who, unqualified, usurps the seat of judgment, remember the fate of those who laid their unholy hands upon the ark, and were smitten with God's anger for their presumption!

Sen∴. Insp∴. Judge not, that thou mayest not be judged: for whatever judgment thou renderest against the errors and offences of others, shall God pronounce against thine!

Ill∴. M∴. My Brother, hear and consider! Thus warned, do you still desire to proceed?

Cand∴. . . . I do.

Ill∴. M∴. Bro∴. Master of Cer∴., since this Bro∴., thus warned, hath such confidence in himself that he is willing to proceed, you will conduct him to the Holy Altar, and cause him to kneel there, in proper position to take upon himself the solemn obligation of Provost and Judge.

[The Candidate is conducted to the Altar, and caused to kneel on both knees, with his hands upon the roll of parchment that represents the Holy Bible, while the Sen∴. Warden lays the blade of a naked sword upon his head: in which position he repeats the following]

OBLIGATION.

I, A . . . . B . . . ., in the presence of the Gr∴. Architect of the Universe, whose Name and Symbol is suspended over me, and praying Him to witness this my obligation, do hereby and hereon most solemnly and sincerely promise and swear, that I will never reveal the secrets of this degree to any person whatsoever, unless it be to one who is duly authorized to receive, when I am duly authorized to communicate them; and at a proper time and in a proper place.

I furthermore promise and swear, that I will decide justly and impartially whatever matters of difference may be submitted to me; and whether in or out of the Lodge; without fear, favour, affection, prejudice, or the hope or promise of reward.

I furthermore promise and swear that I will henceforward most earnestly endeavour to do justice unto all men, whether friends or enemies or indifferent to me; seeking no unfair advantage of any, nor endeavouring to enrich or elevate myself, at the expense of another's fortune, happiness or reputation.

All of which I do most sincerely and solemnly promise and swear; binding myself under the penalty of being despised of all men while living, and my memory execrated after I am dead, and my name ever quoted by way of warning, as that of an unjust and corrupt judge, and unfair and dishonest man, if I wilfully violate this obligation. So help me God, and keep me steadfast in the due performance of the same!

Ill.·. M.·. . . . Arise, my Brother! By the power vested in me, as successor of Azarias the son of Nathan, first Chief Provost and Judge under Solomon the King, I appoint and accept you a Provost and Judge, in the Ancient and accepted Rite of Masonry. Receive now the signs, words and token of this degree.

Sign: . . . Place the ♀ ♒ ♊ ☾ ♉ and ♋ ♀ ♊ ♊ † ☾ fingers of the ‡ hand, on the ‡ side of the ♒ ☿ ♎ ☾.

Answer: . . . Place the ♀ ♒ ♊ ☾ ♉ finger of the ‡ hand on the ♒ ☿ ♎ ☾; the ♈ & ♄ ♋ ♏ under the ♐ & ♀ ♒; thus forming a square.

Token: Interlace the † ♀ ♈ ♈ † ☾ ‡ ♑ ♀ ♒ ♌ ☾ ‡ ♎ of the ‡ & ☉ ♒ ♊, and tap each other mutually, £ times [by ; ; ,], with the ♈ & ♄ ♋ ♏, in the ☋ ☉ † ♋ of the & ☉ ♒ ♊.

Password: . . . ♈ ♀ ♈ ☿ ∴

Sacred Word: . . . ♎ & ☾ ¶ ♀ ♒ ☉ & ∴ or, in French, ♂ ☉ ♐ & ♀ ♒ ☉ ♀ ∴

Other Words: . . . ¶ ♀ * ♀ ∴ ¶ ♄ ♋ ∴ ♎ ♈ ☿ † ¶ ♀ ♒ ∴ ♉ ♀ ♒ ¶ ♄ & ∴ ☡ ♍ ‡ ☉ ♐ & ♀ ☉ & ∴

I now invest you with the apron, collar and jewel of this degree. The latter represents the key of the Chief Provost and Judge, wherewith he unlocked the box of Ebony that contained the Records of the Tribunal. It teaches you to lock carefully up in your heart the secrets of Masonry, and to keep the key ever in your own possession: and it is especially emblematical of that justice and uprightness that alone can unlock to you the mysteries contained in the higher degrees, and enable you to advance towards perfection.

The triangle that hangs above your head is emblematical, here, as elsewhere in Masonry, of the Deity; of His Omnipresence, Omnipotence and Omniscience; and hath His Holy Name in the centre: and it is also emblematical of the three great requisites of a judge, possessed by Him in their perfection and infinitude; and with which, though in an infinitely less degree, every human judge should be invested;—Justice, Equity, and Impartiality. Let that emblem and the balance be ever before your eyes, and remind you of the obligation which you have taken in this Degree; of the duties which devolve upon you; of the responsibilities which rest upon you; and which, with God's eye ever fixed on you, you cannot evade or avoid.

Listen now to the Lecture of this degree.

LECTURE.

It is said that King Solomon, after the death of Hiram Abi, in order that justice might be administered among the workmen upon the Temple, their disputes be decided and their complaints heard, appointed seven Provosts and Judges, to adjust their demands, listen to their complaints, and settle any disputes and differences that might arise among them. He appointed Azarias the Son of Nathan to be the Chief Provost and Judge, Elihoreph and Ahia, the Sons of Sisa, to be Masters of the Records, with the title of Inspectors, and four others, learned in the laws of Moses, to complete the number, and constitute the Tribunal. They held their sittings in the Middle Chamber of the Temple, where the records of the Tribunal were kept, in a box of Ebony, the Key of which was committed to the Chief Provost and Judge; and there they considered and adjusted the demands and differences of the workmen, and determined all appeals from the judgment of a single Provost and Judge; administering the same laws to the Phœnician as to the Hebrew; and endeavouring to do entire justice, according to the law of Moses, between man and man.

Such is the brief account which has come down to us, of the establishment of this degree. The lesson which it inculcates is justice in decision and judgment, and in our intercourse and dealing with other men.

In a country where trial by jury is known, every intelligent man is liable to be called on to act as a judge, either of fact alone, or of fact and law mingled ; and to assume the heavy responsibilities which belong to that character.

Those who are invested with the power of judgment, should judge the causes of all persons uprightly and impartially, without any personal consideration of the power of the mighty, or the bribe of the rich, or the needs of the poor. That is the cardinal rule, which no one will dispute ; though many fail to observe it. But they must do more. They must divest themselves of prejudice and preconception. They must hear patiently, remember accurately, and weigh carefully the facts and the arguments offered before them. They must not leap hastily to conclusions, nor form opinions before they have heard all. They must not presume crime or fraud ; but decide that it exists, only when, and not until, it is proven. They must neither cherish and indulge a stubborn pride of opinion, nor be too facile and yielding to the views and arguments of others. In deducing the motive from the proven act, they must not assign to the act either the best or the worst motive, but that which they would think it just and fair for the world to assign to it, if they themselves had done it : nor must they endeavour to make many little circumstances that weigh nothing separately, weigh much together, to prove their own acuteness and sagacity.

In our intercourse with others, there are two kinds of injustice ; the first, of those who offer an injury ; the second, of those who have it in their power to avert an injury from those to whom it is offered ; and yet do it not. So active injustice may be done in two ways—by force and by fraud,—of which force is lion-like, and fraud fox-like,—both utterly repugnant to social duty, but fraud the more detestable.

Every wrong done by one man to another, whether it affect his person, his property, his happiness or his reputation, is an offence against the law of justice. The field of this degree is therefore a wide and vast one ; and Masonry seeks for the most impressive mode of enforcing the law of justice, and the most effectual means of preventing wrong and injustice.

To this end it teaches this great and momentous truth : that wrong and injustice once done cannot be undone ; but are eternal in their consequences ; once committed, are numbered with the irrevocable Past : that the wrong that is done, *contains* its own retributive penalty, as surely and as naturally, as the acorn contains the oak. Its consequences are its punishment ; it needs no other, and can have no heavier ; they are involved in its commission, and cannot be separated from it. A wrong done to another is an injury done to our own Nature, an offence against our own souls, a disfiguring of the image of the Beautiful and Good. Punishment is not the execution of a sentence, but the occurrence of an effect. It is ordained to follow guilt, not by the decree of God as a judge, but by a law enacted by Him as the Creator and Legislator of the Universe. It is not an arbitrary and artificial annexation, but an ordinary and logical consequence ; and therefore must be borne by the wrong-doer alone.

There can be no interference with, or remittance of, or protection from, the natural effects of our wrongful acts. God will not interpose between the cause and its consequence ; and in that sense there can be no forgiveness of sins. The act which has debased our soul may be repented of, may be turned from ; but the injury is done. The debasement may be redeemed by after efforts, the stain obliterated by bitterer struggles and severer sufferings ; but the efforts and the endurance which might have raised the soul to the loftiest heights are now exhausted in merely regaining what it has lost. There must always be a wide difference between him who only ceases to do evil, and him who has always done well.

He will certainly be a far more scrupulous watcher over his conduct, and far more careful of his deeds, who believes that those deeds will inevitably bear their natural consequences, exempt from after intervention ; than he who believes that penitence and pardon will at any time unlink the chain of sequences. Surely we shall do less wrong and injustice, if the conviction is fixed and embedded in our souls, that every thing done is done irrevocably, that even the Omnipotence of God cannot *uncommit* a deed, cannot make that *undone,* which has *been done;* that every act of ours *must* bear its allotted fruit, according to the everlasting laws,— must remain forever ineffaceably inscribed on the tablets of Universal Nature.

If you have wronged another, you may grieve, repent, and resolutely determine against any such weakness in future. You may, so far as it is possible, make reparation. It is well. The injured party may forgive you, according to the meaning of human language ; but the deed is *done;* and all the powers of Nature, were they to conspire in your behalf, could not make it *undone;* the consequences to the body, the consequences to the soul, though no man may perceive them, *are there*, are written in the annals of the Past, and must reverberate throughout all time.

Repentance for a wrong done, bears, like every other act, its own fruit, the fruit of purifying the heart and amending the Future ; but not of effacing the Past. The commission of the wrong is an irrevocable act; but it does not incapacitate the soul to do right for the future. Its consequences cannot be expunged ; but its course need not be pursued. Wrong and evil perpetrated, though ineffaceable, call for no despair, but for efforts more energetic than before. Repentance is still as valid as ever ; but it is valid to secure the Future, not to obliterate the Past.

Even the pulsations of the air, once set in motion by the human voice, cease not to exist with the sounds to which they gave rise. Their quickly attenuated force soon becomes inaudible to human ears. But the waves of air thus raised perambulate the surface of earth and ocean, and in less than twenty hours, every atom of its atmosphere takes up the altered movement due to that infinitesimal portion of primitive motion which has been conveyed to it through countless channels, and which must continue to influence its path throughout its future existence. The air is one vast library, on whose pages is forever written all that man has ever said or even whispered. There, in their mutable, but unerring characters, mixed with the earliest, as well as the latest signs of mortality, stand forever recorded, vows unredeemed, promises unfulfilled; perpetuating, in the united movements of each particle, the testimony of man's changeful will. God reads that book, though we cannot.

So earth, air and ocean are the eternal witnesses of the acts that we have done. No motion impressed by natural causes or by human agency is ever obliterated. The track of every canoe which has yet disturbed the surface of the ocean, remains forever registered in the future movements of all succeeding particles which may occupy its place. Every criminal is by the laws of the Almighty irrevocably chained to the testimony of his crime ; for every atom of his mortal frame, through whatever changes its particles may migrate, will still retain, adhering to it through every combination, some movement derived from that very muscular effort, by which the crime itself was perpetrated.

What if our faculties should be so enhanced in a future life, as to enable us to perceive and trace the ineffaceable consequences of our idle words and evil deeds; and render our remorse and grief as eternal as those consequences themselves? No more fearful punishment to a superior intelligence can be conceived, than to see still in action, with the consciousness that it must continue in action forever, a cause of wrong put in motion by itself ages before.

Thus Masonry by its teachings endeavours to restrain men from the commission of injustice and acts of wrong and outrage. Though it does not endeavour to usurp the place of religion, still its code of morals proceeds upon other principles than the municipal law ; and it frowns upon and punishes offences which neither that law punishes nor public opinion condemns. In the Masonic law, cheating and overreaching in trade are *theft* ; a deliberate lie is *perjury*, the slanderer is an *assassin*, and the seducer worse than a *murderer*. Especially it condemns those wrongs of which the doer induces another to partake. *He* may repent; *he* may, after agonizing struggles, regain the path of virtue ; *his* spirit may re-achieve its purity through much anguish, after many strifes; but the weaker fellow-creature whom he led astray, whom he made a sharer in his guilt, but whom he cannot make a sharer in his repentance and amendment: whose downward course (the first step of which *he* taught), he cannot check, but is compelled to witness,—what forgiveness of sins can avail him there ? *There* is his perpetual, his inevitable punishment, which no repentance can alleviate, and no mercy can remit.

Let us be just also, in judging of other men's motives. We know but little of the real merits or demerits of any fellow-creature. We can rarely say with certainty that this man is more guilty than that, or even that this man is very good or very wicked. The basest men leave often behind them excellent reputations. There is scarcely one of us who has not, at some time in his life been on the edge of the commission of a great crime. We can every one of us look back, and shuddering, see the time when our feet stood upon the slippery crags that overhung the abyss of guilt; and when, if temptation had been a little more urgent, or a little longer continued, if want and penury had pressed us a little harder, or a little more wine had further disturbed our intellect, dethroned our judgment, and aroused our passions, our feet would have slipped and we should have fallen, never to rise again.

We may be able to say ; *this* man has lied; has pilfered, has forged, has embezzled moneys entrusted to him; and *that* man has gone through life with clean hands. But we cannot say that the former has not struggled long, though unsuccessfully, against temptations under which the second would have succumbed without an effort. We can say which has the cleanest *hands* before *man ;* but not which has the cleanest *soul* before God. We may be able to say, *this* man has committed adultery, and *that* man has been ever chaste; but we cannot tell but that the innocence of one may have been due to the coldness of his heart, to the absence of a motive, to the presence of a fear, to the slight degree of the temptation ; nor but that the fall of the other may have been preceded by the most vehement self-contest, caused by the most over-mastering frenzy, and atoned for by the most hallowing repentance. Generosity as well as niggardliness may be a mere yielding to native temperament ; and in the eye of Heaven, a long life of beneficence in one man may have cost less effort, and may indicate less virtue and less sacrifice of interest, than a few rare hidden acts of kindness wrung by duty out of the reluctant and unsympathizing nature of the other. There may be more real merit, more self-sacrificing effort, more of the noblest elements of moral grandeur, in a life of failure, sin and shame, than in a career, to our eyes, of stainless integrity.

When we condemn or pity the fallen, how do we know that, tempted like him, we should not have fallen as soon, and perhaps with less resistance? How can we know what *we* should do if we were out of employment, famine sitting gaunt and hungry at our fireside, and our children wailing for bread ? *We fall not, because we are not tempted.* He that *hath* fallen may be at heart as honest as we. How do we know that our wife or sister or daughter could resist the distress, the temptation, that lost their poor abandoned sister of shame her virtue ? Perhaps *they* also stand, only because they have not been tempted.

Human justice must be ever uncertain. How many judicial murders have been committed, through ignorance of the phenomena of insanity ! How many men been hung for murder, who were no more murderers at heart than the jury that tried, and the judge that sentenced, them ! It may well be doubted whether the administration of human laws, in every country of the Globe, is not one gigantic mass of injustice and wrong. God seeth not as man seeth ; and the most abandoned criminal, black as he is before the world, may yet have continued to keep some little light burning in a corner of his own soul; which would long since have gone out in that of those who walk proudly in the sunshine of immaculate fame, if they had been tried and tempted like the poor outcast.

We do not know even the *outside* life of men. We are not competent to pronounce even on their *deeds.* We do not know half the acts of wickedness or virtue, even of our most immediate fellows. We cannot say with certainty, even of our nearest friend, that he has not committed a particular sin, and broken a particular commandment. Let each man ask his own heart. Of how many of our best and of our worst acts and qualities, are our most intimate associates utterly unconscious ! How many virtues does not the world give us credit for, that we do not possess : or vices condemn us for, of which we are not the slaves ! It is but a small portion of our evil deeds and thoughts that ever comes to light ; and of our few redeeming goodnesses, the largest portion is known to God alone.

We shall therefore be just, in judging of other men, only when we are charitable: and we should assume the prerogative of judging others, only when the duty is forced upon us ; since we are almost so certain to err ; and since the consequences of error are so serious. No man need covet the office of judge ; for in assuming it, he assumes the most serious and oppressive responsibility. You have assumed it. We all assume it ; for man is ever ready to judge, and ever ready to condemn his neighbour ; while upon the same state of case he acquits and absolves himself. See, therefore, that you exercise your office cautiously and charitably, lest in passing judgment upon the criminal, you commit a greater wrong than that for which you condemn him, and the consequences of which will be eternal.

The faults and crimes and follies of other men are not unimportant to us; but form a part of our moral discipline. War and bloodshed at a distance, and frauds which do not affect our pecuniary interests, touch us in our feelings, and concern our moral welfare. They have much to do with all thoughtful hearts. The public eye may look unconcernedly on the miserable victim of vice ; and that shattered wreck of a man may move the multitude to laughter or to scorn. But to the Mason, it is the form of sacred humanity that is before him; it is an erring fellow-being; a desolate, forlorn, forsaken soul; and his thoughts, enfolding the poor wretch, will be far deeper than those of indifference, ridicule or contempt. All human offences, the whole system of dishonesty, evasion, circumventing, forbidden indulgence and intriguing ambition, in which men are struggling with each other, will be looked upon by a thoughtful Mason, not merely as a scene of mean toils and strifes, but as the solemn conflict of immortal minds, for ends vast and momentous as their own being. It is a sad and unworthy strife, and may well be viewed with indignation; but that indignation must melt into pity. For the stakes for which these gamesters play, are not those which they imagine, not those which are in sight. For example, this man plays for a petty office, and gains it; but the real stake he gains, is sycophancy, uncharitableness, slander and deceit.

Good men are too proud of their goodness. They are respectable; dishonour comes not near them; their countenance has weight and influence; their robes are unstained; the poisonous breath of calumny has never been breathed upon their fair name. How easy it is for them to look down with scorn upon the poor degraded offender; to pass him by with a lofty step; to draw up the folds of their garment around them, that they may not be soiled by his touch! Yet the Great Master of Virtue did not so; but descended to familiar inter-course with publicans and sinners.

Many men think themselves better, in proportion as they can detect sins in others? When they go over the catalogue of their neighbour's unhappy derelictions of temper or conduct, they often, amidst much apparent concern, feel a secret exultation, that destroys all their own pretensions to wisdom and moderation, and even to virtue. Many even take actual pleasure in the sins of others; and this is the case with every one whose thoughts are often employed in agreeable comparisons of his own virtues with his neighbours' faults.

The power of gentleness is too little seen in the world; the subduing influences of pity, the might of love, the control of mildness over passion, the commanding Majesty of that perfect character which mingles grave displeasure with grief and pity for the offender. So it is that a Mason should treat his brothers who go astray. Not with bitterness; nor yet with good-natured easiness, nor with worldly indifference, nor with a philosophic coldness, nor with a laxity of conscience, that accounts everything well, that passes under the seal of public opinion.

The human heart will not bow willingly to what is infirm and wrong in human nature. If it yields to us, it must yield to what is divine in us. The wickedness of my neighbour cannot submit to my wickedness; his sensuality, for instance, to my anger against his vices. My faults are not the instruments that are to arrest his faults. And therefore impatient reformers, and denouncing preachers, and hasty reprovers, and angry parents, and irritable relatives generally fail, in their several departments, to reclaim the erring.

A moral offence is sickness, pain, loss, dishonour, in the immortal part of man. It is guilt, and misery added to guilt. It is itself calamity; and brings upon itself, in addition, the calamity of God's disapproval, the abhorrence of all virtuous men, and the soul's own abhorrence. Deal faithfully, but patiently and tenderly, with this evil. It is no matter for petty provocation, nor for personal strife, nor for selfish irritation.

Speak kindly to your erring brother. God pities him: Christ has died for him: Providence waits for him: Heaven's mercy yearns towards him; and Heaven's spirits are ready to welcome him back with joy. Let your voice be in unison with all those powers that God is using for his recovery.

If one defrauds you, and exults at it, he is the most to be pitied of human beings. He has done himself a far deeper injury than he has done you. It is him, and not you, whom God regards with mingled displea-sure and compassion; and His judgment should be your law. Among all the benedictions of the Holy Mount there is not one for this man; but for the merciful, the peace-makers and the persecuted they are poured out freely.

We are all men of like passions, propensities and exposures. There are elements in us all, which might have been perverted, through the successive processes of moral deterioration, to the worst of crimes. The wretch whom the execration of the thronging crowd pursues to the scaffold, is not worse than any one of that multitude might have become, under similar circumstances. He is to be condemned indeed, but also deeply to be pitied.

It does not become the frail and sinful to be vindictive towards even the worst criminals. We owe much to the good Providence of God, ordaining for us a lot more favourable to virtue. We all had that within us, that might have been pushed to the same excess. Perhaps we should have fallen as he did, with less temptation. Perhaps we have done acts, that, in proportion to the temptation or provocation, were less excusable than his great crime. Silent pity and sorrow for the victim should mingle with our detestation of the guilt. Even the pirate who murders in cold blood on the high seas, is such a man as you or I might have been. Orphanage in childhood, or base and dissolute and abandoned parents; an unfriended youth; evil companions; ignorance and want of moral cultivation; the temptations of sinful pleasure or grinding poverty; familiarity with vice; a scorned and blighted name; seared and crushed affections; desperate fortunes; these are steps that might have led any one among us, to unfurl upon the high seas the bloody flag of universal defiance; to wage war with our kind; to live the life and die the death of the reckless and remorseless freebooter. Many affecting relationships of humanity plead with us to pity him. His head once rested on a mother's bosom. He was once the object of sisterly love and domestic endearment. Perhaps his hand, since often red with blood, once clasped another little loving hand at the altar. Pity him then; his blighted hopes and his crushed heart. It is proper that frail and erring creatures like us should do so; should feel the crime, but feel it as weak, tempted and rescued creatures should.. It may be that when God weighs men's crimes, He will take into consideration the temptations and the adverse circumstances that led to them, and the opportunities for moral culture of the offender; and it may be that our own offences will weigh heavier than we think, and the murderer's lighter than according to man's judgment.

On all accounts, therefore, let the true Mason never forget the solemn injunction, necessary to be observed at almost every moment of a busy life: "Judge not, lest ye yourselves be judged: for whatsoever judgment ye measure unto others, the same shall in turn be measured unto you." Such is the lesson taught to every Provost and Judge.

TO CLOSE.

Ill∴ M∴ Bro∴ Sen∴ Inspector, what is the hour?

Sen. Insp. The last hour of the night. The day cometh.

Ill∴ M∴ Why always the same hour?

Sen∴ Insp∴ Because a Provost and Judge must be always ready to dispense justice; and all hours are alike to him.

Ill∴ M∴ Does any duty of this Lodge remain unperformed?

Sen∴ Insp∴ None, Ill∴ Master.

Ill∴ M∴ Then we may rest from our labours in the Lodge, that each may do his individual duty in the world. Bro∴ Jun∴ Insp∴, how should Masons always act?

Jun∴ Insp∴ With *justice*.

Ill∴ M∴ Bro∴ Sen∴ Inspector, how should they deliberate?

Sen∴ Insp∴ With *impartiality*.

Ill∴ M∴ And decide by the rules of *Equity*. So let us ever act, deliberate and decide. My Brethren, aid me to close this Lodge.

[The Ill∴ M∴ gives the sign, and all the Brethren the answer. Then the Ill∴ Master gives the battery [.; ; ,]—which is repeated by the Sen∴ and Jun∴ Wardens, in succession, and then by all the Brethren with their hands; and the Ill∴ M∴ says]:

Ill∴ M∴ My Brethren, the Lodge is closed.

FINIS.

Eighth Degree.

Intendant of the Buildings.

THE LODGE AND ITS DECORATIONS.

The hangings of the Lodge are crimson. It is lighted by 27 lights, arranged in 3 groups, of 9 each, and each group forming a triple triangle.

In front of the Master is the Altar, on which are five other lights.

Over the Master is a blazing star with five points, and in its centre the name of Deity . . . . יהֹ: [Iao].

OFFICERS AND TITLES.

The Lodge regularly consists, and is always supposed to consist, of five members only; representing the five Architects who were appointed superintendents of the building, in the place, for the time being, of the deceased Hiram Abi.

The Master sits in the East, is styled *Most Skilful*, and represents ADONHIRAM the son of Abda, President of the Board of Architects.

The Sen∴ Warden sits in the West and the Junior Warden in the South; the Sen∴ and Jun∴ Deacons in the North. The Sen∴ Warden represents JOABERT, a Phœnician, chief artificer in brass; the Jún∴ Warden, STOLKIN, a Hebrew, Chief Carpenter: the Sen∴ Deacon, SELEC the Giblemite, Chief Stone-Mason; and the Jun∴ Deacon, GAREB the Hebrew, chief worker in Silver and Gold, and Engraver.

During a reception, the Master represents *King Solomon;* the Sen∴ Warden, *Sadoc* the Priest; and the Jun∴ Warden, *Ahishar*, Governor of the House. The Sen∴ Deacon acts as Master of Ceremonies, and represents *Zabud*, the son of Nathan.

ORNAMENTS, JEWEL, ETC.

The cordon of the degree is a broad red ribbon, worn from the right shoulder to the left hip, at the end of which hangs the jewel, attached by a green ribbon.

The jewel is a triangle of gold, or of silver gilt, on one side of which is engraved the word Ben-Khurim, and on the other the word Achar.

The apron is white, lined with red, and bordered with green. In the centre of it is painted or embroidered a nine-pointed star, and over that a balance. On the flap is a triangle, with one of the following letters at each angle ב∴ א∴ שׁ∴ [B∴ A∴ Sh∴], the initials of the words BEN-KHURIM, ACHAR, SHEKINAH.

7

TO OPEN.

M∴ Sk∴. Bro∴ Joabert, what is the hour?

Sen∴ W∴. Day-break, Most Skilful.

M∴ Sk∴. Then it is time to resume our labours, that the workmen upon the Temple may not be delayed for the want of plans and designs. See that we be secure from interruption.

Sen∴ W∴. Bro∴ Gareb, this Lodge is about to be opened. See that we are duly tyled, and direct the Tyler to allow no one to interrupt us in our labours.

[The Jun∴ Deacon goes to the door, informs the Tyler, closes the door, gives the battery [; ; ?] which is answered from without, returns to his place, and reports]:

Jun∴ D∴. Bro∴ Joabert, we are duly tyled.

Sen∴ W∴. M∴ Skilful Master, we are duly tyled, and secure against interruption.

M∴ Sk∴. Bro∴ Jun∴ Deacon, what is your duty in this Lodge?

Jun∴ D∴. Gareb the Hebrew, whom I represent, was the chief worker in silver and gold, and chief engraver after the death of Hiram Abi. As he furnished designs to the workmen under him, so it is my duty to furnish good examples to the Brethren, by the practice of those virtues that adorn and add grace to the character of a Mason.

M∴ Sk∴. Bro∴ Sen∴ Deacon, what is your duty?

Sen∴ D∴. Selec the Giblemite, whom I represent, was the chief stone-mason. As he saw that the foundations and walls of the Temple were built strong and solid, it is my duty to inculcate those noble virtues which give strength and solidity to the character of a Mason; and which alone can make the order perpetual.

M∴ Sk∴. Bro∴ Jun∴ Warden, what is your duty?

Jun∴ W∴. Stolkin, whom I represent, was the chief carpenter, and rose to the highest honours. It is my duty to inculcate and practice those virtues, sobriety, temperance, punctuality and industry, which make labour honourable, and the mechanic the peer of kings.

M∴ Sk∴. Bro∴ Sen∴ Warden, what is your duty?

Sen∴ W∴. Joabert the Phœnician, whom I represent, was the chief artificer in brass, and completed the great works commenced by Hiram Abi. It is my duty to imitate these illustrious men, in their deeds of usefulness, of charity and of devotion to Masonry.

M∴ Sk∴. And it is my duty, representing Adonhiram the son of Abda, President of the Board of Architects, and who, with Joabert, Stolkin, Selec and Gareb were the favourite pupils of Hiram Abi, and from him learned the science of architecture, studied by him in Assyria and Phœnicia, to superintend, correct and approve the work of the Lodge, to encourage the timid and diffident, to repress the forward and impatient, and to reward the worthy and deserving. Bro∴ Sen∴ Warden, since we no longer build Temples and Palaces, what is the chief employment of an Intendant of the buildings?

Sen∴ W∴. To carry onward the great Masonic works of Charity and Benevolence: to found schools and colleges, for the education of the children of the dead and the poor; hospitals for the sick, and houses of refuge for the unfortunate.

M∴ Sk∴. Aid me, then, my Brethren, in opening this Lodge, that we may take counsel together as to that great work; as our ancient Brethren counselled in regard to the work upon the Temple.

[The M∴ gives the sign of surprise: The Brethren all respond with that of admiration.]

M∴ Sk∴. Bro∴ Sen∴ Warden, what is the age of an Intendant of the building?

Sen∴ W∴. That of a Fellow-craft, multiplied by that of an Apprentice—5 multiplied by 3, or 15.

[Then the Master raps [;]—the Sen∴ W∴ [;]—and the Jun∴ W∴ [?]: and the Master says]:

M∴ Sk∴. Brethren, the Lodge is duly opened.

RECEPTION.

The Lodge being opened, the Master clothes himself in a purple robe, with a sceptre and crown, and represents King Solomon. The Sen.·. Warden, wearing a white robe and mitre, represents Sadoc, the Priest, and the Jun.·. Warden, wearing the collar and apron of the degree, represents Ahishar.

The candidate, dressed as a Perfect Master, is brought into the Lodge, and requested to be seated.

M.·. Sk.·. Sadoc, my Brother, give me your counsel and advice. A base and bloody crime has deprived us of the Chief Architect of the Temple, and there is no one among the workmen competent to take his place. There is no one upon whom his mantle has fallen; for he studied architecture in Babylon, in Thebes and in Memphis, as well as in Tyre, and had learned all that the builders of Phœnicia, Egypt and Assyria could teach him. Moreover he was charged with the construction of the secret chamber, intended in case of emergency to contain the sacred treasures, and the Holy Ark of the covenant. I am at a loss how to provide for carrying on the work, which stands still, and the workmen are idle.

Sen.·. W.·. Th.·. Puissant King Solomon, cannot thy brother the King of Tyre send thee another architect to fill the place of our deceased Gr.·. Master?

M.·. Sk.·. He hath none such in his dominions; and where shall we find one like unto him that we have lost?

Sen.·. W.·. Then, Th.·. P.·., I know not what to advise.

Jun.·. W.·. Th.·. P.·. King Solomon, may thy servant Ahishar speak?

M.·. Sk.·. Speak, my Brother, and freely.

Jun.·. W.·. Th.·. Puissant, our lamented Gr.·. Master was fond of the society of the young who were eager to learn, and delighted to communicate to them the arts and sciences which he had studied in the East and in Egypt. His chief favourites were Adonhiram the son of Abda, Joabert the noble Phœnician, Stolkin of the Tribe of Benjamin, Selec the Giblemite, and Gareb of the Tribe of Naphthali, whom he was wont to term his school, and to whom he taught all the learning that he had gathered from the Sacred Books of the Egyptian Priests and those of the Magi of Persia; the sciences of geometry and astronomy, of numbers and of architecture; with the occult learning of the Indians, Assyrians and Etruscans; as well as that of his own People; and the art of working in brass, in wood, and in silver and gold. He often spoke to me of these his scholars, saying that when he was dead, they would be able to take his place; he often entrusted to Adonhiram the superintendence of the whole work, and made Joabert the chief artificer in brass, Stolkin chief of the workers in wood, Selec chief of the stone masons and Gareb chief of the workmen in silver and gold, and the engravers. Why should they not, if it so please my Lord the King, take his place as he intended, now that he is dead?

M.·. Sk.·. Do you believe, my Brother, that these pupils of our deceased Gr.·. Master are competent to fill his place, and to carry on the work upon the Temple?

Jun.·. W.·. Th.·. Puissant, they were greatly trusted by our deceased Gr.·. Master, and he believed them fitted to succeed him. They may at least conduct the work until one can be found fitted in all respects to be appointed Gr.·. Master Architect. They will partially supply the great loss that we have sustained; if they can do no more.

M.·. Sk.·. Are they present here among us?

J.·. W.·. They are.

M.·. Sk.·. They have then attained the rank of Perfect Masters?

Jun.·. W.·. They have.

M.·. Sk.·. Sadoc, my Brother, what thinkest thou of this suggestion of our Brother Ahishar?

Sen.·. W.·. Th.·. Puissant, I have assisted our deceased Gr.·. Master to instruct these pupils; and have often heard him say that they would soon be fit to take his place. They were ever eager to learn, attentive, docile, orderly and obedient. I think the work may safely be entrusted to their hands; at least for the present.

M.·. Sk.·. Let Adonhiram, Joabert, Stolkin, Selec and Gareb approach the East. [The candidate and four Brethren come forward; and one of the Brethren answers]:

M.·. Sk.·. Were you the pupils of our Brother Hiram?

All: . . . We were.

M∴ Sk∴ In what did he instruct you?

Bro∴ In all the arts and sciences known to the Phœnicians, Egyptians and Assyrians, and especially in architecture; and in the mysterious knowledge of the Indians, the Magi and the Etruscans. But, alas, our knowledge, in comparison with his, is nothing.

M∴ Sk∴ He knows much, who is conscious of his ignorance. Are you willing to devote your time, your talents, your attainments, entire and undivided, to the great work which he commenced, but did not live to finish?

Bro∴ Th∴ Puissant, we fear to assume so grave a responsibility, knowing ourselves incompetent.

M∴ Sk∴ If I command?

Bro∴ Then we shall undertake the task with diffidence; and devote ourselves and all our energies to the great work, relying more upon your kind indulgence than upon our own merits.

M∴ Sk∴ Go then with your Brother, our Master of Ceremonies, who will prepare you to be invested with the office which it is our design to confer upon you, if he finds you qualified and worthy. Take with you these Brethren, Bro∴ Master of Ceremonies, with whose skill in architecture we are satisfied, and see whether they are sufficiently instructed in Masonry; and having informed them of the moral qualifications which we require in those whom we advance to rank and honour, bring them again before us for investiture, if you find them qualified and worthy.

[The M∴ of Cer∴ retires with the Candidate and the four Brethren, and in the preparation room carefully examines the Candidate in the work of the 7th Degree, and then puts to him the following questions]:

1°. What lesson was taught you in the Degree of Secret Master?

2°. What lesson was taught you in the Degree of Perfect Master?

3°. What lesson is taught by the Degree of Confidential Secretary?

4°. What virtues were you taught to practice as a Provost and Judge?

[If he fails to answer correctly, he must be dismissed, to receive further instruction, and undergo a longer probation. He may be prompted in the *work*, and his deficiencies in *that* overlooked; but not in the *moral principles* of the Degrees. This rule is imperative. If he answers correctly, the M∴ of Ceremonies says]:

M∴ Cer∴ Such are the lessons of the Preceding Degrees. To become an Intendant of the Buildings it is required that, besides being skilful Architects, and learned in the knowledge of the East and of Egypt, you should be charitable and benevolent, that you may sympathize with the labouring man, relieve his necessities, see to his comfort and that of his family, and smooth for him and for those who depend upon him the rugged pathway of life. Recognizing all men as your Brethren, and yourself as the Almoner of God's bounty, are you willing to perform these duties?

Cand∴ I am.

M∴ Cer∴ And you, my Brethren, do you answer like our Brother Joabert?

Others. We do.

M∴ Cer∴ Prepare, then, to be invested with the office which you seek.

[Each lays aside the clothing and ornaments of a Perfect Master, and puts on a white robe; and the M∴ of Cer∴ then gives the alarm at the door. The Jun∴ Deacon, partly opening it, says]:

Jun∴ D∴ Who comes here?

M∴ Cer∴ The five Brethren, who being found qualified and competent, are about to be invested with the office of Intendant of the Buildings.

Jun∴ D∴ Let them enter.

[The Candidate and the four Brethren then enter, and make the circuit of the room five times, while the Master reads as follows]:

1st Circuit: . . . . Thou shalt not oppress an hired servant or a labouring man that is poor and needy. On the day when he earns it, thou shalt give him his hire, nor shall the sun go down upon it; for he is poor, and it is his life: lest he cry against thee unto the Lord, and God punish thee for this sin.

2d Circuit: If thy brother be waxen poor, and fallen into decay with thee, then thou shalt relieve him, though he be a stranger or a transient person, that he may live with thee. Take of him no usury nor increase: but fear thy God, and let thy brother live.

3d Circuit: . . . . If there be among you a poor man, and one unable to work, of thy brethren within any of thy gates, thou shalt not harden thy heart, nor shut thine hand from thy poor brother; but thou shalt open thine hand unto him, and shalt surely lend him sufficient for his need: and thine eye shalt not be evil against thy poor brother, so that thou give him naught, and he cry unto the Lord against thee, and it be charged against thee as a sin. Thou shalt give him without grudging, and the Lord shall bless thee; for thou art but his Treasurer, to dispense his benefits to the poor.

4th Circuit: . . . . When thou cuttest down thy harvest in thy field, thou shalt not wholly reap the corners of thy field, nor gather the gleanings of thy harvest: and if thou hast forgotten a sheaf in the field, thou shalt not go again to fetch it. It shall be for the stranger, for the fatherless and for the widow; that the Lord thy God may bless thee in all the work of thy hands. When thou beatest thine olive-trees, thou shalt not go over the boughs again. It shall be for the stranger, the fatherless and the widow. When thou gatherest the grapes of thy vineyard, thou shalt not glean it afterwards. It shall be for the stranger, for the fatherless and for the widow.

5th Circuit: . . . . If thy brother be waxen poor, and be compelled to serve thee, thou shalt not rule over him with rigour; but shalt fear thy God. Nor shalt thou discharge those whose labour is their life, because thy profits are not large; nor leave the children of those who have served thee, and are dead, to suffer with want or to grow up in ignorance: but thou shalt be God's almoner; for He hath but lent thee all the wealth thou hast; and thou art but His Trustee for the poor, the suffering and the destitute.

[At the end of the 5th Circuit, the Candidate and the four Brothers are halted in front of the altar; and the Master of Ceremonies gives each of them a branch of evergreen, and directs them to kneel before the Altar, holding the evergreen in the right hand, and placing the left upon the Holy Bible. The Th.·. P.·. then rises and calls up all the brethren, and approaching the altar says]:

M.·. Sk.·. My Brethren, before you can be invested with the office of Intendant of the Building, it is necessary that you should take an obligation faithfully to perform the duties of the office, and the Masonic duties specially inculcated in this degree. You will therefore repeat your names, and say after me:

OBLIGATION.

I, A. . . . B. . . . ., in the presence of the Gr.·. Architect of the Universe, do hereby and hereon most solemnly and sincerely promise and swear; that I will never reveal the secrets of this degree, except at a proper time and in a proper place, to one duly authorized to receive them, and when I am legally authorized to communicate them.

I furthermore promise and swear, that I will endeavour faithfully to perform the duties imposed upon me in this degree, in good faith, and to the best of my capacity and ability.

I furthermore promise and swear that I will practice the duties of benevolence and charity; that I will not oppress nor deal hardly with the labouring man in my employ, nor defraud him of his wages, nor make unjust charges against him; nor abandon him when he is sick and feeble and unable to work; nor refuse to recognize the claim of his children upon me for assistance; nor over-work nor under-pay him; but will ever remember that he is my brother, and is entitled to my sympathy, to my regard and to my assistance.

To all which I do most solemnly and sincerely promise and swear; and may our Common Father so deal gently or harshly with me, as I deal gently or harshly with my brother! Amen!

Arise, my Brethren! I accept and declare you Intendants of the Building, and Chief Architects of the Masonic Temple. As successors of our lamented Gr.·. Master, strive to follow his excellent precepts, and to imitate his illustrious virtues; and see that you prove not unfaithful to the trust confided to you, nor dishonour the rank and title which you now receive.

In this degree there are three signs and a token:

1st Sign: . . . *of Surprise:* . . . Place the ♈&ʒ♋♏♎, one on each ♈☾♋ʓ†☾; the &☉♒□♎ extended in front of the ♑☿‡☾&☾☉♊, and forming a square; as if to protect the ☾♄☾♎ from the †♀♌&♈. In this attitude, take two steps forward, and then ? backward; and say: ♏☾♒¶&ʒ‡♀♋.·.

2d Sign: *of Admiration:* . . . In answer to the first: . . . Interlace the fingers of the two hands in front of the ♑☿‡☾&☾☉♊, and let them fall to a level with the ♃☉♀♎♈; looking upward, and saying: ☉♐&☉‡∴

3d Sign: *of Sorrow:* . . . Each places his ‡¦&☉♒♊ or his &☾☉‡♈, and his †¼&☉♒♊ on his †¾&♀♀: then each balancing himself three times on his ¶♒☾☾♎, one says &♄☉∴ and the other, ♁☉&∴

Token: . . . Each places his ‡¾&☉♒♊ on the &☾☉‡♈ of the other: then each with his right hand takes the other by the ‡¼☾†♏☿♃ and puts his †¼&☉♒♊ on the ‡¼♎&☿♄†♊☾‡ of the other. Then one says ♎&☾¶♀♒☉&∴ and the other ♁☾*☉∴

Passwords: . . . ♏☽♒·¶&♄‡♀♋∴ ☉♐&☉‡∴

Sacred Words: . . . &♄☉∴ ♁☉&∴ ♎&☾¶♀♒☉&∴ ♁☾*☉∴

The Candidate is then invested with the apron, collar and jewel; the Th∴ P∴ saying:

I invest you with the apron of this degree. Let its three colours, white, red and green, teach you to imitate that purity of morals and zeal for the service of Masonry, which have made the memory of our deceased Gr∴ Master immortal in the recollection of men.

I invest you also with the collar and jewel of this degree. You do not need to be told of what the triangle is an emblem. When you wear them, remember that you do so as the successor of Hiram Abi; and be careful that you do no act inconsistent with the character which as such successor it becomes you to maintain.

This is the meaning of the words of this degree: [The candidate is then instructed in the meaning of the words, from the manuscript].

LECTURE.

The History of this degree is fully given in the reception. In it you have represented one of the five architects appointed by King Solomon to conduct the work upon the Temple, in the place of Hiram the Chief Architect, who had been murdered; and you have been taught the important lesson, that none are entitled to advance in the Ancient and Accepted Rite, who have not by study and application made themselves familiar with Masonic learning and jurisprudence. The degrees of this rite are not for those who are content with the mere work and ceremonies, and do not seek to explore the mines of wisdom that lie buried beneath the surface. You still advance towards the light, towards that star, blazing in the distance, which is an emblem of the Divine Truth, given by God to the first men, and preserved amid all the vicissitudes of ages in the traditions and teachings of Masonry. How far you will advance, depends upon yourself alone. Here, as every where in the world, Darkness struggles with Light, and clouds and shadows intervene between you and the truth.

When you shall have become imbued with the morality of Masonry, with which you yet are, and for some time will be exclusively occupied,—when you shall have learned to practice all the virtues which it inculcates; when they become familiar to you as your Household Gods; then will you be prepared to receive its lofty philosophical instruction, and to scale the heights upon whose summit Light and Truth sit enthroned. Step by step men must advance towards Perfection; and each Masonic Degree is meant to be one of those steps. Each is a development of a particular duty; and in the present you are taught charity and benevolence; to be to your brethren an example of virtue; to correct your own faults; and to endeavour to correct those of your brethren.

Here, as in all the degrees, you meet with the emblems and the names of Deity, the true knowledge of whose character and attributes it has ever been a chief object of Masonry to perpetuate. To appreciate His infinite greatness and goodness, to rely implicitly upon His Providence, to revere and venerate Him as the Supreme Architect, Creator and Legislator of the universe, is the first of Masonic duties.

The Battery of this Degree, and the five circuits which you made around the Lodge allude to the 5 points of fellowship; and are intended to recall them vividly to your mind. To go upon a Brother's errand or to his relief, even bare-foot and upon flinty ground: to remember him in your supplications to the Deity: to clasp him to your heart, and protect him against misfortune and slander: to uphold him when about to stumble and fall: and to give him prudent, honest and friendly counsel; are duties plainly written upon the pages of God's great code of laws, and first among the ordinances of Masonry.

The first sign of the Degree is expressive of the diffidence and humility with which we inquire into the nature and attributes of the Deity; the second, of the profound admiration and reverence with which we contemplate His glories; and the third, of the sorrow with which we reflect upon our insufficient observance of our duties and compliance with His statutes.

The distinguishing property of man is to search for and follow after truth. Therefore, when relaxed from our necessary cares and concerns, we then covet to see, to hear and to learn somewhat; and we esteem knowledge of things, either obscure or wonderful, to be the indispensable means of living happily. Truth, Simplicity, and Candour are most agreeable to the nature of mankind. Whatever is virtuous consists either in Sagacity, and the perception of Truth; or in the preservation of Human Society, by giving to every man his due, and observing the faith of contracts; or in the greatness and firmness of an elevated and unsubdued mind; or in observing order and regularity in all our words and in all our actions; in which consist moderation and temperance.

Masonry has in all times religiously preserved that enlightened faith from which flow sublime devotedness, the sentiment of Fraternity fruitful of good works, the spirit of indulgence and peace, of sweet hopes and effectual consolations; and inflexibility in the accomplishment of the most painful and arduous duties. It has always propagated it with ardour and perseverance; and therefore it labours at the present day more zealously than ever. Scarcely a Masonic discourse is pronounced, that does not demonstrate the necessity and advantages of this faith, and especially recall the two constitutive principles of religion, that make all religion,— love of God, and love of our neighbour. Masons carry these principles into the bosoms of their families and of society. While the Sectarians of former times enfeebled the religious spirit, Masonry, forming one great People over the whole globe, and marching under the great banner of Charity and Benevolence, preserves that religious feeling, strengthens it, extends it in its purity and simplicity, as it has always existed in the depths of the human heart, as it existed even under the dominion of the most ancient forms of worship, but where gross and debasing superstition forbade its recognition.

A Masonic Lodge should resemble a bee-hive, in which all the members work together with ardour for the common good. Masonry is not made for cold souls and narrow minds, that do not comprehend its lofty mission and sublime apostolate. Here the anathema against lukewarm souls applies. To comfort misfortune, to popularize knowledge, to teach whatever is true and pure in religion and philosophy, to accustom men to respect order and the proprieties of life, to point out the way to genuine happiness, to prepare for that fortunate period, when all the fractions of the Human Family, united by the bonds of Toleration and Fraternity, shall be but one household,—these are labours that may well excite zeal and even enthusiasm.

We do not now enlarge upon or elaborate these ideas. We but utter them to you briefly, as hints, upon which you may at your leisure reflect. Hereafter, if you continue to advance, they will be unfolded, explained and developed.

For the present, as we have said, we are occupied solely with the moral code of Masonry. It utters no impracticable and extravagant precepts; certain, because they are so, to be disregarded. It asks of its initiates nothing that is not possible and even easy for them to perform. Its teachings are eminently practical; and its statutes can be obeyed by every just, upright and honest man, no matter what his faith or creed. Its object is to attain the greatest practical good, without seeking to make men perfect. It does not meddle with the domain of religion, nor inquire into the mysteries of regeneration. It teaches those truths that are written by the finger of God upon the heart of man; those views of duty which have been wrought out by the meditations of the studious, confirmed by the allegiance of the good and wise, and stamped as sterling by the response they find in every uncorrupted mind. It does not dogmatize, nor vainly imagine dogmatic certainty to be attainable.

Masonry does not occupy itself with crying down this world, with its splendid beauty, its thrilling interests, its glorious works, its noble and holy affections; nor exhort us to detach our hearts from this earthly life, as empty, fleeting and unworthy, and fix them upon Heaven, as the only sphere deserving the love of the loving or the meditation of the wise. It teaches that man has high duties to perform, and a high destiny to fulfil, on this earth: that this world is not merely the portal to another; and that this life, though not our only one, is an integral one, and the particular one with which we are here meant to be concerned: that the Present is our scene of action; and the Future for speculation and for trust: that man was sent upon the earth to live in it, to enjoy it, to study it, to love it, to embellish it, to make the most of it. It is his country, on which he should lavish his affections and his efforts. It is here his influences are to operate. It is his house, and not a tent; his home, and not merely a school. He is sent into this world, not to be constantly hankering after, dreaming of, preparing for another; but to do his duty and fulfil his destiny on this earth; to do all that lies in his power to improve it, to render it a scene of elevated happiness to himself, to those around him, to those that are to come after him.

And thus, Masonry teaches us, will man best prepare for that Future which he hopes for. The Unseen cannot hold a higher place in our affections than the Seen and the Familiar. The law of our being is Love of Life, and its interests and adornments; love of the world in which our lot is cast, engrossment with the interests and affections of earth. Not a low or sensual love; not love of wealth, of fame, of ease, of power, of splendour. Not low worldliness; but the love of Earth as the garden on which the Creator has lavished such miracles of beauty, as the habitation of humanity, the arena of its conflicts, the scene of its illimitable progress, the dwelling-place of the wise, the good, the active, the loving and the dear; the place of opportunity for the development, by means of sin and suffering and sorrow, of the noblest passions, the loftiest virtues and the tenderest sympathies.

They take very unprofitable pains, who endeavour to persuade men that they are obliged wholly to despise this world, and all that is in it, even whilst they themselves live here. God hath not taken all that pains in forming and framing and furnishing and adorning the world, that they who were made by Him to live in it should despise it. It will be enough, if they do not love it too immoderately. It is useless to attempt to extinguish all those affections and passions which are and always will be inseparable from human nature. As long as the world lasts, and honour and virtue and industry have reputation in the world, there will be ambition and emulation and appetite in the best and most accomplished men in it; and if there were not, more barbarity and vice and wickedness would cover every nation of the world, than it now suffers under.

Those only who feel a deep interest in, and affection for, this world, will work resolutely for its amelioration. Those who undervalue this life, naturally become querulous and discontented, and lose their interest in the welfare of their fellows. To serve them, and so to do our duty as Masons, we must feel that the object is worth the exertion; and be content with this world in which God has placed us, until He permits us to remove to a better one.

It is a serious thing to defame and belie a whole world; to speak of it as the abode of a poor, toiling, drudging, ignorant, contemptible race. You would not so discredit your family, your friendly circle, your village, your city, your country. The world is not a wretched and a worthless one; nor is it a misfortune, but a thing to be thankful for, to be a man.

In society itself, in that living mechanism of human relationships that spreads itself over the world, there is a finer essence within, that as truly moves it, as any power, heavy or expansive, moves the sounding manufactory or the swift-flying car. The man-machine hurries to and fro upon the earth, stretches out its hands on every side, to toil, to barter, to unnumbered labours and enterprises; and almost always the motive, that which moves it, is something that takes hold of the comforts, affections and hopes of social existence. True, the mechanism often works with difficulty, drags heavily, grates and screams with harsh collision. True, the essence of finer motive, becoming intermixed with baser and coarser ingredients, often clogs, obstructs, jars and deranges the free and noble action of social life. But he is neither grateful nor wise, who looks cynically on all this, and loses the fine sense of social good in its perversions. That I can be a *friend*, that I can *have* a friend, though it were but one in the world ; that fact, that wondrous good fortune, we may set against all the sufferings of our social nature. That there is such a place on earth as a *home*, that resort and sanctuary of in-walled and shielded joy, we may set against all the surrounding desolations of life. That one can be a true, social man, can speak his true thoughts, amidst all the janglings of controversy and the warring of opinions ; that fact from within, outweighs all facts from without.

In the visible aspect and action of society, often repulsive and annoying, we are apt to lose the due sense of its invisible blessings. As in Nature it is not the coarse and palpable, not soils and rains, nor even fields and flowers, that are so beautiful, as the invisible spirit of wisdom and beauty that pervades it ; so in society, it is the invisible, and therefore unobserved, that is most beautiful.

What nerves the arm of toil? If man minded himself alone, he would fling down the spade and axe, and rush to the desert ; or roam through the world as a wilderness, and make that world a desert. His home, which he sees not, perhaps, but once or twice in a day, is the invisible bond of the world. It is the good, strong and noble faith that men have in each other, which gives the loftiest character to business, trade and commerce. Fraud occurs in the rush of business ; but it is the exception. Honesty is the rule ; and all the frauds in the world cannot tear the great bond of human confidence. If they could, commerce would furl its sails on every sea, and all the cities of the world would crumble into ruins. The bare character of a man on the other side of the world, whom you never saw, whom you never will see, you hold good for a bond of thousands. The most striking feature of the political state is not governments, nor constitutions, nor laws, nor enactments, nor the judicial power, nor the police ; but the universal will of the people to be governed by the common weal. Take off that restraint, and no government on earth could stand for an hour.

Of the many teachings of Masonry, one of the most valuable is, that we should not depreciate this life. It does not hold, that when we reflect on the destiny that awaits man on earth, we ought to bedew his cradle with our tears ; but, like the Hebrews, it hails the birth of a child with joy, and holds that its birth-day should be a festival.

It has no sympathy with those who profess to have proved this life, and found it little worth ; who have deliberately made up their minds that it is far more miserable than happy ; because its employments are tedious, and their schemes often baffled, their friendships broken, or their friends dead, its pleasures palled, and its honours faded, and its paths beaten, familiar and dull.

Masonry deems it no mark of great piety towards God, to disparage, if not despise, the state that He has ordained for us. It does not absurdly set up the claims of another world, not in comparison merely, but in competition, with the claims of this. It looks upon both as parts of one system. It holds that a man may make the best of this world and of another at the same time. It does not teach its initiates to think better of other works and dispensations of God, by thinking meanly of these. It does not look upon life as so much time lost ; nor regard its employments as trifles unworthy of immortal beings ; nor tell its followers to fold their arms, as if in disdain of their state and species : but it looks soberly and cheerfully upon the world, as a theatre of worthy action, of exalted usefulness, and of rational and innocent enjoyment.

It holds that, with all its evils, life is a blessing. To deny that, is to destroy the basis of all religion, natural and revealed. The very foundation of all religion is laid on the firm belief that God is good : and if this life is an evil and a curse, no such belief can be rationally entertained. To level our satire at humanity and human existence, as mean and contemptible ; to look on this world as the habitation of a miserable race, fit only for mockery and scorn ; to consider this earth as a dungeon or a prison, which has no blessing to offer but escape from it, is to extinguish the primal light of faith and hope and happiness, to destroy the basis of religion, and Truth's foundation in the goodness of God. If it indeed be so, then it matters not what else is true or not true ; speculation is vain and faith is vain ; and all that belongs to man's highest being is buried in the ruins of misanthropy, melancholy, and despair.

Our love of life ; the tenacity with which, in sorrow and suffering, we cling to it ; our attachment to our home, to the spot that gave us birth, to any place, however rude, unsightly or barren, on which the history of our years has been written, all show how dear are the ties of kindred and society. Misery makes a greater impression upon us than happiness ; because the former is not the habit of our minds. It is a strange, unusual guest, and we are more conscious of its presence. Happiness lives with us, and we forget it. It does not excite us,

8

nor disturb the order and course of our thoughts. A great agony is an epoch in our life. We remember our afflictions, as we do the storm and earthquake; because they are out of the common course of things. They are like disastrous events, recorded because extraordinary; and with whole and unnoticed periods of prosperity between. We mark and signalize the times of calamity; but many happy days and unnoted periods of enjoyment pass, that are unrecorded either in the book of memory, or in the scanty annals of our thanksgiving. We are little disposed and less able to call up from the dim remembrances of our past years, the peaceful moments, the easy sensations, the bright thoughts, the quiet reveries, the throngs of kind affections in which life flowed on, bearing us almost unconsciously upon its bosom, because it bore us calmly and gently.

Life is not only good; but it has been glorious in the experience of millions. The glory of all human virtue clothes it. The splendours of devotedness, beneficence and heroism are upon it; the crown of a thousand martyrdoms is upon its brow. The brightness of the soul shines through this visible and sometimes darkened life; through all its surrounding cares and labours. The humblest life may feel its connection with its Infinite Source. There is something mighty in the frail inner man: something of immortality in this momentary and transient being. The mind stretches away, on every side, into infinity. Its thoughts flash abroad, far into the boundless, the immeasurable, the infinite; far into the great, dark, teeming future; and become powers and influences in other ages. To know its wonderful Author, to bring down wisdom from the Eternal Stars, to bear upwards its homage, gratitude, and love, to the Ruler of all worlds, to be immortal in our influences projected far into the slow-approaching Future, makes life most worthy and most glorious.

Life is the wonderful creation of God. It is light, sprung from void darkness; power, waked from inertness and impotence; being created from nothing; and the contrast may well enkindle wonder and delight. It is a rill from the Infinite, overflowing goodness; and from the moment when it first gushes up unto the light, to that when it mingles with the ocean of Eternity, that Goodness attends it and ministers to it. It is a great and glorious gift. There is gladness in its infant voices; joy in the buoyant step of its youth; deep satisfaction in its strong maturity; and peace in its quiet age. There is good for the good; virtue for the faithful; and victory for the valiant. There is, even in this humble life, an infinity for those whose desires are boundless. There are blessings upon its birth; there is hope in its death; and eternity in its prospect. Thus earth, which binds many in chains, is to the Mason the starting place and goal of immortality. Many it buries in the rubbish of dull cares and wearying vanities: but to the Mason it is the lofty mount of meditation, where Heaven, and Infinity and Eternity are spread before him and around him. To the lofty-minded, the pure and the virtuous, this life is the beginning of Heaven, and the threshold of immortality.

God hath appointed one remedy for all the evils in the world; and that is a contented spirit. We may be reconciled to poverty and a low fortune, if we suffer contentedness and equanimity to make the proportions. No man is poor that doth not think himself so; but if, in a full fortune, with impatience he desires more, he proclaims his wants and his beggarly condition. This virtue of contentedness was the sum of all the old moral philosophy, and is of most universal use in the whole course of our lives, and the only instrument to ease the burdens of the world and the enmities of sad chances. It is the great reasonableness of complying with the Divine Providence, which governs all the world, and hath so ordered us in the administration of his great Family. It is fit that God should dispense His gifts as He pleases; and if we murmur here, we may, at the next melancholy, be troubled that He did not make us to be angels or stars.

We ourselves make our fortunes good or bad; and when God lets loose a Tyrant upon us, or a sickness, or scorn, or a lessened fortune, if we fear to die, or know not how to be patient, or are proud, or covetous, then the calamity sits heavy on us. But if we know how to manage a noble principle, and fear not death so much as a dishonest action, and think impatience a worse evil than a fever, and pride to be the greatest disgrace as well as the greatest folly, and poverty far preferable to the torments of avarice, we may still bear an even mind and smile at the reverses of fortune and the ill-nature of Fate.

If thou hast lost thy land, do not also lose thy constancy: and if thou must die sooner than others, or than thou didst expect, yet do not die impatiently. For no chance is evil to him that is content, and to a man nothing is miserable unless it be unreasonable. No man can make another man to be his slave, unless that other hath first enslaved himself to life and death, to pleasure or pain, to hope or fear: command these passions, and you are freer than the Parthian Kings.

When an enemy reproaches us, let us look on him as an impartial relator of our faults; for he will tell us truer than our fondest friend will, and we may forgive his anger, while we make use of the plainness of his declamation. The ox, when he is weary, treads truest ; and if there be nothing else in abuse, but that it makes us to walk warily, and tread sure for fear of our enemies, that is better than to be flattered into pride and carelessness.

If thou fallest from thy employment in public, take sanctuary in an honest retirement, being indifferent to thy gain abroad, or thy safety at home. When the north wind blows hard, and it rains sadly, we do not sit down in it and cry; but defend ourselves against it with a warm garment, or a good fire and a dry roof. So when the storm of a sad mischance beats upon our spirits, we may turn it into something that is good, if we resolve to make it so; and with equanimity and patience may shelter ourselves from its inclement pitiless pelting. If it develope our patience, and give occasion for heroic endurance, it hath done us good enough to recompense us sufficiently for all the temporal affliction : for so a wise man shall overrule his stars; and have a greater influence upon his own content, than all the constellations and planets of the firmament.

Compare not thy condition with the few above thee, but to secure thy content. Look upon those thousands with whom thou wouldest not, for any interest, change thy fortune and condition. A soldier must not think himself unprosperous, if he be not successful as Alexander or Wellington ; nor any man deem himself unfortunate that he hath not the wealth of Rothschild : but rather let the former rejoice that he is not lessened like the many generals who went down horse and man before Napoleon, and the latter that he is not the beggar who, bareheaded in the bleak winter wind holds out his tattered hat for charity. There may be many who are richer and more fortunate ; but many thousands who are very miserable, compared to thee.

After the worst assaults of Fortune, there will be something left to us,—a merry countenance, a cheerful spirit and a good conscience, the Providence of God, our hopes of Heaven, our charity for those who have injured us ; perhaps a loving wife, and many friends to pity, and some to relieve us ; and light and air, and all the beauties of Nature ; we can read, discourse and meditate ; and having still these blessings, we should be much in love with sorrow and peevishness to lose them all, and prefer to sit down on our little handful of thorns.

Enjoy the blessings of this day, if God sends them, and the evils of it bear patiently and calmly; for this day only is ours : we are dead to yesterday, and we are not yet born to the morrow. When our fortunes are violently changed, our spirits are unchanged, if they always stood in the suburbs and expectation of sorrows and reverses. The blessings of immunity, safeguard, liberty and integrity deserve the thanksgiving of a whole life. We are quit from a thousand calamities, every one of which, if it were upon us, would make us insensible of our present sorrow, and glad to receive it in exchange for that other greater affliction.

Measure your desires by your fortune and condition, not your fortunes by your desires : be governed by your needs, not by your fancy; by nature, not by evil customs and ambitious principles. It is no evil to be poor, but to be vicious and impatient. Is that beast better, that hath two or three mountains to graze on, than the little bee that feeds on dew or manna, and lives upon what falls every morning from the store-houses of Heaven, clouds and Providence ?

There are some instances of fortune and a fair condition that cannot stand with some others ; but if you desire this, you must lose that, and unless you be content with one, you lose the comfort of both. If you covet learning, you must have leisure and a retired life ; if honours of State and political distinctions, you must be ever abroad in public, and get experience, and do all men's business, and keep all company, and have no leisure at all. If you will be rich, you must be frugal ; if you will be popular, you must be bountiful ; if a philosopher, you must despise riches. If you would be famous as Epaminondas, accept also his poverty ; for it added lustre to his person, and envy to his fortune, and his virtue without it could not have been so excellent. If you would have the reputation of a martyr, you must needs accept his persecution ; if of a benefactor of the world, the world's injustice.

God esteems it one of his glories, that he brings good out of evil ; and therefore it were but reason we should trust Him to govern His own world as he pleases ; and that we should patiently wait until the change cometh, or the reason is discovered.

But a Mason's contentedness must by no means be a mere contented selfishness, like his who, comfortable himself, is indifferent to the discomfort of others. There will always be in this world wrongs to forgive, suffering to alleviate, sorrows asking for sympathy, necessities and destitution to relieve; and ample occasion for the exercise of active charity and benevolence. And he who sits unconcerned amidst it all, perhaps enjoying his own comforts and luxuries the more, by contrasting them with the hungry and ragged destitution, and shivering misery of his fellows, is not contented, but unfeeling and brutal.

It is the saddest of all sights upon this earth, that of a man, lazy and luxurious, or hard and penurious, to whom want appeals in vain, and suffering cries in an unknown tongue. The man whose hasty anger hurries him into violence and crime, is not half so unworthy to live. He is the faithless steward, that embezzles what is given him in trust for the penniless and impoverished among his brethren. The true Mason must be, and must have a right to be, content with himself; and he can be so only when he lives, not for himself alone, but for others who need his assistance and have a claim upon his sympathy.

The particulars of mercy or alms cannot be narrower than men's needs are. He that gives alms, must do it in mercy, that is, out of a true sense of the calamity of his brother, first feeling it in himself, in some proportion, and then endeavouring to ease himself and the other of their common calamity. Against this rule they offend who give alms merely out of custom; or to upbraid the poverty of the other; or to make him mercenary and lay him under obligation; or with any unhandsome circumstances.

He that gives alms must do it with a single eye and heart, without designs to get the praise of men. He who hath done a good turn, should so forget it, as not to speak of it; but he that boasts it or upbraids it, hath paid himself, and lost the nobleness of the charity.

Give, looking for nothing again, without consideration of future advantages: give to children, to old men, to the unthankful, and the dying, and to those you shall never see again; for else your alms or courtesy is not charity, but traffic and merchandise: and omit not to relieve the needs of your enemy and him who does you injury.

Charity is the great channel, through which God passes all his mercy upon mankind. For we receive absolution of our sins in proportion to our forgiving our brother. This is the rule of our hopes, and the measure of our desire in this world; and on the day of death and judgment, the great sentence upon mankind shall be transacted according to our alms, which is the other part of charity. God Himself is Love; and every degree of charity that dwells in us, is the participation of the Divine Nature.

These principles Masonry reduces to practice. By them it expects you hereafter to be guided and governed. It especially inculcates them upon him who employs the labour of others, forbidding him to discharge them, when to want employment is to starve, or to contract for the labour of man or woman at so low a price that by over-exertion they must sell him their blood and life at the same time with the labour of their hands.

Such are the lessons of this degree. Reflect upon them well, my Brother, before you again apply to advance in Masonry.

TO CLOSE.

M.·. Sk.·. Bro.·. Sen.·. Warden, what is the hour?

Sen.·. W.·. Most Skilful Master, it is the twelfth hour of the day.

M.·. Sk.·. Then it is time for us to rest. Give notice, Bro.·. Sen.·. Warden, that I am about to close this Lodge.

Sen.·. W.·. Bro.·. Jun.·. Warden, give notice to the Brethren that the Most Skilful Master is about to close this Lodge, that they may take notice, and aid him in doing so.

Jun.·. W.·. [Rapping ;]: Brethren, the Most Skilful Master is about to close this Lodge, and desires you to assist him in so doing.

M.·. Sk.·. Together, my Brothers.

[The Master gives the Sign of Surprise, and all the Brethren that of Admiration. Then the M.·. raps [;]—the Sen.·. W.·. [;]—and the Jun.·. W.·. [?]—and the Master says]:

M.·. Sk.·. Go forth into the world, my Brethren, and be charitable and benevolent, that ye may be content. This Lodge is closed.

FINIS.

Ninth Degree.

Knight Elu of Nine.

Bodies of this Degree are called *Chapters.* The hangings are black, strewed with flames, with red and white columns at intervals. There are nine great lights, eight forming an octagon around the altar, which is in the centre; and one placed half way between the altar and the east.

The altar is covered with black, and on it are two swords crossed, and a dagger.

OFFICERS, TITLES, ETC.

The Chapter consists regularly of nine members, who represent the first Nine Knights Elu, appointed by King Solomon. The officers are:

The President, who is styled *Illustrious*, and sits in the East:

The Sen∴ and Jun∴ Inspectors, styled *Excellent*, who sit in the West:

The Orator, in the North:

The Secretary and Treasurer, on the right and left of the President:

The Hospitaller, on the right of the Inspectors:

The Standard-bearer, on their left:

The Master of Ceremonies, in front of the President, on the right.

During a reception these officers are arranged as follows:

The President represents King *Solomon*, and sits in the East.

The *Sen∴ Inspector* represents King *Hiram*, and sits on his right.

The *Jun∴ Inspector*, in the West, represents *Adonhiram* the Son of Abda.

The *Orator* represents *Zabud*, the King's friend, and sits in the North.

The *Secretary* represents *Sadoc* the Priest, and sits on the right of the two Kings:

The *Treasurer* represents *Josaphat*, Son of Ahilud, the Chancellor, and sits on their left.

The *Hospitaller* represents *Ahisar*, Governor of the House.

The *Standard bearer* represents *Banaias*, Son of Joiada, Commander in Chief of the Army.

The Master of Ceremonies represents the Stranger who gave information of the hiding place of Abiram the murderer.

The battery is [; ; ;].

The age is ; times £—or ? , complete.

CLOTHING, ORNAMENTS AND JEWELS.

The apron is white, spotted with red, and lined and bordered with black. On the flap is painted or embroidered an arm holding a dagger; and in the middle of the apron an arm holding a bloody head by the hair.

The cordon is a broad black watered ribbon, worn from the right shoulder to the left hip. At the lower end of this are nine red rosettes, four on each side and one at the bottom; and from the end of the cordon hangs the jewel, which is a dagger, its hilt of gold, and its blade of silver.

During a reception, the President and Sen∴ Inspector wear royal robes, with crown and sceptre; and the Secretary wears the robes and mitre of the High Priest.

TO OPEN.

The President raps once, and says:

Pres∴ Brethren, I am about to open this Chapter of Knights Elu of 9. If there be any one present who has not attained that degree, he is requested to withdraw.

[He raps twice, and the Hospitaller rises]:

Hosp∴ Bro∴ Hospitaller, see that the entrance to the Chapter is duly guarded, that we may not be disturbed in our deliberations.

[The Hospitaller goes out, returns, raps [; ; ;] which is answered from without, returns to his place, and says]:

Hosp∴ Ill∴ President, the entrances to the Chapter are duly guarded, and we are secure.

Pres∴ Thanks, my Brother. Bro∴ Sen∴ Inspector, are you a Knight Elu?

Sen∴ Ins∴ Ill∴ Pres∴, a cavern received me, a lamp gave me light, and a fountain refreshed me.

Qu∴ What saw you in the cavern, besides?

Ans∴ A murderer sleeping, grasping a dagger.

Qu∴ Where were you received a Knight Elu?

Ans∴ In the Audience Chamber of King Solomon, in the presence of all his Court.

Qu∴ How many Elus were first received?

Ans∴ Nine, including Joabert, whom I afterwards represented.

Qu∴ What was the first duty assigned you?

Ans∴ To search for and apprehend the murderers of our Gr∴ Master Hiram Abi, that they might be tried and punished.

Qu∴ Did you find them?

Ans∴ One of them only; Abiram, their Chief and leader.

Qu∴ Where found you him?

Ans∴ In the Mountains east of Joppa, in a cavern whose mouth was overgrown with bushes.

Qu∴ Who conducted you?

Ans∴ A stranger.

Qu∴ By what route?

Ans∴ By a difficult and dangerous path over the mountains.

Qu∴ So men attain freedom. Did you succeed?

Ans∴ We took the murderer alive, and delivered him to King Solomon.

Qu∴ Did he resist?

Ans∴ With desperation, knowing his life was forfeit; like a wild beast hemmed in his lair, crying at every blow *Necum.*

Qu∴ What did that mean?

Ans∴ *Revenge:* the signal agreed upon between him and his companions, who had taken the alarm and fled.

Qu∴ Of what is Abiram the type, to the Knights Elu?

Ans∴ Of Tyranny, chief assassin of Free Thought.

Qu∴ What does the Stranger represent?

Ans∴ The Genius of Civilization, that points out the way to the brave hearts that assail Despotism in its strong-holds.

Qu∴ What does the arm grasping the dagger represent?

Ans∴ The arm of Tyranny threatening prostrate Freedom; and that of Brutus the avenger.

Qu∴ What does the hand holding the bloody head represent?

Ans∴ The punishment by law and after fair trial of those that trample on human liberty; which better suits the People's Majesty than the dagger of Brutus.

Qu∴ What is the cause to which the Knights Elu are now devoted?

Ans∴ That of the oppressed against the oppressor every where.

Qu∴ At what hour did the Nine Elus set forth upon their search?

Ans∴ At the first hour of the night.

Qu∴ At what hour did they return?

Ans∴ At the 12th hour of the night.

Qu∴ What is your age?

Ans∴ ; times £—or?, years complete.

Qu∴ What is the hour?

Ans∴ The hour of the departure of the Nine Elect upon their journey.

Pres∴ Cause then the brethren to assemble round the altar; that, renewing our pledges to each other, we may open this Chapter of Knights Elu of Nine.

Sen∴ Insp∴ [Rapping;]: Brethren and Knights, you will please assemble round the altar, that this Chapter may be opened in due and ancient form.

[The Brethren assemble round the altar, in a circle, including the President and all the officers; and all with drawn swords. They raise their swords at an angle of 45 degrees, all the points meeting in the centre; and repeat as follows:

Hospit∴ *To the cause of all who defend Right and Justice against the tyranny of Kings or the despotism of Popular Opinion!*

Jun∴ Insp∴ *To the cause of Patriotism, warring against corruption and the tyranny of Party!*

Sen∴ Insp∴ *To the cause of Toleration against proscription for opinion's sake!*

Presid∴ *To the cause of every man and every people that protest against any usurpation of Power!*

All: . . *We devote ourselves, our hands, our hearts, our intellects!*

Presid∴ Now, HENCEFORWARD AND FOREVER!

All: . . AMEN!

[All return to their places: The President gives the sign, and all the Brethren the answer. Then the President raps [;]—the Senior Inspector [;]—and the Junior Inspector [;]—and the President says]:

Presid∴ This Chapter of Knights Elu of Nine is open.

RECEPTION.

The officers being properly clothed and seated, the candidate is received in the Preparation Room, clothed as a Perfect Master; and carefully examined by the Hospitaller in the work and principles of the 8th Degree. If the examination be satisfactory, he is conducted into the Chapter, and directed to take his seat, in the same attitude as the Brethren; all of whom sit with the right elbow on the right knee, their heads resting on their right hands; their hats pressed over their eyes; and the black side of the apron outwards. The nine lights are also extinguished.

Presid∴ My Brethren, we still lament the death of our Excellent Gr∴ Master Hiram Abi; and the demands of justice are still unsatisfied. The most strenuous exertions have been made without effect, to discover the murderers; and we fear that they have found means to escape beyond the limits of the kingdom; and that so justice will be defrauded, and the blood of our Brother cry aloud in vain to heaven.

Sec'y∴ Most Potent King Solomon, wherever the murderers go, their consciences bear them company and torture them. God is wise and just, and will most surely punish them; for the murderer cannot hide from Him, nor escape from his own remorse. If it be the will of God, that others, and not we, shall be his instruments to punish them, let us submit to His will and be content.

Sen∴ Insp∴ My Brother, something tells me that the murderers have not escaped, but will yet be discovered; and that we shall be the instruments of Heaven to punish them as they deserve. For murder will not be hid, and Providence ever makes the murderer's efforts to conceal himself, the very means of his detection.

[The M∴ of Ceremonies, without, dressed as a traveller, and without Masonic clothing or jewel, raps [; ; ;] at the door.]

Hosp∴ M∴ Potent King Solomon, there is an alarm at the door of the Audience Chamber.

Pres∴ Attend to that alarm, and see what rash man dares to disturb us while in Council.

[The Hospitaller goes to the door, opens it, and asks]:

Hosp∴ Who rashly ventures to disturb the Council in its deliberations?

M∴ Cer∴ A stranger, just now arrived from Joppa, who has important information to communicate to the King his Lord.

Hosp∴ What is that information?

M∴ Cer∴ He will make that known to no one, save in the presence of the King.

Hosp∴ Let him wait, then, until his request is communicated to the King, and his will ascertained.

[The Hospitaller closes the door, and goes to the East, where the same questions are asked by King Solomon, and like answers returned, as at the door]:

Pres∴ Then let this Stranger come before us: but let him see to it, that his information be sufficiently important to warrant his intrusion.

[The Hospitaller opens the door, and says]:

Hosp∴ It is the pleasure of the Most Potent King that the Stranger enter: but let him see to it that his information be sufficiently important to warrant his intrusion, lest the anger of our Lord the King consume him.

[The M∴ of Cerem∴ enters, advances to the East, kneels in front of King Solomon, rises again, and stands with his arms crossed on his breast]:

Pres∴ Who and whence art thou?

M∴ Cer∴ Pharos, the Son of Miamin, a poor herdsman of Joppa.

Pres∴ What is the information that thou hast to give us?

M∴ Cer∴ Most Potent King, my herds feed on the mountains east of Joppa. Three days ago, searching for one that had strayed, I penetrated by paths before unknown into the deepest recesses of the hills. I found in a narrow valley the slain carcass of the animal I sought; and following the track of him who had killed it, I came upon a cavern in the steep side of a mountain, its mouth overgrown with bushes; and hiding myself near it, among the rocks, I saw at nightfall three persons enter, coming from the valley. Then I crept near, and listened, and from their conversation learned that they were the murderers of the Chief Architect of the Temple, of whom thy officers had been in search. Having heard this, I cautiously withdrew, and came hither with all speed on foot, to give the information.

Sen∴ Insp∴ Said I not, my Brother, that the murderers would be discovered? Had they not slain this poor man's kine, they might have escaped the search of human justice.

Pres∴ It is the Will of Providence that I should be the instrument to punish them. Pharos, Son of Miamin, canst thou conduct my officers to the cavern in which these wretches have taken refuge?

M∴ Cer∴ I can, Oh King; for I noted well the way by which I came.

Pres∴ Go then and refresh thyself, that thou mayest be ready to depart at nightfall. Abizar, see that food and wine be set before this stranger, and let him sleep and be refreshed after his journey until evening.

Sen∴ Insp∴ Whom wilt thou send, my Brother, to apprehend the murderers?

Pres∴ Most of my guards are already absent on the search. I will send such as freely offer to go. My Brethren, who among you, for the love of his deceased Gr∴ Master, will voluntarily go to arrest his murderers?

[The Brethren all rise, each crying: "*I will go*"].

Pres∴ I will send but nine. And since all offer, and I would make no invidious distinction, they shall be chosen by lot. Bro∴ Adonhiram, place in an urn the names of all the Brethren who are Perfect Masters, and let the High Priest Sadoc draw forth in succession the names of nine; and they so drawn shall go upon this expedition.

[The Sen∴ Inspector places several strips of paper in an urn, and the Secretary draws forth nine in succession, reading as he does so the following names: . . . *Joabert* . . . *Stolkin* . . . *Zerbal* . . . *Benhur* . . . *Ahinadab* . . . *Bendecar* . . . *Baana* . . . *Semei* . . . *Guber*].

Pres∴ Let the Brethren who have been named, advance.

[The candidate and eight brethren advance to the East, and the President says to them]:

Pres∴ My Brethren, the lot has fallen on you to undertake this service. Accompany the stranger by the way he came, to the place where he discovered the murderers. Let not the law and justice be defrauded of their due; but taking the assassins alive, bring them hither to be tried, and punished according to their deserts. If you succeed, you shall receive new honours, and your names, as the Nine Elect, be magnified in Israel. Go and refresh yourselves, and prepare to set forth at night-fall.

[The candidate and the eight brethren retire to the preparation room, and the lights in the chapter are put out. In the preparation room, the nine lay aside their Masonic clothing and jewels, and each is armed with a sword. Then, preceded by the M∴ of Ceremonies, they enter the Chapter-room, and make the circuit of it several times, the candidate being led by the M∴ of Cer∴ and meeting many obstacles. After some time he is led through a narrow winding passage, at the end of which is a light, and a representation of a cavern, being a room, the door of which is covered with branches of trees. In sight of this, the M∴ of Cer∴ halts, and says]:

M∴ Cer∴ Are we alone? Your companions must have lost us in the darkness. The cavern is in sight. Shall we go forward, or wait for our companions?

[He waits a while. Shouts are heard in the distance, and he says]:

M∴ Cer∴ They must have found the murderers. Let us press onward to the cavern, and if there be no one there, return to our companions.

[They go on, and enter the room, which is lighted only by a single lamp set on the floor, by the side of a bed of leaves, on which lies a brother representing Abiram, sleeping, and grasping a dagger in his right hand. The room is so arranged and painted as to represent a cave; and in one corner is a basin into which water is dripping as from a fountain. After hesitating a moment, the M∴ of Ceremonies says]:

M∴ Cer∴ He is asleep. Let us spring upon him and bind him.

[The M∴ of Cer∴ steps forward quickly, stumbles over the branches at the entrance, and falls. The Brother on the bed springs up, brandishing the dagger, darts towards the candidate, crying "*Betrayed*," and strikes at him with the dagger, crying at each blow "*Nekum*." The candidate grapples with him, and the Brother gives back to the bed, and allows himself to be pressed down upon it. The Master of Ceremonies, rising, rushes forward, and seizes upon him, and he and the candidate bind him.

The other brethren then approach and enter; and one of them, who represents Stolkin, says]:

Stol∴ Joabert has been more fortunate than we. He has captured one of the assassins.

M∴ Cer∴ We should have taken him sleeping; but my foot caught in the bushes, and as I fell, I awoke him.

Stol∴ Did he resist?

M∴ Cer∴ Desperately; exclaiming that he was betrayed, and striking fiercely with his dagger: crying aloud, as if for a signal, at every blow, *Nekum*.

Stol∴ No doubt a signal. We came upon two others, and pursued them; but knowing the mountain better than we, they escaped; and guided by the light we came hither.

M∴ Cer∴ It is useless to pursue them, among these rocks and mountains.

Stolk∴ Then we had best return. [By this time the M∴ of Cer∴ has poured a liquid representing blood over the garments of the candidate, and upon the dagger, as well as upon the hands of the Brother who represents Abiram]. But Joabert is wounded. Slay the miscreant who has shed his blood.

Another: Hold, my Brother. Remember the command of our Lord the King, that we should by no means slay the murderers, but take them to him alive, that they may be tried and punished. We should ourselves do murder to slay him here. Joabert is but slightly wounded. Let us drink at the fountain and return.

[All drink at the basin; and return by the way they came, to the Preparation room, leading Abiram, whom they there deliver to the Guards, and give the alarm of [; ; ;] at the door; which is opened by the Hospitaller, who says]:

Hosp∴ . .Who desire admission to the Council?

M∴ Cer∴ The Nine Elect who went in search of the murderers of our Gr∴ Master Hiram.

[The Hospitaller closes the door, and reports. The President orders them to be admitted, and they enter. The Chapter is now lighted, and still represents the Court of Solomon; but the nine lights remain extinguished. The left arm of Joabert has been placed in a sling, and he enters, holding the bloody dagger of Abiram in his right hand. As they approach the East, King S∴ says]:

Pres∴ What mean the bloody dagger, and the stains upon your garments? Have you dared, Joabert, to usurp the law's prerogative and that of God, and slay the murderer, whom you were ordered to bring before me alive?

Stolk∴ Not so, my Liege. We followed the stranger through the most difficult and dangerous ways, until we came near the cavern, in the mountains East of Joppa; and there, in the darkness, we lost sight of him and Joabert. Soon after, we saw two men prowling among the rocks, and pursued, but could not overtake them; for, knowing the mountains well, they outran us and escaped. In the mean time we heard, higher up the mountain, a loud voice cry several times *Nekum*, as if by way of signal; and guided by the voice, and afterwards by a glimmering light, we found the cavern, which the Stranger and Joabert had already entered, and discovered Abiram, the leader of the murderers, asleep. But the Stranger stumbling over the bushes at the entrance, and so falling, Abiram awoke, and springing to his feet fought desperately, crying as he struck at Joabert with his dagger, *Nekum*, as a signal to his comrades whom we had chased. He wounded Joabert, who, notwithstanding, seized and overpowered him, took from him his bloody dagger, and with the Stranger's aid bound him hand and foot. Finding it useless to pursue the others, and without waiting to rest, we returned the way we came, bringing with us Abiram, whom we have delivered to thy Guards; though we were sorely tempted to slay him on the spot, for his new attempt to murder; when we saw the blood of Joabert on his dagger.

Pres∴ It is well ye did not; for he who slays without commission from the law, is himself a murderer; and ye had none, but order to the contrary. Whither, think you, have the other two escaped?

Stolk∴ My Lord, we know not. They must still lurk among the mountains.

Pres∴ God will yet give them into our hands. Baanias, give order to your Guards that their Prisoner be loaded with chains and committed to the deepest dungeon; and there let him remain until his accomplices are taken. They shall then be tried, and punished as they deserve. Josaphat, give to the Stranger a talent of gold, and let him return to his family in Joppa; and whatever other favour he asks of us, it shall be granted him. My brother Hiram, how shall we reward these Brethren, and especially Joabert, for their courage, fidelity and obedience?

Sen∴ Insp∴ I know not how to answer, my Brother. Let them decide. If they will have wealth, let my exchequer furnish it. If honours, let us jointly confer them. What sayest thou, Joabert, and thy companions? Will ye choose wealth or honour?

Stolk∴ Honour, my Lord the King: Thy good opinion, and that of our Lord King Solomon.

Sen∴ Insp∴ Then let us make the Knight Elu of Nine a Hebrew and Phœnician Order of Nobility, and a new Degree in Masonry, of which thou and I and these nine shall be the first members; and which shall hereafter be conferred as a high reward for distinguished services done our respective realms.

Pres∴ It pleases me well. Let such new order be created, and patents thereof issued to these nine, Joabert being the first President: and let it be devoted to bravery, devotedness and patriotism. Advance, my

Brethren, and stand around the Altar, raising your right hands to Heaven, to assume an obligation appropriate to this new degree. Brethren, assemble around these Brethren, and form over them the roof of steel.

[The nine Brethren stand around the altar in a circle, laying their left hands on the cross-swords, and the dagger which Joabert is directed to place upon the swords, and raising their right hands towards Heaven. All the other Brethren, and all the officers place the points of their swords together over them; and they repeat the following obligation]:

OBLIGATION.

I, A.... B....., in the presence of the Grand Architect of the Universe, and under this roof of steel, raised to protect or punish, do most solemnly and sincerely promise and swear, that I will never reveal the secrets of this degree of Knights Elu of Nine to any person in the world, unless it be at a proper time and in a proper place, to one legally authorized to receive them, and when I am duly and legally authorized to communicate them.

I furthermore promise and swear that I will ever maintain the cause of the oppressed against the oppressor; of every people that struggles against Tyranny, and is fit to be free; of all who defend Right and Justice and Free Thought against the Despotism of Popular Opinion; of Patriotism, warring against the tyranny of Party; of Toleration against Proscription for opinion's sake; of every Man and every People that protest against any Usurpation of Power; of Free Thought, Free Conscience and Free Speech: and will thereto devote my hand, my heart and my intellect.

I furthermore promise and swear that I will not hesitate to shed my blood, if necessary, in defence of my country, its rights, its honour, its laws and its institutions; nor ever fail to obey the dictates of a profound devotion to her welfare, and an unselfish Patriotism.

All which I do most solemnly and sincerely promise and swear; under no less penalty than that of being expelled in disgrace from this order, denounced in every country on earth as forsworn and dishonourable, and held unworthy of the friendship of man or love of woman, if I should ever, under any temptation, how great soever, be guilty of wilfully violating this my solemn obligation. So help me God, and keep me steadfast in the due performance of the same!

[The swords are now lowered, and their blades laid upon the heads of the nine brethren: and the President says]:

Presid.'. I pronounce you, my brethren, to be duly invested with the Honourable Degree and rank of Knights Elu of Nine. Ever remembering its motto, may you be always brave, devoted and patriotic! Light now, my Brethren, the Nine Great Lights of this Chapter; and as you do so, remind these our newly made Brethren of the knightly virtues which those lights represent to us, and by which their feet are to be hereafter guided. And do you, my Brethren, listen and remember!

[The nine lights are accordingly lighted, by the nine officers; each as he lights one pronouncing a single word, as follows]:

1st Light . . . M.'. of Cer.'. . . . . DISINTERESTEDNESS!
2d Light . . . Standard Bearer . . DUTY!
3d Light . . . Hospitaller . . .'. . DEVOTION!
4th Light . . . Treasurer . . . . . . FIRMNESS!
5th Light . . . Secretary . . . . . . FRANKNESS!
6th Light . . . Orator . . . . SINCERITY!
7th Light . . . Jun.'. Inspector . . . SELF-DENIAL!
8th Light . . . Sen.'. Inspector . . . HEROISM!

9th (the single) Light: President . . PATRIOTISM! . . . And may it and all these knightly virtues ever animate and inspire us all, to perform whatever duties Masonry and our country require!

All: . . So mote it be! Amen!

Pres.'. . . Receive now the signs, words and Token of this Degree.

Sign: . . . Strike with the right hand, as if with a ⎕⊙♌♌☾‡, first at the ♈♉‡☾&☾⊙⎕, and then at the &☾⊙‡♈ of the other; saying ♒☾¶♌♒∴

Answer: . . . Pass the right hand over the ♈♉‡☾&☾⊙⎕, as if to see if it is bloody; and then place it on the &☾⊙♈, and say ♒☾¶⊙&∴

Token: . . . Close the ♈♀♒♌☾‡≏‡♈♈♈♉&☾‡‡|&⊙♒⎕, and present it to the other, with the ♈&♉♋♍ raised. He takes the ♈&♉♋♍ in his ‡|&⊙♒⎕, closing his own ♈♀♒♌☾‡≏, and raising his ♈&♉♋♍. There are thus ♊ ♈♀♒♌☾‡≏ closed, and a ♈&♉♋♍ raised, representing the ♑☾†♌∴

Pass-words . . . One says ♒☾¶♌♒∴—the other answers, ♂♉⊙♍☾‡♈∴—Then the first says ⊙♍♀‡⊙♒∴—the other answers, ⊙¶♀‡♉♑∴

Sacred Word: . . ♌☾♍♌‡·¶&♀†∴

The President then invests the candidate with the apron, collar and jewel, saying:

I invest you with the *apron* of this degree. Its color, white spotted with red, lined and bordered with black, is an emblem of Masonry and Truth sprinkled with the blood of those who have been persecuted for the sake of both; and of the darkness of ignorance and error and intolerance wherewith the world is shrouded, and through which Masonry moves like a star, dispensing light and knowledge and toleration.

The *arm* holding a *dagger*, embroidered on the flap, while it reminds us of that of Tyranny, ever raised to strike at prostrate and struggling freedom; also reminds us of that of Brutus the avenger, who struck at the despotism that oppressed Rome in the person of Cæsar.

The *hand* holding the bloody *head* represents the punishment by due course of law and after fair trial before the regular Tribunal, of those that trample on Human Liberty; which better comports with the People's Majesty, than doth the dagger of Brutus.

I invest you with the *cordon* of this Degree. Its color reminds us ever to lament the prevalence in the world of oppression, usurpation, proscription and uncharitable opinion; and to strive to overcome them by means of the nine excellent qualities of a Knight Elu, of which the nine rosettes, like the nine great lights, are emblems.

The *jewel*, suspended to the cordon, with its hilt of gold and its blade of silver, is no emblem of the poniard of the assassin, but of the weapons of legitimate warfare which a Knight Elu may lawfully use; and especially of the two-edged sword of Truth, with which every Mason should be armed.

My Brother, may you wear these insignia as worthily as they were worn by Joabert whom you have represented. Go now to the Orator, and receive the Lecture of this Degree.

LECTURE.

My Brother, the ceremonies of this Degree need no explanation. Its History is fully told in the incidents of your reception. Originally created to reward the fidelity, obedience and devotion of Joabert and his eight companions, it was consecrated to bravery, devotedness and patriotism: and your obligation has made known to you the duties which you have assumed. They are summed up in the simple mandate; Protect the oppressed against the oppressor; and devote yourself to the honour and interests of your Country.

Masonry is not speculative, but experimental; not sentimental, but practical. It requires self-renunciation and self-control. It wears a stern face towards men's vices, and interferes with many of our pursuits and our fancied pleasures. It penetrates beyond the regions of vague sentiment; beyond the regions where moralizers and philosophers have woven their fine theories, and elaborated their beautiful maxims; to the very depths of the heart, rebuking our littlenesses and meannesses, arraigning our prejudices and passions, and warring against the armies of our vices.

It wars against the passions that spring out of the bosom of a world of fine sentiments, a world of admirable sayings and foul practices, of good maxims and bad deeds; whose darker passions are not only restrained by custom and ceremony, but hidden even from itself by a veil of beautiful sentiments. This terrible solecism has existed in all ages. Romish sentimentalism has often covered infidelity and vice : Protestant straightness often lauds spirituality and faith, and neglects homely truth, candor and generosity; and ultra-liberal refinement soars to heaven in its dreams, and wallows in the mire of earth in its deeds.

There may be a world of Masonic sentiment; and yet a world of little or no Masonry. In many minds there is a vague and general sentiment of Masonic charity, generosity and religious reverence, but no particular virtue, nor habitual kindness, veneration or liberality. Masonry plays about them like the cold though brilliant lights that flash and eddy over Northern skies. There are occasional flashes of generous and reverential feeling, transitory splendours and momentary gleams of just and noble thought, and transient coruscations, that light the Heaven of their imagination ; but there is no vital warmth in the heart; and it remains as cold and sterile as the regions of the Northern Pole. They do nothing: they gain no victories over themselves ; they make no progress; they are still in the North East corner of the Lodge, as when they first stood there as apprentices ; and they do not cultivate Masonry, with a cultivation, determined, resolute and regular, like their cultivation of their estate, profession or knowledge. Their Masonry takes its chance in general and inefficient sentiment, mournfully barren of results.

Most men have *sentiments*, but not *principles*. The former are temporary impressions, the latter permanent and controlling impressions of goodness and virtue. The former are general and involuntary, and do not rise to the character of virtue. Every one feels them. They flash up spontaneously in every heart. The latter are rules of action, and shape and control our conduct; and it is they that Masonry insists upon.

We approve the right; but pursue the wrong. It is the old story of human deficiency. No one abets or deifies injustice, fraud, oppression, covetousness, revenge, envy or slander; and yet how many who condemn these things, are themselves guilty of them. It is no rare thing, for him whose indignation is kindled at a tale of wicked injustice, cruel oppression, base slander, or misery inflicted by unbridled indulgence ; whose anger flames in behalf of the injured and ruined victims of wrong ; to be in some relation unjust, or oppressive, or envious, or self-indulgent, or a careless talker of others. How wonderfully indignant the penurious man often is, at the stinginess or want of public spirit of another!

A great Preacher well said, " Therefore thou art inexcusable, O Man, whosoever thou art, that judgest: for wherein thou judgest another, thou condemnest thyself: for thou that judgest, doest the same things." It is amazing to see how men can talk of virtue and honour, whose life denies both. It is curious to see with what a marvellous facility many bad men quote Scripture. It seems to comfort their evil consciences, to use good words ; and to gloze over bad deeds with holy texts, wrested to their purpose. Often, the more a man talks about Charity and Toleration, the less he has of either; the more he talks about virtue, the smaller stock he has of it. The mouth speaks out of the abundance of the heart; but often the very reverse of what the man practises. And the vicious and sensual often express, and in a sense feel, strong disgust at vice and sensuality.

Here, in the Lodge, virtue and vice are matters of reflection and feeling only. There is little opportunity here, for the practice of either; and Masons yield to the argument here, with facility and readiness; because nothing is to follow. It is easy and safe, here, to *feel* upon these matters. But to-morrow, when they breathe the atmosphere of worldly gains and competitions, and the passions are again stirred at the opportunities of unlawful pleasure, all their fine emotions about virtue, all their generous abhorrence of selfishness and sensuality, melt away like a morning cloud.

For the time, their emotions and sentiments are sincere and real. Men may be really in a certain way, interested in Masonry, while fatally deficient in virtue. It is not always hypocrisy. Men pray most fervently and sincerely; and yet are constantly guilty of acts so bad and base, so ungenerous and unrighteous, that the crimes that crowd the dockets of our courts are scarcely worse.

A man may be a good sort of man in general, and yet a very bad man in particular: good in the Lodge and bad in the world; good in public, and bad in his family; good at home, and bad on a journey or in a strange city. Many a man earnestly desires to be a good Mason. He says so, and is sincere. But if you require him to resist a certain passion, to sacrifice a certain indulgence, to control his appetite at a particular feast, or to keep his temper in a dispute, you will find that he does not wish to be a good Mason, *in that particular case.*

The *duties* of life are more than life. The law imposeth it upon every citizen, that he prefer the urgent service of his country before the safety of his life. If a man be commanded, saith a great writer, to bring ordnance or munition to relieve any of the King's towns that are distressed, then he cannot for any danger of tempest justify the throwing of them overboard; for there it holdeth which was spoken by the Roman, when the same necessity of weather was alleged to hold him from embarking: Necesse est ut eam, non ut vivam: it needs that I go: that I live it doth not need.

How ungratefully he slinks away, that dies, and does nothing to reflect a glory to Heaven? How barren a tree he is, that lives, and spreads, and cumbers the ground, yet leaves not one seed, not one good work to generate another after him. All cannot leave alike; yet all may leave something, answering their proportion and their kinds. Those are dead and withered grains of corn, out of which there will not one ear spring. He will hardly find the way to Heaven, that desires to go thither alone.

Industry is never wholly unfruitful. If it bring not joy with the incoming profit, it will yet banish mischief from thy busied gates. There is a kind of good angel waiting upon Diligence that ever carries a laurel in his hand to crown her. How unworthy was that man of the world that never did aught, but only lived and died! That we have liberty to do anything, we should account it a gift from the favouring Heavens: that we have minds sometimes inclining us to use that liberty well, is a great bounty of the Deity.

Masonry is action, and not inertness. It requires its initiates to work, actively and earnestly, for the benefit of their brethren, their country and mankind. It is the patron of the oppressed, as it is the comforter and consoler of the unfortunate and wretched. It seems to it a worthier honour to be the instrument of advancement and reform, than to enjoy all that rank and office and lofty titles can bestow. It is the advocate of the common people in those things which concern the best interests of mankind. It hates insolent power and impudent usurpation. It pities the poor, the sorrowing, the disconsolate; it would raise and improve the ignorant, the sunken and the degraded.

Its fidelity to its mission will be accurately evidenced, by the extent of the efforts it employs, and the means it sets on foot, to improve the people at large and to better their condition; chiefest of which, within its reach, is to aid in the education of the children of the poor. An intelligent people, informed of its rights, will soon come to know its power, and cannot long be oppressed: and if there be not a sound and virtuous populace, the elaborate ornaments at the top of the pyramid of society will be a wretched compensation for the want of solidity at the base. It is never safe for a nation to repose on the lap of ignorance: and if there ever was a time when public tranquillity was ensured by the absence of knowledge, that season is past. Unthinking stupidity cannot sleep, without being appalled by phantoms and shaken by terrors. The improvement of the mass of the people is the grand security for popular liberty; in the neglect of which, the politeness, refinement and knowledge accumulated in the higher orders and wealthier classes will some day perish like dry grass in the hot fire of popular fury.

But it is not the mission of Masonry to engage in plots and conspiracies against the Civil Government. It is not the fanatical propagandist of any creed or theory; nor does it proclaim itself the enemy of Kings, nor the Apostle of political liberty, fraternity and equality. It is no more the High Priest of Republicanism than of Monarchy. It contracts no entangling alliances with any sect of theorists, dreamers or philosophers. It sits apart from all, in its own calm dignity and simplicity, the same in a Republic as under a King; the same in Turkey as at the Rock of Plymouth; the same now, as when it laid the foundations of the first Temple at Jerusalem.

It gives no countenance to anarchy and licentiousness; and no illusion of glory or extravagant emulation of the Ancients inflames it with a thirst for ideal liberty. It teaches that in rectitude of life and sobriety of habits is the only true and safe road to real liberty; and it is chiefly the soldier of the sanctity of the laws and the rights of conscience.

It recognizes the truth of the proposition, that necessity, as well as abstract right, plays a part in the making of laws, the administration of government, and the regulation of relations in Society. It sees, indeed, that it rules in all the affairs of men. It knows that where any man, or number or race of men, are so degraded, so imbecile of intellect, so incapable of self-control, as to be unfit to be free, and as that it would be injurious to themselves or dangerous to the peace of the community or country for them to be free, the great law of necessity requires that they remain under the control of those of larger intellect and superior wisdom. It trusts and believes that God will, in His own good time, work out His own great and wise purposes; and is willing to wait, where it does not see its own way clear to do some certain good.

It hopes and longs for the day when, like other evils that afflict the earth, pauperism and bondage, of hireling and slave, shall cease and disappear; and all men, become fit to be free, shall be so, from voluntary or involuntary servitude. But it does not preach sedition; nor encourage rebellion by workman or servant, which can only end in disaster and defeat; or, if successful, in bloodshed and barbarism, followed by a more degrading bondage.

But wherever a people is fit to be free, and generously strives to be so, there go all its sympathies. It hates and detests the Tyrant, the lawless oppressor, and him who abuses a lawful Power. It frowns upon cruelty and wanton disregard of the rights of Humanity. It abhors the ferocious master and the selfish employer: and it exerts its influence to lighten the chains which the interest of society forbid should be broken, and to foster that humanity and kindness which man owes to his brother, even when that brother is his slave.

It can never be employed, in any country under Heaven, to teach a toleration for cruelty, to weaken moral hatred for guilt, or to deprave and brutalize the human mind. The dread of punishment will never make a Mason an accomplice in so corrupting his countrymen, and a teacher of depravity and barbarity. If, any where, as has heretofore happened, a Tyrant should send a Satirist on his tyranny to be convicted and punished as a libeller, in a court of justice, a Mason, if a juror in such a case, though in sight of the scaffold streaming with the blood of the innocent, and within hearing of the clash of the bayonets meant to overawe the court, would rescue the intrepid Satirist from the Tyrant's fangs, and send his officers out from the court with defeat and disgrace.

Even if all law and liberty were trampled under the feet of a military banditti, and great crimes were perpetrated with a high hand against all who were deservedly the objects of public veneration: if the People, overthrowing law, roared like a sea round the courts of justice, and demanded the blood of those who, during its temporary fit of insanity and drunken delirium had chanced to become odious to it, for true words frankly spoken, the Masonic juror, unawed alike by the single or the many-headed Tyrant, would consult the dictates of duty alone, and stand with a noble firmness between the human tiger and his prey.

The Mason would much rather pass his life hidden in the recesses of the deepest obscurity, feeding his mind even with the visions and imaginations of good deeds and noble actions, than to be placed on the most splendid throne of the universe, tantalized with a denial of the practice of all which can make the greatest situation any other than the greatest curse. And if he has been enabled to lend the slightest step to any great and laudable designs; if he has had any share in any measure giving quiet to private property and to private conscience, making lighter the yoke of poverty and dependence, or relieving deserving men from oppression; if he has aided in securing to his countrymen the best possession, peace; if he has joined in reconciling the different sections of his own country to each other, and the people to the government of their own creating; and in teaching the citizen to look for his protection to the laws of his country, and for his comfort to the good-will of his countrymen; if he has thus taken his part with the best of men in the best of their actions, he may well shut the book, even if he might wish to read a page or two more. It is enough for his measure. He has not lived in vain.

Masonry teaches that all power is delegated for the good, and not for the injury of the People; and that, when it is perverted from the original purpose, the compact is broken, and the right ought to be resumed: that resistance to power usurped is not merely a duty which man owes to himself and to his neighbour, but a duty which he owes to his God, in asserting and maintaining the rank which He gave him in the creation. This principle neither the rudeness of ignorance can stifle nor the enervation of refinement extinguish. It makes it base for a man to suffer when he ought to act; and, tending to preserve to him the original destinations of Providence, spurns at the arrogant assumptions of Tyrants and vindicates the independent quality of the race of which we are a part.

The wise and well-informed Mason will not fail to be the votary of Liberty and Justice. He will be ready to exert himself in their defence, wherever they exist. It cannot be a matter of indifference to him when his own liberty and that of other men, with whose merits and capacities he is acquainted, are involved in the event of the struggle to be made; but his attachment will be to the cause, as the cause of man; and not merely to the country. Wherever there is a people that understands the value of political justice, and is prepared to assert it, that is his country; wherever he can most contribute to the diffusion of these principles and the real happiness of mankind, that is his country. Nor does he desire for any country any other benefit than justice.

The true Mason identifies the honour of his country with his own. Nothing more conduces to the beauty and glory of one's country than the preservation against all enemies of its civil and religious liberty. The world will never willingly let die the names of those patriots who in her different ages have received upon their own breasts the blows aimed by insolent enemies at the bosom of their country. Evermore will men remember Leonidas who with his three hundred held Thermopylæ against the Persian Myriads; Hannibal, who for Carthage defied the power of Rome; Cincinnatus, who left his plough to put on the purple and command Rome's armies; and the thousand patriots who in every age have held their lives to be their country's property, and of small account compared with her interest or honour.

But also it conduces, and in no small measure, to the beauty and glory of one's country, that justice should be always administered there to all alike, and neither denied, sold, or delayed to any one; that the interest of the poor should be looked to, and none starve, nor be houseless, nor clamour in vain for work; that the child and the feeble woman should not be overworked, nor the slave of an inferior race, unfit to be free, be stinted of food, or overtasked, or unmercifully scourged by brutal master or overseer; and that God's great Laws, of Mercy, Humanity and Compassion should be every where enforced, not only by the laws, but also by the power of public opinion. And he who labours, often against reproach and obloquy, and oftener against indifference and apathy, to bring about that fortunate condition of things, when that great Code of Divine Law shall be every where and punctually obeyed, is no less a patriot than he who bares his bosom to the hostile steel in the ranks of his Country's Soldiery.

For fortitude is seen resplendent, not only in the field of battle and amid the clash of arms, but displays its energy under every difficulty and against every assailant. He who wars against cruelty, oppression and hoary abuses, fights for his country's honour, which those things soil; and her honour is as important as her existence. Often, indeed, the warfare against those abuses which disgrace one's country is quite as hazardous and more discouraging than that against her enemies in the field; and merits equal, if not greater reward.

For those Greeks and Romans who are the objects of our admiration employed hardly any other virtue in the extirpation of tyrants, than that love of liberty, which made them prompt in seizing the sword, and gave them strength to use it. With facility they accomplished the undertaking, amid the general shout of praise and joy; nor did they engage in the attempt so much as an enterprise of perilous and doubtful issue, as in a contest the most glorious in which virtue could be signalized; which infallibly led to present recompense; which bound their brows with wreaths of laurel, and consigned their memories to immortal fame.

But he who assails hoary abuses, regarded perhaps with a superstitious reverence, and around which old laws stand as ramparts and bastions to defend them; who denounces acts of cruelty and outrage on humanity which make every perpetrator thereof his personal enemy, and perhaps make him looked upon with suspicion by the people among whom he lives, as the assailant of an established order of things of which he assails only the abuses, and of laws of which he attacks only the violations,—he can scarcely look for present recompense, nor that his living brows will be wreathed with laurel. And if, contending against a dark array of long-received opinions, superstitions, obloquy and fears, which most men dread more than they do an army terrible with banners, the Mason overcomes and emerges from the contest victorious; or if he does not conquer, but is borne down and swept away by the mighty current of prejudice, passion and interest, in either case, the loftiness of spirit which he displays merits for him more than a mediocrity of fame.

He has already lived too long, who has survived the ruin of his country; and he who can enjoy life after such an event, deserves not to have lived at all. Nor does he any more deserve to live, who looks contentedly upon abuses that disgrace, and cruelties that dishonour, and scenes of misery and destitution and brutalization that disfigure his country, and makes no effort to remedy or to prevent either.

Not often is a country at war; nor can every one be allowed the privilege of offering his heart to the enemy's bullets. But in these patriotic labours of peace, in preventing, remedying and reforming evils, oppressions, wrongs, cruelties and outrages, every Mason can unite: and every one can effect something, and share the honour and glory of the result.

For the cardinal names in the history of the human mind are few and easily to be counted up: but thousands and tens of thousands spend their days in the preparations which are to speed the predestined change, in gathering and amassing the materials which are to kindle and give light and warmth, when the fire from heaven shall have descended on them. Numberless are the sutlers and pioneers, the engineers and artisans, who attend the march of intellect. Many more forward in detachments, and level the way over which the chariot is to pass, and cut down the obstacles that would impede its progress; and these too have their reward. If they labour diligently and faithfully in their calling, not only will they enjoy that calm contentment which diligence in the lowliest task never fails to win; not only will the sweat of their brows be sweet, and the sweetener of the rest that follows; but, when the victory is at last achieved, they will come in for a share in the glory; even as the meanest soldier who fought at Marathon or at King's Mountain became a sharer in the glory of those saving days; and within his own household circle, the approbation of which approaches the nearest to that of an approving conscience, was looked upon as the representative of all his brother heroes; and could tell such tales as made the tear glisten on the cheek of his wife, and lit up his boy's eyes with an unwonted sparkling eagerness. Or, if he fell in the fight, and his place by the fireside and at the table at home was thereafter vacant, that place was sacred; and he was often talked of there in the long winter evenings; and his family was deemed fortunate in the neighbourhood, because it had had a hero in it, who had fallen in defence of his country.

∴ Remember, my Brother, that life's length is not measured by its hours and days, but by that which we have done therein for our country and our kind. An useless life is short, if it last a century: but that of Hannibal was long as the life of oaks, though he died at the age of thirty-five. We may do much in a few years; and we may do nothing in a life-time. If we but eat and drink and sleep, and let every thing go on around us as it pleases; or if we live but to amass wealth, or gain offices, or wear titles, we might as well not have lived at all.

Forget not, therefore, to what you have devoted yourself in this Degree: defend weakness against strength, the friendless against the Great, the oppressed against the oppressor: and be ever vigilant and watchful of the interests and honour of your country: and may the Gr∴ Architect of the Universe give you that strength and wisdom which shall enable you well and faithfully to perform these high duties!

TO CLOSE.

[The President raps once, and says]:

Pres∴ Bro∴ Sen∴ Inspector, what is the hour?

Sen∴ Ins∴ The hour of the return of the Knights Elu of Nine with the murderer Abiram; since which time the nine lights burn in our Chapter.

Pres∴ The hour of rest has come. Cause the Brethren to assemble round the altar, that, renewing our pledges to one another, we may close this Chapter of Knights Elu of Nine.

Sen∴ Insp∴ [Rapping;]: Brethren, you will please assemble around the altar, that this Chapter may be closed in due and ancient form.

[The Brethren assemble round the altar, and the same ceremonies are performed as in opening. Then all return to their places. The President gives the sign, and all the Brethren the answer. Then the Pres.˙. raps [;]—the Sen.˙. Insp.˙. [;]—and the Jun.˙. Insp.˙. [;]—and the President declares],

Pres.˙.   This Chapter of Knights Elu of Nine is closed.

FINIS.

Tenth Degree.

Illustrious Elu of Fifteen.

THE LODGE, ITS DECORATIONS, ETC.

The hangings are black, sprinkled with red and white tears.

There are fifteen lights, five in the east, and five before each Warden.

OFFICERS, TITLES, ETC.

The officers are the same as in the 9th Degree; and represent the same persons during the reception.

The number of members is regularly fifteen and no more.

ORNAMENTS AND JEWELS.

The apron is white, lined, edged and fringed with black, and the flap black. In the middle are painted or embroidered three gates, and over each gate a head.

The cordon is a black ribbon or sash, worn from right to left, on the front of which are painted or embroidered three heads.

The jewel is a dagger, its hilt gold, and its blade silver, hanging at the end of the sash.

During a Reception, the President, Sen∴ Inspector and Secretary are dressed as in the 9th Degree.

The *battery* is ‖ raps at equal distances.

The *age* ‖ times ‖ or ? ‖ years.

The *hour* for opening is the 6th hour of the night: that for closing, the 6th hour of the day.

TO OPEN.

[The 15 Lights are not burning. The President gives one rap, and says]:

Pres∴ Brethren, I am about to open this Chapter of Illustrious Elus of 15. If there be any one present, who has not attained that degree, he is requested to withdraw.

[He raps twice, and the Hospitaller rises] :

Pres.·. Bro.·. Hospitaller, see that the entrance to the Chapter is duly guarded, that we may not be disturbed in our deliberations.

[The Hospitaller goes out, returns, raps 5 equal raps, which is answered from without, returns to his place, and says] :

Hosp.·. Th.·. Ill.·. President, the entrances to the Chapter are duly guarded, and we are secure.

Pres.·. Ill.·. Bro.·. Sen.·. Inspector, you will see that all present are Ill.·. Elus of Fifteen, by receiving, with the aid of the Ill.·. Bro.·. Jun.·. Inspector, the Pass-word from each.

[The two Inspectors go round, one by the north and the other by the south, receive the Pass-word from each Bro.·., and the Jun.·. Insp.·. then communicates it to the Sen.·. Insp.·., who returns to his place and says] :

Sen.·.Ins.·. All present are Ill.·. Elus of Fifteen, Th.·. Ill.·.

Pres.·. Ill.·. Bro.·. Sen.·. Inspector, how did you become an Ill.·. Elu of Fifteen?

Sen.·. Ins.·. My zeal and indefatigable exertions procured me that great honour, far above my deserts.

Qu.·. Where were you received as such?

Ans.·. In the Audience Chamber of King Solomon, and by himself, in the presence of his Court.

Qu.·. How many Elus were at first received?

Ans.·. Fifteen, including Joabert, whom I afterwards represented.

Qu.·. On what occasion were they received?

Ans.·. When King Solomon despatched them to search for and apprehend the two murderers of our Gr.·. Master Hiram Abi, who still remained at large.

Qu.·. Whither were they despatched?

Ans.·. To the country near Gath, a city of the Philistines, where they had taken refuge, after they fled from the mountains east of Joppa when Abiram was taken.

Qu.·. By whom was it discovered that they had taken refuge there?

Ans.·. By Bendecar, one of the Nine Elus, and afterwards appointed Viceroy over that portion of Palestine.

Qu.·. What steps did King Solomon take to have them apprehended?

Ans.·. He sent thither the Fifteen Elus, bearing a letter to Maacha, tributary King of Gath, with a sufficient escort.

Qu.·. To whom was the letter committed?

Ans.·. To Zerbal, Captain of the Guard and one of the Nine Elus.

Qu.·. Did the Fifteen succeed in apprehending the murderers?

Ans.·. They did, with the assistance furnished them by Maacha.

Qu.·. Where did they discover them?

Ans.·. In a quarry between Gath and Saphir, in which they had taken refuge.

Qu.·. By whom were they discovered?

Ans.·. By Joabert and Zerbal, two of the Elus of Fifteen.

Qu.·. What was done with the murderers?

Ans.·. They were taken to Jerusalem, and together with Abiram tried, condemned and executed.

Qu.·. Of what are the two murderers, Nebo and Zabad the types, to the Ill.·. Elus of Fifteen?

Ans.·. Of Fanaticism and Ignorance.

Qu.·. What do the three heads upon the apron and collar represent?

Ans.·. Tyranny, Fanaticism and Ignorance: the three enslavers of mankind, smitten by the sword of Freedom.

Qu.·. What is the cause to which the Ill.·. Elus of Fifteen are now devoted?

Ans.·. That of the oppressed against the oppressor, of Toleration against Fanaticism, of Knowledge against Ignorance, and of Civilization against brutal Barbarism.

Qu.·. When did the Fifteen Elus depart from Jerusalem?

Ans∴. On the 15th day of the month Tammuz, answering to the month of June.

Qu∴. When did they arrive at Gath?

Ans∴. On the 18th day of the same month.

Qu∴. What is your age?

Ans∴. ‖ times ‖ — or ? ‖ years complete.

Qu∴. What is the hour?

Ans∴. The sixth hour of the night.

Qu∴. Cause then the Brethren to assemble around the altar, that, renewing our pledges to one another, we may open this Chapter of Ill∴. Elus of Fifteen.

Sen∴. Insp∴. [Rapping 3]: Brethren, you will please assemble around the altar, that this Chapter may be opened in due and ancient form.

[The Brethren all assemble around the altar in a circle, including the President and all the officers, with their swords drawn. They raise their swords and place the points together in the centre, at an angle of 45 degrees; and repeat as follows]:

Hosp∴. To the cause of every People that struggles against Oppression and Tyranny, and is fit to be free!

Sec'y∴. To the cause of all who defend Right and Justice and Free Thought against the tyranny of popular opinion!

Treas∴. To the cause of the labourer, asking fair wages for his fair day's work!

Jun∴. Ins∴. To the cause of Patriotism, warring against the Tyranny of Party!

Orator∴. To the cause of Toleration against Fanaticism.

Sen∴. Ins∴. To the cause of civilization, instruction and enlightenment against Barbarism, Error and Ignorance!

Pres∴. To the cause of Free Thought, Free Conscience and Free Speech!

All∴. WE DEVOTE OURSELVES, OUR HANDS, OUR HEARTS, OUR INTELLECTS.

Pres∴. Now, HENCEFORWARD AND FOREVER.

All∴. AMEN!

[All return to their places. The President gives the sign, and all the Brethren the answer. Then the President raps ‖ — and a Brother lights the five lights in the East; the President saying]:

Pres∴: As these lights shine in this Chapter, so shall the great light of Freedom blaze in the world!

[The Sen∴. Insp∴. raps ‖ — and a brother lights the five lights in front of him; the Sen∴. Insp∴. saying]:

Sen∴. Ins∴. As my lights shine in this Chapter, so shall the light of religious and political Toleration rise upon the world.

[The Jun∴. Insp∴. raps ‖ — and a Brother lights the 5 lights in front of him; the Jun∴. Insp∴. saying]:

Jun∴. Insp∴. As my lights shine in this Chapter, so shall the light of Education and Intelligence yet shine in all the corners of the Earth.

Pres∴. So mote it be! My Brethren, this Chapter is duly opened in due and ancient form.

RECEPTION.

The officers being properly clothed and seated, the candidate, clothed as an Elu of Nine, is received in the Preparation room, and carefully examined by the Hospitaller, in the work and principles of the 9th Degree. If the examination be satisfactory, he is conducted into the Chapter, and directed to take a seat.

Pres∴. My Brethren, we still lament the death of our Ill∴. Gr∴. Master Hiram Abi; and the demands of justice remain unsatisfied. Excellent Sadoc, what sayeth the law as to him who slayeth his Brother?

Sec∴. Whoso sheddeth man's blood, by man shall his blood be shed; for in the image of God made he man. At the hand of every man's Brother will I require the life of man. If any man hate his neighbour, and lie in wait for him, and rise up against him, and smite him mortally, that he die, then thine eye shall not pity him, but his blood shall purify the land of that innocent blood that he hath shed. He is accursed that smiteth his neighbour secretly, or taketh reward to slay an innocent person.

Pres∴ Such is the law; and the land of Israel is not yet purified of the innocent blood of our Brother, shed upon the floor of the Temple, and the stains whereof still remain to bear witness against his murderers. One in his dungeon awaits his trial and the swift punishment that shall follow it; but two remain at large, nor have they yet been traced from their retreat in the mountains east of Joppa. Samaria and Galilee have been searched in vain, and all the land of Dan and Judah, and the country upon both shores of the Dead Sea, without success; and I fear they have escaped by sea to Egypt, or into Syria or the mountains of Phœnicia, and are beyond our reach.

Sec∴ Most Potent King, doubt not that the Lord will at length give them into thy hand, even as he did Abiram, when thou didst despair of discovering his retreat.

Pres∴ The Nine Elus have even now returned from Galilee and the confines of Phœnicia, and found no trace whatever of the fugitives: Ben-hesed and Ben-abinadab, from the shores of the Dead Sea; Bana and Achimaas from Samaria, and Ben-gaber and Josaphat from Idumea. I know not what further steps to take.

[The M∴ of Ceremonies, who represents Bendecar, one of the Elus of Nine, raps ‖ at the door].

Hosp∴ Th∴ Potent King Solomon, there is an alarm at the entrance of the audience chamber.

Pres∴ See who applies to enter, my Brother, and what his errand is; and if it be not urgent, let him depart.

[The Hospitaller goes to the door, opens it, and asks]:.

Hosp∴ Who is it that applies to enter here?

M∴ Cer∴ Bendecar, one of the Nine Knights Elect, who desires to have speech with our Lord the King.

Hosp∴ Our Lord the King hath said, "See who applies to enter, and what his errand is; and if it be not urgent, let him depart."

M∴ Cer∴ My errand *is* urgent; and I bring tidings that will gladden the heart of our Lord the King. I crave permission to approach him.

Hosp∴ Wait, then, my Brother, while I inform him of thy request.

[He closes the door and approaches the East].

Pres∴ Who is it, Ahisar, that applies to enter?

Hosp∴ Bendecar, one of the Nine Knights Elu, who desires to have speech with thee; and craves permission to approach thy footstool.

Pres∴ What is his errand?

Hosp∴ He saith not, but declares that it is urgent; and that he bears tidings which will gladden thy heart.

Pres∴ Then let him enter and make known his tidings.

[The Hospitaller opens the door, and the M∴ of Cer∴ enters, approaches the East, kneels, rises, and stands with his hands folded across his breast].

Pres∴ What is thine errand, my Brother, and the tidings that thou bringest?

M∴ Cer∴ Th∴ Potent King Solomon, returning from Galilee with my companions, and while they explored the river Jordan from the Sea of Tiberias to Naarath near the Dead Sea, I, leaving them at Zarthan, traversed the mountains to Ekron, and thence to Ascalon upon the Great Sea, and returned hither by the way of Gath-Rimmon, Gibeah and Bethlehem. At Ekron and again at Ashdod I came upon the track of the fugitives, finding those who had seen and could describe them. I traced them unto Saphir; but beyond that could hear nought of them, in Gath or in its suburbs; and having no means to procure assistance in the search, nor being accredited to Maacha, King of Gath, I was perforce compelled to return hither, to inform my Lord the King that the fugitives have taken refuge in the land of Gath.

Pres∴ Thou thinkest so?

M∴ Cer∴ I feel assured that they have taken refuge there. I could not trace them further. They cannot escape by sea; and the large rewards offered for their apprehension have closed against them all the outlets leading into Idumea and towards the sea that covers Sodom.

Pres∴ Bendecar, thou hast done well; and thy reward shall not be wanting. I will forthwith send messengers to my servant Maacha, with letters requiring his assistance in searching out and capturing the fugitives. Let Josaphat our Chancellor write such letters, and the Nine Knights Elu prepare to set forth with sufficient escort. And lest their number be too small, let six others go forth with them, selected by lot from among our servants, making fifteen in all. Place thou in an urn, my Brother Adonhiram, the names of all our Perfect Masters, other than the Nine Elu, and let Sadoc the High Priest draw forth six names; and let those so drawn, with the Nine, go forth upon this expedition.

[The Sen.·. Insp.·. places several names in an urn, upon slips of paper, and the Secretary draws forth six in succession, reading as he does so, the following names: .. *Ben-hesed ... Ben-abinadab ... Achimaas ... Bana ... Josaphat the son of Pharue ... Benyaber*].

Pres.·. Let the Nine Knights Elu, and the six Brethren named advance.

[The candidate and fourteen Brothers, including the M.·. of Cer.·., advance to the East, and the President says to them]:

Pres.·. My Brethren, it devolves on you to perform an important duty. I place you under the command of Zerbal, who shall bear our letters to Maacha our servant, King of Gath. Go thither speedily, and aided by the King our servant, search his dominions for these murderers, even the whole country between the Salt Lake of Sodom and the Great Sea, and into Idumea. If you discover the assassins, take them alive, and bring them hither to be tried and punished; for justice clamors for its due. If you succeed, be sure you shall be rewarded, and your names, as the Fifteen Elus, be glorious. Go and refresh yourselves, and prepare to set forth at mid-day.

[The Candidate and several brothers retire to the ante-room, and lay aside their Masonic clothing and jewels, and each arms himself with a sword. In the mean time all the furniture of the Lodge room is removed, except the lights. A Brother who represents Zerbal then enters, conducting the Candidate, and the other brothers follow. They make several times the circuit of the room, while the lights behind the Candidate as he travels, are put out by degrees, until the room is dark. Obstacles are then placed in his way, and several more circuits are made, and then he is conducted to the ante-room, where Zerbal says]:

Zerb.·. My Brethren, we are now near the City of Gath. Remain here, while I enter the city and present to King Maacha the letters of his Sovereign Lord the King.

[He then goes out, and remains some time; then returns and says]:

Zerb.·. Be of good cheer, my Brethren! The King of Gath has received with reverence the letters of our Lord the King, and hath sent out his guards to scour the country in all directions, in search of the fugitives. They may have taken refuge in the quarries between Gath and Saphir. Let us proceed thither.

[They again enter the Chapter room, and makes several circuits as before. Then Zerbal says]:

Zerb.·. Here is the entrance to a quarry. I will explore it with Joabert and Stolkin, while the rest keep watch without, and guard the other outlets, if there be any.

[The Candidate with the Brothers who represent Zerbal and Stolkin then pass through a narrow passage, so low as to compel them to stoop; and emerge into a small room, representing a quarry in the rocks, lighted by two or three dim lamps, and in which are two men, roughly dressed, and with miners' tools in their hands]:

Zerb.·. Behold the murderers!

The Two: We are lost!

[The two men throw down their tools, draw their daggers, and rush upon the three Brothers. Zerbal and the Candidate seize one, who submits, and they take his dagger from him. The other is seized by Stolkin, but breaks away and escapes through the passage, and is taken by the brothers without. Zerbal, Stolkin and the Candidate then return through the passage, rejoin the others, and all proceed to the ante-room, where they deliver the two prisoners to the Guards. In the mean time the Chapter room is lighted, and the officers seated as before. The M.·. of Cer.·. now raps ‖ at the door, which is answered by the Hospitaller within, who opens the door and asks]:

Hosp.·. Who apply to enter here?

M.·. Cer.·. The fifteen Knights Elect, who were sent to the land of Gath in search of the murderers of our deceased Gr.·. Master.

Hosp.·. The King hath ordered that upon your return, you at once appear before him. Enter.

[The Candidate and the other Brothers enter, advance to the East, kneel, rise, cross their arms upon their breasts and stand in silence].

Pres.∴ Speak, Zerbal! Hast thou succeeded?

Zerb.∴ My liege, we have. We journeyed hence with all speed, and by the shortest route, to the City of Gath, where, my brethren remaining without the walls, I entered the city, obtained immediate audience of the King, and laid before him thy letters. He received them with all reverence, and most courteously entreated me, and forthwith despatched his guards in every direction, to seek and apprehend the fugitives. Returning to my companions, we hastened to the quarries between Gath and Saphir, where I suspected the murderers were concealed; and coming to the entrance of one, I, with Joabert and Stolkin entered, and found two men at work, whom I recognized as the murderers. We sprang upon them, Joabert and I upon one, and Stolkin upon the other. They defended themselves with their daggers, but one we overpowered and bound, while the other, breaking away, fled through the entrance, and was taken by our comrades who remained without. Then, having sent this information and our thanks to King Maacha, we forthwith returned, and have delivered the two fugitives to thy Guards.

Pres.∴ Thanks be to God, who hath delivered these wretches into the hands of justice. Let them be chained, and consigned to separate dungeons till the morrow. And let our Royal Warrant issue, constituting Adonhiram the son of Abda, Ahisar, Governor of the House, Zabud the son of Nathan, Azarias the son of Nathan, Azarias the son of Sadoc, and Elihoreph and Ahia the Scribes, a High Court, in which Josaphat our Chancellor shall preside, to try these prisoners, and determine on their guilt or innocence. Let them have fair trial, be confronted with the witnesses against them, have opportunity to produce evidence in their own behalf, and be heard in their own defence. If innocent, or if it be doubtful whether they are guilty, let them go free; but if, after fair trial and on due deliberation, they are found guilty, then let them be forthwith hanged, and afterwards beheaded, and their heads set upon the East, West and South gates of the city as a terror to all evil-doers. And let the Court convene at the third hour of the day to-morrow, and proceed speedily with the trial. Have I said well, my Brother?

Sen.∴ Insp.∴ Most well and wisely, my Brother.

Pres.∴ So will the land be purified of innocent blood, crime punished, and justice satisfied, and severity still be tempered with humanity. Zerbal, I will reward you and your companions as you deserve. I make you the members of a new order of nobility, and a new degree in Masonry, to be styled the Illustrious Elu of Fifteen, of which I and my Brother Hiram will deem it a high honour to be elected members; and which none shall receive hereafter by our gift, but only by your unanimous vote. Place yourselves around the altar, my Brethren, and assume an obligation appropriate to the new degree.

[The 15 Brothers stand around the altar in a circle, placing their left hands on the cross swords and cross-daggers which are upon it. The other Brothers encircle them and form the roof of steel over them. In this position the Brothers repeat the following obligation:

OBLIGATION.

I, A . . . . B . . . . in the presence of the Grand Architect of the Universe, and under these swords, drawn to protect or punish, do hereby and hereon most solemnly and sincerely promise and swear, that I will never reveal the secrets of this degree of Ill.∴ Elu of Fifteen to any person in the world, unless it be at a time when, and in a place where, it may be lawfully done, and to a person duly authorized to receive them, and when I am duly authorized to communicate them.

I furthermore promise and swear that I will evermore keep and punctually observe my obligation as a Knight Elu of Nine; and again to the same causes as by my obligation in that degree I did, and to the cause of Toleration and Liberality against Fanaticism and Persecution political and religious, and to that of Education, Instruction and Enlightenment against Error, Barbarism, and Ignorance, I hereby irrevocably and forever devote my hand, my heart and my intellect; under the same penalty which I invoked in that degree. So help me God; and keep me steadfast in the due performance of the same!

[The swords are lowered, and one laid on the head of each of the Brothers; and the President says]:

Pres.∴ I therefore declare you to be duly invested with the rank and dignity of Ill.∴ Elu.∴ of Fifteen: which degree I declare to be devoted, now and always hereafter, to Toleration, Liberality and Enlightenment; and I invest you with its collar, apron and jewel, which need no explanation.

Receive now, my brethren, the signs, words and token of this degree:

Sign: . . . Make the motion of bringing a ⁑☿♒♀☉‡♊ up under the ♐&♀♒, &♀†♈ upwards, and strike perpendicularly ♊☿ ♃♒♃☉‡♊, as if opening your ☉♏♊☿♏☾♒.

Answer: . . . Make the ☉⁑⁑‡☾♒♈♀♐☾♎ sign, with the ♑♀♒♌☾‡♎ closed and the ♈&♄♋♏ raised.

Token: . . . Close the ♑♀♒♌☾‡♎ and raise the ♈&♄♋♏ of the ‡&☉♒♊: Then, with that ♈&♄♋♏ close to the ♏☿♊♄ of the other, make a transverse motion as if cutting across his ☉♏♊☿♋☾♒. He does the same to you. As you do it, you say ♍☾‡♏☉† ∴ As he does it, he says ☉†-¶&☉♒☉♒ ∴

Pass-word: . . . . ♍☾‡♏☉† ∴

Sacred Word: . . . . ☉†-¶&☉♒☉♒ ∴

Go now, my Brethren, to the orator; and receive the lecture of this degree.

LECTURE.

This Degree, my Brother, as you have learned by your obligation, is devoted to the same objects as those of the Elu of Nine; and also to the cause of Toleration and Liberality against Fanaticism and Persecution, political and religious; and to that of Education, Instruction and Enlightenment against Error, Barbarism and Ignorance. To these objects you have irrevocably and forever devoted your hand, your heart and your intellect; and whenever in your presence a Chapter of this Degree is opened, you will be most solemnly reminded of your solemn vows here taken at the altar.

Toleration, holding that every other man has the same right to his opinion and faith that we have to ours: and Liberality, holding that as no human being can say with certainty, in the clash and conflict of hostile faiths and creeds, what is Truth, or that he is surely in possession thereof, so every one should feel that it is quite possible that another, equally honest and sincere with himself, and yet holding the contrary opinion, may himself be in possession of the Truth; and that whatever one firmly and conscientiously believes, is truth to him; are the mortal enemies of that Fanaticism which persecutes for opinion's sake; and initiates crusades against whatever it, in its imaginary holiness, deems to be contrary to the law of God.

And Education, Instruction and Enlightenment are the most certain means by which Fanaticism and Intolerance can be rendered powerless.

No true Mason scoffs at honest convictions, and an ardent zeal in the cause of Truth and Justice. But he absolutely denies the right of any man to assume the prerogative of Deity, and condemn his Brother's faith and opinions as heretical and deserving to be punished. Nor does he approve the course of those who endanger the peace of great nations and the best interests of their own race by indulging in a chimerical and visionary philanthropy; a luxury which they can only enjoy by drawing their robes around them to avoid contact with their fellows, and proclaiming themselves holier than they.

For he knows that intolerance and bigotry have been infinitely greater curses to mankind than ignorance and error. Better any error than persecution! Better any belief or opinion than the thumbscrew, the rack and the stake! And he knows also how unspeakably absurd it is, for a creature to whom he himself and every thing around and within him are mysteries, to torture and kill others, because they do not think as he does in regard to the profoundest of those mysteries; which it is utterly beyond the comprehension of either to understand.

We may well be tolerant of each other's creed; for in every faith there are excellent moral precepts. Far in the South of Asia, Zoroaster taught this doctrine: On commencing a journey, the Faithful should turn his thoughts towards Ormuzd, and confess him, in the purity of his heart, to be King of the World; he should love Him, do him homage, and serve him. He must be upright and charitable, despise the pleasures of the body, and avoid pride and haughtiness, and vice in all its forms, and especially falsehood, one of the basest sins of which man can be guilty. He must forget injuries and not avenge himself. He must honour the memory of his parents and relatives. At night, before retiring to sleep, he should rigorously examine his conscience, and repent of the faults which weakness or ill-fortune had caused him to commit. He was required to pray for strength to persevere in the Good, and to obtain forgiveness for his errors. It was his duty to confess his faults to a magus, or to a layman renowned for his virtues, or to the sun. Fasting and maceration were prohibited: and, on the contrary, it was his duty suitably to nourish the body and to maintain its vigour, that his soul might be strong to resist the Genius of Darkness; that he might more attentively read the Divine Word, and have more courage to perform noble deeds.

And in the North of Europe the Druids taught devotion to friends, indulgence for reciprocal wrongs, love of deserved praise, prudence, humanity, hospitality, respect for old age, disregard of the future, temperance, contempt of death, and a chivalrous deference to woman. Listen to these maxims from the Hava Maal, or Sublime Book of Odin:

"If thou hast a friend, visit him often: the path will grow over with grass, and the trees soon cover it, if thou dost not constantly walk upon it. He is a faithful friend, who, having but two loaves, gives his friend one. Be never first to break with thy friend: sorrow wrings the heart of him, who has no one save himself, with whom to take counsel. There is no virtuous man who has not some vice, no bad man who has not some virtue. Happy he who obtains the praise and good-will of men; for all that depends on the will of another is hazardous and uncertain. Riches flit away in the twinkling of an eye: they are the most inconstan: of friends: flocks and herds perish, parents die, friends are not immortal, thou thyself diest: I know but one thing that doth not die, the judgment that is passed upon the dead. Be humane towards those whom thou meetest on the road. If the guest that cometh to thy house is a-cold, give him fire: the man who has journeyed over the mountains needs food and dry garments. Mock not at the aged; for words full of sense come often from the wrinkles of age. Be moderately wise, and not over prudent. Let no one seek to know his destiny, if he would sleep tranquilly. There is no malady more cruel than to be discontented with our lot. Rise early, if thou wouldst become rich, or overcome an enemy: the wolf that sleeps takes no prey; the man that sleeps gains no victory. The glutton eats his own death; and the wise man laughs at the fool's greediness. Nothing is more injurious to the young than excessive drinking: the more one drinks, the more he loses his reason; the bird of forgetfulness sings before those who intoxicate themselves, and wiles away their souls. Man devoid of sense believes he will live always if he avoids war; but, if the lances spare him, old age will give him no quarter. Better live well than live long. When a man lights a fire in his house, death comes before it goes out.".

And thus said the Indian books: "Honour thy father and mother. Never forget the benefits thou hast received. Learn while thou art young. Be submissive to the laws of thy country. Seek the company of virtuous men. Speak not of God but with respect. Live on good terms with thy fellow-citizens. Remain in thy proper place. Speak ill of no one. Mock at the bodily infirmities of none. Pursue not unrelentingly a conquered enemy. Strive to acquire a good reputation. The best bread is that for which one is indebted to his own labour. Take counsel with wise men. The more one learns, the more he acquires the faculty of learning. Knowledge is the most permanent wealth. As well be dumb as ignorant. The true use of knowledge is to distinguish good from evil. Be not a subject of shame to thy parents. What one learns in youth endures like the engraving upon a rock. He is wise who knows himself. Let thy books be thy best friends. When thou attainest an hundred years, cease to learn. Wisdom is solidly planted, even on the shifting ocean. Deceive no one, not even thine enemy. Wisdom is a treasure that every where commands its value. Modesty is the most beautiful ornament of a woman. One is nowhere well lodged but in his own house. Speak mildly, even to the poor. It is sweeter to forgive than to take vengeance. Concord is the finest ornament of a family. First procure the wagon, and then set thyself about finding the oxen. Gaming and quarrels lead to misery. There is no true merit without the practice of virtue. To honour our mother is the most fitting homage we can pay the Divinity. There is no tranquil sleep without a clear conscience. One cannot always have milk to drink: we must conform ourselves to circumstances. He badly understands his interest who breaks his word."

Twenty-four centuries ago, this was the Chinese Ethics.

"The Philosopher said, ' San ! my doctrine is simple, and easy to be understood.' Thseng-Tseu replied, ' that is certain.' The Philosopher having gone out, the disciples asked what their master had meant to say. Thseng-Tseu responded, ' The doctrine of our Master consists solely in being upright of heart, and loving our neighbour as we love ourself.' "

About a century later, the Hebrew law said, " If any man hate his neighbour . . . then shall ye do unto him, as he had thought to do unto his brother . . . Better is a neighbour that is near, than a brother afar off . . . Thou shalt love thy neighbour as thyself."

In the same fifth century before Christ, Socrates the Grecian said, " Thou shalt love thy neighbour as thyself."

Three generations earlier, Zoroaster had said to the Persians : " Offer up thy grateful prayers to the Lord, the most just and pure Ormuzd, the supreme and adorable God, who thus declared to his Prophet Zerdusht : ' Hold it not meet to do unto others what thou wouldst not desire done unto thyself: do that unto the people, which, when done to thyself, is not disagreeable unto thee.' "

The same doctrine had been long taught in the schools of Babylon and Jerusalem. A Pagan declared to the Pharisee Hillel that he was ready to embrace the Jewish religion, if he could make known to him in a few words a summary of the whole law of Moses. " That which thou likest not done to thyself, said Hillel, do it not unto thy neighbour. Therein is all the law : the rest is nothing but the commentary upon it."

" Nothing is more natural," said Confucius, " nothing more simple, than the principles of that morality which I endeavour, by salutary maxims, to inculcate in you . . . It is humanity ; which is to say, that universal charity among all of our species, without distinction. It is uprightness ; that is, that rectitude of spirit and of heart, which makes one seek for truth in every thing, and desire it, without deceiving one's self or others. It is finally sincerity or good faith ; which is to say, that frankness, that openness of heart, tempered by self-reliance, which excludes all feints and all disguising, as much in speech as in action."

To diffuse useful information, to further intellectual refinement, sure forerunner of moral improvement, to hasten the coming of the great day, when the dawn of general knowledge shall chase away the lazy, lingering mists, even from the base of the great social pyramid, is indeed a high calling, in which the most splendid talents and consummate virtue may well press onward, eager to bear a part. From the Masonic ranks ought to go forth those whose genius and not their ancestry ennoble them, to open to all ranks the temple of science, and by their own example to make the humblest men emulous to climb steps no longer inaccessible, and enter the unfolded gates burning in the sun.

The highest intellectual cultivation is perfectly compatible with the daily cares and toils of working men. A keen relish for the most sublime truths of science belongs alike to every class of mankind. And, as philosophy was taught in the sacred groves of Athens, and under the Portico, and in the old Temples of Egypt and India, so in our Lodges ought Knowledge to be dispensed, the Sciences taught, and the Lectures become like the teachings of Socrates and Plato, of Agassiz and Cousin.

Real knowledge never permitted either turbulence or unbelief ; but its progress is the forerunner of liberality and enlightened toleration. Whoso dreads these may well tremble ; for he may be well assured that their day is at length come, and must put to speedy flight the evil spirits of tyranny and persecution, which haunted the long night now gone down the sky. And it is to be hoped that the time will soon arrive, when, as men will no longer suffer themselves to be led blindfold in ignorance, so will they no more yield to the vile principle of judging and treating their fellow-creatures, not according to the intrinsic merit of their actions, but according to the accidental and involuntary coincidence of their opinions.

Whenever we come to treat with entire respect those who conscientiously differ from ourselves, the only practical effect of a difference will be, to make us enlighten the ignorance on one side or the other, from which it springs, by instructing them, if it be theirs ; ourselves, if it be our own ; to the end that the only kind of unanimity may be produced which is desirable among rational beings,—the agreement proceeding from full conviction after the freest discussion.

The Knight Elu of Fifteen ought therefore to take the lead of his fellow-citizens, not in frivolous amusements, not in the degrading pursuits of the ambitious vulgar; but in the truly noble task of enlightening the mass of his countrymen, and of leaving his own name encircled, not with barbaric splendor, or attached to courtly gewgaws, but illustrated by the honors most worthy of our rational nature; coupled with the diffusion of knowledge, and gratefully pronounced by a few, at least, whom his wise beneficence has rescued from ignorance and vice.

We say to him, in the words of the great Roman: "Men in no respect so nearly approach to the Deity, as when they confer benefits on men. To serve and do good to as many as possible,—there is nothing greater in your fortune than that you should be able, and nothing finer in your nature, than that you should be desirous to do this." This is the true mark for the aim of every man and Mason who either prizes the enjoyment of pure happiness, or sets a right value upon a high and unsullied renown. And if the benefactors of mankind, when they rest from their noble labours, shall be permitted to enjoy hereafter, as an appropriate reward of their virtue, the privilege of looking down upon the blessings with which their exertions and charities, and perhaps their toils and sufferings have clothed the scene of their former existence, it will not, in a state of exalted purity and wisdom, be the founders of mighty dynasties, the conquerors of new empires, the Cæsars, Alexanders and Tamerlanes; nor the mere Kings and Counsellors, Presidents and Senators, who have lived for their party chiefly, and for their country only incidentally, often sacrificing to their own aggrandizement or that of their faction the good of their fellow-creatures;—it will not be they who will be gratified by contemplating the monuments of their inglorious fame; but those will enjoy that delight and march in that triumph, who can trace the remote effects of their enlightened benevolence in the improved condition of their species, and exult in the reflection, that the change which they at last, perhaps after many years, survey, with eyes that age and sorrow can make dim no more,—of Knowledge become Power,—Virtue sharing that Empire—Superstition dethroned, and Tyranny exiled, is, if even only in some small and very slight degree, yet still in some degree, the fruit, precious if costly, and though late repaid yet long enduring, of their own self-denial and strenuous exertion, of their own mite of charity and aid to education wisely bestowed, and of the hardships and hazards which they encountered here below.

But Masonry requires of its initiates and votaries nothing that is impracticable. It does not demand that they should undertake to climb to those lofty and sublime peaks of a theoretical and imaginary unpractical virtue, high and cold and remote as the eternal snows that wrap the shoulders of Chimborazo, and at least quite as inaccessible as they. It asks that alone to be done, which is easy to be done. It overtasks no one's strength, and asks no one to go beyond his means or his capacities. It does not expect one whose business or profession yields him little more than the wants of himself and his family require, and whose time is necessarily occupied by his daily avocations, to abandon or neglect the avocation by which he and his children live, and devote himself and his means to the diffusion of knowledge among men. It does not expect him to publish books for the people, or to lecture to the injury of his business, or to found academies and colleges, build up libraries and entitle himself to statues.

But it does require and expect every man of us to do something, within and according to his means: and there is no Mason who cannot do something; if not alone, then by combination and association. If all the Masons of a State choose, they may, by a moderate but permanent annual contribution levied upon themselves, furnish annually a sum equivalent to the interest on a large capital, and therewith build and endow a college. Lodges can unite and aid in the erection and establishment of a school or an academy: and it is the saddest of all Masonic sights when the Brethren of a jurisdiction rebel against a contribution for these purposes, imposed by themselves through their constituted and accredited representatives; and thus make known to a scoffing world what is *their* deliberate opinion of the value of Masonry.

And if a Lodge cannot aid in founding a school or an academy, it can still do something. It can educate one boy or girl, at least, the child of some poor or departed Brother. And let it never be forgotten that in the poorest unregarded child that seems abandoned to ignorance and vice, may slumber the virtues of a Socrates, the intellect of a Bacon, the genius of a Shakspeare, the capacity to do good to mankind of a Washington; and that, in rescuing him from the mire in which he is plunged, and giving him the means of education and development, the Lodge that does it may be the direct and immediate means of conferring upon the world as great a blessing as that given it by John Faust the boy of Mentz, by Fulton, or Arkwright or Morse; may perpetuate the liberties of our own country, and change the destinies of nations, and write a new Chapter in the History of the World.

For we never know the importance of the act we do. The Daughter of Pharaoh little thought what she was doing for the human race, and the vast, unimaginable consequences that depended on her charitable act, when she drew the little child of a Hebrew woman from among the rushes that grew along the bank of the Nile, and determined to rear it as her own.

How often has an act of charity, costing the doer little, given to the world a great painter, a great musician, a great inventor! How often has such an act developed the ragged boy into the great benefactor of his race! On what small and apparently unimportant circumstances have turned and hinged the fates of the world's great conquerors, the Napoleons and Cromwells. There is no law that limits the returns that shall be reaped from a single good deed. The widow's mite may not only be as acceptable to God, but may produce as great results as the rich man's costly offering. The poorest boy, helped by benevolence, may come to lead armies, to decide on peace and war, to control Senates, to dictate to Cabinets; and exercise influences as vast as those of England's great Statesmen, past and present, as the Great Commoner of our own Country, who was once the mill-boy of the Slashes of Hanover, and the mighty Orator and Statesman, once the son of a poor farmer of New Hampshire, but whose magnificent thoughts and noble words will be law many years hereafter to millions of men yet unborn.

But the opportunity to effect a great good does not often occur to any one. It is worse than folly for one to lie idle and inert, and expect the accident to befall him, by which his influences shall live forever. He can expect that to happen, only in consequence of one or many or all of a long series of acts. He can expect to benefit the world only as men attain other results; by continuance, by persistence, by a steady and uniform habit of labouring for the enlightenment of the world, to the extent of his means and capacity.

For it is, in all instances, by dint of steady labour, by giving enough of application to our work, and having enough of time for the doing of it, by regular pains-taking, and the plying of constant assiduities, and not by any process of legerdemain, that we secure the strength and the staple of real excellence. It was thus that Demosthenes, clause after clause, and sentence after sentence, elaborated to the uttermost his immortal orations. It was thus that Newton pioneered his way, by the steps of an ascending geometry, to the mechanism of the Heavens.

It is a most erroneous opinion that those who have left the most stupendous monuments of intellect behind them, were not differently exercised from the rest of the species, but only differently gifted: that they signalized themselves only by their talent, and hardly ever by their industry: for it is in truth to the most strenuous application of those common place faculties which are diffused among all, that they are indebted for the glories which now encircle their remembrance and their name.

We must not imagine it to be a vulgarizing of genius, that it should be lighted up in any other way than by a direct inspiration from Heaven; nor overlook the steadfastness of purpose, the devotion to some single but great object, the unweariedness of labour that is given, not in convulsive and preternatural throes, but by little and little as the strength of the mind may bear it; the accumulation of many small efforts, instead of a few grand and gigantic, but perhaps irregular movements, on the part of energies that are marvellous; by which former alone the great results are brought out that write their enduring records on the face of the earth and in the history of nations and of man.

We must not overlook these elements, to which genius owes the best and proudest of her achievements; nor imagine that qualities so generally possessed as patience and pains-taking, and resolute industry, have no share in upholding a distinction so illustrious as that of the benefactor of his kind.

We must not forget that great results are most ordinarily produced by an aggregate of many contributions and exertions: as it is the invisible particles of vapour, each separate and distinct from the other, that, rising from the Atlantic and its bays and gulfs, and from wide morasses and overflowed plains, float away in clouds, and distil upon the earth in dew, and fall in showers and rains upon the broad prairies and rude mountains, and make the great navigable rivers that are the arteries along which flows the life-blood of our country.

And so Masonry can do much, if each Mason be content to do his share, and if their united efforts are directed by wise counsels to a common purpose. A man would wonder at the mighty things which have been done by degrees and gentle augmentations. Diligence and moderation are the best steps whereby to climb to any excellency; and it is rare if there be any other way. The Heavens send not down their rain in floods, but by drops and dewy distillations. A man is neither good, nor wise, nor rich at once; yet, softly creeping up these hills, he shall every day better his prospect, until at last he gains the summit. It is for God and for Omnipotency to do mighty things in a moment; but by degrees to grow to greatness is the course that he hath left for man.

If Masonry will but be true to her mission, and Masons to their promises and obligations;—if, re-entering vigorously upon a career of beneficence, she and they will but pursue it earnestly and unfalteringly, remembering that our contributions to the cause of charity and education then deserve the greatest credit when it costs us something, the curtailing of a comfort or the relinquishment of a luxury to make them: if we will but give aid to Masonry's great schemes for human improvement, not fitfully and spasmodically, but regularly and incessantly, as the vapours rise, and the springs run, and as the sun rises and the stars come up into the Heavens, then wo may be sure that great results will be attained and a great work done. And then it will most surely be seen that Masonry is not effete or impotent. It will betoken it not degenerated, nor drooping to a fatal decay; but casting off the old and wrinkled skin of routine and inertia, to wax young again, entering the glorious ways of Truth and prosperous Virtue, destined to become great and honorable in these latter ages. And foreseeing this glad result, we may see in our minds our noble and puissant Order rousing herself like a strong man after sleep, and shaking her invincible locks; may see her as an eagle mewing her mighty youth, and kindling her undazzled eyes at the full mid-day beam; purging and unscaling her long-abused sight at the fountain itself of heavenly radiance; while the whole noise of timorous and flocking birds, with those also that love the twilight, flutter about, amazed at what she means, and in their envious gabble would prognosticate disastrous failure and ignominious downfall; unstirred by which and untroubled, she wings her strong way towards the stars, and bathes leisurely in the broad light of Divine Truth and ever-increasing knowledge.

TO CLOSE.

Pres.∴ Bro.∴ Sen.∴ Inspector, what is the hour?

Sen.∴ Insp.∴ Th.∴ Ill.∴, the hour when the Fifteen Elus returned to Jerusalem.

Pres.∴ The hour of rest has come. Cause the Brethren to assemble round the altar, that, renewing our pledges to one another, we may close this Chapter of Ill.∴ Elu of Fifteen.

Sen.∴ Insp.∴ [Rapping 3]: Brethren, you will please assemble around the altar, that this Chapter may be closed in due and ancient form.

[The Brethren assemble round the altar; and the same ceremonies are performed as in opening. Then all return to their places. The President gives the sign; and all the Brethren the answer. Then the President raps ‖ and the lights in front of him are extinguished; the Sen.∴ Inspector ‖ and the lights in front of him are extinguished; the Jun.∴ Insp.∴ ‖ and the lights in front of him are extinguished; and the Pres.∴ says]:

Pres.∴ This Chapter of Ill.∴ Elu of Fifteen is closed.

FINIS.

Eleventh Degree.

Prince Ameth, or Sublime Elu of Twelve.

THE LODGE, ITS DECORATIONS, ETC.

This Lodge is also called a Chapter, and it is decorated like that of the 10th Degree, with the same hangings.

It is lighted, however, by 12 lights, by threes, in the East, West, North and South.

OFFICERS, TITLES, ETC.

The Presiding Officer is styled Th∴ Ill∴ *Prince President:* and all the other officers and members *Princes.*

The two Wardens are styled *Inspectors,* and sit in the West.

The Orator sits in the South.

The Treasurer and Secretary on the right and left of the Prince President.

The Deacons are styled *Auditors,* and sit as in the Symbolic Lodge.

The Master of Ceremonies is styled *Marshal.*

The Chapter regularly consists of 12 members only.

CLOTHING, ORNAMENTS AND JEWELS.

The apron is white, lined, edged and fringed with black, and the flap black. In the middle of the apron is painted or embroidered a flaming heart.

The cordon is a black sash or ribbon, worn from right to left. Over the heart is painted or embroidered upon it a flaming heart; and over that the words, *Vincere aut Mori.*

The jewel is a sword, worn suspended to the cordon.

Battery ... [‖ ,]

Age ... z ✕ ; or ? £ years.

TO OPEN.

Th∴ Ill∴ [Rapping once]: Bro∴ Sen∴ Inspector, I am about to open this Chapter of Princes Ameth, or Sublime Elu of Twelve, in this place for the dispatch of business. Please see, through the proper officer, that the entrance to the Chapter is duly guarded, that we may not be disturbed.

Sen∴ Insp∴ Bro∴ Marshal, the Th∴ Ill∴ Prince President is about to open this Chapter of Princes Ameth, or Sublime Elu of Twelve. Please see that the entrance to the Chapter is duly guarded, that we may not be disturbed.

[The Marshal goes out, returns, raps [‖ ,] which is answered from without, returns to his place and says] :

Marsh∴ Ill∴ Prince Sen∴ Inspector, the entrance to the Chapter is duly guarded, and we are secure from intrusion.

Sen∴ Insp∴ Th∴ Ill∴ Prince President, the entrance to the Chapter is duly guarded, and we are secure from intrusion.

Th∴ Ill∴ Then we may safely proceed. Bro∴ Sen∴ Inspector, are all present Princes Ameth and Sublime Elus of Twelve? Inform yourself by requiring the word.

[The Sen∴ Insp∴ goes round, receives the word, and reports] :

Sen∴ Insp∴ Th∴ Ill∴, all present are Princes Ameth and Elus of Twelve.

Th∴ Ill∴ Bro∴ Sen∴ Inspector, are you a Sublime Elu of Twelve?

Sen∴ Insp∴ My name will satisfy you that I am.

Qu∴ What is your name?

Ans∴ Ameth.

Qu∴ What does it signify?

Ans∴ A True Man; just, fair, sincere, faithful, fearing God.

Qu∴ Where were you received a Prince Ameth or Elu of Twelve?

Ans∴ In a place representing the audience chamber of King Solomon?

Qu∴ How many compose a chapter of Sublime Elu of Twelve?

Ans∴ Twelve or more.

Qu∴ When composed of twelve only, of whom does it consist?

Ans∴ The Th∴ Ill∴ Prince President, the Princes Sen∴ and Jun∴ Inspector, the Prince Orator, the Prince Treasurer and Secretary, the Princes First and Second Auditor, the Prince Marshal, and three Brothers; besides the Tyler.

Th∴ Ill∴ Give me the sign of a Prince Ameth.

[He gives it.]

Th∴ Ill∴ What does it signify?

Ans∴ That my faith cannot be shaken, and my confidence is in God.

Qu∴ What are the characteristics of a Prince Ameth?

Ans∴ Earnestness, Straight-forwardness, Integrity, Fairness, Sincerity and Reliability: which make up the character of a True Man.

Qu∴ Who were the first Elus of Twelve?

Ans∴ The twelve whom King Solomon made Princes and Governors in Israel.

Qu∴ What were their duties?

Ans∴ To provide supplies for the King and for his household, each one his month in the year; to see that the taxes were fairly assessed; to superintend the collection of the revenue; and to protect the People against the rapacity and extortion of the tax-gatherers and farmers of the revenue.

Qu∴ What are now the duties of a Prince Ameth?

Ans∴ To be earnest, true, reliable and sincere: to protect the People against illegal impositions and exactions, to contend for their political rights, and to see, as far as is in his power, that those bear the burthens, who reap the benefits of the Government.

Qu∴ What is the age of a Prince Ameth?

Ans.·. The cube of ; — ? £ years complete.

Qu.·. What is the hour?

Ans.·. The sixth hour of the day.

Th.·. Ill.·. Cause then the Princes to assemble around the altar, that, renewing our pledges to each other, we may open this Chapter of Princes Ameth, or Sublime Elu of Twelve.

[The Brethren form a circle round the altar, with swords drawn, elevating which at an angle of 45 degrees and placing the points together in the centre, they repeat as follows]:

Orator: . . *That the People among whom we live may be protected against illegal impositions and exactions:*

Jun.·. Insp.·. *That they may be secured in the enjoyment of their political rights:*

Sen.·. Insp.·. *That the burthens of the government may be equally apportioned, so that those shall bear most, who reap most benefit from it:*

All: . . WE ARE, AND WILL FOREVER REMAIN, UNITED.

Orator: . . *We will be true unto all men:*

Jun.·. Insp.·. *We will be frank and sincere in all things:*

Sen.·. Insp.·. *We will be earnest in doing that which it is our duty to do:*

Th.·. Ill.·. *No man shall repent that he has relied upon our resolves, our professions, or our word.*

All: . . AND TO THIS WE PLEDGE OURSELVES AS MASONS AND AS TRUE MEN.

[The Brethren return to their places. The Th.·. Ill.·. says, "Together, my Brethren!"; and all give the sign. Then the Th.·. Ill.·. raps ‖, — the Sen.·. Insp.·. ‖, — the Jun.·. Insp.·. ‖, — and all the Brethren ‖, — with their hands; and the Th.·. Ill.·. says]:

Th.·. Ill.·. This Chapter of Princes Ameth is duly opened.

RECEPTION.

The Lodge represents the Court of King Solomon, as in the two preceding degrees; the Th.·. Ill.·. representing King Solomon; the Sen.·. Insp.·., King Hiram; the Jun.·. Insp.·., Adonhiram; the Orator, Zabud; the Secretary, Sadoc the Priest; the Treasurer, Josaphat the Chancellor; the 1st Auditor, Ahisar, and the 2d Auditor Banaias, Commander in Chief. The last is not present when the Candidate enters.

The Candidate represents Bendecar, who discovered where the two murderers had taken refuge. He wears the clothing and jewel of an Elu of Fifteen, and is received in the ante-room by the Marshal, conducted into the Chapter, and requested to be seated.

Immediately afterwards, the Second Auditor enters, approaches the East, and makes his obeisance to King Solomon, who asks:

Th.·. Ill.·. Welcome, Banaias! Are the demands of justice satisfied?

2d Audit.·. They are, my liege. According to the sentence of the Court, the three murderers of our Gr.·. Master have been executed, confessing their guilt in the hearing of all the People, upon the scaffold, and proclaiming that their punishment was just: and their heads, struck off after life was extinct, have been set over the East, West and South gates of the City.

Th.·. Ill.·. It is well. Justice is satisfied, and the land purified of the innocent blood which was shed in the Temple. The majesty of the law is vindicated. Let the stains which yet remain upon the floor of the Temple be washed out. The murderers have atoned for their crime. We will not war upon the dead. At night-fall let their three heads be taken from above the gates, and buried with their bodies in an undistinguished grave. They have gone to meet God's judgment; and to that we will leave them. It is enough that none will lament their death or love their memories.

Hereafter let our deceased Brother and revered Grand Master be unto us and unto all Masons the type and personification of Virtue, of Goodness, of Intelligence and Truth; and his murderers, of Ignorance, Violence and Treachery: so that the murder and its punishment may teach Masons in all ages, the great moral lesson that God will not permit crime to go unpunished; but justice will surely overtake the guilty, and the offence be unerringly followed by its consequence.

12

My Brethren, the affairs of the living, too long neglected in our sorrow for the dead and our pursuit of the murderers, now demand our attention. Many complaints in connection with the revenue have accumulated, and much wrong and oppression is charged to exist, to which I invite your consideration. Our Chancellor will make known to you the nature of these complaints.

Chanc∴ M∴ Potent King Solomon, from all portions of the realm there have come up complaints in regard to the collection of the revenue. The People of Salebim, Elon and Bethanin complain that the tax-gatherers who have been sent among them do practice extortion, and take from them much moneys over and above the sums for which they account to thy Treasury. The people of the Country of Argob in Basan complain that those who collect the tribute do for bribes compound with the great and wealthy, and levy the deficiency on the poor. The people of Thanac and Bethsan complain that the troops are illegally quartered upon them, and they taxed to feed both men and horses. The people of Aruboth and the land of Epher, that their young men are against law impressed to serve in the army, as a means of extorting money: and like complaints come up from every quarter of the land.

Banaias: . . Thy Captains in Manaim, Mageddo and Socho complain that while the people are assessed beyond their means, and the farmers of the revenue grow rich, they are ill supplied with food for themselves and provender for their horses.

Ahisar: . . . The accounts of the collectors of the revenue in the land of Galand, Issachar and Benjamin, and the tribute of Sehon King of the Amorrhites are largely and long in arrears and unsettled.

Sadoc: . . . The contributions for the service of the Temple, from Benhur and Bethsames, from the towns of Jair, and from Manaim and Nephtali remain unpaid for many months.

Adonhiram: . . The contributions for the labourers upon Mount Libanus, from Aser and Baloth, from Og the King of Basan, and from all Bethsan remain unpaid.

King Sol∴ And in the mean time my people groan under the unjust burthen of their taxation, and send up their complaints to be laid at the foot of my throne; while my own table and household, the labourers upon Mount Libanus, my army and the Holy Temple are unprovided for. This must no longer be so. But how shall the evil be remedied? My Brother Hiram, aid me with your counsel and advice.

King Hiram: . . My Brother, if thou farmest out thy revenues, and hast thine army and household supplied by contributions, thy people will ever be oppressed, thy house and army ill-supplied, and those who collect the tribute will grow rich apace. If thou wouldest have thy Treasury overflow and thy people be contented, let all share the burthen alike, each in proportion to his means. Let thine own officers collect the tribute, for certain compensation. Place in each Province of the Kingdom thy representative to superintend the collection of the tribute, and let them in turn account to certain officers at Jerusalem, and they to thee. Then, punishing severely all illegal exaction and extortion, all bribery and corruption, and setting apart fixed sums for thy house, the army, the Temple, thy government and thy labourers, thou wilt protect thy People, and thy revenues be certain and abundant.

K∴ Sol∴ Is this thy system, my Brother?

K∴ Hir∴ It is, and hath been many years.

K∴ Sol∴ Then it shall be mine likewise; and I thank thee, my Brother, for thy counsel. Whom shall we set over this work, my Brother Sadoc?

Sadoc: My Lord the King, thou hast fifteen Knights Elu, whose merits entitle them to promotion and greater honour: and thou hast many Princes and servants whom to advance to be Knights Elu would be but fit reward for faithful service rendered.

K∴ Sol∴ Thou hast well said, my Brother. To reward the deserving is the noblest prerogative of a King. I commit the administration of the revenue to Joabert, henceforward, with supreme control, and the title of Minister of Finance. Stolkin and Zerbal I appoint to be his assistants; and to the three I give rank above the other nobles of my household. We will hereafter by ordinance define their duties and their compensation. Their twelve companions I make Governors in Israel, with the title of Princes Ameth; giving them in charge the revenues of my realm, and supreme control, each in his Province, as my vicegerents and immediate representatives. Let such of them as are now present approach the East!

[The candidate, and eleven Brothers, or as many as there are to do so, repair to the East, and stand in front of the Th∴ Ill∴, who says]:

Th∴ Ill∴. My Brethren, are you willing to take upon yourselves the duties of Governors in Israel and Chiefs over the tribute, with the resolution to discharge those duties, onerous as they may prove, well, faithfully and impartially?

All : . ∴ We are.

Th∴ Ill∴. Will you promise to deal honestly and fairly by all men, to exact nothing, for yourselves or for the State, that is not legally and justly due, to know no distinction of persons, and to see that none are subjected to exaction, extortion, or unjust imposition of burthens, beyond their strength or their fair proportion?

All : . . We will.

Th∴ Ill∴. Let then our chancellor write this decree: We do appoint and commission these twelve to be Governors in Israel, and chiefs over the tribute; and we thus assign to them the land of Israel:

To *Ben-Hur*, Prince Ameth; we assign Mount Ephraim.

To *Ben-Decar;* Macces and Salebim, Bethsames, Elon and Bethanan.

To *Ben-Hesed;* Aruboth, Socho, and all the land of Epher.

To *Ben-Abinadab;* all Nephath-Dor.

To *Bana*, the son of Ahilud; Thanac, Mageddo, and all Bethsan.

To *Ben-Gaber;* Ramoth Galaad, and all the country of Argob, in Basan.

To *Ahinadab*, the son of Addo; the land of Manaim.

To *Achimaas;* the land of Naphtali.

To *Baana* the son of Husi; the land of Aser and Baloth.

To *Josaphat*, the son of Pharue; the land of Issachar.

To *Semei* the son of Ela; the land of Benjamin.

To *Gaber*, the son of Uri; the land of Galaad, and that of Sehon, King of the Amorrhites, and that of Og, King of Basan.

And we give to them, each within his jurisdiction, supreme control over the revenue of their Provinces, with power to judge and punish all who are guilty of extortion and oppression; and to remove, displace and appoint all officers under them; making them our representatives and vicegerents, each in his Province, to be honoured and obeyed accordingly.

Go therefore, my Brethren, and at the altar assume the obligation appropriate to the rank and dignity of Princes Ameth and Rulers over the Tribute.

[The Candidate and the eleven brothers surround the altar, each placing his left hand on the cross-swords, and raising his right towards Heaven. The other brothers encircle them, and form the Arch of Steel over their heads, and those in the inner circle repeat the following]:

OBLIGATION.

I, A . . . . B . . . ., in the presence of the Gr∴ Architect of the Universe, and under these swords, raised to protect or punish, do hereby and hereon most solemnly and sincerely promise and swear, that I will never reveal the secrets of this degree of Princes Ameth, or Sublime Elu of Twelve, to any person in the world, unless at a proper time and in a proper place, to one duly authorized to receive them, and when I am legally authorized to communicate them.

I furthermore promise and swear, that I will ever, to the best of my ability and with all my power, protect the people against illegal impositions and exactions, secure them in the enjoyment of their political rights, and cause the burthens of government to be equally apportioned, in proportion to the benefit received therefrom.

I furthermore promise and swear that I will be ever true to the just cause in which I may engage; frank and sincere in all things; earnest in doing what it is right for me to do; and firm in adhering to my purposes and promises; that those who rely upon me and put trust in me may not be disappointed.

All of which I do most sincerely promise and solemnly swear, binding myself under no less penalty, than that of being deemed by all men false to my word, faithless and dishonourable. So help me God, and keep me steadfast in the due performance of the same!

Th.·. Ill.·. Arise, Princes Ameth and Governors in Israel, and receive the sign, tokens, and words of this degree.

SIGN: . . . Cross the ☉‡♋♎ upon the ↿&☾♎♈, with the ♑♀♒♌☾‡♎⫳↿†☾♒↿&☾♊ and ♈&♄♋♏ raised.

FIRST TOKEN: . . . Each presents to the other the ♈&♄♋♏ of the ‡⫳&☉♒♊, with the ♑♀♒♌☾‡♎⫳↿†☿♎☾♊. One takes the ♈&♄♋♏ of the other; and they turn the ♃‡♀♎♈; times—saying, alternately, as they do so, ♏☾‡♀♈&.·. ♒☾♊☾‡.·. ♎&☾†☿♋♀♈&.·.

SECOND TOKEN: . . . Take the ‡⫳&☉♒♊ of a brother, and tap; times with your ♈&♄♋♏ on the ⫳&☉†☉♒♌☾ of the ♋♀♊♊†☾⫳♑♀♒♌☾‡.

PASS-WORD: . . . ☉♋☾♈&.·.

SACRED WORD: . . . ☉♊☿♒☉♀.·.

Th.·. Ill.·. I invest you, my brother, with the apron, collar and jewel of this Degree. Remember that you wear them as the successor and representative of a Prince Ameth of the Court of King Solomon; and that your conduct and conversation must be such as becomes one invested with so high an honour. The flaming hearts are symbols of that zeal and devotedness that ought to animate you; and the motto is your pledge, that you will rather die than betray the cause of the People, or be overcome through your own fear or fault. Receive now from the Brother Orator the lecture of this Degree.

LECTURE.

The History of this Degree has been fully given in your reception. I need not now repeat it or enlarge upon it.

The duties of a Prince Ameth are, to be earnest, true, reliable and sincere; to protect the People against illegal impositions and exactions; to contend for their political rights, and to see, as far as he may or can, that those bear the burthens, who reap the benefits of the Government.

You are to be true unto all men.

You are to be frank and sincere in all things.

You are to be earnest in doing whatever it is your duty to do.

And no man must repent that he has relied upon your resolve, your profession or your word.

The great distinguishing characteristic of a Mason is sympathy with his kind. He recognizes in the Human Race one Great Family, all connected with himself by those invisible links, and that mighty network of circumstance, forged and woven by God.

Feeling that sympathy, it is his first Masonic duty to serve his fellow-man. At his first entrance into the order, he ceases to be isolated, and becomes one of a great brotherhood, assuming new duties towards every Mason that lives, as every Mason at the same moment assumes new duties towards him.

Nor are those duties on his part confined to Masons alone. He assumes many in regard to his country, and especially towards the great, suffering inarticulate common people; for they too are his brothers. By all proper means, of persuasion and influence, and otherwise if the occasion and emergency require, he is bound to defend them against oppression, and tyrannical and illegal exactions.

He labours equally to defend and to improve the People. He does not flatter them, to mislead them, nor fawn upon them to rule them, nor conceal his opinions to humour them, nor tell them that they can never err, and that their voice is the voice of God. He knows that the safety of every free government, and its continuance and perpetuity, depend upon the virtue and intelligence of the common People: and that, unless their liberty is of such a kind as arms can neither procure nor take away; unless it is the fruit of piety, of justice, of temperance, and unadulterated virtue; unless, being such, it has taken deep root in the minds and hearts of the people at large, there will not long be wanting those who will snatch from them by treachery, what they have acquired by arms.

He knows that if, after being released from the toils of war, the people neglect the arts of peace; if their peace and liberty be a state of warfare; if war be their only virtue, and the summit of their praise, they will soon find peace the most adverse to their interests. It will be only a more distressing war; and that which they imagined liberty will be the worst of slavery. For, unless by the means of knowledge and morality, not frothy and loquacious, but genuine, unadulterated and sincere, they clear the horizon of the mind from those mists of error and passion which arise from ignorance and vice, they will always have those who will bend their necks to the yoke as if they were brutes; who, notwithstanding all their triumphs, will put them up to the highest bidder, as if they were mere booty made in war; and find an exuberant source of wealth and power, in the people's ignorance, prejudices and passions.

The people that does not subjugate the propensity of the wealthy to avarice, ambition and sensuality, expel luxury from them and their families, keep down pauperism, diffuse knowledge among the poor, and labour to raise the abject from the mire of vice and low indulgence, and to keep the industrious from starving in sight of luxurious festivals, will find that it has cherished, in that avarice, ambition, sensuality, selfishness and luxury of the one class, and that degradation, misery, drunkenness, ignorance and brutalization of the other, more stubborn and intractable despots at home, than it ever encountered in the field: and even its very bowels will be continually teeming with the intolerable progeny of tyrants.

These are the first enemies to be subdued: this constitutes the campaign of Peace: these are triumphs, difficult indeed, but bloodless; and far more honourable than those trophies which are purchased only by slaughter and rapine: and if not victors in this service, it is in vain to have been victorious over the despotic enemy in the field.

For if any people thinks that it is a more grand, a more beneficial, or a more wise policy, to invent subtle expedients for increasing the revenue, to multiply its naval and military force, to rival in craft the ambassadors of foreign States, to plot and plan the seizure and swallowing up of foreign territory, to form skilful treaties and alliances, than to administer unpolluted justice to the People, to relieve the condition and raise the estate of the great dumb suffering masses, to redress the injured and succour the distressed, and speedily to restore to every one his own, then that people is involved in a cloud of Error; and will too late perceive, when the illusion of those mighty benefits has vanished, that in neglecting these, which it thought inferior considerations, it has only been precipitating its own ruin and despair.

Unfortunately, every age presents its special problem, most difficult, and often impossible, to solve: and that which this age offers, and forces upon the consideration of all thinking men, is this,—How in a populous and wealthy country, blessed with free institutions and a constitutional government, are the great masses of the manual-labouring class to be enabled to have steady work at fair wages, be kept from starvation, and their children from vice and debauchery, and furnished with that degree of knowledge, at least, that shall fit them intelligently to exercise the privileges of freemen, and especially the right of suffrage?

For, though we do not know why God has so ordered it, it seems to be unquestionably His law, that even in civilized and Christian countries, the large mass of the population shall be fortunate, if during their whole life, from infancy to old age, in health and sickness, they have enough of the commonest and coarsest food to keep themselves and their children from being hungry,—enough, of the commonest and coarsest clothing, to protect themselves and their children from indecent exposure and the bitter cold; and if over their heads they have the rudest shelter.

And He seems to have enacted this law, which no human community has yet found the means to abrogate,—that when a country becomes populous, capital shall tend to concentrate in the hands of a limited number of persons, and labour shall become more and more dependent, and more and more at the mercy of capital; until mere manual labour eventually ceases, in every populous country, to command more than a bare subsistence; and in great cities and large sections of country, it ceases to command even that, and goes about starving, and begging for employment. While every ox and horse can find work, and is worth being fed, it is not always so with man. To be employed, to have a chance to work, at any thing like fair wages, becomes the great engrossing object of a man's life. The capitalist can live without employing the labourer, and discharges him whenever that labour ceases to be profitable. At the moment when the weather is most inclement, provisions dearest and rents highest, he turns him off to starve. If the day-labourer is taken sick, his wages stop. When old, he has no pension to retire upon. His children cannot be sent to school; for before their bones are hardened they must get to work lest they starve. The man, strong and able bodied, works for a shilling or two a day: and the woman, shivering over her little pan of coals, when the mercury drops far below zero, after her hungry children have wailed themselves to sleep, sews by the dim light of her lonely candle, for a bare pittance, selling her life to him who bargained only for the work of her needle.

Fathers and mothers slay their children, to have the burial fees, that with the price of one child's life they may continue life in those that survive. Little girls with bare feet sweep the street crossings, when the winter wind pinches them, and beg piteously for pennies of those who wear warm furs. Children grow up in squalid misery and brutal ignorance; want compels virgin and wife to prostitute themselves; women starve and freeze, and lean up against the walls of workhouses, like bundles of foul rags, all night long, and night after night, when the cold rain falls, and there chances to be no room for them within: and hundreds of families are crowded into a single building, rife with horrors and teeming with foul air and pestilence; where men, women and children huddle together in their filth; of all ages and all colors sleeping indiscriminately together: while, in a great, free, Republican State, in the full vigor of its youth and strength, one person in every seventeen is a pauper receiving charity.

How to deal with this apparently inevitable evil and mortal disease, is the most important of all social problems. What is to be done with pauperism and superabundance of labour; and how is the Country to be preserved, if Brutality and Ignorance are by their votes to fill our offices and control our Government; if not wisdom and authority, but turbulence and low vice are to exalt the vilest miscreants from tavern and brothel to the rank and dignity of Senators.

Masonry will do all in its power, by direct exertion and co-operation, to improve and inform, as well as to protect the people; to better their physical condition, relieve their miseries, supply their wants and minister to their necessities. Let every Mason, in this great work, do all that may be in *his* power.

For it is true now, as it always was and always will be, that to be free is the same thing as to be pious, to be wise, to be temperate and just, to be frugal and abstinent, and to be magnanimous and brave; and to be the opposite of all these is to be the same as to be a slave. And it usually happens, by the appointment, and, as it were, retributive justice of the Deity, that that people which cannot govern themselves, and moderate their passions, but crouch under the slavery of their lusts and vices, are delivered up to the sway of those whom they abhor, and made to submit to an involuntary servitude.

And it is also sanctioned by the dictates of justice and by the constitution of Nature, that he who, from the imbecility or derangement of his intellect, is incapable of governing himself, should, like a minor, be committed to the government of another.

Above all things let us never forget that mankind constitutes one great brotherhood; all born to encounter suffering and sorrow, and therefore bound to sympathize with each other.

For no tower of Pride was ever yet high enough, to lift its possessor above the trials and fears and frailties of humanity. No human hand ever built the wall, nor ever shall, that will keep out affliction, pain and infirmity. Sickness and sorrow, trouble and death are dispensations that level everything. They know none high nor low. The chief wants of life, the great and grave necessities of the human soul, give exemption to none. They make all poor, all weak. They put supplication in the mouth of every human being, as truly as in that of the meanest beggar.

But the principle of misery is not an evil principle. We err, and the consequences teach us wisdom. All elements, all the laws of things around us, minister to this end; and through the paths of painful error and mistake, it is the design of Providence to lead us to truth and happiness. If erring only taught us to err; if mistakes confirmed us in imprudence; if the miseries caused by vicious indulgence had a natural tendency to make us more abject slaves of vice, then suffering would be wholly evil. But, on the contrary, all tends and is designed to produce amendment and improvement. Suffering is the discipline of virtue; of that which is infinitely better than happiness, and yet embraces in itself all essential happiness. It nourishes, invigorates and perfects it. Virtue is the prize of the severely contested race and hard-fought battle; and it is worth all the fatigue and wounds of the conflict. Man should go forth with a brave and strong heart, to battle with calamity. He is to master it, and not let it become *his* master. He is not to forsake the post of trial and of peril; but to stand firmly in his lot, until the great word of Providence shall bid him fly, or bid him sink. With resolution and courage the Mason is to do the work which it is appointed him to do; looking through the dark cloud of human calamity, to the end that rises high and bright before him. The lot of sorrow is great and sublime. None suffer forever, nor for naught, nor without purpose. It is the ordinance of God's wisdom, and of His Infinite Love, to procure for us infinite happiness and glory.

Virtue is the truest liberty; nor is he free that stoops to passions; nor he in bondage that serves a noble master. Examples are the best and most lasting lectures; virtue the best example. He that hath done good deeds and set good precedents, in sincerity, is happy. Time shall not outlive his worth. He lives truly after death, whose good deeds are his pillars of remembrance; and no day but adds some grains to his heap of glory. Good works are seeds, that after sowing return us a continual harvest: and the memory of noble actions is more enduring than monuments of marble.

Life is a school. The world is neither prison nor penitentiary, nor a palace of ease, nor an amphitheatre for games and spectacles; but a place of instruction, and a school. Life is given for moral and spiritual learning: and the entire course of the great school of life is an education for virtue, happiness, and a future existence. The Periods of Life are its terms; all human conditions, its forms; all human employments, its lessons. Families are the primary departments of this moral education: the various circles of society, its advanced stages; Kingdoms and Republics, its universities.

Riches and Poverty, Gayeties and Sorrows, marriages and funerals, the ties of life bound or broken, fit and fortunate, or untoward and painful, are all lessons. Events are not blindly and carelessly flung together. Providence does not school one man, and screen another from the fiery trial of its lessons. It has neither rich favorites nor poor victims. One event happeneth to all. One end and one design concern and urge all men.

The prosperous man has been at school. Perhaps he has thought that it was a great thing, and he a great personage; but he has been merely a pupil. He thought, perhaps, that he was Master, and had nothing to do, but to direct and command; but there was ever a Master above him, the Master of Life. He looks not at our splendid state, or our many pretensions, nor at the aids and appliances of our learning; but at our learning itself. He puts the poor and the rich upon the same form; and knows no difference between them, but their progress.

If from prosperity we have learned moderation, temperance, candour, modesty, gratitude to God, and generosity to man, then we are entitled to be honoured and rewarded. If we have learned selfishness, self-indulgence, wrong-doing and vice, to forget and overlook our less fortunate brother, and to scoff at the providence of God, then we are unworthy and dishonoured, though we have been nursed in affluence, or taken our degrees from the lineage of an hundred noble descents; as truly so, in the eye of Heaven, and all right-thinking men, as though we lay, victims of beggary and disease, in the hospital, by the hedge, or on the dung-hill. The most ordinary human equity looks not at the school, but the scholar; and the equity of Heaven will not look beneath that mark.

The poor man also is at school. Let him take care that he learn, rather than complain. Let him keep his integrity, his candour and his kindness of heart. Let him beware of envy, and of bondage, and keep his self-respect. The body's toil is nothing. Let him beware of the mind's drudgery and degradation. While he betters his condition if he can, let him be more anxious to better his soul. Let him be willing, while poor, and even if always poor, to learn poverty's great lessons, fortitude, cheerfulness, contentment, and implicit confidence in God's Providence. With these, and patience, calmness, self-command, disinterestedness and affectionate kindness, the humble dwelling may be hallowed, and made more dear and noble than the loftiest palace. Let him, above all things, see that he lose not his independence. Let him not cast himself, a creature poorer than the poor, an indolent, helpless, despised beggar, on the kindness of others. Every man should choose to have God for his Master, rather than man; and escape not from this school, either by dishonesty or alms-taking, lest he fall into that state, worse than disgrace, where he can have no respect for himself.

The ties of Society teach us to love one another. That is a miserable society, where the absence of affectionate kindness is sought to be supplied by punctilious decorum, graceful urbanity, and polished insincerity; where ambition, jealousy and distrust rule, in place of simplicity, confidence and kindness.

So, too, the social state teaches modesty and gentleness; and from neglect, and notice unworthily bestowed on others, and injustice, and the world's failure to appreciate us, we learn patience and quietness, to be superior to society's opinion, not cynical and bitter, but gentle, candid and affectionate still.

Death is the great Teacher, stern, cold, inexorable, irresistible; whom the collected might of the world cannot stay or ward off. The breath, that parting from the lips of King or beggar, scarcely stirs the hushed air, cannot be bought, or brought back for a moment, with the wealth of Empires. What a lesson is this, teaching our frailty and feebleness, and an Infinite Power beyond us! It is a fearful lesson, that never becomes familiar. It walks through the earth in dread mystery, and lays its hands upon all. It is a universal lesson, that is read everywhere and by all men. Its message comes every year and every day. The past years are crowded with its sad and solemn mementos; and Death's finger traces its handwriting upon the walls of every human habitation.

It teaches us Duty; to act our part well; to fulfil the work assigned us. When one is dying, and after he is dead, there is but one question: *Has he lived well?* There is no evil in death but that which life makes.

There are hard lessons in the school of God's Providence: and yet the school of life is carefully adjusted, in all its arrangements and tasks, to man's powers and passions. There is no extravagance in its teachings; nor is anything done for the sake of present effect. The whole course of human life is a conflict with difficulties; and, if rightly conducted, a progress in improvement. It is never too late for man to learn. Not part only, but the whole, of life, is a school. There never comes a time, even amidst the decays of age, when it is fit to lay aside the eagerness of acquisition, or the cheerfulness of endeavour. Man walks, all through the course of life, in patience and strife, and sometimes in darkness; for, from patience is to come perfection; from strife, triumph is to issue; from the cloud of darkness the lightning is to flash that shall open the way to eternity.

Let the Mason be faithful in the school of life, and to all its lessons. Let him not learn nothing; nor care whether he learns or not. Let not the years pass over him, witnesses of only his sloth and indifference; or see him zealous to acquire every thing but virtue. Nor let him labour only for himself; nor forget that the humblest man is his brother and hath a claim on his sympathies and kind offices; and that beneath the rough garments which labour wears may beat hearts as noble as throb under the stars of Princes. For,

> Who shall judge a man from nature?
> Who shall know him by his dress?
> Paupers may be fit for princes,
> Princes fit for something less.
> Crumpled shirt and dirty jacket
> May beclothe the golden ore
> Of the deepest thought and feeling—
> Satin vest could do no more.

There are springs of crystal nectar,
  Ever welling out of stone :
There are purple buds and golden
  Hidden, crushed and overgrown.
God who counts by souls, not dresses,
  Loves and prospers you and me :
While He values thrones the highest
  But as pebbles on the sea.

Man, upraised above his fellows,
  Oft forgets his fellows then ;
Masters—rulers—lords, remember
  That your meanest hands are men !
Men of labor, men of feeling,
  Men by thought and men by fame,
Claiming equal rights to sunshine,
  In a man's ennobling name.
There are foam-embroidered oceans,
  There are little weed-clad rills,
There are feeble inch-high saplings,
  There are cedars on the hills ;
God, who counts by souls, not stations,
  Loves and prospers you and me ;
For to Him all vain distinctions
  Are as pebbles on the sea.

Toiling hands alone are builders
  Of a nation's wealth and fame ;
Titled laziness is pensioned,
  Fed and fattened on the same ;
By the sweat of other's forehead,
  Living only to rejoice,
While the poor man's outraged freedom
  Vainly lifteth up its voice.
Truth and justice are eternal,
  Born with loveliness and light ;
Secret wrong shall never prosper
  While there is a starry night.
God, whose world-heard voice is singing
  Boundless love to you and me,
Sinks oppression with its titles,
  As the pebbles on the sea.

Nor are the other duties inculcated in this degree, of less importance. Truth, a Mason is early told, is a Divine attribute and the foundation of every virtue : and frankness, reliability, sincerity, straight-forwardness, plain-dealing, are but different modes in which Truth developes itself. The dead, the absent, the innocent, and those that trust him, no Mason will deceive willingly. To all these he owes a nobler justice, in that they are the most certain trials of human Equity. Only the most abandoned of men, said Cicero, will deceive him, who would have remained uninjured if he had not trusted. All the noble deeds that have beat their marches through succeeding ages have all proceeded from men of truth and genuine courage. The man that is always true is both virtuous and wise: and thus possesses the greatest guards of safety; for the law has not power to strike the virtuous; nor can fortune subvert the wise.

The bases of Masonry being morality and.virtue, it is by studying one and practising the other, that the conduct of a Mason becomes irreproachable. The good of Humanity being its principal object, disinterestedness is one of the first virtues that it requires of its members; for it is the source of justice and beneficence.

To pity the misfortunes of others; to be humble but without meanness; to abjure every sentiment.of hatred and revenge; to show himself magnanimous and liberal without ostentation and without profusion; to be the enemy of vice; to pay homage to wisdom and virtue; to respect innocence; to be constant and patient in adversity and modest in prosperity; to avoid every irregularity which stains the soul and distempers the body; it is by following these precepts that a Mason will become a good citizen, a faithful husband, a tender father, an obedient son and a true brother: will honor friendship, and fulfil with ardor the duties which virtue and the social relations impose upon him.

It is because Masonry imposes upon us these duties, that it is properly and significantly styled *work:* and he who imagines that he becomes a Mason by merely taking the two or three first degrees; and that he may, having leisurely stepped upon that small elevation, thenceforward wear the honors of Masonry worthily, without labour or exertion, and that there is nothing to be done in Masonry, is most strangely deceived.

Is it true that nothing remains to be done in Masonry?

Does one brother no longer proceed by law against another Brother of his Lodge, in regard to matters that could be easily settled within the Masonic family circle?

Has the duel, that hideous heritage of barbarism, interdicted among Brethren by our fundamental laws, and denounced by the municipal code, yet disappeared from the soil we inhabit? Do Masons of high rank religiously refrain from it; or do they not, bowing to a corrupt public opinion, submit to its arbitrament, despite the scandal which it occasions to the Order, and in violation of the feeble restraint of their oath?

Do Masons no longer form uncharitable opinions of their Brethren, enter harsh judgments against them, and judge themselves by one rule and their brethren by another?

Has Masonry any well regulated system of charity? Has it done that which it should have done for the cause of education? Where are its schools, its academies, its colleges, its hospitals and infirmaries?

Are political controversies now conducted with no violence and bitterness?

Do Masons refrain from defaming and denouncing their Brethren who differ with them in religious or political opinions?

What grand social problems or useful projects engage our attention at our communications? Where in our Lodges are lectures habitually delivered for the real instruction of the brethren? Do not our sessions pass in the discussion of minor matters of business, the settlement of points of order and questions of mere administration, and the admission and advancement of Candidates, whom after their admission we take no pains to instruct?

In what Lodge are our ceremonies explained and elucidated; corrupted as they are by time, until their true features can scarcely be distinguished; and where are those great primitive truths of revelation taught, which Masonry has preserved to the world?

We have high dignities and sounding titles. Do their possessors qualify themselves to enlighten the world in respect to the aims and objects of Masonry? Descendants of those Initiates who governed empires, does your influence enter into practical life and operate efficiently in behalf of well regulated and constitutional liberty?

Your debates should be but friendly conversations. You need concord, union and peace. Why then do you retain among you men who excite rivalries and jealousies; why permit great and violent controversy and ambitious pretensions? How do your own words and acts agree? If your Masonry is a nullity, how can you exercise any influence on others?

Continually you praise each other, and utter elaborate and high-wrought eulogies upon the Order. Every where you assume that you are what you should be, and no where do you look upon yourselves as you are. Is it true that all our actions are so many acts of homage to virtue? Explore the recesses of your hearts:

let us examine ourselves with an impartial eye, and make answer to our own questioning. Can we bear to ourselves the consoling testimony that we always rigidly perform our duties?

Let us away with this odious self-flattery! Let us be men, if we cannot be sages! The laws of Masonry, above others excellent, cannot wholly change men's natures. They enlighten them, they point out the true way; but they can lead them in it, only by repressing the fire of their passions. Alas, these often conquer, and Masonry is forgotten.

After praising each other all our lives, there are always excellent brothers who, over our coffins, shower unlimited eulogies. Every one of us who dies has been a model of all the virtues, a very child of the celestial light. In Egypt, among our old masters, where Masonry was more cultivated than vanity, no one could gain admittance to the sacred asylum of the tomb until he had passed under the most solemn judgment. A grave Tribunal sat in judgment upon all, even the kings. They said to the dead, "Whoever thou art, give account to thy country of thy actions. What hast thou done with thy time and life? The law interrogates thee, thy country hears thee, Truth sits in judgment on thee." Princes came there to be judged, escorted only by their virtues and their vices. A public accuser recounted the history of the dead man's life, and threw the blaze of the torch of truth on all his actions. If it were adjudged that the deceased had led an evil life, his memory was condemned in the presence of the nation, and his body was denied the honors of sepulture. Lo, what a lesson the old Masonry gave to the sons of the People!

Is it true that Masonry is effete; that the acacia, withered, affords no shade; that Masonry no longer marches in the advance guard of Truth? No. Is freedom yet universal? Have ignorance and prejudice disappeared from the earth? Are there no longer enmities among men? Do cupidity and falsehood no longer exist? Do toleration and harmony prevail among sects religious and political? There are yet left for Masonry to accomplish works greater than the twelve labours of Hercules: to advance ever, resolutely and steadily; to enlighten the minds of the people, to re-construct society, to reform the laws, and improve the public morals. The eternity in front of it, is as infinite as the one behind. And it cannot cease to labor in the cause of social progress, without ceasing to be true to itself; without ceasing to be Masonry.

TO CLOSE.

Th∴ Ill∴ Bro∴ Sen∴ Insp∴, what is the hour?

Sen∴ Insp∴ The 12th hour of the day, Th∴ Ill∴

Th∴ Ill∴ Then it is time to close this Chapter of Princes Ameth. Cause the Princes to assemble around the altar, that, renewing our pledges to each other, we may close in due and ancient form.

Sen∴ Insp∴ Brethren, you will please assemble around the altar, and assist the Th∴ Ill∴ Prince President to close this Chapter in due and ancient form.

[The Brethren assemble around the altar. The same ceremonies are performed as in opening. Then they return to their places. The Th∴ Ill∴ says, "The sign, my Brethren!" All give the sign: the Th∴ Ill∴, the Sen∴ and Jun∴ Inspectors, and all the Brethren rap [‖ ,] in succession; and the Th∴ Ill∴ says]:

Th∴ Ill∴ My Brethren, this Chapter is closed in due and ancient form.

FINIS.

Twelfth Degree.

Grand Master Architect.

THE LODGE, ITS DECORATIONS, ETC.

Bodies in this degree are styled Chapters.

The hangings are white, strewed with crimson flames.

Behind the Master, in the East, are five columns, each of a different order of Architecture—Tuscan, Doric, Ionic, Corinthian and Composite.

In the North is painted the North Star, and a little below it the Seven Stars of the Great Bear. In the East, behind the columns, is a luminous Star, representing Jupiter, rising in the East as the Morning Star.

Upon the Altar, which is in the centre of the room, are the Holy Bible, and on it all the instruments contained in a case of mathematical instruments.

The Chapter is lighted by three Great Lights, one in the East, one in the West, and one in the South.

Over the Columns, in the East, hangs a Triangle, enclosing the word אדני [Adoni].

OFFICERS, TITLES, ETC.

The Master is styled Th.·. Ill.·. Gr.·. Master.

The Wardens, Ill.·. Sen.·. and Jun.·. Gr.·. Wardens. They sit in the West.

The Gr.·. Orator sits in the South.

The Deacons are styled Ill.·. Sen.·. and Jun.·. Gr.·. Experts.

There is also a Gr.·. Master of Ceremonies.

CLOTHING, ORNAMENTS, AND JEWEL.

The apron is white, lined and bordered with blue, and fringed with gold. On it are painted or embroidered, a protractor on the flap, and in the middle a plain scale, a sector and the compasses, so arranged as to form a triangle.

The cordon is a broad blue watered ribbon, worn from the left shoulder to the right hip.

The jewel is a heptagonal medal of gold. In each angle, on one side, is a star, enclosed by a semicircle. In the centre, on the same side, is an equilateral triangle, formed by arcs of circles, in the centre of which is the letter A.·. On the reverse side are five columns, of the different orders of architecture, with the initial letter of the proper order below each, in old English letters, arranged from left to right: . . Tuscan . . Doric . . Ionic . . Corinthian . . Composite. Above these columns are a sector and a slide rule: below them, the three kinds of compasses, the plain scale, and parallel ruler; and between the 2d and 3d and 3d and 4th columns are the letters ٦.∵ . . . . ٦.∵ . . . . [R.∴ B.∴].

In front of each Brother is a small table; and on it a case of instruments, with paper, and other articles for drafting.

The Battery is ‖ ?

The age of a Gr.∴ M.∴ Architect is the square of ; × ‖ — or ! ‖ years.

TO OPEN.

The Gr.∴ Master, giving one rap, and then two together, says:

Th.∴ Ill.∴. Brethren, I am about to open this Chapter of Gr.∴ Master Architects in this place, that we may proceed with our labours. Bro.∴ Sen.∴ Gr.∴ Warden, see that all present are Gr.∴ Master Architects, by causing the Bre.∴ Gr.∴ Experts to receive the Sacred Word from each Bro.∴ and bring it up to you in the West.

S.∴ G.∴ W.∴. Bre.∴ Sen.∴ and Jun.∴ Gr.∴ Experts, receive the Sacred Word on the North and on the South, beginning in the East, and bring it up to me in the West.

[The Experts receive the word from each Brother as directed. Then the Jun.∴ Gr.∴ Expert gives it to the Sen.∴ Gr.∴ Expert, and he to the Sen.∴ Gr.∴ W.∴., who thereupon says]:

S.∴ G.∴ W.∴. Th.∴ Ill.∴ Gr.∴ Master, all present are Gr.∴ Master Architects; for the word has come up aright to me in the West.

Th.∴ Ill.∴. Thanks, my Brother. Bro.∴ Jun.∴ Gr.∴ Expert, our first care is to see that we are duly tyled, and secure against intrusion. Attend to that duty, and inform the Gr.∴ Tyler, that we are about to open this Chapter of Gr.∴ Master Architects for the despatch of business, and direct him to tyle accordingly.

[The Jun.∴ Gr.∴ Expert goes out, returns, raps ‖ ? which is answered from without, and reports]:

J.∴ G.∴ Exp.∴. Th.∴ Ill.∴ Gr.∴ Master, we are duly tyled.

Th.∴ Ill.∴. How?

J.∴ G.∴ Exp.∴. By a Bro.∴ Gr.∴ Master Architect without, armed and resolute.

Th.∴ Ill.∴. His duty there?

J.∴ G.∴ Exp.∴. To guard us against intrusion, and see that none enter here who are not entitled to do so, and with your permission.

Th.∴ Ill.∴, Thanks, my Brother. Brethren, assume your stations. Bro.∴ Sen.∴ Gr.∴ Warden, are you a Gr.∴ Master Architect?

S.∴ G.∴ W.∴. I have studied mathematics, and am familiar with the instruments used by a Gr.∴ Master Architect.

Qu.∴. What are those instruments?

Ans.∴. The plain compasses, the bow compasses, the drawing compasses, the drawing pen, the parallel ruler, the protractor, the plain scale, the sector, and the slide rule.

Qu.∴. For what purposes does a Gr.∴ Master Architect use the different compasses?

Ans.∴. To bi-sect lines and angles, to draw and erect perpendiculars, make angles equal to given angles, describe circles, construct triangles and rectangles, and project ellipses and ovals.

Qu.∴. What lesson do they teach us in this degree?

Ans.∴. That our life and all Time are but a point in the centre of Eternity; while the diameter of the circle of God's attributes is infinite: and that we, as His finite creatures, should be patient, submissive, moderate in our desires, and contented with our fortunes.

Qu.∴. For what purposes does a Gr.∴ Master Architect use the parallel ruler?

Ans.·. To draw parallel lines, to make angles equal to given angles, to find proportionals to lines, to inscribe squares in triangles, and to reduce plane figures to others of equal area.

Qu.·. What lesson does it teach us in this degree?

Ans.·. That we should be consistent, firm, unwavering, and of that equanimity of mind and temper which befits a Mason.

Qu.·. For what purposes does a Grand Master Architect use the Protractor?

Ans.·. To measure and lay down angles, draw parallel lines, erect and let fall perpendiculars, divide angles, inscribe circles in triangles, and polygons on circles, construct polygons on lines, and describe circles within and without polygons.

Qu.·. What lesson does it teach us in this degree?

Ans.·. That we should be upright and sincere, frank in all our dealings, reliable, moderate in our professions, and exact and punctual in performance.

Qu.·. For what purpose does a Gr.·. M.·. Architect use the Plain Scale?

Ans.·. To lay off distances, serve the purposes of the Protractor, apportion the areas of circles, and determine the diameters of circles of given areas.

Qu.·. What lesson does it teach us in this degree?

Ans.·. That we should not live only or chiefly for ourselves, but partly and even largely for others; apportioning our time, our labour, our acquirements and our intellect, so as in just and proper measure to serve ourselves, our families, our friends, our neighbours and our country.

Qu.·. For what purposes does the Gr.·. M.·. Architect use the Sector?

Ans.·. To divide lines into equal parts, to find proportionals to numbers, to multiply and divide numbers, to square and cube them, and extract the square and cube roots, to make and measure angles, to find and measure chords, sines, tangents, and secants of given angles, to construct polygons, and measure heights and distances by means of the angles, horizontal, of depression and of elevation.

Qu.·. What lesson does it teach us in this degree?

Ans.·. That we should multiply our good deeds, divide that which we can spare of our substance among those who need it more than we, extract the good that is intended to benefit and bless us, from the reverses, the unhappiness and the calamities of life; and, from the data which God has given us in his works, endeavour to approximate to an appreciation of His infinite Wisdom, Beneficence, and Bounty.

Qu.·. For what purposes does a Gr.·. M.·. Architect use the slide-rule?

Ans.·. To serve the purposes of the Sector, to measure the surfaces of quadrilaterals, triangles, parabolas, circles, cycloids, ellipses, prisms, cylinders, pyramids, cones and spheres; to duplicate cubes and globes, by determination of their diameter and side, to measure the contents of vessels and the weight of solids.

Qu.·. What lesson does it teach us in this degree?

Ans.·. That we should strive to grasp and solve the great problems presented by the Universe, and involved in our existence; to know and understand the lofty truths of Philosophy; and to communicate freely of our knowledge unto others, not hiding our talents in the earth like sordid misers, but diffusing light and information among the ignorant and uninformed.

Qu.·. Where were you received and made a Gr.·. Master Architect?

Ans.·. In a place representing the Chamber of Designs, assigned to our Gr.·. Master Hiram Abi, in King Solomon's Temple.

Qu.·. At what hour?

Ans.·. When the day-star had risen in the East, and the North Star looked down upon the Seven that ever circle round him and point him out to the mariner.

Qu.·. Of what is the North Star a symbol to the Mason?

Ans.·. Of Truth and Right, the Pole-Stars that guide Masons over the stormy Seas of Time.

Qu.·. Of what are the Seven Stars the symbol?

Ans.·. Of a Mason's Loyalty to Truth and Right, to his Order, and to his Country.

Qu.·. What do the Five Columns in the East teach us?

Ans∴. That Masonry, in all its orders and degrees, like architecture, is one; the same in all countries and in all ages.

Qu∴. What does the Star signify, rising in the East, behind the Columns?

Ans∴. That the day-light of Perfection approaches.

Qu∴. What is the hour?

Ans∴. That Star has risen.

Qu∴. What is the age of a Gr∴. Master Architect?

Ans∴. ♑♀ * ☾ times the square of ; — or ! ‖ years.

Th∴. Ill∴. The hour of work has arrived. Give notice to the Gr∴. Masters, that I am about to open this Chapter of Gr∴. Master Architects, that they may aid me in so doing.

J∴. G∴. W∴. Brethren in the South, the Th∴. Ill∴. Gr∴. Master is about to open this Chapter of Gr∴. M∴. Architects, and desires your assistance; since the hour of work has arrived.

S∴. G∴. W∴. Brethren in the North, &c. &c.

Th∴. Ill∴. The Sign, my Brethren.

[All give the sign. Then the Gr∴. Master and the Sen∴. and Jun∴. Gr∴. Wardens rap in succession ‖? — and all the Brethren the same with their hands; and the Gr∴. Master says]:

Th∴. Ill∴. I therefore declare this Chapter duly opened.

RECEPTION.

The Candidate, in the clothing and with the jewel of the 11th Degree is received in the ante-room by the Gr∴. Master of Ceremonies, who examines him in the work of that Degree, and in its principles; and if he finds him well informed, conducts him to the door of the Chapter, and raps [‖?]. The Jun∴. Gr∴. Expert opens the door, and asks:

J∴. G∴. Exp∴. Who comes here, and what is his desire?

M∴. Cer∴. A. . . . B. . . ., a Prince Ameth, and Sublime Elu of Twelve, who desires to receive the degree of Gr∴. Master Architect.

J∴. G∴. Exp∴. Does he well understand and has he been true to, the pledges which as a Knight Elu of Nine, Ill∴. Elu of Fifteen, and Sublime Elu of Twelve, he has made to his brethren?

M∴. Cer∴. He does, and has.

J∴. G∴. Exp∴. Why does he desire to receive the Degree of Gr∴. Master Architect?

M∴. Cer∴. That he may increase in knowledge, and be the better fitted to discharge the duties of a good Mason.

J∴. G∴. Exp∴. It is well; let him wait with patience until the Th∴. Ill∴. Gr∴. Master is informed of his request, and his answer returned.

[The Jun∴. Gr∴. Expert closes the door and advances to the East; and the same questions are there asked, and like answers returned, as at the door].

Th∴. Ill∴. Then let him enter and be received in due form.

[The door is opened, and the candidate enters, conducted by the Gr∴. M∴. of Cer∴., and is led 3 times around the chapter; while the Jun∴. Gr∴. Warden reads as follows]:

1st Circuit: . . He that rejecteth wisdom and discipline is unhappy; and their hope is vain, and their labours without fruit, and their works unprofitable. The fruit of good labours is glorious; and the root of wisdom never faileth. Wisdom is better than strength, and a wise man than a strong man. Wisdom is glorious, and never fadeth away, and is easily seen by them that love her, and is found by them that seek her.

2d Circuit: . . . She preventeth them that covet her, so that she first showeth herself unto them. He that awaketh early to seek her shall not labour: for he shall find her sitting at his door. To think upon her is perfect understanding; and he that watcheth for her shall quickly be secure. For she goeth about seeking such as are worthy of her; and she showeth herself to them cheerfully in the ways, and meeteth them with all Providence.

3d Circuit: . . . The multiplied brood of the wicked shall not thrive; and bastard slips shall not take deep root nor any fast foundation. And if they flourish in branches for a time, yet, standing not fast, they shall be shaken with the wind; and through the force of the winds they shall be rooted out. For the branches, not being perfect, shall be broken; and their fruits shall be unprofitable, and sour to eat and fit for nothing.

[At the end of the 3d Circuit, the candidate is halted in front of the Jun∴ Gr∴ Warden, who asks]:

J∴ G∴ W∴ Whom bring you with you, Bro∴ Gr∴ Master of Ceremonies?

M∴ Cer∴ A . . . . B . . . , a Prince Ameth, who desires to obtain the Degree of Gr∴ Master Architect.

J∴ G∴ W∴ Why does he desire to receive that Degree?

M∴ Cer∴ That he may increase in knowledge, and be the better fitted to discharge the duties of a good Mason. -

J∴ G∴ W∴ My Bro∴, dost thou well remember thy pledges to thy Brethren, made by thee as a Knight Elu of Nine?

Cand∴ I do.

J∴ G∴ W∴ Repeat them.

[The Candidate must repeat these pledges, as made in opening and closing in the 9th Degree. If he cannot do so, he must be withdrawn, and his reception postponed until he can do it. Therefore, in the preparation room, the M∴ of Cer∴ must see that he can repeat them, before he asks for his admission].

J∴ G∴ W∴ Hast thou endeavoured faithfully to fulfil these pledges?

Cand∴ I have.

J∴ G∴ W∴ Then thou hast my permission to pass on for further examination: and may thy search for wisdom prove successful!

[The Candidate is then conducted twice more around the room; while the Sen∴ Gr∴ Warden reads as follows]:

4th Circuit: . . . I wished, and understanding was given me: and I called upon God, and the spirit of wisdom came upon me: and I preferred her before Kingdoms and Thrones, and esteemed riches nothing in comparison to her. Neither did I compare unto her any precious stones: for all gold, in comparison of her is a little sand; and silver, in respect to her, is to be counted as clay. I loved her above health and beauty: and chose to have her instead of light; for her light cannot be put out.

5th Circuit: . . . She is an infinite treasure to men; which they that use become the friends of God. In her is the spirit of understanding; holy, one, manifold, subtile, eloquent, active, undefiled, sure, sweet, loving that which is good, quick, which nothing hindereth, beneficent, gentle, kind, steadfast, assured, secure, having all power, overseeing all things and containing all spirits: flowing from the power of God, and a pure emanation of the Glory of the Almighty God, unalloyed with anything base; the brightness of Eternal Light, the unspotted mirror of God's Majesty, and the image of His Goodness.

[At the end of the 5th Circuit, the Candidate is halted in front of the Sen∴ Gr∴ Warden, who asks]:

S∴ G∴ W∴ Whom bring you hither, Bro∴ Gr∴ Master of Ceremonies?

M∴ Cer∴ A . . . . B . . . . ., a Prince Ameth, who desires to obtain the Degree of Gr∴ Master Architect; and being examined by the Jun∴ Gr∴ Warden, hath by him been suffered to pass, and come hither for further examination.

S∴ G∴ W∴ Why does he desire to receive this degree?

M∴ Cer∴ That he may increase in knowledge, and be the better fitted to discharge the duties of a good Mason.

S∴ G∴ W∴ My Bro∴, dost thou well remember thy pledges to thy Brethren, made by thee as an Ill∴ Elu of Fifteen?

Cand∴ I do.

S∴ G∴ W∴ Repeat them.

[The Candidate does so, or must be withdrawn.]

S∴ G∴ W∴ Hast thou endeavoured faithfully to fulfil these pledges?

Cand∴ I have.

S∴ G∴ W∴ Then thou hast my permission to pass on for further examination: and may thy search for wisdom prove successful!

[The Candidate is then conducted twice more around the room; while the Th∴ Ill∴ reads]:

6th Circuit: . . . No evil can overcome wisdom. She glorifieth her Nobility by being conversant with God: and the Lord of all things loveth her. For it is she that teacheth the knowledge of God, and is the expounder of His works. If a man love justice, her labours have great virtues; for she teacheth temperance and prudence, and justice and fortitude; which are such things as man can have nothing more profitable in life.

7th Circuit: . . . She knoweth things past, and judgeth of things to come: she knoweth the subtilties of speeches, and the solutions of arguments: she knoweth signs and wonders before they be done; and the events of times and ages. She will communicate to us of her good things, and be a comfort in our cares and grief. By means of her we shall have immortality, and shall leave behind us an everlasting memory to them that come after us.

[At the end of the 7th Circuit, the Candidate is halted in front of the Th∴ Ill∴, who asks]:

Th∴ Ill∴ Whom bring you hither, Bro∴ Gr∴ M∴ of Ceremonies?

M∴ Cer∴ A . . . B . . ., a Prince Ameth, who desires to obtain the degree of Gr∴ Master Architect; and being examined by the Jun∴ and Sen∴ Gr∴ Wardens, hath by them been suffered to pass, and to come hither for further examination.

Th∴ Ill∴ Why does he desire to receive this degree?

M∴ Cer∴ To increase in knowledge, and be the better fitted to discharge the duties of a good Mason.

Th∴ Ill∴ My Bro∴, dost thou well remember thy pledges to thy Brethren, made by thee as a Prince Ameth?

Cand∴ I do.

Th∴ Ill∴ Repeat them.

[He does so; or is withdrawn.]

Th∴ Ill∴ It is well. Of what art thou in search?

Cand∴ Of wisdom.

Th∴ Ill∴ It is the true Masonic Light. He who obeys the Masonic law shall find it. The degree which you now seek was first conferred upon Adonhiram the Son of Abda, when he was appointed Chief Architect of the Temple, and as such, the successor of the Gr∴ Master Hiram, after having been for a time the chief of the five Intendants of the building: and after his skill and science as an architect had been thoroughly tested, and he found to be superior to the other four Intendants.

———— It was but the ceremony of his investiture with that office. Afterwards it became an honorary degree, conferred first upon the other Intendants, and then upon the Elu, as a mark of honor and distinction.

———— As he advanced, the Ancient Freemason ceased to work with the instruments of the labourer, the Square, the Level, the Plumb and the Trowel: and assumed those of the Architect and Geometrician. As he advanced, also, he passed from that branch of Geometry and Mathematics which occupies itself with the Earth, its surface, and the things that belong to it, with right lines and angles and all the figures formed thereby, to the mathematics of the heavens and the spheres.

———— We no longer occupy ourselves with geometry and mathematics as sciences, nor expect of our initiates a knowledge of their problems, or even of their terms. To us the instruments of the Geometrician, and all the figures, plain and spherical, drawn by these instruments, have a symbolical meaning. By means of the morality of Masonry, we advance towards its philosophy; and every degree is a step in that direction.

————If you would succeed to the rank held by Adonhiram, you must assume the obligation which it imposes. Are you willing to do so?

Cand∴ I am.

Th∴ Ill∴ Bro∴ Sen∴ Gr∴ Expert, you will conduct this brother to the Altar of Masonry, and place him in proper position to assume the obligation of a Gr∴ Master Architect.

[The candidate is conducted to the Altar, and made to kneel on both knees, with his hands upon the Holy Bible and the instruments which are upon it; in which position he repeats the following]

OBLIGATION.

I, A . . . . B . . . ., in the presence of the Gr.·. Architect of the Universe and of this Chapter of Gr.·. Master Architects, do hereby and hereon most solemnly and sincerely promise and swear, that I will never reveal the secrets of this degree to any person in the world, unless it be in a place where, and at a time when, the same may lawfully be done, and to a person duly authorized to receive them, and when I am legally authorized and empowered to communicate them.

——I furthermore promise and swear that during all the rest of my life, within the Lodge and Chapter and without, I will earnestly endeavour to conduct and behave myself in a manner suitable to the character of one, who assumes to be the successor and representative of those men, illustrious for their virtues and excellencies, who were the chief architects of the Temple built by Solomon.

——I furthermore promise and swear that I will hereafter strive to practise all the virtues of which the instruments before me are the symbols in this degree, as they shall be hereafter explained to me, to the end of my life, and so far as human frailty and infirmity will allow.

——To all of which I do most solemnly and sincerely promise and swear, binding myself under the penalty of being deserted and abandoned by my friends and denounced and hunted down by my enemies, and of forfeiting all claim to assistance in danger, comfort in calamity and support in difficulty from any Mason in the world; if I should ever be guilty of wilfully and intentionally violating this my solemn obligation of a Gr.·. Master Architect. So help me God; and keep me steadfast in the due performance of the same!

Th.·. Ill.·. By the authority in me vested, as successor of Adonhiram the son of Abda and Hiram Abi our Gr.·. Master, I declare you to be duly elevated to the degree of Gr.·. Master Architect. Arise, and receive the Sign, Token and Words of this Degree.

SIGN: Lay the ‡♀♌&♈⅟&⊙♒♊ in the middle of the †☾♑♈. Pause a moment; and then ↑†☿♎☾ the ♑♀♒♌☾‡♎ of the ‡⅟&⊙♒♊, and with the ♈&♄♋♏ seem to trace a plan or figure in the palm of the †☾♑♈; looking at the Gr.·. Master, as if receiving directions from him.

TOKEN: ♀♒♈☾‡†⊙↑☾ the ♑♀♒♌☾‡♎ of the ‡⅟&⊙♒♊♎, and place each his other &⊙♒♊ on his &♀⅋.

PASS-WORD: ‡⊙♏-♏☾♒♀♒.·.

SACRED WORD: ⊙♊☿♒⊙♀.·.

I invest you with the apron, collar and jewel of this Degree. Their colours, white and blue, will remind you of what is commonly styled *Symbolic Masonry*, or the *Blue Degrees;* the foundation, but not, as many pretend, the completion and perfection of Masonry. Upon the apron and jewel you see the five orders of architecture, and the instruments of a Grand Master Architect; the symbolic meaning of which you have yet to learn.

——I now present you with the instruments with which a Grand Master Architect works. Listen, and you shall learn their uses, and of what they are the symbols to us in this Degree. Bro.·. Sen.·. Gr.·. Warden, what are the instruments used by a Gr.·. Master Architect.

[The Th.·. Ill.·. and the Sen.·. Gr.·. Warden repeat the questions and answers, in the opening ceremony, in regard to the purposes for which the several instruments are used, and the lessons which are taught by them in this degree, from the compasses to the slide-rule inclusive].

Th∴ Ill∴ Such are the uses of the instruments of a Gr∴ Master Architect, and such the lessons which they teach us. Forget not that you have solemnly sworn to practise all the virtues which they symbolically teach, for thus only can you deserve, how proudly soever you may wear, the title of Gr∴ Master Architect.

———Go now to the Gr∴ Orator, and sitting at his feet receive the Lecture of this Degree.

LECTURE.

My Brother, the history of this Degree is brief, as its ceremonies are simple. After the murderers of our Gr∴ Master Hiram Abi had been discovered, apprehended, tried and punished; his monument and mausoleum completed by the Board of Intendants of the Building; and the matters which concerned the revenue of the realm provided for, King Solomon, to assure uniformity in the work, and vigour in its prosecution, and to reward the superior and eminent science and skill of Adonhiram the son of Abda, appointed him to be Chief Architect of the Temple, with the title of Gr∴ Master Architect, and invested him with that office, as sole successor and representative of the deceased Grand Master Hiram Abi; and at the same time made him Gr∴ Master of Masons, and the Masonic Peer of himself and King Hiram of Tyre. Afterwards the title was conferred upon other Princes of the Jewish Court as an honorarium, and thus the degree became established.

You have heard what are the lessons taught by the working instruments of a Grand Master Architect; and I shall not now enlarge upon those lessons. The great duties which they inculcate, demanding so much of us, and taking for granted the capacity to perform them faithfully and fully, bring us at once to reflect upon the dignity of human nature, and the vast powers and capacities of the human soul; and to that theme we invite your attention in this degree.

Evermore the human soul struggles towards the light, towards God and the Infinite. It is especially so in its afflictions. Words go but a little way into the depths of sorrow. The thoughts that writhe there in silence, that go into the silence of Infinitude and Eternity, have no emblems. Thoughts enough come there, such as no tongue ever uttered. They do not so much want human sympathy, as higher help. There is a loneliness in deep sorrow which the Deity alone can relieve. Alone, the mind wrestles with the great problem of calamity, and seeks the solution from the Infinite Providence of Heaven, and thus is led directly to God.

There are many things in us of which we are not distinctly conscious. To waken that slumbering consciousness into life, and so to lead the soul up to the Light, is one office of every great ministration to human nature, whether its vehicle be the pen, the pencil, or the tongue. We are unconscious of the intensity and awfulness of the life within us. Health and sickness, joy and sorrow, success and disappointment, life and death, are familiar words upon our lips; and we do not know to what depths they point within us.

We seem never to know what any thing means until we have lost it. Many an organ, nerve, and fibre in our bodily frame performs its silent part for years, and we are quite unconscious of its value. It is not until it is injured that we discover that value, and find how essential it was to our happiness and comfort. We never know the full significance of the words, property, ease and health; the wealth of meaning in the fond epithets, parent, child and friend, until the thing or the person is taken away; until, in place of the bright, visible being, comes the awful and desolate shadow, where nothing is: where we stretch out our hands in vain, and strain our eyes upon dark and dismal vacuity. Yet, in that vacuity, we do not *lose* the object that we loved. It becomes only the more real to us. Our blessings not only brighten when they depart, but are fixed in enduring reality; and friendship receives its everlasting seal under the cold impress of death.

A dim consciousness of infinite mystery and grandeur lies beneath all the common-place of life. There is an awfulness and a majesty around us, in all our little worldliness. The rude peasant from the Apennines, asleep at the foot of a pillar in a majestic Roman church, seems not to hear or see, but to dream only of the herd he feeds or the ground he tills in the mountains. But the choral symphonies fall softly upon his ear, and the gilded arches are dimly seen through his half-slumbering eyelids.

So the soul, however given up to the occupations of daily life, cannot quite lose the sense of where it is, and of what is above it and around it. The scene of its actual engagements may be small; the path of its steps, beaten and familiar; the objects it handles, easily spanned, and quite worn out with daily uses. So it may be, and amidst such things, that we all live. So we live our little life; but Heaven is above us; and Eternity is before us and behind us; and suns and stars are silent witnesses and watchers over us. We are enfolded by Infinity. Infinite Powers and Infinite spaces lie all around us. The dread arch of Mystery spreads over us, and no voice ever pierced it. Eternity is enthroned amid Heaven's myriad starry heights; and no utterance or word ever came from those far-off and silent spaces. Above, is that awful majesty; around us, every where, it stretches off into infinity: and beneath it is this little struggle of life, this poor day's conflict, this busy ant-hill of Time.

- But from that ant-hill, not only the talk of the streets, the sounds of music and revelling, the stir and tread of a multitude, the shout of joy and the shriek of agony go up into the silent and all-surrounding Infinitude; but also, amidst the stir and noise of visible life, from the inmost bosom of the visible man, there goes up an imploring call, a beseeching cry, an asking, unuttered and unutterable, for revelation, wailingly and in almost speechless agony praying the dread arch of mystery to break, and the stars that roll above the waves of mortal trouble, to speak; the enthroned majesty of those awful heights to find a voice; the mysterious and reserved heavens to come near; and all to tell us what they alone know; to give us information of the loved and lost; to make known to us what we are, and whither we are going.

Man is encompassed with a dome of incomprehensible wonders. In him and about him is that which should fill his life with majesty and sacredness. Something of sublimity and sanctity has thus flashed down from heaven into the heart of every one that lives. There is no being so base and abandoned but hath some traits of that sacredness left upon him; something, so much perhaps in discordance with his general repute, that he hides it from all around him: some sanctuary in his soul, where no one may enter; some sacred enclosure, where the memory of a child is, or the image of a venerated parent, or the echo of some word of kindness once spoken to him; an echo that will never die away.

Life is no negative, or superficial or worldly existence. Our steps are evermore haunted with thoughts, far beyond their own range, which some have regarded as the reminiscences of a pre-existent state. So it is with us all, in the beaten and worn track of this worldly pilgrimage. There is more here, than the world we live in. It is not all of life, to live. An unseen and infinite presence is here; a sense of something greater than we possess; a seeking, through all the void wastes of life, for a good beyond it; a crying out of the heart for interpretation; a memory of the dead, touching continually some vibrating thread in this great tissue of mystery.

We all not only have better intimations, but are capable of better things than we know. The pressure of some great emergency would develope in us powers, beyond the worldly bias of our spirits; and Heaven so deals with us, from time to time, as to call forth those better things. There is hardly a family so selfish in the world, but that, if one in it were doomed to die—one, to be selected by the others,—it would be utterly impossible for its members, parents and children, to choose out that victim; but that each would say, "I will die; but I cannot choose." And in how many, if that dire extremity had come, would one and another step forth, freed from the vile meshes of ordinary selfishness, and say, like the Roman father and son, "let the blow fall on me!" There are greater and better things in us all, than the world takes account of, or than we take note of; if we would but find them out. And it is one part of our Masonic culture to *find* these traits of power and sublime devotion, to revive these faded impressions of generosity and self-sacrifice, the almost squandered bequests of God's love and kindness to our souls; and to induce us to yield ourselves to their guidance and control.

Upon all conditions of men presses down one impartial law. To all situations, to all fortunes, high or low, the *mind* gives their character. They are, in effect, not what they are in themselves, but what they are to the feeling of their possessors. The King may be mean, degraded, miserable; the slave of ambition, fear, voluptuousness, and every low passion. The Peasant may be the real Monarch, the moral master of his fate, a free and lofty being, more than a Prince in happiness, more than a King in honour.

Man is no bubble upon the sea of his fortunes, helpless and irresponsible upon the tide of events. Out of the same circumstances, different men bring totally different results. The same difficulty, distress, poverty, or misfortune, that breaks down one man, builds up another and makes him strong. It is the very attribute and glory of a man, that he can bend the circumstances of his condition to the intellectual and moral purposes of his nature; and the power and mastery of his will chiefly distinguish him from the brute.

The faculty of moral will, developed in the child, is a new element of his nature. It is a new power brought upon the scene, and a ruling power, delegated from Heaven. Never was a human being sunk so low that he had not, by God's gift, the power to rise. Because God commands him to rise, it is certain that he *can* rise. Every man has the power, and should use it, to make all situations, trials and temptations instruments to promote his virtue and happiness; and is so far from being the creature of circumstances, that *he* creates and controls *them*, making them to be all that they are, of evil or of good, to him as a moral being.

Life is what we make it, and the world is what we make it. The eyes of the cheerful and of the melancholy man are fixed upon the same creation; but very different are the aspects which it bears to them. To the one, it is all beauty and gladness; the waves of ocean roll in light, and the mountains are covered with day. Life, to him, flashes, rejoicing, upon every flower and every tree that trembles in the breeze. There is more to him, everywhere, than the eye sees; a presence of profound joy, on hill and valley and bright, dancing water. The other idly or mournfully gazes at the same scene, and everything wears a dull, dim and sickly aspect. The murmuring of the brooks is a discord to him, the great roar of the sea has an angry and threatening emphasis, the solemn music of the pines sings the requiem of his departed happiness, the cheerful light shines garishly upon his eyes and offends him. The great train of the seasons passes before him like a funeral procession; and he sighs, and turns impatiently away. The eye makes that which it looks upon; the ear makes its own melodies and discords; the world without reflects the world within.

Let the Mason never forget that life and the world are what we make them by our social character; by our adaptation, or want of adaptation to the social conditions, relationships and pursuits of the world. To the selfish, the cold and the insensible, to the haughty and presuming, to the proud, who demand more than they are likely to receive, to the jealous ever afraid they shall not receive enough, to those who are unreasonably sensitive about the good or ill opinions of others, to all violators of the social laws, the rude, the violent, the dishonest and the sensual,—to all these, the social condition, from its very nature, will present annoyances, disappointments, and pains, appropriate to their several characters. The benevolent affections will not revolve around selfishness; the cold-hearted must expect to meet coldness; the proud, haughtiness; the passionate, anger; and the violent, rudeness. Those who forget the rights of others, must not be surprised if their own are forgotten; and those who stoop to the lowest embraces of sense must not wonder, if others are not concerned to find their prostrate honour, and lift it up to the remembrance and respect of the world.

To the gentle, many will be gentle: to the kind, many will be kind. A good man will find that there is goodness in the world: an honest man will find that there is honesty in the world; and a man of principle will find principle and integrity in the hearts of others.

There are no blessings which the mind may not convert into the bitterest of evils; and no trials which it may not transform into the noblest and divinest blessings. There are no temptations, from which assailed virtue may not gain strength, instead of falling before them, vanquished and subdued. It is true that temptations have a great power, and virtue often falls: but the might of these temptations lies not in themselves, but in the feebleness of our own virtue, and the weakness of our own hearts. We rely too much on the strength of our ramparts and bastions, and allow the enemy to make his approaches, by trench and parallel, at his leisure. The offer of dishonest gain and guilty pleasure makes the honest man more honest, and the pure man more pure. They raise his virtue to the height of towering indignation. The fair occasion, the safe opportunity, the tempting chance become the defeat and disgrace of the tempter. The honest and upright man does not wait until temptation has made its approaches and mounted its batteries on the last parallel.

But to the impure, the dishonest, the false-hearted, the corrupt and the sensual, occasions come every day, and in every scene, and through every avenue of thought and imagination. He is prepared to capitulate before the first approach is commenced; and sends out the white flag when the enemy's advance comes in sight of his walls. He *makes* occasions; or, if opportunities come not, evil *thoughts* come, and he throws wide open the gates of his heart and welcomes those bad visitors, and entertains them with a lavish hospitality.

The business of the world absorbs, corrupts and degrades one mind, while in another it feeds and nurses the noblest independence, integrity and generosity. Pleasure is a poison to some, and a healthful refreshment to others. To one, the world is a great harmony, like a noble strain of music with infinite modulations: to another, it is a huge factory, the clash and clang of whose machinery jars upon his ears and frets him to madness. Life is substantially the same thing to all who partake of its lot. Yet some rise to virtue and glory; while others, undergoing the same discipline, and enjoying the same privileges, sink to shame and perdition.

Thorough, faithful and honest endeavour to improve, is always successful, and the highest happiness. To sigh sentimentally over human misfortune, is fit only for the mind's childhood; and the mind's misery is chiefly its own fault; and appointed, under the good Providence of God, as the punisher and corrector of its fault. In the long run, the mind will be happy, just in proportion to its fidelity and wisdom. When it is miserable, it has planted the thorns in its own path: it grasps them, and cries out in loud complaint; and that complaint is but the louder *confession* that the thorns which grew there, *it* planted.

A certain kind and degree of spirituality enter into the largest part of even the most ordinary life. You can carry on no business, without some faith in man. You cannot even dig in the ground, without a reliance on the unseen result. You cannot think or reason or even step, without confiding in the inward, spiritual principles of your nature. All the affections and bonds, and hopes and interests of life centre in the spiritual; and you know that if that central bond were broken, the world would rush to chaos.

Believe that there is a God; that He is our Father; that He has a paternal interest in our welfare and improvement; that he has given us powers by means of which we may escape from sin and ruin; that he has destined us to a future life of endless progression towards perfection and a knowledge of himself;—believe this, as every Mason should, and you can live calmly, endure patiently, labour resolutely, deny yourselves cheerfully, hope steadfastly, and be conquerors in the great struggle of life. Take away any one of these principles, and what remains for us. Say that there is no God; or no way opened for hope and reformation and triumph, no heaven to come, no rest for the weary, no home in God's bosom for the afflicted and disconsolate soul; and we are but the sport of chance, and the victims of despair; hapless wanderers upon the face of a desolate and forsaken earth; surrounded by darkness, struggling with obstacles, toiling for barren results and empty purposes, distracted with doubts, and misled by false gleams of light; wanderers with no way, no prospect, no home; doomed and deserted mariners on a dark and stormy sea, without compass or course, to whom no stars appear, tossing helmless upon the crashing waves, with no haven in the distance to invite us to its welcome rest.

The religious faith thus taught by Masonry is indispensable to the attainment of the great ends of life; and must therefore have been designed to be a part of it. We are made for this faith; and there must be something, somewhere, for us to believe in. We cannot grow healthfully, nor live happily, without it. It is therefore *true*. If we could cut off from any soul all the principles taught by Masonry, the faith in a God, in immortality, in virtue, in essential rectitude, that soul would sink into sin, misery, darkness and ruin. If we could cut off all sense of these truths, the man would sink at once to the grade of the animal.

Society, in its great relations, is as much the creation of Heaven, as is the system of the Universe. If that bond of gravitation that holds all worlds and systems together, were suddenly severed, the universe would fly into wild and boundless chaos. And if we were to sever all the moral bonds that hold society together; if we could cut off from it every conviction of Truth and Integrity, of an authority above it, and of a conscience within it, it would immediately rush to disorder and frightful anarchy and ruin. The religion we teach is therefore as really a principle of things, and as certain and true, as gravitation.

Faith in moral principles, in virtue and in God, is as necessary for the guidance of a man, as instinct is for the guidance of an animal. And therefore this faith, as a principle of man's nature, has a mission as truly authentic in God's Providence, as the principle of instinct. The pleasures of the soul, too, must depend on certain principles. They must recognize a soul, its properties and responsibilities, a conscience, and the sense of an authority above us: and these are the principles of faith. No man can suffer and be patient, can struggle and conquer, can improve and be happy, without conscience, without hope, without a reliance on a just, wise and beneficent God. We must of necessity embrace the great truths taught by Masonry, and live by them, to live happily. Every thing in the universe has fixed and certain laws and principles for its action;—the star in its orbit, the animal in its activity, the physical man in his functions. And he has likewise fixed and certain laws and principles as a spiritual being. His soul does not die for want of aliment or guidance. For the rational soul there is ample provision. From the lofty pine, rocked in the darkening tempest, the cry of the young raven is heard, and it would be most strange if there were no answer for the cry and call of the soul, tortured by want and sorrow and agony. The total rejection of all moral and religious belief would strike out a principle from human nature, as essential to it as gravitation to the stars, instinct to animal life, the circulation of the blood to the human body.

God has ordained that life shall be a social condition. We are members of a civil community. The life of that community depends upon its moral condition. Public spirit, intelligence, uprightness, temperance, kindness, domestic purity, will make it a happy community, and give it prosperity and continuance. Widespread selfishness, dishonesty, intemperance, libertinism, corruption and crime, will make it miserable, and bring about dissolution and speedy ruin. A whole people lives one life: one mighty heart heaves in its bosom; it is one great pulse of existence that throbs there. One stream of life flows there, with ten thousand intermingled branches and channels, through all the homes of human love. One sound as of many waters, a rapturous jubilee or a mournful sighing comes up from the congregated dwellings of a whole nation.

The Public is no vague abstraction; nor should that which is done against that Public, against public interest, law or virtue, press but lightly on the conscience. It is but a vast expansion of individual life; an ocean of tears, an atmosphere of sighs, or a great whole of joy and gladness. It suffers with the suffering of millions: it rejoices with the joy of millions. What a vast crime does he commit,—private man or public man, agent or contractor, legislator or magistrate, Secretary or President, who dares, with indignity and wrong, to strike the bosom of the Public Welfare, to encourage venality and corruption and shameful sale of the elective franchise, to sow dissension, and to weaken the bonds of amity that bind the Nation together! What a huge iniquity, he who, with vices like the daggers of a parricide, dares to pierce that mighty heart, in which the ocean of existence is flowing!

What an unequalled interest lies in the virtue of every one whom we love! In his virtue, nowhere but in his virtue, is garnered up the incomparable treasure. What care we for brother, husband or friend, compared with what we care for his honour, his fidelity, his reputation, his kindness? How venerable is the rectitude of a parent! How sacred his reputation! No blight that can fall upon a child, is like his parent's dishonour. Heathen or Christian, every parent would have his child do well; and pours out upon him all the fulness of parental love, in the one desire that he may do well; that he may be worthy of his cares, and his freely bestowed pains; that he may walk in the way of honour and happiness. In that way he cannot walk one step without virtue. Such is life, in its relationships. A thousand ties embrace it, like the fine nerves of a delicate organization; like the strings of an instrument capable of sweet melodies, but easily wounded, lacerated and broken, by rudeness, anger, and guilty indulgence.

If life could, by any process, be made insensible to pain and pleasure; if the human heart were hard as adamant, then avarice, ambition and sensuality might channel out their paths in it, and make it their beaten way; and none would wonder or protest. If we could be patient under the load of a mere worldly life; if we could bear that burthen as the beasts bear it; then, like beasts, we might bend all our thoughts to the earth; and no call from the great Heavens above us would startle us from our plodding and earthly course.

But we are not insensible brutes, who can refuse the call of reason and conscience. The soul is capable of remorse. When the great dispensation of life presses down upon us, we weep, and suffer and sorrow. And sorrow and agony desire other companionships than worldliness and irreligion. We are not willing to bear those burthens of the heart, fear, anxiety, disappointment and trouble, without any object or use. We are not willing to suffer, to be sick and afflicted, to have our days and months lost to comfort and joy, and overshadowed with calamity and grief, without advantage or compensation: to barter away the dearest treasures, the very sufferings, of the heart; to sell the life-blood from failing frame and fading cheek, our tears of bitterness and groans of anguish, for nothing. Human nature, frail, feeling, sensitive and sorrowing, cannot afford to suffer for nothing.

Every where, human life is a great and solemn dispensation. Man, suffering, enjoying, loving, hating, hoping and fearing; now soaring to Heaven and exploring the far recesses of the universe, and now sinking to the grave, is ever the creature of a high and stupendous destiny. In his bosom is wrapped up a momentous and vast experience, to be unfolded in ages and worlds unknown. Around this great action of existence the curtains of Time are drawn; but there are openings through them which give us glimpses of Eternity. God from on high looks down upon this scene of human probation. The wise and the good in all ages, and above all the Great Master, have interposed for it, with their teachings and their blood. Every thing that exists around us, every movement in Nature, every counsel of Providence, every interposition of God, centres upon one point,—the fidelity of man.

And though the ghosts of the departed and the remembered should come at midnight through the barred doors of our dwellings; though the sheeted dead should glide through the aisles of our churches, and people our Masonic Temples, their teachings would be no more powerful than the dread realities of Life; than those memories of mis-spent years, those ghosts of departed opportunities, that, pointing to our consciences and to Eternity, ever cry in our ears, "Work while the day lasts, for the night of death cometh, in which no man can work."

There are no tokens of public mourning for the calamity of the soul. Men weep when the body dies; and when it is borne to its last rest, they follow it with sad and mournful procession. But for the dying soul, there is no open lamentation; for the lost soul there are no obsequies.

And yet the mind and soul of man have a value which nothing else has. They are worth a care which nothing else is worth; and to the single, solitary individual, they ought to possess an interest which nothing else possesses. The stored treasures of the heart, the unfathomable mines that are in the soul to be wrought, the broad and boundless realms of Thought, the freighted argosy of man's hopes and best affections, are brighter than gold and dearer than treasure.

And yet the mind is in reality little known or considered. It is *all* which man permanently *is*, his inward being, his divine energy, his immortal thought, his boundless capacity, his infinite aspiration; and nevertheless, few value it for what it is worth. Few see a brother-mind in others, through the rags with which poverty has clothed it, beneath the crushing burthens of life, amidst the close pressure of worldly troubles, wants and sorrows. Few acknowledge and cheer it in that humble lot, and feel that the nobility of earth, and the commencing glory of Heaven is there.

Men do not feel the worth of their own souls. They are proud of their mental powers: but the intrinsic, inner, infinite *worth* of their own minds they do not perceive. The poor man, admitted to a palace, feels, lofty and immortal being as he is, like a mere ordinary thing amid the splendours that surround him. He sees the carriage of wealth roll by him, and forgets the intrinsic and eternal dignity of his own mind, in a poor and degrading envy, and feels as an humbler creature, because others are above him, not in mind, but in mensuration. Men respect themselves, according as they are more wealthy, higher in rank or office, loftier in the world's opinion.

The difference among men is not so much in their nature and intrinsic power, as in the faculty of communication. Some have the capacity of uttering and embodying in words their thoughts. All men, more or less, *feel* those thoughts. The glory of genius and the rapture of virtue, when rightly revealed, are diffused and shared among unnumbered minds. When eloquence and poetry speak; when those glorious arts, statuary, painting and music, take audible or visible shape; when patriotism, charity and virtue speak with a thrilling power, the hearts of thousands glow with a kindred joy and ecstasy. If it were not so, there would be no eloquence; for eloquence is that to which other hearts respond; it is the faculty and power of *making* other hearts respond. No one is so low or degraded, as not sometimes to be touched with the beauty of goodness. No heart is made of materials so base, as not sometimes to respond, through every chord of it, to the call of honour, patriotism, generosity and virtue. The poor African Slave will die for the master or mistress, or in defence of the children, whom he loves; and such love in him is common. The poor, abandoned, outcast woman will, without expectation of reward, nurse those who are dying on every hand, utter strangers to her, with a contagious and horrid pestilence. The pickpocket will scale burning walls to rescue child or woman, unknown to him, from the ravenous flames.

Most glorious is this capacity! A power to commune with God and His Angels; a reflection of the Uncreated Light; a mirror that can collect and concentrate upon itself all the moral splendours of the Universe. It is the soul alone that gives any value to the things of this world; and it is only by raising the soul to its just elevation above all other things, that we can look rightly upon the purposes of this earth. No sceptre nor throne, nor structure of ages, nor broad empire, can compare with the wonders and grandeurs of a single thought. That alone, of all things that have been made, comprehends the Maker of all. That alone is the key, which unlocks all the treasures of the Universe; the power that reigns over Space, Time and Eternity. That, under God, is the Sovereign Dispenser to man of all the blessings and glories that lie within the compass of possession, or the range of possibility. Virtue, Heaven and Immortality exist not, nor ever will exist for us, except as they exist and will exist, in the perception, feeling and thought of the glorious mind.

Return now, my Brother, to the Th∴ Ill∴ Gr∴ Master, and receive from him the final instruction of this Degree.

CLOSING INSTRUCTION.

Th∴ Ill∴ My Brother, in the hope that you have listened to and understood the Instruction and Lecture of this degree, and that you feel the dignity of your own nature and the vast capacities of your own soul for good or evil, I proceed briefly to communicate to you the remaining instruction of this Degree.

The Hebrew word suspended in the East, over the five columns, is ADONAI, one of the names of God, usually translated *Lord;* and which, in reading, the Jews always substitute for *His True Name,* which they are forbidden to pronounce.

The five columns, in the five different orders of architecture, are emblematical to us of the five different divisions of the Ancient and Accepted Rite :

The *Tuscan;* of the three Blue Degrees, or the primitive Masonry.

The *Doric;* of the Ineffable Degrees, from the 4th to the 14th inclusive.

The *Ionic;* of the 15th and 16th, or the Council Degrees.

The *Corinthian;* of the 17th and 18th, or the Chapter Degrees.

The *Composite;* of the High Degrees, from the 19th to the 32d inclusive.

And they also symbolize to us the five principal Rites of Masonry: The Tuscan, the *York* Rite; the Doric, the *Rit Moderne,* or *French* Rite; the Ionic, the Rite of *Misraim;* the Corinthian, the Rite of *Perfection;* and the Composite, the *Ancient and Accepted* or *Scotch* Rite, uniting the excellencies and rejecting the defects of the others.

The North Star represents the point within the circle, or the Deity in the centre of the Universe.

The *Seven Stars* that circle around it, are symbols of the seven living, self-subsistent, ever active, hypostatized Powers or Emanations, which were held by Basilides to have been evolved from one unrevealed God: viz: the four Intellectual Powers; NOUS, *the Mind;* LOGOS, *the Reason;* PHRONESIS, *the Thinking Power;* and SOPHIA, *Wisdom:* the Operative Power, DUNAMIS, *Might, accomplishing the purposes of Wisdom:* and the Moral Attributes; DIKAIOSUNE, *Moral Perfection;* and EIRENE, *Inward Tranquillity:* which seven Powers, with the Primal Grand one, out of which they were evolved, constituted in his system *the* FIRST OGDOADE, or OCTAVE, the Root of all Existence; from which were evolved other gradations of spiritual existence, each lower one the impression and ante-type of the immediate higher one; and in all, 365 in number, represented by the mystical word ABRAXAS.

The Morning Star, rising in the East, is an emblem to us of the ever-approaching dawn of Perfection and Masonic Light.

The three Great Lights of the Lodge, are symbols to us of the POWER, WISDOM and BENEFICENCE of the Deity.

For the present, my Brother, let this suffice. We welcome you among us, to this peaceful retreat of Virtue, to a participation in our privileges, to a share in our joys and our sorrows: and we invite you to be seated with us as a member of this Chapter.

TO CLOSE.

Th∴ Ill∴. [Giving one rap, and then two] : Bro∴ Sen∴ Gr∴ Warden, what is the hour ?

S∴ G∴ W∴. The Sun has set, and the Evening Star has risen.

Th∴ Ill∴. The hour for rest has arrived : Give notice to the Gr∴ Masters that I am about to close this Chapter of Gr∴ Master Architects, that they may aid me in so doing.

J∴ G∴ W∴. Brethren in the South, the Th∴ Ill∴ Gr∴ Master is about to close this Chapter of Gr∴ M∴ Architects, and desires your assistance, since the hour of rest has arrived.

S∴ G∴ W∴. Brethren in the North, &c.

Th∴ Ill∴. The sign, my Brethren !

[All give the sign. Then the Gr∴ Master and the Sen∴ and Jun∴ Gr∴ Wardens rap in succession ‖ ? — and all the Brethren the same with their hands, and the Gr∴ Master says] :

Th∴ Ill∴. This Chapter is duly closed.

FINIS.

Thirteenth Degree.

Royal Arch.

THE CHAPTER, ITS DECORATIONS, ETC.

Bodies of this Degree are styled *Chapters*. The Lodge Room represents the Audience Chamber of King Solomon; its hangings, decorations and arrangements being the same as in the Elu Degrees.

There is also an apartment representing a subterranean vault, really under ground, if possible, and at all events without door or window, and into which one descends by an opening overhead, large enough only for a man to pass through. There is however a private entrance for the members of the Chapter. The distance from the opening overhead to the bottom should be as great as possible, and the apartment in which that opening is, should be strewed with rubbish and fragments of rock, to represent the ruins of an ancient building. The opening is closed by a trap-door, representing a flat stone, with an iron ring by which to raise it.

The subterranean apartment is painted to represent a chamber hewn in the rock. There are no lights, so that it is profoundly dark, except when the pedestal and cubical stone are uncovered.

In the middle of the apartment is a triangular pedestal, apparently of white marble, but of some transparent substance, and hollow, so that lights may be placed within it. Upon it is a cube ten inches square, being an imitation of a cubical block of agate, encrusted with glass of different colours, like precious stones. On the top of this is a triangular plate of gold, or some other metal gilded, sunk into the cube, and in the middle of the triangular plate, in black letters, the word יהוה. The light shining through the pedestal should be brilliant enough to enable this to be seen. At the commencement of the reception, the whole is covered with a thick cloth, entirely concealing the light.

OFFICERS, TITLES, ETC.

The Presiding Officer represents King Solomon, and is styled Th∴ Puissant Gr∴ Master. He sits upon a throne in the East, crowned, with a sceptre in his hand, under a rich canopy.

The Sen∴ Warden is styled Gr∴ Warden, and represents Hiram King of Tyre. He sits on the left hand of the Th∴ Puissant, crowned and holding a sceptre.

The Jun∴ Warden is styled Gr∴ Inspector. He sits in the West, and represents Adonhiram the Son of Abda, holding a drawn sword, and wearing his hat.

There is a Gr∴ Treasurer, who represents Joabert, and sits, covered, in the North.

Also a Gr∴ Secretary, representing Stolkin, who sits in the South, covered.

There is also a Master of Ceremonies.

CLOTHING, ORNAMENTS AND JEWELS.

The Th∴ Puissant wears a yellow robe, and a chasuble lined with blue satin, the sleeves coming as low as the elbows. He wears also a broad purple ribbon from the right shoulder to the left hip, to which is suspended a triangle of gold.

The Gr∴ Warden wears a purple robe and a yellow chasuble. The collar and jewel are like those of the Th∴ Puissant.

The Gr∴ Inspector wears the same collar and jewel, and a white robe, without the chasuble.

The Gr∴ Treasurer wears a white robe, the same collar and jewel, and from his button-hole a key of gold suspended by a white ribbon. On the key are the letters . . . . I∴ O∴ L∴ V∴ I∴

The Gr∴ Secretary wears the same robe, ribbon and jewel.

The Brethren who are not officers wear the same collar, and an apron of crimson velvet, on which is embroidered a triangle, surrounded with rays, and in the centre of it the sacred word יהוה. The jewel of the Brethren is a medal of gold, around which, on one side, are the initials of the following words: *Regnante Salomone Rege Sapientissimo, Thesaurum Pretiosissimum Sub Ruinis Invenerunt Adonhiram, Joabert, et Stolkin: . . . Anno Enochi* 2995. On the same side is engraved an aperture in the earth, over which stand two persons, their foreheads touching, lowering a third person into it by a rope. On the reverse side is a triangle surrounded with rays, and in the middle of it the sacred word יהוה. This medal is worn upon the chest, suspended by a white ribbon.

The battery of this Degree is ‖ ;

The age of a Royal Arch Mason is £ times the square of ; or : ; years.

TO OPEN.

[The Th∴ P∴ gives one rap, and says]:

Th∴ P∴ My Brethren, I am about to open this Chapter of Royal Arch Masons. Bro∴ Gr∴ Inspector, satisfy yourself that all present are Masons of the Royal Arch Ecossais, by receiving the Pass-word from each.

[The Gr∴ Inspector does so, and reports]:

Gr∴ Ins∴ Th∴ P∴, all present are Masons of the Royal Arch Ecossais.

Th∴ P∴ Welcome, my Brethren! Bro∴ M∴ of Ceremonies, it is our first duty to see that we are secure against intrusion. Attend to that duty, and inform the Tyler that we are about to open here this Chapter of the Royal Arch, that he may see that none approach without permission.

[The M∴ Cer∴ goes out, returns, raps ‖ ;— which is answered from without, and reports]:

M∴ Cer∴ Th∴ P∴, the Tyler is duly notified and at his post, and we are in security.

Th∴ P∴ Thanks, my Brother! Bro∴ Gr∴ Inspector, are you a Mason of the Royal Arch Ecossais?

Gr∴ Insp∴ I am that which I was and shall be. My name is Adonhiram.

Qu∴ Where did you entitle yourself to become such?

Ans∴ In a vault deep under ground, hollowed in the solid rock by the Patriarch Enoch.

Qu∴ How came you to enter therein?

Ans∴ By exploring the ruins of the Ancient Temple of Enoch, and passing through the nine arches.

Qu∴ What found you there?

Ans∴ A Pedestal, or cubical block of agate, and a plate of gold upon the cube.

Qu∴ What saw you upon that plate?

Ans∴ The Mysterious and Ineffable Name of the Gr∴ Architect of the Universe.

Qu∴ What is that Name?

Ans∴ I know its letters. None but the Grand, Elect, Ancient, Perfect and Sublime Masons know its true pronunciation.

Qu∴ Of what is the Cubical Stone an emblem?

Ans∴ Of Perfection.

Qu∴ To what do you now aspire?

Ans∴ To that degree, the summit of Ancient Masonry, the knowledge of the True Word.

Qu∴ What is your age?

Ans∴ ⚊☾*☾♒ times the square of ; — or : ; years complete.

Qu∴ What is the hour?

Ans∴ Sunrise.

Th∴ P∴ Let us then open this Chapter; since by Work only we can attain Perfection.

[The Th∴ P∴ raps ‖; — The Gr∴ Warden does the same]:

Gr∴ Insp∴ Come to order, my Brethren!

[All the Brethren repeat ‖; with their hands. The Th∴ P∴ and Gr∴ Warden give the sign of admiration; all the Brethren repeat it. Then the two Kings kneel: the Th∴ P∴ rises first, and taking the Gr∴ Warden by the arm, assists him to rise. All the Brethren kneel, and each in turn, beginning on the right, helps the other to rise].

Th∴ P∴ My Brethren, this Chapter of Masons of the Royal Arch Ecossais is open.

RECEPTION.

[Not less than three candidates can be received at once, in this degree. If there are not so many applicants, and the case is deemed *really* emergent, one or more Brothers who have already received the degree may act as candidates; but in that case the ceremonies proceed *in all respects* as if *all* were candidates.

The three candidates, in the clothing and jewels of Gr∴ Master Architects, are received in the preparation room by the Master of Ceremonies, and conducted to the door of the Chapter, where they meet the Tyler, who asks]:

Tyler: Who come here, Bro∴ M∴ of Ceremonies?

M∴ Cer∴ Three zealous Brothers, who having regularly received all the preceding Degrees, seek now to be advanced to the Degree of Royal Arch Ecossais; that they may hereafter attain that of Perfection.

Tyler: Wait, then, until I announce them to the Grand Inspector.

[The Tyler raps ‖; —and the door is opened by the Gr∴ Inspector, who asks]:

Gr∴ Insp∴ What is your desire, Bro∴ Tyler?

Tyler: The M∴ of Cer∴ waits, with three zealous Brethren, who, having regularly received all the preceding Degrees, seek now to be advanced to the Degree of Royal Arch Ecossais, that they may hereafter attain that of Perfection.

Gr∴ Insp∴ God alone is Perfect, and can confer Perfection on His Creatures. There is no vacancy in the Chapter; and they cannot be admitted.

[He closes the door: and the Tyler says]:

Tyler∴ You have heard, Bro∴ Master of Ceremonies.

M∴ Cer∴ I have heard; but I do not despair. The wish of these Brethren shall be made known to the Gr∴ Warden.

[The M∴ Cer∴ then raps ‖; —and the door is again opened by the Gr∴ Inspector].

Gr∴ Insp∴ What is your desire, Bro∴ M∴ of Ceremonies?

M∴ Cer∴ I bring with me three zealous Brethren, who, having regularly received all the preceding Degrees, seek now to be advanced to the Degree of Royal Arch Ecossais, that they may hereafter attain that of Perfection.

Gr∴ Insp∴ I have said that God alone is perfect, and can confer Perfection on his creatures. There is no vacancy in the Chapter.

M∴ Cer∴ These are true men and upright Masons, worthy to be advanced, and who have complied with all their pledges given at the altar. I demand that their request be made known to the Gr∴ Warden and Gr∴ Master.

Gr∴ Insp∴ Do you vouch for their proficiency in the preceding degrees?

M∴ Cer∴ I do. They know the duties of a Gr∴ Master Architect, and the lessons taught by the instruments he uses.

Gr∴ Insp∴ I will make known their wish to the Gr∴ Warden and the Th∴ ₋P∴ Gr∴ Master. They may perhaps consent, if the Brethren be proficients, as you say.

[He closes the door, goes to the East, and says]:

Gr∴ Insp∴ Th∴ P∴ Gr∴ Master and Ill∴ Gr∴ Warden, Three zealous Brethren, who have received all the preceding degrees, seek now to be advanced to the degree of Royal Arch Ecossais, that they may hereafter attain that of Perfection.

Th∴ P∴ Hast thou not given them to know that our numbers are complete?

Gr∴ Insp∴ I have; but our Bro∴ the Master of Ceremonies has prayed me to make known their wish to you, declaring them to be true men and upright Masons, worthy to be advanced, and who have complied with all their pledges given at the altar.

Th∴ P∴ Does he vouch for their proficiency in the preceding degrees?

Gr∴ Insp∴ He does; saying that they know the duties of a Gr∴ Master Architect, and the lessons taught by the instruments he uses.

Th∴ P∴ My Brethren, you hear. Is it your will that our number shall be increased?

[The Brethren raise the right hand in token of assent].

Th∴ P∴ Since the Brethren consent, let the Master of Ceremonies, and those who come with him enter.

[The Gr∴ Inspector goes to the door, opens it, and says]:

Gr∴ Insp∴ The Brethren consent that their number shall be increased: and the Gr∴ Master orders that these Brethren be allowed to enter.

[They enter, conducted by the M∴ of Cer∴ and advance to the East].

Th∴ P∴ My Brethren, you desire to be advanced to the degree of Royal Arch. When this degree was conferred upon Adonhiram, Joabert and Stolkin, who first received it, and in whose behalf it was created, they had earned the right to it by a singular service done to Masonry. For, sent to explore the ruins of the ancient Temple built by the Patriarch Enoch, they discovered and fearlessly explored a deep shaft sunk perpendicularly in the earth; and descending through nine arches sealed up from mortal eyes for centuries, they reached the cell, hewn in the solid rock, far under ground, in which a sacred treasure had been hidden before the flood. If you would see that treasure, you must descend as they did into the deep vault where it remains deposited, and so entitle yourselves to attain the degree you seek. Do you consent to do so?

Cand∴ We do.

Th∴ P∴ Go then with him who brought you hither, to the place which represents the ruins of the ancient Temple, explore the vault, and bring hither the sacred treasure.

[The candidates retire, accompanied by the Master of Ceremonies and two or three other Brothers, and are conducted to the room representing the ruins, and directed to remove the stones and rubbish from the place where the trap is. They do so, and the iron ring is discovered. They are directed to raise the trap, and do so].

M∴ Cer∴ Who among you will first descend?

[One offering to do so, is prepared by a strong rope fitted with loops for his feet, and fastened round his middle. He is then told that, if he meets with any obstacle, and desires to re-ascend, he can shake the rope, and will be drawn up; but if he reaches the bottom safe, he is to cast loose the rope. He is then lowered for some distance, in perfect darkness, and when near the bottom, a brother below interposes an obstacle, preventing him from going lower; and he is drawn up.

Another candidate is lowered and drawn up in the same way. Then the third is lowered, being furnished with a torch, and told to remain quiet if he reaches the bottom, until the others come to him. No obstacle being interposed, he reaches the bottom, and casts off the rope. The others are then lowered down, and when all have reached the bottom, some rubbish is thrown down upon them, and at the same moment a brother, unseen by them, extinguishes the light, and they are in utter darkness.

[*A Voice in a remote part of the cell*] : DARKNESS, and DEATH, and the GRAVE, are reserved for all men !

[*Another Voice*] : One FATE comes alike to all; the NIGHT of DEATH, after the short day of Life !

[*Another Voice*] : After Death and the Grave, come the Resurrection, and Light, and Life Eternal. [Immediately a Brother lifts the cloth that covers the pedestal; and discloses it to their eyes].

[*A Voice*] : Kneel, feeble and erring mortals, and adore the Great Ineffable name of GOD !

[They kneel, and a Brother comes forward and raises each by the arm; and says] :

Bro∴. Take now this sacred treasure, the Cubical Stone hidden deep in the Earth by Enoch the Patriarch, and return with it whence ye came.

. [They take the cubical stone from the Pedestal, are drawn up, one after the other, and return to the Chapter. In the mean time the lights in the Pedestal are extinguished, and the Brothers that were in the vault return by the private way to the Chapter. At the door of the Chapter, the M∴ of Cer∴ raps ‖ ; —and the door is opened by the Gr∴ Inspector, who asks] :

Gr∴ Insp∴. Who seek admission here?

M∴ Cer∴. Three zealous Brethren, who, as Adonhiram, Joabert and Stolkin did before them, have descended through the nine arches, into the subterranean vault, hewn in the solid rock, and have brought thence the cubical stone, there deposited by Enoch the Patriarch, which they desire to lay before the Gr∴ Master.

Gr∴ Insp∴. I will make known to him their desire.

[He closes the door, goes to the East, and says] :

Gr∴ Insp∴. Th∴ P∴ Gr∴ Master, three zealous Brethren wait without; who, as Adonhiram, Joabert and Stolkin did before them, have descended through the nine arches, into the subterranean vault, hewn in the solid rock, and have brought thence, and desire to lay before you, the cubical stone there deposited by Enoch the Patriarch.

Th∴ P∴. Let them enter, my Brother.

[The door is opened. The Gr∴ Master raps 3, and all the Brothers rise and uncover their heads, and stand with their arms raised towards heaven. The candidates enter, bearing the cubical agate, and place it, by direction, upon a pedestal of white marble, which has been set in the centre of the room; and remain standing by it. Then the Th∴ P∴ says] :

. Th∴ P∴. Behold, my Brethren, the Ineffable Name of Deity, engraved by Enoch, and discovered by the three first Masons of the Royal Arch.

[He then raps once, and all the Brothers kneel, himself and the candidates included. Then he raises the Gr∴ Warden, and the Brothers raise each other, and three brothers raise the candidates].

Th∴ P∴. My Brethren, you having, like the three Illustrious Masters who first received this degree, descended through the nine arches, into the subterranean vault hewn in the solid rock, and brought thence the Ineffable Name deposited there by Enoch the Patriarch, the Brethren consent that you shall be advanced to be Masons of the Royal Arch Ecossais. But to be received among us, it is necessary that you first assume a solemn and binding obligation. Are you prepared to do so?

[The Th∴ P∴ raps 3, and all the Brethren rise, and surround the candidates. Three Brothers, standing in front of each candidate, present their swords, with the points placed together, at his breast, and his hands are placed upon the blades. In this attitude, standing, each repeats the following]

OBLIGATION.

I, A. . . . B. . . ., in the presence of the Almighty, Terrible, Just and Merciful Creator of the Universe, do, upon these blades, promise and vow to Him, and solemnly pledge my honour to my Brethren, that I will never reveal the secrets of this degree to any person in the world, except to those who are legally entitled to receive them, when I am legally authorized to communicate them; and at such time, and in such place and manner as it may legally be done.

16

——— I furthermore promise, vow and pledge my honour, that I will never communicate the words of this degree, unless to or in the presence of three brethren, I being one; or unless I have a commission or patent which authorizes me to do so, for the purpose of forming a new Chapter of the Royal Arch.

——— I furthermore promise, vow, and pledge my honour, that I will never receive or assist in receiving, or be present at, or consent to, the reception of a brother in this degree, unless he shall have received all the preceding degrees by regular authority; nor unless he is at the time a regular member in good standing, of a regular Lodge of Master Masons, and has been Master or Warden of such a Lodge; nor unless he has proven his zeal and devotion to Masonry; nor unless he is a man of intelligence and information, charitable and benevolent, true, honest, sincere and upright; so far as I may know or have the means of judging.

——— I furthermore promise, vow and pledge my honour, that I will redouble my own zeal in the cause of Masonry, and my charity and friendship towards my Brethren; and that honour and duty shall be the lights by which my course shall be directed during my whole life.

——— All which I promise and vow, and thereunto pledge my honour, under no less a penalty than that of sinking so low in the estimation of my Brethren and the world, that my name shall be the synonym of degradation and dishonour; my violated faith become a by-word; and I, fallen below contempt, be looked upon with pity by every man and every woman in the world. So help me God! and keep me steadfast in the due performance of this, my solemn promise, vow and pledge of a Royal Arch Ecossais!

Th.·. P.·. My Brethren, as the successor and representative of Solomon, King of Israel, I receive and accept you as Masons of the Royal Arch Ecossais, and as the Liegemen of Honour and Duty, henceforward and forever. Receive now the Signs, Words and Token of this Degree.

1st Sign: *Of Admiration:* . . . ‡⊙♀♎☾‡ ♏☿♈&‡&⊙♒♊♎ towards Heaven; the &☾⊙♊ inclined to the left and the ‡‡¶♒☾☾ on the ground.

2d Sign: *Of Adoration:* . . . ♑⊙††. upon both ¶♒☾☾♎, bring the †‡&⊙♒♊ down from the †‡♎&☿ ♑†♊☾‡ to the ‡‡&♀‡: and place, at the same time, the †‡&⊙♒♊ ♏☾&♀♒♊ the ♏⊙‡¶.

Token: . . . Place your hands under the ⊙‡♋‡♀♈♎ of the Brother, as if to help him to rise.

Pass-word: . . . &⊙♋☾†☾¶ ¶&☾♏†♀♋.·.

Sacred Word: . . . This, my Brother, is the Ineffable Word, engraved upon the plate of Gold which is upon the Cube of Agate. Its pronunciation is known to the Grand, Elect, Perfect and Sublime Masons only, and cannot now be communicated to you. You can receive and communicate it only by its letters, and as one of three brethren, repeating these letters alternately. They are *Yod. . He . . Vav . . He* . , meaning, I am that which I was and shall be.

———There are nine names of Deity, used as words in this Degree, in place of, and as synonyms of the Ineffable Name, and appropriated, one to each of the Arches; and all of which are to be demanded in succession, when it is desired thoroughly to test a Brother. They were used by the different nations of antiquity, and are as follows:

1st Arch: . .	⊙♈&☿♋.·.	Egyptian:
2d "	⊙♋♑♒.·.	Egyptian:
3d "	♏☾†.·.	Phœnician:
4th "	⊙†&♀♋.·.	Hebrew:
5th "	⊙♊☿♒⊙♀.·. . .	Hebrew:
6th "	⊙♑♋.·.	Indian:
7th "	⊙♎♎♑‡.·.	Assyrian:
8th "	♎⊙♒.·.	Assyrian:
9th "	♄⊙*.·.	Assyrian.

These are styled the covering words: because they cover and conceal from the Profane the True Name of God, known to the first men, and revealed by God to Moses.

I invest you with the apron of this Degree. Its crimson colour denotes the zeal and devotedness of a Royal Arch Mason. Upon it you see the Triangle, emblem of the Deity, or Infinite Wisdom, Infinite Power and Infinite Harmony, surrounded by rays of glory, and with the Ineffable Name in the centre.

I invest you also with the purple collar and the jewel, of this Degree. Upon the face of the jewel you see a representation of the first three recipients of this degree, two of them lowering the third into the subterranean vault. Around this device you see the initials of the following words: *Regnante Salomone Rege Sapientissimo, Thesaurum Pretiosissimum Sub Ruinis Invenerunt Adonhiram, Joabert Et Stolkin.* . . *Anno Enochi, 2995.* * . . On the reverse side you again behold the luminous triangle and the Ineffable Name. Let them ever remind you that the good Mason reveres and adores the Gr∴ Architect of the Universe, and endeavours, by pursuing the path of Honour and Duty, to perform well and faithfully the part assigned him in this world. Go now to the Gr∴ Inspector, and listen to the Legend and History of this Degree.

LEGEND AND HISTORY.

My Brethren, this is the Legend and History of this Degree, as it has come to us, partly in the Jewish writings, and partly by Masonic tradition.

Enoch, the son of Jared, was the sixth in descent from Adam, the father of the human race. Filled with the fear and love of God, while the world grew wicked around him, he adored and revered Him, and obeyed His laws, and strove to lead men in the way of Honour and Duty. He dreamed that the Deity appeared to him in visible shape, and said to him, "Enoch, thou hast longed to know my True Name. Arise, and follow me, and thou shalt learn it." Then it seemed to Enoch that he was taken up, and in an instant transported to a mountain, whose summit was hid among the clouds, and seemed to reach the stars, and there he saw upon the clouds, in letters of brilliant light, the awful and mysterious name יהוה; whose pronunciation was then whispered in his ear, and he prohibited from uttering it to any man. Instantly he seemed to be transported from the mountain, and to descend perpendicularly into the earth, passing through nine subterranean apartments, one below the other, and each roofed with arches; in the ninth and lowest of which he saw, upon a triangular plate of gold, surrounded by brilliant rays of light, the same Ineffable Name which he had seen upon the mountain; and thereupon he awoke.

Enoch, accepting his dream as an inspiration, journeyed in search of the mountain which he had seen in his dream, until, weary of the search, he stopped in the land of Canaan, then already populous with the descendants of Adam; and there employing workmen, and with the help of his son Methuselah, he excavated nine apartments in the earth, one above the other, and each roofed with arches, as he had seen them in his dream, the lowest being hewn out of the solid rock. In the crown of each arch he left a narrow aperture, closed with a square stone, and over the upper one he built a modest temple, roofless, and of huge unhewn stones, to the Gr∴ Architect of the Universe. Upon a triangular plate of gold, inlaid with many precious gems, he engraved the Ineffable Name of God, and sank the plate into one face of a cube of agate, which he then placed upon a pedestal of white alabaster, in the lowest of the nine apartments. The pedestal was triangular and hollow, and into it, from a crevice in the rock, flowed a stream of inflammable air, that burned continually with a brilliant light, until after it was discovered in the reign of Solomon.

None knew of his deposite of this precious treasure; and that it might remain undiscovered, and survive the flood which, it was made known to him, would soon overwhelm all the known world in one vast sea of ruin, he covered the aperture and the stone that closed it, and the great ring of iron, used to raise the stone, with the granite pavement of his primitive temple.

Then, fearing that all knowledge of the arts and sciences would be lost in the universal flood, he built two great columns upon a high hill, one of brass, to resist water, and one of granite to resist fire. Upon the

---

* [In the reign of Solomon, wisest of Kings, Adonhiram, Joabert and Stolkin found under the ruins a most precious treasure].

granite column he engraved, in the hieroglyphics which Misraim afterwards carried into Egypt, a description of the subterranean apartments, and of the treasure there deposited: and on that of brass, the rudiments of all the arts and sciences then known, and the great truths familiar to the antediluvian Masons.

The granite column was overturned and swept away, and worn to a shapeless mass by the great Deluge, and the characters upon it wholly obliterated; but that of brass, by God's Providence, stood firm, and was afterwards found by Noah, who sought in vain for that of granite; the purport of the inscription upon which he knew from Methuselah his grandfather, but not the place of the Temple or the subterranean apartments, to which that inscription would, he knew, have guided him.

Thenceforward the true name of God remained unknown, until He said unto Moses, in Egypt, when He ordered him to go unto Pharaoh, and cause him to send forth the children of Israel out of Egypt, "*I am that which I was and shall be. I am the God of thy Fathers, the God of Abraham, of Isaac and of Jacob. Thus shalt thou say to the children of Israel, He who is hath sent me unto you. I am the Lord that appeared to Abraham, to Isaac and to Jacob, by my name Al-Shedi; but my name* יהוה *I did not show them.*"

That Ineffable Name, meaning The Eternal, Self-Existent Being, Independent, Infinite, without Beginning, End or Change, the Source of all other Beings, Moses engraved upon a plate of gold, and placed it in the ark of the covenant, where it remained for many years, during the whole time of Joshua, and unto the time of the Judges who succeeded him. Forbidden to make known its true pronunciation to the people, he communicated it to Aaron and to Joshua only; and it was afterwards made known to the Chief Priests alone. The Word being composed of consonants only, so that its true pronunciation could only be communicated orally, it was wholly lost in the revolutions and disasters that ensued after the death of Joshua and his immediate successors.

But the Word still remained in the ark, engraved on the plate of gold; and in the time of Othniel, the son of Cenez, the younger brother of Caleb, in a battle against Chusan-Rasathaim, King of Syria, those who bore the ark were slain by an ambush in a forest, and the ark fell upon the ground. The enemy, attacked and defeated in their turn, were driven from the place before they had time to plunder it; and after the battle, the men of Israel, searching for it, were led to it by the roaring of a Lion, which, couching by it, had guarded it, holding the golden key in his mouth. Upon the approach of the High Priest and Levites, he laid down the key, and withdrew in peace, allowing them to take away the ark; taught by the Deity himself that the Israelites were his chosen people, entitled to the custody of that which contained his Sacred Name. Hence, upon the golden key worn by our Gr∴ Treasurer, you see the initials of these words: *In Ore Leonis, Verbum Inveni: In the Lion's mouth I found the Word.*

When the Philistines took the ark, in the time of Samuel, and Ophni and Phineas, the sons of Eli, were slain defending it, those who took it melted down the plate of gold, and made of it an image of Dagon: and thenceforward no man saw that Ineffable Name, until the reign of Solomon, King of Israel.

The Jews, as a nation, did not believe in the existence of one sole God, until a late period in their history. Their early and popular ideas of the Deity were eminently coarse, low and unworthy. While Moses was receiving the law upon Mount Sinai, they forced Aaron to mould or cast an image of the Egyptain God Apis, and fell down and worshipped and adored it. They were ever ready to return to the worship of the Gods of Egypt; and soon after the death of Joshua they became devout worshippers of Bel, Chemosh and Astarte, and the multitude of other Gods adored by the Moabites, the Ammonites, the Syrians and the Phœnicians.

Among them, as among all other nations, the conceptions of God formed by individuals varied according to their intellectual and spiritual capacities; poor and imperfect, and investing God with the commonest attributes of humanity, among the ignorant and coarse; but pure and lofty, among the virtuous and richly gifted. These conceptions gradually improved and became purified and ennobled, as the Hebrews advanced in civilization; being lowest in the Historical Books, amended in the Prophetic writings, and reaching their highest elevation among the Poets. Terah, the father of Abraham and the father of Nachor served other Gods. The Elohim, or subordinate Deities, are represented in the commencement of the Book of Genesis, as creating the universe. Laban, a near relative of Abraham, and whose sister was selected as a wife for Isaac, pursued Jacob for having stolen his Gods; and Jacob collected the strange Gods worshipped by his household, and hid them under an oak.

In the mind of Moses, an intellectual and highly educated man, versed in all the learning of the Egyptians, the conceptions of the God of Israel reached a sublime simplicity of expression ; and yet he admitted the existence of other Gods, not asserting that He was the sole God ; but only that He was superior to all others.

Among the People, the God of the wise and the God of the ignorant, the God of the Priests and the God of the Prophets, were the embodiments of two very different classes of ideas. The God of Exodus and Numbers is represented as partial, unstable, revengeful and deceitful ; while the ideas of Deity contained in the book of Job, the nobler Psalms, in Ezekiel and Daniel, are magnificent, simple and sublime. The idea of the One Living and True God was a plant of slow and gradual growth in the Hebrew mind ; and if Moses, the Patriarchs or the Priests had a true and adequate knowledge of Him and His attributes, they utterly failed to communicate that knowledge to the People at large. It was not until a late day in their history, that the Jewish writers were heard to say, "Will God in very deed dwell on the earth? Behold, the Heaven and the Heaven of Heavens cannot contain Thee : how much less this House that I have builded? Whither shall I go from Thy Spirit? or whither shall I flee from Thy presence? . . . Oh יהוה, my God, thou art very great ; thou art clothed with honour and majesty : who coverest thyself with light as with a garment ; who stretchest out the Heavens like a curtain ; who layeth the beams of his chambers in the waters ; who maketh the clouds his chariot ; who walketh upon the wings of the wind. . . . I know that whatsoever God doeth, it shall be forever : nothing can be put to it, nor any thing taken from it . . . The strength of Israel will not lie nor repent : for He is not a man that He should repent . . . For the word of the Lord is right ; and all his works are done in Truth. He loveth righteousness and judgment. Lying lips are an abomination to the Lord ; but they that deal truly are his delight. Thou desirest not sacrifice, else would I give it : thou delightest not in burnt offering. He hath shewed thee, O man, what is good : and what doth יהוה require of thee, but to do justly, to love mercy, and to walk humbly with thy God."

There is therefore a deeper meaning than appears upon the surface, in the attempts of the ancient Israelites and of the initiates of Masonry, to ascertain the True name of the Deity and its pronunciation. It is an allegory, in which are represented the people's ignorance of the true nature and attributes of God, their proneness to worship other Deities, their low and erroneous notions of the Grand Architect of the Universe, of which all partook except a few favored persons ; for even Solomon built altars and sacrificed to Chemosh and Astarte ; and the people were for many ages idolaters at heart. The True Nature of God was unknown to them, like His Name ; and with the knowledge of the true pronunciation of that Name, they lost the knowledge of the Deity Himself, and worshipped the false gods of the surrounding nations.

David intended to build a Temple to God, and prepared much of the material ; but bequeathed the enterprise to Solomon his son. Solomon selected for its site a level plain near Jerusalem, and his workmen commenced to excavate the foundations ; but finding the overthrown columns of the Cyclopean Temple of Enoch, and supposing it to have been a place of worship erected to the false Gods of the Canaanites, the King returned to the place upon Mount Moriah, which had before-time been the threshing floor of Ornan or Areunah the Jebusite, and which David had purchased from him, and there had erected an altar to the Lord, while the Ark still remained at the high place of Gabaon.

There Solomon built the Temple. Under it he caused to be excavated a Secret Vault, the approach to which was through eight other vaults or apartments in succession, all under ground, and to which a long and narrow passage led from under the King's Palace. In the ninth apartment was placed a great column of white marble, called the Pillar of Beauty, on which it was intended to place the Ark ; and in this apartment he held his private conferences with King Hiram of Tyre and Hiram Abi ; they only, beside himself, knowing the way by which it was approached.

The Sacred Name, lost to the Jewish People, was retained in the Ancient Mysteries, in which Joseph and Moses had been initiated ; and it thus came to Samuel, and from him to David and to Solomon. But after the Ark was taken by the Philistines, it was forbidden to the Initiates of the Mysteries again to write the Word. It was made known by Solomon to Hiram King of Tyre and Hiram Abi ; and they agreed that it should never be communicated by them to any one, unless all three were present. After the death of Hiram Abi, the two Kings refrained from visiting the secret vault, in which everything so vividly reminded them of the

Brother and Companion they had lost; and resolved not again to do so, until they should have selected one to fill his place.

While they were yet undetermined whom to choose, Solomon proposed to erect a public edifice for the administration of justice, upon the site of the ancient Temple of Enoch; and to that end directed that the fallen columns and the rubbish should be removed. Adonhiram the Chief Architect, with Joabert and Stolkin, two of the Intendants of the Building, were directed to go thither, and survey the ground and lay off the foundations for the proposed building. In doing so, they removed some of the shattered fragments of the columns and of the old broken pavement, and discovered a large ring, attached to a square slab of granite, raising which by their united strength, an aperture was disclosed, like a deep well sunk in the earth. Joabert offered to explore it, and furnishing himself with a torch, was lowered into the opening by his Companion. After descending for some distance he came to a floor, and discovered in the centre of it a slab of granite with an iron ring, like that above, and raising the slab he saw another aperture, through which he descended to another floor, and thence in like manner to another. Weary by his long suspension, and his torch nearly extinguished, he made known to his Companions, by shaking the rope, that he desired to be drawn up. Arriving at the surface, he informed them of his discoveries, and his belief that there were other apartments still below.

Stolkin then offered to descend; and reaching the third floor, discovered a similar stone and ring, and afterwards two others in succession, and reaching the sixth floor, wearied with the exertion, and his torch nearly failing, he gave the signal to ascend, and was drawn up, without discovering that there were still other apartments below the sixth.

Adonhiram then descended, and passing through three more openings, reached the ninth apartment. As he reached it, his companions dislodged some rubbish above, which falling upon him bruised him and extinguished his torch; and he then discovered in the centre of the apartment a luminous triangular pedestal of white alabaster, hollow, and lighted by an undying fire within; and upon which sat a cube of agate, into one face of which was sunk a plate of gold, thickly encrusted with precious gems that glittered in the light; and enamelled on the plate the word יהוה, the Ineffable name of Deity; as the same had been placed there by Enoch the Patriarch.

Since the time of Samuel that word had not been written in the copies of the law of Moses; but wherever it occurred, the word ADONAI had been substituted; so that Adonhiram knew not the meaning of the word; but struck with admiration at the sight; astounded at the perpetual light, fed by no human hand for many centuries, and which seemed to him to indicate the immediate presence of the Deity; and penetrated with gratitude to God for allowing him to make so wonderful a discovery, he fell upon one knee, and raising his hands uttered his thanks to that God whom yet he knew only by his name ADONAI, or AL-SHEDI; by which only he was known to the Patriarchs; and then, without rising, placed his right hand behind him, and seizing the rope, gave his companions the signal, and was drawn by them to the surface.

After informing his companions of that which he had seen and discovered, Adonhiram proposed that they should procure ladders of rope, and descend together into the vault, on the ensuing day. To this they gladly assented; and making known to no one what they had discovered, they procured ladders, and returning the next morning, descended together to the ninth apartment. At the sight of the luminous pedestal and Cube of Agate, Joabert and Stolkin, affected like Adonhiram with astonishment, awe, and gratitude, fell, as he also did again, upon their knees, and raising their hands to Heaven, thanked God for all his mercies, and especially for allowing them to discover these marvels.

Adonhiram and Stolkin first arose, and seeing Joabert, who was a Phœnician, and originally a Stone Mason, from the city of Gebal, still upon his knees, they placed their hands under his arms, and assisted him to rise; Adonhiram saying to him, in consequence of their great friendship, *Hamalek Kheblim;* meaning "Chief of the United Brotherhood." Then examining the Cube of Agate, and not knowing the meaning of the Word upon it, they resolved to carry it to King Solomon and Hiram King of Tyre, who had then consummated their new and closer alliance; thinking that they might know the meaning of the mysterious Word.

Ascending therefore, with the Cube of Agate, they closed the entrance carefully and repaired to the Palace, where they found the two Kings conferring together. King Solomon, immediately on beholding the

Cube and the inscription upon it, exclaimed to the King of Tyre, " My Brother, behold the True and Ineffable Name of the Eternal, Self-Existent and Almighty God, the Grand Architect of the Universe ;" and he and King Hiram both fell upon their knees, raised their hands to Heaven, and thanked God for all his mercies, and especially for again allowing them to see his Ineffable Name.

Then rising, King Solomon inquired of the three Brethren whence came the marvellous stone; and they thereupon recounted to him their whole adventure, even to the words spoken by Adonhiram, upon raising Joabert from his knees. Then Solomon, reflecting for a time, said, " My Brother of Tyre, I remember well " to have heard from my father David a tradition that the Patriarch Enoch, inspired by a dream, in which " he saw this Sacred Name, and knowing that the world was shortly to be overwhelmed by a flood, made " such a vault as this that hath been discovered, and there deposited, upon a plate of gold, set in a great " Agate, the Ineffable Name of God; and afterwards engraved upon a granite column, which the flood " swept away and wore to a shapeless mass, directions in the Sacred Characters how to discover the place " in which the Ineffable Name was so deposited. None were ever enabled to discover it; but it hath now " most certainly been found, and we may now make the Word known to those whose eminent merits shall " entitle them to receive it, for it is the True Word of a Mason and the True Name of the Great Archi- " tect of the Universe, known to thee and me, and to our deceased Brother Hiram Abi."

Then King Solomon said to the three Brethren ; " My brethren, the Gr.·. Architect of the Universe has " bestowed upon you a signal mark of his favour, by selecting you to be the discoverers of the precious " treasures of Masonry. I rejoice with you upon this your great good fortune. Wear henceforth the title of " Masons of the Ninth or Royal Arch, as a high honour and order of Nobility. I make it a degree in Masonry ; " into which my Brother Hiram and myself will seek to be admitted ; and which shall hereafter be conferred " only at your pleasure, and as a high mark of distinction for eminent services rendered to the State or to " Masonry. I have fixed upon a place in which to deposite this sacred treasure ; and when it is so deposited, " you shall be present, and shall then learn the pronunciation of this Great and Ineffable Word; and the " profound mysteries which it involves."

King Solomon then fixed upon the Signs, Token, and Pass-word of the degree; the signs imitating the actions of the three brethren upon first seeing the luminous Pedestal and Cube; the token representing the mode in which Adonhiram and Stolkin raised Joabert; and the pass-word being the expression of affection and friendship addressed by Adonhiram to him in doing so. And he then said: " The Sacred Word of this Degree " shall be the Great Ineffable Name: but in this degree it shall never be pronounced. I had received it orally " from my father David, and made it known to my brother Hiram the King and my brother Hiram Abi. We " agreed never to communicate it unless when we were all present. The Ill.·. Hiram Abi died rather than " divulge it. Long disused, and the name ADONAI substituted for it in the Sacred Books, its true characters " once again greet our eyes, and we shall perhaps be authorized to communicate it to others. In this Degree " it shall be communicated only by its letters, and that only in the presence of three Brethren: and I so " communicate it to you."

Then he repeated to them the letters of which the word is composed, as you have already received them: and he also made known to them the nine names of Deity in different languages, which are the covering words of this degree, and to be used instead of the Ineffable Name.

Afterwards the two Kings, with Adonhiram, Joabert and Stolkin, deposited the cube of agate in the place prepared for its reception ; and the degree of Grand, Elect, Perfect and Sublime Mason was then created and established, and received by them as the first five members of the degree of Perfection : and Adonhiram, Joabert and Stolkin then received the true pronunciation and explanation of the Sacred Name, and learned the true nature and attributes of the Deity ; to whom, until that time, they had ascribed human attributes exaggerated, and a nature assimilated to that of man.

After the Temple had been completed and dedicated, King Solomon selected the Twelve Princes Ameth, the nine most eminent Ill.·. Elus of Fifteen, and Zerbal, who succeeded Adonhiram as Grand Master Architect; all of them Masons eminently distinguished by their talents and their virtues ; and conferred upon them first the degree of Royal Arch, and then that of Perfection, and assigned them special duties. There were thus 27 Grand, Elect, Perfect and Sublime Masons.

But there were also 3568 Ancient Masons, who had aided in building the Temple, and who envied the 25 Brothers who had been so associated with the two Kings. Jealous of the superior honour shown them, these envious Masons sent a deputation to King Solomon, to lay their complaints before him. He heard them patiently to the end, and mildly answered, that the 25 Brothers of whom they were jealous had merited the preference shown them, by their extraordinary zeal and eminent services, for which they had deserved to be especially loved and honoured by him; and he said: "Your time is not yet come. Continue to perform your "duties as Masons, and wait patiently and contentedly; and in due time, if you are found deserving, you will "receive the same reward."

One of the Deputation, not satisfied with this mild and gentle answer, but giving way to his anger, insolently replied, "We are Master Masons, and do not need to receive the higher degrees created for the "King's favourites. We know how the Word has been changed: and we will travel as Masters, and as such "earn and receive our wages." The King, astonished at this intemperate response, but not moved to anger, mildly answered: "Those for whom the sublime degree of Perfection was first created, had deserved it by "descending into the bowels of the earth, and bringing thence a treasure inestimable to Masons, and which "alone was needed to complete the Temple of the living God. Go in peace. Do as those Brothers did. Let "your services in the cause of Masonry be as valuable, and your zeal and devotedness as great as theirs; and "I, in my justice, will reward you as amply as you shall deserve."

The Deputies, returning, reported to those who sent them the responses of the King. Most of the Masons were satisfied, and acknowledged his justice, and strove by the strict performance of their duty to merit his favour, and to attain to the degree of Perfection. But a small number, vain, jealous, and haughty men, resolved to explore the ruins, where they understood the treasure had been found, in the hope of discovering other treasures; and intending, if they found any, to escape with them into foreign countries.

Accordingly, some twenty or more in number, they went to the ruins, and at daybreak readily discovered an iron ring, and near it the ladders by which the three discoverers had descended. They raised the stone, while some of their companions who in vain endeavoured to dissuade them from their purpose remained at a distance watching them, and then they, one after the other, descended into the vault. A short time only elapsed, when those who followed them and remained at a distance, saw a flame of fire leap into the air from the aperture, and the roar of an explosion followed, that shook the earth all around, and was heard even in the city, and all the arches were shattered and fell in, crushing and burying those who had descended; and thus their haughty insolence received its due reward. It was supposed that, finding in the ninth vault the luminous pedestal, and supposing it to contain valuable treasures, they had broken it to pieces, and that the flame had flashed out and filled the vault and thus produced the explosion. Nothing remained of the nine apartments, except a chasm in the earth nearly filled with rubbish, which was afterwards filled up by order of King Solomon, and the proposed building erected over it.

Such is the Legend and History of this Degree. Whether it is historically true, or but an allegory, containing in itself a deeper truth and a profounder meaning, we do not undertake to decide; nor is it at all important we should do so. We know that the Hebrews were forbidden to pronounce the sacred name; that wherever it occurred, they read in place of it the word ADONAI; and that under it, when the Masoretic points, which represented the vowels, came to be used, they placed those which belonged to the latter word. The possession of the true pronunciation was held to confer on him who had it, extraordinary and supernatural powers; and the word itself, worn upon the person, was regarded as an amulet, a protection against personal danger, sickness, and evil spirits. We know that all this was a mere vain superstition, natural to a rude and uncivilized people; necessarily disappearing as the intellect of man became enlightened; and wholly unworthy of a Mason. It was common to all the ancient nations. The sacred word Honover was supposed by the ancient Persians to be pregnant with a mysterious power: and they taught that by its utterance the universe was created. Among the Hindoos it was forbidden to pronounce the word Aum or Oum, the Sacred name of the Supreme Deity. These superstitious notions in regard to the efficacy of The Word, and the prohibition against pronouncing it, could, being errors, have formed no part of the pure primitive religion, nor of the esoteric doctrines taught by Moses, and the full knowledge of which was confined to the Priests. They grew up in the minds of the people, like other errors and fables, not only among the Jews, but among all other ancient nations, out of original truths misunderstood; most of them being at the beginning allegories intended as vehicles of truth, and becoming errors by being literally accepted.

It is true that, before the Masoretic points were used, the pronunciation of a word in the Hebrew language could not be known from the characters in which it was written. It was therefore easy for that of the Name of the Deity to be forgotten and lost. It is certain its true pronunciation is not at all represented by the word JEHOVAH; and therefore that that is not the true name of Deity, nor the Ineffable Word. The pronunciation of the Word, and the Word itself would be lost when the knowledge of the true nature and attributes of God faded out of the minds of the Jewish people, and they adopted as their gods, Bel, Chemosh, Amun, Astarte, and other Deities worshipped by the different nations by which they were successively subjugated. When they lost that knowledge, and then only, would they or could they forget the name of God. So long as they worshipped the True God, they would undoubtedly recollect His Name.

Among all the ancient nations, those who were enlightened and intelligent and educated, had one faith and one idea of the Deity; while the common People had another. To this rule the Hebrews were no exception. JEHOVAH, to the mass of the People, was like the Gods of the nations round-about, except that He was the *peculiar* God, first of the family of Abraham, of that of Isaac and of that of Jacob, and afterwards the *national* God; and, as they believed, *more powerful* than the other Gods of the same nature worshipped by their neighbours.

Jethro, the father-in-law of Moses, said to him [18 Exod. 11]: "Now I know that יהוה is greater than all the Elohim; for in the very matter wherein they prided themselves, He proved Himself their superior."

So it is said [22 Exod. 28], "Thou shalt not revile the Elohim; nor curse the Ruler of thy People." So [97 Psalms, 7] "Worship Him, all ye Elohim." And the Witch of Endor said to Saul, "I saw Elohim ascending out of the Earth."

The Deity of the early Jews talked to Adam and Eve in the garden; He conversed with Cain; He sat with Abraham in his tent; that Patriarch required a visible token, before he would believe in His positive promise; He allowed Himself to be expostulated with, and his determination in regard to Sodom changed, by Abraham; He showed to Moses his person, though not his face; He is represented as dictating the minutest police regulations to the Israelites; He required and delighted in sacrifices and burnt offerings; He was angry, jealous, and revengeful, as well as wavering and irresolute; He allowed Moses to reason Him out of His fixed resolution to destroy the Israelites entirely: He commanded the performance of the most horrid and shocking acts of cruelty and barbarity; the murder of men and women, and the violation of innocent virgins. Such were the popular notions of the Deity; and no more unworthy and degraded ideas of God's nature were entertained by any people of antiquity. Either the priests took little trouble to correct these notions; or else the popular interest was not sufficiently enlarged to enable them to entertain any loftier conceptions of the Almighty.

But such were not the ideas entertained by the intellectual and enlightened few among the Hebrews. It is certain that they possessed a knowledge of the true character, nature and attributes of God; as did the same class of men among the Egyptians and Phœnicians; as did Zoroaster and Confucius, and Socrates and Plato. But their doctrines on this subject were esoteric: they did not communicate them to the people at large, but only to a favoured few; as they were communicated in Egypt, Phœnicia, Greece and Samothrace in the Greater Mysteries, to the Initiates. The communication of this knowledge constituted Masonry among the Jews. That was *the Lost Word*, which was made known to the Grand, Elect, Perfect and Sublime Masons. It would be folly to pretend that the *forms* of Masonry were the same then as now. Probably the very name of the order is a much later creation. The present titles, and the names of the degrees now in use were not then known. But, by whatever name it *was* then known, Masonry existed then as it exists now, the same in spirit and at heart.

The Supreme, Self-Existent, Eternal, All-Wise, All-Powerful, Infinitely Good, Beneficent and Merciful Creator of the universe, was the same, by whatever name he was called, to the intellectual and enlightened men of all nations. To communicate true and correct ideas in regard to Him, was the object of the Mysteries. There Hiram the King of Tyre and Hiram Abi obtained their knowledge of Him and His nature. There it was taught to Moses and Pythagoras.

17

Hence many Masons regard the Legend of this degree as but an allegory, representing the perpetuation of the knowledge of the True God by means of the Mysteries. By the subterranean vault they understand the place of initiation, which in the ancient ceremonies was generally underground. The Temple itself presented a symbolic image of the universe; and resembled in its arrangements all the Temples of such of the ancient nations as practised the mysteries. The system of numbers was intimately connected with their religions and worship, and has come down to us in Masonry; though the esoteric meaning with which the numbers used by us are pregnant, is scarcely known to most of those who use them. Those numbers were especially employed, that had a reference to the Deity, represented His attributes, or figured in the frame-work of the world, in time and space, and formed more or less the basis of that frame-work. These numbers were universally regarded as sacred, being the expression of Order and Intelligence, the utterances of Divinity Himself.

The Holy of Holies of the Temple formed a cube. It corresponded with the number four, by which the ancients represented nature, it being the number of substance or corporeal forms, and of the elements, the cardinal points and seasons. The number three represented everywhere the Supreme Being. And hence the name of Deity, written upon the triangular plate, and that sunken into the cube of agate, taught the ancient Mason, and teaches us, that the true knowledge of God, His nature, essence and attributes, is written by Him upon the leaves of the great book of universal nature, and may be read there by all who are endowed with the requisite amount of intellect and intelligence. *This knowledge of God, so written there, and of which Masonry in all ages has been the interpreter, is the* MASTER MASON'S WORD.

Within the Temple, all the arrangements were mystically and symbolically connected with the same system. The vault or ceiling, starred like the firmament, was supported by twelve columns, representing the twelve months of the year. The border that ran around the columns represented the zodiac, and one of the twelve celestial signs was appropriated to each column. The brazen sea was supported by twelve oxen, three looking to each cardinal point of the compass.

And so in our day every Masonic Lodge represents the Universe. Each extends, we are told, from the rising to the setting sun, from the South to the North, from the surface of the Earth to the Heavens, and from the same to the centre of the globe. In it are represented the sun, moon and stars: three great torches in the East, West and South, forming a triangle, give it light, and like the Delta or Triangle suspended in the East, and enclosing the Ineffable Name, indicate, by the mathematical equality of the angles and sides, the beautiful and harmonious proportions which govern in the aggregate and details of the Universe; while those sides and angles represent, by their number, three, the Trinity of Power, Wisdom and Harmony, which presided at the building of this marvellous work. These three great lights also represent the great mystery of the three principles, of creation, dissolution or destruction, and reproduction or regeneration, consecrated by all creeds in their numerous Trinities.

The luminous pedestal, lighted by the perpetual and undying flame within, is a symbol of that light of Reason, given by God to man, by which he is enabled to read in the book of nature the record and revelation of the attributes and essence of the Deity:

The three Masters, Adonhiram, Joabert and Stolkin, are types of the true Mason, who seeks for knowledge from pure motives, and that he may be the better enabled to serve and benefit his fellow-men; while the discontented and presumptuous Masters who were buried in the ruins of the arches, represent those who strive to acquire it for unholy purposes, to subjugate their fellows, and to gratify their pride, their vanity or their ambition.

The Lion that guarded the Ark and held in his mouth the key wherewith to open it, figuratively represents Solomon, the Lion of the Tribe of Judah, who preserved and communicated the key to the true knowledge of God, of his laws, and of the profound mysteries of the moral and physical universe.

The column of brass, erected by Enoch, and which survived the flood, allegorically represents the Mysteries and Masonry; from the earliest times the custodians and depositaries of the great moral and religious truths unknown to the world at large, and handed down from age to age by an unbroken current of tradition, embodied in symbols, emblems and allegories.

Thus, my Brother, do we interpret the Legend of this Degree. How it may have been founded is, after all, of little importance. To us its value consists in the lessons which it inculcates, and the duties which it prescribes to those who receive it and assume its obligations.

Masonry teaches its initiates that the pursuits and occupations of this life, its activity, care and ingenuity, the predestined developments of the Nature given us by God, tend to promote His great design in making the world; and are not at war with the great purpose of life. It teaches, that everything is beautiful in its time, in its place, in its appointed office; that every thing which man is put to do, if rightly and faithfully done, naturally helps to work out his salvation; that if he obeys the genuine principles of his calling, he will be a good man; and that it is only by neglect and non-performance of the tasks set for him by Heaven, by wandering into idle dissipation, or by violating their beneficent and lofty spirit, that he becomes a bad man. The appointed action of life is the great training of Providence; and if man yields himself to it, he will need neither churches nor ordinances, except for the *expression* of his religious homage and gratitude.

For there is a religion of toil. It is not all drudgery, a mere stretching of the limbs and straining of the sinews to tasks. It has a meaning and an intent. A living heart pours life-blood into the toiling arm; and warm affections inspire and mingle with man's labours. They are the *home* affections. Labour toils a-field, or plies its task in cities, or urges the keels of commerce over wide oceans; but home is its centre; and thither it ever goes with its earnings, with the means of support and comfort for others; offerings sacred to the thought of every true man, as a sacrifice at a golden shrine. Many faults there are amidst the toils of life; many harsh and hasty words are uttered; but still the toils go on, weary and hard and exasperating as they often are. For in that home is age or sickness, or helpless infancy, or gentle childhood, or feeble woman, that must not want. If man had no other than mere selfish impulses, the scene of labour which we behold around us would not exist.

The advocate who fairly and honestly presents his case, with a feeling of true self-respect, honour and conscience, to help the tribunal on towards the right conclusion, with a feeling that God's justice reigns there, is acting a religious part, leading that day a religious life; or else right and justice are no part of religion. Whether, during all that day, he has once appealed, in form or in terms, to his conscience, or not; whether he has once spoken of religion and God, or not; if there has been the inward purpose, the conscious intent and desire, that sacred justice should triumph, he has that day led a good and religious life, and made a most essential contribution to that religion of life and of society, the cause of equity between man and man, and of truth and right action in the world.

Books, to be of religious tendency in the Masonic sense, need not be books of sermons, of pious exercises, or of prayers. Whatever inculcates pure, noble and patriotic sentiments, or touches the heart with the beauty of virtue, and the excellence of an upright life, accords with the religion of Masonry, and is the Gospel of literature and art. That Gospel is preached from many a wall and book, from many a poem and fiction, and Review and Newspaper; and it is a painful error and miserable narrowness, not to recognize these wide-spread agencies of Heaven's providing; not to see and welcome these many-handed coadjutors, to the great and good cause.

There is also a religion of society. In business, there is much more than sale, exchange, price, payment: for there is the sacred faith of man in man. When we repose perfect confidence in the integrity of another; when we feel that he will not swerve from the right, frank, straight-forward, conscientious course, for any temptation; his integrity and conscientiousness are the image of God to us; and when we believe in *it*, it is as great and generous an act, as when we believe in the rectitude of the Deity.

In gay assemblies for amusement, the good affections of life gush and mingle. If *they* did not go up to these gathering-places, they would be as dreary and repulsive as the caves and dens of outlaws and robbers. When friends meet, and hands are warmly pressed, and the eye kindles and the countenance is suffused with gladness, there is a religion between their hearts; and each loves and worships the True and Good that is in the other. It is not policy that spreads such a charm around that meeting, but the halo of bright and beautiful affection.

The same splendour of kindly liking, and affectionate regard, shines like the soft over-arching sky, over all the world; over all places where men meet, and walk or toil together; not over lovers' bowers and marriage-altars alone, not over the homes of purity and tenderness alone; but over all tilled fields and busy workshops, and dusty highways, and paved streets. There is not a worn stone upon the sidewalks, but has been the altar of such offerings of mutual kindness: nor a wooden pillar or iron railing against which hearts beating with affection have not leaned. How many soever other elements there are in the stream of life, that is flowing through these channels, *that* is surely here and every where: honest, heartfelt, disinterested, inexpressible affection.

So every Masonic Lodge is a Temple of Religion; its officers, ministers of religion; its teachings, instruction in religion. For here we inculcate charity, hope and faith, disinterestedness, affection, toleration, patriotism, devotedness, and all the virtues. Here we meet as brothers, and learn to know and love each other. Here we greet each other with joy, are lenient to each other's faults, regardful of each other's feelings, ready to aid each other's wants. And that is the true religion revealed to the Ancient Patriarchs; which Masonry taught many centuries ago; and which it *will* teach as long as Time endures. If unworthy passions and selfish, bitter or revengeful feelings, contempt, dislike, hatred, enter here, they are intruders, and most unwelcome:—strangers, and not guests.

Certainly there are many evils and bad passions, and much hate and contempt and unkindness every where in the world. We can not refuse to see the evil that is in life. But *all* is not evil. We still see God in the world. There is good amidst the evil. The hand of Mercy leads wealth to the hovels of poverty and sorrow. Truth and simplicity live amid many wiles and sophistries. There are good hearts beneath gay robes, and beneath tattered garments also. Love clasps the hand of love, amid all the envyings and distortions of showy competition; and fidelity, piety, sympathy hold the long night-watch by the bedside of the suffering neighbour, amidst all surrounding poverty and misery. Noble and large-hearted men and women go from city to city to nurse those who are prostrated by the awful pestilence that depopulates; and poor lost women join them in this pious duty, and risk their lives for strangers, with the most unselfish heroism. Masonry still binds together its great brotherhood, and with Odd-Fellowship and other kindred Orders makes men love each other, feeds the hungry, clothes the naked, relieves the destitute, watches with the sick and buries the dead. God bless the kindly office, the pitying thought, the loving heart, wherever they are! and they are every where.

There is an element of good in all men's lawful pursuits and a divine spirit breathing in all their lawful affections. The ground on which they tread is holy ground. There is a natural religion of life, answering, with however many a broken tone, to the religion of nature. There is a beauty and glory in Humanity, in man, answering, with however many a mingling shade, to the loveliness of soft landscapes, and swelling hills, and the wondrous glory of the starry heavens.

Men may be virtuous, self-improving, and religious *in* their employments. Precisely for that, those employments were made. All their social relations, friendship, love, the ties of family, were made to be holy. They may be religious, not by a kind of protest and resistance against their several vocations; but by conformity to their true spirit. Those vocations do not *exclude* religion; but *demand* it, for their own perfection. They may be religious labourers, whether in field or factory; religious physicians, lawyers, sculptors, poets, painters, and musicians. They may be religious in all the toils and in all the amusements of life. Their life may be a religion; the broad earth its altar; its incense the very breath of life; its fires ever kindled by the brightness of Heaven.

Bound up with our poor, frail life, is the mighty thought that spurns the narrow span of all visible existence. Ever the soul reaches outward, and asks for freedom. It looks forth from the narrow and grated windows of sense, upon the wide immeasurable creation; it knows that around it and beyond it lie outstretched the infinite and everlasting paths.

Everything within us and without us is entitled to stir our minds to admiration and wonder. We are a mystery encompassed with mysteries. The connection of mind with matter is a mystery; that wonderful telegraphic communication between the brain and every part of the body. How does the nerve in the finger know of the will that moves it? What is that will; and how does its commanding act originate? It is all mystery. Within this folding veil of flesh, within these dark channels, every instant's action is a history of miracles. Every familiar step is more than a story in a land of enchantment. If a marble statue were suddenly endowed with our self-moving power, it would be intrinsically no more wonderful than is the action of every being around us.

The infinite variety of the human countenance is a wonder; and every familiar face around us, bears mysteries and marvels in every look. What is it that holds together, and secures on its firm foundation the very house we dwell in ? Joint to joint, beam to beam, every post to its socket, is swathed and fastened by the same mighty bands that hold millions of worlds in their orbits. All active motion and all seeming rest are determined by unnumbered, nicely balanced, immeasurable influences and attractions. Universal harmony springs from infinite complication. The momentum of every step we take in our dwelling, contributes its part to the order of the Universe.

We live in a system of things, and dwell in a palace, whose dome is spread out in the boundless skies, whose lights are hung in the wide arches of Heaven, whose foundations are longer than the earth and broader than the sea ; and yet we are connected by ties of thought, and even of matter, with its whole boundless extent; and every stamp of our foot has its influence upon the motion of that Universe. We are borne onward among the celestial spheres ; rolling worlds are around us; bright, starry abodes fill all the coasts and skies of Heaven; we are borne on and kept, by powers, silent and unperceived indeed, but real and boundless as the immeasurable universe.

Nor is the small and finite less mysterious than the infinite. The humblest object beneath our eye as completely defies our scrutiny, as the economy of the most distant star. Every blade of grass holds within itself secrets, which no human penetration ever fathomed. Its internal organization, its channels for the vital juices to flow in, its instruments to secrete the nutriment flowing upward from the soil, and gathered from the atmosphere, its whole mechanism, more curious than any ever framed by the ingenuity of man, present us questions which the profoundest philosopher cannot answer. No man can tell what is the principle of Life, without which, though the whole organization remains, the plant dies. None knows what is that wonderful power of secretion. There are inscrutable mysteries wrapped up in the foldings of that humble spire of grass.

You take your pen, and sit down to spread out your account of the insignificance of human life. First pause, and tell us how that pen was formed, with which you would write, and the table on which your paper lies. You can tell neither. The very instruments you use to record your thoughts, startle you into astonishment. Wherever we place our hand, we lay it on the locked bosom of mystery. Step where we will, we tread upon a land of wonder. The furrows of the field, the clods of the valley, the dull, beaten path, the insensible rock, are traced over and in every direction, with this handwriting, more significant and sublime than all the frowning ruins, and all the overthrown or buried cities, that past generations have left upon the earth. It is the handwriting of the Almighty.

The history of the humblest human life is a tale of marvels. There is no dull or unmeaning thing in existence, did we but understand it. There is not one of our employments, or of our states of mind, that is not, if we could but interpret it, as significant, though not as instructive, as Holy Writ. Experience, sensation, feeling, suffering, rejoicing ; a world of meaning and of wonder lies in the modes and changes, and strugglings and soarings of the life in which these are bound up.

There is a vision like that of Eliphaz, stealing upon us, if we would mark it, through the veils of every evening's shadows, or coming in the morning, with the mysterious revival of thought and consciousness; there is a message whispering in the stirred leaves, or starting beneath the clods of the field, in the life that is every where bursting from its bosom. Every thing around us images a spiritual life ; all forms, modes, processes, changes, though we discern them not. A Mason's great business with life is so to read the book of its teaching; to find that life is not the doing of drudgeries, but the hearing of oracles. The old mythology is but a leaf in that book; for it peopled the world with spiritual natures; and science, many-leaved, still spreads before us the same tale of wonder.

We shall be just as happy hereafter, as we are pure and upright, and no more ; just as happy as our character prepares us to be, and no more: our moral, like our mental character is not formed in a moment; it is the habit of our minds ; and it is the result of many thoughts and feelings and efforts, bound together by many natural and strong ties. The great law of Retribution is, that all coming experience is to be affected by every present feeling; every future moment of being must answer for every present moment; one moment, sacrificed to vice, or lost to improvement, is *for ever* sacrificed and lost; an hour's delay to enter the right path, is to put us back so far, in the everlasting pursuit of happiness ; and every sin, even of the best men, is to be thus answered for, if not according to the full measure of its ill-desert, yet according to a rule of unbending rectitude and impartiality.

The law of retribution presses upon every man; whether he thinks of it, or not. It pursues him through all the courses of life, with a step that never falters nor tires, and with an eye that never sleeps nor slumbers. If it were not so, God's government would not be impartial; there would be no discrimination; no moral dominion; no light shed upon the mysteries of Providence.

Whatsoever a man soweth, that, and not something else, shall he reap. That which we are doing, good or evil, grave or gay; that which we do to-day and shall do to-morrow; each thought, each feeling, each action, each event; every passing hour, every breathing moment; all are contributing to form the character, according to which we are to be judged. Every particle of influence that goes to form that aggregate,—our character,—will, in that future scrutiny, be sifted out from the mass; and, particle by particle, with ages perhaps intervening, fall a distinct contribution to the sum of our joys or woes. Thus every idle word and idle hour will give answer in the judgment.

Let us take care, therefore, what we sow. An evil temptation comes upon us; the opportunity of unrighteous gain, or of unhallowed indulgence, either in the sphere of business or of pleasure, of society or solitude. We yield; and plant a seed of bitterness and sorrow. To-morrow it will threaten discovery. Agitated and alarmed, we cover the sin, and bury it deep in falsehood and hypocrisy. In the bosom where it lies concealed, in the fertile soil of kindred vices, that sin dies not, but thrives and grows; and other and still other germs of evil gather around the accursed root; until, from that single seed of corruption, there springs up in the soul all that is horrible in habitual lying, knavery or vice. Loathingly, often, we take each downward step; but a frightful power urges us onward; and the hell of debt, disease, ignominy or remorse gathers its shadows around our steps even on earth; and are yet but the beginnings of sorrows. The evil deed may be done in a single moment; but conscience never dies, memory never sleeps; guilt never can become innocence; and remorse can never whisper peace.

Beware then, thou who art tempted to evil; beware what thou layest up for the future! Beware what thou layest up in the Archives of Eternity! Wrong not thy neighbour; lest the thought of him thou injurest, and who suffers by thy act, be to thee a pang which long years will not deprive of its bitterness. Break not into the house of innocence to rifle it of its treasure; lest, when many years have passed over thee, the moan of its distress may not have died away from thine ear. Build not the desolate throne of ambition in thy heart; nor be busy with devices and circumventings, and selfish schemings; lest desolation and loneliness be on thy path, as it stretches into the long futurity. Live not a negligent and irreligious life; for, bound up with that life is the immutable principle of an endless retribution, and elements of God's creating, which shall never spend their force, but shall continue ever to unfold with the ages of Eternity. Be not deceived! God has formed thy nature, thus to answer to the future. His law can never be abrogated; nor His justice eluded; and forever and ever it will be true, that "*whatsoever a man soweth, that shall he also reap.*"

TO CLOSE.

Th.∴ P.∴ [Rapping 3]: Br.∴ Gr.∴ Inspector, what is the hour?

Gr.∴ Insp.∴ Sunset, Th.∴ Puissant.

Th.∴ P.∴ It is time then to close this Chapter; that by rest we may prepare for the labours of the morrow. Give notice therefore to the Brethren that the labours of this day are at an end, and that this Chapter is about to be closed.

Gr.∴ Insp.∴ [Rapping 3]: Brethren, the labours of this day are at an end, and this Chapter is about to be closed.

[The Th.∴ P.∴ raps ‖ — the Gr.∴ Warden; — The Gr.∴ Insp.∴ ‖ — the Gr.∴ Treasurer; — the Gr.∴ Secretary ‖ and all the other Brethren; with their hands. Then the Th.∴ P.∴ and the Gr.∴ Warden give the sign of admiration. All the Brethren repeat it: then the two Kings kneel: the Th.∴ P.∴ rises first, and assists the Gr.∴ Warden to rise. All the Brethren then kneel, and each in turn, beginning on the right, helps the other to rise].

Th.∴ P.∴ This Chapter of Royal Arch Masons is duly closed.

FINIS.

Fourteenth Degree.

Grand, Elect, Perfect and Sublime Mason.

THE LODGE, ITS DECORATIONS, ETC.

This Lodge represents a subterranean apartment, without opening to admit the light. It ought regularly to be a perfect cube; that is, its length, breadth and height should be exactly equal. The hangings are crimson, with columns at regular intervals.

In the East is a transparency, on which is painted a luminous triangle, having in its centre the word יהוה. It should be large and brilliant.

In front of the Master's seat in the East are two large gilded columns; and between them a transparent triangular pedestal, lighted within, and representing alabaster, on which is the Cube of Agate, having upon its upper face the Ineffable Name upon a triangular plate of gold. Around the sides of the plate, in the character of the degree, are the nine names of Deity in different languages, as given in the Royal Arch degree.

In front of the Jun.∙. Warden in the West are 3 lights; in front of the Sen.∙. Warden, in the North, 5; in front of the Orator, in the South, 7; and in front of the Master, in the East, and between him and the columns, 9. Those in front of the Jun.∙. Warden form a triangle; those in front of the Sen.∙. Warden, a pentagon; those in front of the Orator, a heptagon; and those in front of the Master, three equilateral triangles in one line.

The Lodge room should be approached by a long and narrow passage, lighted by a single lamp, hanging from above, half way its length.

The Lodge is styled *The Sacred Vault.*

OFFICERS, TITLES, ETC.

The Presiding Officer is styled *Th.∙. Puissant Gr.∙. Master.*

The Sen.∙. and Jun.∙. Wardens are styled *Sen.∙. and Jun.∙. Grand Wardens.*

The Grand Treasurer sits in the East, on the right of the Gr.∙. Master. Before him is the altar of incense, which is four-square, with a gilded horn at each corner, and covered by a plate of metal of the colour of gold. Upon it is an urn, filled with perfumes for burning.

The Gr.∙. Secretary sits in the East, on the left of the Th.∙. P.∙. Before him is a table, covered with a white linen cloth, on which are a basket containing twelve small loaves of bread, and a cup of red wine.

The Deacons are styled *Gr.∙. Sen.∙. and Jun.∙. Experts.*

There is also a Gr∴ Master of Ceremonies.

In the passage-way are three Sentinels, each with a sword in his hand; one at the further door of the passage, one half-way, and one at the door of the Lodge.

Upon the altar of incense is a small silver vessel containing perfumed oil, and a little trowel of gold. When there is a reception, all the jewels for the candidates are placed on the table in front of the Gr∴ Secretary, with a ring for each. This ring is a plain one, of gold, with this motto engraved on the inside: *Virtus junxit: Mors non separabit.*

In front of the Sen∴ Warden is a short column, on which is a brazen basin, filled with pure water.

CLOTHING, ORNAMENTS, AND JEWEL.

The Th∴ P∴ wears a purple robe, with the collar and jewel of the degree. All the other members, the collar, apron and jewel.

The apron is of white sheepskin, lined with crimson, and edged with blue. Around it, on the inside of the edging of blue, is a delicate embroidery in crimson, representing a wreath of flowers. In the middle of the apron is painted or embroidered the jewel; and on the flap is a representation of a flat square stone, to which is attached a ring.

The collar is of crimson velvet.

The jewel is a compass, opened upon a quarter of a circle, and surmounted by a pointed crown. Within the compass is a medal, representing, on one side the Sun, and on the other a Star, in the centre of which is a triangle, and on that the Sacred Word יהוה. This jewel is suspended from the collar.

The dress of the Brethren should be black, with black gloves; and each wears a sword.

The battery is ; ‖ £ and ; times ;

The age is the cube of ; or square of z — or $,

TO OPEN.

Th∴ P∴ [Rapping 1]: My Brethren, I am about to open this Lodge of Perfection. I pray you to give me your attention and assistance.

[The officers assume their stations; and the Th∴ P∴ raps 2, and says]:

Th∴ P∴ Respectable Bro∴ Jun∴ Gr∴ Expert, are all present Gr∴, El∴, Perf∴ and Subl∴ Masons?

[If the Jun∴ Gr∴ Expert knows all the Brothers, he answers in the affirmative. If he does not, he says]:

J∴ Gr∴ Exp∴ Th∴ P∴, I am not certain.

Th∴ P∴ In that case, Bros∴ Sen∴ and Jun∴ Gr∴ Experts, you will receive the first [or any other he fixes on] covered word from each one present, and carry it up to the Most Excellent Bro∴ Jun∴ Gr∴ Warden, and he to the M∴ Ex∴ Bro∴ Sen∴ Gr∴ Warden, that it may come to me in the East.

[The two Experts receive the word from all except the Th∴ P∴ and the two Wardens. Then the Jun∴ Gr∴ Expert gives it to the Sen∴ Gr∴ Expert. He goes and gives it to the Jun∴ Gr∴ Warden, and he to the Sen∴ Gr∴ Warden, who goes and gives it to the Th∴ P∴ in the East].

Th∴ P∴ The word has come up to the East aright. Bro∴ Jun∴ Gr∴ Expert, it is our first duty to see that the approach to this sacred vault is duly guarded. Attend to that duty; see that the sentinels are duly posted; and advise them that this Lodge of Perfection is about to be opened, and that they must allow none to approach without the proper pass-words.

[The Jun∴ Gr∴ Expert goes out, returns, and says]:

J∴ Gr∴ Exp∴ Th∴ P∴ Gr∴ Master, the sentinels are duly posted, and your orders made known to them.

Th∴ P∴ Thanks, my Brother! Let us, my Brethren, return our thanks to the Gr∴ Architect of the Universe for the many blessings and comforts with which He has surrounded us, and implore His aid to enable us to perform our duties.

[All kneel; and the Gr∴ Master reads the following]

PRAYER.

Sovereign Architect of this vast universe! to whom each thought we think and every word we speak is known; we pay to Thee the sincere homage of our most earnest thanks and fervent gratitude for all the blessings and the comforts which Thy infinite goodness has bestowed upon us; for life, and health and strength; for our exemption from extreme penury and destitution; for the faculty and capacity of enjoying the delights and beauties of the natural world, with which Thou hast surrounded us; for the bright Heavens, for light and the delicious air, and the green leaves and lovely flowers, and running water; for the love of those who are near and dear to us, and the faithfulness of friends, and the sympathy of the kind-hearted, and the good opinion of the just and upright; and for every thing within us and without us, that adds to our comfort and enjoyment, or calls into exercise the manly and heroic virtues, and so fits us for a brighter and a better world. We beseech Thee to purify our hearts by the sacred fire of Thy love; to guide and direct us in the ways of virtue; to cast out from among us all impiety and perversity, and to aid us in advancing towards Perfection. Let Peace, Charity, and the love of Humanity form the chain of our union; and cause us in this Lodge faintly to imitate the state and condition of Thy Elect in Thy Holy and Spiritual Kingdom. Enable us in all things to discern and adopt the good, and reject the evil! Let us not be deceived by pretended zeal and devotion, nor deceive ourselves as to our own weaknesses and errors! And aid us in advancing the purposes and attaining the objects of true and genuine Masonry, and thus to serve our fellows and assist in carrying forward Thy great designs; to effect which Thou didst create the universe and endow man with reason. Amen!

[After this prayer, the Brethren remain for a moment or two in profound silence. Then the Th∴ P∴ raps 3, and they all rise, and remain standing. He then asks]:

Th∴ P∴ M∴ Excellent Sen∴ Gr∴ Warden, what brought you hither?

Sen∴ Gr∴ W∴ My obligation, my love for Masonry, and my earnest desire to approach Perfection.

Qu∴ What do you bring hither with you?

Ans∴ True Friendship, and a sincere love for virtue.

Qu∴ What are the characteristics of a Gr∴, El∴, Perf∴ and Sub∴ Mason?

Ans∴ That he frees himself from the dominion of iniquity, injustice, revenge, envy and jealousy; that he is active in doing good; and speaks of his brethren, only to praise them.

Qu∴ What should be your deportment in this place?

Ans∴ That of profound respect and perfect decorum.

Qu∴ How is it that here Princes and Subjects, the master and the employed, the rich and the poor, become friends, brothers and equals?

Ans∴ By the influence of that, of which the Triangle over you is an emblem; of a Power infinitely greater than yours or any other on earth.

Qu∴ What does the Triangle represent?

Ans∴ It contains the Ineffable Name, and represents the Great Creator of the Universe; in comparison with whom all men are so infinitely small and powerless, that the difference between the highest and the lowest is insignificant.

Qu∴ What are you, my Brother?

Ans∴ I *am* your Brother; a Gr∴, El∴, Perf∴ and Sub∴ Mason; who have undergone all the tests and trials, and obtained the reward of my labours.

Qu∴ What is that reward?

Ans∴ The knowledge of the True God; a faint but true appreciation of His nature and infinite attributes; a confidence in His wisdom and justice, His benevolence and love for his feeble creatures; securing me against scepticism and despair.

Qu∴ Have you the True Word of a Gr∴, El∴, Perf∴ and Sublime Mason?

Ans∴ I have.

Qu∴ What is it?

Ans∴ That knowledge and confidence; of which the visible word is but a symbol.

Qu∴ What is your Masonic age?

Ans∴ The square of z or S, years complete.

Qu∴ What contract did you enter into, on receiving this degree?

Ans∴ I devoted myself to virtue, and to the cause of Humanity; and became the firm ally of the virtuous and good.

Qu∴ What is the token of that contract?

Ans∴ This ring, symbol of Eternity and of unbroken friendship.

Qu∴ What is the hour?

Ans∴ Noon; the sun is in the zenith.

Qu∴ What does the arrival of that hour require of us?

Ans∴ That we renew our labours for the benefit of our fellows, our country and mankind, while it is yet day; for that the night soon cometh, in which no man can work.

Qu∴ Where shall we find materials with which to work?

Ans∴ In the virtues of our Brethren, and in our own intellect and energy, regulated and directed by the square and compasses of Reason.

Th∴ P∴ Then, that we may so work while it is day, as the brethren desire, let us open this Lodge! Announce to the Brethren that we will forthwith open this Lodge of Gr∴ El∴ Perf∴ and Subl∴ Masons, by the mysterious numbers [;] [‖] [£] and [z].

Sen∴ Gr∴ Ward∴ Brethren in the North and South, the Th∴ P∴ Gr∴ Master, with your assistance, is about to open this Lodge of Gr∴ Elect, Perfect and Sublime Masons, that we may renew our labours; and prays that you will aid him in doing so.

[The Jun∴ Gr∴ Warden raps; at equal intervals]:

[The Sen∴ Gr∴ Warden raps ‖ at equal intervals]:

[The Th∴ P∴ raps £ at equal intervals]:

[Then follows a short but profound silence]:

[The Th∴ P∴ raps; slowly and at equal intervals]:

[All the Officers and Brothers give the 1st sign]:

[The Th∴ P∴ again raps; as before]:

[All give the 2d sign]:

[The Th∴ P∴ again raps; as before]:

[All give the 3d sign]:

Th∴ P∴ Most excellent Brothers Sen∴ and Jun∴ Gr∴ Wardens, this Lodge of Perfection is opened.

Sen∴ Gr∴ W∴ Brethren in the North, this Lodge of Perfection is opened.

Jun∴ Gr∴ W∴ Brethren in the South, this Lodge of Perfection is opened.

[Then the Th∴ P∴ gives the sign of simple admiration. The two Gr∴ Wardens repeat it together, and then all the Brethren do so. Then the Th∴ P∴ salutes the Lodge by the 1st sign: all the Brothers repeat it. The Th∴ P∴ gives one rap; and all cover themselves, and take their seats].

RECEPTION.

The Candidate being in an apartment beyond the narrow passage leading to the Lodge Room, clothed as a Royal Arch Mason, the Master of Ceremonies conducts him to the door entering into the passage, and informs him what pass-word he is to give to the first Sentinel within, and directs him to rap; ‖ and £ at the door. The luminous pedestal is covered with a thick cloth.

The Guard, first answering by the same battery, opens the door and asks: [bringing down the point of his sword] :

Guard: . . Who comes here?

M∴ Cer∴. A Mason, with the first pass-word.

Guard: Advance Bro∴ Mason, and give the pass-word.

[The Candidate gives it] :

Guard: The word is right. Pass, my Brother.

[The M∴ of Cer∴ then communicates to the Candidate the second pass-word, and directs him to give the same battery on approaching the second Sentinel. That pass-word is demanded and received in the same way].

[Then the M∴ of Cer∴ communicates to the Candidate the third pass-word, and directs him to give the same battery on approaching the third Sentinel. That pass-word is demanded and received in the same way].

[Then the M∴ Cer∴ raps ; ‖ £ and z at the door of the Lodge Room. The battery is repeated from within, and the Jun∴ Gr∴ Expert partly opens the door, and asks] :

J∴ Gr∴ Exp∴. Who comes here ?

M∴ Cer∴. A Mason of the Royal Arch, who having ever been true to the demands of Honour and the dictates of Duty, is desirous to be admitted into the Sacred Vault, that he may pray the Th∴ Puissant Gr∴ Master and the Brethren to confer upon him the Degree of Perfection.

J∴ Gr∴ Exp∴. I will advise the Th∴ P∴ Gr∴ Master of his request, and return his answer.

[He closes the door, and goes to the East, where the Th∴ P∴ asks the same question, and the same answer is given, as at the door].

Th∴ P∴. Let this Mason of the Royal Arch enter, and be received in due and ancient form.

[The M∴ of Cer∴ having instructed the Candidate how to give the sign of admiration, conducts him into the Lodge. As he enters, the Jun∴ Gr∴ Warden meets him, and places the point of his sword against his chest. The M∴ of Cer∴ does the same, and he is then led up to the East; where, directed by the M∴ of Cer∴ he gives the sign of admiration ; after which there is a profound silence for some moments. Then the Th∴ P∴ asks] :

Th∴ P∴. What request have you to prefer, my Brother ?

Cand∴. [The M∴ of Cer∴ dictating the answer]: Th∴ P∴ Gr∴ Master, I desire to be permitted to receive the degree of Perfection.

Th∴ P∴. My Brother, before your request can be granted, or the assent of the brethren asked, there are certain questions which I must put to you, and which you must answer. Should you fail to do so, your request will be denied.

Th∴ P∴. Are you a Mason?

Cand∴. My Brethren know me to be such.

Qu∴. Can you give to our Brother the Jun∴ Gr∴ Warden the sign, word and token of the first degree ?

Ans∴. I can. [He gives them].

Qu∴. Are you a fellow-craft Mason ?

Ans∴. I have seen the letter G., and I know the Pass-word.

Th∴ P∴. Give, then, to the Jun∴ Gr∴ Warden the sign, word and token of that degree. [He gives them].

Qu∴. Are you a Master Mason ?

Ans∴. I have seen the body of our Gr∴ Master disinterred.

Th∴ P∴. Give the sign, word and token of a Master Mason to the Jun∴ Gr∴ Warden. [He does so. When he pronounces the word, all the Brethren present their swords at his breast: and the Th∴ P∴ says: " Beware, my Brother. You cause us to tremble when you pronounce that word aloud. You might do so elsewhere, and be heard by the Profane. We pardon you ; but be careful never again to be guilty of a like indiscretion].

Th∴ P∴. Are you a Secret Master ?

Cand∴. I have passed from the Square to the Compass: I have seen the Tomb of our Gr∴ M∴ Hiram Abi, and in company with my Brethren I have shed tears thereon.

Qu.˙. What was the lesson taught you in that degree?

Ans.˙. Secrecy . . Obedience . . and *Fidelity*.

Qu.˙. Are you a Perfect Master?

Ans.˙. I have seen the three circles, enclosing the square, upon the two crossed columns.

Qu.˙. What lesson were you taught in that degree?

Ans.˙. Honesty, sincerity, frankness, straightforwardness and *good faith*.

Qu.˙. Are you a Confidential Secretary?

Ans.˙. My zeal was mistaken for curiosity; and my life was for a time in danger.

Qu.˙. What lesson were you taught in that degree?

Ans.˙. To be *zealous* and *faithful, disinterested* and *benevolent*, and to act the *peace-maker*.

Qu.˙. Are you a Provost and Judge?

Ans.˙. I dispense impartial justice to the workmen.

Qu.˙. What lesson were you taught in that degree?

Ans.˙. To *decide justly and impartially*, and *to do justice* to all men, seeking no undue advantage of any, nor endeavouring to enrich or elevate myself at the expense of another's fortune, happiness or reputation.

Qu.˙. Are you an Intendant of the Building?

Ans.˙. I was a pupil of our Gr.˙. Master Hiram Abi; and with four others was thought worthy to take his place.

Qu.˙. What lesson was taught you in that degree?

Ans.˙. *Benevolence* and *charity*, and *brotherly sympathy* for those in my employ.

Qu.˙. Are you an Elu of Nine?

Ans.˙. A cavern received me, a lamp gave me light, and a fountain refreshed me.

Qu.˙. What lesson was taught you in that degree?

Ans.˙. To *protect* the *oppressed* against the oppressor, and *Free Thought, Free Conscience* and *Free Speech* against usurpation and invasion.

Qu.˙. Are you an Ill.˙. Elu of Fifteen?

Ans.˙. My zeal and indefatigable exertions procured me that great honour, far above my deserts.

Qu.˙. Against what do you contend as an Elu of Fifteen?

Ans.˙. *Tyranny, Fanaticism,* and *Ignorance.*

Qu.˙. Are you a Sublime Elu of Twelve?

Ans.˙. My name will satisfy you that I am.

Qu.˙. What is that name?

Ans.˙. AMETH, a true man. It is my name and my profession.

Qu.˙. What are the duties of a Prince Ameth?

Ans.˙. To be *earnest, true, reliable* and *sincere*; and to be the *advocate* and *champion* of *the rights of the People*.

Qu.˙. Are you a Gr.˙. Master Architect?

Ans.˙. I have studied mathematics, and am familiar with the instruments used by a Gr.˙. Master Architect.

Qu.˙. Of what is the North Star the symbol to you?

Ans.˙. Of TRUTH and RIGHT; the pole-stars that guide Masons over the stormy seas of Time.

Qu.˙. Are you a Royal Arch Mason Ecossais?

Ans.˙. I have descended through the nine arches into the subterranean vault, and seen the luminous pedestal, the cube of agate, and THE GREAT WORD.

Qu.˙. To what did you pledge yourself as a Royal Arch Mason?

Ans.˙. Ever to be guided and directed by HONOUR and DUTY.

Th.˙. P.˙. Give to the Gr.˙. Jun.˙. Warden the words, signs and token of a Mason of the Royal Arch. [He does so].

Qu.˙. Can you pronounce the Sacred Word?

Ans.˙. I cannot. I have come hither in hopes to obtain that secret.

[The Th.˙. P.˙. gives the sign of admiration, and says]:

Th∴ P∴ You ask a boon which I alone am not competent to grant. These Brethren must be satisfied and unanimously consent that you shall receive the degree you seek. Answer me yet again: Since you have been a Mason, have you ever endeavoured to conduct yourself with frankness and sincerity towards your brethren? Have you ever attempted to injure a Brother in his person, his property, his domestic relations or his reputation? Have you ever refused to comply with your Masonic obligations to the widow or orphans of a Brother? Does your conscience reproach you with the violation of any portion of any one of your Masonic obligations, of which violation you have not repented; or with any wrong done by you, for which you have not earnestly endeavoured to make amends? Have you ever found in those obligations any thing contrary to the duties you owe yourself, your family, your friends, your country or your God; or to the feelings of a good man and a man of honour?

[The candidate answers each question *separately.* Then the Th∴ P∴ says]:

Th∴ P∴ My Brother, you will now please to retire. But first, if you wish to explain any answer you have made, you are at liberty to do so.

[If he makes any explanation, it is listened to, and then, or if he makes none, the Gr∴ Master says]:

Th∴ P∴ Retire then, my Brother, while we consult together; and place entire confidence in the justice and impartiality of your Brethren.

[The candidate retires; and the Gr∴ Master says]:

Th∴ P∴ My Brethren, do you consent that this Mason of the Royal Arch shall be admitted to the degree of Perfection?

[Those who agree, hold up the right hand].

Th∴ P∴ Do any object?

[Those who object extend the right hand before them, as if repelling a person. If any object, the candidate is so informed, and sent away. If none, the Gr∴ Master says]:

Th∴ P∴ Then let us applaud, my Brethren, by z £ ‖ and ;

[The Brethren all so applaud; hearing which, the M∴ of Cer∴ re-conducts the candidate into the room, and places him between the two Wardens].

Th∴ P∴ My Brother, the Brethren assent to your receiving the degree of Perfection. Remember that you are in the immediate presence of the Gr∴ Architect of the Universe, who knows every secret thought of your heart; and that, though you may deceive us, you cannot deceive Him. If you have not answered us truly, withdraw. And fear to lie unto us and to your Maker, by approaching our altar with false or feigned professions on your lips, with indifference and carelessness; without a fixed resolution to perform faithfully and heartily all the duties which you may assume. Learn also that this eminent degree will bind you to us more firmly than before, by new and additional duties and obligations. If you are prepared ever to fulfil these duties with firmness and fidelity; if you are satisfied that we will impose upon you no duty and require of you the performance of no act that will not exalt and ennoble the character: if you are firmly resolved that we shall never have reason to repent having conferred upon you this degree; and if you are willing to form an indissoluble connection of amity and brotherhood with us, in the cause of THE JUST, THE RIGHT, and THE TRUE, answer that you are willing to assume the obligation of this degree.

Cand∴ I am willing.

Th∴ P∴ First go, then, to the station of our Sen∴ Gr∴ Warden, and wash your hands in the brazen laver, as a token of the purity of your intentions and the sincerity of your purposes, and that you here lay aside all ignoble passions and unworthy desires, and dedicate yourself to Truth and Virtue.

[The candidate is conducted to the laver, where he washes his hands, and returns to his former place between the Wardens. Then the Th∴ P∴ says to him]:

Th∴ P∴ My Brother, you will now approach the altar by the steps of a Gr∴ El∴ Perf∴ and Sub∴ Mason, and kneel to receive the obligation of this degree:

[The candidate is conducted to the altar of incense, which he is made to reach by S quick steps and one slow. Then he kneels upon both knees, and gives the sign of adoration of a Royal Arch Mason, and with his hands takes hold of two of the horns of the altar, and in that position repeats the following]

OBLIGATION.

I, A . . . . B . . . ., in the presence of the Gr∴ Architect of the Universe, kneeling before this altar raised to Him, and holding thereto, in token of my dependence upon Him and my trust in Him, do hereby and hereon most solemnly and sincerely promise and swear, that I will never reveal the secrets of this degree, nor any thing that may occur in a Lodge thereof, except at such time, and in such place and manner as I may lawfully do so, and to those only who may be duly authorized to receive, while I am legally authorized to communicate and make known the same.

I furthermore promise and swear that I will never take up arms against my country, nor side with her enemies, nor enter directly or indirectly into any plot, plan or conspiracy against her, her honour or her welfare; but will make known and defeat every such plot, plan or conspiracy, whenever it may be in my power.

I furthermore promise and swear, that I will pay equal regard and consideration to all my Brethren of this degree, no matter of what rank or condition, or whether rich or poor; knowing no other distinction among them than that of superior merit and virtue; and recognizing them all as my Brethren, if they are honest men; and that I will assist them in their poverty, rescue them from danger, and comfort and console them in misfortune.

I furthermore promise and swear, that I will visit my Brethren when they are sick; and in every case of necessity will aid and assist them with my counsel, my purse and my person.

I furthermore promise and swear that I will never knowingly have illicit connexion with the wife, mother, daughter, sister, or any other near relative of a Brother.

I furthermore promise and swear, that, if there be a Lodge of this degree within the distance of fifty miles, I will visit it at least twice in each year, on the 27th of December and the 24th of June, if it be in my power; and oftener if my business and my duty to my family permit.

I furthermore promise and swear, that I will never vote for the admission of a candidate to this degree, unless I have a previous personal knowledge of his good conduct and good morals; nor agree to confer it upon any one who is not at the time a member in good standing of a regularly constituted Master's Lodge, or who has not been Master or Warden of such a Lodge.

I furthermore promise and swear that I will never consent to, or be present at, the admission of a Brother to this degree, unless he has been duly elected thereto by a unanimous vote of the brethren of the Lodge; nor even then, if I know that any absent brother, a member of the Lodge, would have voted against him, if he had been present.

I furthermore promise and swear, that I will ever hereafter strive to maintain the character, and deserve the name, of a Grand, Elect, Perfect and Sublime Mason; doing and abiding by, in all emergencies, that which is Just, Right and True, and that only, without regard to consequences, or consideration of success or reward.

And I consent, in case I should ever wilfully or intentionally violate this my solemn obligation, to be held and deemed by all men as perjured, base and infamous, a moral leper, offensive to God and man; to touch whom would be defilement, and to associate with whom, dishonour. So help me God! and keep me steadfast in the due performance of the same!

[The moment the obligation is concluded, the incense upon the altar is lighted, and the cloth covering the pedestal and cube of agate is removed; and all the Brothers, falling upon their knees, give the 3d sign, and then rise. The Master of Ceremonies (the candidate still kneeling) brings the vessel of oil and the trowel, while the Jun∴ Gr∴ Warden uncovers the side over the heart of the candidate. The Th∴ P∴ then, taking a little oil upon the trowel, anoints the candidate's eyes, lips and side over the heart; and says, as he does so]:

Th∴ P∴ By the power vested in me as Master of this Lodge, and, in that character, Successor and Representative of Solomon, King of Israel, I devote and consecrate you to the service of that which is Just,

Right and True, to Honour and Duty, and to all the excellencies and virtues which go to make up the character of a Perfect Mason!

Orator: JUSTICE *is immutable!*

J.˙. Gr.˙. W.˙. The RIGHT *is omnipotent!*

Sen.˙. Gr.˙. W.˙. TRUTH *is immortal!*

Th.˙. P.˙. And thou art henceforth their sworn knight and soldier. Arise, my Brother!

[The candidate rises, and is conducted to the table of bread and wine, where the Th.˙. P.˙. hands him of each, and says]:

Th.˙. P.˙. Eat of this bread, my Brother, and drink from the same cup with me, as a pledge of brotherhood; and let this ceremony ever remind you that Hospitality is a truly Masonic virtue; and that every one of us owes to his brother kind services, and graceful courtesies, and prompt and cheerful assistance and relief.

[The candidate eats and drinks; after which all the brothers do the same; after which the Th.˙. P.˙. takes the cup, goes to the altar, and pours what wine remains upon the incense, saying]:

Th.˙. P.˙. I pour out this libation to the memory of our departed Brethren; and as an acknowledgment that it is our duty to pour comfort and consolation into the hearts of the distressed, the afflicted and the destitute; and that the thanks and gratitude of the widow and orphan are a Mason's most acceptable offering to his God.

[Then the Th.˙. P.˙. puts the ring upon the third finger of the right hand of the candidate, saying]:

Th.˙. P.˙. My Brother, this plain ring is a visible mark of the compact that you have now made. Its motto is, *Virtus junxit, mors non separabit:* [*Virtue has united us, and death shall not separate us*]. Promise me that you will wear it during your lifetime, and that you will provide that, after your death, it shall go into the hands of no other person than your widow, your eldest son, or the friend whom of all others you most love.

Cand.˙. I promise.

Th.˙. P.˙. I now invest you with the apron of this degree. Of its three colours, *white*, like the snowy purity of the ermine, represents JUSTICE; *blue*, the colour of the perfectly symmetrical and changeless arch of the sky, represents RIGHT; and *crimson*, the colour of fire which tries and purifies all things, represents TRUTH.

Th.˙. P.˙. I also invest you with the collar and jewel of this degree. The compasses remind us that science, united to honour and virtue, made the architects of the Temple the companions of Kings; and that the men of intellect and learning, the Great Kings of Thought, are in this age the rulers of the world. The sun, source of light to our system, and once worshipped as a god, and the star, type of the myriad suns that light other and countless systems of worlds, are emblems of that Masonic Light in search of which every Mason travels; the correct knowledge of the Deity and of his laws that control the universe.

Th.˙. P.˙. We have in this degree three signs, three tokens, three covered words, three pass-words, and a Grand Ineffable Word.

1ST SIGN: . . . Bring the ‡⁑&☉≈□ quickly and &☿‡♀♍☿≈♈☉††♄ from the left side of the ☉♏□☿-♋☾≈ to the right, as if cutting it open.

2D SIGN: . . . Place the ☿⁑☾≈⁑‡⁑&☉≈□ upon the †⁑♐&☾☾¶, as if to protect it from the heat of the fire, holding the ‡⁑☾†♏☿♃ with the †☾♑♈&☉≈□. Then change, and put the †⁑&☉≈□ before the ‡⁑♐&☾☾¶, holding the †⁑☾†♏☿♃ with the ‡⁑&☉≈□.

3D SIGN: . . . Raise the ♈♃☿⁑&☉≈□♎, ☿§☾≈, towards Heaven, the head inclining backward and the ☾♄☾♎⁑‡☉♀♎☾□: and then put the ?♑♀‡♎♈⁑♑♀≈♌☾‡♎ of the ‡⁑&☉≈□ on the †♀§♎.

1ST TOKEN: . . . Take each other by the right hand, and ♈♑‡≈ the &☉≈□♎ ☿*☾‡; times—saying, alternately . . ♏☾‡♀♈&.˙. ≈☾□☾‡.˙. ♎&⁑†☿♋♀♈&.˙.

2D TOKEN: . . . Begin with the ♋☉♎♈☾‡♎⁑♌‡♀§. One asks "♐☉≈⁑♄☿♑⁑♌☿⁑♑♑‡♈&☾‡." The other replies by passing, first to the ♋♀□□†☾ of the ♑☿‡☾-☉‡♋, and then to the ☾†♏☿♃ of the other, ♑≈□☾‡≈☾☉♈&. The other does the same. Then each puts his †☾♑♈⁑&☉≈□ on the other's ‡⁑♎&☿-♑†□☾†, and advances his ‡♀♌&♈⁑♑☿☿♈ so as to pass it beyond the †☾♑♈⁑♑☿☿♈ of the other; and they then ♏☉†☉≈♐☾; ♈♀♋☾♎

3D TOKEN: . . . Each takes the other by the ⊣ℂⲙ𝒷𝒵 with his ⊣⅃&⊙≈□, and puts his ⊣⅃&⊙≈□⅃ ⲙℂ&♀≈□ the other's ⲙ⊙𝒇¶; as if to □⊣⊙𝒵 him 𝒇⊣𝒷⌒ℂ to himself.

COVERED WORDS: . .
{
1st. . . ⌠&ℂⲙ⊹♀☉∴
2d. . . ☎⊙&⊙ⲙℂ≈♀∴
3d. . . ⊙□𝒷≈⊙♀∴
}

PASS-WORDS: . . . . .
{
1st. . . ⌒&♀ⲙⲙ𝒷⊹ℂ♈&∴
2d. . . ⊙⊹⌠&⊙≈⊙≈∴
3d. . . ☎⊙⊹⊙&⌐☎☉ ⅃⊹⊙ⲙ⊹ℂ𝒇∴
}

GRAND SACRED WORD: . . . . יהוה∴ The true pronunciation of which word I give you in a whisper, in which way only I can communicate it to you, or you to another person. . . . . [♀&⅃&]. . .

My Brother, I salute you as a Grand, Elect, Perfect and Sublime Mason, duly created and constituted. It remains for you to learn what meanings are involved in the legend and symbolism of this Degree. Go therefore to the Brother the Gr∴ Orator, and receive his instruction.

LEGEND, HISTORY, ETC.

My Brother, you were informed in the Royal Arch Degree, that King Solomon builded a Secret Vault, the approach to which was through eight other vaults or apartments in succession, all under ground, and to which a long and narrow passage led from under his palace; that the ninth vault was immediately under the Holy of Holies of the Temple; that, in that apartment King Solomon held his private conferences with King Hiram of Tyre, and Hiram Abi; and that, after the death of Hiram Abi, the two Kings ceased to visit it, resolving not to do so again, until they should have selected one to fill his place; and that, until that time, they would make known the Sacred Name to no one.

After Adonhiram, Joabert and Stolkin had discovered the cube of agate and the Mysterious Name, as you have heard, and had delivered it to King Solomon, the two Kings, after much deliberation, determined to deposit it in the secret vault, and to permit the three Masters who had discovered it to be present, and then to make known to them the true pronunciation of the Ineffable Word, creating a new degree, the last of Ancient Masonry, of which those three Masters and themselves should be the first members, to be called the Degree of Perfection, and its recipients, Grand, Elect, Perfect and Sublime Masons.

Accordingly, after some days, the cube of agate was so deposited in the Secret Vault (which was thereafter styled the *Sacred* Vault); being set upon the summit of the column of white marble, called the Pillar of Beauty. Then all knelt, and returned thanks to God for his multiplied favours shown to them and to the Jewish People. Then the correct pronunciation of the Sacred Name was given to the three Masters, and the degree of Perfection, with its signs, words and tokens, was instituted; and thus the zeal and devotedness of Adonhiram, Joabert and Stolkin were rewarded.

After the twelve Princes Ameth, the first Nine of the Ill∴ Elus of Fifteen, and the Chief Architect, were admitted to this degree, the Nine Elus of Fifteen were assigned to the duty of guarding the approaches to the sacred vault, the eldest being stationed at the entrance of that vault, and the others respectively, at the entrances of the other eight. But that has long been dispensed with in our ceremonies; and three sentinels only are required, each of whom has his especial pass-word.

The private entrance to the Secret Vault having been constructed by Hiram Abi, with the aid of certain Phœnician Architects and Masons; who, being initiates of the Mysteries, and solemnly sworn to secrecy as to its existence, had returned to their homes; none others knew of it, except the two Kings, and those who were made Gr∴ Elect, Perfect and Sublime Masons. To none others was the True Word communicated; all of inferior degrees knowing only the substitute, adopted at the death of Hiram Abi, as the Master Mason's Word.

The Temple is said to have been completed in the year 3000; six years, six months and ten days after King Solomon had laid the first stone; and its completion was celebrated with the greatest pomp, and the most splendid magnificence.

It was after these ceremonies were performed, and the Temple was dedicated, that King Solomon conferred this degree on the twenty-five whom we have mentioned. During three days he gave audience to the Brethren. The twenty-five to whom he gave this degree, he received in the Sacred Vault, exacting from each of them a solemn promise to live in peace, union and concord; to practise, like their deceased Gr∴ Master, Charity and Beneficence; like him to make wisdom, justice and equity the rule of their life and conduct; to be profoundly secret as to the mysteries of this degree, and never to confer them on any one who should not have proven himself worthy thereof, by his zeal, fervour and constancy; to assist each other in their labours, distresses, difficulties and calamities, and to punish treason, perfidy and injustice. When they had so promised, he gave them his benediction; showed them the ark of the covenant, whence issued the oracles of God; offered up sacrifice and incense; united with them in a libation: and then, having embraced each of them, and presented each with a ring, as a token of the covenant which each had entered into with virtue and the virtuous, and bestowed upon them many other marks of honour; he gave them permission to remain at his Court, or to travel into foreign countries, as they might prefer.

The second day, he gave audience to all Masons from the degree of Master up to that of Royal Arch. He filled all the vacancies in the different degrees, created by the exaltation of the twenty-five Brothers to that of Perfection, and made many honorary members of the Degree of Grand Master Architect, and the other degrees; engaging them never to forget the principles of honour, uprightness and virtue which they had been and then were taught in the different degrees; always to live united in harmony, and to aid and comfort one another in their necessities and distresses. This was done in the Holy of Holies of the Temple. He gave them the jewels and decorations of the different degrees which he conferred; and bound them by solemn obligations to be faithful and discreet guardians of the mysteries of their respective degrees, and never to communicate them to any but the deserving; and having showed them many other marks of favour, he invited them to remain at his Court; giving them permission to travel in foreign countries, if they saw fit; and to those who were of Tyre, to return to their own homes.

The third day he devoted to the Fellow-crafts and Apprentices, raising those of the former who were worthy, to the degree of Master, and passing such of the latter as deserved it by fidelity and obedience, to the degree of Fellow-craft. He caused them to enter into like obligations, and gave them permission to remain at Jerusalem or return to their homes, giving the Intendants of the Building orders to furnish them money for their expenses, in case they should see fit to return to their own countries.

Afterwards this great King, renowned for his wisdom, and long the faithful servant of God, became deaf to the voice of duty; and, filled with haughty pride at the glory he had gained, vain of his great wealth, and intoxicated with flattery, he forgot the lessons which he had taught to others, multiplied the number of his wives and concubines, and gave himself up to shameless and indecent luxury; and, yielding to the blandishments of lascivious women, he built Temples to the Gods of other nations, and profanely offered up to them the incense which should have been offered to the True God alone, in the Holy of Holies of the Temple.

These acts of the King and their Grand Master, covered all good Masons with shame, and afflicted them with the profoundest grief. Far from following his example, they lamented his infatuation, and devoted themselves to bringing up their children in the true principles of virtue; pointing them by way of warning to the shameful and irregular life led by the King, as an example to be avoided. The people, following their Monarch's example, frequented the Temples of the false Gods, and sacrificed upon their altars, indulging in all the obscene and indecent rites of the worship of Moloch and Astarte. The Masons long contended against this inroad of vice and evil; but finding their efforts unavailing, and remembering the punishment that similar excesses and crimes had often brought upon their ancestors, they foresaw the future desolation of Jerusalem, and the destruction of the Temple, and that the descendants of the Jews would expiate in captivity the monstrous sins of their ancestors; and therefore determined to flee into other countries, and avoid the impending disaster.

They were of necessity extremely careful as to the admission of new members into the Masonic Order; making merit, and merit alone, the test of qualification: and the Gr∴ El∴ Perf∴ and Sub∴ Masons especially received no one until after long probation and by many trials he had been proven worthy.

Upon the completion of the Temple, many Masons of the inferior degrees, and some of the Gr∴ El∴ Perf∴ and Sub∴ Masons journeyed into other countries. Still more followed them, after the excesses of the King became intolerable; and in a few years the Jewish Architects and Free Masons were to be found in every part of the world. They admitted many into the order, made known to them its truths, and taught them its duties. For a long time they were wisely cautious to admit none but proper persons, who could appreciate the true purposes and objects of the Royal Craft. But by degrees the inferior grades of Masonry so spread abroad, that men were indiscriminately admitted without due inquiry; and it was forgotten that Masonry was not a popular, but a select and exclusive institution. Improper men gained admission. It became no privilege, nor any mark of honour, to be even a Master Mason; dissensions grew rife among the members; ambition, entering in, coveted rank and honours, the secrets were improperly divulged, and Blue Masonry fell into contempt.

But the Gr∴ El∴ Perf∴ and Sub∴ Masons did not fall into these errors. They carefully concealed their secrets from the vulgar gaze, kept strict watch at the doors of their Temples, and refused to multiply the number of their initiates. They strove to arrest the downward progress of the Symbolic Degrees, and refused to confer any degree above that of Master, on those who conducted themselves imprudently and unmasonically. But they could not close the door against innovations and irregularities. Masonry continued to degenerate; candidates were admitted without due inquiry, and for the sake of revenue alone; the degrees were conferred with too great rapidity, and without a knowledge of the principles, or even of the work of the preceding degrees, on the part of the Candidates; men of little intellect and information swarmed in the order, and debased and degraded it; others joined it merely through idle curiosity, and wholly disregarded and set at naught their obligations; frivolous ceremonies were multiplied and new degrees invented, and large bodies of men calling themselves Masons threw off their allegiance, pretended to a knowledge of the True Word, and invented new Rites; so that the Temple of Symbolical Masonry became a mere arena of strife and house of contention.

The crimes and follies of the Jewish People at length produced their natural consequences. Immediately upon King Solomon's death they were divided into two kingdoms, Israel and Judah; the people of the former of which, after no great lapse of time, were carried into captivity, ceased to exist as a people, and their descendants have never yet been discovered. The descendants of Solomon reigned for many years over Judah; but at length in the reign of Zedekiah, Nebuchadnezzar, King of Assyria, conquered Judah, and Jerusalem was destroyed by Nebuzaradan his general, the Temple razed to the ground, and the treasures and most of the people of Jerusalem and Judah carried away to Babylon. This occurred four hundred and seventy years after the dedication of the Temple.

Some Gr∴ El∴ Perf∴ and Subl∴ Masters had still remained at Jerusalem. They fought bravely in its defence, and many lost their lives upon the walls and in the streets. After the city was taken and the King's Palace and the Temple demolished, they bethought themselves of the Sacred Vault and the inestimable treasure it contained; and feared lest it should have been discovered and the treasure carried away. During the reign of one of the impious descendants of Solomon, the secret passage leading to it from the King's Palace had been walled up, and the original descent into it from the Holy of Holies opened. Repairing to the ruins of the Temple, at night, and eluding the parties of the victors that patrolled the streets, they discovered that the way which led down to the vault had not been discovered, nor the slab of marble that covered it disturbed: but upon it they found the dead body of Galahad, son of Sephoris, an eminent Brother of the Degree of Perfection, and Chief of the Levites. He had been entrusted with the custody of the Sacred Vault, and the care of the lamps that burned continually within the pedestal of alabaster, on which stood the cube of agate, upon which, inscribed on the triangular plate of gold, was the Ineffable Word. He, like Hiram Abi, who lost his life rather than reveal this Word, preferred to be buried under the ruins of the falling Temple, rather than, by escaping, to risk the discovery of the sacred treasures, never yet profaned by unholy hands.

Removing the body, and descending into the vault, they erased the sacred letters from the plate of gold, and broke the plate in pieces, placed the cube of agate in a corner of the vault, and covered it with rubbish, extinguished the lamps and overturned the pedestal. Then ascending, they conveyed the body of Galahad into the vault, and laid it down by the overturned pedestal, clad in his Masonic clothing and wearing the insignia and jewel of a Gr∴ El∴ Perf∴ and Sublime Mason, and performed over him a brief and solemn ceremony of Masonic burial. Then they ascended again, replaced the slab of marble that covered the entrance, and heaped upon it heavy stones and beams of timber, that it might not be discovered until the Temple should at some future time be rebuilt.

They then departed, determining not to make known to any one what they had done, except to those who should afterwards be permitted to become Gr∴ El∴ Perf∴ and Sublime Masons; and not again to *write* the name, but to hand it down by tradition only, and that only by spelling in syllables, without ever pronouncing the entire word. That practice was afterwards observed, when the temple had been rebuilt by permission of King Cyrus; and has come down to us; the true pronunciation being confided to none but those who receive this degree; and then in a whisper, and with a prohibition against ever pronouncing it aloud, or even in a whisper, except when confiding it to a new Initiate. Once in each year, the Word was repeated by syllables in the Temple, the Brothers forming a circle, and the High Priest, in the centre, repeating the syllables to a Brother, who repeated them to the one next him, and so they passed round the circle, and returned to the High Priest; while a great noise was made without the Temple, with trumpets, and instruments of music, that none might hear the Sacred Syllables; and in that manner the true pronunciation has come down to us.

Such is the Legend of the Degree. We do not know how far, in its details, it is historically true. That the true name of the Deity was thus cautiously communicated, we know; and that its true pronunciation was lost to the Jewish People. And we also know that the Legend has a double meaning. To those whom Solomon initiated in the final degree of the Mysteries, afterwards called the Degree of Perfection of Free Masonry, he taught the true doctrine in regard to the being, nature and attributes of God, the true history of the creation of the Universe, the explanation of the great problem of the existence of suffering and evil, and the doctrine of the immortality of the soul, and of a future spiritual existence, in which it would ever advance towards that perfection of which this degree is but a faint and imperfect symbol. In the care taken to conceal the Word from their conquerors and from the people, we see that which was habitually taken to conceal these doctrines, and to expound and develope them to the favoured few alone, who became enrolled among the Masons of this Degree.

After the destruction of the City and Temple, some of the Grand Elect, Perfect and Sublime Masons were carried away captive into Babylon: others escaped into Egypt, Phœnicia, Syria, the Desert of the Thebaid; and wandered even into India. At a later day they penetrated, conveyed thither in Phœnician ships, into England, Scotland and Ireland. Wheresoever they went, they spread Free-Masonry, and inculcated its pure, peaceful and benevolent doctrines, substituting, in place of the legend of Osiris and Typhon, which was represented in the Egyptian Mysteries, that of Hiram Abi, slain by the three assassins, whose names, in time, became so corrupted as scarcely to be recognized. They commended themselves and their order to the favourable consideration of Princes, Nobles and People, by the purity of its principles, the virtues which they practised, and the great and splendid edifices which they erected everywhere. Admitting into the order good and true men of all ranks and degrees, they were careful not unnecessarily to multiply the number of those who received the Degree of Perfection. Making an architect and worker in brass their type of the Principle of good, of honor and incorruptible integrity and fidelity, they paid no regard to rank; but made virtue, capacity and intellectual attainments the sole test of fitness to receive this Degree.

From them the Essenes and their great Teacher John the Baptist received their pure and profound doctrines: from them Philo Judaeus learned them in the schools of Alexandria. They were the Masters of the Druids, the Brahmins and the Magi, and inspired Confucius, Zoroaster, Pythagoras and Plato.

Christ appeared, and made public the true doctrines, until his time confined to a select few, and even by them in many instances added to, perverted and corrupted. After his death, Jewish traditions and the tenets of the Greek Philosophy were interpolated into his pure religion: and the creed taught by the Great Teacher was overlaid with follies and fictions. The religious mind indulged in the fantastic vagaries of Gnosticism; and the idolatry of Saints and images recalled to mind the worship of idols in the days of Solomon.

When the Powers of Christendom united to conquer from the followers of the Crescent, Jerusalem and the Holy Land, the Masons, then numerous in every Christian country, eager to participate in the glorious enterprise, offered their services to the confederated Princes. Under leaders elected by themselves, and known only in the hour of battle, they joined the standards of the invading armies, and on every disorderly march of the motley forces that entered Palestine, they preserved good order, scrupulously performed their military duties, and at all times practised those principles of heroism, honour, morality and virtue, which they had been taught by their fathers; treating each other as brothers, living in the same harmony as when the world was at peace, and occupying the same tents without distinction of rank.

It would be impossible to relate all their acts of heroism and bravery in the different battles which were fought during the Crusades. Without them, Palestine would not have been recovered, nor a Christian King have been seated on the Throne of Jerusalem. They fronted the most imminent danger, and ever sought to receive the first shock of the battle. Often they turned the scale in favour of the Christian hosts. Their counsels were heard with respect; and they were ever ready to assist and succour the unfortunate, to nurse the sick and care for the wounded soldier of every Nation. Their blood was poured out like water at Acre and Ascalon. They were the foremost to mount the walls of Jerusalem, and to plant upon them the standard of the Cross; and when the city was taken, they, entering among the foremost, strove to stay the carnage which ensued, saving the wounded, the old and the unfortunate, and at the hazard of their lives protecting the women from violation.

Their disinterestedness, generosity and charity, their close and perfect union with and devotion to one another, and their undaunted bravery and contempt of danger and death, attracted the attention and excited the admiration of the Christian leaders and Princes; who, finding that they had some secret bond of union, and one leader whose slightest order was obeyed by all, and whose will was communicated instantaneously as it were, and in some unknown mode, to all his forces, sought to penetrate the mystery. Learning that they constituted a particular order, in which all, even to the humblest soldier, were equals, they sought to become members of it, and were admitted. But they were first informed, that wisdom, justice, probity, honour, morality, friendship, equality and union were the fundamental laws of the Order; that rank and dignity gave no one a claim to enter it; and that if they did so, they must thereafter regard every Mason as their equal, if he were an honourable, honest and upright man, no matter what his rank or title. Some of the Princes, governed by prejudice and pride of birth, declined to enter the order; but the eminent, virtuous and distinguished among them did so with joy, and were in due time advanced to the degree of Gr.·. Elect, Perf.·. and Sublime Mason. Received as Fellow-Crafts, they embraced the Venerable Brothers who surrounded and accepted them, and many of whom were but private soldiers, thanking them for displaying to their eyes the mysteries of Masonry, and for their distinguished services in the common cause of Christendom. They were told that their gratitude was due to the Gr.·. Architect of the Universe alone; for that, their fathers having been driven from the Holy Land, the Masons could not but unite in the common enterprise, and deserved no thanks for assisting to recover their country from the hands of the Infidel. Such is the feeling which should animate all Masons; since, in complying with our obligations, and practising the virtues here inculcated, we but perform our duty.

Thus was new vigour given to Masonry. Carried, by those returning from Palestine, into every country, it was protected by the Christian Princes, and became a Power in every State. Connecting itself with Chivalry and the Knightly Orders, by new Degrees, it everywhere taught the practice of the noble and heroic virtues; and continued to flourish amid all the revolutions and vicissitudes of Empires, the downfall of Dynasties, and the overthrow of Thrones. It crossed the ocean to America, it penetrated the primeval forests, it was scattered even among the Indian tribes. Itself undergoing many changes in forms and ceremonies, it divided into different rites, practised in different countries; but the cardinal principles of Masonry remained unchanged in all. Let us hope, my Brother, that they may so continue, until time shall be no more. Go now to the Sen∴ and Jun∴ Gr∴ Wardens, and receive from them the Catechism of this Degree.

CATECHISM.

Sen∴ Gr∴ W∴. What are you?

Jun∴ Gr∴ W∴. A Gr∴ El∴ Perf∴ and Sub∴ Mason. - I have learned the Great Secret.

Sen∴ Gr∴ W∴. Where were you received as such?

Jun∴ Gr∴ W∴. In a place where the light of the Sun and Moon was not needed.

Qu∴. Where is that place?

Ans∴. Under the Holy of Holies, in a secret place called the Sacred Vault.

Qu∴. Who received you there?

Ans∴. The Successor and Representative of Solomon, King of Israel.

Qu∴. Whom did *you* represent?

Ans∴. Adonhiram the son of Abda.

Qu∴. How did you enter the Sacred Vault?

Ans∴. Through a long and narrow passage, and eight arched apartments underground.

Qu∴. How did your entrance thereunto commence?

Ans∴. By ; raps.

Qu∴. What did they signify?

Ans∴. The term of my Apprenticeship, and the ; Masters, ⊙⊓☿♒⚹♀‡⊙♋‡♂☿⊙♏☾‡♈⸪⊙♒⊓⸬⌂♈☿†¶♀♒, who descended into the earth, and bore thence to King Solomon the Sacred Treasure, placed there before the Deluge by Enoch the Patriarch.

Qu∴. What followed these ; raps?

Ans∴. ‖ others.

Qu∴. What did they signify?

Ans∴. The term of my service as a Fellow Craft, and the first Gr∴ Elect, Perfect and Sublime Masons.

Qu∴. Who were they?

Ans∴. The same ; Masters, with the two Kings, Solomon and Hiram of Tyre.

Qu∴. What followed these ‖ raps?

Ans∴. £ others.

Qu∴. What did they signify?

Ans∴. The age of a Master Mason: the £ §‡☿✳☿⌂♈⌂‡⊙♒⊓⸬♂☿⊓♌☾⌂, and the £ years occupied in ♏☿♀†⊓♀♒♌‡♈⅋☾⸬♈♈☾♋§†☾.

Qu∴. What followed these £ raps?

Ans∴. Z others.

Qu∴. What did they signify?

Ans∴. The age of a Perfect Master; the square of which is the age of a Gr∴ El∴ Perf∴ and Subl∴ Mason.

Qu∴. What did this alarm procure you?

Ans∴. The ninth arch was opened to me, and, by the aid of the pass-words, I penetrated into the Sacred Vault.

Qu∴. What was unveiled to you during your reception?

Ans∴. A brilliant light, within a pedestal of alabaster, which dazzled my eyes, and filled my soul with admiration.

Qu∴. What saw you by that light?

Ans∴. A cube of agate upon the pedestal; sunk into one side whereof was a triangular plate of gold; and engraved on that the Holy and Ineffable Name of Deity.

Qu∴. How came that treasure thither?

Ans.·. It was taken by the three Masters from a vault hewn in the solid rock, to which they descended through nine arched apartments, one above the other.

Qu.·. When and by whom was it placed there?

Ans.·. Before the Deluge, by the Patriarch Enoch.

Qu.·. Will you give me that Word?

Ans.·. I cannot. It is forbidden.

Qu.·. How then shall I know that you have it?

Ans.·.· ♋⊙&⊙♏☿♒☾& was substituted in its place, after the death of Hiram Abi.

Qu.·. What does that mean?

Ans.·. *What! is this the Builder?*

Qu.·. What at last became of the plate of gold and the name upon it?

Ans.·. After the Temple was destroyed by Nabuzaradan, certain faithful Gr.·., Elect, Perf.·. and Subl.·. Masons erased the name and broke up the plate, that it might not fall into the hands of the idolatrous Assyrians.

Qu.·. When you became a Prince Ameth, what did you see?

Ans.·. Twelve great lights.

Qu.·. What did they signify?

Ans.·. The twelve Ill.·. Elus of Fifteen who were appointed by Solomon the King to be Governors over Israel, and charged with the collection of the revenues of the realm.

Qu.·. What were their names?

Ans.·. Ben-Hur, Ben-Decar, Ben-Hesed, Ben-Abinadab, Bana, Ben-Gaber, Ahinadab, Achimaas, Baana, Josaphat, Semei and Gaber; who, with Joabert, Stolkin and Zerbal, were the first Ill.·. Elus of Fifteen; and of whom Ben-Hur, Ahinadab, Ben-Decar, Baana, Semei and Gaber, with Joabert, Stolkin and Zerbal, were the first Elus of Nine.

Qu.·. What signifies, to us, as Gr.·., El.·., Perf.·. and Subl.·. Masters, the key of ivory of a Secret Master?

Ans.·. That we are the depositaries of the True Word, the Great Secret, and the Ancient Doctrines of Masonry; that we must lock them up in our hearts, and keep them inviolable, always so regulating our life and conduct as not to prove unworthy of the great trust reposed in us.

Qu.·. What signification, to us, have the tomb and monument erected to our deceased Gr.·. Master Hiram Abi?

Ans.·. That the memories of its great and good men are the noblest treasures of a nation, standing, like mountain-tops above the Deluge, high above the dark and wintry ocean of the Past, to invite us to leave *our* names and memories as worthy legacies to our country.

Qu.·. What, to us, signifies the balance of the Provost and Judge?

Ans.·. That we are to weigh carefully the qualifications of those who desire to be admitted among us; and reject them without hesitation, if any sordid vice, or ignoble passion, or selfishness, ingratitude or want of Honour weighs down the scale against them.

Qu.·. What signify the swords upon whose points you were received, when you entered the Sacred Vault?

Ans.·. Contempt and Pity; the punishments which Masons inflict on those who are base enough to violate their obligations.

Qu.·. What does the inflamed heart signify, in the degree of Sub.·. Elu of Twelve or Prince Ameth?

Ans.·. Ardent devotion to the cause of Masonry and the welfare of our Brothers.

Qu.·. What is the Sacred Word of a Knight Elu of Nine?

Ans.·. ♌☾♏♄‡-♈&♀†.·.

Qu.·. What does it signify?

Ans.·. Hero of Might, or Mighty and Distinguished Man.

Qu.·. What are the pass-words of that degree?

Ans.·. ♒☾♐♄♋, meaning *vengeance*, the signal agreed upon by the fugitives who had murdered our Gr.·. Master, and the exclamation of the Chief Assassin when his retreat was discovered: ♁☿⊙♏☾‡♈ .·. ⊙♏♀‡⊙♋ .·. and ⊙♈♀‡☿♑.·.

Qu∴. What do the nine lights signify, in the Chapter of Knights Elu of Nine ; eight together, and one by itself?

Ans∴. The Nine Elect who were sent to search for the murderers, and one of whom captured Abiram Akirop their leader.

Qu∴. What was the name of the stranger who made known to Solomon the place where the murderer Akirop was concealed?

Ans∴. Pharos, the son of Miamin, a herdsman of Joppa.

Qu∴. What became of him, after the murderer was captured?

Ans∴. Liberally rewarded by King Solomon, he returned to Joppa.

Qu∴. What became of the two companions of Akirop?

Ans∴. Escaping the Nine Elect in the mountains near Joppa, they fled into the country of Gath, and took refuge in a quarry between Gath and Saphir.

Qu∴. By whom was their place of refuge discovered?

Ans∴. By Ben-Decar, one of the Nine Elus, and afterwards appointed Governor over that part of Palestine, as one of the Elus of Twelve, or Princes Ameth.

Qu∴. What steps did King Solomon take, to have them apprehended?

Ans∴. He sent thither the fifteen Elus, bearing a letter to Maacha, Tributary King of Gath, with a sufficient escort.

Qu∴. To whom was the letter committed?

Ans∴. To Zerbal, Captain of the Guards, and one of the Nine Elus.

Qu∴. Did the Fifteen succeed in apprehending the murderers?

Ans∴. They did, with the assistance furnished them by King Maacha.

Qu∴. By whom were they discovered?

Ans∴. By Joabert and Zerbal, two of the Elus of Fifteen.

Qu∴. What was done with the murderers?

Ans∴. They were taken to Jerusalem ; and, with Abiram, tried, condemned and executed.

Qu∴. What were the names of the other two murderers?

Ans∴. Nebo and Zabad.

Qu∴. Of what are they the types to us?

Ans∴. Of Fanaticism and Ignorance.

Qu∴. How were they punished?

Ans∴. They were first hanged, and afterwards beheaded.

Qu∴. What do the three heads represent, upon the apron and collar of an Ill∴. Elu of Fifteen?

Ans∴. Tyranny, Fanaticism and Ignorance; the three enslavers of mankind, smitten by the hand of Freedom.

Qu∴. What are the words of an Elu of Fifteen?

Ans∴. ♍ ℂ ♏ ☉ † and ☉ † -¶ ☍ ☉ ♒ ☉ ♒ ∴.

Qu∴. What did you next become, after you had been received an Ill∴. Elu of Fifteen?

Ans∴. A Sub∴. Elu of Twelve, or Prince Ameth.

Qu∴. Did you advance further?

Ans∴. Like Adonhiram, I became Gr∴. Master Architect.

Qu∴. What is the pass-word of a Gr∴. Master Architect?

Ans∴. ‡ ☉ ♏ - ♏ ℂ ♒ ? ♒ ∴. — Chief of the Architects.

Qu∴. What further honour did you receive?

Ans∴. Like the three Masters who descended into the vault of Enoch, and bore thence to King Solomon the Sacred Treasure, I was made a Royal Arch Mason.

Qu∴. Who were first received Masons of the Royal Arch?

Ans∴. Adonhiram, Joabert and Stolkin, with Solomon, and Hiram King of Tyre.

Qu∴. To what were you devoted, as a Royal Arch Mason?

Ans∴. To Honour and Duty.

Qu.∴ Are you a Gr.∴ El.∴ Perf.∴ and Sublime Mason?

Ans.∴ I have entered into the most Secret and Sacred place.

Qu.∴ What is it called?

Ans.∴ The Sacred Vault.

Qu.∴ Where do the Gr.∴ El.∴ Perf.∴ and Subl.∴ Masons work?

Ans.∴ Under ground.

Qu.∴ Where under ground?

Ans.∴ Under the Holy of Holies of the Temple.

Qu.∴ What are their works?

Ans.∴ To keep in profound secrecy the Mysteries of Masonry; to practise the purest morality, and to assist and relieve their brothers.

Qu.∴ What do they know?

Ans.∴ All that men have ever known as to the nature and attributes of the Deity, the laws of harmony which govern the Universe, and the immortality of the soul.

Qu.∴ Whither do they travel?

Ans.∴ To the four quarters of the globe.

Qu.∴ With what object?

Ans.∴ To make known the truth, and teach the pure morality of Masonry.

Qu.∴ What did the Sacred Vault contain?

Ans.∴ The Ineffable Name, or True Word of a Mason, engraved on a plate of gold, upon a cube of agate.

Qu.∴ What is your name?

Ans.∴ ♌⊙♍⊙☿♒.

Qu.∴ What does it signify?

Ans. An elevated place.

Qu.∴ How many signs has a Grand El.∴ Perf.∴ and Sub.∴ Mason?

Ans.∴ Three indispensable to be known, and six others.

Qu.∴ Give me the three principal signs.

Ans.∴ [He gives them].

Qu.∴ Give me the six others.

Ans.∴ [They are given thus]:

4th Sign: . . Bear upon the ♈☿☾ of the †‡♑☿☿♈, raising the heel. At the same time raise the ☾♄☾♎‡⊙♒♊‡⊙‡♋♎ to Heaven. This is the sign of *Admiration*.

5th Sign: . . Of *Distress*. . . Interlace the fingers of your hands, and put them on the ♈|☿♃ of your &☾⊙♊, ♃⊙†♋♎ upward.

6th Sign: . . Give the 4th Sign, each turning his back on the other. Then †☿☿¶|⊙♈‡☾⊙‡& other, over the ♎&☿ ȝ†♊☾‡∴

7th Sign: . . ‡†⊙♃ your ‡‡&⊙♒♊ on your &☾⊙‡♈: raise the same ⊙‡♋ towards &☾⊙*☾♒, and bringing it down, ♎♈‡♀¶☾ with it your ‡‡&♉♃.

8th Sign: . . Place your ‡‡&⊙♒♊ on your ♋☿ ȝ♈&, as if to pull out your ♈☿♒♌ȝ☾, and thence carry it quickly to your &☾⊙‡♈.

9th Sign: . . As if holding a ♊⊙♌♌☾‡, ♎♈‡♀¶☾‡⊙♈ the Brother's ♑☿‡☾&☾⊙♊; then ‡†⊙♃ your †‡&⊙♒♊ to your own ♑☿†☾&☾⊙♊.

Qu.∴ How many tokens are there?

Ans.∴ Three principal ones.

Qu.∴ Give them to me.

Ans.∴ [He gives them].

Qu.∴ How many Pass-words are there?

Ans.∴ Three principal ones.

Qu.∴ Give them.

Ans.·. [He does so].

Qu.·. How many covered words ?

Ans.·. Three likewise.

Qu.·. Give them.

Ans.·. [He does so].

Qu.·. What are the working tools of the Grand, Elect, Perfect and Sublime Mason ?

Ans.·. The Crow, the Mattock and the Spade.

Qu.·. To what uses have they been put ?

Ans.·. To discover and raise the square stone, which covered the entrance to the vaults of Enoch; to open a way to the Sacred Vault, after the Temple was destroyed; and to break in pieces the pedestal therein.

Qu.·. What did those Masons who entered the Sacred Vault, after the destruction of the Temple, find when they discovered the entrance ?

Ans.·. The corpse of Galahad.

Qu.·. Who was he ?

Ans.·. The son of Sephoris, a Gr.·. Elect, Chief of the Levites, and Special Guardian of the Sacred Vault; who died at his post, buried under the ruins of the Temple.

Qu.·. What disposition did they make of the corpse ?

Ans.·. They placed it in the Sacred Vault, clothed in his insignia, and wearing the jewel of a Gr.·. Elect.

Qu.·. What did King Solomon become, after the completion of the Temple ?

Ans.·. A libertine and an idolater; sacrificing to Chemosh, Moloch and Astarte; which caused many Masons to abandon Judea, fearful of the ruin which they believed his sins would bring upon his kingdom.

Qu.·. How long did he reign ?

Ans.·. Forty years, dying at the age of 58.

Qu.·. Who succeeded him ?

Ans.·. His kingdom was divided into those of Judah and Israel. Rehoboam his Son reigned over the former only.

Qu.·. When did his race cease to reign ?

Ans.·. When Nabuzaradan, General of the Assyrian armies, took Jerusalem, destroyed the Temple, and carried Zedekiah the King away captive unto Babylon: when the surviving Gr.·. Elect entered the Sacred Vault, erased the Ineffable Name, broke up the golden plate, and overturned the pedestal.

Qu.·. How long did the captivity last ?

Ans.·. Seventy years; and the war, two.

Qu.·. Who restored the Jews to freedom ?

Ans.·. Cyrus, King of Persia.

Qu.·. What other favour did he show them ?

Ans.·. He gave them permission to rebuild the city and Temple of the Lord, and restored to them most of the ornaments and vessels of the ancient Temple.

Qu.·. What are the characteristics of a Gr.·. El.·. Perf.·. and Sub.·. Mason ?

Ans.·. That he frees himself from the dominion of iniquity, injustice, revenge, envy and jealousy: that he is active in doing good; and speaks of his brethren only to praise them.

Qu.·. What is your reward ?

Ans.·. The knowledge of the True God; a faint, but true appreciation of His nature and Infinite attributes; a confidence in His wisdom and justice; an implicit trust in His beneficence and love for his creatures, securing me against scepticism and despair.

Qu.·. What is your Masonic age ?

Ans.·. The square of z—or $, years complete.

Qu.·. What contract did you enter into, on receiving this degree ?

Ans.·. I devoted myself to Virtue, and to the cause of Humanity; and became the firm ally of the Virtuous and the Good.

Qu.·. What is the token of that contract ?

20

Ans.·. This ring, symbol of Eternity, and of unbroken friendship.

Qu.·. By what light does a Gr.·. Elect work?

Ans.·. By the light of Truth, which emanates from Him whose Holy Name glitters upon the Triangular plate of gold, and lights our Lodge.

Sen.·. Gr.·. Ward.·. Return now, my Brother, to the Th.·. P.·. Gr.·. Master, and receive from him the closing instruction of this degree.

LECTURE.

My Brother, you have received the last degree in Ancient Masonry; and it is my duty to give you the concluding instruction in that degree, that you may be prepared to advance, if you desire, through the still higher degrees of the Ancient and Accepted Rite.

It is for each individual Mason to discover the secret of Masonry, by reflecting on its emblems, and upon what is said and done in the work. Seek and ye shall find. The great object of Masonry being the physical and moral amelioration of every individual in particular, and of society in general, there are important truths to be substituted in public opinion in the place of many errors and injurious prejudices; and among these moral maladies are some whose treatment requires courage and at the same time much prudence and discretion. The Masonic Secret manifests itself without speech revealing it, to him who well comprehends all the degrees, in proportion as he receives them, and particularly to those who advance to the highest degrees of the Ancient and Accepted Rite. That Rite raises a corner of the veil even in the degree of Apprentice; for in that it declares that Masonry is a worship.

Never intermeddling with points of doctrine, in politics or religion, Masonry labours to improve the social order, by enlightening men's minds, by warming men's hearts with love of the good, by inspiring them with the great principle of human fraternity, by requiring of its disciples, that their language and actions shall conform to that principle, that they shall enlighten one another, triumph over their passions, abhor vice, and pity the vicious man, as one afflicted with a deplorable malady.

It is the universal, eternal, immutable religion, such as God planted it in the heart of universal humanity. Its ministers are all Masons who comprehend it and are devoted to it: its offerings to God are good works; the sacrifice of the base and disorderly passions; and perpetual efforts to attain to all the moral perfection of which man is capable.

That enlightened faith, from which as from a living spring flow sublime devotedness, the sentiment of fraternity fruitful of good works, the spirit of indulgent kindness and gentle peace, sweet hopes, effectual consolation, and inflexible resolution to accomplish the most arduous and painful duties, Masonry has in all times religiously preserved. Ardently and perseveringly it has propagated it in all ages; and in our own day more zealously than ever. Scarcely a Masonic discourse is pronounced or a Masonic lesson read, by the highest officer or the humblest lecturer, that does not demonstrate the necessity and advantages of this faith, and earnestly teach the two constitutive principles of religion, the two great tenets that make all true religion,— Love of God, and Love of our neighbor. These two principles Masons carry into the bosom of their families, and into society. The Sectarians of former days substituted intolerance for charity and persecution for love: and did not love God, because they hated their neighbour. "Thou shalt love the Lord thy God with all thy "heart, soul, strength and mind, and thy neighbour as thyself; this do, and thou shalt live . . Suffer little "children to come unto me, for of such is the Kingdom of Heaven, into which ye shall not enter, except ye "be converted and become as little children . . He that loveth not his brother knoweth not God, for God is "love . . Whosoever hateth his brother is a murderer and abideth in death and darkness." Such is the true religion, and whatever is contrary to it is falsehood; and that true religion is the very spirit of Masonry. Forming one great people over the whole globe, it preserves that religion, strengthens it, extends it in its purity and simplicity, and makes it the rule and guide of the life and conduct of its members.

To make honour and duty the steady beacon-lights that shall guide your life-vessel over the stormy seas of Time; to do that which it is right to do, not because it will insure you success, or bring with it a reward, or gain the applause of men, or be most prudent and most advisable; but because it is right, and therefore *ought* to be done; to war always against error, ignorance, intolerance and vice; and yet to pity those who err, to teach the ignorant, to be yourself tolerant even of intolerance, and to strive to reclaim the vicious; are some of the duties of a Mason.

A good Mason is one that can look upon death, and see its face with the same countenance with which he hears its story; that can endure all the labours of his life with his soul supporting his body; that can equally despise riches when he hath them and when he hath them not; that is not sadder if they are in his neighbour's exchequer, nor more lifted up if they shine round about his own walls: one that is not moved with good fortune coming to him, nor going from him; that can look upon another man's lands with equanimity and pleasure, as if they were his own; and yet look upon his own and use them too, just as if they were another man's; that neither spends his goods prodigally and foolishly, nor yet keeps them avariciously and like a miser; that weighs not benefits by weight and number, but by the mind and circumstances of him that confers them; that never thinks his charity expensive, if a worthy person be the receiver; that does nothing for opinion's sake, but every thing for conscience, being as careful of his thoughts as of his acting in markets and theatres, and in as much awe of himself as of a whole assembly; that is bountiful and cheerful to his friends, and charitable and apt to forgive his enemies; that loves his country, consults its honour, and obeys its laws, and desires and endeavours nothing more than that he may do his duty and honour God. And such a Mason may reckon his life to be the life of a man, and compute his months, not by the course of the sun, but by the zodiac and circle of his virtues.

The whole world is but one Republic, of which each nation is a family and every individual a child. The sublime art of Masonry, not in any wise derogating from the different duties which the diversity of States requires, tends to create a new People, which, composed of many nations, shall all be bound together by the bonds of science, morality and virtue.

Essentially philanthropic, philosophical and progressive, it has for its bases the existence of God and the immortality of the soul; for its object, the study of universal morality, the sciences and the arts, and the practice of all the virtues. In every age its device has been, Liberty, Equality, Fraternity.

It is neither a political party nor a religious sect. It embraces all parties and all sects, to form from among them all a vast fraternal-association. It recognizes the dignity of man, and his right to freedom whenever he is fitted for it; and it knows nothing that should place one man below another, except debasement, ignorance and crime.

It is philanthropic; for it recognizes the great truth that all men are of the same origin, have common interests, and should co-operate together to the same end.

Therefore it teaches its members to love one another, to give to each other mutual assistance and support in all the circumstances of life, to share each other's pains and sorrows, as well as their joys and pleasures; to guard the reputations, respect the opinions, and be perfectly tolerant of the errors, of each other, in matters of faith and beliefs.

It is philosophical, because it teaches the great Truths concerning the nature and existence of one Supreme Deity, and the existence and immortality of the soul. It revives the Academe of Plato, and the wise teachings of Socrates. It reiterates the maxims of Pythagoras, Confucius and Zoroaster, and reverentially enforces the sublime lessons of Him who died upon the Cross.

The ancients thought that universal humanity acted under the influence of two opposing Principles, the Good and the Evil: of which the Good urged men towards Truth, Independence and Devotedness; and the Evil towards Falsehood, Servility and Selfishness. Masonry represents the Good Principle and constantly wars against the evil one. It is the Hercules, the Osiris, the Apollo, and the Ormuzd, at everlasting and deadly feud with the demons of ignorance, brutality, baseness, falsehood, slavishness of soul, intolerance, superstition, tyranny, meanness, the insolence of wealth, and bigotry.

When Despotism and Superstition ruled everywhere and seemed invincible, it invented, to avoid persecution, the Mysteries, that is to say, the Allegory, the Symbol and the Emblem, and transmitted its doctrines by the secret mode of initiation. Now, retaining its ancient ceremonies, and absolutely forbidding innovation, it openly displays in every civilized country its banner, on which its principles are written in letters of living light.

Man's views in regard to God, will contain only so much positive truth as the human mind is capable of receiving; whether that truth is attained by the exercise of reason, or communicated by revelation. It must necessarily be both limited and alloyed, to bring it within the competence of finite human intelligence. Being finite, we can form no correct or adequate idea of the Infinite: being material, we can form no clear conception of the Spiritual. We do believe in and know the infinity of Space and Time, and the spirituality of the Soul; but the *idea* of that infinity and spirituality eludes us. Even Omnipotence cannot infuse infinite conceptions into finite minds; nor can God, without first entirely changing the conditions of our being, pour a complete and full knowledge of His own nature and attributes into the narrow capacity of a human soul. Human intelligence could not grasp it, nor human language express it.

The consciousness of the individual reveals *itself* alone. His knowledge cannot pass beyond the limits of his own being. His conceptions of other things and other beings *are only his conceptions*. They are not those things or beings *themselves*. The living principle of a living Universe must be INFINITE; while all *our* ideas and conceptions are *finite*, and applicable only to finite beings. The Deity is thus not an object of *knowledge*, but of *faith*: not to be approached by the *understanding*, but by the *moral sense*; not to be *conceived*, but to be *felt*. All attempts to embrace the Infinite in the conception of the Finite, are and must be only accommodations to the frailty of man. Shrouded from human comprehension in an obscurity from which a chastened imagination is awed back, and Thought retreats in conscious weakness, the Divine Nature is a theme on which man is little entitled to dogmatize. Here the philosophic Intellect becomes most painfully aware of its own insufficiency.

And yet it is here that man most dogmatizes, classifies and describes God's attributes, makes out his map of God's nature, and his inventory of God's qualities, feelings, impulses and passions; and then hangs and burns his brother, who, as dogmatically as he, makes out a different map and inventory. The common understanding has no humility. *Its* God is an *incarnate* Divinity. Imperfection imposes its own limitations on the Illimitable, and clothes the Inconceivable Spirit of the Universe in forms that come within the grasp of the senses and the intellect, and are derived from that finite and imperfect nature which is but God's creation.

We are *all* of us, though not all *equally*, mistaken. The cherished dogmas of each of us are not, as we fondly suppose, the pure truth of God; but simply our own special form of error, the fragmentary and refracted ray of light which has fallen on our own minds.

> Our little systems have their day;
>   They have their day, and cease to be:
>   They are but broken lights of Thee,
> And Thou, O Lord, art more than they.

Thus perfect Truth is not attainable anywhere. We fondly style this Degree, that of Perfection; and yet that which it teaches is imperfect and defective. Still we are not to relax in the pursuit of Truth, nor contentedly acquiesce in error. It is our duty ever to press forward in the search; for though absolute Truth is unattainable, yet the amount of error in our views is capable of progressive and perpetual diminution; and thus it is that Masonry is a continual struggle towards the Light.

All errors are not equally innocuous; and to entertain unworthy conceptions of the nature and Providence of God, is what Masonry symbolizes by ignorance of the True Word. Not the entire and perfect and absolute Truth in regard to God; but the highest and noblest conception of Him that our minds are capable of forming, is the True Word of a Mason; and it is Ineffable, because one man cannot communicate to another his own conception of Deity.

For every man's conception of God must vary with his mental cultivation and mental powers. If any one contents himself with any *lower* image than his intellect is capable of grasping, then he contents himself with that which is false *to him*, as well as false *in fact*. If lower than he can reach, he must needs *feel* it to be false. The negro's idea of God, true to him, is false to me, because I feel it to be unworthy and inadequate. And if we, of the nineteenth century after Christ, adopt the conceptions of the nineteenth century before him; if *our* conceptions of God are those of the ignorant, narrow-minded and vindictive Israelite; then we think worse of God, and have a lower, meaner and more limited view of His nature, than the faculties which he has bestowed are capable of grasping. The highest view we can form is nearest to the truth. If we acquiesce in any lower one, we acquiesce in an untruth. We feel that it is an affront and an indignity to Him, to conceive of Him as cruel, short-sighted, capricious and unjust; as a jealous, an angry, a vindictive Being. When we examine our conceptions of His character, if we can conceive of a loftier, nobler, higher, more beneficent, glorious and magnificent character, then this latter is to us the true conception of Deity; *for nothing can be imagined more excellent than He.*

Religion, to obtain currency and influence with the great mass of mankind, must needs be alloyed with such an amount of error, as to place it far below the standard attainable by the higher human capacities. A religion as pure as the loftiest and most cultivated human reason could discern, would not be comprehended by, or effective over, the less-educated portion of mankind. What is Truth to the philosopher, would not be Truth, nor have the effect of Truth, to the peasant. The religion of the many must necessarily be more incorrect than that of the refined and reflective few, not so much in its essence as in its forms, not so much in the spiritual idea which lies latent at the bottom of it, as in the symbols and dogmas in which that idea is embodied. The truest religion would, in many points, not be comprehended by the ignorant, nor consolatory to them, nor guiding and supporting for them. The doctrines of the Bible are often not clothed in the language of strict truth, but in that which was fittest to convey to a rude and ignorant people the practical essentials of the doctrine. A perfectly pure faith, free from all extraneous admixtures, a system of noble theism and lofty morality, would find too little preparation for it in the common mind and heart, to admit of prompt reception by the masses of mankind; and Truth might not have reached us, if it had not borrowed the wings of Error.

We cannot read literally the views of God contained in the Hebrew writings. To *us* their inner meaning is different from their words; and we read them thus:

"I am the God of Abraham, the God of Isaac and the God of Jacob; the Absolute, Uncreated Existence, that which was and shall be. This is my Eternal Name, and my memorial unto all generations.

"I demand the veneration and adoration due me from mankind. By the inflexible law of cause and effect which I have enacted, the consequences of the vices and iniquities of the fathers descend and are visited upon their children through many generations of those that set my laws at defiance; and those only escape, who love me and follow my law.

"God is merciful and gracious, indulgent and abundant in goodness and truth, showing mercy to thousands, forgiving iniquity, transgression and sin, but requiring repentance, reformation and atonement from the guilty.

"The Lord יהוה is one God. He is the only God, the Eternal Truth, by whose immutable laws the good deed involves in itself its reward, and the sin its punishment. He protects the fatherless and the widow, and loves the stranger, and gives him food and raiment."

Many parts of these writings contain views of Deity, of God, and of Man's relations to him, as pure and lofty as the Human Intellect can grasp; but others, quite as numerous and characteristic, depict feelings and opinions, on these topics, as low, meagre, and unworthy, as ever took their rise in savage and uncultivated minds. They would require us to believe that the Pure, Spiritual, Supreme, Ineffable, Immutable Creator of the universe, infinite in wisdom, consistency, justice and mercy, who permits his frail creatures to call Him Father, so mistook in the creation of man, as to repent, and grieve, and find it necessary to destroy his own work: that he permits the existence of a rival though inferior God; and allows him to gain the dominion over this world, and to people Hell with God's creatures: that He selected one favoured people from the rest of His children, and commissioned them to devastate and destroy; that He sanctioned fraud, commanded cruelty, contended, and long in vain, with the magic of other Gods, hardened the heart of Pharaoh that He might punish him and his people, and slay them in multitudes, because their King was thus hardened to resist His will; that he wrestled in the body with one Patriarch and supped with another, sympathized with and shared in human passions, became enraged, formed rash and cruel resolutions, and was persuaded to abandon them;—

and all this they would require, because these coarse conceptions prevailed some thousands of years ago, among a People, whose History, as written by themselves, is not of a nature to inspire us with any extraordinary confidence in either their virtues or their intellect.

The Mason regards God as a Moral Governor, as well as an Original Creator; as a God at hand, and not merely one afar off in the distance of infinite space, and in the remoteness of Past or Future Eternity. He conceives of Him as taking a watchful and presiding interest in the affairs of the world, and as influencing the hearts and actions of men.

To him, God is the great Artificer of the World of Life and Matter; and man, with his wonderful corporeal and mental frame, His direct work. He believes that God has made men with different intellectual capacities; and enabled some, by superior intellectual power, to see and originate truths which are hidden from the mass of men. He believes that when it is His will that mankind should make some great step forward, or achieve some pregnant discovery, He calls into being some intellect of more than ordinary magnitude and power, to give birth to new ideas, and grander conceptions of the Truths vital to Humanity.

We hold that God has so ordered matters in this beautiful and harmonious, but mysteriously-governed Universe, that one great mind after another will arise, from time to time, as such are needed, to discover and flash forth before the eyes of men the truths that are wanted, and the amount of truth that can be borne. He so arranges, that nature and the course of events shall send men into the world, endowed with that higher mental and moral organization, in which grand truths, and sublime gleams of spiritual light will spontaneously and inevitably arise.

Whatever Hiram Abi really was, he is the type, perhaps an imaginary type, to us, of humanity in its highest phase; an exemplar of what man may and should become, in the course of ages, in his progress towards the realization of his destiny; an individual gifted with a glorious intellect, a noble soul, a fine organization, and a perfectly balanced moral being; an earnest of what humanity may be, and what we believe it will hereafter be in God's good time; *the possibility of the race made real.*

The Mason believes that God has arranged this glorious but perplexing world with a purpose, and on a plan. He holds that every man sent upon this earth, and especially every man of superior capacity, has a duty to perform, a mission to fulfil, a baptism to be baptized with: that every great and good man possesses some portion of God's truth, which he must proclaim to the world, and which must bear fruit in his own bosom. In a true and simple sense, he believes all the pure, wise and intellectual to be inspired, and to be so for the instruction, advancement and elevation of mankind. That kind of inspiration, like God's omnipresence, is not limited to the few writers claimed by Jews, Christians or Moslems, but is co-extensive with the race. It is the consequence of a faithful use of our faculties. Each man is its subject, God is its source, and Truth its only test. It differs in degrees, as the intellectual endowments, the moral wealth of the soul, and the degree of cultivation of those endowments and faculties differ. It is limited to no sect, age or nation. It is wide as the world, and common as God. It was not given to a few men, in the infancy of mankind, to monopolize inspiration, and bar God out of the soul. You and I are not born in the dotage and decay of the world. The stars are beautiful as in their prime; the most ancient Heavens are fresh and strong. God is still everywhere in nature wherever a heart beats with love, wherever Faith and Reason utter their oracles, there is God, as formerly in the hearts of seers and prophets. No soil on earth is so holy as the good man's heart; nothing is so full of God. This inspiration is not given to the learned alone, not alone to the great and wise, but to every faithful child of God. Certain as the open eye drinks in the light, do the pure in heart see God; and he that lives truly, feels Him as a presence not to be put by.

Truths that are written by the finger of God upon the heart of man, are definite enough for the Mason. Views of religion and duty, wrought out by the meditations of the studious, confirmed by the allegiance of the good and wise, stamped as sterling by the response they find in every uncorrupted mind, are sure enough for him. He does not cling to dogmatic certainty, nor vainly imagine such certainty attainable. He is willing to rest the hopes which animate him, and the principles which guide him, on the deductions of reason and the convictions of instinct. He believes that no surer foundation can be discovered for religious belief, than the deductions of the intellect and the convictions of the heart. Reason proves to him the existence and attributes of God; those spiritual instincts, which he believes to be the voice of God in the soul, infuse into his mind a sense of his relation to God, and a hope of future existence; and his reason and conscience alike irresistibly point to virtue as the highest good, and the destined end and aim of man.

He studies the wonders of the Heavens, the frame-work and revolutions of the Earth, the mysterious beauties and adaptations of animal existence, the moral and material constitution of the human creature, so fearfully and wonderfully made; and is satisfied that God *is;* and that a Wise and Good Being is the author of the starry Heavens above him, and of the moral world within him: and his mind finds an adequate foundation for its hopes, its worship, its principles of action, in the far-stretching universe, in the glorious firmament, in the deep, full soul, bursting with unutterable thoughts.

These are truths which every reflecting mind will unhesitatingly receive, as not to be surpassed, nor capable of improvement; and fitted, if obeyed, to make earth indeed a Paradise, and man only a little lower than the angels. The worthlessness of ceremonial observances, and the necessity of active virtue: the enforcement of purity of heart as the security for purity of life, and of the government of the thoughts, as the originators and forerunners of action; universal philanthropy, requiring us to love all men, and to do unto others that and that only which we should think it right, just and generous for them to do unto us; forgiveness of injuries; the necessity of self-sacrifice in the discharge of duty; humility; genuine sincerity, and *being* that which we *seem* to be; all these sublime precepts need no miracle, no voice from the clouds, to recommend them to our allegiance, or to assure us of their divine origin. They command obedience by virtue of their inherent rectitude and beauty; and have been, and are, and will be the law in every age and every country of the world.

To the Mason, God is our Father in Heaven,—to be whose especial children is the best reward of the peace-makers—to see whose face is the highest hope of the pure in heart:—who is ever at hand to strengthen His true worshippers—to whom are due our heartiest love, our humblest submission—whose most acceptable worship is a holy heart—in whose constant presence our life is passed,—to whose merciful disposal we are resigned by that death which we hope is to make known to us His great Creation-Thought; and whose severe decrees forbid a living man to lap his soul in an Elysium of mere indolent content.

As to our feelings towards Him, and our conduct towards man, Masonry teaches little about which men can differ, and little from which they can dissent. He is our *Father;* and we are all *brethren.* This much lies open to the most ignorant and busy, as fully as to those who have most leisure and are most learned. This needs no Priest to teach it, and no authority to endorse it; and if every man did that only which is consistent with it, it would exile barbarity, cruelty, intolerance, uncharitableness, perfidy, treachery, revenge, selfishness, and all their kindred vices and bad passions, beyond the confines of the world.

The true Mason, sincerely holding that a Supreme God created and governs this world, believes also that He governs it by laws, which, though wise, just and beneficent, are yet steady, unwavering, inexorable. He believes that his agonies and sorrows are not specially ordained for *his* chastening, *his* strengthening, *his* elaboration and development; but are incidental and necessary results of the operation of laws, the best that could be devised for the happiness and purification of the species, and to give occasion and opportunity for the practice of all the virtues, from the homeliest and most common, to the noblest and most sublime; or perhaps not even that, but the best adapted to work out the vast, awful, glorious, eternal designs of the Great Spirit of the universe. He believes that the ordained operations of nature, which have brought misery to him, have, from the very unswerving tranquillity of their career, showered blessings and sunshine upon many another path; that the unrelenting chariot of Time, which has crushed or maimed him in its allotted course, is pressing onward to the accomplishment of those serene and mighty purposes, to have contributed to which, even as a victim, is an honour and a recompense. He takes this view of Time and Nature and God, and yet bears his lot without murmur or distrust; because it is a portion of a system, the best possible, because ordained by God. But he does not believe that God loses sight of him, while superintending the march of the great harmonies of the universe; nor that it was not foreseen, when the universe was created, its laws enacted, and the long succession of its operations pre-ordained, that in the great march of those events, he would suffer pain and undergo calamity. He believes that his individual good entered into God's consideration, as well as the great cardinal results to which the course of all things is tending.

Thus believing, he has attained an eminence in virtue, the highest, amid *passive* excellence, which humanity can reach. He finds his reward and his support in the reflection that he is an unreluctant and self-sacrificing co-operator with the Creator of the Universe; and in the noble consciousness of being worthy and capable of so sublime a conception, yet so sad a destiny. He is then truly entitled to be called a Grand, Elect, Perfect and Sublime Mason. He is content to fall early in the battle, if his body may but form a stepping-stone for the future conquests of humanity.

It cannot be that God, who, we are certain, is perfectly good, can choose us to suffer pain, unless either we are ourselves to receive from it an antidote to what is evil in ourselves, or else as such pain is a necessary part in the scheme of the universe, which as a whole is good. In either case, the Mason receives it with submission. He would not suffer unless it was ordered so. Whatever his creed, if he believes that God is, and that He cares for his creatures, he cannot doubt that; nor that it would not have been so ordered, unless it was either better for himself, or for some other persons, or for some things. To complain and lament is to murmur against God's will, and worse than unbelief.

The Mason, whose mind is cast in a nobler mould than those of the ignorant and unreflecting, and is instinct with a diviner life,—who loves truth more than rest, and the peace of Heaven rather than the peace of Eden,—to whom a loftier being brings severer cares,—who knows that man does not live by pleasure or content alone, but by the presence of the power of God,—must cast behind him the hope of any other repose or tranquillity, than that which is the last reward of long agonies of thought; he must relinquish all prospect of any Heaven save that of which trouble is the avenue and portal; he must gird up his loins, and trim his lamp, for a work which cannot be put by, and must not be negligently done. If he does not like to live in the furnished lodgings of tradition, he must build his own house, his own system of faith and thought, for himself.

The hope of success, and not the hope of reward, should be our stimulating and sustaining power. Our object, and not ourselves, should be our inspiring thought. Selfishness is a sin, when temporary, and for time: Spun out to eternity, it does not become celestial prudence. We should toil and die, not for Heaven or Bliss, but for Duty.

In the more frequent cases, where we have to join our efforts to those of thousands of others, to contribute to the carrying forward of a great cause; merely to till the ground or sow the seed for a very distant harvest, or to prepare the way for the future advent of some great amendment; the amount which each one contributes to the achievement of ultimate success, the portion of the price which justice should assign to each as his especial production, can never be accurately ascertained. Perhaps few of those who have laboured, in the patience of secrecy and silence, to bring about some political or social change, which they felt convinced would ultimately prove of vast service to humanity, may live to see the change effected, or the anticipated good flow from it. Fewer still of them will be able to pronounce what appreciable weight their several efforts contributed to the achievement of the change desired. Many will doubt, whether, in truth, these exertions have any influence whatever; and, discouraged, cease all active effort.

Not to be thus discouraged, the Mason must labour to elevate and purify his *motives*, as well as sedulously cherish the conviction, assuredly a true one, that in this world there is no such thing as effort thrown away; that in all labour there is profit; that all sincere exertion, in a righteous and unselfish cause, is necessarily followed, in spite of all appearance to the contrary, by an appropriate and proportionate success; that no bread cast upon the waters can be wholly lost; that no seed planted in the ground can fail to quicken in due time and measure; and that, however we may, in moments of despondency, be apt to doubt, not only whether our cause will triumph, but whether, if it does, we shall have contributed to its triumph,—there is One, who has not only seen every exertion we have made, but who can assign the exact degree in which each soldier has assisted to gain the great victory over social evil.

The Grand, Elect, Perfect and Sublime Mason will in nowise deserve that honorable title, if he has not that strength, that will, that self-constraining energy; that Faith, that feeds upon no earthly hope, nor ever thinks of victory, but, content in its own consummation, combats because it ought to combat, rejoicing fights, and still rejoicing falls.

The Augean Stables of the World; the accumulated uncleanness and misery of centuries, require a mighty river to cleanse them thoroughly away; every drop we contribute aids to swell that river and augment its force, in a degree appreciable by God, though not by man; and he whose zeal is deep and earnest, will not be over-anxious that his individual drops should be distinguishable amid the mighty mass of cleansing and fertilizing waters; far less that, for the sake of distinction, it should flow in ineffective singleness away. He will not be careful that his name should be inscribed upon the mite which he casts into the Treasury of God. It suffices the Mason to know, that, if he has laboured, with purity of purpose, in any good cause, he *must* have contributed to its success; that the *degree* in which he has contributed, is a matter of infinitely small concern; and still more, that the consciousness of having so contributed, however obscurely and unnoticed, is his sufficient, even if it be his sole, reward. Let every Grand, Elect, Perfect and Sublime Mason cherish this faith. It is a duty. It is the brilliant and never dying light that shines within and through the symbolic pedestal of alabaster, on which reposes the cube of agate, symbol of duty, inscribed with the Divine name of God. He who sows and reaps is a good labourer, and worthy of his hire. But he who sows that which shall be reaped by others, who know not of and care not for the sower, is a labourer of a nobler order, and worthy of a loftier guerdon.

The Mason does not exhort others to an ascetic undervaluing of this life, as an insignificant and unworthy portion of existence; for that demands feelings which are unnatural, and which therefore, if attained, must be morbid, and if merely professed, insincere; and it teaches us to look rather to a future life for the compensation of social evils, than to this life for their cure; and so does injury to the cause of virtue and to that of social progress. Life is real, and is earnest, and it is full of duties to be performed. Those only who feel a deep interest and affection for this world will work resolutely for its amelioration: those whose affections are transferred to Heaven, easily acquiesce in the miseries of earth, giving them up as hopeless, as befitting, and as ordained; and console themselves with the idea of the amends which are one day to be theirs. It is a sad truth, that those most decidedly given to spiritual contemplation, and to making religion rule in their hearts, are often most apathetic towards all improvement of this world's systems, and in many cases virtual conservatives of evil, and hostile to political and social reform, as diverting men's energies from eternity.

The Mason does not war with his own instincts, macerate the body into weakness and disorder, disparage what he sees to be beautiful, knows to be wonderful, and feels to be unspeakably dear and fascinating. He does not put down the nature which God has given him, to struggle after one which He has *not* bestowed. He knows that man is sent into the world, not a spiritual, but a composite being, made up of body and mind, the body having, as is fit and needful in a material world, its full, rightful and allotted share. His life is guided by a full recognition of this fact. He does not deny it in bold words, and admit it in weaknesses and inevitable failings. He believes that his spirituality will come in the next stage of his being, when he puts on the spiritual body: that his body will be dropped at death: and that, until then, God meant it to be commanded and controlled, but not neglected, despised or ignored by the soul, under pain of heavy consequences.

Yet the Mason is not indifferent as to the fate of the soul, after its present life, as to its continued and eternal being, and the character of the scenes in which that being will be fully developed. These are to him topics of the profoundest interest, and the most ennobling and refining contemplation. They occupy much of his leisure; and as he becomes familiar with the sorrows and calamities of this life, as his hopes are disappointed and his visions of happiness here fade away; when life has wearied him in its race of hours; when he is harassed and toil-worn, and the burthen of his years weighs heavy on him, the balance of attraction gradually inclines in favour of another life; and he clings to his lofty speculations with a tenacity of interest which needs no injunction, and will listen to no prohibition. They are the consoling privilege of the aspiring, the wayworn, the weary and the bereaved.

To him the contemplation of the Future lets in light upon the Present, and develops the higher portions of his nature. He endeavours rightly to adjust the respective claims of heaven and earth upon his time and thought, so as to give the proper proportions thereof to performing the duties and entering into the interests of this world, and to preparation for a better; to the cultivation and purification of his own character, and to the public service of his fellow-men.

"*Thy brother shall live again.*" Thy Brother: not some undefined spirituality, some new and strange being; but thy brother *himself*. Not so spiritually changed as to be forever lost to thee. Not re-absorbed into

21

the Parent-Soul, nor living again in a vague, indefinite, unremembering existence; but *the same* life, in its character, affections, and spiritual identity. What noble and consoling words, to be uttered amidst the wrecks of Time, the memorials of buried Nations, the earth-mounds every where rising above the silent dust of all that has ever lived and breathed in the visible creation! They come from beyond the regions of all visible life. From the dark earth under our feet, no voice issues; from the silent stars no word is uttered. Here are but silence, dust and death. The Earth entombs us, and the Heavens crush us, until these words come to us, sent from Heaven, uttered from the great realm of invisible life.

There is life for us, *somewhere;* and we ask not where. We can wait God's time for *that*. Somewhere in His great Universe we shall find our lost ones, and be with them evermore. The Mason believes that there is that within us, which shall never die: that the soul is essentially immortal, and immortally blessed; and that no dark eclipse shall come over it, between death and the resurrection, to bury it in the gloom of utter unconsciousness, or cause it to wander like a shadow in the dim realms of an intermediate state.

In that future existence, the Mason believes that his perceptions of God's presence will be clearer, and his insight into His nature incalculably deeper. When the soul at death emerges from the body, he hopes to lay down at once and forever all those temptations with which in this life the senses beset the soul, all that physical weakness which has clogged and bounded the exertions of the intellect, all that obscurity with which our material nature has too often clouded our moral vision. But he does not hope to attain perfection at once. He believes that, according to the point which each soul has reached on earth, will be its starting point in Heaven; that through long ages of self-elaborating effort, it must win its way up nearer and nearer to the Throne of God; and that occupation can never fail, nor its interest ever flag, even through everlasting being: for, infinite as may be its duration, it will ever be surpassed by the infinity of God's perfection, and of the created Universe: nor does he fear that eternity will exhaust the contemplations of him to whom will lie open, not only the systems and firmaments we read of and can dimly see, but that larger, remoter, more illimitable Universe which we cannot even dream of here.

And he hopes that, at length,—when, in the course of those endless gradations of Progress, through which our spiritual faculties will ever advance towards full development, we shall have begun to know God our Father with something of the same cognizance wherewith we know our fellow-creatures here, we shall so learn to love Him, that Love will absorb into itself all the elements and constituents of that immortal life.

And even in regard to this, the Mason does not dogmatize, but entertaining and uttering his own convictions, he leaves every one else free to do the same; and only hopes that the time will come, even if after the lapse of unimaginable ages, when all men shall form one great family of brothers, and one law alone shall govern God's whole Universe, and that law the law of Love.

Believe as you may, my Brother; if the Universe is not, to you, without a God, and if man is not like the beast that perishes, but hath an immortal soul, we welcome you among us; to wear, as we wear, with humility and a strong consciousness of your own demerits and short-comings, the title of Gr∴ Elect, Perf∴ and Sublime Mason.

TO CLOSE.

[The Th∴ P∴ raps 3, and says]:

Th∴ P∴ Whence come you, Most Exc∴ Sen∴ Gr∴ Warden?

S∴ G∴ W∴ From Judea.

Qu∴ What bring you thence?

Ans∴ The precious treasure of a Gr∴ Elect, engraven on my heart, and which I desire to communicate to you.

Th∴ P∴ Approach, and do so, my Brother!

[The Sen∴ Gr∴ W∴ approaches the East, giving the sign of admiration; and whispers the Word, by its letters, in the ear of the Th∴ P∴]

Th∴ P∴ My Brethren, you will form in a circle upon my right and left, to receive this Treasure.

[They do so; and place their ☌☉♒□♎ on their ☌☾☉□♎, in the attitude of the 5th sign. The Th∴ P∴

whispers the word, by the letters, to the Bro∴ on his right, and he to the next on the right; and so it goes round the circle, and returns to the Th∴ P∴].

Th∴ P∴. My Brethren, the Gr∴ Architect of the Universe having allowed us to receive the Ineffable Word, let us, that it may ever remain engraved upon our hearts, that we may not again be plunged in darkness, purify our souls of all impurities, and pray for His aid and support.

[All kneel: and the Th∴ P∴ repeats the following]

PRAYER.

Direct us, Oh יהוה, Supreme Ruler of the Universe! Keep us from falling into the pits which our enemies dig for us! Animate us with thy Divine Spirit! Extend over us Thy beneficent Providence, and by means of Thy gifts and favours enable us to assist the poor and relieve the needy! Bless and sanctify our works, that they may produce good fruit! Strengthen us with Thy Holy Power; and, that we may add to Thy glory, help us to perform our Masonic duties, and to practise all the Masonic virtues! Amen!

[All rise].

Th∴ P∴. Bro∴ Sen∴ Gr∴ W∴, what is the hour?

Ans∴. Midnight.

Qu∴. What then remains for us to do?

Ans∴. To rest.

Qu∴. What motive brought you hither?

Ans∴. The desire of practising virtue, charity and justice with my Brethren.

Qu∴. What other purpose had you?

Ans∴. That of contemplating the brilliant Triangle.

Qu∴. Why does that so often occupy us here?

Ans∴. Because it is an emblem of the Gr∴ Architect of Heaven and Earth.

Qu∴. What fruit do you expect to receive from that contemplation?

Ans∴. Light, Truth and Knowledge.

Qu∴. What knowledge?

Ans∴. That entrusted to Masons in the earliest ages, and which Masonry has handed down to us; the knowledge of the Deity, His creatures and His works.

Qu∴. Have you attained that knowledge?

Ans∴. In part. I hope to know more as I advance towards Perfection beyond the grave.

Th∴ P∴. So mote it be! Announce, my Brother, that I am about to close this Lodge by the Mysterious Numbers.

S∴ G∴ W∴. Brethren in the North and South, the Th∴ P∴ Gr∴ Master is about to close this Lodge by the Mysterious Numbers. Be pleased to give him your assistance.

[The Th∴ P∴ salutes the assembly by the 1st sign. They respond by the same].

Th∴ P∴. M∴ Ex∴ Sen∴ and Jun∴ Gr∴ Wardens, and Ex∴ Officers and B thren of this Venerable Lodge of Perfection, we are about to close the same, that you may retire in peace, and continue to do good, and to live virtuously in the presence of the Gr∴ Architect of the Universe. Attend!

[The Jun∴ Gr∴ W∴ raps; — the Sen∴ Gr∴ W∴ ‖ — and the Th∴ P∴ £ — Then there is silence for a moment or two. Then

> The Th∴ P∴ raps; —
> All the Bros∴ give the 1st sign.
> He raps; again.
> They give the 2d sign.
> He raps; again.
> And they give the 3d sign].

Th∴ P∴. The Lodge is closed. My Brethren, go in peace!

FINIS.

Fifteenth Degree.

Knights of the Sword, of the East, or of the Eagle.

THE LODGE, ITS DECORATIONS, AND FURNITURE.

This degree requires a preparation room, and two principal apartments, styled "*Hall of the East,*" and "*Hall of the West:*" between which must be an ante-chamber or passage.

The preparation room is plain, without furniture or ornaments.

The Hall of the East, or first apartment, represents the Council-Chamber of Cyrus King of Persia, at Babylon. It is hung with green, from the ceiling to the floor. On the South, West and North there must be a space of at least six feet between the hangings and the wall. It is brilliantly lighted, by no particular number or arrangement of lights. In the East is a superb Throne. In the West are two arm-chairs; in the North and South, seats for the brethren. The Throne is elevated by two steps, and adorned with gold-lace and fringe.

Behind the throne is a transparency representing the dream of Cyrus, to wit: a roaring lion ready to spring upon him: above it a brilliant glory, surrounded with luminous clouds; and in the centre of the glory the Ineffable Name of God, in Hebrew letters. Out of the clouds an eagle emerges, bearing in his beak a pennant, upon which are the words: "*Restore liberty to the captives.*" Below the luminous clouds are Nebuchadnezzar and Belshazzar, loaded with chains, the former on all fours, eating grass.

Inside of the hangings, with room for the brethren to sit between, must be a wall of canvass, about three feet high, painted to represent bricks, commencing on each side of the throne, and going entirely around the North, South and West sides of the room, inclosing within it the two chairs in the West. At each of the four corners, and midway the Northern, Southern and Western sides, is a tower, also painted like brick-work: and, except that midway the Western side, five or six feet high. The other must be at least seven feet high, and large enough to contain a man. It must have two doors, one opening on the inside, and the other on the outside of the hangings. At the latter door, in the space between the hangings and the wall, must be two sentinels, armed with pikes and swords. The hangings must fit closely to the sides of this tower, so that one can pass in and out of the tower, without being seen by those within the hangings; and there must be no passage for the light, from one door of the tower to the other.

The wall may extend along the East, behind the Throne. When the Brethren are standing, they are inside, and when sitting, outside, of the wall.

The door leading into the ante-chamber, should be near the East.

In the ante-chamber separating the two apartments, must be a solid wooden bridge; under which a representation of running water with dead bodies and dismembered limbs floating in it. Near it should be a

1.A

watch-fire. The approach to it must be guarded by several armed men, and the further end should reach to the door of the second apartment. The river is a representation of the River Jordan, above the Dead Sea, upon the route from Babylon on the Euphrates to Jerusalem.

The third chamber, called the Chamber or Hall of the West, or the second apartment, represents the encampment of the Masons among the ruins of Jerusalem. The hangings are crimson. The room is lighted by 70 lights, disposed in 10 groups of 7 each. One in each group is lighted all the time. The others will be lighted at the proper period of the work. There is no Throne; but simply a seat in the East at the time of reception.

A curtain at the West end of the Hall conceals a blazing glory and an altar. This curtain will be raised or drawn aside at the time directed: and, at the same time, green hangings will take the place of the crimson, leaving the crimson festoons, and changing only the lower portion of the hangings; which may be so arranged as to fold over each other.

The middle of the Hall represents the Temple demolished, and the column Boaz broken; with the working tools of Masonry scattered about in disorder. Along the sides of the hall will be represented, as if in stone-work, the ruined walls of Jerusalem.

OFFICERS, TITLES, ORNAMENTS, AND JEWELS.

In the First Apartment.

The *Sov∴ Master* presides, representing CYRUS, King of Persia.

The *Sen∴ Warden* is styled *Gr∴ Master of Cavalry*, and represents the General highest in rank, named SISINNA.

The *Jun∴ Warden* is styled *Gr∴ Master of Infantry*, and represents the General second in rank, named NABUZARADIN.

The Orator is styled *Gr∴ M∴ of the Palace*, and represents DANIEL.

The Keeper of the Seals represents RATIM, and is styled *Gr∴ Master of the Chancery*.

The Treasurer is styled *Gr∴ M∴ of the Finances*, and represents MITHRIDATES.

The Secretary is styled *Gr∴ M∴ of Despatches*, and represents SCHEMEL.

The *Gr∴ Master of Ceremonies* represents ABAZAR.

The other Brothers are styled *Knights*.

The Sov∴ Master bears a sceptre. The officers wear over the neck, as a collar, a broad, green, watered ribbon, falling upon the stomach, and without any jewel. The Master wears a similar collar, fringed and bordered with gold, and with a small tassel of gold at the bottom; on the breast of which are embroidered, crosswise, a sword, and a sceptre surmounted by a small sun; all in gold.

The Knights wear a broad, green, watered ribbon, as a baldrick, from left to right, without jewel.

The apron is white, edged and lined with green, and the flap down. On the flap must be painted or embroidered the knot of Solomon, badly tied; and in the middle of the main apron two sabres crossed. On the reverse side are the emblems of a Grand Elu Ecossais.

In the Second Apartment.

Here the Master is styled *Th∴ Excellent;* the Wardens, *Excellent;* and the other Brothers, *Venerable.* All wear a scarf of water-colored silk, both edges fringed with gold. It is worn around the body as a girdle; the ends falling down over the skirts of the coat; and on the ends a bridge embroidered in gold, on which are, upon its arch, the letters ℵ.·. ℧.·. ℧.·. The scarf is embroidered throughout, with human heads, mutilated limbs, crowns, and swords whole and broken. The apron is crimson velvet, edged with green. On the flap are embroidered, in gold, a bleeding head; and two swords crossed. In the centre of the main apron, three triangles formed of chains with triangular links.

The jewel is three triangles, one within the other, diminishing in size, and enclosing two naked swords, crossed, hilts downward, resting on the base of the inner triangle.

Under the swords, within the triangle, the Master wears a square, the Sen.·. Warden a level, the Jun.·. Warden a plumb. The other officers wear in like manner their ordinary jewel of the Symbolic Lodge, within the triangle and under the swords.

Each Knight wears a silver trowel with an ebony handle, suspended by a red ribbon from his girdle, on his right side.

The term Knight will be added to all titles except the Master's; as Exc.·. Kt.·. Sen.·. Warden: and the brothers who are not officers will be addressed as Ven.·. Kt.·. A.·. . B . . ., &c.

The jewels are entirely of gold.

The Battery is £ — by ‖ and ?

The Step; to advance boldly, by ‖ long steps, sword in hand, and the arm raised as if to engage in combat.

The Age of a Knight of the East is £. years.

The Plaudit; *Glory to God! Health to our Sovereign Master!*

TO OPEN.

The Knights being all in their places in the first apartment [the Council Chamber of King Cyrus], except the Sov.·. Master (who does not enter until after he is announced by a stamp of the foot upon the floor, near the entrance), the M.·. of Cavalry says:

M.·. Cav.·. The Sov.·. Master has ordered us to assemble here, to hold a council extraordinary. Be attentive, Knights! He approaches!

[The Sov.·. Master enters, escorted by the two Guards of the Tower, with drawn swords. After he takes his place, they return].

[The Sov.·. Master gives one rap with the hilt of his sword, and salutes the Knights. They, following the M.·. of Cav.·., respond by laying the right hand on the heart, and bowing].

Sov.·. M.·. Exc.·. Kt.·. M.·. of Cav.·., what is the duty of a true Knight?

M.·. Cav.·. To see to the security of the Council; that none may enter but true Knights.

Sov.·. M.·. Exc.·. Kts.·. Masters of Cav.·. and Inf.·., proceed to make your inspection.

[The two Wardens examine both doors of the Tower, see that the Guards are at their posts; return to their own stations; and the Sen.·. W.·. reports]:

M.·. Cav.·. Th.·. Exc.·. Sov.·. M.·., the Guards surround the Palace, and the Council may deliberate in safety.

Sov.·. M.·. Does that suffice?

M.·. Cav.·. It is necessary to know whether all who are present are entitled to sit in the Council.

Sov.·. M.·. Assure yourselves of that.

[They do so, by receiving the Pass-word, and the Sen.·. W.·. reports]:

M.·. Cav.·. All who are present are Knights good and true.

Sov∴ M∴. What is the hour?

M∴ Cav∴. The end of the ten weeks of the years of captivity.

Sov∴ M∴. Ex∴ Kts∴ Masters of Cav∴ and Inf∴, since that is the hour, announce that the Council is about to be opened.

[Each makes the announcement to those on his side of the Lodge: the Sov∴ M∴ raps ‖ ? — and each Warden repeats it].

Sov∴ M∴. Together, my Brethren!

[All the Knights, simultaneously with the Sov∴ M∴, applaud once, saying; *Glory to God! Health to the Sov∴ Master !*]:

Sov∴ M∴. This Council of Knights of the East or of the Sword is open, and its labours are resumed.

[The Wardens repeat this. The Sov∴ M∴ gives one rap, and says, " Be seated, Sir Kts∴."].

RECEPTION.

The first part of the reception takes place in the second apartment, which represents the ruins of Jerusalem.

The Junior Deacon prepares the Candidate, who is to be dressed as a Gr∴ El∴ Per∴ and Subl∴ Mason, and conducts him to the door, where he raps z times by; ; ;

Sen∴ D∴. Most Exc∴, there is an alarm at the door.

M∴ Exc∴. Attend to the alarm, and see who comes there.

[The Sen∴ Deacon responds with the same alarm, opens and says, " Who comes here ?"]

Jun∴ D∴. A Mason, who having attained the Degree of Perfection of the Ancient and Accepted Rite, solicits the honour of being created a Knight of the East.

Sen∴ D∴. Is it of his own free will and accord he makes this request?

Jun∴ D∴. It is.

Sen∴ D∴. Is he duly and truly prepared, and worthy and well-qualified ?

Ans∴. He is.

Qu∴. Has he made suitable proficiency in the preceding degrees?

Ans∴. He has.

Qu∴. By what further means does he expect to obtain the privilege he seeks ?

Ans∴. By means of the true word of a Perfect Mason.

Qu∴. Has he that true word?

Ans∴. He has; and with your assistance we will communicate it.

[The three Brothers form three triangles: one with their right feet; one with their left arms and hands; and one with their right arms and hands: and raising the upper one, composed of their right arms and hands, above their heads; whisper under it, alternately . . . . *Cand∴* ♄ ☿ ♉: . . . . *Jun∴ D∴* & ☽ . . . . *Sen∴ D∴* *☉*: . . . . . *Cand∴* & ☽ . . . .].

Sen∴ D∴. Who is this that comes with THE TRUE WORD; and whence doth he bring it ?

Jun∴ D∴. Zerubbabel, a Prince of the House of Judah, and one of the Captivity; who cometh from Babylon, from the Court of Cyrus the King, upon a pilgrimage to the ruins of the Temple and the Holy City, bearing with him THE TRUE WORD received from the High Priest at Babylon

Sen∴ D∴. What is his desire ?

Jun∴ D∴. To see the ruins of the Temple, and to offer his services to the Council of those of his Brethren who have returned hither from Egypt.

Sen∴ D∴. Let him wait then with patience, until the M∴ Exc∴ Master can be informed of his request.

[The Sen∴ D∴ reports to the M∴ Exc∴; the same questions being asked and like answers returned as at the door; except that, in answer to the question, if he has the word, the answer is, " He has, and with the proper assistance has given it"].

M∴ Exc∴. Admit the Noble Prince, and receive him with due honour.

[The Sov∴ M∴ raps 3 times. The Brothers all rise. The Jun∴ Deacon enters with the Candidate, who is received by the Sen∴ D∴ and led to the centre of the room, where he halts, facing the M∴ Exc∴]:

M∴ Exc∴ Most Noble Prince Zerubbabel, this Council has been selected to govern that remnant of the children of Israel which returned hither from Egypt, whereto they had been carried by Johanan the son of Kareah, after the destruction of the City and Temple by Nebuchadnezzar King of the Chaldeans. The walls of the Holy City remain in ruins, and the grass and weeds still grow over and hide the wreck of the Temple. The hands of the Heathen are against us, and we hardly maintain ourselves against their assaults. We cannot receive you as befits your rank; for we are distressed and poor and discouraged. Yet we welcome you hither. We rejoice that you have thought of your brethren in their distresses; and we thank you for your offer of assistance.

Sen∴ Ward∴ M∴ Exc∴, thus hath the Lord said by his Prophet Jeremiah: " I will be the God of all the families of Israel, and they shall be my people. Again I will build thee and thou shalt be built, O virgin of Israel! Thou shalt yet plant vines upon the mountain of Samaria. For there shall be a day when the watchmen upon the Mount Ephraim shall cry, Arise ye, and let us go up to Zion, unto the Lord our God. He that scattered Israel will gather him, and keep him as a shepherd does his flock: for the Lord hath redeemed Jacob, and ransomed him from the hand that was stronger than his."

Sen∴ Deac∴ It is the first year of Cyrus King of Persia; and the Lord hath stirred up his spirit, and he hath promised to rebuild the Lord's House in Jerusalem. But the memory of kings is frail and treacherous; and he delayeth, and hath forgotten his promise; until the hearts of your Brethren in Captivity are very heavy; and I have come hither at their request to pray unto the God of Israel that he will cause Cyrus the King to remember his promise, and set free the children of Israel, and rebuild the Temple of the Lord.

M∴ Exc∴ Let us offer up our prayers, my Brethren!

[All kneel; and the M∴ Exc∴ repeats the following]

PRAYER.

Remember, O Lord! what is come upon us: consider, and behold our reproach! Our inheritance is given to strangers, and our homes to aliens. We are orphans and fatherless; our mothers are as widows. Our necks are under the yoke of persecution. We labour and have no rest. We have become bondmen to the Egyptians and the Assyrians, to be satisfied with bread. Our fathers have sinned and have gone, and we bear the burthen of their iniquities and of our own. Servants rule over us; and none delivereth us out of their merciless hands. Because of the swords of the Sons of the Wilderness, we gain our bread with our lives. Our skins became dark because of the terrible famine. They ravished our women in Zion, and our maids in all the cities of Judah. Our Princes they hanged up by the hands; and they dishonoured the faces of our Elders. They made our young men grind their corn; and our children were crushed under heavy burthens of wood. Our elders sit no longer at the gate, and the music of our young men has ceased. The joy of our heart is gone; our dances are turned into mourning. Our crowns have fallen from our heads. Wo unto us, for we have sinned; and our hearts are faint therefor, and our eyes dim! The mountain of Zion is a desert, and none disturb the foxes that infest it. Thou, O Lord, remainest forever: thy throne endures beyond all generations! Forget us not forever: for Thou hast forsaken us for many years! Turn unto us again, O our Father! Incline the heart of the King to remember his promise! Send thine angels to him in his dreams; that he may perform his vow, and rebuild thy Holy City and Temple! Be no longer angered with Thy People; but forgive them, and renew our days as of old! Amen!

Sen∴ D∴ M∴ Exc∴ Master, after I shall have visited the ruins of the Temple and wept over the distresses of our people, I return to Babylon, whence I have come hither by permission of Cyrus the King. Like us, he worships one God. His word has ever been held sacred; and he hath ever been distinguished for his virtue and honour. If I can but obtain a hearing, I feel assured that he will remember and fulfil his promise; that he will release our captive brethren, and allow us to rebuild the House of the Lord. I will embrace the earliest opportunity, even at the risk of his displeasure, to remind him of his promise and urge him to its performance.

M∴ Exc∴ Most noble Prince, we receive your promise with thanks and gratitude. Accept our poor hospitality, until you are prepared to return; and we will then furnish you with safe escort to the Persian frontier; and follow you with earnest and devout prayers for your safety and success. May God incline the heart of the King to grant your request and perform his promise! Partake with us now of our frugal repast.

[A table is then set with bread, wine and meats. The Knights all partake. After it is over, the M.·. Exc.·. says]:

M.·. Exc.·. Exc.·. Sen.·. Warden, take with you an escort of sufficient strength, and after the noble Prince has visited the ruins of the Temple and the city, accompany him to the Persian frontier. Meanwhile let him be thy guest: and when he departs, watch with thy life over his safety; for he bears with him the hopes and fortunes of Israel. My Brethren, the Council is adjourned.

[The candidate is now conducted to the preparation room; where he is received by the Master of Ceremonies. He retains the collar and apron of the 14th Degree, but wears no arms, ornament or jewel. He is to be bareheaded, his neck and hands bound with three chains of triangular links, fastened to the three angles of a large link of the same shape; and they must be long enough for him to be able to stretch out his arms at full length. His head is then to be covered with a sack-cloth strewed with ashes. He is then led to the outer door of the tower, with his hands over his face; where the guards search him thoroughly before he enters the Tower.

In the mean time, the Brethren have repaired to the first apartment, representing the Court of King Cyrus, and all are in their proper places, and properly clothed.

After searching the candidate, the guards interrogate him as follows, the M.·. of Ceremonies replying]:

Qu.·. What do you desire?

Ans.·. To know whether it is possible to have speech of your Sovereign.

Qu.·. Who are you?

Ans.·. Zerubbabel, a Prince of the House of Judah: the first among my equals; a Mason by rank; but a captive and slave by misfortune.

Qu.·. What is your age?

Ans.·. ♎☾*☾♒♈♄ years.

Qu.·. Whence came you?

Ans.·. From Jerusalem.

Qu.·. What brings you hither?

Ans.·. The tears and miseries of my Brethren.

Guard: Wait, then. We will endeavour to have speech allowed you with the Sovereign.

[One of the Guards raps ‖ ? at the inner door of the Tower. The M.·. of Inf.·. gives the same alarm: then the M.·. of Cavalry; and the Sov.·. Master gives one rap].

M.·. Inf.·. A guard raps at the door of the Tower with the alarm of a Knight of the Sword.

M.·. Cav.·. Sov.·. M.·., a guard gives the alarm of a Knight of the Sword at the door of the Tower.

Sov.·. M.·. Let him enter.

[The M.·. of Inf.·. goes to the door of the Tower, raps, opens, and conducts the Guard to the West; who, leaving his pike, crossing his arms, and bowing, says: "One who claims to be the first among Masons, his equals, and ♎☾*☾♒♈♄ years of age, desires to have speech of the Sovereign."]

M.·. of Cav.·. Let him be introduced into the Tower of the Palace. We will interrogate him.

[The Guard again bows, retires, causes the candidate to enter the Tower, shuts him up there, and returns to his post. Then the M.·. of Cavalry questions the candidate through the door, which should remain closed]

M.·. Cav.·. With what purpose come you hither?

M.·. Cer.·. I come to ask for justice, and to appeal to the goodness of the Sovereign.

M.·. Cav.·. In what matter?

M.·. Cer.·. To implore his mercy for my Brethren of the House of Israel, who have now been captive seventy years.

Qu.·. Who then are you?

Ans.·. A Mason, first among my equals: a Prince by birth; a captive and slave by misfortune: my name Zerubbabel.

Qu∴ What favour would you ask of the Sovereign?

Ans∴ That which he has promised the Grand Architect of the Universe: that his justice would give us our liberty, and suffer us to return to Jerusalem, and there, with the aid of the remnant of our people, rebuild the City and Temple of the Lord our God.

M∴ Cav∴ The Sov∴ Master shall be informed of your request.

[The M∴ of Cav∴ then returns to the West; and says]:

M∴ Cav∴ Sov∴ Master, one is in the Tower of the Palace, who asks for justice, and desires to appeal to the goodness of his Sovereign.

Sov∴ M∴ In what matter?

Ans∴ To implore your mercy for his Brethren, the countrymen of the Ex∴ Master of the Palace, the Captive Children of Israel.

Qu∴ Who is he?

Ans∴ Zerubbabel, a Mason: first among his equals; a Prince by birth, a captive and slave by misfortune.

Qu∴ What boon does he ask of me?

Ans∴ That which he says thou didst promise the Grand Architect of the Universe: that thou wouldst be just, and restore to his captive Brethren their freedom; suffering them to return to Jerusalem, there to rebuild their City and Temple.

Sov∴ M∴ Since motives so praiseworthy have brought him hither, let permission to appear before us with his face uncovered be accorded to him.

[The Guards open the door of the Tower; and the Master of Ceremonies receives the Candidate, conducts him to the East, and causes him to kneel on one knee before the Sov∴ Master].

Sov∴ M∴ This is indeed Zerubbabel, who fought by my side against the idolatrous Elymeans, and saved my life at the risk of his own. Arise, my friend, and fearlessly prefer your request.

M∴ Cer∴ Sov∴ Master, the tears and lamentations of my fellow Captives and the remnant of our people at Jerusalem have compelled me to appeal to your justice and mercy. Those languish here in slavery; and all pine for the day to arrive when the Holy City and Temple shall be rebuilt: and they have prayed me to gain access to your Majesty's presence and implore your clemency: that you will be pleased to restore to freedom those who are held here in your dominions in bondage, and permit them to join their countrymen in Jerusalem, there to rebuild the City and Temple of the Lord.

Sov∴ M∴ Zerubbabel, I have often heard of your fame as a wise and accomplished Mason. I have myself a profound veneration for that ancient and honorable Institution, and a sincere desire to become a member thereof, and I will this moment grant your request, on condition that you will reveal to me the secrets of Masonry, which distinguish the Architects of the Jews from those of all other nations.

M∴ Cer∴ Sov∴ M∴, when our Gr∴ Master, Solomon, King of Israel, first instituted the fraternity of Free and Accepted Masons, he taught us that Equality lay at the foundation of the whole system. Here that does not reign. Your rank, your titles, your superiority and your court are wholly incompatible with the ceremonies by which our mysteries are taught. Moreover he instructed us, that Truth was a Divine attribute, and the foundation of every virtue. To be good men and true, and faithfully to keep our secrets, is the first lesson we are taught in Masonry. My engagements are sacred and inviolable. If I can obtain your favour only at the expense of my integrity, the Temple must remain in ruins; and for myself I am ready to accept an honourable exile or a glorious death, or still to wear the chains of slavery.

Sov∴ M∴ I admire the fidelity and incorruptible virtue of Zerubbabel. He who is so faithful to his Masonic engagements cannot but be faithful to his Monarch. Zerubbabel, you are free. My Guards will free you from those chains and that garb of slavery, and clothe you in garments suited to your rank and deserved by your virtues: and may those badges of servitude never again disgrace the hands of a Mason, and more particularly those of a Prince of the House of Judah! [The chains and sackcloth are taken off.] We assign you a seat of rank and honour among the Princes and Lords of Persia.

M∴ Cer∴ Sov∴ Master, permit thy servant to thank thee for thy clemency and thy royal favour. And be not angry with thy servant if he again urges the prayers and entreaties of his countrymen pining in bondage. Thou didst promise to set them free, and allow them to return to their own land, where their God hath promised that they shall be gathered together, and shall dwell in the midst of Jerusalem, and be his people, and He will be their God, in Truth and Righteousness. Wilt thou not hear His voice, and obey His will, that thou mayst reign long upon the Throne that He hath given thee?

Sov∴ M∴. Generals, Princes and Knights, I long since resolved to set free the Hebrews whom we have so many years held in captivity. They, like us, worship one God, and detest idolatry. I weary of seeing them pining in their chains. Other matters of serious import caused me to forget them; but I have been suddenly reminded of my duty as a just and merciful Monarch. Last night I dreamed that I saw a roaring lion ready to spring upon and devour me. Alarmed at the sight thereof, I endeavoured to escape his jaws by flight, but my feet refused to obey. Then I saw Nebuchadnezzar and Belshazzar the Kings of Babylon prostrate, and loaded with chains, and above them, in a bright glory, the Ineffable Name of the God of the Hebrews: and from the glory and the luminous clouds around it came an Eagle, that seemed to utter words, the meaning of which was, that I should restore the captives to their liberty, or my crown should pass into the hands of strangers. Then, amazed and in terror I awoke.

Excellent Master of the Palace, in whom are light and understanding and wisdom, who didst interpret the dreams of Nebuchadnezzar the King, and read the handwriting that announced to Belshazzar the end of his kingdom, explain to me my dream, and with thy wisdom advise me what I shall do.

M∴ Pal∴. Sov∴ Master, thus spoke the Lord by the mouth of Isaiah his Prophet: "Thus saith the Lord to his Anointed, to Cyrus, whose right hand I have holden, to subdue nations before him: and I will loose the loins of Kings, to open before him the two-leaved gates, and the gates shall not be shut. I will go before thee and make the crooked places straight. I will break in pieces the gates of brass, and cut in sunder the bars of iron. And I will give thee the treasures of darkness, and hidden riches of secret places; that thou mayest know that I, the Lord, who call thee by thy name, am the God of Israel. For Jacob my servant's sake, and Israel my Elect, I have even called thee by thy name. I have surnamed thee, though thou hast not known me. I am the Lord; and there is none else, no God, besides me. I have surnamed thee, though thou hast not known me. Woe unto him that striveth with his Maker!"

Sov∴ Master, the voice which you heard in your dream was that of the Gr∴ Architect of the Universe, who long since through his Prophets foretold your coming, and gave you the dominion of the East. The captives are the children of Israel who were brought hither by Nebuchadnezzar, and have now been seventy years in slavery. The Gr∴ Architect commands you to give them freedom and restore them to their homes, to return to them their treasures, and to aid them in rebuilding their City and His Holy Temple, in more than its original splendour. The chains upon the kings who reigned here in Babylon before you, warn you of the fate which will fall upon you, if you disobey His commands. And the lion represents His anger, that will swiftly overtake and destroy you if you remain deaf to his warning voice. For that it was that Babylon fell. For thus said the Lord, by his Prophet Jeremiah: "Call together the Archers against Babylon: all ye that bend the bow, camp against it round about: let none escape: recompense her according to her work: according to all that she hath done, do unto her: for she hath been proud against the Lord, against the Holy One of Israel. . . The children of Israel and the children of Judah were oppressed together; and all that took them captives held them fast; they refused to let them go. Their Redeemer is strong. The God of Armies is his name. He shall thoroughly plead their cause. I will punish Bel in Babylon, and her whole land shall be confounded, and all her slain shall fall in the midst of her; for the spoilers will come unto her from the North; saith the Lord." Even so, O great King, will He do unto thee; and more also, if thou obey not his voice.

Sov∴ M∴. Wise Master of the Palace, I will obey the voice. Zerubbabel, I give you permission to rebuild your Temple. I here decree and ordain that every captive of Judah and Israel in my dominions is from this moment free. Gr∴ Master of the Chancery, cause to be proclaimed throughout all my kingdom, and put in writing, these words: "Thus saith Cyrus King of Persia: The Supreme God hath given me all the Kingdoms of the Earth; and he hath charged me to build Him an house at Jerusalem, which is in Judah. Who is among you of all his people? His God be with him; and let him go up to Jerusalem which is in Judah, and build the House of the Lord God of Israel [the only God], in Jerusalem. And whosoever remaineth in any place where he sojourneth, let the men of his place help him with silver, and with gold, and with goods, and with beasts, besides the free-will offering for the House of God in Jerusalem." Gr∴ Master of the Finances, bring forth the vessels of the House of the Lord which Nebuchadnezzar brought forth out of Jerusalem, and put in the House of his Gods; and deliver them unto whomsoever Zerubbabel shall appoint. Let the House be builded, the place where they offered sacrifices, and let the foundations thereof be strongly laid, and let the expenses be given out of the King's House. And let the golden and silver vessels of the House of God be restored, and brought again unto the Temple at Jerusalem, each to its place, and put them in the House of God. Zerubbabel, be thou Chief among thy equals. I will give orders that you be obeyed in every place through which you may pass, and that all supplies and assistance be furnished you, as they would be to myself. Draw near, my friend!

[The candidate is conducted to the foot of the Throne: where the Sov∴ M∴ returns him his sword; saying]:

Sov∴ M∴. As a distinctive mark of your superiority over your people, and of your supreme power and authority next to myself, I arm you with this sword, taken from you by my guards. I am persuaded that you will never draw it in the cause of injustice and oppression; but only in defence of your Countrymen or other just and virtuous cause.

And as a mark of my esteem, I also invest you with this collar and apron, which I have adopted, in imitation of those worn by the Mason-builders of your Temple. They are accompanied by no mysteries; but I confer them only on the Princes of my Court, and as the highest mark of honour and distinction. I now commit you to the charge of Nabuzaradin, my General, who will furnish escorts to conduct you and those who go with you, and your sacred treasures, safely to Jerusalem. So do I decree.

[The Gr∴ M∴ of Cavalry takes the candidate, causes him to enter the Tower, and leaves him there, until the Knights pass silently into the other apartment].

CEREMONIES IN THE SECOND APARTMENT.

As soon as the brethren are all arranged, the Master of Ceremonies goes to the Tower, and conducts the candidate along the rear of the hangings, to the bridge, where the Guards stop him, and attempt to prevent his passage; but he forces his way and puts them to flight, and so reaches the door of the 2d apartment; losing his collar and apron in the melée.

Here the M∴ of Ceremonies gives the alarm of ‖ ? When it is heard, each brother takes from his girdle the trowel that hangs there, and holds it in his left hand, and his sword in his right. Then the Jun∴ W∴ gives the alarm of ‖ ? — the Sen∴ W∴ the same, and the M∴ Exc∴ responds with one rap.

Sen∴ W∴. M∴ Ex∴ Master, there is an alarm at the door of the Lodge.

M∴ Exc∴. Ex∴ Sen∴ W∴, see who makes the alarm, and on what business he comes.

[The Jun∴ W∴ goes to the door, and inquires, "Who comes here, and upon what mission?"]

M∴ Cer∴. Zerubbabel, Prince of the House of Judah, and Commander under Cyrus the King, of all the People of Israel; with other Princes who have come with him from Babylon, bearing news that the captives are set free, and orders given to rebuild the House of the Lord.

[The Junior Warden reports to the Sen∴ Warden, and he to the M∴ Exc∴.]

Sov∴ M∴. My Brethren, Zerubbabel is of right our Prince, and the Ruler of those who are to rebuild the Temple. Let him be admitted, and received with acclamation and due honour.

[The brothers rise, and as the candidate enters, they salute him, and say, "Health to Zerubbabel, Prince of Judah!" He enters and approaches the East].

Sen∴ W∴. M∴ Ex∴ Master, behold Zerubbabel, our Prince, who comes to be received into the bosom of our fraternity.

M∴ Exc∴. Zerubbabel, the brethren await anxiously for information of your mission, and how you have succeeded in its objects.

M∴ Cer∴. M∴ Exc∴ Master, the King having given me permission to appear at the foot of his Throne,

2A

was touched with the miseries of the captives, and remembered his promise, which in a dream God had ordered him to fulfil. He hath set free all the captives, and ordered that the Temple be rebuilt in more than its former splendour, with the aid of his royal treasury; and he hath restored to us the holy vessels of silver and gold, carried away by Nebuchadnezzar. Me he hath appointed to rule over the People and direct the work. He armed me with this sword to protect and defend my brethren, honoured me with the title of Brother in the company of his Lords and Princes, and invested me with the insignia of an order established by him in imitation of Masonry. Then his General Nabuzaradin gave me an escort to conduct me hither: but at the crossing of the river Jordan we were assailed by our enemies, whom we overcame, and forced our way across the bridge, I losing in the contest the insignia of the Persian order given me by the King.

M∴ Exc∴ My brother, you have lost but the worthless insignia of another order, while you have preserved all that belongs to genuine Masonry. In the place of that which you have lost, we will confer upon you the honours of a new degree in Masonry, composed of those who are to rebuild the Temple; and to which none others can be admitted. But before I can communicate to you its secrets, which have been faithfully preserved since the captivity, we must needs be assured that your long residence in another land, among men of another faith, has not diminished your regard for the tenets, and obscured your knowledge of the mysteries, of Free Masonry.

M∴ Cer∴ Interrogate me, M∴ Exc∴, and I will answer.

M∴ Exc∴ To what degree have you advanced in Masonry?

Ans∴ To that of Perfection.

Qu∴ Give me the signs of that degree.

[The Cand∴ gives them].†

Qu∴ Give me the grips and words.

[He gives them].

M∴ Exc∴ Brother Knights, is it your opinion that the Prince Zerubbabel is entitled to be admitted to the Mysteries of this Degree?

[The Brothers assent, by rising, and elevating the points of their swords].

M∴ Exc∴ Ex∴ Sen∴ Warden, cause the candidate to advance by three steps of a Master, to the front, the last bringing him to the altar; there to enter into such engagements as we shall require.

[The candidate advances, kneels at the altar, and takes the following obligation]:

OBLIGATION.

I, A . . . . B . . . ., do hereby and hereon solemnly promise and swear, that I will never reveal the secrets of this degree to any person of an inferior degree, or to a Profane, nor make them known at any time or in any place, except when duly authorized so to do in conferring this degree, or to one who has received it by due authority.

I furthermore promise and swear that I will not be present at, or aid or assist in, the conferring of this degree on any person who has not regularly received the 14th Degree of the Ancient and Accepted Rite of Free Masonry.

I furthermore promise and swear that I will obey a summons from a Lodge of this Degree, when delivered to me by the hands of a brother, or by letter, if I am within the distance of forty miles; natural infirmities, sickness of my family or friends, and unavoidable accidents alone preventing me.

I furthermore promise and swear that I will assist, protect and defend my brethren of this degree by all lawful means consistent with the character of a true Mason: and will even go the distance of forty miles to relieve their distresses or minister to their necessities, if I can do so without injury to those who have a prior claim upon me.

To all of which I swear, under the penalty of being consigned to a hopeless captivity, my chains being never broken, and my body buried hopelessly in a dungeon, without light to my eyes, or a human voice to cheer me while I live. So help me God, and keep me steadfast!

[The candidate rises; and the M∴ Exc∴ says to him]:

M∴ Exc∴ My Brother, the destruction of the Temple having subjected Masons to so great misfortunes, we have feared lest those who were carried away to Babylon, and their descendants, might, in their dispersion, have forgotten their obligations; and ceased to perform the duties, while remembering the words, signs and tokens of Masonry. This has constrained us, while awaiting the time of rebuilding the Temple, to create a new Degree, with secrets known to ourselves alone, in which we preserve the ancient memorials of the Craft. Here we allow none to enter save those whom we know to be true and sincere Masons: judging them not merely by their signs, words and tokens, but by their actions and their morals. When these are found to be right and good, we with pleasure accept them among us, and make known to them our mode of recognition.

[The curtain is now drawn aside, displaying the Glory, and the altar furnished with all the implements of Masonry and the Book of the Law. The hangings are also suddenly changed from red to green, and all the lights are lighted].

M∴ Exc∴. Behold, my Brother, the glory of the Second Temple: the Book of the Law, long lost and lately found; and the glorious Light that is an emblem of Masonic Truth. The object of our labours is the rebuilding of the Second Temple. The sword given you by Cyrus the King must be used to defend your Brethren engaged in that labour, and to punish those who may profane our work. Receive now the signs, tokens and words of this Degree.

SIGN: . . . Bring the ‡⅓&⊙♒♊ to the †⅔♎&☿ ♁†♊☾‡, and thence with a ♍♀♌♍⊙♌ motion to the ‡⅔&♀§, imitating the waves of a river.

ANSWER: . . . Place the ‡⅓&⊙♒♊ upon the †¼&♀§, and then bring it across the ♏☿♊♄ to the ‡⅔&♀§.

TOKEN: . . . Take each other by the †☾♑♈¼&⊙♒♊, ♑♀♒♌☾‡♎ ♀♒♈☾‡†⊙↿☾♊, the †¼⊙‡♋ raised and extended, as if ♑☿‡↿♀♒♌¼♏⊙↿¶ an enemy, and forcing a passage: and then place each the §☿♀♒♈ of his ♎♃☿‡♊ against the other's &☾⊙‡♈. In this attitude, one says ♁♁♊⊙&∴ and the other, ♏☾♒♁⊙♋♀♒∴

PASS-WORDS: . . . †♀♏☾†♈⊙♎∴ &⊙*⊙‡♀♒-&⊙♋♀♋∴

GRAND WORD: . . . ♎&⊙†⊙†∴ ♎&⊙†♁♋∴ ⊙♏♀∴

M∴ Exc∴. My brother, after giving you liberty, Cyrus the King conferred upon you an order in imitation of Masonry; and appointed you Prince and Ruler over Israel. In honour of yourself, and that it may take the place of the honour so conferred upon you, this degree shall be henceforward called Knights of the East, or of the Sword. And as a token of your new dignity, and the peculiar emblem of this degree, I now present you with the Trowel; with which in one hand and the Sword in the other, our enemies compel us to labour in rebuilding the Temple.

I also present you with the Scarf of the Degree. It is to be worn by you in all Lodges: as one should ever be proud to wear the insignia which he has never dishonoured. I also present you with the jewel of the Degree. The triangles are an emblem of that Justice, Equity and Mercy which go to make the perfect Mason: and the cross-swords teach us that a life of virtue is not a life of ease, but of constant warfare against vice and ignorance, superstition and error.

And now my Brother, I proclaim you duly advanced to the degree of Knight of the East or of the Sword, the Fifteenth Degree of the Ancient and Accepted rite. My Brethren, do you, his equals, ratify the appointment of this our Brother, to be a Prince and Ruler over Israel, and to conduct the work of re-building the Temple? If so, give me the sign of assent.

[The brethren assent by elevating their swords perpendicularly, and then lowering the points].

M∴ Exc∴. It is well. Pass, Prince and Brother, to the Throne of the Sovereigns of our Lodges. Serve as a triangular stone for the edifice, and rule wisely over the workmen, as our former Grand Master did at the building of the first Temple.

[The Brethren all clap their hands 3 times; cry *Zerubbabel*, 3 times, and all are seated. Then follows the Lecture].

LECTURE.

"Now, in the first year of Cyrus, King of Persia," says the Compiler of the Sacred Book of Chronicles, "(that the word of the Lord by the mouth of Jeremiah might be accomplished,) the Lord stirred up the Spirit of Cyrus, King of Persia, that he made a Proclamation throughout all his Kingdom, and also in writing, saying: Thus saith Cyrus, King of Persia: All the kingdoms of the Earth hath the Lord God of Heaven given me: and he hath charged me to build him an House in Jerusalem, in Judea. Who among you are of his People? The Lord his God be with him, and let him go up."

The dream which you have heard described in the ceremonies of this Degree, and the earnest solicitations of Zerubbabel, a Prince of the House of Judah, and one of those held in captivity in Persia, (who had served in the Persian wars, and on one occasion had saved the life of Cyrus in his youth, and who had recently returned from a pilgrimage to Jerusalem), coupled with the interpretation of the dream by the Prophet Daniel, the Chief of the Presidents set by Darius over the one hundred and twenty Princes of Persia, who denounced against the King the anger of God, and his own speedy destruction, if he dared to disobey the mandate conveyed to him in his dream, produced this Proclamation—the liberty of the captives and the restoration of the Holy vessels.

Ten chiefs of the Hebrews accompanied Zerubbabel to Jerusalem; among whom were Joshua, the son of Jozadak, Nehemiah and Mordecai. And in all there went from Persia and Assyria, at that time, to Jerusalem, forty-two thousand three hundred and sixty Hebrews, besides servants and their maids.

Zerubbabel, with the chiefs who accompanied him, and a large force of the People, reached in safety the river that separates Assyria from Judea. He threw a bridge over it; but was attacked in crossing, by the people who had seized on the larger portion of Judea when the Hebrews were carried away captive; and a bloody battle ensued, resulting in the defeat of the enemy and the safe passage of the Jews. Zerubbabel lost in the battle the marks of honour which Cyrus had given him, as badges of his rank and dignity as a Satrap of Persia and Viceroy of Judea.

After the destruction of the city by Nebuchadnezzar, Nebuzaradin his General left many of the poorer people, who had nothing, in the land of Judah, and assigned them vineyards and fields. He also liberated Jeremiah the Prophet, and gave him permission to remain at Jerusalem, giving him the means whereby to live. He made Gedaliah the son of Ahikam Governor over the cities of Judah, and placed him over the poorer classes that were not carried away to Babylon. After the Assyrian forces had marched homeward, the Jewish troops that had been in the field and at posts at a distance from the city, and all the Jews that had sought refuge from the storm of Assyrian War in Moab, and among the Ammonites, and in Edom, and elsewhere, returned to Judea, and gathered wine and summer fruits, on which to live.

After Ishmael, of the blood royal, had murdered Gedaliah, after eating bread with him, and had also killed the Assyrian kings that had been left as guards for the viceroy, and had then himself fled to the Ammonites, Johanan the son of Kareah succeeded to the command over the people, and removed them near to the frontier of Egypt, fearing the anger of the Assyrian King whose troops had been treacherously murdered. And soon afterwards, notwithstanding the urgent advice of Jeremiah, who warned them that, if they went into Egypt, they should die by the sword, by the famine and by the pestilence, Johanan and the other captains led the whole remnant of the People into Egypt. There they embraced the worship of the Goddess Neith, and sacrificed to her. But Nebuchadnezzar invaded Egypt with a great army; and conquered it, and shattered the images and burned the Temples of the Gods, and destroyed most of the Israelites who had fled. A small number escaped, and returning to Judea, settled about Jerusalem, and there remained, wretched and miserable, and exposed to constant attacks from furious enemies on all sides.

There, while Ezekiel was seeing visions and prophesying on the banks of the Chaldean river Chebar, and Daniel was being educated at the Court of Babylon, the few fugitives at Jerusalem increased continually by the arrival of other fugitives; but leaving little record of their suffering, their disasters and their successes, struggled to maintain a national existence. Among them were a few Elect and Perfect Masons, who, recognizing each other, met in secret to lament the misfortunes of their people, and to practise the ceremonies of Masonry. They explored the ruins until they discovered the entrance of the Sacred Vault, entering which, they penetrated as far as the pedestal, and found the plate of gold under the cubical stone. Determined entirely to prevent a future discovery of the Secret Word by the Profane, they broke up the triangular plate and melted it down, and shattered the cubical Agate into fragments; and thenceforward they and their successors transmitted the mysteries orally. Animated with the hope of one day seeing their labours upon the Temple renewed, they organized a government, by the election of a chief or captain of the People, who exercised the Executive Power. The law of Moses was lost, except so far as it existed in tradition; and such brief laws were enacted by the Elus, as were absolutely indispensable to civil order, and organization for defence.

When the captivity ended, Ananias was the chief or captain of this unfortunate and poor people. He received Zerubbabel into the fraternity, upon the ruins of the Temple, and surrendered to him, as Viceroy of Cyrus, the Executive power over the remnant of the Jewish nation.

When the labours upon the Temple were commenced, they were continually harassed by enemies on every side, were compelled to be every moment prepared to defend themselves, and worked at all times with their arms by them: so that they were, by a natural exaggeration, said to labour with the Sword in one hand and the Trowel in the other.

After the return from the captivity, in the seventh month, Joshua the son of Jozadak and his brethren the Priests, and Zerubbabel the son of Shealtiel, and his brethren rebuiled the Altar of God, and kept the Feast of the Tabernacles, and offered burnt-offerings, of the new moons and regular feasts, from the first day of the Seventh Month. They hired masons and carpenters; and employed men from Tyre and Sidon in Phœnicia, as Solomon had done, to bring cedars from Lebanon to Joppa.

In the second year after their return, they laid the foundation of the Second Temple; and set the Priests in order, in their regalia, with trumpets, and the Levites with cymbals, to praise the Lord; and sang together, praising and thanking the Lord, for his goodness, and his eternal mercy. And all the People shouted with a great shout when they praised the Lord, because the foundation of the House of the Lord was laid. And many Priests and Levites, and chiefs of the Fathers who were old men, and had seen the first Temple, wept aloud when they saw the foundation laid, and many of them shouted for joy.

The Prophets had said: "This is the Word of the Lord unto Zerubbabel, saying, Not by might, nor by power, but by my Spirit, saith the God of Armies. Who art thou, O great Mountain? Before Zerubbabel, a plain: and he shall bring forth the Keystone, while the people shout, *Success, success unto it!* The hands of Zerubbabel have laid the foundation of this House: his hands shall finish it also: and ye shall know that the God of Armies hath sent me unto you. . . Be strong, O Zerubbabel! saith the Lord: Be strong, O Joshua, son of Josadak, the High Priest: be strong all ye people of the land, saith the Lord, and work; for I am with you, saith the God of Armies. The glory of this latter House shall be greater than that of the former; and in this place will I give peace. In that day will I take thee, O Zerubbabel, my servant, son of Shealtiel, and will make thee as a signet: for I have chosen thee, saith the God of Armies. Take silver and gold, and make crowns, and set one upon the head of Joshua the son of Josadak, the High Priest: and say, thus saith the God of Armies; Behold the man whose name is The Branch; he shall grow up out of his place, and build the Temple of the Lord; and he shall bear the glory, and shall sit and rule upon his throne; and he shall be a Priest upon his Throne. . . Execute true judgment, and show mercy and compassion every man to his brother: and oppress not the widow, nor the fatherless, the stranger nor the poor; and do none of you imagine evil against your brother in your heart. I am returned unto Zion, and will dwell in the midst of Jerusalem: and Jerusalem shall be called a City of Truth; and the Mountain of the God of Armies, our Holy Mountain. There shall yet old men and old women dwell in the streets of Jerusalem, and every man with his staff in his hand for very age. Speak ye every man the truth to his neighbour: execute the judgment of truth and peace in your gates. And let none of you imagine evil in his heart against his neighbour: and love no false oath: for all these I hate, saith the Lord."

Notwithstanding these promises, and the endeavours of the people to obey these laws, the people of the land weakened the hands of the people of Judah, and troubled them in building, and hired counsellors against them to frustrate their purpose, all the days of Cyrus King of Persia, even until the reign of Darius King of Persia. These troubles and the ultimate success of the enterprise will be more particularly alluded to in the degree which you are next to receive, constituting, indeed, correctly speaking, the second part of one and the same degree. For the present we pause here in our history.

This degree, like all others in Masonry, is symbolical. Based upon historical truth and authentic tradition, it is still an allegory. The leading lesson of this degree is Fidelity to obligation, and Constancy and Perseverance under difficulties and discouragement.

Masonry is engaged in her crusade,—against ignorance, intolerance, fanaticism, superstition, uncharitableness and error. She does not sail with the trade-winds upon a smooth sea, with a steady free breeze, fair for a welcoming harbor; but meets and must overcome many opposing currents, baffling winds and dead calms.

The chief obstacles to her success are the apathy and faithlessness of her own selfish children, and the supine indifference of the world. In the roar and crush and hurry of life and business, and the tumult and uproar of politics, the quiet voice of Masonry is unheard and unheeded. The first lesson which one learns, who engages in any great work of reform or beneficence, is, that men are essentially careless, lukewarm and indifferent, as to every thing that does not concern their own personal and immediate welfare. It is to single men, and not to the united efforts of many, that all the great works of man, struggling toward perfection, are owing. The enthusiast, who imagines that he can inspire with his own enthusiasm the multitude that eddies around him, or even the few who have associated themselves with him as co-workers, is grievously mistaken; and most often the conviction of his own mistake is followed by discouragement and disgust. To do all, to pay all, and to suffer all, and then, when despite all obstacles and hindrances, success is accomplished, and a great work done, to see those who opposed or looked coldly on it, claim and reap all the praise and reward, is the common and almost universal lot of the benefactor of his kind.

He who endeavours to serve, to benefit and improve the world, is like a swimmer, who struggles against a rapid current, in a river lashed into angry waves by the winds. Often they roar over his head, often they beat him back and baffle him. Most men yield to the stress of the current, and float with it to the shore: and only here and there the stout, strong heart and vigorous arms struggle on towards ultimate success.

It is the motionless and stationary that most fret and impede the current of progress; the solid rock or stupid dead tree, rested firmly on the bottom, and around which the river whirls and eddies: the Masons that doubt and hesitate and are discouraged: that disbelieve in the capability of man to improve: that are not disposed to toil and labour for the interest and well-being of general humanity: that expect others to do all, even of that which they do not oppose or ridicule; while they sit, applauding and doing nothing, or perhaps prognosticating failure.

There were many such at the re-building of the Temple. There were prophets of evil and misfortune— the lukewarm and the indifferent and the apathetic; those who stood by and sneered; and those who thought they did God service enough if they now and then faintly applauded. There were ravens croaking ill omen, and murmurers who preached the folly and futility of the attempt. The world is made up of such; and they were as abundant then as they are now.

But gloomy and discouraging as was the prospect, with lukewarmness within and bitter opposition without, our ancient brethren persevered. Let us leave them engaged in the good work; and whenever to us, as to them, success is uncertain, remote and contingent, let us still remember that the only question for us to ask, as true men and Masons, is, what does duty require; and not what will be the result and our reward if we do our duty.

Masonry teaches that God is a Paternal Being, and has an interest in his creatures, such as is expressed in the title *Father;* an interest unknown to all the systems of Paganism, untaught in all the theories of philosophy; an interest not only in the glorious beings of other spheres, the Sons of Light, the dwellers in Heavenly worlds, but in us, poor, ignorant and unworthy; that He has pity for the erring, pardon for the guilty, love for the pure, knowledge for the humble, and promises of immortal life for those who trust in and obey him.

Without a belief in Him, life is miserable, the world is dark, the universe disrobed of its splendours, the intellectual tie to nature broken, the charm of existence dissolved, the great hope of being lost; and the mind, like a star struck from its sphere, wanders through the infinite desert of its conceptions, without attraction, tendency, destiny or end.

Masonry teaches, that, of all the events and actions, that take place in the universe of worlds and the eternal succession of ages, there is not one, even the minutest, which God did not forever foresee, with all the distinctness of immediate vision.

It teaches that the soul of man is formed by Him for a purpose; that, built up in its proportions, and fashioned in every part, by infinite skill, an emanation from His spirit, its nature, necessity and design is virtue. It is so formed, so moulded, so fashioned, so exactly balanced, so exquisitely proportioned in every part, that sin introduced into it is misery; that vicious thoughts fall upon it like drops of poison; and guilty desires, breathing on its delicate fibres, make plague-spots there, deadly as those of pestilence upon the body. It is made for virtue, and not for vice; for purity, as its end, rest and happiness. Not more vainly would we attempt to make the mountain sink to the level of the valley, the waves of the angry sea turn back from its shores and cease to thunder upon the beach, the stars to halt in their swift courses, than to change any one law of our own nature. And one of those laws, uttered by God's voice, and speaking through every nerve and fibre, every power and element, of the moral constitution he has given us, is that we must be virtuous; that if tempted we must resist: that we must govern our unruly passions. And this is not the dictate of an arbitrary will, nor of some stern and impracticable law; but it is part of the great firm law of harmony that binds the universe together.

We know that God is good, and that what He does is right. This known, the works of creation, the changes of life, the destinies of eternity, are all spread before us, as the dispensations and counsels of infinite love. This known, we then know that the love of God is working to issues, like itself, beyond all thought and imagination, good and glorious; and that the only reason why we do not understand it, is that it is too glorious for us to understand. God's love takes care for all, and nothing is neglected. It watches over all, provides for all, makes wise adaptations for all; for age, for infancy, for maturity, for childhood; in every scene of this or another world; for want, weakness, joy, sorrow, and even for sin. All is good and well and right; and shall be so forever. Through the eternal ages the light of God's beneficence shall shine hereafter, disclosing all, consummating all, rewarding all that deserve reward. Then we shall see, what now we can only believe. The cloud will be lifted up, the gate of mystery be passed, and the full light shine forever; the light of which that of the Lodge is a symbol. Then that which caused us trial shall yield us triumph; and that which made our heart ache shall fill us with gladness; and we shall then feel that there, as here, the only true happiness is to learn, to advance, and to improve; which could not happen unless we had commenced with error, ignorance and imperfection.

Go, now, my Brother, to the Sen∴ and Jun∴ Wardens, and listen to the Catechism of this Degree.

CATECHISM.

Sen∴ W∴ Are you a Knight of the East?

Jun∴ W∴ I have knelt before King Cyrus in chains, and gone forth from his presence free and ennobled.

Qu∴ How did you attain this degree?

Ans∴ By resolution and perseverance, when others were apathetic and discouraged.

Qu∴ In what work are we engaged in this degree?

Ans∴ In re-building the Temple of the Lord.

Qu∴ What do the Temple and its re-construction signify to us?

Ans∴ The establishment of that universal religion of primitive truth which men call Masonry; and of that state of toleration, peace, equality and liberty, which will make of this Earth a fit Temple for a God of mercy and equity.

Qu.·. Who first re-built the Temple?

Ans.·. Zerubbabel, a Prince of the House of Judah, born in Persia during the captivity.

Qu.·. Of what is he the type to us?

Ans.·. Of the strong swimmer that stems the furious current, and never yields to it, though often beaten back and baffled: of the Leader of Men, who encourages the disheartened, incites the indolent, inspires the lukewarm, and cheers the timid and despondent: who, with his strong will and clear perceptions, forces the stupid, the stationary and the laggard to aid in his great purposes, despite their reluctance; and hurls out of his path all who oppose and thwart him.

Qu.·. Of what else is he the type?

Ans.·. Of stern and incorruptible fidelity to his engagements; since he preferred that the Temple should remain forever in ruins, rather than degrade and dishonour himself by betraying the secrets of Masonry; impressively teaching us the lesson that none should ever do evil, even to effect a great and good work.

Qu.·. Of what are the ruins of the ancient walls of the City of Jerusalem and the Temple, an emblem to us?

Ans.·. Of the dismembered fragments of the primitive religion, embedded in the different creeds of antiquity, and buried among the follies and fables of which they were composed: and of the condition of the human intellect, degraded by idolatry, superstition, and ignorance.

Qu.·. How did our Masonic Brethren labour at re-building the Temple?

Ans.·. With the Sword in one hand and the Trowel in the other.

Qu.·. What does that typify to us?

Ans.·. That while the good Mason smites with the edge of the sword the demons of vice, brutality, rapacity and oppression, he builds steadily the walls of the Temple of Truth and Toleration in which all men may worship who believe in a God.

Qu.·. To what do the 70 lights of the Lodge allude?

Ans.·. To the 70 years of the captivity: and the threescore and ten years of human life.

Qu.·. What do the green and gold of this degree teach us?

Ans.·. The green, that Masonry, like the soul of man, is immortal,—the old Truth, the old Faith, the old Morality, coeval with time, and known before the flood. The gold, that the honours of Masonry are more precious than the gifts of kings.

Qu.·. Of what are the chains of the captives, with their triangular links, an emblem?

Ans.·. Of the three powers that have in all ages imposed fetters on the human intellect, and gyves and manacles on the limbs of the people whom God made free;—the Kings, Priests and Nobles,—or TYRANNY, SUPERSTITION and PRIVILEGE.

Qu.·. Of what are the broken columns and disarranged implements of Masonry an emblem?

Ans.·. Of the schisms and disturbances that spring up when Brethren contend for offices and honours; when jurisdiction usurps upon jurisdiction, and the dissensions of Masons are exposed to the eyes of the Profane.

Qu.·. Of what is the defeat of those who assailed Zerubbabel and his company at the crossing of the river an emblem?

Ans.·. Of the disastrous overthrow and discomfiture of all who attack and persecute Masonry, and resist its attempts to pass the frontiers guarded by ignorance and error.

Qu.·. Of what are the three triangles, one within the other, a symbol?

Ans.·. Of the three principal infinite Attributes of Deity; POWER, INTELLIGENCE and GOODNESS.

Qu.·. Of what are the two cross-swords a symbol?

Ans.·. Of TRUTH and JUSTICE: the chief Masonic weapons; armed with which we need never dread or anticipate defeat.

Qu.·. What art do you profess?

Ans.·. Free-Masonry.

Qu.·. What do you build?

Ans∴ Temples and Tabernacles.

Qu∴ Where?

Ans∴ In the heart.

Qu∴ Which way do you travel?

Ans∴ From Babylon to Jerusalem; from the darkness of Error to the light of Truth; from the sandy deserts of Ignorance and mental Bondage, to the green hills and fertile plains of Knowledge and intellectual Liberty.

Qu∴ What is your age?

Ans∴ Threescore and ten: the full age of man: because he who has faithfully performed all his Masonic duties, has lived the full term of life, though he dies young.

TO CLOSE.

[The M∴ Exc∴ gives one rap].

M∴ Exc∴ Ex∴ Bro∴ Sen∴ Warden, what are you?

Sen∴ W∴ A Free-Mason and a Knight.

M∴ Exc∴ How do you work?

Sen∴ W∴ With the sword in one hand and the trowel in the other.

M∴ Exc∴ Whence come you?

Sen∴ W∴ From the East.

M∴ Exc∴ What do you bring with you?

Sen∴ W∴ Permission to work.

M∴ Exc∴ What is your work?

Sen∴ W∴ To rebuild the true Masonic Temple of the Gr∴ Architect.

M∴ Exc∴ What is your age?

Sen∴ W∴ Threescore and ten years.

M∴ Exc∴ What is the time?

Sen∴ W∴ The moment of laying the foundation of the New Temple.

M∴ Exc∴ Since that time has arrived and we are allowed to work, and since we have now only to execute what we have already determined on, give notice, Bros∴ Sen∴ and Jun∴ Wardens, that this Council of Knights of the East or the Sword is about to be closed; and our ordinary labours to be recommenced.

Sen∴ W∴ Exc∴ Bro∴ Jun∴ Warden, it is the pleasure of the M∴ Exc∴ Master that this Council be now closed, and that the Brethren repair to their ordinary labours. This you will please proclaim and make known.

Jun∴ W∴ Ven∴ Brethren and Knights, it is the pleasure of the M∴ Exc∴ Master, that this Council be now closed; and that each of us repair to his ordinary labours. You will take due notice of this, and act accordingly.

[The M∴ Exc∴ raps ‖ ? Each Warden repeats]:

M∴ Exc∴ Together, my Brethren!

[All the Knights, guided by the M∴ Exc∴, give the sign, applaud, and cry: *Glory to God and the Sovereign!*]

[The M∴ Exc∴ says: "The Council is closed." Each Warden repeats: The M∴ Exc∴ gives one rap: Each Warden repeats; and the Knights retire in silence.]

FINIS.

Sixteenth Degree.

Princes of Jerusalem.

THE LODGE, ITS DECORATIONS, ETC.

There are two apartments. The first represents the Court of Zerubbabel, King or Viceroy of Jerusalem. The hangings are saffron-colour; and it is lighted by 25 lights, in groups of 5.

The second apartment represents the Court of Darius, King of Persia. The hangings are green; the Throne and canopy saffron-colour.

In the centre of the first apartment is an altar: on which lie a roll of parchment representing the Book of the Law, a square, compasses, plumb and level, a sword and a balance. Over the M.·. Ill.·. in the East is a large gilded triangle; and in the centre of it the Ineffable Name in Hebrew characters.

OFFICERS, AND THEIR TITLES.

In the second apartment, the same as in the second apartment (or Hall of the East) in the Degree of Knights of the East; the Presiding Officer representing King Darius.

In the first, he represents ZERUBBABEL, the Viceroy of Darius; and is styled *Most Illustrious Tirshatha.*

The Sen.·. Warden represents NEHEMIAH; and is styled *Illustrious Scribe.*

The Jun.·. Warden represents ISHUA, and is styled *Wise and Venerable Priest.*

The Senior Deacon is styled *Captain of the Tribes.*

The Junior Deacon is styled *Captain of the Guards.*

The three principal officers sit together in the East.

The Princes are styled *Valiant:* and Bodies in this Degree are styled COUNCILS OF PRINCES OF JERUSALEM.

The battery is ? ‖ — by ♑♀*☾♎ at equal intervals.

DRESS, DECORATIONS, ETC.

The *apron* is crimson, lined and edged with saffron-colour. On the flap is an equal balance, held by a hand of Justice. In the middle of the apron, a representation of the Second Temple; on one side of which is a sword lying across a buckler; and on the other, a square and triangle. The letter ﬢ is on one side, and ﭏ on the other.

The *cordon* is of saffron-coloured silk, at least four inches wide, and bordered with gold. On it are embroidered a balance, a hand of Justice (holding a sword), a poniard, five stars, and two small crowns.

The *jewel* is a medal of gold. On one side is engraved a hand, holding an equal balance; and on the other a double-edged sword, surrounded by five stars; on one side of which is the letter D.·. and on the other the letter Z.·.

The *gloves* are crimson.

The *order* is worn from the right shoulder to the left hip.

TO OPEN.

[The Counsel is opened and closed in the first apartment].

[The M.·. Ill.·. raps ‖ and says]:

M.·. Ill.·. Ill.·. Scribe, what is the hour?

Sen.·. W.·. The Sun is risen, M.·. Ill.·. Tirshatha.

M.·. Ill.·. M.·. Wise and Venerable Priest, return thanks to God, for this Council, that He hath sent his great gift of Light once more upon the earth. Kneel, Princes, and let us offer up our orisons to God!

PRAYER.

Jun.·. D.·. O Lord our God! we bless thee for ever and ever! Blessed be Thy Glorious Name, which is exalted above all blessing and praise! Thou, Thou art the only God. Thou hast made Heaven, the Heaven of Heavens, with all their Armies of Stars, the Earth and all therein; and Thou preservest them all; and the Armies of Light worship Thee! Thou art a gracious and merciful God, Great, Mighty and Terrible, who keepest covenant and mercy; and didst preserve our ancient brethren, a remnant, in all the trouble that came upon them, on their Kings, their Princes, their Priests, their Prophets, their Fathers, and all thine elected People, since the time of the Kings of Assyria until that of the rebuilding of the Temple. Since the days of their fathers they were wrong-doers, and for their sins they, their Kings and their Priests were delivered into the hands of the Assyrian Kings, to the sword, to captivity and to great spoliation and misery: from all which do Thou be pleased, O our Father, to save us in Thine Infinite Mercy. For afterwards Thou didst show them favour, and didst permit a remnant to return, and to occupy Thy Holy City, and didst give Light to their eyes, and relief from their bondage, that they might set again upon its foundations Thy House, and repair its desolation, as we would do with the Temple of Masonry, and fortify themselves in the Holy City: and now again Thou performest Thy daily miracle, and makest the Great Sun, Thy Central Light, to rise again in the East, and gladden the world, and renew the life of all creatures that lay dead in sleep since the evening.

We thank Thee, we praise Thee, we magnify Thee, for Thy great gift of Light, which is the Life of all the Universe; and we pray Thee to let also the Dawn of Masonry, which is the True Light, coeval with the world, shine again in the souls and intellects of all mankind, and conquer the whole world to its religion of Love and Peace and Toleration! Amen!

M.·. Ill.·. Ill.·. Scribe, how goes on the work?

Sen.·. W.·. M.·. Ill.·., as the People of the land weakened the hands of our ancient brethren, and troubled them in building, and hired counsellers against them, and frustrated their purposes, all the days of Cyrus King of Persia, and in the reigns of Ahasuerus and Artaxerxes, and even unto the second year of Darius the King; even so, for many years did enemies without and indolence and apathy within, weaken the hands of the Brethren of the Ancient and Accepted Rite, and trouble them in their work, and frustrate their purposes; until our Rite became almost disused, and the work almost ceased; as the chiefs of the Samaritans, from the days of Artaxerxes and his decree against our ancient brethren, caused their work to cease by violence and force. But the sun is now risen, and the darkness disappears.

M∴ Ill∴. What said the Prophets to our ancient brethren, when the clouds lowered upon their hopes, and the elements around them seemed gloomy and threatening?

Jun∴ D∴. Thus said Haggai the Prophet, on the first day of the 6th month: "Thus saith the God of Armies, 'Go up to the mountain and bring timbers, and build the House; and I will take pleasure in it, and I will be glorified. I am with you,' saith the Lord."

Sen∴ D∴. On the one and twentieth day of the seventh month, thus said Haggai the Prophet: "Be strong, O Zerubbabel! and be strong, O Joshua, the son of Josadak the High Priest! and be strong, all ye people of the land, and work! For I am with you, saith the Lord of Hosts. The glory of this latter House shall be greater than that of the former, and in this place will I give peace."

Jun∴ W∴. Thus said Haggai the Prophet, on the four and twentieth day of the ninth month: "In that day, saith the God of Armies, will I take thee, O Zerubbabel, my servant, the son of Shealtiel, and will make thee as a signet: for I have chosen thee, saith the Lord of Hosts."

Sen∴ W∴. Thus said Zechariah, the son of Iddo, on the four and twentieth day of the month Sebat; "Thus saith the Lord, 'I am returned to Jerusalem with mercies: my House shall be built in it, and a line shall be stretched forth upon Jerusalem. Sing and rejoice, O Daughter of Zion! for, lo! I come, and I will dwell in the midst of Thee, saith the Lord. Who art thou, O great mountain?—before Zerubbabel a plain; and he shall bring forth the Key-stone, while the People cry, 'Stability and continuance unto it!' The hands of Zerubbabel have laid the foundation of this House. His hands shall also finish it: and ye shall know that the Lord of Armies hath sent me unto you."

M∴ Ill∴. My Brethren, as our Ancient Brethren arose, encouraged by the Prophets, let us rise up, and begin to build anew the Temple of Masonry. For we, like them, dwell too long in our ceiled houses, while that House falls into decay and lieth waste. We, like them, have sown much and reaped little. We eat and are still hungry; we drink and are still a-thirst: we clothe ourselves, and are not warm; we earn wages, and put them in a sack with holes. Because the Temple of our Rite lieth waste, and we run every man to his own house; and we neglect the interests of Masonry, which are the interests of all humanity.

My Brethren, let this Council be now opened, and our labours upon the Masonic Temple resumed. Ill∴ Captain of the Tribes, let all the brethren be arrayed for the work which we have to do, that it may no more be hindered or delayed.

S∴ W∴. Princes and Brethren, it is the pleasure of the M∴ Ill∴ Master, that this Council be now opened, and that our labours on the Masonic Temple recommence. Let all therefore be prepared for whatever work there is to do; as our ancient Brethren worked with sword and trowel when they rebuilt God's House at Jerusalem.

[The Capt∴ of the Guards raps ▌ — and the Capt∴ of the Tribes, the Jun∴ W∴, the Sen∴ W∴ and the M∴ Ill∴ do each the same in succession].

M∴ Ill∴. Together, my Brethren!

[The Brethren all give the sign; clap the hands ▌ times, applaud, saying Laus Deo; and the M∴ Ill∴ says]:

M∴ Ill∴. My Brethren, this Council is open.

RECEPTION.

The Brethren being in the second apartment, dressed and decorated as in the Hall of King Cyrus or Court of Cyrus, in the 15th Degree, the Master of Ceremonies and three other Brethren receive the candidate in the preparation room. The five are all dressed alike, in the dress and with the ornaments and jewel of a Knight of the East; and the Master of Ceremonies bears a roll of parchment, tied with a green ribbon, and sealed with a large seal.

The M∴ of Cer∴ gives the alarm at the door, by ? ▌

M∴ Inf∴. Prince M∴ of Cav∴, there is an alarm at the door of the Palace.

M∴ Cav∴. Attend to that alarm, my Brother, and learn who approach, and their request.

M∴ Inf∴ [Going to and opening the door]: Who approach the presence of Darius the Great King, and what is their request?

M∴ Cer∴ Seraiah, Reelaiah, Mordecai, Bilshan, and Mispar, Princes of Judah and Knights of the East, with letters to the King from Tatnai, Governor beyond the river, and from Satabazanes, crave an audience.

[The M∴ Inf∴ reports to the M∴ Cav∴; who repairs to the East, and makes the same report].

Sov∴ M∴ Permit the messengers to appear in our presence.

[The M∴ Cer∴, the candidate and the three brothers enter, advance to the East, and kneel on one knee. The M∴ of Despatches advances and receives the letter].

Sov∴ M∴ Rise, Princes and Knights, and declare your wishes to the King.

M∴ Cer∴ Sov∴ Master, Great King Darius, in the first year of Cyrus the King, he made proclamation throughout all his Kingdom, that God had charged him to build unto Him a house at Jerusalem; and said unto our people in Persia, "Who among you are of the People of Israel? Their God be with them, and let them go up to Jerusalem, which is in Judah, and build the House of the Lord God of Israel [the one True God], in Jerusalem." And he set free our people, and restored to them the Holy Vessels of the Temple; and they returned to Jerusalem and laid the foundations of the Temple. But the people that dwelt round about them hindered and interrupted them during the whole reign of Cyrus the King, and even until now. And in the days of Artaxerxes the King, the people whom the Assyrian had put into the cities of Samaria, beyond the river, sent letters unto the King, saying unto him that Jerusalem was a rebellious and bad city, and that if the same were builded again, and the walls set up once more, our people would refuse to pay toll, tribute or custom, and the revenue of the King be thereby endamaged. Which false testimony the King believing, he sent an answer unto those of Samaria, beyond the river, declaring that search had been made, and it was found that Jerusalem of old time had made insurrection against the Kings, and rebellion and sedition had occurred therein. Wherefore he commanded them to cause the work to cease, and to let not the city be builded, until other order. Whereupon Rehum the Chancellor and Shimshai the Scribe, and their People, went up in haste unto Jerusalem, and made the work to cease, by force and power: and so it hath ceased until now. But now the Prophets have made known that it is the will of God that His House shall be builded, and Zerubbabel the Viceroy, and Joshua the High Priest, have begun to build the House, and the Prophets of God do help them. And Tatnai, Governor beyond the river, and Satabazanes and their companions have come unto them, and inquired of them who directed the building of the Temple and the walls of the city: and it hath been agreed that the work shall not cease until the matter be made known unto thee, and thy sovereign pleasure be declared: and we have brought with us the letter of Tatnai and Satabazanes concerning the matter, being sent unto thee by Zerubbabel the Viceroy.

Sov∴ M∴ Read thou the letter, our Gr∴ Master of Despatches.

M∴ Desp∴ "Tatnai, Governor beyond the river, and Satabazanes, unto Darius the Great King, Health and Peace! Be it known unto the King that we went into the Province of Judea, to the House of the Great God, which is builded with great stones, and timber is laid on the walls, and the work goeth fast on; and prospereth in their hands. Then asked we the leaders of the Jews, and said unto them, Who commanded you to build this House, and to set up these walls? We asked their names also, that we might write and send unto thee the names of the men that were leaders among them.

"And thus they returned us answer, saying: 'We are the servants of the God of Heaven and Earth, and we build the House that was builded many years ago, which a Great King of Israel builded and set up. But after our fathers incurred the anger of the God of Heaven, he gave them into the hand of Nebuchadnezzar, King of Babylon, the Chaldean, who destroyed God's House, and carried away the People into Babylon. But in the first year of Cyrus the King, he made a decree to build the House. And the vessels of gold and silver, of the House, which the King of Babylon took out of the Temple at Jerusalem, and put in the Temple of Bel in Babylon, these did Cyrus the King take out of the Temple of Bel, and they were delivered unto Sheshbazzar; whom he had made Governor; to whom he said, 'take these vessels, and go carry them unto the Temple in Jerusalem, and let the House of God be builded in its old place.'

"Then came Sheshbazzar [whom we call Zerubbabel], and laid the foundation of the House of God in Jerusalem; and from that time until now it hath been in building, and is yet not finished."

"Now therefore, if it seem good to the King, let there be search made in the Royal Archives at Babylon, whether it be true that a decree was made by Cyrus the King, to build this House of God at Jerusalem; and let the King send his pleasure to us, concerning this matter."

Sov∴ M∴ Our Gr∴ Master of the Chancery, let search be forthwith made, if there be such a decree. [The Keeper of the Seals goes out, and remains a little while].

Sov∴ M∴ Ye Princes of Judah, who is this God that ye worship?

M∴ Cer∴ Sov∴ Master, the One, true, only God, invisible, omnipotent, who created the world, and whom no man hath seen at any time: to whom all time is now and all space is near; from whom is Life and Light; and who at first existed alone, with Time and Space, Infinite and Eternal as they.

Sov∴ M∴ Are ye not worshippers of the sun, or of idols and images?

M∴ Cer∴ Sov∴ Master, this commandment gave our God unto Moses our Lawgiver. "Thou shalt have no other Gods before me. Thou shalt not make unto thee any graven image, or any likeness of any thing in heaven, or on the earth, or in the water, or under the earth: nor shalt thou bow down to them nor serve them. Ye shall destroy their altars, break their images and cut down their groves. Ye shall worship no other God, but the God whose name no man shall pronounce. Lift not up your eyes unto heaven, to worship and adore the sun and the moon and the stars, even all the glorious Armies of Heaven, whose light God hath bestowed upon all the nations of the earth. Ye shall utterly destroy all the places wherein the nations which ye shall possess worship their Gods, upon the high mountains, and the hills, and under every green tree. Ye shall overthrow their altars, and break their columns, and burn their groves with fire: and ye shall hew down the graven images of their Gods, and utterly obliterate their names and memories."

Sov∴ M∴ Such also are the commands of our law. [The Keeper of the Seals here enters, bringing with him a roll of parchment]: Gr∴ Master of the Chancery, hast thou discovered the decree?

M∴ Chan∴ Sov∴ Master, I find it thus written upon a roll in the Royal Archives: "Thus saith Cyrus the King of Persia: The Lord God of Heaven hath given me all the Kingdoms of the Earth; and he hath charged me to build him an house at Jerusalem in Judah. Who among you is of his People? His God be with him; and let him go up to Jerusalem, in Judah, and build the House of the Lord God of Israel (the only God) in Jerusalem."

Sov∴ M∴ It is enough. Let the decree of Cyrus the Great King be fulfilled! Prepare such decree as is suitable, and send it by these Princes of Judah to Tatnal and Satabazanes, that it may be punctually obeyed: and meantime give to these ambassadors fit entertainment; for they, like us, worship the True God, and do not bow down to images and idols. Princes, the audience is over!

[The candidate and the four brothers then return to the preparation room; and after a little delay, during which time the Brethren pass into the other apartment, they approach the door of that apartment, and the M∴ Cer∴ gives the alarm by || raps.]

Jun∴ War∴ M∴ Ill∴, there is an alarm at the entrance to the Council.

M∴ Ill∴ Attend to that alarm, and see who approaches!

Jun∴ W∴ [Opening the door]: Who approaches this Council among the ruins of Jerusalem?

M∴ Cer∴ Seraiah, Reelaiah, Mordecai, Bilshan and Mispar, Ambassadors to Darius the Great King, bringing with them his decree, and good tidings to the People of the Lord.

[The Jun∴ W∴ reports to the Sen∴ Warden, and he to the M∴ Ill∴].

M∴ Ill∴ Open wide the doors, and invite the Ambassadors to enter!

[They enter and approach the East].

M∴ Ill∴ Welcome, Princes, to Jerusalem! We give thanks to God for your safe return: and wait anxiously to hear how you have fared in your mission.

M∴ Cer∴ M∴ Ill∴, after the Council did us the great honour to select us to bear its petition and the letter of Tatnal and Satabazanes to the foot of the Throne of Darius the King, we set forth on our way; and notwithstanding that we were attacked by the Samaritans on this side the river, whom we resisted and put to flight, we reached Babylon in safety, and obtained audience of the King; who received us graciously and ordered the letter to be read, and thereupon directed search to be made in the Royal Archives for the decree made by Cyrus the King in the first year of his reign. In the meantime he inquired of us what God the Jews adored, and whether they bowed down to images and idols, or adored the Armies of Heaven; to which we having made answer in the words of the law of Moses, the Gr∴ Master of the Chancery brought before him the roll, found in the House of the Rolls, at Achmetha, in the Palace, in the Province of Media, with the decree of Cyrus the King recorded therein: which being read and heard, he declared that he did confirm and would execute the same; and ordered fit decree to be prepared, and sent by us to Tatnai and Satabazanes, that it might be punctually obeyed: and was also pleased to order for us fit entertainment; saying that we, like the Persians, worshipped the True God, and bowed not down to images and idols: after which we were dismissed with honours and rewards, and have returned in safety hither, bringing with us the letter of the King. The People have met us without the city, and accompanied us hither, singing songs of joy and praise for our happy return, and doing us great honour.

Sov∴ M∴ We too, my Brethren, return sincere thanks to God for your safety. Resume now your seats in the Council; first delivering the letter of the King to our Secretary, who will read the same.

[The candidate and the others are seated; and the Secretary opens the roll, and reads]:

" Thus saith Darius the King: We have caused search to be made for, and have found, the decree made by Cyrus the King in the first year of his reign, commanding that the Temple of God at Jerusalem should be rebuilt, and the vessels thereof restored; and are pleased to confirm that decree: Now therefore, Tatnai, Governor beyond the river, Satabazanes, and your people, meddle no more therewith; but let the work of this House of God alone. Let the Governor of the Jews and the Elders of the Jews build this House of God in its proper place. Moreover I decree what ye shall do to the Elders of these Jews, for the building of this House of God; that of the Royal revenues, of the tribute beyond the river, means be furnished them, that the work be not delayed: and whatever they need for the sacrifices, and wheat, salt, wine and oil, upon the requisition of the Priests at Jerusalem, let it be given them daily without fail: that they may offer acceptable oblations to the God of Heaven, and pray for the life of the King and of his sons.

" Also I decree, that whosoever shall disobey this decree, let timber be pulled down from his house, and set up for a gallows, and he be hanged thereon; and his house for his offence be made a pile of rubbish. And may the God that dwelleth, and whose Name is worshipped, at Jerusalem, destroy all rulers and all people that shall endeavour to hinder or destroy the House of God at Jerusalem! Thus do I, Darius the King, decree: and let all promptly obey!"

Sov∴ M∴ GLORY BE TO GOD THE HIGHEST FOR HIS MERCIES! AND HONOUR AND PROSPERITY AND LENGTH OF DAYS TO THE SOVEREIGN! Join me, my Brethren, in the acclamation!

[All clap their hands ♃♀*☽ times, and cry once, " *Glory to God, and honour to the Sovereign!*"]

Sov∴ M∴ My Brother, Captain of the Tribes, cause it to be proclaimed throughout the City unto the People, that Darius the King has graciously granted our requests, and commanded that the work upon the House of the Lord shall not longer be hindered or delayed: and bid them rejoice; for the end of the sorrow and suffering of Israel approaches.

[The Sen∴ Deacon goes out].

Sov∴ M∴ Princes and Brethren, our Messengers to the Court of Darius the King deserve our thanks and gratitude. The faithful servant earneth his reward. Ill∴ Scribe, and M∴ Wise and Ven∴ Priest, with what new honour shall we distinguish our brave and faithful brethren, Seraiah, Reelaiah, Mordecai, Bilshan and Mispar?

Sen∴ W∴ M∴ Ill∴, I am at great loss what to answer. M∴ Wise and Ven∴ Priest, can you not aid us with your advice?

Jun∴ W∴ M∴ Ill∴, the People dispute with each other, and there is none to sit in judgment between them. Those who have returned from the captivity claim lands of those who have possessed them many years; and there is no Tribunal to decide. And the People clamour and are divided, and dissensions are rife among them. Let the messengers our brethren be made judges between the people, to administer Justice and Equity. So shall they receive honour and distinction, and do the Lord and his people good service.

M∴ Ill∴ M∴ Wise and Ven∴, it shall even be as thou sayest. Approach, my Brethren! [They approach the Throne]. By the advice and consent of the Council, I do hereby create and constitute a Tribunal to be composed of five Judges, who shall judge between man and man, and administer justice and equity, and whose judgment shall be without appeal. And I appoint thee, Selaiah, to be Chief of that Tribunal, and Reelaiah, Mordecai, Bilshan and Mispar to sit with thee in judgment. Go now, and kneel at the Holy altar of Sacrifice, and assume the obligation appropriate to your office.

OBLIGATION.

I, A . . . B . . ., in the presence of the Gr∴ Architect of the Universe, and of this Gr∴ Council of the Princes of Jerusalem, do hereby and hereon most solemnly and sincerely promise and swear, that I will never reveal or make known the secrets of this degree, to any person in the known world, except to those to whom the same may lawfully belong, and to them only when I am duly allowed and authorized to do so.

I furthermore promise and swear, that whenever I am called upon to judge and decide between my brethren, I will do so with Justice and Equity, without favour or partiality, and leaning neither to the right hand nor to the left.

I furthermore promise and swear, that I will endeavour to reconcile all differences and disputes between my brethren, and to persuade them not to go to law with each other; and will exert all my influence to restore and promote peace, harmony and kind feeling between those who may be estranged, or about to become estranged, from each other.

I furthermore promise and swear that I will be courteous to all men, and will lead an honest and irreproachable life.

I furthermore promise and swear that I will never insult, deride or ridicule a Bro∴ Prince of Jerusalem; nor give or send him a challenge, nor accept one from him; nor strike or wound him, except in absolute self-defence; nor injure him in his person, property, reputation or feelings.

I furthermore promise and swear that I will never abandon a Brother, in whatever adversity he may be, in combat, or in sickness, or in prison; but will aid him with my counsel, my friends, my sword and my purse.

To all of which I do most solemnly promise and sincerely swear, binding myself under no less a penalty, than that of having my house pulled down, and the timbers thereof set up as a gallows, and I hanged thereon. So help me God! and keep me steadfast to keep and perform the same!

Sov∴ M∴ Arise, my Brethren, Princes of Jerusalem and Judges! Your superior merit has not only made you my equals, but has placed you above me. For you are Princes and Judges by election and a general proclamation, and have the right and power to judge me, who am a Prince by birth alone.

Prince Selaiah, I now invest thee with this apron, which shall hereafter be appropriate to this degree. Its colours are emblematical of that fervency and zeal which have procured you this honour; and of the day of Hope that now by your means dawns on Israel. Its different blazonings are emblematical of that equity and justice by which you have sworn to be ever guided.

Masons in this and the higher degrees wear the apron, that they may never forget that they attained their high rank and dignity by means of Masonic labour alone; and that, remembering their first estate, they may be courteous and kind to Masons of the inferior degrees.

If there be a controversy between men, and they come unto judgment that ye may judge them, then ye shall justify the righteous and condemn the wicked.

Thou shalt not have in thine house divers measures, a great and a small: thou shalt have a perfect and just weight, a perfect and just measure; that thy days may be lengthened in the land which the Lord thy God giveth thee.

He shall be accursed that removeth his neighbor's land-mark; and he that perverteth the judgment of the stranger, the fatherless, and the widow.

Ye shall do no unrighteousness in judgment: Ye shall not respect the person of the poor, nor honour the person of the mighty; but in righteousness shall ye judge your neighbour.

Blessings are upon the head of the just; but violence covereth the mouth of the wicked. The memory of the just is blessed; but the name of the wicked shall rot.

4A

Receive also this collar, whose color also symbolizes the dawn of that new day for which all true Masons rejoice. The balance upon it is a symbol of impartiality; the hand and sword, of that severity which crime sometimes makes a stern necessity; the poniard, of the fate that shall swiftly overtake the oppressor and the unjust judge; the stars, of the number of your members; and the crowns, of the supremacy of your judgments and authority.

Receive also this jewel, emblematic of the same; and the initials engraved thereon will ever remind you of the gracious clemency of Darius, and the gratitude of Zerubbabel for your services and fidelity.

Receive also the sign, words and token of a Prince of Jerusalem.

SIGN: . . . Advance boldly, with the ♎♃☿‡♊⁑‡☉♀♎☽♊, as if to engage in a combat; the †⁑&☉♒♊ on the †⁑&♀§.

ANSWER: . . . ♎♈‡☾♈↑&‡☿♄♈ the ☉‡♋ at the height of the ♎&☿♄†♊☾‡, as if to commence the combat; the ‡⁑♑☿☿♈ forming a ♎♓♄☉‡☾ with the §☿♀♒♈ of the †☾♑♈.

TOKEN: . . . ♈☉§ each other mutually with the ‡⁑♈&♄♋♏ on the ♉☿♀♒♈ of the †♀♈♈†☾‡♑♀-♒♌☾‡ of the ‡⁑&☉♒♊—‖ ♈☉§♎—thus—, and ♈♃♀↑☾? At the same time place the ‡♀♌&♈‡♑☾☾♈ together at the §☿♀♒♈♎, forming a straight line; and let the ¶♒☾☾♎ touch each other. Then reciprocally place the †☾♑♈⁑&☉♒♊ on the ♎&☿♄†♊☾‡ of the other, ☿§☾♒♒♌ the ♑♀♒♌☾‡♎. One says ♈♃☾♒♈♄, and the other, ♈♃☾♒♈♄-♈&‡☾☾. Then form a square with the †☾♑♈‡♃‡♀♎♈ on the ‡♀♌&♈—let go the &☉♒♊♎, bring the §☿♀♒♈ of the ‡⁑♑☿☿♈ to the †⁑&☾☾†, and salute each other by bowing.

PASS-WORD: . . . ♈☾♏☾♈∴

SACRED WORD: . . . ☉♊☉‡∴

The Israelites re-entered into Jerusalem, after their captivity in Babylon, on the 20th day of Tebet or Tebeth, the 10th month of the year; and their thanksgiving, after the completion of the second temple, took place on the 23d day of Adar, the 12th month of the 6th year of the reign of Darius. The temple had been finished on the 3d day of the same month; and, on the 14th day of the following month, the Passover was celebrated in it.

Hear now, my brother, the History and Lecture of this Degree.

HISTORY AND LECTURE.

The historical incidents commemorated in this degree are so fully detailed in the ceremonies, as to need no further repetition. It remains only to allude to those which followed the return of the embassy from Babylon, and the action of the Tribunal of the Five Princes of Jerusalem.

Tatnai, Governor of the Jewish side of the River, and Satabazanes and their People, obeyed the mandate of Darius. And the Elders of the Jews builded, and they prospered through the prophesying of Haggai the Prophet, and Zechariah the son of Iddo: and they builded and finished the Temple, according to the commandment of the God of Israel, and according to the orders of Cyrus, Darius and Artaxerxes, Kings of Persia.

It was finished on the third day of the month Adar, in the sixth year of the reign of Darius. On the 20th day of that month, the children of Israel, the Priests and the Levites and the rest of the children of the

Captivity kept the dedication of the House of God with joy and sacrifices; and the Priests and Levites were then assigned to their several duties, in accordance with the law of Moses.

In the fifth month of the seventh year of Artaxerxes the King, Ezra came from Babylon to Jerusalem. He was a lineal descendant of Aaron, and well read in the Mosaic law and sacred traditions, and a favourite of the King, who readily granted his request to be allowed to return to Jerusalem and unite again with his people; and issued in his favour a decree to this effect: "Artaxerxes, King of Kings, unto Ezra the Priest, a Teacher of the Law of the God of Heaven, Health and Peace! I decree that all Jews and their Priests and Levites, in my realm, who are disposed of their own free will to return to Jerusalem, may do so with thee. And I, by the advice of my Council of Seven, do send thee to enforce the Law of God, which is in thy keeping, in Judah and Jerusalem: and to carry thither the silver and gold which we and our Council have freely offered unto Israel's God in Jerusalem; and whatever may be given thee in our Province of Babylon, as a voluntary gift from the People and the Priests for the House of God in Jerusalem, wherewith to purchase animals for your sacrifices, and any residue to dispose of as your God may direct. I give to thee the remaining vessels for the service of the Temple, to be placed therein; and whatsoever more may be needed therefor shall be furnished by the Royal Treasury. And I command all my Receivers of the Revenue beyond the river to pay to you, upon your requisition, to the extent of an hundred talents of silver, an hundred measures of wheat, an hundred baths of wine, an hundred baths of oil, and whatever salt is required. Whatsoever is required by the God of Heaven, let it be diligently done for His House, that His displeasure may not fall upon our realm.

"It shall not be lawful to impose tax, toll, tribute or custom on the Priests, Levites, Minstrels, Porters, Nethinims or Ministers of the Temple. And thou, Ezra, to enforce the Law of God, whereof thou hast a copy, appoint magistrates and judges, for all the people beyond the River that know that law, and teach it to them who know it not. And if any one disobey that law or the law of the King, let him without delay be condemned to suffer death, or to exile, confiscation of property or imprisonment."

Collecting together 1506 men, with their women and children, and ashamed to ask an escort of the King, because he had assured him that God would protect and defend them on the way, Ezra set forth from Babylon on the first day of the first month, of the seventh year of the reign of Artaxerxes, prepared to enforce as well as obey the law of God, and to legislate and administer the law to the people of Israel.

At the river of Ahava he encamped and remained three days, and there sent for and was joined by 262 Levites and Nethinims whose duty it was to serve the Levites. Then he held a fast, delivered the sacred vessels into the custody of the Priests, and again moved on the twelfth day of the first month. Safely through the hostile forces that lay in wait for him by the way he passed, protected by God; and reached Jerusalem on the first day of the fifth month, having occupied four months in the journey: and there delivered the mandates of the King to his Lieutenants and Governors, and they furthered the people and the House of God.

In the ninth month, on the 20th day of the month, all the People assembled at Jerusalem, in obedience to his peremptory summons commanding their attendance on pain of exile and confiscation of goods: and there they sat in the streets, in a great rain, trembling with fear and shivering with cold. Then he commenced the work of reform by compelling all who had married among the unbelieving people of the country to put away their wives.

After Nehemiah was appointed Governor, and the walls of the city were completely rebuilt, and on the first day of the seventh month, a solemn feast was held, and the whole People came together. Then Ezra brought forth the book of the Law of Moses, and read it to the People, and with the aid of the Priests and Levites expounded it to them for seven days, during which time they rejoiced and feasted, as they had not done since the time of Joshua the son of Nun and successor of Moses; and on the eighth day a solemn assembly was held according to the ancient custom, at which many were initiated into the mysteries.

And on the 24th day there was a fast; and the people entered into and sealed a solemn covenant; by which they bound themselves, confirming it by an oath, to walk in God's law, which was given by Moses the servant of God, and to observe and keep all God's commandments, and his judgments and his statutes, and to pay tax and tithe and the first fruits, and observe the seventh day and the seventh year.

Thus was the Temple rebuilt, the work of our ancient brethren completed, and the old law restored. The Samaritans, ancient enemies of the Jews, compelled by the power of the Kings of Persia to submit and pay tribute to the children of Israel, troubled them no longer. The cities were rebuilt, and for a time peace and prosperity reigned in Jerusalem. Masonry again flourished as in the days of its first glory, and the number of its initiates largely increased. But this period of peace and glory was of short duration. Seventy years after the Christian era the Romans invaded Judea, took Jerusalem and razed it to the ground, burnt the Temple and almost annihilated the people.

A few Architects escaping remained in the vicinity of the beloved city, and there preserved in the strictest secrecy the ancient mysteries and instruction. Adopting yet greater precautions, they admitted none until after the most thorough tests and a long probation. Under the Romans, and afterwards under the Saracens, they waited for some fortunate chance that should again put them in possession of the land of their fathers, and enable them again to rebuild the Temple.

Others, at the dispersion of the People, fled to the desert for safety. After a time they reappeared at the ruins of the Temple, assembling under the banner of fraternal charity and love for humanity. On the very site of the House of God they founded an hospital for the pilgrims who came to visit the wreck of the Holy City. They became a religious order, bound by vows of strict observance, pledged to celibacy, and devoted to the relief of the poor, as well by alms as by the fruits of the earth which the new Masters of Judea allowed them to cultivate. Afterwards, becoming a religious soldiery, their swords changed their precarious possession into a title.

Hope sprang up anew, when Peter the Hermit, an obscure but zealous fanatic, preached throughout Europe the first crusade. The rumor of that Holy War, flying abroad upon the wings of the wind, reached the remotest regions of the world. The religious soldiery, chiefly inhabiting the deserts of the Thebaid, emerged from their solitudes. Eager to distinguish themselves, they hastened to unite with their brethren at Jerusalem. They found them the allies of the Architects; all having as their object, though with different views, the restoration of the Temple. Laying aside their prejudices, they adopted the same rites, and disguised under the same symbolism of a speculative architecture a glorious purpose. Determining to join the Crusaders, they resolved to serve under chiefs elected by themselves, whom they elected from among the military Brethren, as being best qualified by experience and long service.

They then adopted an established ritual, substituting in place of the old ceremonial of the Mysteries, more ancient than Solomon or Hiram, or even than Moses himself, a formula, symbols and allegories referring to the building of the first Temple, and thus always reminding them of their great purpose of rebuilding the Temple, and restoring the Holy Land to the descendants of Judah and Benjamin. Thus they kept themselves apart from the mass of the Crusaders, and secured the enlistment and perpetual allegiance of a large body of loyal and obedient recruits.

In a vast army composed of many thousands, speaking different languages, and gathered from all quarters of Europe, and many of them rapacious, degraded and brutal, and equally as dangerous to them as the Infidel enemy, caution and prudence were indispensable. To ensure themselves against surprise, they adopted words, signs and tokens for mutual recognition even when at great distances apart, and to preserve their secrets against curiosity, treason and imprudence. And taking the name of Free Masons [as independent auxiliaries], they joined the Armies of the Cross, and soon gained distinction and renown.

The Architects who had built and still maintained their hospital upon the ruins of the Temple, did not remain idle. They too, leaving a small number of their more aged members to perform the duties of hospitality, relief and charity, took up arms, elected a leader, who afterwards became their Grand Master, and joined the Christian armies. Several orders, rising in like manner from small beginnings, increased in stature, and became numerous, wealthy and powerful. The Templars, the Order of St. John, and the Teutonic Knights, sprang up in succession, reached the height of wealth, power and greatness, and were in succession despoiled and annihilated.

During the several crusades, the Order of Free Masons naturally increased in numbers, and itself became powerful and influential, though in secret; for none but the initiated knew that such an order existed. Men of all Christian countries joined the Order, and it spread throughout the different States of Europe, and

XVI . . 11

flourished alike under the shadow of the Mosque and the Vatican. After the first successes, and when a Christian King sat upon the throne of Jerusalem, and Christian Lords held Principalities and Dukedoms in Palestine, eighty-one Masons repaired to Sweden, with letters to the Bishop of Upsal, whom they initiated into their mysteries, to secure his assistance in reanimating the zeal of the confederated Princes.

The attempt to conquer the Holy Land was renewed, but proved unsuccessful. The Masons then sent again 81 members to Upsal, to deliver to the Prelate their manuscripts and jewels and other Masonic treasures, sealed up in a coffer. He received it, and deposited it in a marble tomb, sealed with firm seals, buried in a deep cavern under the Tower of the Four Crowns; from which, at a later period, those precious archives were recovered.

After this deposit, the 81 Brothers returned to Jerusalem; but the victories of the Sultan of Egypt destroying the last lingering hope of rebuilding the Temple, they resolved to abandon their country, desolated by the Infidel, and to form new establishments in remote regions: and many years had not elapsed until their Lodges, Chapters, Councils and Preceptories were found in every country in Europe.

We no longer expect, my Brother, to rebuild the Temple at Jerusalem. To us it has become but a symbol. To us the whole world is God's Temple, as is every upright heart. To establish all over the world, the New Law and Reign of Love, Peace, Charity and Toleration, is to build that Temple, most acceptable to God, in erecting which Masonry is now engaged. No longer needing to repair to Jerusalem to worship, nor to offer up sacrifices and shed blood to propitiate the Deity, man may make the woods and mountains his Churches and Temples, and worship God with a devout gratitude, and works of charity and beneficence to his fellow-men. Wherever the humble and contrite heart silently offers up its adoration, under the overarching trees, in the open level meadows, on the hill-side, in the glen, or in the city's swarming streets; there is God's House and the New Jerusalem.

The Princes of Jerusalem no longer sit as magistrates to judge between the People; nor is their number limited to five. But their duties still remain substantially the same, and their insignia and symbols retain their old significance. Justice and Equity are still their characteristics. To reconcile disputes and heal dissensions, to restore amity and peace, to soothe dislikes and soften prejudices are their peculiar duties, and they know that the peace-makers are blessed.

Their emblems have been already explained. They are part of the language of Masonry; the same now as it was when Moses learned it from the Egyptian Hierophants.

Still we observe the spirit of the Divine law, as thus enunciated to our ancient brethren, when the Temple was rebuilt, and the book of the law again opened:

Execute true judgment; and show mercy and compassion every man to his brother. Oppress not the widow nor the fatherless, the stranger nor the poor; and let none of you imagine evil against his brother in his heart. Speak ye every man the truth to his neighbour; execute the judgment of Truth and Peace in your gates; and love no false oath; for all these I hate, saith the Lord.

"Let those who have power rule in righteousness, and Princes in judgment. And let him that is a judge be as an hiding place from the wind, and a covert from the tempest; as rivers of water in a dry place; as the shadow of a great rock in a weary land. Then the vile person shall no more be called liberal; nor the churl bountiful: and the work of justice shall be peace; and the effect of justice, quiet and security; and wisdom and knowledge shall be the stability of the times. Walk ye righteously and speak uprightly: despise the gains of oppression, shake from your hands the contamination of bribes: stop not your ears against the cries of the oppressed, nor shut your eyes that you may not see the crimes of the great; and you shall dwell on high, and your place of defence be like munitions of rocks."

Forget not these precepts of the old Law: and especially do not forget, as you advance, that every Mason, however humble, is your brother, and the labouring man your peer. Remember always that all Masonry is work, and that the trowel is an emblem of the degrees in this Council. Labour, when rightly understood, is both noble and ennobling, and intended to develope man's moral and spiritual nature, and not to be deemed a disgrace or a misfortune.

Everything around us is, in its bearings and influences, moral. The serene and bright morning, when we recover our conscious existence from the embraces of sleep; when, from that image of Death God calls us to a new life, and again gives us existence, and his mercies visit us in every bright ray and glad thought, and call for gratitude and content: the silence of that early dawn, the hushed silence, as it were, of expectation: the holy eventide, its cooling breeze, its lengthening shadows, its falling shades, its still and sober hour: the sultry noontide and the stern and solemn midnight: and Spring-time, and chastening Autumn; and Summer, that unbars our gates, and carries us forth amidst the ever-renewed wonders of the world; and Winter, that gathers us around the evening hearth:—all these, as they pass, touch by turns the springs of the spiritual life in us, and are conducting that life to good or evil. The idle watch-hand often points to something within us; and the shadow of the gnomon on the dial often falls upon the conscience.

A life of labour is not a state of inferiority or degradation. The Almighty has not cast man's lot beneath the quiet shades, and amid glad groves and lovely hills, with no task to perform; with nothing to do but to rise up and eat, and to lie down and rest. He has ordained that *Work* shall be done, in all the dwellings of life, in every productive field, in every busy city and on every wave of every ocean. And this he has done, because it has pleased Him to give man a nature destined to higher ends than indolent repose and irresponsible profitless indulgence; and because, for developing the energies of such a nature, work was the necessary and proper element. We might as well ask why He could not make two and two be six, as why He could not develope these energies without the instrumentality of work. They are equally impossibilities.

This, Masonry teaches, as a great Truth; a great moral landmark, that ought to guide the course of all mankind. It teaches its toiling children that the scene of their daily life is all spiritual, that the very implements of their toil, the fabrics they weave, the merchandise they barter, are designed for spiritual ends; that so believing, their daily lot may be to them a sphere for the noblest improvement. That which we do in our intervals of relaxation, our church-going and our book-reading, are specially designed to prepare our minds for the *Action* of Life. We are to hear and read and meditate, that we may *act* well: and the Action of Life is itself the great field for spiritual improvement. There is no task of industry or business, in field or forest, on the wharf, the ship's deck or the exchange, but has spiritual ends. There is no care or cross of our daily labour, but was especially ordained, to nurture in us patience, calmness, resolution, perseverance, gentleness, disinterestedness, magnanimity. Nor is there any tool or implement of toil, but is a part of the great spiritual instrumentality.

All the relations of life, those of parent, child, brother, sister, friend, associate, husband, wife, are moral, throughout every living tie and thrilling nerve that binds them together. They cannot subsist a day nor an hour, without putting the mind to a trial of its truth, fidelity, forbearance, and disinterestedness.

A great city is one extended scene of moral action. There is no blow struck in it, but has a purpose, ultimately good or bad, and therefore moral. There is no action performed, but has a motive; and motives are the special jurisdiction of morality. Equipages, houses and furniture are symbols of what is moral, and they in a thousand ways minister to right or wrong feeling. Everything that belongs to us, ministering to our comfort or luxury, awakens in us emotions, of pride or gratitude, of selfishness or vanity, thoughts of self-indulgence, or merciful remembrances of the needy and the destitute.

Everything acts upon and influences us. God's great law of sympathy and harmony is potent and inflexible as His law of gravitation. A sentence embodying a noble thought stirs our blood; a noise made by a child frets and exasperates us, and influences our actions.

A world of spiritual objects, influences and relations lies around us all. We all vaguely deem it to be so; but he only lives a charmed life, like that of genius and poetic inspiration, who communes with the spiritual scene around him, hears the voice of the spirit in every sound, sees its signs in every passing form of things, and feels its impulse in all action, passion and being. Very near to us lie the mines of wisdom: unsuspected they lie all around us. There is a secret in the simplest things, a wonder in the plainest, a charm in the dullest.

We are all naturally seekers of wonders. We travel far to see the majesty of old ruins, the venerable forms of the hoary mountains, great water-falls, and galleries of art. And yet the world-wonder is all around us; the wonder of setting suns, and evening stars, of the magic spring-time, the blossoming of the trees, the strange transformations of the moth; the wonder of the Infinite Divinity and of his boundless revelation. There is no splendour beyond that which sets its morning throne in the golden East; no dome sublime as that of Heaven; no beauty so fair as that of the verdant, blossoming earth; no place, however invested with the sanctities of old time, like that home which is hushed and folded within the embrace of the humblest wall and roof.

And all these are but the symbols of things far greater and higher. All is but the clothing of the spirit. In this vesture of time is wrapped the immortal nature; in this show of circumstance and form stands revealed the stupendous reality. Let man but be, as he is, a living soul, communing with himself and with God, and his vision becomes eternity; his abode, infinity; his home, the bosom of all-embracing love.

The great problem of Humanity is wrought out in the humblest abodes; no more than this is done in the highest. A human heart throbs beneath the beggar's gabardine; and that and no more stirs with its beating the Prince's mantle. The beauty of Love, the charm of Friendship, the sacredness of Sorrow, the heroism of Patience, the noble Self-sacrifice, these and their like, alone, make life to be life indeed, and are its grandeur and its power. They are the priceless treasures and glory of humanity; and they are not things of condition. All places and all scenes are alike clothed with the grandeur and charm of virtues such as these.

The million occasions will come to us all, in the ordinary paths of our life, in our homes, and by our firesides, wherein we may act as nobly, as if, all our life long, we visited beds of sickness and pain. Varying every hour, the million occasions will come in which we may restrain our passions, subdue our hearts to gentleness and patience, resign our own interest for another's advantage, speak words of kindness and wisdom, raise the fallen, cheer the fainting and sick in spirit, and soften and assuage the weariness and bitterness of their mortal lot. To every Mason there will be opportunity enough for these. They cannot be written on his tomb; but they will be written deep in the hearts of men, of friends, of children, of kindred all around him, in the book of the great account, and, in their eternal influences, on the great pages of the universe.

To such a destiny, at least, my Brethren, let us all aspire! These laws of Masonry let us all strive to obey! And so may our hearts become true temples of the Living God! And may He encourage our zeal, sustain our hopes, and assure us of success!

TO CLOSE.

M∴ Ill∴ Ill∴ Scribe, what is the hour?

Sen∴ W∴ High noon, M∴ Ill∴

M∴ Ill∴ The walls of Jerusalem again encircle the Holy City, and the Temple is rebuilt: The book of the law is read again in the hearing of the People; and the new reign of Justice and Equity has commenced. M∴ Wise and Ven∴ Priest, may we not now cease from our labours?

Jun∴ W∴ M∴ Ill∴, Duty is eternal; and Masonic labours *cease* only when we reach the grave, where the wicked cease from troubling, and the weary are at rest. But we may *rest* from our labours for a time, and by refreshing ourselves gain strength to resume them with renewed vigour.

M∴ Ill∴ Let us then close this council, that we may refresh ourselves, and afterwards sleep until the dawn of another day summons us to labour for the good of humanity!

[The Capt∴ of the Guards raps ‖ — the Captain of the Tribes, Jun∴ W∴ and Sen∴ W∴ and then the M∴ Ill∴ each do the same in succession].

M∴ Ill∴ Together, my Brethren!

[The Brothers all give the sign, clap ‖ times, and applaud, crying: LAUS DEO!]

M∴ Ill∴ My Brethren, the council is closed.

DUTIES AND PRIVILEGES OF PRINCES OF JERUSALEM.

1st. Princes of Jerusalem are chiefs in Masonry. They have a right to inspect all Lodges of the degrees from the 1st to the 14th, and Councils of Knights of the East; and can revoke and annul whatever work may be done therein, which they find to violate the constitution and laws of the ancient and accepted rite.

2*d*. When a Prince visits a Lodge, or a Council of the 15th Degree, he must wear the proper clothing, order and jewel, or he is not entitled to be recognized. When he applies for admission, the Presiding Officer must depute a Brother, who is a Prince, if there be any such in the Lodge or Council, to try and examine him; and if there be none other, must do it himself, if he himself be a Prince. If he proves himself, then the doors are thrown open, the Presiding Officer calls to order, the arch of steel is formed, and the visitor seated in the East on the right, with all the appropriate honours. This is in a Council.

If he visits a Symbolic Lodge, and there be no brother who is a Prince, the word of honour of the visitor, proving himself a Master, will suffice. Then the Master deputes four of the most eminent members of the Lodge [not officers], who receive and accompany the visitor. The door is thrown open, and the arch of steel formed. The visitor is conducted to the East; and if the Master be not a Prince, he must offer him his seat and mallet; which the visitor may accept or decline. When he retires from the Lodge, the same ceremonies are observed as at his entrance.

3*d*. If a Prince of Jerusalem presents himself at the door of a Lodge, wherein there is no Brother who has attained this degree, and without his certificate as Prince of Jerusalem, the Master must depute a committee of expert and enlightened Brothers to examine him in the degrees in which the Lodge works. After examination, he must give his Masonic Word of Honor, that he is a Prince of Jerusalem; and he is then to be received with the honours mentioned in the 2d article.

4*th*. The Princes of Jerusalem are entitled to inspect the work of all inferior bodies, and to examine their Constitutions, Statutes, and Laws; and to the exercise of this power no one can object. When five of them sit together, they are Judges in the last resort of all questions referred to them from inferior bodies; and from their decision there is no appeal. That is the power which was given to their predecessors by the People of Jerusalem. They have a right to be covered in all inferior bodies, and to address the presiding officer without rising or asking permission.

5*th*. These rights were conferred on the first Princes by way of reward for their eminent services, rendered to the People of Jerusalem, and their profound and thorough knowledge of Masonry. In rank they were next below Zerubbabel the Viceroy. Wherefore the Princes should be careful to admit none among them who are not at all points worthy to succeed the first Princes, and sit in the places which they occupied with so much honour to themselves.

6*th*. Princes of Jerusalem must be upright, courteous, and strict observers of Masonic Rules, enforcing justice to be done, and good order to be preserved in Lodges.

7*th*. If a Prince of Jerusalem does not lead an irreproachable life, and deal honestly by all men, he shall suffer such punishment as a majority of the Princes of his Council shall determine.

8*th*. If one Prince of Jerusalem insults or ridicules another, he shall be prohibited from sitting in his Council for three successive meetings.

9*th*. If one Prince challenges or accepts a challenge from another, he shall be forever expelled from the Council, and his name erased; and notice thereof given to the Supreme Council, and to all corresponding Councils and Symbolic Lodges.

10*th*. If any Prince shall solicit votes for himself or for any other Prince, for any office, he shall be forever expelled.

11*th*. The Grand Feast of the Princes of Jerusalem is on the 23d day of the 12th month of the Jewish calendar; on which day the People of Israel returned thanks to God that the Temple was rebuilt. On the same day is the regular annual election of all officers. A feast should also be celebrated on the 20th day of the 10th month of the same calendar, in commemoration of the triumphal entry of the ambassadors, who on that day arrived at Jerusalem.

FINIS.

Seventeenth Degree.

Knight of the East and West.

THE LODGE, ITS DECORATIONS, ETC.

The Lodge Room is in the shape of a Heptagon, hung with crimson, sprinkled with stars of gold. In each angle is a square column; on the capitals of which, beginning at the South East, and going round by the South, West and North, in regular succession, to the North East corner, are the initials respectively, of the following words: . . . Beauty . . . Divinity . . . Wisdom . . . Power . . . Honour . . . Glory . . . and Force: . . . and on their bases, of these, . . . Friendship . . . Union . . . Resignation . . . Discretion . . . Fidelity . . . Prudence . . and Temperance.

On each of these columns should be a brilliant lamp or transparency.

In the East is an altar, upon a platform to which you ascend by 7 steps. The platform is supported by four winged oxen, with the heads, respectively, of a Lion, an Ox, a Man and an Eagle.

Around the room are twenty-four Thrones or Seats, richly decorated. On the ceiling are the Sun and Moon: and over the seat of the Master in the East hangs a two-edged sword, surrounded by seven stars.

Upon the platform, in front of the altar, is a Throne, that is always vacant, and in front of it a footstool. The Seat of the Master is at the foot of the Platform, in front.

On the altar is a silver basin with perfumed water, a chafing-dish with live coals, and a large Bible, sealed with seven great seals, of green wax, at least two inches in diameter, attached to red ribbons, that at the other end pass through holes in one lid, the seals lying upon the other lid, and being slightly attached to it by a drop of wax, so as to be easily separated, leaving the seal whole.

The Tracing Board of the Degree is a Heptagon, with the seven words whose initials are on the capitals of the columns, on the outside, and the other seven on the inside, on each side respectively.

In the centre is the figure of a man in a long white robe, with a golden girdle round his waist, and long hair and beard as white as snow: his right hand stretched out and holding seven stars, his head encircled by a glory, his eyes blazing with light, and a two-edged sword in his mouth. Around him stand seven golden candlesticks, and on each, one of these letters: E∴ S∴ P∴ T∴ S∴ P∴ L∴ [*Ephesus* . . *Smyrna* . . *Pergamos* . . *Thyatira* . . *Sardis* . . . *Philadelphia* . . . *Laodicea*]: The Sun and Full Moon also appear on the Tracing Board; and the basin and chafing-dish.

OFFICERS, TITLES, DECORATIONS, ETC.

Bodies in this Degree are called *Preceptories.* A Preceptory should be composed of 24 Members.

The Master is styled *Venerable:* the two Wardens *Zealous,* and the other Brothers *Faithful.* The other officers are a *Lecturer,* an *Examiner,* a *Sen∴ Deacon,* a *Jun∴ Deacon, Treasurer, Secretary,* and a *Guard* of the inner, and one of the outer door.

1u

The Master represents John the Baptist. The Officers and Members, his most eminent disciples among the Essenes.

The apron is of yellow silk, triangular in shape, and lined and edged with crimson. On it, in the centre, is the Tetractys, in dots of gold.

The order is a broad white ribbon worn from right to left, crossed by a black one of equal width, worn from left to right. The jewel is suspended from the latter.

The jewel is a heptagonal medal, part gold, part silver or mother-of-pearl. On one side are engraved, at the angles, the same letters as are upon the square columns, with a star over each. In the centre of it, on the same side, is a lamb, lying on a book with seven seals, on which seals are respectively the same letters. On the reverse side are two swords cross-wise, points upward, and the hilts resting on an even balance: in the corners, the initials of the seven churches.

Each Brother wears under the jewel, order and apron a long white robe, and on his head a circlet of gold or gilded metal, like a coronet.

The battery is £ — by : and ,

TO OPEN.

The Ven.·. Master, having on a table near him the Sealed Book, and his hand resting upon it, raps once, and asks:

V.·. M.·. Faithful Bro.·. Jun.·. Deacon, the first duty of Knights of the East and West in Council?

Jun.·. D.·. To see that they are secure from intrusion, Ven.·. Master.

Ven.·. M.·. See to that, my Bro.·., and caution the Inner and Outer Guards to sleep not upon their posts, but be vigilant; for we are about to open this Preceptory, and must not be disturbed by the Profane or the Pharisees.

[The Jun.·. Deacon goes out, returns, gives the Pass-word for the night to the two Guards, and reports]:

Jun.·. D.·. Ven.·. M.·., the Guards are posted at the inner and the outer door, and have the Pass-word for the night, and we are secure from intrusion.

Ven.·. M.·. It is well. Brother Jun.·. Deacon, what is your duty as a Kt.·. of the East and West?

Jun.·. D.·. To work, to reflect, and to pray.

Ven.·. M.·. Faithful Brother Sen.·. Deacon, what is your duty as a Kt.·. of the East and West?

Sen.·. D.·. To hope, to trust, and to believe.

Ven.·. M.·. Faithful Bro.·. Examiner, what is your duty as a Knight of the East and West?

Exam.·. To be vigilant; that the bad, the base, and the selfish gain no admittance into the ranks of the Faithful.

Ven.·. M.·. Faithful Bro.·. Lecturer, your duty as such?

Lec.·. To teach the truths that lie hid in allegories.

Ven.·. M.·. Zealous Bro.·. Jun.·. Warden, your duty?

Jun.·. W.·. To revere God and love men: to be just and humane: to be true to all men.

Ven.·. M.·. Zealous Bro.·. Sen.·. Warden, your duty?

Sen.·. W.·. To bear persecution with patience, and affliction with resignation: to despise Death; and to minister to the wants of my brethren.

Ven.·. M.·. The duty of the Ven.·. Master?

Sen.·. W.·. To preach the Truth in the desert of Human Life: to proclaim the coming of the New Law: to instruct and baptize the accepted candidate: to judge with justice: and to expound in its true sense the old law.

Ven.·. M.·. I recognize the duty. Zealous Bro.·. Sen.·. Warden, what is the hour?

Sen∴ W∴ Before day. The Morning Star glitters in the East, on the shoulders of the hills, over the desert ; and the Seven are low in the North.

Ven∴ M∴ My Brethren, the dawn of the new day approaches, bringing with it Light and the New Law. The Time cometh, and the Man. To your knees, my Brethren !

[The Brethren all kneel [facing the East], on both knees. The Ven∴ M∴ repeats the following prayer, the Brethren all making the responses] :

PRAYER.

Hear us, our Father, God of the Ancient Patriarchs, whom they adored on the Plains of Chaldæa !

Resp∴ Be gracious unto us, our Father !

———— We wander in the Desert in darkness, and turn anxiously to the East, and look longingly for the promised Light.

Resp∴ Send us the Dawn of Day, our Father !

———— We sit in the shadow of death, and our feet tread the margin of the sea that covers Sodom, and our tents whiten the Desert upon its sterile shores. Send us Thy Light, our Father, Thy Light promised to our Fathers ! Thy Light, to guide our feet into the way of Peace !

Resp∴ Thy Light, to be the Life of Men !

———— Send us the New Law of Love, for which the world pines and languishes ; and make war and bloodshed to cease among the nations, and strife and dissension in the Cities, and heart-burnings in the Desert among the Faithful !

Resp∴ Help us to love Thee and one another, our Father !

———— Save us from our enemies and from the hand of all that hate us ! And help us to serve Thee without fear, in Holiness and Righteousness before Thee, all the days of our life !

Resp∴ Amen ! *So mote it be !* AMEN !

[The organ then plays, and the Brethren sing the following hymn] :

HYMN.

Day-spring of eternity !
　Dawn on us this morning-tide !
Light from Light's exhaustless sea !
　Now no more thy radiance hide ;
With thy new glories put to flight
The shades and cares of lingering night !

Let the morning dew of love
　On our sleeping conscience rain !
Gentle comfort from above
　Flow through life's long parchéd plain :
Flood the earth with peace and joy ;
And all the Powers of Wrong destroy !

————

Ven∴ M∴ Zealous Bro∴ Sen∴ W∴, announce to the Brethren, through the Zealous Bro∴ Jun∴ W∴, that the first faint blush of Dawn dims the light of the Morning Star, and this Preceptory is about to be opened ; charging them according to the ancient custom.

Sen∴ W∴ Zealous Bro∴ Jun∴ Warden, the first faint blush of Dawn dims the light of the Morning Star, and this Preceptory is about to be opened. Announce this to the Brethren, with the ancient charge.

Jun∴ W∴ [Rapping thrice, at which all rise] : Faithful Brethren, Essenes that wait for the Light and the new Law, the first faint blush of the coming Dawn, long waited for, begins to dim the splendour of the Morning Star. The glittering Seven fade into the far North, and the day cometh, and this Preceptory is now about to be opened.

Jun∴ W∴ Ye shall keep my Sabbaths and reverence my Sanctuary.

Sen∴ W∴ Ye shall obey my judgments and keep my ordinances and my statutes.

V∴ M∴ Ye shall not profane the name of your God.

J∴ W∴ Ye shall love and venerate every man his father and mother.

S∴ W∴ Ye shall not glean your vineyards, nor gather every grape, nor wholly reap the corners of your fields; but leave something for the poor and the stranger.

V∴ M∴ Nor steal, nor deal falsely, nor lie one to another.

J∴ W∴ Nor defraud nor despoil your neighbours.

S∴ W∴ Nor go up and down as tale-bearers among the People.

V∴ M∴ Thou shalt not hate thy brother in thy heart; nor suffer thy neighbour to go astray for want of warning.

J∴ W∴ Nor take revenge, nor feed and nurse old grudges; but love thy neighbour as thyself.

S∴ W∴ Ye shall rise up respectfully before the hoary head, and honour the presence of the aged man, and fear your God.

V∴ M∴ Ye shall not vex the stranger in your land, but shall love him as yourselves; for ye were strangers in the land of Egypt.

S∴ W∴ If thy brother be waxen poor, and fallen into decay with thee, thou shalt relieve him, even if he be a stranger or sojourner, that he may live with thee. Thou shalt not give him thy money upon usury, nor lend him thy victuals for increase.

V∴ M∴ These are the statutes, and judgments and laws of the Lord your God. Whatsoever He hath commanded you, observe and do it; nor add thereto, nor diminish from it, and it shall be well with you and your children. Together, my Brethren!

[The Brethren all give the sign. Then the Ven∴ raps ? — the Sen∴ W∴ ? — the Jun∴ W∴ ? — and the Ven∴ [,] Then the Brethren clap : , with their hands, and cry once ☿☋↑&☽☉&∴]

V∴ M∴ This Preceptory is opened in due form. Bro∴ Jun∴ Deacon, inform the Guards.

RECEPTION.

The Candidate is received in the preparation room by the Examiner, who divests him of his regalia and jewel, if he wear any. He is then made to bare his feet and place them in slippers, and a hair cloth is thrown over his shoulders, fastened together in front at the throat, and confined round the waist by a girdle of leather. He is then conducted to the door of the Lodge.

The Lodge room is thus prepared for his reception. The Brethren put off their regalia and jewels, and appear in their white robes only: The book with seven seals is placed upon the altar, and white curtains are let down from the ceiling to the floor, in front of the altar and platform, and of the hangings, all around the room, concealing the seats of all except the Ven∴ Master, who alone sits, while all the other brothers stand. The small table, which was at the right of the Master, is placed in the centre of the room, and covered with white linen, and on it are set the chafing dish, the basin of perfumed water, and a little vase with perfumed oil. The columns are also concealed.

The Examiner raps : , at the door, and it is partly opened by the Junior Warden, who asks:

J∴ W∴ Who seeks admission here, and with what purpose?

Exam∴ A weary traveller, who, having crossed the desert, wanders on the shore of the Dead Sea in darkness, seeking for light.

S∴ W∴ What does he desire?

Ex∴ To be admitted to know the Mysteries of the Twenty-Four Elders.

Qu.·. Whence comes he?

Ans.·. From the Schools of the Philosophers of Greece and Egypt, and from sitting at the feet of the Pharisees and Kabbalists.

Qu.·. By what title does he expect to gain admission here?

Ans.·. By being a Mason, a Prince of Jerusalem, and a patient and humble searcher after Truth.

Qu.·. Do you vouch for this?

Ans.·. I do.

J.·. W.·. Then let him wait, with patience and humility, until the Elders are informed of his request.

[The Jun.·. Warden closes the door, and reports to the Sen.·. Warden, where the same questions are asked and like answers returned as at the door, except the last question and answer. The Sen.·. Warden reports to the Ven.·. Master, the same questions being asked and the same answers given. Upon receiving the answers, the Ven.·. Master says]:

V.·. M.·. Zealous Bro.·. Examiner, go to this Candidate and strictly examine if he be a Mason, and if his principles be such that we may fitly admit him among us.

[The Examiner goes to the Candidate, and questions him as follows]:

Qu.·. 1. . . . Do you declare that, uninfluenced by curiosity, or the desire of worldly advantage, or any base, low or unworthy motive, and as an honest and earnest seeker after Truth, you have come hither?

Ans.·. . . . I do.

Qu.·. 2. . . . Are you a Mason?

Ans.·. . . . I am.

Qu.·. 3. . . . To what degree have you attained?

Ans.·. . . . To that of Prince of Jerusalem.

Qu.·. 4. . . . Give me the Pass-word of a Prince of Jerusalem.

Ans.·. . . . ♈☾♏☾♈·.

Qu.·. 5. . . . The Sacred Word?

Ans.·. . . . ☉⬛☉✝·.

Qu.·. 6. . . . The sign.

[He gives it.]

Qu.·. 7. . . . The grip.

[He gives it.]

Qu.·. 8. . . . I accept and recognize you as a Brother. What found you in the Schools of Philosophy?

Ans.·. . . . Empty babblings and vain janglings of words, and a confused mass of incoherent ideas.

Qu.·. 9. . . . What found you among the Kabbalists?

Ans.·. . . . The rhapsodies and extravagances of insanity and delirium.

Qu.·. 10. . . . What found you in the Desert?

Ans.·. . . . Patience and Submission.

Qu.·. 11. . . . What lesson have you learned on the shores of the Dead Sea?

Ans.·. . . . Humility, and Veneration.

Qu.·. 12. . . . What do you expect to find among us?

Ans.·. . . . The True Light.

Qu.·. 13. . . . It is not yet Day. We have but reached Truth's threshold. But we advance. Would you advance with us?

Ans.·. . . . I would.

Qu.·. 14. . . . Have you hitherto, to the best of your ability, been mindful of your Masonic obligations, and striven to comply with them in spirit and in truth?

Ans.·. . . . I have.

Qu.·. 15. . . . Have you ever wronged a brother, or allowed him to be wronged, when you could have prevented it; without afterwards repenting and making reparation?

Ans.·. . . . I have not.

Qu.·. 16. . . . Have you any dissension or quarrel with a Bro.·. Prince of Jerusalem unreconciled?

Ans∴ . . . . I have not.

Exam∴. It is well. Wait again with patience, until the Elders are informed of the answers you have made.

[The Bro∴ Examiner enters the Preceptory, advances to the East, and says] :

Exam∴. Ven∴ Master, the Candidate has satisfactorily answered the sixteen questions.

Ven∴ M∴. My Brethren, you hear the report of our Faithful Brother Examiner. Shall the Candidate be received ? If you assent, give me the sign.

[All who assent give the sign by putting the right hand to the forehead. If it is unanimously assented to, the Ven∴ M∴ says] :

V∴ M∴. Faithful Bro∴ Lecturer, you will please receive and introduce the Candidate.

[The Lecturer goes out, and leads in the Candidate. The room is now lighted dimly, by one or two candles on the table in the centre, the lights on the columns burning low and being shaded. The Brethren, except the Master, stand facing the East. The Lecturer conducts him seven times around the room, the officers repeating at each circuit as follows] :

1st Circuit : . . . . . . He that hath an ear, let him hear what the spirit saith unto the churches: To him that overcometh will I give to eat of the tree of life, which is in the midst of the Paradise of God.

2d Circuit : . . . . . . He that hath an ear, let him hear what the spirit saith unto the churches: He that overcometh shall not be hurt of the second death.

3d Circuit : . . . . To him that overcometh will I give to eat of the hidden manna; and I will give him a white stone, and in the stone a new name written, which no man shall know but he that shall receive it.

4th Circuit : . . . . . . He that overcometh, and laboureth in my service until the end, to him will I give power over the nations, and his influences shall control and guide them, and I will give him the Morning Star.

5th Circuit : . . . . . He that overcometh shall be clothed in robes of white : and I will not erase his name from the Book of Life ; but I will own him as mine before my Father and all his Angels.

6th Circuit : . . . . . Him that overcometh will I make a pillar in the Temple of my God, and he shall remain there forever: and I will write upon him the name of God, and the name of the City of God, the New Jerusalem, which cometh down out of Heaven from God ; and mine own new name.

7th Circuit : . . . . . . To Him that overcometh will I grant to sit with me near my Throne, even as I also overcame, and am seated with my Father near His Throne. As many as I love, I rebuke and chasten : be zealous therefore, and repent !

[The Lecturer and Candidate then halt in front of the Ven∴ M∴; who asks] :

Ven∴ M∴. Bro∴ Examiner, whence come you, and whither do you travel ?

Lect∴. From the desert and the darkness, towards the Light.

Ven∴ M∴. Have you yet found the Light ?

Lect∴. Ven∴ Master, no : but the Seven Stars sink low in the North ; the Pleiades and Orion are in the Zenith ; the Morning Star grows pale ; the Dawn, long expected, approaches.

Ven∴ M∴. Light comes from God. When clouds and darkness are around us, we should implore His aid. Let us do so, my Brethren !

[All kneel ; and the Ven∴ M∴ repeats the following]

PRAYER.

Our Father, who, when darkness brooded upon the face of the vast chaos, and the universe lay a confused mass of struggling forces, without form and void, didst move upon it, and said, *Let there be light !*—and light was: Thou who didst set the Light against the Darkness, and call one Day, and the other Night: Thou who didst set the Greater and Lesser Lights in the Heavens: Thou who bringest forth Mazzaroth in his season, and guidest Arcturus with his sons: enable this Candidate to find the light for which he seeketh ! Let the dawn of the New Day arise, and shine upon the clouds of Error, and cause the darkness of ignorance and superstition to flee away and be seen no more forever. Amen !

——————— ———————

V∴ M∴ My Brother, the innocent and pure of heart alone can be admitted to our mysteries. [A brother brings a basin of pure water and a white towel, and places them on the table]. In token of that innocence and purity; and as a pledge to us that your hands shall henceforward never be defiled by covetousness, unjust gain, tyranny, oppression, injustice, baseness or fraud, you will wash them in the pure water before you.

[The Candidate does so; and the Ven∴ M∴ proceeds]:

V∴ M∴ The living know that they shall die: but the dead know not anything; neither have they any more a reward; for the memory of them is forgotten. Also their love and their hatred and their envy is now perished; neither have they any more a portion forever in anything done under the sun.

Remember now thy Creator in the days of thy youth, while the evil days come not, nor the years draw nigh when thou shalt say, I have no pleasure in them: while the sun, or the light, or the moon or the stars are not darkened; and the clouds pass away after the rain:

In the day when the limbs are not yet trembling with age, nor the head bowed with sorrow, nor the eyes dim with weeping: before thou goest to thy long home, and the mourners go about the streets; before the silver cord is loosed and the golden bowl broken, and the pitcher shivered at the spring, and the wheel shattered at the cistern: before the dust returns to the earth as it was, and the spirit unto God who gave it.

My Brother, when you became a Mason, you placed your trust in God. Do you still continue to do so?

Cand∴ I do.

V∴ M∴ Do you firmly believe that there is but one God, Supreme, Infinite, Eternal, Unchangeable; that He is infinitely good, wise, just and true; and that evil and pain, and sorrow and misery are but parts of the plan of Infinite Wisdom, working together to produce infinite good? and that the soul is immortal?

Cand∴ I do.

V∴ M∴ Kneel, then, and be consecrated to the service of Truth!

[He kneels in front of the Ven∴ Master, as he stands near the table, while the Brethren form a circle around him. Then the Ven∴ M∴ takes in his hand a small quantity of perfumed water from the basin, and pours it on his head, saying]:

V∴ M∴ In imitation of our Ancient Masters, the Egyptians, and as a token and solemn pledge that you here, henceforth and forever, renounce all that is vicious, sordid and base, I pour upon thy head this pure water; and I devote and consecrate thee to the service of Truth, Justice, Virtue and Benevolence. I do this as a symbol of repentance and reformation; but One cometh hereafter, whose shoes I am not worthy to unloose. He shall baptize you with the Holy Spirit and with fire. His fan will be in his hand, and he will thoroughly sweep his threshing floor, and gather his wheat into his granary, and burn up the chaff with a devouring fire. His axe is prepared for the trees; and every tree that beareth not good fruit will be cut down and cast into the fire. [A Brother puts live coals in the chafing-dish, or in some other way produces a heat over his head, that he sensibly feels]. Lo! a symbol of that baptism, with the Spirit and with fire; purified by which, man becomes God's soldier, to war against Fanaticism, Intolerance, Bigotry, Falsehood, and the whole brood of kindred fiends, that so long have made a hell of our earth, which was created a paradise: symbol also of that suffering and pain; and wo and want, and sharp ingratitude, and bitter injustice, that are God's baptism of fire, by which He strengthens the human soul, and gives occasion and incentive to the noblest virtues; and thus purifying it, lifts it above humanity. To suffer is the noblest lot of man here below; for none but those who suffer doth God baptize with fire and with his Spirit.

My Brother, you have been baptized with water and with fire: and you are clad in hair-cloth, and a girdle of leather, as a token of sorrow and penitence. Are you prepared to suffer and endure in the cause of Masonry and for the good of your fellow-men?

Cand∴ I am.

V∴ M∴ My Brethren, who among you is worthy to open the Book with Seven Seals? [There is no reply: and, laying his hand on the head of the candidate, he says]: My Brother, Socrates drank the hemlock, when the doors of his prison were open, that he might not set the example of disobeying the laws of his ungrateful country. Curtius leaped, in his armour, into the gulf that could thus only be closed, and else would swallow Rome. Daniel prayed three times a day, openly, to God, knowing that the penalty was exposure, naked, to hungry lions: and an army of martyrs have offered up their lives, a willing sacrifice, to prove their faith or benefit mankind. None other can open the Great Book with Seven Seals, and learn the mysteries that are hidden therein. Are you prepared to shed your blood, in proof of your fidelity and courage, and even for those who may have wronged you, because God made men your Brethren?

Cand.·. I am.

V.·. M.·. Prepare him, then, for the last trial, my Brethren!

[He is blindfolded, and seated in a chair. His right arm is bandaged, a slight incision made near the vein with a lancet, so as to draw a little blood, and tepid water is poured upon it in a small stream, and falls into a basin on the floor, to produce the impression that he is bleeding. After this has been continued some minutes, that arm is freed from the bandage, and the same process gone through with the left arm. Then the Ven.·. M.·. says]:

V.·. M.·. Enough, my Brethren! The cause of Humanity does not now require our Brother's life. Whenever it shall, let him be ready to lay it upon the altar of his God, of friendship, of his country, or of the human race. Bind up his wounds!

[Both arms are dressed and bandaged, as after bleeding. In the mean time the Brethren have assumed their regalia, the white curtains are removed or rolled up, and all the lights are lighted. The table is placed again to the right of the Master's seat, and the little vessel of oil upon the altar].

V.·. M.·. My Brother, thou hast wandered long in the desert of this world, and sought for Light in the darkness of Philosophy, on the shores of the Dead Sea of Human Life. Dost thou still pray for Light?

Cand.·. I do.

V.·. M.·. My Brethren, he also is your Brother, for he seeks to find the Truth. Give him light!

[The bandage is removed from his eyes; and he is then led by the Ven.·. Master to the Platform, to which he ascends, and stands near the altar. He is then made to kneel, on both knees, with both hands on the Book with Seven Seals, and repeats the following]

OBLIGATION.

I, A . .·. . . . B . . . . ., in the presence of the One God, Creator of the Universe, and calling upon these Brethren as witnesses, do, upon this Sacred Book, most solemnly promise and sincerely swear, that I will never reveal the secrets of this Degree or the mode of my admission, to any person in the world, to whom the same may not lawfully belong, and only when I am authorized to communicate them.

I furthermore promise and swear that I will be ever ready to expose, and if necessary to yield up, my life, in the cause of Friendship, my Country, or of Common Humanity.

I furthermore promise and swear, that I will never fight or combat with a Brother of this Degree, except in the extremest and clearest case of self-defence: and that I will, at all times, when he has justice on his side, be ready to aid and support him against any who seek his life, or to destroy his honour, reputation, peace of mind or estate; that I never will slander, revile or speak slightingly of a Brother, or endeavour to bring him into contempt or to cast ridicule upon him: nor suffer others to assail his character in his absence, without resenting it myself, or informing him thereof at the earliest opportunity: and that I will on all occasions consult his honour and his interest.

I furthermore promise and swear, that I will hereafter be just and upright, benevolent to my fellow-men, and indulgent of their errors.

I furthermore promise and swear, that I will pay due respect and obedience to the superior authorities of the Ancient and Accepted Rite; and especially to the Knights Kadosch, Sublime Princes of the Royal Secret, and Sovereign Gr.·. Inspectors General of the 33d Degree, within whose jurisdiction I may be; and that I will in every thing assist and support them in all proper and justifiable measures for the good of Masonry, according to the constitutions of the Supreme Council.

To all which I do most solemnly promise and swear, invoking the just anger of the Deity, if I wilfully violate this my solemn, deliberate and voluntary obligation. So help me God, and keep me steadfast to perform the same!

V∴ M∴ My Brother, arise! I accept and receive you as a Brother of this Degree; and I now further devote you to its duties and to Masonry.

[Saying this, he takes the vessel of oil, and with the tip of his finger anoints his Head, Eyes, Mouth, Heart, the tip of his right Ear, his right Hand, and right Foot; and says]:

V∴ M∴ Your brain, sight, speech, passions, hearing, and powers of work and action, instruments to man for good or evil, I hereby forever devote to Good; and charge you hereafter to let them aid in no base, dishonest or vicious thought, word or action! Thus devoted, pledged and sworn, and having sealed your covenant with us with your blood, you are worthy to open the Book with Seven Seals. Approach, and open the first seal!

[He opens the first seal. The organ plays a few notes; and the Ven∴ M∴ takes from behind the altar a bow, a quiver filled with arrows, and a coronet, and gives them to a Brother, and says to him]: "Depart and continue the conquest! And I saw, and lo! a white horse; and he that sat on him held a bow; and a crown was given unto him: and he went forth conquering and to conquer. Open now the second seal!"

He does so: and the Ven∴ M∴ takes from behind the altar a naked sword; [Music is heard here, and as each seal is opened]; and gives it to another Brother, saying: "Go forth and create strife and dissension among the Profane and Wicked, that they may destroy each other; and smite thou unsparingly the vices, the superstitions and the errors that infest and afflict the world! For there went out another horse that was red; and it was given to him that sat thereon to banish peace from the earth, and that the wicked should slay one another; and there was given unto him a great sword. Open now the third seal!"

He does so: and the Ven∴ M∴ takes from behind the altar a pair of balances, and gives them to another Brother; and says: "Go thou and administer Justice and Equity, and see that the poor be no longer oppressed with false weights and false measures; and that their wages be punctually paid them; that they may no longer starve! Open now the fourth seal!"

He does so: and the Ven∴ M∴ takes from behind the altar a human skull, and gives it to another Brother, saying: "Go thou and teach mankind that the soul which sins shall die; that they may learn humility and the vanity of all earthly things!—for lo! a pale horse; and his name that sits on him is Death; and after death the judgment: and power is given to him to slay with the sword, and with starvation, and with sickness, and the beasts of the earth. Open now the fifth seal!"

He does so: and the Ven∴ M∴ takes from behind the altar a linen cloth, stained with much blood, and gives it to another Brother, saying: "Go thou and accuse those who have persecuted and slain them who have come on earth to reform and be the benefactors of mankind! For under the altar are the souls of those who have been slain because they taught God's Truth, and condemned the errors of those who ruled over the consciences of men: and they cry with a voice that ascends to God's footstool, 'How long, O Lord, Holy and True, wilt Thou refrain from judging and avenging our blood upon these monsters of cruelty and oppression under whom the earth groans and mankind are crushed and trampled down?' And white robes are given unto them; and they are told to be patient yet a little while, until all who, like them, shall endeavour to serve mankind, shall, like them, be tortured and slain, and the great purposes of God in His time be fulfilled. Open now the sixth seal!"

He does so: and immediately there is a crash of loud music from the organ, thunder rolls near the Lodge, and the lights are all darkened.

V∴ M∴ Lo! a great earthquake; and the sun is eclipsed and the moon becomes red as blood; and the stars of Heaven fall to the earth, as a fig-tree casteth her unripe figs, when shaken by a mighty wind: and the Heaven vanishes as a scroll is rolled together: and the mountains and islands are moved out of their places: and earth's rulers, the great, the rich, the captains of armies, the powerful, the bondmen and the free, hide themselves in the caves, and take refuge among the rocks upon the mountains, and call upon them, crying, "Fall upon us, and hide us from the face of Him that sitteth on the Throne, and from the anger of God; for the great day of his wrath is come, and who shall be able to stand."

The Ven∴ M∴ then, with a liquid of the colour of blood, marks a Tau cross upon the forehead of the candidate, and says: "Hurt not the earth, nor the sea nor the trees, until we have sealed the servants of God upon their foreheads! Glory to God who sitteth upon the Throne, and unto his Son, who as a Lamb for the sacrifice shall take away the sins of the world!"

2B

The Brethren all kneel, and bow their heads to the floor, and say together, "Amen! Blessing and glory, and wisdom and thanksgiving, and honour and power and might be unto our God, forever and ever: Amen!"

Then the Ven∴ M∴ takes from the candidate his girdle and hair-cloth, and puts upon him a white linen robe; and says; "And one of the Elders said unto me, 'who are these that are arrayed in white robes? and whence came they?' and I said unto him, 'Ven∴, thou knowest.' And he said unto me, 'These are they who have been purified by sorrow and suffering, and by the intercession and blood of the Redeemer. Therefore stand they before God's throne, and serve him day and night in his Temple: and he that sitteth on the Throne shall dwell among them; and they shall hunger no more, neither thirst any more; nor shall the sun scorch them, nor the fire again torture them. For the Lamb who sitteth upon his Throne shall sustain them, and shall lead them to the living springs of truth; and God shall wipe away all tears from their eyes.' Open now the Seventh Seal."

He does so: and for a time there is a perfect silence. Then the Ven∴ Master takes from behind the altar seven trumpets, and gives them to the two Wardens, the Lecturer and Examiner, the Secretary and Treasurer and the Senior Deacon; and to the Jun∴ Deacon a gilded censer, and incense, which he lights and places upon the altar. After it has burned a time, he takes it, and flings down the contents upon a place prepared to receive them. Immediately the 1st trumpet sounds.

V∴ M∴ Hail and fire, mingled with blood shall be cast upon the earth; and the third part of the trees, and all the green grass shall be burned up.

[The 2d Trumpet sounds].

V∴ M∴ A great mountain vomiting fire shall be torn up and flung into the sea; and the third part of the oceans shall become blood; and the third part of all living creatures in the sea shall die, and the third part of the ships thereon be destroyed.

[The 3d Trumpet sounds].

V∴ M∴ A great star shall fall from Heaven, burning like a lamp; and a third part of the waters of all the rivers and of the living springs that feed the rivers, shall become bitter as wormwood: and all who drink thereof shall die.

[The 4th Trumpet sounds].

V∴ M∴ A third part of the sun, moon and stars shall be eclipsed and darkened; and by day there shall be but a dim light, and the night shall be dark and gloomy.

[The 5th Trumpet sounds].

V∴ M∴ The first woe shall come upon the Earth; the reign of the Spirit of Evil; and the locusts of Ignorance, Fanaticism and Superstition, whose leader is Abaddon.

[The 6th Trumpet sounds].

V∴ M∴ Then the four Demons, that came among men while yet they had not gone abroad from the banks of the Euphrates, Bigotry, Intolerance, Ambition and Selfishness shall be let loose, and with fire and the sword and all manner of savage torture shall slay one third of mankind; and yet the others shall not repent. And God's servants shall endeavour to reform the People, and Thought and Speech and Conscience shall struggle to be free: but those who would reform mankind, and free the world from slavery and oppression, shall be slain; and their dead bodies, denied burial, shall be flung to rot upon the earth, which shall then be one great Sodom. But Truth shall still struggle with Error; and the great earthquake of Thought shall at length shake the Souls of Nations; and the second woe shall cease.

[The 7th Trumpet sounds].

V∴ M∴ The Kingdoms of this world shall become the Kingdoms of God and His Anointed; and he shall reign forever and ever. The long war between the Evil and the Good, between Michael and his angels and the Dragon and his angels shall end; and the Serpent and his angels shall be overcome, and shall pass away and be seen no more forever; and salvation and strength, and the Kingdom of God, which is Truth, shall come, and thenceforward remain forever: and sorrow and evil shall disappear; and the labours of those who have borne testimony to the Truth, and given up their lives to benefit the world shall not have been in vain; but they shall have eternal fame and glory and honour, when the names of all conquerors and kings shall have faded out of the memories of men.

J∴ & S∴ W∴. We give Thee thanks, O Lord God Omnipotent! who art Eternal, and to whom the Past, the Present and the Future are One; because Thou wilt in due time assert Thy Power, and vindicate Thy Justice, Thy Wisdom and Thy Goodness, when Evil shall reign no longer.

V∴ M∴. For Thou wilt in due time judge all men, and reward Thy servants and those who have loved and served mankind, the Known and the Unknown, the Lofty and the Low; and those who have vexed and plagued the Earth Thou wilt reward according to their evil works. And then shall Thy Temple be rebuilt in the Heavens; and those who wear Thy Name written upon their foreheads, and Thy Law engraven in their hearts, shall inhabit its courts forever. Blessed, henceforward, are the dead, who fall in the cause of Truth: for they shall then rest from their labours and their sorrows, and their works shall follow them!

[The organ plays an exulting and triumphant air; and the Ven∴ M∴ and the Candidate descend from the Platform; the Ven∴ having first opened the Great Book, and laid upon it the Square and the Compasses. They halt at the Master's seat; when the music ends, and the Ven∴ M∴ invests the Candidate with the collar, apron, jewel, and sword of the Degree; saying]:

"I invest you with the apron of this Degree. Its color is emblematical of the Dawn; its shape of the Deity, of Justice, of Equality, of Equanimity; the Tetractys upon it, of the Universe, with the Deity in its centre.

"I invest you with the order of this Degree. Its two colors, white and black, are emblematical of the contest between the Principles of Good and Evil.

"I invest you with the jewel of this Degree. Its heptagonal shape will be hereafter explained to you, as also will the devices upon it. Its material, gold and silver or mother of pearl, symbolizes the Sun and Moon, the Great Lights of the Day and Night, themselves Emblems of Strength and Beauty, the two pillars at the Threshold of Masonry.

"Receive now the Signs, Tokens and Words of this Degree.

Sign: . . . Look at your ‡♀♌&♈⸸♎&☿ ƨ †♊☾‡.·.

Answer: . . . Look at the †☾♑♈⸸♎&☿ ƨ †♊☾‡: one says ☉♏☉♊♊☿♒.·. the other ♄☉&-♏☉†♀♒.

First Token: . . . Put the †☾♑♈⸸&☉♒♊ in a brother's ‡♀♌&♈: He ♐☿*☾‡♎ yours with his †☾♑.♈: Then look mutually at the ‡⸸♎&☿ ƨ †♊☾‡.

Second Token: . . . ♈☿ ƨ ♐& with your †☾♑♈⸸&☉♒♊ the †⸸♎&☿ ƨ †♊☾‡ of the Brother; who answers by ♈☿ ƨ ♐&♀♒♌ your ‡⸸♎&☿ ƨ †♊☾‡ with his ‡⸸&☉♒♊.

Sign to enter the Lodge: . . . Put the ‡⸸&☉♒♊ upon the ♑☿‡☾&☾☉♊.

Pass-Word: . . . ♄☉ &-♏☉†♀♒.·.

Covered Word: . . . ☉♏☉♊♊☿♒.·.

V∴ M∴ . I finally present you with this coronet, in token of your present rank in Masonry. Remember that it, like the other insignia of the Ancient and Accepted Rite, is honourable, only so long as it is worn with honour. On the brow of the dishonest, the dissipated, the vicious or the base, honours undeserved are the extremest disgrace. See, therefore, that you wear it worthily and well!

[The Candidate is now directed to be seated in front of the Ven∴ M∴, and receives from the Lecturer the following History and Instruction]:

HISTORY.

This, my Brother, is the first of the Philosophical degrees of the Ancient and Accepted Rite; and the beginning of a course of instruction which will fully unveil to you the heart and inner mysteries of Masonry. Do not despair because you have often seemed-on the point of attaining the inmost light, and have as often been disappointed. In all time, truth has been hidden under symbols, and often under a succession of allegories: where veil after veil had to be penetrated, before the true Light was reached, and the essential truth stood revealed.

We are about to approach those ancient Religions which once ruled the minds of men, and whose ruins encumber the plains of the great Past, as the broken columns of Palmyra and Tadmor lie bleaching on the sands of the desert. They rise before us, those old, strange, mysterious creeds and faiths, shrouded in the mists of antiquity, and stalk dimly and undefined along the line which divides Time from Eternity; and forms of strange, wild, startling beauty mingle in the vast throng of figures with shapes monstrous, grotesque and hideous.

The religion taught by Moses, which, like the laws of Egypt, enunciated the principle of exclusion, borrowed, at every period of its existence, from all the creeds with which it came in contact. While, by the studies of the learned and wise, it enriched itself with the most admirable principles of the religions of Egypt and Asia, it was changed, in the wanderings of the People, by everything that was most impure or seductive in the pagan manners and superstitions. It was one thing in the times of Moses and Aaron, another in those of David and Solomon, and still another in those of Daniel and Philo.

At the time when John the Baptist made his appearance in the desert, near the shores of the Dead Sea, all the old philosophical and religious systems were approximating towards each other. A general lassitude inclined the minds of all towards the quietude of that amalgamation of doctrines for which the expeditions of Alexander and the more peaceful occurrences that followed, with the establishment in Asia and Africa of many Grecian dynasties and a great number of Grecian colonies, had prepared the way. After the intermingling of different nations, which resulted from the wars of Alexander in three-quarters of the globe, the doctrines of Greece, of Egypt, of Persia and of India met and intermingled everywhere. All the barriers that had formerly kept the nations apart, were thrown down; and while the People of the West readily connected their faith with those of the East, the people of the Orient hastened to learn the traditions of Greece and the legends of Athens. While the Philosophers of Greece, all, (except the disciples of Epicurus), more or less Platonicians, seized eagerly upon the beliefs and doctrines of the East; the Jews and Egyptians, before then the most exclusive of all peoples, yielded to that eclectism which prevailed among their masters, the Greeks and Romans.

Under the same influences of toleration, even those who embraced Christianity, mingled together the old and the new, Christianity and Philosophy, the Apostolic teachings, and the traditions of Mythology. The man of intellect, devotee of one system, rarely displaces it with another in all its purity. The people take such a creed as is offered them. Accordingly, the distinction between the esoteric and the exoteric doctrine, immemorial in other creeds, easily gained a foothold among many of the Christians; and it was held by a vast number, even during the preaching of Paul, that the writings of the Apostles were incomplete; that they contained only the germs of another doctrine, which must receive from the hands of philosophy, not only the systematic arrangement which was wanting, but all the development which lay concealed therein. The writings of the Apostles, they said, in addressing themselves to mankind in general, enunciated only the articles of the vulgar faith; but transmitted the mysteries of knowledge to superior minds, to the Elu,— mysteries handed down from generation to generation in esoteric traditions; and to this science of the mysteries they gave the name of Γνῶσις [Gnōsis].

The Gnostics derived their leading doctrines and ideas from Plato and Philo, the Zend-avesta and the Kabbala, and the Sacred books of India and Egypt; and thus introduced into the bosom of Christianity the cosmological and theosophical speculations, which had formed the larger portion of the ancient religions of the Orient, joined to those of the Egyptian, Greek and Jewish doctrines, which the Neo-Platonists had equally adopted in the Occident.

Emanation from the Deity of all spiritual beings, progressive degeneration of these beings from emanation to emanation, redemption and return of all to the purity of the Creator; and, after the re-establishment of the primitive harmony of all; a fortunate and truly divine condition of all, in the bosom of God; such were the fundamental teachings of Gnosticism. The genius of the Orient, with its contemplations, irradiations and intuitions, dictated its doctrines. Its language corresponded to its origin. Full of imagery, it had all the magnificence, the inconsistencies and the mobility of the figurative style.

Behold, it said, the light, which emanates from an immense centre of Light, that spreads everywhere its benevolent rays: so do the spirits of Light emanate from the Divine Light. Behold all the springs which nourish, embellish, fertilize and purify the Earth: they emanate from one and the same ocean: so from the bosom of the Divinity emanate so many streams, which form and fill the universe of Intelligences. Behold numbers, which all emanate from one primitive number, all resemble it, all are composed of its essence, and still vary infinitely; and utterances, decomposable into so many syllables and elements, all contained in the primitive word, and still infinitely various; so the world of Intelligences emanated from a Primary Intelligence, and they all resemble it, and yet display an infinite variety of existences.

It revived and combined the old doctrines of the Orient and the Occident: and it found in many passages of the Gospels and the Pastoral letters, a warrant for doing so. Christ himself spoke in parables and allegories, John borrowed the enigmatical language of the Platonists, and Paul often indulged in incomprehensible rhapsodies, the meaning of which could have been clear to the initiates alone.

It is admitted that the cradle of Gnosticism is probably to be looked for in Syria, and even in Palestine. Most of its expounders wrote in that corrupted form of the Greek used by the Hellenistic Jews, and in the Septuagint and the New Testament: and there was a striking analogy between their doctrines and those of the Egyptian Philo, of Alexandria, the seat of three schools, at once philosophic and religious—the Greek, the Egyptian, and the Jewish.

Pythagoras and Plato, the most mystical of the Grecian Philosophers, (the latter heir to the doctrines of the former), and who had travelled, the latter in Egypt, and the former in Phœnicia, India, and Persia, also taught the esoteric doctrine, and the distinction between the initiated and the profane. The dominant doctrines of Platonism were found in Gnosticism. Emanation of Intelligences from the bosom of the Deity; the going astray in error and the sufferings of spirits, so long as they are remote from God, and imprisoned in matter; vain and long-continued efforts to arrive at the knowledge of the Truth, and re-enter into their primitive union with the Supreme Being; alliance of a pure and divine soul with an irrational soul, the seat of evil desires; angels or demons who dwell in and govern the planets, having but an imperfect knowledge of the ideas that presided at the creation; regeneration of all beings by their return to the κόσμος νοητός, [kosmos noetos], the world of Intelligences, and its Chief, the Supreme Being; sole possible mode of re-establishing that primitive harmony of the creation, of which the music of the spheres of Pythagoras was the image; these were the analogies of the two systems: and we discover in them some of the ideas that form a part of Masonry; in which, in the present mutilated condition of the symbolic degrees, they are disguised and overlaid with fiction and absurdity, or present themselves as casual hints that are passed by wholly unnoticed.

The distinction between the esoteric and exoteric doctrines, (a distinction purely Masonic), was always and from the very earliest times preserved among the Greeks. It remounted to the fabulous times of Orpheus; and the mysteries of Theosophy were found in all their traditions and myths. And after the time of Alexander, they resorted for instruction, dogmas and mysteries, to all the schools, to those of Egypt and Asia, as well as those of Ancient Thrace, Sicily, Etruria, and Attica.

The Jewish-Greek School of Alexandria is known only by two of its Chiefs, Aristobulus and Philo, both Jews of Alexandria in Egypt. Belonging to Asia by its origin, to Egypt by its residence, to Greece by its language and studies, it strove to show that all truths embedded in the philosophies of other countries were transplanted thither from Palestine. Aristobulus declared that all the facts and details of the Jewish Scriptures were so many allegories, concealing the most profound meanings, and that Plato had borrowed from them all his finest ideas. Philo, who lived a century after him, following the same theory, endeavored to show that the Hebrew writings, by their system of allegories, were the true source of all religious and philosophical doctrines. According to him, the literal meaning is for the vulgar alone. Whoever has meditated on philosophy, has purified himself by virtue, and raised himself by contemplation, to God and the intellectual world, and received their inspiration, pierces the gross envelope of the letter, discovers a wholly different order of things, and is initiated into mysteries, of which the elementary or literal instruction offers but an imperfect image. A historical fact, a figure, a word, a letter, a number, a rite, a custom, the parable or vision of a prophet, veil the most profound truths: and he who has the key of science will interpret all according to the light he possesses.

Again we see the symbolism of Masonry, and the search of the Candidate for light. "Let men of narrow minds withdraw," he says, "with closed ears. We transmit the divine mysteries to those who have received the sacred initiation, to those who practise true piety, and who are not enslaved by the empty trappings of words or the preconceived opinions of the pagans."

To Philo, the Supreme Being was the Primitive Light, or the Archetype of Light, Source whence the rays emanate that illuminate Souls. He was also the Soul of the Universe, and as such acted in all its parts. He Himself fills and limits his whole Being. His Powers and Virtues fill and penetrate all. These Powers, [Δυνάμεις, dunameis] are Spirits distinct from God, the Ideas of Plato personified. He is without beginning, and lives in the prototype of Time, [αιων, aion].

His image is THE WORD [Λογος], a form more brilliant than fire; that not being the pure light. This Logos dwells in God; for the Supreme Being makes to Himself within his Intelligence the types or ideas of everything that is to become reality in this World. The Logos is the vehicle by which God acts on the Universe, and may be compared to the speech of man.

The Logos being the World of Ideas [κοσμος νοητος], by means whereof God has created visible things, He is the most ancient God, in comparison with the World which is the youngest production. The Logos, *Chief of Intelligences*, of which He is the general representative, is named *Archangel, type* and *representative* of all spirits, even those of mortals. He is also styled the man-type and primitive man.

God only is Wise. The wisdom of man is but the reflection and image of that of God. He is the Father; and His WISDOM the mother of creation: for He united Himself with WISDOM [Σοφια, Sophia], and communicated to it the germ of creation, and it brought forth the material world. He created the ideal world only, and caused the material world to be made real after its type, by His Logos, which is His speech, and at the same time the Idea of Ideas, the Intellectual World. The Intellectual City was but the Thought of the Architect, who meditated the creation, according to that plan of the Material City.

The Word is not only the Creator, but occupies the place of the Supreme Being. Through Him all the Powers and Attributes of God act. On the other side, as first representative of the Human Family, He is the Protector of men and their Shepherd.

God gives to man the Soul or Intelligence, which exists before the body, and which he unites with the body. The reasoning Principle comes from God through the Word, and communes with God and with the Word; but there is also in man an irrational Principle, that of the inclinations and passions which produce disorder, emanating from inferior spirits who fill the air as ministers of God. The body, taken from the Earth, and the irrational Principle that animates it concurrently with the rational Principle, are hated by God, while the rational soul which he has given it, is, as it were, captive in this prison, this coffin, that encompasses it. The present condition of man is not his primitive condition, when he was the image of the Logos. He has fallen from his first estate. But he may raise himself again, by following the directions of WISDOM [Σοφια] and of the Angels which God has commissioned to aid him in freeing himself from the bonds of the body, and combating Evil, the existence whereof God has permitted, to furnish him the means of exercising his liberty. The souls that are purified, not by the Law but by light, rise to the Heavenly regions, to enjoy there a perfect felicity. Those that persevere in evil go from body to body, the seats of passions and evil desires. The familiar lineaments of these doctrines will be recognized by all who read the Epistles of St. Paul, who wrote after Philo, the latter living in the reign of Caligula, and being the cotemporary of Christ.

And the Mason is familiar with these doctrines of Philo: that the Supreme Being is a centre of Light whose rays or emanations pervade the Universe; for that is the Light for which all Masonic journeys are a search, and of which the sun and moon in our Lodges are only emblems: that Light and that Darkness, chief enemies from the beginning of Time, dispute with each other the empire of the world; which we symbolize by the candidate wandering in darkness and being brought to light: that the world was created, not by the Supreme Being, but by a secondary agent, who is but His Word, [the Λογος], and by types which are but his ideas, aided by an Intelligence, or Wisdom [Σοφια], which is one of His Attributes; in which we see the occult meaning of the necessity of recovering the Word; and of our two columns of Strength and Wisdom, which are also the two parallel lines that bound the circle representing the Universe: that the visible world is the image of the invisible world; that the essence of the Human Soul is the image of God, and it existed before the body; that the object of its terrestrial life is to disengage itself of its body or its sepulchre; and that it will ascend to the Heavenly regions whenever it shall be purified; in which we see the meaning, now almost forgotten in our Lodges, of the mode of preparation of the candidate for apprenticeship, and his tests and purifications in all the degrees.

Philo incorporated in his eclectism neither Egyptian nor Oriental elements. But there were other Jewish Teachers in Alexandria who did both. The Jews of Egypt were slightly jealous of, and a little hostile to those of Palestine, particularly after the erection of the sanctuary at Leontopolis by the High Priest Onias; and therefore they admired and magnified those sages, who, like Jeremiah, had resided in Egypt. The wisdom of Solomon was written at Alexandria, and, in the time of St. Jerome, was attributed to Philo; but it contains principles at variance with his. It personifies Wisdom, and draws between its children and the Profane, the same line of demarcation that Egypt had long before taught to the Jews. That distinction existed at the beginning of the Mosaic creed. Moses himself was an initiate in the mysteries of Egypt, as he was compelled to be, as the adopted son of the daughter of Pharaoh, *Thouoris*, daughter of *Sesostris-Ramses*; who, as her tomb and monuments show, was, in the right of her infant husband, Regent of Lower Egypt or the Delta at the time of the Hebrew Prophet's birth, reigning at Heliopolis. She was also, as the reliefs on her tomb show, a Priestess of Hathor and Neith, the two great primeval goddesses. As her adopted son, living in her Palace and presence forty years, and during that time scarcely acquainted with his brethren the Jews, the law of Egypt compelled his initiation: and we find in many of his enactments the intention of preserving, between the common people and the initiates, the line of separation which he found in Egypt. Moses and Aaron his brother, the whole series of High Priests, the Council of the 70 Elders, Solomon and the entire succession of Prophets, were in possession of a higher science; and of that science Masonry is, at least, the lineal descendant. It was familiarly known as the knowledge of the Word.

Amun, at first the God of Lower Egypt only, where Moses was reared, was the Supreme God. He was styled *the Celestial Lord, who sheds Light on hidden things.* He was the source of that divine life, of which the crux ansata is the symbol; and the source of all Power. He united all the attributes that the Ancient Oriental Theosophy assigned to the Supreme Being. He was the πληρωμα (Pleroma), or *Fulness of things*, for He comprehended in Himself everything; and the Light; for he was the Sun-God. He was unchangeable in the midst of everything phenomenal in his worlds. He created nothing; but everything emanated from him; and of Him all the other Gods were but manifestations.

The Ram was his living symbol; which you see reproduced in this degree, lying on the book with seven seals on the tracing-board. He caused the creation of the world by the Primitive *Thought* [Εννοια, Ennoia], or *Spirit* [Πνευμα, Pneuma], that issued from him by means of his *Voice* or the Word; and which *Thought or Spirit* was personified as the Goddess Neith. She, too, was a divinity of *Light*, and mother of the Sun; and the Feast of Lamps was celebrated in her honour at Sais. The Creative Power, another manifestation of Deity, proceeding to the creation conceived of in Her, the Divine Intelligence, produced with its word the universe, symbolized by an egg issuing from the mouth of KnEph; from which egg came Ptha, image of the Supreme Intelligence as realized in the world, and the type of that manifested in man; the principal agent, also, of Nature, or the creative and productive Fire. Phre or Re, the Sun, or Celestial Light, whose symbol was ☉, the point within a circle, was the son of Ptha: and Tiphé, his wife, or the celestial firmament, with the seven celestial bodies, animated by spirits or genii that govern them, was represented on many of the monuments, clad in blue or yellow, her garments sprinkled with stars, and accompanied by the sun, moon and five planets; and she was the type of Wisdom, and they of the Seven Planetary Spirits of the Gnostics, that with her presided over and governed the sublunary world.

In this degree, unknown for a hundred years to those who have practised it, these emblems reproduced refer to these old doctrines. The lamb, the yellow hangings strewed with stars, the seven columns, candlesticks and seals all recall them to us.

The Lion was the symbol of ATHOM-RE, the Great God of Upper Egypt, the Hawk of RA or PHRE, the Eagle of MENDES, the Bull of APIS; and three of these are seen under the platform on which our altar stands.

The first HERMES was the INTELLIGENCE or WORD of God. Moved with compassion for a race living without law, and wishing to teach them that they sprang from his bosom, and to point out to them the way that they should go, [the books which the first Hermes had written on the mysteries of divine science, in the sacred characters, being unknown to those who lived after the flood], God sent to man OSIRIS and ISIS, accompanied by THOTH, the incarnation or terrestrial repetition of the first HERMES; who taught men the arts, science, and the ceremonies of religion; and then ascended to Heaven or the Moon. OSIRIS was the Principle of Good. TYPHON, like AHRIMAN, was the principle and source of all that is evil in the moral and physical order. Like the Satan of Gnosticism, he was confounded with matter.

From Egypt or Persia the new Platonists borrowed the idea, and the Gnostics received it from them, that man, in his terrestrial career, is successively under the influence of the Moon, of Mercury, of Venus, of the Sun, of Mars, of Jupiter, and of Saturn, until he finally reaches the Elysian Fields; an idea again symbolized in the Seven Seals.

The Jews of Syria and Judea were the direct precursors of Gnosticism; and in their doctrines were ample oriental elements. These Jews had had with the Orient, at two different periods, intimate relations, familiarizing them with the doctrines of Asia, and especially of Chaldea and Persia;—their forced residence in Central Asia under the Assyrians and Persians; and their voluntary dispersion over the whole East, when subjects of the Seleucidæ and the Romans. Living near two-thirds of a century, and many of them long afterwards, in Mesopotamia, the cradle of their race; speaking the same language, and their children reared with those of the Chaldeans, Assyrians, Medes and Persians, and receiving from them their names (as the case of Daniel, who was called Belteshazzar, proves), they necessarily adopted many of the doctrines of their conquerors. Their descendants, as Ezra and Nehemiah show us, hardly desired to leave Persia, when they were allowed to do so. They had a special jurisdiction, and governors and judges taken from their own people; many of them held high office, and their children were educated with those of the highest nobles. Daniel was the friend and minister of the King, and the Chief of the College of the Magi at Babylon; if we may believe the book which bears his name, and trust to the incidents related in its highly figurative and imaginative style. Mordecai, too, occupied a high station, no less than that of Prime Minister, and Esther his cousin was the Monarch's wife.

The Magi of Babylon were expounders of figurative writings, interpreters of nature, and of dreams; astronomers and divines; and from their influences arose among the Jews, after their rescue from captivity, a number of sects, and a new exposition, the mystical interpretation, with all its wild fancies and infinite caprices. The Eons of the Gnostics, the Ideas of Plato, the Angels of the Jews and the Demons of the Greeks, all correspond to the Ferouers of Zoroaster.

A great number of Jewish families remained permanently in their new country; and one of the most celebrated of their schools was at Babylon. They were soon familiarized with the doctrine of Zoroaster, which itself was more ancient than Cyrus. From the system of the Zend-Avesta they borrowed, and subsequently gave large development to, everything that could be reconciled with their own faith; and these additions to the old doctrine were soon spread by the constant intercourse of commerce, into Syria and Palestine.

In the Zend-Avesta, God is Illimitable Time. No origin can be assigned to Him. He is so entirely enveloped in his glory, His nature and attributes are so inaccessible to human Intelligence, that He can be only the object of a silent Veneration. Creation took place by emanation from Him. The first emanation was the primitive Light, and from that the King of Light, ORMUZD. By the WORD, Ormuzd created the world pure. He is its preserver and judge: a Being Holy and Heavenly; Intelligence and Knowledge; the First-born of Time without limits; and invested with all the Powers of the Supreme Being.

Still he is, strictly speaking, the Fourth Being. He had a Ferouer, a pre-existing Soul, [in the language of Plato, a type or ideal]; and it is said of Him, that he existed from the beginning, in the primitive Light. But, that Light being but an element, and his Ferouer a type, he is, in ordinary language, the First-born of

ZEROUANE-AKHERENE. Behold, again, THE WORD of Masonry; the *Man*, on the Tracing Board of this Degree; the LIGHT towards which all Masons travel.

He created after his own image, six Genii called *Amshaspands*, who surround his Throne, are his organs of communication with inferior spirits and men, transmit to Him their prayers, solicit for them his favours, and serve them as models of purity and perfection. Thus we have the *Demiourgos* of Gnosticism, and the six *Genii* that assist him.

The names of these *Amshaspands* are Bahman, Ardibehest, Schariver, Sapandomad, Khordad and Amerdad.

The fourth, the Holy SAPANDOMAD, created the first man and woman.

Then ORMUZD created 28 *Izeds*, of whom MITHRAS is the chief. They watch, with *Ormuzd* and the *Amshaspands*, over the happiness, purity and preservation of the world, which is under their government: and they are also models for mankind and interpreters of men's prayers. With *Mithras* and *Ormuzd*, they make a *pleroma* [or complete number] of 30, corresponding to the 30 *Eons* of the Gnostics, and to the *ogdoade*, *dodecade* and *decade* of the Egyptians. *Mithras* was the Sun-God, invoked with, and soon confounded with him, becoming the object of a special worship, and eclipsing *Ormuzd* himself.

The third order of pure spirits is more numerous. They are the *Ferouers*, the THOUGHTS of Ormuzd, or the IDEAS which he conceived before proceeding to the creation of things. They too are superior to men. They protect them during their life on earth; they will purify them from evil at their resurrection. They are their tutelary genii, from the fall to the complete regeneration.

AHRIMAN, second-born of the Primitive Light, emanated from it, pure like ORMUZD; but, proud and ambitious, yielded to jealousy of the First-born. For his hatred and pride, the Eternal condemned him to dwell, for 12,000 years, in that part of space where no ray of light reaches; the black empire of darkness. In that period the struggle between *Light* and *Darkness*, *Good* and *Evil*, will be terminated.

AHRIMAN scorned to submit, and took the field against ORMUZD. To the good spirits created by his Brother, he opposed an innumerable army of Evil Ones. To the seven *Amshaspands* he opposed seven *Archdevs*, attached to the seven Planets; to the *Izeds* and *Ferouers* an equal number of *Devs*, which brought upon the world all moral and physical evils. Hence *Poverty, Maladies, Impurity, Envy, Chagrin, Drunkenness, Falsehood, Calumny*, and their horrible array.

The image of Ahriman was the Dragon, confounded by the Jews with Satan and the Serpent-Tempter. After a reign of 3000 years, Ormuzd had created the Material World, in 6 periods, calling successively into existence the Light, Water, Earth, plants, animals and Man. But Ahriman concurred in creating the earth and water; for darkness was already an element, and Ormuzd could not exclude its Master. So also the two concurred in producing Man. Ormuzd produced, by his Will and Word, a Being that was the type and source of universal life for everything that exists under Heaven. He placed in man a pure principle, or Life, proceeding from the Supreme Being. But Ahriman destroyed that pure principle, in the form wherewith it was clothed; and when Ormuzd had made, of its recovered and purified essence, the first man and woman, Ahriman seduced and tempted them with wine and fruits; the woman yielding first.

Often, during the three latter periods of 3000 years each, Ahriman and Darkness are, and are to be triumphant. But the pure souls are assisted by the Good Spirits; the Triumph of Good is decreed by the Supreme Being, and the period of that triumph will infallibly arrive. When the world shall be most afflicted with the evils poured out upon it by the spirits of perdition, three Prophets will come to bring relief to mortals. SOSIOSCH, the principal of the Three, will regenerate the earth, and restore to it its primitive beauty, strength and purity. He will judge the good and the wicked. After the universal resurrection of the good, he will conduct them to a home of everlasting happiness. Ahriman, his evil demons, and all wicked men will also be purified in a torrent of melted metal. The law of Ormuzd will reign everywhere; all men will be happy; all, enjoying unalterable bliss, will sing with Sosiosch the praises of the Supreme Being.

These doctrines, the details of which were sparingly borrowed by the Jews, were much more fully adopted by the Gnostics; who taught the restoration of all things, their return to their original pure condition, the happiness of those to be saved, and their admission to the feast of Heavenly Wisdom.

The doctrines of Zoroaster came originally from Bactria, an Indian Province of Persia. Naturally, therefore, it would include Hindoo or Buddhist elements, as it did. The fundamental idea of Buddhism was, matter subjugating the intelligence, and intelligence freeing itself from that slavery. Perhaps something came to Gnosticism from China. "Before the chaos which preceded the birth of Heaven and Earth," says Lao-Tseu, "a single Being existed, immense and silent, immovable and ever active—the mother of the universe. I know not its name: but I designate it by the word *Reason*. Man has his *type* and *model* in the Earth; Earth in Heaven; Heaven in Reason; and Reason in Itself." Here again are the *Ferouers*, the *Ideas*, the *Eons*,—the REASON or INTELLIGENCE [Εννοια], SILENCE [Σιγή], WORD [Λογος] and WISDOM [Σοφια] of the Gnostics: *Ennoia, Sigé, Logos* and *Sophia*.

The dominant system among the Jews after their captivity was that of the Pheroschim or Pharisees. Whether their name was derived from that of the Parsees, or followers of Zoroaster, or from some other source, it is certain that they had borrowed much of their doctrine from the Persians. Like them they claimed to have the exclusive and mysterious knowledge, unknown to the mass. Like them they taught that a constant war was waged between the Empire of Good and that of Evil. Like them they attributed the sin and fall of man to the demons and their chief; and like them they admitted a special protection of the righteous by inferior beings, agents of Jehovah. All their doctrines on these subjects were at bottom those of the Holy Books; but singularly developed; and the Orient was evidently the source from which those developments came.

They styled themselves *Interpreters*; a name indicating their claim to the exclusive possession of the true meaning of the Holy Writings, by virtue of the oral tradition which Moses had received on Mount Sinaï, and which successive generations of Initiates had transmitted, as they claimed, unaltered, unto them. Their very costume, their belief in the influences of the stars, and in the transmigration of souls, their system of angels and their astronomy, were all foreign.

Sadduceeism arose merely from an opposition essentially Jewish, to these foreign teachings, and that mixture of doctrines, adopted by the Pharisees, and which constituted the popular creed.

We come at last to the *Essenes* and *Therapeuts*, with whom this degree is particularly concerned. That intermingling of oriental and occidental rites, of Persian and Pythagorean opinions, which we have pointed out in the doctrines of Philo, is unmistakable in the creeds of these two sects.

They were less distinguished by metaphysical speculations than by simple meditations and moral prac-tices. But the latter always partook of the Zoroastrian principle, that it was necessary to free the soul from the trammels and influences of matter; which led to a system of abstinence and maceration entirely opposed to the ancient Hebraic ideas, favourable as they were to physical pleasures. In general, the life and manners of these mystical associations, as Philo and Josephus describe them, and particularly their prayers at sunrise, seem the image of what the Zend-Avesta prescribes to the faithful adorer of Ormuzd; and some of their observances cannot otherwise be explained.

The Therapeuts resided in Egypt, in the neighbourhood of Alexandria; and the Essenes in Palestine, in the vicinity of the Dead Sea. But there was nevertheless a striking co-incidence in their ideas, readily explained by attributing it to a foreign influence. The Jews of Egypt, under the influence of the School of Alexandria, endeavoured in general to make their doctrines harmonize with the traditions of Greece; and thence came, in the doctrines of the Therapeuts, as stated by Philo, the many analogies between the Pytha-gorean and Orphic ideas, on one side, and those of Judaism on the other: while the Jews of Palestine, having less communication with Greece, or contemning its teachings, rather imbibed the Oriental doctrines, which they drank in at the source, and with which their relations with Persia made them familiar. This attachment was particularly shown in the Kabbala, which belonged rather to Palestine than to Egypt, though as extensively known in the latter; and furnished the Gnostics with some of their most striking theories.

It is a significant fact, that while Christ spoke often of the Pharisees and Sadducees, he never once men-tioned the Essenes, between whose doctrines and his there was so great a resemblance, and, in many points, so perfect an identity. Indeed, they are not named, nor even distinctly alluded to, anywhere in the New Testament.

John, the son of a Priest who ministered in the Temple at Jerusalem, and whose mother was of the family of Aaron, was in the deserts until the day of his showing unto Israel. He drank neither wine nor strong drink. Clad in hair-cloth, and with a girdle of leather, and feeding upon such food as the desert afforded, he preached, in the country about Jordan, the baptism of repentance, for the remission of sins; that is, the necessity of repentance and reformation. He taught the people charity and liberality; the publicans, justice, equity, and fair dealing; the soldiery, peace, truth, and contentment; to do violence to none, accuse none falsely, and be content with their pay. He inculcated the necessity of a virtuous life, and the folly of trusting to their descent from Abraham.

He denounced both Pharisees and Sadducees as a generation of vipers, threatened with the anger of God. He baptized those that confessed their sins. He preached in the desert; and therefore in the country where the Essenes lived, professing the same doctrines. He was imprisoned before Christ began to preach. Matthew mentions him without preface or explanation; as if, apparently, his history was too well known to need any. "In those days," he says, "came John the Baptist, preaching in the wilderness of Judea." His disciples frequently fasted; for we find them with the Pharisees, coming to Jesus to inquire why *his* disciples did not fast as often as they; and he did not denounce *them*, as his habit was to denounce the Pharisees; but answered them kindly and gently.

From his prison, John sent two of his disciples to inquire of Christ: "Art thou he that is to come, or do we look for another?" Christ referred them to his miracles as an answer; and declared to the people that John was a prophet, and more than a prophet, and that no greater man had ever been born; but that the humblest Christian was his superior. He declared him to be Elias, who was to come.

John had denounced to Herod his marriage with his brother's wife as unlawful; and for this he was imprisoned, and finally executed to gratify her. His disciples buried him; and Herod and others thought he had risen from the dead and appeared again in the person of Christ. The people all regarded John as a prophet; and Christ silenced the Priests and Elders by asking them whether he was inspired. They feared to excite the anger of the people by saying that he was not. Christ declared that he came "in the way of right. ousness;" and that the lower classes believed him, though the Priests and Pharisees did not.

Thus John, who was often consulted by Herod, and to whom that monarch showed great deference, and was often governed by his advice; whose doctrine prevailed very extensively among the people and the publicans, taught *some* creed older than Christianity. That is plain: and it is equally plain, that the very large body of the Jews that adopted his doctrines, were neither Pharisees nor Sadducees, but the humble, common people. They must, therefore, have been Essenes. It is plain, too, that Christ applied for baptism as a sacred rite, well known and long practised. It was becoming to him, he said, to fulfil all righteousness.

In the 18th chapter of the Acts of the Apostles we read thus: "And a certain Jew, named Apollos, born at Alexandria, an eloquent man, and mighty in the Scriptures, came to Ephesus. This man *was instructed in the way of the Lord,* and, being fervent in spirit, *he spake and taught diligently the things of the Lord, knowing only the baptism of John;* and he began to speak boldly in the synagogue; whom, when Aquila and Priscilla had heard, they took him unto them, and expounded unto him *the way of God* more perfectly.".

Translating this from the symbolic and figurative language into the true ordinary sense of the Greek text, it reads thus: "And a certain Jew, named Apollos, an Alexandrian by birth, an eloquent man, and of extensive learning, came to Ephesus. He had learned in the mysteries the true doctrine in regard to God; and, being a zealous enthusiast, he spoke and taught diligently the truths in regard to the Deity, having received no other baptism than that of John." He knew nothing in regard to Christianity; for he had resided in Alexandria, and had just then come to Ephesus; being, probably, a disciple of Philo, and a Therapeut.

"That, in all times," says St. Augustine, "is the Christian religion, which to know and follow is the most sure and certain health, called according to that name, but not according to the thing itself, of which it is the name; for the thing itself, which is now called the Christian religion, *really was known to the Ancients,* nor was wanting at any time from the beginning of the human race, until the time when Christ came in the flesh; from whence the true religion, which had previously existed, began to be called Christian; and this in our days is the Christian religion, not as having been wanting in former times, but as having, in later times, received this name."

The Wandering or Itinerant Jews or Exorcists, who assumed to employ the Sacred Name in exorcising evil spirits, were no doubt Therapeutæ or Essenes.

"And it came to pass," we read in the 19th Chapter of the Acts, verses 1 to 4, "that while Apollos was at Corinth, Paul, having passed through the upper parts of Asia Minor, came to Ephesus; and finding certain disciples, he said to them, Have ye received the Holy Ghost since ye became Believers? And they said unto him, We have not so much as heard that there is any Holy Ghost. And he said to them, In what, then, were you baptized? And they said, in John's Baptism. Then said Paul, John indeed baptized with the baptism of repentance, saying to the people that they should believe in him who was to come after him, that is, in Jesus Christ. When they heard this, they were baptized in the name of the Lord Jesus."

This faith, taught by John, and so nearly Christianity, could have been nothing but the doctrine of the Essenes; and there can be no doubt that John belonged to that sect. The place where he preached, his macerations and frugal diet, the doctrines he taught, all prove it conclusively. There was no other sect to which he could have belonged; certainly none so numerous as his, except the Essenes.

We find, from the two letters written by Paul to the brethren at Corinth, that City of Luxury and Corruption, that there were contentions among them. Rival sects had already, about the 57th year of our era, reared their banners there, as followers, some of Paul, some of Apollos and some of Cephas. [1st Cor. Ch. 1, v. 11, 12, Ch. 3, v. 4, 5, 6, 21, 22]. Some of them denied the resurrection: [Id. Ch. 15, v. 12]. Paul urged them to adhere to the doctrines taught by himself, and had sent Timothy to them to bring them afresh to their recollection.

According to Paul, Christ was to come again. He was to put an end to all other Principles and Powers, and finally to Death, and then He Himself once more merged in God; who should then be all in all.

The forms and ceremonies of the Essenes were symbolical. They had, according to Philo the Jew, four degrees; the members being divided into two Orders, the *Practici* and *Therapeutici;* the latter being the contemplative and medical Brethren; and the former the active, practical, business men. They were Jews by birth; and had a greater affection for each other than the members of any other sect. Their brotherly love was intense. They fulfilled the Christian law, "Love one another." They despised riches. No one was to be found among them, having more than another. The possessions of one were intermingled with those of the other; so that they all had but one patrimony, and were brethren. Their piety towards God was extraordinary. Before sunrise they never spake a word about profane matters; but put up certain prayers which they had received from their forefathers. At dawn of day, and before it was light, their prayers and hymns ascended to Heaven. They were eminently faithful and true, and the Ministers of Peace. They had mysterious ceremonies, and initiations into their mysteries; and the Candidate promised that he would ever practise fidelity to all men, and especially to those in authority, "because no one obtains the government without God's assistance."

Whatever they said, was firmer than an oath; but they avoided swearing, and esteemed it worse than perjury. They were simple in their diet and mode of living, bore torture with fortitude, and despised death. They cultivated the science of medicine and were very skilful. They deemed it a good omen to dress in white robes. They had their own courts, and passed righteous judgments. They kept the Sabbath more rigorously than the Jews.

Their chief towns were Engaddi, near the Dead Sea, and Hebron. Engaddi was about 30 miles southeast from Jerusalem, and Hebron about 20 miles south of that city. Josephus and Eusebius speak of them as an ancient sect; and they were no doubt the first among the Jews to embrace Christianity: with whose faith and doctrine their own tenets had so many points of resemblance, and were indeed in a great measure the same. Pliny regarded them as a very ancient people.

In their devotions they turned towards the rising sun; as the Jews generally did towards the Temple. But they were no idolaters; for they observed the law of Moses with scrupulous fidelity. They held all things in common, and despised riches, their wants being supplied by the administration of Curators or Stewards. The Tetractys, composed of round dots instead of jods, was revered among them. This being a Pythagorean symbol, evidently shows their connection with the school of Pythagoras: but their peculiar tenets more resemble those of Confucius and Zoroaster : and probably were adopted while they were prisoners in Persia ; which explains their turning towards the Sun in prayer.

Their demeanour was sober and chaste. They submitted to the superintendence of governors whom they appointed over themselves. The whole of their time was spent in labour, meditation and prayer ; and they were most sedulously attentive to every call of justice and humanity, and every moral duty. They believed in the unity of God. They supposed the souls of men to have fallen, by a disastrous fate, from the regions of purity and light, into the bodies which they occupy ; during their continuance in which they considered them confined as in a prison. Therefore they did not believe in the resurrection of the body ; but in that of the soul only. They believed in a future state of rewards and punishments ; and they disregarded the ceremonies or external forms enjoined in the law of Moses to be observed in the worship of God ; holding that the words of that lawgiver were to be understood in a mysterious and recondite sense, and not according to their literal meaning. They offered no sacrifices, except at home ; and by meditation they endeavoured, as far as possible, to isolate the soul from the body, and carry it back to God.

Eusebius broadly admits " that the ancient Therapeutæ were Christians ; and that their ancient writings were our Gospels and Epistles."

The Essenes were of the Eclectic Sect of Philosophers, and held Plato in the highest esteem ; they believed that true philosophy, the greatest and most salutary gift of God to mortals, was scattered, in various portions, through all the different Sects ; and that it was, consequently, the duty of every wise man to gather it from the several corners where it lay dispersed, and to employ it, thus re-united, in destroying the dominion of impiety and vice.

The great festivals of the Solstices were observed in a distinguished manner by the Essenes ; as would naturally be supposed, from the fact that they reverenced the Sun, not as a God, but as a symbol of light and fire ; the fountain of which the Orientals supposed God to be. They lived in continence and abstinence, and had establishments similar to the monasteries of the early Christians.

The writings of the Essenes were full of mysticism, parables, enigmas and allegories. They believed in the esoteric and exoteric meanings of the Scriptures ; and, as we have already said, they had a warrant for that in the Scriptures themselves. They found it in the Old Testament, as the Gnostics found it in the New. The Christian writers, and even Christ himself recognized it as a truth, that all Scripture had an inner and outer meaning. Thus we find it said as follows, in one of the Gospels :

" Unto you it is given to know the mystery of the Kingdom of God ; but unto men *that are without*, all these things are done in parables ; that seeing, they may see and not perceive, and hearing, they may hear and not understand. . . And the disciples came and said unto him, Why speakest Thou the truth in parables ? He answered and said unto them, Because it is given unto you to know the mysteries of the Kingdom of Heaven, but to them it is not given."

Paul, in the 4th Chapter of his Epistle to the Galatians, speaking of the simplest facts of the Old Testament, asserts that they are *an allegory*. In the 3d Chapter of the 2d letter to the Corinthians he declares himself a minister of the New Testament, appointed by God ; " Not of the letter, but of the spirit ; for the letter killeth." Origen and St. Gregory held that the Gospels were not to be taken in their literal sense ; and Athanasius admonishes us that " Should we understand sacred writ according to the letter, we should fall into the most enormous blasphemies."

Eusebius said, " those who preside over the Holy Sepulchres, philosophize over them, and expound their literal sense by allegory."

The sources of our knowledge of the Kabbalistic doctrines, are the books Jezirah and Sohar, the former drawn up in the 2d Century, and the latter a little later ; but containing materials much older than themselves. In their most characteristic elements, they go back to the time of the exile. In them, as in the teachings of Zoroaster, everything that exists emanated from a source of infinite LIGHT. Before everything, existed THE ANCIENT OF DAYS, the KING OF LIGHT ; a title often given to the Creator in the *Zend-Avesta* and the code of the *Sabeans*. With the idea so expressed is connected the pantheism of India. THE KING OF LIGHT, THE ANCIENT, is ALL THAT IS. He is not only the real cause of all Existences ; he is Infinite [ENSORU]. He is HIMSELF : there is nothing in Him that He can call *Thou*.

In the Indian doctrine, not only is the Supreme Being the real cause of all, but he is the only real Existence : all the rest is illusion. In the Kabbala, as in the Persian and Gnostic doctrines, He is the Supreme Being unknown to all, the Unknown Father. The world is his revelation, and subsists only in Him. His attributes are reproduced there, with different modifications, and in different degrees, so that the Universe is His Holy Splendour : it is but His Mantle ; but it must be revered in silence. All beings have emanated from the Supreme Being : The nearer a being is to Him, the more perfect it is ; the more remote in the scale, the less its purity.

A ray of Light, shot from the Deity, is the cause and principle of all that exists. It is at once Father and Mother of All, in the sublimest sense. It penetrates everything ; and without it nothing can exist an instant. From this double Force, designated by the two first letters of the word I.·. H.·. U.·. H.·. emanated the First-born of God, the Universal Form, in which are contained all beings, the Persian and Platonic Archetype of things, united with the Infinite by the primitive ray of Light.

This First-Born is the Creative Agent, Conservator and animating Principle of the Universe. It is the Light of Light. It possesses the three Primitive Forces of the Divinity, Light, Spirit and Life ; [Φῶς, Πνεῦμα´ and Ζωη]. As it has received what it gives, Light and Life, it is equally considered as the generative and conceptive Principle, the Primitive Man, Adam Kadmon. As such, it has revealed itself in ten emanations or *Sephiroth*, which are not ten different beings, nor even beings at all ; but sources of life, vessels of Omnipotence, and types of Creation. They are *Sovereignty, Wisdom, Prudence, Magnificence, Sternness, Beauty, Victory, Glory, Permanency* and *Empire*. These are attributes of God ; and this idea, that God reveals Himself by His attributes, and that the human mind cannot perceive or discern God Himself, in his works, but only his mode of manifesting Himself, is a profound Truth.

To each of these attributes was given one of the most sacred names of the Supreme Being. *Wisdom* they termed Jeh ; *Prudence*, Ihuh ; *Magnificence*, El ; *Sternness*, Elohim ; *Victory* and *Glory*, Zabaoth ; and *Empire*, Adonai. *Sovereignty* was also styled Or, which is the Our of the Sabean system, that is Light.

Wisdom was also called Nous and Logos, [Νοῦς and Λογος], Intellect or the Word. *Prudence*, source of the oil of anointing, responds to the Holy Ghost of the Christian Faith.

Beauty is represented by green and yellow. *Victory* is Ihuh-Zabaoth, the column on the right hand, the column *Jachin*: *Glory* is the column *Boaz*, on the left hand. And thus our symbols appear again in the Kabbala. And again the Light, the object of our labours, appears as the creative power of Deity. The circle, also, was the special symbol of the first of the *Sephiroth*.

We do not further follow the Kabbala, its four Worlds of Spirits, *Aziluth, Briah, Jezirah*, and *Asiah*, or of *emanation, creation, formation*, and *fabrication*, one inferior to and one emerging from the other, the superior always enveloping the inferior ; its doctrine that, in all that exists, there is nothing purely material ; that all comes from God, and in all He proceeds by irradiation ; that everything subsists by the Divine ray that penetrates creation ; and all is united by the Spirit of God, which is the life of life ; so that all is God ; the Existences that inhabit the four worlds, inferior to each other in proportion to their distance from the Great King of Light : the contest between the good and evil Angels and Principles, to endure until the Eternal Himself comes to end it and re-establish the primitive harmony ; the four distinct parts of the Soul of Man ; and the migrations of impure souls, until they are sufficiently purified to share with the Spirits of Light the contemplation of the Supreme Being whose Splendour fills the Universe.

The Word was also found in the Phœnician Creed. As in all those of Asia, a Word of God, written in starry characters, by the planetary Divinities, and communicated by the Demi-Gods, as a profound mystery, to the higher classes of the human race, to be communicated by them to mankind, created the world. The faith of the Phœnicians was an emanation from that ancient worship of the Stars, which, in the creed of Zoroaster alone, is connected with a faith in one God. Light and Fire are the most important agents in the Phœnician faith. There is a race of children of the Light. They adored the Heaven with its lights, deeming it the Supreme God.

Everything emanates from a Single Principle, and a Primitive Love, which is the Moving Power of All and governs all. Light, by its union with Spirit, whereof it is but the vehicle or symbol, is the Life of everything; and penetrates everything. It should therefore be respected and honoured everywhere; for everywhere it governs and controls.

The Chaldaic and Jerusalem Paraphrasts endeavoured to render the phrase, Iɴᴜᴏ-Dᴇʙᴀʀ . . [רבר יהוה], the Word of God, a personalty, wherever they met with it. The phrase, "And God created man," is, in the Jerusalem Targum, "And the Word of Iɴᴜᴏ created man."

So, in xxviii Gen. 20, 21, where Jacob says; if God, [יהיה אלהים, Iᴜɪᴏ Aʟᴏɪᴍ], will be with me . . . then shall Iɴᴜᴏ be my Aʟᴏɪᴍ: והיה יהוה לי לאלהים; Uᴀɪᴏ Iɴᴜᴏ Lɪ Lᴀʟᴏɪᴍ]; and this stone shall be God's House [יהיה כיח ארהם . . Iᴜɪᴏ Bɪᴛᴏ Aʟᴏɪᴍ]: Onkelos paraphrases it, "If the Word of Iɴᴜᴏ will be my help . . . then the Word of Iᴜᴜᴏ shall be my God."

So, in iii Gen. 8, for "The Voice of the Lord God," [יהוה אלהים, Iɴᴜᴏ Aʟᴏɪᴍ], we have, "The voice of the Word of Iɴᴜᴏ."

In ix Wisdom 1, "O God of my Fathers and Lord of Mercy! who hast made all things with thy Word . . ἐν λόγου σου."

And in xviii Wisdom 15, "Thine Almighty Word [Λογος] leaped down from Heaven."

Philo speaks of the Word as being the same with God. So in several places he calls it δεύτερος Θεὸς Λόγος, the Second Divinity; ἐικὼν τοῦ Θεόυ, the Image of God: the Divine Word that made all things: the ὕπαρχος, substitute, of God; and the like.

Thus, when John commenced to preach, had been for ages agitated, by the Priests and Philosophers of the East and West, the great questions concerning the eternity or creation of matter: immediate or intermediate creation of the universe by the Supreme God; the origin, object, and final extinction of evil; the relations between the intellectual and material worlds, and between God and man; and the creation, fall, redemption and restoration to his first estate, of man.

The Jewish doctrine, differing in this from all the other oriental creeds, and even from the Elohistic legend with which the book of Genesis commences, attributed the creation to the immediate action of the Supreme Being. The Theosophists of the other Eastern Peoples interposed more than one intermediary between God and the world. To place between them but a single Being, to suppose for the production of the world but a single intermediary, was, in their eyes, to lower the Supreme Majesty. The interval between God, who is perfect Purity, and matter, which is base and foul, was too great for them to clear it at a single step. Even in the Occident, neither Plato nor Philo could thus impoverish the Intellectual World.

Thus Cerinthus of Ephesus, with most of the Gnostics, Philo, the Kabbala, the Zend-Avesta, the Puranas, and all the Orient, deemed the distance and antipathy between the Supreme Being and the material world too great, to attribute to the former the creation of the latter. Below, and emanating from, or created by, the Ancient of Days, the Central Light, the Beginning or First Principle [Αρχή], one, two or more Principles, Existences or Intellectual Beings were imagined, to some one or more of whom, [without any immediate creative act on the part of the Great Immovable, Silent Deity], the immediate creation of the material and mental universe was due.

We have already spoken of many of the speculations on this point. To some, the world was created by the Logos or Word, first manifestation of, or emanation from, the Deity. To others, the beginning of creation was by the emanation of a ray of Light, creating the principle of *Light* and *Life*. The Primitive Thought, creating the inferior Deities, a succession of Iɴᴛᴇʟʟɪɢᴇɴᴄᴇs, the Iynges of Zoroaster, his *Amshaspands*, *Izeds*, and *Ferouers*, the *Ideas* of Plato, the *Æons* of the Gnostics, the *Angels* of the Jews, the *Nous*, the *Demiourgos*, the Dɪᴠɪɴᴇ Rᴇᴀsoɴ, the *Powers* or *Forces*, of Philo, and the Elohim, Forces or Superior Gods of the ancient legend with which Genesis begins,—to these and other intermediaries the creation was owing. No restraints were laid on the Fancy and the Imagination. The veriest Abstractions became Existences and Realities. The attributes of God, personified, became Powers, Spirits, Intelligences.

God was the *Light of Light*, *Divine Fire*, *the Abstract Intellectuality*, the *Root* or *Germ* of the universe. *Simon Magus*, founder of the Gnostic faith, and many of the early Judaizing Christians, admitted that the manifestations of the Supreme Being, as Fᴀᴛʜᴇʀ, or Jᴇʜoᴠᴀʜ, Soɴ or Cʜʀɪsᴛ, and Hoʟʏ Sᴘɪʀɪᴛ, were only so many different *modes* of Existence, or *Forces* [δυναμεις] of the same God. To others they were, as were the multitude of Subordinate Intelligences, real and distinct beings.

The oriental imagination revelled in the creation of these Inferior Intelligences, Powers of Good and Evil, and Angels. We have spoken of those imagined by the Persians and the Kabbalists. In the Talmud, every star, every country, every town and almost every tongue has a Prince of Heaven as its Protector. JEHUEL is the guardian of fire, and MICHAEL of water. Seven spirits assist each; those of fire being *Seraphiel*, *Gabriel*, *Nitriel*, *Tammael*, *Tchimschiel*, *Hadarniel* and *Sarniel*. These seven are represented by the square columns of this degree, while the columns JACHIN and BOAZ represent the angels of fire and water. But the columns are not representatives of these alone.

To Basilides, God was without name, uncreated, at first containing and concealing in Himself the Plenitude of his Perfections; and when these are by him displayed and manifested, there result as many particular Existences, all analogous to Him, and still and always Him. To the Essenes and the Gnostics, the East and the West both devised this faith: that the Ideas, Conceptions or Manifestations of the Deity were so many Creations, so many Beings, all God, nothing without Him, but more than what we now understand by the word *ideas*. They emanated from and were again merged in God. They had a kind of middle existence between our modern ideas, and the intelligences or ideas, elevated to the rank of genii, of the oriental mythology.

These personified attributes of Deity, in the theory of Basilides, were the Πρωτόγονος or *First-born*, Νοῦς [*Nous* or *Mind*]: from it emanates Λόγος [*Logos*, or THE WORD]: from it Φρόνησις [*Phronesis*, *Intellect*]: from it Σοφία [*Sophia*, *Wisdom*]: from it Δύναμις [*Dunamis*, *Power*]: and from it Δικαιοσύνη [*Dikaiosune*, *Righteousness*]: to which latter the Jews gave the name of Ειρηνη [*Eirene*, *Peace* or *Calm*], the essential characteristic of Divinity, and harmonious effect of all His perfections. The whole number of successive emanations was 365, expressed by the Gnostics, in Greek letters, by the mystic word ΑΒΡΑΞΑΣ: [*Abraxas*]; designating God as manifested, or the aggregate of his manifestations; but not the Supreme and Secret God Himself. These 365 Intelligences compose altogether the Fulness or *Plenitude* [Πληρωμα] of the Divine Emanations.

With the Ophites, a sect of the Gnostics, there were seven inferior spirits [inferior to Ialdabaoth, the Demiourgos or Actual Creator]: *Michaël*, *Suriël*, *Raphaël*, *Gabriel*, *Thauthabaoth*, *Erataoth* and *Athaniel*, the genii of the stars called the Bull, the Dog, the Lion, the Bear, the Serpent, the Eagle, and the Ass that formerly figured in the constellation Cancer, and symbolized respectively by those animals; as *Ialdabaoth*, *Iao*, *Adonaï*, *Eloï*, *Oraï* and *Astaphaï* were the genii of Saturn, the Moon, the Sun, Jupiter, Venus and Mercury.

The WORD appears in all these creeds. It is the *Ormuzd* of Zoroaster, the *Ensoph* of the Kabbala, the *Nous* of Platonism and Philonism, and the *Sophia* or *Demiourgos* of the Gnostics.

And all these creeds, while admitting these different manifestations of the Supreme Being, held that His identity was immutable and permanent. That was Plato's distinction between the Being always the same, [τὸ ὄν] and the perpetual flow of things incessantly changing, the Genesis.

The belief in dualism, in some shape, was universal. Those who held that everything emanated from God, aspired to God and re-entered into God, believed that, among those emanations were two adverse Principles, of Light and Darkness, Good and Evil. This prevailed in Central Asia and in Syria; while in Egypt it assumed the form of Greek speculation. In the former, a second Intellectual Principle was admitted, active in its Empire of Darkness, audacious against the Empire of Light. So the Persians and Sabeans understood it. In Egypt, this second Principle was Matter, as the word was used by the Platonic School, with its sad attributes, Vacuity, Darkness and Death. In their theory, matter could be animated only by the low communication of a principle of divine-life. It resists the influences that would spiritualize it. That resisting Power is Satan, the rebellious Matter, Matter that does not partake of God.

To many there were two Principles; the Unknown Father, or Supreme and Eternal God, living in the centre of the Light, happy in the perfect purity of his being; the other, eternal Matter, that inert, shapeless, darksome mass, which they considered as the source of all evils, the mother and dwelling-place of Satan.

To Philo and the Platonists, there was a Soul of the world, creating visible things, and active in them, as agent of the Supreme Intelligence; realizing therein the ideas communicated to Him by that Intelligence, and which sometimes excel his conceptions, but which He executes without comprehending them.

The Apocalypse or Revelations, by whomever written, belongs to the Orient and to extreme antiquity. It reproduces what is far older than itself. It paints, with the strongest colours that the Oriental genius ever employed, the closing scenes of the great struggle of Light, and Truth, and Good, against Darkness, Error and Evil; personified in that between the New Religion on one side, and Paganism and Judaism on the other. It is a particular application of the ancient myth of Ormuzd and his Genii against Ahriman and his Devs; and it celebrates the final triumph of Truth against the combined powers of men and demons. The ideas and imagery are borrowed from every quarter; and allusions are found in it to the doctrines of all ages. We are continually reminded of the Zend-Avesta, the Jewish Codes, Philo and the Gnosis. The Seven Spirits surrounding the Throne of the Eternal, at the opening of the Grand Drama, and acting so important a part throughout, everywhere the first instruments of the Divine Will and Vengeance, are the Seven Amshaspands of Parsism; as the Twenty-four Ancients, offering to the Supreme Being the first supplications and the first homage, remind us of the Mysterious Chiefs of Judaism, foreshadow the Eons of Gnosticism, and reproduce the 24 Good Spirits created by Ormuzd and inclosed in an egg.

The Christ of the Apocalypse, First-born of Creation and of the Resurrection, is invested with the characteristics of the Ormuzd and Sosiosch of the Zend-Avesta, the Ensoph of the Kabbala and the Carpistes [Καρπιστης] of the Gnostics. The idea that the true Initiates and Faithful become Kings and Priests, is at once Persian, Jewish, Christian and Gnostic. And the definition of the Supreme Being, that he is at once Alpha and Omega, the beginning and the end—he that was, and is, and is to come, i. e. Time illimitable; is Zoroaster's definition of Zerouane-Akherene.

The depths of Satan which no man can measure: his triumph for a time, by fraud and violence; his being chained by an angel; his reprobation and his precipitation into a sea of metal; his names of The Serpent and the Dragon; the whole conflict of the Good Spirits or celestial armies against the bad; are so many ideas and designations found alike in the Zend-Avesta, the Kabbala and the Gnosis.

We even find in the Apocalypse that singular Persian idea, which regards some of the lower animals as so many Devs or vehicles of Devs.

The guardianship of the earth by a good angel, the renewing of the earth and heavens, and the final triumph of pure and holy men, are the same victory of Good over Evil, for which the whole Orient looked.

The gold, and white raiments, of the twenty-four Elders are, as in the Persian faith, the signs of a lofty perfection and divine purity.

Thus the Human mind laboured and struggled and tortured itself for ages, to explain to itself what it felt, without confessing it, to be inexplicable. A vast crowd of indistinct abstractions, hovering in the imagination, a train of words embodying no tangible meaning, an inextricable labyrinth of subtleties, was the net result.

But one grand idea ever emerged and stood prominent and unchangeable over the weltering chaos of confusion. God is great, and good and wise. Evil and pain and sorrow are temporary, and for wise and beneficent purposes. They must be consistent with God's goodness, purity and infinite perfection; and there must be a mode of explaining them, if we could but find it out; as, in all ways we will endeavour to do. Ultimately, Good will prevail, and Evil be overthrown. God alone can do this, and He will do it, by an Emanation from Himself, assuming the Human form and redeeming the world.

Behold the object, the end, the result, of the great speculations and logomachies of antiquity: the ultimate annihilation of evil, and restoration of Man to his first estate, by a Redeemer, a Christos, the incarnate Word, Reason or Power of Deity.

This Redeemer is the Word or Logos, the Ormuzd of Zoroaster, the Ensoph of the Kabbala, the Nous of Platonism and Philonism: he that was in the Beginning with God, and was God, and by whom everything was made. That He was looked for by all the People of the East is abundantly shown by the Gospel of John and the Letters of Paul; wherein scarcely anything seemed necessary to be said in proof that such a Redeemer was to come; but all the energies of the writers are devoted to showing that Jesus was that Christos whom all the nations were expecting.

In this degree the great contest between good and evil, in anticipation of the appearance and advent of the Word or Redeemer is symbolized; and the mysterious esoteric teachings of the Essenes and the Cabalists.

4B

Of the practices of the former we gain but glimpses in the ancient writers; but we know that, as their doctrines were taught by John the Baptist, they greatly resembled those of greater purity and more perfect, taught by Jesus; and that not only Palestine was full of John's disciples, so that the Priests and Pharisees did not dare to deny John's inspiration; but his doctrine had extended into Asia Minor, and had made converts in luxurious Ephesus, as it also had in Alexandria in Egypt: and that they readily embraced the Christian faith, of which they had before not even heard.

These old controversies have died away, and the old faiths have faded into oblivion. But Masonry still survives, vigorous and strong, as when philosophy was taught in the schools of Alexandria and under the Portico; teaching the same old truths as the Essenes taught by the Shores of the Red Sea, and as John the Baptist preached in the Desert: truths imperishable as the Deity, and undeniable as Light. Those truths were gathered by the Essenes from the doctrines of the Orient and the Occident, from the Zend-Avesta and the Vedas, from Plato and Pythagoras, from India, Persia, Phœnicia and Syria, from Greece and Egypt, and from the Holy Books of the Jews. Hence we are called Knights of the East and West, because their doctrines came from both. And these doctrines, the wheat sifted from the chaff, the Truth separated from Error, Masonry has garnered up in her heart of hearts, and through the fires of persecution, and the storms of calamity, has brought them and delivered them unto us. That God is One, immutable, unchangeable, infinitely just and good; that Light will finally overcome Darkness; Good Conquer Evil, and Truth be victor over Error;—these, rejecting all the wild and useless speculations of the Zend-Avesta, the Kabbala, the Gnostics, and the Schools, are the religion and Philosophy of Masonry.

Those speculations and fancies it is useful to study; that knowing in what worthless and unfruitful investigations the mind may engage, you may the more value and appreciate the plain, simple, sublime, universally acknowledged truths, which have in all ages been the Light by which Masons have been guided on their way, the wisdom and strength that like imperishable columns have sustained and will continue to sustain its Glorious and Magnificent Temple.

TO CLOSE.

V∴ M∴ Bro∴ J∴ Warden, what is the hour?

J∴ W∴ Ven∴ Master, the Dawn is bright in the East, and the Sun is about to rise.

V∴ M∴ The Dawn of Hope and the Sun of Righteousness!—My Brethren, we may rest from our labours. Bro∴ Examiner, are any poor brethren unrelieved?

Ex∴ None, Ven∴ Master.

V∴ M∴ Bro∴ Lecturer, doth any offence of a Brother remain unreproved, that hath been made known to us?

Lect∴ None, Ven∴ Master.

V∴ M∴ What then, my Brethren, remains to be done?

J∴ W∴ To be patient.

S∴ W∴ To watch.

J∴ W∴ To meditate.

S∴ W∴ To pray.

V∴ M∴ Let us pray then, my Brethren, in silence. [He raps 3: all rise].

[There is a few minutes' silence: and the Ven∴ M∴ says]:

V∴ M∴ Faithful Brethren,—Essenes that have long waited for the Light and the new Law, the Sun is about to rise upon the waters of the Dead Sea. Aid me to close this Preceptory. Together, my Brethren!

[All give the sign: Then the Ven∴ raps?—the S∴ W∴?—the J∴ W∴?—and the Ven∴ ,—. Then the Brothers clap :, with their hands, and all cry Hoscheah!].

V∴ M∴ The Preceptory is closed.

FINIS.

Eighteenth Degree.

Knight, or Sovereign Prince of Rose Croix, of Heredon.

THE CHAPTER, ITS ROOMS, DECORATIONS, ETC.

Bodies in this degree are styled CHAPTERS. There must be four rooms.

The *first* is a mere ordinary reception room, of small size, where the Candidate is first received.

The *second*, in which the ceremonies of reception commence, is hung with black sprinkled with white tears; and paved in Mosaic, of black and white squares. It is lighted by 33 lights, upon 3 candlesticks, each with eleven branches. Each light is to be enclosed in a small tin box, with a hole in the side, not more than an inch in diameter, shaped like a star, through which alone the light shines.

In the East, South and North corners of this Room are three columns, one in each, from 5 feet 8 inches to 6 feet in height. Upon them must appear, in large transparent characters, the following words: on that in the East, FAITH: on that in the South, HOPE: and on that in the North, CHARITY.

In the eastern extremity of the room must be an altar, to which one ascends by three steps. It is covered with a black cloth, strewed with white flames. Above the altar must be a large transparency, on which are painted three very large crosses, on the centre one of which, about midway its length, is the mystic rose, enclosed in a crown of thorns. Upon the altar are two large candles of yellow wax. Two large black curtains conceal the altar, which, parting in the middle, are drawn aside at the proper time during the ceremony of reception.

At the foot of the steps, on the right, should be a small table, covered with a black cloth; and upon it the Holy Bible, square and compasses, a triangle, a black collar and a habit for the candidate.

The Very Wise Master sits in front of this table. The Senior and Junior Wardens are in the West, the former on the North and the latter on the South side. There is no table before them. The Secretary sits in the East, at the foot of the steps on the south side, the lower step serving him for a table. All the other officers and members are seated where they please, indiscriminately around the room; and, as every one, even the Master, is supposed to sit upon the ground, the benches on which they sit must not be more than six inches high.

Upon the altar, between the two lights, is a skull.

The altar, the table and the three columns should all be of a triangular shape.

The *third* chamber represents Hell. All the punishments and tortures described by Dante are seen there, in the midst of fire, painted on a transparency that covers all the walls; besides which there is no light. On each side of the door, on the inside, is a human skeleton, holding an arrow in its right hand.

The *fourth* chamber is hung with crimson, and brilliantly decorated. The three candlesticks with the 33 lights [the boxes removed] are placed there, in the same relative positions, and arranged, as in the second apartment. Under the canopy, in the East, is a serpent forming a circle, with a Crux Ansata in the centre, on which is inscribed in letters of Gold, the Word I∴ N∴ R∴ I∴. In the West, over the Wardens a resplendent Glory, with a blazing star in the centre, and in the star the Hebrew Word . . . . . . יהוה.

The altar should be splendidly decorated, and illuminated with transparent lights, with an open Bible, the Square and Compasses, and a Crux Ansata of Gold upon it.

In front of the Master are two triangular columns, of pure white. On the one upon the right is inscribed in large letters of Gold, the Word INFINITY: and on the one upon the left, IMMORTALITY. In front of the Wardens are two similar columns. On the one upon the right is inscribed REASON: and on that upon the left, NATURE.

In the South is an Organ.

DRESS, ORNAMENTS, AND JEWELS.

In the Second Apartment.

The Knights are all dressed in black, and should wear [though that may be dispensed with], a very short Chasuble of silk stuff, edged all round with black silk or velvet two inches wide. On the breast is a crimson cross, upright, and two inches wide.

The *Cordon* is plain black, at least three inches wide. Upon one side of it a crimson cross, and a crimson rosette at the bottom. It is worn as a collar. Or, if worn across the body, there must be a crimson cross on the breast.

The *Apron* is of black silk or velvet, plain, and with a large crimson cross in the centre.

The *Master* wears a blazing star over his heart, in the centre of which is the letter JOD; and at the five points the letters *F.*, [FAITH], *H.*, [HOPE], *C.*, [CHARITY], *V.*, [VIRTUE], and *T.*, [TRUTH]. The Sen∴ Warden wears the Triangle, and the Jun∴ W∴ the Square and the Compasses, crosswise. All these jewels are covered with crape. The principal jewel of the degree is not worn in this apartment.

All the Knights wear swords.

The Battery of the Degree is £ by [: ,]. The Age ; ; years: The Cry of Acclamation Hoscuean—not to be confounded with *Huzza*.

In the Fourth Apartment.

The *Cordon* is of crimson silk or velvet, worn across the body, and at least three inches wide. There may also be a Collar of ribbon of the same color, at the bottom of which is a black rosette, on which the jewel of the degree reposes. The Apron is of white silk or velvet, with the jewel of the degree painted or embroidered on it. It should be edged with red.

The *Jewel* is a compass, the points resting on a segment of one-fourth of a circle. On the upper part of it is a rose, in bloom. Lower down is a crimson cross, showing on both sides. At the bottom, on one side, an eagle, with his wings extended and head depressed, and on the other a pelican, piercing its breast to feed its young, who are in a nest below it. Between the eagle and pelican springs a branch of Acacia. On the summit of the Compass is an antique crown. On the segment of the circle, on one side, is the Word, and on the other the Pass-word, in the hieroglyphics of the degree.

The Jewel should be of gold. The Pelican, the Eagle, and the Rose of silver.

The Jewels of the Master and Wardens are uncovered.

All the Knights wear Swords and Chapeaux.

Each Brother, at his reception, adopts as his own, some characteristic, the choice of which is left to himself, as *Prudence, Valour,* &c. Those of the three first officers and M.·. of Ceremonies are always the same; *Wisdom, Strength, Beauty,* and *Alarm.* A Kt. Rose ☩, in writing his name should write the *consonants* only, and an *unequal* number, if there are more than two. The date is, from *the Orient of Heroden,* adding the degree of latitude and longitude, or, under the vault of the zenith, &c.

OFFICERS.

The Officers of a Chapter of Knights Rose ☩ are twelve in number; but only the three first are indispensable.

They are *The Very Wise Master,* the *Very Exc.·. Sen.·. and Jun.·. Wardens,* the *Chancellor,* the *Grand Orator,* the *Kt.·. Hospitaller* or *Almoner,* the *Secretary,* styled *Master of Dispatches,* the Treasurer, styled *Comptroller,* the *Standard-bearer,* the *M.·. of Ceremonies,* the *Pursuivant . . . . . .* and the *Guardian of the Temple.*

The Master is in the East; the Wardens in the West; the Chancellor on the right and the Hospitaller on the left of the Master, the Gr.·. Orator in the South; the Pursuivant on the inside, and the Guardian of the Temple on the outside of the door; the Comptroller on the right, in front, and the Master of Dispatches on the left in front of the Master: the Standard-bearer on the right of the Wardens, and the Master of Ceremonies on the left of the Wardens.

TITLES.

The Presiding Officer is styled *Very Wise and Perfect Master:*
The Wardens, *Very Excellent and Perfect:*
The other Officers, *Very Potent and Perfect:*
And the Knights, *Very Worshipful and Perfect.*
In the *Second* apartment, the Word *Perfect* is omitted in all the titles.
The Chapter is opened in the second apartment; and closed in the fourth.

DRAUGHTS, OR TRACING BOARDS.

Of the Second Apartment: . . An oblong square surrounded by triple lines equidistant from each other.

Upon the three lines on each side are the words Wisdom, Strength, Beauty, on the outer, middle and inner lines respectively, and between each the denticulated tassel. Within the lines, the whole Eastern portion represents the Celestial Vault sprinkled with stars, but the sun and moon obscured with clouds. In the extreme East, among the clouds, an eagle hovers. In the centre of the plan is the representation of a mountain, on the summit of which is a cubical stone, and on it a rose, with the letter jod in the centre. Around the mountain, clouds and darkness hang, and further to the West are all the ancient tools and implements of Masonry, with the two columns prostrate, and broken in several pieces.

Of the Fourth Apartment: An oblong square surrounded by four lines, equidistant from each other. On the lines are written Faith, Hope, Charity, Truth. In the body of the plan, the whole East represents the sun and moon shining in a sky that glitters with stars. In the extreme East is seen in the sky a cross surrounded by a glory, and a bright cloud in which appear the heads of seven angels. On the cross a rose in full bloom, and in its centre the letter jod. In the centre of the plan a representation of a mountain, on the summit of which is a blazing star with seven luminous points, and in the centre of that the letter jod. In the body of the draught, in the South, a pelican on her nest, from whose breast flow seven streams of blood, with which she feeds seven young that surround her. In the North an eagle hovering in the air, and on the Western side of the mountain an open tomb. Between the lines on the North are the compasses, the tracing-board, the crow-bar, the trowel and the square : between the lines on the South, the cubical stone, the gavel, the rule and the level ; and between those on the West, the rough ashlar, the stone-hammer, the mallet, the chisel and the plumb-line or perpendicular.

TO OPEN.

The Master is seated on the third step of the altar, his head leaning on his hand. He gives one rap on the little table by his side, which the Wardens repeat ; and says :

V∴ W∴ It is time to commence our labours. Very Excellent Senior and Junior Wardens, request all the Very Worshipful Knights to be pleased to assist me in opening this Sovereign Chapter of Rose Croix.

[Each Warden says, on his side] : " Very Worshipful Brethren and Kts∴, be pleased to assist our Very Wise Master in opening the Chapter. To order, Knights and Brethren !

[The Knights rise and align themselves in two ranks, bareheaded and with swords drawn].

V∴ W∴ Very Excellent Sen∴ and Jun∴ Wardens, are all the brethren in order?

Both : . . They are.

V∴ W∴ Very Excellent Brother Senior Warden, what is your present duty ?

S∴ W∴ To see that the Chapter is well tyled, and whether all the Brethren here present are Knights of the Rose Croix.

V∴ W∴ Very Excellent Brethren Sen∴ and Jun∴ Wardens, assure yourselves of that.

[The Sen∴ W∴ receives the signs, grips, ward and pass-word from the Master of Ceremonies, and then says to him] :

Sen∴ W∴ Very Potent Brother, see whether the Chapter is well tyled.

[The M∴ of Ceremonies goes out to do so, and when he returns, he reports to the Jun∴ W∴ Immediately the two Wardens, each on his side, proceed to receive from each brother the signs, words and grips of the degree, and report to the Master. Then returning to their stations, and the M∴ of Ceremonies having reported the Chapter well tyled, the Jun∴ W∴ gives a rap on the table of the Sen∴ W∴ and says to him] :

Jun∴ W∴ Very Excellent Brother Sen∴ W∴, this Chapter is well tyled.

[The Sen∴ W∴ raps one ; and the Master responding, the Sen∴ W∴ says to him] :

Sen∴ W∴ Very Wise Master, the Chapter is well tyled.

V∴ W∴ Very Excellent Brother Sen∴ W∴, what is the hour?

Sen∴ W∴ The instant when the veil of the Temple was rent asunder ; when darkness overspread the face of the earth ; when the light of the stars was obscured ; when the columns and working tools of Masonry were broken ; when the blazing star disappeared, the cubical stone sweated blood and water, and the Word was lost.

V∴ W∴ Since Masonry is in so exceeding great tribulation, let us employ all our energies, my brethren, in new labours to recover the lost Word ; and to that end let us open our Chapter.

[The Wardens, each at his column, say] :

W∴ W∴ Very Potent and Worshipful Brethren, the Very Wise Master is about to open the Chapter. Be pleased to unite with him in doing so.

[The V∴ Wise strikes £ raps. The Wardens each repeat].

V∴ W∴ Very Ex∴ Sen∴ and Jun∴ Wardens, what is the first duty that we should perform?

W∴ W∴ To respect the decrees and mandates of the Most High ; to pay to Him the profoundest homage, and to humble ourselves unceasingly before Him.

V∴ W∴ Let us perform our duties.

[The V∴ Wise gives the questioning sign : and all the brothers the response. Then they take each his sword in his right hand, and give the sign of the Good Shepherd, so that the sword of each rests on his left arm, point upwards].

V.·. W.·. My brethren, let us bend the knee devoutly to Him who hath given us being!

[Saying this, he rises, and all the knights follow his example. All turn to the East, give the sign, and kneel on one knee. After a moment the V.·. Wise rises, and the others do so likewise. Then all clap their hands *£* times, and say three times, *Hoscheah! Hoscheah! Hoscheah!*].

V.·. W.·. Very Excellent, Potent, and Worshipful Knights, this Chapter is duly opened.

RECEPTION.

A Kt.·. of the E.·. and W.·. who desires this degree must present a petition in the following form.

"*To the Very Wise Master, Wardens and Knights of ——— Chapter of Rose ✠.·.*

Bro.·. A .... B .... , who is a Knight of the East, Prince of Jerusalem, and Kt.·. of the East and West, earnestly desires to receive the degree of Rose Croix in your Sovereign Chapter. If it shall please you to admit him among you, he faithfully promises ever to obey your laws and statutes, to live and demean himself as becomes a Kt.·. of that Ill.·. Degree, and ever to have at heart the interest and good of the order, performing faithfully and diligently whatever service of charity and good works may be required of him.

A .... B .... .''

This petition being received, if the candidate is unanimously elected, a day is appointed on which he shall receive the degree, and he is notified of it.

When the reception commences, the Chapter occupies the second apartment. The candidate should be dressed in black, with the regalia and jewel of a Kt.·. of the East and West, or Gr.·., El.·., Perf.·. and Sub.·. Mason; with a sword by his side, a chapeau on his head, and his eyes uncovered. The Master of Ceremonies finds him in the reception room, which is the first apartment, hung with black, with no furniture but a small table and a chair, and on the table a Bible and several human bones. The light is only from one candle set in a human skull. He is left there alone for some minutes, and then the M.·. of C.·. enters, and says to him:

M.·. Cer.·. My Brother, there are several questions that you must answer sincerely and truly, before I can attempt to introduce you into this Sovereign Chapter of Knights of Rose Croix.

1st. What is your religious belief?

2d. Do you respect the character of every Reformer that has in the different periods of the world's history appeared on earth to teach men virtue and morality?

3d. Do you regard with toleration the religious opinions of other men?

4th. Are you willing to meet in the Masonic Temple, and to recognize as Brothers, all good Masons who believe in one God and the Immortality of the Soul, whether they have received that belief from the teachings of Moses, of Zoroaster, of Bouddha, of Mahomet, or of the founder of the Christian religion?

5th. Do you recognize the fact that all the emblems, forms and ceremonies of Masonry are symbolical of certain great primitive truths, which each one is at liberty to interpret in accordance with his own faith?

6th. Are you willing to unite in ceremonies which those of another faith may regard as peculiarly applicable to the events recorded in their own sacred books, they leaving to you the perfect right to apply the same ceremonies to your own, or to give them a more general or more narrow interpretation as you may choose?

[If these questions are all answered in the affirmative, the M.·. of Ceremonies proceeds. If any one is answered in the negative, he informs the candidate that it is not possible for him to receive this degree, and permits him to retire. If all are answered in the affirmative, he says]:

M.·. Cer.·. My Brother, if such be your views, you may unite with us in a degree in which the Christian sees manifest allusions to a Divine Teacher, perhaps the Deity Himself, or the Son of Deity, that became man and suffered the pains of death to redeem the world; the Follower of the teachings of Moses, to a Messiah yet to come; and others of other creeds, to that Saviour of the world whom all Nations in all ages have expected, in whose supposed advent many Nations have rejoiced, and for whom many still continue to look.

My Brother, all our Temples are demolished, our working tools are broken, and our columns cast down and shattered. Notwithstanding all our precautions, the Sacred Word is again lost. We labour day and night; but in vain: for we know not how to re-discover the Word, nor the means of recognizing each other. Our order is in the greatest consternation, and we have no hope except in the mercy and goodness of Him of whom the whole universe of worlds is but one.Thought. If you are willing to aid us in this emergency, and to assist in recovering the lost Word, you will follow me.

[He then conducts him to the door of the second apartment, and gives the alarm of a Kt∴ Rose Croix. The Sen∴ Warden opens the door and asks, "Who comes here, and what is your desire?"]

M∴ Cer∴ A Mason, Knight of the East and West, long lost, and wandering alone through thick forests and among the mountains; and who, having lost the Word at the destruction of the Temple, with your assistance seeks to recover it.

[The door is then closed: the Jun∴ W∴ questioned by the Sen∴ W∴ makes the same answers as are made at the door: and he reports in the same words to the Very Wise, who inquires]:

V∴ W∴ My Brethren, do you consent that this Knight of the East and West shall be permitted to enter?

·[The Knights all give their assent by stretching forth their right hand: and immediately seat themselves on the floor, as if in gloomy meditation, each with his right hand on his neck, his head bent down, and his left hand covering his face, his elbows resting on his knees].

V∴ W∴ Very Exc∴ Bro∴ Jun∴ Warden, the Brethren consent that the candidate shall be introduced. Receive him, therefore, and place him in the West.

[The Sen∴ Warden goes to the door and receives the candidate, saying to him : "Enter, my Brother, into this place where melancholy and sadness reign and all the brethren are in lamentation." He conducts him to the West, places him, standing, between himself and the Jun∴ Warden, and gives the alarm of a Rose Croix. The Very Wise responds with the same alarm].

Sen∴ W∴ Very Wise Master, a worthy Knight of the East and West presents himself to this Sovereign Chapter, to obtain the favour of admittance to the sublime degree of Rose Croix.

V∴ W∴ Of whom and where was he born?

Sen∴ W∴ Of noble parents, and in the Tribe of Judah.

V∴ W∴ What is his country?

Sen∴ W∴ Judea.

V∴ W∴ What art does he profess?

Sen∴ W∴ Masonry.

V∴ W∴ Worthy Knight, you find us overwhelmed with sorrow: and from the consternation that prevails here you may judge what confusion reigns upon the Earth. All is changed, and the chief support of Masonry is no more. Our work has become corrupted and we find it no longer possible to labour. The Veil of the Temple is rent in twain; [at this moment the curtain is drawn aside from before the altar]; the stars have disappeared, the light of the sun and moon is obscured, and darkness has fallen upon the face of the whole Earth. The Blazing Star is seen no more, the Cubical Stone sweats blood and water, and the Sacred Word is again lost: so that it is not in our power to communicate it to you. Nevertheless we will not remain idle and inactive. We will with all our energies endeavour to recover the Word, that light may shine once more, and Masonry revive. ⁓ Is it your desire to assist us?

Cand∴ It is.

V∴ W∴ Very Potent Master of Ceremonies, inform this Brother of the nature of the task which he is about to undertake.

M∴ Cer∴ My Brother, you are still engaged, as a Mason, in the search for Light and Truth; of which search the many journeys that you have made in the different degrees are symbolical. But your search is not for the truth of any particular creed or religion. That search would be in vain; for what is truth to one man is not truth to another. Not often by argument and evidence, but almost always by the accidents of birth, education and circumstance our religious belief is formed; and argument and testimony strike the mind of man, when aimed at his religious creed and faith, only to glance off and leave no impression. They never penetrate the atmosphere of repulsion that surrounds it, but roll over it, as quicksilver over glass.

"It is the great primitive Truths, revealed by God to the first men, that we seek to find. Mutilated and disfigured, mingled with a thousand errors, misunderstood and perverted only, have they come down to the world at large. Masonry has preserved them, and teaches them under symbols and ceremonies, concerning herself exclusively with the great, leading, cardinal, indispensable truths, which all Masons of whatever creed may admit and receive; and leaving each free to make such further and particular application of her symbols as shall best suit the faith that he professes.

"The object of Masonry was not in any time merely to preserve the true pronunciation of the name of the Deity; in finding which you have been so long, and perhaps unsuccessfully engaged. That, itself, is but a symbol. By what name the Great Creator is called, it is not essential to know. The time has long since passed, when it was believed that the possession of that name conferred peculiar and wondrous powers upon the fortunate men to whom it had been revealed.

"Our symbols and ceremonies envelop the great primitive truths, known to the first men that lived. With whatever *particular* meaning they may have, peculiar or believed to be peculiar to particular creeds, and differing as the faith differs of those who receive them, we have nothing to do.

"The great enigma of all ages to the human mind has been the existence of Sin and Evil. The antagonism of the Good and Evil principles, and the necessity and certainty of the coming, at some time, of a Warrior, a Hero, a Saviour or a Redeemer, who should conquer and destroy the Genius, the Demon, the Giant, the Principle of Evil, has been an article in all creeds, from the earliest ages of the world.

"It is the great problem of human existence,—this, whether any Power of Good has already commenced or will hereafter commence that combat with the Principle and Power of Evil that is ultimately to destroy it;—whether sin and sorrow, and calamity and pain are hereafter to disappear from the universe, and all be thenceforward light and joy and happiness and content;—whether there is another life, in which the power and influence of the Demon of Evil will be unfelt, and where reparation will be made for the sufferings of virtue and the calamities of the good in this life: for it is the great problem whether there be any light; whether there is a Great, Good, Fatherly, Beneficent Deity, who will in his own good time connect together all the thousand links of circumstance into one good and excellent result, and by divine patent and commission arm, if He has not already armed, the Power and Principle of Good with authority to take captive, disarm and slay outright the Power and Principle of Evil.

"We are about to conduct you through certain forms and ceremonies—to display to you certain symbols and emblems. We do not give you in advance their interpretation; but only indicate to you their general tendency. We place the thread in your hands, that will guide you through the labyrinth. It is for you to apply and interpret the symbols and ceremonies of the degree in such manner as may seem to you truest and most appropriate.

"A vast multitude of men believe that the Redeemer, before whom Evil is ultimately to recede and fall prostrate, has already appeared upon the earth. Many believe he was a man, many, the Son of God, and many, the Deity incarnate. A vaster multitude still wait for the Redeemer. Each will apply our symbols and ceremonies according to his faith. But to us as Masons, is it not the most important inquiry, not whether the Redeemer has appeared, but whether, in the combat to be waged, the Principle of Good is ultimately to prevail, the Principle of Evil to be prostrated, and another world to exist, both for those who have died, and for those that are yet to be born, in which sin and shame, and pain and sorrow shall be known no more forever?

"Kneel with us, then, my Brother, and unite with us in imploring the assistance, protection and support of Him to whom we owe our Being; and who alone can make Darkness Light, and bring the tyranny of Evil to an end.

PRAYER.

Great and Dread Being, Father, who wast, when beside Thee there were Time and Space alone; a single Thought of whom shaped itself into an Universe of Suns and Worlds, and infinite myriads upon myriads of living creatures; Eternal as Time, and Infinite as Space; to whom all the PAST and all the FUTURE now IS, and ever will be PRESENT: Thou who dost uphold, sustain and govern the Universe by the law of Harmony that Thou hast made its instinct: and by whom no creature that lives is forgotten or unregarded: look with favour upon us and upon this our Dear Brother! Deign to bless him, to protect him, and to make his labours fortunate! Watch over him that he may do nothing to displease Thee, or that may make him unworthy of the rank in Masonry to which he now aspires! Illuminate his mind with wisdom, that he may understand our symbols; and teach him to trust in Thy beneficence, and the final overthrow of Evil, Wrong and Misery, in Thine own appointed Time! Amen.

V∴ W∴ Very Excellent Jun∴ Warden, cause this Brother to travel for 33 years; and let him learn how to count them in such sense as he may think most consistent with Truth.

[The Junior Warden takes the Candidate by the hand, and causes him slowly to make the Circuit of the Room three times. At each time he kneels before the altar, and inclines his head; and on each Circuit he is made to halt before each of the columns, and is addressed by the Junior W∴ as follows]:

On the 1st Circuit:

Jun∴ W∴ [At the 1st Column]: My Brother, what word do you read upon this Column?

Cand∴ FAITH.

Jun∴ W∴ Faith in God: that He is good and wise and merciful: that He is not a tyrant, but a Father; that under His direction and guidance, all the Universe is one harmonious Whole, governed by one wise and loving law of harmony, to work out a great result; to which, unseen by us, all Sin, all Pain, all Evil, all Wrong, and all Violence tend.

Jun∴ W∴ [At the 2d Column]: My Brother, what word do you read upon this column?

Cand∴ HOPE.

Jun∴ W∴ Hope: in the ultimate fulfilment of human expectation in all ages: Hope in the final victory of a Redeemer, already come or yet to appear, God, Demi-God or Man, representative of the Principle of Good; who shall overthrow the Principle of Evil, and vindicate the Infinite Justice, Truth and Goodness of God.

Jun∴ W∴ [At the 3d Column]: My Brother, what word do you read upon this column?

Cand∴ CHARITY.

Jun∴ W∴ Charity: taught us by Faith and Hope: Charity for those who differ with us in opinion; whether we or they believe that the Redeemer, the Saviour, the Word, the Principle of Light and Good, the Christ or the Messiah, who is to dethrone the Principle of Evil, is yet to appear or has already come upon the earth. Charity for them, and for their faith; and even for their errors: for they have equal right with us, to hold their own opinions true and ours erroneous: since what any man believes, is Truth, to *him:* and none can say with certainty that he hath the same possession of Truth as of a chattel.

Jun∴ W∴ On the 2d Circuit:

[At the 1st Column]: My Brother, what read you still upon this Column?

Cand∴ FAITH.

Jun∴ W∴ Faith in human nature: Confidence in our own kind; in the honesty of men's purposes and intentions; in man's capability for improvement and advancement: the same faith in others that we would have them place in us; and to withhold which from us, we feel to be a wrong.

Jun∴ W∴ [At the 2d column]: My Brother, what read you still upon this column?

Cand∴ HOPE.

Jun∴ W∴ Hope, in the continual advancement towards perfection of the human race: in the ultimate triumph of Masonry, that shall make of all men one family and household: hope in the cessation of war and bloodshed; in the advent of peace and liberty; in the disappearance of error, wrong and crime; and in the final enfranchisement of the human heart and intellect in every clime and country of the world.

Jun∴ W∴ [At the 3d column]: My Brother, what read you still on this column?

Cand∴ CHARITY.

Jun∴ W∴ That charity which relieves the distresses of other men; feeds the hungry, clothes the naked, protects the widow and orphan, nurses the sick, and gives decent sepulture to the dead.

On the 3d Circuit:

Jun∴ W∴ [At the 1st column]: My Brother, what read you still on this column?

Cand∴ FAITH.

Jun∴ W∴ Faith in Ourselves: in our power to do good, and to exert a beneficial influence upon our fellow-men: faith, that if we are but right and true and honest, we can become immortal in our good influences living after us; and strike a hard blow at wrong and ignorance and error:—that noble and modest confidence in ourselves, which is the secret of all success, and the parent of all great and noble actions.

Jun∴ W∴ [At the 2d column]: My Brother, what read you still on this column?

Cand∴ HOPE.

Jun∴ W∴ Hope in a Hereafter; where man, immortal, shall be happy: where we shall see and understand the perfect symmetry, proportion and harmony of all God's works; and comprehend the great mystery of His government of the world.

Jun∴ W∴ [At the 3d column]: My Brother, what read you still on this column?

Cand∴ CHARITY.

Jun∴ W∴ Charity for the faults and shortcomings of our Brethren: that merciful judgment upon the acts of others, that we pass upon our own; believing that they are better than they seem, as we are conscious that we ourselves deserve not the world's harsh judgment: and that love which teaches us to do unto all men that only which we should desire them to do unto us.

[The candidate is then conducted to the East, where the Master says to him, "My Brother, what have you seen and learned on your journey?"]

Jun∴ W∴ The triangular columns, and three virtues, Faith, Hope and Charity.

V∴ W∴ Is it your purpose hereafter to practise these virtues more zealously, and thus become (as thus alone you can become) a true and perfect Mason?

Cand∴ It is.

V∴ W∴ My Brother, the Temple erected to the glory of the Gr∴ Architect of the Universe has been destroyed. The Spirit of Evil has invaded and possessed the fair world which God made fit to be his Temple and Church, its every mountain an altar, and all men and every living thing His worshippers. In the rebuilding of that Temple we and all good Masons are engaged. The columns which you have seen are the bases on which we desire to found it. If you wish to unite with us in this great work, you must first bind yourself to us by a solemn obligation, as we are all bound to each other. Are you willing to do so?

Cand∴ I am.

V∴ W∴ Kneel then at the altar and assume it.

[The candidate kneels at the altar. The Master raps once, and the Brethren all rise. The hands of the candidate are placed upon the Holy Bible, and he takes the following]

OBLIGATION.

I, A . . . . . B . . . . ., do, by the most sacred and solemn form of oath known to me, most solemnly and sincerely swear, never, either directly or indirectly to reveal the mysteries of this Degree of Sovereign Prince of Rose Croix, to any Brother of an Inferior degree, or to any other person in the world, who shall not be justly and lawfully entitled to the same: under the penalty of being forever deprived of the True Word, and remaining perpetually in darkness, my blood running constantly from my body, and I suffering without intermission the most cruel pangs of remorse; the bitterest gall, mingled with vinegar, being my constant drink, the sharpest thorns my pillow, and death upon the cross completing my punishment.

I furthermore promise and swear that I will observe and obey all the rules and laws of this order of Knights of the Rose Croix, and the decrees and mandates that may be transmitted to me by the Sov∴ Inspectors Gen∴ in Sup∴ Council of the 33d Degree in whose jurisdiction I may reside: that I will never reveal the place where I have been received, nor by whom, nor the ceremonies used at my reception, to any person in the world, except to a lawful Knight of the Rose Croix; and that I will never initiate, or assist at the initiation of any person in this degree, except under a lawful patent obtained for that purpose from the proper authority. So help me God, and keep me steadfast to perform and keep this my solemn obligation! Amen!

V∴ W∴ ALL IS ACCOMPLISHED !

[At these words, the Brethren all rise, and resume their former position on the floor, except the Wardens, who continue with the Master and the Candidate. The Master and Wardens divest him of his sword, apron, collar and jewel. Then the Master puts upon him the chassuble, and the black collar and apron, saying to him :]

V∴ W∴ This new habit, symbol of the mingled good and evil in the world and in human nature, reminds us, and must remind you, of the duties we owe and the virtues we are to practise. Its black bordering, also a symbol of darkness, itself a type of Evil and Death, indicates our sorrow at the loss of the True Word, and at the continued dominion of the Principle of Darkness, Evil and Death in this fair world. The black collar and apron are emblems of sorrow and repentance, fit for one who knows his own weakness and frailties, and who laments the sad condition and untoward fate of his fellows.

My Brother, you have undertaken to aid us in our Search for the Sacred Word. Return therefore to the West, and prepare to follow us.

[When the Wardens and Candidate reach the West, the Master says] :

V∴ W∴ Very∴ Exc∴ Wardens, how may we again find the Sacred Word ?

Sen∴ W∴ By travelling three days in darkness.

V∴ W∴ Travel then, my Brethren, from the East to the West, and from the North to the South.

[All arise, and travel in silence seven times around the Chapter; each making, at each circuit, a genuflection before the altar.]

At the 3d Circuit, the V∴ Wise passes into the 4th apartment: at the 4th Circuit, the two Wardens: at the 5th, all the other officers: at the 6th, all the Knights.

At the 7th Circuit, the M∴ of Ceremonies, finding himself alone with the Candidate, approaches the door leading into the 4th apartment, but stops short, and says, "You cannot enter here, my Brother, unless you can give the Sentinel the True Word. Have you found it?

Cand∴ I have not.

[Immediately the door of the 4th apartment, which was partly open, is closed with a loud noise : and the Knights in that apartment proceed to change their dress, &c., and invest themselves in the full regalia and decorations for that apartment].

M∴ Cer∴ My Brother, you must pass through other trials, and humble yourself still more, before you can attain to the True Word. I must deprive you of your insignia as a Mason, and invest you in sackcloth and ashes ; for thus only, by humility and penitence, can fallen and sinful man recover the favour of Deity.

[He takes off his collar, apron and chasuble, and covers him with a black cloth, strewed with tears, or sprinkled with ashes, so that he can see nothing, and says to him] :

M∴ Cer∴ I am now about to conduct you into a place of darkness and gloomy horror. Only by obscure and intricate paths can we arrive there ; but thence and thence alone shall the Word triumphantly emerge at the appointed time, to give glory to Masonry and light and life to the World.

[He then leads him, by roundabout ways, and in silence, to the third apartment, where he restores him to sight, and leads him several times around the room, saying to him] :

M∴ Cer∴ Behold, my Brother, that which to many is the actual representation, and to others but the symbol, of the fate reserved for those who offend against God's laws and mock at His power and justice. Whatever your creed, profoundly reflect upon the lesson it teaches you. The justice of God is certain, and punishment, here or hereafter, is the inevitable result and effect of sin and wrong. In what shape to be inflicted, it is not material to us to know. It is sufficient to be certain that by the inflexible law, crime and error must be followed by pain and sorrow and remorse, the fires that torture the soul; if not by that flame here represented, that tortures the body. Here too are symbolized those passions that make the heart of man a hell;—ambition, avarice, lust, anger, envy, hatred, revenge; against which Masonry wages war. Are you willing to become the soldier of Faith, Hope and Charity, (for such is every true Knight of the Rose Croix), and enlist in this new crusade against the powers of evil, and all the wrongs that vex and afflict humanity?

Cand∴ I am.

M∴ Cer∴ I shall then re-conduct you to the place from whence we came hither, and endeavour to gain admission into the sacred place of light, where what you desire to learn will be made known. Be careful to remember the instruction which I am about to give you, for I can render you no further assistance.

[The M∴ of C∴ then repeats to him the four first questions which he will be asked, and the answers, covers his eyes again with the cloth, leads him back into the second apartment, and gives the alarm of a Kt∴ Rose ✠ at the door of the 4th apartment. The Jun∴ Warden responds with the same, and reports an alarm to the Sen∴ W∴, who reports to the Master:]

V∴ W∴. Bro∴ Sen∴ Warden, send and see who makes the alarm.

[The Sen∴ Warden gives the order to the Jun∴ Warden, who goes to the door, opens it a little, and asks]:

Jun∴ W∴. Who comes here?

M∴ Cer∴. A Bro∴ Knight of the East and West, who, having journeyed through the darkest and most difficult places in search of the True Word, and seen the place of punishment beyond the grave, hopes by the aid of your labour and instruction to gain that ample reward of his exertions and toils.

[The Jun∴ W∴ closes the door, and reports the answer to the Sen∴ W∴, who reports it in the same words to the Master].

V∴ W∴. Let the Knight be admitted and placed in the West.

[The candidate is then introduced, and placed, standing, between the Wardens, still being covered with the cloth].

V∴ W∴. Sir Knight of the East and West, what read you on the column on my right? He is in darkness, Sir Knight M∴ of Cer∴. Let him read with your eyes.

Cand∴. INFINITY. [He is prompted in these answers, by the M∴ of Cer∴.].

V∴ W∴. [Giving the sign, to which all the Knights respond]: THE INFINITY OF GOD! Of His *Power*, His *Wisdom*, His *Knowledge*, His *Justice*, His *Mercy* and His *Love*. To Him be all Honour and Glory forever!

Sen∴ W∴. Sir Knight of the East and West, what read you on the column on my left?

Cand∴. NATURE.

V∴ W∴. NATURE, THE VISIBLE THOUGHT OF GOD! Beneficent Nature, Great Mother of us all; through which we know God, and adore Him in His works: the great book written by Him, in which we may read His Wisdom and Goodness; the Universal Harmony of all that is!

Jun∴ W∴. Sir Knight of the East and West, what read you on the column upon my right?

Cand∴. REASON.

V∴ W∴. REASON! THE SUPREME AND INFINITE INTELLIGENCE OF THE DIVINITY: the WORD by which He created the Universe; the Spirit of God that moved upon the face of the Waters: Reason, breathed by Him into man, and whereby man became a living soul.

—————— Sir Knight of the East and West, what read you on the column on my left?

Cand∴. IMMORTALITY.

V∴ W∴. THE IMMORTALITY OF THE SOUL OF MAN; his lofty destiny and correspondent duties; a firm and settled Faith in which is the Corner Stone of Masonry. ‡⊂‡⊂⊙�, Sir Knight, ♀〰‡𝖄&⊂}⌐⊙⊙⊂{𝖄‡Ⅱ‐⊂{‡𝖄‡⊂‡♀〰♀𝖄♀⊙⌐⌐ of the 𝖄𝖄 ⅃ ‡‡𝖄⫽𝖄 ‡Ⅱ⌐ you have ‡⊂‡⊂⊙𝖄 ⊂Ⅱ.

[He does so].

V∴ W∴. [Giving three raps; at which all the Knights rise and give the sign]: Give thanks to God, my Brethren! The *Word* is recovered. Let our Brother therefore be restored to light.

[The eyes of the Candidate are uncovered. As soon as that is done, all the Brothers give the Rose ✠ battery with their hands, and seven times cry HOSCULAH!].

V∴ W∴. Cry Hosanna in the Highest! Peace on earth, and good-will towards men! The cubical stone is changed into the Mystic Rose; the blazing Star re-appears in all its splendour; the columns of the Temple are replaced, and the working tools of Masonry are restored: the Stars again shine forth; the True Light that lighteth every one that cometh into the world hath dispelled the Darkness; and the New Law begins to rule upon earth!

[The music immediately plays the following anthem, which is sung by all the Knights] . . . . .

Grateful notes and numbers bring,
While the praise of God we sing:
Holy, Holy, Holy Lord!
Be thy glorious name adored!
Chorus: . . . Men on earth, and saints above!
Sing the great Redeemer's love!
Lord! thy mercies never fail!
Hail, Celestial Goodness, hail!

While on earth ordained to stay,
Guide our footsteps in thy way!
Mortals! raise your voices high,
Till they reach the echoing sky!
Chorus: . . . Men on earth, &c.

V∴ W∴ Very Exc∴ Wardens, you will please conduct the Candidate to the East, that he may receive his reward.

[Both Wardens conduct him to the East.]

V∴ W∴ My Brother, from a place of Horror and Darkness, emblematic of the condition of the world under the dominion of the Principle of Evil, you have passed into this Temple, an emblem of what that world shall be, in the day for which men in all ages and every clime have looked and longed; when Typhon, Ahriman, the Serpent, the Principle of Evil shall be overcome and destroyed. That victory is the True Masonic Light, of which we have so many symbols. Hoping that you will hereafter steadily practice those virtues by which alone you can aid in hastening the coming of that day, I shall now proceed to communicate to you the secrets of this Degree.

By the signs, words, and grips you will be enabled to make yourself known, and to know your Brethren.

First Sign: . . . Lift the eyes to Heaven; ♀♒♈☾‡†☉↥☾ at the same time the ♑♀♒♌☾‡♎ of the &☉♒♊♎, ‡☉♀♎☾ them to the ♑☿‡☾&☾☉♊, turn the §☉†♋♎ upwards, and let them ♑☉†† upon the ♏☾††♄.

Answer: . . . Raise the ‡♃&☉♒♊ as high as the ♑☿‡☾&☾☉♊, the ♈&♄♋♏♃☉♒♊♃♑☿♒♌☾‡♎, (except the ♑♀‡♎♈♃♑♀♒♌☾‡), ↥†☿♎☾♊: the meaning of which is, that there is but one God, Sovereign and Eternal.

Sign of Distress: . . . ↥‡☿♎♎ the †☾♌♎, the left ♏☾&♀♒♊. The answer is the same.

Token: . . . ↥‡☿♎♎ the &☉♒♊♎ on the ♏‡☾☉♎♈, left uppermost.

Answer: . . . The same: after which the Brother who demanded the sign, ↥‡☿♎♎☾♎ his &☉♒♊♎ again, and puts the left hand on the ‡♀♌&♈♃♏‡☾☉♎♈ of the other, without ♄♒↥‡☿♎♎♀♒♌ the ☉†♋♎: in which position the pass-word is given.

Pass-Word: . . . ☾♋☉♒♄☾†∴ . . . . . General Word: . . . ‡☾§&-☽♊☿♒∴

Sacred Word: . . . ♀♒‡♀∴

V∴ W∴ Go now, my Brother, and make yourself known to all the Brethren of this Sovereign Chapter: and then return to me.

[He goes round, and whispers the Pass-word to each: and then returning, kneels before the altar. All the Knights place their right hands upon him. The Master invests him with the collar and jewel; and then lays his naked sword upon his head, and says]:

V∴ W∴ By virtue of the power which I have received from this Sovereign Chapter, and by the consent of these Knights, my Brothers and Equals, I do admit, receive and constitute you, to be now and forever Knight, Prince of the Eagle and of the Pelican, Perfect Freemason of Heredon, under the title of Sovereign of Rose Croix: to enjoy all titles and prerogatives of Prince and Perfect Mason, wheresoever in the world there are Masons. Virtue and humility are the foundations of this Degree. Henceforward be you, therefore, virtuous, modest and unpresuming; and so live that you may not disgrace or dishonour the name that you have earned, and the jewel that you are now entitled to wear.

The Sovereign Master then raises the Candidate, and gives him the grip; which is, each ⚷♑ ♈♎ his ‡⚳♌&♈⚷&⊙♒□ on the other's ‡⚳♌&♈⚷♎&♉♑ †□☾‡, and his † on the other's †⚷♎&♉♑ †□☾‡; and in that position one ¶♀♎♎☾♎ the other's ♑♀‡☾&☾⊙□, and says ☾♎⊙♒♑ ☾†∴ and the other says ⚷⊙♉‡✱☿♏♀♎∴

The Acolyte is then placed in the South, and the following lecture is read to him:

LECTURE.

My Brother, each of us makes such application to his own faith and creed, of the symbols and ceremonies of this degree, as seems to him proper. With these special interpretations we have here nothing to do. Like the legend of our Grand Master Hiram, in which some see figured the condemnation and sufferings of Christ; others those of the unfortunate Grand Master of the Templars; others those of the first Charles, King of England; and others still the annual descent of the Sun at the winter Solstice to the regions of darkness, the basis of many an ancient legend; so the ceremonies of this degree receive different explanations; each interpreting them for himself, and being offended at the interpretation of no other.

In no other way could Masonry possess its character of Universality: that character which has ever been peculiar to it from its origin; and which enabled two Kings, worshippers of different Deities, to sit together as Grand Masters, while the walls of the first temple arose; and the men of Gebal, bowing down to the Phœnician Gods, to work by the side of the Hebrews to whom those Gods were abomination; and sit with them in the same Lodge as brethren.

You have already learned that these ceremonies have one general significance, to every one, of every faith, who believes in God, and the soul's immortality.

The primitive men met in no Temples made with human hands. "God," said Stephen, the first Martyr, "dwelleth not in Temples made with hands." In the open air, under the overarching mysterious sky, in the great World-Temple, they uttered their vows and thanksgivings, and adored the God of Light; of that Light that was to them the type of Good, as darkness was the type of Evil.

All antiquity solved the enigma of the existence of Evil, by supposing the existence of a Principle of Evil, of Demons, fallen Angels, an Ahriman, a Typhon, a Siva, a Lok or a Satan, that, first falling themselves, and plunged in misery and darkness, tempted man to his fall, and brought sin into the world. All believed in a future life, to be attained by purification and trials: in a State or Successive States of reward and punishment; and in a Mediator or Redeemer, by whom the Evil Principle was to be overcome, and the Supreme Deity reconciled to his creatures. The belief was general, that he was to be born of a Virgin, and suffer a painful death. The Indians called him Chrishna; the Chinese, Kioun-tse; the Persians, Sosiosch; the Chaldeans, Dhouvanai; the Egyptians, Horus; Plato, Love; and the Scandinavians, Balder.

Chrishna, the Hindoo Redeemer, was cradled and educated among Shepherds. A Tyrant, at the time of his birth, ordered all the male children to be slain. He performed miracles, say his legends, even raising the dead. He washed the feet of the Brahmins, and was meek and lowly of spirit. He was born of a Virgin;

descended to Hell, rose again, ascended to Heaven, charged his disciples to teach his doctrines, and gave them the gift of miracles.

The first Masonic Legislator whose memory is preserved to us by history, was Bouddha, who, about a thousand years before the Christian era, reformed the religion of Manous. He called to the Priesthood all men, without distinction of caste, who felt themselves inspired by God to instruct men. Those who so associated themselves formed a Society of Prophets under the name of Samaneans. They recognized the existence of a single uncreated God, in whose bosom everything grows, is developed and transformed. The worship of this God reposed upon the obedience of all the beings he created. His feasts were those of the Solstices. The doctrines of Bouddha pervaded India, China, and Japan. The Priests of Brahma, professing a dark and bloody creed, brutalized by Superstition, united together against Bouddhism, and with the aid of Despotism, exterminated its followers. But their blood fertilized the new doctrine which produced a new Society under the name of Gymnosophists : and a large number, fleeing to Ireland, planted their doctrines there, and there erected the round towers, which were their temples, and some of which still stand, solid and unshaken as at first, visible monuments of the remotest ages.

The Phœnician Cosmogony, like all others in Asia, was the Word of God, written in astral characters, by the planetary Divinities, and communicated by the Demi-gods, as a profound mystery, to the brighter intelligences of Humanity, to be propagated by them among men. Their doctrines resembled the Ancient Sabeism, and being the faith of Hiram the King and his namesake the Artist, are of interest to all Masons. With them, the First Principle was half material, half spiritual, a dark air, animated and impregnated by the spirit ; and a disordered chaos, covered with thick darkness. From this came the WORD, and thence creation and generation ; and thence a race of men, children of light, who adored Heaven and its Stars as the Supreme Being ; and whose different Gods were but incarnations of the Sun, the Moon, the Stars and the Ether. *Chrysor* was the great igneous power of Nature, and *Baal* and *Melkarth* representations of the Sun.

Man had fallen, but not by the tempting of the serpent. For, with the Phœnicians, the Serpent was deemed to partake of the Divine Nature, and was sacred, as he was in Egypt. He was deemed to be immortal, unless slain by violence, becoming young again in his old age, by entering into and consuming himself. Hence the Serpent in a circle, holding his tail in his mouth, was an emblem of Eternity. With the head of a hawk he was of a Divine Nature, and a symbol of the sun. Hence one Sect of the Gnostics took him for their good genius, and hence the brazen serpent reared by Moses in the Desert, on which the Israelites looked and lived.

" Before the chaos, that preceded the birth of Heaven and Earth," said the Chinese Lao-Tseu, " a single Being existed, immense and silent, immutable and always acting ; the mother of the universe. I know not the name of that Being, but I designate it by the word Reason. Man has his model in the earth, the earth in Heaven, heaven in Reason, and Reason in itself."

" I am," says Isis, " Nature ; parent of all things, the sovereign of the Elements, the primitive progeny of Time, the most exalted of the Deities, the first of the Heavenly Gods and Goddesses, the Queen of the Shades, the uniform countenance ; who dispose with my rod the numerous lights of Heaven, the salubrious breezes of the sea, and the mournful silence of the dead ; whose single Divinity the whole world venerates in many forms, with various rites and by many names. The Egyptians, skilled in ancient lore, worship me with proper ceremonies, and call me by my true name, Isis the Queen."

The Hindu Vedas thus define the Deity :

" He who surpasses speech, and through whose power speech is expressed, know thou that He is Brahma ; and not these perishable things that man adores.

" He whom Intelligence cannot comprehend, and He alone, say the sages, through whose Power the nature of Intelligence can be understood, know thou that He is Brahma ; and not these perishable things that man adores.

" He who cannot be seen by the organ of sight, and through whose power the organ of seeing sees, know thou that He is Brahma ; and not these perishable things that man adores.

" He who cannot be heard by the organ of hearing, and through whose power the organ of hearing hears, know thou that He is Brahma ; and not these perishable things that man adores.

"He who cannot be perceived by the organ of smelling, and through whose power the organ of smelling smells, know thou that He is Brahma; and not these perishable things that man adores."

"When God resolved to create the human race," said *Arius*, "He made a Being that He called The WORD, The Son, *Wisdom*, to the end that this Being might give existence to men." This WORD is the *Ormuzd* of Zoroaster, the *Ensoph* of the Kabbala, the Νοῦς of Plato and Philo, the *Wisdom* or *Demiourgos* of the Gnostics.

That is the True Word, the knowledge of which our ancient brethren sought as the priceless reward of their labours on the Holy Temple: the Word of Life, the Divine Reason, in whom was Life, and that Life the Light of men; which long shone in darkness, and the darkness comprehended it not; the Infinite Reason that is the Soul of Nature, immortal, of which the Word of this degree reminds us; and to believe wherein and revere it is the peculiar duty of every Mason.

"In the beginning," says the extract from some older work, with which John commences his Gospel, "was the Word, and the Word was with God, and the Word was God. All things were made by Him, and without Him was not anything made that was made. In Him was Life, and the life was the Light of man; and the light shineth in darkness, and the darkness did not contain it."

It is an old tradition that this passage was from an older work. And Philostorgius and Nicephorus state, that when the Emperor Julian undertook to rebuild the Temple, a stone was taken up, that covered the mouth of a deep square cave, into which one of the labourers being let down by a rope, he found in the centre of the floor a cubical pillar, on which lay a roll or book, wrapped in a fine linen cloth, in which, in capital letters, was the foregoing passage.

However this may have been, it is plain that John's Gospel is a polemic against the Gnostics; and, stating at the outset the current doctrine in regard to the creation by the Word, he then addresses himself to show and urge that this Word was Jesus Christ.

And the first sentence, fully rendered into our language, would read thus: When the process of emanation, of creation or evolution of existences inferior to the Supreme God began, the Word came into existence and was: and this Word was [προς τον Θεον] *near to* God; i. e. the immediate or first emanation from God: and it was God Himself, developed or manifested in that particular mode, and in action. And by that Word everything that is was created. And thus Tertullian says that God made the World out of nothing, by means of His Word, Wisdom or Power.

To Philo the Jew, as to the Gnostics, the Supreme Being was the *Primitive Light*, or *Archetype of Light, Source* whence the rays emanate that illuminate Souls. He is the Soul of the World, and as such acts everywhere. He himself fills and bounds his whole existence, and his forces fill and penetrate everything. His Image is the WORD [Logos], a form more brilliant than fire, which is not pure light. This WORD dwells in God; for it is within His Intelligence that the Supreme Being frames for Himself the Types of Ideas of all that is to assume reality in the Universe. The WORD is the Vehicle by which God acts on the Universe, the World of Ideas, by means whereof God has created visible things, the more Ancient God, as compared with the Material World, Chief and General Representative of all Intelligences, the Archangel, type and representative of all spirits, even those of Mortals, the type of Man, the primitive man himself. These ideas are borrowed from Plato. And this WORD is not only the Creator, [*by Him was everything made that was made*], but acts in the place of God; and through him act all the Powers and Attributes of God. And also, as first representative of the human race, he is the protector of Men and their Shepherd.

The actual condition of Man is not his primitive condition, that in which he was the image of the Word. His unruly passions have caused him to fall from his original lofty estate. But he may rise again, by following the teachings of Heavenly Wisdom, and the Angels whom God commissions to aid him in escaping from the entanglements of the body, and by fighting bravely against Evil, the existence of which God has allowed solely to furnish him with the means of exercising his free will.

The Supreme Being of the Egyptians was *Amun*, a secret and concealed God, the Unknown Father of the Gnostics, the Source of Divine Life, and of all force, the Plenitude of all, comprehending all things in Himself, the original Light. He *creates* nothing; but everything *emanates* from Him: and all other Gods are but his Manifestations. From Him, by the utterance of a Word, emanated *Neith*, the Divine Mother of all things, the Primitive Thought, the Force that puts everything in movement, the Spirit everywhere extended, *the Deity of Light and Mother of the Sun.*

Of this Supreme Being, *Osiris* was the image, Source of all Good in the moral and physical world, and constant foe of Typhon, the Genius of Evil, the Satan of Gnosticism, brute matter, deemed to be always at feud with the spirit that flowed from the Deity: and over whom Horus, the Redeemer, Son of Isis and Osiris, is finally to prevail.

In the Zend-Avesta of the Persians, the Supreme Being is *Time without limit,* Zeruane Akherene.—No origin could be assigned to Him; for He was enveloped in His own Glory, and His Nature and Attributes were so inaccessible to human Intelligence, that He was but the object of a silent veneration. The commencement of Creation was by emanation from Him. The first emanation was the Primitive Light, and from this Light emerged *Ormuzd*, the *King of Light*, who, by the Word, created the World in its purity, is its Preserver and Judge, a Holy and Sacred Being, Intelligence and Knowledge, Himself Time without limit, and wielding all the powers of the Supreme Being.

In this Persian faith, as taught many centuries before our era, and embodied in the Zend-Avesta, there was in man a pure Principle, proceeding from the Supreme Being, produced by the Will and Word of Ormuzd. To that was united an impure principle, proceeding from a foreign influence, that of Ahriman, the Dragon, or principle of Evil. Tempted by Ahriman, the first man and woman had fallen; and for twelve thousand years there was to be war between *Ormuzd* and the Good Spirits created by him, and *Ahriman* and the Evil Ones whom he had called into existence.

But pure Souls are assisted by the Good Spirits, the triumph of the Good Principle is determined upon in the decrees of the Supreme Being, and the period of that triumph will infallibly arrive. At the moment when the earth shall be most afflicted with the evils brought upon it by the Spirits of perdition, three Prophets will appear to bring assistance to mortals. Sosiosch, Chief of the Three, will regenerate the world, and restore to it its primitive Beauty, Strength and Purity. He will judge the good and the wicked. After the universal resurrection of the Good, the pure Spirits will conduct them to an abode of eternal happiness. Ahriman, his evil Demons, and all the world, will be purified in a torrent of liquid burning metal. The Law of Ormuzd will rule everywhere: all men will be happy: all, enjoying an unalterable bliss, will unite with Sosiosch in singing the praises of the Supreme Being.

These doctrines, with some modifications, were adopted by the Kabbalists and afterwards by the Gnostics.

Apollonius of Tyana says: "We shall render the most appropriate worship to the Deity, when to that God whom we call the First, who is One, and separate from all, and after whom we recognize the others, we present no offerings whatever, kindle to Him no fire, dedicate to Him no sensible thing; for he needs nothing, even of all that natures more exalted than ours could give. The earth produces no plant, the air nourishes no animal, there is in short nothing, which would not be impure in his sight. In addressing ourselves to Him, we must use only the higher word, that, I mean, which is not expressed by the mouth,—the silent inner word of the spirit. . . . From the most Glorious of all Beings, we must seek for blessings, by that which is most glorious in ourselves; and that is the spirit, which needs no organ."

Strabo says: "This one Supreme Essence is that which embraces us all, the water and the land, that which we call the Heavens, the World, the Nature of things. This Highest Being should be worshipped, without any visible image, in sacred groves. In such retreats the devout should lay themselves down to sleep, and expect signs from God in dreams."

Aristotle says: "It has been handed down in a mythical form, from the earliest times to posterity, that there are Gods, and that The Divine compasses entire nature. All besides this has been added, after the mythical style, for the purpose of persuading the multitude, and for the interest of the laws and the advantage of the State. Thus men have given to the Gods human forms, and have even represented them under the figure of other beings, in the train of which fictions followed many more of the same sort. But if, from all this, we separate the original principle, and consider it alone, namely, that the first Essences are Gods, we shall find that this has been divinely said; and since it is probable that philosophy and the arts have been several times, so far as that is possible, found and lost, such doctrines may have been preserved to our times as the remains of ancient wisdom."

Porphyry says : " By images addressed to sense, the ancients represented God and his powers—by the visible they typified the invisible for those who had learned to read, in these types, as in a book, a treatise on the Gods. We need not wonder if the ignorant consider the images to be nothing more than wood or stone ; for just so, they who are ignorant of writing see nothing in monuments but stone, nothing in tablets but wood, and in books but a tissue of papyrus."

Apollonius of Tyana held, that birth and death are only in appearance : that which separates itself from the *one* substance, (the *one* Divine essence), and is caught up by matter, seems to be born ; that, again, which releases itself from the bonds of matter, and is reunited with the one Divine Essence, seems to die. There is, at most, an alternation between becoming visible and becoming invisible. In all there is, properly speaking, but the one essence, which alone acts and suffers, by becoming all things to all ; the Eternal God, whom men wrong, when they deprive him of what properly can be attributed to him only, and transfer it to other names and persons.

The New Platonists substituted the idea of the Absolute, for the Supreme Essence itself ;—as the first, simplest principle, anterior to all existence ; of which nothing determinate can be predicated ; to which no consciousness, no self-contemplation can be ascribed ; inasmuch as to do so, would immediately imply a quality, a distinction of subject and object. This Supreme Entity can be known only by an intellectual intuition of the Spirit, transcending itself, and emancipating itself from its own limits.

This mere logical tendency, by means of which men thought to arrive at the conception of such an absolute, the ὄν, was united with a certain mysticism, which, by a transcendent state of feeling, communicated, as it were, to this abstraction what the mind would receive as a reality. The absorption of the Spirit into that superexistence (τὸ ἐπέκεινα τῆς οὐσίας), so as to be entirely identified with it, or such a revelation of the latter to the spirit raised above itself, was regarded as the highest end which the spiritual life could reach.

The New Platonists' idea of God, was that of One Simple Original Essence, exalted above all plurality and all becoming : the only true Being ; unchangeable, eternal [Εἷς ὢν ἐν τῷ νῦν τὸ ἀεὶ πεπλήρωκε καὶ μόνον ἔστι τὸ κατὰ τοῦτον ὄντως ὤν] : from whom all Existence in its several gradations has emanated—the world of Gods, as nearest akin to Himself, being first, and at the head, of all. In these Gods, that perfection, which in the Supreme Essence was enclosed and unevolved, is expanded and becomes knowable. They serve to exhibit in different forms the image of that Supreme Essence, to which no soul can rise, except by the loftiest flight of contemplation ; and after it has rid itself from all that pertains to sense—from all manifoldness. They are the mediators between man (amazed and stupefied by manifoldness), and the Supreme Unity.

Philo says : " He who disbelieves the miraculous, simply as the miraculous, neither knows God, nor has he ever sought after Him ; for otherwise he would have understood, by looking at that truly great and awe-inspiring sight, the miracle of the universe, that these miracles (in God's providential guidance of his people) are but child's play for the Divine Power. But the truly miraculous has become despised through familiarity. The universal, on the contrary, although in itself insignificant, yet, through our love of novelty, transports us with amazement."

In opposition to the anthropopathism of the Jewish Scriptures, the Alexandrian Jews endeavoured to purify the idea of God from all admixture of the Human. By the exclusion of every human passion, the idea of God was sublimated to a something devoid of all attributes, and wholly transcendental ; and the mere Being [ὄν], the Good, in and by itself, the Absolute of Platonism, was substituted for the personal Deity [יהוה] of the Old Testament. By soaring upward, beyond all created existence, the mind, disengaging itself from the Sensible, attains to the intellectual intuition of this Absolute Being ; of whom, however, it can predicate nothing but existence, and sets aside all other determinations as not answering to the exalted nature of the Supreme Essence.

Thus Philo makes a distinction between those who are in the proper sense Sons of God, having by means of contemplation raised themselves to the highest Being, or attained to a knowledge of Him, in His immediate self-manifestation, and those who know God only in his mediate revelation through his operation—such as He declares Himself in creation—in the revelation still veiled in the letter of Scripture—

those, in short, who attach themselves simply to the Logos, and consider this to be the Supreme God; who are the sons of the Logos, rather than of the True Being, (ὅν).

"God," says Pythagoras, "is neither the object of sense, nor subject to passion, but invisible, only intelligible, and supremely intelligent. In his body he is like the *light*, and in his soul he resembles truth. He is the universal *spirit* that pervades and diffuseth itself over all nature. All beings receive their *life* from him. There is but one only God, who is not, as some are apt to imagine, seated above the world, beyond the orb of the universe; but being himself all in all, he sees all the beings that fill his immensity; the only Principle, the *Light* of Heaven, the Father of all. He *produces everything*; He orders and disposes everything; He is the REASON, the LIFE, and the MOTION of all being."

"I am the LIGHT of the world; he that followeth me shall not walk in DARKNESS, but shall have the LIGHT of LIFE." So said the Founder of the Christian Religion, as his words are reported by John the Apostle.

God, say the sacred writings of the Jews, appeared to Moses in a FLAME of FIRE, in the midst of a bush, which was not consumed. He descended upon Mount Sinai, as the smoke of a *furnace*: He went before the children of Israel, by day, in a pillar of cloud, and, by night, in a pillar of *fire*, to give them *light*. "Call you on the name of *your* Gods," said Elijah the Prophet to the Priests of Baal, "and I will call upon the name of ADONAI; and the God that answereth *by fire*, let him be God."

According to the Kabbala, as according to the doctrines of Zoroaster, everything that exists has emanated from a source of infinite light. Before all things, existed the *Primitive Being*, THE ANCIENT OF DAYS, *the Ancient King of Light*; a title the more remarkable, because it is frequently given to the Creator in the Zend-Avesta, and in the Code of the Sabeans, and occurs in the Jewish Scriptures. To this idea the Kabbala united the pantheism of India. *The King of Light*, THE ANCIENT, is everything that *is*. He is not only the real cause of existences: He is infinite [Ensoph]. He is HIMSELF: [I AM THAT WHICH I AM]: there is nothing in Him that can be called *Thou*. He cannot be known. He is a closed eye: *the unknown* FATHER. And his different names represent his attributes. The Kabbalists termed his *wisdom*, JEH; his *providence*, JEHOVAH; his *magnificence*, EL; his *severity*, ELOHIM; his *victory* and *glory*, ZABAOTH; and his *dominion*, ADONAI: and another of his attributes was LIGHT, [OUR], from the Hebrew word אור. The world was His Revelation, God revealed, and subsisted only in Him. His attributes were there reproduced with various modifications and in different degrees; so that the universe was his Holy Splendour, his Mantle. He was to be adored in silence; and perfection consisted in a nearer approach to Him.

Before the creation of worlds, the PRIMITIVE LIGHT filled all space, so that there was no void. When the Supreme Being, existing in this Light, resolved to display his perfections, or manifest them in worlds, he withdrew within Himself, formed around him a void space, and shot forth his first emanation, a ray of light; the cause and principle of everything that exists, uniting both the generative and conceptive power, which penetrates everything, and without which nothing could subsist for an instant. Represented by the two first letters of the word I. II. U. II., from it emanated the firstborn of God, the Archetype of the Persians and Platonists, the universal form from which all existences are evolved; the Creative Agent, Preserver and Animating Principle of the world; the Light of Light; possessed of the three Primitive Forces of Divinity, Light, Spirit and Life; the Φῶς, Πνευμα and Ζωή of the Gnostics.

Man fell, seduced by the Evil Spirits most remote from the Great King of Light, those of the fourth world of spirits, Asiah, whose chief was Belial. They wage incessant war against the pure Intelligences of the other worlds, who, like the Amshaspands, Izeds and Ferouers of the Persians are the tutelary guardians of man. In the beginning, all was unison and harmony; full of the same divine light and perfect purity. The Seven Kings of Evil fell, and the Universe was troubled. Then the Creator took from the Seven Kings the principles of Good and of Light, and divided them among the four worlds of Spirits, giving to the three first the Pure Intelligences, united in love and harmony, while to the fourth were vouchsafed only some feeble glimmerings of light.

When the strife between these and the good angels shall have continued the appointed time, and these Spirits enveloped in darkness shall long and in vain have endeavoured to absorb the Divine light and life, then will the Eternal Himself come to correct them. He will deliver them from the gross envelopes of matter that hold them captive, will re-animate and strengthen the ray of light or spiritual nature which they have preserved, and re-establish throughout the Universe that primitive Harmony which was its bliss.

Marcion, the Gnostic, said, "The Soul of the True Christian, adopted as a child by the Supreme Being, to whom it has long been a stranger, receives from Him the Spirit and Divine Life. It is led and confirmed, by this gift, in a pure and holy life, like that of God; and if it so completes its earthly career, in charity, chastity, and sanctity, it will one day be disengaged from its material envelope, as the ripe grain is detached from the straw, and as the young bird escapes from its shell. Like the angels, it will share in the bliss of the Good and Perfect Father, re-clothed in an aerial body or organ, and made like unto the Angels in Heaven."

You see, my Brother, what is the meaning of Masonic Light. You see why the East of the Lodge, where the initial letter of the Name of the Deity overhangs the Master, is the place of Light. Light, as contradistinguished from darkness, is Good, as contradistinguished from Evil: and it is that Light, the true knowledge of Deity, the Eternal Good, for which Masons in all ages have sought. Still Masonry marches steadily onward towards that Light that shines in the great distance, the Light of that day when Evil, overcome and vanquished, shall fade away and disappear forever, and Life and Light be the one law of the Universe, and its eternal Harmony.

The degree of Rose ☩ teaches but three things;—the unity, immutability and goodness of God; the immortality of the Soul; and the ultimate defeat and extinction of evil and wrong and sorrow, by a Redeemer or Messiah, yet to come, if he has not already appeared.

It replaces the three pillars of the old Temple, with three that have been already explained to you,—Faith [in God, mankind, and man's self]; Hope, [in the victory over evil, the advancement of Humanity, and in a hereafter], and Charity [relieving the wants, and tolerant of the errors and faults of others]. To be trustful, to be hopeful, to be indulgent; these, in an age of selfishness, of ill opinion of human nature, of harsh and bitter judgment, are the most important Masonic Virtues, and the true supports of every Masonic Temple. And they are the old pillars of the Temple under different names. For he only is wise who judges others charitably; he only is strong who is hopeful; and there is no beauty like a firm faith in God, our fellows and ourself.

The second apartment, clothed in mourning, the columns of the Temple shattered and prostrate, and the brethren bowed down in the deepest dejection, represent the world under the tyranny of the Principle of Evil; where virtue is persecuted and vice rewarded; where the righteous starve for bread, and the wicked live sumptuously and dress in purple and fine linen; where insolent ignorance rules, and learning and genius serve; where King and Priest trample on liberty and the rights of conscience; where Freedom hides in caves and mountains, and sycophancy and servility fawn and thrive; where the cry of the widow and the orphan starving for want of food, and shivering with keen cold, ever climbs up to heaven from a million miserable hovels; where men, willing to labour, and starving, they and their children and the wives of their bosom, beg plaintively for work, when the pampered capitalist stops his mills; where the law punishes her who starving steals a loaf, and lets the seducer go free; where the success of a party justifies murder, and violence and rapine go unpunished; and he who with many years' cheating and grinding the faces of the poor grows rich, receives office and honour in life, and after death brave funeral and a splendid mausoleum;—this world, where, since its making, war has never ceased, nor man paused in the sad task of torturing and murdering his brother; and of which ambition, avarice, envy, hatred, lust, and the rest of Abriman's and Typhon's army make a Pandemonium: this world, sunk in sin, reeking with baseness, clamorous with sorrow and misery. If any see in it also a type of the sorrow of the Craft for the death of Hiram, the grief of the Jews at the fall of Jerusalem, the misery of the Templars at the ruin of their order and the death of De Molay, or the world's agony and pangs of wo at the death of the Redeemer, it is the right of each to do so.

The third apartment represents the consequences of sin and vice, and the hell made of the human heart by its fiery passions. If any see in it also a type of the Hades of the Greeks, the Gehenna of the Hebrews, the Tartarus of the Romans or the Hell of the Christians, or only of the agonies of remorse and the tortures of an upbraiding conscience, it is the right of each to do so.

The fourth apartment represents the universe, freed from the insolent dominion and tyranny of the Principle of Evil, and brilliant with the true Light that flows from the Supreme Deity; when sin and wrong, and pain and sorrow, remorse and misery shall be no more forever; when the great plans of Infinite Eternal Wisdom shall be fully developed; and all God's creatures, seeing that all apparent evil and individual suffering and wrong were but the drops that went to swell the great river of infinite goodness, shall know that vast as is the power of Deity, his goodness and beneficence are infinite as his power. If any see in it a type of the peculiar mysteries of any faith or creed, or an allusion to any past occurrence, it is their right to do so. Let each apply its symbols as he pleases. To all of us they typify the universal rule of Masonry,—of its three chief virtues, Faith, Hope and Charity, of brotherly love and universal benevolence. We labour here to no other end. These symbols need no other interpretation.

The obligations of our Ancient Brethren of the Rose ⚲ were, to fulfil all the duties of friendship, cheerfulness, charity, peace, liberality, temperance and chastity: and scrupulously to avoid impurity, haughtiness, hatred, anger, and every other kind of vice. They took their philosophy from the old Theology of the Egyptians, as Moses and Solomon had done, and borrowed its hieroglyphics and the cyphers of the Hebrews. Their principal rules were, to exercise the profession of medicine charitably and without fee, to advance the cause of virtue, enlarge the sciences, and induce men to live as in the primitive times of the world.

When this degree had its origin, it is not important to inquire; nor with what different rites it has been practised in different countries and at various times. Even to-day its ceremonies differ with the degrees of latitude and longitude, and it receives variant interpretations. If we were to examine all the different ceremonials, their emblems, and their formulas, we should see that all that belongs to the primitive and essential elements of the order, is respected in every sanctuary. All alike practise virtue, that it may produce fruit. All labour, like us, for the extirpation of vice, the purification of man, the development of the arts and sciences, and the relief of humanity.

None admit an adept to their lofty philosophical knowledge, and mysterious sciences, until he has been purified at the altar of the symbolic degrees. Of what importance are differences of opinion as to the age and genealogy of the degree, or variances in the practice, ceremonial and liturgy, or the shade of colour of the banner under which each tribe of Israel marched, if all revere the Holy Arch of the symbolic degrees, first and unalterable source of Free-Masonry; if all revere our conservative principles, and are with us in the great purposes of our organization?

If, anywhere, brethren of a particular religious belief have been excluded from this degree, it merely shows how gravely the purposes and plan of Masonry may be misunderstood. For whenever the door of any degree is closed against him who believes in one God and the soul's immortality, on account of the other tenets of his faith, that degree is Masonry no longer. No Mason has the right to interpret the symbols of this degree for another, or to refuse him its mysteries, if he will not take them with the explanation and commentary superadded.

Listen, my Brother, to our explanation of the symbols of the degree, and then give them such further interpretation as you think fit.

The Cross has been a sacred symbol from the earliest Antiquity. It is found upon all the enduring monuments of the world, in Egypt, in Assyria, in Hindostan, in Persia, and on the Bouddhist towers of Ireland. Bouddha was said to have died upon it. The Druids cut an oak into its shape and held it sacred, and built their temples in that form. Pointing to the four quarters of the world, it was the symbol of universal nature. It was on a cruciform tree that Chrishna was said to have expired, pierced with arrows. It was revered in Mexico.

But its peculiar meaning in this degree, is that given to it by the Ancient Egyptians. Thoth or Phtha is represented on the oldest monuments carrying in his hand the Crux Ansata, or Ankh, [a Tau cross, with a ring or circle over it]. He is so seen on the double tablet of Shufu, and Noh Shufu, builders of the greatest of the Pyramids, at Wady Meghara, in the peninsula of Sinai. It was the hieroglyphic for life, and with a triangle prefixed meant life-giving. To us therefore it is a symbol of Life—of that life that emanated from the Deity, and of that Eternal Life for which we all hope, through our faith in God's infinite goodness.

The Rose was anciently sacred to Aurora and the Sun. It is a symbol of Dawn, of the resurrection of Light and the renewal of life, and therefore of the dawn of the first day, and more particularly of the resurrection: and the Cross and Rose together are therefore hieroglyphically to be read, *the Dawn of Eternal Life* which all Nations have hoped for by the advent of a Redeemer.

The *Pelican* feeding her young is an emblem of the large and bountiful beneficence of Nature, of the Redeemer of fallen man, and of that humanity and charity that ought to distinguish a Knight of this degree.

The *Eagle* was the living Symbol of the Egyptian God *Mendes* or *Menthra*, whom *Sesostris-Ramses* made one with *Amun-Re*, the God of Thebes and Upper Egypt, and the representative of the Sun, the word RE meaning *Sun* or *King*.

The *Compasses* surmounted with a *crown* signify that notwithstanding the high rank attained in Masonry by a Knight of the Rose Croix, equity and impartiality are invariably to govern his conduct.

To the word INRI, inscribed on the Crux Ansata over the Master's Seat, many meanings have been assigned. The Christian Initiate reverentially sees in it the initials of the inscription upon the cross on which Christ suffered—*Jesus Nazarenus Rex Judæorum*. The sages of Antiquity connected it with one of the greatest secrets of Nature, that of universal regeneration. They interpreted it thus, *Igne Natura renovatur integra;* [entire nature is renovated by fire]: The Alchemical or Hermetic Masons framed for it this aphorism, *Igne nitrum roris invenitur.* And the Jesuits are charged with having applied to it this odious axiom, *Justum necare reges impios.* The four letters are the initials of the Hebrew words that represent the four elements—*Iammim*, the seas or water; *Nour*, fire; *Rouach*, the air, and *Iebeschah*, the dry earth.

To us it has this general meaning: In the hieroglyphic language of Egypt, the *Crux Ansata* meant *life*, and it formed part of the character that represented the word ENH—*living*. RE, was the *Sun*, or *King*: and ENH-RE, the *living King* or GOD OF LIGHT. Thus it represents to us the Eternal Deity, who is LIFE and LIGHT; and unites the two great Symbols, the Cross, and the Circle with a Point in the centre—ETERNAL LIFE, GOD, and NATURE.

The *Crux Ansata* surrounded by a Serpent in a Circle, is a Symbol of Eternity and immortality.

The battery alludes to the six days or periods in which God created the world, and to the day or period of rest.

The 33 lights, disposed by elevens, represent the Sacred numbers 3 and 5. For 33 is equal to $3 + 3 + 5 \times 3$.

The solemn feast of this degree, which is held on Holy Thursday, commemorates the feast of the Passover observed by the Jews; thus ordered:

"On the tenth of this month [the first Jewish month in the year], they shall take to them every man a lamb, . . . a lamb for an house; and if the household be too little for the lamb, let him and his neighbour next unto his house take it, according to the number of the souls. Your lamb shall be without blemish, a male of the first year . . . And ye shall keep it up until the fourteenth day of the same month, and the whole assembly of the congregation of Israel shall kill it in the evening . . . and they shall eat the flesh in that night, roasted with fire . . . and ye shall let nothing of it remain until the morning; nor break any bone of it; and that which remaineth of it until the morning ye shall burn with fire. And thus shall ye eat it; with your loins girded, your shoes on your feet, and your staff in your hand; and ye shall eat it in haste; it is the Lord's Passover. And this day shall be unto you for a memorial, and ye shall keep it as a feast to the Lord throughout your generations, a feast by an ordinance forever."

This feast, and the bread and wine of which we partake at every assembly, are to us symbols of fraternity and brotherly affection; and of that perfect union that must ever subsist among Brother Knights of the Rose ✠.

Thus the Degree of Rose ✠ is devoted to and symbolizes the final triumph of truth over falsehood, of liberty over slavery, of light over darkness, of life over death, and of good over evil. The great truth it inculcates is, that notwithstanding the existence of Evil, God is infinitely wise, just and good: that though the affairs of the world proceed by no rule of right and wrong known to us in the narrowness of our views, yet all is right, for it is the work of God; and all evils, all miseries, all misfortunes, are but as drops in the vast current that is sweeping onward, guided by Him, to a great and magnificent result: that, at the appointed time, He will redeem and regenerate the world, and the Principle, the Power and the existence of Evil will then cease; that this will be brought about by such means and instruments as He chooses to employ; whether by the merits of a Redeemer that has already appeared, or a Messiah that is yet waited for; by an incarnation of Himself, or by an inspired prophet, it does not belong to us as Masons to decide. Let each judge and believe for himself.

In the mean time, we labour to hasten the coming of that day. The morals of antiquity, of the law of Moses and of Christianity are ours. We recognize every teacher of Morality, every Reformer, as a Brother in this great work. The Eagle is to us the symbol of Liberty, the Compasses of Equality, the Pelican of Humanity, and our Order of Fraternity. Labouring for these, with Faith, Hope and Charity as our armor, we will wait with patience for the final triumph of Good and the complete manifestation of the Word of God.

No one Mason has the right to measure for another, within the walls of a Masonic Temple, the degree of veneration which he shall feel for any Reformer, or the Founder of any Religion. We teach a belief in no particular creed, as we teach unbelief in none. Whatever higher attributes the Founder of the Christian Faith may, in our belief, have had or not have had, none can deny that he taught and practised a pure and elevated morality, even at the risk and to the ultimate loss of his life. He was not only the benefactor of a disinherited people, but a model for mankind. Devotedly he loved the children of Israel. To them he came, and to them alone he preached that Gospel which his disciples afterwards carried among foreigners. He would fain have freed the chosen People from their spiritual bondage of ignorance and degradation. As a lover of all mankind, laying down his life for the emancipation of his Brethren, he should be to all, to Christian, to Jew and to Mahometan, an object of unceasing gratitude and veneration.

The Roman world felt the pangs of approaching dissolution. Paganism, its Temples shattered by Socrates and Cicero, had spoken its last word. The God of the Hebrews was unknown beyond the limits of Palestine. The old religions had failed to give happiness and peace to the world. The babbling and wrangling philosophers had confounded all men's ideas, until they doubted of everything and had faith in nothing: neither in God nor in his goodness and mercy, nor in the virtue of man, nor in themselves. Mankind was divided into two great classes,—the master and the slave; the powerful and the abject, the high and the low, the tyrants and the mob; and even the former were satiated with the servility of the latter, sunken by lassitude and despair to the lowest depths of degradation.

When, lo, a voice, in the inconsiderable Roman Province of Judea proclaims a new Gospel—a new God's word, to crushed, suffering, bleeding humanity. Liberty of Thought, Equality of all men in the eye of God, universal Fraternity! a new doctrine, a new religion; the old Primitive Truth uttered once again!

Man is once more taught to look upward to his God. No longer to a God hid in impenetrable mystery, and infinitely remote from human sympathy, emerging only at intervals from the darkness to smite and crush humanity: but a God, good, kind, beneficent and merciful: a father, loving the creatures he has made, with a love immeasurable and exhaustless; who feels for us, and sympathizes with us, and sends us pain and want and disaster only that they may serve to develope in us the virtues and excellencies that befit us to live with Him hereafter.

Jesus of Nazareth, the Deity incarnate, or the Son of God, or an inspired prophet, or a pure, noble-hearted wise man, (whichever according to your faith and mine he may have been), is the expounder of the new Law of Love. He calls to him the humble, the poor, the Pariahs of the world. The first sentence that he pronounces blesses the world, and announces the new gospel: "Blessed are they that mourn, for they shall be comforted." He pours the oil of comfort upon every crushed and bleeding heart. Every sufferer is his proselyte. He shares our sorrows, and sympathizes with all our afflictions.

He raises up the sinner and teaches him to hope for forgiveness. He pardons the woman taken in adultery. He selects his disciples not among the Pharisees or the Philosophers, but among the low and humble, even of the fishermen of Galilee. He heals the sick and feeds the poor. He lives among the destitute and the friendless. "Suffer little children," he said, "to come unto me; for of such is the kingdom of Heaven. Blessed are the humble-minded, for theirs is the kingdom of Heaven; the meek, for they shall inherit the Earth; the merciful, for they shall obtain mercy; the pure in heart, for they shall see God; the peace-makers, for they shall be called the children of God. First be reconciled to thy brother, and then come and offer thy gift at the altar. Give to him that asketh thee, and from him that would borrow of thee turn not away. Love your enemies: bless them that curse you: do good to them that hate you; and pray for them which despitefully use you and persecute you. All things whatsoever ye would that men should do to you, do ye also unto them; for this is the law and the Prophets. He that taketh not his cross, and followeth after me, is not worthy of me. A new commandment I give unto you, that ye love one another: as I have loved you, that ye also love one another: by this shall all know that ye are my disciples. Greater love hath no man than this, that a man lay down his life for his friends."

That Gospel of Love he sealed with his life. The cruelty of the Jewish Priesthood, and the Roman indifference to barbarian blood, nailed him to the cross, and he expired uttering blessings upon humanity.

Dying thus, he bequeathed his teachings to man as an inestimable inheritance. Perverted and corrupted, they have served as a basis for many creeds, and been even made the warrant for intolerance and persecution. We here teach them in their purity. They are our Masonry; for to them good men of all creeds can subscribe.

That God is good and merciful, and loves and sympathizes with the creatures he has made; that his finger is visible in all the movements of the moral, intellectual and material universe; that we are his children, the objects of his paternal care and regard; that all men are our brothers, whose wants we are to supply, their errors to pardon, their opinions to tolerate, their injuries to forgive; that man has an immortal soul, a free will, a right to freedom of thought and action; that all men are equal in God's sight; that we best serve God by humility, meekness, gentleness, kindness, and the other virtues which the lowly can practise as well as the lofty; this is the new Law, the Word, for which the world had waited and pined so long: and every true Knight of the Rose ⳾ will revere the memory of Him who taught it, and look indulgently even on those who assign to him a character far above his own conceptions or belief, even to the extent of deeming him Divine.

Hear Philo, the Greek Jew. "The contemplative soul, unequally guided, sometimes towards abundance and sometimes towards barrenness, though ever advancing, is illuminated by the primitive ideas, the rays that emanate from the Divine Intelligence, whenever it ascends towards the Sublime Treasures. When, on the contrary, it descends, and is barren, it falls within the domain of those Intelligences that are termed Angels... for, when the soul is deprived of the light of God, which leads it to the knowledge of things, it no longer enjoys more than a feeble and secondary light, which gives it, not the understanding of things, but that of words only, as in this baser world. . . .

·.·Let the narrow-souled withdraw, having their ears sealed up! We communicate the divine mysteries to those only who have received the sacred initiation, to those who practise true piety, and who are not enslaved by the empty pomp of words, or the doctrines of the pagans. . . . ·

. O, ye Initiates, ye whose ears are purified, receive this in your souls, as a mystery never to be lost! Reveal it to no Profane! Keep and contain it within yourselves, as an incorruptible treasure, not like gold or silver, but more precious than everything beside; for it is the knowledge of the Great Cause, of Nature, and of that which is born of both. And if you meet an Initiate, besiege him with your prayers, that he conceal from you no new mysteries that he may know, and rest not until you have obtained them! For me, although I was initiated in the Great Mysteries by Moses, the Friend of God, yet, having seen Jeremiah, I recognized him not only as an Initiate, but as a Hierophant; and I follow his school."

We, like him, recognize all Initiates as our Brothers. We belong to no one creed or school. In all religions there is a basis of Truth; in all there is pure Morality. All that teach the cardinal tenets of Masonry we respect; all teachers and reformers of mankind we admire and revere.

Masonry has too her mission to perform. With her traditions reaching to the earliest times, and her symbols dating further back than even the monumental history of Egypt extends, she invites all men of all religions to enlist under her banners and to war against evil, ignorance and wrong. You are now her knight, and to her service your sword is consecrated. May you prove a worthy soldier in a worthy cause!

TO CLOSE.

The Master raps three times. Each Warden repeats, and the Knights all rise.

V∴ W∴ Very Ex∴ and Perf∴ Sen∴ Warden, the name of the first column?

Sen∴ W∴ Infinity.

7B ·

V∴ W∴ Of the second?

Sen∴ W∴ Nature.

V∴ W∴ Of the third?

Sen∴ W∴ Reason.

V∴ W∴ Of the fourth?

Sen∴ W∴ Immortality.

V∴ W∴ What word do the initials of these four disclose to us?

Sen∴ W∴ I cannot pronounce it without your assistance.

V∴ W∴ I∴

Sen∴ W∴ N∴

V∴ W∴ R∴

Sen∴ W∴ I∴

V∴ W∴ What does it signify?

Sen∴ W∴ The Infinite God of Light and Life.

V∴ W∴ How did you arrive at the knowledge of this Sacred Word?

Sen∴ W∴ By the practice of the three Divine Virtues, Faith, Hope and Charity.

V∴ W∴ Do you know the Pelican?

Sen∴ W∴ I do, Very Wise and Perfect Master.

V∴ W∴ Of what is it the symbol?

S∴ W∴ Of the mercy of God, the mediation of a Redeemer, and the humanity of a true Mason.

V∴ W∴ Of what is the Eagle, hovering in the East, a symbol?

Sen∴ W∴ Of the Deity; and of that Liberty and Free Thought to which He has given mankind the right.

V∴ W∴ Of what are the Compasses a symbol?

S∴ W∴ Equality and impartial Justice.

V∴ W∴ What do the Cross and Rose signify to us?

S∴ W∴ The approaching dawn of the reign of good; eternal life, and the immortality of the soul. They also teach us humility and modesty.

V∴ W∴ What are we taught in this degree?

Sen∴ W∴ That God, our Father, is infinitely wise and good: that everything in the universe is ordered by Him for wise and good purposes, consistent with His nature and divine attributes: that sin and wrong and suffering are parts of his plan, and work together in ways unknown to us, to evolve that great result: that the reign of evil is but temporary, and at the appointed time the Evil Principle will be overcome and annihilated, and Good thenceforward rule forever: and that there is another and an eternal life of happiness, to which we may attain by the beneficence of God, and a strict performance of our duties.

V∴ W∴ What, then, are the duties of a Knight of the Rose Croix?

Sen∴ W∴ To have faith in God, his fellows and himself; to hope for the end of evil, the redemption of the world, and life everlasting; to be charitable in act, word and opinion; to aid his brethren in their distresses, and comfort them in their affliction; to be modest and humble; to be true, upright, frank and sincere; to labour for the improvement of mankind, and to perform all the other duties of a good Mason.

V∴ W∴ Very Ex∴ and Perf∴ Sen∴ Warden, what is the hour?

Sen∴ W∴ The moment when the Word was recovered; when the cubical stone was changed into a mystical rose; when the blazing Star re-appeared in all its splendour; when the columns of the Temple were replaced, and the working tools of Masonry restored; when the Stars again shone forth, the True Light dispelled the darkness, and the New Law began to rule upon the Earth.

V∴ W∴ Since that is the hour, we may close this Chapter and retire in peace. Very Ex∴ and Perf∴ Sen∴ and Jun∴ Wardens, give notice to the Knights accordingly.

[The Wardens in succession, announce that the Very W∴ and Perf∴ Master is about to close the Chapter: and all the Knights return their Swords, and arrange themselves in a line in the South, the Wardens on the east of the line. The Master leaves his place, and embraces all the Knights, commencing on the east, and saying to each, Peace be unto you: and they all salute in like manner in return. Then the Master returns to his place, and says] :

V∴ W∴ Very Worshipful and Perf∴. Knights, the labours of this Sovereign Chapter are ended. Let us perform our last duty !

[All the Knights, looking at him, give the sign, he also giving it. Then, still imitating him, all give the battery with their hands, and cry £ times, Иосипеаи !].

V∴ W∴ This Sov∴. Chapter is closed.

THE SOLEMN BANQUET.

When this ceremony is to be performed, the V∴ W∴ does not close the Chapter, but merely suspends, after asking the hour and receiving the answer, in the closing ceremony. Then he and all the Knights put on their shoes slip-shod, take each a white rod or reed, and proceed to the place where the banquet is prepared.

In the middle of the room is a round table, covered with a white cloth. On it is a loaf of bread in a plate, and a large cup of wine; and in the middle of the table three yellow candles. All the Brethren arrange themselves round this table with their heads bare.

The V∴ Wise makes the following prayer, which all the brethren repeat after him.

Sovereign Creator of all things, and Source of Life and Light, who providest for all our necessities, bless the nourishment for the body which we are about to take ; and make it to give us strength to labour for Thy Glory and for the advancement of all the great interests of humanity—Amen !

The V∴ W∴ takes the bread, breaks off a piece, and passes it to the Brother on his right. All do the same in turn, and they eat in silence. Then the V∴ W∴ takes the wine in his left hand, makes the sign with his right, drinks, and passes the cup to the Brother on his right: and so all drink in succession.

The Very W∴ then carefully takes all the remnants and crumbs, and, accompanied by all the Brethren, goes and casts them in the fire, kneeling on one knee, by way of offering. Then all rise, and the V∴ W∴ gives the kiss of peace to the Bro∴ on his right, saying, Peace be unto you. This is done in turn by each, until the kiss is returned to the Master, each one responding.

The last Knight admitted performs the duties of Servitor. During the repast, the most profound silence is maintained.

The Grand Feast day of the order is Holy Thursday—[the Thursday of Holy Week]. That feast is indispensable to a Rose ⳽⳾, even if he be alone. He must, in spirit at least, feast that day with his Brethren.

A young lamb, roasted, is to be eaten at the feast. It must be white, and without spot or blemish. One of the Brethren must prepare it ; and the head and feet must be cut off and burned as an offering. He must be killed with a single blow of a knife.

ORDERS AT THE BANQUET.

[These are used only at the regular feast, or other banquet of the Knights ; and not when they partake of he bread and wine].

ORDERS.

Flag across!
Right hand to the Chalice!
Raise Chalice!
Draw in three times!
Chalice to the left shoulder!
Horizontally to the right shoulder!
To the front!
Perpendicularly down, and deposite in three times!
  [Which forms a Cross].
The battery [followed by the word of applause, Hoscheah!].

CALLING TO REFRESHMENT.

V∴ W∴. To the glory of the Gr∴. Architect of the Universe, in the name and under the auspices of the Gr∴. Consistory of Sub∴. Princes of the Royal Secret 32d Degree of the Ancient and Accepted Rite, for the State of   ; under the Jurisdiction of the Supreme Council of Sov∴. Gr∴. Insp∴. of the 33d Degree for the Southern Jurisdiction of the United States of America; and by virtue of the power conferred on me by this Sovereign Chapter of Kts∴. of the Rose ✠, I call this meeting from labour to refreshment. Join me, my Brethren!

The V∴. W∴. gives the sign of recognition. The Kts∴. return the sign of answer: then all strike with their hands : , — and say three times, Hoscheah!

V∴ W∴. This Chapter is now called to refreshment. Before we part, let us eat together the bread earned by our labours, and thank our Heavenly Father for furnishing us with the means of sustaining life. Bro∴. M∴. of Ceremonies, visit the avenues, and see if there be any brother or even any Profane, who suffers from hunger or thirst; and if there be, bring him in, for whoever he may be, he is our Brother, and we will gladly divide with him our bread and wine.

The M∴. of Cerem∴. goes out, visits the avenues, returns and reports. Then the Kts∴. take their places at the Table prepared for the ceremony of the Supper.

CEREMONY OF THE TABLE, OR SUPPER.

In the middle of the Lodge, in front of the Wardens, a Table is prepared, covered with a white cloth. On it is a plate containing a loaf of white bread. The plate is in the centre of a triangle formed by three candlesticks, in which must be candles of white or yellow wax. Near the plate is a decanter filled with white wine, and a goblet: and also a paper on which is written in capital letters, the Word. The paper is triangular in shape. A pan of burning coals is near.

All the Knights take their places round the Table; the V∴. W∴. facing the West, with the Chancellor on his right and the Orator on his left. Opposite the V∴. W∴. are the Wardens, with the Initiate between them.

When the Circle is formed, the V∴. W∴. takes a piece of bread, eats it, and passes the plate to the Chancellor, saying, "Take and eat, and give to the hungry!" The Music plays as the plate passes round, and each Kt∴. takes and eats a piece of the bread. When the plate returns to the V∴. W∴. he places it on the Table, and the Music stops.

Then the V∴. W∴. fills the goblet with wine, drinks, and passes it to the Chancellor; saying, "Take and drink, and give to the thirsty."

As the Goblet passes round, the music plays. When it returns to the V∴. W∴., he throws what wine is left into the fire, and then burns the paper, saying, ♀∴ ♏∴ ♃∴ ♀∴.— after which—"Order, my brethren !" The music plays, and the Kts∴ place themselves under the sign of the Good Shepherd, and face the West.

Then the V∴ W∴ taps gently on the shoulder of the Chancellor, who faces him. The V∴ W∴ gives the sign of recognition, and the Chancellor returns the answering sign : and vice versa.

The V∴ W∴ gives the token, and they pronounce the Sacred Word in the usual manner.

The Chancellor performs the same ceremony with the Kt∴ on his right ; and so on, until the Word returns to the V∴ W∴ * The music stops, and the V∴ W∴ says :

My Brethren, we may now retire : But first I must require your oath not to reveal any of this day's proceedings. [Music plays].

Then the V∴ W∴ presents the hilt of his sword. The Orator passes before him, places his right hand on the hilt of the sword, and says, "I swear." All the Knights follow in turn, and do the same, until they arrive again at their respective places.

Then the music ceases. The V∴ W∴ says : "Peace be unto you !" all answer §⊙♉ *♉♍♀♎♐♌♒∴. and retire in silence.

CEREMONY OF EXTINGUISHING THE SEVEN LIGHTS.

This ceremony invariably takes place on every Thursday before Easter, after the ceremony of the Table, at the moment when the Word is returned to the V∴ Wise, and when all have resumed their positions, and the music ceases.

For that purpose a candlestick is set at the west end of the Table, with seven branches of unequal size, so as to form a triangle ; the middle one being uppermost, and forming the summit of the triangle.

All the Kts∴ surround the Table, and at a sign from the V∴ W∴, the M∴ of Despatches proceeds towards the candlestick, on which burn seven wax candles, and says :

M∴ Desp∴ He came to regenerate Humanity ; but they knew him not, and put him to death.

He then extinguishes the lowest light on the left, and returns to his place.

The Kt∴ Hospitaller follows, and says :

Kt∴ Hosp∴ He desired that all men should be brethren ; but his brethren knew him not ; and put him to death.

The Kt∴ Hospitaller then extinguishes the lowest light on the right, and retires to his place.

The Orator follows, and says :

Orator : . . His sublime teachings were intended to insure happiness to mankind ; but they knew him not, and put him to death.

He extinguishes the second light on the left, and retires to his place.

The Chancellor follows, and says :

Chan∴ He came to put Truth in the place of Error, and Love in the place of Hatred ; but those whom he loved knew him not, and put him to death.

He extinguishes the second light on the right, and retires to his place.

The Jun∴ Warden follows and says :

Jun∴ W∴ He taught that every man should do that only unto his Brother which he would wish his Brother to do unto him ; but they understood him not, and put him to death.

He extinguishes the third light on the left, and retires to his place.

The Sen∴ W∴ follows and says :

Sen∴ W∴ He endeavoured to relieve his brethren from the bonds of Tyranny, to protect the weak and feeble, and to bring back to the paths of duty the oppressors of Humanity ; but they listened not unto him, and nailed him on a cross.

He extinguishes the third light on the right, and retires to his place.

---

* Here, on the Thursday before Easter, the ceremony of extinguishing the Seven Lights commences.

The V∴ W∴ comes last and says:

V∴ W∴ Yes, my Brethren, the Apostle of Liberty, Equality and Fraternity fell a victim to priestly arrogance and despotic power. Fanaticism, aided by Ignorance and Superstition, inflicted the punishment of a slave and malefactor upon the Emancipator of Mankind, the Friend of the Poor and the Destitute, the Comforter, who, sheltering with his love the lowest of the low, opened to them that home of eternal happiness, prepared for them by the Father from all Eternity.

Guests of one day, and shelterless the next! Your Friend is dead! Your Benefactor is no more! Mourn! lament! and cry Wo unto us! For Error triumphs, Truth disappears, and Ignorance has extinguished the Light of Philosophy!

Then the V∴ W∴ extinguishes the last light, and says:

V∴ W∴ Yet, my Brethren, be of good cheer! Let us go in search of the Word, the Word of regeneration and immortal life! We shall recover it; and then, disciples of a crucified Master, let us proclaim it, as he did, at the peril of our lives! Redeemed from mental and moral bondage by his teachings, let us labour to deserve his munificent gift, by labouring, as he did, for the progress and advancement of Humanity!

Work, henceforward, as those who know the responsibility that rests upon them! And he who died for you and for all men shall be your witness, and will aid and assist you in the hour of difficulty and peril. His hand will support and sustain you, and make you to triumph in the great contest with those enemies that assailed him as they have always assailed the truth, and hated him as they have always hated the light.

Peace be with you! Be ye blessed! The peace of our Master be with you always!

My Brethren, we may now retire; but I must first require your oath, [&c., as in closing the Table ceremony].

HONOURS.

When a Kt∴ Rose ☩ is announced at the door of a Lodge, the Master sends 3 stars and 3 swords to meet and introduce him. These mean 3 brethren, bearing each a light in one hand and a sword in the other.

When the Chapter is in mourning, instead of striking with their hands and saying Hoscheah, the Kts∴ strike 6 — 1 — with the right hand on the forearm, and say 3 times " Wo unto us!"

A Kt∴ K—H∴ is entitled to 5 stars and 5 swords.

A S∴ P∴ R∴ S∴ to 7 stars and 7 swords.

The Gr∴ Commander of the Gr∴ Consistory to 9 stars and 9 swords.

A Sov∴ Gr∴ Ins∴ Gen∴ to 11 stars and 11 swords.

When a S∴ P∴ R∴ S∴ or Sov∴ Gr∴ Insp∴ Gen∴ is introduced, the gavels of the three officers must bent: and the V∴ W∴, after the introduction, must leave his seat, meet the visitor, and present him with his gavel.

The Gr∴ Com∴ of the Gr∴ Consistory, the Sov∴ Gr∴ Commander of the Sup∴ Council at Charleston, or his special delegate, are also entitled to the steel vault.

Statutes and Regulations for the Sob∴ Chapters of Knights of the Rose ✠

UNDER

THE JURISDICTION OF THE SUP∴ COUNCIL, 33ᴰ

AT CHARLESTON, IN SOUTH CAROLINA.

TO THE GLORY OF THE HOLY OF HOLIES, AND TO ALL WHO KNOW THE BRILLIANT LIGHT.

STATUTES AND REGULATIONS.

CHAPTER I.

ART. I.

A Knight of the Rose ✠ is qualified to take the mallet in any symbolic Lodge or Lodge of Perfection, or Council of Princes of Jerusalem, if it is offered to him. If, as is courteous, he declines to take it, he is entitled to seat himself by the Presiding officer, without waiting for an invitation.

ART. II.

A Knight of Rose ✠ must not present himself in his Chapter, or in any inferior body, without being fully clothed as a Knight, and wearing his cordon and jewel. If he present himself otherwise in a Chapter he must be refused admission; and if in an inferior body, he is not to be recognized as a Knight.

ART. III.

When a Knight enters a Chapter, after having performed his first devoirs to the East, he will salute the Master, and then take the lowest place, so as to interfere with no one, and come to order like the other Knights.

ART. IV.

A Knight Rose ✠ must never sign any paper connected with Masonry, without adding his rank; nor do anything contrary to rule, or which may infringe upon the prerogatives of the Supreme Council.

ART. V.

When, in any City or place there is a Chapter well and regularly established, all the Knights who compose it must assemble at least five times a year; to wit: on each of the four annual Feasts, and on Holy Thursday; and they must in no wise omit celebrating the Feasts of St. John with the inferior brethren.

ART. VI.

If a Knight learns that there is another Knight within two leagues of his residence, and there is no Chapter established in the place where he resides, he must go and visit such Knight, and invite him to unite with him in the Feast of Holy Thursday; and in such case they will meet half-way.

ART. VII.

If a Knight finds himself alone in his Degree, he must hold by himself the regular feast of Holy Thursday, uniting in the spirit with his Brother Knights: and this, even if he be on a journey; that feast being indispensable.

ART. VIII.

A Knight cannot excuse himself from attending the Chapter when he has information of an assembly, except on account of sickness of himself or his family or friend: but he must attend and present his excuse in every other case, and then retire; or, if the distance be too great for him to attend, he must send the excuse in writing.

ART. IX.

If a Knight is three times absent from his Chapter, in succession, without offering a legitimate excuse for his absence; or if he attends another Chapter in preference to his own, his Chapter may omit to notify him to attend for the future, and regard him as a mere visitor.

ART. X.

A Knight Rose ✠ visiting a Symbolic Lodge or Lodge of Perfection is entitled to the regular honours. If they are not paid him, he will seat himself on the floor near the Jun∴ Warden; in which case all work must cease until he is properly received.

ART. XI.

If a Knight falls sick, he is to be visited by all the Knights, and especially by the Kt∴ Hospitaller, Kt∴ Comptroller and Kt∴ Chancellor: who shall take great care that he shall want for nothing.

ART. XII.

If a Knight dies, all the Kts∴ must attend his funeral, wearing their dress and jewel. His jewel is to be buried with him, upon his breast, unless he leave a son or near relative worthy to be received a Knight, in which case the Chapter will retain the jewel, and give it to such son or relative, at his reception.

ART. XIII.

The Knight who takes the place of the deceased must wear mourning for him for the space of three months, by shrouding the jewel with crape.

ART. XIV.

At the first meeting after a funeral, a Kt∴ appointed for that purpose must deliver a funeral oration in regard to the deceased; or a special annual meeting may be held at a regular fixed time in each year, at which orations must be delivered in honour of the memory of all Knights who have died during the preceding year.

ART. XV.

The names of deceased Knights will never be erased from the roll on which they have been inscribed; but below or opposite their names will be drawn a death's head and cross-bones.

ART. XVI.

Every Knight who dies in want of means, must be buried at the expense of the Order.

CHAPTER II.

ART. I.

A Chapter can be constituted by three Knights, at its commencement, for want of a larger number; to wit, the Very Wise and the two Wardens; in which case the Junior Warden will perform the duties of Secretary until the number of members is increased.

ART. II.

A Chapter should regularly consist of not less than 12 nor more than 24 members. But this rule is not peremptory.

ART. III.

The Master, Wardens and other officers will be elected annually, at the assembly on Holy Thursday.

ART. IV.

The officers elected shall immediately enter on the discharge of their duties.

ART. V.

As we are all obliged, according to our means, to aid and assist all needy Masons, a Chapter must never be held without taking a contribution for charitable purposes; and a discourse must always be pronounced for the edification of the Brethren.

ART. VI.

All Chapters must be exceedingly circumspect not to give to any one whatever the degree of Knight Rose ✠, until after strict examination and inquiry into his life and morals. He must be a Knight of the East and West, and 33 years of age, both which facts must be stated in his petition: and he must be balloted for at two successive meetings, receiving each time an unanimous vote.

ART. VII.

If a Chapter becomes too numerous, it may be divided into two or more classes, by vote of the Chapter; which two or more classes or chambers shall thenceforward have three officers in common,—a President, a Grand Chancellor, and a Secretary General; who, whenever the good of the Chapter requires, may convene the two chambers in single assembly.

ART. VIII.

The officers of each Chamber must be elected by the whole Chapter.

ART. IX.

The Chapter when convoked on the regular days, must never close without the banquet.

ART. X.

In all assemblies, each Kt.·. has an equal vote, except the Presiding Officer, who has the casting vote.

Nineteenth Degree.

Grand Pontiff, or Sublime Scotch Mason.

THE LODGE ROOM, AND ITS DECORATIONS.

The hangings are blue, sprinkled with stars of gold. The whole Lodge is lighted by one large spherical transparency, behind the Master's seat in the East.

In the East is a throne, and over it a blue canopy.

Around the room are twelve columns, two in the East, [one on each side of the Master], two in the West, [one on each side of the Warden], four on the North side, and four on the South side, of the Lodge; on their capitals are the English initials of the names of the Twelve Tribes, in the following order, beginning with the column on the right hand of the Master, and going round by the North, West and South: . . . Ephraim . . . Benjamin . . . Issachar . . . Judah . . . Naphtali . . . Asher . . . Dan . . . Manasseh . . . Zebulon . . . Reuben . . . Simeon . . . Gad. Under these, in the same order, are the zodiacal signs . . ♉ . . . ♊ . . . ♋ . . . ♌ . . . ♍ . . . ♎ . . . ♏ . . . ♐ . . . ♑ . . . ♒ . . . ♓ . . . ♈; and under these, again, in the same order, the following names and titles of the Deity: . . . אלהים . . . יהו . . . גמל . . . מלך . . . אל-חי . . . עין . . . אלוה . . . ארד . . . אל . . . אצ-נבה . . . אדני . . . ידזה.

On the base of each column is the initial, in the same order, of the name of one of the Apostles of Christ: John . . . Peter . . . Andrew . . . James . . . Philip . . . Bartholomew . . . Thomas . . . Matthew . . . James, son of Alpheus . . . Lebbeus, surnamed Thaddeus . . . Simon the Canaanite . . . and Matthias.

DRAUGHT OR TRACING BOARD.

The Tracing Board has a mountain in the foreground. A city, four-square, appears descending from the sky; (in which are neither sun, moon, stars nor clouds, but only the azure vault on which the light from the city reflects). Below is a representation of Jerusalem overturned and in ruins. Around the descending city is a wall of jasper, the foundation of which is laid with the precious stones of twelve different kinds and colours, that appear on the Pontiff's breast plate. All the buildings are of gold. The architecture of the city is oriental, and there is no Temple. There are twelve gates of pearl, three on each side. A great glory in the centre gives it light.

On the six gates that show in the painting are the first three and the last three initials of the names of the Tribes, and the first and last three names of Deity given above: and on the foundation under those gates, the initials of the first three and last three names of the Apostles.

A sparkling river runs through the city; and upon it, in the centre of the city, stands a tree, loaded with fruits, leaves and blossoms. Its roots are on each side of the stream.

Beneath the ruins of the overturned city lies writhing a serpent with three heads, bound with brazen chains.

OFFICERS, DRESS, ETC.

The Master is styled *Th∴ Puissant.* He wears a white satin robe, and holds a sceptre in his hand. On his breast is the Jewish High Priest's breast plate, or the Aurim and Thummim.

There is but one Warden; who sits in the West, opposite the Th∴ P∴ holding a gilded rod. There are also an Orator, two Deacons, and a Master of Ceremonies.

All the members, except the Th∴ P∴ wear robes of white linen; and a fillet of sky-blue satin round the forehead, with twelve stars embroidered on it in gold.

The cordon is crimson, bordered with white, worn from left to right. On it are twelve stars embroidered in gold, and the letters A . . Ω . .

The jewel is an oblong square, with the letter א engraved on one side, and ת on the other.

The battery is , ? at equal intervals.

TO OPEN.

Th∴ P∴ Brethren, Gr∴ Pontiffs, Sub∴ Scottish Masons, I propose to open this Lodge. Aid me to do so. Bro∴ Jun∴ Deacon, see that we are properly tyled.

[The Jun∴ Deacon goes out, returns, gives the battery of , ? equal raps, which is answered from without, returns to his place, and says] :

J∴-D∴ Th∴ Puissant, we are properly tyled.

Th∴ P∴ How?

J∴ D∴ By a Sublime Scottish Mason without, armed and vigilant.

Th∴ P∴ It is well. Bro∴ Warden, what is the hour?

W∴ The time foretold to all nations. The Sun of Truth has risen over the Desert. The last struggle between Good and Evil, Light and Darkness, commences. The cubical Stone has become a mystic Rose, and the lost Word is recovered.

Th∴ P∴ Be grateful to God, my Brethren! And let us proceed to open this Lodge, that we may labour together for His glory and the improvement of mankind. Together, my Brethren!

[All give the sign. Then the Th∴ P∴ raps , — the Warden , — and so on alternately to , ? — Then the Brethren all clap , ? with their hands, and cry ; times Носснкан!].

Th∴ P∴ The sun is up, and this Lodge is open.

RECEPTION.

The Candidate is clothed in the dress, jewel and ornaments of a Kt∴ Rose ☩, received by the M∴ of Ceremonies, and conducted to the door of the Lodge. The M∴ Cer∴ raps , ? — and the door is slightly opened by the J∴ D∴, and the following conversation ensues:

J∴ D∴ Who hails?

M∴ Cer∴ A Knight of the Rose ☩, who desires to attain the degree of Gr∴ Pontiff.

J∴ D∴ How long hath he served?

M∴ Cer∴ Three years.

Qu∴ Where?

Ans∴ In the ranks of Truth.

Qu∴ How armed?

Ans∴ With Charity, Hope and Faith.

Qu∴ Against what enemies?

Ans∴ Intolerance and Oppression.

Qu∴ Why doth he now desire to attain the degree of Sublime Ecossais?

Ans∴ That he may be the better qualified to serve the cause of Truth and Light.

Qu∴ What other weapon does he need, than Charity, Hope and Faith?

Ans∴ Patience: to be content to wait.

J∴ D∴ Then let him take his first lesson now; and wait with patience until the Th∴ Puissant is informed of his request and his will ascertained.

[The J∴ D∴ closes the door, returns to the Lodge, and reports to the Th∴ P∴; the same questions being asked, and answers returned, as at the door; except the last order of the J∴ D∴ to be patient and wait: instead of which the Th∴ P∴ says]:

Th∴ P∴ Since his desires are so commendable, Bro∴ J∴ Deacon, you will permit him to enter.

[The door is opened, and the candidate enters, conducted by the M∴ of Ceremonies. As he enters, the organ plays, and the Brethren sing the following ode, all standing up]:

ODE.

Truth dawns upon the human soul,
  And Error disappears:
No longer darkness hath control,
From Heaven's blue face the storm-clouds roll,
  And all the glittering years
No longer for men's sorrow groan,
  Their sin, their shame, their tears;
But still and stately, past God's Throne,
March onward, where Love reigns alone.

That Sun is risen, is HERE; that Day
  Is Now, to GOD... *We WAIT...*
The world and stars wait... The array
Of ages stretching far away,
  The Angels at God's gate,
And ancient Time ... all wait the Light,
  Sure as God's Truth, though late;
When sin no more the world shall blight,
But endless day dethrone the night.

———

[When the ode is concluded, the candidate is led 12 times around the Lodge, halting at one of the columns at each circuit, and his attention being directed to the Initials upon its capital and base; the M∴ of Ceremonies saying at each respectively as follows]:

At the 4th Column: Judah shall return again to his first estate, when the Empire of Evil ends. Light and not darkness is eternal: Truth and not Error is immortal.

At the 3d Column: Issachar shall once more be free, when Sin and Suffering are known no longer. Far in the Future unto us, that day of Light is *now* to God. Time is a succession of points, each in the centre of Eternity. Evil lasts only during Time. The reign of God is measured by Eternity.

At the 9th Column: ... Zebulon shall find peace; as ships that come out of great storms, and furl their sails and let drop their anchors in quiet harbours. For Peace shall be the Universal Law to all the children of a common Father.

At the 10*th Column:* . . . Reuben, like all mankind, has wandered far into the darkness. The steps of the Ages ring in their stately march, down the long slopes of Time; and ever the Dawn draws nearer. Men are God's instruments to accelerate its coming. Work then, my Brother, be patient, wait!

At the 11*th Column:* . . . Simeon shall be reconciled to God; when Intolerance no longer persecutes, and Bigotry no longer hates: when man, brother of man, shall no longer be his torturer, his dread, his Fate. The waves of Eternity roll ever nearer to us, on the narrow sands of Life, that crumble under our weary feet. Those on whose ears the roar of the same surges smites, and whom the next wave will engulf together, should have in their hearts a prayer to God, and not hatred for their brother.

At the 12*th Column:* . . . Gad shall overcome at last; though a troop of Evils long overcome *him*, as they overcome us all. The Serpent is still unchained. The Giants still assail the battlements of Heaven, and scarce recoil before its lightnings. Typhon and Ahriman march with the port of conquerors. But with them march the Ages, majestic in their silence, and calm as fate. Centuries are the moments of Truth's twilight.

At the 1*st Column:* . . . Ephraim hath strayed from home. He shall return, in tears and penitent, and find eternal rest. From God all souls have emanated, and to him all return. The wanderings of none can be eternal; for then would Evil be immortal and a God; and pain and sorrow, misery and crime would have seized upon and hold in fee a portion of God's Sovereignty.

At the 8*th Column:* . . . Manasseh shall be restored to sight. We are all blind swimmers in the currents of a mighty sea that hath no shore. We see as in a dream, the effects, and not the causes. The simplest things are miracles to us. We do not see the flower that is within the seed, nor the towering oak enveloped in the acorn, nor the smells and colours in the tasteless, colourless, invisible air and limpid water and rank dark earth, from which the seed extracts them, by its mysterious chemistry. When the Divine Light cometh, we shall see and know.

At the 2*d Column:* . . . Benjamin shall be redeemed, and come back from exile and captivity. For they, like pain and poverty and sorrow, are blessings. Without them, there would be scant excellence in human nature;—neither fortitude nor self-denial, nor industry nor patience, nor charity nor tolerance, magnanimity nor generosity, heroism nor gratitude. Our exile from the presence of the Deity, our captivity by Sin and Sorrow, are the means, offered us by God, to purify the heart and ennoble the soul.

At the 7*th Column:* . . . Dan shall obey the new Law,—the law of Love. *He prayeth best that loveth best all things, both great and small; for the great God that loveth us, He made and loveth all.* All things, all souls are but the tones of one great harmony, in which sin and pain, and sorrow mingle as its discords, that but add grandeur to the anthem; they and the concords leading by infinite modulations to the grand, final, perfect chord, that is to resound through all the infinities of space, forever.

At the 6*th Column:* . . . Asher shall pluck the fruit of the Tree of Life, that towers above the golden spires, and overlooks the jasper walls of the new Jerusalem. For he and all men shall learn to know the true God, the Infinity of Infinite attributes; not angry and jealous, nor implacable and vindictive; but kind and indulgent to human feebleness and frailty; loving and forgiving; a benefactor, a friend, a father.

At the 5*th Column:* . . . Naphtali believes, hopes waits and is patient. *Believes* that all death is new life; all destruction and dissolution, recombination and reproduction; and all evil and affliction but the modes of this great genesis, that shall not be eternal. *Hopes* for the time when this incessant flux and change shall cease, and the new Law of Love and Light rule in all spheres and over all existences; and *waits* with patience the fulfilment of the inviolable promises of God.

[At this moment a thick cloth is flung over the Candidate's head; and he is immediately seized by several brothers, and hurried into a small room that is perfectly dark. Leaving the cloth so that he can remove it at pleasure, they place him, sitting on the floor, in the middle of the room, and retire. This room should have no furniture, and be entirely hung with black. Apertures must be so arranged, that, without admitting the least light, the voice of one speaking outside may be heard. It must also be so arranged, that, by means of electricity or otherwise, sudden and momentary flashes of light may be produced, succeeded by intense darkness.

The candidate is left for five minutes in entire solitude and perfect silence. Then a Bro∴ says, in his hearing]:

1st Bro∴ All who will not worship the Beast with seven heads and ten horns, and upon his horns ten crowns, and the mysterious name upon his forehead, shall be slain. All men, the high and the low, the rich and the poor, freemen and slaves, shall receive upon their right hand, or on their forehead, his mark, his name, and the number of his name, which is six hundred threescore and six; or they shall neither buy nor sell; for his is power, dominion, and the authority of the great dragon. Man, helpless and in darkness, wilt thou receive his mark, that thou mayest emerge to light?

2d Brother . . . Fear God; and give glory to Him; for the hour of his judgment is come! And worship Him that made heaven and earth, and the sea, and the springs of waters; for He alone hath the True sign. If any man worship the Beast and his image, and receive his mark on his forehead or in his hand, he shall drink the wine of God's indignation, and be banished from the presence of the Holy Angels and of the Word that is the Redeemer. Remorse shall torture them, and they shall have no rest, who worship the Beast and his image, and receive the mark of his name.

3d Brother . . . Have patience, oh! thou, who, though in darkness, art still our brother! Keep the commandments of God, and thy faith in His justice and infinite goodness! Blessed are the dead that die in the Lord. They rest from their labours, and their influences live after them.

[There is silence again for a little while; and then the Brethren on the outside proceed]:

1st Bro∴ The first Angel hath poured his vial on the earth; and a foul and horrible plague hath fallen on all who wear the mark of the Beast, and have worshipped his image. [Light flashes into the room].

2d Bro∴ The second Angel hath poured his vial upon the sea; and it hath become like the blood of a dead man; and everything therein hath died. [Flash].

3d Bro∴ The third Angel hath poured his vial upon the rivers, the brooks, and the living springs; and they have become blood. [Flash].

Thou art just and righteous, O God, the Infinite and Eternal, in all Thy judgments! For Thou hast given to them blood to drink, who have persecuted their Brethren for their faith, and usurped Thy power and prerogative of judgment, and shed the blood of the virtuous and good.

1st Bro∴ The fourth Angel hath poured his vial upon the sun; and the wicked are scorched with great heat, and yet will not repent. [Flash].

2d Bro∴ The fifth Angel hath poured his vial upon those who worship the Beast. His kingdom is shrouded in darkness; and his followers howl for pain and terror, and blaspheme, and still do not repent. [Flashes].

3d Bro∴ The sixth Angel hath poured out his vial upon the great rivers of the Orient, and they are dried up: and the spirits of Falsehood, Fraud and Evil marshal their armies for the great battle, to be fought on the great day of the Almighty God. Unexpectedly, before men see its dawn, that day will come. See that ye be not found unprepared; but wear evermore the armour of Charity, Hope and Faith; lest it come suddenly and find you naked and defenceless! [Flash].

1st Bro∴ The seventh Angel hath poured his vial into the air. It is done! [Upon this, thunder is heard without, and frequent flashes light the cell. Then there are loud noises, voices, and a crash representing a city destroyed by an earthquake].

1st Bro∴ The cities of the nations have fallen; and Intolerance, that Great Babylon, is no more. The chains imposed by fraud upon the human mind, the manacles and fetters fastened by force upon Free Thought have fallen. The towers and battlements, the bastions and the ramparts, that Power, and Fraud and Falsehood thought impregnable, have fallen; and they shall no longer be drunk with the blood of the Saints and Martyrs of the Truth.

2d Bro∴ Salvation, glory, honour and power to the Eternal God and Infinite Father! True and righteous are His judgments. Let all His creatures, and the great voices of the ocean and His thunders cry rejoicingly; The Lord God Omnipotent reigneth, and Sin and Evil are dethroned! Blessed are they that obey his law, and trust in his goodness, that they may have right to the Tree of Life, and may enter in through the gates into the city. Brother, who art in darkness, wilt thou obey that law, and trust in that Infinite Goodness, and be patient, though the appointed time may seem to draw no nearer during thy life, nor thy labours and exertions to produce any fruit?

Cand.·. I will.

2d Bro.·. Wilt thou be neither weary nor discouraged; satisfied to sow the seed, and that those who come after thee may reap, if God so wills it?

Cand.·. I will.

1st Bro.·. Come, then, with us to the abode of Light!

[The door is opened, and the Candidate received by several brethren, and conducted into the Lodge. The draft or tracing-board is seen displayed; and after he enters, the officers read as follows]:

Orator: I saw a new Heaven and a new Earth: for the first heaven and the first earth were passed away, and there was no more sea. I saw the Holy City, the New Jerusalem, coming down from God out of Heaven. Henceforth He will dwell with men, and be their Father, and they his obedient loving children. He will wipe the tears from all eyes: and there shall be no more death, nor fraud nor falsehood. There shall be no more sin and shame, nor remorse nor affliction; nor sickness and death any more: for the ancient wrong and evil have passed away forever.

Ward.·. He that sits upon the Throne saith; I make all things new. Write! for these words are true. To him that thirsts I give freely the waters of the Spring of Life. He that overcometh shall inherit all things. I will be his Father, and will love my child.

Th.·. P.·. In the Heavenly City there shall be no Temple: for the Lord God Almighty and the Redeemer are its Temple. Nor sun nor moon shall be needed there:. for the Primitive Light shall shine therein and give it light. In that light shall all nations walk; and there shall all the splendours of the Universe have their spring and centre. Therein shall be no night, nor wickedness nor falsehood: but the light and everlasting Life and Truth of God shall reign there forever. He is Alpha and Omega, the beginning and the end, the First and the Last; from whom all things come, and to whom all return.

My Brother, if you believe in these promises, go now to the Holy Altar, and there assume the obligations of this Degree.

[The Candidate kneels at the Altar and, with his hands upon the Holy Bible, assumes the following]

OBLIGATION.

I, A . . . . B . . . . . , in the presence of Almighty God, and believing in his Justice and Mercy, do hereby and hereon most solemnly and sincerely promise and swear, that I will never reveal any of the secrets of this degree to any person in the world, except to him to whom the same may lawfully belong, and then only when I am duly authorized and empowered so to do.

I furthermore promise and swear, that I will obey the by-laws, rules and regulations of any Lodge of this degree to which I may belong; and the Edicts, laws and mandates of the Consistory of Sub.·. Princes of the Royal Secret under whose jurisdiction it may be holden, as well as those of the Sup.·. Council of the 33d Degree within whose jurisdiction I may reside, so far as the same may come to my knowledge: and that I will always recognize the Sup.·. Council of the 33d Degree at Charleston as the only true and legitimate Supreme Body for the Southern jurisdiction of the United States, of the Ancient and Accepted Rite of Masonry, and bear to it true faith and due allegiance, so far as its mandates and edicts conform to the ancient constitutions and the Landmarks of Masonry.

I furthermore promise and swear, That I will devote myself, my heart, my hand, my speech and my intellect, to the cause of Justice, Truth and Toleration; and will endeavour to do something for the benefit of my Country and the world, that shall live after I am dead: and that I will henceforward consider only what it is right and just, and noble and generous for me to do; and not whether any benefit to myself or mine will result therefrom; or whether I shall receive therefor thanks or ingratitude.

All of which I do most solemnly and sincerely promise and swear, binding myself under no less a penalty than that of being held false Knight and faithless Soldier, by every true Knight and honest man in Christendom. So help me God! and keep me steadfast in the due and punctual performance of the same!

Th.·. P.·. Malki-Tsedek, King of Salem, whose name signifies Just and Equitable King, was the Priest of the Most High God. He met Abraham returning from the slaying of the Kings, and blessed him: and Abraham gave unto him the tenth of the spoils.

[He anoints the Candidate with a little oil, on the crown of the head, and says]:

Th.·. P.·. Be thou a Priest forever, after the order of Malki-Tsedek, virtuous, sincere, equitable, true, Minister of Justice and Priest of Toleration! Be faithful to God, thy duty, and thyself; and thus deserve the title of Sublime Pontiff or Scottish Mason, which you are henceforward entitled to wear. Rise now, my Brother, and receive the Sign, Token and Words of this Degree.

Sign: Raise the ‡♀♌&♈‡&☉♒♊ to a &☿‡♀♍☿♒♈☉† §☿♎♀♈♀☿♒, the ♑♀♒♌☾‡♎ extended; and then drop the; †☉♎♈‡♑☿♒♌☾‡♎ perpendicularly.

Token: . . Place reciprocally the ‡☉†♋ of the ‡‡&☉♒♊ on the ♑☿‡☾&☾☉♊ of the other. . . . The first says &☉††☾†♑-♄☉&∴ . . . The second, ‡‡☉♀♎☾‡♄☾‡♈&☾‡†☿‡♊∴ . . . The first, ☉♋♒♑-☉†∴ . . . The second, ♋☉♄‡♌☿♊‡☉♎♎♀♎♈‡♑♎∴ . . . And both say, ☉♋☾♒∴

Pass-word: . . ☉♋♒♑-☉†∴

Sacred Word: . . &☉††☽†♑-♄☉&.

[Every brother then advances in turn to the Candidate, and gives him the Token: and the Th.·. P.·. then invests him with the insignia of the degree; saying, as he does so]:

The *robe* of white linen, with which I now invest you, is emblematical of that equity and purity which should characterize one who is consecrated to the service of Truth; and reminds us also of the vesture of the one hundred and forty-four thousand who refused to wear the mark of the beast upon their foreheads.

This *cordon* of crimson, bordered with white, teaches you that the zeal and ardour of a Knight and Pontiff ought to be set off by the greatest purity of morals and perfect charity and beneficence. The twelve stars upon it and upon the fillet allude to the twelve gates of the New City, the twelve signs of the Zodiac, the twelve fruits of the Tree of Life, the twelve Tribes of Israel and the twelve Apostles; the initials of whose names appear upon the gates and foundations of the New City, and on the twelve columns of the Lodge.

This *fillet* is the peculiar emblem of your Pontificate. And as the slightest contact with earth will soil its spotless purity, remember that so the least indiscretion will soil the exalted character that you have now voluntarily assumed.

Receive this *jewel:* and let the letters upon it and the cordon, the first and last of the Greek and Hebrew Alphabets, ever remind you of the love and veneration which you owe to that Great Being, the source of all existance, the Alpha and Omega, the First and the Last; on whose promises we rely with perfect confidence, in whose mercy and goodness we implicitly trust, and for the fulfilment of whose wise purposes we are content to wait.

[The Warden now displays to the Candidate the Tracing Board; and the Th.·. P.·. continues]:

Th.·. P.·. My Brother, after the ceremonies of this degree, this painting needs but little explanation; and most of that may be found in the closing chapters of the Apocalypse.

To us as Masons, the City overturned represents the Empire of Evil, finally overwhelmed and destroyed in the last great conflict between the Principles of Light and Darkness: which event mankind has in all ages expected, and the Holy Books of every Ancient Nation have foretold. The City descending from Heaven is the New Empire of Light and Truth, for which we wait and hope. The Tree of Life is emblematical of Truth, the basis of all the virtues represented by its fruits. The buildings of gold and walls of precious stones, and gates of pearl, are symbols of the glory that shall invest and make magnificent the Universe, when sickness and sin and pain and sorrow and guilt and evil shall disappear forever, and leave the world again a paradise, the splendid Temple of a God of Mercy and Beneficence. The River, to the dwellers in Eastern Deserts, was the symbol of purity, of generosity, of plenty: the tree, with its leaves and flowers and fruits, of Nature, who bestows her bounties and her many blessings, without waiting for men's thanks.

The twelve Tribes, whose initials adorn the columns, and are seen on the pearl gates of the City, are emblematical of the human race: and the twelve Apostles, whose initials are also on the bases of the columns, and on the foundations of the City, are to us the type of all those who have laboured to reform, instruct and elevate mankind.

The signs of the Zodiac, upon the columns, accompany the initials of those Tribes, respectively, to which they were assigned among the Hebrews: . . The Lion, to Judah . . Cancer, formerly the Asses, to Issachar . . Capricorn, to Zebulon . . Aquarius, to Reuben . . Pisces, to Simeon . . Aries, to Gad . . Taurus, to Ephraim . . Sagittarius, to Manasseh . . Gemini, to Benjamin . . Scorpio, once the Eagle, to Dan . . Libra, to Asher . . and Virgo, to Naphtali.

The Serpent, writhing in chains, has to us a peculiar signification. It was promised that the offspring of the woman should bruise the Serpent's head. Fulfil thou the prophecy!

[The candidate is caused to step in succession on the three heads: and as he does so, the Th∴ P∴ says, at each step respectively]:

> *So shall the foot of* Truth *crush* Error!
> *So* Honesty *and* Honour *trample on* Falsehood!
> *So* Charity *tread in the dust* Intolerance!

Th∴ P∴ The Hebrew characters upon the twelve columns are the twelve Great Names and Titles of Deity, upon the breast-plate of the High Priest. Beginning with the column of Judah, and in the order given above, they are: Melec; King or Sovereign: . . Gemel; Dispenser of Rewards and Punishments: . . Adar; Fire or Splendour: . . Aluh; the Adored: . . Ain; the Eye, or All-Seeing: . . Al-Khi; the Living God, or Life: . . Alhim; the Creative Deities, or the Aggregate of the Forces of Nature: . . Al; the Ancient Semitic Nature-God; the Elevated: . . Ihu; Life: . . Aish-Gebah; Majesty of Fire: . . Adonai; Lords: Sovereign: . . . and IHUH; Abstract Existence; The Self-Existent.

Go now, my Brother, and listen to the Lecture of this Degree.

LECTURE.

My Brother, the true Mason labours for the benefit of those that are to come after him, and for the advancement and improvement of his race. That is a poor ambition which contents itself within the limits of a single life. All men who deserve to live, desire to survive their funerals, and to live afterwards in the good that they have done mankind, rather than in the marble of men's memories. Most men desire to leave some work behind them that may outlast their own day and brief generation. That is an instinctive impulse, given by God, and often found in the rudest human heart; the surest proof of the soul's immortality, and of the fundamental difference between man and the wisest brutes. To plant the trees that after we are dead shall shelter our children, is as natural as to love the shade of those our fathers planted. The rudest unlettered husbandman, painfully conscious of his own inferiority, the poorest widowed mother, giving her life-blood to those who pay only for the work of her needle, will toil and stint themselves to educate their child, that he may take a higher station in the world than they; and of such children are the world's greatest benefactors.

In his influences that survive him, man becomes immortal, before the general resurrection. The Spartan mother, that, giving her son his shield, said, "With it, or upon it!" afterwards shared the government of Lacedæmon with the legislation of Lycurgus; for she too made a law, that lived after her; and she led the Spartan soldiery that afterwards demolished the walls of Athens, and aided Alexander to conquer the Orient. The widow that gave Marion the fiery arrows to burn her own house, that it might no longer shelter the enemies of her infant country, the house where she had lain upon her husband's bosom, and where her children had been born, legislated more effectually for her State than Locke or Shaftesbury, or than many a Legislature has done, since that State won her freedom.

It was of slight importance to the Kings of Egypt and the Monarchs of Assyria and Phœnicia, that the son of a Jewish woman, a foundling, adopted by the daughter of Sesostris Ramses, slew an Egyptian that oppressed a Hebrew slave, and fled into the desert, to remain there forty years. But Moses, who might otherwise have become Regent of Lower Egypt, known to us only by a tablet on a tomb or monument, became the deliverer of the Jews, and led them forth from Egypt to the frontiers of Palestine, and made for them a law, out of which grew the Christian faith; and so has shaped the destinies of the world. He and the old Roman lawyers, with Alfred of England, the Saxon Thanes and Norman Barons, the old judges and chancellors, and the makers of the canons, lost in the mists and shadows of the Past,—these are our legislators; and we obey the laws that they enacted.

Napoleon died upon the barren rock of his exile. His bones, borne to France by the son of a King, rest in the Hôpital des Invalides, in the great city on the Seine. His Thoughts still govern France. He, and not the People, dethroned the Bourbon, and drove the last King of the House of Orleans into exile. He, in his coffin, and not the People, voted the crown to the Third Napoleon; and he, and not the Generals of France and England, led their united forces against the grim Northern Despotism.

Mahomet announced to the Arabian idolaters the new creed, *There is but one God, and Mahomet, like Moses and Christ, is his apostle.* For many years unaided, then with the help of his family and a few friends, then with many disciples, and last of all with an army, he taught and preached the Koran. The religion of the wild Arabian enthusiast converting the fiery Tribes of the Great Desert, spread over Asia, built up the Saracenic dynasties, conquered Persia and India, the Greek Empire, Northern Africa and Spain, and dashed the surges of its fierce soldiery against the battlements of Northern Christendom. The law of Mahomet still governs a fourth of the human race; and Turk and Arab, Moor and Persian, still obey the Prophet, and pray with their faces turned towards Mecca; and he, and not the living, rules and reigns in the fairest portions of the Orient.

Confucius still enacts the law for China; and the thoughts of Peter the Great govern Russia. Plato and the other great Sages of Antiquity still reign as the Kings of Philosophy, and have dominion over the human intellect. The great Statesmen of the Past still preside in the Councils of Nations. Burke still lingers in the House of Commons, and Webster's grave accents yet ring in the American Senate.

Washington sleeps calmly in his tomb at Mount Vernon; which has become the Mecca, and the Potomac the highway, of the Pilgrims of Freedom. But his influences still live, and rule in the hearts of twenty-three millions of people; sway and direct the Councils of a great Nation; determine its foreign policy; and sanction or condemn its diplomacy and legislation. He has a truer and more absolute veto than the President; for he exercises his power through the People, who are Supreme, and who decide as he directs.

It has been well said, that when Tamerlane had built his pyramid of fifty thousand human skulls, and wheeled away with his vast armies from the gates of Damascus, to find new conquests, and build other pyramids, a little boy was playing in the streets of Mentz, son of a poor artisan, whose apparent importance in the scale of beings was, compared with that of Tamerlane, as that of a grain of sand to the giant bulk of the earth: but Tamerlane and all his shaggy legions, that swept over the East like a hurricane, have passed away, and become shadows; while the wonderful invention of John Faust the boy of Mentz, has exerted a greater influence on man's destinies and overturned more thrones and dynasties than all the victories of all the blood-stained conquerors that from Nimrod downward have afflicted God's fair world.

Long ages ago, the Temple built by Solomon and our Ancient Brethren sank into ruin, when the Assyrian Armies sacked Jerusalem. The Holy City is a mass of hovels cowering under the dominion of the Crescent; and the Holy Land a desert. The Kings of Egypt and Assyria, who were cotemporaries of Solomon, are forgotten, and their histories mere fables. The Ancient Orient is a shattered wreck bleaching on the shores of Time. The Wolf and the Jackal howl among the ruins of Thebes and of Tyre, and the sculptured images of the Temples and Palaces of Babylon are dug from their ruins and carried into strange lands. But the quiet and peaceful Order, of which the Son of a poor Phœnician Widow was one of the Grand Masters, with the Kings of Israel and Tyre, has continued to increase in stature and influence, defying the angry waves of time and the storms of persecution. Age has not weakened its wide foundations, nor shattered its columns, nor marred the beauty of its harmonious proportions. Where rude barbarians, in the time of Solomon, peopled inhospitable howling wildernesses, in France and Britain, and in that New World, not known to Jew or Gentile, until the glories of the Orient had faded, that Order has builded new Temples, and teaches to its million of Initiates those lessons of peace, good-will, and toleration, of reliance on God and confidence in man, which it learned when Hebrew and Giblemite worked side by side on the slopes of Lebanon; and the Servant of Jehovah and the Phœnician Worshipper of Bel sat with the humble artisan in Council at Jerusalem.

It is the Dead, that govern. The Living only obey. And if the Soul sees, after death, what passes on this earth, and watches over the welfare of those it loves; then must its greatest happiness consist in seeing the current of its beneficent influences widening out from age to age, as rivulets widen into rivers, and aiding to shape the destinies of individuals, families, States, the World: and its bitterest punishment, in seeing its evil influences causing mischief and misery, and cursing and afflicting men, long after the frame it dwelt in has become dust, and when both name and memory are forgotten.

We know not who among the Dead control our destinies. The universal human race is linked and bound together by those influences, which in the truest sense do make men's fates. Humanity is the unit, of which man is but a fraction. What other men in the Past have done, said, thought, makes the great iron network of circumstance that environs and controls us all. We take our faith on trust. We think and believe as the Old Lords of Thought command us; and Reason is powerless before Authority.

We would make or annul a particular contract; but the Thoughts of the dead Judges of England, living when their ashes have been cold for centuries, stand between us and that which we would do, and utterly forbid it. We would settle our estate in a particular way; but the prohibition of the English Parliament, its uttered Thought when the first or second Edward reigned, comes echoing down the long avenues of time, and tells us we shall not exercise the power of disposition as we wish. We would gain a particular advantage of another; and the thought of the old Roman lawyer who died before Justinian, or that of Rome's great orator Cicero, annihilates the act, or makes the intention ineffectual. This act, Moses forbids; that, Alfred. We would sell our land; but certain marks on a perishable paper tell us that our father or remote ancestor ordered otherwise: and the arm of the dead, emerging from the grave, with peremptory gesture prohibits the alienation. About to sin or err, the thought or wish of our mother, told us when we were children, by words that died upon the air in the utterance, and many a long year were forgotten, flashes on our memory, and holds us back with a power that is resistless.

Thus we obey the dead: and thus shall the living, when we are dead, for weal or wo obey us. The Thoughts of the Past are the laws of the Present and the Future. That which we say and do, if its effects last not beyond our lives, is unimportant. That which shall live when we are dead, as part of the great body of law enacted by the dead, is the only act worth doing, the only Thought worth speaking. The desire to do something that shall benefit the world, when neither praise nor obloquy will reach us where we sleep soundly in the grave, is the noblest ambition entertained by man.

It is the ambition of a true and genuine Mason. Knowing the slow processes by which the Deity brings about great results, he does not expect to reap as well as sow, in a single lifetime. It is the inflexible fate and noblest destiny, with rare exceptions, of the great and good, to work, and let others reap the harvest of their labours. He who does good, only to be repaid in kind, or in thanks and gratitude, or in reputation and the world's praise, is like him who loans his money, that he may, after certain months, receive the principal back with interest. To be repaid for eminent services with slander, obloquy or ridicule, or at best with stupid indifference or cold ingratitude, as it is common, so it is no misfortune, except to those who lack the wit to see or sense to appreciate, or the nobility of soul to thank and reward with eulogy, the benefactor of his kind. His influences live, and the great Future will obey; whether it recognize or disown the lawgiver.

Miltiades was fortunate that he was exiled; and Aristides that he was ostracized, because men wearied of hearing him called The Just. Not the Redeemer was unfortunate; but those only who repaid him for the inestimable gift he offered them, and for a life passed in toiling for their good, by nailing him upon the cross, as though he had been a slave or malefactor. The persecutor dies and rots, and Posterity utters his name with execration: but his victim's memory he has unintentionally made glorious and immortal.

If not for slander and persecution, the Mason who would benefit his race must look for apathy and cold indifference in those whose good he seeks, in those who ought to seek the good of others. Except when the sluggish depths of the Human Mind are broken up and tossed as with a storm, when at the appointed time a great Reformer comes, and a new Faith springs up and grows with supernatural energy, the progress of Truth is slower than the growth of oaks; and he who plants need not expect to gather. The Redeemer, at his death, had twelve disciples, and one betrayed and one deserted and denied him. It is enough for us to know that the fruit will come in its due season. When; or who shall gather it, it does not in the least concern us to know. It is our business to plant the seed. It is God's right to give the fruit to whom he pleases; and if not to us, then is our action by so much the more noble.

To sow, that others may reap; to work and plant for those that are to occupy the earth when we are dead; to project our influences far into the future, and live beyond our time; to rule as the Kings of Thought, over men who are yet unborn; to bless with the glorious gifts of Truth and Light and Liberty those who will neither know the name of the giver, nor care in what grave his unregarded ashes repose, is the true office of a Mason and the proudest destiny of a man.

All the great and beneficent operations of Nature are produced by slow and often imperceptible degrees. The work of destruction and devastation only is violent and rapid. The Volcano and the Earthquake, the Tornado and the Avalanche leap suddenly into full life and fearful energy, and smite with an unexpected blow. Vesuvius buried Pompeii and Herculaneum in a night; and Lisbon fell prostrate before God in a breath, when the earth rocked and shuddered: the Alpine village vanishes and is erased at one bound of the avalanche; and the ancient forests fall like grass before the mower, when the mad tornado is hurled upon them. Grim Pestilence slays its thousands in a day, and the storm in a night strews the sand with shattered navies.

The Gourd of the Prophet Jonah grew up, and was withered, in a night. But many years ago, before the Norman Conqueror stamped his mailed foot on the neck of prostrate Saxon England, some wandering barbarian, of the continent then unknown to the world, in mere idleness, with hand or foot, covered an acorn with a little earth, and passed on regardless, on his journey to the dim Past. He died and was forgotten; but the acorn lay there still, the mighty force within it acting in the darkness. A tender shoot stole gently up; and fed by the light and air and frequent dews, put forth its little leaves, and lived, because the elk or buffalo chanced not to place his foot upon and crush it. The years marched onward, and the shoot became a sapling, and its green leaves went and came with Spring and Autumn. And still the years came and passed away again, and William the Norman Bastard parcelled England out among his Barons, and still the sapling grew, and the dews fed its leaves, and the birds builded their nests among its small limbs for many generations. And still the years came and went, and the Indian hunter slept in the shade of the sapling, and Richard Lion-Heart fought at Acre and Ascalon, and John's bold Barons wrested from him the Great Charter; and lo! the sapling had become a tree; and still it grew, and thrust its great arms wider abroad, and lifted its head still higher towards the Heavens: strong-rooted, and defiant of the storms that roared and eddied through its branches: and when Columbus ploughed with his keels the Western Ocean, and Cortez and Pizarro bathed the cross in the blood of many thousand Mexican and Peruvian hearts; and when the Puritan, the Huguenot, the Cavalier and the follower of Penn sought a refuge and a resting-place beyond the ocean, the Great Oak still stood, firm-rooted, vigorous, stately, haughtily domineering over all the forest, heedless of all the centuries that had hurried past since the wild Indian planted the little acorn in the forest;—a stout and hale old tree, with wide circumference shading many a rood of ground; and fit to furnish timbers for a ship, to carry the thunders of the Great Republic's guns around the world. And yet, if one had sat and watched it every instant, from the moment when the feeble shoot first pushed its way to the light until the eagles built among its branches, he would never have seen the tree or sapling *grow*.

Many long centuries ago, before the Chaldean Shepherds watched the Stars or Shufu built the Pyramids, one could have sailed in a seventy-four where now a thousand islands gem the surface of the Indian Ocean; and the deep sea lead would no where have found any bottom. But below those waves were myriads upon myriads, beyond the power of Arithmetic to number, of little minute existences, each a perfect living creature, made by the Almighty Creator, and fashioned by Him for the work it had to do. There they toiled beneath the waters, each doing its allotted work, and wholly ignorant of the result which God intended. They lived and died, incalculable in numbers and almost infinite in the succession of their generations, each adding his mite to the gigantic work that went on there under God's direction. Thus hath He chosen to create great Continents and Islands; and still the coral-insects live and work, as when they made the rocks that underlie the valley of the Ohio.

Thus God hath chosen to create. Where now is firm land, once chafed and thundered the great primeval ocean. For ages upon ages the minute shields of infinite myriads of infusoria, and the stony stems of encrinites sunk into its depths, and there, under the vast pressure of its waters, hardened into limestone. Raised slowly from the Profound by His hand, its quarries underlie the soil of all the continents, hundreds of feet in thickness; and we, of these remains of the countless dead, build tombs and palaces, as the Egyptians, whom we call ancient, built their pyramids.

On all the broad lakes and oceans the Great Sun looks earnestly and lovingly, and the invisible vapors rise ever up to meet him. No eye but God's beholds them as they rise. There, in the upper atmosphere, they are condensed to mist, and gather into clouds, and float and swim around in the ambient air. They sail with its currents, and hover over the ocean, and roll in huge masses round the stony shoulders of great mountains. Condensed still more by change of temperature, they drop upon the thirsty earth in gentle showers, or pour upon it in heavy rains, or storm against its bosom at the angry Equinoctial. The shower, the rain and the storm pass away, the clouds vanish, and the bright stars again shine clearly upon the glad earth. The rain-drops sink into the ground, and gather in subterranean reservoirs, and run in subterranean channels, and bubble up in springs and fountains; and from the mountain-sides and heads of valleys the silver threads of water begin their long journey to the ocean. Uniting, they widen into brooks and rivulets, then into streams and rivers; and, at last, a Nile, a Ganges, an Amazon, or a Mississippi rolls between its banks, mighty, majestic and resistless, creating vast alluvial valleys to be the granaries of the world, ploughed by the thousand keels of commerce and serving as great highways, and as the impassable boundaries of rival nations; ever returning to the ocean the drops that rose from it in vapor, and descended in rain and snow and hail upon the level plains and lofty mountains; and causing him to recoil for many a mile before the headlong rush of their great tide.

So it is with the aggregate of Human endeavour. As the invisible particles of vapour combine and coalesce to form the mists and clouds that fall in rain on thirsty continents, and bless the great green forests and wide grassy prairies, the waving meadows and the fields by which men live; as the infinite myriads of drops that the glad earth drinks are gathered into springs and rivulets and rivers, to aid in levelling the mountains and elevating the plains, and to feed the large lakes and restless oceans; so all Human Thought, and Speech and Action, all that is done and said and thought and suffered upon the Earth combines together, and flows onward in one broad resistless current towards those great results to which they are determined by the will of God.

We build slowly and destroy swiftly. Our Ancient Brethren who built the Temples at Jerusalem, with many myriad blows felled, hewed, and squared the cedars, and quarried the stones, and carved the intricate ornaments, which were to be the Temples. Stone after stone, by the combined effort and long toil of Apprentice, Fellow-Craft and Master, the walls arose; slowly the roof was framed and fashioned; and many years elapsed, before, at length, the Houses stood finished, all fit and ready for the Worship of God, gorgeous in the sunny splendours of the atmosphere of Palestine. So they were built. A single motion of the arm of a rude, barbarous Assyrian Spearman, or drunken Roman or Gothic Legionary of Titus, moved by a senseless impulse of the brutal will, flung in the blazing brand; and, with no further human agency, a few short hours sufficed to consume and melt the Temple to a smoking mass of black unsightly ruin.

Be patient, therefore, my Brother, and wait!

The issues are with God: To do,
Of right belongs to us.

Therefore faint not, my Brother, nor be weary in well doing. Be not discouraged at men's apathy, nor disgusted with their follies, nor tired of their indifference. Care not for returns and results; but see only what there is to do, and do it, leaving the results to God. Soldier of the Cross! Sworn Knight of Justice, Truth, and Toleration! Good Knight and True! be patient and work!

TO CLOSE.

Th∴P∴ Bro∴ Warden, what is the hour?

W∴ Th∴P∴ the hour is accomplished.

Th∴P∴ What then remains to be done?

W∴ To work, to wait, and to be patient.

Th∴P∴ Work then, my Brethren, while it is yet Day; for the night cometh in which no man can work. For what do we wait, Bro∴ Warden?

W∴ For the Light of Noon-day.

Th∴P∴ Let us then close this Lodge, and be patient. Bro∴ Warden, inform the Knights and Pontiffs, that I am about to close this Lodge, if they consent; in order that each may go forth into the world, and do his duty as Soldier and Priest of Truth, Light and Toleration.

W∴ . . . . Brother Knights and Pontiffs, the Th∴ Puissant Master is about to close this Lodge, if you consent, that we may all go forth into the world and labour to elevate and ennoble humanity, as true Soldiers and Priests of Light, Truth and Toleration. If you consent, give me the sign!

[All give the sign. The Th∴P∴ and W∴ rap , ? as in opening. Then all the Brethren clap , ? with their hands, and cry ; times HOSCHEAH!]

Th∴P∴ The Sun climbs towards the Zenith; and this Lodge is closed.

FINIS.

Twentieth Degree.

Venerable Grand Master of all Symbolic Lodges; or Master ad Vitam.

THE LODGE, ITS DECORATIONS, ETC.

The hangings are blue and gold; [the blue and gold of the clouds in which God appeared to Moses].

In the East is a Throne, which you ascend by nine steps, under a canopy. Before it is an altar, on which are an open Bible, Square and Compasses, Sword, Mallet, &c., as in Symbolic Lodges. The Lodge is lighted by nine lights, in a candlestick with nine branches, between the Altar and the South.

Over the Ven∴ Master in the East is a glory, surrounding a Triangle, in the centre of which are the words, *Fiat Lux.*

In the middle of the room are three columns, forming a triangle, on which are these words: on that in the East, TRUTH: on that in the West, JUSTICE: on that in the South, TOLERATION.

This Lodge cannot be opened with less than nine members.

The lights in the great candlestick are arranged in three triangles, one within the other. There are other lights in different parts of the Lodge, all arranged in squares and triangles; but those in the great candlestick should be of yellow wax, and very large.

OFFICERS, DRESS, ETC.

The Presiding officer is styled Ven∴ Gr∴ Master; and sits in the East.

The Gr∴ Sen∴ and Gr∴ Jun∴ Wardens are, the former in the West, and the latter in the South. The Gr∴ Sen∴ and Gr∴ Jun∴ Deacons sit as the Deacons do in Symbolic Lodges. The Orator sits in the North. The Pursuivant guards the door, within.

All the Brethren wear their hats.

The cordon is a broad ribbon of yellow and sky-blue; or two, one of each color, worn crossing each other.

The apron is yellow, bordered and lined with sky-blue. Upon it, in the centre, are three triangles, equilateral, one within the other, with the initial letters of the nine Great Lights in the corners, thus arranged: in the corners of the outer Triangle, . . at the apex, C∴: at the right hand corner below, G∴ and at the left hand corner, V∴ . . . . Of the middle Triangle . . at the apex, IL∴; and at the right and left hand corners, P∴ and H∴ . . . . And of the inner Triangle, at the apex, T∴, and at the right and left hand corners, T∴ and J∴.

In the centre of the inner triangle is the Tetragrammaton: and across it, from below upwards, the words, FIAT LUX∴.

The tracing Board is an Octagon, with a square raised on each of five sides, and an equilateral triangle

1D

on each of the three others: with the initials of the twenty-nine Virtues of a Mason in the corners of the Squares and Triangles.

The jewel is of gold; like the triangles on the apron, with the same words and letters; or like the tracing-board.

The Battery is , ?

TO OPEN.

[The Ven∴ Gr∴ Master gives one rap; and says]:

V∴ M∴ Gr∴ Masters and Brethren, the hour has come for this Gr∴ Lodge to convene. Be pleased to clothe yourselves and repair to your appropriate stations. Bro∴ Gr∴ Jun∴ Deacon, see that the doors are duly guarded.

[The Jun∴ Deacon goes out, returns, gives the alarm [, ?] — and reports]:

Jun∴ D∴ Ven∴ Gr∴ Master, the doors are duly guarded.

Ven∴ M∴ Bro∴ Gr∴ Sen∴ Warden, ascertain whether all present are Gr∴ Masters.

[The Sen∴ W∴ goes round, receives the word from each, returns, and reports]:

Sen∴ W∴ Ven∴ Gr∴ Master, all present have the word, and prove themselves Gr∴ Masters.

Ven∴ M∴ Bro∴ Gr∴ Jun∴ Deacon, what compose the first Masonic Square?

Jun∴ D∴ *Prudence, Temperance, Chastity* and *Sobriety.*

Ven∴ M∴ Bro∴ Gr∴ Sen∴ Deacon, what compose the second Masonic Square?

Sen∴ D∴ *Heroism, Firmness, Equanimity* and *Patience.*

Ven∴ M∴ Bro∴ Gr∴ Secretary, what compose the third Masonic Square?

Sec∴ *Purity, Honour, Fidelity* and *Punctuality.*

Ven∴ M∴ Bro∴ Gr∴ Treasurer, what compose the fourth Masonic Square?

Treas∴ *Charity, Kindness, Generosity* and *Liberality.*

Ven∴ M∴ Bro∴ Gr∴ Orator, what compose the fifth Masonic Square?

Orat∴ *Disinterestedness, Mercy, Forgiveness* and *Forbearance.*

V∴ M∴ Bro∴ Gr∴ Jun∴ Warden, what is the first great Masonic Triangle?

J∴ W∴ *Veneration, Devotedness* and *Patriotism.*

V∴ M∴ Bro∴ Gr∴ Sen∴ Warden, what is the second great Masonic Triangle?

S∴ W∴ *Gratitude to God; Love of mankind;* and *Confidence in Human Nature.*

V∴ M∴ And the third great Triangle is composed of TRUTH, which includes *Frankness, Plain-dealing* and *Sincerity;* JUSTICE, which includes *Equity* and *Impartiality;* and TOLERATION. My Brethren, these are the appropriate jewels of a Grand Master; compared with which, silver and gold and precious stones are valueless as the common earth from which they came. [Raps , ?] Brethren in the South, what seek you to attain in Masonry?

Jun∴ W∴ LIGHT! The Light of *Knowledge, Science* and *Philosophy.*

Ven∴ M∴ [Raps , ?] Brethren in the North, what seek you to attain in Masonry?

Orator: . . LIGHT! The Light of *Liberty, Free Thought, Free Speech* for all mankind: Free *Conscience,* Free *Action,* within Law the same for all.

Ven∴ M∴ [Raps , ?]. Brethren in the West, what seek you to attain in Masonry?

Sen∴ W∴ LIGHT! The Great Light of God's Divine *Truth,* Eternal as Himself; and of *Virtue,* immortal as the Soul.

Ven∴ M∴ Aid me then, my Brethren, to open this Lodge; that we may together seek the True Masonic Light. The sign, my Brethren!

[The Brethren all give the sign].

Ven∴ M∴ My Brethren, let the Great Lights of the Lodge be lighted!

[Each officer advances in turn, and lights one of the lights in the great candlestick, and then returns to his station; saying, as he lights the candle, as follows]:

Pursuivant: Let *Veneration* for the Deity burn in this Lodge as its first Great Light!

Jun∴ Deacon: Let the Light of *Charity* shine in this Lodge!

Sen∴ Deacon: Let the light of *Generosity* be lifted up in this Lodge!

Secretary: Let the light of *Heroism* blaze like the Day among us!

Treasurer: Let the Light of *Honour* ever direct our footsteps!

Orator: Let the Light of *Patriotism* shine in our souls as in the Lodge!

Jun∴ Warden: Let the Great Light of *Justice* burn steadily upon our altars!

Sen∴ Warden: Let the Great Light of *Toleration* dim the fires of Persecution!

Ven∴ Master: Let the Great Light of TRUTH illumine our Souls, and complete the Great Triangles of Perfection!

[Then all clap their hands [, ?] — and cry *Fiat Lux!*].

Ven∴ M∴ My Brethren, the Nine Great Lights are burning in our Lodge, and it is duly opened.

RECEPTION.

[The Candidate for this Degree, wearing the collar and jewel of a Gr∴ Pontiff, and the jewel of a Rose ✠, is received by the Sen∴ Deacon, and conducted to the door of the Lodge-Room; in which the Nine great Lights are extinguished. The Sen∴ Deacon raps [, ?], which the Jun∴ Deacon answers from within, opens the door and enquires]:

J∴ Deac∴ Who seeks admission here?

Sen∴ D∴ A Mason, who having attained the 19th Degree, desires to be here qualified to preside over all Symbolic Lodges; that he may still further advance in Masonry.

S∴ D∴ Is it not through mere idle curiosity, or for the sake of distinction among his fellows, that he prefers this request?

Sen∴ D∴ It is not.

J∴ D∴ Is he of that number of Masons, who, having obtained the degrees, repose thereafter in contented indolence, indifferent to the evils that demand to be redressed?

Sen∴ D∴ He is not.

J∴ Deac∴ Is he of that class of Masons who utter beautiful sentiments, and press on others the performance of Masonic duty; and with that remain content?

Sen∴ D∴ He is not.

J∴ Deac∴ Is he of that class of Masons who spare their own purse, and levy liberal contributions on those of others, for works of charity and the welfare of the Order?

Sen∴ D∴ He is not.

J∴ D∴ If he be one of these, let him speedily withdraw. For such Masons we have here no room, no need, no use. Do you vouch for him that he is none of these?

Sen∴ D∴ I do.

Jun∴ D∴ It is well. Let him wait with patience until the Ven∴ Gr∴ Master, informed of his request, ascertains the will of the Brethren.

[The Jun∴ Deacon reports to the Sen∴ Warden, the same questions being asked, and like answers returned as at the door; except the last answer; instead of which the Sen∴ Warden says " It is well:" and reports to the Ven∴ Master, the same questions being asked, and like answers returned, except the last].

Ven∴ M∴ It is well. My Brethren, you hear. Is it your pleasure that this Candidate shall be admitted? If so, give me the affirmative sign.

[The affirmative sign is, to raise the right hand above the head].

Ven∴ M∴ If any are of another opinion, give me the negative sign.

[The negative sign is, to stretch out the right hand to the front, palm open and outwards, as if repelling a person. If the votes are all in the affirmative, the Ven∴. M∴. says, "Let the Candidate be admitted." He is introduced, and placed in the centre of the Triangle formed by the Three Columns, and in front of the altar; where the Sen∴. Deacon leaves him by himself].

Ven∴. M∴. My Brother, you have often kneeled before the altar of Masonry; and you now stand before it again, enclosed in the great triangle formed by the three great columns which support this Lodge. What name do you read upon the column in the South?

Cand. TOLERATION.

Ven∴. M∴. No man has the right to dictate to another in matters of belief or Faith. No man can say that he has possession of Truth, as he has of a chattel. It is no merit in any one to entertain that faith which his birth-place, his education or habit have imposed upon him, without examination and investigation into the evidences on which it is based. When man persecutes for opinion's sake, he usurps the prerogative of God. Do you admit the truth of these principles?

Cand∴. I do..

Ven∴. M∴. What name do you read upon the column in the West?

Cand∴. JUSTICE.

Ven∴. M∴. Man should judge others as he judges himself; believe others honest and sincere as he believes himself; find for their actions the excuses that he readily finds for his own; and look always for a good rather than a bad motive. Justice and Equity are like the Light and Air. God made them common to all; and he who denies justice to his Brother, or wrongs him in his estate, his affections, or his reputation, is a plunderer unfit to live. Do you recognize the truth of these principles?

Cand∴. I do.

Ven∴. M∴. What name do you read upon the column in the West?

Cand∴. TRUTH.

Ven∴. M∴. He who lies is a coward. No falsehood can be other than an evil. To lie, expressly or by implication, is base and dishonourable. Without Truth, there can be no virtue: and he who professes an opinion he does not entertain, originates a falsehood or a slander, or receives and passes it, as he receives and passes coin, is an utterer of spurious moneys, deserving to be branded as a malefactor and forger. God is PERFECT TRUTH, and every lie, prevarication, misrepresentation, colouring or concealment is an offence against HIM, and disgraceful to a Mason. Do you recognize the truth of these principles?

Cand∴. I do.

Ven∴. M∴. Will you make them hereafter the inflexible rule of your life, conduct and conversation, letting no inducement, temptation or necessity, however stringent, persuade you to swerve from them?

Cand∴. I will.

Ven∴. M∴. Kneel then at the Altar, and assume the obligation appropriate to the rank and degree which you desire to receive.

[The Candidate kneels, and repeats the following]

OBLIGATION.

I, A. . . . . B. . . . . ., do hereby and hereon, in the presence of the God of Truth, Justice and Mercy, and appealing to Him for the uprightness of my intentions, most solemnly and sincerely swear, and to each Gr∴. Master here present, and elsewhere in existence, do most sincerely promise, pledge myself and vow; That I will never reveal any of the Secrets of this Degree to any person in the known world, except to one who is duly authorized to receive them, and when I am fully authorized to communicate them.

. . . . . I furthermore promise and swear that I will henceforward forever make those virtues which compose the five Masonic Squares and three Masonic Triangles of this Lodge the rule and guide of my life, conduct and conversation; and will endeavour by all means in my power to extend and increase the practice of them among men: and particularly, that my steps shall ever be guided and directed by the Nine Great Lights of a Gr∴. Master, as I shall be informed thereof hereafter.

. . . . . . I furthermore promise and swear that I will not govern any Lodge or other Masonic Body, over which I may be called to preside, in a haughty or arbitrary manner; but with gentleness, urbanity and courtesy; and that I will use my best endeavours to preserve peace and harmony among the members thereof and all Masons everywhere.

I furthermore promise and swear, that I will never assist in, be present at, or consent to, the conferring of this degree and dignity upon any Mason who will not and does not answer, and, as I believe, truly, heartily and sincerely, all the questions asked of me at the door, and here before the Altar and within the columns.

To all of which I do most solemnly and sincerely swear; binding myself under no less a penalty, than that of being despised and execrated by all Masons, and detested by all whom I hold most dear on earth. So help me God! and keep me steadfast! Amen!

[The Ven∴ M∴ then raises the Candidate, and gives him the signs, words and tokens; as follows]:

FIRST SIGN: ... Form four ⟨cipher⟩, thus: Place the ⟨cipher⟩ on the ⟨cipher⟩, the ⟨cipher⟩, the ⟨cipher⟩ raised: thus making with the ⟨cipher⟩ one ⟨cipher⟩, and with the ⟨cipher⟩ one. Place the ⟨cipher⟩ on the ⟨cipher⟩, making a similar ⟨cipher⟩ with the ⟨cipher⟩; and with the ⟨cipher⟩ of the ⟨cipher⟩ form a ⟨cipher⟩.

SECOND SIGN: ⟨cipher⟩ on both ⟨cipher⟩; and place the ⟨cipher⟩ on the ⟨cipher⟩, leaning the head a little to the left.

THIRD SIGN: ∴ Cross the ⟨cipher⟩ on the ⟨cipher⟩ and ⟨cipher⟩ and ⟨cipher⟩ uppermost. The ⟨cipher⟩ and ⟨cipher⟩ thus form four ⟨cipher⟩: then place the ⟨cipher⟩ in a ⟨cipher⟩.

TOKEN: .. Take each the ⟨cipher⟩ of the other with the ⟨cipher⟩ the ⟨cipher⟩ on the ⟨cipher⟩, and the fingers closed together on the ⟨cipher⟩: ⟨cipher⟩ the ⟨cipher⟩ thus ! ⟨cipher⟩—then ⟨cipher⟩ the ⟨cipher⟩ down as far as the ⟨cipher⟩, as if to ⟨cipher⟩ each other the ⟨cipher⟩: then raise the; ⟨cipher⟩, and ⟨cipher⟩ with the ⟨cipher⟩ the ⟨cipher⟩ of each other.

TOKEN UPON INTRODUCTION: .. Take each other by the right hand, with the ⟨cipher⟩ upon the ⟨cipher⟩ of the ⟨cipher⟩, and ⟨cipher⟩ your ⟨cipher⟩ that of the other, to the ⟨cipher⟩ of the ⟨cipher⟩.

PASS-WORD: ... ⟨cipher⟩∴
ANSWER: ... ⟨cipher⟩∴

2d PASS-WORD: ... ⟨cipher⟩∴
ANSWER: ... ⟨cipher⟩∴

3d PASS-WORD: ... ⟨cipher⟩∴

SACRED WORD: .. ⟨cipher⟩∴

[The Ven∴ M∴ then invests the candidate with the collar, apron and jewel of the degree; and then says]:

V∴ M∴ My Brother, as the presiding officer of a Lodge, it will be your particular duty to dispense light and knowledge to the Brethren. That duty is not performed, nor is that which the old charges require, that at opening and closing the Master shall give or cause to be given, a lecture, or part of a lecture, for the instruction of the Brethren, by asking and receiving the answers to three or four merely formal and trivial questions.

On the contrary, that duty is far higher and more important: and it behooves the Master to be prepared to perform it: nor should any one accept the office of Master, until, by acquaintance and familiarity with the history, morals, and philosophy of Masonry, he is fitted to enlighten and instruct his brethren. That you may ever remember that duty, you will now proceed symbolically to perform it, by restoring to us the splendor of our Nine Great Lights in Masonry.

[Directed by the Sen∴ W∴, the candidate lights each of the nine lights in succession: the V∴ M∴ saying, before and after each is lighted, and the candidate repeating, as follows]:

V∴ M∴ *Let the Great Light of* VENERATION *shine in our Lodge!* Veneration of God, the Supreme Father: not a slavish fear and adulation, but a loving reverence for a Deity infinitely wise, good, beneficent, and merciful. FIAT LUX! [The candidate lights the first candle]. The light shines! Let us applaud, my Brethren! [All clap with their hands ,? and cry LUX EST!]. Say after me, my Brother! *So let the Light of Veneration shine in me!* [The candidate repeats this].

Let the Great Light of CHARITY *shine in our Lodge!* Charity; to relieve misery and distress, and condole with the broken-hearted; charity, to forgive the errors and judge kindly of the motives of our Brother. *Fiat Lux!* [The candidate lights the 2d]. The light shines! let us applaud, my Brethren! [They applaud as before]. My Brother, say after me . . . *So let the Light of Charity shine in me!*

Let the Great Light of GENEROSITY *shine in our Lodge;* that generous nobility of soul that overlooks injuries, and scorns to punish wrongs; that will rather confer than receive favours; and that doubles the value of its gifts by the graceful mode in which it makes them. *Fiat Lux!* [The 3d is lighted]. The light shines! Let us applaud! my Brethren! [Appl∴]. My Bro∴, say after me . . . *So let the Light of Generosity shine in me!*

Let the Great Light of HEROISM *shine in our Lodge:* that noble Heroism, inspired by which, men die at obscure posts of duty, when none are their witnesses save God: which sustains the martyr at the stake, upholds the humble missionary among savages, strengthens the fireman's arm, and actuates the patient watcher with the sick, when the air is thick with pestilence! *Fiat Lux!* [The 4th is lighted]. The light shines! Let us applaud, my Brethren! [Appl∴]. My Bro∴, say after me . . . *So may the Light of Heroism shine in me!*

Let the Great Light of HONOUR *shine in our Lodge!* that true Honour, incapable of baseness, treachery, or deceit: that never breaks its word to man or woman; that guards its ermine from the slightest spot or stain; and fears the act far more than the disgrace that follows it. *Fiat Lux!* &c. &c. . . . *So may the Light of Honour shine in me!*

Let the Great Light of PATRIOTISM *shine in our Lodge:* Patriotism, willing to sacrifice itself for the common good, even when neither thanks nor honour follow it: that asks not whether what the country's weal requires will or will not be popular; but does the right without regard to consequences: the patriotism of Leonidas, who died to hold Thermopylæ; of Curtius, who leaped into the yawning gulf; of Winkelried, who turned the Burgundian spear-points towards his heart; of Socrates, who died because the law willed it, rather than escape; of all who love the soil that gave them birth, enough to die for it unwept, unhonoured, and unsung. *Fiat Lux!* &c. &c. . . . *So may the Light of Patriotism shine in me!*

Let the Great Light of JUSTICE *shine in our Lodge!* Justice, that gives to every man his due, and pronounces righteous judgment even when its possessor is plaintiff or defendant; that takes bribes neither from friendship nor dislike; that is not rash nor censorious; nor hates sin so much as to come to love mankind too little. *Fiat Lux!* &c. &c. . . *So may the Light of Justice shine in me!*

Let the Great Light of TOLERATION *shine in our Lodge:* Toleration, that fears to usurp God's prerogative, remembering the warning; *Judge not, lest ye be judged:* and holds that every man has an estate in fee in his opinions, and the absolute, ample right of free enjoyment. *Fiat Lux,* &c. &c. . . *So may the Light of Toleration shine in me!*

Let the Great Light of TRUTH, *greatest and crowning Light of all, shine in our Lodge!* Truth, the Imperial and Divine! The Infinite Attribute of God! Truth, that rebukes and abhors evasion, prevarication, and mental reservation. Truth, that rejoices in the light—itself and Light twin emanations from the Deity. *Fiat Lux!* &c. &c. . . . *So may the Divine Light of Truth shine in me!* [Cand∴ repeats]. . . . Seal, now, and perfect your obligation as Gr∴ Master of all symbolic Lodges: [says, and cand∴ repeats] . . . *and when these great lights cease to illumine my soul, direct my conduct, and guide my footsteps, may I, as false Mason and worthless man, cease to exist, and be remembered only to be despised; so help me God!*

[The Ven∴ M∴ then displays to the candidate the tracing board, and says to him]:

V∴ M∴ My Brother, behold the 5 Great Squares and 3 Great Triangles of Masonry: composed as follows:

The square at the bottom of the octagon, that surrounds the Ineffable Name, and the 7 letters of the words with which He created Light,—of *Prudence, Temperance, Chastity* and *Sobriety.*

The first square on the right,—of *Heroism, Firmness, Equanimity* and *Patience.*

The first square on the left,—of *Probity, Honour, Fidelity* and *Punctuality.*

The upper square on the right, of *Disinterestedness, Mercy, Forgiveness* and *Forbearance.*

The upper square on the left,—of *Charity, Kindness, Generosity* and *Liberality.*

The Triangle on the right,—of *Gratitude* to God; *Love* of Mankind; and *Confidence* in Human Nature.

The Triangle on the left,—of *Veneration, Devotedness* and *Patriotism:* Veneration of God; Devotedness to family and friends; and ardent Love for our country.

And the Triangle in the centre,—of TRUTH, which includes *Frankness, Plain-dealing* and *Sincerity;* JUSTICE, which includes *Equity* and *Impartiality;* and *Toleration.*

[The Orator then reads the following Lecture]:

LECTURE.

The true Mason, my Brother, is a practical Philosopher, who, under religious emblems, in all ages adopted by wisdom, builds upon plans traced by nature and reason the moral edifice of knowledge. He ought to find, in the symmetrical relation of all the parts of this rational edifice, the principle and rule of all his duties, the source of all his pleasures. He improves his moral nature, becomes a better man, and finds in the reunion of virtuous men, assembled with pure views, the means of multiplying his acts of beneficence. Masonry and Philosophy, without being one and the same thing, have the same object, and propose to themselves the same end, the worship of the Gr∴ Architect of the Universe, acquaintance and familiarity with the wonders of nature, and the happiness of humanity, attained by the constant practice of all the virtues.

As Gr∴ Master of all Symbolic Lodges, it is your especial duty to aid in restoring Masonry to its primitive purity. You have become an instructor. Masonry long wandered in error. Instead of improving, it degenerated from its primitive simplicity, and retrograded towards a system, distorted by stupidity and ignorance, which, unable to construct a beautiful machine, made a complicated one. Less than two hundred years ago, its organization was simple, and altogether moral, its emblems, allegories and ceremonies easy to be understood, and their purpose and object readily to be seen. It was then confined to a very small number of degrees. Its constitutions were like those of a Society of Essenes, written in the first century of our era. There could be seen the primitive Christianity, organized into Masonry, the school of Pythagoras without incongruities or absurdities; a Masonry simple and significant, in which it was not necessary to torture the mind to discover reasonable interpretations; a Masonry at once religious and philosophical, worthy of a good citizen and an enlightened philanthropist.

Innovators and inventors overturned that primitive simplicity. Ignorance engaged in the work of making degrees; and trifles and gewgaws and pretended mysteries, absurd or hideous, usurped the place of Masonic Truth. The picture of a horrid vengeance, the poniard and the bloody head, appeared in the peaceful Temple of Masonry, without sufficient explanation of their symbolic meaning. Oaths, out of all proportion with their object, shocked the candidate, and then became ridiculous, and were wholly disregarded. Acolytes were exposed to tests, and compelled to perform acts, which, if real, would have been abominable; but being mere chimeras, were preposterous, and excited contempt and laughter only. Eight hundred degrees of one kind and another were invented: Infidelity, Hermeticism, Jesuitry were taught under the mask of Masonry.

The rituals, even of the respectable degrees, copied and mutilated by ignorant men, became nonsensical and trivial; and the words so corrupted that it has hitherto been found impossible to recover many of them at all. Candidates were made to degrade themselves, and to submit to insults not tolerable to a man of spirit and honour.

Hence it was, that, practically, the largest portion of the degrees claimed by the Ancient and Accepted Rite, and the Rites of Perfection and Misraim, fell into disuse, were merely communicated, and their rituals became jejune and insignificant. These Rites resembled those old palaces and baronial castles, the different parts of which, built at different periods remote from one another, upon plans and according to tastes that greatly varied, formed a discordant and incongruous whole. Judaism and chivalry, superstition and philosophy, philanthropy and insane hatred and longing for vengeance, a pure morality and unjust and illegal revenge, were found strangely mated, and standing hand in hand within the Temples of Peace and Concord: and the whole system was one grotesque commingling of incongruous things, of contrasts and contradictions, of shocking and fantastic extravagances, of parts repugnant to good taste, and fine conceptions overlaid and disfigured by absurdities engendered by ignorance, fanaticism and a senseless mysticism.

An empty and sterile pomp, impossible indeed to be carried out, and to which no meaning whatever was attached, with far-fetched explanations that were either so many stupid platitudes or themselves needed an interpreter; lofty titles, arbitrarily assumed, and to which the inventors had not condescended to attach any explanation that should acquit them of the folly of assuming temporal rank, power, and titles of nobility, made the world laugh, and the Initiate feel ashamed.

Some of these titles we retain; but they have with us meanings entirely consistent with that Spirit of Equality which is the foundation and peremptory law of its being of all Masonry. The *Knight*, with us, is he who devotes his hand, his heart, his brain to the Science of Masonry, and professes himself the Sworn Soldier of Truth: the *Prince* is he who aims to be *Chief* [*Princeps*], *first, leader*, among his equals, in virtue and good deeds: The *Sovereign* is he who, one of an order whose members are all Sovereigns, is Supreme only because the law and constitutions are so, which he administers, and by which he, like every brother, is governed. The Titles, *Puissant, Potent, Wise, and Venerable*, indicate that power of Virtue, Intelligence, and Wisdom which those ought to strive to attain who are placed in high office by the suffrages of their brethren: and all our other titles and designations have an esoteric meaning, consistent with modesty and equality, and which those who receive them should fully understand. As Master of a Lodge it is your duty to instruct your Brethren that they are all so many constant lessons, teaching the lofty qualifications which are required of those who claim them, and not merely idle gewgaws worn in ridiculous imitation of the times when the Nobles and Priests were masters and the People slaves: and that, in all true Masonry, the Knight, the Pontiff, the Prince, and the Sovereign are but the first among their equals: and the cordon, the clothing and the jewel but symbols and emblems of the virtues required of all good Masons.

The Mason kneels, no longer to present his petition for admittance, or to receive the answer, no longer to a man as his superior, who is but his brother, but to his God; to whom he appeals for the rectitude of his intentions, and whose aid he asks to enable him to keep his vows. No one is degraded by bending his knee to God at the altar, or to receive the honour of Knighthood as Bayard and Du Guesclin knelt. To kneel for other purposes, Masonry does not require. God gave to man a head to be borne erect, a port upright and majestic. We assemble in our Temples to cherish and inculcate sentiments that conform to that loftiness of bearing which the just and upright man is entitled to maintain, and we do not require those who desire to be admitted among us, ignominiously to bow the head. We respect man, because we respect ourselves, that he may conceive a lofty idea of his dignity as a human being, free and independent. If modesty is a virtue, humility and obsequiousness to man are base; for there is a noble pride which is the most real and solid basis of virtue. Man should humble himself before the Infinite God; but not before his erring and imperfect brother.

As Master of a Lodge, you will therefore be exceedingly careful that no Candidate, in any Degree, be required to submit to any degradation whatever; as has been too much the custom in some of the Degrees: and take it as a certain and inflexible rule, to which there is no exception, that Masonry requires of no man anything to which a Knight and Gentleman cannot honourably and without feeling outraged or humiliated, submit.

The Supreme Council for the Southern Jurisdiction of the United States at length undertook the indispensable and long delayed task of revising and reforming the work and rituals of the thirty degrees under its jurisdiction. Retaining the essentials of the degrees and all the means by which the members recognize one another, it has sought out and developed the leading idea of each degree, rejected the puerilities and absurdities with which many of them were disfigured, and made of them a connected system of moral, religious and philosophical instruction. Sectarian of no creed, it has yet thought it not improper to use the old allegories, based on occurrences detailed in the Hebrew and Christian books, and drawn from the Ancient Mysteries of Egypt, Persia, Greece, India, the Druids and the Essenes, as vehicles to communicate the Great Masonic Truths; as it has used the legends of the Crusades, and the ceremonies of the orders of Knighthood

It retains none of the revolting and odious representations of a criminal and wicked vengeance. It has not allowed Masonry to play the assassin; to avenge the death, either of Hiram Abi, Charles the 1st, or Jacques De Molay and the Templars. The Ancient and Accepted Rite of Masonry has now become, what Masonry at first was meant to be, a Teacher of Great Truths, inspired by an upright and enlightened reason, a firm and constant wisdom, and an affectionate and liberal philanthropy.

It is no longer a system, over the composition and arrangement of the different parts of which, want of reflection, chance, ignorance, and perhaps motives still more ignoble presided; a system unsuited to our habits, our manners, our ideas, or the world-wide philanthropy and universal toleration of Masonry; or to bodies small in number, whose revenues should be devoted to the relief of the unfortunate, and not to empty show: no longer a vicious aggregate of Degrees, shocking by its anachronisms and contradictions, powerless to disseminate light, information, and moral and philosophical ideas.

As Master, you will teach those who are under you, and to whom you will owe your office, that the decorations of many of the degrees are to be dispensed with, whenever the expense would interfere with the duties of charity, relief and benevolence; and to be indulged in only by wealthy bodies that will thereby do no wrong to those entitled to their assistance. The essentials of all the degrees may be procured at slight expense; and it is at the option of every Brother to procure or not to procure as he pleases, the dress, decorations and jewels of any degree other than the 14th, 18th, 30th and 32d.

We teach the truth of none of the legends we recite. They are to us but parables and allegories, involving and enveloping Masonic instruction; and vehicles of useful and interesting information. They represent the different phases of the human mind, its efforts and struggles to comprehend nature, God, the government of the Universe, the permitted existence of sorrow and evil. To teach us wisdom, and the folly of endeavouring to explain to ourselves that which we are not capable of understanding, we reproduce the speculations of the Philosophers, the Kabbalists, the Mystagogues and the Gnostics. Every one being at liberty to apply our symbols and emblems as he thinks most consistent with truth and reason and with his own faith, we give them such an interpretation only as may be accepted by all. Our degrees may be conferred in France or Turkey, at Pekin, Ispahan, Rome or Geneva, on Plymouth Rock, in the City of Penn or in Catholic Louisiana, upon the subject of an absolute government or the citizen of a Free State, upon Sectarian or Theist. To honour the Deity, to regard all men as our Brethren, as children, equally dear to him, of the Sup∴ Creator of the Universe, and to make himself useful to society and himself by his labour, are its teachings to its initiates in all the degrees.

Preacher of Liberty, Fraternity and Equality, it desires them to be attained by making men fit to receive them, and by the moral power of an intelligent and enlightened People. It lays no plots and conspiracies. It hatches no premature revolutions; it encourages no people to revolt against the constituted authorities; but recognizing the great truth that freedom follows fitness for freedom as the corollary follows the axiom, it strives to *prepare* men to govern themselves.

Where domestic slavery exists, it recognizes it as an institution allowed by God, for purposes of infinite wisdom and benevolence, and which He will remove in his own good time, as He gave Liberty to the Israelites enslaved four hundred years in Egypt, to the slaves of Imperial Rome and the Helots of Sparta, to the Peasants of France, and the thralls and serfs of Saxon and Norman England; and as he will give it to the serfs of Russia, the Coolies of India and the Peons of Mexico. It inculcates upon the Master, care and kindness for the slave whom God has placed in his power and under his protection; and whose unfitness to be free, and certain annihilation if he were liberated, create an irresistible necessity for keeping him in bondage. It teaches him humanity and the alleviation of the condition of his slave, and moderate correction and gentle discipline; as it teaches them to the master of the apprentice: and as it teaches to the employers of other men, in mines, manufactories and workshops, consideration and humanity for those who depend upon their labour for their bread, and to whom want of employment is starvation, and overwork is fever, consumption and death.

As Master of a Lodge, you are to inculcate these duties on your brethren. Teach the employed to be honest, punctual and faithful, as well as respectful and obedient to all proper orders: but also teach the employer that every man who desires to work, has a right to have work to do; and that they, and those who from sickness or feebleness, loss of limb or of bodily vigour, old age or infancy, are not able to work, have a right to be fed, clothed and sheltered from the inclement elements: that he commits an awful sin against Masonry and in the sight of God, if he closes his workshops or factories, or ceases to work his mines, when they do not yield him what he regards as sufficient profit, and so dismisses his workmen and workwomen to starve; or when he reduces the wages of man or woman to so low a standard that they and their families cannot be clothed and fed and comfortably housed; or by overwork must give him their blood and life in exchange for the pittance of their wages: and that his duty as a Mason and Brother peremptorily requires him to continue to employ those who else will be pinched with hunger and cold, or resort to theft and vice: and to pay them fair wages, though it may reduce or annul his profits or even eat into his capital: for God hath but loaned him his wealth, and made him His almoner and agent to invest it.

The Degrees of which the Supreme Council of the South has jurisdiction are divided into seven classes.

The 1st Class is composed of the 3 Symbolic Degrees, which the Supreme Council, for the sake of peace and harmony, has for the present relinquished to the Grand Lodges of the York Rite, reserving always the right to re-take them at pleasure; but in the mean time commencing with the 4th Degree, and requiring those who desire to receive it, to have first obtained the three first in a York Lodge, and to be in good standing as a York Mason. Still it has established the Rituals of those Degrees according to its own work and system, and requires them to be referred to continually for explanation, and permits and indeed recommends that they be regularly conferred, before the 4th, on those who have already received them in the York Rite, in the mutilated, corrupt and imperfect state in which they have long existed in that Rite, especially since the creation almost within our own times, of the Mark Master and Royal Arch Degrees.

The 2d Class includes the 4th, 5th, 6th, 7th and 8th Degrees. The 1st Class is that of *The Builders:* the 2d, being the 1st Class of the *Capitular* Order, is that of *Instructors.*

The 3d Class includes the 9th, 10th and 11th Degrees. It is the second of the Capitular Order, and is the Class of *Directors of the Work.*

The 4th Class includes the 12th, 13th and 14th Degrees. It is the third of the Capitular Order, and the Class of *Architects.*

The 5th Class includes the 15th, 16th, 17th and 18th Degrees. It is the fourth and last of the Capitular Order, and the Class of *Knights.*

The 6th Class includes the Degrees from the 19th to the 27th inclusive. It is the 1st Class of the *Areopagus;* and is styled the Class of *Pontiffs.*

The 7th and last Class includes the Degrees from the 28th to the 33d inclusive. It is the 2d Class of the *Areopagus,* and is styled the class of *the Grand Elect.*

Except as mere symbols of the moral virtues and intellectual qualities, the tools and implements of Masonry belong exclusively to the three first degrees. They also, however, serve to remind the Mason who has advanced further, that his new rank is based upon the humble labours of the symbolic degrees, as they are improperly termed, inasmuch as all the Degrees are symbolic.

Thus the initiates are inspired with a just idea of Masonry, to wit, that it is essentially WORK; both teaching and practising LABOUR; and that it is altogether emblematic. Three kinds of work are necessary to the preservation and protection of man and society: manual labour, specially belonging to the three blue

Degrees; labour in arms, symbolized by the intermediate Knightly Degrees; and intellectual labour, belonging particularly to higher Masonry.

We have preserved and multiplied such emblems as have a true and profound meaning. We reject many of the old and senseless explanations. We have not reduced Masonry to a cold metaphysics that exiles everything belonging to the domain of the imagination. The ignorant, and those half-wise in reality but over-wise in their own conceit, may assail our symbols with sarcasms; but they are nevertheless ingenious veils that cover the Truth, respected by all who know the means by which the heart of man is reached and his feelings enlisted. The Great Moralists often had recourse to allegories, in order to instruct men without repelling them. But we have been careful not to allow our emblems to be too obscure, so as to require far-fetched and forced interpretations. In our days, and in the enlightened land in which we live, we do not need to wrap ourselves in veils so strange and impenetrable, as to prevent or hinder instruction instead of furthering it; or to induce the suspicion that we have concealed meanings which we communicate only to the most reliable adepts.

The leading ideas in the Second Class, or that of *Instructors*, are:

In the 4th Degree; silence and discretion; the first and indispensable qualifications for one who would advance in the Ancient and Accepted Rite.

In the 5th; the honour and respect due to the memory of departed excellence; and that it alone should be the model for a Mason's conduct.

In the 6th; that no man is allowed to advance in Masonry, who seeks to do so, through an idle curiosity alone, and mere profane motives, with no zeal to arrive at the truth: for such a man will be a mere dead limb in Masonry, worthless to it and to himself.

In the 7th; that every Mason should be just, and keep his passions in proper subjection. This is indicated by the balance. Ever ready to find excuses for himself, he is taught that he ought to be a Provost and Severe Judge of his own conduct and motives.

In the 8th; that the duty of a Mason is to improve and assist his Brethren. Therefore it is, that the Candidate ascends the Seven Steps of exactitude, and has explained to him and enforced upon him the five points of fellowship: to work, to intercede, to pray, to love his brethren and to sustain them.

———— In the third Class: or that of *Directors of the Work:*

In the 9th Degree; That Masonry is the implacable antagonist of the three great evils that afflict humanity; the three great powers of darkness and evil, Falsehood, Fanaticism and Ignorance; and that its mission upon earth is ultimately to exterminate the first, that inciter of the second, and of whom the third is the blind and stupid instrument.

In the 10th; that when falsehood is destroyed, Fanaticism and Ignorance will share its fate, and cease to afflict humanity.

In the 11th; that those who have extinguished in their own souls these three Powers of Evil, are alone entitled to be selected to rule and govern men; that Providence is the certain avenger of crime, no place hiding the guilty from its eye; and punishment, by torture of the body or of the soul being, by the inflexible law of God, the certain result and consequence of vice and iniquity.

———— In the 4th Class, or that of *Architects:*

In the 12th Degree; That the five orders of Architecture, and the different working-tools of the three Degrees have a symbolic meaning, and constitute a complete code of Ethics; by which the upright Mason must square and regulate his conduct.

In the 13th; that resolution, patience, and perseverance are indispensable to him who would arrive at the knowledge of Truth; which is attained only by long and laborious investigation, and by overcoming many impediments, nine of which are indicated; *Indolence . . Preconceived opinion . . Blind reliance on authority . . Inaccurate discrimination . . . Superficial investigation . . Self-conceit . . Rash haste in reaching conclusions . . . Self-interest . . and Want of moral principle . . .* which passed, man enters the 9th vault, where Truth is revealed to Him: and thus those who seek knowledge as a mere instrument to serve their ambition, their avarice or their vices, perish by it, like those jealous and ambitious Masons who were overwhelmed by the ruins in which they dug.

In the 14*th;* That virtue is the true Perfection, and all virtuous men are brothers: that he who assists his brethren, visits the sick, obeys the dictates of love and charity, and knows no other distinction among men than that between the virtuous and the vicious, obeys God's law, and has discovered the True Word, which the selfish, the unfeeling and the malicious can never discover or comprehend. And the rank and honour conferred by this degree are emblems of that reward which all nations have believed awaits the virtuous in another world.

———— In the 5th Class; or that of the *Knights:*

In the 15*th Degree;* That Patriotism, and Devotion to the interests, and love for the institutions, of our Country, are indispensable to the Perfect Mason; and, combined with fidelity and incorruptible integrity, entitle the possessor to be invested with the highest honours.

In the 16*th;* that Masonry rewards those only who are ready to risk their lives in defence of their country; and commits the power of judging to those only who have proved their impartiality and their quick sense of Justice and Equity.

We need not recall to your mind the leading ideas of the 17th, 18th and 19th Degrees, which you cannot yet have forgotten.

The Duties of the Class of *Instructors*, are, particularly, to perfect the younger Masons in the words, signs and tokens and other work of the degrees they have received; to explain to them the meaning of the different emblems, and to expound the moral instruction which they convey. And upon their report of proficiency alone can their pupils be allowed to advance and receive an increase of wages.

The Directors of the Work are to report to the Chapters upon the regularity, activity and proper direction of the work of bodies in the lower degrees, and what is needed to be enacted for their prosperity and usefulness. In the Symbolic Lodges, they are particularly charged to stimulate the zeal of the workmen, to induce them to engage in new labours and enterprises for the good of Masonry, their country and mankind; and to give them fraternal advice when they fall short of their duty; or, in cases that require it, to invoke against them the rigor of Masonic law.

The Architects should be selected from none but Brothers well instructed in Symbolic Masonry, zealous, and capable of discoursing upon that Masonry, illustrating it, and discussing the simple questions of moral philosophy. And one of them, at every communication, should be prepared with a lecture, communicating useful knowledge or giving good advice to the Brethren.

The Knights wear the sword. They are bound to prevent and repair, as far as may be in their power, all injustice, both in the world and in Masonry, to protect the weak and to bring oppressors to justice. Their works and lectures must be in this spirit. They should inquire whether Masonry fulfils, as far as it ought and can, its principal purpose, which is to succour the unfortunate. That it may do so, they should prepare propositions to be offered in the Symbolic Lodges, calculated to attain that end, to put an end to abuses, and prevent or correct negligence. Those in the Symbolic Lodges who have attained the rank of Knights are most fit to be appointed Almoners, and charged to ascertain and make known who need and are entitled to the charity of the order.

In the sixth class those only should be received who have sufficient reading and information to discuss the great questions of philosophy. From them the Orators of the Lodges should be selected, as well as those of the Councils and Chapters. They are charged to suggest such measures as are necessary to make Masonry entirely faithful to the spirit of its institution, both as to its charitable purposes, and the diffusion of light and knowledge; such as are needed to correct abuses that have crept in, and offences against the rules and general spirit of the order; and such as will tend to make it, as it was meant to be, the great Teacher of Mankind.

As Master of a Lodge, Council or Chapter, it will be your duty to impress upon the minds of your Brethren these views of the general plan and separate parts of the Ancient and Accepted Rite; of its spirit and design; its harmony and regularity; of the duties of the officers and members; and of the particular lessons intended to be taught by each degree.

Especially you are not to allow any assembly of the body over which you may preside, to close, without recalling to the mind of the Brethren the Masonic virtues and duties which are represented upon the Tracing

Board of this Degree. That is an imperative duty. Forget not that, more than three thousand years ago, ZOROASTER said; *Be good, be kind, be humane and charitable; love your fellows; console the afflicted; pardon those who have done you wrong.* Nor that more than two thousand three hundred years ago CONFUCIUS repeated, also quoting the language of those who had lived before himself; *Love thy neighbour as thyself: Do not to others what thou wouldst not wish should be done to thyself: Forgive injuries. Forgive your enemy, be reconciled to him, give him assistance, invoke God in his behalf.*

Let not the morality of your Lodge be inferior to that of the Persian or Chinese Philosopher.

Urge upon your Brethren the teaching and the unostentatious practice of the morality of the Lodge, without regard to times, places, religions, or peoples.

Urge them to love one another, to be devoted to one another, to be faithful to the country, the Government and the laws: for to serve the country is to pay a dear and sacred debt:

To respect all forms of worship, to tolerate all political and religious opinions; not to blame, and still less to condemn the religion of others: not to seek to make converts; but to be content if they have the religion of Socrates; a veneration for the Creator, the religion of good works, and grateful acknowledgment of God's blessings:

To fraternize with all men; to assist all who are unfortunate; and to cheerfully postpone their own interests to that of the Order:

To make it the constant rule of their lives, to think well, to speak well, and to act well:

To place the sage above the soldier, the noble or the Prince; and take the wise and good as their models.

To see that their professions and practice, their teachings and conduct do always agree:

To make this also their motto: Do that which thou oughtest to do; let the result be what it will.

Such, my Brother, are some of the duties of that office which you have sought to be qualified to exercise. May you perform them well; and in so doing gain honour for yourself, and advance the great cause of Masonry, Humanity, and Progress.

TO CLOSE.

Ven∴ M∴ Bro∴ Sen∴ Warden, have you anything in the West, to bring before this Lodge of Gr∴ Masters?

Sen∴ W∴ Nothing, Ven∴ Gr∴ Master.

Ven∴ M∴ Bro∴ Jun∴ Warden, have you anything in the South?

Jun∴ W∴ Nothing, Ven∴ Gr∴ Master.

Ven∴ M∴ Bro∴ Orator, have you anything in the North?

Orator: . . Nothing, Ven∴ Gr∴ Master.

Ven∴ M∴ Has any Gr∴ Master anything to suggest, offer or propose to this Lodge, for the benefit of a Br∴ Mason, of this Lodge, of his Country, or of Humanity?

Ans∴ . . . .

Ven∴ M∴ Br∴ Sen∴ Warden, what is the hour?

Sen∴ W∴ The world waits for the Light.

Ven∴ M∴ Then it is time for us to close; that the Great Lights of this Lodge may be borne into and illuminate the world. The Sign, my Brethren!

[The Brethren give the 1st Sign: Then the Ven∴ M∴ raps , ? — the Sen∴ W∴ , ? — the Jun∴ W∴ , ? — and then all the Brethren clap , ? with their hands; and cry LUX EST].

Ven∴ M∴ Wherever the nine great lights are, there is this Lodge. Let the great Light of *Veneration* go forth from hence, and shine in the world! [The Pursuivant takes one of the Lights, and goes out].

Ven∴ M∴ Let the great Light of *Charity* go forth into and inspire the world! [The Jun∴ Deacon takes one and goes out].

Ven∴ M∴ Let the Great Light of *Generosity* go forth into and ennoble the world! [The Sen∴ Deacon takes one, and goes out].

Ven∴ M∴ Let the great Light of *Heroism* go forth into the world and burn in the spirits of men! [The Secretary takes one and goes out].

Ven∴ M∴ Let the Great Light of *Honour* go forth into the world, and Baseness skulk and hide from its presence! [The Treasurer takes one and goes out].

Ven∴ M∴ Let the Great Light of *Patriotism* go forth and shine in the world! [The Orator takes one and goes out].

Ven∴ M∴ Let the Great Light of *Justice* go forth and blaze upon the altars of all men's hearts! [The Jun∴ Warden takes one and goes out].

Ven∴ M∴ Let the Great Light of *Toleration* go forth, and dim the fires of Persecution! [The Sen∴ Warden takes one and goes out].

Ven∴ M∴ I bear the Light of TRUTH into the world, to overcome Falsehood and Error; and this Lodge is closed until the Lights return! [He goes out with the last Light; and the remaining Brethren follow; which closes the Lodge].

FINIS.

Twenty-First Degree.

Noachite; or Prussian Knight.

THE CHAPTER: ITS DECORATIONS, ETC.

Orders of this Degree are styled *Grand Chapters.*

A Gr∴ Chapter must be held in a retired place, on the night of the full moon, in each lunar month. The place is lighted by a large window or opening, so arranged as to admit the rays of the moon, the only light allowed, at as early an hour of the night as practicable.

The presiding officer sits facing the moonlight, and the Knights in front of him and on either hand, in no particular place or order.

The *officers* are . . . a Knight Lieutenant Commander, Knight Official, Knight Introducer, Knight Orator, Knight of the Chancery, Knight of the Finances, and Knight Warden. The other members are styled *Knight Masons.*

The *dress* is entirely black, except the gloves and apron; with swords, spurs, and black masks.

The *order* is a broad black ribbon, worn from right to left; and the *jewel* is a silver full moon, suspended from the third button-hole of the vest, or a golden triangle traversed by an arrow, point downward, suspended from the collar. On the jewel is an arm upraised, holding a naked sword, and around it the motto, FIAT JUS-TITIA, RUAT COELUM. The *apron* and *gloves* are yellow.

On the upper part of the apron is an arm, naked and upraised, holding a naked sword; and under it a human figure, erect, with wings, with the forefinger of his right hand on his lips, and the other arm hanging by his side, holding a key in the left hand; being the Egyptian figure of Silence.

The battery is; raps, at equal intervals.

TO OPEN.

[The Lieutenant Commander gives; raps, and says]:

Lt∴ Com∴ Kt∴ Official, the full moon is half-way between the horizon and the zenith. The hour for this Gr∴ Chapter to convene has arrived. Let the Kt∴ Warden post the Sentinels and Patrols, that no spy may gain admission among us.

Kt∴ Off. Kt∴ Warden, post the Sentinels, and send forth the Patrols on all the approaches to this Holy Place, that no spy may witness our deliberations.

[The Kt∴ Warden goes out, remains a short time, returns, and reports: "Sir Official, the Sentinels are at their posts, and the Patrols occupy all the avenues of the forest."]

Kt∴. Official. Ill∴. Lt∴. Commander, the Sentinels and Patrols are properly disposed; and we are in security.

Lt∴. Com∴. Sir Official, you will then examine every person present, and receive from each the Pass-word, that we may know we have no spy or traitor among us.

[The Official receives the Pass-word from each, and reports: "Ill∴. Lt∴. Commander, none but true Knights are present."].

Lt∴. Com∴. Sir Official, are you a Prussian Knight?

Off∴. I am.

Lt∴. Com∴. How were you received a Prussian Knight?

Off∴. By the light of the full moon, like our ancient brethren, initiated in the Temple of Belus.

Lt∴. Com∴. Whence come we to-night?

Off∴. From the four quarters of the globe.

Lt∴. Com∴. What come we here to do?

Off∴. To hear and consider the complaints of the oppressed, who cry out for justice upon their tyrants: to judge those denounced to us for crime: to devise measures for the relief of struggling humanity.

Lt∴. Com∴. Knights and Brethren, if these be your objects, give me the Token.

[All rise, draw their swords, and clash them together once].

Lt∴. Com∴. Sir Introducer, whence come you?

Kt∴. Introd∴. From the shores of Europe.

Lt∴. Com∴. What left you there?

Kt∴. Intr∴. Want and distress: Women that wail for bread, and men for work: the hovel peopled with stolid misery, under the shadows of the palace tenanted by Luxury: Starvation and Despair in Cities and in the Country; and by their side Affluence and Pomp.

Lt∴. Com∴. What come you here to do?

Kt∴. Intr∴. To aid in remedying these evils.

Lt∴. Com∴. Sir Orator, whence come you?

Kt∴. Orat∴. From the plains of Chaldea and the banks of the Nile.

Lt∴. Com∴. What left you there?

Kt∴. Orat∴. Ignorance, barbarity, slavery, and superstition.

Lt∴. Com∴. What come you here to do?

Kt∴. Orator∴. To punish crime, to rebuke intolerance, and to labour for the good of men.

Lt∴. Com∴. Sir Warden, whence come you?

Ward∴. From the forests of the New World.

Lt∴. Com∴. What left you there?

Ward∴. Liberty and Free Thought.

Lt∴. Com∴. What come you here to do?

Ward∴. To labour to make them common to all, as the air and light of Heaven.

Lt∴. Com∴. Knights and Brethren, if these be your objects, give me the token.

[All rise, and clash their swords together twice].

Lt∴. Com∴. Sir Almoner, what of the Treasury?

Alm∴. Ill∴. Lt∴. Commander, it is rich to overflowing with the grateful tears of widows, the thanks of orphans, and the blessings of the poor, the distressed and the destitute.

Kt∴. Lt∴. C∴. Amen! So mote it be forever!

[The Knights all clash their swords together thrice].

Lt∴. Com∴. Such being our duties, let this Chapter be opened. Brethren, the Sign!

[All the Knights raise their arms towards Heaven, the Sword in the right hand, and turn towards the Moon: then, they dropping their arms, and facing the Lt∴. Commander, he says: "This Grand Chapter is open in due form. Sir Warden, make Proclamation that all who demand justice may draw near."]

Kt∴. Ward∴. Whosoever hath been wronged by the great or oppressed by the powerful; whosoever hath been unjustly accused or his household outraged: whosoever hath fallen into the hands of corrupt judges: whosoever hath suffered by bribery or extortion ; let him come freely forward and prefer his complaint; and right shall be done him by this Grand Chapter of Prussian Knights, from whose judgment there is no appeal.

RECEPTION.

The Candidate is brought to the door of the Chapter, without a sword or collar, with his head bare, in ordinary garments, wearing a plain white apron and white gloves. The Knight Introducer, who is with him, gives ; distinct, slow knocks upon the door. The Warden on the inside answers by a single rap, opens the door, and asks "Who desire to enter this Grand Chapter?" The Introducer answers, "The Knight Introducer, having the signs, words and grips; with a Master Mason, descended from Adoniram, and who has received the 20th Degree."

[The Warden receives the signs, words and grips, and says, "Remain, my Brother, until I learn the will of the Ill.·. Lt.·. Commander ;" and closes the door. He goes to the Kt.·. Official, and whispers in his ear that the Kt.·. Introducer, with a Master descended from Adoniram, and who has attained the degree of Grand Master of all Symbolic Lodges, desires to enter].

The Kt.·. Official says aloud, "Ill.·. Lt.·. Commander, the Kt.·. Introducer, with a Master Mason, descendant of Adoniram, and Grand Master of all Symbolic Lodges, clothed in a white apron and white gloves, desires to enter"].

Kt.·. Com.·. Demand of the Kt.·. Introducer what this Mason, descendant of Adoniram the Son of Abda, desires.

[The Kt.·. Official goes to the door, and gives one rap. The Kt.·. Introducer answers with ; slow. The Kt.·. Warden opens the door].

Kt.·. Off.·. What is the desire of our Brother, descendant of Adoniram, and Grand Master of all Symbolic Lodges ?

Kt.·. Intr.·. He comes to demand justice.

Off.·. Against whom ?

Intr.·. He will make that known to the Ill.·. Lt.·. Commander.

Off.·. Upon what charge ?

Intr.·. Oppression and injustice.

Off.·. Do you vouch for the sincerity and good faith of the Brother ?

Intr.·. I do.

Off.·. It is well. Wait again with patience until I learn the will of the Ill.·. Lt.·. Commander.

[The Kt.·. Official returns near the Lt.·. Commander].

Lt.·. C.·. Sir Official, what does the brother demand?

Kt.·. Off.·. Justice.

Lt.·. C.·. On whom ?

K.·. O.·. He will make that known only to you.

Lt.·. C.·. Upon what charge ?

K.·. O.·. Injustice and oppression.

Lt.·. Com.·. Against such demands, the doors of our Chapter are never closed. Hasten to admit the Kt.·. Introducer and the Brother !

Kt.·. Off.·. Sir Warden, admit the Kt.·. Introducer and the Brother !

[They enter, and advance to the Lt.·. Commander, and the candidate kneels before him. The Introducer, speaking for him, says]: "Most Noble and Ill.·. Lt.·. Commander Noachite, I demand doom and judgment of Count Reinfred of Loegria and the Bishop of Vienne; who, the one falsely claiming, and the other corruptly judging, have taken from me my inheritance, and after divided the same between themselves: to the Count half, and half to the Church."

Lt.·. Com.·. Arise, my Brother ! Thou needest not kneel for justice; to which the humblest man hath a right as he hath to air; and which, like air, is neither to be bought nor sold. Who art thou, and what proof dost thou offer that thy charge is true?

Cand∴ I am known as Adolf the Saxon, a man of humble birth, a Master Mason and Knight of the Rose Croix; and I have fought for the Cross in the Holy Land. My patrimony lay between the domain of the Count Reinfred and the estates of the Church; and the Bishop and the Count coveted them. So while I was absent in the Holy Land, they had a monk who was a cunning penman to forge a deed, and my own seal thereto, by which, for moneys (it was said) loaned me by the Count on my departure, I did convey unto him all my patrimony. Then the Count, before the Bishop's Court, preferred his claim, the which was speedily determined in his favour; and I afterwards returning, find my patrimony shared between the Count and Church, one half to each; and all appeal or other way of redress denied me. To this I pledge my Masonic word: and moreover, Th∴ Ill∴, let but the Count produce the parchment, and I will find the means to prove it false.

Lt∴ Com∴ The Count is here, a Mason and a Noachite. Stand forth, Sir Count, Knight and Mason, and answer!

[A brother rises, comes forward and says, "On my Masonic word, the charge is false"].

Lt∴ Com∴ Hast thou the parchment?

Reinf∴ It is here. [He hands a roll of parchment to the Lt∴ Com∴].

Lt∴ Com∴ Adolf the Saxon, it is *his* Masonic word against *thine own*. What other proof hast thou to offer?

Cand∴ Command, Th∴ Ill∴ Lt∴ Commander, the Count Reinfred to make me answer to three questions, and no more.

Lt∴ Com∴ Count Reinfred, answer; and truly, remembering that thou art a Mason!

Cand∴ Upon what day, and in what year hath this conveyance date?

Reinf∴ Of the nativity of St. John the Baptist, in the year 1187.

Cand∴ That day was I at Mayence, with the Emperor Frederic Barbarossa. What witnesses attest that I did seal it?

Reinf∴ John of Seis, and Theobald, the Bishop's almoner.

Cand∴ And in what place did I seal the same and they attest it?

Reinf∴ Even in my audience-chamber, at the castle.

Cand∴ That day, I say, was I at Mayence. Sir Knight Introducer, is it not so?

Kt∴ Intr∴ It is; I saw thee there.

Cand∴ That day the Almoner lay sick at Marburg. A Knight here knoweth it.

Kt∴ Orat∴ 'Tis true. I found him there and gave him aid.

Cand∴ And on the parchment is the vender's private mark; a key, in the upper right hand corner. It is the mark of Isaac the Jew of Vienna: and he adopted it after Frederic the Emperor died; having before then stamped his parchment with a crown.

Kt∴ of Chan∴ It is most true. I know the Jew, these many years.

Lt∴ Com∴ The mark is here. Count Reinfred, what hast thou to answer? . . . He standeth mute. Brethren, your judgment. Is this Knight innocent or guilty?

[All answer, "guilty, upon our words."].

Lt∴ Com∴ Most guilty and most wicked! Forsworn and perjured Knight and Mason! I banish thee forever from this Order. Dare never more to enter Lodge or Chapter. Put off thy Knightly badges; and go forth, condemned, disgraced, degraded. Within three days restore this brother his possessions; or look thou to thy head. And for thy use thereof, pay him forthwith an hundred marks! Go and obey! Brethren, is this your judgment?

[All the Knights clash their swords. The sentenced Knight puts off his order and jewel, and goes forth in silence].

Lt∴ Com∴ And for the haughty Bishop, see, Sir Chancellor, that with all speed the arrow and the writing summon him to make restitution or prepare to abide the judgment of this Grand Chapter. For none shall be so high or haughty that he shall plunder and oppress the feeble with impunity. *Adolf the Saxon, art thou satisfied?*

Cand.·. Most amply, Th.·. Ill.·.

Introd.·. Th.·. Ill.·. Lt.·. Com.·., the place of Count Reinfred in our Grand Chapter is vacant. I have served with the good Knight Adolf under Frederick the Emperor and Richard of England. Good Knight and true is he, and faithful Mason, and I propose him to the brethren for their suffrages.

Lt.·. Com.·. Adolf, is this thine own desire?

Cand.·. It is my most earnest wish.

Lt.·. Com.·. Brother Knights, if it be your pleasure that Adolf the Saxon shall fill the place in this Grand Chapter, made vacant by the degradation of Count Reinfred, give me the token.

[All clash their swords].

Lt.·. Com.·. Adolf, the Brethren consent to receive you into this Grand Chapter; but I am yet required to exact of you certain pledges. Dost thou agree and promise that thou wilt be just and righteous, and in all things strive to emulate and equal that Patriarch from whom we take the name of Noachites; who alone, with his family, was found worthy to be saved, when God destroyed mankind with the Deluge?

Cand.·. I do.

Lt.·. Com.·. Dost thou promise to avoid idleness, to live honestly, to deal fairly by all men, and to discourage strife and contention?

Cand.·. I do.

Lt.·. Com.·. Dost thou promise that thou wilt be neither haughty nor vain-glorious; nor obsequious to the great, nor insolent to thy inferiors?

Cand.·. I do.

Lt.·. Com.·. Dost thou promise that thou wilt be humble and contrite before the Deity; and ever bear in mind the fate of Phaleg and his followers, who endeavoured to build a tower whereby they might climb beyond the reach of another Deluge, and defy the Omnipotence of God?

Cand.·. I do.

Lt.·. Com.·. Dost thou promise, as a member of this Tribunal, to give righteous judgment only, against all persons whatsoever; to be impartial between the high and the low; to be cautious and slow to determine, and prompt to execute; to smite the oppressor and the wrong-doer, and protect the widow, the orphan, the poor and the helpless; to be swayed neither by bribe nor fear, nor favour nor affection; and still to temper justice with mercy; remembering that there is no man who doth not err and sin?

Cand.·. I do.

Lt.·. Com.·. Kneel then, and assume the solemn obligation of a Patriarch Noachite, or Prussian Knight.

[The Candidate kneels on both knees, grasping with both hands the hilt of a sword, handed him by a brother, which hilt must be in the shape of a cross, and the sword held perpendicularly, the point upon the floor. In this attitude he repeats the following obligation]:

OBLIGATION.

I, A. . . . B. . . ., upon the sacred word of a Master Mason, and Knight of the Rose Croix, do most solemnly promise and vow, that I will faithfully keep the secrets of this degree, and will reveal them to no person in the world, unless to one who shall be legally authorized to receive them.

I furthermore promise and vow that I will evermore give just and upright judgment, to the best of my knowledge and ability; looking upon men's deeds with charity, and condemning no one unheard: that I will listen patiently to his defence, weigh impartially his statements, and decide for innocence in case of doubt.

I furthermore promise and vow, that I will aid in executing the judgments of this Grand Chapter; and if myself accused, will promptly and cheerfully submit to its jurisdiction.

I furthermore promise and vow to be merciful and compassionate; and ever to remember that I am a man, and that all men are my brothers. And furthermore, that I will be humble and modest in all my conduct, and carefully avoid all haughtiness and insolence in my demeanour and conversation. So help me God and keep me steadfast to perform faithfully this my vow!

The Lt.·. Commander directs him to bow three times to the ground, in token of his humility; and then raises him, and communicates the Signs, Words and Tokens.

Sign: . . . Raise ♏☿♈&⁑&☉♒♊♎ with the ♑♀♒♌☾‡♎ ☾♉♈☾♒♊☾♊, the ♈&♑♋♏♎ opposite the ☾☉‡♎: and at the same time make; ♌☾♒♑ ♑†☾↑♈♀☿♒♎ with the †‡¶♒☾☾.

Pass-word: ⁑&☉†☾♌.·. pronounced; times, slowly and in a melancholy tone.

Sacred Word: . . . ♎&☾♋.·. . . . ¶&☾♋.·. . . . ♄☉⁑☾♈&.·.; given only thus: . . .

Token: . . . One brother takes the ♑☿‡☾♑♀♒♌☾‡ of a Brother between his own ♈&♑♋♏‡☉♒♊ ⁑♑☿‡☾♑♀♒♌☾‡, and ⁑‡☾♎♎☾♎ it; saying ♎&☾♋: the other responds by like ⁑‡☾♎♎♑‡☾ of the ♑☿‡☾♑♀♒♌☾‡ of the first brother, saying ¶&☾♋.·. and the first again ⁑‡☾♎♎☾♎ the ♑☿‡☾♑♀♒♌☾‡ of the second, saying ♄☉⁑☾♈&.·.

To enter a Chapter, a brother &☿†♊♎⁑♑⁑‡;♑♀♒♌☾‡♎. The Sentinel or Guardian does the same. The Brother then gives the sign, takes the; ♑♀♒♌☾‡♎ of the Sentinel or Guardian, and says— ♑‡☾♊☾‡♀↑ ♏☉‡♏☉‡☿♎♎☉. The other responds; times ♒☿☉¶&.·. and the first says; times, ⁑&☉†☾♌.·.

[The Kt. Commander then invests the Candidate with the apron, collar and jewel of the Degree, and directs him to kneel on both knees; when he strikes him lightly with his sword on the right and left shoulder and on the head, saying: "By virtue of the authority vested in me by this Grand Chapter, I do constitute and create you a Mason Noachite, and Prussian Knight, and I do devote you, henceforward forever, to the cause of every one who hath been wronged by the great or oppressed by the powerful; of every one who hath been unjustly accused or his household outraged: of every one who hath fallen into the hands of corrupt judges: of every one who hath suffered by bribery or extortion; of the oppressed, the widow, the orphan, the poor, the distressed and the destitute. Arise, Knight and Soldier of Struggling and Suffering Humanity, and be armed for the combats that await you!]

[He rises, and the Kt.·. Official buckles on his spurs, and the Kt.·. Commander hands him a sword; and the latter says]:

Kt.·. Com.·. You are now prepared to do the duties of a True Knight: and the Kt.·. Orator will, on the first convenient occasion, make known to you the history and final instruction of this Degree. [This the Kt.·. Orator may do out of the Chapter, in private].

HISTORY.

The Knights of this Order originally united themselves together in the times of the Crusades; when, in consequence of the general disorder that prevailed all over Europe, and the multitude of Estates and Titles left to be disputed, wrong and violence went unrebuked, and became superior to the law. Composed at first of a few Masons, who had learned the rules of justice from the teachings of the Order, they exerted only a moral influence, owing to the purity of their lives, and the justice of their opinions. They called themselves

Nonchite Masons; because they strove to imitate the primeval justice and purity of the beloved Patriarch. Finding that where their influence was most needed, mere advice and exhortation, addressed to the rude Barons and haughty rapacious Priesthood, had no effect, they assumed the power to enforce performance of their judgments; and through the common people and a multitude of the poorer Knights who had found the benefit of their protection, and who revered their justice, they found a ready means of compelling obedience, and inflicting punishment. Their number was limited, and their persons unknown. They met always at night, when the moon was full; and the more perfectly to remain unknown, allowed no light but hers.

Lest their own members should become haughty and vain-glorious on account of the mysterious power they possessed, they inculcated humility, and incessantly reminded each other of that haughtiness and pride which led the descendants of Noah to erect the Tower of Babel; and of the miseries of Phaleg, who suggested the idea of its building; and who therefor condemned himself to a rigorous penitence, and buried himself in the vast solitudes of Northern Germany, in what is now the kingdom of Prussia, where he is said to have builded a temple in the shape of a Delta, and therein to have passed his life imploring the mercy of God.

The Order, in several parts of Germany, was popularly known as the Holy Vehme: and even kings trembled at its judgments. It continued to exercise its vast powers, until law and civilization rendered them no longer necessary; but the Order still continued to exist, deciding Masonic controversies only; and inflicting no other than Masonic punishments. As it continued more particularly to flourish in Prussia, where Frederic of Brunswick, King of Prussia, became the Grand Master General of the Order, the members took the name of Prussian Knights, out of gratitude to that Monarch, whose ancestors were for three hundred years its Patrons.

The Chapters of this Degree are no longer Tribunals to try and punish for offences committed without the limits of Masonry. They claim no jurisdiction except between their own members, and exercise none between those of the inferior degrees, except by their consent. And in all their judgments it is their rule and duty to judge of other men's motives and actions by the same rules by which they judge their own; to believe others equally as honest in their views as themselves; and to find for the conduct of others the same excuses that they find for their own; for this alone is justice. And they prove their humility by their tolerance; which causes them to believe that their opinions are as likely to be erroneous as the opinions of others to the contrary, and that the Deity alone knows what is truth.

They meet only on the nights of the full moon; and allow no other light than hers; because such was the ancient custom of the order, derived from the mysteries of Ceres and the old worship of Isis. In the Heavenly host they admire the work of the Supreme Creator, and the universal laws of harmony and motion, the two first laws that emanated from God.

You are especially charged in this Degree to be modest and humble, and not vain-glorious nor filled with self conceit. Be not wiser in your own opinion than the Deity, nor find fault with his works, nor endeavour to improve upon what he has done. Be modest also in your intercourse with your fellows, and slow to entertain evil thoughts of them, and reluctant to ascribe to them evil intentions. A thousand presses, flooding the country with their evanescent leaves, are busily and incessantly engaged in maligning the motives and conduct of men and parties, and in making one man think worse of another; while, alas, scarcely one is found that ever, even accidentally, labours to make man think better of his fellow.

Slander and the Spirit of Lies never stalked as boldly over any country in open daylight, as they do at this day over ours. The most retiring disposition, the most unobtrusive demeanour, is no shield against the arrows of these demons. The most eminent public service only makes the hounds of vituperation and invective more eager and more unscrupulous, when he who has done such service presents himself as a candidate for the People's Suffrages.

The evil is wide-spread and universal. No man, no woman, no household is sacred, or safe from this new Inquisition. No act is so pure or so praiseworthy, that the unscrupulous vender of lies who lives by his lies and by pandering to a corrupt and morbid public appetite will not proclaim it as a crime. No motive is so innocent or so laudable, that he will not hold it up as villainy. Journalism sneaks about and pries into the interior of private houses, gloats over the details of domestic tragedies of sin and shame, and deliberately invents and industriously circulates the most unmitigated and baseless falsehoods, to coin money for those who pursue it as a trade, or to effect a temporary result in the wars of faction.

We need not enlarge upon these evils. They are apparent to us all: and it is the duty of a Mason to do all that may be in his power to lessen, if not to remove them. With the errors and even sins of other men, that do not personally affect us or ours, and need not our condemnation to be odious, we have nothing to do: and the journalist has no patent that makes him the Censor of Morals. There is no obligation resting on us to trumpet forth our disapproval of every wrongful or injudicious or improper act that every other man commits.

One ought, in truth, to write or speak against no other one in this world. Each man in it has enough to do, to watch and keep guard over himself. Each of us is sick enough in this great Lazaretto: and journalism and polemical writing constantly remind us of a scene once witnessed in a little hospital; where it was horrible to hear how the patients mockingly reproached each other with their disorders and infirmities: how one, who was wasted by consumption, jeered at another who was bloated by dropsy: how one laughed at another's cancer of the face; and this one again at his neighbour's locked-jaw or squint; until at last the delirious fever-patient sprang out of his bed, and tore away the coverings from the wounded bodies of his companions; and nothing was to be seen but hideous misery and mutilation. Such is the revolting work in which journalism and political partisanship, and all the world outside of Masonry, are engaged.

Very generally, the censure bestowed upon men's acts, by those who have appointed and commissioned themselves Custodes Morum, Keepers of the Public Morals, is undeserved. Often it is not only undeserved, but praise is deserved instead of censure, and, when the latter is not undeserved, it is always extravagant, and therefore unjust.

A Mason will wonder what spirit they are endowed withal, that can basely libel at a man, even, that is fallen. If they had any nobility of soul, they would with him condole his disasters, and drop some tears in pity of his folly and wretchedness: and if they were merely human and not brutal, Nature did grievous wrong to a human body, to curse it with a soul so cruel as to strive to add to a wretchedness already intolerable. When a Mason hears of any man that hath fallen into public disgrace, he should have a mind to commiserate his mishap, and not to make him more disconsolate. To envenom a name by libels, that already is openly tainted, is to add stripes with an iron rod to one that is flayed with whipping; and to every well tempered mind will seem most inhuman and diabolical.

Not most diabolical, nevertheless: because there is a lower deep, into which journalism and partisanship daily plunge, and seem refreshed as one might be who indulges in the luxury of a cool and perfumed bath. Even the man who does wrong and commits errors often has a quiet home, a fireside of his own, a gentle loving wife and innocent children, who perhaps do not know of his past errors and lapses—past and long repented of; or if they do, do love him the better, because, being mortal, he hath erred, and being in the image of God, he hath repented. That every blow at this husband and father strikes full upon the pure and tender bosoms of that wife and those daughters, is a consideration that doth not concern or stay the hand of the base and brutal journalist and partisan: but he strikes home at the shuddering, shrinking, quivering, innocent, tender bosom; and then goes out upon the great arteries of cities, where the current of life pulsates, and holds his head erect, and calls on his fellows to laud him and admire him for the noble, generous, manly act he hath done, in striking his Malay dagger through one heart into another tender and trusting one.

If you seek for high and strained carriages, you shall, for the most part, meet with them in low men. Arrogance is a weed that ever grows on a dunghill. It is from the rankness of that soil that she hath her height and spreadings. To be modest and unaffected with our superiors is duty; with our equals, courtesy; with our inferiors, nobleness. There is no arrogance so great as the proclaiming of other men's errors and faults, by those who understand nothing but the dregs of actions, and who make it their business to besmear deserving fames. Public reproof is like striking a deer in the herd. It not only wounds him, to the loss of blood, but betrays him to the hound, his enemy.

The occupation of the spy hath been ever held dishonourable; and it is none the less so, now that, with rare exceptions, every editor and every partisan has become a perpetual spy upon the actions of other men. Their malice makes them nimble-eyed, apt to note a fault and publish it, and, with a strained construction, to deprave those things that the doer's intents have told his soul were honest. Like the crocodile, they slime the way of others, to make them fall; and when that has happened, they feed their insulting envy on the life-blood of the prostrate. They set the vices of other men on high, for the gaze of the world, and place their virtues under ground, that none may note them. If they cannot wound upon proofs, they will do it upon likelihoods: and if not upon them, they manufacture lies, as God created the world, out of nothing; and so corrupt the fair temper of men's reputations; knowing that the multitude will believe them, because affirmations are apter to win belief, than negatives to uncredit them; and that a lie travels faster than an eagle flies, while the contradiction lags after it at a snail's pace, and, halting, never overtakes it. Nay, it is contrary to the morality of journalism, to allow a lie to be contradicted in the journal that spawned it. And even if that great favour is ever conceded, a slander once raised will scarce ever die, or fail of finding many that will allow it both a harbour and trust.

This is, beyond any other, the age of falsehood. Once, to be suspected of equivocation was enough to soil a gentleman's escutcheon; but now it has become a strange merit in a partisan or public man, always and scrupulously to tell the truth. Lies are part of the regular ammunition of all campaigns and controversies, valued according as they are profitable and effective; and are stored up and have a market price, like saltpetre and sulphur.

My brother, if men weighed the imperfections of humanity, they would breathe less condemnation. Ignorance gives disparagement a louder tongue than knowledge does. Wise men had rather know, than tell. Frequent dispraises are but the faults of uncharitable wit: and it is from where there is no judgment, that the heaviest judgment comes; for self-examination would make all judgments charitable. If we even do know vices in men, we can scarce show ourselves in a nobler virtue, than in the charity of concealing them; if that be not a flattery, persuading to continuance. And it is the basest office man can fall into, to make his tongue the defamer of the worthy man.

There is but one rule for the Mason in this matter. If there be virtues, and he is called upon to speak of him that owns them, let him tell them forth impartially. And if there be vices mixed with them, let him be content the world shall know them by some other tongue than his. For if the evil-doer deserves no pity, his wife, his parents or his children, or other innocent persons who love him may: and the bravo's trade, practised by him who stabs the defenceless for a price paid by individual or party, is really no more respectable now than it was a hundred years ago, in Venice. Where we want experience, Charity bids us think the best, and leave what we know not to the Searcher of Hearts: for mistakes, suspicions and envy often injure a clear fame; and there is least danger in a charitable construction.

And, finally, the Mason should be humble and modest towards the Grand Architect of the Universe, and not impugn his Wisdom, nor set up his own imperfect sense of Right against His Providence and Dispensations, nor attempt too rashly to explore the Mysteries of God's Infinite Essence and inscrutable plans, and of that Great Nature which we are not made capable to understand.

From all those vain philosophies let him steer far away, which endeavour to account for all that is, without admitting that there is a God, separate and apart from the Universe which is his work: that erect Universal Nature into a God, and worship it alone: that annihilate Spirit, and believe no testimony except that of the bodily senses: that by logical formulas and dextrous collocation of words make the actual, living, guiding and protecting God fade into the dim mistiness of a mere abstraction and unreality, itself a mere logical formula.

Nor let him have any alliance with those theorists who chide the delays of Providence and busy themselves to hasten the slow march which it has imposed upon events: who neglect the practical, to struggle after impossibilities: who are wiser than Heaven; know the aims and purposes of the Deity, and can see a shorter and more direct means of attaining them, than it pleases Him to employ: who would have no discords in the great harmony of the Universe of things; but equal distribution of property, no subjection of one man to the will of another, no compulsory labour, and still no starvation nor destitution nor pauperism.

Let him not spend his life, as they do, in building a new tower of Babel; in attempting to change that which is fixed by an inflexible law of God's enactment: but let him, yielding to the Superior Wisdom of Providence, content to believe that the march of events is rightly ordered by an Infinite Wisdom, and leads, though we cannot see it, to a great and perfect result,—let him, my Brother, be satisfied to follow the path pointed out by that Providence, and to labour for the good of the human race in that mode in which God has chosen to enact that that good shall be effected: and above all, let him build no Tower of Babel, under the belief that, by ascending he will mount so high that God will disappear or be superseded by a great monstrous aggregate of material forces, or a mere glittering logical formula: but, evermore, standing humbly and reverently upon the earth and looking with awe and confidence towards Heaven, let him be satisfied that there is a *real* God, a *person*, and not a formula, a Father and a Protector, who loves and sympathizes, and compassionates; and that the eternal ways by which He rules the world are infinitely wise, no matter how far they may be above the feeble comprehension and limited vision of man.

The blazonry of this degree is: . . 1st. Azure, a Moon Argent, surrounded with stars or. . . 2d. Sable, an equilateral triangle traversed by an arrow or.

The Statutes of the Order forbid holding a Table Lodge.

TO CLOSE.

[The Lt∴ Com∴ gives ; raps, and says]:

Lt∴ Com∴ Sir Official, the Moon is passing from us. The hour for this Gr∴ Chapter to close has arrived. Give notice to the Knights that our labours are about to end.

[The Kt∴ Official gives one rap, and says]:

Kt∴ Off∴ Brethren and Knights, prepare to close this Gr∴ Chapter. The light by which we work is about to be obscured.

Kt∴ Com∴ Sir Official, we have heard the complaints of the oppressed; we have judged those denounced to us as criminals; we have administered Justice and regarded Mercy. What more remains to be done?

Kt∴ Off∴ To go forth and labour in the cause of struggling humanity: to imitate in our conduct and conversation the righteous Patriarch; and thus to become true Noachites.

Kt∴ Com∴ And is there no more?

Kt∴ Orator∴ Phaleg! Phaleg! Phaleg!

Kt∴ Off∴ True! To remember the fate of Phaleg; and warned thereby, to be modest and humble, and not boastful, vain-glorious, or wise in our own conceit.

Kt∴ Com∴ It is well. Go forth, my Brethren, and perform these duties. Sir Official, give notice to the Knights that this Grand Chapter is darkened.

Off∴ Knights and Brethren, this Gr∴ Chapter is darkened, and its labours end. The Sign and Word, my Brethren!

[All the Brethren give the Sign and repeat the Pass-word, as directed].

Kt∴ Com∴ The light has departed. Farewell!

FINIS.

Twenty-Second Degree.

Knight of the Royal Axe, or Prince of Libanus.

Bodies of this degree are styled *Colleges*. There are two apartments. The first is a plain room, of moderate dimensions, without any fixed number of lights, and prepared to represent a carpenter's workshop on Mount Lebanon. The second is hung with red, and lighted by 36 lights, arranged by sixes and each six by twos. It represents the Council Room of the Round Table. In the centre of the Room is such a table, around which the brethren sit. The altar is in the East, and upon it are an open Bible, the Square and Compasses, and an Axe.

The officers are a Chief Prince, who is styled *Th∴ Puissant;* a Sen∴ and Jun∴ Grand Warden, and a Sen∴ and Junior Deacon.

The *Order* is a broad, rainbow-colored ribbon, worn as a collar. It may be worn as a sash, from right to left; and is lined with purple. The jewel, suspended to the collar, is an axe and handle of gold. On the top or end of the handle are the letters N∴ and S∴ . . . . On one side of the handle, L∴ . . . . On the other, Ts∴ . . . . On one side of the blade, A∴ C∴ D∴ Z∴ N∴ E∴ ∴ . . On the other, Sn∴ Kn∴ Y∴ M∴ A∴ B∴

The letters on the top are the initials of the words *Noah* and *Solomon:* those on the handle, of *Lebanon* and *Tsidunians:* those on the first side of the blade, of *Adoniram, Cyrus, Darius, Zerubbabel, Nehemiah,* and *Ezra:* and those on the other side, of *Shem, Khem, Yaphet, Moses, Ahliab* and *Betsel-Al.*

The *Apron* is white, lined and bordered with purple. On the middle a round table is embroidered, on which are mathematical instruments, and plans unrolled. On the flap is a serpent with three heads.

The *Tracing Board* is a view of the mountain and forests of Lebanon, the summit of the mountain covered with snow; and of the Temple erected of its cedars and pines. It is in the form of an axe.

In the workshop the Sen∴ Warden presides, and is styled *Master Carpenter.* He and all the Brethren wear frocks or blouses and aprons.

The *battery* is : by ♈♃☿♎ — but there is no particular alarm or battery in the workshop.

TO OPEN.

[The Ch∴ Prince gives one rap, and says] : " My Brethren, the day-star has risen in the East. It is time to arouse the workmen; that they may prepare for their labours. Brother Sen∴ Gr∴ Warden, are all the Princes present?"

4D

Sen∴ G∴ W∴ Th∴ Puissant, they are.

Th∴ P∴ Announce to them, my brother, through the Jun∴ Gr∴ Warden, that I am about to open this College; that directions may be given to the workmen, their complaints be heard, and justice administered.

S∴ G∴ W∴ Bro∴ Jun∴ Gr∴ Warden, the Th∴ Puissant is about to open this College of Princes of Libanus. Make proclamation that all who desire instruction, and those who have complaints to prefer or justice to demand may come forward and be heard.

Jun∴ G∴ W∴ Brethren, it is made known to me that the Th∴ Puissant is about to open this College of Princes of Libanus. Let those who have instructions to ask, complaints to prefer, or justice to demand, draw near and they shall be heard.

Th∴ P∴ My Brethren, unite with me in imploring the blessing of the Supreme Deity upon our labours!
[All the Knights repeat the following prayer]:

PRAYER.

Thou who didst create the universe, and hast builded it in infinite magnificence, as Thou art infinite in skill and wisdom, bless us in our daily labours, and prosper and look indulgently upon the work of our hands! Teach us and all men that labour is honourable, and that to work well in our vocation is the noblest destiny of man! Improve, O beneficent God, the condition of the toiling millions! Teach the rich and the haughty, compassion for those over whom they have control; and hasten the coming of the day when idleness will no longer be a privilege to boast of, nor labour be deemed ignoble; and when all men shall acknowledge the great truth, that to work well and faithfully in our appointed sphere, is the most acceptable prayer that erring man can offer up to Thee! Amen!

Th∴ P∴ Brother Jun∴ Gr∴ Warden, arouse the workmen, by the usual alarm.

The Jun∴ Gr∴ W∴ raps ? — the Sen∴ Gr∴ Warden ? — and the Th∴ P∴ ? — Then, after a moment's silence, the Th∴ P∴ gives the sign, which all answer: and he says, " The cedars upon Mount Libanus wait to be felled ; and this College is open."

RECEPTION.

The Candidate, in the dress, insignia, and jewels of a Prussian Knight, or Rose ⊕, with sword and other apparel complete, is brought to the door of the second apartment, in which the officers and brethren are seated around the table, on which are plans and mathematical instruments. The Senior Deacon having charge of the candidate raps : by ♈ ♃ ☿ ♎. The Junior Deacon opens the door a little, and asks, " Who comes here?"

Sen∴ D∴ A worthy Prussian Knight and Knight of the Rose Croix, who desires to obtain the Degree. of Prince of Libanus, and to that end hath travelled hither from afar.

Jun∴ Deac∴ Has he received all the preceding degrees ?

Sen∴ Deac∴ He has.

Jun∴ Deac∴ Hath he approved himself a true Knight and a just Judge ?

Sen∴ Deac∴ He has.

Jun∴ Deac∴ What further claim hath he to this privilege ?

Sen∴ Deac∴ The claim of birth; and rank in Masonry.

Jun∴ Deac∴ I will advise the College of his request. Let him patiently await their answer. . . . [He closes the door].

Ch∴ Pr∴ Brother Junior Deacon, who seeks admittance to the College ?

Jun∴ Deac∴ A Knight of the Rose Croix and Prussian Knight; who desires to obtain the degree of Prince of Libanus; in charge of the Knight our Senior Deacon.

Ch∴ Prince∴ Has he received all the preceding degrees ?

Jun∴ Deac∴ The Senior Deacon answers that he has.

Ch∴ Pr∴ Hath he approved himself a true Knight and a just Judge?

Jun∴ Deac∴ The Senior Deacon answers that he has.

Ch∴ Pr∴ What further claim hath he to this privilege?

Jun∴ Deac∴ The claim of birth, and rank in Masonry.

Ch∴ Pr∴ The claim is not sufficient. But let him be admitted.

[He is admitted, and advances to the Table; and the Th∴ Puissant addresses him thus]:

Ch∴ Pr∴ Is it your desire, my Brother, to obtain the degree of Prince of Libanus?

Cand∴ It is.

Ch∴ Pr∴ We know the grounds on which you claim it: but birth is not regarded here; and rank in Masonry does not of itself suffice. We are all workmen in our several vocations. You see us now engaged in preparing plans for the labourers; and studying the calculations of astronomy. None can, by our constitutions, be admitted to the high privileges of this degree, unless he hath first wrought one year in the workshop; and obtained the unanimous suffrage of the workmen. Is your desire for this degree sufficient to induce you to lay aside your insignia, your sword and jewels, for a time, and join the Sons of Labour, who represent the toiling millions?

Cand∴ It is.

Ch∴ Pr∴ Go, then, my Brother, obtain their suffrages, and return to us.

[The Candidate withdraws, with the Senior Deacon, and goes to the door of the first apartment, where they give three or four raps. The door is opened, and they enter. The workmen are hewing, sawing, planing, mortising, &c., and the master-workman copying designs from a tracing-board. As the Candidate enters, he gives one loud rap, and the workmen pause].

M∴ Carp∴ Whom have you there, Brother Senior Deacon?

Sen∴ Deac∴ A Knight of the Rose Croix and Prussian Knight, who desires your suffrages, that he may obtain the degree of Prince of Libanus.

M∴ Carp∴ Our suffrages are given to those that *work.* Hath *he* yet learned to work?

Sen∴ Deac∴ Nay; but desires to do so; and hath for that come hither.

M∴ Carp∴ Doth he acknowledge the dignity of labour; and that it is no curse, but a privilege, for man to be allowed to earn his sustenance by the exercise of his strong arms and sturdy muscles?

Sen∴ Deacon. He does.

M∴ Carp∴ Does he admit that the honest labouring man, upright and independent, is, in nature's heraldry, the peer of Kings; and that not labour, but idleness, is disgraceful?

Sen∴ Deac∴ He does.

M∴ Carp∴ Art thou willing to eat only what thou earnest; patiently to receive instruction; and to recognize and treat these humble workmen as thy brethren and thy equals?

Cand∴ I am.

M∴ Carp∴ Then, as thou wast divested of thy outward garments, upon thy first entry into a Masonic Lodge, divest thyself now of thy insignia and jewels, and assume the dress and apron of a workman.

[The Candidate puts off his regalia, and is clothed in a blouse and coarse apron, and directed to saw a long plank in two lengthwise. When he has finished, the Master Carpenter says]: "My Brother, the *saw,* the *plane,* and the *hewing-axe* are the working tools of a Prince of Libanus. The saw symbolizes that steady patience, and persevering determination, by which the resolute man makes his way to the object of his endeavour through all obstacles; and teaches us that Masons, labouring for the improvement of the world and the great cause of human progress, must be content to advance—certainly, though never so painfully and slowly, towards success. As the PLANE cuts down the inequalities of surfaces, it is symbolical of Masonry, which cuts off the prejudices of ignorance, and the absurdities of superstition, and aids to polish and civilize mankind. The AXE is the great agent of civilization and improvement. It is the troops, armed with that weapon, that have conquered barbarism. Under its blows the primeval forests disappear, and the husbandman displaces the wild hunter, and to the rude barbarism of the early ages succeed settled society and laws, and all the arts that refine and elevate mankind. The axe is nobler than the sword. And as the sturdy pioneer, armed with the axe, strides onward in the front of civilization; and as the stout oak, and pine, and ash, and elm fall, never to rise again before him, so Masonry hews at those mighty Upas-trees, Intolerance, Bigotry, Superstition, Uncharitableness, and Idleness; and lets in the light of truth and reason upon the human mind, which these Vices have overshadowed and darkened for centuries."

[The Candidate is then made to use the plane; and then a brother brings him a piece of dry bread and a cup of water; and the Master Carpenter says to him], "Eat, my brother, of the labourer's food. It is thine own; for thou hast earned it; and no one suffers because thou dost eat."

[He is then made to use the axe. Then the Master Carpenter says]: "My Brethren, this Knight, by his ready acquiescence in our rules, and his cheerful conformity to our customs, has shown a true appreciation of the dignity of labour. We may require him to toil with us a year; or, at our option, we may at once give him our suffrages. If no one wishes otherwise, we will proceed to vote upon his request to be admitted among the Princes of Libanus."

[The vote is taken by ballot; and, it being declared white, the Candidate is informed that he is duly elected to receive the degree, and that he will repair to the second apartment. He is again invested with his insignia and jewels, during which time the Brethren go out one by one, and repair to the second chamber, dressed in the insignia and jewel of this degree].

[The Senior Deacon gives the alarm: raps, by ♈ ♏ ♉ ♎—and the Junior Deacon asks], "Who comes here?"

Sen∴ Deac∴ A Knight of the Rose Croix and Prussian Knight; who having wrought cheerfully in the workshop, and learned the use of the saw, plane and axe, has received the suffrages of the workmen, and demands to be received a Prince of Libanus.

[The Junior Deacon repeats the same to the Th∴ P∴, who orders him to be admitted. The three principal officers are now in their proper seats].

Sen∴ Deac∴ Th∴ Puissant Chief Prince, I present to you this Knight, who has toiled in the workshop, and received the unanimous suffrages of the Brethren.

Th∴ P∴ My Brother, do you still persist in your desire to enter this association of labourers?

Cand∴ I do.

Th∴ P∴ Are you not deterred by the hazard of such toil and fare as you experienced in the workshop?

Cand∴ I am not.

Th∴ P∴ Go, then, and kneel at the altar, and receive the obligation of this Degree.

He kneels upon both knees, with his hands upon the axe and Bible, and takes this obligation:

OBLIGATION.

I, A. . . . . . B. . . . . ., of my own free will and accord, in the presence of the Supreme Architect of the Universe, and this Illustrious College of Princes of Libanus, do hereby and hereon, most solemnly and sincerely promise and swear, that I will never communicate the secrets of this degree to any person or persons whatsoever, unless he or they shall be lawfully entitled to the same, by having legally received all the preceding degrees, in the proper and legally constituted bodies, or from a legally authorized Inspector-General or Deputy Inspector; nor then, without due authority for so doing from a legal and duly established Supreme Council of the 33d Degree.

I furthermore promise and swear, that I will ever hereafter use my best endeavours to elevate the character of the labouring classes, and to improve their condition, to disseminate the blessings of education among their children, and to give to themselves their due and proper social and political weight; and recognizing labour as honourable, I will regard the labouring man as my peer and equal, so far as his honesty, virtue, and intelligence may entitle him to it.

All which I promise and swear, under the penalty of exposure on the highest pinnacle of Mount Libanus, there miserably to perish in its perpetual snows. So help me God; and aid me to keep and observe the same!

[The Th∴ P∴ raises him, and communicates the signs and words].

Sign: ∴ Raise ⎓⎓ [cipher] towards the [cipher], the [cipher] [cipher] as much as possible, and let them [cipher] upon the [cipher], as if [cipher] with an [cipher]. It alludes to [cipher] the [cipher] of Libanus.

Answer: . . . . Raise [cipher] to the [cipher] of the [cipher], [cipher], and let them [cipher] together, in front.

Token: . . . Take [cipher] each other's [cipher], [cipher] them, in sign of good faith.

Pass-words: . . . [cipher]∴ [cipher]∴ [cipher]∴ [cipher]∴ [cipher]∴ [cipher]∴

Sacred Words: [cipher]∴ [cipher]∴

[The Candidate is then invested with the apron, collar, and jewel of the degree: and the Th∴ P∴ explains to him the initials upon the jewel; concluding by saying]: "The Serpent with three heads, upon the flap of the apron, is Idleness, the body from which issue the three vices symbolized by the heads: Drunkenness, Impurity, and Gaming: by which so many Youths have been lost, and so many great Nations have sunk into ignoble imbecility and shameful bondage."

The Th∴ P∴ then recites to him the following History and Lecture:

HISTORY AND LECTURE.

The Tsidunians or Phœnicians were ever ready to aid the Israelites in their holy enterprises. The tie between them was the mysteries, into which the principal persons of both Nations were initiated; Moses having necessarily received them in Egypt, before he could marry the daughter of a priest of On. These mysteries, modified by Solomon, or perhaps at an earlier day by Joshua or even Moses, to suit the genius and manners of the Jewish People, became Masonry, such as it was practised at the building of the Temple, and such as it has in part come down to us. Hiram King of Tyre in Phœnicia, and Hiram Abi, also a Phœnician and not a Jew, were also initiates; and hence the intimate connection between them and Solomon, as Masons. The people of Tsidun, a city of Phœnicia, were employed by Noah to cut cedars on Mount Libanus, of which to build the Ark, under the superintendence of Japhet. His descendants repeopled Tsidun and Phœnicia, and procured and furnished the cedar from Lebanon to build the Ark of the Covenant; and at a later day his posterity, under Adoniram, cut in the same forests cedars for King Solomon: and at a time still later, they felled timber on the same mountains to construct the second Temple.

Upon the same mountain they established Colleges of Artificers, like those in Etruria and afterwards at Rome; from which latter many deduce Masonry. But the Etrurians, who emigrated from Assyria to Egypt and afterwards to Etruria; better known as the Hyksos, from Resen [R. S. N.] on the Tigris, or as the Shepherd Kings, carried with them the same mysteries, which went also with them into Phœnicia; and the Etrurian and Roman Colleges were in all respects like those of Mt. Libanus. These Artificers everywhere adored the Grand Architect of the Universe; and had their signs and words, by which to recognize each other. Solomon himself, whose wisdom necessarily gave him a true idea of the dignity of labour, built a small palace on the mountain, to which he often repaired to inspect the progress of the work. The names of the Patriarchs who were the Inspectors and Conductors of the workmen on the mountain at different periods are preserved in our pass-words. The institution of Colleges upon Mount Libanus was perpetuated by the Druses, from whom the Crusaders obtained a knowledge of this degree.

Sympathy with the great labouring classes, respect for labour itself, and resolution to do some good *work* in our day and generation, these are the lessons of this Degree; and they are purely Masonic. Masonry has made a working man and his associates the Heroes of her principal legend, and himself the companion of Kings. The idea is as simple and true as it is sublime. From first to last, Masonry is *work.* It venerates the Grand *Architect* of the Universe. It commemorates the *building* of a Temple. Its principal emblems are *the working tools* of Masons and Artisans. It preserves the name of the first *worker* in *brass* and *iron* as one of its pass-words. When the Brethren meet together, they are *at labour.* The Master is the *over-seer* who sets the craft *to work* and gives them proper instruction. Masonry is the apotheosis of WORK.

It is the hands of brave forgotten men that have made this great, populous, cultivated world a world for *us.* It is *all* work, and *forgotten* work. The *real* conquerors, creators and eternal proprietors of every great and civilized land are all the heroic souls that ever were in it, each in his degree; all the men that ever felled a forest-tree or drained a marsh, or contrived a wise scheme, or did or said a true or valiant thing therein. Genuine work alone, done faithfully,—*that* is eternal, even as the Almighty Founder and World-builder Himself. All work is noble: a life of ease is not for any man, nor for any God. The Almighty Maker is not like one who, in old immemorial ages, having made his machine of a Universe, sits ever since, and sees it *go.* Out of that belief comes Atheism. The faith in an Invisible, Unnameable, Directing Deity, present everywhere in all that we see and work and suffer, is the essence of all faith whatsoever.

The life of all Gods figures itself to us as a Sublime Earnestness,—of Infinite battle against Infinite labour. Our highest religion is named the Worship of Sorrow. For the Son of Man there is no noble crown, well worn, or even ill-worn, but is a crown of thorns. Man's highest destiny is not to be happy, to love pleasant things and find them. His only true unhappiness should be that he cannot work, and get his destiny as a man fulfilled. The day passes swiftly over, our life passes swiftly over, and the night cometh, wherein no man can work. That night once come, our happiness and unhappiness are vanished, and become as things that never were. But our work is not abolished, and has not vanished. It remains, or the want of it remains, for endless Times and Eternities. It is in our influences after death that we are immortal.

Whatsoever of morality and intelligence; what of patience, perseverance, faithfulness, of method, insight, ingenuity, energy; in a word, whatsoever of STRENGTH a man has in him, will lie written in the WORK he does. To work is to try himself against Nature and her unerring, everlasting laws; and they will return true verdict as to him. The noblest Epic is a mighty Empire slowly built together, a mighty series of heroic deeds, a mighty conquest over chaos. Deeds are greater than words. They have a life, mute, but undeniable; and grow. They people the vacuity of Time, and make it green and worthy.

Labour is the truest emblem of God, the Architect and Eternal Maker; noble Labour, which is yet to be the King of this Earth, and sit on the highest Throne. Men without duties to do, are like trees planted on precipices; from the roots of which all the earth has crumbled. Nature owns no man who is not also a Martyr. She scorns the man who sits screened from all work, from want, danger, hardship, the victory over which is work; and has all his work and battling done by other men: and yet there are men who pride themselves that they and theirs have done no work, time out of mind.

The chief of men is he who stands in the van of men, fronting the peril which frightens back all others, and if not vanquished would devour them. Hercules was worshipped for twelve labours. The Czar of Russia became a toiling shipwright, and worked with his axe in the docks of Saardam: and something came of that. Cromwell worked, and Napoleon; and effected somewhat.

There is a perennial nobleness and even sacredness in work. Be he never so benighted and forgetful of his high calling, there is always hope in a man that actually and earnestly works: in Idleness alone is there perpetual Despair. Man perfects himself by working. Jungles are cleared away. Fair seed-fields rise instead, and stately cities; and withal, the man himself first ceases to be a foul unwholesome jungle and desert thereby. Even in the meanest sort of labour, the whole soul of man is composed into a kind of real harmony, the moment he begins to work. Doubt, Desire, Sorrow, Remorse, Indignation, and even Despair shrink murmuring far off into their caves, whenever the man bends himself resolutely against his task. Labour is life. From the inmost heart of the worker rises his God-given Force, the Sacred Celestial Life-essence, breathed into him by Almighty God; and awakens him to all nobleness, as soon as work fitly begins. By it man learns Patience, Courage, Perseverance, Openness to light, readiness to own himself mistaken, resolution to do better and improve. Only by labour will man continually learn the virtues. There is no Religion in stagnation and inaction; but only in activity and exertion. There was the deepest truth in that saying of the old monks, *laborare est orare*. "He prayeth best who loveth best all things both great and small;" and can man love except by working earnestly to benefit that being whom he loves?

"Work; and therein have well-being," is the oldest of Gospels; unpreached, inarticulate, but ineradicable and enduring forever. To make Disorder, wherever found, an eternal enemy; to attack and subdue him, and make order of him, the subject not of Chaos, but of Intelligence and Divinity, and of ourselves; to attack ignorance, stupidity and brute-mindedness, wherever found, to smite it wisely and unweariedly, to rest not while we live and it lives, in the name of God, this is our duty as Masons; commanded us by the Highest God. Even He, with his unspoken voice, awfuller than the thunders of Sinai, or the syllabled speech of the Hurricane, speaks to us. The Unborn Ages; the old Graves, with their long-mouldering dust speak to us. The deep Death-Kingdoms, the Stars in their never resting course, all Space and all Time, silently and continually admonish us, that we too must work while it is called to-day. Labour, wide as the Earth, has its summit in Heaven. To toil, whether with the sweat of the brow, or of the brain or heart, is worship,—the noblest thing yet discovered beneath the Stars. Let the weary cease to think that labour is a curse and doom pronounced by Deity. Without it there could be no true excellence in human nature. Without it and pain and sorrow, where would be the human virtues? Where Patience, Perseverance, Submission, Energy, Endurance, Fortitude, Bravery, Disinterestedness, the noblest excellencies of the Soul?

Let him who toils complain not, nor feel humiliated. Let him look up, and see his fellow-workmen there, in God's Eternity; they *alone* surviving there. Even in the weak human memory they long survive, as Saints, as Heroes and as Gods: they *alone* survive, and people the unmeasured solitudes of Time.

To the primeval man, whatsoever good came, descended on him (as in mere fact, it ever does), direct from God; whatsoever duty lay visible for him, this a Supreme God had prescribed. For the primeval man, in whom dwelt Thought, this Universe was all a Temple, life everywhere a Worship.

Duty is with us ever: and evermore forbids us to be idle. To work with the hands or brain, according to our acquirements and our capacities, to do that which lies before us to do, is more honourable than rank and title. Ploughers, spinners and builders, inventors and men of science, poets, advocates and writers, all stand upon one common level, and form one grand innumerable host, marching ever onward since the beginning of the world; each entitled to our sympathy and respect, each a man and our brother.

It was well to give the earth to man as a dark mass, whereon to labour. It was well to provide rude and unsightly materials in the ore-bed and the forest, for him to fashion into splendour and beauty. It was well, not because of that splendour and beauty; but because the act creating them is better than the things themselves; because exertion is nobler than enjoyment; because the labourer is greater and more worthy of honour than the idler. Masonry stands up for the nobility of labour. It is Heaven's great ordinance for human improvement. It has been broken down for ages; and Masonry desires to build it up again. It has been broken down, because men toil only because they must, submitting to it as, in some sort, a degrading necessity; and desiring nothing so much on earth as to escape from it. They fulfil the great law of labour in the letter; but break it in the spirit: they fulfil it with the muscles, but break it with the mind.

Masonry teaches that every idler ought to hasten to some field of labour, manual or mental, as a chosen and coveted theatre of improvement; but he is not impelled to do so, under the teachings of an imperfect civilization. On the contrary, he sits down, folds his hands, and blesses and glorifies himself in his idleness. It is time that this opprobrium of toil were done away. To be ashamed of toil; of the dingy workshop and dusty labour-field; of the hard hand, stained with service more honourable than that of war; of the soiled and weather-stained garments, on which Mother Nature has stamped, midst sun and rain, midst fire and steam, her own heraldic honours; to be ashamed of these tokens and titles, and envious of the flaunting robes of imbecile idleness and vanity; is treason to Nature, impiety to Heaven, a breach of Heaven's great Ordinance. Toil, of brain, heart or hand, is the only true manhood and genuine nobility.

Labour is a more beneficent ministration than man's ignorance comprehends, or his complainings will admit. Even when its end is hidden from him, it is not mere blind drudgery. It is all a training, a discipline, a development of energies, a nurse of virtues, a school of improvement. From the poor boy that gathers a few sticks for his mother's hearth, to the strong man who fells the oak or guides the ship or the steam-car, every human toiler, with every weary step and every urgent task, is obeying a wisdom far above his own wisdom, and fulfilling a design far beyond his own design.

The great law of human industry is this; that industry, working, either with the hand or the mind, the application of our powers to some task, to the achievement of some result, lies at the foundation of all human improvement. We are not sent into the world like animals, to crop the spontaneous herbage of the field, and then to lie down in indolent repose: but we are sent to dig the soil and plough the sea; to do the business of cities and the work of manufactories. The world is the great and appointed school of industry. In an artificial state of society, mankind are divided into the idle and the labouring classes; but such was not the design of Providence.

Labour is man's great function, his peculiar distinction and his privilege. From being an animal, that eats and drinks and sleeps only, to become a worker, and with the hand of ingenuity to pour his own thoughts into the moulds of Nature, fashioning them into forms of grace and fabrics of convenience, and converting them to purposes of improvement and happiness, is the greatest possible step in privilege.

The Earth and the Atmosphere are man's laboratory. With spade and plough, with mining-shafts and furnaces and forges, with fire and steam; amidst the noise and whirl of swift and bright machinery, and abroad in the silent fields, man was made to be ever working, ever experimenting. And while he and all his dwellings of care and toil are borne onward with the circling skies, and the splendours of heaven are around him, and their infinite depths image and invite his thought, still in all the worlds of philosophy, in the universe of intellect, man must be a worker. He is nothing, he can be nothing, can achieve nothing, fulfil nothing, without working. Without it, he can gain neither lofty improvement nor tolerable happiness. The idle must hunt down the hours as their prey. To them Time is an enemy, clothed with armour; and they must kill him, or themselves die. It never yet did answer, and it never will answer, for any man to do nothing, to be exempt from all care and effort, to lounge, to walk, to ride and to feast alone. No man can live in that way. God made a law against it: which no human power can annul, no human ingenuity evade.

The idea that a property is to be acquired in the course of ten or twenty years, which shall suffice for the rest of life; that by some prosperous traffic or grand speculation, all the labour of a whole life is to be accomplished in a brief portion of it; that by dexterous management, a large part of the term of human existence is to be exonerated from the cares of industry and self-denial, is founded upon a grave mistake, upon a misconception of the true nature and design of business, and of the conditions of human well-being. The desire of accumulation for the sake of securing a life of ease and gratification, of escaping from exertion and self-denial, is wholly wrong, though very common.

It is better for the Mason to live while he lives, and enjoy life as it passes; to live richer and die poorer. It is best of all for him to banish from the mind that empty dream of future indolence and indulgence; to address himself to the business of life, as the school of his earthly education; to settle it with himself now, that independence, if he gains it, is not to give him exemption from employment. It is best for him to know, that, in order to be a happy man, he must always be a labourer, with the mind or the body, or with both; and that the reasonable exertion of his powers, bodily and mental, is not to be regarded as mere drudgery, but as a good discipline, a wise ordination, a training in this primary school of our being, for nobler endeavours, and spheres of higher activity hereafter.

There are reasons why a Mason may lawfully, and even earnestly desire a fortune. If he can fill some fine palace, itself a work of art, with the productions of lofty genius; if he can be the friend and helper of humble worth; if he can seek it out, where failing health or adverse fortune presses it hard, and soften or stay the bitter hours that are hastening it to madness or to the grave; if he can stand between the oppressor and his prey, and bid the fetter and the dungeon give up their victim; if he can build up great institutions of learning, and academies of art; if he can open fountains of knowledge for the people, and conduct its streams in the right channels; if he can do better for the poor than to bestow alms upon them—even to think of them, and devise plans for their elevation in knowledge and virtue, instead of forever opening the old reservoirs and resources for their improvidence; if he has sufficient heart and soul to do all this, or part of it; if wealth would be to him the handmaid of exertion, facilitating effort, and giving success to endeavour; then may he lawfully, and yet warily and modestly, desire it. But if it is to do nothing for him, but to minister ease and indulgence, and to place his children in the same bad school; then there is no reason why he should desire it.

What is there glorious in the world, that is not the product of labour, either of the body or of the mind? What is history, but its record? What are the treasures of genius and art, but its work? What are cultivated fields, but its toil? The busy marts, the rising cities, the enriched empires of the world are but the great treasure-houses of labour. The pyramids of Egypt, the castles and towers and temples of Europe, the buried cities of Italy and Mexico, the canals and railroads of Christendom, are but tracks, all round the world, of the mighty footsteps of labour. Without it, antiquity would not have been. Without it, there would be no memory of the past and no hope for the future.

Even utter indolence reposes on treasures that labour at some time gained and gathered. He that does nothing, and yet does not starve, has still his significance; for he is a standing proof that *somebody* has at *some time* worked. But not to such does Masonry do honour. It honours the Worker, the Toiler; him who produces and not alone consumes; him who puts forth his hand to add to the treasury of human comforts, and not alone to take away. It honours him who goes forth amid the struggling elements to fight his battle, and who shrinks not, with cowardly effeminacy, behind pillows of ease. It honours the strong muscle and the manly nerve, and the resolute and brave heart, the sweating brow and the toiling brain. It honours the great and beautiful offices of humanity; manhood's toil and woman's task; paternal industry, and maternal watching and weariness; wisdom teaching and patience learning; the brow of care that presides over the State, and many-handed labour that toils in workshop, field and study, beneath its mild and beneficent sway.

God has not made a world of rich men; but rather a world of poor men; or of men, at least, who must toil for a subsistence. That is, then, the best condition for man, and the grand sphere of human improvement. If the whole world could acquire wealth, (and one man is as much entitled to it as another, when he is born); if the present generation could lay up a complete provision for the next, as some men desire to do for their children; the world would be destroyed at a single blow. All industry would cease with the necessity for it; all improvement would stop with the demand for exertion; the dissipation of fortunes, the mischiefs of which are now countervailed by the healthful tone of society, would breed universal disease, and break out into universal license; and the world would sink into the grave of its own loathsome vices.

Almost all the noblest things that have been achieved in the world, have been achieved by poor men; poor scholars, poor professional men; poor artisans and artists; poor philosophers, poets and men of genius. A certain staidness and sobriety, a certain moderation and restraint, a certain pressure of circumstances, are good for man. His body was not made for luxuries. It sickens, sinks and dies under them. His mind was not made for indulgence. It grows weak, effeminate and dwarfish, under that condition. And he who pampers his body with luxuries and his mind with indulgence, bequeaths the consequences to the minds and bodies of his descendants, without the wealth which was their cause. For wealth, without a law of entail to help it, has always lacked the energy even to *keep* its own treasures. They drop from its imbecile hand. The third generation almost inevitably goes down the rolling wheel of fortune, and there learns the energy necessary to rise again, if it rises at all; heir, as it is, to the bodily diseases and mental weaknesses and the soul's vices of its ancestors, and *not* heir to their wealth. And yet we are, almost all of us, anxious to put our children, or to ensure that our grand-children shall be put, on this road to indulgence, luxury, vice, degradation and ruin; this heirship of hereditary disease, soul-malady and mental leprosy.

If wealth were employed in promoting mental culture at home, and works of philanthropy abroad; if it were multiplying studies of art, and building up institutions of learning around us; if it were in every way raising the intellectual character of the world, there could scarcely be too much of it. But if the utmost aim, effort and ambition of wealth be, to procure rich furniture, and provide costly entertainments, and build luxurious houses, and minister to vanity, extravagance and ostentation, there could scarcely be too little of it. To a certain extent it may laudably be the minister of elegancies and luxuries, and the servitor of hospitality and physical enjoyment: but just in proportion as its tendencies, divested of all higher aims and tastes, are running that way, they are running to peril and evil.

Nor does that peril attach to individuals and families alone. It stands, a fearful beacon, in the experience of Cities, Republics and Empires. The lessons of past times, on this subject, are emphatic and solemn. The history of wealth has always been a history of corruption and downfall. The people never existed that could stand the trial. Boundless profusion is too little likely to spread for any people the theatre of manly energy, rigid self-denial and lofty virtue. You do not look for the bone and sinew and strength of a country, its loftiest talents and virtues, its martyrs to patriotism or religion, its men to meet the days of peril and disaster, among the children of ease, indulgence and luxury.

In the great march of the races of men over the earth, we have always seen opulence and luxury sinking before poverty and toil and hardy nurture. That is the law which has presided over the great processions of empire. Sidon and Tyre, whose merchants possessed the wealth of princes; Babylon and Palmyra, the seats of Asiatic luxury; Rome, laden with the spoils of a world, overwhelmed by her own vices more than by the hosts of her enemies; all these, and many more are examples of the destructive tendencies of immense and unnatural accumulation: and men must become more generous and benevolent, not more selfish and effeminate, as they become more rich, or the history of modern wealth will follow in the sad train of all past examples.

All men desire distinction, and feel the need of some ennobling object in life. Those persons are usually most happy and satisfied in their pursuits, who have the loftiest ends in view. Artists, mechanicians and inventors, all who seek to find principles or develop beauty in their work, seem most to enjoy it. The farmer who labours for the beautifying and scientific cultivation of his estate is more happy in his labours, than one who tills his own land for a mere subsistence. This is one of the signal testimonies which all human employments give to the high demands of our nature. To gather wealth never gives such satisfaction as to bring the humblest piece of machinery to perfection; at least, when wealth is sought for display and ostentation, or mere luxury and ease and pleasure; and not for ends of philanthropy, the relief of kindred, or the payment of just debts, or as a means to attain some other great and noble object.

With the pursuits of multitudes is connected a painful conviction, that they neither supply a sufficient object, nor confer any satisfactory honour. Why work, if the world is soon not to know that such a being ever existed; and when one can perpetuate his name, neither on canvas nor on marble, nor in books, nor by lofty eloquence or statesmanship?

The answer is, that every man has a work to do in himself, greater and sublimer than any work of genius; and works upon a nobler material than wood or marble—upon his own soul and intellect; and may so attain the highest nobleness and grandeur, known on earth or in heaven; may so be the greatest of artists and of authors; and his life, which is far more than speech, may be eloquent.

The great author or artist only portrays what every man should *be*. He *conceives*, what we should *do*. He conceives and represents moral beauty, magnanimity, fortitude, love, devotion, forgiveness, the soul's greatness. He portrays virtues, commended to our admiration and imitation. To embody those portraitures in our lives, is the practical realization of those great ideals of art. The magnanimity of Heroes, celebrated on the historic or poetic page; the constancy and faith of Truth's martyrs; the beauty of love and pity glowing on the canvas; the delineations of Truth and Right, that flash from the lips of the Eloquent, are, in their essence, only that which every man may feel and practise in the daily walks of life. The work of virtue is nobler than any work of genius: for it is a nobler thing to *be* a hero than to *describe* one, to *endure* martyrdom than to *paint* it, to *do* right than to *plead* for it. Action is greater than writing. A good man is a nobler object of contemplation than a great author. There are but two things worth living for; to do what is worthy of being written; and to write what is worthy of being read; and the greater of these is *the doing*.

Every man has to do the noblest thing that any man can do or describe. There is a wide field for the courage, cheerfulness, energy and dignity of human existence. Let therefore no Mason deem his life doomed to mediocrity or meanness, to vanity or unprofitable toil, or to any ends less than immortal. No one can truly say that the grand prizes of life are for others, and he can do nothing. No matter how magnificent and noble an act the author can describe or the artist paint. It will be still nobler for you to go and *do* that which one describes, or *be* the model which the other draws.

The loftiest action that ever was described is not more magnanimous than that which we may find occasion to do, in the daily walks of life; in temptation, in distress, in bereavement, in the solemn approach to death. In the great Providence of God, in the great ordinances of our being, there is opened to every man a sphere for the noblest action. It is not even in extraordinary situations, where all eyes are upon us, where all our energy is aroused and all our vigilance is awake, that the highest efforts of virtue are usually demanded of us; but rather in silence and seclusion, amidst our occupations and our homes; in wearing sickness, that makes no complaint; in sorely-tried honesty, that asks no praise; in simple disinterestedness, hiding the hand that resigns its advantage to another.

Masonry seeks to ennoble common life. Its work is to go down into the obscure and unsearched records of daily conduct and feeling; and to portray, not the ordinary virtue of an extraordinary life; but the more extraordinary virtue of ordinary life. What is done and borne in the shades of privacy, in the hard and beaten path of daily care and toil, full of uncelebrated sacrifices; in the suffering, and sometimes insulted suffering, that wears to the world a cheerful brow; in the long strife of the spirit, resisting pain, penury and neglect, carried on in the inmost depths of the heart;—what is done and borne, and wrought and won there, is a higher glory, and shall inherit a brighter crown.

On the volume of Masonic life one bright word is written, from which on every side blazes an ineffable splendour. That word is Dutr.

To aid in securing to all labour permanent employment and its just reward: to help to hasten the coming of that time when no one shall suffer from hunger or destitution, because, though willing and able to work, he can find no employment, or because he has been overtaken by sickness in the midst of his labour, are part of your duties as a Knight of the Royal Axe. And if we can succeed in making some small nook of God's creation a little more fruitful and cheerful, a little better and more worthy of Him,—or in making some one or two human hearts a little wiser, and more manful and hopeful and happy, we shall have done *work*, worthy of Masons, and acceptable to our Father in Heaven.

TO CLOSE.

[The Ch∴ Prince gives one rap: and says: "Bro∴ Sen∴ Grand Warden, what is the hour?"]

S∴ G∴ W∴ Th∴ Puissant, the sun has set.

Th∴ P∴ It is time then to call the workmen from their labours, that they may rest. Announce to the Princes that this College is about to be closed.

S∴ G∴ W∴ Bro∴ Jun∴ Gr∴ Warden, the Th∴ Puissant is about to close this College of Princes of Libanus. You will communicate the same to the Brethren.

J∴ G∴ W∴ Brethren, the Th∴ Puissant is about to close this College of Princes of Libanus.

Th∴ P∴ Brother Jun∴ Gr∴ Warden, we will call the workmen from their labours by the usual alarm.

[The J∴ G∴ W∴ raps?—the S∴ G∴ W∴?—and the Th∴ P∴?—and the sign is given and answered as at opening.]

Th∴ P∴ The cedars of Mount Libanus are felled; and this College is closed.

FINIS.

Twenty-Third Degree.

Chief of the Tabernacle.

Lodges in this Degree are styled *Assemblies*. The hangings are white, supported by red and black columns, by twos, placed here and there, according to the taste of the architect. In the eastern part of the room, a sanctuary is separated from the rest of the room, by a balustrade, and a crimson curtain in front of the balustrade, looped up on each side.

In the East of the sanctuary is a throne, to which you ascend by seven steps. Before the throne is a table covered with a crimson cloth. On this is the roll of the Book of the Law, and by that a poniard.

Above the throne is a representation of the Ark of the Covenant, crowned with a glory, in the centre whereof is the Tetragrammaton in Hebrew characters; and on either side of the Ark are the Sun and the Moon.

To the right of the first table, and more to the West, is the horned altar of sacrifices. To the left, and more to the West, the altar of perfumes. In the West are two chandeliers, each with five branches; and in the East one with two branches.

During a reception, there is a dark apartment, with an altar in the centre of it, near which are placed a light and three skulls. In front of the altar is a human skeleton.

The Presiding Officer sits upon the throne. He represents Aaron, the High Priest, and is styled *M∴ Excellent High Priest*. The Wardens sit in front of the altar, and represent his two sons, Eleazar and Ithamar. They are styled *Excellent Priests*; and all the other members, *Worthy Levites*.

The High Priest wears a large red tunic, over which is placed a shorter one of white, without sleeves. On his head is a close mitre of cloth of gold; on the front of which is a painted or embroidered delta, enclosing the Ineffable Name in Hebrew characters. Over the dress he wears a black sash, with silver fringe, from which hangs by a red rosette a dagger. The sash is worn from left to right. Suspended on his breast is the breast-plate, or Urim and Thummim.

The two Wardens have the same dress, except the delta on the mitre, and the breast-plate.

The Levites wear a white tunic, cinctured with a red belt, fringed with gold. From this belt, by a black rosette, is suspended a censer, of silver, which is the jewel of the Degree.

The *apron* is white, lined with deep scarlet, and bordered with red, blue and purple ribbons. In the middle it has a gold chandelier, with seven branches; and on the flap a myrtle-tree of violet colour.

The Battery of the Degree is £ — by ? ? ?,

TO OPEN.

The H.'. P.'. gives two raps, and says: "Eleazar, my son, what is the hour?"

Eleaz.'. My father, it is the hour to replenish the fire that burns continually upon the altar of burnt-offering, and to prepare for the morning sacrifice.

H.'. P.'. Bro.'. Jun.'. Deacon, what is the first care of the Chiefs of the Tabernacle when about to assemble?

Jun.'. Deac.'. To see that the Tabernacle is duly guarded; that none may approach thereto, save those to whom its care and service are entrusted.

H.'. P.'. Attend to that duty, and inform the Captain of the Guards that we are about to open this Assembly, to carry forth the ashes from the altar, and to prepare for the morning sacrifice; and instruct him to see that none approach, save those appointed for that service, lest they die.

[The Jun.'. Deacon goes out, returns again, and says]: "M.'. Exc.'. H.'. Priest, the Tabernacle is duly guarded, and none can approach but those that have the proper Pass-word."

H.'. P.'. Eleazar, my son, are all present Chiefs of the Tabernacle?

Elea.'. My father, all present have been initiated in the first degree, and know the sacred name of the God of Israel, of which the letters only can be pronounced.

H.'. P.'. What is that name?

Elea.'. The Ineffable, at which the fallen angels tremble.

H.'. P.'. Will you give it to me?

Elea.'. I cannot. It is forbidden to pronounce it, except once each year by the High Priest, and in conformity to the ancient usage.

M.'. Exc.'. Pronounce the letters, then, with Ithamar.

[The Wardens pronounce alternately, YOD . . . HE . . . VAV . . . HE.'.].

M.'. Exc.'. Great is ADONI, Lord of the ALHIM, who was known to our fathers only by His name AL SHEDI: the only True God, that Is that which HE WAS and SHALL BE: Father and Lord of Earth and Heaven! Ithamar, my son, give notice to the Levites that I am about to open this Assembly, that they may prepare to discharge the duties for which they have been set apart.

Jun.'. W.'. My Brethren, the M.'. Exc.'. H.'. Priest is about to open this Assembly of Chiefs of the Tabernacle. You will take due notice, and prepare to discharge your appropriate duties.

M.'. Exc.'. The sign, my children!

[All give the sign. The M.'. Exc.'. raps?—the Sen.'. W.'.?—the Jun.'. W.'.?—and the M.'. Exc.'.,—and the M.'. Exc.'. declares the Assembly open].

RECEPTION.

The Candidate represents *Eliasaph*, the son of Lael, Chief of the House of Gershon, the son of Levi. The Sen.'. Deacon, who represents Moses, prepares him, by bandaging his eyes, and leads him to the door of the Lodge, where he gives £ raps, by ??? and ,—and the door is opened by the Jun.'. Deacon, representing Joshua, who inquires, "Who comes here?"

Sen.'. Deac.'. Eliasaph, the son of Lael, and Chief of the House of Gershon, the son of Levi; who desires to be prepared to do the service of the people of the Lord in the Tabernacle of the Congregation, and to make an atonement for the children of Israel.

Jun.'. Deac.'. Does he of his own accord and cheerfully make this request?

Sen.'. D.'. He does.

Jun.'. D.'. Is he duly prepared and worthy to receive so great an honour?

Sen.'. D.'. He is.

Jun.'. D.'. Is his soul prepared to receive and digest the truth?

Sen.'. D.'. It is.

Jun∴ D∴ By what further right does he expect to obtain so great a privilege ?

Sen∴ D∴ Because the Lord has given him, and those numbered with him, as a gift to Aaron and his sons, from among the children of Israel; and he and his brethren have been taken by the Lord, instead of all the first-born among the children of Israel.

Jun∴ D∴ It is well. Let him wait a time with patience, until the M∴ Excellent High Priest is informed of his request, and his answer received.

[The Jun∴ Deacon closes the door, goes to the East and raps 6, 1; and the same questions are asked and like answers returned as at the door].

H∴ P∴ It is well; since he comes endowed with these necessary qualifications, let him be conducted to the cell of probation and purification.

[The Jun∴ Deacon goes to the door, and repeats this order. The candidate is then conducted to the dark apartment, and seated upon the floor, in front of the altar and skeleton. The apartment must be entirely without light. The Sen∴ Deacon says to him: " My Brother, I leave you for a time. After you have counted 3, 5, 7 and 9, remove the bandage from your eyes, and await with patience and fortitude whatever shall befall you." He then goes out, and closes the door, leaving him alone.

After a little time a loud crash of thunder is imitated, near the door of the apartment, succeeded by a profound silence. This is repeated three times; and then, in the profound stillness one cries with a loud voice, " Korah, Dathan and Abiram, and their company have put fire in their censers, and laid incense thereon, and stood in the door of the Tabernacle, before the Lord: and the Lord hath done a new thing, for the Earth hath opened her mouth, and hath swallowed them up, for their presumption, with all that appertained to them; and they have gone down alive into the chasm, and the earth has closed upon them, and they have perished from among the congregation."

Another voice cries aloud: " Flee, children of Israel, for there hath come a fire from the Lord, and consumed the two hundred and fifty men that offered incense."

Another voice cries; " The children of Israel have murmured against the Lord, and against Moses and Aaron, for the death of Korah and his company; and He hath sent the plague upon them, and many thousands have died thereof; and the whole people is about to be destroyed."

A profound silence continues for some minutes, and then, by means of a wicket prepared for the purpose, at the bottom of the door, a single feeble light is introduced, and the wicket silently closed again. Immediately a gong is sounded loudly by the door; it thunders again, and chains are rattled together and dashed loudly on the floor. This is followed by groans and cries as of persons in extreme agony; and then by silence. Then the wicket is partly opened, and one in a disguised voice says to the candidate, through the wicket, " Hast thou repented of thy sins ?"]

Cand∴ I have.

Voice∴ Pray then to the God of Israel for mercy and forgiveness, lest he consume thee with fire, as he hath consumed Nadab and Abihu, the sons of Aaron the High Priest.

[After a pause of a few minutes, the voice asks, " Hast thou bowed thee to the earth and prayed?"

If the candidate answers in the affirmative (and if he does not, the question is repeated at intervals, until he does), the door is opened, and the Sen∴ Deacon enters, and says to him; " My Brother, thou hast heard of the awful punishment with which God hath visited those who, not being duly qualified, have presumptuously intermeddled with holy things. Take heed that thou do not so likewise; for as God hath said that no stranger, not of the seed of Aaron, shall approach to offer incense before the Lord, that he be not dealt with as Korah and his company; even so, if thou approachest our mysteries, except with a pure heart, thy sins repented of, and a sincere desire to serve God and thy fellow-men, will their fate or a worse overtake thee. Dost thou now dare to proceed?

The candidate assenting, the Sen∴ Deacon sprinkles him with water, and cuts off a lock of his hair, saying " I sprinkle thee with this pure water in token of that purity of heart and blamelessness of life which must hereafter characterize thee as a Levite without guile : and as I sever from thy head this lock of hair, even so must thou divest thyself of every selfish and sordid feeling, and devote thyself hereafter to the service of God, and the welfare, happiness, and improvement of mankind."

He then clothes him in a white tunic and white drawers, with sandals on his feet, and a white cloth over his head, covering his eyes so as to prevent him from seeing, and then conducts him to the door of the Assembly, where, rapping ? ? ? , he is admitted. Upon entering. the ·Jun.·. Warden meets him, opens the tunic, and marks the sign of the cross upon his breast, saying. "Upon thy entrance into this Holy Place, thou art marked with the sign of the cross, which, pointing to the four quarters of the compass, is a symbol of the Universe of which God is the Soul; and it teaches you how insignificant is man, and how continually he should humble himself in the presence of that Great Being who knows his inmost thoughts."

He is then conducted three times around the room, from East to West, by the way of the South, while the H.·. P.·. reads :

"O Mighty and Inscrutable Being, greater than Brahma, and of whom Bel and Amun are but personifications of an attribute; we bow down before Thee as the Primitive Creator, that with a thought didst from Thyself utter all the worlds! Eternal Father, of whose thought the Universe is but a mode! Infinite in attributes, of which each is infinite! Incorruptible! coeval with Time, and co-extensive with space! The ancient Absolute, and sole original Existence; whose laws of Harmony guide the motions of the suns and stars! Thou art the All; and in Thee all things exist."

At the end of the 3d Circuit, the Sen.·. Deacon and the Candidate halt in the East, where the Sen.·. D.·. gives ? ? ? , raps; and the H.·. P.·. asks] :

H.·. P.·. Whom bring you hither with you, worthy Sen.·. Deacon ?

Sen.·. Dea.·. Eliasaph the son of Lael, Chief of the House of Gershon son of Levi; whom God has given as a gift to thee and to thy sons, from among the children of Israel; to do the service of the children of Israel in the Tabernacle of the Congregation; and to make atonement for the children of Israel.

H.·. P.·. Hath he prayed in the silence and darkness of the cell of probation and purification ?

Sen.·. D.·. He has.

H.·. P.·. Hath he heard the thunder of the Lord, and the roar of the Earthquake; and repented of his sins ?

Sen.·. D.·. He has.

H.·. P.·. Hath he been sprinkled with the water of purification, and passed through the other necessary ceremonies to prepare him to receive the mysteries ?

Sen.·. D.·. He has.

H.·. P.·. Hast thou been warned that thou must enter here, and seek to know our mysteries, with a pure heart, and a sincere desire to serve God and thy fellow-men ?

Cand.·. I have.

H.·. P.·. And art thou willing henceforward to devote thyself to that service; to eschew and avoid vice and iniquity, and practice virtue, charity and truth ?

Cand.·. I am, M.·. Excellent.

H.·. P.·. Bro.·. Sen.·. Deacon, why do you travel from the East to the West, by the way of the South ?

Sen.·. D.·. We copy the example of the Sun; and follow his beneficent course.

H.·. P.·. It is well. He is the fountain of light, and an emblem of the kind beneficence of the Deity. Like him, let this Candidate hereafter shine among men, blessing all within his sphere of action, and returning good for evil. Return now to the West; and thence approach the altar by seven regular steps, and place the Candidate in due position to receive the obligation of a Levite or Chief of the Tabernacle.

The Candidate is re-conducted to the West, and made to reach the altar by seven steps, stepping first with the left foot; at the altar he kneels, with his hands open upon the Holy Bible, Square and Compasses, the right wrist over the left at right angles, forming a cross. The brethren surround him, each crossing his arms upon his breast; and he repeats the following

OBLIGATION.

I, A . . . . . B . . . . ., in the presence of the God of Israel, do hereby and hereon most solemnly and sincerely promise and swear, that I will never reveal any of the Secrets of this Degree to any person not legally authorized to receive them, nor without due authority warranting me to do so.

I furthermore promise and swear that I will be tractable and obedient to my superiors; that I will keep my body pure, and receive obediently the doctrines and mysteries of this Order.

I furthermore promise and swear that I will henceforth, to the best of my ability and knowledge, obey the laws of God, and serve, and labour to do good to, my fellow-men.

To all of which I do most solemnly swear; binding myself under no less a penalty than that of having the earth open under my feet, and being swallowed up alive, like Korah, Dathan and Abiram. So help me God; and keep me steadfast!

————————

One of the Brethren places the sharp point of a sword against the Candidate's left breast: and the H∴ P∴ asks: "My brother, what feelest thou?" Upon hearing his answer he says, "It is the sword of Vengeance in the hand of a Brother: and as it now pains the flesh, remember that if thou dost violate thine obligation, the sharp arrows of conscience and keen remorse will pierce thee through, and torture thee forever. To whom dost thou look for strength to enable thee to keep thy vows and escape this punishment?"

Cand∴. To God.

H∴ P∴. It is well. In Him alone, and not in our own fleeting and evanescent resolution there is safety. What now dost thou desire?

Cand∴. Light.

H∴ P∴. Light is the gift of God, and common to all men. Be thou henceforth a Son of Light.

Sen∴ W∴. God is one; unapproachable, single, eternal and unchanging; and not that supposed God of Nature, Dionusos, Sabazius, Zagreus or Zeus, whose manifold power was imagined to be immediately revealed to the Senses in the incessant round of movement, life and death.

Jun∴ W∴. The Manifold is an infinite illustration of the One. The forces of Nature are the laws enacted by the Absolute Uncreated Existence. In the absence of Creation by Him, no attribute could have been appended to His Name. By the emanations of His Omnipotence we become conscious of His Abstract Being: and the Elohim, by means of which he created all that is, are His Creative Powers, and a portion of those Emanations.

Sen∴ W∴. Al and Bel and Chemosh and Osiris, and all the other Gods of the Heathen are false idols; because, being but men's attributes enlarged and personified, they are wholly unreal and have no existence. There is but one God, Infinite and Incomprehensible, to whom no human attribute can be assigned, even when imagined to be infinite: one God, to attain to a conception of whom all ideas of all other supposed Gods are but ineffectual attempts, falling infinitely more short of the mark at which they aim than an arrow shot at the Sun.

Jun∴ W∴. The world is not God, but the work of God: nor are the Sun and Moon and the Starry Armies of Heaven, Gods or Elohim, but creatures of God, moulded by His Powers out of matter created by Him. The Powers of God are not Persons nor Beings separate from Him, but His Thoughts, immaterial as our Thoughts, and existing in Him as Thought exists in our own Souls.

Sen∴ W∴. God is the Soul of the World, separate from and superior to the universe of things, as the Soul of Man is separate from and superior to his frail body.

Jun∴ W∴. He is neither jealous nor revengeful, nor changeable. He doth not hate nor repent nor give way to anger; but remains in ever undisturbed serenity and repose: and what is otherwise said of Him is but language accommodated to the rude intellects of the Common People, who demand a God with their own passions and infirmities; and to whom any other is an unreality.

Sen∴ W∴. There is no rival God ever at war with the Ineffable; nor any independent and Self-existent Evil Principle in rebellion against Him. The universe is a great whole, in which everything tends to good result, through an infinite series of things, like a great harmony in which discords and concords mingle, and which without either would be imperfect.

Jun∴ W∴. Man, too feeble of intellect to comprehend these mysteries, must believe: and simple faith is wiser than all the vain speculations of Philosophy. Believe that God is a Spirit, the Soul of the Great Universe; its Creator, Ruler and Preserver: that one great law of Harmony governs all things: that all evil Deities and Demons are but imaginary: and all the vulgar ideas of God, mere idle and feeble attempts to conceive of Him and His Attributes.

Sen.·. W.·. Believe this; and trust in Him, and in his Goodness and Mercy. Be sincere and true, and humble and patient; and thou shalt hereafter, in His good time, learn the meaning of the great mystery and riddle of existence.

[The cloth is now removed from the Brother's eyes; and being raised he receives the Sign, Token and Words.

SIGN: . . . Advance the †‡♑☿ ☿ ♈ and with the right hand make a motion as if taking something from ♈&☾‡†☾♑♈. It alludes to the manner in which the H.·. Priest bore the Holy Oil to feed the Sacred fire, when he entered the Tabernacle to perform the sacrifices.

TOKEN: . . . Mutually take the †‡☾†♏☿♃ of each other with the ‡‡&⊙♒♊, ⊙‡↑&♀♒♌‡♈&☾‡ ⊙‡♎, so as to form a kind of circle.

PASS-WORDS: . . . One says ⊙♅‡♀-⊙†.·. The other answers, ♈⊙♏☾‡♒⊙↑†☾ ☿♑ ‡☾✱☾⊙†☾♊ ♈‡♅ ♈&.·.

SACRED WORD: . . ♄☾&☿ ♅⊙&.·.

M.·. Exc.·. I accept and receive you, my Brother, as a Levite and Chief of the Tabernacle, and consecrate and devote you henceforth to the Service of The Children of Light; and I now invest you with the tunic and belt, the jewel and apron of this degree. The jewel, or censer of silver, is ever to remind you to offer up unceasingly to God the incense of good deeds and charitable actions dictated by a pure and upright heart.

The three colours, crimson, blue and purple, with which the white apron is bordered, are symbols—the first [from ארם, red, splendid] of the splendour and glory of God: the second, [from תכלת, blue, the same as תכלית, perfection], of His infinite Perfection: and the third, [from ארגכן, the Imperial Colour], of His Infinite Majesty and Power.

The Candlestick with seven branches, upon the apron, represents what were anciently known as the seven planets or principal Heavenly Bodies, Saturn, Jupiter, Mars, the Sun, Moon, Venus and Mercury: and the Seven Angels that the Hebrews assigned to their government: . . To Saturn, Michael, [MIC-AL]: to Jupiter, Gabriel [Gebri-AL]: To Mars, Auriel [Auri-AL]: to the Sun, Zerachiel [Zerekhi-AL]: to the Moon, Saphiel [Tsaph-AL]: to Venus, Hamaliel [Khmali-AL]: and to Mercury, Raphael [Reph-AL]: signifying, in Hebrew, respectively, the Semblance, the Strength, the Fire, the Rising, the Messenger, the Mercy and the Healing, of AL, the great Semitic God of the Ancient Patriarchs: as to whom and these planets and Angels, and their connection with Masonry, you will be more fully instructed as you advance.

The myrtle-tree, of violet colour, embroidered on the flap of the apron, is a symbol of the immortality of the Soul; a doctrine not found in the books of Moses; but taught to the initiates, in the Hebrew, as it was in the Egyptian, Indian, Phœnician, Samothracian and Eleusinian Mysteries.

Hear now the Lecture of this Degree.

LECTURE.

Among most of the Ancient Nations there was, in addition to their public worship, a private one styled the Mysteries; to which those only were admitted who had been prepared by certain ceremonies called initiations.

The most widely disseminated of the ancient worships were those of Isis, Orpheus, Dionusos, Ceres and Mithras. Many barbarous nations received the knowledge of the mysteries in honour of these divinities from the Egyptians, before they arrived in Greece: and even in the British Isles the Druids celebrated those of Dionusos, learned by them from the Egyptians.

The Mysteries of Eleusis, celebrated at Athens in honour of Ceres, swallowed up, as it were, all the others. All the neighbouring nations neglected their own, to celebrate those of Eleusis; and in a little while all Greece and Asia Minor were filled with the initiates. They spread into the Roman Empire, and even beyond its limits, "those holy and august Eleusinian Mysteries," said Cicero, "in which the people of the remotest lands are initiated." Zosimus says that they embraced the whole human race; and Aristides termed them the common temple of the whole world.

There were, in the Eleusinian feasts, two sorts of Mysteries, the great and the little. The latter were a kind of preparation for the former; and everybody was admitted to them. Ordinarily there was a novitiate of three, and sometimes of four years.

Clemens of Alexandria says that what was taught in the great mysteries concerned the universe, and was the completion and perfection of all instruction; wherein things were seen as they were, and nature and her works were made known.

The ancients said that the Initiates would be more happy after death than other mortals; and that, while the souls of the Profane, on leaving their bodies, would be plunged in the mire and remain buried in darkness, those of the Initiates would fly to the Fortunate Isles, the abode of the Gods.

Plato said that the object of the mysteries was to re-establish the soul in its primitive purity, and in that state of perfection which it had lost. Epictetus said, "whatever is met with therein, has been instituted by our Masters, for the instruction of man and the correction of morals."

Proclus held that initiation elevated the soul, from a material, sensual and purely human life, to a communion and celestial intercourse with the Gods: and that a variety of things, forms and species were shown initiates representing the first generation of the Gods.

Purity of morals and elevation of soul were required of the Initiates. Candidates were required to be of spotless reputation, and irreproachable virtue. Nero, after murdering his mother, did not dare to be present at the celebration of the mysteries: and Antony presented himself to be initiated, as the most infallible mode of proving his innocence of the death of Avidius Cassius.

The initiates were regarded as the only fortunate men. "It is upon us alone," says Aristophanes, "shineth the beneficent day-star. We alone receive pleasure from the influence of his rays; we, who are initiated, and who practise towards citizen and stranger every possible act of justice and piety." And it is therefore not surprising that, in time, initiation came to be considered as necessary, as baptism afterwards was to the Christians; and that not to have been admitted to the Mysteries was held a dishonour.

"It seems to me," says the great orator, philosopher, and moralist, Cicero, "that Athens, among many excellent inventions, divine, and very useful to the human family, has produced none comparable to the Mysteries; which for a wild and ferocious life have substituted humanity, and urbanity of manners. It is with good reason they use the term *initiation;* for it is through them that we in reality have learned the first principles of life; and they not only teach us to live in a manner more consoling and agreeable, but they soften the pains of death by the hope of a better life hereafter."

Where the Mysteries originated is not known. It is supposed that they came from India, by the way of Chaldea, into Egypt, and thence were carried into Greece. Wherever they arose, they were practised among all the ancient nations; and, as was usual, the Thracians, Cretans and Athenians each claimed the honour of invention, and each insisted that they had borrowed nothing from any other people.

In Egypt and the East, all religion, even in its most poetical forms, was more or less a mystery; and the chief reason why in Greece a distinct name and office were assigned to the mysteries, was because the superficial popular theology left a want unsatisfied, which religion in a wider sense alone could supply. They were practical acknowledgments of the insufficiency of the popular religion to satisfy the deeper thoughts and aspirations of the mind. The vagueness of symbolism might perhaps reach what a more palpable and conventional creed could not. The former, by its indefiniteness, acknowledged the abstruseness of its subject; it treated a mysterious subject mystically; it endeavoured to illustrate what it could not explain, to excite an appropriate feeling, if it could not develop an adequate idea, and made the image a mere subordinate convey-ance for the conception which itself never became too obvious or familiar.

The instruction now conveyed by books and letters was of old conveyed by symbols; and the priest had to invent or to perpetuate a display of rites and exhibitions, which were not only more attractive to the eye than words, but often to the mind more suggestive and pregnant with meaning.

Afterwards, the institution became rather moral and political, than religious. The civil magistrates shaped the ceremonies to political ends in Egypt: the sages who carried them from that country to Asia, Greece and the North of Europe, were all kings or legislators. The chief magistrate presided at those of Eleusis, represented by an officer styled *King:* and the Priest played but a subordinate part.

The Powers revered in the Mysteries were all in reality Nature-Gods; none of whom could be consistently addressed as mere heroes, because their nature was confessedly super-heroic. The Mysteries, only in fact a more solemn expression of the religion of the ancient poetry, taught that doctrine of the Theocracia or Divine Oneness, which even poetry does not entirely conceal. They were not in any open hostility with the popular religion, but only a more solemn exhibition of its symbols; or rather a part of itself in a more impressive form. The essence of all mysteries, as of all polytheism, consists in this, that the conception of an unap-proachable Being, single, eternal and unchanging, and that of a God of Nature whose manifold power is immediately revealed to the senses in the incessant round of movement, life and death, fell asunder in the treatment, and were separately symbolized. They offered a perpetual problem to excite curiosity, and contri-buted to satisfy the all-pervading religious sentiment, which, if it obtain no nourishment among the simple and intelligible, finds compensating excitement in a reverential contemplation of the obscure.

Nature is as free from dogmatism as from tyranny; and the earliest instructors of mankind not only adopted her lessons, but as far as possible adhered to her method of imparting them. They attempted to reach the understanding through the eye; and the greater part of all religious teaching was conveyed through this ancient and most impressive mode of "exhibition" or demonstration. The Mysteries were a sacred drama, exhibiting some legend significant of nature's change, of the visible universe in which the Divinity is revealed, and whose import was in many respects as open to the Pagan as to the Christian. Beyond the current traditions or sacred recitals of the temple, few explanations were given to the spectators, who were left, as in the school of nature, to make inferences for themselves.

The method of indirect suggestion, by allegory or symbol, is a more efficacious instrument of instruction than plain didactic language; since we are habitually indifferent to that which is acquired without effort: "The initiated are few, though many bear the thyrsus." And it would have been impossible to provide a lesson suited to every degree of cultivation and capacity, unless it were one framed after Nature's example, or rather a representation of Nature herself, employing her universal symbolism instead of technicalities of language, inviting endless research, yet rewarding the humblest inquirer, and disclosing its secrets to every one in proportion to his preparatory training and power to comprehend them.

Even if destitute of any formal or official enunciation of those important truths, which even in a culti-vated age it was often found inexpedient to assert except under a veil of allegory, and which moreover lose their dignity and value in proportion as they are learned mechanically as dogmas, the shows of the mysteries certainly contained suggestions if not lessons, which in the opinion not of one competent witness only but of many, were adapted to elevate the character of the spectators, enabling them to augur something of the purposes of existence, as well as of the means of improving it, to live better and to die happier.

Unlike the religion of books or creeds, these mystic shows and performances were not the reading of a lecture, but the opening of a problem, implying neither exemption from research, nor hostility to philosophy: for on the contrary, philosophy is the great Mystagogue or Arch-Expounder of symbolism: though the inter-pretations by the Grecian Philosophy of the old myths and symbols were in many instances as ill-founded, as in others they are correct.

No better means could be devised to rouse a dormant intellect, than those impressive exhibitions, which addressed it through the imagination; which instead of condemning it to a prescribed routine of creed, invited it to seek, compare and judge. The alteration from symbol to dogma is as fatal to beauty of expression, as that from faith to dogma is to truth and wholesomeness of thought.

The first philosophy often reverted to the natural mode of teaching; and Socrates, in particular, is said to have eschewed dogmas, endeavouring, like the mysteries, rather to awaken and develop in the minds of his hearers the ideas with which they were already endowed or pregnant, than to fill them with ready-made adventitious opinions.

So Masonry still follows the ancient manner of teaching. Her symbols are the instruction she gives; and the lectures are but often partial and insufficient one-sided endeavours to interpret those symbols. He who would become an accomplished Mason, must not be content merely to hear or even to understand the lectures, but must, aided by them, and they having as it were marked out the way for him, study, interpret, and develop the symbols for himself.

The earliest speculation endeavoured to express far more than it could distinctly comprehend; and the vague impressions of the mind found in the mysterious analogies of phenomena their most apt and energetic representations. The Mysteries, like the symbols of Masonry, were but an image of the eloquent analogies of Nature; both those and these revealing no new secret to such as were or are unprepared, or incapable of interpreting their significancy.

Everywhere in the Old Mysteries, and in all the symbolism and ceremonial of the Hierophant was found the same mythical personage, who, like Hermes or Zoroaster, unites human Attributes with Divine, and is himself the God whose worship he introduced, teaching rude men the commencements of civilization through the influence of song, and connecting with the symbol of his death, emblematic of that of Nature, the most essential consolations of religion.

The Mysteries embraced the three great doctrines of Ancient Theosophy. They treated of God, Man and Nature. Dionusos, whose Mysteries Orpheus is said to have founded, was the God of Nature, or of the moisture which is the life of Nature, who prepares in darkness the return of life and vegetation, or who is himself the Light and Change evolving their varieties. He was theologically one with Hermes, Prometheus and Poseidon. In the Egean Islands he is Butes, Dardanus, Himeros, or Imbros. In Crete he appears as Iasius or Zeus, whose worship remaining unveiled by the usual forms of mystery betrayed to profane curiosity the symbols which if irreverently contemplated, were sure to be misunderstood. In Asia he is the long-stoled Bassareus coalescing with the Sabazius of the Phrygian Corybantes; the same with the mystic Iacchus, nursling or son of Ceres, and with the dismembered Zagreus, son of Persephone.

In symbolical forms the mysteries exhibited THE ONE, of which THE MANIFOLD is an infinite illustration, containing a moral lesson, calculated to guide the soul through life and to cheer it in death. The story of Dionusos was profoundly significant. He was not only creator of the world, but guardian, liberator, and saviour of the soul. God of the many-coloured mantle, he was the resulting manifestation personified, the all in the many, the varied year, life passing into innumerable forms.

The spiritual regeneration of man, was typified in the Mysteries by the second birth of Dionusos as offspring of the Highest; and the agents and symbols of that regeneration were the elements that effected Nature's periodical purification—the air, indicated by the mystic fan or winnow; the fire, signified by the torch; and the baptismal water; for water is not only cleanser of all things, but the genesis or source of all.

These notions clothed in ritual suggested the soul's reformation and training, the moral purity formally proclaimed at Eleusis. He only was invited to approach, who was "of clean hands and ingenuous speech, free from all pollution, and with a clear conscience." "Happy the man," say the initiated in Euripides and Aristophanes, "who purifies his life, and who reverently consecrates his soul in the thiasus of the God. Let him take heed to his lips that he utter no profane word; let him be just and kind to the stranger and to his neighbour; let him give way to no vicious excess, lest he make dull and heavy the organs of the spirit. Far from the mystic dance of the thiasus be the impure, the evil speaker, the seditious citizen, the selfish hunter after gain, the traitor; all those, in short, whose practices are more akin to the riot of Titans than to the regulated life of the Orphici, or the Curetan order of the Priests of Idæan Zeus."

The votary, elevated beyond the sphere of his ordinary faculties, and unable to account for the agitation which overpowered him, seemed to become divine in proportion as he ceased to be human, to be a dæmon or god. Already, in imagination, the initiated were numbered among the beatified. They alone enjoyed the true life, the Sun's true lustre, while they hymned their God beneath the mystic groves of a mimic Elysium, and were really renovated or regenerated under the genial influence of their dances.

"They whom Proserpina guides in her mysteries," it was said, "who imbibe her instruction and spiritual nourishment, rest from their labours and know strife no more. Happy they who witness and comprehend these sacred ceremonies! They are made to know the meaning of the riddle of existence by observing its aim and termination as appointed by Zeus; they partake a benefit more valuable and enduring than the grain bestowed by Ceres; for they are exalted in the scale of intellectual existence, and obtain sweet hopes to console them at their death."

No doubt the ceremonies of Initiation were originally few and simple. As the great truths of the primitive revelation faded out of the memories of the masses of the People, and wickedness became rife upon the earth, it became necessary to discriminate, to require longer probation and satisfactory tests of the candidates, and by spreading around what at first were rather schools of instruction than mysteries, the veil of secrecy, and the pomp of ceremony, to heighten the opinion of their value and importance.

Whatever pictures later and especially Christian writers may draw of, the Mysteries, they must, not only originally, but for many ages, have continued pure; and the doctrines of natural religion and morals there taught, have been of the highest importance; because both the most virtuous as well as the most learned and philosophic of the ancients speak of them in the loftiest terms. That they ultimately became degraded from their high estate, and corrupted, we know.

The rites of Initiation became progressively more complicated. Signs and tokens were invented by which the Children of Light could with facility make themselves known to each other. Different degrees were invented, as the number of initiates enlarged, in order that there might be in the inner apartment of the Temple a favoured few, to whom alone the more valuable secrets were entrusted, and who could wield effectually the influence and power of the Order.

Originally the mysteries were meant to be the beginning of a new life of reason and virtue. The initiated or esoteric companions were taught the doctrine of the One Supreme God, the theory of death and eternity, the hidden mysteries of Nature, the prospect of the ultimate restoration of the soul to that state of perfection from which it had fallen, its immortality, and the states of reward and punishment after death. The uninitiated were deemed Profane, unworthy of public employment or private confidence, sometimes proscribed as Atheists, and certain of everlasting punishment beyond the grave.

All persons were initiated into the lesser mysteries; but few attained the greater, in which the true spirit of them, and most of their secret doctrines were hidden. The veil of secrecy was impenetrable, sealed by oaths and penalties the most tremendous and appalling. It was by initiation only that a knowledge of the Hieroglyphics could be obtained, with which the walls, columns and ceilings of the Temples were decorated, and which, believed to have been communicated to the Priests by revelation from the celestial deities, the youth of all ranks were laudably ambitious of deciphering.

The ceremonies were performed at dead of night, generally in apartments under ground, but sometimes in the centre of a vast pyramid, with every appliance that could alarm and excite the candidate. Innumerable ceremonies, wild and romantic, dreadful and appalling, had by degrees been added to the few expressive symbols of primitive observance, under which there were instances in which the terrified aspirant actually expired with fear.

The pyramids were probably used for the purposes of initiation, as were caverns, pagodas and labyrinths; for the ceremonies required many apartments and cells, long passages and wells. In Egypt a principal place for the mysteries was the island of Philæ on the Nile, where a magnificent Temple of Osiris stood, and his relics were said to be preserved.

With their natural proclivities, the Priesthood, that select and exclusive class, in Egypt, India, Phœnicia, Judea and Greece, as well as in Britain and Rome, and wherever else the mysteries were known, made use of them to build wider and higher the fabric of their own power. The purity of no religion continues long. Rank and dignities succeed to the primitive simplicity. Unprincipled, vain, insolent, corrupt and venal men put on God's livery to serve the Devil withal; and luxury, vice, intolerance and pride depose frugality, virtue.

gentleness and humility; and change the altar where they should be servants, to a throne on which they reign.

But the Kings, Philosophers and Statesmen, the wise and great and good who were admitted to the mysteries, long postponed their ultimate self-destruction, and restrained the natural tendencies of the Priesthood. And accordingly Zosimus thought that the neglect of the mysteries after Dioclesian abdicated, was the chief cause of the decline of the Roman Empire; and in the year 364, the Proconsul of Greece would not close the mysteries, notwithstanding a law of the Emperor Valentinian, lest the people should be driven to desperation, if prevented from performing them; upon which, as they believed, the welfare of mankind wholly depended. They were practised in Athens until the 8th century, in Greece and Rome for several centuries after Christ; and in Wales and Scotland down to the 12th century.

The inhabitants of India originally practised the Patriarchal religion. Even the later worship of Vishnu was cheerful and social; accompanied with the festive song, the sprightly dance, and the resounding cymbal, with libations of milk and honey, garlands, and perfumes from aromatic woods and gums.

There perhaps the mysteries commenced: and in them, under allegories, were taught the primitive truths. We cannot, within the limits of this lecture, detail the ceremonies of initiation; and shall use general language, except where something from those old mysteries still remains in Masonry.

The Initiate was invested with a cord of three threads, so twined as to make three times three, and called *zennar*. Hence comes our cable-tow. It was an emblem of their tri-une Deity, the remembrance of whom we also preserve in the three chief officers of our Lodges, presiding in the three quarters of that Universe which our Lodges represent; in our three greater and three lesser lights, our three moveable and three immoveable jewels, and the three pillars that support our Lodges.

The Indian mysteries were celebrated in subterranean caverns and grottos hewn in the solid rock; and the Initiates adored the Deity, symbolized by the solar fire. The Candidate, long wandering in darkness, truly wanted Light, and the worship taught him was the worship of God, the Source of Light. The vast Temple of Elephanta, perhaps the oldest in the world, hewn out of the rock, and 135 feet square, was used for initiations; as were the still vaster caverns of Salsette, with their 300 apartments.

The periods of initiation were regulated by the increase and decrease of the moon. The mysteries were divided into four steps or degrees. The Candidate might receive the first at eight years of age, when he was invested with the zennar. Each degree dispensed something of perfection. "Let the wretched man," says the Hitopadesa, "practise virtue, whenever he enjoys one of the three or four religious degrees; let him be even-minded with all created things, and that disposition will be the source of virtue."

After various ceremonies, chiefly relating to the unity and trinity of the Godhead, the Candidate was clothed in a linen garment without a seam, and remained under the care of a Brahmin until he was twenty years of age, constantly studying and practising the most rigid virtue. Then he underwent the severest probation for the second degree, in which he was sanctified by the sign of the cross, which, pointing to the four quarters of the compass, was honoured as a striking symbol of the universe by many nations of antiquity, and was imitated by the Indians in the shape of their temples.

Then he was admitted to the Holy Cavern, blazing with light, where, in costly robes, sat, in the East, West and South, the three chief Hierophants, representing the Indian tri-une Deity. The ceremonies there commenced with an anthem to the Great God of Nature; and then followed this apostrophe: "O mighty Being! greater than Brahma! we bow down before Thee as the primal Creator! Eternal God of Gods! The World's Mansion! Thou art the Incorruptible Being, distinct from all things transient! Thou art before all Gods, the Ancient Absolute Existence, and the Supreme Supporter of the Universe! Thou art the Supreme Mansion; and by Thee, O Infinite Form, the Universe was spread abroad."

The Candidate, thus taught the first great primitive truth, was called upon to make a formal declaration, that he would be tractable and obedient to his superiors; that he would keep his body pure; govern his tongue, and observe a passive obedience in receiving the doctrines and traditions of the order; and the firmest secrecy in maintaining inviolable its hidden and abstruse mysteries. Then he was sprinkled with water (whence our *baptism*); certain words, now unknown, were whispered in his ear; and he was divested of his shoes, and made to go three times around the cavern. Hence our three circuits; hence we were neither barefoot nor shod; and the words were the Pass-words of that Indian degree.

The Gymnosophist Priests came from the banks of the Euphrates into Ethiopia, and brought with them their sciences and their doctrines. Their principal College was at Meroe, and their mysteries were celebrated in the Temple of Amun, renowned for his oracle. Ethiopia was then a powerful State, which preceded Egypt in civilization, and had a theocratic government. Above the King was the Priest; and could put him to death in the name of the Deity. Egypt was then composed of the Thebaid only. Middle Egypt and the Delta were a gulf of the Mediterranean. The Nile by degrees formed an immense marsh, which, afterwards drained by the labour of man, formed Lower Egypt; and was for many centuries governed by the Ethiopian Sacerdotal Caste, of Arabic origin; afterwards displaced by a dynasty of warriors. The magnificent ruins of Axoum, with its obelisks and hieroglyphics, temples, vast tombs and pyramids, around ancient Meroe, are far older than the pyramids near Memphis.

The Priests, taught by Hermes, embodied in books the occult and hermetic sciences, with their own discoveries and the revelations of the Sibyls. They studied particularly the most abstract sciences, discovered the famous geometrical theorems which Pythagoras afterwards learned from them, calculated eclipses, and regulated, nineteen centuries before Cæsar, the Julian year. They descended to practical investigations as to the necessities of life, and made known their discoveries to the people; they cultivated the fine arts, and inspired the people with that enthusiasm which produced the avenues of Thebes, the Labyrinth, the Temples of Karnac, Denderah, Edfou, and Philœ, the monolithic obelisks, and the great Lake Moeris, the fertilizer of the country.

The wisdom of the Egyptian Initiates, the high sciences and lofty morality which they taught, and their immense knowledge, excited the emulation of the most eminent men, whatever their rank and fortune; and led them, despite the complicated and terrible trials to be undergone, to seek admission into the mysteries of Osiris and Isis.

From Egypt, the mysteries went to Phœnicia, and were celebrated at Tyre. Osiris changed his name, and became Adoni or Dionusos, still the representative of the Sun; and afterwards these mysteries were introduced successively into Assyria, Babylon, Persia, Greece, Sicily, and Italy. In Greece and Sicily, Osiris took the name of Bacchus, and Isis that of Ceres, Cybele, Rhea and Venus.

Bar Hebraeus says; "Enoch was the first who invented books and different sorts of writing. The ancient Greeks declare that Enoch is the same as Mercury Trismegistus [Hermes], and that he taught the sons of men the art of building cities, and enacted some admirable laws. . . He discovered the knowledge of the Zodiac, and the course of the Planets; and he pointed out to the sons of men, that they should worship God, that they should fast, that they should pray, that they should give alms, votive offerings and tenths. He reprobated abominable foods and drunkenness, and appointed festivals for sacrifices to the Sun, at each of the Zodiacal Signs."

Manetho extracted his history from certain pillars which he discovered in Egypt, whereon inscriptions had been made by Thoth, or the first Mercury, [or Hermes], in the sacred letters and dialect: but which were after the flood, translated from that dialect into the Greek tongue, and laid up in the private recesses of the Egyptian Temples. These pillars were found in subterranean caverns, near Thebes and beyond the Nile, not far from the sounding statue of Memnon, in a place called Syringes; which are described to be certain winding apartments underground; made, it is said, by those who were skilled in ancient rites; who, foreseeing the coming of the Deluge, and fearing lest the memory of their ceremonies should be obliterated, built and contrived vaults, dug with vast labour, in several places.

From the bosom of Egypt sprang a man of consummate wisdom, initiated in the secret knowledge of India, of Persia and of Ethiopia, named Thoth or Phtha by his compatriots, Taaut by the Phœnicians, Hermes Trismegistus by the Greeks, and Adris by the Rabbins. Nature seemed to have chosen him for her favourite, and to have lavished on him all the qualities necessary to enable him to study her and to know her thoroughly. The Deity had, so to say, infused into him the sciences and the arts, in order that he might instruct the whole world.

He invented many things necessary for the uses of life, and gave them suitable names; he taught men how to write down their thoughts and arrange their speech; he instituted the ceremonies to be observed in the worship of each of the Gods; he observed the courses of the stars; he invented music, the different bodily exercises, arithmetic, medicine, the art of working in metals, the lyre with three strings; he regulated the three tones of the voice, the *sharp*, taken from autumn, the *grave* from winter and the *middle* from spring, there being then but three seasons. It was he who taught the Greeks the mode of interpreting terms and things, whence they gave him the name of 'Ερμης [*Hermes*] which signifies *Interpreter*.

In Egypt he instituted hieroglyphics: he selected a certain number of persons whom he judged fittest to be the depositaries of his secrets, of such only as were capable of attaining the throne and the first offices in the mysteries; he united them in a body, created them *Priests of the Living God*, instructed them in the sciences and arts, and explained to them the symbols by which they were veiled. Egypt, 1500 years before the time of Moses, revered in the mysteries ONE SUPREME GOD, called the ONLY UNCREATED. Under Him it paid homage to seven principal deities. It is to Hermes, who lived at that period, that we must attribute the concealment or *veiling* [*velation*] of the Indian worship, which Moses *unveiled* or *revealed*, changing nothing of the laws of Hermes, except the plurality of his mystic Gods.

The Egyptian Priests related that Hermes, dying, said: "Hitherto I have lived an exile from my true country: now I return thither. Do not weep for me: I return to that celestial country whither each goes in his turn. There is God. This life is but a death." This is precisely the creed of the old Buddhists or Samaneans, who believed that from time to time God sent Buddhas on earth, to reform men, to wean them from their vices, and lead them back into the paths of virtue.

Among the sciences taught by Hermes, there were secrets which he communicated to the Initiates only upon condition that they should bind themselves, by a terrible oath, never to divulge them, except to those who, after long trial, should be found worthy to succeed them. The Kings even prohibited the revelation of them on pain of death. This secret was styled the Sacerdotal Art, and included alchemy, astrology, magism [magic], the science of spirits, &c. He gave them the key to the Hieroglyphics of all these secret sciences, which were regarded as sacred, and kept concealed in the most secret places of the Temple.

The great secrecy observed by the initiated Priests, for many years, and the lofty sciences which they professed, caused them to be honoured and respected throughout all Egypt, which was regarded by other nations as the college, the sanctuary, of the sciences and arts. The mystery which surrounded them strongly excited curiosity. Orpheus metamorphosed himself, so to say, into an Egyptian. He was initiated into Theology and Physics. And he so completely made the ideas and reasonings of his teachers his own, that his Hymns rather bespeak an Egyptian Priest than a Grecian Poet: and he was the first who carried into Greece the Egyptian fables.

Pythagoras, ever thirsty for learning, consented even to be circumcised, in order to become one of the Initiates: and the occult sciences were revealed to him in the innermost part of the sanctuary.

The Initiates in a particular science, having been instructed by fables, enigmas, allegories, and hieroglyphics, wrote mysteriously whenever in their works they touched the subject of the Mysteries, and continued to conceal science under a veil of fictions.

When the destruction by Cambyses of many cities, and the ruin of nearly all Egypt, in the year 528 before our era, dispersed most of the Priests into Greece and elsewhere, they bore with them their sciences, which they continued to teach enigmatically, that is to say, ever enveloped in the obscurities of fables and hieroglyphics; to the end that the vulgar herd, seeing, might see nothing, and hearing might comprehend nothing. All the writers drew from this source: but these mysteries, concealed under so many unexplained envelopes, ended in giving birth to a swarm of absurdities, which from Greece, spread over the whole Earth.

In the Grecian Mysteries, as established by Pythagoras, there were three degrees. A preparation of five years' abstinence and silence was required. If the candidate were found to be passionate or intemperate, contentious, or ambitious of worldly honours and distinctions, he was rejected.

In his lectures, Pythagoras taught the mathematics, as a medium whereby to prove the existence of God from observation and by means of reason; grammar, rhetoric and logic, to cultivate and improve that reason; arithmetic, because he conceived that the ultimate benefit of man consisted in the science of numbers; and geometry, music and astronomy, because he conceived that man is indebted to them for a knowledge of what is really good and useful.

He taught the true method of obtaining a knowledge of the Divine laws; to purify the soul from its imperfections, to search for truth, and to practise virtue; thus imitating the perfections of God. He thought his system vain, if it did not contribute to expel vice and introduce virtue into the mind. He taught that the two most excellent things were, to speak the truth, and to render benefits to one another. Particularly he inculcated Silence, Temperance, Fortitude, Prudence and Justice. He taught the immortality of the soul, the Omnipotence of God, and the necessity of personal holiness to qualify a man for admission into the Society of the Gods.

Thus we owe the particular mode of instruction in the Degree of Fellow-Craft to Pythagoras; and that degree is but an imperfect reproduction of his lectures. From him, too, we have many of our explanations of the symbols. He arranged his assemblies due East and West, because he held that Motion began in the East and proceeded to the West. Our Lodges are said to be due East and West, because the Master represents the rising Sun, and of course must be in the East. The pyramids, too, were built precisely by the four cardinal points. And our expression, that our Lodges extend upwards to the Heavens, comes from the Persian and Druidic custom of having to their Temples no roofs but the sky.

Plato developed and spiritualized the philosophy of Pythagoras. Even Eusebius the Christian admits, that he reached to the vestibule of Truth, and stood upon its threshold.

The Druidical ceremonies undoubtedly came from India; and the Druids were originally Buddhists. The word *Druidh*, like the word *Magi*, signifies wise or learned men; and they were at once philosophers, magistrates and divines.

There was a surprising uniformity in the Temples, Priests, doctrines and worship of the Persian Magi and British Druids. The Gods of Britain were the same as the Cabiri of Samothrace. Osiris and Isis appeared in their Mysteries, under the names of Hu and Ceridwen; and like those of the primitive Persians, their Temples were enclosures of huge unhewn stones, some of which still remain, and are regarded by the common people with fear and veneration. They were generally either circular or oval. Some were in the shape of a circle to which a vast serpent was attached. The circle was an Eastern symbol of the Universe, governed by an Omnipotent Deity whose centre is everywhere, and his circumference nowhere: and the egg was a universal symbol of the world. Some of the Temples were winged, and some in the shape of a cross; the winged ones referring to Kneph, the winged Serpent-Deity of Egypt; whence the name of *Narestock*, where one of them stood. Temples in the shape of a cross were also found in Ireland and Scotland. The length of one of these vast structures, in the shape of a serpent, was nearly three miles.

The grand periods for initiation into the Druidical mysteries, were quarterly; at the equinoxes and solstices. In the remote times when they originated, these were the times corresponding with the 13th of February, 1st of May, 19th of August, and 1st of November. The time of annual celebration was May-Eve, and the ceremonial preparations commenced at midnight, on the 29th of April. When the initiations were over, on May-Eve, fires were kindled on all the cairns and cromlechs in the island, which burned all night to introduce the sports of May-day. The festival was in honour of the Sun. The initiations were performed at midnight; and there were three degrees.

The Gothic mysteries were carried Northward from the East, by Odin; who, being a great warrior, modelled and varied them to suit his purposes and the genius of his people. He placed over their celebration twelve Hierophants, who were alike Priests, Counsellors of State, and Judges from whose decision there was no appeal.

He held the numbers three and nine in peculiar veneration; and was probably himself the Indian Buddha. Every thrice-three months, thrice-three victims were sacrificed to the tri-une God.

The Goths had three great festivals; the most magnificent of which commenced at the winter Solstice, and was celebrated in honour of Thor, the Prince of the Power of the Air. That being the longest night in the year, and the one after which the Sun comes Northward, it was commemorative of the Creation; and they termed it mother-night, as the one in which the creation of the world and light from the primitive darkness took place. This was the *Yule*, *Juul* or *Yeol* feast, which afterwards became Christmas. At this feast the initiations were celebrated. Thor was the Sun, the Egyptian Osiris and Kneph, the Phœnician Bel or Baal. The initiations were had in huge intricate caverns, terminating, as all the Mithriac caverns did, in a spacious vault, where the Candidate *was brought to light.*

Joseph was undoubtedly initiated. After he had interpreted Pharaoh's dream, that Monarch made him his Prime Minister, let him ride in his second chariot, while they proclaimed before him, ABRECH!; and set him over the land of Egypt. In addition to this, the King gave him a new name, Tsaphnath-Paäneach, and married him to As'nath, daughter of Potipherah a Priest of On or Hieropolis, where was the Temple of Athom-Re, the Great God of Egypt; thus completely naturalizing him. He could not have contracted this marriage, nor have exercised that high dignity, without being first initiated in the mysteries. When his Brethren came to Egypt the second time, the Egyptians of his court could not eat with them, as that would have been abomination; though they ate with Joseph; who was therefore regarded not as a foreigner, but as one of themselves: and when he sent and brought his brethren back, and charged them with taking his cup, he said, "Know ye not that a man like me practises divination?" thus assuming the Egyptian of high rank initiated into the mysteries, and as such conversant with the occult sciences.

So also must Moses have been initiated: for he was not only brought up in the court of the King, as the adopted son of the King's daughter, until he was forty years of age; but he was instructed in all the learning of the Egyptians, and married afterwards the daughter of Jethro, a Priest of On likewise. Strabo and Diodorus both assert that he was himself a Priest of Heliopolis. Before he went into the Desert there were intimate relations between him and the Priesthood; and he had successfully commanded, Josephus informs us, an army sent by the King against the Ethiopians. Simplicius asserts that Moses received from the Egyptians, in the mysteries, the doctrines which he taught to the Hebrews: and Clement of Alexandria and Philo say that he was a Theologian and Prophet, and interpreter of the Sacred Laws. Manetho, cited by Josephus, says he was a Priest of Heliopolis, and that his true and original (Egyptian) name was Asersaph or Osarsiph.

And in the institution of the Hebrew Priesthood, in the powers and privileges, as well as the immunities and sanctity which he conferred upon them, he closely imitated the Egyptian institutions; making *public* the worship of that Deity whom the Egyptian Initiates worshipped in private; and strenuously endeavouring to keep the people from relapsing into their old mixture of Chaldaic and Egyptian superstition and idol-worship, as they were ever ready and inclined to do; even Aaron, upon their first clamorous discontent, restoring the worship of Apis, as an image of which Egyptian God he made the golden calf.

The Egyptian Priests taught in their great mysteries, that there was one God, Supreme and Unapproachable, who had *conceived* the Universe by His Intelligence, before He *created* it by his Power and Will. They were no Materialists nor Pantheists; but taught that Matter was not eternal or co-existent with the great First Cause, but created by Him.

The early Christians, taught by the founder of their Religion, but in greater perfection, those primitive truths that from the Egyptians had passed to the Jews, and been preserved among the latter by the Essenes, received also the institution of the Mysteries; adopting as their object the building of the symbolic Temple, preserving the old Scriptures of the Jews as their sacred book, and as the fundamental law, which furnished the new veil of Initiation with the Hebraic words and formulas, which, corrupted and disfigured by time and ignorance, appear in many of our degrees.

Such, my Brother, is the doctrine of the first degree of the Mysteries, or that of Chief of the Tabernacle, to which you have now been admitted: and the moral lesson of which is, devotion to the service of God, and disinterested zeal and constant endeavour for the welfare of men. You have here received only hints of the true objects and purposes of the Mysteries. Hereafter, if you are permitted to advance, you will arrive at a more complete understanding of them and of the sublime doctrines which they teach. Be content, therefore, with that which you have seen and heard, and await patiently the advent of the greater light.

TO CLOSE.

H.·. P.·. Eleazer, my son, what is the hour?

Ele.·. The sacrifices are concluded, and the fire burns brightly upon the altar of burnt-offering.

H.·. P.·. Of what are the sacrifices symbolical?

Elea.·. Of the sacrifice of our personal feelings and of our pleasures upon the altar of Duty.

H.·. P.·. Of what is the ever-burning fire symbolical?

Elea.·. Of the never-ceasing mercy and goodness of God; and of that zeal and devotion to his service and the welfare of men, which ought never to burn low or feebly in the bosom of a Chief of the Tabernacle.

H.·. P.·. Of what is the Tabernacle symbolical?

Elea.·. Of the Universe: in which God dwells, as the soul of man dwelleth in his body.

H.·. P.·. Of what are the six branches of the candlestick of gold symbolical?

Elea.·. Of the six months of light; and the six days in which God created the Universe.

H.·. P.·. Of what are the seven lamps symbolical?

Elea.·. Of the 7 planets; and of the 7 great stars that pointed the people of Israel to the North.

H.·. P.·. What are the colours of the hangings of the Tabernacle?

Elea.·. White, blue, purple and scarlet.

H.·. P.·. Of what are these colours the symbols to the Chiefs of the Tabernacle?

Sen.·. W.·. White of the candour, innocence and purity, which are indispensable to a Levite: and Red of the Glory and Splendour, Blue of the Infinite Perfection, and Purple of the Majesty and Power of that Great Deity to whose service the Levite is dedicated.

H.·. P.·. What now remains to be done?

Sen.·. W.·. To meditate in silence, and prepare for the duties of the morrow.

H.·. P.·. That we may retire and do so, let this Assembly now be closed. The sign, my Sons!

[The sign is given, and the battery as at opening; and the H.·. P.·. declares the Chapter closed].

FINIS.

Twenty-Fourth Degree.

Prince of the Tabernacle.

The Lodge consists of two apartments, the first of which proceeds directly into the second, and is called *the Vestibule*, where the brethren clothe themselves. It is furnished at all points like a Master's Lodge.

The second apartment is made completely circular, by means of a suite of hangings. The decorations of this vary, as will be stated hereafter, according to the three points of reception. In the centre is placed a candlestick with seven branches, each holding seven lights.

The dress is a blue silk tunic or alb; the collar of which is decorated with rays of gold representing a glory; and the body of it sprinkled with stars of gold. Upon the head is a close crown encircled with stars, and surmounted by a delta.

The sash or cordon is a broad watered scarlet ribbon, worn as a collar, or as a sash from right to left. The apron is white, lined with deep scarlet, and bordered with green; with the flap sky-blue. In the middle of the apron is a representation of the first Tabernacle, built by Moses.

The jewel is the letter א, worn from a collar of broad crimson ribbon.

The Lodge is styled *Assembly*. The Chief Prince is styled *Th.·. Puissant:* and there are three Wardens, who are styled *Puissant*. The first Warden represents AARON the High Priest, and sits in the West. The second represents BETSEL-AL [Bezaleel], and sits in the South. The third represents AHLI-AB [Aholiab], and sits in the North.

The Ch.·. Prince represents MOSES: and the Candidate represents ELEAZAR the son of Aaron.

The battery is ? ? ? ,

TO OPEN.

Th.·. P.·. Puissant Warden in the North, I am about to open this Assembly of Princes of the Tabernacle, that we may take counsel for the welfare of the Order. Are we well guarded, so that none save those who are entitled to do so can approach the Tabernacle?

3d Ward.·. Th.·. Puissant Chief Prince, the Tabernacle is guarded on all sides, and we are in security.

Th.·. P.·. Puissant Warden in the West, are all present Princes of the Tabernacle?

1st Ward.·. All are Princes of the Tabernacle, Th.·. P.·., and have seen the Perfection of the Holy Mysteries of the Hebrews.

Th.·. P.·. What are the duties of a Prince of the Tabernacle?

1st Ward.·. To labour incessantly for the glory of God, the honour of his Country and the happiness of his Brethren.

Th.·. P.·. Puissant Warden in the North, whom dost thou represent?

3d Ward.·. Ahli-Ab, Th.·. P.·., who aided in building the first Tabernacle.

Th.·. P.·. How did he labour upon the Tabernacle of the Lord?

3d Ward.·. As an engraver; beautifying the vessels thereof; and as an embroiderer in blue and purple, and scarlet and fine linen.

Th.·. P.·. What does his occupation teach thee, in morals?

3d Ward.·. To engrave upon my heart, and ever recollect, the Laws of God and the Statutes of Righteousness, Virtue and Truth; and to make my life beautiful with the embroidery of good actions.

Th.·. P.·. Puissant Warden in the South, whom dost thou represent?

2d Ward.·. Betsel-Al. Th.·. P.·., who aided in building the first Tabernacle.

Th.·. P.·. How did he labour upon the Tabernacle of the Lord?

2d Ward.·. In gold and silver and brass; in the cutting of stones, and in the carving of wood.

Th.·. P.·. What does his occupation teach thee in morals?

2d Ward.·. Ever to strive to attain perfection, and to be patient and persevering in every good work.

Th.·. P.·. Puissant Warden in the West, Most Excellent High Priest, what is your duty in the Tabernacle?

1st Ward.·. To offer up prayers and thanks to the Deity, in lieu of Sacrifices; and to aid you with my counsel and advice.

Th.·. P.·. It is time to proceed to discharge our duties. Aid me, Princes, to open this Assembly! The Sign, my Brethren!

[Each gives the Second Sign. The Th.·. P.·. raps ? ? ?,—each Warden successively the same: and the Th.·. P.·. declares the Assembly open].

RECEPTION.

[The Candidate, representing Eleazar, the son of Aaron, is clothed in a white tunic, without ornaments or insignia, and conducted to the door of the vestibule, in charge of the Sen.·. Deacon, who enters with him without ceremony. This room is furnished in every respect like a Master Mason's Lodge, except that, instead of the Bible, a roll of parchment, representing the Book of the Law, lies upon the Altar: and the Hebrew letter Yod is in the East, instead of the letter G. Here the Sen.·. Deacon addresses him thus]:

Sen.·. D.·. Bro.·. Eleazar, thou hast been chosen to be anointed, consecrated, and sanctified, to minister unto the Lord in the Priest's office. But before thou canst enter upon the Mysteries of Consecration, thou must in the most solemn manner give assurance that no unworthy motive prompts thee to seek to know those Ancient Mysteries which were instituted among the Patriarchs; and the knowledge of which is indispensable to him who would become a Priest in Israel. Kneel, therefore, and place thy hand on the Book of the Law, and make true answer to such questions as shall be asked thee.

1st. Dost thou, now representing Eleazar the son of Aaron, solemnly declare that in seeking to know the hidden Ancient Mysteries, thou art not actuated by any spirit of idle curiosity, or the pride of knowledge; but by a sincere desire thereby to be the better able to serve God, your Country and your Brethren, and more effectually to labour for the reformation and improvement of mankind?

Cand.·. I do.

2d. In the character of Chief of the Tabernacle, hast thou earnestly striven to discharge all the duties required of thee, and to live worthily, act justly, and fear God?

Cand.·. I have.

3d. Hast thou, while a Chief of the Tabernacle, done wrong to any one, without making reparation, as far as was in thy power?

Cand.·. I have not.

4th. Dost thou solemnly swear, upon the Holy Book of the law, and with thy heart open before God, and all its thoughts legible to Him, that these answers are true and sincere, without equivocation or double meaning, or any mental reservation whatsoever? If thou dost, say, "*I swear,*" and kiss the Book of the Law.

Cand∴ I swear.

[The Sen∴ Deacon then raises him, and directs him to wash himself in a vessel prepared for the purpose; after which he instructs him in regard to the emblems and furniture of the Lodge room as follows]:

Sen∴ D∴ I am charged, my Brother, to explain to you the meaning of the several symbols with which you are now surrounded.

The Triangle with the letter Yod in the centre, suspended in the East, is an Emblem of the Deity, and of equity; because its sides are equal, and it is the first perfect figure that can be formed with straight lines.

The Square upon the Altar is an emblem of rectitude of intention and action, and of obedience to Constituted Authority: The Compasses, of Command, of the Motion of the Heavenly bodies, of harmony and of Eternity.

The three lights on the East, West and South of the Altar, represent the Summer Solstice and the Vernal and Autumnal equinoxes; the three persons of the Indian Godhead, the Creator, Preserver and Destroyer; the three Egyptian Gods, Osiris, Isis and Horus: and, to us, the absolute REASON, the creative POWER, and the Protecting INTELLIGENCE that constitute the Godhead.

The two columns at the entrance represent the two solstices, and are the parallel lines between which is the circle with a point in the centre, representing the Sun. The circle also represents the Deity, in the centre of the universe; and the two columns those erected by Enoch to perpetuate the history of the times before the flood.

The plumb is a symbol of decision, firmness and independence: of truth, and straight-forward simplicity.

The level is a symbol of equality and equanimity; and teaches us that all men are equal in the sight of God and in the Mysteries.

The blazing star represents Sirius or Sothis, the dog-star, announcing the approach of the inundation of the Nile, to the forefathers of the Hebrews, when they toiled upon its banks.

The rough stone or ashlar represents the Profane who is ignorant of the Mysteries; and the perfect cube is a symbol of the Enlightened to whom they are known.

To many of these symbols there are other meanings which it should be your study to discover for yourself. Often they are indicated to the initiate by a hint or a suggestion only; in order that, obtaining Masonic light by thought and investigation, he may the more highly value it. And, as many of the explanations given in the three symbolic degrees embody the most common-place ideas, inventions of men of no capacity, after the true interpretation of these symbols had long been lost, it is the more incumbent on you, by reflection and study, to learn the true meaning for yourself.

[This instruction being concluded, the Sen∴ Deacon blindfolds the Candidate, takes him by the hand, and leads him to the door of the second apartment.

This apartment, circular in shape, is now hung with scarlet: and around it, in front of the hangings are 12 columns, each having painted on it in brilliant letters one of the signs of the zodiac, which thus follow each other in regular progression. The Presiding Officer (Moses) sits in the East, clothed with all his insignia, between the columns on which are the signs *Taurus* and *Aries*: The 1st Warden, (Aaron) sits in the West, between the signs *Libra* and *Scorpio;* The 2d Warden in the South, between the signs *Capricornus* and *Aquarius;* and the 3d Warden in the North, between the signs *Cancer* and *Leo.* In the centre of the room, by the chandelier, is a triangular altar.

The Sen∴ Deacon raps at the door [???,]. It is opened by the Jun∴ Deacon, who inquires: "Who seeks admission to this inner chamber of the Mysteries?"]

Sen∴ D∴ Eleazar the son of Aaron, who having been appointed to minister unto God in the Priest's office, desires first to know the Mysteries and receive the indispensable degree of Prince of the Tabernacle.

Jun∴ D∴ Has he attained the degree of Chief of the Tabernacle?

Sen∴ D∴ He has.

Jun∴ D∴ In that character, has he earnestly striven to discharge all the duties required of him, and to live worthily, act justly and fear God ?

Sen∴ D∴ He has.

Jun∴ D∴ Has he, while such, done wrong to any one, without afterwards making reparation, as far as hath been in his power?

Sen∴ D∴ He hath not.

Jun∴ D∴ Eleazar, art thou actuated, in seeking to know the Mysteries, by a sincere desire to be thereby better able to serve God, your country and your brethren, and more efficiently to labour for the good of man ?

Cand∴ I am.

Jun∴ D∴ Art thou not induced to come hither through idle curiosity or the pride of knowledge, and a desire to become superior to thy brothers and fellows?

Cand∴ I am not.

Jun∴ D∴ By what further right does he expect to gain admission here ?

Sen∴ D∴ By the Sacred Word.

Jun∴ D∴ Has he the Sacred Word?

Sen∴ D∴ He has.

Jun∴ D∴ Let him give it.

Sen∴ D∴ He cannot, except with our assistance.

Jun∴ D∴ Let him begin then.

Cand∴ Yod. . . *Sen∴ D∴* He. . *Jun∴ D∴* Vav. . . *Cand∴* He.

Jun∴ D∴ The word is right. Let him wait until the Th∴ P∴ Ch∴ Pr∴ is informed of his request.

[The Jun∴ Deac∴ closes the door, goes to the centre of the circle, and gives the battery; and the Th∴ P∴ asks the same questions, in substance, as were asked at the door; and like answers are returned; until the Th∴ Puissant asks if the Candidate has the word; to which the Jun∴ Deac∴ answers: "He has, and with my aid and that of his guide our Sen∴ Deacon, he has given it."]

Th∴ P∴ It is well. Since he comes endowed with these necessary qualifications, let him enter, and be received in due form.

[This is announced to the candidate, and he enters. When within the circle, he is stopped by the Jun∴ Deacon, who bares his right arm, and holds a candle near enough to it to cause him to feel the heat and a slight pain; and the Jun∴ Deacon says]: "I test you by FIRE: and let this present pain ever remind you that he who rashly assumes to perform offices for which he is unfit, deserves the fate of Nadab and Abihu, who were consumed by fire from Heaven, when they offered strange fire before the Lord in the wilderness of Sinai."

[The candidate is then led 3 times around the room; while the Th∴ P∴ reads]:

Th∴ P∴ "And the Lord spake unto Moses, saying, Bring the Tribe of Levi near, and present them before Aaron the Priest, that they may minister unto him. And they shall keep his charge, and the charge of the whole congregation before the tabernacle of the congregation, to do the service of the tabernacle. And thou shalt give the Levites unto Aaron and his sons. They are wholly given unto him out of the children of Israel. And thou shalt appoint Aaron and his sons, and they shall wait on their Priests' office; and the stranger that cometh nigh shall be put to death."

[The candidate is then halted in the South, by the 2d Warden's station, who pours a small quantity of water on his head, and says]: "Thou hast reached the South. I test thee with WATER, the second test. Let it ever remind thee that none but the pure of heart can be admitted to the Holy Tabernacle in the Heavens; where God, who is Infinite Purity, presides; and that it is reformation and repentance, and not the blood of animals sacrificed, that wash out sin; of which reformation the lavation of the body is a symbol."

[Then the candidate is again led 3 times around the room, while the 1st Warden reads]:

1st W∴ "At the door of the tabernacle of the congregation I will meet with the children of Israel; and I will sanctify the tabernacle of the congregation and the altar: I will sanctify also both Aaron and his sons, to minister to me in the Priest's office: and I will dwell among the children of Israel, and I will be their God: and they shall know that I am the Lord their God, that brought them forth out of the land of Egypt, that I might dwell among them; I, the Lord their God."

[The candidate is then halted in the West, by the 1st Warden's station; who causes him to kneel upon a place prepared for the occasion with sand and gravel; and says]: "Thou hast reached the West. I test thee with EARTH. It is the common mother, and to it our frail bodies return. It is well to kneel upon its bosom when we would implore the mercy and forgiveness of God. Let the beneficence of the earth, which produceth generously and liberally, even for the unworthy, teach thee generosity, and that the open hand is a fit companion of the pure heart."

[Then the candidate is again led 3 times round the circle, while the 2d Warden reads]:

2d W.·. "Ye shall do no unrighteousness in judgment: thou shalt not respect the person of the poor, nor honour the person of the mighty; in righteousness thou shalt judge thy neighbour. Thou shalt not hate thy brother in thy heart. Thou shalt not seek revenge, nor bear ill-will against the children of thy people; but thou shalt love thy neighbour as thyself. Thou shalt not glean thy vineyard, nor gather every grape. Thou shalt leave some for the poor and the stranger. Ye shall be holy, for I, Adonai, am holy. Ye shall keep my Sabbaths, and reverence my sanctuary. Thou shalt rise up in the presence of the hoary head, and honour the face of the aged, and fear thy God. If thy brother be waxen poor and fallen in decay with thee, then shalt thou relieve him, even if he be a stranger or a sojourner, that he may live with thee. Thou shalt not lend him money upon usury, nor victuals for increase. Thou shalt open thine hand wide unto thy brother, to thy poor and to thy needy in the land."

[The candidate is then halted in the East, at the station of the Th.·. Puissant; who says to him, while the brethren, with fans, make a wind about him]: "Thou hast reached the East. I test thee with AIR, the life of all men, the free, inestimable gift of God. Like Him it is mighty, but invisible. Like Him it blesses us ever. Be thou liberal and generous as the air: for, if God freely gives thee light and air, and asks in return nothing but gratitude and whispered thanks, thou mayest well afford to share thy plenty with thy destitute, afflicted and unfortunate brother. Bro.·. Sen.·. Deacon, whence come you?"

Sen.·. Deac.·. Out of the darkness.

Th.·. P.·. And whither go you?

Sen.·. Deac.·. To the East, the place of Light, and cradle of the Mysteries.

Th.·. P.·. Thou art already there. What is thy desire?

Sen.·. Deac.·. That this aspirant may go the way that we have gone before him, and attain unto the new life.

Th.·. P.·. The soul is immortal; but for the body, life comes only out of death. If he would see the light, conduct him to the Holy Altar, and let him there assume the proper obligation.

[The Candidate is led to the altar, where he kneels (advancing to it from the West by six equal and one long step), and, with his hands upon the book of the Law, repeats the following obligation]:

OBLIGATION.

I, A. . . . . B. . . . ., in the presence of the God of Abraham, Isaac and Jacob, and knowing that he is now reading the thoughts of my heart, do hereby and hereon, most solemnly and sincerely promise and swear, that I will never reveal to any person in the world the secrets of this degree of Prince of the Tabernacle, unless it be to one who is legally authorized to receive them; and when I am legally authorized to communicate them to him.

I furthermore promise and swear, that I will pay due obedience to all the laws, rules and regulations which appertain to this degree, or may be regularly made and enacted by the superior authority.

I furthermore promise and swear, that I will remember and observe the lessons which I have received in this degree; that I will be generous and liberal to the poor and needy, and just and impartial in public and private judgment, even when deciding between myself and another; that I will not harbor malice nor seek revenge, but will love my neighbour like myself, so far as human infirmity will allow: that I will not entirely glean my wheat-field nor my vineyard, but will leave something for the hungry and the stranger; and that I will not oppress or take usury of a brother. And should I wilfully violate this my obligation, I admit that I shall deserve to be consumed with fire from Heaven, like Nadab and Abihu, and that my ashes should be flung into the air, to be blown to the four corners of the earth by the winds: and may God aid me faithfully to keep and perform this, my obligation!

[The Candidate is then told to rise. He does so, and remains standing blindfolded before the altar. A brother in the vestibule reads in a gloomy voice as follows]:

"Hebel became a keeper of sheep, but Cayin was a tiller of the ground. In process of time it came to pass that Cayin brought, of the fruit of the ground, an offering unto the Lord. And Hebel, he also brought, of the firstlings of his flock, and of the fat thereof. And the Lord had regard unto Hebel and to his offering. But unto Cayin and his offering he had not regard. And Cayin was very wroth, and his countenance was downcast. And the Lord said unto Cayin, 'Why art thou wroth, and why is thy countenance downcast? If thou doest well, canst thou not lift it up? but if thou doest not well, sin coucheth at the door. Though unto thee be its desire, thou shouldest rule over it.' Cayin spoke with Hebel his brother; and it came to pass, when they were in the field, that Cayin rose up against Hebel, his brother, and slew him."

[In the mean time, all the lights are extinguished, except a single lamp or candle: and, as the reading concludes, three brethren, clothed in black and wearing black masks, rush in, seize the Candidate, in silence, tear the bandage from his eyes, and hurry him into the vestibule, where they force him into a coffin, placed on the floor in the middle of the room. They then throw a black cloth over his body, leaving the face uncovered, and withdraw. Both apartments are now entirely dark. All is silent for a time, and then mournful voices are heard in the second apartment, saying, from different quarters of the room, as follows]:

1st Voice: . . . Osiris, the God of Light, is slain. The Spirit of Evil hath conquered, and darkness is about to prevail over the earth.

2d Voice: . . . Typhon hath flung the body in a coffin upon the waters; and Iris and Horus go in search of it, mourning, over the earth.

3d Voice: . . . Cama is slain by Iswara, and committed to the waves. The wintry constellations laugh for joy; and the earth is wrinkled with cold, and shudders at the darkness.

4th Voice: . . . Ahriman has prevailed over Ormuzd. The Six Evil Devs cry aloud for joy; and the three thousand years of evil, sorrow and darkness commence.

5th Voice: . . . Atys is slain in Phrygia, and his body remains without sepulture, while all the land is cursed with barrenness, and Cybele seeks him weeping, on the plains and among the mountains that resound with the clashing of her cymbals.

6th Voice: . . . Thammuz, mutilated by the wintry boar in Phœnicia, has descended to the shades, and left the world to mourn. Astarte, wearing the crescent, sitting with veiled head on Mount Libanus, besieges heaven with prayers for his return.

7th Voice: . . . Dionusos is slain by the Giants; and the women mourn his death in the Etruscan forests and upon the Syrian mountains; and all the Malignant Signs of the Zodiac rejoice.

8th Voice: . . Mithras is dead, is dead. His body lies in the tomb, and the Magi weep over it, and chant their funereal hymns, while the shadows of night gather over them, and all Persia and Armenia mourn: but his suffering shall be the safety of the disconsolate.

1st Voice: . . Let us cry unto the Lord. Adoni-Alhim, give us Light!

2d Voice: . . See our tears, Al-Shedi, Most Mighty and Victorious! Save us from the darkness, and restore us to thy favour!

3d Voice: . . Have mercy upon us, Adon-Tsbauth, Lord of the Starry Hosts of Heaven, and Author of our Existence! Have mercy, Al-Khanan, Lord of Mercy!

4th Voice: . . Thou art the Most High, O Aliun! Thou art the Fire, O AL, whose titles are Adar and Aish-Gebar! Thou art the Light, O Melec-Alhim! Lift upon us the light of thy countenance!

5th Voice: . . Guide our footsteps, and direct us in the right path, O Lord our God. Io Nissi! Be merciful unto us, and with Thy great Light drive back the Powers of Darkness!

[During these lamentations and cries, resounding from different directions, in mournful and piercing tones, the coffin is taken up and carried into the second apartment, and placed upon the floor in the centre. By this time the room will have been changed, by dropping hangings entirely black on the inside of the columns.

There is still but a single dim light. At the head of the coffin is set an artificial tree of the thorny tamarisk or the acacia.

The Princes now assume their seats, in perfect silence, all covered with black robes or mantles, entirely concealing their jewels and regalia. Then the Th∴ Puissant speaks]:

Th∴ P∴ My Brethren, the Power of Darkness has prevailed over the Prince of Light. The Earth mourns and is wrinkled with frost. The leaves fall from the trees; snow shrouds the mountains, and cold winds sweep over the shuddering skies. All Nature laments; and we share the common sorrow. Excellent First Warden, let prayers be offered up in the Tabernacle for the return of Light and the re-ascension of the Sun, and of that Moral and Spiritual Light of which he is the type.

1st Ward∴ Th∴ Puissant, all the Nations of the Earth do fast and pray. Our ancient taskmasters on the banks of the Nile mourn for Osiris. The Chaldeans lament for Bel, and the Phœnicians for Thammuz. The Phrygian women clash their cymbals and weep for Atys: on the Syrian hills and over the Etruscan plains the Virgins lament for Dionusos: while far in India the Brahmins pray for the return of Cama; and in Persia the Magi predict the resurrection of Mithras. The dead will rise again, as the wheat grows from the grain; and all the world will then rejoice.

Th∴ P∴ We, like our Ancient Masters, mourn Osiris; the type to us of the Sun, of Light, of Life. The Scorpion and the Serpent rule the winter waves, on which the frail ark tosses that contains his body. Weep, my Brethren, for Osiris! Weep for Light lost, and Life departed, and the Good and Beautiful oppressed by Evil! Man hath fallen from his first Estate, and is lost, as the sun hath sunken into the icy arms of winter. Weep for Osiris, type of the Good, the True, the Beautiful! How shall his body be recovered from the embraces of the hungry sea; and earth again be gladdened by his presence?

2d Ward∴ Th∴ Puissant, nine Princes offer to go forth and search for the body of Osiris.

Th∴ P∴ Let them go forth, my Brother, by threes, to the East, the West and the South, and make diligent search; while we continue in fasting and prayer.

[The Brethren walk round, as if searching for the body, and after a time they gather round the coffin: and one says]: "Behold, my brethren, the body of Osiris under this spreading tamarisk." Each of the Brethren makes the first sign; and says, "*God wills it.*" Then a brother says, "Cover the face, my brethren, and let us hasten to the Th∴ P∴ Ch∴ Prince, and make known to him that the body is found."

[They cover the face, and return to the Station of the 2d Warden; and the Jun∴ Deacon says: "Puissant 2d Warden, Prince Betsel-Al, we have found the body of Osiris cast on shore at Byblos, and concealed by a tamarisk-tree, which by the wonderful virtue of the body has grown up around it in a night"].

2d Ward∴ Th∴ P∴ Ch∴ Prince, the body of Osiris has been found at Byblos, where it hath been cast ashore, concealed by a tamarisk-tree, which by the wonderful virtue of the body has grown up around it.

Th∴ P∴ Summon the Princes, my brother, to attend us while we repair thither: for it is promised that the dead shall rise again.

2d Ward∴ Princes and brethren, the body of Osiris is found, at Byblos; and the Ch∴ Prince goeth thither, and summons you to bear him company.

[The Brethren again surround the coffin. In the mean time, the room is hung with red as before, and the lights are lighted. The Th∴ P∴ says, "My Brethren, assist me to raise this body." He takes off the covering, grasps the right hand of the Candidate with his right, and the left with his left, and with the assistance of the three other officers, raises him to his feet].

3d Warden: Osiris is risen again, and prevails against the Powers of Darkness. Orpheus and Dionusos return from the Shades. Cama and Atys rise again; and Adoni reigns henceforth in Heaven.

2d Ward∴ The Sun turns back from the South, and darkness flees before him. To-day is the great feast of the Winter Solstice.

1st Ward∴ The reign of Light and Life has recommenced. The feet of the young Spring shine afar off upon the Mountains; and the Bull and Ram lead on the glittering constellations: Let all the world rejoice! The reign of Evil ends; and the Good Principle is victorious. Let Earth and Heaven be glad!

3d Ward∴ The seed dies, and out of its death springs the young shoot of the new wheat, to produce an hundred-fold.

2d Ward∴ The worm dies in its narrow prison-house, woven by itself, and out of its death springs the brilliant moth, emblem of immortality.

1st Ward∴ The deadly serpent dies, and self-renews its own existence; and out of the death of Night's sleep, the minor mystery, comes the renewed life of the morning.

Th∴ P∴ . . . Now, as ever, out of Death springs Life: out of Darkness ever comes the Light; and to Evil, in eternal circle Good succeeds. Hence the profound truth of the Indian idea of the Godhead; God, three in One; the Creator, the Preserver and the Destroyer: the three sides of the Triangle; the One Only Absolute; developing Himself in three Modes, and those modes one harmony.

[The Candidate is now seated; and the Th∴ P∴ proceeds, addressing him]:

Th∴ P∴ "My Brother, the allegory in which you have performed a part, we will shortly endeavour more fully to explain to you. As an initiate of the time of Moses, you have represented the different personifications of the Sun among the Ancient Nations, and the Principle of Light and of Good, warring with and victorious over that of Darkness and Evil.

"When the Hebrew Initiate, whom you have represented, had been raised as you have, from his simulated and allegorical death, he was briefly taught the meaning and application of the ceremony through which he had passed. History is silent as to the language of that explanation. Hear however its substance, as spoken in the Deserts four thousand years ago.

"'You are taught by this Mystery,' it was said to him, 'that the Heathen Gods are Unrealities, and mere ideal personifications either of the heavenly bodies, of the Powers of Nature, or of the Principles of Light and Darkness, and Good and Evil. The Egyptians, Phœnicians, Chaldeans and Philistines have thus given to the Sun, the Moon, the Stars, Heaven, Earth, the Sky, Light, Fire, the Air and the Sea, personal characteristics and names. They worship the Powers of Nature in the Constellations, and the Constellations in the animals imaged there. The idol is mere wood and stone, the representation of an unreal ideality. Our People, prone to idol-worship are forbidden to make to themselves any symbol or idol of the Deity. There is but one Only True God, who hath no bodily shape, nor hath been seen of any man. He is not the Light, nor Fire, but pure Absolute Intellect and Existence, the Soul and Spirit of the Universe, which He created with a thought. The Past, the Present and the illimitable Future, the infinite series of events and successions of time in both directions, are all present to Him at one and the same moment. There is to Him no Future and no Past. Present everywhere, there is to Him neither *There* nor *Elsewhere*. Everything to Him is *Here* and *Now*. He is unchangeable, immutable, infinitely just, wise and powerful. He can neither be angry nor repent. What we term his punishments are but the inevitable results, that by his great laws of cause and effect, the corollaries from universal harmony, flow from and follow sin and crime.

"The soul is immortal. The body, perishing, dissolves into atoms infinitely small and mingles again with nature, and forms new bodies, of man, and living things below man, and the vegetable creation. The soul, a spark of the Universal Soul, imprisoned in the body, becomes sordid with the body's imperfections; and must be purified before it can return and mingle again with the Universal Source. It is immortal, not of necessity, but unless God pleases, as it and all things emanated from Him, to absorb it again into Himself. No sin that man commits will go unpunished, and after death the soul will feel the results of its sins and errors here, by a law as inflexible as that which holds the stars to their courses.

"You are also taught how constant is the struggle in every man's nature between the Divine Will, implanted in every man by God, and the natural will, prone to vice and error, and caused by the frailty of the flesh. Osiris and Typhon, Ormuzd and Ahriman, Vishnu and Siva, make of every human soul, as they do of the world and universe, a battle-field. All the universe coheres. The struggle between material light and darkness is more than a *symbol* of that between good and evil. It is in the truest sense *the same*. Such is the law of harmony. The contest is *One:* and it goes on under different forms, in the universe and all its parts.

"It will henceforward be your duty to seek full instruction in these great mysteries, which the mass of the people are incapable of understanding. To them, material images of God will ever be indispensable. One religion after another will spring up, and grow for a time, and decay and die, and give place to another; the framers and a select few will know the great primitive truths which must be the foundations of all religions; but the people will ever worship idols and images, either carved of wood and stone, or found on earth or in the heavens, or the gross material ideas and images which in their own minds they will form and enthrone as representations of the Deity. He will ever be to them only an ideal aggregate of their own mental faculties and their passions, as unreal as an image in a mirror.

"To you it will be given to understand these truths; and the esoteric meaning of the allegories and fables which are taught the people; and which, without their knowing it, contain all truth. We hope that you will zealously avail yourself of the opportunities which we shall gladly give you, to learn from us all that we ourselves know of the true essence and relations of the Deity and Nature.' Such, in substance, were the lessons taught to the Hebrew Initiate; whom you are yet for a while to represent, while you are finally consecrated, as he was, to the service of God, as a Priest before Him, and to that of man, as a Teacher and Benefactor. Make bare thy right foot, and kneel before me!"

The candidate kneels, with his right foot naked. The Th.·. P.·. takes in his left hand a small vessel of perfumed oil; and says: "I will sanctify the Tabernacle of the congregation, and the Altar. I will sanctify also both Aaron and his sons, to minister to me in the Priest's office. In the Tabernacle of the congregation without the vail, which is before the testimony, Aaron and his sons shall order it from evening to morning before the Lord. It shall be a statute forever unto their generations, on behalf of the children of Israel. And thou shalt anoint Aaron and his sons, and consecrate them, that they may minister unto me in the Priest's office." [He pours a little of the oil on the head of the candidate, and says]: "Eleazar, son of Aaron, I do anoint thee and consecrate thee to the service of truth and virtue, which is the service of the Lord; to minister unto Him and unto thy fellow-men in this world, which is His truest Tabernacle and Temple."

He then takes a small vessel, with a liquid resembling blood, and using a small brush or pencil, suiting the action to the word, says: "With the blood of the ram slain for a burnt offering I touch the tip of thy right ear, the thumb of thy right hand, and the great toe of thy right foot, and with the same blood I sprinkle thy garments, and do sanctify thee and them. Thine ear is hereafter to be ever open to the cry of distress, the prayer of want, the moan of suffering, the supplication of the penitent, and the call of duty: thy hand is henceforth to be opened wide in charity, and ready to labour in every good work: and thy feet are to stand firmly wherever duty places thee, however dangerous the post; nor ever to slide upon the slippery paths of Temptation."

He raises him and gives him the signs, token and words, and invests him with the insignia and jewel of the Degree; and then says: "Brethren, behold a new Priest of the Tabernacle, to be instructed and prepared to fulfil all his duties as a Prince of Well-Doers in this Tabernacle of clay, that he may be raised on the great day of account, a shining monument of God's glory, in the Tabernacle not made with hands, eternal in the Heavens."

1st Sign: *of Recognition:* . . . Raise the eyes to Heaven, and ↥☿*☾‡ ♈&☾♋ ♃♀♈& the †⁑&☉♒♊, ☿⁑☾♒, as if to ⁑‡☿♈☽↥♈ them from ♀♒♈☾♒♎☾ ⁑†♀♌&♈. At the same time, place the ‡⁑&☉♒♊ on the †⁑♏‡☾☉♎♈, inclining the &☾☉♊ towards the †⁑♎&☿♄†♊☾‡: then ♊‡☉♃ the ‡⁑&☉♒♊ ♊☿♃♒ ♊♀☉♌☿♒☉††♄ to the ‡⁑&♀⁑.

2d. The Grand Sign: . . Place both hands ♄⁑☿♒ the &☾☉♊, with the ♈&♄♋♏♎ and ♑☿‡☾♑♀♒♌☾‡♎ ☾♉♈☾♒♊☾♊, and joining so as to form a triangle; the ⁑☿♀♒♈♎ of the ♑☿‡☾♑♀♒♌☾‡♎ above.

3d Sign: *of closing:* . . . Make a similar triangle with the ♑☿‡☾♑♀♒♌☾‡♎, the ☉‡♋♎ extended and the ♈&♄♋♏♎ turned ♊☿♃♒♃☉‡♊: the body being the base, the ☉‡♋♎, &☉♒♊♎ and ♑☿‡☾♑♀♒♌☾‡♎ the sides, and the ♋☾☾♈♀♒♌ of the ⁑☿♀♒♈♎ of the latter the apex, of the Triangle.

Token: . . . Mutually take each other's hands; the ‡ with the ‡ and the † with the †☾♑♈, ↥‡☿♎♎ ♀♒♌ them—and give the Pass-word.

Pass-word: ♊☾‡☾¶-♄☾&♄☉&.·. [Substitute for the latter word, ☉♊☿♒♀]: . . or, in English, ♈&☾ ♁☿♄‡♒☾♄ ☿♑ ♌☿♊.

SACRED WORD; ♄☾¶&⊙♃☾♈♎♄☾&♑⊙& [substitute ⊙♊☿♒♀] . . . or in English, ♌☿♊ ♃♀♓♎ ♀♈.

[The following lecture is then read to the Initiate]:

LECTURE.

Symbols were the almost universal language of ancient theology. They were the most obvious method of instruction; for, like nature herself, they addressed the understanding through the eye; and the most ancient expressions denoting communication of religious knowledge, signify ocular exhibition. The first teachers of mankind borrowed this method of instruction; and it comprised an endless store of pregnant hieroglyphics. These lessons of the olden time were the riddles of the Sphynx, tempting the curious by their quaintness, but involving the personal risk of the adventurous interpreter. "The Gods themselves," it was said, "disclose their intentions to the wise, but to fools their teaching is unintelligible;" and the King of the Delphic Oracle was said not to *declare*, nor on the other hand to *conceal;* but emphatically "*intimate* or *signify*."

The Ancient Sages, both barbarian and Greek, involved their meaning in similar indirections and enigmas; their lessons were conveyed either in visible symbols, or in those "parables and dark sayings of old," which the Israelites considered it a sacred duty to hand down unchanged to successive generations. The explanatory tokens employed by man, whether emblematical objects or actions, symbols or mystic ceremonies, were like the mystic signs and portents either in dreams or by the wayside, supposed to be significant of the intentions of the Gods; both required the aid of anxious thought and skilful interpretation. It was only by a correct appreciation of analogous problems of nature, that the will of Heaven could be understood by the Diviner, or the lessons of Wisdom become manifest to the Sage.

The mysteries were a series of symbols; and what was *spoken* there consisted wholly of accessory explanations of the act or image; sacred commentaries, explanatory of established symbols; with little of those independent traditions embodying physical or moral speculation, in which the elements or planets were the actors, and the creation and revolutions of the world were intermingled with recollections of ancient events: and yet with so much of that also, that nature became her own expositor through the medium of an arbitrary symbolical instruction; and the ancient views of the relation between the human and divine received dramatic forms.

There has ever been an intimate alliance between the two systems, the symbolic and the philosophical, in the allegories of the monuments of all ages, in the symbolic writings of the priests of all nations, in the rituals of all secret and mysterious societies: there has been a constant series, an invariable uniformity of principles, which come from an aggregate, vast, imposing and true, composed of parts that fit harmoniously only there.

Symbolical instruction is recommended by the constant and uniform usage of antiquity; and it has retained its influence throughout all ages, as a system of Mysterious Communication. The Deity, in his revelations to man, adopted the use of material images for the purpose of enforcing sublime truths; and Christ taught by symbols and parables. The mysterious knowledge of the Druids was embodied in signs and symbols. Taliesin, describing his initiation, says, "The secrets were imparted to me by the old Giantess (*Ceridwen*, or *Isis*), without the use of audible language." And again he says, "I am a *silent* proficient."

Initiation was a school, in which were taught the truths of primitive revelation, the existence and attributes of one God, the immortality of the Soul, rewards and punishments in a future life, the phenomena of Nature, the arts, the sciences, morality, legislation, philosophy and philanthropy, and what we now style psychology and metaphysics, with animal magnetism and the other occult sciences.

All the ideas of the Priests of Hindostan, Persia, Syria, Arabia, Chaldea, Phœnicia, were known to the Egyptian Priests. The rational Indian philosophy, after penetrating Persia and Chaldea, gave birth to the Egyptian Mysteries. We find that the use of Hieroglyphics was preceded in Egypt by that of the easily understood symbols and figures, from the mineral, animal and vegetable kingdoms, used by the Indians, Persians and Chaldeans to express their thoughts: and this primitive philosophy was the basis of the modern philosophy of Pythagoras and Plato.

All the philosophers and legislators that made Antiquity illustrious were pupils of the initiation; and all the beneficent modifications in the religions of the different people instructed by them were owing to their institution and extension of the mysteries. In the chaos of popular superstitions, those mysteries alone kept man from lapsing into absolute brutishness. Zoroaster and Confucius drew their doctrines from the mysteries. Clemens of Alexandria, speaking of the Great Mysteries, says, "Here ends all instruction. Nature and all things are seen and known." Had moral truths alone been taught the Initiate, the mysteries could never have deserved or received the magnificent eulogiums of the most enlightened men of Antiquity,—of Pindar, Plutarch, Isocrates, Diodorus, Plato, Euripides, Socrates, Aristophanes, Cicero, Epictetus, Marcus Aurelius and others;—philosophers hostile to the Sacerdotal Spirit, or historians devoted to the investigation of Truth. No: All the sciences were taught there: and those oral or written traditions briefly communicated, which reached back to the first age of the world.

Socrates said, in the Phædo of Plato; "It well appears that those who established the mysteries, or secret assemblies of the Initiated, were no contemptible personages, but men of great genius, who, in the early ages strove to teach us, under enigmas, that he who shall go to the invisible regions, without being purified, will be precipitated into the abyss; while he who arrives there, purged of the stains of this world, and accomplished in virtue, will be admitted to the dwelling-place of the Deity. . . The initiated are certain to attain the company of the Gods."

Pretextatus, Proconsul of Achaia, a man endowed with all the virtues, said, in the 4th century, that to deprive the Greeks of those Sacred Mysteries which bound together the whole human race, would make life insupportable.

Initiation was considered to be a mystical death; a descent into the infernal regions, where every pollution, and the stains and imperfections of a corrupt and evil life were purged away by fire and water; and the perfect *Epopt* was then said to be *regenerated, new-born*, restored to a *renovated* existence of *life, light* and *purity;* and placed under the Divine Protection.

A new language was adapted to these celebrations,—and also a language of hieroglyphics, unknown to any but those who had received the highest Degree. And to them ultimately were confined the learning, the morality and the political power of every people among which the mysteries were practised. So effectually was the knowledge of the hieroglyphics of the highest degree hidden from all but a favoured few, that in process of time their meaning was entirely lost, and none could interpret them. If the same hieroglyphics were employed in the higher as in the lower degrees, they had a different and more abstruse and figurative meaning. It was pretended, in later times, that the sacred hieroglyphics and language were the same that were used by the Celestial Deities. Everything that could heighten the mystery of initiation was added, until the very name of the ceremony possessed a strange charm, and yet conjured up the wildest fears. The greatest rapture came to be expressed by the word that signified to pass through the mysteries.

The Priesthood possessed one-third of Egypt. They gained much of their influence by means of the Mysteries, and spared no means to impress the people with a full sense of their importance. They represented them as the beginning of a new life of reason and virtue: the initiated, or esoteric companions were said to entertain the most agreeable anticipations respecting death and eternity, to comprehend all the hidden mysteries of Nature, to have their souls restored to the original perfection from which man had fallen; and at their death to be borne to the celestial mansions of the Gods. The doctrines of a future state of rewards and punishments formed a prominent feature in the mysteries; and they were also believed to assure much temporal happiness and good fortune, and afford absolute security against the most imminent dangers by land and sea. Public odium was cast on those who refused to be initiated. They were considered profane, unworthy of public employment or private confidence; and held to be doomed to eternal punishment as impious. To betray the secrets of the Mysteries, to wear on the stage the dress of an Initiate, or to hold the Mysteries up to derision, was to incur death at the hands of public vengeance.

It is certain that up to the time of Cicero, the mysteries still retained much of their original character of sanctity and purity. And at a later day, as we know, Nero, after committing a horrible crime, did not dare, even in Greece, to aid in the celebration of the Mysteries ; nor at a still later day was Constantine, the Christian Emperor, allowed to do so, after his murder of his relatives.

Everywhere, and in all their forms, the Mysteries were funereal ; and celebrated the mystical death and restoration to life of some divine or heroic personage : and the details of the legend and the mode of the death varied in the different Countries where the Mysteries were practised.

Their explanation belongs both to astronomy and mythology ; and the Legend of the Master's Degree is but another form of that of the Mysteries, reaching back, in one shape or other, to the remotest antiquity.

Whether Egypt originated the legend, or borrowed it from India or Chaldea, it is now impossible to know. But the Hebrews received the Mysteries from the Egyptians ; and of course were familiar with *their* legend,—known as it was to those Egyptian Initiates, Joseph and Moses. It was the fable (or rather the *truth* clothed in allegory and figures) of Osiris, the Sun, Source of Light and Principle of Good, and Typhon, the Principle of Darkness and Evil. In all the histories of the Gods and Heroes lay couched and hidden astronomical details and the history of the operations of visible Nature ; and those in their turn were also symbols of higher and profounder truths. None but rude uncultivated intellects could long consider the Sun and Stars and the Powers of Nature as Divine, or as fit objects of Human Worship ; and *they* will consider them so while the world lasts ; and ever remain ignorant of the great Spiritual Truths of which these are the hieroglyphics and expressions.

A brief summary of the Egyptian legend will serve to show the leading idea on which the Mysteries among the Hebrews were based.

Osiris, said to have been an ancient King of Egypt, was the Sun ; and Isis, his wife, the Moon : and his history recounts, in poetical and figurative style, the annual journey of the Great Luminary of Heaven through the different Signs of the Zodiac.

In the absence of Osiris, Typhon, his Brother, filled with Envy and Malice, sought to usurp his throne ; but his plans were frustrated by Isis. Then he resolved to kill Osiris. This he did, by persuading him to enter a coffin or sarcophagus, which he then flung into the Nile. After a long search, Isis found the body, and concealed it in the depths of a forest ; but Typhon, finding it there, cut it into fourteen pieces, and scattered them hither and thither. After a tedious search, Isis found thirteen pieces, the fishes having eaten the other (the privates), which she replaced of wood, and buried the body at Philæ ; where a temple of surpassing magnificence was erected in honour of Osiris.

Isis, aided by her son Orus or Horus warred against Typhon, slew him, reigned gloriously, and at her death was re-united to her husband, in the same tomb.

Typhon was represented as born of the earth ; the upper part of his body covered with feathers, in stature reaching the clouds, his arms and legs covered with scales, serpents darting from him on every side, and fire flashing from his mouth. Horus, who aided in slaying him, became the God of the Sun, answering to the Grecian Apollo ; and Typhon is but the anagram of Python, the great serpent slain by Apollo.

The word Typhon, like Eve, signifies *a serpent*, and *life*. By its form the serpent symbolizes life, which circulates through all nature. When, towards the end of autumn, the Woman (Virgo), in the constellations seems (upon the Chaldean sphere) to crush with her heel the head of the serpent, this figure foretells the coming of winter, during which life seems to retire from all beings, and no longer to circulate through nature. This is why Typhon signifies also a serpent, the symbol of winter, which, in the Catholic Temples, is represented surrounding the Terrestrial Globe, which surmounts the heavenly cross, emblem of redemption. If the word Typhon is derived from *Tupoul*, it signifies a tree which produces apples (*mala*, evils), the Jewish origin of the fall of man. Typhon means also one who supplants, and signifies the human passions, which expel from our hearts the lessons of wisdom. In the Egyptian Fable, Isis wrote the sacred word for the instruction of men, and Typhon effaced it as fast as she wrote it. In morals, his name signifies *Pride, Ignorance* and *Falsehood*.

When Isis first found the body, where it had floated ashore near Byblos, a shrub of *erica* or tamarisk near it had, by the virtue of the body, shot up into a tree around it, and protected it ; and hence our sprig of acacia. Isis was also aided in her search by Anubis, in the shape of a dog. He was Sirius or the Dog-Star, the friend and counsellor of Osiris, and the inventor of language, grammar, astronomy, surveying, arithmetic, music and medical science ; the first maker of laws ; and who taught the worship of the Gods, and the building of Temples.

In the Mysteries, the nailing of the body of Osiris up in the chest or ark was termed the *aphanism*, or disappearance [of the Sun at the Winter Solstice, below the Tropic of Capricorn], and the recovery of the different parts of his body by Isis, the *Euresis*, or finding. The Candidate went through a ceremony representing this, in all the Mysteries everywhere. The main facts in the fable were the same in all countries ; and the prominent Deities were everywhere a male and a female.

In Egypt they were Osiris and Isis : in India, Mahadeva and Sita : in Phœnicia, Thammuz (or Adonis) and Astarte (or Venus) : in Phrygia, Atys and Cybele : in Persia, Mithras and Asis : in Samothrace and Greece, Dionusos or Sabazeus and Rhea : in Britain, Hu and Ceridwen ; and in Scandinavia, Woden and Frea : and in every instance these Divinities represented the Sun and the Moon.

The Mysteries of Osiris, Isis and Horus, seem to have been the model of all the other ceremonies of initiation subsequently established among the different peoples of the old world. Those of Atys and Cybele, celebrated in Phrygia ; those of Ceres and Proserpine, at Eleusis and many other places in Greece, were but copies of them. This we learn from Plutarch, Diodorus Siculus, Lactantius and other writers ; and in the absence of direct testimony should necessarily infer it from the similarity of the adventures of these Deities ; for the ancients held that the Ceres of the Greeks was the same as the Isis of the Egyptians ; and Dionusos or Bacchus as Osiris.

In the legend of Osiris and Isis, as given by Plutarch, are many details and circumstances other than those that we have briefly mentioned ; and all of which we need not repeat here. Osiris married his sister Isis : and laboured publicly with her to ameliorate the lot of men. He taught them agriculture, while Isis invented laws. He built temples to the Gods, and established their worship. Both were the patrons of artists and their useful inventions ; and introduced the use of iron for defensive weapons and implements of agriculture, and of gold to adorn the temples of the Gods. He went forth with an army to conquer men to civilization, teaching the people which he overcame to plant the vine and sow grain for food.

Typhon, his brother, slew him when the sun was in the sign of the Scorpion, that is to say, at the autumnal equinox. They had been rival claimants, says Synesius, for the throne of Egypt, as Light and Darkness contend ever for the empire of the world. Plutarch adds, that at the time when Osiris was slain, the moon was at its full ; and therefore it was in the sign opposite the Scorpion, that is, the Bull, the sign of the vernal equinox.

Plutarch assures us that it was to represent these events and details that Isis established the mysteries, in which they were reproduced by images, symbols, and a religious ceremonial, whereby they were imitated : and in which lessons of piety were given, and consolations under the misfortunes that afflict us here below. Those who instituted these mysteries meant to strengthen religion and console men in their sorrows by the lofty hopes found in a religious faith, whose principles were presented to them covered by a pompous ceremonial, and under the sacred veil of allegory.

Diodorus speaks of the famous columns erected near Nysa, in Arabia, where, it was said, were two of the tombs of Osiris and Isis. On one was this inscription : " I am Isis, Queen of this country. I was instructed by Mercury. No one can destroy the laws which I have established. I am the eldest daughter of Saturn, most ancient of the Gods. I am the wife and sister of Osiris the King. I first made known to mortals the use of wheat. I am the mother of Orus the King. In my honour was the city of Bubaste built. Rejoice, O Egypt, rejoice, land that gave me birth !" . . . And on the other was this : " I am Osiris the King, who led my armies into all parts of the world, to the most thickly inhabited countries of India, the North, the Danube, and the Ocean. I am the eldest son of Saturn : I was born of the brilliant and magnificent egg, and my substance is of the same nature as that which composes light. There is no place in the universe where I have not appeared, to bestow my benefits and make known my discoveries." The rest was illegible.

To aid her in the search for the body of Osiris, and to nurse her infant child Horus, Isis sought out and took with her Anubis, son of Osiris, and his sister Nephté. He, as we have said, was Sirius, the brightest star in the Heavens. After finding him, she went to Byblos, and seated herself near a fountain, where she had learned that the sacred chest had stopped which contained the body of Osiris. There she sat, sad and silent, shedding a torrent of tears. Thither came the women of the Court of Queen Astarte, and she spoke to them, and dressed their hair, pouring upon it deliciously perfumed ambrosia. This known to the Queen, Isis was engaged as nurse for her child, in the palace, one of the columns of which was made of the erica or tamarisk, that had grown up over the chest containing Osiris, cut down by the King, and, unknown to him, still enclosing the chest: which column Isis afterwards demanded, and from it extracted the chest and the body, which, the latter wrapped in thin drapery and perfumed, she carried away with her.

Blue Masonry, ignorant of its import, still retains among its emblems one of a woman weeping over a broken column, holding in her hand a branch of acacia, myrtle, or tamarisk, while Time, we are told, stands behind her combing out the ringlets of her hair. We need not repeat the vapid and trivial explanation there given, of this representation of *Isis*, weeping at Byblos, over the column torn from the palace of the King, that contained the body of Osiris, while Horus, the God of Time, pours ambrosia on her hair.

Nothing of this recital was historical; but the whole was an allegory or sacred fable, containing a meaning known only to those who were initiated into the mysteries. All the incidents were astronomical, with a meaning still deeper lying behind *that* explanation, and so hidden by a double veil. The mysteries, in which these incidents were represented and explained, were like those of Eleusis in their object, of which Pausanias, who was initiated, says that the Greeks, from the remotest antiquity, regarded them as the best calculated of all things to lead men to piety: and Aristotle says they were the most valuable of all religious institutions, and thus were called mysteries par excellence; and the Temple of Eleusis was regarded as, in some sort, the common sanctuary of the whole earth, where religion had brought together all that was most imposing and most august.

The object of all the mysteries was to inspire men with piety, and to console them in the miseries of life. That consolation, so afforded, was the hope of a happier future, and of passing, after death, to a state of eternal felicity.

Cicero says that the initiates not only received lessons which made life more agreeable, but drew from the ceremonies happy hopes for the moment of death. Socrates says that those who were so fortunate as to be admitted to the mysteries, possessed, when dying, the most glorious hopes for eternity. Aristides says that they not only procure the initiates consolations in the present life, and means of deliverance from the great weight of their evils, but also the precious advantage of passing after death to a happier state.

Isis was the Goddess of Sais; and the famous Feast of Lights was celebrated there in her honour. There were celebrated the mysteries, in which were represented the death and subsequent restoration to life of the God Osiris, in a secret ceremony and scenic representation of his sufferings, called the Mysteries of Night.

The Kings of Egypt often exercised the functions of the Priesthood; and they were initiated into the sacred science as soon as they attained the throne. So at Athens, the First Magistrate, or Archon-King superintended the mysteries. This was an image of the union that existed between the Priesthood and Royalty, in those early times when legislators and kings sought in religion a potent political instrument.

Herodotus says, speaking of the reasons why animals were deified in Egypt: "If I were to explain these reasons, I should be led to the disclosure of those holy matters which I particularly wish to avoid, and which, but from necessity, I should not have discussed at all." So he says, "The Egyptians have at Sais the tomb of a certain personage, whom I do not think myself permitted to specify. It is behind the Temple of Minerva." [The latter, so called by the Greeks, was really Isis, whose was the often-cited enigmatical inscription, "I am what was and is and is to come. No mortal hath yet unveiled me."] So again he says: "Upon this lake are represented by night the accidents which happened to him whom I dare not name. The Egyptians call them their mysteries. Concerning these, at the same time that I confess myself sufficiently informed, I feel myself compelled to be silent. Of the ceremonies also in honour of Ceres, I may not venture to speak, further than the obligations of religion will allow me."

It is easy to see what was the great object of initiation and the mysteries; whose first and greatest fruit was, as all the ancients testify, to civilize savage hordes, to soften their ferocious manners, to introduce among them social intercourse, and lead them into a way of life more worthy of men. Cicero considers the establishment of the Eleusinian mysteries to be the greatest of all the benefits conferred by Athens on other commonwealths; their effects having been, he says, to civilize men, soften their savage and ferocious manners, and teach them the true principles of morals, which *initiate* man into the only kind of life worthy of him. The same philosophic orator, in a passage where he apostrophizes Ceres and Proserpina, says that mankind owes these Goddesses the first elements of moral life, as well as the first means of sustenance of physical life; knowledge of the laws, regulation of morals, and those examples of civilization which have improved the manners of men and cities.

Bacchus in Euripides says to Pentheus, that his new institution (the Dionysiac Mysteries) deserved to be known, and that one of its great advantages was, that it proscribed all impurity: that these were the Mysteries of Wisdom, of which it would be imprudent to speak to persons not initiated: that they were established among the Barbarians, who in that showed greater wisdom than the Greeks, who had not yet received them.

This double object, political and religious,—one teaching our duty to men, and the other, what we owe to the Gods; or rather, respect for the Gods calculated to maintain that which we owe the laws, is found in that well-known verse of Virgil, borrowed by him from the ceremonies of initiation: "Teach me to respect Justice and the Gods." This great lesson, which the Hierophant impressed on the initiates, after they had witnessed a representation of the Infernal regions, the Poet places after his description of the different punishments suffered by the wicked in Tartarus, and immediately after the description of that of Sisyphus.

Pausanias, likewise, at the close of the representation of the punishments of Sisyphus and the daughters of Danaus, in the Temple at Delphi, makes this reflection; that the crime or impiety which in them had chiefly merited this punishment, was the contempt which they had shown for the Mysteries of Eleusis. From this reflection of Pausanias, who was an initiate, it is easy to see that the Priests of Eleusis, who taught the dogma of punishment in Tartarus, included among the great crimes deserving these punishments, contempt for and disregard of the Holy Mysteries; whose object was to lead men to piety, and thereby to respect for justice and the laws, chief object of their institution, if not the only one, and to which the needs and interest of religion itself were subordinate; since the latter was but a means to lead more surely to the former: for the whole force of religious opinions being in the hands of the legislators to be wielded, they were sure of being better obeyed.

The Mysteries were not merely simple lustrations and the observation of some arbitrary formulas and ceremonies; nor a means of reminding men of the ancient condition of the race prior to civilization: but they led men to piety by instruction in morals and as to a future life; which at a very early day, if not originally, formed the chief portion of the ceremonial.

Symbols were used in the ceremonies, which referred to agriculture, as Masonry has preserved the ear of wheat in a symbol and in one of her words: but their principal reference was to astronomical phenomena. Much was no doubt said as to the condition of brutality and degradation in which man was sunk before the institution of the Mysteries; but the allusion was rather metaphysical, to the ignorance of the uninitiated, than to the wild life of the earliest men.

The great object of the Mysteries of Isis, and in general of all the Mysteries, was a great and truly politic one. It was to ameliorate our race, to perfect its manners and morals, and to restrain society by stronger bonds than those that human laws impose. They were the invention of that ancient science and wisdom which exhausted all its resources to make legislation perfect; and of that philosophy which has ever sought to secure the happiness of man, by purifying his soul from the passions which can trouble it, and as a necessary consequence introduce social disorder. And that they were the work of genius is evident from their employment of all the sciences, a profound knowledge of the human heart, and the means of subduing it.

It is a still greater mistake to imagine that they were the inventions of charlatanism, and means of deception. They may in the lapse of time have degenerated into imposture and schools of false ideas; but they were not so at the beginning; or else the wisest and best men of antiquity have uttered the most wilful falsehoods. In process of time the very allegories of the Mysteries themselves, Tartarus and its punishments, Minos and the other judges of the dead, came to be misunderstood, and to be false because they were so; while at first they were true, because they were recognized as merely the arbitrary forms in which truths were enveloped.

The object of the Mysteries was to procure for man a real felicity on earth by the means of virtue: and to that end he was taught that his soul was immortal; and that error, sin and vice must needs, by an inflexible law, produce their consequences. The rude representation of physical torture in Tartarus was but an image of the certain, unavoidable, eternal consequences that flow by the law of God's enactment from the sin committed and the vice indulged in. The poets and mystagogues laboured to propagate these doctrines of the soul's immortality and the certain punishment of sin and vice, and to accredit them with the people, by teaching them, the former in their poems, and the latter in the sanctuaries; and they clothed them with the charms, the one of poetry, and the other of spectacles and magic illusions.

They painted, aided by all the resources of art, the virtuous man's happy life after death, and the horrors of the frightful prisons destined to punish the vicious. In the shades of the sanctuaries, these delights and horrors were exhibited as spectacles, and the initiates witnessed religious dramas, under the name of *initiation* and *mysteries*. Curiosity was excited by secrecy, by the difficulty experienced in obtaining admission, and by the tests to be undergone. The candidate was amused by the variety of the scenery, the pomp of the decorations, the appliances of machinery. Respect was inspired by the gravity and dignity of the actors and the majesty of the ceremonial; and fear and hope, sadness and delight, were in turns excited.

The Hierophants, men of intellect, and well understanding the disposition of the people and the art of controlling them, used every appliance to attain that object, and give importance and impressiveness to their ceremonies. As they covered those ceremonies with the veil of Secrecy, so they preferred that Night should cover them with its wings. Obscurity adds to impressiveness, and assists illusion; and they used it to produce an effect upon the astonished initiate. The ceremonies were conducted in caverns dimly lighted: thick groves were planted around the Temples, to produce that gloom that impresses the mind with a religious awe.

The very word *mystery*, according to Demetrius Phalereus, was a metaphorical expression that denoted the secret awe which darkness and gloom inspired. The night was almost always the time fixed for their celebration; and they were ordinarily termed *nocturnal* ceremonies. Initiations into the Mysteries of Samothrace took place at night; as did those of Isis, of which Apuleius speaks. Euripides makes Bacchus say, that *his* mysteries were celebrated at night, because there is in night something august and imposing.

Nothing excites men's curiosity so much as Mystery, concealing things which they desire to know: and nothing so much increases curiosity as obstacles that interpose to prevent them from indulging in the gratification of their desires. Of this the Legislators and Hierophants took advantage, to attract the people to their sanctuaries, and to induce them to seek to obtain lessons from which they would perhaps have turned away with indifference, if they had been pressed upon them. In this spirit of mystery they professed to imitate the Deity, who hides Himself from our senses, and conceals from us the springs by which He moves the Universe. They admitted that they concealed the highest truths under the veil of allegory, the more to excite the curiosity of men, and to urge them to investigation. The secrecy in which they buried their mysteries, had that end. Those to whom they were confided, bound themselves, by the most fearful oaths, never to reveal them. They were not allowed even to speak of these important secrets with any others than the initiated; and the penalty of death was denounced against any one indiscreet enough to reveal them, or found in the Temple without being an initiate: and any one who had betrayed those secrets, was avoided by all, as excommunicated.

Aristotle was accused of impiety, by the Hierophant Eurymedon, for having sacrificed to the manes of his wife, according to the rite used in the worship of Ceres. He was compelled to flee to Chalcis; and to purge his memory from this stain, he directed, by his will, the erection of a Statue to that Goddess. Socrates, dying, sacrificed to Esculapius, to exculpate himself from the suspicion of Atheism. A price was set on the head of Diagoras, because he had divulged the Secret of the Mysteries. Andocides was accused of the same crime, as was Alcibiades, and both were cited to answer the charge before the inquisition at Athens, where the People were the judges. Æschylus the Tragedian was accused of having represented the mysteries on the stage; and was acquitted only on proving that he had never been initiated.

Seneca, comparing Philosophy to initiation, says that the most sacred ceremonies could be known to the adepts alone: but that many of their precepts were known even to the Profane. Such was the case with the doctrine of a future life, and a state of rewards and punishments beyond the grave. The ancient legislators clothed this doctrine in the pomp of a mysterious ceremony, in mystic words and magical representations, to impress upon the mind the truths they taught, by the strong influence of such scenic displays upon the senses and imagination.

In the same way they taught the origin of the soul, its fall to the earth past the spheres and through the elements, and its final return to the place of its origin, when, during the continuance of its union with earthly matter, the sacred fire, which formed its essence, had contracted no stains, and its brightness had not been marred by foreign particles, which denaturalizing it, weighed it down and delayed its return. These metaphysical ideas, with difficulty comprehended by the mass of the initiates, were represented by figures, by symbols, and by allegorical analogies; no idea being so abstract that men do not seek to give it expression by, and translate it into, sensible images.

The attraction of Secrecy was enhanced by the difficulty of obtaining admission. Obstacles and suspense redoubled curiosity. Those who aspired to the initiation of the Sun and in the Mysteries of Mithras in Persia, underwent many trials. They commenced by easy tests and arrived by degrees at those that were most cruel, in which the life of the Candidate was often endangered. Gregory Nazianzen terms them *tortures* and mystic *punishments*. No one can be initiated, says Suidas, until after he has proven, by the most terrible trials, that he possesses a virtuous soul, exempt from the sway of every passion, and as it were impassible. There were twelve principal tests; and some make the number larger.

The trials of the Eleusinian initiations were not so terrible; but they were severe; and the suspense, above all, in which the aspirant was kept for several years [the memory of which is retained in Masonry by the *ages* of those of the different degrees], or the interval between admission to the *inferior* and initiation in the *great* mysteries, was a species of torture to the curiosity which it was desired to excite. Thus the Egyptian Priests tried Pythagoras before admitting him to know the secrets of the sacred science. He succeeded, by his incredible patience and the courage with which he surmounted all obstacles, in obtaining admission to their society and receiving their lessons. Among the Jews, the Essenes admitted none among them, until they had passed the tests of several degrees.

By initiation, those who before were *fellow-citizens* only, became *brothers*, connected by a closer bond than before, by means of a religious fraternity, which bringing men nearer together, united them more strongly: and the weak and the poor could more readily appeal for assistance to the powerful and the wealthy, with whom religious association gave them a closer fellowship.

The initiate was regarded as the favourite of the Gods. For him alone Heaven opened its treasures. Fortunate during life, he could, by virtue and the favour of Heaven, promise himself after death an eternal felicity.

The Priests of the Island of Samothrace promised favourable winds and prosperous voyages to those who were initiated. It was promised them that the Cabiri, and Castor and Pollux, the Dioscuri, should appear to them when the storm raged, and give them calms and smooth seas: and the Scholiast of Aristophanes says that those initiated in the mysteries there were just men, who were privileged to escape from great evils and tempests.

The initiate in the mysteries of Orpheus, after he was purified, was considered as released from the empire of evil, and transferred to a condition of life which gave him the happiest hopes. "I have emerged from evil," he was made to say, "and have attained good." Those initiated in the mysteries of Eleusis believed that the Sun blazed with a pure splendour for them alone. And, as we see in the case of Pericles, they flattered themselves that Ceres and Proserpine inspired them and gave them wisdom and counsel.

Initiation dissipated errors and banished misfortune: and after having filled the heart of man with joy during life, it gave him the most blissful hopes at the moment of death. We owe it to the Goddesses of Eleusis, says Socrates, that we do not lead the wild life of the earliest men: and to them are due the flattering hopes which initiation gives us for the moment of death and for all eternity. The benefit which we reap from these august ceremonies, says Aristides, is not only present joy, a deliverance and enfranchisement from the old ills; but also the sweet hope which we have in death of passing to a more fortunate state. And Theon says that participation in the mysteries is the finest of all things, and the source of the greatest blessings. The happiness promised there was not limited to this mortal life; but it extended beyond the grave. There a new life was to commence, during which the initiate was to enjoy a bliss without alloy and without limit. The Corybantes promised eternal life to the initiates of the mysteries of Cybele and Atys.

Apuleius represents Lucius, while still in the form of an ass, as addressing his prayers to Isis, whom he speaks of as the same as Ceres, Venus, Diana and Proserpine, and as illuminating the walls of many cities simultaneously with her feminine lustre, and substituting her quivering light for the bright rays of the Sun. She appears to him in his vision as a beautiful female, " over whose divine neck her long thick hair hung in graceful ringlets." Addressing him, she says, " The parent of Universal nature attends thy call. The mistress of the Elements, initiative germ of generations, Supreme of Deities, Queen of departed Spirits, first inhabitant of Heaven, and uniform type of all the Gods and Goddesses, propitiated by thy prayers, is with thee. She governs with her nod the luminous heights of the firmament, the salubrious breezes of the ocean, the silent deplorable depths of the shades below; one Sole Divinity under many forms, worshipped by the different nations of the Earth under many titles, and with various religious rites."

Directing him how to proceed, at her festival, to re-obtain his human shape, she says : " Throughout the entire course of the remainder of thy life, until the very last breath has vanished from thy lips, thou art devoted to my service . . . . Under my protection will thy life be happy and glorious ; and when, thy days being spent, thou shalt descend to the shades below, and inhabit the Elysian fields, there also, even in the subterranean hemisphere, shalt thou pay frequent worship to my propitious portion : and yet further ; if, through sedulous obedience, religious devotion to my ministry, and inviolable chastity, thou shalt prove thyself a worthy object of divine favour, then shalt thou feel the influence of the power that I alone possess. The number of thy days shall be prolonged beyond the ordinary decrees of fate."

In the procession of the festival, Lucius saw the image of the Goddess, on either side of which were female attendants, that, " with ivory combs in their hands, made believe, by the motion of their arms and the twisting of their fingers, to comb and ornament the Goddess' royal hair." Afterwards, clad in linen robes, came the initiated. " The hair of the women was moistened by perfume, and enveloped in a transparent covering ; but the men, terrestrial stars, as it were, of the great religion, were thoroughly shaven, and their bald heads shone exceedingly."

Afterwards came the Priests, in robes of white linen. The first bore a lamp in the form of a boat, emitting flame from an orifice in the middle : the second, a small altar : the third, a golden palm-tree : and the fourth displayed the figure of a left hand, the palm open and expanded, " representing thereby a symbol of equity and fair-dealing, of which the left hand, as slower than the right hand, and more void of skill and craft, is therefore an appropriate emblem."

After Lucius had, by the grace of Isis, recovered his human form, the Priest said to him, " Calamity hath no hold on those whom our Goddess hath chosen for her service, and whom her majesty hath vindicated." And the people declared that he was fortunate to be " thus after a manner born again, and at once betrothed to the service of the Holy Ministry."

When he urged the Chief Priest to initiate him, he was answered that there was not " a single one among the initiated, of a mind so depraved, or so bent on his own destruction, as, without receiving a special command from Isis, to dare to undertake her ministry rashly and sacrilegiously, and thereby commit an act certain to bring upon himself a dreadful injury." " For," continued the chief Priest, " the gates of the shades below, and the care of our life being in the hands of the Goddess,—*the ceremony of initiation into the Mysteries is*, as it were, *to suffer death*, with the precarious chance of resuscitation. Wherefore the Goddess, in the wisdom of her Divinity, hath been accustomed to select as persons to whom the secrets of her religion can with propriety be entrusted, those who, standing as it were on the utmost limit of the course of life they have completed, *may through her Providence be in a manner born again*, and commence the career of a new existence."

When he was finally to be initiated, he was conducted to the nearest baths, and after having bathed, the Priest first solicited forgiveness of the Gods, and then sprinkled him all over with the clearest and purest water, and conducted him back to the Temple ; where, says Apuleius, " after giving me some instruction that mortal tongue is not permitted to reveal, he bade me for the succeeding ten days restrain my appetite, eat no animal food, and drink no wine."

These ten days elapsed, the Priest led him into the inmost recesses of the Sanctuary. "And here, studious reader," he continues, "peradventure thou wilt be sufficiently anxious to know all that was said and done, which, were it lawful to divulge, I would tell thee; and, wert thou permitted to hear, thou shouldst know. Nevertheless, although the disclosure would affix the penalty of rash curiosity to my tongue as well as thy ears, yet will I, for fear thou shouldst be too long tormented with religious longing, and suffer the pain of protracted suspense, tell the truth notwithstanding. Listen then to what I shall relate. *I approached the abode of death; with my foot I pressed the threshold of Proserpine's Palace. I was transported through the elements, and conducted back again. At midnight I saw the bright light of the sun shining. I stood in the presence of the Gods, the Gods of Heaven and of the Shades below; ay, stood near and worshipped.* And now have I told thee such things that, hearing, thou necessarily canst not understand; and being beyond the comprehension of the Profane, I can enunciate without committing a crime."

After night had passed, and the morning had dawned, the usual ceremonies were at an end. Then he was consecrated by twelve stoles being put upon him, clothed, crowned with palm-leaves, and exhibited to the people. The remainder of that day was celebrated as his birthday and passed in festivities: and on the third day afterwards, the same religious ceremonies were repeated, including a religious breakfast, "*followed by a final consummation of ceremonies.*"

A year afterwards, he was warned to prepare for initiation into the mysteries of "the Great God, Supreme Parent of all the other Gods, the invincible Osiris." "For," says Apuleius, "although there is a strict connexion between the religions of both Deities, AND EVEN THE ESSENCE OF BOTH DIVINITIES IS IDENTICAL, the ceremonies of the respective initiations are considerably different."

Compare with this hint the following language of the prayer of Lucius, addressed to Isis; and we may judge what doctrines were taught in the mysteries, in regard to the Deity: " O Holy and Perpetual Preserver of the Human Race! ever ready to cherish mortals by Thy munificence, and afford thy sweet maternal affection to the wretched under misfortune; whose bounty is never at rest, neither by day nor by night, nor throughout the very minutest particle of duration; thou who stretchest forth thy health-bearing right hand over the land and over the sea for the protection of mankind, to disperse the storms of life, to unravel the inextricable entanglement of the web of fate, to mitigate the tempests of fortune, and restrain the malignant influences of the stars,—*the Gods in Heaven adore thee, the Gods in the shades below do thee homage, the stars obey thee, the Divinities rejoice in thee, the elements and the revolving seasons serve thee!* At thy nod the winds breathe, clouds gather, seeds grow, buds germinate: *in obedience to Thee the Earth revolves* AND THE SUN GIVES HIS LIGHT. IT IS THOU WHO GOVERNEST THE UNIVERSE AND TREADEST TARTARUS UNDER THY FEET."

Then he was initiated into the nocturnal mysteries of Osiris and Serapis: and afterwards into those of Ceres at Rome: but of the ceremonies in these initiations, Apuleius says nothing.

Under the Archonship of Euclid, bastards and slaves were excluded from initiation: and the same exclusion obtained against the Materialists or Epicureans who denied Providence and consequently the utility of initiation. By a natural progress, it came at length to be considered that the gates of Elysium would open only for the initiates, whose souls had been purified and regenerated in the sanctuaries. But it was never held, on the other hand, that initiation alone sufficed. We learn from Plato, that it was also necessary for the soul to be purified from every stain: and that the purification necessary was such as gave virtue, truth, wisdom, strength, justice and temperance.

Entrance to the Temples was forbidden to all who had committed homicide, even if it were involuntary. So it is stated by both Isocrates and Theon. Magicians and Charlatans, who made trickery a trade, and impostors pretending to be possessed by evil spirits, were excluded from the sanctuaries. Every impious person and criminal was rejected; and Lampridius states that before the celebration of the mysteries, public notice was given, that none need apply to enter but those against whom their consciences uttered no reproach, and who were certain of their own innocence.

It was required of the initiate that his heart and hands should be free from any stain. Porphyry says that man's soul, at death, should be enfranchised from all the passions, from hate, envy and the others; and, in a word, *be as pure as it is required to be in the mysteries.* Of course it is not surprising that parricides and perjurers, and others who had committed crimes against God or man, could not be admitted.

In the Mysteries of Mithras, a lecture was repeated to the initiate on the subject of Justice. And the great moral lesson of the mysteries, to which all their mystic ceremonial tended, expressed in a single line by Virgil, was *to practice Justice and revere the Deity;*—thus recalling men to justice, by connecting it with the justice of the Gods, who require it and punish its infraction. The initiate could aspire to the favours of the Gods, only because and while he respected the rights of society and those of humanity. "The sun," says the chorus of Initiates in Aristophanes, "burns with a pure light for us alone, who, admitted to the mysteries, observe the laws of piety in our intercourse with strangers and our fellow-citizens." The rewards of initiation were attached to the practice of the social virtues. It was not enough to be initiated merely. It was necessary to be faithful to the *laws* of initiation, which imposed on men duties in regard to their kind. Bacchus allowed none to participate in his mysteries, but men who conformed to the rules of piety and justice. Sensibility, above all, and compassion for the misfortunes of others, were precious virtues, which initiation strove to encourage. "Nature," says Juvenal, "has created us compassionate, since it has endowed us with tears. Sensibility is the most admirable of our senses. What man is truly worthy of the torch of the mysteries; the man such as the Priest of Ceres requires him to be, if he regards the misfortunes of others as wholly foreign to himself?"

All who had not used their endeavours to defeat a conspiracy; and those who had on the contrary fomented one; those citizens who had betrayed their country, who had surrendered an advantageous post or place, or the vessels of the State, to the enemy; all who had supplied the enemy with money; and in general, all who had come short of their duties as honest men and good citizens, were excluded from the mysteries of Eleusis. To be admitted there, one must have lived equitably, and with sufficient good fortune not to be regarded as hated by the Gods.

Thus the Society of the Initiates was, in its principle, and according to the true purpose of its institution, a society of virtuous men, who laboured to free their souls from the tyranny of the passions, and to develop the germ of all the social virtues. And this was the meaning of the idea, afterwards misunderstood, that entry into Elysium was only allowed to the initiates: because entrance to the sanctuaries was allowed to the virtuous only, and Elysium was created for virtuous souls alone.

The precise nature and details of the doctrines as to a future life, and rewards and punishments there, developed in the mysteries, is in a measure uncertain. Little direct information in regard to it has come down to us. No doubt, in the ceremonies, there was a scenic representation of Tartarus and the judgment of the dead, resembling that which we find in Virgil: but there is as little doubt that these representations were explained to be allegorical. It is not our purpose here to repeat the descriptions given of Elysium and Tartarus. That would be aside from our object. We are only concerned with the great fact that the Mysteries taught the doctrine of the soul's immortality, and that, in some shape, suffering, pain, remorse and agony, ever follow sin as its consequences.

Human ceremonies are indeed but imperfect symbols; and the alternate baptisms in fire and water intended to purify us into immortality, are ever in this world interrupted at the moment of their anticipated completion. Life is a mirror which reflects only to deceive, a tissue perpetually interrupted and broken, an urn forever fed, yet never full.

All initiation is but introductory to the great change of death. Baptism, anointing, embalming, obsequies by burial or fire, are preparatory symbols, like the initiation of Hercules before descending to the Shades, pointing out the mental change which ought to precede the renewal of existence. Death is the true initiation, to which sleep is the introductory or minor mystery. It is the final rite which united the Egyptian with his God, and which opens the same promise to all who are duly prepared for it.

The body was deemed a prison for the soul; but the latter was not condemned to eternal banishment and imprisonment. The Father of the Worlds permits its chains to be broken, and has provided in the course of Nature the means of its escape. It was a doctrine of immemorial antiquity, shared alike by Egyptians, Pythagoreans, the Orphici, and by that characteristic Bacchic Sage, "the Preceptor of the Soul," Silenus, that death is far better than life; that the real death belongs to those who on earth are immersed in the Lethe of its passions and fascinations, and that the true life commences only when the soul is emancipated for its return.

And in this sense, as presiding over life and death, Dionusos is in the highest sense *the* LIBERATOR: since, like Osiris, he frees the soul, and guides it in its migrations beyond the grave, preserving it from the risk of again falling under the slavery of matter or of some inferior animal form, the purgatory of Metempsychosis; and exalting and perfecting its nature through the purifying discipline of his mysteries. "The great consummation of all philosophy," said Socrates, professedly quoting from traditional and mystic sources, "is *Death:* He who pursues philosophy aright, *is studying how to die.*"

All soul is part of the Universal Soul, whose totality is Dionusos; and it is therefore he who, as Spirit of Spirits, leads back the vagrant spirit to its home, and accompanies it through the purifying processes, both real and symbolical, of its earthly transit. He is therefore emphatically the *Mystes* or Hierophant, the great Spiritual Mediator of Greek religion.

The human soul is itself δαιμονιος, a God *within* the mind, capable through its own power of rivalling the canonization of the Hero, of making itself immortal by the practice of the good, and the contemplation of the beautiful and true. The removal to the Happy Islands could only be understood mythically; everything earthly must die; Man, like Œdipus, is wounded from his birth; his real elysium can exist only beyond the grave. Dionusos died and descended to the Shades. His passion was the great Secret of the Mysteries; as Death is the Grand Mystery of existence. His death, typical of Nature's Death, or of her periodical decay and restoration, was one of the many symbols of the *palingenesia* or second birth of man.

Man, descended from the elemental Forces or Titans [Elohim], who fed on the body of the Pantheistic Deity creating the Universe by self-sacrifice, commemorates in sacramental observance this mysterious passion; and while partaking of the raw flesh of the victim, seems to be invigorated by a fresh draught from the fountain of universal life, to receive a new pledge of regenerated existence. Death is the inseparable antecedent of life; the seed dies in order to produce the plant, and earth itself is rent asunder and dies at the birth of Dionusos. Hence the significancy of the *phallus*, or of its inoffensive substitute the obelisk, rising as an emblem of resurrection by the tomb of buried Deity at Lerna or at Sais.

Dionusos-Orpheus descended to the Shades to recover the lost Virgin of the Zodiac, to bring back his mother to the sky as Thyone; or what has the same meaning, to consummate his eventful marriage with Persephone, thereby securing, like the nuptials of his father with Semele or Danaë, the perpetuity of Nature. His under-earth office is the depression of the year, the wintry aspect in the alternations of bull and serpent, whose united series makes up the continuity of Time, and in which, physically speaking, the stern and dark are ever the parents of the beautiful and bright.

It was this aspect, sombre for the moment but bright by anticipation, which was contemplated in the mysteries: the human sufferer was consoled by witnessing the severer trials of the Gods; and the vicissitudes of life and death, expressed by apposite symbols, such as the sacrifice or submersion of the Bull, the extinction and re-illumination of the torch, excited corresponding emotions of alternate grief and joy, that play of passion which was present at the origin of Nature, and which accompanies all her changes.

The greater Eleusiniæ were celebrated in the month Boëdromion, when the seed was buried in the ground, and when the year, verging to its decline disposes the mind to serious reflection. The first days of the ceremonial were passed in sorrow and anxious silence, in fasting and expiatory or lustral offices. On a sudden, the scene was changed: sorrow and lamentation were discarded, the glad name of Iacchus passed from mouth to mouth, the image of the God crowned with myrtle and bearing a lighted torch was borne in joyful procession from the Ceramicus to Eleusis, where during the ensuing night, the initiation was completed by an imposing revelation. The first scene was in the προναος, or outer court of the sacred enclosure, where amidst utter darkness, or while the mediating God, the star illuminating the Nocturnal Mystery, alone carried an unextinguished torch, the candidates were overawed with terrific sounds and noises, while they painfully groped their way as in the gloomy cavern of the soul's sublunar migration; a scene justly compared to the passage of the Valley of the Shadow of Death. For by the immutable law exemplified in the trials of Psyche, man must pass through the terrors of the under-world, before he can reach the height of Heaven. At length the gates of the *adytum* were thrown open, a supernatural light streamed from the illuminated statue of the Goddess, and enchanting sights and sounds, mingled with songs and dances, exalted the communicant to a rapture of supreme felicity, realizing, as far as sensuous imagery could depict, the anticipated reunion with the Gods.

In the dearth of direct evidence as to the detail of the ceremonies enacted, or of the meanings connected with them, their tendency must be inferred from the characteristics of the contemplated deities with their accessory symbols and mythi, or from direct testimony as to the value of the Mysteries generally.

The ordinary phenomena of vegetation, the death of the seed in giving birth to the plant, connecting the sublimest hopes with the plainest occurrences, was the simple yet beautiful formula assumed by the great mystery in almost all religions, from the Zend-Avesta to the Gospel. As Proserpina, the divine power is as the seed decaying and destroyed; as Artemis, she is the principle of its destruction; but Artemis Proserpina is also Core Soteira, the Saviour, who leads the Spirits of Hercules and Hyacinthus to Heaven.

Many other emblems were employed in the mysteries,—as the dove, the myrtle-wreath, and others, all significant of life rising out of death, and of the equivocal condition of dying yet immortal man.

The horrors and punishments of Tartarus, as described in the Phædo and the Æneid, with all the ceremonies of the judgments of Minos, Eacus and Rhadamanthus, were represented, sometimes more and sometimes less fully, in the Mysteries; in order to impress upon the minds of the initiates this great lesson,—that we should be ever prepared to appear before the Supreme Judge, with a heart pure and spotless; as Socrates teaches in the Gorgias. For the soul stained with crimes, he says, to descend to the Shades, is the bitterest ill. To adhere to Justice and Wisdom, Plato holds, is our duty, that we may some day take that lofty road that leads towards the heavens, and avoid most of the evils to which the soul is exposed in its subterranean journey of a thousand years. And so in the Phædo, Socrates teaches that we should seek here below to free our soul of its passions, in order to be ready to enter our appearance, whenever Destiny summons us to the Shades.

Thus the Mysteries inculcated a great moral truth, veiled with a fable of huge proportions and the appliances of an impressive spectacle, to which, exhibited in the sanctuaries, art and natural magic lent all they had that was imposing. They sought to strengthen men against the horrors of death and the fearful idea of utter annihilation. Death, says the author of the dialogue entitled *Axiochus*, included in the works of Plato, is but a passage to a happier state: but one must have lived well, to attain that most fortunate result. So that the doctrine of the immortality of the soul was consoling to the virtuous and religious man alone: while to all others it came with menaces and despair, surrounding them with terrors and alarms that disturbed their repose during all their life.

For the material horrors of Tartarus, allegorical to the initiate, were real to the mass of the Profane; nor in latter times, did, perhaps, many initiates read rightly the allegory. The triple-walled prison, which the condemned soul first met, round which swelled and surged the fiery waves of Phlegethon, wherein rolled roaring huge blazing rocks; the great gate with columns of adamant which none save the Gods could crush; Tisiphone, their warder, with her bloody robes; the lash resounding on the mangled bodies of the miserable unfortunates: their plaintive groans, mingled in horrid harmony with the clashings of their chains; the Furies, lashing the guilty with their snakes; the awful abyss where Hydra howls with its hundred heads, greedy to devour; Tityus, prostrate, and his entrails fed upon by the cruel vulture; Sisyphus, ever rolling his rock; Ixion on his wheel; Tantalus tortured by eternal thirst and hunger, in the midst of water and with delicious fruits touching his head; the daughters of Danaus at their eternal, fruitless task; beasts biting and venomous reptiles stinging; and devouring flame eternally consuming bodies ever renewed in endless agony: all these sternly impressed upon the people the terrible consequences of sin and vice, and urged them to pursue the paths of honesty and virtue.

And if, in the ceremonies of the Mysteries, these material horrors were explained to the initiates as mere symbols of the unimaginable torture, remorse and agony that would rend the immaterial soul and rack the immortal spirit, they were feeble and insufficient in the same mode and measure only, as all material images and symbols fall short of that which is beyond the cognizance of our senses: and the grave Hierophant, the imagery, the paintings, the dramatic horrors, the funereal sacrifices, the august mysteries, the solemn silence of the sanctuaries, were none the less impressive, because they were known to be but symbols, that with material shows and images made the imagination to be the teacher of the intellect.

So, too, it was represented, that except for the gravest sins there was an opportunity for expiation; and the tests of *water, air* and *fire* were represented; by means of which, during the march of many years, the soul could be purified, and rise towards the ethereal regions; that ascent being more or less tedious and laborious, according as each soul was more or less clogged by the gross impediments of its sins and vices. Herein was shadowed forth, (how distinctly taught the initiates we know not), the doctrine that pain and sorrow, misfortune and remorse, are the inevitable *consequences* that flow from sin and vice, as effect flows from cause; that by each sin and every act of vice the soul drops back and loses ground in its advance towards perfection; and that the ground so lost is and will be in reality never so recovered as that the sin shall be as if it never had been committed; but that throughout all the eternity of its existence, each soul shall be conscious that every act of vice or baseness it did on earth has made the distance greater between itself and ultimate perfection.

We see this truth glimmering in the doctrine, taught in the Mysteries, that though slight and ordinary offences could be expiated by penance, repentance, acts of beneficence and prayers, grave crimes were mortal sins, beyond the reach of all such remedies. Eleusis closed her gates against Nero; and the Pagan Priests told Constantine that among all their modes of expiation there was none so potent as could wash from *his* soul the dark spots left by the murder of his wife, and his multiplied perjuries and assassinations.

The object of the ancient initiations being to ameliorate mankind and to perfect the intellectual part of man, the nature of the human soul, its origin, its destination, its relations to the body and to universal nature, all formed part of the mystic science; and to them in part the lessons given to the initiate were directed. For it was believed that initiation tended to his perfection, and to preventing the divine part within him, overloaded with matter gross and earthy, from being plunged into gloom, and impeded in its return to the Deity. The soul, with them, was not a mere conception or abstraction; but a reality including in itself life and thought; or, rather, of whose essence it was to live and think. It was material; but not brute, inert, inactive, lifeless, motionless, formless, lightless matter. It was held to be active, reasoning, thinking; its natural home in the highest regions of the universe, whence it descended to illuminate, give form and movement to, vivify, animate, and carry with itself the baser matter; and whither it unceasingly tends to reascend, when and as soon as it can free itself from its connection with that matter. From that substance, divine, infinitely delicate and active, essentially luminous, the souls of men were formed, and by it alone, uniting with and organizing their bodies, men *lived*.

This was the doctrine of Pythagoras, who learned it when he received the Egyptian Mysteries: and it was the doctrine of all who by means of the ceremonial of initiation thought to purify the soul. Virgil makes the spirit of Anchises teach it to Æneas: and all the expiations and lustrations used in the mysteries were but symbols of those intellectual ones by which the soul was to be purged of its vice-spots and stains, and freed of the incumbrance of its earthly prison, so that it might rise unimpeded to the source from which it came.

Hence sprung the doctrine of the transmigration of souls; which Pythagoras taught as an allegory, and those who came after him received literally. Plato, like him, drew his doctrines from the East and the mysteries, and undertook to translate the language of the symbols used there, into that of philosophy; and to prove by argument and philosophical deduction, what, *felt* by the consciousness, the mysteries taught by symbols as an indisputable fact,—the immortality of the soul. Cicero did the same; and followed the mysteries in teaching that the Gods were but mortal men, who for their great virtues and signal services had deserved that their souls should, after death, be raised to that lofty rank.

It being taught in the Mysteries, either by way of allegory, the meaning of which was not made known except to a select few; or, perhaps only at a later day, as an actual reality, that the souls of the vicious dead passed into the bodies of those animals to whose nature their vices had most affinity, it was also taught that the soul could avoid these transmigrations, often successive and numerous, by the practice of virtue, which would acquit it of them, free it from the circle of successive generations, and restore it at once to its source. Hence nothing was so ardently prayed for by the initiates, says Proclus, as this happy fortune, which, delivering them from the empire of Evil, would restore them to their true life, and conduct them to the place of final rest. To this doctrine probably referred those figures of animals and monsters which were exhibited to the initiate, before allowing him to see the sacred light for which he sighed.

Plato says, that souls will not reach the term of their ills, until the revolutions of the world have restored them to their primitive condition, and purified them from the stains which they have contracted by the contagion of fire, earth and air. And he held that they could not be allowed to enter Heaven, until they had distinguished themselves by the practice of virtue in some one of three several bodies. The Manicheans allowed five: Pindar, the same number as Plato; as did the Jews.

And Cicero says, that the ancient soothsayers, and the interpreters of the will of the Gods, in their religious ceremonies and initiations, taught that we expiate here below the crimes committed in a prior life; and for that are born. It was taught in these mysteries, that the soul passes through several states, and that the pains and sorrows of this life are an expiation of prior faults.

This doctrine of transmigration of souls obtained, as Porphyry informs us, among the Persians and Magi. It was held in the East and the West, and that from the remotest antiquity. Herodotus found it among the Egyptians, who made the term of the circle of migrations from one human body, through animals, fishes and birds, to another human body, three thousand years. Empedocles even held that souls went into plants. Of these, the laurel was the noblest, as of animals the lion; both being consecrated to the Sun, to which it was held in the Orient, virtuous souls were to return. The Curds, the Chinese, the Kabbalists, all held the same doctrine. So Origen held, and the Bishop Synesius, the latter of whom had been initiated, and who thus prayed to God; "O Father, grant that my soul, reunited to the light, may not be plunged again into the defilements of earth!" So the Gnostics held; and even the Disciples of Christ inquired if the man who was born blind, was not so punished for some sin that he had committed before his birth.

Virgil, in the celebrated allegory in which he develops the doctrines taught in the mysteries, enunciated the doctrine, held by most of the ancient philosophers, of the pre-existence of souls, in the eternal fire from which they emanate; that fire which animates the stars, and circulates in every part of Nature: and the purifications of the soul, by fire, water and air, of which he speaks, and which three modes were employed in the Mysteries of Bacchus, were symbols of the passage of the soul into different bodies.

The relations of the human soul with the rest of nature were a chief object of the science of the mysteries. The man was there brought face to face with entire nature. The world, and the spherical envelope that surrounds it, were represented by a mystic egg, by the side of the image of the Sun-God whose mysteries were celebrated. The famous Orphic egg was consecrated to Bacchus in his mysteries. It was, says Plutarch, an image of the Universe, which engenders everything, and contains everything in its bosom. "Consult," says Macrobius, "the initiates of the mysteries of Bacchus, who honour with special veneration the sacred egg." The rounded and almost spherical form of its shell, he says, which encloses it on every side, and confines within itself the principles of life, is a symbolic image of the world; and the world is the universal principle of all things.

This symbol was borrowed from the Egyptians, who also consecrated the egg to Osiris, germ of Light, himself born, says Diodorus, from that famous egg. In Thebes, in Upper Egypt, he was represented as emitting it from his mouth, and causing to issue from it the first principle of heat and light, or the Fire-God, Vulcan, or Phtha. We find this egg even in Japan, between the horns of the famous Mithriac Bull, whose attributes Osiris, Apis and Bacchus all borrowed.

Orpheus, author of the Grecian Mysteries, which he carried from Egypt to Greece, consecrated this symbol: and taught that matter, uncreated and informous, existed from all eternity, unorganized, as chaos; containing in itself the Principles of all Existences confused and intermingled, light with darkness, the dry with the humid, heat with cold; from which, it after long ages taking the shape of an immense egg, issued the purest matter, or first substance, and the residue was divided into the four elements, from which proceeded heaven and earth and all things else. This grand Cosmogonic idea he taught in the mysteries; and thus the Hierophant explained the meaning of the mystic egg, seen by the initiates in the Sanctuary.

Thus entire Nature, in her primitive organization, was presented to him whom it was wished to instruct in her secrets and initiate in her mysteries; and Clemens of Alexandria might well say that initiation was a real physiology.

So Phanes, the Light-God, in the Mysteries of the New Orphics, emerged from the egg of chaos: and the Persians had the great egg of Ormuzd. And Sanchoniathon tells us that in the Phœnician theology, the matter of chaos took the form of an egg; and he adds: "Such are the lessons which the Son of Thabion, first Hierophant of the Phœnicians, turned into allegories, in which physics and astronomy intermingled, and which he taught to the other Hierophants, whose duty it was to preside at orgies and initiations; and who, seeking to excite the astonishment and admiration of mortals, faithfully transmitted these things to their successors and the initiates."

In the mysteries was also taught the division of the Universal Cause into an Active and a Passive cause; of which two, Osiris and Isis,—the heavens and the earth, were symbols. These two First Causes, into which it was held that the great Universal First Cause at the beginning of things divided itself, were the two great Divinities, whose worship was, according to Varro, inculcated upon the initiates at Samothrace. "As is taught," he says, "in the initiation into the mysteries at Samothrace, Heaven and Earth are regarded as the two first Divinities. They are the potent Gods worshipped in that Island, and whose names are consecrated in the books of our Augurs. One of them is male and the other female; and they bear the same relation to each other as the soul does to the body, humidity to dryness." The Curetes, in Crete, had builded an altar to Heaven and to Earth; whose mysteries they celebrated at Gnossus, in a cypress grove.

These two Divinities, the Active and Passive Principles of the Universe, were commonly symbolized by the generative parts of man and woman; to which in remote ages, no idea of indecency was attached; the *Phallus* and *Cteis*, emblems of generation and production, and which, as such, appeared in the mysteries. The Indian Lingam was the union of both, as were the boat and mast, and the point within a circle; all of which expressed the same philosophical idea as to the Union of the two great Causes of Nature, which concur, one actively and the other passively, in the generation of all beings: which were symbolized by what we now term *Gemini*, the Twins, at that remote period when the Sun was in that Sign at the Vernal Equinox, and when they were Male and Female; and of which the Phallus was perhaps taken from the generative organ of the Bull, when about twenty-five hundred years before our era he opened that equinox, and became to the Ancient World the symbol of the creative and generative Power.

The initiates at Eleusis commenced, Proclus says, by invoking the two great causes of nature, the Heavens and the Earth, on which in succession they fixed their eyes, addressing to each a prayer. And they deemed it their duty to do so, he adds, because they saw in them the Father and Mother of all generations. The concourse of these two agents of the universe was termed in theological language a *marriage*. Tertullian, accusing the Valentinians with having borrowed these symbols from the Mysteries of Eleusis, yet admits that in those Mysteries they were explained in a manner consistent with decency, as representing the powers of nature. He was too little of a philosopher to comprehend the sublime esoteric meaning of these emblems, which will, if you advance, in other Degrees be unfolded to you.

The Christian Fathers contented themselves with reviling and ridiculing the use of these emblems. But as they in the earlier times created no indecent ideas, and were worn alike by the most innocent youths and virtuous women, it will be far wiser for us to seek to penetrate their meaning. Not only the Egyptians, says Diodorus Siculus, but every other people that consecrate this symbol (the Phallus), deem that they thereby do honour to the Active Force of the universal generation of all living things. For the same reason, as we learn from the geographer Ptolemy, it was revered among the Assyrians and Persians. Proclus remarks that in the distribution of the Zodiac among the twelve great Divinities, by ancient astrology, six signs were assigned to the male and six to the female principle.

There is another division of nature, which has in all ages struck all men, and which was not forgotten in the Mysteries; that of Light and Darkness, Day and Night, Good and Evil; which mingle with, and clash against, and pursue or are pursued by each other throughout the universe. The Great Symbolic Egg distinctly reminded the initiates of this great division of the world. Plutarch, treating of the dogma of a Providence, and of that of the two principles of Light and Darkness, which he regarded as the basis of the Ancient Theology, of the Orgies and the Mysteries, as well among the Greeks as the Barbarians,—a doctrine whose origin, according to him, is lost in the night of time,—cites, in support of his opinion, the famous Mystic Egg of the disciples of Zoroaster and the initiates in the Mysteries of Mithras.

To the initiates in the Mysteries of Eleusis was exhibited the spectacle of these two principles, in the successive scenes of Darkness and Light which passed before their eyes. To the profoundest darkness, accompanied with illusions and horrid phantoms, succeeded the most brilliant light, whose splendour blazed round the statue of the Goddess. The candidate, says Dion Chrysostomus, passed into a mysterious temple, of astonishing magnitude and beauty, where were exhibited to him many mystic scenes; where his ears were stunned with many voices; and where Darkness and Light successively passed before him. And Themistius in like manner describes the initiate, when about to enter into that part of the sanctuary tenanted by the Goddess, as filled with fear and religious awe, wavering, uncertain in what direction to advance through the profound darkness that envelopes him. But when the Hierophant has opened the entrance to the inmost sanctuary, and removed the robe that hides the Goddess, he exhibits her to the initiate, resplendent with divine light. The thick shadow and gloomy atmosphere which had environed the candidate vanish; he is filled with a vivid and glowing enthusiasm, that lifts his soul out of the profound dejection in which it was plunged; and the purest light succeeds to the thickest darkness.

In a fragment of the same writer, preserved by Stobæus, we learn that the initiate, up to the moment when his initiation is to be consummated, is alarmed by every kind of sight: that astonishment and terror take his soul captive; he trembles; cold sweat flows from his body; until the moment when the Light is shown him,—a most astounding Light,—the brilliant scene of Elysium, where he sees charming meadows overarched by a clear sky, and festivals celebrated by dances; where he hears harmonious voices, and the majestic chants of the Hierophants; and views the sacred spectacles. Then, absolutely free, and enfranchised from the dominion of all ills, he mingles with the crowd of initiates, and crowned with flowers celebrates with them the holy orgies, in the brilliant realms of ether, and the dwelling-place of Ormuzd.

In the Mysteries of Isis, the candidate first passed through the dark valley of the shadow of death; then into a place representing the elements or sublunary world, where the two principles clash and contend; and was finally admitted to a luminous region, where the sun, with his most brilliant light, put to rout the shades of night. Then he himself put on the costume of the Sun-God, or the Visible Source of Ethereal Light, in whose mysteries he was initiated; and passed from the empire of darkness to that of light. After having set his feet on the threshold of the palace of Pluto, he ascended to the Empyrean, to the bosom of the Eternal Principle of Light of the Universe, from which all souls and intelligences emanate.

Plutarch admits that this theory of two Principles was the basis of all the Mysteries, and consecrated in the religious ceremonies and mysteries of Greece. Osiris and Typhon, Ormuzd and Ahriman, Bacchus and the Titans and Giants, all represented these principles. Phanes, the luminous God that issued from the Sacred Egg, and Night, bore the sceptres in the Mysteries of the New Bacchus. Night and Day were two of the eight Gods adored in the Mysteries of Osiris. The sojourn of Proserpine and also of Adonis, during six months of each year in the upper world, abode of light, and six months in the lower or abode of darkness, allegorically represented the same division of the Universe.

The connexion of the different initiations with the Equinoxes which separate the Empire of the Nights from that of the Days, and fix the moment when one of these principles begins to prevail over the other, shows that the Mysteries referred to the continual contest between the two principles of light and darkness, each alternately victor and vanquished. The very object proposed by them shows that their basis was the theory of the two principles and their relations with the soul. "We celebrate the august Mysteries of Ceres and Proserpine," says the Emperor Julian, "at the autumnal Equinox, to obtain of the Gods that the soul may not experience the malignant action of the Power of Darkness that is then about to have sway and rule in Nature." Sallust the Philosopher makes almost the same remark as to the relations of the soul with the periodical march of light and darkness, during an annual revolution; and assures us that the mysterious festivals of Greece related to the same. And in all the explanations given by Macrobius of the Sacred Fables in regard to the Sun, adored under the names of Osiris, Horus, Adonis, Atys, Bacchus, &c., we invariably see that they refer to the theory of the two Principles, Light and Darkness, and the triumphs gained by one over the other. In April was celebrated the first triumph obtained by the light of day over the length of the nights; and the ceremonies of mourning and rejoicing had, Macrobius says, as their object the vicissitudes of the annual administration of the world.

This brings us naturally to the tragic portion of these religious scenes, and to the allegorical history of the different adventures of the Principle, Light, victor and vanquished by turns, in the combats waged with darkness during each annual period. Here we reach the most mysterious part of the ancient initiations, and that most interesting to the Mason who laments the death of his Grand Master Hiram. Over it Herodotus throws the august veil of mystery and silence. Speaking of the Temple of Minerva, or of that Isis who was styled the Mother of the Sun-God, and whose Mysteries were termed *Isiac*, at Sais, he speaks of a Tomb in the Temple, in the rear of the Chapel and against the wall; and says, "It is the tomb of a man, whose name respect requires me to conceal. Within the Temple were great obelisks of stone, [*phalli*], and a circular lake paved with stones and revetted with a parapet. It seemed to me as large as that at Delos," [where the Mysteries of Apollo were celebrated]. "In this lake the Egyptians celebrate, during the night, what they style the Mysteries, in which are represented the sufferings of the God of whom I have spoken above." This God was Osiris, put to death by Typhon, and who descended to the Shades and was restored to life; of which he had spoken before.

We are reminded, by this passage, of the Tomb of Hiram, his death, and his raising from the grave, symbolical of restoration of life; and also of the brazen Sea in the Temple at Jerusalem. Herodotus adds: "I impose upon myself a profound silence in regard to these Mysteries, with most of which I am acquainted. As little will I speak of the initiations of Ceres, known among the Greeks as Thesmophoria. What I shall say will not violate the respect which I owe to religion."

Athenagoras quotes this passage to show that not only the Statue but the Tomb of Osiris was exhibited in Egypt, and a tragic representation of his sufferings; and remarks that the Egyptians had mourning ceremonies in honour of their Gods, whose deaths they lamented; and to whom they afterwards sacrificed as having passed to a state of immortality.

It is, however, not difficult, combining the different rays of light that emanate from the different Sanctuaries, to learn the genius and the object of these secret ceremonies. We have hints, and not details.

We know that the Egyptians worshipped the Sun, under the name of Osiris. The misfortunes and tragical death of this God were an allegory relating to the Sun. Typhon, like Ahriman, represented Darkness. The sufferings and death of Osiris in the Mysteries of the Night were a mystic image of the phenomena of Nature, and the conflict of the two great principles which share the empire of Nature, and most influence our souls. The Sun is neither born, dies nor is raised to life: and the recital of these events was but an allegory, veiling a higher truth.

Horus, son of Isis, and the same as Apollo or the Sun, also died and was restored again to life and to his mother; and the priests of Isis celebrated these great events by mourning and joyous festival succeeding each other.

In the mysteries of Phœnicia, established in honour of Thammuz or Adoni, also the Sun, the spectacle of his death and resurrection was exhibited to the initiates. As we learn from Meursius and Plutarch, a figure was exhibited representing the corpse of a young man. Flowers were strewed upon this body; the women mourned for him; a tomb was erected to him. And these feasts, as we learn from Plutarch and Ovid, passed into Greece.

In the mysteries of Mithras, the Sun-God, in Asia Minor, Armenia and Persia, the death of that God was lamented, and his resurrection was celebrated with the most enthusiastic expressions of joy. A corpse, we learn from Julian Firmicus, was shown the initiates, representing Mithras dead; and afterwards his resurrection was announced; and they were then invited to rejoice that the dead God was restored to life, and had by means of his sufferings secured their salvation. Three months before, his birth had been celebrated, under the emblem of an infant, born on the 25th of December, or the 8th day before the Kalends of January.

In Greece, in the mysteries of the same God, honoured under the name of Bacchus, a representation was given of his death, slain by the Titans; of his descent into hell, his subsequent resurrection, and his return towards his Principle or the pure abode whence he had descended to unite himself with matter. In the islands of Chios and Tenedos, this death was represented by the sacrifice of a man, actually immolated.

The mutilation and sufferings of the same Sun-God, honoured in Phrygia under the name of Atys, caused the tragic scenes that were, as we learn from Diodorus Siculus, represented annually in the mysteries of

Cybele, mother of the Gods. An image was borne there, representing the corpse of a young man, over whose tomb tears were shed, and to whom funeral honours were paid.

At Samothrace, in the mysteries of the Cabiri or great Gods, a representation was given of the death of one of them. This name was given to the Sun, because the Ancient Astronomers gave the name of Gods Cabiri and of Samothrace to the two Gods in the Constellation Gemini; whom others term Apollo and Hercules, two names of the Sun. Athenion says that the young Cabirus so slain was the same as the Dionusos or Bacchus of the Greeks. The Pelasgi, ancient inhabitants of Greece, and who settled Samothrace, celebrated these mysteries, whose origin is unknown: and they worshipped Castor and Pollux as patrons of navigation.

The tomb of Apollo was at Delphi, where his body was laid, after Python, the Polar Serpent that annually heralds the coming of autumn, cold, darkness and winter, had slain him, and over whom the God triumphs, on the 25th of March, on his return to the lamb of the vernal equinox.

In Crete, Jupiter Ammon, or the Sun in Aries, painted with the attributes of that equinoctial sign, the Ram or Lamb;—that Ammon who, Martianus Capella says, is the same as Osiris, Adoni, Adonis, Atys, and the other Sun-Gods,—had also a tomb, and a religious initiation; one of the principal ceremonies of which consisted in clothing the initiate with the skin of a white lamb. And in this we see the origin of the apron of white sheep-skin, used in Masonry.

All these deaths and resurrections, these funereal emblems, these anniversaries of mourning and joy, these cenotaphs raised in different places to the Sun-God, honoured under different names, had but a single object, the allegorical narration of the events which happen here below to the Light of Nature, that sacred fire from which our souls were deemed to emanate, warring with matter and the dark principle resident therein, ever at variance with the Principle of Good and Light poured upon itself by the Supreme Divinity. All these mysteries, says Clemens of Alexandria, displaying to us murders and tombs alone, all these religious tragedies, had a common basis, variously ornamented: and that basis was the fictitious death and resurrection of the Sun, Soul of the World, principle of life and movement in the Sublunary World, and source of our intelligences, which are but a portion of the Eternal Light blazing in that Star, their chief centre.

It was in the Sun that Souls, it was said, were purified; and to it they repaired. It was one of the gates of the soul, through which the theologians, says Porphyry, say that it re-ascends towards the home of Light and the Good. Wherefore, in the Mysteries of Eleusis, the Dadoukos (the first officer after the Hierophant, who represented the Grand Demiourgos or Maker of the Universe), who was posted in the interior of the Temple, and there received the Candidates, represented the Sun.

It was also held that the vicissitudes experienced by the Father of Light had an influence on the destiny of souls; which, of the same substance as he, shared his fortunes. This we learn from the Emperor Julian and Sallust the Philosopher. They are afflicted when he suffers: they rejoice when he triumphs over the Power of Darkness which opposes his sway and hinders the happiness of Souls, to whom nothing is so terrible as darkness. The fruit of the sufferings of the God, father of light and Souls, slain by the Chief of the Powers of Darkness, and again restored to life, was received in the mysteries. "His death works your Salvation;" said the High Priest of Mithras. That was the great secret of this religious tragedy, and its expected fruit;— the resurrection of a God, who, repossessing himself of his dominion over Darkness, should associate with him in his triumph those virtuous Souls that by their purity were worthy to share His glory; and that strove not against the divine force that drew them to Him, when he had thus conquered.

To the initiate was also displayed the spectacle of the chief agents of the Universal Cause, and of the distribution of the world, in the detail of its parts arranged in most regular order. The Universe itself supplied man with the model for the first Temple reared to the Divinity. The arrangement of the Temple of Solomon, the symbolic ornaments which formed its chief decorations, and the dress of the High Priest,—all, as Clemens of Alexandria, Josephus and Philo state, had reference to the order of the world. Clemens informs us that the Temple contained many emblems of the Seasons, the Sun, the Moon, the planets, the constellations Ursa Major and Minor, the zodiac, the elements, and the other parts of the world.

Josephus, in his description of the High Priest's Vestments, protesting against the charge of impiety brought against the Hebrews by other nations, for contemning the Heathen Divinities, declares it false, because, in the construction of the Tabernacle, in the vestments of the Sacrificers and in the Sacred vessels, the whole World was in some sort represented. Of the three parts, he says, into which the Temple was divided, two represent Earth and Sea, open to all men, and the third, Heaven, God's dwelling-place, reserved for Him alone. The twelve loaves of Shew-bread signify the twelve months of the year. The Candlestick represented the twelve signs through which the Seven Planets run their courses; and the seven lights, those planets; the veils, of four colours, the four elements; the tunic of the High Priest, the earth; the hyacinth, nearly blue, the Heavens; the ephod, of four colours, the whole of nature; the gold, Light; the breast-plate, in the middle, this earth in the centre of the world; the two Sardonyxes, used as clasps, the Sun and Moon; and the twelve precious stones of the breast-plate arranged by threes, like the Seasons, the twelve months, and the twelve signs of the zodiac. Even the loaves were arranged in two groups of six, like the zodiacal signs above and below the Equator. Clemens, the learned Bishop of Alexandria, and Philo, adopt all these explanations.

Hermes calls the Zodiac, the Great Tent,—Tabernaculum. In the Royal Arch Degree of the American Rite, the Tabernacle has four veils, of different colours, to each of which belongs a banner. The colours of the four are White, Blue, Crimson and Purple, and the banners bear the images of the Bull, the Lion, the Man and the Eagle, the Constellations answering 2500 years before our era to the Equinoctial and Solstitial points: to which belong four stars, Aldebaran, Regulus, Fomalhaut and Antares. At each of these veils there are three words: and to each division of the Zodiac, belonging to each of these Stars, are three Signs. The four signs, Taurus, Leo, Scorpio and Aquarius, were termed the *fixed* signs, and are appropriately assigned to the four veils.

So the Cherubims, according to Clemens and Philo, represented the two hemispheres; their wings, the rapid course of the firmament, and of time which revolves in the zodiac. "For the Heavens fly;" says Philo, speaking of the wings of the Cherubim: which were winged representations of the Lion, the Bull, the Eagle and the Man; of two of which, the human-headed, winged bulls and lions, so many have been found at Nimroud; adopted as beneficent symbols, when the Sun entered Taurus at the vernal equinox and Leo at the summer solstice: and when, also, he entered Scorpio, for which, on account of its malignant influences, Aquila, the eagle, was substituted, at the autumnal equinox; and Aquarius (the water-bearer) at the winter solstice.

So, Clemens says, the candlestick with seven branches represented the seven planets, like which the seven branches were arranged and regulated, preserving that musical proportion and system of harmony of which the sun was the centre and connection. They were arranged, says Philo, by threes, like the planets above and those below the sun; between which two groups was the branch that represented him, the mediator or moderator of the celestial harmony. He is, in fact, the fourth in the musical scale, as Philo remarks, and Martianus Capella in his hymn to the Sun.

Near the candlestick were other emblems representing the heavens, earth, and the vegetative matter out of whose bosom the vapours arise. The whole temple was an abridged image of the world. There were candlesticks with four branches, symbols of the elements and the seasons; with twelve, symbols of the signs; and even with three hundred and sixty, the number of days in the year, without the supplementary days. Imitating the famous Temple of Tyre, where were the great columns consecrated to the winds and fire, the Tyrian artist placed two columns of bronze at the entrance of the porch of the temple. The hemispherical brazen sea, supported by four groups of bulls, of three each, looking to the four cardinal points of the compass, represented the bull of the vernal equinox, and at Tyre were consecrated to Astarte; to whom Hiram, Josephus says, had builded a temple, and who wore on her head a helmet bearing the image of a bull. And the throne of Solomon, with bulls adorning its arms, and supported on lions, like those of Horus in Egypt and of the Sun at Tyre, likewise referred to the vernal equinox and summer solstice.

Those who in Thrace adored the sun, under the name of Saba-Zeus, the Grecian Bacchus, builded to him, says Macrobius, a temple on Mount Zelmisso, its round form representing the world and the sun. A circular aperture in the roof admitted the light, and introduced the image of the sun into the body of the sanctuary, where he seemed to blaze as in the heights of Heaven, and to dissipate the darkness within that temple which was a representative symbol of the world. There the passion, death and resurrection of Bacchus were represented.

So the Temple of Eleusis was lighted by a window in the roof. The sanctuary so lighted, Dion compares to the universe, from which he says it differed in size alone; and in it the great lights of nature played a great part and were mystically represented. The images of the Sun, Moon and Mercury were represented there, (the latter the same as Anubis who accompanied Isis); and they are still the three lights of a Masonic Lodge; except that for Mercury, the Master of the Lodge has been absurdly substituted.

Eusebius names as the principal Ministers in the Mysteries of Eleusis, first, the *Hierophant*, clothed with the attributes of the Grand Architect (Demiourgos) of the Universe. After him came the *Dadoukos*, or torch-bearer, representative of the Sun: then the altar-bearer, representing the Moon: and last, the *Hieroceryx*, bearing the caduceus, and representing Mercury. It was not permissible to reveal the different emblems and the mysterious pageantry of initiation to the Profane; and therefore we do not know the attributes, emblems and ornaments of these and other officers; of which Apuleius and Pausanias dared not speak.

We know only that everything recounted there was marvellous; everything done there tended to astonish the initiate; and that eyes and ears were equally astounded. The Hierophant, of lofty height, and noble features, with long hair, of a great age, grave and dignified, with a voice sweet and sonorous, sat upon a throne, clad in a long trailing robe; as the Motive-God of Nature was held to be enveloped in His work, and hidden under a veil which no mortal can raise. Even his name was concealed, like that of the Demiourgos, whose name was ineffable.

The Dadoukos also wore a long robe, his hair long, and a bandeau on his forehead. Callias, when holding that office, fighting on the great day of Marathon, clothed with the insignia of his office, was taken by the Barbarians to be a King. The Dadoukos led the procession of the initiates, and was charged with the puri-fications.

We do not know the functions of the *Epibomos* or assistant at the altar, who represented the moon. That planet was one of the two homes of souls, and one of the two great gates by which they descended and re-ascended. Mercury was charged with the conducting of souls through the two great gates; and in going from the sun to the moon, they passed immediately by him. He admitted or rejected them as they were more or less pure, and therefore the Hieroceryx or Sacred Herald, who represented Mercury, was charged with the duty of excluding the Profane from the Mysteries.

The same officers are found in the procession of initiates of Isis, described by Apuleius. All clad in robes of white linen, drawn tight across the breast, and close-fitting down to the very feet, came, first, one bearing a lamp in the shape of a boat; second, one carrying an altar; and third one carrying a golden palm-tree and the caduceus. These are the same as the three officers at Eleusis, after the Hierophant. Then one carrying an open hand, and pouring milk on the ground from a golden vessel in the shape of a woman's breast. The hand was that of justice: and the milk alluded to the Galaxy or Milky Way, along which souls descended and remounted. Two others followed, one bearing a winnowing-fan, and the other a water-vase; symbols of the purification of souls by air and water: and the third purification, by earth, was represented by an image of the animal that cultivates it, the cow or ox, borne by another officer.

Then followed a chest or ark, magnificently ornamented, containing an image of the organs of genera-tion of Osiris, or perhaps of both sexes: emblems of the original generating and producing powers. When Typhon, said the Egyptian fable, cut up the body of Osiris into pieces, he flung his genitals into the Nile, where a fish devoured them. Atys mutilated himself, as his Priests afterwards did in imitation of him; and Adonis was in that part of his body wounded by the boar: all of which represented the loss by the Sun of his vivifying and generative power, when he reached the autumnal equinox (the Scorpion that on old monu-ments bites those parts of the Vernal Bull), and descended toward the region of darkness and winter.

Then, says Apuleius, came "one who carried in his bosom an object that rejoiced the heart of the bearer, a venerable effigy of the Supreme Deity, neither bearing resemblance to man, cattle, bird, beast, or any living creature: an exquisite invention, venerable from the novel originality of the fashioning: a wonderful, ineffable symbol of religious mysteries, to be looked upon in profound silence. Such as it was, its figure was that of a small urn of burnished gold, hollowed very artistically, rounded at the bottom, and covered all over the out-side with the wonderful hieroglyphics of the Egyptians. The spout was not elevated, but extended laterally, projecting like a long rivulet; while on the opposite side was the handle, which, with similar lateral extension, bore on its summit an asp, curling its body into folds, and stretching upward its wrinkled, scaly, swollen throat."

The salient basilisk, or royal ensign of the Pharaohs, often occurs on the monuments—a serpent in folds, with his head raised erect above the folds. The basilisk was the phœnix of the serpent-tribe: and the vase or urn was probably the vessel, shaped like a cucumber, with a projecting spout, out of which, on the monuments of Egypt, the priests are represented pouring streams of the *crux ansata* or Tau Cross, and of *sceptres* over the kings.

In the Mysteries of Mithras, a sacred cave, representing the whole arrangement of the world, was used for the reception of the initiates. Zoroaster, says Eubulus, first introduced this custom of consecrating caves. They were also consecrated, in Crete, to Jupiter; in Arcadia, to the Moon and Pan; and in the Island of Naxos, to Bacchus. The Persians, in the cave where the Mysteries of Mithras were celebrated, fixed the seat of that God, Father of Generation, or Demiourgos, near the equinoctial point of Spring, with the Northern portion of the world on his right, and the Southern on his left.

Mithras, says Porphyry, presided over the Equinoxes, seated on a Bull, the symbolical animal of the Demiourgos, and bearing a sword. The equinoxes were the gates through which souls passed to and fro, between the hemisphere of light and that of darkness. The milky way was also represented, passing near each of these gates; and it was, in the old theology, termed the pathway of souls. It is, according to Pythagoras, vast troops of souls that form that luminous belt.

The route followed by souls, according to Porphyry, or rather their progressive march in the world, lying through the fixed stars and planets, the Mithriac cave not only displayed the zodiacal and other constellations, and marked gates at the four equinoctial and solstitial points of the zodiac, whereat souls enter into and escape from the world of generations; and through which they pass to and fro between the realms of light and darkness; but it represented the seven planetary spheres which they needs must traverse, in descending from the heaven of the fixed stars to the elements that envelop the earth: and seven gates were marked, one for each planet, through which they pass, in descending or returning.

"We learn this from Celsus, in Origen; who says that the symbolic image of this passage among the Stars, used in the Mithriac Mysteries, was a ladder, reaching from earth to heaven, divided into seven steps or stages, to each of which was a gate, and at the summit an eighth, that of the fixed stars. The first gate, says Celsus, was that of Saturn, and of lead, by the heavy nature whereof his dull slow progress was symbolized. The second, of tin, was that of Venus, symbolizing her soft splendor and easy flexibility. The third, of brass, was that of Jupiter, emblem of his solidity and dry nature. The fourth, of iron, was that of Mercury, expressing his indefatigable activity and sagacity. The fifth, of copper, was that of Mars, expressive of his inequalities and variable nature. The sixth, of silver, was that of the Moon; and the seventh, of gold, that of the Sun. This order is not the real order of these Planets; but a mysterious one, like that of the days of the Week consecrated to them, commencing with Saturday, and *retrograding* to Sunday. It was dictated, Celsus says, by certain harmonic relations; those of the fourth.

"Thus there was an intimate connexion between the Sacred Science of the Mysteries, and ancient astronomy and physics; and the grand spectacle of the Sanctuaries was that of the order of the Known Universe, or the spectacle of nature itself, surrounding the soul of the initiate, as it surrounded it when it first descended through the planetary gates, and by the equinoctial and solstitial doors, along the Milky Way, to be for the first time immured in its prison-house of matter. But the mysteries also represented to the Candidate, by sensible symbols, the invisible forces which move this visible universe, and the virtues, qualities and powers attached to matter, and which maintain the marvellous order observed therein. Of this Porphyry informs us.

The world, according to the philosophers of antiquity, was not a purely material and mechanical machine. A great Soul, diffused everywhere, vivified all the members of the immense body of the universe; and an Intelligence, equally great, directed all its movements, and maintained the eternal harmony that resulted therefrom. Thus the Unity of the Universe, represented by the symbolic egg, contained in itself two unities, the Soul and the Intelligence, which pervaded all its parts; and they were to the Universe, considered as an animated and intelligent being, what intelligence and the soul of life are to the individuality of man.

The doctrine of the Unity of God, in this sense, was taught by Orpheus. Of this his hymn or palinode is a proof; fragments of which are quoted by many of the Fathers, as Justin, Tatian, Clemens of Alexandria, Cyril and Theodoret, and the whole by Eusebius, quoting from Aristobulus. The doctrine of the Logos (word) or the Noos (intellect), his incarnation, death, resurrection or transfiguration; of his union with matter, his division in the visible world, which he pervades, his return to the original Unity, and the whole theory relative to the origin of the soul and its destiny, were taught in the mysteries, of which they were the great object.

The Emperor Julian explains the Mysteries of Atys and Cybele by the same metaphysical principles, respecting the demiurgical Intelligence, its descent into matter, and its return to its origin: and extends this explanation to those of Ceres. And so likewise does Sallust the Philosopher, who admits in God a secondary intelligent Force, which descends into the generative matter to organize it. These mystical ideas naturally formed a part of the sacred doctrine and of the ceremonies of initiation, the object of which, Sallust remarks, was to unite man with the World and the Deity; and the final term of perfection whereof was, according to Clemens, the contemplation of nature, of real beings and of causes. The definition of Sallust is correct. The mysteries were practised as a means of perfecting the soul, of making it to know its own dignity, of reminding it of its noble origin and immortality, and consequently of its relations with the Universe and the Deity.

What was meant by *real* beings, was *invisible* beings, *genii*. the *faculties* or *powers* of nature; everything not a part of the *visible* world, which was called by way of opposition, *apparent* existence. The theory of Genii, or Powers of Nature, and its Forces, personified, made part of the Sacred Science of initiation, and of that religious spectacle of different beings exhibited in the Sanctuary. It resulted from that belief in the providence and superintendence of the Gods, which was one of the primary bases of initiation. The administration of the Universe by Subaltern Genii, to whom it is confided, and by whom good and evil are dispensed in the world, was a consequence of this dogma, taught in the Mysteries of Mithras, where was shown that famous egg, shared between Ormuzd and Ahriman, each of whom commissioned twenty-four Genii to dispense the good and evil found therein; they being under twelve Superior Gods, six on the side of Light and Good, and six on that of Darkness and Evil.

This doctrine of the Genii, depositaries of the Universal Providence, was intimately connected with the Ancient Mysteries, and adopted in the sacrifices and initiations both of Greeks and Barbarians. Plutarch says that the Gods, by means of Genii, who are intermediates between them and men, draw near to mortals in the ceremonies of initiation, at which the Gods charge them to assist, and to distribute punishment and blessing. Thus not the Deity, but his ministers, or a Principle and Power of Evil, were deemed the authors of vice and sin and suffering: and thus the Genii or angels differed in character like men, some being good and some evil; some Celestial Gods, Archangels, Angels, and some Infernal Gods, Demons and fallen Angels.

At the head of the latter was their Chief, Typhon, Ahriman or Shaitan, the Evil Principle; who, having wrought disorder in nature, brought troubles on men by land and sea, and caused the greatest ills, is at last punished for his crimes. It was these events and incidents, says Plutarch, which Isis desired to represent in the ceremonial of the mysteries, established by her in memory of her sorrows and wanderings, whereof she exhibited an image and representation in her Sanctuaries, where also were afforded encouragements to piety and consolation in misfortune. The dogma of a Providence, he says, administering the Universe by means of intermediary Powers, who maintain the connection of man with the Divinity, was consecrated in the mysteries of the Egyptians, Phrygians and Thracians, of the Magi and the Disciples of Zoroaster; as is plain by their initiations, in which mournful and funereal ceremonies mingled. It was an essential part of the lessons given the initiates, to teach them the relations of their own souls with Universal Nature, the greatest lessons of all, meant to dignify man in his own eyes, and teach him his place in the universe of things.

Thus the whole system of the Universe was displayed in all its parts to the eyes of the initiate; and the symbolic cave which represented it was adorned and clothed with all the attributes of that Universe. To this world so organized, endowed with a double force, active and passive, divided between light and darkness, moved by a living and intelligent Force, governed by Genii or Angels who preside over its different parts, and whose nature and character are more lofty or low in proportion as they possess a greater or less portion of dark matter, —to this world descends the soul, emanation of the ethereal fire, and exiled from the luminous region above the world. It enters into this dark matter, wherein the hostile Principles, each seconded by his troops of

Genii, are ever in conflict, there to submit to one or more organizations in the body which is its prison, until it shall at last return to its place of origin, its true native country from which during this life it is an exile.

But one thing remained,—to represent its return, through the constellations and planetary spheres, to its original home. The celestial fire, the philosophers said, soul of the world and of fire, an universal principle, circulating above the Heavens, in a region infinitely pure and wholly luminous, itself pure, simple and unmixed, is above the world by its specific lightness. If any part of it (say a human soul) descends, it acts against its nature in doing so, urged by an inconsiderate desire of the intelligence, a perfidious love for matter which causes it to descend, to know what passes here below, where good and evil are in conflict. The Soul, a simple substance, when unconnected with matter, a ray or particle of the Divine Fire, whose home is in Heaven, ever turns towards that home, while united with the body, and struggles to return thither.

Teaching this, the mysteries strove to recall man to his divine origin, and point out to him the means of returning thither. The great science acquired in the mysteries was knowledge of man's self, of the nobleness of his origin, the grandeur of his destiny, and his superiority over the animals, which can never acquire this knowledge, and whom he resembles so long as he does not reflect upon his existence and sound the depths of his own nature.

By doing and suffering, by virtue and piety and good deeds, the soul was enabled at length to free itself from the body and ascend, along the path of the Milky Way, by the gate of Capricorn and by the seven spheres, to the place whence by many gradations and successive lapses and enthralments it had descended. And thus the theory of the spheres, and of the signs and intelligences which preside there, and the whole system of astronomy were connected with that of the soul and its destiny; and so were taught in the mysteries, in which were developed the great principles of physics and metaphysics as to the origin of the soul, its condition here below, its destination and its future fate.

The Greeks fix the date of the establishment of the Mysteries of Eleusis at the year 1423 B. C., during the reign of Erechtheus at Athens. According to some authors, they were instituted by Ceres herself; and according to others, by that Monarch, who brought them from Egypt, where, according to Diodorus of Sicily, he was born. Another tradition was, that Orpheus introduced them into Greece, together with the Dionisiac ceremonies, copying the latter from the Mysteries of Osiris, and the former from those of Isis.

Nor was it at Athens only, that the worship and Mysteries of Isis, metamorphosed into Ceres, were established. The Bœotians worshipped the Great or Cabiric Ceres, in the recesses of a sacred grove, into which none but initiates could enter; and the ceremonies there observed, and the sacred traditions of their mysteries, were connected with those of the Cabiri in Samothrace.

So in Argos, Phocis, Arcadia, Achaia, Messenia, Corinth, and many other parts of Greece, the Mysteries were practised, revealing everywhere their Egyptian origin, and everywhere having the same general features; but those of Eleusis, in Attica, Pausanius informs us, had been regarded by the Greeks, from the earliest times, as being as far superior to all the others, as the Gods are to mere Heroes.

Similar to these were the Mysteries of Bona Dea, the Good Goddess, whose name, say Cicero and Plutarch, it was not permitted to any man to know, celebrated at Rome from the earliest times of that city. It was these Mysteries, practised by women alone, the secrecy of which was impiously violated by Clodius. They were held at the Kalends of May; and, according to Plutarch, much of the ceremonial greatly resembled that of the Mysteries of Bacchus.

The Mysteries of Venus and Adonis belonged principally to Syria and Phœnicia, whence they passed into Greece and Sicily. Venus or Astarte was the Great Female Deity of the Phœnicians, as Hercules, Melkarth or Adoni was their Chief God. Adoni, called by the Greeks Adonis, was the lover of Venus. Slain by a wound in the thigh inflicted by a wild boar in the chase, the flower called anemone sprang from his blood. Venus received the corpse, and obtained from Jupiter the boon that her lover should thereafter pass six months of each year with her, and the other six in the Shades with Proserpine; an allegorical description of the alternate residence of the Sun in the two hemispheres. In these Mysteries, his death was represented and mourned, and after this maceration and mourning were concluded, his resurrection and ascent to Heaven were announced.

Ezekiel speaks of the festivals of Adonis under the name of those of Thammuz, an Assyrian Deity whom every year the women mourned, seated at the doors of their dwellings. These Mysteries, like the others, were celebrated in the Spring, at the Vernal Equinox, when he was restored to life; at which time, when they were instituted, the Sun (ADON, Lord, or Master) was in the Sign Taurus, the domicile of Venus. He was represented with horns; and the hymn of Orpheus in his honour styles him "the two-horned God;" as in Argos Bacchus was represented with the feet of a bull.

Plutarch says that Adonis and Bacchus were regarded as one and the same Deity; and that this opinion was founded on the great similarity in very many respects between the Mysteries of these two Gods.

The Mysteries of Bacchus were known as the Sabazian, Orphic and Dionysiac Festivals. . They went back to the remotest antiquity among the Greeks, and were attributed by some to Bacchus himself, and by others to Orpheus. The resemblance in ceremonial between the observances established in honour of Osiris in Egypt, and those in honour of Bacchus in Greece, the mythological traditions of the two Gods, and the symbols used in the festivals of each, amply prove their identity. Neither the name of Bacchus, nor the word *orgies* applied to his feasts, nor the sacred words used in his mysteries, are Greek, but of foreign origin. Bacchus was an Oriental Deity, worshipped in the East, and his orgies celebrated there, long before the Greeks adopted them. In the earliest times he was worshipped in India, Arabia and Bactria.

He was honoured in Greece with public festivals, and in simple or complicated mysteries, varying in ceremonial in various places; as was natural, because his worship had come thither from different countries and at different periods. The people who celebrated the complicated mysteries were ignorant of the meaning of many words which they used, and of many emblems which they revered. In the Sabazian Feasts, for example [from Saba-Zeus, an oriental name of this Deity], the words EVOI, SABOI, were used, which are in nowise Greek; and a serpent of gold was thrown into the bosom of the initiate, in allusion to the fable that Jupiter had, in the form of a serpent, had connection with Proserpine, and begotten Bacchus, the Bull; whence the enigmatical saying, repeated to the initiates, that a bull engendered a dragon or serpent, and the serpent in turn engendered the bull, who became Bacchus: the meaning of which was, that the Bull (Taurus, which then opened the Vernal Equinox, and the Sun in which Sign, figuratively represented by the Sign itself, was Bacchus, Dionusos, Saba-Zeus, Osiris, &c.), and the Serpent, another constellation, occupied such relative positions in the Heavens, that when one rose the other set, and *vice versa*.

The serpent was a familiar symbol in the mysteries of Bacchus. The initiates grasped them with their hands, as Ophiucus does on the celestial globe: and the Orpheo-telestes, or Purifier of Candidates, did the same, crying, as Demosthenes taunted Eschines with doing in public at the head of the women whom his mother was to initiate, EVOI, SABOI, HYES, ATTÊ, ATTÊ, HYES!

The initiates in these mysteries had preserved the ritual and ceremonies that accorded with the simplicity of the earliest ages, and the manners of the first men. The rules of Pythagoras were followed there. Like the Egyptians, who held wool unclean, they buried no initiate in woollen garments. They abstained from bloody sacrifices; and lived on fruits or vegetables or inanimate things. They imitated the life of the contemplative Sects of the Orient; thus approximating to the tranquillity of the first men, who lived exempt from trouble and crimes in the bosom of a profound peace. One of the most precious advantages promised by their initiation was, to put man in communion with the Gods, by purifying his soul of all the passions that interfere with that enjoyment, and dim the rays of divine light that are communicated to every soul capable of receiving them, and that imitates their purity. One of the degrees of initiation was the state of inspiration to which the adepts were claimed to attain. The initiates in the mysteries of the Lamb, at Pepuza, in Phrygia, professed to be inspired, and prophesied: and it was claimed that the soul, by means of these religious ceremonies, purified of all stain, could see the Gods in this life, and certainly, in all cases, after death.

The sacred gates of the Temple, where the ceremonies of initiation were performed, were opened but once in each year, and no stranger was ever allowed to enter it. Night threw her veil over these august mysteries, which could be revealed to no one. There the sufferings of Bacchus were represented, who, like Osiris, died, descended to hell and rose to life again; and raw flesh was distributed to the initiates, which each ate, in memory of the death of the Deity, torn in pieces by the Titans.

These mysteries also were celebrated at the vernal equinox; and the emblem of generation, to express the active energy and generative power of the Divinity was a principal symbol. The initiates wore garlands and crowns of myrtle and laurel.

In these mysteries, the aspirant was kept in terror and darkness three days and nights; and was then made to perform the Αφανισμος, or ceremony representing the death of Bacchus, the same mythological personage with Osiris. This was effected by confining him in a close cell, that he might seriously reflect, in solitude and darkness, on the business he was engaged in; and his mind be prepared for the reception of the sublime and mysterious truths of primitive revelation and philosophy. This was a symbolic death; the deliverance from it, regeneration; after which he was called διφυης or twin-born. While confined in the cell, the pursuit of Typhon after the mangled body of Osiris, and the search of Rhea or Isis for the same, were enacted in his hearing; the initiated crying aloud the names of that Deity derived from the Sanscrit. Then it was announced that the body was found; and the aspirant was liberated amid shouts of joy and exultation.

Then he passed through a representation of Hell and Elysium. "Then," said an ancient writer, "they are entertained with hymns and dances, with the sublime doctrines of sacred knowledge, and with wonderful and holy visions. And now become perfect and initiated, they are FREE, and no longer under restraint; but, crowned and triumphant, they walk up and down the regions of the blessed, converse with pure and holy men, and celebrate the sacred mysteries at pleasure." They were taught the nature and objects of the mysteries, and the means of making themselves known, and received the name of *Epopts;* were fully instructed in the nature and attributes of the Divinity, and the doctrine of a future state; and made acquainted with the unity and attributes of the Grand Architect of the Universe, and the true meaning of the fables in regard to the Gods of Paganism: the great Truth being often proclaimed, that "Zeus is the primitive Source of all things; there is ONE God; ONE power, and ONE ruler over all." And after full explanation of the many symbols and emblems that surrounded them, they were dismissed with the barbarous words Κοyξ and Ομπαξ, corruptions of the Sanscrit words, *Kanska aum Pakscha;* meaning, *object of our wishes, God, Silence,* or *Worship the Deity in Silence.*

Among the emblems used was the rod of Bacchus; which once, it was said, he cast on the ground, and it became a serpent; and at another time he struck the rivers Orontes and Hydaspes with it, and the waters receded and he passed over dry-shod. Water was obtained, during the ceremonies, by striking a rock with it. The Bacchæ crowned their heads with serpents, carried them in vases and baskets, and at the Ευρησις, or finding, of the body of Osiris, cast one, alive, into the aspirant's bosom.

The Mysteries of Atys in Phrygia, and those of Cybele his mistress, like their worship, much resembled those of Adonis and Bacchus, Osiris and Isis. Their Asiatic origin is universally admitted, and was with great plausibility claimed by Phrygia, which contested the palm of antiquity with Egypt. They, more than any other people, mingled allegory with their religious worship, and were great inventors of fables; and their sacred traditions as to Cybele and Atys, whom all admit to be Phrygian Gods, were very various. In all, as we learn from Julius Firmicus, they represented by allegory the phenomena of nature, and the succession of physical facts, under the veil of a marvellous history.

Their feasts occurred at the equinoxes, commencing with lamentation, mourning, groans and pitiful cries for the death of Atys; and ending with rejoicings at his restoration to life.

We shall not recite the different versions of the legend of Atys and Cybele, given by Julius Firmicus, Diodorus, Arnobius, Lactantius, Servius, Saint Augustine and Pausanias. It is enough to say that it is in substance this: that Cybele, a Phrygian Princess, who invented musical instruments and dances, was enamoured of Atys, a youth; that either he in a fit of frenzy mutilated himself, or was mutilated by her in a paroxysm of jealousy; that he died, and afterwards, like Adonis, was restored to life. It is the Phœnician fiction as to the Sun-God, expressed in other terms, under other forms and with other names.

Cybele was worshipped in Syria, under the name of Rhea. Lucian says that the Lydian Atys there established her worship, and built her a temple. The name of Rhea is also found in the ancient cosmogony of the Phœnicians by Sanchoniathon. It was Atys the Lydian, says Lucian, who, having been mutilated, first established the Mysteries of Rhea, and taught the Phrygians, the Lydians and the people of Samothrace to celebrate them. Rhea, like Cybele, was represented drawn by lions, bearing a drum, and crowned with towers. According to Varro, Cybele represented the earth. She partook of the characteristics of Minerva, Venus, the

Moon, Diana, Nemesis and the Furies; was clad in precious stones; and her High Priest wore a robe of purple and a tiara of gold.

The Grand Feast of the Syrian Goddess, like that of the Mother of the Gods at Rome, was celebrated at the vernal equinox. Precisely at that equinox the Mysteries of Atys were celebrated, in which the initiates were taught to expect the rewards of a future life; and the flight of Atys from the jealous fury of Cybele was described, his concealment in the mountains and in a cave, and his self-mutilation in a fit of delirium; in which act his priests imitated him. The feast of the passion of Atys continued three days; the first of which was passed in mourning and tears; to which afterwards clamorous rejoicings succeeded; by which, Macrobius says, the Sun was adored under the name of Atys. The ceremonies were all allegorical, some of which, according to the Emperor Julian, could be explained, but more remained covered with the veil of mystery. Thus it is that symbols outlast their explanations, as many have done in Masonry, and ignorance and rashness substitute new ones.

In another legend, given by Pausanias, Atys dies, wounded like Adonis by a wild boar in the organs of generation; a mutilation with which all the legends ended. The pine-tree under which he was said to have died, was sacred to him; and was found upon many monuments, with a bull and a ram near it; one the sign of exaltation of the Sun, and the other of that of the Moon.

The worship of the Sun under the name of Mithras belonged to Persia, whence that name came, as did the erudite symbols of that worship. The Persians, adorers of Fire, regarded the Sun as the most brilliant abode of the fecundating energy of that element, which gives life to the earth, and circulates in every part of the universe, of which it is, as it were, the soul. This worship passed from Persia into Armenia, Cappadocia and Cilicia, long before it was known at Rome. The Mysteries of Mithras flourished more than any others in the imperial city. The worship of Mithras commenced to prevail there under Trajan. Adrian prohibited these Mysteries, on account of the cruel scenes represented in their ceremonial: for human victims were immolated therein, and the events of futurity looked for in their palpitating entrails. They reappeared in greater splendour than ever under Commodus, who with his own hand sacrificed a victim to Mithras: and they were still more practised under Constantine and his successors, when the Priests of Mithras were found everywhere in the Roman Empire, and the monuments of his worship appeared even in Britain.

Caves were consecrated to Mithras, in which were collected a multitude of astronomical emblems; and cruel tests were required of the initiates.

The Persians built no temples; but worshipped upon the summits of hills, in enclosures of unhewn stones. They abominated images, and made the Sun and Fire emblems of the Deity. The Jews borrowed this from them, and represented God as appearing to Abraham in a flame of fire, and to Moses as a fire at Horeb and on Sinai.

With the Persians, Mithras, typified in the Sun, was the invisible Deity, the Parent of the Universe, the Mediator. In Zoroaster's cave of initiation, the Sun and Planets were represented over-head, in gems and gold, as also was the Zodiac. The Sun appeared emerging from the back of Taurus. Three great pillars, Eternity, Fecundity and Authority, supported the roof; and the whole was an emblem of the universe.

Zoroaster, like Moses, claimed to have conversed face to face, as man with man, with the Deity; and to have received from him a system of pure worship, to be communicated only to the virtuous, and those who would devote themselves to the study of Philosophy. His fame spread over the world, and pupils came to him from every country. Even Pythagoras was his scholar.

After his novitiate, the candidate entered the cavern of initiation, and was received on the point of a sword presented to his naked left breast, by which he was slightly wounded. Being crowned with olive, anointed with balsam of benzoin, and otherwise prepared, he was purified with fire and water, and went through seven stages of initiation. The symbol of these stages was a high ladder with seven rounds or steps. In them, he went through many fearful trials, in which darkness played a principal part. He saw a representation of the wicked in Hades; and finally emerged from darkness into light. Received in a place representing Elysium, in the brilliant assembly of the initiated, where the Archimagus presided, robed in blue, he assumed the obligations of secrecy, and was entrusted with the Sacred Words, of which the Ineffable Name of God was the chief.

Then all the incidents of his initiation were explained to him: he was taught that these ceremonies brought him nearer the Deity; and that he should adore the consecrated Fire, the gift of that Deity and His visible residence. He was taught the sacred characters known only to the initiated; and instructed in regard to the creation of the world, and the true philosophical meaning of the vulgar mythology; and especially of the legend of Ormuzd and Ahriman, and the symbolic meaning of the six Amshaspands created by the former: *Bahman*, the Lord of Light; *Ardibehest*, the Genius of Fire; *Shariver*, the Lord of Splendour and Metals; *Stapandomad*, the Source of Fruitfulness; *Khadad*, the Genius of Water and Time; and *Amerdad*, the Protector of the Vegetable World, and the prime cause of growth. And finally he was taught the true nature of the Supreme Being, Creator of Ormuzd and Ahriman, the Absolute First Cause, styled ZERUANE AKHERENE.

In the Mithriac initiation were several degrees. The first, Tertullian says, was that of Soldier of Mithras. The ceremony of reception consisted in presenting the Candidate a crown, supported by a sword. It was placed near his head, and he repelled it, saying " Mithras is my crown." Then he was declared the soldier of Mithras, and had the right to call the other initiates fellow-soldiers, or companions in arms. Hence the title *Companions* in the Royal Arch Degree of the American Rite.

Then he passed, Porphyry says, through the degree of the Lion,—the constellation Leo, domicil of the Sun and symbol of Mithras, found on his monuments. These ceremonies were termed at Rome Leontic and Heliac; and *Coracia* or *Hiero-Coracia*, of the Raven, a bird consecrated to the Sun, and a sign placed in the Heavens below the Lion, with the Hydra, and also appearing on the Mithriac monuments.

Thence he passed to a higher degree, where the initiates were called *Perses* and children of the Sun. Above them were the *Fathers*, whose chief or Patriarch was styled Father of Fathers, or *Pater Patratus*. The initiates also bore the title of *Eagles* and *Hawks*, birds consecrated to the Sun in Egypt, the former sacred to the God Mendes, and the latter the emblem of the Sun and Royalty.

The little island of Samothrace was long the depository of certain august mysteries, and many went thither from all parts of Greece to be initiated. It was said to have been settled by the ancient Pelasgi, early Asiatic colonists in Greece. The Gods adored in the Mysteries of this island were termed CABIRI, an oriental word, from *Cabar*, great. Varro calls the Gods of Samothrace, *Potent Gods*. In Arabic, Venus is called *Cabar*. Varro says that the Great Deities whose mysteries were practised there, were Heaven and Earth. These were but symbols of the Active and Passive Powers or Principles of universal generation. The two Twins, Castor and Pollux, or the Dioscuri, were also called the Gods of Samothrace; and the Scholiast of Apollonius, citing Mnaseas, gives the names of Ceres, Proserpine, Pluto and Mercury, as the four Cabiric Divinities worshipped at Samothrace, as Axieros, Axiocersa, Axiocersus and Casmillus. Mercury was, there as everywhere, the minister and messenger of the Gods; and the young servitors of the altars, and the children employed in the Temples were called Mercuries or Casmilli; as they were in Tuscany, by the Etrusci and Pelasgi, who worshipped the Great Gods.

Tarquin the Etruscan was an initiate of the Mysteries of Samothrace; and Etruria had its Cabiri as Samothrace had. For the worship of the Cabiri spread from that island into Etruria, Phrygia and Asia Minor: and it probably came from Phœnicia into Samothrace: for the Cabiri are mentioned by Sanchoniathon; and the word *Cabar* belongs to the Hebrew, Phœnician and Arabic languages.

The Dioscuri, tutelary Deities of Navigation, with Venus, were invoked in the Mysteries of Samothrace. The constellation Auriga, or Phaëton, was also honoured there with imposing ceremonies. Upon the Argonautic expedition, Orpheus, an initiate of these Mysteries, a storm arising, counselled his companions to put into Samothrace. They did so, the storm ceased, and they were initiated into the Mysteries there, and sailed again with the assurance of a fortunate voyage, under the auspices of the Dioscuri, patrons of sailors and navigation.

But much more than that was promised the initiates. The Hierophants of Samothrace made something infinitely greater to be the object of their initiations; to wit, the consecration of men to the Deity, by pledging them to virtue; and the assurance of those rewards which the justice of the Gods reserve for initiates after death. This, above all else, made these ceremonies august, and inspired everywhere so great a respect for them, and so great a desire to be admitted to them. That originally caused the island to be styled *Sacred*. It was respected by all nations. The Romans, when masters of the world, left it its liberty and laws. It was

12D

an asylum for the unfortunate and a sanctuary inviolable. There men were absolved of the crime of homicide, if not committed in a temple.

Children of tender age were initiated there, and invested with the sacred robe, the purple cincture and the crown of olive, and seated upon a throne, like other initiates. In the ceremonies was represented the death of the youngest of the Cabiri, slain by his brothers, who fled into Etruria, carrying with them the chest or ark that contained his genitals: and there the Phallus and the sacred ark were adored. Herodotus says that the Samothracian initiates understood the object and origin of this reverence paid the Phallus, and why it was exhibited in the Mysteries. Clemens of Alexandria says that the Cabiri taught the Tuscans to revere it. It was consecrated at Heliopolis in Syria, where the Mysteries of a Divinity having many points of resemblance with Atys and Cybele were represented. The Pelasgi connected it with Mercury; and it appears on the monuments of Mithras; always and everywhere a symbol of the life-giving power of the Sun at the Vernal Equinox.

In the Indian Mysteries, as the Candidate made his three circuits, he paused each time he reached the South, and said, "I copy the example of the Sun, and follow his beneficent course." Blue Masonry has retained the Circuits, but has utterly lost the explanation; which is, that in the Mysteries the Candidate invariably represented the Sun, descending Southward towards the reign of the Evil Principle, Ahriman, Siva, or Typhon, (darkness and winter); there figuratively to be slain, and after a few days to rise again from the dead, and commence to ascend to the Northward.

Then the death of Sita was bewailed; or that of Cama, slain by Iswara, and committed to the waves on a chest, like Osiris and Bacchus; during which the Candidate was terrified by phantoms and horrid noises.

Then he was made to personify Vishnu, and perform his avatars, or labours. In the two first he was taught in allegories the legend of the Deluge: In the 1st he took three steps at right angles, representing the three huge steps taken by Vishnu in that avatar; and hence the three steps in the Master's degree, ending at right angles.

The nine avatars finished, he was taught the necessity of faith, as superior to sacrifices, acts of charity, or mortifications of the flesh. Then he was admonished against five crimes, and took a solemn obligation never to commit them. He was then introduced into a representation of Paradise; the Company of the Members of the Order, magnificently arrayed, and the Altar with a fire blazing upon it, as an emblem of the Deity.

Then a new name was given him, and he was invested in a white robe and tiara, and received the signs, tokens and lectures. A cross was marked on his forehead, and an inverted level, or the Tau Cross, on his breast. He received the sacred cord, and divers amulets or talismans; and was then invested with the sacred Word or Sublime Name, known only to the Initiated, the Triliteral A. U. M.

Then the multitude of emblems was explained to the Candidate; the arcana of science hidden under them, and the different virtues of which the mythological figures were mere personifications. And he thus learned the meaning of those symbols, which, to the uninitiated, were but a maze of unintelligible figures.

The third degree was a life of seclusion, after the Initiate's children were capable of providing for themselves; passed in the forest, in the practice of prayers and ablutions, and living only on vegetables. He was then said to be born again.

The fourth was absolute renunciation of the world, self-contemplation and self-torture; by which Perfection was thought to be attained, and the soul merged in the Deity.

In the second degree, the Initiate was taught the Unity of the Godhead, the happiness of the patriarchs, the destruction by the Deluge, the depravity of the heart and the necessity of a mediator, the instability of life, the final destruction of all created things, and the restoration of the world in a more perfect form. They inculcated the Eternity of the Soul, explained the meaning of the doctrine of the Metempsychosis, and held the doctrine of a state of future rewards and punishments: and they also earnestly urged that sins could only be atoned for by repentance, reformation and voluntary penance; and not by mere ceremonies and sacrifices.

The Mysteries among the Chinese and Japanese came from India, and were founded on the same principles and with similar rites. The word given to the new initiate was O-MI-TO Fo, in which we recognize the original name A. U. M., coupled at a much later time with that of Fo, the Indian Buddha, to show that he was the Great Deity himself.

The equilateral triangle was one of their symbols; and so was the mystical Y; both alluding to the Tri-une God, and the latter being the ineffable name of the Deity. A ring supported by two serpents was em-blematical of the world protected by the power and wisdom of the Creator; and that is the origin of the two parallel lines (into which time has changed the two serpents), that support the circle in our Lodges.

Among the Japanese, the term of probation for the highest degree was twenty years.

The main features of the Druidical Mysteries resembled those of the Orient.

The ceremonies commenced with a hymn to the sun. The candidates were arranged in ranks of *threes*, *fives* and *sevens*, according to their qualifications; and conducted nine times around the Sanctuary, from East to West. The Candidate underwent many trials, one of which had direct reference to the legend of Osiris. He was placed in a boat, and sent out to sea alone, having to rely on his own skill and presence of mind to reach the opposite shore in safety. The death of Hu was represented in his hearing, with every external mark of sorrow, while he was in utter darkness. He met with many obstacles, had to prove his courage, and expose his life against armed enemies; represented various animals, and at last, attaining the permanent light, he was instructed by the Arch-Druid in regard to the Mysteries, and in the morality of the Order, incited to act bravely in war, taught the great truths of the immortality of the soul and a future state, solemnly en-joined not to neglect the worship of the Deity, nor the practice of rigid morality; and to avoid sloth, conten-tion, and folly.

The aspirant attained only the exoteric knowledge in the two first degrees. The third was attained only by a few, and they persons of rank and consequence, and after long purification, and study of all the arts and sciences known to the Druids, in solitude, for nine months. This was the symbolical death and burial of these Mysteries.

The dangerous voyage upon the actual open sea, in a small boat covered with a skin, on the evening of the 29th of April, was the last trial, and closing scene, of initiation. If he declined this trial, he was dis-missed with contempt. If he made it and succeeded, he was termed thrice-born, was eligible to all the digni-ties of the State, and received complete instruction in the philosophical and religious doctrines of the Druids.

The Greeks also styled the Εποπτης, Τρυγογος, thrice-born; and in India perfection was assigned to the Yogee who had accomplished many births.

The general features of the Initiations among the Goths were the same as in all the mysteries. A long probation, of fasting and mortification, circular processions, representing the march of the celestial bodies, many fearful tests and trials, a descent into the infernal regions, the killing of the God *Balder* by the Evil Principle, *Lok*, the placing of his body in a boat and sending it abroad upon the waters; and, in short, the Eastern Legend, under different names, and with some variations.

The Egyptian Anubis appeared there, as the dog guarding the gates of death. The Candidate was immured in the representation of a tomb; and when released, goes in search of the body of Balder, and finds him, at length, restored to life, and seated upon a throne. He was obligated upon a naked sword, (as is still the custom in the *Rit Moderne*), and *sealed* his obligation by drinking mead *out of a human skull.*

Then all the ancient primitive truths were made known to him, so far as they had survived the assaults of time: and he was informed as to the generation of the Gods, the creation of the world, the deluge, and the resurrection, of which that of Balder was a type.

He was marked with the sign of the cross, and a ring was given to him as a symbol of the Divine Pro-tection; and also as an emblem of Perfection; from which comes the custom of giving a ring to the Aspirant in the 14th Degree.

The point within a Circle, and the Cube, emblem of Odin, were explained to him; and lastly, the nature of the Supreme God, " the author of everything that existeth, the Eternal, the Ancient, the Living and Awful Being, the Searcher into concealed things, the Being that never changeth;" with whom Odin the Conqueror was by the vulgar confounded: and the Tri-une God of the Indians was reproduced, as ODIN, the Almighty FATHER, FREA, (*Rhea* or *Phre*), his wife (emblem of universal *matter*), and *Thor* his son, (the Mediator).

Here we recognize *Osiris, Isis,* and *Hor* or *Horus.* Around the head of Thor, as if to show his eastern origin, twelve stars were arranged in a circle.

He was also taught the ultimate destruction of the world, and the rising of a new one, in which the brave and virtuous shall enjoy everlasting happiness and delight: as the means of securing which happy fortune, he was taught to practise the strictest morality and virtue.

The initiate was prepared to receive the great lessons of all the Mysteries, by long trials, or by abstinence and chastity. For many days he was required to fast and be continent, and to drink liquids calculated to diminish his passions and keep him chaste.

Ablutions were also required, symbolical of the purity necessary to enable the soul to escape from its bondage in matter. Sacred baths and preparatory baptisms were used, lustrations, immersions, lustral sprinklings, and purifications of every kind. At Athens they bathed in the Ilissus, which thence became a sacred river; and before entering the Temple of Eleusis, all were required to wash their hands in a vase of lustral water placed near the entrance. Clean hands and a pure heart were required of the Candidates. Apuleius bathed seven times in the sea, symbolical of the Seven Spheres through which the Soul must re-ascend: and the Hindus must bathe in the sacred river Ganges.

Clemens of Alexandria cites a passage of Menander, who speaks of a purification by sprinkling three times with salt and water. Sulphur, resin and the laurel also served for purification, as did air, earth, water and fire. The initiates at Heliopolis, in Syria, says Lucian, sacrificed the sacred lamb, symbol of Aries, then the sign of the Vernal Equinox; ate his flesh, as the Israelites did at the Passover; and then touched his head and feet to theirs, and knelt upon the fleece. Then they bathed in warm water, drank of the same, and slept upon the ground.

There was a distinction between the lesser and greater mysteries. One must have been for some years admitted to the former, before he could receive the latter, which were but a preparation for them, the Vestibule of the Temple, of which those of Eleusis were the Sanctuary. There, in the lesser mysteries, they were prepared to receive the holy truths taught in the greater. The initiates in the lesser were called simply *Mystes,* or Initiates; but those in the greater, *Epoptes,* or Seers. An ancient poet says that the former were an imperfect shadow of the latter, as sleep is of Death. After admission to the former, the initiate was taught lessons of morality, and the rudiments of the sacred science, the most sublime and secret part of which was reserved for the Epopt, who saw the Truth in its nakedness, while the Mystes only viewed it through a veil and under emblems fitter to excite than to satisfy his curiosity.

Before communicating the first secrets and primary dogmas of initiation, the priests required the Candidate to take a fearful oath never to divulge the secrets. Then he made his vows, prayers and sacrifices to the Gods. The skins of the victims consecrated to Jupiter were spread on the ground, and he was made to set his feet upon them. He was then taught some enigmatic formulas, as answers to questions, by which to make himself known. He was then enthroned, invested with a purple cincture, and crowned with flowers, or branches of palm or olive.

We do not certainly know the time that was required to elapse between the admission to the Lesser and Greater Mysteries of Eleusis. Most writers fix it at five years. It was a singular mark of favour when Demetrius was made Mystes and Epopt in one and the same ceremony. When at length admitted to the degree of perfection, the initiate was brought face to face with entire nature, and learned that the soul was the whole of man; that earth was but his place of exile; that Heaven was his native country; that for the soul, to be born is really to die; and that death was for it the return to a new life. Then he entered the sanctuary; but he did not receive the whole instruction at once. It continued through several years. There were, as it were, many apartments, through which he advanced by degrees, and between which thick veils intervened. There were Statues and Paintings, says Proclus, in the inmost sanctuary, showing the forms assumed by the Gods. Finally the last veil fell, the sacred covering dropped from the image of the Goddess, and she stood revealed in all her splendour, surrounded by a divine light, which, filling the whole sanctuary, dazzled the eyes and penetrated the soul of the initiate. Thus is symbolized the final revelation of the true doctrine as to the nature of Deity and of the soul, and of the relations of each to matter.

This was preceded by frightful scenes, alternations of fear and joy, of light and darkness; by glittering lightning and the crash of thunder, and apparitions of spectres, or magical illusions, impressing at once the eyes and ears. This Claudian describes, in his poem on the rape of Proserpine, where he alludes to what passed in her mysteries. "The temple is shaken," he cries; "fiercely gleams the lightning, by which the Deity announces his presence. Earth trembles; and a terrible noise is heard in the midst of these terrors. The Temple of the Son of Cecrops resounds with long-continued roars; Eleusis uplifts her sacred torches; the serpents of Triptolemus are heard to hiss; and fearful Hecate appears afar."

The celebration of the Greek Mysteries continued, according to the better opinion, for nine days.

On the first, the initiates met. It was the day of the full moon, of the month Boëdromion; when the moon was full at the end of the sign Aries, near the Pleiades and the place of her exaltation in Taurus.

The second day, there was a procession to the sea, for purification by bathing.

The third was occupied with offerings, expiatory sacrifices and other religious rites, such as fasting, mourning, continence, &c. A mullet was immolated, and offerings of grain and living animals made.

On the fourth, they carried in procession the mystic wreath of flowers, representing that which Proserpine dropped when seized by Pluto, and the Crown of Ariadne in the Heavens. It was borne on a triumphal car drawn by oxen; and women followed bearing mystic chests or boxes, wrapped with purple cloths, containing grains of sesame, pyramidal biscuits, salt, pomegranates and the mysterious serpent, and perhaps the mystic phallus.

On the fifth, was the superb procession of torches, commemorative of the search for Proserpine by Ceres; the initiates marching by trios, and each bearing a torch; while at the head of the procession marched the Dadoukos.

The sixth was consecrated to Iacchus, the young Light-God, son of Ceres, reared in the sanctuaries and bearing the torch of the Sun-God. The chorus in Aristophanes terms him the luminous star that lights the nocturnal initiation. He was brought from the sanctuary, his head crowned with myrtle, and borne from the gate of the Ceramicus to Eleusis, along the sacred way, amid dances, sacred songs, every mark of joy, and mystic cries of *Iacchus*.

On the seventh there were gymnastic exercises and combats, the victors in which were crowned and rewarded.

On the eighth was the feast of Æsculapius.

On the ninth the famous libation was made for the souls of the departed. The Priests, according to Athenæus, filled two vases, placed one in the East and one in the West, towards the gates of day and night, and overturned them, pronouncing a formula of mysterious prayers. Thus they invoked Light and Darkness, the two great principles of nature.

During all these days no one could be arrested, nor any suit brought, on pain of death, or at least a heavy fine: and no one was allowed, by the display of unusual wealth or magnificence, to endeavour to rival this sacred pomp. Everything was for religion.

Such were the Mysteries; and such the Old Thought, as in scattered and widely separated fragments it has come down to us. The human mind still speculates upon the great mysteries of nature, and still finds its ideas anticipated by the ancients, whose profoundest thoughts are to be looked for, not in their philosophies, but in their symbols, by which they endeavoured to express the great ideas that vainly struggled for utterance in words, as they viewed the great circle of phenomena,—Birth, Life, Death or Decomposition, and New Life out of Death and Rottenness,—to them the greatest of mysteries. Remember, while you study their symbols, that they had a profounder sense of these wonders than we have. To them the transformations of the worm were a greater wonder than the stars; and hence the poor dumb scarabæus or beetle was sacred to them. Thus their faiths are condensed into symbols or expanded into allegories, which they understood, but were not always able to explain in language; for there are thoughts and ideas which no language ever spoken by man has words to express.

Thus ends the instruction of this Degree; and we reserve the further explanation of the symbols and ceremonies of the Mysteries, especially as connected with astronomy, for the next Degree.

TO CLOSE.

Th∴ P∴ Puissant Warden in the West, what is the hour?

1st W∴ Th∴ P∴, it is time for the evening sacrifice.

Th∴ P∴ Puissant Warden in the North, Prince Ahli-Ab, what tidings hast thou in the North?

3d W∴ Th∴ Puissant, Balder, slain by Lok, has arisen from the dead; and the nations of the North rejoice, for the long nights of winter grow shorter.

Th∴ P∴ Puissant Warden in the South, Prince Betsel-Al, what tidings hast thou in the South?

2d W∴ Th∴ Puissant, Osiris slain by Typhon is restored to life; and the dwellers on the banks of the Nile are glad, for light begins to prevail against darkness.

Th∴ P∴ Puissant Warden in the West, Excellent High Priest, what tidings hast thou in the West?

1st W∴ Th∴ Puissant, Hu, slain by Ceridwen and cast upon the stormy waters, is again alive; and the people of the Western Islands celebrate the winter solstice, and the triumph of the Powers of Light over those of Darkness.

Th∴ P∴ And so everywhere the Principle of Good prevails over that of Evil, and men rejoice. My Brethren, the fast is over, and the feasts commence. It is time to close this Assembly of Princes of the Tabernacle. Assist me, my Brethren, to do so, by giving me the sign of closing.

[The sign is given; the Th∴ P∴ raps [: ,]—each Warden in succession the same—and the Th∴ P∴ declares the Assembly closed.]

Twenty-Fifth Degree.

Knight of the Brazen Serpent.

THE LODGE: ITS DECORATIONS, ETC.

The Lodge, in this Degree, is styled *The Council;* and represents that held near Mount Sinai; when the New Moon occurred at the Vernal Equinox, in the last year of the journeying of the children of Israel in the desert. The hangings are red and blue. In the East is a throne, over which is a transparency; and on that is painted a burning bush, having in its centre the word יהוה. Besides this transparency, the Lodge has seven lights, extending from East to West, and the centre one being a great globular light in the centre of the room, representing the sun. The other lights are of wax, three on each side of the central light; and over the seven are suspended the following emblems, arranged from East to West: . . ♄ . . . ♃ . . . ♂ : . . ☉ . . . ♀ . . ☿ . . . ☽ . . . that is, . . . SATURN, JUPITER, MARS, THE SUN, VENUS, MERCURY, THE MOON. Around the Lodge are twelve columns, each having on its capital one of the zodiacal signs, commencing in the East with Taurus, and going round by the North, West and South in regular order.

In the North is a painting, representing Mount Sinai, with the tents of the Hebrews in the foreground. The Lodge is supposed to be in the open air, at daybreak, in front of the tent of Moses, where he gave audience to the people who came to prefer their complaints and grievances. The arched ceiling overhead should represent the morning sky.

Over the seat of the Presiding Officer is a winged globe encircled by a Serpent: and on each side of him is a short column on which is a Serpent, his body coiled in folds, and his head and neck erect above the folds.

The Presiding Officer represents MOSES and OSIRIS, and is styled *Most Potent Leader.* He sits in the East. The Senior Warden represents JOSHUA and HORUS, and sits on his right. The Junior Warden represents CALEB, or ANUBIS, and sits in the West. He is styled *Lieutenant Commander,* and the Sen∴ Warden, *Commander of the Host.* The Orator is styled *High Priest,* represents ELEAZAR and ORION, and sits in the South. The Secretary is styled *Register,* and sits on the right of Joshua. The Treasurer sits on the left of the Presiding officer. The Sen∴ Deacon is styled *Examiner,* and the Junior Deacon, *Archer.*

The order is a crimson ribbon, on which are embroidered the words, one under the other, . . OSIRIS . . ORMUZD ∴ OSARSIPH . . MOSES . . and under them a Bull, with a disk, surmounted by a crescent, between his horns. This is worn from left to right: and across it, from right to left, is worn a broad, white, watered ribbon; on which are the words . . ISIS . : CERES . . over a dog's head and a crescent. On the right breast, on the left breast, and at the crossing of these orders is a star of gold. Under that on the right breast is the letter A∴ [for *Aldebaran*]: under that on the left breast the letter A∴ [for *Antares*]: and under that at the crossing of the orders, the letter F∴ [for *Fomalhaut*]. On the crimson cordon is the word גבורה [GBURH—*Valor*]; and on the white, און [AUN—*Virtus*] . . meaning *Active* Energy, or *Generative* power, and Passive Energy or *Capacity to produce.*

The jewel is a Tau Cross surmounted by a circle,—the *Crux Ansata,*—round which a serpent is entwined.

On the cross is engraved the word חלתי [KnaLaTI; *He has suffered or been wounded*], on the upright part of the cross : and on the arms the word נחשתן, [NεKnuSnTaN . . the brazen serpent].

The apron is white, lined and edged with black; the white side spotted with golden stars, and the black side with silver ones. Those on the white side represent, by their positions and distances, the *Pleiades*, the *Hyades*, *Orion* and *Capella*. Those on the black side represent the stars of *Perseus*, *Scorpio* and *Bootes*. In the middle of the white side is a triangle in a glory, in the centre of which is the word יהוה. On the flap is a serpent in a circle, with his tail in his mouth, and in the centre of the circle so formed, a scarabæus or beetle. Over this is a star of gold, with the letter R∴ [*Regulus*] over it: on the right side of the apron another, with the letter A∴ [*Aldebaran*] over it; on the left side another, with the letter A∴ [*Antares*] over it: and at the bottom of the apron another, with the letter F∴ [*Fomalhaut*] over it.

The battery is z — by ‖ slow ; quick and ,

TO OPEN.

M∴P∴ Brethren, Princes of the Tabernacle and Knights of the Brazen Serpent, if the day and the hour have arrived, I propose to open here a Council of Knights of the Brazen Serpent, for mutual instruction and the performance of the necessary duties. Be clothed; and await, each in his place or station, the customary orders.

[The brethren are clothed, and the officers assume their stations].

M∴P∴ Bro∴ Examiner, it is our first duty to see that we are secure from intrusion. See that the guards are set, and inform them that we are about to open this Council, that they may keep watch and ward as they should do.

Sen∴D∴ Bro∴ Archer, set the guards without the doors of the Council, and advise them that it is about to be opened; that they may keep watch and ward as they should do, and allow none who are not entitled to approach.

[The Archer goes out, returns, gives the alarm of the degree, which is answered from without, and reports]:

Jun∴D∴ Most Respectable Examiner, the guards are posted, and duly informed as to their duties, and we are secure against intrusion.

Sen∴D∴ M∴ Potent Leader, the guards are posted, and duly informed as to their duties; and we are secure against intrusion.

M∴P∴ Bro∴ Lt∴ Commander, are all present Knights of the Brazen Serpent? Be certain of that, by receiving the pass-word from each.

[The Jun∴ Warden goes round, receives the pass-word from each Brother, returns to his place, and says] :

Jun∴W∴ M∴P∴ Leader, all present have the Pass-word, and I recognize them as Knights of the Brazen Serpent.

M∴P∴ Thanks, my Brother! Bro∴ Commander of the Host, what is the hour?

Sen∴W∴ Most Potent Leader, it is the break of day, of the morning of the Vernal Equinox. The God-like child sits upon the waters in the gates of the Orient, not yet arisen; while the Earth awaits to rejoice at the blessing of his smiles. The Circle surmounted by the Crescent shines in the Heavens; and in the sign of the Celestial Bull, House of Venus and place of the Moon's Exaltation, the Sun, mighty with a new life, and the New Moon are in conjunction, and open the New Year and the Chaldean Saros: while, blushing and reluctant, the beautiful Star Amalthea rises with the Sun in the East.

M∴P∴ If that be the hour, it is time to open this Council. Whom does our brother Eleazar represent here ?

Sen∴W∴ Orion, whom Zoroaster dying invoked; on whose shoulders glitter Bellatrix and Betelgueux, Rigel at his feet, and in his belt three Kingly Stars, known of old time to mariner and husbandman: Orion, visible to all the habitable world; who follows the Celestial Bull, and with him comes to the Meridian, ever in vain pursuit, enamored of Merope, who with her sister Pleiads ever flees before her ardent lover.

M∴ P∴ Whom does our brother Caleb represent here?

Sen∴ W∴ SIRIUS, called by the Egyptians ANUBIS and SOTHIS, and by the Hebrews CALEB ANUBACH; who, as the Sun enters the Celestial Bull and meets the joyous Pleiades, sweet Virgins of the Spring, rises with the King of Day, and doubles the activity of his fires and his solstitial ardour; who, rising with Cancer, will at the Summer Solstice bring enervating heat, fever and hydrophobia, and the Etesian winds; and with his setting, sharp cold, and frosts, wrinkling earth's haggard face, and chilling the blood in all her ancient veins.

M∴ P∴ And whom do you, my Brother, represent here?

Sen∴ W∴ HORUS, the son of Isis and Osiris; before whom Typhon the Malignant Serpent of the Northern Pole and Power of Evil flees aghast, and sinks in the dark Western Ocean, as Aldebaran leads the starry armies of Heaven up the sky's eastern slope, and the dogs of Orion climb upward, straining at the leash, while the foul Scorpion shudders on the world's western edge, and hears the loud bay of Orion's hounds, Sirius and Procyon, urging her to the fatal plunge.

M∴ P∴ Whom does the Most Potent Leader represent?

Sen∴ W∴ OSIRIS, King of the Starry influences of Light and Life; ORMUZD, Great Principle of Good; ATYS, ADONIS, DIONUSOS, BACCHUS, APOLLO;—all Deities that in all ages have represented with most feeble expression the Divine Source of good, the Eternal, Infinite, Incomprehensible, Father of Light and Life.

M∴ P∴ Alas! I am his most feeble and inconsiderable creature; and even as I am, so is the Sun of Spring, that the Ancients deemed a God and the Source of life and generation; and so were Osiris, Ormuzd, Atys, Saba-Zeus, Bel and Amun, and all the mighty Deities imagined by those who watched the stars in Ethiopia and Egypt, on the Chaldean plains and upon the slopes of the Himalayan Mountains. I am but a poor, feeble, erring, fallible man, who need your aid, my brethren, your countenance, your encouragement, your counsel, to enable me to perform aright the duties that here devolve upon me. Bro∴ Com∴ of the Host, are you a Knight of the Brazen Serpent?

Sen∴ W∴ M∴ Potent, I know the meaning of the Cross around which twines the Serpent, and of the coiled basilisc.

M∴ P∴ Where obtained you that degree?

Sen∴ W∴ In a legal Council of Knights of the Brazen Serpent, held in a place representing the open space in front of the Tent of Moses near Mount Sinai.

M∴ P∴ When was the first Council of Knights of the Brazen Serpent held?

Ans∴ In the fortieth year of the journeying of the people of Israel, at the Vernal Equinox, when the days of Moses were almost an hundred and twenty years, and the end of his pilgrimage drew nigh; and when the people of Israel murmured and complained that he had brought them up from Egypt to die there in the wilderness.

Qu∴ At what hour?

Ans∴ At the first dawn of day; when Aldebaran, preceded by Orion and his dogs, led up the glittering host of Heaven in the East, and Capella gleamed also on the Eastern margin of the Desert; while low in the West Antares shone malignant, and Fomalhaut in the South looked calmly on the land of Canaan:—when the people were gathering the manna, and the cloud still rested on the Tabernacle.

Qu∴ What are our duties, as Knights of the Brazen Serpent?

Ans∴ To purify the soul of its alloy of earthliness, that through the gate of Capricorn and the seven spheres it may at length ascend to its eternal home beyond the Stars; and to preserve and perpetuate the great truths enveloped in the symbols and allegories of the Ancient Mysteries.

M∴ P∴ That we may perform these duties, Valiant Commander of the Host, it is my pleasure that this Council be now opened. This you will make known to the Exc∴ Lt∴ Commander, and he to the Knights, that all may have due notice.

Sen∴ W∴ Exc∴ Lt∴ Commander, it is the pleasure of the M∴ Potent Leader, that this Council be now opened, in order that the duties incumbent upon us here may be performed. This you will make known to the Knights, that they, having due notice, may aid in opening the same.

Jun∴ W∴ [Rapping;] Knights and Masons, you will be pleased to give due attention, while the M∴ Potent Leader with our aid opens this Council; that we may here proceed to perform the duties that devolve upon us.

M∴ P∴ Let the Seven Mystic Lights dispel the darkness of the Council!

[The Jun∴ Warden lights in succession the three lights on the West of the Central Light, saying, as he lights each, beginning on the West, as follows]:

Jun∴ W∴ The Moon shines in our Council; and over it presides the Archangel Tsapu-Al, the messenger of God:

———Mercury shines in our Council; and over it presides the Archangel Repu-Al, the Healing Influence of God:

———Venus shines in our Council; and over it presides the Archangel Kumali-Al, the Merciful Kindness of God.

[The Sen∴ Warden then lights in succession the three lights on the East of the Central Light, saying, as he lights each, beginning in the East, as follows]:

Sen∴ W∴ Saturn shines in our Council; and over it presides the Archangel Micu-Al, the Semblance and Image of God:

———Jupiter shines in our Council; and over it presides the Archangel Gedir-Al, the Strength and Mightiness of God:

———Mars shines in our Council; and over it presides the Archangel Auri-Al, the Light and Fire of God,

[Then the M∴ P∴ advances and lights the Central Light, saying]:

M∴ P∴ The Sun, the newly risen Osiris, the beneficent Ormuzd, Type of the Principle of Good and Light, and feeble and imperfect image of the Deity, shines in our Council; and over it presides the Archangel Zerekhi-Al, the Rising of God, the Sun of Righteousness.

[Then the M∴ P∴ returns to his place, and says, "The Sign, my Brethren!" All give the sign: then the M∴ P∴ raps ‖ slow —; quick and , — and each Warden does the same in succession; and the M∴ P∴ declares the Council to be duly opened].

RECEPTION.

The Candidate is prepared in the ante-room, by being dressed in a plain garb, without insignia or jewel, and loaded with chains.

The Examiner (having first satisfied himself as to his proficiency in the preceding degrees), accompanies him to the door of the Lodge, and gives the alarm [‖ slow —; quick — and ,]; which is answered by one rap from within, and the Archer opens the door and asks,

Arch∴ Who comes here, and upon what mission?

Exam∴ One of the people of Israel, to announce to the M∴ P∴ Leader a great misfortune that has befallen the people; and to implore at his hands relief and assistance.

Arch∴ Who is the applicant, and by what right does he claim admission here?

Ex∴ Eliab, the son of Pallu, of the Tribe of Reuben; loaded with chains, in token of the penitence of the People, who flee in terror before the venomous springing serpents that Adonai hath sent to punish them.

[The Archer directs the Candidate to wait a time, until the Most Potent Leader is informed of his request, closes the door, and reports to the Lt∴ Commander, who reports to the M∴ Potent, who directs that the applicant be admitted. He enters, and is led up in front of the M∴ P∴, where he kneels, and the Examiner answers for him].

M∴ P∴ Who art thou that comest thus, loaded with chains?

Ex∴ Eliab, of the Tribe of Reuben, sent in behalf of the People, who dare not come before you, Adonai being angered with them.

M∴ P∴ Ah! disobedient and stiff-necked race! How have they again tempted His anger?

Ex∴ M∴ Potent Leader, the soul of the People was much discouraged, because of the way, journeying from Mount Hor, by the way of the Red Sea, to compass the land of Edom; and coming hither unto Punon, they spake against Adonai, calling him the Power of Evil, and against you, saying: "Why hath Al-Schedi and his servant Moses brought us up out of Egypt, to die in the wilderness? There is no bread, nor any water, and our souls loathe this unsubstantial manna. We go to and fro, lo! now almost these forty years, and as Aaron, who gave back to us the worship of the celestial Bull hath died in the Desert, so also shall we all die here. Let us put trust in Adonai no longer; but let us call on the Great Gods Amun and Astarte, Osiris and Isis, to deliver us from this bondage of misery." And as they cried aloud on those Gods, and many among them invoked Typhon, the Power of Darkness and Evil, lo! Adonai sent venomous springing serpents among them, who dart upon the people, curling round and biting them, and by their venom much people of Israel hath already died. And those that remain have repented, and say "We have sinned; for we have spoken against Adonai and his servant Moses." And they said unto me, "Put heavy chains upon thy neck in token of our penitence, and go for us unto Moses our Leader, and beseech him to pray unto Adonai that he take away the serpents from us;" and I have done as they desired.

M∴ P∴ Hast thou also murmured, and called upon the false Gods of the Egyptians and Phœnicians?

Ex∴ Because I refused, and withstood the people, and rebuked them in the name of Adonai, Lord of Tsbauth, they sought to slay me; but repenting they sent me hither, because I had not sinned like them.

M∴ P∴ Thou hast done well, arise! Relieve him of his chains, and give him a seat of honour; for that he hath not forgotten his duty to his God. And ye, my Brethren, remain here with patience, until I pray unto the God of Israel again to forgive and save his People that he hath chosen.

[The M∴ P∴, who represents a very feeble old man, rises, assisted by two brethren, and is absent for a time. When he returns, he brings with him a serpent of brass entwined round a Tau Cross, with his head elevated above it: and after taking his seat, he says]:

M∴ P∴ I have prayed for the People, and Adonai hath said unto me, "Make thee an image of a venomous springing serpent, and set it upon a pole; and it shall come to pass that every one that is bitten, when he looketh upon it, shall live." Take thou therefore, Eleazar the High Priest, this Serpent and Cross, and place it upon a pole, and set in the middle of the camp; and make proclamation that those who look upon it, confessing their sins, and having faith in the Most High God, though they have been bitten by the venomous springing serpents, shall not die, but live; for Adonai is AL-KHANAN, the God of Mercy.

[Eleazar takes the serpent, and goes out. After a time he returns and says]:

Orator: . . M∴ Potent Leader, great is ADONAI, AL-KHANAN, the God of Mercy! for he hath had mercy on His People Israel: and every one that hath beheld the serpent, owning his sin and doing homage to the Most High, is healed, and liveth; and the plague of the serpent is stayed.

M∴ P∴ Praise ye the Lord, ADONAI, AL יהרה L'AL ALIUN, my children, the Supporter of the Heavens and the Earth!—for He is Great, and His mercy endureth forever, and He hath forgiven His people Israel.

———The plague of Serpents is stayed; and as they have fled to their caves in the rocks, so the Celestial Serpent flees, with the Scorpion, before the glittering stars of Orion. The great festival of the vernal equinox approaches, my Brethren, and it is time to prepare ourselves by purification for the passover. Light will soon prevail once more over darkness; and the pulses of life again beat in the bosom of earth, long chilled by the wintry frosts. My brethren, what signs indicate the approach of the Great Festival?

Com∴ of H∴ The twenty-seven stars of the Husbandman, by the mystic numbers, one, two, and three, have disappeared during the glancings of the Dawn. The Celestial Ram, clear in the East at the morning twilight, announces the approaching entry of the Great Light of Heaven into Taurus; and the Celestial Twins, chief Cabiri of Samothrace and Gods of Mariners, plunged in the solar fires, accompany the sun across the upper Heavens, and go down with him into the dark bosom of the waters when he sets.

Lt∴ Com∴ The Pleiades prepare to lead up the Sabæan year: the Heavenly Watchers, Succoth-Beneth, Virgins of Spring and daughters of Atlas and Hesperia, whose lost sister, wedded to a mortal lover, weeps with dishevelled hair, afar off in the Heavens.

Orator: . . The Sun, flushed with victory, and marching towards the Celestial Lion of the Summer Solstice, will to-morrow meet the new Moon in the Sign of the Celestial Bull, and Earth will rejoice and thrill with happiness through all her veins and arteries, at the new life which the fortunate conjunction promises. To-morrow with him will rise the Pleïades, and the rainy Hyades, in whose van marches the brilliant Aldebaran, Leader of all the Heavenly armies.

Com∴ of H∴. With him will rise Orion's Dogs,—Sothis, the Star of Isis, whose light glitters many-coloured, like that of the diamond, and whom Ormuzd set over the celestial host; and Procyon, both straining at the leash up the blue slope of Heaven; and behind them Orion, known to the Assyrians as Nimrod, who taught mortals the chase and to worship the eternal fire: Orion, before whom Perseus far to the westward flees; and who with his bright stars glittering on his shoulders and in his belt will unite with Horus, and rising heliacally with the Celestial Bull, will conquer Typhon, and plunge him in the dark western ocean over which ever broods eternal night.

M∴ P∴. Thus shall Osiris conquer Typhon, and Ormuzd, Ahriman. Thus again, in the ever-revolving circle of change, shall the Empire of Light prevail against that of Darkness, and the Principle of Evil flee before the Principle of Good. And evermore through the bright gate of Capricorn shall the souls of men ascend to their old starry home; until the final victory of Light, when Winter and Darkness and Evil shall be no more forever; but in all God's universe, as now among the stars that circle around His Throne in solemn harmony, eternal Light, undying Happiness, and everlasting Spring. Therefore, my children, prepare by continence and fasting and the proper purifications, as the soul is prepared to ascend to Heaven, for the Great Festival of the Passover, which and the opening spring it celebrates are types to us and to all initiates of the Sacred Mysteries, of that eternal spring of Light and Happiness, which God has promised, and for which we humbly but confidently hope.

Lt∴ Com∴. Most Potent, what shall be done with the brazen image of the Serpent and the Cross, which thou didst cause to be set up before the people?

M∴ P∴. I give it you, my Brethren, that it may be evermore a symbol of Faith, Repentance and Mercy; which are the great mysteries of man's destiny. And lest the knowledge of its true symbolic meaning should be lost, and the people of Israel should hereafter, following the example of the Egyptians and Phœnicians, imagine this mere emblem and symbol of healing and divination to be a Divinity, and invent for it a history, and make of it a new God, as they are ever prone to do, ye shall perpetuate the remembrance of this day's occurrences, and the true meaning of the Serpent and the Cross, and of our other symbols, and of the fables of Osiris and Ormuzd, as a part and the last degree of those Sacred Mysteries which Joseph, the son of Jacob, like myself, learned from the Egyptians; and which I have taught to you, such as our forefathers, before the days of Abraham and the Pharaohs, practised them upon the plains of Chaldea.

———Kneel, therefore, my children, and with me swear, in the presence of the Most High God, faithfully to keep and perpetuate the true meaning thereof, and the secrets of the last degree of these our Mysteries; and to teach and practise the virtues which our symbols illustrate and represent.

[All kneel, including the Candidate; and all repeat the following]

OBLIGATION.

I do solemnly promise and swear, before the Most High God, by His names, ADONAI, Lord of Heaven and Earth, and AL-KHANAN, a God full of Mercy and Compassion, that I will never reveal the secrets of this Degree of Knight of the Brazen Serpent, nor by my presence aid in revealing them, to any person who shall not be entitled to receive them, by having passed through all the previous degrees of the Ancient and Accepted Rite; nor without due authority lawfully obtained.

I furthermore promise and swear that I will perpetuate the true meaning of the Tau Cross entwined with a Serpent, and of the other symbols of Masonry, and of the ancient fables of Osiris and Ormuzd, so far as I may be capable of doing so; and will prevent them, if in my power, from being the occasion of the worship of new idols and images, visible or mental.

I furthermore promise and swear that I will at all times earnestly endeavour to practise all the virtues which the symbols of Masonry represent and illustrate; and repenting of my sins, my errors and my vices, I will strive to reform whatever in my conduct and conversation may be amiss.

And should I wilfully and knowingly fail or neglect to keep and perform any part of this my obligation, I consent to be deemed unworthy of Divine mercy or human kindness; and that the fiery serpents of remorse and an accusing conscience shall torture me forever. So help me God, and aid me to keep these promises!

[The M.·. P.·. then takes his seat, and says]:

M.·. P.·. My son Eliab, approach and receive the Signs, Words and Tokens of this Degree.

[The Candidate is caused to approach the East by *z* serpentine steps, advancing first the right foot; and the M.·. Potent then communicates to him the Signs, Words and Tokens].

Due-Guard: . . . ♀♒↥†♀♒☾ the &☾☉♊, and with the forefinger §☿ ♀♒♈‡☉♈ some object on the ♌‡☿♑♒♊ . . . or, ☾♉♈☾♒♊ the ‡&☉♒♊ and ☉‡♋ to a distance before you, looking forward, as if descrying some object afar off, and §☿ ♀♒♈♀♒♌‡♈☿‡♀♈.

1st Sign: . . . Place the †♃‡♀♎♈ in the ‡&☉♒♊, forming a ↥‡☿♎: they lay ♏☿♈& on the ♎♈☿♋☉↥& and ♏☿♃.

2d Sign: . . . Place the †&☉♒♊ over the &☾☉‡♈, inclining the ♏☿♊♄ to the same side, as if you ♑☾†♈ a ♎&☉‡§ §☉♀♒ there.

3d Sign: . . . Make the ♎♀♌♒ of the ↥‡☿♎ on ♄☿♑‡♎☾†♑, as a ↥☉♈&☿†♀↥ does.

Token: . . . Place yourself upon the right of the person to be examined, and take his †♃‡♀♎♈ with your †&☉♒♊.

Answer: . . . He takes your ‡♃‡♀♎♈ with his ‡&☉♒♊.

2d Token: . . . ↥†☾♒↥& the ♑♀♒♌☾‡♎ of each other's &☉♒♊♎, and put the ♈&♑♋♏♎ against each other, so as to form a ♈‡♀☉♒♌†☾.

Pass-word: . . . ¶&☉†☉♈♀.·.

Sacred Word: . . . ☉†-¶&☉♒☉♒.·.

[The M.·. Potent then invests the Candidate with the apron, collar and jewel of the Degree, saying]:

M.·. P.·. I now accept and receive you a Knight of the Brazen Serpent; and I invest you with the apron, collar and jewel of the Degree. Their blazonry, so far as you do not already understand it, will be fully explained in the lecture of this Degree, which you will receive from the Brother Orator, to whose seat you will now repair.

LECTURE.

My Brother, we have represented before you the incidents upon which this Degree was founded; and you understand its objects and purposes. It is both philosophical and moral. While it teaches the necessity of reformation as well as repentance, as a means of obtaining mercy and forgiveness, it is also devoted to an explanation of the symbols of Masonry: and especially to those which are connected with that ancient and universal legend, of which that of Hiram Abi is but a variation; that legend which, representing a murder or a death, and a restoration to life, by a drama in which figure Osiris, Isis and Horus, Atys and Cybele, Adonis and Venus, the Cabiri, Dionusos, and many another representative of the active and passive Powers of Nature, taught the initiates in the Mysteries that the rule of Evil and Darkness is but temporary, and that that of Light and Good will be eternal.

Maimonides says: "In the days of Enos, the son of Seth, men fell into grievous errors, and even Enos himself partook of their infatuation. Their language was, that since God has placed on high the heavenly bodies, and used them as his ministers, it was evidently his will, that they should receive from man the same veneration as the servants of a great prince justly claim from the subject multitude. Impressed with this notion, they began to build temples to the Stars, to sacrifice to them, and to worship them, in the vain expectation that they should thus please the Creator of all things. At first, indeed, they did not suppose the Stars to be the only Deities, but adored in conjunction with them the Lord God Omnipotent. In process of time, however, that great and venerable Name was totally forgotten, and the whole human race retained no other religion than the idolatrous worship of the Host of Heaven."

The first learning in the world consisted chiefly in symbols. The wisdom of the Chaldeans, Phœnicians, Egyptians, Jews; of Zoroaster, Sanchoniathon, Pherecydes, Syrus, Pythagoras, Socrates, Plato, of all the ancients, that is come to our hand, is symbolic. It was the mode, says Serranus on Plato's Symposium, of the Ancient Philosophers, to represent truth by certain symbols, and hidden images.

"All that can be said concerning the Gods," says Strabo, "must be by the exposition of old opinions and fables: it being the custom of the ancients to wrap up in enigma and allegory their thoughts and discourses concerning Nature; which are therefore not easily explained."

As you learned in the 24th Degree, my brother, the ancient philosophers regarded the soul of man as having had its origin in Heaven. That was, Macrobius says, a settled opinion among them all; and they held it to be the only true wisdom, for the soul, while united with the body, to look ever towards its source, and strive to return to the place whence it came. Among the fixed stars it dwelt, until, seduced by the desire of animating a body, it descended to be imprisoned in matter. Thenceforward it has no other resource than recollection, and is ever attracted towards its birth-place and home. The means of return are to be sought for in itself. To re-ascend to its source, it must do and suffer in the body.

Thus the mysteries taught the great doctrine of the divine nature and longings after immortality of the soul, of the nobility of its origin, the grandeur of its destiny, its superiority over the animals who have no aspirations Heavenward. If they struggled in vain to express its *nature*, by comparing it to Fire and Light,— if they erred as to its original place of abode, and the mode of its descent, and the path which, descending and ascending, it pursued among the stars and spheres, these were the accessories of the Great Truth, and mere allegories designed to make the idea more impressive and as it were tangible, to the human mind.

Let us, in order to understand this old Thought, first follow the soul in its descent. The sphere or Heaven of the fixed stars was that Holy Region, and those Elysian Fields, that were the native domicil of souls, and the place to which they re-ascended, when they had recovered their primitive purity and simplicity. From that luminous region the soul set forth, when it journeyed towards the body; a destination which it did not reach until it had undergone three degradations, designated by the name of Deaths; and until it had passed through the several spheres and the elements. All souls remained in possession of Heaven and of happiness, so long as they were wise enough to avoid the contagion of the body, and to keep themselves from any contact with matter. But those who, from that lofty abode, where they were lapped in eternal light, have looked longingly towards the body, and towards that which we here below call *life*, but which is to the soul a real death; and who have conceived for it a secret desire,—those souls, victims of their concupiscence, are attracted by degrees towards the inferior regions of the world, by the mere weight of the thought and of that terrestrial desire. The soul, perfectly incorporeal, does not at once invest itself with the gross envelope of the body, but little by little, by successive and insensible alterations, and in proportion as it removes further and further from the simple and perfect substance in which it dwelt at first. It first surrounds itself with a body composed of the substance of the stars; and afterwards, as it descends through the several spheres, with ethereal matter more and more gross, thus by degrees descending to an earthly body; and its number of degradations or deaths being the same as that of the spheres which it traverses.

The Galaxy, Macrobius says, crosses the zodiac in two opposite points, Cancer and Capricorn, the tropical points in the sun's course, ordinarily called the Gates of the Sun. These two tropics, before his time, corresponded with those constellations, but in his day with Gemini and Sagittarius, in consequence of the precession of the equinoxes; but the *signs* of the Zodiac remained unchanged; and the Milky Way crossed at the *signs* Cancer and Capricorn, though not at those *constellations*.

Through these *gates* souls were supposed to descend to earth and re-ascend to Heaven. One, Macrobius says, in his Dream of Scipio, was styled the Gate of Men; and the other, the Gate of the Gods. Cancer was the former, because souls descended by it to the earth; and Capricorn the latter, because by it they re-ascended to their seats of immortality, and became Gods. From the Milky Way, according to Pythagoras, diverged the route to the dominions of Pluto. Until they left the Galaxy, they were not deemed to have commenced to descend towards the terrestrial bodies. From that they departed, and to that they returned. Until they reached the sign Cancer, they had not left it, and were still Gods. When they reached Leo, they commenced their apprenticeship for their future condition; and when they were at Aquarius, the sign opposite Leo, they were furthest removed from human life.

The soul, descending from the celestial limits, where the Zodiac and Galaxy unite, loses its spherical shape, the shape of all Divine Nature, and is lengthened into a cone, as a point is lengthened into a line; and then, an indivisible monad before, it divides itself and becomes a duad—that is, unity becomes division, disturbance and conflict. Then it begins to experience the disorder which reigns in matter, to which it unites itself, becoming as it were intoxicated by draughts of grosser matter; of which inebriation the cup of Bacchus, between Cancer and Leo, is a symbol. It is for them the cup of forgetfulness. They assemble, says Plato, in the fields of oblivion, to drink there the water of the river Ameles, which causes men to forget everything. This fiction is also found in Virgil. "If souls," says Macrobius, "carried with them into the bodies they occupy all the knowledge which they had acquired of divine things, during their sojourn in the Heavens, men would not differ in opinion as to the Deity; but some of them forget more, and some less, of that which they had learned."

We smile at these notions of the ancients; but we must learn to look through these material images and allegories, to the ideas, struggling for utterance, the great speechless thoughts which they envelope: and it is well for us to consider whether we ourselves have yet found out any *better* way of representing to ourselves the soul's origin and its advent into this body, so entirely foreign to it; if, indeed, we have ever thought about it at all; or have not ceased to think, in despair.

The highest and purest portion of matter, which nourishes and constitutes divine existences, is what the poets term *nectar*, the beverage of the Gods. The lower, more disturbed and grosser portion, is what intoxicates souls. The ancients symbolized it as the River Lethe, dark stream of oblivion. How do *we* explain the soul's forgetfulness of its antecedents, or reconcile that utter absence of remembrance of its former condition, with its essential immortality. In truth, we for the most part dread and shrink from any attempt at explanation of it to ourselves.

Dragged down by the heaviness produced by this inebriating draught, the soul falls along the zodiac and the milky way, to the lower spheres, and in its descent not only takes, in each sphere, a new envelope of the material composing the luminous bodies of the planets, but receives there the different faculties which it is to exercise while it inhabits the body.

In Saturn, it acquires the power of reasoning and intelligence, or what is termed the logical and contemplative faculty. From Jupiter it receives the power of action. Mars gives it valour, enterprise and impetuosity. From the Sun it receives the senses and imagination, which produce sensation, perception and thought. Venus inspires it with desires. Mercury gives it the faculty of expressing and enunciating what it thinks and feels. And, on entering the sphere of the Moon, it acquires the force of generation and growth. This lunary sphere, lowest and basest to Divine bodies, is first and highest to terrestrial bodies. And the lunary body there assumed by the soul, while as it were the sediment of celestial matter, is also the first substance of animal matter.

The celestial bodies, Heaven, the Stars and the other Divine elements, ever aspire to rise. The soul, reaching the region which mortality inhabits, tends towards terrestrial bodies, and is deemed to die. Let no one, says Macrobius, be surprised that we so frequently speak of the *death* of this soul, which yet we call immortal. It is neither annulled nor destroyed by such death; but merely enfeebled for a time; and does not thereby forfeit its prerogative of immortality; for afterwards, freed from the body, when it has been purified from the vice-stains contracted during that connection, it is re-established in all its privileges, and returns to the luminous abode of its immortality.

On its return, it restores to each sphere through which it ascends, the passions and earthly faculties received from them: to the Moon, the faculty of increase and diminution of the body; to Mercury, fraud, the architect of evils; to Venus, the seductive love of pleasure; to the Sun, the passion for greatness and empire; to Mars, audacity and temerity; to Jupiter, avarice; and to Saturn, falsehood and deceit: and at last, relieved of all, it enters naked and pure into the eighth sphere or highest Heaven.

All this agrees with the doctrine of Plato, that the soul cannot re-enter into Heaven, until the revolutions of the universe shall have restored it to its primitive condition, and purified it from the effects of its contact with the four elements.

This opinion of the pre-existence of souls, as pure and celestial substances, before their union with our bodies, to put on and animate which they descend from Heaven, is one of great antiquity. A modern Rabbi, Manasseh Ben Israel, says it was always the belief of the Hebrews. It was that of most philosophers who admitted the immortality of the soul: and therefore it was taught in the Mysteries; for, as Lactantius says, they could not see how it was possible that the soul should exist *after* the body, if it had not existed *before* it, and if its nature was not independent of that of the body. The same doctrine was adopted by the most learned of the Greek Fathers, and by many of the Latins; and it would probably prevail largely at the present day, if men troubled themselves to think upon this subject at all, and to inquire whether the soul's immortality involved its prior existence.

Some philosophers held that the soul was incarcerated in the body, by way of punishment for sins committed by it in a prior state. How they reconciled this with the same soul's unconsciousness of any such prior state, or of sin committed there, does not appear. Others held that God, of his mere will, sent the soul to inhabit the body. The Kabbalists united the two opinions. They held that there are four worlds, *Aziluth, Briarth, Jezirath* and *Aziath ;* the world of *emanation,* that of *creation,* that of *forms,* and the *material* world; one above and more perfect than the other, in that order, both as regards their own nature and that of the beings who inhabit them. All souls are originally in the world Aziluth, the Supreme Heaven, abode of God and of pure and immortal spirits. Those who descend from it without fault of their own, by God's order, are gifted with a divine fire, which preserves them from the contagion of matter, and restores them to Heaven so soon as their mission is ended. Those who descend through their own fault, go from world to world, insensibly losing their love of Divine things, and their self-contemplation; until they reach the world Aziath, falling by their own weight. This is a pure Platonism, clothed with the images and words peculiar to the Kabbalists. It was the doctrine of the Essenes, who, says Porphyry "believe that souls descend from the most subtile ether, attracted to bodies by the seductions of matter." It was in substance the doctrine of Origen ; and it came from the Chaldeans, who largely studied the theory of the Heavens, the spheres, and the influences of the signs and constellations.

The Gnostics made souls ascend and descend through eight Heavens, in each of which were certain Powers that opposed their return, and often drove them back to earth, when not sufficiently purified. The last of these Powers, nearest the luminous abode of souls, was a serpent or dragon.

In the ancient doctrine, certain genii were charged with the duty of conducting souls to the bodies destined to receive them, and of withdrawing them from those bodies. According to Plutarch, these were the functions of Proserpine and Mercury. In Plato, a familiar genius accompanies man at his birth, follows and watches him all his life, and at death conducts him to the tribunal of the Great Judge. These genii are the media of communication between man and the Gods ; and the soul is ever in their presence. This doctrine is taught in the oracles of Zoroaster: and these Genii were the Intelligences that resided in the planets.

Thus the secret science and mysterious emblems of initiation were connected with the Heavens, the Spheres and the Constellations: and this connection must be studied by whomsoever would understand the ancient mind, and be enabled to interpret the allegories, and explore the meaning of the symbols, in which the old sages endeavoured to delineate the ideas that struggled within them for utterance, and could be but insufficiently and inadequately expressed by language, whose words are images of those things alone that can be grasped by and are within the empire of the senses.

It is not possible for us thoroughly to appreciate the feelings with which the ancients regarded the Heavenly bodies, and the ideas to which their observation of the Heavens gave rise; because we cannot put ourselves in their places, look at the stars with their eyes in the world's youth, and divest ourselves of the knowledge which even the commonest of us have, that makes us regard the Stars and Planets and all the Universe of Suns and Worlds, as a mere inanimate machine and aggregate of senseless orbs, no more astonishing except in degree, than a clock or an orrery. *We* wonder and are amazed at the Power and Wisdom, (to most men it seems only a kind of Infinite *Ingenuity*), of the MAKER: *they* wondered at the *Work*, and endowed *it* with Life and Force and mysterious Powers and mighty Influences.

Memphis, in Egypt, was in Latitude 29° 5″ North, and in Longitude 30° 18′ East. Thebæ, in Upper Egypt, in Latitude 25° 45′ North, and Longitude 32° 43′ East. Babylon was in Latitude 32° 30′ North, and Longitude 44° 23′ East: while Saba, the ancient Sabæan capital of Ethiopia, was about in Latitude 15° North.

Through Egypt ran the great River Nile, coming from beyond Ethiopia, its source in regions wholly unknown, in the abodes of heat and fire, and its course from South to North. Its inundations had formed the alluvial lands of Upper and Lower Egypt, which they continued to raise higher and higher, and to fertilize by their deposits. At first, as in all newly-settled countries, those inundations, occurring annually and always at the same period of the year, were calamities: until, by means of levees and drains and artificial lakes for irrigation, they became blessings, and were looked for with joyful anticipation, as they had before been awaited with terror. Upon the deposit left by the Sacred River, as it withdrew into its banks, the husbandman sowed his seed; and the rich soil and the genial sun ensured him an abundant harvest.

Babylon lay on the Euphrates, which ran from Southeast to Northwest, blessing, as all rivers in the Orient do, the arid country through which it flowed; but its rapid and uncertain overflows bringing terror and disaster.

To the ancients, as yet inventors of no astronomical instruments, and looking at the Heavens with the eyes of children, this earth was a level plain of unknown extent. About its boundaries there was speculation, but no knowledge. The inequalities of its surface were the irregularities of a plane. That it was a globe, or that anything lived on its under surface, or on what it rested, they had no idea. Every twenty-four hours the sun came up from beyond the Eastern rim of the world, and travelled across the sky, over the earth, always South of, but sometimes nearer and sometimes further from the point overhead; and sunk below the world's Western rim. With him went light, and after him followed darkness.

And every twenty-four hours appeared in the Heavens another body, visible chiefly at night, but sometimes even when the sun shone, which likewise, as if following the sun at a greater or less distance, travelled across the sky; sometimes as a thin crescent, and thence increasing to a full orb resplendent with silver light; and sometimes more and sometimes less to the Southward of the point overhead, within the same limits as the Sun.

Man, enveloped by the thick darkness of profoundest night, when everything around him has disappeared, and he seems alone with himself and the black shades that surround him, feels his existence a blank and nothingness, except so far as memory recalls to him the glories and splendours of light. Everything is dead to him, and he, as it were, to Nature. How crushing and overwhelming the thought, the fear, the dread, that *perhaps*, that darkness may be eternal, and that day may possibly never return; if it ever occurs to his mind, while the solid gloom closes up against him like a wall! What then can restore him to life, to energy, to activity, to fellowship and communion with the great world which God has spread around him, and which perhaps in the darkness may be passing away? LIGHT restores him to himself and to nature which seemed lost to him. Naturally, therefore, the primitive men regarded light as the principle of their real existence, without which life would be but one continued weariness and despair. This necessity for light, and its actual creative energy, were felt by all men: and nothing was more alarming to them than its absence. It became their first Divinity, a single ray of which, flashing into the dark tumultuous bosom of chaos, caused man and all the universe to emerge from it. So all the poets sung who imagined Cosmogonies; such was the first dogma of Orpheus, Moses and the Theologians. Light was Ormuzd, adored by the Persians, and Darkness Ahriman, origin of all evils. Light was the life of the universe, the friend of man, the substance of the Gods and of the Soul.

14D

. The sky was to them a great solid concave arch; a hemisphere of unknown material, at an unknown distance above the flat level earth; and along it journeyed in their courses the Sun, the Moon, the Planets and the Stars.

The Sun was to them a great globe of fire, of unknown dimensions, at an unknown distance. The Moon was a mass of softer light; the stars and planets lucent bodies, armed with unknown and supernatural influences.

. It could not fail to be soon observed, that at regular intervals the days and nights were equal; and that two of these intervals measured the same space of time as elapsed between the successive inundations, and between the returns of spring-time and harvest. Nor could it fail to be perceived that the changes of the moon occurred regularly; the same number of days always elapsing between the first appearance of her silver crescent in the West at evening and that of her full orb rising in the East at the same hour : and the same again, between that and the new appearance of the crescent in the West.

. It was also soon observed that the Sun crossed the Heavens in a different line each day, the days being longest and the nights shortest when the line of his passage was furthest North, and the days shortest and nights longest when that line was furthest South; that his progress North and South was perfectly regular, marking four periods that were always the same,—those when the days and nights were equal, or the Vernal and Autumnal Equinoxes: that when the days were longest, or the Summer Solstice; and that when they were shortest, or the Winter Solstice.

With the Vernal Equinox, or about the 25th of March of our Calendar, they found that there unerringly came soft winds, the return of warmth, caused by the Sun turning back to the northward from the middle ground of his course, the vegetation of the new year, and the impulse to amatory action on the part of the animal creation. Then the Bull and the Ram, animals most valuable to the agriculturist, and symbols themselves of vigorous generative power, recovered their vigor, the birds mated and builded their nests, the seeds germinated, the grass grew, and the trees put forth leaves. With the Summer Solstice, when the Sun reached the extreme northern limit of his course, came great heat, and burning winds, and lassitude and exhaustion ; then vegetation withered, man longed for the cool breezes of Spring and Autumn and the cool water of the wintry Nile or Euphrates, and the Lion sought for that element far from his home in the desert.

With the Autumnal Equinox came ripe harvests, and fruits of the tree and vine, and falling leaves, and cold evenings presaging wintry frosts ; and the Principle and Powers of Darkness, prevailing over those of Light, drove the Sun further to the South, so that the nights grew longer than the days. And at the Winter Solstice the earth was wrinkled with frost, the trees were leafless, and the Sun reaching the most Southern point in his career, seemed to hesitate whether to continue descending, to leave the world to darkness and despair, or to turn upon his steps and retrace his course to the Northward, bringing back seed-time and spring, and green leaves and flowers and all the delights of love.

Thus, naturally and necessarily, time was divided, first into days, and then into moons or months, and years; and with these divisions and the movements of the Heavenly bodies that marked them, were associated and connected all men's physical enjoyments and privations. Wholly agricultural, and in their frail habitations greatly at the mercy of the elements and the changing seasons, the primitive people of the Orient were . most deeply interested in the recurrence of the periodical phenomena presented by the two great luminaries of Heaven, on whose regularity all their prosperity depended.

And the attentive observer soon noticed that the smaller lights of Heaven were, apparently, even more regular than the Sun and Moon, and foretold with unerring certainty, by their risings and settings, the periods of recurrence of the different phenomena and seasons on which the physical well-being of all men depended. They soon felt the necessity of distinguishing the individual stars or groups of stars, and giving them names, that they might understand each other, when referring to and designating them. Necessity produced designations at once natural and artificial. Observing that, in the circle of the year, the renewal and periodical appearance of the productions of the earth were constantly associated, not only with the courses of the Sun, but also with the rising and setting of certain Stars, and with their position relatively to the Sun, the centre to which they referred the whole starry host, the mind naturally connected the celestial and terrestrial objects that were *in fact* connected; and they commenced by giving to particular Stars or groups of Stars the names of those terrestrial objects which seemed connected with them; and for those which still remained unnamed by this nomenclature, they, to complete a system, assumed arbitrary and fanciful names.

Thus the Ethiopian of Thebes or Saba styled those Stars under which the Nile commenced to overflow, Stars of Inundation, or that *poured out water* [Aquarius].

Those Stars among which the Sun was, when he had reached the Northern Tropic and began to *retreat* Southward, were termed, from his retrograde motion, the Crab (Cancer).

As he approached, in Autumn, the middle point between the Northern and Southern extremes of his journeying, the days and nights became equal; and the Stars among which he was then found, were called Stars of the Balance (Libra).

. Those Stars among which the Sun was, when the Lion, driven from the Desert by thirst, came to slake it at the Nile, were called Stars of the Lion (Leo).

Those among which the Sun was at harvest, were called those of the Gleaning Virgin, holding a Sheaf of Wheat (Virgo).

Those among which he was found in February, when the Ewes brought their young, were called Stars of the Lamb (Aries).

Those in March, when it was time to plough, were called Stars of the Ox (Taurus).

Those under which hot and burning winds came from the desert, venomous like poisonous reptiles, were called Stars of the Scorpion (Scorpio).

Observing that the annual return of the rising of the Nile was always accompanied by the appearance of a beautiful Star, which at that period showed itself in the direction of the sources of that river, and seemed to warn the husbandman to be careful not to be surprised by the inundation, the Ethiopian compared this act of that Star to that of the Animal which by barking gives warning of danger, and styled it the Dog (Sirius).

Thus commencing, and as astronomy came to be more studied, imaginary figures were traced all over the Heavens, to which the different Stars were assigned. Chief among them were those that lay along the path which the Sun travelled as he climbed towards the North and descended to the South: lying within certain limits and extending to an equal distance on each side of the line of equal nights and days. This belt, curving like a Serpent, was termed the Zodiac, and divided into twelve Signs.

At the vernal equinox, 2455 years before our Era, the Sun was entering the sign and constellation Taurus, or the Bull; having passed through, since he commenced, at the Winter Solstice, to ascend Northward, the Signs Aquarius, Pisces and Aries; on entering the first of which he reached the lowest limit of his journey Southward.

From Taurus, he passed through Gemini and Cancer, and reached Leo when he arrived at the terminus of his journey Northward. Thence through Leo, Virgo and Libra he entered Scorpio at the Autumnal Equinox, and journeyed Southward through Scorpio, Sagittarius and Capricornus to Aquarius, the terminus of his journey South.

The path by which he journeyed through these signs, became the *Ecliptic;* and that which passes through the two equinoxes, the *Equator.*

They knew nothing of the immutable laws of nature; and whenever the Sun commenced to tend Southward, they feared lest he might continue to do so, and by degrees disappear forever, leaving the earth to be ruled forever by darkness, storm and cold.

Hence they rejoiced when he commenced to re-ascend after the Winter Solstice, struggling against the malign influences of Aquarius and Pisces, and amicably received by the Lamb. And when at the Vernal Equinox he entered Taurus, they still more rejoiced at the assurance that the days would again be longer than the nights, that the season of seed-time had come, and the Summer and harvest would follow.

And they lamented when, after the Autumnal Equinox, the malign influence of the venomous Scorpion, the vindictive Archer and the filthy and ill-omened He-Goat dragged him down towards the Winter Solstice.

Arriving there, they said he had been slain, and had gone to the realm of darkness. Remaining there three days, he rose again, and again ascended Northward in the heavens; to redeem the earth from the gloom and darkness of Winter, which soon became emblematical of sin and evil and suffering; as the Spring, Summer and Autumn became emblems of happiness and immortality.

Soon they personified the Sun, and worshipped him under the name of Osiris, and transmuted the legend of his descent among the Winter Signs, into a fable of his death, his descent into the infernal regions, and his resurrection.

The Moon became Isis, the wife of Osiris; and winter, as well as the desert or the ocean into which the Sun descended, became Typhon, the Spirit or Principle of Evil, warring against and destroying Osiris.

From the journey of the Sun through the twelve signs came the legend of the twelve labours of Hercules, and the incarnations of Vishnu and Bouddha. Hence came the legend of the murder of Hiram Abi, representative of the Sun, by the three fellow-crafts, symbols of the three winter signs, Capricornus, Aquarius and Pisces, who assailed him at the three gates of Heaven and slew him at the winter solstice. Hence the search for him by the nine fellow-crafts, the other nine signs, his finding, burial and resurrection.

The Celestial Taurus, opening the new year, was the Creative Bull of the Hindús and Japanese, breaking with his horn the egg out of which the world is born. Hence the bull Apis was worshipped by the Egyptians, and reproduced as a golden calf by Aaron in the desert. Hence the cow was sacred to the Hindús. Hence, from the sacred and beneficent signs of Taurus and Leo, the human-headed winged lions and bulls in the palaces at Kouyounjik and Nimroud, like which were the Cherubim set by Solomon in his Temple: and hence the twelve brazen or bronze oxen, on which the laver of brass was supported.

The Celestial Vulture or Eagle, rising and setting with the Scorpion, was substituted in its place, in many cases, on account of the malign influences of the latter: and thus the four great periods of the year were marked by the Bull, the Lion, the Man (Aquarius) and the Eagle; which were upon the respective standards of Ephraim, Judah, Reuben and Dan; and still appear on the shield of American Royal Arch Masonry.

Afterwards the Ram or Lamb became an object of adoration, when, in his turn, he opened the equinox, to deliver the world from the wintry reign of darkness and evil.

Around the central and simple idea of the annual death and resurrection of the Sun, a multitude of circumstantial details soon clustered. Some were derived from other astronomical phenomena; while many were merely poetical ornaments and inventions.

Besides the Sun and Moon, those ancients also saw a beautiful Star, shining with a soft, silvery light, always following the Sun at no great distance when he set, or preceding him when he rose. Another of a red and angry colour, and still another more kingly and brilliant than all, early attracted their attention, by their free movements among the fixed hosts of Heaven: and the latter by his unusual brilliancy, and the regularity with which he rose and set. These were Venus, Mars and Jupiter. Mercury and Saturn could scarcely have been noticed in the world's infancy, or until astronomy began to assume the proportions of a science.

In the projection of the celestial sphere by the astronomical priests, the zodiac and constellations, arranged in a circle, presented their halves' in diametrical opposition; and the hemisphere of winter was said to be adverse, opposed, contrary, to that of summer. Over the angels of the latter ruled a king (Osiris or Ormuzd), enlightened, intelligent, creative and beneficent. Over the fallen angels or evil genii of the former, the demons or Devs of the subterranean empire of darkness and sorrow, and its stars, ruled also a chief. In Egypt the Scorpion first ruled, the sign next the Balance, and long the chief of the winter signs; and then the Polar Bear or Ass, called Typhon, that is, deluge, on account of the rains which inundated the earth while that constellation domineered. In Persia, at a later day, it was the Serpent, which, personified as Ahriman, was the Evil Principle of the religion of Zoroaster.

The Sun does not arrive at the same moment in each year at the equinoctial point on the equator. The explanation of his anticipating that point belongs to the science of astronomy; and to that we refer you for it. The consequence is, what is termed the precession of the equinoxes, by means of which the Sun is constantly changing his place in the zodiac, at each vernal equinox; so that now, the signs retaining the names which they had 300 years before Christ, they and the constellations do not correspond; the Sun being now in the constellation Pisces, when he is in the sign Aries.

The annual amount of precession is 50 seconds and a little over [50" 1.]. The period of a complete Revolution of the Equinoxes, 25,856 years. The precession amounts to 30° or a sign, in 2155.6 years. So that, as the sun now enters Pisces at the Vernal Equinox, he entered Aries at that period, 300 years B. C., and Taurus 2455 B. C. And the division of the Ecliptic, now *called* Taurus, lies in the Constellation Aries ; while the *sign* Gemini is in the *Constellation* Taurus. Four thousand six hundred and ten years before Christ, the sun entered Gemini at the Vernal Equinox.

At the two periods, 2455 and 300 years before Christ, and now, the entrances of the sun at the Equinoxes and Solstices into the signs, were and are as follows :

B. C. 2455.

Vern. Equinox, he entered Taurus . . .	from Aries.
Summer Solstice . . . Leo	from Cancer.
Autumnal Equinox . . Scorpio . . .	from Libra.
Winter Solstice . . . Aquarius . .	from Capricornus.

B. C. 300.

Vern. Eq. . . . . . Aries	from Pisces.
Summer Sols. . . . . Cancer . . .	from Gemini.
Autumn. Eq. . . . . . Libra	from Virgo.
Winter Sol. . . . . . Capricornus . .	from Sagittarius.

1856.

Vern. Eq. . . . . . Pisces	from Aquarius.
Sum. Sols. . . . . . Gemini . . .	from Taurus.
Aut. Eq. . . . . . . Virgo	from Leo.
Winter Solst. . . . . Sagittarius . .	from Scorpio.

From confounding *signs* with *causes* came the worship of the sun and stars. "If," says Job, "I beheld the sun when it shined, or the moon progressive in brightness ; and my heart hath been secretly enticed, or my mouth hath kissed my hand, this were an iniquity to be punished by the Judge ; for I should have denied the God that is above."

Perhaps we are not, on the whole, much wiser than those simple men of the old time. For what do we know of *effect* and *cause*, except that one thing regularly or habitually *follows* another ?

So, because the heliacal rising of Sirius *preceded* the rising of the Nile, it was deemed to *cause* it ; and other stars were in like manner held to *cause* extreme heat, bitter cold, and watery storm.

A religious reverence for the zodiacal Bull [Taurus] appears, from a very early period, to have been pretty general,—perhaps it was universal, throughout Asia ; from that chain or region of Caucasus to which it gave name, and which is still known under the appellation of Mount Taurus, to the Southern extremities of the Indian Peninsula ; extending itself also into Europe, and through the Eastern parts of Africa.

This evidently originated during those remote ages of the world, when the colure of the vernal equinox passed across the stars in the head of the sign Taurus, [among which was Aldebaran] ; a period when, as the most ancient monuments of all the oriental nations attest, the light of arts and letters first shone forth.

The Arabian word Al-de-baran, means the *foremost*, or *leading*, star : and it could only have been so named, when it *did* precede, or *lead*, all others. The year then opened with the sun in Taurus ; and the multitude of ancient sculptures, both in Assyria and Egypt, wherein the bull appears with lunette or crescent horns, and the disk of the sun between them, are direct allusions to the important festival of the first new moon of the year: and there was everywhere an annual celebration of the festival of the first new moon, when the year opened with Sol and Luna in Taurus.

David sings: "Blow the trumpet in *the New Moon; in* the time appointed; on our solemn feast-day: for this is a statute unto Israel, and a law of the God of Jacob. This he ordained to Joseph, for a testimony, when he came out of the land of Egypt."

The reverence paid to Taurus continued long after, by the precession of the Equinoxes, the colure of the vernal equinox had come to pass through Aries. The Chinese still have a temple, called "The Palace of the horned Bull;" and the same symbol is worshipped in Japan and all over Hindostan. The Cimbrians carried a brazen bull with them, as the image of their God, when they overran Spain and Gaul; and the representation of the Creation, by the Deity in the shape of a bull, breaking the shell of an egg with his horns, meant Taurus, opening the year, and bursting the symbolical shell of the annually-recurring orb of the new year.

Theophilus says that the Osiris of Egypt was supposed to be dead or absent fifty days in each year. Landseer thinks that this was because the Sabæan priests were accustomed to see, in the lower latitudes of Egypt and Ethiopia, the first or chief stars of the Husbandman [BoÖTES] sink achronically beneath the Western horizon; and then to begin their lamentations, or hold forth the signal for others to weep: and when his prolific virtues were supposed to be transferred to the vernal sun, bacchanalian revelry became devotion.

Before the colure of the vernal Equinox had passed into Aries, and after it had left Aldebaran and the Hyades, the Pleiades were, for seven or eight centuries, the leading stars of the Sabæan year. And thus we see, on the monuments, the disk and crescent, symbols of the sun and moon in conjunction, appear successively,—first on the head, and then on the neck and back of the Zodiacal Bull, and more recently on the forehead of the Ram.

The diagrammatical character or symbol, still in use to denote Taurus, ♉, is this very crescent and disk: a symbol that has come down to us from those remote ages when this memorable conjunction in Taurus, by marking the commencement, at once of the Sabæan year and of the cycle of the Chaldean Saros, so pre-eminently distinguished that sign, as to become its characteristic symbol. On a bronze bull from China, the crescent is attached to the *back* of the Bull, by means of a cloud, and a curved groove is provided for the occasional introduction of the disk of the sun, when solar and lunar time were coincident and conjunctive, at the commencement of the year, and of the lunar cycle. When that was made, the year did not open with the stars in the *head* of the Bull, but when the colure of the vernal Equinox passed across the middle or later degrees of the asterism Taurus, and the Pleiades were, in China, as in Canaan, the leading stars of the year.

The crescent and disk combined always represent the conjunctive Sun and Moon; and when placed on the head of the Zodiacal Bull, the commencement of the cycle termed SAROS by the Chaldeans, and Metonic by the Greeks; and supposed to be alluded to in Job, by the phrase, "Mazzaroth in his season;" that is to say, when the first new Moon and new Sun of the year were coincident, which happened once in eighteen years and a fraction.

On the sarcophagus of Alexander, the same symbol appears on the head of a Ram, which, in the time of that monarch, was the leading sign. So too in the sculptured temples of the Upper Nile, the crescent and disk appear, not on the head of Taurus, but on the forehead of the Ram or the Ram-headed God, whom the Grecian Mythologists called Jupiter Ammon, really the Sun in Aries.

If we now look for a moment at the individual stars which composed and were near to the respective constellations, we may find something that will connect itself with the symbols of the Ancient Mysteries and of Masonry.

It is to be noticed that when the Sun is *in* a particular constellation, no part of that constellation will be seen, except just before sunrise and just after sunset; and then only the edge of it: but the constellations *opposite* to it will be visible. When the Sun is in Taurus, for example, that is, when Taurus *sets with* the Sun, Scorpio rises as he sets, and continues visible through the night. And if Taurus rises and sets with the Sun to-day, he will, six months hence, rise at sunset and set at sunrise; for the stars thus gain on the Sun two hours a month.

Going back to the time when, watched by the Chaldean shepherds, and the husbandmen of Ethiopia and Egypt,

"The milk-white Bull with golden horns
Led on the new-born year,"

we see in the neck of TAURUS, the Pleiades, and in his face the Hyades, "which Grecia from their shower-ing names," and of whom the brilliant Aldebaran is the chief; while to the southwestward is that most splendid of all the constellations, Orion, with Betelgueux in his right shoulder, Bellatrix in his left shoulder, Rigel on the left foot, and in his belt the three stars known as the Three Kings, and now as the Yard and Ell. Orion, ran the legend, persecuted the Pleiades; and to save them from his fury, Jupiter placed them in the Heavens, where he still pursues them, but in vain. They, with Arcturus and the Bands of Orion, are men-tioned in the Book of Job. They are usually called the Seven Stars, and it is said there *were* seven, before the fall of Troy; though now only six are visible.

The Pleiades were so named from a Greek word signifying *to sail*. In all ages they have been observed for signs and seasons. Virgil says that the sailors gave names to "the Pleiades, Hyades and the Northern Car; *Pleiadas, Hyadas, Claramque Lycaonis Arcton.*" And Palinurus, he says,—

Arcturum, pluviasque Hyadas, Geminosque Triones,
Armatumque auro circumspicit Oriona,—

studied Arcturus and the rainy Hyades and the Twin Triones, and Orion cinctured with gold.

Taurus was the prince and leader of the celestial host for more than two thousand years: and when his head set with the Sun about the last of May, the Scorpion was seen to rise in the Southeast.

The Pleiades were sometimes called *Vergiliæ*, or the Virgins of Spring; because the Sun entered this cluster of stars in the season of blossoms. Their Syrian name was *Succoth*, or *Succoth-beneth*, derived from a Chaldean word, signifying to *speculate* or *observe*.

The *Hyades* are five stars in the form of a V, 11° southeast of the Pleiades. The Greeks counted them as seven. When the vernal equinox was in Taurus, Aldebaran led up the starry host; and as he rose in the East, Aries was about 27° high.

When he was close upon the meridian, the Heavens presented their most magnificent appearance. Capella was a little further from the meridian, to the north; and Orion still further from it to the southward. Procyon, Sirius, Castor and Pollux had climbed about halfway from the horizon to the meridian. Regulus had just risen upon the ecliptic. The Virgin still lingered below the horizon. Fomalhaut was halfway to the meridian in the Southwest; and to the Northwest were the brilliant constellations, Perseus, Cepheus, Cassiopeia and Andromeda; while the Pleiades had just passed the meridian.

ORION is visible to all the habitable world. The equinoctial line passes through the centre of it. When Aldebaran rose in the East, the Three Kings in Orion followed him; and as Taurus set, the Scorpion, by whose sting it was said Orion died, rose in the East.

Orion rises at noon about the 9th of March. His rising was accompanied with great rains and storms, and it became very terrible to mariners.

In Boötes, called by the ancient Greeks *Lycaon*, from *lukos*, a wolf, and by the Hebrews, Caleb Anubach, the Barking Dog, is the Great Star ARCTURUS, which, when Taurus opened the year, corresponded with a season remarkable for its great heat.

Next comes GEMINI, the Twins, two human figures, in the heads of which are the bright Stars CASTOR and POLLUX, the Dioscuri, and the Cabiri of Samothrace, patrons of navigation: while South of Pollux are the brilliant Stars SIRIUS and PROCYON, the greater and lesser Dog; and still further South, Canopus, in the Ship Argo.

Sirius is apparently the largest and brightest Star in the Heavens. When the Vernal Equinox was in Taurus, he rose heliacally, that is, just before the Sun, when, at the Summer Solstice, the Sun entered Leo, about the 21st of June, fifteen days previous to the swelling of the Nile. The heliacal rising of Canopus was also a precursor of the rising of the Nile. Procyon was the forerunner of Sirius, and rose before him.

There are no important Stars in CANCER. In the Zodiacs of Esne and Dendera and in most of the astrological remains of Egypt, the sign of this constellation was a beetle (*Scarabæus*), which thence became sacred, as an emblem of the gate through which souls descended from Heaven. In the crest of Cancer is a cluster of Stars formerly called *Præsepe*, the Manger, on each side of which is a small Star, the two of which were called *Aselli*, little asses.

In *Leo* are the splendid Stars, REGULUS, directly on the ecliptic, and DENEBOLA in the Lion's tail. Southeast of Regulus is the fine Star COR HYDRÆ.

The combat of Hercules with the Nemæan lion was his first labour. It was the first sign into which the Sun passed, after falling below the Summer Solstice; from which time he struggled to re-ascend.

The Nile overflowed in this sign. It stands first in the Zodiac of Dendera, and is in all the Indian and Egyptian Zodiacs.

In the left hand of VIRGO (Isis or Ceres) is the beautiful Star SPICA Virginis, a little South of the Ecliptic. VINDEMIATRIX, of less magnitude, is in the right arm; and Northwest of Spica, in Boötes (the husbandman, Osiris), is the splendid Star ARCTURUS.

The division of the first Decan of the Virgin, Aben Ezra says, represents a beautiful Virgin with flowing hair, sitting in a chair, with two ears of corn in her hand, and suckling an infant. In an Arabian MSS. in the Royal Library at Paris, is a picture of the Twelve Signs. That of Virgo is a young girl with an infant by her side. Virgo was Isis; and her representation, carrying a child (Horus) in her arms, exhibited in her temple, was accompanied by this inscription: "I AM ALL THAT IS, THAT WAS, AND THAT SHALL BE; and the fruit which I brought forth is the Sun."

Nine months after the Sun enters Virgo, he reaches the Twins. When Scorpio begins to rise, Orion sets: when Scorpio comes to the meridian, Leo begins to set, Typhon reigns, Osiris is slain, and Isis (the Virgin) his sister and wife, follows him to the tomb, weeping.

The Virgin and Boötes, setting heliacally at the autumnal equinox, delivered the world to the wintry constellations, and introduced into it the genius of Evil, represented by Ophiucus, the Serpent.

At the moment of the Winter Solstice, the Virgin rose heliacally (*with* the Sun), having the Sun (Horus) in her bosom.

In LIBRA are four Stars of the second and third magnitude, which we shall mention hereafter. They are Zuben-es-Chamali, Zuben-el-Gemabi, Zuben-hak-rabi, and Zuben-el-Gubi. Near the last of these is the brilliant and malign Star, ANTARES in Scorpio.

In SCORPIO, ANTARES, of the 1st magnitude, and remarkably red, was one of the four great Stars, FOMALHAUT, in Cetus, ALDEBARAN in Taurus, REGULUS in Leo, and ANTARES, that formerly answered to the Solstitial and Equinoctial points, and were much noticed by astronomers. This sign was sometimes represented by a Snake, and sometimes by a Crocodile, but generally by a Scorpion, which last is found on the Mithriac Monuments and on the Zodiac of Dendera. It was considered a sign accursed, and the entrance of the Sun into it commenced the reign of Typhon.

In Sagittarius, Capricornus and Aquarius there are no stars of importance.

Near Pisces is the brilliant Star FOMALHAUT. No sign in the Zodiac is considered of more malignant influence than this. It was deemed indicative of *Violence* and *Death*. Both the Syrians and Egyptians abstained from eating fish, out of dread and abhorrence; and when the latter would represent anything as odious, or express hatred by Hieroglyphics, they painted a fish.

In Auriga is the bright Star CAPELLA, which to the Egyptians never set.

And, circling ever round the North Pole are Seven Stars, known as Ursa Major, or the Great Bear, which have been an object of universal observation in all ages of the world. They were venerated alike by the Priests of Bel, the Magi of Persia, the Shepherds of Chaldea and the Phœnician navigators, as well as by the astronomers of Egypt. Two of them, MERAK and DUBHE, always point to the North Pole.

The Phœnicians and Egyptians, says Eusebius, were the first who ascribed divinity to the Sun, Moon and Stars, and regarded them as the sole causes of the production and destruction of all beings. From them went abroad over all the world all known opinions as to the generation and descent of the Gods. Only the Hebrews looked beyond the visible world to an invisible Creator. All the rest of the world regarded as Gods those luminous bodies that blaze in the firmament, offered them sacrifices, bowed down before them, and raised neither their souls nor their worship above the visible Heavens.

The Chaldeans, Canaanites and Syrians, among whom Abraham lived, did the same. The Canaanites consecrated horses and chariots to the Sun. The inhabitants of Emesa in Phœnicia adored him under the name of Elagabalus; and the Sun, as Hercules, was the great Deity of the Tyrians. The Syrians worshipped, with fear and dread, the Stars of the Constellation Pisces, and consecrated images of them in their Temples. The Sun as Adonis was worshipped in Byblos and about Mount Libanus. There was a magnificent Temple of the Sun at Palmyra, which was pillaged by the soldiers of Aurelian, who rebuilt it and dedicated it anew. The Pleiades, under the name of Succoth-Beneth, were worshipped by the Babylonian colonists who settled in the country of the Samaritans. Saturn, under the name of Remphan, was worshipped among the Copts. The planet Jupiter was worshipped, as Bel or Baal; Mars as Malec, Melech or Moloch; Venus as Ashtaroth or Astarte, and Mercury as Nebo, among the Syrians, Assyrians, Phœnicians and Canaanites.

Sanchoniathon says that the earliest Phœnicians adored the Sun, whom they deemed sole Lord of the Heavens; and honoured him under the name of BEEL-SAMIN, signifying *King of Heaven*. They raised columns to the elements, fire and air or wind, and worshipped them; and Sabeism or the worship of the Stars flourished everywhere in Babylonia. The Arabs, under a sky always clear and serene, adored the Sun, Moon and Stars. Abulfaragius so informs us, and that each of the twelve Arab Tribes invoked a particular Star as its Patron. The Tribe Hamyar was consecrated to the Sun; the Tribe Cennah to the Moon; the Tribe Misa was under the protection of the beautiful Star in Taurus, Aldebaran; the Tribe Tai, under that of Canopus; the Tribe Kais, of Sirius; the Tribes Lachamus and Idamus, of Jupiter; the Tribe Asad, of Mercury; and so on. The Saracens, in the time of Heraclius, worshipped Venus, whom they called CABAR, or The Great; and they swore by the Sun, Moon and Stars. Shahristan, an Arabic author, says that the Arabs and Indians before his time had temples dedicated to the seven Planets. Abulfaragius says that the seven great primitive nations, from whom all others descended, the Persians, Chaldeans, Greeks, Egyptians, Turks, Indians and Chinese, all originally were Sabeists, and worshipped the Stars. They all, he says, like the Chaldeans, prayed, turning towards the North pole, three times a day, at Sunrise, Noon and Sunset, bowing themselves three times before the Sun. They invoked the Stars and the Intelligences which inhabited them, offered them sacrifices, and called the fixed stars and planets Gods. Philo says that the Chaldeans regarded the stars as sovereign arbiters of the order of the world, and did not look beyond the visible causes to any invisible and intellectual being. They regarded NATURE as the Great Divinity, that exercised its powers through the action of its parts, the Sun, Moon, Planets and Fixed Stars, the successive revolutions of the seasons, and the combined action of Heaven and Earth. The great feast of the Sabeans was when the Sun reached the vernal equinox: and they had five other feasts at the times when the five minor planets entered the signs in which they had their exaltation.

Diodorus Siculus informs us that the Egyptians recognized two great Divinities, primary and eternal, the Sun and Moon, which they thought governed the world, and from which everything receives its nourishment and growth: that on them depended all the great work of generation, and the perfection of all effects produced in nature. We know that the two great Divinities of Egypt were Osiris and Isis, the greatest agents of nature; according to some, the Sun and Moon, and according to others, Heaven and Earth, or the active and passive principles of generation.

And we learn from Porphyry, that Chæremon, a learned priest of Egypt, and many other learned men of that nation, said that the Egyptians recognized as gods, the stars composing the zodiac, and all those that by their rising or setting marked its divisions; the subdivisions of the signs into decans, the horoscope and the stars that presided therein, and which were called Potent Chiefs of Heaven: that considering the Sun as the Great God, Architect and Ruler of the World, they explained not only the fable of Osiris and Isis, but generally all their sacred legends, by the stars, by their appearance and disappearance, by their ascension, by the phases of the moon, and the increase and diminution of her light; by the march of the sun, the division of time and the heavens into two parts, one assigned to darkness and the other to light; by the Nile; and, in fine, by the whole round of physical causes.

Lucian tells us that the bull Apis, sacred to the Egyptians, was the image of the celestial Bull, or

Taurus; and that Jupiter Ammon, horned like a ram, was an image of the constellation Aries. And Clemens of Alexandria assures us that the four principal sacred animals, carried in their processions, were emblems of the four signs or cardinal points which fixed the seasons at the equinoxes and solstices, and divided into four parts the yearly march of the sun. They worshipped fire also, and water, and the Nile, which river they styled Father, Preserver of Egypt, sacred emanation from the Great God Osiris; and in their hymns to which they called it the god crowned with millet (which grain, represented by the *pschent*, was part of the head-dress of their kings), bringing with him abundance. The other elements were also revered by them: and the Great Gods, whose names are found inscribed on an ancient column, are, the Air, Heaven, the Earth, the Sun, the Moon, Night and Day. And, in fine, as Eusebius says, they regarded the Universe as a great Deity, composed of a great number of gods, the different parts of itself.

The same worship of the Heavenly Host extended into every part of Europe, into Asia Minor, and among the Turks, Scythians, and Tartars. The ancient Persians adored the Sun as Mithras, and also the Moon, Venus, Fire, Earth, Air and Water; and, having no statues or altars, they sacrificed on high places to the Heavens and to the Sun. On seven ancient *pyrea* they burned incense to the Seven Planets, and considered the elements to be divinities. In the Zend-Avesta we find invocations addressed to Mithras, the stars, the elements, trees, mountains, and every part of nature. The Celestial Bull is invoked there, to which the Moon unites herself; and the four great stars, Taschter, Satevis, Haftorang, and Venant, the great Star Rapitan, and the other constellations which watch over the different portions of the earth.

The Magi, like a multitude of ancient nations, worshipped fire, above all the other elements and powers of nature. In India, the Ganges and the Indus were worshipped, and the Sun was the Great Divinity. They worshipped the Moon also, and kept up the sacred fire. In Ceylon, the Sun, Moon, and other planets were worshipped: in Sumatra, the Sun, called Iri, and the Moon, called Handa. And the Chinese built Temples to Heaven, the Earth, the genii of the air, of the water, of the mountains and of the stars, to the sea-dragon, and to the planet Mars.

The celebrated Labyrinth was built in honour of the Sun; and its twelve palaces, like the twelve superb columns of the Temple at Hieropolis, covered with symbols relating to the twelve signs and the occult qualities of the elements, were consecrated to the twelve Gods or tutelary genii of the signs of the Zodiac. The figure of the pyramid and that of the obelisk, resembling the shape of a flame, caused these monuments to be consecrated to the Sun and to Fire. And Timæus of Locria says: "The equilateral triangle enters into the composition of the pyramid, which has four equal faces and equal angles, and which in this is like fire, the most subtle and mobile of the elements." They and the obelisks were erected in honour of the Sun, termed in an inscription upon one of the latter, translated by the Egyptian Hermapion, and to be found in Ammianus Marcellinus, "Apollo the strong, Son of God, he who made the world, true Lord of the diadems, who possesses Egypt and fills it with his glory."

The two most famous divisions of the Heavens, by seven, which is that of the planets, and by twelve, which is that of the signs, are found on the religious monuments of all the people of the ancient world. The twelve Great Gods of Egypt are met with everywhere. They were adopted by the Greeks and Romans; and the latter assigned one of them to each sign of the Zodiac. Their images were seen at Athens, where an altar was erected to each; and they were painted on the porticos. The People of the North had their twelve *Azes*, or Senate of twelve great Gods, of whom Odin was chief. The Japanese had the same number, and like the Egyptians divided them into classes, seven, who were the most ancient, and five, afterwards added: both of which numbers are well known and consecrated in Masonry.

There is no more striking proof of the universal adoration paid the stars and constellations, than the arrangement of the Hebrew camp in the Desert, and the allegory in regard to the twelve Tribes of Israel, ascribed in the Hebrew legends to Jacob. The Hebrew camp was a quadrilateral, in sixteen divisions, of which the central four were occupied by images of the four elements. The four divisions at the four angles of the quadrilateral exhibited the four signs that the astrologers call *fixed*, and which they regard as subject to the influence of the four great Royal Stars, Regulus in Leo, Aldebaran in Taurus, Antares in Scorpio, and Fomalhaut in the mouth of Pisces, on which falls the water poured out by Aquarius; of which constellations the Scorpion was represented in the Hebrew blazonry by the Celestial Vulture or Eagle, that rises at the same time with it and is its paranatellon. The other signs were arranged on the four faces of the quadrilateral, and in the parallel and interior divisions.

There is an astonishing coincidence between the characteristics assigned by Jacob to his sons, and those of the signs of the Zodiac, or the planets that have their domicil in those signs.

Reuben is compared to running water, unstable and that cannot excel; and he answers to Aquarius, his ensign being a man. The water poured out by Aquarius flows towards the South Pole, and it is the first of the four Royal Signs, ascending from the winter Solstice.

The Lion (Leo) is the device of *Judah;* and Jacob compares him to that animal, whose constellation in the Heavens is the domicil of the Sun; the Lion of the Tribe of Judah; by whose grip when that of apprentice and that of fellow-craft,—of Aquarius at the winter Solstice and of Cancer at the vernal equinox,—had not succeeded in raising him, Hiram was lifted out of the grave.

Ephraim, on whose ensign appears the Celestial Bull, Jacob compares to the ox. *Dan,* bearing as his device a Scorpion, he compares to the Cerastes or horned Serpent, synonymous in astrological language, with the vulture or pouncing eagle; and which bird was often substituted on the flag of Dan, in place of the venomous scorpion, on account of the terror which that reptile inspired, as the symbol of Typhon and his malign influences; wherefore the Eagle, as its paranatellon, that is, rising and setting at the same time with it, was naturally used in its stead. Hence the four famous figures in the sacred pictures of the Jews and Christians, and in Royal Arch Masonry, of the Lion, the Ox, the Man and the Eagle, the four creatures of the Apocalypse, copied there from Ezekiel, in whose reveries and rhapsodies they are seen revolving around blazing circles.

The Ram, domicil of Mars, chief of the Celestial Soldiery and of the twelve Signs, is the device of *Gad,* whom Jacob characterizes as a warrior, chief of his army.

Cancer, in which are the stars termed *Aselli,* or little asses, is the device of the flag of *Issachar,* whom Jacob compares to an ass.

Capricorn, of old represented with the tail of a fish, and called by astronomers the Son of Neptune, is the device of *Zebulon,* of whom Jacob says that he dwells on the shore of the sea.

Sagittarius, chasing the Celestial Wolf, is the emblem of *Benjamin,* whom Jacob compares to a hunter: and in that constellation the Romans placed the domicil of Diana the huntress. Virgo, the domicil of Mercury, is borne on the flag of *Naphtali,* whose eloquence and agility Jacob magnifies, both of which are attributes of the Courier of the Gods. And of *Simeon* and *Levi* he speaks as united, as are the two fishes that make the Constellation Pisces which is their armorial emblem.

Plato, in his Republic, followed the divisions of the Zodiac and the planets. So also did Lycurgus at Sparta, and Cecrops in the Athenian Commonwealth. Chun, the Chinese legislator, divided China into twelve Tcheou, and specially designated twelve mountains. The Etruscans divided themselves into twelve Cantons. Romulus appointed twelve Lictors. There were twelve tribes of Ishmael and twelve disciples of the Hebrew Reformer. The New Jerusalem of the Apocalypse has twelve gates.

The Souciet, a Chinese book, speaks of a palace composed of four buildings, whose gates looked towards the four corners of the world. That on the East was dedicated to the new moons of the months of Spring; that on the West, to those of Autumn; that on the South to those of Summer; and that on the North to those of Winter: and in this palace the Emperor and his grandees sacrificed a lamb, the animal that represented the Sun at the vernal equinox.

Among the Greeks, the march of the Choruses in their theatres represented the movements of the Heavens and the planets, and the Strophe and Anti-Strophe imitated, Aristoxenes says, the movements of the Stars. The number five was sacred among the Chinese, as that of the planets other than the Sun and Moon. Astrology consecrated the numbers twelve, seven, thirty and three hundred and sixty; and everywhere *seven,* the number of the planets, was as sacred as *twelve,* that of the signs, the months, the oriental cycles, and the sections of the horizon. We shall speak more at large hereafter, in another degree, as to these and other numbers, to which the ancients ascribed mysterious powers.

The Signs of the Zodiac and the Stars appeared on many of the ancient coins and medals. On the public seal of the Locrians-Ozoles was Hesperus or the planet Venus. On the medals of Antioch on the Orontes was the ram and crescent; and the Ram was the special Deity of Syria, assigned to it in the division of the earth among the twelve signs. On the Cretan coins was the Equinoctial Bull; and he also appeared on those of the Mamertins and of Athens. Sagittarius appeared on those of the Persians. In India the twelve signs appeared upon the ancient coins. The Scorpion was engraved on the medals of the Kings of Comagena, and Capricorn on those of Zeugma, Anazorba and other cities. On the medals of Antoninus are found nearly all the signs of the Zodiac.

Astrology was practised among all the ancient nations. In Egypt, the book of Astrology was borne reverentially in the religious processions; in which the few sacred animals were also carried, as emblems of the equinoxes and solstices. The same science flourished among the Chaldeans, and over the whole of Asia and Africa. When Alexander invaded India, the astrologers of the Oxydraces came to him to disclose the secrets of their science of Heaven and the Stars. The Brahmins whom Apollonius consulted, taught him the secrets of Astronomy, with the ceremonies and prayers whereby to appease the Gods and learn the future from the stars. In China, astrology taught the mode of governing the State and families. In Arabia it was deemed the mother of the sciences; and old libraries are full of Arabic books on this pretended science. It flourished at Rome. Constantine had his horoscope drawn by the astrologer Valens. It was a science in the middle ages, and even to this day is neither forgotten nor unpractised. Catharine de Medici was fond of it. Louis XIV. consulted his horoscope, and the learned Casini commenced his career as an astrologer.

The ancient Sabæans established feasts in honour of each planet, on the day, for each, when it entered its place of *exaltation*, or reached the particular degree in the particular sign of the zodiac, in which astrology had fixed the place of its exaltation; that is, the place in the Heavens where its influence was supposed to be greatest, and where it acted on Nature with the greatest energy. The place of exaltation of the sun was in Aries, because, reaching that point, he awakens all Nature, and warms into life all the germs of vegetation; and therefore his most solemn feast among all nations, for many years before our Era, was fixed at the time of his entrance into that sign. In Egypt, it was called the Feast of Fire and Light. It was the Passover, when the Paschal Lamb was slain and eaten, among the Jews, and Neurouz among the Persians. The Romans preferred the place of *domicil* to that of exaltation; and celebrated the feasts of the planets under the signs that were their *houses*. The Chaldeans, whom, and not the Egyptians, the Sabæans followed in this, preferred the places of exaltation.

Saturn, from the length of time required for his apparent revolution, was considered the most remote, and the Moon the nearest planet. After the Moon came Mercury and Venus, then the Sun, and then Mars, Jupiter and Saturn.

So the risings and settings of the Fixed Stars, and their conjunctions with the Sun, and their first appearance as they emerged from his rays, fixed the epochs for the feasts instituted in their honour; and the Sacred Calendars of the ancients were regulated accordingly.

In the Roman games of the circus, celebrated in honour of the Sun and of entire Nature, the Sun, Moon, Planets, Zodiac, Elements, and the most apparent parts and potent agents of Nature were personified and represented, and the courses of the Sun in the Heavens were imitated in the Hippodrome; his chariot being drawn by four horses of different colours, representing the four elements and seasons. The courses were from East to West, like the circuits round the Lodge, and seven in number, to correspond with the number of planets. The movements of the Seven Stars that revolve around the pole were also represented, as were those of Capella, which by its heliacal rising at the moment when the Sun reached the Pleiades, in Taurus, announced the commencement of the annual revolution of the Sun.

The intersection of the Zodiac by the colures at the Equinoctial and Solstitial points, fixed four periods, each of which has, by one or more nations, and in some cases by the same nation at different periods, been taken for the commencement of the year. Some adopted the Vernal Equinox, because then day began to prevail over night, and light gained a victory over darkness. Sometimes the Summer Solstice was preferred; because then day attained its maximum of duration, and the acme of its glory and perfection. In Egypt, another reason was, that then the Nile began to overflow, at the heliacal rising of Sirius. Some preferred the Autumnal Equinox, because then the harvests were gathered, and the hopes of a new crop were deposited in the bosom of the earth. And some preferred the Winter Solstice, because then, the shortest day having arrived, their length commenced to increase, and Light began the career destined to end in victory at the Vernal Equinox.

The Sun was figuratively said to *die* and be *born again* at the Winter Solstice; the games of the Circus, in honour of the invincible God-Sun, were then celebrated, and the Roman year, established or reformed by Numa, commenced. Many peoples of Italy commenced their year, Macrodius says, at that time; and represented by the four ages of man the gradual succession of periodical increase and diminution of day, and the light of the Sun; likening him to an infant born at the Winter Solstice, a young man at the Vernal Equinox, a robust man at the Summer Solstice, and an old man at the Autumnal Equinox.

This idea was borrowed from the Egyptians, who adored the Sun at the Winter Solstice, under the figure of an infant.

The image of the Sign in which each of the four seasons commenced, became the form under which was figured the Sun of that particular season. The Lion's skin was worn by Hercules; the horns of the Bull adorned the forehead of Bacchus; and the autumnal serpent wound its long folds round the Statue of Serapis, 2500 years before our era; when those Signs corresponded with the commencements of the Seasons. When other constellations replaced them at those points, by means of the precession of the Equinoxes, those attributes were changed. Then the Ram furnished the horns for the head of the Sun, under the name of Jupiter Ammon. He was no longer born exposed to the waters of Aquarius, like Bacchus, nor enclosed in an urn like the God Canopus; but in the Stables of Augeas or the Celestial Goat. He then completed his triumph, mounted on an ass, in the constellation Cancer which then occupied the Solstitial point of Summer.

Other attributes the images of the Sun borrowed from the constellations which, by their rising and setting fixed the points of departure of the year, and the commencements of its four principal divisions.

First the Bull and afterwards the Ram (called by the Persians the Lamb), was regarded as the regenerator of Nature, through his union with the Sun. Each, in his turn, was an emblem of the Sun overcoming the winter darkness, and repairing the disorders of Nature, which every year was regenerated under these Signs, after the Scorpion and Serpent of Autumn had brought upon it barrenness, disaster and darkness. Mithras was represented sitting on a Bull; and that animal was an image of Osiris: while the Greek Bacchus armed his front with its horns, and was pictured with its tail and feet.

The Constellations also became note-worthy to the husbandman, which by their rising or setting, at morning or evening, indicated the coming of this period of renewed fruitfulness and new life. Capella, or the Kid Amalthea, whose horn is called that of abundance, and whose place is over the equinoctial point, or Taurus; and the Pleiades, that long indicated the Seasons, and gave rise to a multitude of poetic fables, were the most observed and most celebrated in antiquity.

The original Roman year commenced at the Vernal equinox. July was formerly called *Quintilis*, the 5th month, and August *Sextilis*, the 6th, as *September* is still the 7th month, *October* the 8th, and so on. The Persians commenced their year at the same time, and celebrated their great feast of Neurouz when the Sun entered Aries and the Constellation Perseus rose,—Perseus, who first brought down to earth the heavenly fire consecrated in their temples: and all the ceremonies then practised reminded men of the renovation of Nature and the triumph of Ormuzd, the Light-God, over the powers of Darkness and Ahriman their Chief.

The Legislator of the Jews fixed the commencement of their year in the month Nisan, at the Vernal Equinox, at which season the Israelites marched out of Egypt and were relieved of their long bondage; in commemoration of which Exodus, they ate the Paschal Lamb at that Equinox. And when Bacchus and his army had long marched in burning deserts, they were led by a Lamb or Ram into beautiful meadows, and to the Springs that watered the Temple of Jupiter Ammon. For to the Arabs and Ethiopians, whose great Divinity Bacchus was, nothing was so perfect a type of Elysium as a Country abounding in springs and rivulets.

Orion, on the same meridian with the Stars of Taurus, died of the sting of the celestial Scorpion, that rises when he sets; as dies the Bull of Mithras in autumn: and in the Stars that correspond with the autumnal equinox we find those malevolent genii that ever war against the Principle of good, and that take from the Sun and the Heavens the fruit-producing power that they communicate to the earth.

With the vernal equinox, dear to the sailor as to the husbandman came the Stars that, with the Sun, open navigation, and rule the stormy Seas. Then the Twins plunge into the solar fires, or disappear at setting, going down with the Sun into the bosom of the waters. And these tutelary Divinities of mariners, the Dioscuri or Chief Cabiri of Samothrace, sailed with Jason to possess themselves of the golden-fleeced ram, or Aries, whose rising in the morning announced the Sun's entry into Taurus, when the Serpent-bearer Jason rose in the evening, and, in aspect with the Dioscuri, was deemed their brother. And Orion, son of Neptune, and most potent controller of the tempest-tortured ocean, announcing sometimes calm and sometimes tempest, rose after Taurus, rejoicing in the forehead of the new year.

The Summer Solstice was not less an important point in the Sun's march than the Vernal Equinox, especially to the Egyptians, to whom it not only marked the end and term of the increasing length of the days and of the domination of light, and the *maximum* of the Sun's elevation ; but also the annual recurrence of that phenomenon peculiar to Egypt, the rising of the Nile, which, ever accompanying the Sun in his course, seemed to rise and fall as the days grew longer and shorter, being lowest at the Winter Solstice, and highest at that of Summer. Thus the Sun seemed to regulate its swelling ; and the time of his arrival at the solstitial point being that of the first rising of the Nile, was selected by the Egyptians as the beginning of a year which they called the Year of God, and of the Sothiac Period, or the period of Sothis, the Dog-Star, who, rising in the morning, fixed that epoch, so important to the people of Egypt. This year was also called the Heliac, that is the Solar year, and the Canicular year ; and it consisted of three hundred and sixty-five days, without intercalation ; so that, at the end of four years, or of four times three hundred and sixty-five days, making 1460 days, it needed to add a day, to make four complete revolutions of the Sun. To correct this, some Nations made every fourth year consist, as we now do, of 366 days : but the Egyptians preferred to add nothing to the year of 365 days, which, at the end of 120 years, or of 30 times 4 years, was short 30 days or a month ; that is to say, it required a month more to complete the 120 revolutions of the Sun, though so many were counted, that is, so many years. Of course the commencement of the 121st year would not correspond with the Summer Solstice, but would precede it by a month : so that, when the Sun arrived at the Solstitial point whence he at first set out, and whereto he must needs return, to make in reality 120 years, or 120 complete revolutions, the first month of the 121st year would have ended.

Thus, if the commencement of the year went back 30 days every 120 years, this commencement of the year, continuing to recede, would, at the end of 12 times 120 years, or of 1460 years, get back to the Solstitial point, or primitive point of departure of the period. The Sun would then have made but 1459 revolutions, though 1460 were counted ; to make up which, a year more would need to be added. So that the Sun would not have made his 1460 revolutions until the end of 1461 years of 365 days each,—each revolution being in reality not 365 days exactly, but 365¼.

This period of 1461 years, each of 365 days, bringing back the commencement of the Solar year to the Solstitial point, at the rising of Sirius, after 1460 complete Solar revolutions, was called in Egypt the *Sothiac* period, the point of departure whereof was the Summer Solstice, first occupied by the Lion and afterwards by Cancer, under which sign is Sirius, which opened the period. It was, says Porphyry, at this Solstitial New Moon, accompanied by the rising of Seth or the Dog Star, that the beginning of the year was fixed, and that of the generation of all things, or, as it were, the natal hour of the world.

Not Sirius alone determined the period of the rising of the Nile. Aquarius, his urn, and the stream flowing from it, in opposition to the sign of the Summer Solstice then occupied by the Sun, opened in the evening the march of Night, and received the full Moon in his cup. Above him and with him rose the feet of Pegasus, struck wherewith, the waters flow forth that the Muses drink. The Lion and the Dog, indicating, were supposed to *cause* the inundation, and so were worshipped. While the Sun passed through Leo, the waters doubled their depth ; and the sacred fountains poured their streams through the heads of lions. Hydra, rising between Sirius and Leo, extended under three signs. Its head rose with Cancer, and its tail with the feet of the Virgin and the beginning of Libra ; and the inundation continued while the Sun passed along its whole extent.

The successive contest of light and darkness for the possession of the lunar disk, each being by turns victor and vanquished, exactly resembled what passed upon the earth by the action of the Sun and his journeys from one Solstice to the other. The lunary revolutions presented the same periods of light and darkness as the year, and was the object of the same religious fictions. Above the Moon, Pliny said, everything is pure, and filled with eternal light. There ends the cone of shadow which the earth projects, and which produces night; there ends the sojourn of night and darkness; to it the air extends; but there we enter the pure substance.

The Egyptians assigned to the Moon the demiurgic or creative force of Osiris, who united himself to her in the spring, when the Sun communicated to her the principles of generation which she afterwards disseminated in the air and all the elements. And the Persians considered the Moon to have been impregnated by the Celestial Bull, first of the signs of spring. In all ages, the Moon has been-supposed to have great influence upon vegetation, and the birth and growth of animals, and the belief is as widely entertained now as ever, and that influence regarded as a mysterious and inexplicable one. Not the astrologers alone, but Naturalists like Pliny, Philosophers like Plutarch and Cicero, Theologians like the Egyptian Priests, and Metaphysicians like Proclus, believed firmly in these lunar influences.

"The Egyptians," says Diodorus Siculus, "acknowledged two great Gods, the Sun and Moon, or Osiris and Isis, who govern the world and regulate its administration by the dispensation of the seasons . . . Such is the nature of these two great Divinities, that they impress an active and fecundating force, by which the generation of beings is effected; the Sun, by heat and that spiritual principle that forms the breath of the winds; the Moon by humidity and dryness; and both by the forces of the air which they share in common. By this beneficial influence everything is born, grows and vegetates. Wherefore this whole huge body in which nature resides, is maintained by the combined action of the Sun and Moon, and their five qualities,—the principles spiritual, fiery, dry, humid and airy."

So five primitive powers, elements or elementary qualities, are united with the Sun and Moon in the Indian theology,—air, spirit, fire, water and earth; and the same five elements are recognized by the Chinese. The Phœnicians, like the Egyptians, regarded the Sun and Moon and Stars as sole causes of generation and destruction here below.

The Moon, like the Sun, changed continually the track in which she crossed the Heavens, moving ever to and fro between the upper and lower limits of the Zodiac: and her different places, phases and aspects there, and her relations with the Sun and the Constellations, have been a fruitful source of mythological fables.

All the planets had what astrology termed their *houses*, in the Zodiac. The House of the Sun was in Leo, and that of the Moon in Cancer. Each other planet had two signs; Mercury had Gemini and Virgo; Venus, Taurus and Libra; Mars, Aries and Scorpio; Jupiter, Pisces and Sagittarius; and Saturn, Aquarius and Capricornus. From this distribution of the signs also came many mythological emblems and fables; as also many came from the places of exaltation of the planets. Diana of Ephesus, the Moon, wore the image of a crab on her bosom, because in that sign was the Moon's domicil; and lions bore up the throne of Horus, the Egyptian Apollo, the Sun personified, for a like reason; while the Egyptians consecrated the tauriform scarabæus to the Moon, because she had her place of exaltation in Taurus: and for the same reason Mercury is said to have presented Isis with a-helmet like a bull's head.

A further division of the Zodiac was of each sign into three parts, of 10° each, called Decans, or, in the whole Zodiac, 36 parts; among which the seven planets were apportioned anew, each planet having an equal number of decans, except the first, which opening and closing the series of planets five times repeated, necessarily had one decan more than the others. This sub-division was not invented until after Aries opened the vernal equinox; and accordingly Mars, having his house in Aries, opens the series of decans and closes it; the planets following each other, five times in succession, in the following order, Mars, the Sun, Venus, Mercury, the Moon, Saturn, Jupiter, Mars, &c.; so that to each sign are assigned three planets, each occupying 10 degrees. To each Decan a God or Genius was assigned, making thirty-six in all, one of whom, the Chaldeans said, came down upon earth every ten days, remained so many days, and re-ascended to Heaven. This division is found on the Indian sphere, the Persian, and that Barbaric one which Aben Ezra describes. Each genius of the Decans had a name and special characteristics. They concur and aid in the effects produced by the Sun, Moon and other planets charged with the administration of the world; and the doctrine in regard to them, secret and august as it was held, was considered of the gravest importance; and its principles, Firmicus says, were not entrusted by the ancients, inspired as they were by the Deity, to any but the initiates, and to them only with great reserve, and a kind of fear, and when cautiously enveloped with an obscure veil, that they might not come to be known by the profane.

With these Decans were connected the *paranatellons*, or those stars *outside* of the Zodiac, that rise and set at the same moment with the several divisions of 10° of each sign. As there were anciently only forty-eight celestial figures or constellations, of which twelve were in the Zodiac, it follows that there were, outside of the Zodiac, thirty-six other asterisms, paranatellons of the several thirty-six Decans. For example, as when Capricorn set, Sirius and Procyon, or Canis Major and Canis Minor rose, they were the Paranatellons of Capricorn, though at a great distance from it in the heavens. The rising of Cancer was known from the setting of Corona Borealis and the rising of the Great and Little Dog, its three paranatellons.

The risings and settings of the Stars are always spoken of as connected with the Sun. In that connection there are three kinds of them, cosmical, achronical and heliacal, important to be distinguished by all who would understand this ancient learning.

When any Star rises or sets with the same degree of the same sign of the Zodiac that the Sun occupies at the time, it rises and sets simultaneously with the Sun, and this is termed rising or setting *cosmically;* but a star that so rises and sets can never be seen, on account of the light that precedes, and is left behind by the Sun. It is therefore necessary, in order to know *his* place in the Zodiac, to observe stars that rise just before, or set just after him.

A Star that is in the east when night commences, and in the west when it ends, is said to rise and set *achronically.* A Star so rising or setting was in *opposition* to the Sun, rising at the end of evening twilight, and setting at the beginning of morning twilight, and this happened to each Star but once a year, because the Sun moves from West to East, with reference to the Stars, one degree a day.

When a Star rises as night ends in the morning, or sets as night commences in the evening, it is said to rise or set *heliacally,* because the Sun (*Helios*) seems to touch it with his luminous atmosphere. A Star thus re-appears after a disappearance, often, of several months, and thenceforward it rises an hour earlier each day, gradually emerging from the Sun's rays, until at the end of three months it precedes the Sun six hours and rises at midnight. A Star sets heliacally, when no longer remaining visible above the western horizon after sunset, the day arrives when they cease to be seen setting in the West. They so remain invisible, until the Sun passes so far to the Eastward as not to eclipse them with his light; and then they re-appear, but in the East, about an hour and a half before sunrise; and this is their *heliacal* rising. In this interval, the cosmical rising and setting take place.

Besides the relations of the Constellations and their paranatellons with the houses and places of exaltation of the Planets, and with their places in the respective Signs and Decans, the Stars were supposed to produce different effects according as they rose or set, and according as they did so either cosmically, achronically or heliacally; and also according to the different seasons of the year in which these phenomena occurred; and these differences were carefully marked on the old Calendars; and many things in the ancient allegories are referable to them.

Another and most important division of the Stars was into good and bad, beneficent and malevolent. With the Persians, the former, of the Zodiacal Constellations, were from Aries to Virgo, inclusive; and the latter from Libra to Pisces inclusive. Hence the good Angels and Genii, and the bad Angels, Devs, Evil Genii, Devils, Fallen Angels, Titans and Giants of the Mythology. The other thirty-six Constellations were equally divided, eighteen on each side, or, with those of the Zodiac, twenty-four.

Thus the symbolic Egg, that issued from the mouth of the invisible Egyptian God KNEPH; known in the Grecian Mysteries as the Orphic Egg; from which issued the God CNUMONG of the Coresians, and the Egyptian OSIRIS, and PHANES, God and Principle of Light; from which, broken by the Sacred Bull of the Japanese the world emerged; and which the Greeks placed at the feet of BACCHUS TAURI-CORNUS; the Magian Egg of ORMUZD, from which came the Amshaspands and Devs; was divided into two halves, and equally apportioned between the Good and Evil Constellations and Angels. Those of Spring, as for example Aries and Taurus, Auriga and Capella, were the beneficent stars; and those of Autumn, as the Balance, Scorpio, the Serpent of Ophiucus and the Dragon of the Hesperides, were types and subjects of the Evil Principle, and regarded as malevolent causes of the ill effects experienced in autumn and winter. Thus are explained the mysteries of the journeyings of the human soul through the spheres, when it descends to the earth by the Sign of the Serpent, and returns to the Empire of light by that of the Lamb or Bull.

The creative action of Heaven was manifested, and all its demiurgic energy developed, most of all at the vernal equinox, to which refer all the fables that typify the victory of Light over Darkness, by the triumphs of Jupiter, Osiris, Ormuzd and Apollo. Always the triumphant God takes the form of the Bull, the Ram or the Lamb. Then Jupiter wrests from Typhon his thunderbolts, of which that malignant Deity had possessed himself during the winter. Then the God of Light overwhelms his foe, pictured as a huge Serpent. Then Winter ends; the Sun, seated on the Bull and accompanied by Orion blazes in the Heavens. All nature rejoices at the victory; and Order and Harmony are everywhere re-established, in place of the dire confusion that reigned while gloomy Typhon domineered, and Ahriman prevailed against Ormuzd.

The universal Soul of the World, motive power of Heaven and of the Spheres, it was held, exercises its creative energy chiefly through the medium of the Sun, during his revolution along the signs of the Zodiac, with which signs unite the paranatellons that modify their influence, and concur in furnishing the symbolic attributes of the Great Luminary that regulates Nature and is the depositary of her greatest powers. The action of this Universal Soul of the World is displayed in the movements of the Spheres, and above all in that of the Sun, in the successions of the risings and settings of the Stars, and in their periodical returns. By these are explainable all the metamorphoses of that Soul, personified as Jupiter, as Bacchus, as Vishnu or as Buddha, and all the various attributes ascribed to it; and also the worship of those animals that were consecrated in the ancient Temples, representatives on earth of the Celestial Signs, and supposed to receive by transmission from them the rays and emanations which in them flow from the Universal Soul.

All the old Adorers of Nature, the Theologians, Astrologers and Poets, as well as the most distinguished Philosophers, supposed that the Stars were so many animated and intelligent beings, or eternal bodies, active causes of effects here below, animated by a living principle, and directed by an intelligence that was itself but an emanation from and a part of the life and universal intelligence of the world: and we find in the hierarchical order and distribution of their eternal and divine Intelligences, known by the names of Gods, Angels and Genii, the same distributions and the same divisions as those by which the ancients divided the visible universe and distributed its parts. And the famous divisions by seven and by twelve, appertaining to the planets and the signs of the zodiac, is everywhere found in the hierarchical order of the Gods, the Angels, and the other Ministers that are the depositaries of that Divine Force which moves and rules the world.

These, and the other Intelligences assigned to the other Stars have absolute dominion over all parts of Nature; over the elements, the animal and vegetable kingdoms, over man and all his actions, over his virtues and vices, and over the good and evil which divide between them his life. The passions of his soul and the maladies of his body,—these and the entire man are dependent on the heavens and the genii that there inhabit, who preside at his birth, control his fortunes during life, and receive his soul or active and intelligent part when it is to be re-united to the pure life of the lofty Stars. And all through the great body of the world are disseminated portions of the universal Soul, impressing movement on everything that seems to move of itself, giving life to the plants and trees, directing by a regular and settled plan the organization and development of their germs, imparting constant mobility to the running waters and maintaining their eternal motion, impelling the winds and changing their direction or stilling them, calming and arousing the ocean, unchaining the storms, pouring out the fires of volcanoes, or with earthquakes shaking the roots of huge mountains and the foundations of vast continents; by means of a force that, belonging to Nature, is a mystery to man.

And these invisible Intelligences, like the stars, are marshalled in two great divisions, under the banners of the two Principles of Good and Evil, Light and Darkness; under Ormuzd and Ahriman, Osiris and Typhon. The Evil Principle was the motive-power of brute matter; and it, personified as Ahriman and Typhon, had its hosts and armies of Devs and Genii, Fallen Angels and Malevolent Spirits, who waged continual war with the Good Principle, the Principle of Empyreal Light and Splendour, Osiris, Ormuzd, Jupiter or Dionusos, with his bright hosts of Amshaspands, Izeds, Angels and Archangels; a warfare that goes on from birth until death, in the soul of every man that lives.

We have heretofore, in the 24th Degree, recited the principal incidents in the legend of Osiris and Isis, and it remains but to point out the astronomical phenomena which it has converted into mythological facts.

The Sun, at the vernal equinox, was the fruit-compelling star that by his warmth provoked generation and poured upon the sublunary world all the blessings of Heaven; the beneficent God, tutelary genius of universal vegetation, that communicates to the dull earth new activity, and stirs her great heart, long chilled by winter and his frosts, until from her bosom burst all the greenness and perfume of spring, making her rejoice in leafy forests and grassy lawns and flower-enamelled meadows, and the promise of abundant crops of grain and fruits and purple grapes in their due season.

He was then called Osiris, Husband of Isis, God of Cultivation and Benefactor of Men, pouring on them and on the earth the choicest blessings within the gift of the Divinity. Opposed to him was Typhon, his antagonist in the Egyptian mythology, as Ahriman was the foe of Ormuzd, the Good Principle, in the theology of the Persians.

The first inhabitants of Egypt and Ethiopia, as Diodorus Siculus informs us, saw in the Heavens two first eternal causes of things, or great Divinities, one the Sun, whom they called Osiris, and the other the Moon, whom they called Isis; and these they considered the causes of all the generations of earth. This idea, we learn from Eusebius, was the same as that of the Phœnicians. On these two great Divinities the administration of the world depended. All sublunary bodies received from them their nourishment and increase, during the annual revolution which they controlled, and the different seasons into which it was divided.

To Osiris and Isis, it was held, were owing civilization, the discovery of agriculture, laws, arts of all kinds, religious worship, temples, the invention of letters, astronomy, the gymnastic arts, and music; and thus they were the universal benefactors. Osiris travelled to civilize the countries which he passed through, and communicate to them his valuable discoveries. He built cities, and taught men to cultivate the earth. Wheat and wine were his first presents to men. Europe, Asia and Africa partook of the blessings which he communicated, and the most remote regions of India remembered him, and claimed him as one of their great Gods.

You have learned how Typhon, his brother, slew him. His body was cut into pieces, all of which were collected by Isis, except his organs of generation, which had been thrown into and devoured in the waters of the river that every year fertilized Egypt. The other portions were buried by Isis, and over them she erected a tomb. Thereafter she remained single, loading her subjects with blessings. She cured the sick, restored sight to the blind, made the paralytic whole, and even raised the dead. From her Horus or Apollo learned divination and the science of medicine.

Thus the Egyptians pictured the beneficent action of the two luminaries that, from the bosom of the elements, produced all animals and men, and all bodies that are born, grow and die in the eternal circle of generation and destruction here below.

When the Celestial Bull opened the new year at the vernal equinox, Osiris, united with the Moon, communicated to her the seeds of fruitfulness which she poured upon the air, and therewith impregnated the generative principles which gave activity to universal vegetation. Apis, represented by a Bull, was the living and sensible image of the Sun or Osiris, when in union with Isis or the Moon at the vernal equinox, concurring with her in provoking everything that lives to generation. This conjunction of the Sun with the Moon at the vernal equinox, in the constellation Taurus, required the Bull Apis to have on his shoulder a mark resembling the Crescent Moon. And the fecundating influence of these two luminaries was expressed by images that would now be deemed gross and indecent, but which then were not misunderstood.

Everything good in Nature comes from Osiris,—order, harmony, and the favourable temperature of the seasons and celestial periods. From Typhon come the stormy passions and irregular impulses that agitate the brute and material part of man; maladies of the body, and violent shocks that injure the health and derange the system; inclement weather, derangement of the seasons, and eclipses. Osiris and Typhon were the Ormuzd and Ahriman of the Persians; principles of good and evil, of light and darkness, ever at war in the administration of the universe.

Osiris was the image of generative power. This was expressed by his symbolic statues, and by the sign into which he entered at the vernal equinox. He especially dispensed the humid principle of Nature, generative element of all things; and the Nile and all moisture were regarded as emanations from him, without which there could be no vegetation.

That Osiris and Isis were the Sun and Moon, is attested by many ancient writers; by Diogenes Laertius, Plutarch, Lucian, Suidas, Macrobius, Martianus Capella and others. His power was symbolized by an Eye over a Sceptre. The Sun was termed by the Greeks, the Eye of Jupiter, and the Eye of the World; and his is the All-Seeing Eye in our Lodges. The oracle of Claros styled him King of the Stars and of the Eternal Fire, that engenders the year and the seasons, dispenses rain and winds, and brings about daybreak and night. And Osiris was invoked as the God that resides in the Sun and is enveloped by his rays, the invisible and eternal force that modifies the sublunary world by means of the Sun.

Osiris was the same God known as Bacchus, Dionusos and Serapis. Serapis is the author of the regularity and harmony of the world. Bacchus, jointly with Ceres (identified by Herodotus with Isis) presides over the distribution of all our blessings; and from the two emanates everything beautiful and good in Nature. One furnishes the germ and principle of every good; the other receives and preserves it as a deposit; and the latter is the function of the Moon in the theology of the Persians. In each theology, Persian and Egyptian, the Moon acts directly on the earth; but she is fecundated, in one by the Celestial Bull and in the other by Osiris, with whom she is united at the vernal equinox, in the sign Taurus, the place of her exaltation or greatest influence on the earth. The force of Osiris, says Plutarch, is exercised through the Moon. She is the passive cause, relatively to him, and the active cause relatively to the earth, to which she transmits the germs of fruitfulness received from him.

In Egypt the earliest movement in the waters of the Nile began to appear at the vernal equinox, when the new Moon occurred at the entrance of the Sun into the constellation Taurus; and thus the Nile was held to receive its fertilizing power from the combined action of the equinoctial Sun and the new Moon, meeting in Taurus. Osiris was often confounded with the Nile, and Isis with the earth; and Osiris was deemed to act on the earth, and to transmit to it his emanations, through both the Moon and the Nile; whence the fable that his generative organs were thrown into that river. Typhon, on the other hand, was the principle of aridity and barrenness; and by his mutilation of Osiris was meant that drought which caused the Nile to retire within his bed and shrink up in autumn.

Elsewhere than in Egypt, Osiris was the symbol of the refreshing rains that descend to fertilize the earth; and Typhon the burning winds of autumn; the stormy rains that rot the flowers, the plants and leaves; the short, cold days; and everything injurious in Nature, and that produces corruption and destruction.

In short, Typhon is the principle of corruption, of darkness, of the lower world from which come earthquakes, tumultuous commotions of the air, burning heat, lightning and fiery meteors, and plague and pestilence. Such too was the Ahriman of the Persians; and this revolt of the Evil Principle against the Principle of Good and Light, has been represented in every cosmogony, under many varying forms. Osiris, on the contrary, by the intermediation of Isis, fills the material world with happiness, purity and order, by which the harmony of Nature is maintained. It was said that he died at the autumnal equinox, when Taurus or the Pleiades rose in the evening, and that he rose to life again in the Spring, when vegetation was inspired with new activity.

Of course the two signs of Taurus and Scorpio will figure most largely in the mythological history of Osiris, for they marked the two equinoxes, 2500 years before our Era; and next to them the other constellations, near the equinoxes, that fixed the limits of the duration of the fertilizing action of the Sun; and it is also to be remarked that Venus, the Goddess of Generation, has her domicil in Taurus, as the Moon has there her place of exaltation.

When the Sun was in Scorpio, Osiris lost his life, and that fruitfulness which, under the form of the Bull he had communicated, through the Moon, to the Earth. Typhon, his hands and feet horrid with serpents, and whose habitat in the Egyptian planisphere was under Scorpio, confined him in a chest and flung him into the Nile, under the 17th degree of Scorpio. Under that sign he lost his life and virility; and he recovered them in the spring, when he had connection with the Moon. When he entered Scorpio, his light diminished, Night re-assumed her dominion, the Nile shrunk within its banks, and the earth lost her verdure and the trees their leaves. Therefore it is that on the Mithriac Monuments, the Scorpion bites the testicles of the Equinoctial Bull, on which sits Mithras, the Sun of Spring and God of Generation : and that, on the same monuments, we see two trees, one covered with young leaves, and at its foot a little bull and a torch burning; and the other loaded with fruit, and at its foot a Scorpion, and a torch reversed and extinguished.

· Ormuzd or Osiris, the beneficent Principle that gives the world light, was personified by the Sun, apparent source of light. Darkness, personified by Typhon or Ahriman, was his natural enemy. The Sages of Egypt described the necessary and eternal rivalry or opposition of these principles, ever pursuing one the other, and one dethroning the other in every annual revolution, and at a particular period, one in the Spring, under the Bull, and the other in Autumn under the Scorpion, by the legendary history of Osiris and Typhon, detailed to us by Diodorus and Synesius ; in which history were also personified the Stars and constellations Orion, Capella, the Twins, the Wolf, Sirius and Hercules, whose risings and settings noted the advent of one or the other equinox.

Plutarch gives us the positions in the Heavens of the Sun and Moon, at the moment when Osiris was murdered by Typhon. The Sun, he says, was in the Sign of the Scorpion, which he then entered at the autumnal equinox. The moon was full, he adds; and consequently, as it rose at sunset, it occupied Taurus, which, opposite to Scorpio, rose as it and the Sun sank together, so that she was then found alone in the sign Taurus, where, six months before she had been in union or conjunction with Osiris, the Sun, receiving from him those germs of universal fertilization which he communicated to her. It was the sign through which Osiris first ascended into his empire of light and good. It rose with the Sun on the day of the Vernal Equinox; it remained six months in the luminous hemisphere, ever preceding the Sun and above the horizon during the day; until in autumn, the Sun arriving at Scorpio, Taurus was in complete opposition with him, rose when he set, and completed its entire course above the horizon during the night; presiding, by rising in the evening, over the commencement of the long nights. Hence in the sad ceremonies commemorating the death of Osiris, there was borne in procession a golden bull covered with black crape, image of the darkness into which the familiar sign of Osiris was entering, and which was to spread over the Northern regions, while the Sun, prolonging the nights, was to be absent, and each to remain under the dominion of Typhon, Principle of Evil and Darkness.

Setting out from the sign Taurus, Isis, as the Moon, went seeking for Osiris through all the superior signs, in each of which she became full in the successive months from the autumnal to the vernal equinox, without finding him in either. Let us follow her in her allegorical wanderings.

Osiris was slain by Typhon his rival, with whom conspired a Queen of Ethiopia, by whom, says Plutarch, were designated the winds. The paranatellons of Scorpio, the sign occupied by the Sun when Osiris was slain, were the Serpents, reptiles which supplied the attributes of the Evil Genii and of Typhon, who himself bore the form of a serpent in the Egyptian planisphere. And in the division of Scorpio is also found Cassiopeia, Queen of Ethiopia, whose setting brings stormy winds.

Osiris descended to the shades or infernal regions. There he took the name of Serapis, identical with Pluto, and assumed his nature. He was then in conjunction with Serpentarius, identical with Æsculapius, whose form he took in his passage to the lower signs, where he takes the names of Pluto and Ades.

Then Isis wept the death of Osiris, and the golden bull covered with crape was carried in procession. Nature mourned the impending loss of her summer glories, and the advent of the empire of night, the withdrawing of the waters, made fruitful by the Bull in spring, the cessation of the winds that brought rains to swell the Nile, the shortening of the days and the despoiling of the earth. Then Taurus, directly opposite the Sun, entered into the cone of shadow which the earth projects, by which the Moon is eclipsed at full, and with which, making night, the Bull rises and descends as if covered with a veil, while he remains above our horizon.

The body of Osiris, enclosed in a chest or coffin, was cast into the Nile. Pan and the Satyrs, near Chemmis, first discovered his death, announced it by their cries, and everywhere created sorrow and alarm. Taurus, with the full Moon, then entered into the cone of shadow, and under him was the Celestial River, most properly called the Nile, and below, Perseus, the God of Chemmis, and Auriga, leading a she-goat, himself identical with Pan, whose wife Aiga the she-goat was styled.

Then Isis went in search of the body. She first met certain children who had seen it, received from them their information, and gave them in return the gift of divination. The second full Moon occurred in Gemini, the Twins who presided over the oracles of Didymus, and one of whom was Apollo, the God of Divination.

She learned that Osiris had, through mistake, had connection with her sister Nephte, which she discovered by a crown of leaves of the melilot, which he had left behind him. Of this connection a child was born, whom Isis, aided by her dogs, sought for, found, reared, and attached to herself, by the name of Anubis, her faithful guardian. The third full Moon occurs in Cancer, domicil of the Moon. The paranatellons of that sign are, the crown of Ariadne or Proserpine, made of leaves of the melilot, Procyon and Canis Major, one star of which was called the Star of Isis, while Sirius himself was honoured in Egypt under the name of Anubis.

Isis repaired to Byblos, and seated herself near a fountain, where she was found by the women of the Court of a King. She was induced to visit his Court, and became the nurse of his son. The fourth full Moon was in Leo, domicil of the Sun, or of Adonis, King of Byblos. The paranatellons of this sign are the flowing water of Aquarius, and Cepheus, King of Ethiopia, called Regulus, or simply The King. Behind him rise Cassiopeia his wife, Queen of Ethiopia, Andromeda his daughter and Perseus his son-in-law, all paranatellons in part of this sign, and in part of Virgo.

Isis suckled the child, not at her breast, but with the end of her finger, at night. She burned all the mortal parts of its body, and then, taking the shape of a swallow, she flew to the great column of the palace, made of the tamarisk-tree that grew up round the coffin containing the body of Osiris, and within which it was still enclosed. The fifth full Moon occurred in Virgo, the true image of Isis, and which Eratosthenes calls by that name. It pictured a woman suckling an infant, the son of Isis, born near the winter solstice. This sign has for paranatellons the mast of the Celestial Ship, and the swallow-tailed fish or swallow above it, and a portion of Perseus, son-in-law of the King of Ethiopia.

Isis, having recovered the sacred coffer, sailed from Byblos in a vessel with the eldest son of the King, towards Boutos, where Anubis was, having charge of her son Horus; and in the morning dried up a river, whence arose a strong wind. Landing, she hid the coffer in a forest. Typhon, hunting a wild boar by moonlight, discovered it, recognized the body of his rival, and cut it into fourteen pieces, the number of days between the full and new Moon, and in every one of which days the Moon loses a portion of the light that at the commencement filled her whole disk. The sixth full Moon occurred in Libra, over the divisions separating which from Virgo are the Celestial Ship, Perseus, son of the King of Ethiopia, and Boötes, said to have nursed Horus. The river of Orion that sets in the morning is also a paranatellon of Libra, as are Ursa Major, the Great Bear or Wild Boar of Erymanthus, and the Dragon of the North Pole, or the celebrated Python from which the attributes of Typhon were borrowed. All these surround the full Moon of Libra, last of the Superior Signs, and the one that precedes the new Moon of Spring, about to be reproduced in Taurus, and there be once more in conjunction with the Sun.

Isis collects the scattered fragments of the body of Osiris, buries them, and consecrates the phallus, carried in pomp at the *Pamylia* or feasts of the vernal equinox, at which time the congress of Osiris and the Moon was celebrated. Then Osiris had returned from the shades, to aid Horus his son and Isis his wife against the forces of Typhon. He thus reappeared, say some, under the form of a wolf, or, others say, under that of a horse. The Moon, fourteen days after she is full in Libra, arrives at Taurus and unites herself to the Sun, whose fires she thereafter for fourteen days continues to accumulate on her disk from new Moon to full. Then she unites with herself all the months in that superior portion of the world where light always reigns, with harmony and order, and she borrows from him the force which is to destroy the germs of evil that Typhon had, during the winter, planted everywhere in nature. This passage of the Sun into Taurus, whose attributes he assumes on his return from the lower hemisphere or the shades, is marked by the rising in the evening of the Wolf and the Centaur, and by the heliacal setting of Orion, called the Star of Horus, and which thenceforward is in conjunction with the Sun of Spring, in his triumph over the darkness or Typhon.

Isis, during the absence of Osiris, and after she had hidden the coffer in the place where Typhon found it, had rejoined that malignant enemy; indignant at which, Horus her son deprived her of her ancient diadem, when she rejoined Osiris as he was about to attack Typhon: but Mercury gave her in its place a helmet shaped like the head of a bull. Then Horus, as a mighty warrior, such as Orion was described, fought with and defeated Typhon; who in the shape of the Serpent or Dragon of the Pole had assailed his father. So, in Ovid, Apollo destroys the same Python, when Io, fascinated by Jupiter, is metamorphosed into a cow, and placed in the sign of the Celestial Bull, where she becomes Isis. The equinoctial year ends at the moment when the Sun and Moon, at the vernal equinox, are united with Orion, the Star of Horus, placed in the Heavens under Taurus. The new Moon becomes young again in Taurus, and shows herself as a crescent, for the first time, in the next sign, Gemini, the domicil of Mercury. Then Orion, in conjunction with the Sun, with whom he rises, precipitates the Scorpion, his rival, into the shades of night, causing him to set whenever he himself reappears on the eastern horizon, with the Sun. Day lengthens and the germs of evil are by degrees eradicated: and Horus (from *Aur*, Light) reigns triumphant, symbolizing, by his succession to the characteristics of Osiris, the eternal renewal of the Sun's youth and creative vigour at the vernal equinox.

Such are the coincidences of astronomical phenomena with the legend of Osiris and Isis; sufficing to show the origin of the legend, overloaded as it became at length with all the ornamentation natural to the poetical and figurative genius of the Orient.

Not only into this legend, but into those of all the ancient nations, enter the Bull, the Lamb, the Lion, and the Scorpion or the Serpent; and traces of the worship of the Sun yet linger in all religions. Everywhere, even in our Order, survive the equinoctial and solstitial feasts. Our ceilings still glitter with the greater and lesser luminaries of the Heavens, and our lights, in their number and arrangement, have astronomical references. In all churches and chapels, as in all Pagan temples and pagodas, the altar is in the East; and the ivy over the east windows of old churches is the Hedera Helix of Bacchus. Even the cross had an astronomical origin; and our Lodges are full of the ancient symbols.

The learned author of the Sabæan Researches, Landseer, advances another theory in regard to the legend of Osiris; in which he makes the constellation Boötes play a leading part. He observes that, as none of the stars were visible at the same time with the Sun, his actual place in the zodiac, at any given time, could only be ascertained by the Sabæan astronomers by their observations of the stars, and of their heliacal and achronical risings and settings. There were many solar festivals among the Sabæans, and part of them agricultural ones; and the concomitant signs of those festivals were the risings and settings of the stars of the Husbandman, Bear-driver or Hunter, Boötes. His stars were, among the Hierophants, the established nocturnal indices or signs of the Sun's place in the ecliptic at different seasons of the year: and the festivals were named, one, that of the *Aphanism*, or disappearance; another, that of the *Zetesis*, or search, &c., of Osiris or Adonis, that is, of *Boötes*.

The returns of certain stars, as connected with their concomitant seasons of spring (or seed-time) and harvest, seemed to the ancients, who had not yet discovered that gradual change, resulting from the apparent movement of the stars in longitude, which has been termed the precession of the equinoxes, to be eternal and immutable; and those periodical returns were to the initiated, even more than to the vulgar, celestial oracles, announcing the approach of those important changes, upon which the prosperity, and even the very existence of man must ever depend: and the oldest of the Sabæan constellations seem to have been, an astronomical *Priest*, a *King*, a *Queen*, a *Husbandman* and a *Warrior;* and these more frequently recur on the Sabæan cylinders than any other constellations whatever. The *King* was *Cepheus* or *Chepheus* of Ethiopia; the *Husbandman, Osiris, Bacchus, Sabazeus, Noah* or *Boötes*. To the latter sign, the Egyptians were nationally, traditionally and habitually grateful; for they conceived that from Osiris all the greatest of terrestrial enjoyments were derived. The stars of the Husbandman were the signal for those successive agricultural labours on which the annual produce of the soil depended; and they came in consequence to be considered and hailed, in Egypt and Ethiopia, as the genial stars of terrestrial productiveness; to which the oblations, prayers and vows of the pious Sabæan were regularly offered up.

Landseer says that the stars in Boötes, reckoning down to those of the 5th magnitude inclusive, are *twenty-six*, which seeming achronically to disappear in succession, produced the fable of the cutting of Osiris into twenty-six pieces by Typhon. There are more stars than this in the constellation; but no more that the ancient votaries of Osiris, even in the clear atmosphere of the Sabæan climates, could observe without telescopes.

Plutarch says Osiris was cut into *fourteen* pieces: Diodorus, into *twenty-six;* in regard to which, and to the whole legend, Landseer's ideas, varying from those commonly entertained, are as follows:—

Typhon, Landseer thinks, was the *ocean,* which the ancients fabled or believed surrounded the Earth, and into which all the stars in their turn appear successively to sink: [perhaps it was DARKNESS personified, which the ancients called TYPHON. He was hunting by moonlight, says the old legend, when he met with Osiris].

The ancient Saba must have been near latitude 15° north. Axoum is nearly in 14°, and the Western Saba or Meroë is to the north of that. Forty-eight centuries ago, Aldebaran, the leading star of the year, had, at the vernal equinox, attained at daylight in the morning, an elevation of about 14 degrees, sufficient for him to have ceased to be *combust,* that is, to have emerged from the sun's rays, so as to be visible. The ancients allowed *twelve* days for a star of the first magnitude to emerge from the solar rays: and there is less twilight, the further South we go.

At the same period, too, Cynosura was not the pole-star; but Alpha Draconis was; and the stars rose and set with very different degrees of obliquity from those of their present risings and settings. By having a globe constructed with circumvolving poles, capable of any adjustment with regard to the colures, Mr. Landseer ascertained that, at that remote period, in lat. 15° north, the 26 stars in Boötes, or 27, including Arcturus, did not set achronically in succession: but several set simultaneously in couples, and six by threes simultaneously; so that, in all, there were but *fourteen* separate settings or disappearances, corresponding with the fourteen pieces into which Osiris was cut, according to Plutarch. Kappa, Iota and Theta, in the uplifted western hand, disappeared together, and last of all. They really skirted the horizon; but were invisible in that low latitude, for the three or four days mentioned in some of the versions; while the *Zetesis* or search was proceeding, and the women of Phœnicia and Jerusalem sat weeping for the Wonder, Thammuz: after which they immediately reappeared, below and to the eastward of α Draconis.

And, on the very morning after the achronical departure of the last star of the Husbandman, Aldebaran rose heliacally, and became visible in the East in the morning before day.

And precisely at the moment of the heliacal rising of Arcturus, also rose Spica Virginis. One is near the middle of the Husbandman, and the other near that of the Virgin: and Arcturus may have been the part of Osiris, which Isis did not recover with the other pieces of the body.

At Dedan and Saba it was thirty-six days, from the beginning of the *aphanism,* i. e. the *disappearance* of these stars, to the heliacal rising of Aldebaran. During these days, or forty at Medina, or a few more at Babylon and Byblos, the stars of the Husbandman successively sank out of sight, during the *crepusculum* or short-lived morning twilight of those Southern climes. They disappeared during the glancings of the dawn, the special season of ancient sidereal observation.

Thus the forty days of mourning for Osiris were measured out by the period of the departure of his Stars. When the last had sunken out of sight, the vernal season was ushered in; and the Sun arose with the splendid Aldebaran, the Tauric leader of the Hosts of Heaven; and the whole East rejoiced and kept holiday.

With the exception of the Stars κ, ι and θ, Boötes did not begin to reappear in the Eastern quarter of the Heavens till after the lapse of about four months. Then the Stars of Taurus had declined Westward, and Virgo was rising heliacally. In that latitude, also, the Stars of Ursa Major [termed anciently the Ark of Osiris] set; and Benetnasch, the last of them, returned to the Eastern horizon, with those in the head of Leo, a little before the Summer Solstice. In about a month, followed the Stars of the Husbandman: the chief of them, Ras, Mirach and Arcturus being very nearly simultaneous in their heliacal rising.

Thus the Stars of Boötes rose in the East immediately after Vindemiatrix, and as if under the genial influence of its rays: He had his annual career of prosperity: He revelled orientally for a quarter of a year, and attained his meridian altitude with Virgo; and then, as the Stars of the Water-Urn rose, and Aquarius began to pour forth his annual deluge, he declined Westward, preceded by the Ark of Osiris. In the East, he was the Sign of that happiness in which Nature, the great Goddess of passive production, rejoiced. Now, in the West, as he declines towards the Northwestern horizon, his generative vigour gradually abates: the Solar year grows old: and as his Stars descend beneath the Western Wave, Osiris dies, and the world mourns.

The Ancient Astronomers saw all the great Symbols of Masonry in the Stars. Sirius still glitters in our

Lodges as the Blazing Star, (*l'Etoile Flamboyante*). The Sun is still symbolized by the point within a Circle; and, with the Moon and Mercury or Anubis, in the three Great Lights of the Lodge. Not only to these, but to the figures and numbers exhibited by the Stars, were ascribed peculiar and divine powers. The veneration paid to numbers had its source there. The three Kings in Orion are in a straight line, and equidistant from each other, the two extreme Stars being 3°.apart, and each of the three distant from the one nearest it 1° 30'. And as the number *three* is peculiar to Apprentices, so the straight line is the first principle of Geometry, having length but no breadth, and being but the extension of a point, and an emblem of Unity, and thus of Good, as the divided or broken line is of Duality or Evil. Near these Stars are the Hyades, *five* in number, appropriate to the Fellow-Craft; and close to them the Pleiades, of the Master's number, *seven*: and thus these three sacred numbers, consecrated in Masonry as they were in the Pythagorean philosophy, always appear together in the Heavens, when the Bull, emblem of fertility and production, glitters among the Stars, and Aldebaran leads the Hosts of Heaven (*Tsbauth*).

Algenib in Perseus and Almaach and Algol in Andromeda form a right-angled triangle, illustrate the 47th problem, and display the Grand Master's square upon the skies. Denebola in Leo, Arcturus in Boötes and Spica in Virgo form an equilateral triangle, universal emblem of Perfection, and the Deity with His Trinity of Infinite Attributes, Wisdom, Power and Harmony; and that other, the generative, preserving and destroying Powers. The Three Kings form, with Rigel in Orion, two triangles included in one: and Capella and Menkalina in Auriga, with Bellatrix and Betelgueux in Orion, form two isosceles triangles with β Tauri, that is equidistant from each pair; while the four first made a right-angled parallelogram,—the oblong square so often mentioned in our degrees.

Julius Firmicus, in his description of the mysteries, says, "But in those funerals and lamentations which are annually celebrated in honour of Osiris, their defenders pretend a physical reason. They call the seeds of fruit, Osiris; the Earth, Isis; the natural heat, Typhon: and because the fruits are ripened by the natural heat, and collected for the life of man, and are separated from their marriage to the earth, and are sown again when Winter approaches, this they would have to be the death of Osiris: but when the fruits, by the genial fostering of the earth, begin again to be generated by a new procreation, this is the finding of Osiris."

No doubt the decay of vegetation and the falling of the leaves, emblems of dissolution and evidences of the action of that Power that changes Life into Death, in order to bring Life again out of Death, were regarded as signs of that Death that seemed coming upon all Nature; as the springing of leaves and buds and flowers in the spring was a sign of restoration to life: but these were all secondary, and referred to the Sun as first cause. It was *his* figurative death that was mourned, and not theirs; and with that death, as with his return to life, many of the stars were connected.

We have already alluded to the relations which the twelve signs of the Zodiac bear to the legend of the Master's Degree. Some other coincidences may have sufficient interest to warrant mention.

Hiram was assailed at the East, West and South Gates of the Temple. The two equinoxes were called, we have seen, by all the Ancients, the Gates of Heaven, and the Syrians and Egyptians considered the Fish (the Constellation near Aquarius, and one of the Stars whereof is Fomalhaut) to be indicative of violence and death.

Hiram lay several days in the grave; and, at the Winter Solstice, for five or six days, the length of the days did not perceptibly increase. Then, the Sun commencing again to climb Northward, as Osiris was said to arise from the dead, so Hiram was raised, by the powerful attraction of the Lion (Leo), who waited for him at the Summer Solstice, and drew him to himself.

The names of the three assassins may have been adopted from three Stars that we have already named. We search in vain in the Hebrew or Arabic for the names *Jubelo, Jubela* and *Jubelum*. They embody an utter absurdity, and are capable of no explanation in those languages. Nor are the names *Gibs, Gravelot, Hobhen* and the like, in the Ancient and Accepted Rite, any more plausible, or better referable to any ancient language. But when, by the precession of the Equinoxes, the Sun was in Libra at the Autumnal Equinox, he met, in that sign, where the reign of Typhon commenced, three Stars forming a triangle,—*Zuben-es-Chamali* in the West, *Zuben-Hak-Rabi* in the East, and *Zuben-El-Gubi* in the South, the latter immediately below the Tropic of Capricorn, and so within the realm of Darkness. From these names, those of the murderers have perhaps been corrupted. In Zuben-Hak-Rabi we may see the original of Jubelum Akirop; and in Zuben-El-Gubi, that of Jubelo Gibs: and time and ignorance may even have transmuted the words Es Chamali into one as little like them as Gravelot.

Isis, the Moon personified, sorrowing sought for her husband. Nine or twelve Fellow-Crafts (the Rites vary as to the number), in white aprons, were sent to search for Hiram in the Legend of the Master's Degree; or, in this Rite, the Nine Knights Elu. Along the path that the Moon travels are nine conspicuous Stars, by which nautical men determine their longitude at Sea;—Arietis, Aldebaran, Pollux, Regulus, Spica Virginis, Antares, Altair, Fomalhaut and Markab. These might be well said to accompany Isis in her search.

In the York Rite, *twelve* Fellow-Crafts were sent to search for the body of Hiram and the murderers. Their number corresponds with that of the Pleiades and Hyades in Taurus, among which Stars the Sun was found when Light began to prevail over Darkness, and the Mysteries were held. These Stars, we have shown, received early and particular attention from the astronomers and poets. The Pleiades were the Stars of the ocean to the benighted mariner; the Virgins of Spring, heralding the season of blossoms.

As six Pleiades only are now visible, the number twelve may have been obtained by them, with Aldebaran, and five far more brilliant Stars than any other of the Hyades, in the same region of the Heavens, and which were always spoken of in connection with the Pleiades;—the Three Kings in the belt of Orion, and Bellatrix and Betelgueux on his shoulders; brightest of the flashing starry hosts.

"Canst thou," asks Job, "bind the sweet influences of the Pleiades or loose the bands of Orion?" And in the book of Amos we find these Stars connected with the victory of Light over Darkness: "Seek Him," says that Seer, "that maketh the Seven Stars (the familiar name of the Pleiades), and Orion, AND TURNETH THE SHADOW OF DEATH INTO MORNING."

An old legend in Masonry says that a dog led the Nine Elu to the cavern where Abiram was hid. Boötes was anciently called Caleb Anubach, the Barking Dog; and was personified in Anubis, who bore the head of a dog, and aided Isis in her search. Arcturus, one of his Stars, fiery red, as if fervent and zealous, is also connected by Job with the Pleiades and Orion. When Taurus opened the year, Arcturus rose after the Sun, at the time of the Winter Solstice, and seemed searching him through the darkness, until, sixty days afterwards, he rose at the same hour. Orion then also, at the Winter Solstice, rose at noon, and at night seemed to be in search of the Sun.

So, referring again to the time when the Sun entered the autumnal equinox, there are nine remarkable Stars that come to the meridian nearly at the same time, rising as Libra sets, and so seeming to chase that Constellation. They are Capella and Menkalina in the Charioteer, Aldebaran in Taurus, Bellatrix, Betelgueux, the Three Kings and Rigel in Orion. Aldebaran passes the meridian first, indicating his right to his peculiar title of *Leader*. Nowhere in the heavens are there, near the same meridian, so many splendid Stars. And close behind them, but further South, follows Sirius, the Dog-Star, who showed the nine Elu the way to the murderer's cave.

Besides the division of the signs into the ascending and descending series (referring to the upward and downward progress of the soul), the latter from Cancer to Capricorn, and the former from Capricorn to Cancer, there was another division of them not less important; that of the six superior and six inferior signs; the former, 2455 years before our era, from Taurus to Scorpio, and 300 years before our era, from Aries to Libra; and the latter, 2455 years B. C. from Scorpio to Taurus, and 300 years B. C. from Libra to Aries; of which we have already spoken, as the two Hemispheres, or Kingdoms of Good and Evil, Light and Darkness; of Ormuzd and Ahriman among the Persians, and Osiris and Typhon among the Egyptians.

With the Persians, the six first Genii, created by Ormuzd, presided over the six first signs, Aries, Taurus, Gemini, Cancer, Leo and Virgo: and the six evil Genii, or Devs, created by Ahriman, over the six others, Libra, Scorpio, Sagittarius, Capricornus, Aquarius and Pisces. The soul was fortunate and happy under the Empire of the six first; and began to be sensible of evil, when it passed under the Balance or Libra, the seventh sign. Thus the soul entered the realm of Evil and Darkness when it passed into the Constellations that belong to and succeed the autumnal Equinox; and it re-entered the realm of Good and Light, when it arrived, returning, at those of the Vernal Equinox. It lost its felicity by means of the Balance, and regained it by means of the Lamb. This is a necessary consequence of the premises; and it is confirmed by the authorities and by emblems still extant.

Sallust the Philosopher, speaking of the Feasts of Rejoicing, celebrated at the Vernal Equinox, and those of Mourning, in memory of the rape of Proserpine, at the autumnal equinox, says that the former were celebrated, because then is effected, as it were, the return of the soul towards the Gods: that the time when the principle of Light recovered its superiority over that of Darkness, or day over night, was the most favourable one for souls that tend to re-ascend to their Principle; and that when Darkness and the Night again become victors, was most favourable to the descent of souls towards the infernal regions.

For that reason, the old astrologers, as Firmicus states, fixed the locality of the river Styx in the 8th degree of the Balance. And he thinks that by Styx was allegorically meant the earth.

The Emperor Julian gives the same explanation, but more fully developed. He states, as a reason why the august Mysteries of Ceres and Proserpine were celebrated at the Autumnal Equinox, that at that period of the year men feared lest the impious and dark power of the Evil Principle, then commencing to conquer, should do harm to their souls. They were a precaution and means of safety, thought to be necessary at the moment when the God of Light was passing into the opposite or adverse region of the world; while at the Vernal Equinox there was less to be feared, because then that God, present in one portion of the world, *recalled souls to him*, he says, *and showed himself to be their Saviour.* He had a little before developed that theological idea, of the attractive force which the Sun exercises over souls, drawing them to him and raising them to his luminous sphere. He attributes this effect to him at the feasts of Atys, dead and restored to life, or the feasts of Rejoicing, which at the end of three days succeeded the mourning for that death; and he inquires why those mysteries were celebrated at the Vernal Equinox. The reason, he says, is evident. As the sun, arriving at the equinoctial point of spring, drawing nearer to us, increases the length of the days, that period seems most appropriate for those ceremonies. For, besides that there is a great affinity between the substance of Light and the nature of the Gods, the Sun has that occult force of attraction, by which he draws matter towards himself, by means of his warmth, making plants to shoot and grow, &c.; and why can he not, by the same divine and pure action of his rays, attract and draw to him fortunate souls. Then, as light is analogous to the Divine Nature, and favourable to souls struggling to return to their First Principle, and as that light so increases at the Vernal Equinox, that the days prevail in duration over the nights, and as the Sun has an attractive force, besides the visible energy of his rays, it follows that souls are attracted towards the solar light. He does not further pursue the explanation; because, he says, it belongs to a mysterious doctrine, beyond the reach of the vulgar, and known only to those who understand the mode of action of Deity, like the Chaldean author whom he cites, who had treated of the Mysteries of Light, or the God with seven rays.

Souls, the Ancients held, having emanated from the Principle of Light, partaking of its destiny here below, cannot be indifferent to or unaffected by these revolutions of the Great Luminary, alternately victor and overcome during every Solar revolution.

This will be found to be confirmed by an examination of some of the Symbols used in the Mysteries. One of the most famous of these was THE SERPENT, the peculiar Symbol also of this Degree. The Cosmogony of the Hebrews and that of the Gnostics designated this reptile as the author of the fate of Souls. It was consecrated in the Mysteries of Bacchus and in those of Eleusis. Pluto overcame the virtue of Proserpine under the form of a serpent; and, like the Egyptian God Serapis, was always pictured seated on a serpent, or with that reptile entwined about him. It is found on the Mithriac Monuments, and supplied the attributes of Typhon to the Egyptians. The sacred basilisc, in coil, with head and neck erect, was the royal ensign of the Pharaohs. Two of them were entwined around and hung suspended from the winged Globe on the Egyptian Monuments. On a tablet in one of the Tombs at Thebes, a God with a spear pierces a serpent's head. On a tablet from the Temple of Osiris at Philœ is a tree, with a man on one side, and a woman on the other, and in front of the woman an erect basilisc, with horns on its head and a disk between the horns. The head of Medusa was encircled by winged snakes, which, the head removed, left the Hierogram or Sacred Cypher of the Ophites or Serpent-worshippers. And the Serpent, in connection with the Globe or circle is found upon the monuments of all the Ancient Nations.

Over Libra, the sign through which souls were said to descend or fall, is found, on the Celestial Globe, the Serpent, grasped by Serpentarius, the Serpent-bearer. The head of the reptile is under Corona Borealis, the Northern Crown, called by Ovid, *Libera,* or *Proserpine;* and the two Constellations rise, with the Balance, after the Virgin (or Isis), whose feet rest on the eastern horizon at Sunrise on the day of the equinox. As the Serpent extends over both signs, Libra and Scorpio, it has been the gate through which souls descend, during the whole time that those two signs in succession marked the autumnal equinox. To this alluded the Serpent, which, in the Mysteries of Bacchus Saba-Zeus, was flung into the bosom of the initiate.

And hence came the enigmatical expression; *the Serpent engenders the Bull, and the Bull the Serpent;* alluding to the two adverse constellations, answering to the two equinoxes, one of which rose as the other set, and which were at the two points of the heavens through which souls passed, ascending and descending. By the Serpent of Autumn, souls fell; and they were regenerated again by the Bull on which Mithras sate, and whose attributes Bacchus-Zagreus and the Egyptian Osiris assumed, in their mysteries, wherein were represented the fall and regeneration of souls, by the Bull slain and restored to life.

Afterwards the regenerating Sun assumed the attributes of *Aries* or the Lamb; and in the Mysteries of Ammon, souls were regenerated by passing through that sign, after having fallen through the Serpent.

The Serpent-bearer, or Ophiucus, was Æsculapius, God of Healing. In the Mysteries of Eleusis, that Constellation was placed in the eighth Heaven: and on the eighth day of those Mysteries, the feast of Æsculapius was celebrated. It was also termed Epidaurus, or the feast of the Serpent of Epidaurus. The Serpent was sacred to Æsculapius; and was connected in various ways with the mythological adventures of Ceres.

So the libations to Souls, by pouring wine on the ground, and looking towards the two gates of Heaven, those of day and night, referred to the ascent and descent of Souls.

Ceres and the Serpent, Jupiter Ammon and the Bull, all figured in the Mysteries of Bacchus. Suppose Aries, or Jupiter Ammon occupied by the Sun setting in the West;—Virgo (Ceres) will be on the Eastern horizon, and in her train the Crown, or Proserpine. Suppose Taurus setting;—then the Serpent is in the East; and reciprocally; so that Jupiter Ammon, or the Sun of Aries causes the Crown to rise after the Virgin, in the train of which comes the Serpent. Place reciprocally the Sun at the other equinox, with the balance in the West, in conjunction with the Serpent under the Crown; and we shall see the Bull and the Pleiades rise in the East. Thus are explained all the fables as to the generation of the Bull by the Serpent and of the Serpent by the Bull, the biting of the testicles of the Bull by the Scorpion, on the Mithriac Monuments; and that Jupiter made Ceres with child by tossing into her bosom the testicles of a Ram.

In the Mysteries of the bull-horned Bacchus, the officers held serpents in their hands, raised them above their heads, and cried aloud, "Eva!" the generic oriental name of the serpent, and the particular name of the constellation in which the Persians placed Eve and the serpent. The Arabians call it *Hevan;* Ophiucus himself, *Hawa,* and the brilliant star in his head, *Ras-al-Hawa.* The use of this word *Eva* or *Evoë* caused Clemens of Alexandria to say that the priests in the Mysteries invoked *Eve,* by whom evil was brought into the world.

The mystic winnowing-fan, encircled by serpents, was used in the feasts of Bacchus. In the Isiac Mysteries a basilisc twined round the handle of the mystic vase. The Ophites fed a serpent in a mysterious ark, from which they took him when they celebrated the Mysteries, and allowed him to glide among the sacred bread. The Romans kept serpents in the Temples of Bona Dea and Æsculapius. In the Mysteries of Apollo, the pursuit of Latona by the serpent Python was represented. In the Egyptian Mysteries, the dragon Typhon pursued Isis.

According to Sanchoniathon, TAAUT, the interpreter of Heaven to men, attributed something divine to the nature of the dragon and serpents, in which the Phœnicians and Egyptians followed him. They have more vitality, more spiritual force, than any other creature; of a fiery nature, shown by the rapidity of their motions, without the limbs of other animals. They assume many shapes and attitudes, and dart with extraordinary quickness and force. When they have reached old age, they throw off that age and are young again, and increase in size and strength, for a certain period of years.

The Egyptian Priests fed the sacred serpents in the temple at Thebes. Taaut himself had in his writings discussed these mysteries in regard to the serpent. Sanchoniathon said in another work, that the serpent was immortal, and re-entered into himself: which, according to some ancient theosophists, particularly those of India, was an attribute of the Deity. And he also said that the serpent never died, unless by a violent death.

The Phœnicians called the serpent *Agathodemon* [the good spirit]; and Kneph was the Serpent-God of the Egyptians.

The Egyptians, Sanchoniathon said, represented the serpent with the head of a hawk, on account of the swift flight of that bird: and the chief Hierophant, the sacred interpreter, gave very mysterious explanations of that symbol; saying that such a serpent was a very divine creature, and that, opening his eyes, he lighted with their rays the whole of first-born space: when he closes them, it is darkness again. In reality, the hawk-headed serpent, genius of light, or good genius, was the symbol of the Sun.

In the hieroglyphic characters, a snake was the letter T or DJ. It occurs many times on the Rosetta stone. The horned serpent was the hieroglyphic for a God.

According to Eusebius, the Egyptians represented the world by a blue circle, sprinkled with flames, within which was extended a serpent with the head of a hawk. Proclus says they represented the four quarters of the world by a cross, and the soul of the world, or Kneph, by a serpent surrounding it in the form of a circle.

We read in Anaxagoras, that Orpheus said, that the water, and the vessel that produced it, were the primitive principles of things, and together gave existence to an animated being, which was a serpent, with two heads, one of a lion and the other of a bull, between which was the figure of a God whose name was Hercules or Kronos: that from Hercules came the egg of the world, which produced heaven and earth, by dividing itself into two hemispheres: and that the God Phanes, which issued from that egg, was in the shape of a serpent.

The Egyptian Goddess *Ken*, represented standing naked on a lion, held two serpents in her hand. She is the same as the *Astarte* or *Ashtaroth* of the Assyrians. *Hera*, worshipped in the Great Temple at Babylon, held in her right hand a serpent by the head; and near *Rhea*, also worshipped there, were two large silver serpents.

In a sculpture from Kouyunjik, two serpents attached to poles are near a fire-altar, at which two eunuchs are standing. Upon it is the sacred fire, and a bearded figure leads a wild goat to the sacrifice.

The serpent of the Temple of Epidaurus was sacred to *Æsculapius*, the God of Medicine, and 462 years after the building of the city, was taken to Rome after a pestilence.

The Phœnicians represented the God *Nomu*, (*Kneph* or *Amun-Kneph*) by a serpent. In Egypt, a Sun supported by two asps was the emblem of *Horhat* the good genius; and the serpent with the winged globe was placed over the doors and windows of the Temples as a tutelary God. Antipater of Sidon calls *Amun* "the renowned Serpent," and the Cerastes is often found embalmed in the Thebaid.

On ancient Tyrian coins and Indian Medals, a serpent was represented, coiled round the trunk of a tree. *Python*, the Serpent Deity, was esteemed oracular; and the tripod at Delphi was a triple-headed serpent of gold.

The portals of all the Egyptian Temples are decorated with the hierogram of the Circle and the Serpent. It is also found upon the Temple of Naki-Rustan in Persia; on the triumphal arch at Pechin, in China; over the gates of the great Temple of Chaundi Teeva, in Java; upon the walls of Athens; and in the Temple of Minerva at Tegea. The Mexican hierogram was formed by the intersecting of two great Serpents, which described the circle with their bodies, and had each a human head in its mouth.

All the Buddhist crosses in Ireland had serpents carved upon them. Wreaths of snakes are on the columns of the ancient Hindu Temple at Burwah-Sangor.

Among the Egyptians, it was a symbol of Divine Wisdom, when extended at length; and, with its tail in its mouth, of Eternity.

In the ritual of Zoroaster, the Serpent was a symbol of the Universe. In China, the ring between two Serpents was the symbol of the world governed by the power and wisdom of the Creator. The Bacchanals carried serpents in their hands or round their heads.

The Serpent entwined round an Egg, was a symbol common to the Indians, the Egyptians and the Druids. It referred to the creation of the Universe. A Serpent with an egg in his mouth was a symbol of the Universe containing within itself the germ of all things that the Sun develops.

The property possessed by the Serpent, of casting its skin, and thus apparently renewing its youth, made it an emblem of eternity and immortality. The Syrian women still employ it as a charm against barrenness, as did the devotees of Mithras and Saba-Zeus. The Earth-born civilizers of the early world, Fohi, Cecrops and Erechtheus, were half-man, half-serpent. The snake was the guardian of the Athenian Acropolis. Naheustan, the brazen serpent of the wilderness, became naturalized among the Hebrews as a token of healing power. "Be ye," said Christ, "wise as serpents, and harmless as doves."

The Serpent was as often a symbol of malevolence and enmity. It appears among the emblems of Siva-Roudra, the power of desolation and death: it is the bane of Aëpytus, Idmon, Archemorus and Philoctetes; it gnaws the roots of the tree of life in the Eddas, and bites the heel of unfortunate Eurydice. In Hebrew writers it is generally a type of evil; and is particularly so in the Indian and Persian Mythologies. When the Sea is churned by Mount Mandar rotating within the coils of the Cosmical Serpent Vasouki, to produce the Amrita or water of immortality, the serpent vomits a hideous poison, which spreads through and infects the universe, but which Vishnu renders harmless by swallowing it. Ahriman in serpent-form invades the realm of Ormuzd; and the Bull, emblem of life, is wounded by him and dies. It was therefore a religious obligation with every devout follower of Zoroaster to exterminate reptiles, and other impure animals, especially serpents. The moral and astronomical significancy of the Serpent were connected. It became a maxim of the Zend-Avesta, that Ahriman, the Principle of Evil, made the Great Serpent of Winter, who assaulted the creation of Ormuzd.

A serpent-ring was a well known symbol of time: and to express dramatically how time preys upon itself, the Egyptian priests fed vipers in a subterranean chamber, as it were in the sun's winter abode, on the fat of bulls, or the year's plenteousness. The dragon of winter pursues Ammon, the golden ram, to Mount Casius. The Virgin of the zodiac is bitten in the heel by Serpens, who, with Scorpio, rises immediately behind her; and as honey, the emblem of purity and salvation, was thought to be an antidote to the serpent's bite, so the bees of Aristæus, the emblems of nature's abundance, are destroyed through the agency of the serpent, and regenerated within the entrails of the Vernal Bull.

The Sun-God is finally victorious. Chrishna crushes the head of the serpent Calyia; Apollo destroys Python, and Hercules that Lernæan monster whose poison festered in the foot of Philoctetes, of Mopsus, of Chiron, or of Sagittarius. The infant Hercules destroys the pernicious snakes detested of the gods, and ever, like St. George of England and Michael the Archangel, wars against hydras and dragons.

The eclipses of the sun and moon were believed by the orientals to be caused by the assaults of a dæmon in dragon-form; and they endeavoured to scare away the intruder by shouts and menaces. This was the original Leviathan or Crooked Serpent of old, transfixed in the olden time by the power of Jehovah, and suspended as a glittering trophy in the sky; yet also the Power of Darkness, supposed to be ever in pursuit of Sun and Moon. When it finally overtakes them, it will entwine them in its folds, and prevent their shining. In the last Indian Avatara, as in the Eddas, a serpent vomiting flames is expected to destroy the world. The serpent presides over the close of the year, where it guards the approach to the golden fleece of Aries, and the three apples or seasons of the Hesperides; presenting a formidable obstacle to the career of the Sun-God. The Great Destroyer of snakes is occasionally married to them; Hercules with the northern dragon begets the three ancestors of Scythia; for the Sun seems at one time to rise victorious from the contest with darkness, and at another to sink into its embraces. The northern constellation Draco, whose sinuosities wind like a river through the wintry bear, was made the astronomical cincture of the universe, as the serpent encircles the mundane egg in the Egyptian hieroglyphics.

The Persian Ahriman was called "The old serpent, the liar from the beginning, the Prince of Darkness, and the rover up and down." The Dragon was a well known symbol of the waters and of great rivers; and it was natural that by the pastoral Asiatic Tribes, the powerful nations of the alluvial plains in their neighbourhood, who adored the dragon or Fish, should themselves be symbolized under the form of dragons; and, overcome by the superior might of the Hebrew God, as monstrous Leviathans maimed and destroyed by him. Ophioneus, in the old Greek Theology, warred against Kronos, and was overcome and cast into his proper element, the sea. There he is installed as the Sea-God Oannes or Dragon, the Leviathan of the watery half of creation, the dragon who vomited a flood of water after the persecuted woman of the Apocalypse, the monster who threatened to devour Hesione and Andromeda, and who for a time became the grave of Hercules and Jonah: and he corresponds with the obscure name of *Rahab*, whom Jehovah is said in Job to have transfixed and overcome.

In the spring, the year or Sun-God appears as Mithras or Europa mounted on the Bull; but in the opposite half of the Zodiac he rides the emblem of the waters, the winged horse of Nestor or Poseidon: and the serpent, rising heliacally at the autumnal equinox, besetting with poisonous influence the cold constellation Sagittarius, is explained as the reptile in the path who "bites the horse's heels, so that his rider falls backward." The same serpent, the Oannes Aphrenos or Musaros of Syncellus, was the Midgard Serpent which Odin sunk beneath the sea, but which grew to such a size as to encircle the whole earth.

For these Asiatic symbols of the contest of the Sun-God with the Dragon of darkness and winter were imported not only into the Zodiac, but into the more homely circle of European legend; and both Thor and Odin fight with dragons, as Apollo did with Python the great scaly snake, Achilles with the Scamander and Bellerophon with the Chimæra. In the apocryphal book of Esther, dragons herald "a day of darkness and obscurity;" and St. George of England, a problematic Cappadocian Prince, was originally only a varying form of Mithras. Jehovah is said to have "cut Rahab and wounded the dragon." The latter is not only the type of earthly desolation, the dragon of the deep waters, but also the leader of the banded conspirators of the sky, of the rebellious stars, which, according to Enoch, "came not at the right time;" and his tail drew a third part of the Host of Heaven, and cast them to the earth. Jehovah "divided the sea by his strength, and broke the heads of the Dragons in the waters." And, according to the Jewish and Persian belief, the Dragon would, in the latter days, the winter of time, enjoy a short period of licensed impunity, which would be a season of the greatest suffering to the people of the earth; but he would finally be bound or destroyed in the great battle of Messiah; or, as seems intimated by the Rabbinical figure of being eaten by the faithful, be, like Ahriman or Vasouki, ultimately absorbed by and united with the Principle of good.

Near the image of Rhea, in the Temple of Bel at Babylon, were two large serpents of silver, says Diodorus, each weighing thirty talents; and in the same Temple was an image of Juno, holding in her right hand the head of a serpent. The Greeks called Bel, *Beliar;* and Hesychius interprets that word to mean a dragon or great serpent. We learn from the book of Bel and the Dragon, that in Babylon was kept a great live serpent, which the people worshipped.

The Assyrians, the Emperors of Constantinople, the Parthians, Scythians, Saxons, Chinese and Danes all bore the serpent as a standard; and among the spoils taken by Aurelian from Zenobia were such standards, *Persici Dracones.* The Persians represented Ormuzd and Ahriman by two serpents, contending for the mundane egg. Mithras is represented with a lion's head and human body, encircled by a serpent. In the Sadder is this precept: "When you kill serpents, you shall repeat the Zend-Avesta, and thence you will obtain great merit; for it is the same as if you had killed so many devils."

Serpents encircling rings and globes, and issuing from globes, are common in the Persian, Egyptian, Chinese and Indian monuments. Vishnu is represented reposing on a coiled serpent, whose folds form a canopy over him. Mahadeva is represented with a snake around his neck, one round his hair, and armlets of serpents on both arms. Bhairava sits on the coils of a serpent, whose head rises above his own. Parvati has snakes about her neck and waist. Vishnu is the Preserving Spirit, Mahadeva and Bhairava are names of Siva, the Evil Principle, and Parvati is his consort. The King of Evil Demons was called in Hindû Mythology, *Naga*, the King of Serpents, in which name we trace the Hebrew *Nachash*, serpent.

In Cashmere were seven hundred places where carved images of serpents were worshipped: and in Thibet the great Chinese Dragon ornamented the Temples of the Grand Lama. In China, the dragon was the stamp and symbol of royalty, sculptured in all the Temples, blazoned on the furniture of the houses, and interwoven with the vestments of the chief nobility. The Emperor bears it as his armorial device: it is engraved on his sceptre and diadem, and on all the vases of the imperial palace. The Chinese believe that there is a dragon of extraordinary strength and sovereign power, in heaven, in the air, on the waters, and on the mountains. Their God Fohi is said to have had the form of a man, terminating in the tail of a snake, a combination to be more fully explained to you in a subsequent degree.

The dragon and serpent are the 5th and 6th sign of the Chinese Zodiac; and the Hindus and Chinese believe that, at every eclipse, the sun or moon is seized by a huge serpent or dragon, the serpent *Asootee* of the Hindus, which enfolds the globe; and the constellation Draco; to which also refers "the War in Heaven, when Michael and his Angels fought against the dragon."

Sanchoniathon says that Taaut was the author of the worship of serpents among the Phœnicians. He "consecrated," he says, "the species of dragons and serpents; and the Phœnicians and Egyptians followed him in this superstition." He was "the first who made an image of Cœlus;" that is, who represented the Heavenly Host of Stars by visible symbols; and was probably the same as the Egyptian Thoth. On the Tyrian coins of the age of Alexander, serpents are represented in many positions and attitudes, coiled round trees, erect in front of altars, and crushed by the Syrian Hercules.

The seventh letter of the Egyptian alphabet, called *Zeuta* or *Life*, was sacred to Thoth, and was expressed by a serpent standing on his tail: and that Deity, the God of healing, like Æsculapius, to whom the serpent was consecrated, leans on a knotted stick round which coils a snake. The Isiac tablet, describing the mysteries of Isis, is charged with serpents in every part, as her emblems. The *asp* was specially dedicated to her, and is seen on the heads of her statues, on the bonnets of her priests, and on the tiaras of the Kings of Egypt. Serapis was sometimes represented with a human head and serpentine tail; and in one engraving two minor Gods are represented with him, one by a serpent with a bull's head, and the other by a serpent with the radiated head of a lion.

On an ancient sacrificial vessel found in Denmark, having several compartments, a serpent is represented attacking a kneeling boy, pursuing him, retreating from him, appealed to beseechingly by him, and conversing with him. We are at once reminded of the Sun at the new year represented by a child sitting on a lotus, and of the relations of the Sun of Spring with the Autumnal Serpent, pursued by and pursuing him, and in conjunction with him. Other figures on this vessel belong to the Zodiac.

The base of the *tripod* of the Pythian Priestess was a triple-headed serpent of brass, whose body, folded in circles growing wider and wider towards the ground, formed a conical column, while the three heads, disposed triangularly, upheld the *tripod* of gold. A similar column was placed on a pillar in the Hippodrome at Constantinople, by the founder of that city; one of the heads of which is said to have been broken off by Mahomet the Second, by a blow with his iron mace.

The British God Hu was called "The Dragon—Ruler of the World," and his car was drawn by serpents. His ministers were styled *Adders*. A Druid in a poem of Taliessin says, "I am a Druid, I am an *Architect*, I am a Prophet, I am a *Serpent* (Gnadi)." The Car of the Goddess Ceridwen also was drawn by serpents.

In the elegy of Uther Pendragon, this passage occurs in a description of the religious rites of the Druids: "While the Sanctuary is earnestly invoking *The Gliding King*, before whom *the Fair One* retreats, upon the veil that covers the huge stones; whilst the Dragon moves round over the places which contain vessels of drink-offering, whilst the drink-offering is in *the Golden Horns:*" in which we readily discover the mystic and obscure allusion to the Autumnal Serpent pursuing the Sun along the circle of the Zodiac, to the celestial cup or crater, and the Golden horns of Virgil's milk-white Bull: and, a line or two further on, we find the Priest imploring the victorious *Beli*, the Sun-God of the Babylonians.

With the serpent, in the Ancient Monuments, is very often found associated the Cross. The Serpent upon a Cross was an Egyptian Standard. It occurs repeatedly upon the Grand Staircase of the Temple of Osiris at Philoë: and on the pyramid of Ghizeh are represented two kneeling figures erecting a Cross, on the top of which is a serpent erect. The *Crux Ansata* was a Cross with a coiled Serpent above it; and it is perhaps, the most common of all emblems on the Egyptian Monuments, carried in the hand of almost every figure of a Deity or a Priest. It was, as we learn by the monuments, the form of the iron tether-pins, used for making fast to the ground the cords by which young animals were confined; and as used by shepherds, became a symbol of Royalty to the Shepherd Kings.

A Cross, like a Teutonic or Maltese one, formed by four curved lines within a circle, is also common on the Monuments, and represented the Tropics and the Colures.

The Caduceus, borne by Hermes or Mercury, and also by Cybele, Minerva, Anubis, Hercules Ogmius the God of the Celts, and the personified Constellation Virgo, was a winged wand, entwined by two serpents. It was originally a simple Cross, symbolizing the equator and equinoctial colure, and the four elements proceeding from a common centre. This Cross, surmounted by a circle, and that by a crescent, became an emblem of the Supreme Deity—or of the active power of generation and the passive power of production conjoined,—and was appropriated to Thoth or Mercury. It then assumed an improved form, the arms of the Cross being changed into wings, and the circle and crescent being formed by two snakes, springing from the wand, forming a circle by crossing each other, and their heads making the horns of the crescent; in which form it is seen in the hands of Anubis.

The triple Tau, in the centre of a circle and a triangle, typifies the Sacred Name; and represents the Sacred Triad, the Creating, Preserving and Destroying Powers; as well as the three great lights of Masonry. If to the Masonic point within a Circle, and the two parallel lines, we add the single Tau Cross, we have the Ancient Egyptian Triple Tau.

A column in the form of a cross, with a circle over it, was used by the Egyptians to measure the increase of the inundations of the Nile. The Tau and Triple Tau are found in many Ancient Alphabets.

With the Tau or the Triple Tau may be connected, within two circles, the double cube, or perfection; or the perfect ashlar.

The *Crux Ansata* is found on the sculptures of Khorsabad; on the ivories from Nimroud, of the same age, carried by an Assyrian Monarch; and on cylinders of the later Assyrian period.

As the single Tau represents the one God, so, no doubt, the Triple Tau, the origin of which cannot be traced, was meant to represent the Trinity of his attributes, the three Masonic pillars, WISDOM, STRENGTH and HARMONY.

The Prophet Ezekiel, in the 4th verse of the 9th chapter, says: "And the Lord said unto him, 'Go through the midst of the city, through the midst of Jerusalem, and mark the letter TAU upon the foreheads of those that sigh and mourn for all the abominations that be done in the midst thereof.'" So the Latin Vulgate, and the probably most ancient copies of the Septuagint translate the passage. This *Tau* was in the form of the cross of this degree, and it was the emblem of *life* and *salvation*. The Samaritan *Tau* and the Ethiopic *Tavvi* are the evident prototype of the Greek *τ*; and we learn from Tertullian, Origen and St. Jerome that the Hebrew *Tau* was anciently written in the form of a Cross.

In ancient times the mark *Tau* was set on those who had been acquitted by their judges, as a symbol of innocence. The military commanders placed it on soldiers who escaped unhurt from the field of battle, as a sign of their safety under the Divine Protection.

It was a sacred symbol among the Druids. Divesting a tree of part of its branches, they left it in the shape of a Tau Cross, preserved it carefully, and consecrated it with solemn ceremonies. On the tree they cut deeply the word TAU, by which they meant God. On the right arm of the Cross, they inscribed the word HESUS, on the left BELEN or BELENUS, and on the middle of the trunk THARAMIS. This represented the sacred *Triad*.

It is certain that the Indians, Egyptians and Arabians paid veneration to the sign of the Cross, thousands of years before the coming of Christ. Everywhere it was a sacred symbol. The Hindus and the Celtic Druids built many of their Temples in the form of a Cross, as the ruins still remaining clearly show, and particularly the ancient Druidical Temple at Classerniss in the Island of Lewis in Scotland. The Circle is of 12 Stones. On each of the sides, east, west and south are three. In the centre was the image of the Deity; and on the north an avenue of twice nineteen stones, and one at the entrance. The Supernal Pagoda at Benares is in the form of a Cross; and the Druidical subterranean grotto at New Grange in Ireland.

The Statue of Osiris at Rome had the same emblem. Isis and Ceres also bore it; and the caverns of initiation were constructed in that shape with a pyramid over the *Sacellum*.

Crosses were cut in the stones of the Temple of Serapis in Alexandria; and many Tau Crosses are to be seen in the sculptures of Alabastion and Esné, in Egypt. On coins, the symbol of the Egyptian God Kneph was a Cross within a Circle.

The Crux Ansata was the particular emblem of Osiris, and his sceptre ended with that figure. It was also the emblem of Hermes, and was considered a Sublime Hieroglyphic, possessing mysterious powers and virtues, as a wonder-working amulet.

The Sacred Tau occurs in the hands of the mummy-shaped figures between the forelegs of the row of Sphynxes, in the great avenue leading from Luxor to Karnac. By the Tau Cross the Cabalists expressed the number 10, a perfect number, denoting Heaven, and the Pythagorean Tetractys, or incommunicable name of God. The Tau Cross is also found on the stones in front of the door of the Temple of Amunoth III, at Thebes, who reigned about the time when the Israelites took possession of Canaan : and the Egyptian Priests carried t in all the sacred processions.

Tertullian, who had been initiated, informs us that the Tau was inscribed on the forehead of every person who had been admitted into the Mysteries of Mithras.

As the simple Tau represented Life, so, when the Circle, symbol of Eternity was added, it represented Eternal life.

At the Initiation of a King, the Tau, as the emblem of life and key of the Mysteries, was impressed upon his lips.

In the Indian Mysteries, the Tau Cross, under the name of *Tiluk*, was marked upon the body of the Candidate, as a sign that he was set apart for the Sacred Mysteries.

On the upright tablet of the King, discovered at Nimroud, are the names of thirteen Great Gods (among which are YAV and BEL) ; and the left hand character of every one is a cross composed of two cuneiform characters.

The Cross appears upon an Ancient Phœnician medal found in the ruins of Citium ; on the very ancient Buddhist Obelisk near Ferns in Ross-shire ; on the Buddhist Round Towers in Ireland, and upon the splendid obelisk of the same era at Forres in Scotland.

Upon the façade of a temple at Kalabche in Nubia are three regal figures, each holding à Crux Ansata.

Like the Subterranean Mithriatic Temple at New Grange in Scotland, the Pagodas of Benares and Mathura were in the form of a Cross. Magnificent Buddhist Crosses were erected, and are still standing, at Clonmacnoise, Finglas and Kilcullen in Ireland. Wherever the monuments of Buddhism are found, in India, Ceylon or Ireland, we find the Cross: for Buddha or Boudh was represented to have been crucified.

All the planets known to the Ancients, were distinguished by the Mystic Cross, in conjunction with the solar or lunar symbols ; Saturn by a cross over a crescent, Jupiter by a cross under a crescent, Mars by a cross resting obliquely on a circle, Venus, by a cross under a circle, and Mercury by a cross surmounted by a circle and that by a crescent.

The Solstices, Cancer and Capricorn, the two Gates of Heaven, are the two pillars of Hercules, beyond which he, the Sun, never journeyed: and they still appear in our Lodges, as the two great columns, Jachin and Boaz, and also as the two parallel lines that bound the circle with a point in the centre, emblem of the Sun between the two tropics of Cancer and Capricorn.

The Blazing Star in our Lodges, we have already said, represents Sirius, Anubis, or Mercury, Guardian and Guide of Souls. Our Ancient English brethren also considered it an emblem of the Sun. In the old Lectures they said ; " The Blazing Star or Glory in the centre refers us to that Grand Luminary the Sun, which enlightens the Earth, and by its genial influence dispenses blessings to mankind." It is also said in those lectures to be an emblem of Prudence. The word *Prudentia* means, in its original and fullest signification, *Foresight:* and accordingly the Blazing Star has been regarded as an emblem of Omniscience, or the All-Seeing Eye, which to the Ancients was the Sun.

Even the Dagger of the Elu of Nine is that used in the Mysteries of Mithras; which, with its blade black and hilt white, was an emblem of the two principles of Light and Darkness.

Isis, the same as Ceres, was, as we learn from Eratosthenes, the Constellation Virgo, represented by a woman holding an ear of wheat. The different emblems which accompany her in the description given by Apuleius, a serpent on either side, a golden vase, with a serpent twined round the handle, and the animals that marched in procession, the bear, the ape, and Pegasus, represented the Constellations that rising with the Virgin, when on the day of the Vernal Equinox she stood in the Oriental gate of Heaven, brilliant with the rays of the full moon, seemed to march in her train.

The cup, consecrated in the Mysteries both of Isis and Eleusis, was the Constellation Crater or the Cup. The sacred vessel of the Isiac ceremony finds its counterpart in the Heavens. The Olympic robe presented to the initiate, a magnificent mantle, covered with figures of serpents and animals, and under which were twelve other sacred robes, wherewith he was clothed in the sanctuary, alluded to the starry Heaven and the twelve signs: while the seven preparatory immersions in the sea alluded to the seven spheres, through which the soul plunged, to arrive here below and take up its abode in a body.

The Celestial Virgin, during the three last centuries that preceded the Christian era, occupied the horoscope or Oriental point, and that gate of Heaven through which the Sun and Moon ascended above the horizon at the two equinoxes. Again it occupied it at midnight, at the winter Solstice, the precise moment when the year commenced. Thus it was essentially connected with the march of times and seasons, of the Sun, the Moon, and day and night, at the principal epochs of the year. At the equinoxes were celebrated the greater and lesser Mysteries of Ceres. When souls descended past the Balance, at the moment when the Sun occupied that point, the Virgin rose before him; she stood at the gates of day and opened them to him. Her brilliant Star, Spica Virginis, and Arcturus, in Boütes, northwest of it, heralded his coming. When he had returned to the vernal equinox, at the moment when souls were regenerated, again it was the Celestial Virgin that led the march of the signs of night; and in her stars came the beautiful full moon of that month. Night and Day were in succession introduced by her, when they began to diminish in length; and souls, before arriving at the gates of Hell, were also led by her. In going through these signs, they passed the Styx in the 8th degree of Libra. She was the famous Sibyl who initiated Eneas, and opened to him the way to the infernal regions.

This peculiar situation of the Constellation Virgo, has caused it to enter into all the sacred fables in regard to nature, under different names and the most varied forms. It often takes the name of Isis or the Moon, which, when at its full at the Vernal Equinox, was in union with it or beneath its feet. Mercury (or Anubis) having his domicil and exaltation in the sign Virgo, was, in all the sacred fables and Sanctuaries, the inseparable companion of Isis, without whose counsels she did nothing.

This relation between the emblems and mysterious recitals of the initiations, and the Heavenly bodies and order of the world, was still more clear in the Mysteries of Mithras, adored as the Sun in Asia Minor, Cappadocia, Armenia and Persia, and whose Mysteries went to Rome in the time of Sylla. This is amply proved by the descriptions we have of the Mithriac cave, in which were figured the two movements of the Heavens, that of the fixed Stars and that of the Planets, the Constellations, the eight mystic gates of the spheres, and the symbols of the elements. So on a celebrated monument of that religion, found at Rome, were figured, the Serpent or Hydra under Leo, as in the Heavens, the Celestial Dog, the Bull, the Scorpion, the Seven Planets, represented by seven altars, the Sun, Moon, and emblems relating to Light, to Darkness, and to their succession during the year, where each in turn triumphs for six months.

The Mysteries of Atys were celebrated when the Sun entered Aries; and among the emblems was a ram at the foot of a tree which was being cut down.

. Thus, if not the whole truth, it is yet a large part of it, that the Heathen Pantheon, in its infinite diversity of names and personifications, was but a multitudinous, though in its origin unconscious allegory, of which physical phenomena, and principally the Heavenly Bodies, were the fundamental types. The glorious images of Divinity which formed Jehovah's Host, were the Divine Dynasty or real theocracy which governed the early world; and the men of the golden age, whose looks held commerce with the skies, and who watched the radiant rulers bringing winter and summer to mortals, might be said with poetic truth to live in immediate communication with Heaven, and like the Hebrew Patriarchs, to see God face to face. Then the Gods introduced their own worship among mankind: then Oannes, Oe or Aquarius rose from the Red Sea to impart science to the Babylonians; then the bright Bull legislated for India and Crete; and the Lights of Heaven, personified as Liber and Ceres, hung the Bœotian hills with vineyards, and gave the golden sheaf to Eleusis. The children of men were, in a sense, allied, or married, to those sons of God who sang the jubilee of creation; and the encircling vault with its countless Stars, which to the excited imagination of the solitary Chaldean wanderer appeared as animated intelligences, might naturally be compared to a gigantic ladder, on which, in their rising and setting, the Angel luminaries appeared to be ascending and descending between earth and Heaven. The original revelation died out of men's memories; they worshipped the Creature instead of the Creator; and holding all earthly things as connected by eternal links of harmony and sympathy with the heavenly bodies, they united in one view astronomy, astrology and religion. Long wandering thus in error, they at length ceased to look upon the Stars and external nature as Gods; and by directing their attention to the microcosm or narrower world of self, they again became acquainted with the True Ruler and Guide of the Universe, and used the old fables and superstitions as symbols and allegories, by which to convey and under which to hide the great truths which had faded out of most men's remembrance.

In the Hebrew writings, the term "Heavenly Hosts" includes not only the counsellors and emissaries of Jehovah, but also the celestial luminaries; and the stars, imagined in the East to be animated intelligences, presiding over human weal and woe, are identified with the more distinctly impersonated messengers or angels, who execute the Divine decrees, and whose predominance in heaven is in mysterious correspondence and relation with the powers and dominions of the earth. In Job, the Morning Stars and the Sons of God are identified; they join in the same chorus of praise to the Almighty; they are both susceptible of joy; they walk in brightness; and are liable to impurity and imperfection in the sight of God. The Elohim originally included not only foreign superstitious forms, but also all that host of heaven which was revealed in poetry to the shepherds of the desert, now as an encampment of warriors, now as careering in chariots of fire, and now as winged messengers, ascending and descending the vault of heaven, to communicate the will of God to mankind.

"The Eternal," says the Bereshith Rabba to Genesis, "called forth Abraham and his posterity out of the dominion of the stars; by nature, the Israelite was a servant to the stars, and born under their influence, as are the heathen; but by virtue of the law given on Mount Sinai, he became liberated from this degrading servitude." The Arabs had a similar legend. The Prophet Amos explicitly asserts that the Israelites, in the desert, worshipped, not Jehovah, but Moloch, or a Star-God, equivalent to Saturn. The Gods El or Jehovah were not merely planetary or solar. Their symbolism, like that of every other Deity, was coextensive with nature, and with the mind of man. Yet the astrological character is assigned even to Jehovah. He is described as seated on the pinnacle of the universe, leading forth the Hosts of Heaven, and telling them unerringly by name and number. His stars are His sons and His eyes, which run through the whole world, keeping watch over men's deeds. The stars and planets were properly the angels. In Pharisaic tradition, as in the phraseology of the New Testament, the Heavenly Host appears as an Angelic Army, divided into regiments and brigades, under the command of imaginary chiefs, such as Massaloth, Legion, Karton, Gistra, &c.,—each Gistra being captain of 365,000 myriads of stars. The Seven Spirits which stand before the throne, spoken of by several Jewish writers, and generally presumed to have been immediately derived from the Persian Amshaspands, were ultimately the seven planetary intelligences, the original model of the seven-branched golden candlestick exhibited to Moses on God's mountain. The stars were imagined to have fought in their courses against Sisera. The Heavens were spoken of as holding a predominance over earth, as governing it by signs and ordinances, and as containing the elements of that astrological wisdom, more especially cultivated by the Babylonians and Egyptians.

Each nation was supposed by the Hebrews to have its own guardian angel, and its own providential star. One of the chief of the Celestial Powers, at first Jehovah himself in the character of the Sun, standing in the height of Heaven, overlooking and governing all things, afterwards one of the angels or subordinate planetary genii of Babylonian or Persian mythology, was the patron and protector of their own nation, "the Prince that standeth for the children of thy people." The discords of earth were accompanied by a warfare in the sky; and no people underwent the visitation of the Almighty, without a corresponding chastisement being inflicted on its tutelary angel.

The fallen Angels were also fallen Stars; and the first allusion to a feud among the spiritual powers in early Hebrew Mythology, where Rahab and his confederates are defeated, like the Titans in a battle against the Gods, seems to identify the rebellious Spirits as part of the visible Heavens, where the "high ones on high" are punished or chained, as a signal proof of God's power and justice. God, it is said—

" Stirs the sea with his might—by his understanding He smote Rahab—His breath clears the face of Heaven—His hand pierced the crooked Serpent . . . God withdraws not his anger; beneath him bow the confederates of Rahab."

Rahab always means a sea-monster; probably some such legendary monstrous dragon, as in almost all mythologies is the adversary of Heaven and demon of eclipse, in whose belly, significantly called the belly of Hell, Hercules, like Jonah, passed three days, ultimately escaping with the loss of his hair or rays. Chesil, the rebellious giant Orion, represented in Job as riveted to the sky, was compared to Ninus or Nimrod, the mythical founder of Nineveh (City of Fish) the mighty hunter, who slew lions and panthers before the Lord. Rahab's confederates are probably the " High ones on High," the Chesilim or constellations in Isaiah, the Heavenly Host or Heavenly Powers, among whose number were found folly and disobedience.

" I beheld," says Pseudo-Enoch, " seven stars like great blazing mountains, and like Spirits, entreating me. And the angel said, This place, until the consummation of Heaven and Earth, will be the prison of the Stars and of the Host of Heaven. These are the Stars which over-stepped God's command before their time arrived ; and came not at their proper season; therefore was he offended with them, and bound them, until the time of the consummation of their crimes in the secret year." And again : " These Seven Stars are those which have transgressed the commandment of the Most High God, and which are here bound until the number of the days of their crimes be completed."

The Jewish and early Christian writers looked on the worship of the sun and the elements with comparative indulgence. Justin Martyr and Clemens of Alexandria admit that God had appointed the stars as legitimate objects of heathen worship, in order to preserve throughout the world some tolerable notions of natural religion. It seemed a middle point between Heathenism and Christianity ; and to it certain emblems and ordinances of that faith seemed to relate. The advent of Christ was announced by a Star from the East; and his nativity was celebrated on the shortest day of the Julian Calendar, the day when, in the physical commemorations of Persia and Egypt, Mithras or Osiris was newly found. It was then that the acclamations of the Host of Heaven, the unfailing attendants of the Sun, surrounded, as at the spring-dawn of creation, the cradle of his birth-place, and that, in the words of Ignatius, " a star, with light inexpressible, shone forth in the Heavens, to destroy the power of magic and the bonds of wickedness; for God himself had appeared, in the form of man, for the renewal of eternal life."

But however infinite the variety of objects which helped to develop the notion of Deity, and eventually assumed its place, substituting the worship of the creature for that of the creator; of parts of the body, for that of the soul, of the universe, still the notion itself was essentially one of unity. The idea of one God, of a creative, productive, governing unity resided in the earliest exertion of thought: and this monotheism of the primitive ages, makes every succeeding epoch, unless it be the present, appear only as a stage in the progress of degeneracy and aberration. Everywhere in the old faiths we find the idea of a supreme or presiding Deity. Amun or Osiris presides among the many Gods of Egypt: Pan, with the music of his pipe, directs the chorus of the constellations, as Zeus leads the solemn procession of the celestial troops in the astronomical theology of the Pythagoreans. " Amidst an infinite diversity of opinions on all other subjects," says Maximus Tyrius, " the whole world is unanimous in the belief of one only almighty King and Father of All."

There is always a Sovereign Power, a Zeus or Deus, Mahadeva or Adideva, to whom belongs the maintenance of the order of the Universe. Among the thousand gods of India, the doctrine of Divine Unity is never lost sight of: and the ethereal Jove, worshipped by the Persian in an age long before Xenophanes or Anaxagoras, appears as supremely comprehensive and independent of planetary or elemental subdivisions, as the " Vast One" or " Great Soul" of the Vedas.

But the simplicity of belief of the patriarchs did not exclude the employment of symbolical representations. The mind never rests satisfied with a mere feeling. That feeling ever strives to assume precision and durability as an idea, by some *outward* delineation of its thought. Even the ideas that are above and beyond the senses, as all ideas of God are, require the aid of the senses for their expression and communication. Hence come the representative forms and symbols which constitute the external investiture of every religion ; attempts to express a religious sentiment that is essentially *one*, and that vainly struggles for adequate external utterance, striving to tell to one man, to *paint* to him, an idea existing in the mind of another, and essentially incapable of utterance or description, in a language all the words of which have a sensuous meaning. Thus, the idea being perhaps the same in all, its expressions and utterances are infinitely various, and branch into an infinite diversity of creeds and sects.

All religious expression is symbolism; since we can describe only what we see; and the true objects of religion are unseen. The earliest instruments of education were symbols; and they and all other religious forms differed and still differ according to external circumstances and imagery, and according to differences of knowledge and mental cultivation. To present a visible symbol to the eye of another is not to inform him of the meaning which that symbol has to *you*. Hence the philosopher soon superadded to these symbols, explanations addressed to the ear, susceptible of more precision, but less effective, obvious and impressive than the painted or sculptured forms which he despised. Out of these explanations grew by degrees a variety of narratives, whose true object and meaning were gradually forgotten. And when these were abandoned, and philosophy resorted to definitions and formulas, its language was but a more refined symbolism, grappling with and attempting to picture ideas impossible to be expressed. For the most abstract expression for Deity which language can supply, is but a *sign* or *symbol* for an object unknown, and no more truthful and adequate than the terms Osiris and Vishnu, except as being less sensuous and explicit. To say that He is a *Spirit*, is but to say that He is not matter. *What* spirit is, we can only define as the Ancients did, by resorting, as if in despair, to some sublimized species of matter, as Light, Fire, or Ether.

No symbol of Deity can be appropriate or durable except in a relative or moral sense. We cannot exalt words that have only a sensuous meaning, *above* sense. To call Him a *Power* or a *Force* or an *Intelligence*, is merely to deceive ourselves into the belief that we use words that have a meaning to us, when they have none, or at least no more than the ancient visible symbols had. To call Him *Sovereign, Father, Grand Architect of the Universe, Extension, Time, Beginning, Middle and End, Whose face is turned on all sides, the Source of life and death*, is but to present other men with symbols by which we vainly endeavour to communicate to them the same vague ideas which men in all ages have impotently struggled to express. And it may be doubted whether we have succeeded either in communicating, or in forming in our own minds, any more distinct and definite and true and adequate idea of the Deity, with all our metaphysical conceits and logical subtleties, than the rude ancients did, who endeavoured to symbolize and so to express his attributes, by the Fire, the Light, the Sun and Stars, the Lotus and the Scarabæus; all of them types of what, except by types, more or less sufficient, could not be expressed at all.

The primitive men recognized the Divine Presence under a variety of appearances, without losing their faith in this unity and Supremacy. The invisible God, manifested and on one of His many sides visible, did not cease to be God to him. He recognized him in the Evening breeze of Eden, in the whirlwind of Sinai, in the Stone of Beth-El; and identified Him with the fire or thunder or the immovable rock adored in Ancient Arabia. To him the image of the Deity was reflected in all that was pre-eminent in excellence. He saw Jehovah, like Osiris and Bel, in the Sun as well as in the Stars, which were his children, his eyes, "which run through the whole world, and watch over the Sacred Soil of Palestine, from the year's commencement to its close." He was the sacred fire of Mount Sinai, of the burning bush, of the Persians, those Puritans of Paganism.

Naturally it followed that Symbolism soon became more complicated, and all the powers of Heaven were re-produced on earth, until a web of fiction and allegory was woven, which the wit of man, with his limited means of explanation, will never unravel. Hebrew Theism itself became involved in symbolism and image-worship, to which all religions ever tend. We have already seen what was the symbolism of the Tabernacle, the Temple and the Ark. The Hebrew establishment tolerated not only the use of emblematic vessels, vestments and cherubs, of Sacred Pillars and Seraphim, but symbolical representations of Jehovah himself, not even confined to poetical or illustrative language.

"Among the Adityas," says Chrishna, in the Bagvat Ghita, "I am Vishnu, the radiant Sun among the Stars; among the waters, I am ocean; among the mountains, the Himalaya; and among the mountain-tops, Meru." The Psalms and Isaiah are full of similar attempts to convey to the mind ideas of God, by ascribing to him sensual proportions. He rides on the clouds, and sits on the wings of the wind. Heaven is his pavilion and out of his mouth issue lightnings. Men cannot worship a mere abstraction. They require some outward form in which to clothe their conceptions, and invest their sympathies. If they do not shape and carve or paint visible images, they have invisible ones, perhaps quite as inadequate and unfaithful, within their own minds.

The incongruous and monstrous in the Oriental images came from the desire to embody the Infinite, and, to convey by multiplied, because individually inadequate symbols, a notion of the Divine Attributes to the understanding. Perhaps we should find that we mentally do the same thing, and make within ourselves images quite as incongruous, if judged of by our own limited conceptions, if we were to undertake to analyze and gain a clear idea of the mass of infinite attributes which we assign to the Deity; and even of His Infinite Justice and infinite Mercy and Love.

We may well say, in the language of Maximus Tyrius: " If, in the desire to obtain some faint conception of the Universal Father, the Nameless Lawgiver, men had recourse to words or names, to silver or gold, to animals or plants, to mountain-tops or flowing rivers, every one inscribing the most valued and most beautiful things with the name of Deity, and with the fondness of a lover clinging with rapture to each trivial reminiscence of the Beloved, why should we seek to reduce this universal practice of symbolism, necessary, indeed, since the mind often needs the excitement of the imagination to rouse it into activity, to one monotonous standard of formal propriety? Only let the image duly perform its task, and bring the divine idea with vividness and truth before the mental eye; if this be effected, whether by the art of Phidias, the poetry of Homer, the Egyptian Hieroglyph, or the Persian element, we need not cavil at external differences, or lament the seeming fertility of unfamiliar creeds, *so long as the great essential is attained*, THAT MEN ARE MADE TO REMEMBER, TO UNDERSTAND AND TO LOVE."

Certainly, when men regarded Light and Fire as something spiritual and above all the corruptions and exempt from all the decay of matter; when they looked upon the Sun and Stars and Planets as composed of this finer element, and as themselves great and mysterious Intelligences, infinitely superior to man, living Existences, gifted with mighty powers and wielding vast influences, those elements and bodies conveyed to them, when used as symbols of Deity, a far more adequate idea than they can now do to us, or than we can comprehend, now that Fire and Light are familiar to us as air and water, and the Heavenly Luminaries are lifeless worlds like our own. Perhaps they gave them ideas as adequate as we obtain from the mere *words* by which we endeavour to symbolize and shadow forth the ineffable mysteries and infinite attributes of God.

There are, it is true, dangers inseparable from symbolism, which countervail its advantages, and afford an impressive lesson in regard to the similar risks attendant on the use of language. The imagination, invited to assist the reason, usurps its place, or leaves its ally helplessly entangled in its web. Names which stand for things are confounded with them; the means are mistaken for the end: the instrument of interpretation for the object; and thus symbols come to usurp an independent character as truths and persons. Though perhaps a necessary path, they were a dangerous one by which to approach the Deity; in which "many," says Plutarch, "mistaking the sign for the thing signified, fell into a ridiculous superstition; while others, in avoiding one extreme, plunged into the no less hideous gulf of irreligion and impiety."

All great Reformers have warred against this evil, deeply feeling the intellectual mischief arising out of a degraded idea of the Supreme Being: and have claimed for their own God an existence or personality distinct from the objects of ancient superstition; disowning in His name the symbols and images that had profaned His Temple. But they have not seen that the utmost which can be effected by human effort, is to substitute impressions relatively correct, for others whose falsehood has been detected, and to replace a gross symbolism by a purer one. Every man, without being aware of it, worships a conception of his own mind; for all symbolism, as well as all language, shares the subjective character of the ideas it represents. The epithets we apply to God only recall either visible or intellectual symbols to the eye or mind. The modes or forms of manifestation of the reverential feeling that constitutes the religious sentiment, are incomplete and progressive; each term and symbol predicates a partial truth, remaining always amenable to improvement or modification, and, in its turn, to be superseded by others more accurate and comprehensive.

Idolatry consists in confounding the symbol with the thing signified, the substitution of a material for a mental object of worship, after a higher spiritualism has become possible; an ill-judged preference of the inferior to the superior symbol, an inadequate and sensual conception of the Deity: and every religion and every conception of God is idolatrous, in so far as it is imperfect, and as it substitutes a feeble and temporary idea in the shrine of that Undiscoverable Being who can be known only in part, and who can therefore be honoured, even by the most enlightened among his worshippers, only in proportion to their limited powers of understanding and imaging to themselves His perfections.

Like the belief in a Deity, the belief in the soul's immortality is rather a natural feeling, an adjunct of self-consciousness, than a dogma belonging to any particular age or country. It gives eternity to man's nature, and reconciles its seeming anomalies and contradictions; it makes him strong in weakness and perfectable in imperfection; and it alone gives an adequate object for his hopes and energies, and value and dignity to his pursuits. It is concurrent with the belief in an infinite external Spirit, since it is chiefly through consciousness of the dignity of the mind within us, that we learn to appreciate its evidences in the Universe.

To fortify, and as far as possible to impart this hope, was the great aim of ancient wisdom, whether expressed in forms of poetry or philosophy; as it was of the mysteries, and as it is of Masonry. Life rising out of death was the great mystery, which symbolism delighted to represent under a thousand ingenious forms. Nature was ransacked for attestations to the grand truth which seems to transcend all other gifts of imagination, or rather to be their essence and consummation. Such evidences were easily discovered. They were found in the olive and lotus, in the evergreen myrtle of the *Mystæ* and of the grave of Polydorus, in the deadly but self-renewing serpent, the wonderful moth emerging from the coffin of the worm, the phenomena of germination, the settings and risings of the sun and stars, the darkening and growth of the moon, and in sleep, "the minor mystery of death."

The stories of the birth of Apollo from Latona, and of dead heroes, like Glaucus, resuscitated in caves, were allegories of the natural alternations of life and death in nature, changes that are but expedients to preserve her virginity and purity inviolable in the general sum of her operations, whose aggregate presents only a majestic calm, rebuking alike man's presumption and his despair. The typical death of the Nature-God, Osiris, Atys, Adonis, Hiram, was a profound but consolatory mystery: the healing charms of Orpheus were connected with his destruction; and his bones, those valued pledges of fertility and victory, were by a beautiful contrivance often buried within the sacred precincts of his immortal equivalent.

In their doctrines as to the immortality of the soul, the Greek Philosophers merely stated with more precision ideas long before extant independently among themselves, in the form of symbolical suggestion. Egypt and Ethiopia in these matters learned from India, where, as everywhere else, the origin of the doctrine was as remote and untraceable as the origin of man himself. Its natural expression is found in the language of Chrishna, in the Bagvat Ghita: "I myself never was non-existent, nor thou, nor these princes of the Earth; nor shall we ever hereafter cease to be. . . The soul is not a thing of which a man may say, it hath been, or is about to be, or is to be hereafter; for it is a thing without birth; it is pre-existent, changeless, eternal, and is not to be destroyed with this mortal frame."

According to the dogma of antiquity, the thronging forms of life are a series of purifying migrations, through which the divine principle re-ascends to the unity of its source. Inebriated in the bowl of Dionusos, and dazzled in the mirror of existence, the souls, those fragments or sparks of the Universal Intelligence, forgot their native dignity, and passed into the terrestrial frames they coveted. The most usual type of the spirit's descent was suggested by the sinking of the Sun and Stars from the upper to the lower hemisphere. When it arrived within the portals of the proper empire of Dionusos, the God of this World, the scene of delusion and change, its individuality became clothed in a material form; and as individual bodies were compared to a garment, the world was the investiture of the Universal Spirit. Again the body was compared to a vase or urn, the soul's recipient; the world being the mighty bowl which received the descending Deity. In another image, ancient as the Grottos of the Magi and the denunciations of Ezekiel, the world was as a dimly illuminated cavern, where shadows seem realities, and where the soul becomes forgetful of its celestial origin in proportion to its proneness to material fascinations. By another, the period of the Soul's embodiment is as when exhalations are condensed, and the aerial element assumes the grosser form of water.

But if vapor falls in water, it was held, water is again the birth of vapors, which ascend and adorn the Heavens. If our mortal existence be the death of the spirit, our death may be the renewal of its life; as physical bodies are exalted from earth to water, from water to air, from air to fire, so the man may rise into the Hero, the Hero into the God. In the course of Nature, the soul, to recover its lost estate, must pass through a series of trials and migrations. The scene of those trials is the Grand Sanctuary of Initiations, the world: their primary agents are the elements; and Dionusos, as Sovereign of Nature, or the sensuous world personified, is official Arbiter of the Mysteries, and guide of the soul, which he introduces into the body and dismisses from it. He is the Sun, that liberator of the elements; and his spiritual mediation was suggested by the same imagery which made the Zodiac the supposed path of the spirits in their descent and their return, and Cancer and Capricorn the gates through which they passed.

He was not only Creator of the World, but guardian, liberator and Saviour of the Soul. Ushered into the world amidst lightning and thunder, he became the Liberator celebrated in the Mysteries of Thebes, delivering earth from Winter's chain, conducting the nightly chorus of the Stars and the celestial revolution of the year. His symbolism was the inexhaustible imagery employed to fill up the stellar devices of the Zodiac: he was the Vernal Bull, the Lion, the Ram, the Autumnal Goat, the Serpent: in short, the varied Deity, the resulting manifestation personified, the all in the many, the varied year, life passing into innumerable forms; essentially inferior to none, yet changing with the seasons, and undergoing their periodical decay.

He mediates and intercedes for man, and reconciles the Universal Unseen Mind with the individualized spirit of which he is emphatically the Perfecter; a consummation which he effects, first through the vicissitudes of the elemental ordeal, the alternate fire of Summer and showers of Winter, "the trials or tests of an immortal Nature;" and secondarily and symbolically through the Mysteries. He holds not only the cup of generation, but also that of wisdom or initiation, whose influence is contrary to that of the former, causing the soul to abhor its material bonds, and to long for its return. The first was the Cup of Forgetfulness; while the second is the Urn of Aquarius, quaffed by the returning spirit, as by the returning Sun at the Winter Solstice, and emblematic of the exchange of worldly impressions for the recovered recollection of the glorious sights and enjoyments of its pre-existence. Water nourishes and purifies; and the urn from which it flows was thought worthy to be a symbol of the Deity, as of the Osiris-Canobus who with living water irrigated the soil of Egypt; and also an emblem of Hope that should cheer the dwellings of the dead.

The second birth of Dionusos, like the rising of Osiris and Atys from the dead, and the raising of Hiram, is a type of the spiritual regeneration of man. Psyche (the Soul) like Ariadne, had two lovers, an earthly and an immortal one. The immortal suitor is Dionusos, the Eros-Phanes of the Orphici, gradually exalted by the progress of thought, out of the symbol of Sensuality into the torch-bearer of the Nuptials of the Gods; the Divine Influence which physically called the world into being, and which awakening the soul from its Stygian trance, restores it from earth to Heaven.

Thus the scientific theories of the ancients, expounded in the mysteries, as to the origin of the soul, its descent, its sojourn here below, and its return, were not a mere barren contemplation of the nature of the world, and of the intelligent beings existing there. They were not an idle speculation as to the order of the world, and about the soul, but a study of the means for arriving at the great object proposed,—the perfecting of the soul; and, as a necessary consequence, that of morals and society. This Earth, to them, was not the Soul's home, but its place of exile. Heaven was its home, and there was its birth-place. To it, it ought incessantly to turn its eyes. Man was not a terrestrial plant. His roots were in Heaven. The soul had lost its wings, clogged by the viscosity of matter. It would recover them when it extricated itself from matter and commenced its upward flight.

Matter being, in their view, as it was in that of St. Paul, the principle of all the passions that trouble reason, mislead the intelligence, and stain the purity of the soul, the Mysteries taught man how to enfeeble the action of matter on the soul, and restore to the latter its natural dominion. And lest the stains so contracted should continue after death, lustrations were used, fastings, expiations, macerations, continence, and above all initiations. Many of these practices were at first merely symbolical,—material signs indicating the moral purity required of the initiates; but they afterwards came to be regarded as actual productive causes of that purity.

The effect of initiation was meant to be the same as that of philosophy, to purify the soul of its passions, to weaken the empire of the body over the divine portion of man, and to give him here below a happiness anticipatory of the felicity to be one day enjoyed by him, and of the future vision by him of the Divine Beings.

And therefore Proclus and the other Platonists taught " that the mysteries and initiations withdrew souls from this mortal and material life, to re-unite them to the Gods ; and dissipated for the adepts the shades of ignorance by the splendours of the Deity." Such were the precious fruits of the last degree of the Mystic Science,—to see Nature in her springs and sources, and to become familiar with the causes of things and with real existences.

Cicero says that the soul must exercise itself in the practice of the virtues, if it would speedily return to its place of origin. It should, while imprisoned in the body, free itself therefrom by the contemplation of superior beings, and in some sort be divorced from the body and the senses. Those who remain enslaved, subjugated by their passions and violating the sacred laws of religion and society, will re-ascend to Heaven, only after they shall have been purified through a long succession of ages.

The initiate was required to emancipate himself from his passions, and to free himself from the hindrances of the senses and of matter, in order that he might rise to the contemplation of the Deity, or of that incorporeal and unchanging light in which live and subsist the causes of created natures. " We must," says Porphyry, " flee from everything sensual, that the soul may with ease re-unite itself with God, and live happily with Him." " This is the great work of initiation," says Hierocles,—" to recall the soul to what is truly good and beautiful, and make it familiar therewith, and they its own ; to deliver it from the pains and ills it endures here below, enchained in matter as in a dark prison ; to facilitate its return to the celestial splendours, and to establish it in the Fortunate isles, by restoring it to its first estate. Thereby, when the hour of death arrives, the soul, freed of its mortal garmenting, which it leaves behind it as a legacy to earth, will rise buoyantly to its home among the Stars, there to re-take its ancient condition, and approach towards the Divine nature as far as man may do."

Plutarch compares Isis to knowledge, and Typhon to ignorance, obscuring the light of the sacred doctrine whose blaze lights the soul of the initiate. No gift of the Gods, he holds, is so precious as the knowledge of the Truth, and that of the Nature of the Gods, so far as our limited capacities allow us to rise towards them. The Valentinians termed initiation LIGHT. The initiate, says Psellus, becomes an Epopt, when admitted to see THE DIVINE LIGHTS. Clemens of Alexandria, imitating the language of an initiate in the Mysteries of Bacchus, and inviting this initiate, whom he terms blind like Tiresias, to come to see Christ, who will blaze upon his eyes with greater glory than the Sun, exclaims: "Oh Mysteries most truly holy ! Oh pure Light ! When the torch of the Dadoukos gleams, Heaven and the Deity are displayed to my eyes ! I am initiated, and become holy !" This was the true object of initiation ; to be sanctified, and TO SEE, that is, to have just and faithful conceptions of the Deity, the knowledge of whom was THE LIGHT of the mysteries. It was promised the initiate at Samothrace, that he should become pure and just. Clemens says that by baptism, souls are illuminated, and led to the pure light with which mingles no darkness, nor anything material. The initiate, become an Epopt, was called a SEER. " HAIL, NEW-BORN LIGHT !" the initiates cried in the Mysteries of Bacchus.

Such was held to be the effect of complete initiation. It lighted up the soul with rays from the Divinity, and became for it, as it were, the eye with which, according to the Pythagoreans, it contemplates the field of Truth ; in its mystical abstractions, wherein it rises superior to the body, whose action on it it annuls for the time, to re-enter into itself, so as entirely to occupy itself with the view of the Divinity, and the means of coming to resemble Him.

Thus enfeebling the dominion of the senses and the passions over the soul, and as it were freeing the latter from a sordid slavery, and by the steady practice of all the virtues, active and contemplative, our ancient brethren strove to fit themselves to return to the bosom of the Deity. Let not our objects as Masons fall below theirs. We use the symbols which they used ; and teach the same great cardinal doctrines that they taught, of the existence of an intellectual God, and the immortality of the soul of man. If the details of their doctrines as to the soul seem to us to verge on absurdity, let us compare them with the common notions of our own day, and be silent. If it seems to us that they regarded the symbol in some cases as the thing symbolized, and worshipped the sign as if it were itself Deity, let us reflect how insufficient are our own ideas of Deity, and how we worship those ideas and images formed and fashioned in our own minds, and not the Deity Himself: and if we are inclined to smile at the importance they attached to lustrations and fasts, let us pause and inquire whether the same weakness of human nature does not exist to-day, causing *rites* and ceremonies to be regarded as *actirely* efficient for the salvation of souls.

And let us ever remember the words of an old writer, with which we conclude this lecture: "It is a pleasure to stand on the shore, and to see ships tossed upon the sea: a pleasure to stand in the window of a castle, and see a battle and the adventures thereof: but no pleasure is comparable to the standing on the vantage-ground of TRUTH (a hill not to be commanded, and where the air is always clear and serene), and to see the errors and wanderings, and mists and tempests, in the vale below; *so always that this prospect be with pity, and not with swelling or pride.* Certainly it is Heaven upon Earth to have a man's mind move in charity, rest in Providence, AND TURN UPON THE POLES OF TRUTH."

TO CLOSE.

M∴ P∴ Bro∴ Lt∴ Commander, what is the hour?

Lt∴ Com∴ M∴ Potent Leader, the twilight after Sunset. The Pleiades and Aldebaran and the Three Kings of Orion have sunk in the Western ocean, and Perseus rises with the Scorpion in the East.

M∴ P∴ Then it is time to close this Chapter, until Light, ever alternating with Darkness, as Good with Evil, and Happiness with Sorrow, in this world, again obtains the mastery. How shall we be safe while Evil and Darkness frown from their gloomy thrones upon the Earth?

Lt∴ Com∴ By faith in God's Providence, repentance of our sins, and reformation.

M∴ P∴ Right, my son! Bro∴ Commander of the Host, give notice that this Council is now about to close, in order that the Brethren may rest from their labours.

Com∴ of H∴ Bro∴ Lt∴ Com∴, make known to the Brethren that the M∴ P∴ Leader is now about to close this Council, that, while the Scorpion domineers in Heaven with the Serpent, they may rest from their labours.

Lt∴ Com∴ Brethren, the M∴ P∴ Leader is about to close this Council, that while the Scorpion and Serpent domineer in Heaven, you may rest from your labours. Rest, therefore, until Aldebaran again leads up the Hosts of Heaven.

[The Sen∴ and Jun∴ W∴ and the Master, each in succession, rap as in opening: the sign is given; and the M∴ P∴ declares the Council closed].

FINIS.

Twenty-Sixth Degree.

Prince of Mercy or Scottish Trinitarian.

DECORATIONS, &c.

LODGES of this degree are styled *Chapters*. The hangings are green, supported by nine columns, alternately white and red; upon each of which is a chandelier, holding nine lights. The canopy over the Throne is green, white and red; and before the Throne is a table, covered with a cloth of the same colours. Instead of a gavel, the Presiding officer uses an arrow, the plume of which is red on one side and green on the other, the spear white, and the point gilded.

By the altar is a statue representing TRUTH, clad in the same colours. It is the Palladium of the Order. The altar itself, in the centre, is of a triangular shape, the top being a gilded plate in the shape of a Delta, on which in glittering stones is the Ineffable Name, יהוה, and under it the letters I∴ H∴ Σ∴ on a *Crux Ansata.*

The *officers* are, a *Chief Prince*, styled *Most Excellent*, two *Wardens*, styled *Excellent*, two *Deacons*, a *Sacrificer* and a *Guard of the Palladium*. The other members are styled *Princes.*

The Chief Prince wears a tri-colored tunic, green, white and red, and a crown surmounted with nine points. The other members wear a white tunic. All wear the Order, which is a broad tri-coloured collar, green, white and red.

The apron is red, with a white border. In the middle of it, is an equilateral triangle, embroidered with gold; in the centre of which is the jewel. The flap is sky-blue.

The jewel is an equilateral triangle of gold, in the centre of which is a heart of gold. On the heart are engraved the letters הי. The jewel is suspended from the collar.

The battery is , ‖ raps — by ; — ‖ — and £ — given thus [; — ; ? — ; ; ,].

The Step : . . . Is ; equal steps—the first with the left foot.

The Age : . . . $, years—the square of ; times ;

The Order : . . . Standing; the ‡‡&☉♒♊ on the ‡‡&♀ §

The *tessera*, or mark, given to the Initiate, is a small fish made of silver or ivory; on one side of which is the word יהוה, and on the other, in the Rose Croix cipher, the Pass-word of the degree.

TO OPEN.

Ch∴ Pr∴. Exc∴ Sen∴. Warden, I am about to open this Chapter of Princes of Mercy, in the inner chamber of the Mysteries. Satisfy yourself that all present are entitled to remain.

[The Sen∴ Warden goes round and receives the Pass-word of the Degree from each Brother, returns to his station, and says]:

S∴ W∴ M∴ Exc∴, all present are of the Faithful; and have passed through the three degrees of the Mysteries.

M∴ Exc∴ Bro∴ Jun∴ Deacon, the first duty of a Chapter of Princes of Mercy, when assembled?

J∴ Deac∴ To see that the Chapter is duly guarded, M∴ Exc∴

M∴ Exc∴ That being your duty, see that the Soldiers of the Cross are at their posts; and inform the Captain of the Guards that we are about to open this Chapter of Princes of Mercy; that he may redouble his vigilance.

[The Jun∴ Deacon goes out, returns, closes the door, gives the alarm of the Degree, which is answered from without, returns to his place, and says]:

J∴ Deac∴ M∴ Exc∴, the Guards are at their posts; and their Captain is duly warned that this Chapter is about to be opened.

M∴ Exc∴ Who commands the Guards?

J∴ Deac∴ One who has assumed the name and emulates the fidelity of Ulric the Goth, over whose body the soldiers of Domitian forced their way into a Lodge of Christian Masons.

M∴ Exc∴ We may then safely proceed. Bro∴ Sen∴ Warden, are you a Prince of Mercy?

Sen∴ W∴ I have seen the luminous Delta, and become one of the Faithful by means of the Triple Covenant of which we bear the mark.

M∴ Exc∴ What is that Triple Covenant?

Sen∴ W∴ That made with Noah, when God set his bow in the Heavens: that made with Abraham and his descendants; and that made with all the Earth, that the day should come when Light and Truth and Happiness should be victorious over Darkness, Falsehood and Misery.

M∴ Exc∴ Where did our ancient Brethren meet to celebrate their mysteries which we imitate?

Sen∴ W∴ In the innermost recesses of the great Temple at Elephanta, hewn out of the solid rock, and in the most secret chamber of the vast subterranean Temple of Bouddha at Salsette; within the columns of the roofless fanes of Persia; in the forest Temples of the Druids; in the depths of the Pyramids of Memphis; in the dark vaults of Crete and Samothrace; under the Holy of Holies at Jerusalem; in the great Temple of Eleusis; and in the dark catacombs under Rome, where the Christian Masons met at midnight to avoid the wrath of the persecuting Emperors.

M∴ Exc∴ What does our Lodge represent?

Sen∴ W∴ The catacombs.

M∴ Exc∴ Whom do we imitate in this Degree?

Sen∴ W∴ The Christian Masons, who met when Domitian was Emperor; when the night was dark and gloomy, the night of wo and persecution; when danger and death, like hounds, hung on the footsteps of our Christian brethren, and they were driven to the caverns and quarries for shelter and for safety.

M∴ Exc∴ Rome is a lifeless corpse, and her Emperors are shadows; but Masonry still lives, and the smoke from the fires of Persecution no longer ascends to Heaven. Yet the *spirit* of Persecution lives and is strong, and men forget that all mankind are brethren. Let us take heed, my Brethren, that we fall not into that great sin. Strength to resist temptation comes from God. Let us humbly kneel before him, and confess our errors, and implore his mercy for the helpless and the persecuted.

[All kneel; and M∴ Exc∴ repeats the following]

PRAYER.

Our Father [the Lord's Prayer]. We have sinned against Thee, O our Father, and have broken Thy commandments. We have forgotten Mercy, and practised Intolerance. We have judged our Brother harshly, and condemned him unheard. Soften our hearts towards those who go astray, and teach us Mercy, and help us to look with leniency on their failings, their shortcomings and their errors! If we are not in possession of the Truth, help us to attain it! If we already have it, help us in our waywardness to look with kindness and compassion upon those who are less fortunate than we, and yet perhaps more deserving of Thy Mercy! If those whom we think Heretics and Superstitious are truly in error, and striving honestly to attain the Truth, teach us to pity and not to hate them; and if they are in Error and do *not* strive to reach the Truth, teach us to pity them the more! Help us to resist and subdue our evil passions, our pride of opinion, our bitter and revengeful feelings! Touch the hearts of all Persecutors, and teach them that, as Thou only hast the knowledge unerringly to determine what *is* Truth, so Thou alone hast the right and prerogative to condemn error! Make all men humane and benevolent! Hasten the coming of that promised dawn, when all war and all persecution for opinion's sake shall cease, and all mankind shall feel and know that there is no heresy so monstrous as persecution, and no offence greater in Thy sight than intolerance! Place thy hand between man's life and the cannon's mouth! Send back the sword, the pike and the musket to the furnace, to be forged into the peaceful implements of agriculture and the arts! Let, in Thy good time, Peace and Love and Harmony reign sovereign in the world, and War and Hatred and Discord be known no more forever! Strengthen our faith in Thee and in Thy Goodness and Benevolence! Pardon us our errors, our sins and our presumption; and help and strengthen us to keep our Masonic vows and sacred obligations, as those did whom Domitian persecuted and Nero slew! Amen!

All: . . . So mote it be! Amen!

M.·. Exc.·. Bro.·. Sen.·. Warden, let this Chapter be now opened for the disposal of such business, and for such proper work as may come before it. This you will communicate to the Exc.·. Jun.·. Warden, and he to all the Princes, that they may take due notice thereof, and aid us in the performance of our duties.

Sen.·. W.·. Exc.·. Bro.·. Jun.·. Warden, it is the pleasure of the M.·. Exc.·. Ch.·. Prince, that this Chapter be now opened. You will therefore so announce to all the Princes, that, having due notice, they may aid us in the performance of our duties.

Jun.·. W.·. Brethren, it is the pleasure of the Most Exc.·. Chief Prince, that this Chapter be now opened. You will take due notice thereof, and be prepared to aid us in the performance of our duties.

M.·. Exc.·. Together, my Brethren!

[All give the second sign. Then the Jun.·. W.·. raps ; — the Sen.·. W.·. ‖ — and the M.·. Exc.·. ₤ — Then all the Princes clap with their hands [; ‖ ₤]—and applaud, crying &☿⌂↑&☾☉&].

M.·. Exc.·. The labours of this Chapter are resumed.

RECEPTION.

The Candidate represents a Catechumen, who has received the second degree of the Essenian and early Christian Mysteries. He must be dressed in a plain white robe, reaching from the neck to the feet; and be barefooted, with his eyes bandaged, so as entirely to prevent his seeing. A rope is passed three times around his body. In this condition he is led to the door of the Chapter; where the Examiner, who conducts him, raps [;]—which is answered from within by [‖]—and the Examiner raps [₤]. The door is then partly opened by the Guard of the Palladium: who asks:

Guard: Who comes to disturb the Faithful in their meditations?

Exam.·. A Catechumen, who, having passed through the two first degrees of the Sacred Mysteries, seeks now to be admitted to the full light, and to become one of the Faithful.

Qu.·. Has he passed the regular terms of probation, and undergone the necessary tests and trials?

Ans.·. He has.

Qu.·. Is he of pure morals, and devout; and will he devote himself zealously to the teaching and diffusion of the True Faith?

Ans.·. He will.

Qu.·. Art thou prepared to undergo stripes and persecution, hunger and destitution, and the scoffs and neers of the Profane, in the service of Masonry?

Ans.·. I am.

Qu.·. Has he sufficient discernment to see the Truth under the veil that covers it from Profane eyes? Does he understand that all Masonry is a succession of allegories, and all its teachings symbolic; and can he see, without receiving offence, the performance of ceremonies in which the Hebrew, the Egyptian, the Persian and the Christian behold the embodiment of their peculiar faith, he being left free to apply and interpret the same as he pleases?

Ans.·. He has; he does; he can.

Qu.·. Does he respect the faith of every man that hath a faith in this age of unbelief and universal doubt? Does he revere the character of all Reformers and all the great Teachers of Morality?

Ans.·. He does.

Qu.·. How is he called?

Ans.·. CONSTANS.

Exam.·. Let him wait with patience until his request is made known to this M.·. Exc.·. Chapter of Princes of Mercy, and its will is ascertained.

[He closes the door, and goes to the East; where the same questions are asked, and like answers returned as at the door].

M.·. Exc.·. If he be blind, barefoot and firmly bound, let him be admitted, after he shall have washed his hands in pure water, and received the customary warning.

[The Guard goes again to the door, opens it, and says]:

Guard: It is the will of the Chapter that, if he be blind, barefoot and firmly bound, he be admitted, after he shall have washed his hands in pure water, and received the customary warning.

[The Examiner then places before the Candidate a bowl of pure water, in which he washes his hands, and dries them on a napkin. While he is doing so, the Examiner says]:

Exam.·. While thou dost purify thy outer man, forget not that thou must present thyself here with a pure soul, without which the external cleanliness of the body will by no means be accepted, and of which this lavation is a mere symbol.

[The hands of the Candidate are then confined behind his back; and he is led into the Chapter, which remains in perfect silence, except when that silence is broken by the voice of the M.·. Exc.·. He is led nine times around the Lodge; while the M.·. Exc.·. reads as follows]:

1st Circuit: . . . Thus said the Holy Books of ancient India: There are three Supreme Gods, the three Forms and Aspects of the First, the Supreme, Single, Imperishable, Infinite, Omnipotent, Excellent, Perfect, Incorporeal, Invisible God PARABRAHMA, Omnipresent, the Universal Substance, Cause of all Phenomena, and Soul of the World: and these three, the Powers of *Creation, Preservation* and *Destruction,* distinct in persons, are but one God, the TRIMOURTI, Triple Form of the Supreme, the Word A.·. U.·. M.·., first utterance of the Eternal.

2d Circuit: . . . Chrishna, they said, ninth Incarnation of Vishnu, the second person of the Trimourti, born of a royal virgin, without sin, was chaste and holy. He washed the feet of the Brahmins; he descended into hell; he arose again, and ascended to heaven; he charged his disciples to teach his pure doctrines, and gave them the gift of miracles. He will appear again at the end of the world, the tenth Incarnation of Vishnu. He will become man, and mounted on a white horse, with a sword glittering like a comet, will traverse the world and destroy the guilty. The heavens shall be rolled away, the celestial spheres be confounded and halt in their courses: the sun shall lose his light, and the great serpent breathing torrents of fire shall consume the universe; but the seeds of creation shall be preserved in the lotus; and a new creation and new age of innocence shall commence.

3d Circuit: . . . Above all Existences, said the Ancient Buddhists, is the Spirit, Universal, Indestructible, who during incalculable Time preserves all that is, and remains in repose, until the Laws of Destiny oblige him to create new worlds. From Him flow the Bouddhas, each a Trinity, of INTELLIGENCE, LAW and UNION, each a Redeemer. Maïtreya, born of a virgin, shall come as Sakya did, to regenerate the world. The Stars shall salute Him at his Nativity, the Earth exhale perfumes, the jewels hidden in her bosom rise glittering to the surface, everywhere bloom the lotus, the running waters become clear as crystal, the winds breathe softly, and the sky be pure and serene; the tortures of the wicked shall be suspended, all venomous reptiles and beasts of prey disappear, ferocious men lose their fierce instincts and become good and gentle, the sick and infirm become well and strong, and all mankind unite in Orisons to God.

4th Circuit: . . . From ZERVANÉ AKHERENÉ, the Supreme Divinity and Ancient Unlimited Time, said the old Persians, inaccessible in his glory, his nature and his attributes, and to be worshipped with silent veneration, came Time, that is the Age of the Universe; in whose bosom the Universe reposes. From the Supreme emanated the Pure Light, and Ormuzd, the King of Light, the Mysterious Word HONOVER, the Divine Will, base of all existence and Source of all Good. He will in the fourth age create Sosiosch the Saviour, who shall prepare the human race for the general resurrection. A Great Comet shall dash against the Earth: the good and the bad shall arise and resume their bodies: and all shall be as it was on the first day of the creation. Ahriman, the Spirit of Evil, shall be plunged into thick darkness and covered with a torrent of melted brass. The Earth shall shake like a sick man. The mountains shall melt, and torrents of metal flow from their bosoms, through which all souls shall pass, that thus parting with the defilement of their sins, they may be fitted for the bliss that awaits them. Universal Nature shall be regenerated. A new Earth, more beautiful, more fertile, more delicious than the first, shall become the home of restored mankind. Darkness shall disappear, there shall be no more hell nor torment, Ormuzd shall reign alone; and he with his angels, and Ahriman with his innumerable demons shall together offer up to the Eternal a sacrifice that shall never end.

5th Circuit: . . . MITHRA, it was said in the Ancient Sabean Mysteries, is the Grand Architect of the Universe Himself, appearing in visible shape, the Spirit of the Sun and Light, the Eye of ORMUZD. He rules the harmonious marches of the Stars, makes Nature fruitful, wars against the evils that scourge her, pours out upon the earth the blessings of Heaven, proclaims THE DIVINE WORD, and lives in the souls of the Prophets, who are his echoes. He is Love, King of the living and dead, the Supremely Pure, Holy and Wise. He is Three and One; for his Essence ILLUMINATES, WARMS and MAKES FRUITFUL at once. He is the Incarnate Mediator, bringing back souls to God. Seated in the Middle Chamber, between Light and Darkness, he presides over initiations, crowned with the Sun of Truth and Justice, and bearing the Gavel of gold, Eternal, living, victorious and intelligent.

6th Circuit: . . . The Supreme God ALFADER, said our Ancient Brethren, the Druids of Scandinavia, Germany and Gaul, is Eternal. He made Heaven, Earth and Air, and Men, and gave to men immortal souls. ODIN and FREA, his First-Created, and THOR, their son, are the Supreme Council and Trinity of the Gods. The reign of evil shall draw near to its end. The Great Dragon shall turn in the Ocean and the World be inundated: the earth shall shudder, the trees be uprooted, the mountains topple and fall headlong, the Wolf Fenris devour the Sun, and the Great Dragon vomit torrents of venom. The Stars shall flee away and heaven melt, and the Evil Angels and Giants war against the Gods and Heroes. The Wolf Fenris shall devour Odin and perish; Thor perish by the poison of the expiring Serpent; and fire consume the Universe. A new world shall emerge from the bosom of the flames, beautiful with green meadows. The fields shall produce bountifully without labour, calamity be unknown, and a vast golden palace more brilliant than the Sun receive and be the home of the Just forever. Then the Supreme Being shall come from his dwelling on high, administer Divine Justice, pronounce his decrees, and establish his immutable laws.

7th Circuit: . . . AMUN-RE, said the Ancient Egyptians, the Uncreated, Immutable, Omnipotent God, author, preserver, and soul of Nature is the Supreme Triad, Father, Mother and Son, from whom the long chain of Triads descends to the Incarnations in human form. Osiris, final conqueror of TYPHON the Power of Evil, shall sit in judgment on all the dead. Horus and Anubis shall weigh the actions of each in the unerring scales; Thoth record the result, and Osiris, Supreme Judge, pronounce the final sentence, on each according to his deserts. The irreclaimable depart to the lower hemisphere of darkness, remorse and pain: the imperfect return to earth to inhabit other bodies and expiate their sins; the Just return to the bosom of the Deity, to enjoy eternal happiness in the realm of light and love.

8th Circuit: . . . Thus was it promised unto JUDAH: The sceptre shall not depart from Judah, nor a lawgiver from between his feet, until SHILOH come; and unto Him shall the gathering of the People be. Unto us a child is born; unto us a son is given; and the Government shall be upon his shoulder; and his name. shall be called Wonderful, Counsellor, The Mighty God, The Everlasting Father, The Prince of Peace. Of the increase of his Government and peace there shall be no end, upon the Throne of David, and upon his Kingdom, to order it, and to establish it with judgment and with justice from henceforth even for ever. There shall come forth a Rod out of the stem of Jesse, and a Branch shall grow out of his roots: and the Spirit of God shall rest upon him, the spirit of wisdom and understanding, the spirit of counsel and power, of knowledge and the fear of God: He shall not judge after the sight of his eyes, nor reprove after the hearing of his ears; but with righteousness shall he judge the poor, and reprove with equity for the meek of the earth. The wolf shall dwell with the lamb, and the leopard shall lie down with the kid; and the calf and the young lion and the fatling together, and a little child shall lead them: they shall not hurt nor destroy in all my Holy Mountain; for the Earth shall be full of the knowledge of God, as the waters cover the sea. He will swallow up death in victory, and God will wipe away tears from off all faces. He will feed his flock like a shepherd; and gather the lambs in his arms, and carry them in His bosom, and gently lead those that are with young.. The Sun shall be no more thy light by day, nor shall the Moon shine to give thee light: but the Lord shall be unto Thee an Everlasting Light, and thy God thy Glory.

9th Circuit: . . . In the Beginning was the Word, and the Word was with God, and the Word was God: all things were made by Him: in Him was life, and that life was the light of Mankind: the true Light, which lighteth every man that cometh into the world. And the Word became incarnate, and dwelt among men, and they beheld his glory, the glory of the First-Born of the Father, full of benevolence and truth. Thus said the ancient Christian Masons; and they said also; God so loved the world that he gave his only Son, that whosoever believeth in Him should not perish, but have everlasting life. For He sent not that Son into the world to condemn it; but that through him it might be saved. There are Three that bear record in Heaven; The FATHER, the WORD, and the HOLY SPIRIT, and these Three are one. Love is of God, and every one that loveth is born of God, and knoweth God, and he that loveth not knoweth not God, for God is Love; and hath loved us, and hath sent his Son to be the propitiation for our sins, that we might live through Him; and hath imparted to us His Spirit: and in the dispensation of the fulness of times He will gather together in one all things in Christ, both in heaven and on earth; for it pleased the Father that in him should be the Plenitude of all Perfection; and, having made peace through the blood of his cross, that by him he should reconcile all things unto himself.

[The Candidate is now halted in front of the Jun∴ Warden]:

· J∴ Ward∴ Thus in all ages the golden threads of Truth have gleamed in the woof of error. Fortunate the Mason, who, by the Light of Wisdom, the true Masonic Light, first emanation from the Deity, can discern the golden threads, God's hieroglyphics, written when Time began; and read them aright, as they were read by our ancient Brethren in the early ages!

Sen∴ W∴ Thus in all ages the WORD of God, His THOUGHT, the Great Creative POWER, not spoken through material organs, nor in a voice audible to mortal ears, has sounded in the Souls of Men, and taught them the Great Truths of Reason, Philosophy and Religion. Fortunate the Mason to whom that Word, the Deity manifest, is audible, intelligible, significant: God's THOUGHT, that made the Stars and all that is, and the Great Laws of Harmony and Motion!

M∴ Exc∴ Thus in all ages rosy gleams of light tinging the dark clouds of error have taught mankind that Truth and Light, perfect and glorious, linger below the Horizon of Mortal vision, in time to rise, like the Sun, and fill God's universe with light and glory, at the Dawn of his promised Day. Fortunate the Mason who with firm Faith and Hope accepts these struggling rays that gild the clouds, as ample evidence that in God's good Time his dawn of Day will come, and be eternal!

[The Examiner gives ; raps].

Jun∴ W∴ Brother Examiner, whom have you there, blind and in bondage?

Ex∴ Brother Constans, a worthy Catechumen, who having passed the necessary terms of probation, and undergone the tests and trials, now anxiously desires to see the great light, and to be received among the Faithful.

Jun∴ W∴ Brother Constans, is this request caused, not by idle curiosity, but by a sincere desire to attain unto the Truth, that thereby thou mayst the better perform thy duties both towards God and man?

Cand∴ It is.

Jun∴ W∴ Brother Examiner, dost thou vouch for him, that he is zealous and devout, that he is true and honest, that he can be secret and silent?

Ex∴ I do.

Jun∴ W∴ Then, since thou art his surety, let him see to it, all his life, that he bring no shame upon thee, by making false thy pledge in his behalf. Lead him, my Brother, to the Senior Warden!

[Halting in front of the Sen∴ Warden's station, the Ex∴ gives ‖ raps].

Sen∴ W∴ Bro∴ Examiner, whom have you there, blind and in bondage?

Ex∴ Bro∴ Constans, a worthy Catechumen, &c.

Sen∴ W∴ Bro∴ Constans, is this request, &c.?

Cand∴ It is.

Sen∴ W∴ Bro∴ Examiner, dost thou vouch for him, that he loveth his Brethren, that he is kind and gentle, that he is modest and humble, and not proud, haughty, self-conceited or vain-glorious?

Ex∴ I do.

Sen∴ W∴ Then, since thou dost become his surety, let him see to it, all his life, that he bring thee not to shame, by making false thy pledge in his behalf. Conduct him to the M∴ Excellent in the Orient!

[In front of the M∴ Excellent's seat, the Examiner raps £ by ; ,].

M∴ Ex∴ Bro∴ Ex∴ whom have you there, bound and in bondage?

Ex∴ Bro∴ Constans, a worthy Catechumen, &c.

M∴ Ex∴ Bro∴ Constans, is this request, &c.?

Cand∴ It is.

M∴ Ex∴ Be sure, my Brother, that you answer not hastily or lightly; but upon due and profound reflection and self-examination, and in sincerity and truth. Are you prepared to assume the arduous duties which will devolve upon you as one of the Faithful?

Cand∴ I am.

M∴ Ex∴ Bro∴ Examiner, dost thou vouch for his stability and resolution; for his courage in danger, and his contempt of death; for his truth and sincerity, and that he will be merciful and tolerant?

Ex∴ I do.

M∴ Ex∴ It is well. Let him take heed that he bring not shame upon thee, by making false the pledge which thou hast given for him. Kneel then, my brother, that thou mayst join us in prayer!

[All kneel, and the following prayer and response are repeated]:

PRAYER.

Infinitely Illustrious and Supreme Father, who createst and dost cherish and support all men, infinitely various of counsel, all-pure, all-powerful, all-mighty God, who consumest all things, and again thyself reproducest and repairest them; ever in endless circle bringing life out of death and light out of darkness; who directest the ineffable harmonies that are the law of the boundless Universe! Thou Universal Parent of eternally successive being, Father of Motion, infinitely various in design; whose thought produced the Earth and Starry Heavens; who art everywhere present, co-extensive with Time and Space; of whose essence are justice, mercy and goodness; Author of life and Soul of all that moves; hear our suppliant voices, and be not offended at our prayers! Aid us to keep thy commandments and perform our duties! Keep us from the slippery descents of vice, and help us to stand firm in the ways of duty! Support and strengthen this our Brother, and all Masons everywhere! Fill our souls with love for Thee and gratitude! Save us from persecutors, and teach us and all our Brethren to be tolerant of error, the common lot of man: and send our life a happy, blameless end. O! Father, give us Faith and Understanding, and fit us for admission to the Sublime Mysteries of Heaven!

Our Father, who art in Heaven, &c.! Amen!

[All respond; "So mote it be, now and evermore, in this world, and in the world to come!"]

20D

M∴ Ex∴ Bro∴ Examiner, you will re-conduct this Brother to the Exc∴ Sen∴ Warden, who will place him near the Great Light by the proper steps.

[He is conducted to the West; and the Examiner places him before the Altar, by ; steps, commencing with the left foot: where he kneels and receives the following]

OBLIGATION.

I, A. . . . . B. . . . ., of my own free will and accord, in the presence of the Great Creator of the Universe, and of this Venerable Chapter, do most solemnly promise and swear, that I will never reveal the secrets of this degree to any person in the world, either intentionally or for want of due inquiry, unless it be to one who shall regularly have received all the lower degrees of the Ancient and Accepted Rite, in a regular and constitutional manner. I furthermore promise and swear, that I will never confer or aid in conferring this degree, nor be present at conferring it, upon any one, unless it is so done by virtue of a particular permission or warrant from a regularly established Sup∴ Council of the 33d degree; to whose authority, laws, rules and regulations I now swear true faith, loyalty and allegiance; or by virtue of authority from a Sovereign Inspector General or Deputy Inspector duly authorized: and that even in such case I will not do so, if the Candidate be not a worthy Brother, of pure life and irreproachable manners and morals.

I furthermore promise and swear, that I will be zealous, firm, upright, honest, true, frank, humble, modest, gentle, kind, silent, discreet, merciful and tolerant; and that I will endeavour to obey the New Commandment by loving my Brother.

And should I wilfully or knowingly violate this my obligation, I consent to be condemned, cast out and despised by all men: and may the Ruler of the Universe guide and assist me to keep this my solemn obligation!

[Suddenly there is a disturbance at the door, and the Guard comes in in haste and breathless, and says: "The Soldiery have discovered our retreat. They are too numerous to be resisted, and they approach rapidly." (Arms are clashed together in the ante-room.) "I hear the clash of their arms."]

M∴ Ex∴ Up! my Brethren, and escape by the secret passages. Separate from one another, and let each take care of himself. Away! Away!

[All the members go out, leaving the Candidate kneeling before the altar. A number now rush in at the door, with clash of arms and fierce loud words, and surround the Candidate. One of them represents the Centurion].

Cent∴ Comrades, it is here our Gods are blasphemed, and the rites of sorcery are practised. But the tattered rogues have escaped us again. Search for the passages by which they have fled, and pursue them. Away! Ah, here is one that in their hurry they have left behind, blinded and bound, and kneeling before an altar!

1st Sold∴ Shall I hew the blasphemous Judean in pieces?

2d Sold∴ Stand aside, till I thrust my lance through him.

3d Sold∴ Devote him to the Eternal Gods!

Cent∴ Silence, my men! Domitian needs him for the Amphitheatre and the Lions. What art thou, knave? Dost thou worship the Immortal Gods of Rome?

Cand∴ No.

Cent∴ Not even Jupiter nor Mars?

Cand∴ No.

Cent∴ A rank Judean and an unbeliever! It is said that ye have a WORD by which ye pretend to work miracles. It is here, too, that ye blasphemously imitate the Holy Mysteries. [He places the point of his sword against the Candidate's breast]. Give me that Word, or die!

Cent∴ The Word! dog of a Jew!

Cent.. The Word, the Word, I say; if you would live!

Cent.. Then die! But, no, I will not disgrace a Roman sword with ignoble blood. Call in the Persian slaves with the bowstring!

[A small cord is placed around the Candidate's neck, and twisted so as to hurt him slightly].

Cent.. Wait until I give the signal! Wilt thou not yet speak the Word?

Cent.. Why, what a stubborn knave! Be ready, slaves. . . . . Now!

M.·. Exc.·. Hold, my Brethren! The trial is sufficient. Remove the cord and unbind his hands. Constans, thou art worthy to be accepted among the Faithful. What now dost thou most desire?

Cand.·. Light.

M.·. Exc.·. I am come a Light into the world, that whosoever believeth in me should not abide in darkness. While ye have Light, believe ye in the Light, that ye may be the Children of Light. This is Life Eternal, to know the only True God, and the Word that did create the Universe, in whom is Light, and that Light the Life of men. My Brethren, aid me to bring this newly accepted Brother to Light.

[The bandage is removed, and the M.·. Exc.·. assists him to rise; and says]:

M.·. Exc.·. Behold, the darkness is past, and the True Light now shineth. My Brother, you have before this been brought to Light in Masonry, when the Worshipful Master, with the aid of the Brethren, first made you a Mason. You have been taught to believe in the True God, whom the ancient Patriarchs worshipped. You have passed heretofore through Degrees intended to remind you of the Essenian and Hebrew Mysteries; and in this you see a faint imitation of those practised by the first Christians in the catacombs under Rome. As you were not required to profess a belief in the tenets of the Essenes or the Pharisees, so neither here are you required to believe in the divine mission or character of Jesus of Nazareth. We shadow forth *the Secret Discipline* of the early Christians, as we do the Egyptian, Persian, Grecian, Hebrew and Scandinavian Mysteries, as the diverse and varying and often eccentric forms in which Masonry has developed itself in the different ages of the world. Masonically we know not whether you be Christian, Jew or Moslem. We have no right to *ask*. If you be Christian, you will see in this, as in the 18th Degree, a Christian ceremony; and so you have the right to regard and interpret it. Your Brethren will respect *your* faith, as they have a right to demand that you shall respect *theirs*. If you be not a Christian, you will see in it a mere historical allegory, symbolizing great Truths, acknowledged alike by you and them.

While you were veiled in darkness, you heard repeated by the Voice of the Great Past its most ancient doctrines. None has the right to object, if the Christian Mason sees foreshadowed in Chrishna and Sosiosch, in Mithras and Osiris, the Divine Word that, as he believes, became Man, and died upon the cross to redeem a fallen race. Nor can *he* object if others see reproduced, in the Word of the beloved Disciple, that was in the beginning with God, and that was God, and by whom everything was made, only the Logos of Plato, and the Word or Uttered Thought or First Emanation of Light, or the Perfect Reason of the Great, Silent, Supreme, Uncreated Deity, believed in and adored by all.

We do not undervalue the importance of any Truth. We utter no word that can be deemed irreverent by any one of any faith. We do not tell the Moslem that it is only important for him to believe that there is but one God, and wholly unessential whether Mahomet was his prophet. We do not tell the Hebrew that the Messiah whom he expects was born in Bethlehem nearly two thousand years ago; and that he is a heretic because he will not so believe. And as little do we tell the sincere Christian that Jesus of Nazareth was but a man like us, or his history but the unreal revival of an older legend. To do either is beyond our jurisdiction. Masonry, of no one age, belongs to all time; of no one religion, it finds its great truths in all.

To Every Mason, there is a God; One, Supreme, Infinite in Goodness, Wisdom, Foresight, Justice, and Benevolence; Creator, Disposer and Preserver of all things. How, or by what intermediates He creates and acts, and in what way He unfolds and manifests Himself, Masonry leaves to Creeds and Religions to inquire.

To every Mason, the soul of man is immortal. Whether it emanates from and will return to God, and what its continued mode of existence hereafter, each judges for himself. Masonry was not made to settle that.

To every Mason, Wisdom or Intelligence, Force or Strength, and Harmony, or Fitness and Beauty, are the Trinity of the attributes of God. With the subtleties of Philosophy concerning them Masonry does not meddle, nor decide as to the reality of the supposed Existences which are their Personifications ; nor whether the Christian Trinity be such a personification, or Reality of the gravest import and significance.

To every Mason, the Infinite Justice and Benevolence of God give ample assurance that Evil will ultimately be dethroned, and the Good, the True and the Beautiful reign triumphant and eternal. It teaches, as it feels and knows, that Evil, and Pain and Sorrow exist as part of a Wise and Beneficent plan, all the parts of which work together under God's eye to a result which shall be perfection. Whether the existence of evil is rightly explained in this creed or in that, by Typhon the Great Serpent, by Ahriman and his Armies of Wicked Spirits, by the Giants and Titans that war against Heaven, by the two co-existent Principles of Good and Evil, by Satan's temptation and the fall of Man, by Lok and the Serpent Fenris, it is beyond the domain of Masonry to decide, nor does it need to inquire. Nor is it within its Province to determine how the ultimate triumph of Light and Truth and Good, over Darkness and Error and Evil is to be achieved ; nor whether the Redeemer, looked and longed for by all nations, hath appeared in Judea, or is yet to come.

It reverences all the great reformers. It sees in Moses, the Lawgiver of the Jews, in Confucius and Zoroaster, in Jesus of Nazareth, and in the Arabian Iconoclast, Great Teachers of Morality, and Eminent Reformers, if no more: and allows every brother of the Order to assign to each such higher and even Divine Character as his Creed and Truth require.

Thus Masonry disbelieves no truth, and teaches unbelief in no creed, except so far as such creed may lower its lofty estimate of the Deity, degrade Him to the level of the passions of humanity, deny the high destiny of man, impugn the goodness and benevolence of the Supreme God, strike at the great columns of Masonry, Charity, Hope and Faith, or inculcate immorality, and disregard of the active duties of the Order.

Masonry is a worship ; but one in which all civilized men can unite ; for it does not undertake to explain or dogmatically to settle those great mysteries, that are above the feeble comprehension of our human intellect. It trusts in God, and hopes ; it BELIEVES, like a child, and is humble. It draws no sword to compel others to adopt its belief, or to be happy with its hopes. And it WAITS with patience to understand the mysteries of Nature and Nature's God hereafter.

The greatest mysteries in the Universe are those which are ever going on around us; so trite and common to us that we never note them or reflect upon them. Wise men tell us of the *laws* that regulate the motions of the spheres, which flashing in huge circles and spinning on their axes are also ever darting with inconceivable rapidity through the infinities of Space ; while we atoms sit here, and dream that all was made for us. They tell us learnedly of centripetal and centrifugal *forces*, gravity and attraction, and all the other sounding terms, invented to hide a *want* of meaning. There are other forces in the Universe than those that are mechanical.

Here are two minute seeds, not much unlike in appearance, and two of larger size. Hand them to the learned Pundit, Chemistry, who tells us how combustion goes on in the lungs, and plants are fed with phosphorus and carbon, and the alkalies and silex. Let her decompose them, analyze them, torture them in all the ways she knows. The net result of each is a little sugar, a little fibrin, a little water—carbon, potassium, sodium and the like—one cares not to know what.

We hide them in the ground ; and the slight rains moisten them, and the Sun shines upon them, and little slender shoots spring up and grow ;—and what a miracle is the mere growth !—the force, the power, the *capacity* (which is the true word) by which the little feeble shoot, that a small worm can nip off with a single snap of its mandibles, extracts from the earth and air and water the different elements, so learnedly catalogued, with which it increases in stature, and rises imperceptibly towards the sky ! The slender shoot is a better chemist than Liebig.

One grows to be a slender, fragile, feeble stalk, soft of texture, like an ordinary weed: another a strong bush, of woody fibre, armed with thorns, and sturdy enough to bid defiance to the winds : the third a tender tree, subject to be blighted by the frost, and looked down upon by all the forest ; while another spreads its rugged arms abroad, and cares for neither frost nor ice, nor the snows that for months lie piled around its roots.

But lo ! out of the brown foul earth, and colourless invisible air, and limpid rain-water, the chemistry of the seeds has extracted *colours*—four different shades of green, that paint the leaves which put forth in the spring upon our plants, our shrubs and our trees. Later still come the flowers—the vivid colours of the rose, the beautiful brilliance of the carnation, the modest blush of the apple, and the splendid white of the orange. Whence come the *colours* of the leaves and flowers? By what process of chemistry are *they* extracted from the carbon, the phosphorus and the lime? Is it any greater miracle to make something out of nothing?

Pluck the flowers. Inhale the delicious *perfumes;* each perfect, and all delicious. Whence have *they* come? By what combination of acids and alkalies could the chemist's laboratory produce *them?*

And now on two comes the fruit—the ruddy apple and the golden orange. Pluck them—open them! The texture and fabric how totally different! The *taste* how entirely dissimilar—the *perfume* of each distinct from its flower and from the other. Whence the taste and this new perfume? The same earth and air and water have been made to furnish a different taste to each fruit, a different perfume not only to each fruit, but to each fruit and its own flower.

Is it any more a problem whence come thought and will and perception and all the phenomena of the mind, than this whence come the colours, the perfumes, the taste of the fruit and flower?

And lo! in each fruit new seeds, each gifted with the same wondrous power of reproduction—each with the same wondrous *forces* wrapped up in it to be again in turn evolved. Forces that had lived three thousand years in the grain of wheat found in the wrappings of an Egyptian mummy: forces of which learning and science and wisdom know no more than they do of the nature and laws of action of God. What can *we* know of the nature, and how can *we* understand the powers and mode of operation, of the human soul, when the glossy leaves, the pearl-white flower, and the golden fruit of the orange are a miracle wholly beyond our comprehension?

We but hide our ignorance in a cloud of words;—and the words too often are mere combinations of sounds without any meaning. What is the centrifugal force? A *tendency* to go in a particular direction! What external force, then, produces that tendency?

What force draws the needle round to the north? What force moves the muscle that raises the arm, when the will determines it shall rise? Whence comes the *will* itself? Is it spontaneous—a first cause, or an effect? These too are miracles; inexplicable as the creation, or the existence and self-existence of God.

Who will explain to us the passion, the peevishness, the anger, the memory and affections of the small canary-wren? the consciousness of identity and the dreams of the dog? the reasoning powers of the elephant? the wondrous instincts, passions, government and civil policy and modes of communication of ideas of the ant and bee?

Who has yet made us to understand, with all his learned words, how heat comes to us from the Sun, and light from the remote Stars, setting out upon its journey earth-ward from some, what time the Chaldeans commenced to build the Tower of Babel? Or how the image of an external object comes to and fixes itself upon the retina of the eye; and when there, how that mere empty, unsubstantial image becomes transmuted into the wondrous thing that we call SIGHT? Or how the waves of the atmosphere striking upon the tympanum of the ear—those thin, invisible waves of a compound of oxygen and nitrogen—produce the equally wondrous phenomenon of HEARING, and become the roar of the tornado, the crash of the awful thunder, the mighty voice of the ocean, the chirping of the cricket, the delicate sweet notes and exquisite trills and variations of the wren and mocking-bird, or the magic melody of the instrument of Paganini?

Our senses are mysteries to us, and we are mysteries to ourselves. Philosophy has taught us nothing as to the nature of our sensations, our perceptions, our cognizances, the origin of our thoughts and ideas, but *words.* By no effort or degree of reflection, never so long continued, can man become conscious of a personal identity in himself, separate and distinct from his body and his brain. We torture ourselves in the effort to gain an idea of ourselves, and weary with the exertion. Who has yet made us understand how from the contact with a foreign body, the image in the eye, the wave of air impinging on the ear, particular particles entering the nostrils, and coming in contact with the palate, come sensations in the nerves, and from that, perception in the mind?

What do we know of Substance? Men even doubt yet whether it exists. Philosophers tell us that our senses only make known to us the *attributes* of substance, extension, hardness, colour, and the like; but not *the thing itself* that *is* extended, solid, black or white; as we know the *attributes* of the Soul, its thoughts and its perceptions, and not the Soul itself which perceives and thinks.

What a wondrous mystery is there in heat and light, existing, we know not how, within certain limits, narrow in comparison with infinity, beyond which on every side stretch out infinite space and the blackness of unimaginable darkness, and the intensity of inconceivable cold! Think only of the mighty Power required to maintain warmth and light in the Central point of such an infinity, to whose darkness, that of Midnight, to whose cold that of the last Arctic Island is nothing! And yet GOD is every-where.

And what a mystery are the effects of heat and cold upon the wondrous fluid that we call water! What a mystery lies hidden in every flake of snow and in every crystal of ice, and in their final transformation into the invisible vapor that rises from the ocean or the land, and floats above the summits of the mountains!

What a multitude of wonders, indeed, has chemistry unveiled to our eyes! Think only that if some single law enacted by God were at once repealed, that of attraction or affinity or cohesion, for example, the whole material world, with its solid granite and adamant, its veins of gold and silver, its trap and porphyry, its huge beds of coal, our own frames and the very ribs and bones of this apparently indestructible earth, would instantaneously dissolve, with all Suns and Stars and Worlds throughout all the Universe of God, into a thin invisible vapor of infinitely minute particles or atoms, diffused through infinite space; and with them light and heat would disappear; unless the Deity Himself be, as the Ancient Persians thought, the Eternal Light and the Immortal Fire.

The mysteries of the Great Universe of God! How *can* we with our limited mental vision expect to grasp and comprehend them! Infinite SPACE, stretching out from us every way, without limit: infinite TIME, without beginning or end; and We, HERE, and NOW, in the centre of each. An infinity of suns, the nearest of which only *diminish* in size, viewed with the most powerful telescope: each with its retinue of worlds; infinite numbers of such suns, so remote from us that their light would not reach us, journeying during an infinity of time, while the light that *has* reached us, from some that we *seem* to see, has been upon its journey for fifty centuries: our world spinning upon its axis, and rushing ever in its circuit round the sun; and it, the sun and all our system revolving round some great central point; and that, and suns, stars and worlds ever-more flashing onward with incredible rapidity through illimitable space: and then, in every drop of water that we drink, in every morsel of much of our food, in the air, in the earth, in the sea, incredible multitudes of living creatures, invisible to the naked eye, of a minuteness beyond belief, yet organized, living, feeding, perhaps with consciousness of identity, and memory and instinct.

Such are the mysteries of the great Universe of God! And yet we, whose life and that of the world on which we live form but a point in the centre of infinite Time: we, who nourish animalculæ within, and on whom vegetables grow without, would fain learn how God created this Universe, would understand His Powers, His Attributes, His Emanations, His Mode of Existence and of Action; would fain know the plan according to which all events proceed, that plan profound as God Himself; would know the laws by which he controls His Universe; would fain see and talk to Him face to face, as man talks to man: and we try not to *believe*, because we do not *understand*.

He commands us to love one another, to love our neighbour as ourself; and we dispute and wrangle, and hate and slay each other, because we cannot be of one opinion as to the Essence of His Nature, as to His Attributes; whether He became man born of a woman, and was crucified; whether the Holy Ghost is of the *same* substance with the Father, or only of a *similar* substance; whether a feeble old man is God's Vice-gerent; whether some are elected from all eternity to be saved and others to be condemned and punished; whether punishment of the wicked after death is to be eternal: whether this doctrine or the other be heresy or truth;—drenching the world with blood, depopulating realms, and turning fertile lands into deserts; until, for religious war, persecution and bloodshed, the Earth for many a century has rolled round the Sun, a charnel-house, steaming and reeking with human gore, the blood of brother slain by brother for opinion's sake, that has soaked into and polluted all her veins, and made her a horror to her sisters of the Universe.

And if men were all Masons, and obeyed with all their heart her mild and gentle teachings, that world would be a paradise; while intolerance and persecution make of it a hell. For this is the Masonic Creed: BELIEVE, in God's Infinite Benevolence, Wisdom and Justice: HOPE, for the final triumph of Good over Evil, and for Perfect Harmony as the final result of all the concords and discords of the Universe: and be CHARITABLE as God is, towards the unfaith, the errors, the follies and the faults of men: for all make one great brotherhood.

On being now again brought to light, you see before you the luminous Delta, with three equal sides, in all ages the representation of Deity, the Trinity of Wisdom, Power and Harmony; and upon it THE INEFFABLE NAME, and the Cross, heretofore explained to you, as the *Crux Ansata*, or Egyptian emblem of immortality; with the Greek letters I.·. H.·. Σ.·. which to the Christian are the name of his Redeemer, and will be explained to you hereafter. Receive now the signs, tokens, and words of this Degree.

1st SIGN: . . . *Of Entrance:* . . . Place the ‡⁑&☉♒♊ over the ☾♄☾♎ as if to protect ♈&☾♋ from the †♀♌&♈ of the ♎♑♒.

2d SIGN: . . . *Of the Trinity:* . . . Form a ♈‡♀☉♒♌†☾ with the ?♈&♑♋♏♎ and ?♑☿‡☾♑?♒-♑☾‡♎— and place them over the ♎♈☿♋☉↕&, ♑♒♀♈☾♊ at the ⁑☿ ♀♒♈♎.

3d SIGN: . . . *Of Appeal:* . . . ↕‡☿♎♎ the ?☉‡♋♎ over the &☾☉♊—⁑☉†♋♎ ♑⁑♃☉‡♊ and the &☉♒♊♎ ☿⁑☾♒— and say †?⁑♏☾♒♀⁑☉♋☾♈&.·. ["To ME," (i. e. *Help—à moi!*) "SONS OF THE TRUTH!"].

DUE-GUARD: . . . ‡⁑&☉♒♊ on the ‡⁑&♀⁑.

TOKEN: . . . Press ♏☿ ♈&⁑&☉♒♊♎ lightly on the ♎&☿ ♑†♊☾‡♎ of a brother, pronouncing at the same time the Pass-Word.

PASS-WORD: . . . ♌☿♋☾†.·.

SACRED WORD: . . . יהוה.

[The Brother is then seated and receives the following instruction, by dialogue between the Sen.·. and Jun.·. Wardens].

INSTRUCTION.

Sen.·. W.·. Bro.·. Jun.·. Warden, are you a Prince of Mercy?

Jun.·. W.·. I have seen the Delta and the Holy NAMES upon it, and am an AMETH like yourself, in the TRIPLE COVENANT, of which we bear the mark.

Qu.·. What is the first Word upon the Delta?

Ans.·. The Ineffable Name of Deity, the true mystery of which is known to the Ameth alone.

Qu.·. What do the three sides of the Delta denote to us?

Ans.·. To us, and to all Masons, the three Great Attributes or Developments of the Essence of the Deity; WISDOM, or the Reflective and Designing Power, in which, when there was nought but God, the Plan and Idea of the Universe was shaped and formed: FORCE, or the Executing and Creating Power, which instantaneously acting, realized the Type and Idea framed by Wisdom; and the Universe, and all Stars and Worlds, and Light and Life, and Men and Angels and all living creatures WERE; and HARMONY, or the Preserving Power, Order and Beauty, maintaining the Universe in its State, and constituting the law of Harmony, Motion, Proportion and Progression:—WISDOM, which *thought* the plan; STRENGTH which *created:* HARMONY which *upholds* and *preserves:*—the Masonic Trinity, three Powers and one Essence: the three columns which support the Universe, Physical, Intellectual and Spiritual, of which every Masonic Lodge is a type and symbol:—while to the Christian Mason, they represent the Three that bear record in Heaven, the FATHER, the WORD and the HOLY SPIRIT, which three are ONE.

Qu.·. What do the three Greek letters upon the Delta, I.·. II.·. Σ.·. [*Iota, Eta,* and *Sigma*] represent.

Three of the Names of the Supreme Deity among the Syrians, Phœnicians and Hebrews . . . Iᴀᴜᴴ [יהוה]; *Self-Existence* . . . Eʟ or Aʟ [אל]: *the Nature-God, or Soul of the Universe* . . . Sᴴᴇᴅɪ or Sʜᴀᴅᴅᴀɪ [שדי]; *Supreme Power.* Also three of the Six Chief Attributes of God, among the Kabbalists ;—Wɪsᴅᴏᴍ [Iᴇʜ], the *Intellect* (Νοῦς) of the Egyptians, the *Word* (Λογος) of the Platonists, and the *Wisdom* (Σοφια) of the Gnostics : . . Mᴀɢɴɪғɪᴄᴇɴᴄᴇ [Eʟ], the Symbol of which was the Lion's Head : . . and Vɪᴄᴛᴏʀʏ and Gʟᴏʀʏ [*Sebaoth*], which are the two columns Jᴀᴄʜɪɴ and Bᴏᴀᴢ, that stand in the Portico of the Temple of Masonry. To the Christian Mason they are the three first letters of the name of the Son of God, who died upon the cross to redeem mankind.

Qu.·. What is the first of the Tʜʀᴇᴇ Cᴏᴠᴇɴᴀɴᴛs, of which we bear the mark ?

Ans.·. That which God made with Noah; when He said, " I will not again curse the earth any more for " man's sake, neither will I smite any more everything living as I have done. While the Earth remaineth, " seed-time and harvest, and cold and heat, and winter and summer, and day and night shall not cease. I " will establish my covenant with you, and with your seed after you, and with every living creature. All " mankind shall no more be cut off by the waters of a flood, nor shall there any more be a flood to destroy " the earth. This is the token of my covenant : I do set my bow in the cloud, and it shall be for a token of " a covenant between me and the earth : an everlasting covenant between Me and every living creature on " the earth."

Qu.·. What is the second of the Three Covenants ?

Ans.·. That which God made with Abraham; when he said, " I am the Absolute Uncreated God. I will " make my covenant between me and thee, and thou shalt be the Father of Many Nations, and Kings shall " come from thy loins. I will establish my covenant between Me and thee, and thy descendants after thee, " to the remotest generations, for an everlasting covenant; and I will be thy God and their God, and will give " thee the land of Canaan for an everlasting possession."

Qu.·. What is the third covenant ?

Ans.·. That which God made with all men by His prophets ; when he said : " I will gather all nations " and tongues, and they shall come and see my Glory. I will create new Heavens and a new earth; and the " former shall not be remembered, nor come into mind. The Sun shall no more shine by day, nor the Moon " by night; but the Lord shall be an everlasting light and splendour. His Spirit and his Word shall remain " with men forever. The fourth beast shall be the fourth kingdom upon earth, diverse from all Kingdoms, " and shall lay waste and devastate the earth; and shall speak against the Supreme God, and persecute his " Saints, and think to change his eternal laws; but the Ancient of Days shall judge him, and take away his " dominion, and consume and destroy it unto the end; and the kingdom and dominion, and all power under " Heaven shall be given to the People of the Saints of the Most High, whose kingdom is an everlasting king- " dom, and all men shall serve and obey Him. The Heavens shall vanish away like vapour, and the earth " shall wax old like a garment, and they that dwell therein shall die; but my salvation shall be forever, " and my righteousness shall not end; and there shall be Light among the Gentiles, and salvation unto the " ends of the earth. The redeemed of the Lord shall return, and everlasting joy be on their heads, and sorrow " and mourning shall flee away."

Qu.·. What is the symbol of the Triple Covenant ?

Ans.·. The Triple Triangle.

Qu.·. Of what else is it the symbol to us ?

Ans.·. Of the Trinity of Attributes of the Deity ; and of the triple essence of Man, the Principle of Life, the Intellectual Power, and the Soul or Immortal Emanation from the Deity.

Qu.·. What is the first great Truth of the Sacred Mysteries ?

Ans.·. No man hath seen God at any time. He is One, Eternal, All-Powerful, All-Wise, Infinitely Just, Merciful, Benevolent and Compassionate, Creator and Preserver of all things, the Source of Light and Life, coextensive with Time and Space; Who thought, and with the Thought created the universe and all living things, and the souls of men: Tʜᴀᴛ Is:—the Pᴇʀᴍᴀɴᴇɴᴛ; while everything beside is a perpetual genesis.

Qu.·. What is the second great Truth of the Sacred Mysteries ?

Ans∴ The Soul of Man is Immortal; not the result of organization, nor an aggregate of modes of action of matter, nor a succession of phenomena and perceptions; but an EXISTENCE, one and identical, a living spirit, a spark of the Great Central Light, that hath entered into and dwells in the body; to be separated therefrom at death, and return to God who gave it: that doth not disperse or vanish at death, like breath or a smoke, nor can be annihilated; but still exists and possesses activity and intelligence, even as it existed in God, before it was enveloped in the body.

Qu∴ What is the third great Truth in Masonry?

Ans∴ The impulse which directs to right conduct, and deters from crime, is not only older than the ages of nations and cities, but coeval with that Divine Being who sees and rules both heaven and earth. Nor did Tarquin less violate that Eternal Law, though in his reign there might have been no written law at Rome against such violence; for the principle that impels us to right conduct, and warns us against guilt, springs out of the nature of things. It did not begin to be law when it was first *written*, but when it *originated*, and it is coeval with the Divine Intelligence itself. The consequence of virtue is not to be made the end thereof; and laudable performances must have deeper roots, motives and instigations, to give them the stamp of virtues. If a man shall lay down as the chief good that which has no connection with virtue, and measure it by his own interests, and not according to its moral merit; if such a man shall act consistently with his own principles, and is not sometimes influenced by the goodness of his heart, he can cultivate neither friendship, justice nor generosity. It is impossible for the man to be brave, who shall pronounce pain the greatest evil; or temperate, who shall propose pleasure as the highest good.

Qu∴ What is the fourth great Truth in Masonry?

Ans∴ The moral truths are as absolute as the metaphysical truths. Even the Deity cannot make it that there should be effects without a cause, or phenomena without substance. As little could He make it to be sinful and evil to respect our pledged word, to love truth, to moderate our passions. The principles of Morality are axioms, like the principles of Geometry. The moral laws are the necessary relations that flow from the nature of things, and they are not created by, but have existed eternally in God. Their continued existence does not depend upon the exercise of His WILL. Truth and Justice are of His ESSENCE. Not because we are feeble and God omnipotent, is it our duty to obey his law. We may be forced, but are not under obligation, to obey the stronger. God is the principle of Morality, but not by His mere will, which, abstracted from all other of His attributes, would be neither just nor unjust. Good is the expression of His will, in so far as that will is itself the expression of eternal, absolute, uncreated justice, which is *in* God, which His will did not create; but which it executes and promulgates, as our will proclaims and promulgates and executes the idea of the good which is in us. He has given us the law of Truth and Justice; but He has not arbitrarily instituted that law. Justice is inherent in His will, because it is contained in His intelligence and wisdom, in His very nature and most intimate essence.

Qu∴ What is the fifth great Truth in Masonry?

Ans∴ There is an essential distinction between Good and Evil, what is just and what is unjust; and to this distinction is attached, for every intelligent and free creature, the absolute obligation of conforming to what is good and just. Man is an intelligent and free being,—free, because he is conscious that it is his duty, and because it is *made* his duty, to obey the dictates of truth and justice, and therefore he must necessarily have the power of doing so, which involves the power of *not* doing so;—capable of comprehending the distinction between good and evil, justice and injustice, and the obligation which accompanies it, and of naturally adhering to that obligation, independently of any contract or positive law; capable also of resisting the temptations which urge him towards evil and injustice, and of complying with the sacred law of eternal justice.

That man is not governed by a resistless Fate or inexorable Destiny; but is free to choose between the evil and the good: that Justice and Right, the Good and Beautiful, are of the essence of the Divinity, like His Infinitude; and therefore they are laws to man: that we are conscious of our freedom to act, as we are conscious of our identity, and the continuance and connectedness of our existence; and have the same evidence of one as of the other; and if we can put *one* in doubt, we have no certainty of *either*, and everything is unreal: that we can deny our free will and free agency, only upon the ground that they are in the nature of things impossible; which would be to deny the Omnipotence of God.

Qu.·. What is the sixth great Truth of Masonry?

Ans.·. The necessity of practising the moral truths, is *obligation.* The moral truths, necessary in the eye of reason, are obligatory on the will. The moral obligation, like the moral truth that is its foundation, is *absolute.* As the necessary truths are not more or less necessary, so the obligation is not more or less obligatory. There are degrees of importance among different obligations; but none in the obligation itself. We are not *nearly* obliged, *almost* obliged. We are wholly so, or not at all. If there be any place of refuge to which we can escape from the obligation, it ceases to exist. If the obligation is absolute, it is immutable and universal. For if that of to-day may not be that of to-morrow, if what is obligatory on *me* may not be obligatory on *you,* the obligation would differ from itself, and be variable and contingent. This fact is the principle of all morality. That every act contrary to right and justice, deserves to be repressed by force, and punished when committed, equally in the absence of any law or contract: that man naturally recognizes the distinction between the merit and demerit of actions, as he does that between justice and injustice, honesty and dishonesty; and feels, without being taught, and in the absence of law or contract, that it is wrong for vice to be rewarded or go unpunished, and for virtue to be punished or left unrewarded: and that, the Deity being infinitely just and good, it must follow as a necessary and inflexible law that punishment shall be the result of Sin, its inevitable and natural effect and corollary, and not a mere arbitrary vengeance.

Qu.·. What is the seventh great truth in Masonry?

Ans.·. The immutable law of God requires, that besides respecting the absolute rights of others, and being merely just, we should do good, be charitable, and obey the dictates of the generous and noble sentiments of the soul. Charity is a law, because our conscience is not satisfied nor at ease if we have not relieved the suffering, the distressed and the destitute. It is to *give* that which he to whom you give has no right to *take* or *demand.* To be charitable is obligatory on us. We are the Almoners of God's bounties. But the obligation is not so precise and inflexible as the obligation to be *just.* Charity knows neither rule nor limit. It goes beyond all obligation. Its beauty consists in its liberty. "He that loveth not, knoweth not God; FOR GOD IS LOVE. If we love one another, God dwelleth in us, and His love is perfected in us. God is love; and he that dwelleth in love, dwelleth in God, and God in Him." To be kindly affectioned one to another with brotherly love; to relieve the necessities of the needy, and be generous, liberal and hospitable; to return to no man evil for evil: to rejoice at the good fortune of others, and sympathize with them in their sorrows and reverses; to live peaceably with all men, and repay injuries with benefits and kindness; these are the sublime dictates of the Moral Law, taught from the infancy of the world, by Masonry.

Qu.·. What is the eighth great Truth in Masonry?

Ans.·. That the laws which control and regulate the Universe of God, are those of motion and harmony· We see only the isolated incidents of things, and with our feeble and limited capacity and vision cannot discern their connection, nor the mighty chords that make the apparent discord perfect harmony. Evil is merely apparent, and all is in reality good and perfect. For pain and sorrow, persecution and hardships, affliction and destitution, sickness and death are but the means, by which alone the noblest virtues could be developed. Without them, and without sin and error, and wrong and outrage, as there can be no effect without an adequate cause, there could be neither patience under suffering and distress; nor prudence in difficulty; nor temperance to avoid excess; nor courage to meet danger; nor truth, when to speak the truth is hazardous; nor love, when it is met with ingratitude; nor charity for the needy and destitute; nor forbearance and forgiveness of injuries: nor toleration of erroneous opinions; nor charitable judgment and construction of men's motives and actions; nor patriotism, nor heroism, nor honor, nor self-denial, nor generosity. These and most other virtues and excellencies would have no existence, and even their names be unknown; and the poor virtues that still existed, would scarce deserve the name; for life would be one flat, dead, low level, above which none of the lofty elements of human nature would emerge; and man would lie lapped in contented indolence and idleness, a mere worthless negative, instead of the brave, strong soldier against the grim legions of Evil and rude Difficulty.

Qu.·. What is the ninth great Truth in Masonry?

Ans∴. The great leading doctrine of this Degree;—that the JUSTICE, the WISDOM and the MERCY of God are alike infinite, alike perfect, and yet do not in the least jar or conflict one with the other; but form a Great Perfect Trinity of Attributes, three and yet one: that, the principle of merit and demerit being absolute, and every good action deserving to be rewarded, and every bad one to be punished, and God being as just as He is good; and yet the cases constantly recurring in this world, in which crime and cruelty, oppression, tyranny and injustice are prosperous, happy, fortunate and self-contented, and rule and reign, and enjoy all the blessings of God's beneficence, while the virtuous and good are unfortunate, miserable, destitute, pining away in dungeons, perishing with cold, and famishing with hunger, slaves of oppression, and instruments and victims of the miscreants that govern; so that this world, if there were no existence beyond it, would be one great theatre of wrong and injustice, proving God wholly disregardful of His own necessary law of merit and demerit;—it follows that there must be another life, in which these apparent wrongs shall be repaired: That all the powers of man's soul tend to infinity; and his indomitable instinct of immortality, and the universal hope of another life, testified to by all creeds, all poetry, all traditions, establish its certainty; for man is not an orphan; but hath a Father in heaven: and the day must come when Light and Truth, and the Just and Good shall be victorious, and Darkness, Error, Wrong and Evil be annihilated, and known no more forever: That the universe is one great Harmony, in which, according to the faith of all nations, deep-rooted in all hearts in the primitive ages, Light will ultimately prevail over Darkness, and the Good Principle over the Evil; and the myriad souls that have emanated from the Divinity, purified and ennobled by the struggle here below, will again return to perfect bliss in the bosom of God, to offend against whose laws will then be no longer possible.

Qu∴. What, then, is the one great lesson taught to us, as Masons, in this Degree?

Ans∴. That to that state and realm of Light and Truth and Perfection, which is absolutely certain, all the good men on earth are tending; and if there is a law from whose operation none are exempt, which inevitably conveys their bodies to darkness and to dust, there is another not less certain, nor less powerful, which conducts their spirits to that state of Happiness and Splendour and Perfection, the bosom of their Father and their God. The wheels of Nature are not made to roll backward. Everything presses on to Eternity. From the birth of Time an impetuous current has set in, which bears all the sons of men towards that interminable ocean. Meanwhile, Heaven is attracting to itself whatever is congenial to its nature, is enriching itself by the spoils of the Earth, and collecting within its capacious bosom whatever is pure, permanent and divine, leaving nothing for the last fire to consume but the gross matter that creates concupiscence; while everything fit for that good fortune shall be gathered and selected from the ruins of the world, to adorn that Eternal City.

Let every Mason then obey the voice that calls him thither. Let us seek the things that are above, and be not content with a world that must shortly perish, and which we must speedily quit, while we neglect to prepare for that in which we are invited to dwell forever. While everything within us and around us reminds us of the approach of death, and concurs to teach us that this is not our rest, let us hasten our preparations for another world, and earnestly implore that help and strength from our Father, which alone can put an end to that fatal war which our desires have too long waged with our destiny. When these move in the same direction, and that which God's will renders unavoidable shall become our choice, all things will be ours; life will be divested of its vanity, and death disarmed of its terrors.

Qu∴. What are the symbols of the purification necessary to make us perfect Masons?

Ans∴. Lavation with pure water, or baptism; because to cleanse the body is emblematical of purifying the soul; and because it conduces to the bodily health, and virtue is the health of the soul, as sin and vice are its malady and sickness:—unction, or anointing with oil; because thereby we are set apart and dedicated to the service and priesthood of the Beautiful, the True, and the Good:—and robes of white; emblems of candour, purity and truth.

Qu∴. What is to us the chief symbol of man's ultimate redemption and regeneration?

Ans∴. The fraternal supper, of bread which nourishes, and of wine which refreshes and exhilarates, symbolical of the time which is to come, when all mankind shall be one great harmonious brotherhood; and teaching us these great lessons: that as matter changes ever, but no single atom is annihilated, it is not rational to suppose that the far nobler soul does not continue to exist beyond the grave: that many thousands who have died before us might claim to be joint owners with ourselves of the particles that compose our mortal bodies; for matter ever forms new combinations; and the bodies of the ancient dead, the patriarchs before and since the flood, the kings and common people of all ages, resolved into their constituent elements, are carried upon the wind over all continents, and continually enter into and form part of the habitations of new souls, creating new bonds of sympathy and brotherhood between each man that lives and all his race. And thus, in the bread we eat, and in the wine we drink to-night, *may* enter into and form part of us the identical particles of matter that once formed parts of the material bodies called Moses, Confucius, Plato, Socrates, or Jesus who died upon the cross. In the truest sense, we eat and drink the bodies of the dead; and cannot say that there is a single atom of our blood or body, the ownership of which some other soul might not dispute with us, and produce prior title. It teaches us also the infinite beneficence of God, who sends us seed-time and harvest, each in its season, and makes His showers to fall and His sun to shine alike upon the evil and the good; bestowing upon us unsolicited His innumerable blessings, and asking no return. For there are no angels stationed upon the watch-towers of creation to call the world to prayer and sacrifice; but He bestows His benefits in silence, like a kind friend who comes at night, and leaving his gifts at our door, to be found by us in the morning, goes quietly away and asks no thanks, nor ceases his kind offices for our ingratitude. And thus the bread and wine teach us that our Mortal Body is no more WE than the house in which we live, or the garments that we wear; but the Soul is I, the ONE, identical, unchangeable, immortal emanation from the Deity, to return to God and be forever happy, in His good time; as our mortal bodies, dissolving, return to the elements from which they came, their particles coming and going ever in perpetual genesis. To our Jewish Brethren, this supper is symbolical of the Passover: to the Christian Mason, of that eaten by Christ and his Disciples, when, celebrating the Passover, he broke bread and gave it to them, saying, "Take! eat! this is my body:" and giving them the cup, he said, "Drink ye all of it! for this is my blood of the New Testament, which is shed for many for the remission of sins:" thus symbolizing the perfect harmony and union between himself and the faithful; and his death upon the cross for the salvation of man.

M∴ Exc∴. My Brethren, let us purify this our newly adopted Brother, and devote him to the service of God and virtue.

[A Brother brings a cup of pure water; and the M∴ Exc∴. pours a small quantity upon the head of the Candidate, saying]:

M∴ Exc∴. As the first Christian Masons, in the gloomy catacombs under the Eternal City, baptized their initiates with pure water, as a symbol of regeneration, even so do I pour this water upon thy head, as a symbol of that purification of the soul by suffering and sorrow, by which, parting with the stains of sin and the sordidness of vice, it becomes fit to return to its eternal home in the bosom of the Father who loveth all the children He hath made.

[Then a Brother brings perfumed oil in a cup, and the M∴ Exc∴, dipping his finger in it, marks with it a Tau cross upon the forehead of the Candidate, saying]:

M∴ Exc∴. By this sign I do devote thee henceforward to the cause of Truth. [*The Statue is then unveiled, and he continues*]: Behold the Palladium of this Order. It is no image or idol to be worshipped; neither the Egyptian Isis, nor Astarte of the Phœnicians, nor Ceres, the symbol of nature; but an emblem of Purity and Truth,—TRUTH, which here we worship,—Truth, the antagonist of Error, Fraud and Falsehood, and of which you are now the servant.

[A vessel containing bread, and a vase containing wine, are now placed upon the table in front of the Throne; and the M∴ Exc∴ says]:

M∴ Exc∴. Not in irreverent imitation of the rites of any church, nor as here assuming to administer any sacrament; but to renew our obligations of fraternal kindness and affection, and to express our sincere and heartfelt gratitude to God for His beneficence and His sure promises, let us eat and drink together.

[Each Brother eats a morsel of the bread, and drinks of the wine; and then the M∴ Exc∴ says]:

M∴ Exc∴. Faith in God's Word, and a sincere reliance upon his loving kindness and benevolence, are the true bread of life; and virtue and good deeds, and kindly and genial affections, are the wine that exalts and nourishes the soul. Let these of which we have now partaken ever be symbols to us of Faith and Virtue, and remind us that we are the Brethren of every true and upright Mason on the globe.

[The M∴ Exc∴ then clothes the new Brother in a white tunic, and invests him with the apron, collar and jewel; saying]:

M∴ Exc∴ My Brother, the colours of this Degree are *green, white* and *red*. The *green* is an emblem of the immortality of God, the Soul, and Virtue; the *white*, of Sincerity, Candour and Purity; and the *red*, of Zeal, Fervour and Courage. They are also the symbol of the Holy Trinity; the green, of the Infinite Wisdom and Supreme Intelligence that formed within itself the idea of the universe; the red, of the Word, or efficient Force, by which it sprang into existence; and the white, of the Spirit or perfect Harmony by which it is maintained and all its movements regulated.

By the Holy Name upon the Delta, I charge thee to be true, sincere, merciful and tolerant; and as I press the point of this arrow against thy heart, so may Eternal Truth there penetrate and enter and abide forever! And as the arrow flies straight to its mark, so be thou ever frank, honest and straightforward in all thou sayest and doest, remembering that in this world thou art being prepared for that which is to come! And so I receive thee as one of the Faithful and a Prince of Mercy: and I present thee with this *tessera* or mark, which thou wilt hereafter wear, in evidence that thou art entitled to the privileges and honours of this Degree.

[The following lecture is then read to the new Brother]:

LECTURE.

The history of Masonry is the history of Philosophy. Masons do not pretend to set themselves up for instructors of the human race: but, though Asia produced and preserved the mysteries, Masonry has, in Europe and America, given regularity to their doctrines, spirit and action, and developed the moral advantages which mankind may reap from them. More consistent, and more simple in its mode of procedure, it has put an end to the vast allegorical pantheon of ancient mythologies, and itself become a science.

None can deny that Christ taught a lofty morality. "Love one another: forgive those that despitefully "use you and persecute you: be pure of heart, meek, humble, contented: lay not up riches on earth, but in "heaven: submit to the powers lawfully over you: become like these little children, or ye cannot be saved, "for of such is the Kingdom of Heaven: forgive the repentant; and cast no stone at the sinner, if you too "have sinned: do unto others as ye would have others do unto you:" such, and not abstruse questions of theology, were his simple and sublime teachings.

The early Christians followed in his footsteps. The first preachers of the faith had no thought of domination. Entirely animated by his saying, that he among them should be first, who should serve with the greatest devotion, they were humble, modest and charitable, and they knew how to communicate this spirit of the inner man to the churches under their direction. These churches were at first but spontaneous meetings of all Christians inhabiting the same locality. A pure and severe morality, mingled with religious enthusiasm, was the characteristic of each, and excited the admiration even of their persecutors. Everything was in common among them; their property, their joys and their sorrows. In the silence of night they met for instruction and to pray together. Their love-feasts, or fraternal repasts, ended these reunions, in which all differences in social position and rank were effaced in the presence of a paternal Divinity. Their sole object was to make men better, by bringing them back to a simple worship, of which universal morality was the basis; and to end those numerous and cruel sacrifices which everywhere inundated with blood the altars of the Gods. Thus did Christianity reform the world, and obey the teachings of its founder. It gave to woman her proper rank and influence; it regulated domestic life; and by admitting the slaves to the love-feasts, it by degrees raised them above that oppression under which half of mankind had groaned for ages.

This, in its primitive purity, as taught by Christ himself, was the true primitive religion, as communicated by God to the Patriarchs. It was no new religion, but the reproduction of the oldest of all; and its true and perfect morality is the morality of Masonry, as is the morality of every creed of antiquity.

In the early days of Christianity, there was an initiation like those of the Pagans. Persons were admitted on special conditions only. To arrive at a complete knowledge of the doctrine, they had to pass three degrees of instruction. The initiates were consequently divided into three classes; the first, *Auditors*, the second, *Catechumens*, and the third, *the Faithful*. The Auditors were a sort of novices, who were prepared by certain ceremonies and certain instruction to receive the dogmas of Christianity. A portion of these dogmas was made known to the Catechumens; who, after particular purifications, received baptism, or the initiation of the *theogenesis* (*divine generation*); but in the grand mysteries of that religion, the incarnation, nativity, passion and resurrection of Christ, none were initiated but *the Faithful*. These doctrines, and the celebration of the Holy Sacraments, particularly the Eucharist, were kept with profound secrecy. These mysteries were divided into two parts; the first styled the Mass of the Catechumens; the second, the Mass of the Faithful. The celebration of the Mysteries of Mithras was also styled *a mass;* and the ceremonies used were the same. There were found all the sacraments of the Catholic Church, even the breath of confirmation. The Priest of Mithras promised the initiates deliverance from sin, by means of confession and baptism, and a future life of happiness or misery. He celebrated the oblation of bread, image of the resurrection. The baptism of newly-born children, extreme unction, confession of sins,—all belonged to the Mithriac rites. The candidate was purified by a species of baptism, a mark was impressed upon his forehead, he offered bread and water, pro-nouncing certain mysterious words.

During the persecutions in the early ages of Christianity, the Christians took refuge in the vast catacombs which stretched for miles in every direction under the city of Rome, and are supposed to have been of Etruscan origin. There, amid labyrinthine windings, deep caverns, hidden chambers, chapels and tombs, the persecuted fugitives found refuge, and there they performed the ceremonies of the Mysteries.

The Basilideans, a sect of Christians that arose soon after the time of the Apostles, practised the Mysteries, with the old Egyptian legend. They symbolized Osiris by the Sun, Isis by the Moon, and Typhon by Scorpio; and wore crystals bearing these emblems, as amulets or talismans to protect them from danger; upon which were also a brilliant star and the serpent. They were copied from the talismans of Persia and Arabia, and given to every candidate at his initiation.

Irenæus tells us that the Simonians, one of the earliest sects of the Gnostics, had a Priesthood of the Mysteries.

Tertullian tells us that the Valentinians, the most celebrated of all the Gnostic schools, imitated, or rather perverted, the Mysteries of Eleusis. Irenæus informs us, in several curious chapters, of the mysteries prac-tised by the Marcosians; and Origen gives much information as to the mysteries of the Ophites; and there is no doubt that all the Gnostic sects had mysteries and an initiation. They all claimed to possess a secret doc-trine, coming to them directly from Jesus Christ, different from that of the Gospels and Epistles, and superior to those communications, which, in their eyes, were merely exoteric. This secret doctrine they did not com-municate to every one; and among the extensive sect of the Basilideans hardly one in a thousand knew it, as we learn from Irenæus. We know the name of only the highest class of their initiates. They were styled *Elect* or *Elus* [Εκλέκτοι], and Strangers to the World [ξένοι ἐν κόσμῳ]. They had at least three degrees—the *Material*, the *Intellectual* and the *Spiritual;* and the lesser and greater mysteries: and the number of those who attained the highest degree was quite small.

Baptism was one of their most important ceremonies; and the Basilideans celebrated the 10th of January, as the anniversary of the day on which Christ was baptized in Jordan.

They had the ceremony of laying on of hands, by way of purification; and that of the mystic banquet, emblem of that to which they believed the Heavenly Wisdom would one day admit them, in the fulness of things [Πλήρωμα].

Their ceremonies were much more like those of the Christians than those of Greece; but they mingled with them much that was borrowed from the Orient and Egypt: and taught the primitive truths, mixed with a multitude of fantastic errors and fictions.

The discipline of the secret, was the concealment (*occultatio*) of certain tenets and ceremonies. So says Clemens of Alexandria.

To avoid persecution, the early Christians were compelled to use great precaution, and to hold meetings of the Faithful [*of the Household of Faith*] in private places, under concealment by darkness. They assembled in the night, and they guarded against the intrusion of false brethren and profane persons, spies, who might cause their arrest. They conversed together figuratively, and by the use of symbols, lest cowans and eaves-droppers might overhear: and there existed among them a favoured class, or Order, who were initiated into certain mysteries which they were bound by solemn promise not to disclose, or even converse about, except with such as had received them under the same sanction. They were called *Brethren, the Faithful, Stewards of the Mysteries, Superintendents, Devotees of the Secret,* and ARCHITECTS.

In the *Hierarchiæ,* attributed to St. Dionysius the Areopagite, the first Bishop of Athens, the tradition of the sacrament is said to have been divided into three degrees, or grades, *purification, initiation,* and *accomplishment* or *perfection;* and it mentions also, as part of the ceremony, *the bringing to sight.*

The Apostolic Constitutions, attributed to Clemens, Bishop of Rome, describes the early church, and says: "These regulations must on no account be communicated to all sorts of persons, because of the mysteries contained in them." It speaks of the Deacon's duty to keep the doors, that none uninitiated should enter at the oblation. *Ostiarii,* or doorkeepers, kept guard, and gave notice of the time of prayer and church-assemblies; and also by private signal, in times of persecution, gave notice to those within, to enable them to avoid danger. The mysteries were open to the *Fidèles* or *Faithful* only; and no spectators were allowed at the communion.

Tertullian, who died about A.D. 216, says in his *Apology:* "None are admitted to the religious mysteries without an oath of secrecy. We appeal to your Thracian and Eleusinian mysteries; and we are specially bound to this caution, because if we prove faithless, we should not only provoke Heaven, but draw upon our heads the utmost rigour of human displeasure. And should strangers betray us? They know nothing but by report and hearsay. Far hence, ye Profane! is the prohibition from all holy mysteries."

Clemens, Bishop of Alexandria, born about A.D. 191, says, in his *Stromata,* that he cannot explain the mysteries, because he should thereby, according to the old proverb, put a sword into the hands of a child. He frequently compares the Discipline of the Secret with the heathen Mysteries, as to their internal and recondite wisdom.

Whenever the early Christians happened to be in company with strangers, more properly termed *the Profane,* they never spoke of their sacraments, but indicated to one another what they meant, by means of symbols, and secret watchwords, disguisedly, and as by direct communication of mind with mind, and by enigmas.

Origen, born A.D. 134 or 135, answering Celsus, who had objected that the Christians had a concealed doctrine, said: "Inasmuch as the essential and important doctrines and principles of Christianity are openly taught, it is foolish to object that there are other things that are recondite; for this is common to Christian discipline with that of those philosophers in whose teachings some things were exoteric and some esoteric: and it is enough to say that it was so with some of the disciples of Pythagoras."

The formula which the primitive church pronounced at the moment of celebrating its mysteries, was this: "Depart, ye Profane! Let the Catechumens, and those who have not been admitted or initiated, go forth."

Archelaus, Bishop of Cascara in Mesopotamia, who, in the year 278, conducted a controversy with the Manichæans, said: "These mysteries the church now communicates to him who has passed through the introductory degree. They are not explained to the Gentiles at all; nor are they taught openly in the hearing of Catechumens; but much that is spoken is in disguised terms, that the Faithful [Πιστοι], who possess the knowledge, may be still more informed, and those who are not acquainted with it, may suffer no disadvantage."

Cyril, Bishop of Jerusalem, was born in the year 315, and died in 386. In his *Catechesis* he says: "The Lord spake in parables to his hearers in general; but to his disciples he explained in private the parables and allegories which he spoke in public. The splendour of glory is for those who are early enlightened: obscurity and darkness are the portion of the unbelievers and ignorant. Just so the church discovers its mysteries to those who have advanced beyond the class of Catechumens: we employ obscure terms with others."

St. Basil, the Great Bishop of Cæsarea, born in the year 326, and dying in the year 376, says: "We receive the dogmas transmitted to us by writing, and those which have descended to us from the Apostles, beneath the mystery of oral tradition: for several things have been handed to us without writing, lest the vulgar, too familiar with our dogmas, should lose a due respect for them. . . . This is what the uninitiated are not permitted to contemplate; and how should it ever be proper to write and circulate among the people an account of them?"

St. Gregory Narianzen, Bishop of Constantinople, A. D. 379, says: "You have heard as much of the mystery as we are allowed to speak openly in the ears of all: the rest will be communicated to you in private; and that you must retain within yourself. . . . Our mysteries are not to be made known to strangers."

St. Ambrose, Archbishop of Milan, who was born in 340, and died in 393, says, in his work *De Mysteriis*: "All the mystery should be kept concealed, guarded by faithful silence, lest it should be inconsiderately divulged to the ears of the Profane. . . . It is not given to all to contemplate the depths of our mysteries . . . that they may not be seen by those who ought not to behold them; nor received by those who cannot preserve them." And in another work: "He sins against God, who divulges to the unworthy the mysteries confided to him. The danger is not merely in violating truth, but in telling truth, if he allow himself to give hints of them to those, from whom they ought to be concealed. . . . Beware of casting pearls before swine! . . . Every mystery ought to be kept secret; and, as it were, to be covered over by silence, lest it should rashly be divulged to the ears of the Profane. Take heed that you do not incautiously reveal the mysteries!"

St. Augustin, Bishop of Hippo, who was born in 347, and died in 430, says in one of his discourses: "Having dismissed the Catechumens, we have retained you only to be our hearers; because, besides those things which belong to all Christians in common, we are now to discourse to you of sublime mysteries, which none are qualified to hear, but those who, by the Master's favour, are made partakers of them. . . . To have taught them openly, would have been to betray them." And he refers to the Ark of the Covenant, and says that it signified a mystery, or secret of God, shadowed over by the cherubims of glory, and honoured by being veiled.

St. Chrysostom and St. Augustin speak of initiation more than fifty times. St. Ambrose writes to those who are initiated: and initiation was not merely baptism, or admission into the church, but it referred to initiation into the mysteries. To the baptized and initiated the mysteries of religion were unveiled; they were kept secret from the Catechumens; who were permitted to hear the Scriptures read and the ordinary discourses delivered, in which the mysteries, reserved for the Faithful, were never treated of. When the services and prayers were ended, the Catechumens and spectators all withdrew.

Chrysostom, Bishop of Constantinople, was born in 354, and died in 417. He says: "I wish to speak openly; but I dare not, on account of those who are not initiated. I shall therefore avail myself of disguised terms, discoursing in a shadowy manner. . . . Where the holy mysteries are celebrated, we drive away all uninitiated persons, and then close the doors." He mentions the acclamations of the initiated; "which," he says, "I here pass over in silence; for it is forbidden to disclose such things to the Profane." Palladius, in his life of Chrysostom, records, as a great outrage, that, a tumult having been excited against him by his enemies, they forced their way into the *penetralia*, where the uninitiated beheld what it was not proper for them to see: and Chrysostom mentions the same circumstance in his epistle to Pope Innocent.

St. Cyril of Alexandria, who was made Bishop in 412, and died in 444, says in his 7th Book against Julian: "These mysteries are so profound and so exalted, that they can be comprehended by those only who are enlightened. I shall not, therefore, attempt to speak of what is so admirable in them, lest by discovering them to the uninitiated, I should offend against the injunction not to give what is holy to the impure, nor cast pearls before such as cannot estimate their worth. . . . I should say much more, if I were not afraid of being heard by those who are uninitiated; because men are apt to deride what they do not understand. And the ignorant, not being aware of the weakness of their minds, condemn what they ought most to venerate."

Theodoret, Bishop of Cyropolis in Syria, was born in 393, and made Bishop in 420. In one of his three Dialogues, called the Immutable, he introduces *Orthodoxus*, speaking thus: "Answer me, if you please, in mystical or obscure terms; for perhaps there are some persons present, who are not initiated into the mysteries." And in his preface to Ezekiel, tracing up the secret discipline to the commencement of the Christian era, he says: "These mysteries are so august, that we ought to keep them with the greatest caution."

Minucius Felix, an eminent lawyer of Rome, who lived in 212, and wrote a defence of Christianity, says: "Many of them [the Christians] know each other by tokens and signs (*notis et insignibus*), and they form a friendship for each other, almost before they become acquainted."

The Latin Word, *tessera*, originally meant a square piece of wood or stone, used in making tesselated pavements, afterwards a tablet on which anything was written, and then a cube or die. Its most general use was to designate a piece of metal or wood, square in shape, on which the watch-word of an Army was inscribed; whence *tessera* came to mean the watch-word itself. There was also a *tessera hospitalis*, which was a piece of wood cut into two parts, as a pledge of friendship. Each party kept one of the parts; and they swore mutual fidelity by Jupiter. To break the *tessera* was considered a dissolution of the friendship. The early Christians used it as a Mark, the watch-word of friendship. With them it was generally in the shape of a fish, and made of bone. On its face was inscribed the word Ιχθυς, a fish, the initials of which represented the Greek words, Ιησους Χριστος Θεου Υιος, Σωτηρ; *Jesus Christ, the Son of God, the Saviour.*

St. Augustine, (*de Fide et Symbolis*) says: "This is the faith which in a few words is given to the *Novices* to be kept by a Symbol: these few words are known to all the Faithful: that by believing they may be submissive to God; by being thus submissive, they may live rightly; by living rightly, they may purify their hearts; and with a pure heart may understand what they believe."

Maximus Taurinus says: "The tessera is a symbol and sign, by which to distinguish between the Faithful and the Profane."

The most ancient Trinitarian doctrine on record is that of the Brahmins. The Eternal Supreme Essence, called Parabrahma, Breem, Paratma, produced the Universe by self-reflection, and first revealed himself as Brahma, the *Creating* Power, then as Visuno, the *Preserving* Power, and lastly as Siva, the *Destroying* and *Renovating* power; the three Modes in which the Supreme Essence reveals himself in the material Universe; but which soon came to be regarded as three distinct Deities. These three Deities they styled the Trimurti, or Triad.

The Persians received from the Indians the doctrine of the three principles, and changed it to that of a principle of Life, which was individualized by the Sun, and a principle of Death, which was symbolized by cold and darkness; parallel of the moral world; and in which the continual and alternating struggle between light and darkness, life and death, seemed but a phase of the great struggle between the good and evil principles, embodied in the legend of Ormuzd and Ahriman. Mithras, a Median reformer, was deified after his death, and invested with the attributes of the Sun; the different astronomical phenomena being figuratively detailed as actual incidents of his life; in the same manner as the history of Buddha was invented among the Hindūs.

The Trinity of the Hindūs became among the Ethiopians and Abyssinians Neph-Amon, Phtha, and Neith—the God Creator, whose emblem was a ram—Matter, or the primitive mud, symbolized by a globe or an egg, and Thought, or the Light which contains the germ of everything; triple manifestation of one and the same God, (Athom), considered in three aspects, as the *creative power, goodness* and *wisdom.* Other Deities were speedily invented; and among them Osiris, represented by the Sun, Isis, his wife, by the Moon or Earth, Typhon, his Brother, the Principle of Evil and Darkness, and Horus, son of Osiris and Isis. And this Trinity, of Osiris, Isis and Horus became subsequently the Chief Gods and objects of worship of the Egyptians.

The ancient Etruscans, a race that from the city of Resen on the Tigris, are supposed to have emigrated to Egypt, and to have been known there as the Hyksos, or Shepherd Kings; and who, driven thence, sailed from the shores of Libya to Umbria in Italy; acknowledged only one Supreme God; but they had images for his different attributes, and temples to these images. Each town had one National Temple, dedicated to the three great attributes of God, Strength, Riches and Wisdom, or *Tina, Talna* and *Minerva.* The National Deity was always a Triad under one roof; and it was the same in Egypt, where one Supreme God alone was acknowledged, but was worshipped as a Triad, with different names in each different home. Each city in Etruria might have as many gods and gates and temples as it pleased; but three sacred gates, and one Temple to three Divine Attributes were obligatory, wherever the laws of Tages (or Tauut or Thoth) were received. The only gate that remains in Italy, of the olden time, undestroyed, is the Porta del Circo at Volterra; and it has upon it the three heads of the three National Divinities, one upon the key-stone of its magnificent arch, and one above each side-pillar.

22D

The Buddhists hold that the God SAKYA of the Hindūs, called in Ceylon, GAUTAMA, in India beyond the Ganges, SOMONAKODOM, and in China, CHY-KIA, or Fo, constituted a Trinity [TRIRATNA], of BOUDDHA, DHARMA and SANGA,—*Intelligence*, *Law*, and *Union* or *Harmony*.

The Chinese Sabeans represented the Supreme Deity as composed of CHANG-TI, the *Supreme Sovereign*, TIEN, the *Heavens*, and TAO, the *Universal Supreme Reason* and *Principle of Faith*; and that from Chaos, an immense silence, an immeasurable void, without perceptible forms, alone, infinite, immutable, moving in a circle in illimitable space, without change or alteration, when vivified by the Principle of Truth, issued all Beings, under the influence of TAO, Principle of Faith, who produced one, one produced two, two produced three, and three produced all that is.

The Sclavono-Vendes typified the Trinity by the three heads of the God TRIGLAV; and the Pruczi or Prussians by the Tri-une God, PERKOUN, PIKOLLOS and POTRIMPOS, the Deities of *Light* and *Thunder*, of *Hell* and the *Earth*, its fruits and animals : and the Scandinavians by ODIN, FREA and THOR.

According to Philo of Alexandria, the Supreme Being, Primitive Light or Archetype of Light, uniting with WISDOM [Σοφια], the mother of Creation, forms in Himself the types of all things, and acts upon the Universe through the WORD, [Λογος . . Logos], who dwells in God, and in whom all His powers and attributes develop themselves ; a doctrine borrowed by him from Plato ; while the Kabbalists represented the First-born of INUH, (the Universal Form, containing in Himself all beings), the Creative agent, preserver and animating principle of the world, as containing within Himself the three primitive Forces of the Deity, LIGHT, SPIRIT and LIFE [Φως, Πνευμα and Ζωη . . Phōs, Pneuma and Zōe] ; and as further revealed in the ten Emanations or SEPHIROTH, which are but attributes of God ; SUPREMACY, WISDOM [the Νους or Λογος . . Nous or Logos] ; PRUDENCE [the Φρονησις . . Phronēsis of the Gnostics, or the Συνησις . . Sunēsis of the Platonists] ; MAGNIFICENCE, SEVERITY, BEAUTY, VICTORY, ESTABLISHMENT and DOMINION : designating *Wisdom*, *Prudence*, *Magnificence*, *Severity*, *Victory* and *Glory*, and *Dominion*, by six of the most sacred names of Deity in the Hebrew : . . . JEH . . INUH . . EL . . ELOHIM . . . ZEBAOTH and ADONAI.

Simon Magus and his disciples taught that the Supreme Being or Centre of Light produced first of all, three couples of united Existences, of both sexes, [Συζυγιας . . . Suzugias], which were the origins of all things : REASON and INVENTIVENESS ; SPEECH and THOUGHT ; CALCULATION and REFLECTION : [Νους and Επινοια, Φωνη and Εννοια, Λογισμος and Ενθυμησις . . . Nous and Epinoia, Phōne and Ennoia, Logismos and Enthumēsis] ; of which Ennoia or WISDOM was the first produced, and Mother of all that exists.

Other Disciples of Simon, and with them most of the Gnostics, adopting and modifying the doctrine, taught that the Πληρωμα . . Plerōma, or PLENITUDE of Superior Intelligences, having the Supreme Being at their head, was composed of eight Eons [Αιωνες . . Aiōnes] of different sexes ; . . PROFUNDITY and SILENCE ; SPIRIT and TRUTH ; the WORD and LIFE ; MAN and the CHURCH : [Βυθος and Σιγη ; Πνευμα and Αληθεια ; Λογος and Ζωη ; Ανθρωπος and Εκκλησια. . . . Buthos and Sigē ; Pneuma and Aletheia ; Logos and Zōe ; Anthrūpos and Ekklūsia].

Bardesanes, whose doctrines the Syrian Christians long embraced, taught that the unknown Father, happy in the Plenitude of His Life and Perfections, first produced a Companion for Himself [Συζυγος . . . Suzugos], whom He placed in the Celestial Paradise, and who became, by Him, the Mother of CHRISTOS, Son of the Living God : i. e. (laying aside the allegory), that the Eternal conceived, in the silence of his decrees, the Thought of revealing Himself by a Being who should be His image or His Son : that to the Son succeeded his Sister and Spouse, the Holy Spirit, and they produced four spirits of the elements, male and female, Maio and Jabscho, Nouro and Rucho ; then Seven Mystic Couples of Spirits, and Heaven and Earth, and all that is ; then seven spirits governing the planets, twelve governing the Constellations of the Zodiac, and thirty-six Starry Intelligences whom he called Deacons : while the Holy Spirit [*Sophia-Achamoth*], being both the Holy Intelligence and the Soul of the physical world, went from the Plerōma into that material world and there mourned her degradation, until CHRISTOS her former spouse, coming to her with his Divine Light and Love, guided her in the way to purification, and she again united herself with him as his primitive Companion.

Basilides, the Christian Gnostic, taught that there were seven emanations from the Supreme Being: The

First-born, Thought, the Word, Reflection, Wisdom, Power and Righteousness [Πρωτογονος, Νους, Λογος, Φρονησις, Σοφια, Δυναμις and Δικαιοσυνη . . . Protogonos, Nous, Logos, Phronesis, Sophia, Dunamis and Dikaiosunē]; from whom emanated other Intelligences in succession, to the number, in all, of three hundred and sixty-five; which were God manifested, and composed the Plenitude of the Divine Emanations, or the God Abraxas; of which the Thought [or Intellect, Νους . . Nous] united itself, by baptism in the river Jordan, with the man Jesus, servant [διακονος . . Diakonos] of the human race; but did not suffer with him; and the disciples of Basilides taught that the Νους put on the appearance only of humanity, and that Simon of Cyrene was crucified in his stead and ascended into heaven.

Basilides held that out of the unrevealed God, who is at the head of the world of emanations, and exalted above all conception or designation ['Ο ακατονομαστος, αρρητος], were evolved seven living, self-subsistent, ever-active hypostatized powers:

FIRST: THE INTELLECTUAL POWERS.

1st. Nous . . . . . Νους . . . . . . The Mind.
2d. Logos . . . . . Λογος . . . . . The Reason.
3d. Phronesis . . Φρονησις . . . . The Thinking Power.
4th. Sophia . . . . Σοφια . . . . . Wisdom.

SECOND: THE ACTIVE OR OPERATIVE POWER.

5th. Dunamis . . . Δυναμις . . . . Might, accomplishing the purposes of Wisdom.

THIRD: THE MORAL ATTRIBUTES.

6th. Dikaiosunē . . Δικαιοσυνη . . Holiness or Moral Perfection.
7th. Eirēnē . . . . Ειρηνη . : . . Inward Tranquillity.

These Seven Powers (Δυναμεις . . Dunameis), with the Primal Ground out of which they were evolved, constituted in his scheme the Πρωτη Ογδοας [Prote Ogdoas], or First Octave, the root of all Existence. From this point, the spiritual life proceeded to evolve out of itself continually many gradations of existence, each lower one being still the impression, the *antetype*, of the immediate higher one. He supposed there were 365 of these regions or gradations, expressed by the mystical word Αβραξας [Abraxas].

The αβραξας is thus interpreted, by the usual method of reckoning Greek letters numerically . . . α, 1 . . β, 2 . . ρ, 100 . . α, 1 . . ξ, 60 . . α, 1 . . ς, 200 = 365: which is the whole Emanation-World, as the development of the Supreme Being.

In the system of Basilides, Light, Life, Soul and Good were opposed to Darkness, Death, Matter and Evil, throughout the whole course of the universe.

According to the Gnostic view, God was represented as the immanent, incomprehensible and original source of all perfection; the Unfathomable Abyss, (βύθος . . buthos), according to Valentinus, exalted above all possibility of designation; of whom, properly speaking, nothing can be predicated; the ακατονομαστος of Basilides, the ὠν of Philo. From this incomprehensible Essence of God, an *immediate* transition to finite things is inconceivable. *Self-limitation* is the first beginning of a communication of life on the part of God—the first passing of the hidden Deity into manifestation; and from this proceeds all further self-developing manifestation of the Divine Essence. From this primal link in the chain of life there are evolved in the first place, the manifold powers or attributes inherent in the divine Essence, which, until that first self-comprehension, were all hidden in the Abyss of His Essence. Each of these attributes presents the whole divine Essence under one particular aspect; and to each, therefore, in this respect, the title of God may appropriately be applied. These Divine Powers evolving themselves to self-subsistence, become thereupon the germs and principles of all further developments of life. The life contained in them unfolds and individualizes itself more and more, but in such a way that the successive grades of this evolution of life continually sink lower and lower; the spirits become feebler, the further they are removed from the first link in the series.

The first manifestation, they termed πρωτη καταληψις εαυτου, [protē katalēpsis heautou] or πρωτον καταληπτον του θεου, [proton Katalēpton tou Theou]; which was hypostatically represented in a νους or λογος, [Nous or Logos].

In the Alexandrian Gnosis, the Platonic notion of the ὕλη [Hulè] predominates. This is the dead, the unsubstantial—the boundary that limits from without the evolution of life in its gradually advancing progression, whereby the Perfect is ever evolving itself into the less Perfect. This ὕλη, again, is represented under various images;—at one time as the darkness that exists along-side of the light; at another, as the void [κένωμα, κενον . . . Kenoma, Kenon], in opposition to the Fulness, [Πλήρωμα . . . Pleroma] of the Divine Life; or as the shadow that accompanies the light; or as the chaos, or the sluggish, stagnant, dark water. This matter, dead in itself, possesses by its own nature no inherent tendency; as life of every sort is foreign to it, itself makes no encroachment on the Divine. As, however, the evolutions of the Divine life (the essences developing themselves out of the progressive emanation) become feebler, the further they are removed from the first link in the series; and as their connection with the first becomes looser at each successive step, there arises at the last step of the evolution, an imperfect, defective product, which, unable to retain its connection with the chain of Divine life, sinks from the World of Eons into the material chaos: or, according to the same notion, somewhat differently expressed, [according to the Ophites and to Bardesanes], a drop from the fulness of the Divine life bubbles over into the bordering void. Hereupon the dead matter, by commixture with the living principle, which it wanted, first of all receives animation. But, at the same time, also, the divine, the living, becomes corrupted by mingling with the chaotic mass. Existence now multiplies itself. There arises a subordinate, defective life; there is ground for a new world; a creation starts into being, beyond the confines of the world of emanation. But, on the other hand, since the chaotic principle of matter has acquired vitality, there now arises a more distinct and more active opposition to the God-like—a barely negative, blind, ungodly nature-power, which obstinately resists all influence of the Divine: hence, as products of the spirit of the ὕλη, (of the πνεῦμα ὑλικον . . Pneuma Hulikon), are Satan, malignant spirits, wicked men, in none of whom is there any reasonable or moral principle, or any principle of a rational will; but blind passions alone have the ascendancy. In them there is the same conflict, as the scheme of Platonism supposes, between the soul under the guidance of Divine reason. [the νοῦς . . Nous], and the soul blindly resisting reason—between the πρόνοια [pronoia] and the αναγη [anagê], the Divine Principle and the natural.

The Syrian Gnosis assumed the existence of an active, turbulent kingdom of evil, or of darkness, which, by its encroachments on the kingdom of light, brought about a commixture of the light with the darkness, of the God-like with the ungodlike.

Even among the Platonists, some thought that along with an organized, inert matter, the substratum of the corporeal world, there existed from the beginning a blind, lawless motive power, an ungodlike soul, as its original motive and active principle. As the inorganic matter was organized into a corporeal world, by the plastic power of the Deity, so by the same power, law and reason were communicated to that turbulent, irrational soul. Thus the chaos of the ὕλη was transformed into an organized world, and that blind soul into a rational principle, a mundane soul, animating the Universe. As from the latter proceeds all rational, spiritual life in humanity, so from the former proceeds all that is irrational, all that is under the blind sway of passion and appetite; and all malignant spirits are its progeny.

In one respect *all* the Gnostics agreed: they *all* held, that there was a world purely emanating out of the vital development of God, a creation evolved directly out of the Divine Essence, far exalted above any outward creation produced by God's plastic power, and conditioned by a pre-existing matter. They agreed in holding that the framer of *this lower world* was not the Father of *that higher world* of emanation; but the Demiurge [Δημιουργος], a being of a kindred nature with the universe framed and governed by him, and far inferior to that higher system and the Father of it.

But some, setting out from ideas which had long prevailed among certain Jews of Alexandria, supposed that the Supreme God created and governed the world by His ministering spirits, by the angels. At the head of these angels stood one who had the direction and control of all; therefore called the Artificer and Governor of the World. This Demiurge they compared with the plastic, animating, mundane spirit of Plato and the Platonists [the δεύτερος θεός . . Deuteros Theos; the θεος γεννητος . . Theos Genetos], who, moreover, according to the Timæus of Plato, strives to represent the *Idea* of the Divine Reason; in that which is *becoming*, (as contradistinguished from that which *is*), and temporal. This angel is a representative of the Supreme God, on the lower stage of existence : he does not act independently, but merely according to the ideas inspired in him by the Supreme God ; just as the plastic, mundane soul of the Platonists creates all things after the pattern of the ideas communicated by the Supreme Reason [Νους . . Nous—the ὅ ἐστι ζῷον . . ho esti zoün—the παράδειγμα . . paradeigma, of the Divine Reason hypostatized]. But these ideas transcend his limited essence ; he cannot understand them ; he is merely their unconscious organ ; and therefore is unable himself to comprehend the whole scope and meaning of the work which he performs. As an organ under the guidance of a higher inspiration, he reveals higher truths than he himself can comprehend. The mass of the Jews, they held, recognized not the angel, by whom, in all the Theophanies of the Old Testament, God *revealed* himself ; they knew not the Demiurge in his true relation to the hidden Supreme God, *who never reveals himself* in the sensible world. They confounded the type and the archetype, the symbol and the idea. They rose no higher than the Demiurge ; they took him to be the Supreme God himself. But the spiritual men among them, on the contrary, clearly perceived, or at least *divined*, the ideas veiled under Judaism : they rose beyond the Demiurge, to a knowledge of the Supreme God ; and are therefore properly his worshippers [θεραπευταί . . Therapeutai].

Other Gnostics, who had not been followers of the Mosaic religion, but who had, at an earlier period, framed to themselves an oriental Gnosis, regarded the Demiurge as a being absolutely *hostile* to the Supreme God. He and his angels, notwithstanding their finite nature, were to establish their independence ; they will tolerate no foreign rule within their realm. Whatever of a higher nature descends into their kingdom, they seek to hold imprisoned there, lest it should raise itself above their narrow precincts. Probably, in this system, the kingdom of the Demiurgic Angels corresponded, for the most part, with that of the deceitful Star-Spirits, who seek to rob man of his freedom, to beguile him by various arts of deception, and who exercise a tyrannical sway over the things of this world. Accordingly, in the system of these Sabæans, the seven Planet-Spirits, and the twelve Star-Spirits of the zodiac, who sprang from an irregular connection between the cheated Fetahil and the Spirit of Darkness, play an important part in everything that is bad. The Demiurge is a limited and limiting being, proud, jealous and revengeful ; and this his character betrays itself in the Old Testament, which, the Gnostics held, came from him. They transferred to the Demiurge himself, whatever in the idea of God, as presented by the Old Testament, appeared to them defective. Against his will and rule, the ὕλη was continually rebelling, revolting without control against the dominion which he, the fashioner, would exercise over it ; casting off the yoke imposed on it, and destroying the work he had begun. The same jealous being, limited in his power, ruling with despotic sway, they imagined they saw in nature. He strives to check the germination of the divine seeds of life which the Supreme God of Holiness and Love, who has no connection whatever with the sensible world, has scattered among men. That perfect God was at most known and worshipped in mysteries by a few spiritual men.

The Gospel of St. John is in great measure a polemic against the Gnostics, whose different sects, to solve the great problems, the creation of a material world by an immaterial Being, the fall of man, the incarnation, the redemption and restoration of the spirits called men, admitted a long series of intelligences, intervening in a series of spiritual operations ; and which they designated by the names, *The Beginning, the Word, the Only Begotten, Life, Light* and *Spirit* [Ghost] : in Greek, Ἀρχή, Λόγος, Μονογενής, Ζωή, Φῶς and Πνεῦμα [Archē, Logos, Monogenes, Zōe, Phōs and Pneuma]. St. John, at the beginning of his Gospel, avers that it was Jesus Christ who existed in the Beginning ; that He was the Word of God by which everything was made : that He was the Only Begotten, the Life and the Light, and that he diffuses among men the Holy Spirit [or Ghost], the Divine Life and Light.

So the Pleroma [Πλήρωμα], Plenitude or Fulness, was a favorite term with the Gnostics, and Truth and Grace were the Gnostic Eons : and the Simonians, Doketēs and other Gnostics held that the Eon Christ Jesus was never really, but only apparently clothed with a human body : but St. John replies that the Word did really become Flesh, and dwelt among us ; and that in Him were the Pleroma and Truth and Grace.

The Gospel of St. John commences with these words ; as translated in our version : "In the Beginning was the Word, and the Word was with God, and the Word was God : the same was in the beginning with God." This, a statement of the doctrine of the Gnostics against whom the author of the book was writing, expanded into its full meaning, is as follows. "When the work of Emanation and Creation commenced, and the Supreme God, until then existing alone, in the profundity of his own nature, unmanifested, began to manifest Himself, the WORD, His first Emanation, WAS, commenced to exist. That word was (pros ton Theon) near to, an *immediate* and *primary* emanation from God; and was God Himself manifested in one aspect or mode of development." And then it is declared that by this Word, first and immediate emanation from God, everything was made that was made: all subsequent emanations proceeded from Him: and out of Him came life and the light given unto men. And then the author proceeds to prove that this Word was Jesus Christ.

In the doctrine of Valentinus, reared a Christian at Alexandria, God was a Perfect Being, an Abyss, [Βυθος . . Buthos], which no intelligence could sound, because no eye could reach the invisible and ineffable heights on which he dwelt, and no mind could comprehend the duration of his existence; He has always been; He is the Primitive Father and Beginning [the Προπατωρ and Προαρχη . . Propatōr and Proarchè]: He will BE always, and does not grow old. The development of His Perfections produced the intellectual world. After having passed infinite ages in repose and silence, He manifested Himself by His Thought, source of all His manifestations, and which received from Him the germ of His creations. Being of His Being, His Thought [Εννοια . . Ennoia] is also termed Χαρις [Charis] Grace or Joy, and Σιγη, or Αρρητον, [Sigē or Arrēton,] Silence or the Ineffable. Its first manifestation was Νους [Nous], the Intelligence, first of the Eons, commencement of all things, first revelation of the Divinity, the Μονογενης [Monogenes], or Only Begotten: next, Truth [Αληθεια . . Alētheia], his companion. Their manifestations were the Word [Λογος . . Logos] and Life [Ζωη . . Zoe]; and theirs, Man and the Church [Ανθρωπος and Εκκλησια . . Anthropos and Ekklesia]: and from these, other twelve, six of whom were Hope, Faith, Charity, Intelligence, Happiness and Wisdom; or, in the Hebrew, *Kesten, Kina, Amphe, Ouananim, Thaedes,* and *Oubina.* The harmony of the Eons, struggling to know and be united to the Primitive God, was disturbed, and to redeem and restore them, the Intelligence [Νους] produced Christ and the Holy Spirit his companion; who restored them to their first estate of happiness and harmony; and thereupon they formed the Eon Jesus, born of a Virgin, to whom the Christos united himself in baptism, and who, with his Companion Sophia-Achamoth, saved and redeemed the world.

The Marcosians taught that the Supreme Deity produced by his words the Λογος [Logos] or Plenitude of Eons: His first utterance was a syllable of four letters, each of which became a being; his second of four, his third of ten, and his fourth of twelve; thirty in all, which constituted the Πληρωμα, [Pleroma].

The Valentinians and others of the Gnostics, distinguished three orders of existences:—1st. The divine germs of life, exalted by their nature above matter, and akin to the Σοφια [Sophia], to the mundane soul and to the Pleroma:—the spiritual natures, φυσεις πνευματικαι [Phuseis Pneumatikai]: 2d. The natures originating in the life, divided from the former by the mixture of the υλη,—the psychical natures, φυσεις ψυχικαι [Phuseis Psuchikai]; with which begins a perfectly new order of existence, an image of that higher mind and system, in a subordinate grade; and finally, 3d. The Ungodlike or Hylic Nature, which resists all amelioration, and whose tendency is only to destroy—the nature of blind lust and passion.

The nature of the πνευματικον [pneumatikon], the spiritual, is essential relationship with God (the ὁμοουσιον τῳ θεῳ . . Homoousion tō Theou); hence the life of Unity, the undivided, the absolutely simple (ουσια ἑνικη, μονοειδης . . Ousia henikē, monoeides).

The essence of the ψυχικοι [psuchikoi] is disruption into multiplicity, manifoldness; which, however, is subordinate to a higher unity, by which it allows itself to be guided, first unconsciously, then consciously.

The essence of the υλικοι [Hulikoi], (of whom Satan is the head), is the direct opposite to all unity; disruption and disunion in itself, without the least sympathy, without any point of coalescence whatever for unity; together with an effort to destroy all unity, to extend its own inherent disunion to everything, and to rend everything asunder. This principle has no power to posit anything; but only to negative: it is unable to create, to produce, to form, but only to destroy, to decompose.

By Marcus, the disciple of Valentinus, the idea of a Λογος του οντος [Logos Tou Ontos], of a WORD, manifesting the hidden Divine Essence, in the Creation, was spun out into the most subtle details—the entire creation being, in his view, a continuous *utterance* of the Ineffable. The way in which the germs of divine life [the σπερματα πνευματικα . . spermata pneumatika], which lie shut up in the Eons, continually unfold and individualize themselves more and more, is represented as a spontaneous analysis of the several *names* of the

Ineffable, into their several *sounds*. An *echo* of the Pleroma falls down into the ὑλη [Hylē], and becomes the forming principle of a new, but lower creation.

One formula of the pneumatical baptism among the Gnostics ran thus: " In the NAME which is hidden from all the Divinities and Powers" [of the Demiurge], " The Name of Truth" [the Αληθεια [Aletheia], self-manifestation of the Buthos], which Jesus of Nazareth has put on in the light-zones of Christ, the living Christ, through the Holy Ghost, for the redemption of the angels,—the Name by which all things attain to Perfection." The Candidate then said: " I am established and redeemed ; I am redeemed in my soul from this world, and from all that belongs to it, by the name of יהוי, who has redeemed the Soul of Jesus by the living Christ." The assembly then said: " Peace (or Salvation) to all on whom this name rests !"

The boy Dionusos, torn in pieces, according to the Bacchic Mysteries, by the Titans, was considered by the Manicheans as simply representing the Soul, swallowed up by the powers of darkness,—the divine life rent into fragments by matter:—that part of the luminous essence of the primitive man [the πρωτος ανθρωπος [Protos Anthropos] of Mani, the πρων ανθροπος [Praōn Anthropos] of the Valentinians, the Adam Kadmon ; and the Kaiomorts of the Zendavesta], swallowed up by the powers of darkness ; the Mundane Soul, mixed with matter —the seed of divine life, which had fallen into matter, and had thence to undergo a process of purification and development.

The Γνωσις [Gnosis] of Carpocrates and his son Epiphanes consisted in the knowledge of one Supreme Original being, the highest unity, from whom all existence has emanated, and to whom it strives to return. The finite spirits that rule over the several portions of the Earth, seek to counteract this universal tendency to unity ; and from their influence, their laws and arrangements, proceeds all that checks, disturbs or limits the original communion, which is the basis of nature, as the outward manifestation of that highest Unity. These spirits, moreover, seek to retain under their dominion the souls which, emanating from the highest Unity, and still partaking of its nature, have lapsed into the corporeal world, and have there been imprisoned in bodies, in order under their dominion to be kept within the cycle of migration. From these finite spirits, the popular religions of different nations derive their origin. But the souls which, from a reminiscence of their former condition, soar upward to the contemplation of that higher Unity, reach to such perfect freedom and repose, as nothing afterwards can disturb or limit, and rise superior to the popular deities and religions. As examples of this sort, they named Pythagoras, Plato, Aristotle and Christ. They made no distinction between the latter and the wise and good men of every nation. They taught that any other soul which could soar to the same height of contemplation, might be regarded as equal with him.

The Ophites commenced their system with a Supreme Being, long unknown to the Human race, and still so to the greater number of men ; the Βυθος [Buthos], or Profundity, Source of Light, and of Adam-Kadmon, the Primitive Man, made by the Demiourgos, but perfected by the Supreme God by the communication to him of the Spirit [Πνευμα . . Pneuma]. The first emanation was the Thought of the Supreme Deity, [the Εννοια . . Ennoia], the conception of the Universe in the Thought of God. This Thought, called also Silence (Σιγη . . Sigē), produced the Spirit [Πνευμα . . Pneuma], Mother of the Living, and Wisdom of God. Together with this Primitive Existence, Matter existed also, (the Waters, Darkness, Abyss and Chaos), eternal like the Spiritual Principle. Bythos and His Thought, uniting with Wisdom, made her fruitful by the Divine Light, and She produced a perfect and an imperfect being, *Christos*, and a Second and inferior wisdom, *Sophia-Achamoth*, who falling into chaos remained entangled there, became enfeebled, and lost all knowledge of the Superior Wisdom that gave her birth. Communicating movement to Chaos, she produced Ialdabaoth, the Demiourgos, Agent of Material Creation, and then ascended towards her first place in the scale of creation. Ialdabaoth produced an angel that was his image, and this a second, and so on in succession to the sixth after the Demiourgos : the seven being *reflections* one of the other, yet different and inhabiting seven distinct regions. The names of the six thus produced were IAO, SABAOTH, ADONAI, ELOI, ORAI and ASTAPHAI. Ialdabaoth, to become independent of his mother, and to pass for the Supreme Being, made the world, and man, in his own image ; and his mother caused the Spiritual principle to pass from him into man so made ; and henceforward the contest between the Demiourgos and his mother, between light and darkness, good and evil, was concentrated in man; and the image of Ialdabaoth, reflected upon matter became the Serpent-Spirit, Satan, the Evil Intelligence. Eve, created by Ialdabaoth, had by his Sons children that were angels like themselves. The Spiritual light was withdrawn from man by Sophia, and the world surrendered to the influence of evil; until the Spirit, urged by the entreaties of Wisdom, induced the Supreme Being to send Christos to redeem it. Compelled, despite himself, by his Mother, Ialdabaoth caused the man Jesus to be born of a Virgin, and the Celestial Saviour, uniting with his Sister, Wisdom, descended through the regions of the seven angels, appeared in each under the form of its chief, concealed his own, and entered with his sister into the man Jesus at the baptism in Jordan. Ialdabaoth, finding that Jesus was destroying his empire and abolishing his worship, caused the Jews to hate and crucify him; before which happened, Christos and Wisdom had ascended to the celestial regions. They restored Jesus to life and gave him an ethereal body, in which he remained eighteen months on earth, and receiving from Wisdom the perfect knowledge [Γνωσις . . Gnosis] communicated it to a small number of his apostles, and then arose to the intermediate region inhabited by Ialdabaoth, where, unknown to him, he sits at his right hand, taking from him the Souls of Light purified by Christos. When nothing of the Spiritual world shall remain subject to Ialdabaoth, the redemption will be accomplished, and the end of the world, the completion of the return of Light into the Plenitude will occur.

Tatian adopted the theory of Emanation, of Eons, of the existence of a God too sublime to allow Himself to be known, but displaying Himself by Intelligences emanating from His bosom. The first of these was his Spirit [Πνευμα . . Pneuma], God Himself, God thinking, God conceiving the universe. The second was the Word [Λογος . . Logos] no longer merely the Thought or Conception, but the Creative Utterance, manifestation of the Divinity, but emanating from the Thought or Spirit; the First-Begotten, author of the visible creation. This was the Trinity, composed of the Father, Spirit and Word.

The Elxaïtes adopted the Seven Spirits of the Gnostics; but named them Heaven, Water, Spirit, The Holy Angels of Prayer, Oil, Salt and the Earth.

The opinion of the Doketes as to the human nature of Jesus Christ, was that most generally received among the Gnostics. They deemed the intelligences of the Superior World too pure and too much the antagonists of matter, to be willing to unite with it: and held that Christ, an Intelligence of the first rank, in appearing upon the earth, did not become confounded with matter, but took upon himself only the *appearance of a body*, or at the most used it only as an envelope.

Noëtus termed the Son the first Utterance of the Father; the Word, not by Himself, as an Intelligence, and unconnected with the flesh, a real Son; but a Word, and a perfect Only Begotten; light emanated from the Light; water flowing from its spring; a ray emanated from the Sun.

Paul of Samosata taught that Jesus Christ was the Son of Joseph and Mary; but that the Word, Wisdom or Intelligence of God, the Νους [Nous] of the Gnostics, had united itself with him, so that he might be said to be at once the Son of God, and God Himself.

Arius called the Saviour the first of creatures, non-emanated from God, but really created, by the direct will of God, before time and the ages. According to the Church, Christ was of the same nature as God; according to some dissenters, of the same nature as man. Arius adopted the theory of a nature analogous to both. When God resolved to create the Human race, He made a Being which he called THE WORD, THE SON, WISDOM [Λογος, Υιος, Σοφια . . Logos, Uios, Sophia], to the end that He might give existence to men. This WORD is the Ormuzd of Zoroaster, the Ensoph of the Kabbala, the Νους [Nous] of Platonism and Philonism, and the Σοφια or Δημιουργος [Sophia or Demiourgos] of the Gnostics. He distinguished the Inferior Wisdom, or the daughter, from the Superior Wisdom; the latter being *in* God, inherent in His nature, and incapable of communication to any creature: the second, by which the Son was made, communicated itself to Him, and therefore He Himself was entitled to be called the Word and the Son.

Manes, founder of the Sect of the Manicheans, who had lived and been distinguished among the Persian Magi, profited by the doctrines of Scythianus, a Kabbalist or Judaizing Gnostic of the times of the Apostles; and knowing those of Bardesanes and Harmonius, derived his doctrines from Zoroasterism, Christianity and Gnosticism. He claimed to be the Παρακλητος [Parakletos] or Comforter, in the Sense of a Teacher, organ of the Deity, but not in that of the Holy Spirit or Holy Ghost: and commenced his *Epistola Fundamenti* in these words, "Manes, Apostle of Jesus Christ, elect of God the Father; Behold the Words of Salvation, emanating from the living and eternal fountain." The dominant idea of his doctrine was Pantheism, derived by him from its source in the regions of India and on the confines of China: that the cause of all that exists is in God; and at last, God is all in all. All souls are equal—God is in all, in men, animals and plants. There are two Gods, one of Good and the other of Evil, each independent, eternal, chief of a distinct Empire; necessarily, and of their very natures hostile to one another. The Evil God, Satan, is the Genius of matter alone: The God of Good is infinitely his Superior, the True God; while the other is but the chief of all that is the Enemy of God, and must in the end succumb to His Power. The Empire of Light alone is eternal and true; and this Empire is a great chain of Emanations, all connected with the Supreme Being which they make manifest; all Him, under different forms, chosen for one end, the triumph of the Good. In each of His members lie hidden thousands of ineffable treasures. Excellent in His Glory, incomprehensible in His Greatness, the Father has joined to Himself those fortunate and glorious Eons [Αιωνς . . Aiones], whose Power and Number it is impossible to determine. This is Spinoza's Infinity of Infinite Attributes of God. Twelve Chief Eons, at the head of all, were the Genii of the twelve Constellations of the Zodiac, and called by Manes, Olamin. Satan, also, Lord of the Empire of Darkness, had an Army of Eons or Demons, emanating from his Essence, and reflecting more or less his image, but divided and inharmonious among themselves. A war among them brought them to the confines of the Realm of Light. Delighted, they sought to conquer it. But the Chief of the Celestial Empire created a Power which he placed on the frontiers of Heaven, to protect his Eons, and destroy the Empire of Evil. This was the Mother of Life, the Soul of the World, an Emanation from the Supreme Being, too pure to come in immediate contact with matter. It remained in the highest region; but produced a Son, the first Man [the *Kaiomorts*, Adam-Kadmon, Πρωτος Ανθρωπος [Protos Anthropos], and Hivil-Zivah; of the Zend-Avesta, the Kabbala, the Gnosis and Sabeism]; who commenced the contest with the Powers of Evil; but, losing part of his panoply, of his Light, his Son and many souls born of the Light, who were devoured by the darkness, God sent to his assistance the living Spirit, or the Son of the First Man [Υιός Ανθρώπου . . . Uios Anthropou], or Jesus Christ. The Mother of Life, general Principle of Divine Life, and the first Man, Primitive Being that reveals the Divine Life, are too sublime to be connected with the Empire of Darkness. The Son of Man or Soul of the World, enters into the Darkness, becomes its captive, to end by tempering and softening its savage nature. The Divine Spirit, after having brought back the Primitive Man to the Empire of Light, raises above the world that part of the Celestial Soul that remained unaffected by being mingled with the Empire of Darkness. Placed in the region of the Sun and Moon, this pure soul, the Son of Man, the Redeemer or Christ, labours to deliver and attract to Himself that part of the Light or of the Soul of the First Man, diffused through matter; which done, the world will cease to exist. To retain the rays of Light still remaining among his Eons, and ever tending to escape and return, by concentrating them, the Prince of Darkness, with their consent, made Adam, whose soul was of the Divine Light, contributed by the Eons, and his body of matter, so that he belonged to both Empires, that of Light and that of Darkness. To prevent the light from escaping at once, the Demons forbade Adam to eat the fruit of "knowledge of good and evil," by which he would have known the Empire of Light and that of Darkness. He obeyed; an Angel of Light induced him to transgress, and gave him the means of victory; but the Demons created Eve, who seduced him into an act of Sensualism, that enfeebled him, and bound him anew in the bonds of matter. This is repeated in the case of every man that lives.

To deliver the soul, captive in darkness, the Principle of Light, or Genius of the Sun, charged to redeem the Intellectual World, of which he is the type, came to manifest Himself among men. Light appeared in the darkness, but the darkness comprehended it not; according to the words of St. John. The Light could not unite with the darkness. It but put on the *appearance* of a human body, and took the name of Christ in the Messiah, only to accommodate itself to the language of the Jews. The Light did its work, turning the Jews from the adoration of the Evil Principle, and the Pagans from the worship of Demons. But the Chief of the Empire of Darkness caused him to be crucified by the Jews. Still he suffered in appearance only, and his death gave to all souls the symbol of their enfranchisement. The person of Jesus having disappeared, there was seen in his place a cross of Light, over which a celestial voice pronounced these words: "The cross of

Light is called The Word, Christ, The Gate, Joy, The Bread, The Sun, The Resurrection, Jesus, The Father, The Spirit, Life, Truth and Grace."

With the Priscillianists there were two principles, one the Divinity, the other, Primitive Matter and Darkness; each eternal. Satan is the son and lord of matter; and the secondary angels and demons, children of matter. Satan created and governs the visible world. But the soul of man emanated from God, and is of the same substance with God. Seduced by the evil spirits, it passes through various bodies, until, purified and reformed, it rises to God and is strengthened by His light. These powers of evil hold mankind in pledge; and to redeem this pledge, the Saviour, Christ the Redeemer, came and died upon the cross of expiation, thus discharging the written obligation. He, like all souls, was of the same substance with God, a manifestation of the Divinity, not forming a second person; unborn, like the Divinity, and nothing else than the Divinity under another form.

It is useless to trace these vagaries further; and we stop at the frontiers of the realm of the three hundred and sixty-five thousand emanations of the Mandaïtes from the Primitive Light, Fira or Ferho and Yavar; and return contentedly to the simple and sublime creed of Masonry.

Such were some of the ancient notions concerning the Deity; and taken in connection with what has been detailed in the preceding Degrees, this Lecture affords you a true picture of the ancient speculations. From the beginning until now, those who have undertaken to solve the great mystery of the creation of a material universe by an Immaterial Deity, have interposed between the two, and between God and man, divers manifestations of, or emanations from, or personified attributes or agents of, the Great Supreme God, who is coexistent with Time and coextensive with Space.

The universal belief of the Orient was, that the Supreme Being did not Himself create either the earth or man. The fragment which commences the Book of Genesis, consisting of the first chapter and the three first verses of the second, assigns the creation, or rather the *formation* or *modelling* of the world from matter already existing in confusion, not to IHUH, but to the ELOHIM, well known as Subordinate Deities, Forces or Manifestations, among the Phœnicians. The second fragment imputes it to IHUH-ELOHIM [*Lord of the Elohim*]: and St. John assigns the creation to the Λογος or WORD; and asserts that CHRIST was that WORD, as well as LIGHT and LIFE, other emanations from the Great Primeval Deity, to which other faiths had assigned the work of creation.

An absolute existence, wholly immaterial, in no way within the reach of our senses; a cause, but not an effect, that never was not, but existed during an infinity of eternities, before there was anything else except Time and Space, is wholly beyond the reach of our conceptions. The mind of man has wearied itself in speculations as to His nature, His essence, His attributes; and ended in being no wiser than it began. In the impossibility of conceiving of immateriality, we feel at sea and lost whenever we go beyond the domain of matter. And yet we know that there are Powers, Forces, Causes, that are themselves *not* matter. We give them names, but *what* they really are, and what their essence, we are wholly ignorant.

But, fortunately, it does not follow that we may not *believe* or even *know*, that which we cannot *explain* to ourselves, or that which is beyond the reach of our comprehension. If we believed only that which our intellect can grasp, measure, comprehend, and have distinct and clear ideas of, we should believe scarce anything. The senses are not the witnesses that bear testimony to us of the loftiest truths.

Our greatest difficulty is, that language is not adequate to express our ideas; because our words refer to *things*, and are images of what is substantial and material. If we use the word "*emanation*," our mind involuntarily recurs to something material, *issuing out* of some other thing that is material; and if we *reject* this idea of materiality, nothing is left of the emanation but an unreality. The word "thing" itself suggests to us that which is material and within the cognizance and jurisdiction of the senses. If we cut away from it the idea of materiality, it presents itself to us as *no thing*, but an intangible unreality, which the mind vainly endeavours to grasp. *Existence* and *Being* are terms that have the same colour of materiality; and when we speak of a *Power* or *Force*, the mind immediately images to itself one physical and material thing acting upon another. Eliminate that idea; and the Power or Force, devoid of physical characteristics, seems as unreal as the shadow that dances on a wall, itself a mere *absence* of light; as spirit is to us merely that which is *not matter*.

Infinite space and infinite time, are the two primary ideas. We formulize them thus: add body to body and sphere to sphere, until the imagination wearies; and still there will remain beyond, a void, empty, unoccupied space, limitless, because it *is* void. Add event to event in continuous succession, forever and forever, and there will still remain, before and after, a TIME in which there was and will be no event, and also endless because it too *is* void.

Thus these two ideas of the boundlessness of space and the endlessness of time seem to *involve* the ideas that matter and events are limited and finite. We cannot conceive of an *infinity* of worlds or of events; but only of an *indefinite* number of each; for, as we struggle to conceive of their *infinity*, the thought ever occurs in despite of all our efforts—there must be *space*.in which there are *no* worlds; there must have been *time* when there were no events.

We cannot conceive how, if this earth moves millions of millions of miles a million times repeated, it is still *in the centre of space;* nor how, if we lived millions of millions of ages and centuries, we should still be in the centre of eternity—with still as much *space* on one side as on the other; with still as much *time* before us as behind; for that seems to say that the world has not moved nor we lived at all.

Nor can we comprehend how an infinite series of worlds, added together, is no larger than an infinite series of atoms; or an infinite series of centuries no longer than an infinite series of seconds; both being alike infinite, and therefore one series containing no more or fewer units than the other.

Nor have we the capacity to form in ourselves any idea of that which is *immaterial*. We use the word, but it conveys to us only the idea of the absence and negation of materiality; which vanishing, Space and Time alone, infinite and boundless, seem to us to be left.

We cannot form any conception of an effect without a cause. We cannot but believe, indeed we know, that, how far soever we may have to run back along the chain of effects and causes, it cannot be *infinite;* but we must come at last to *something* which is not an effect, but the first cause: and yet the fact is literally beyond our comprehension. The mind refuses to grasp the idea of *self*-existence, of existence without a beginning. As well expect the hair that grows upon our head to understand the nature and immortality of the soul.

It does not need to go so far in search of mysteries; nor have we any right to disbelieve or doubt the existence of a Great First Cause, itself no effect, because we cannot comprehend it; because the words we use do not even express it to us adequately.

We rub a needle for a little while, on a dark, inert mass of iron ore, that had lain idle in the earth for many centuries. Something is thereby communicated to the steel—we term it a *virtue*, a *power*, or a *quality*—and then we balance it upon a pivot; and, lo! drawn by some invisible, mysterious Power, one pole of the needle turns to the North, and there the same Power keeps the same pole for days and years; will keep it there, perhaps, as long as the world lasts, carry the needle where you will, and no matter what seas or mountains intervene between it and the North Pole of the world. And this Power, thus acting, and indicating to the mariner his course over the trackless ocean, when the stars shine not for many days, saves vessels from shipwreck, families from distress, and those from sudden death, on whose lives the fate of nations and the peace of the world depend. But for it, Napoleon might never have reached the ports of France on his return from Egypt, nor Nelson lived to fight and win at Trafalgar. Men call this Power *Magnetism*, and then complacently think that they have explained it all; and yet they have but given a new *name* to an unknown thing, to *hide* their ignorance. What is this wonderful Power? It is a real, actual, *active* Power: that we know and see. But what its *essence* is, or how it acts, we do not know, any more than we know the essence or the mode of action of the Creative Thought and Word of God.

And again, what *is* that which we term *galvanism* and *electricity*,—which evolved by the action of a little acid on two metals, aided by a magnet, circles the earth in a second, sending from land to land the *Thoughts* that govern the transactions of individuals and nations? The mind has formed no notion of matter, that will include *it;* and no name that we can give it, helps us to understand its essence and its being. It is a Power, like Thought and the Will. We know no more.

What is this power of *gravitation* that makes everything upon the earth tend to the centre? How does it reach out its invisible hands towards the erratic meteor-stones, arrest them in their swift course, and draw them down to the earth's bosom? It *is* a *power*. We know no more.

What is that *heat* which plays so wonderful a part in the world's economy?—that *caloric*, latent everywhere, within us and without us, produced by combustion, by intense pressure, and by swift motion? Is it substance, matter, spirit, or immaterial, a mere Force or State of Matter?

And what is *light?* A *substance,* say the books,—*matter,* that travels to us from the sun and stars, each ray separable into seven, by the prism, of distinct colours, and with distinct peculiar qualities and action. And *if* a substance, what is its essence, and what power is inherent in it, by which it journeys incalculable myriads of miles, and reaches us ten thousand years or more after it leaves the stars.

All power is equally a mystery. Apply intense cold to a drop of water in the centre of a globe of iron, and the globe is shattered as the water freezes. Confine a little of the same limpid element in a cylinder which Enceladus or Typhon could not have riven asunder, and apply to it intense heat; and the vast power that couched latent in the water shivers the cylinder to atoms. A little shoot from a minute seed, a shoot so soft and tender that the least bruise would kill it, forces its way downward into the hard earth, to the depth of many feet, with an energy wholly incomprehensible. What are these mighty forces, locked up in the small seed, and the drop of water?

Nay, what is LIFE itself, with all its wondrous, mighty energies,—that power which maintains the heat within us, and prevents our bodies, that decay so soon without it, from resolution into their original elements? —Life, that constant miracle, the nature and essence whereof have eluded all the philosophers; and all their learned dissertations on it are a mere jargon of words?

No wonder the ancient Persians thought that Light and Life were one,—both emanations from the Supreme Deity, the archetype of light. No wonder that in their ignorance they worshipped the Sun. God breathed into man the spirit of life,—not matter, but an emanation from Himself; not a creature *made* by Him, nor a distinct existence, but a *Power,* like His own Thought: and light, to those great-souled ancients, also seemed no creature, and no gross material substance, but a pure emanation.from the Deity, immortal and indestructible like Himself.

What, indeed, is REALITY? Our dreams are as real, while they last, as the occurrences of the daytime. We see, hear, feel, act, experience pleasure and suffer pain, as vividly and actually in a dream as when awake. The occurrences and transactions of a year are crowded into the limits of a second: and the dream remembered is as real as the past occurrences of life.

The philosophers tell us that we have no cognizance of *substance* itself; but only of its *attributes:* that when we see that which we call a block of marble, our perceptions give us information only of something extended, solid, coloured, heavy, and the like; but not of the very *thing* itself, to which these attributes belong. And yet the attributes do not exist without the substance. They are not substantives, but adjectives. There is no such *thing* or *existence* as hardness, weight or colour, by itself, detached from any subject, moving first here, then there, and attaching itself to this and to the other subject. And yet, they say, the attributes are not the subject.

So Thought, Volition and Perception are not the soul, but its *attributes;* and we have no cognizance of the soul *itself,* but only of *them,* its manifestations. Nor of God; but only of His Wisdom, Power, Magnificence, Truth, and other attributes.

And yet we know that there *is* matter, a soul within our body, a God that lives in the universe.

Take, then, the attributes of the soul. I am conscious that I exist and am the same identical person that I was twenty years ago. I am conscious that my body is not I,—that if my arms were lopped away, this *person* that I call ME, would still remain, complete, entire, identical as before. But I cannot ascertain, by the most intense and long-continued reflection, what I am, nor where within my body I reside, nor whether I am a point, or an expanded substance. I have no power to examine and inspect. I exist, will, think, perceive. *That* I know, and nothing more. I think a noble and sublime Thought. What is that Thought? It is not Matter, nor Spirit. It is not a Thing; but a *Power* and *Force.* I make upon a paper certain conventional marks, that *represent* that Thought. There is no Power or Virtue in the *marks* I write, but only in the Thought which they tell to others. I die, but the Thought still lives. It is a Power. It acts on men, excites them to enthusiasm, inspires patriotism, governs their conduct, controls their destinies, disposes of life and death. The words I speak, are but a certain succession of particular sounds, that by conventional arrangement communicate to others the Immaterial, Intangible, Eternal Thought. The fact that Thought continues to exist an instant, after it makes its appearance in the soul, proves it immortal: for there is nothing conceivable that can destroy it. The spoken words, being mere sounds, may vanish into thin air, and the written ones, mere marks, be burned, erased, destroyed; but the THOUGHT itself lives still, and must live on forever.

A Human Thought, then, is an actual EXISTENCE, and a FORCE and POWER, capable of acting upon and controlling matter as well as mind. Is not the existence of a God, who is the immaterial soul of the Universe, and whose THOUGHT, embodied or not embodied in his WORD, is an Infinite Power, of Creation and production, destruction and preservation, quite as comprehensible as the existence of a Soul, of a Thought separated from the Soul, of the Power of that Thought to mould the fate and influence the Destinies of Humanity?

And yet we know not whence that Thought comes, nor what it is. It is not WE. We do not mould it, shape it, fashion it. It is neither our mechanism nor our invention. It appears spontaneously, flashing, as it were, into the soul, making that soul the involuntary instrument of its utterance to the world. It comes to us, and seems a stranger to us, seeking a home.

As little can we explain the mighty power of the human WILL. Volition, like Thought, seems spontaneous, an effect without a cause. Circumstances *provoke* it, and serve as its *occasion*, but do not *produce* it. It springs up in the soul, like Thought, as the waters gush upward in a spring. Is it the manifestation of the soul, merely making apparent what passes *within* the soul, or an emanation from it, going abroad and acting outwardly, itself a real Existence, as it is an admitted Power? We can but own our ignorance. It is certain that it acts on other souls, controls, directs them, shapes their action, legislates for men and nations: and yet it is not material nor visible; and the laws it writes merely inform one soul of what has passed within another.

God, therefore, is a mystery, only as everything that surrounds us, and as we ourselves are a mystery. We know that there is and must be a FIRST CAUSE. His attributes, severed from Himself, are unrealities. As color and extension, weight and hardness, do not exist apart from matter, as separate existences and substantives, spiritual or immaterial; so the Goodness, Wisdom, Justice, Mercy and Benevolence of God are not independent existences, personify them as men may, but *attributes* of the Deity, the *adjectives* of One Great Substantive. But we know that He must be Good, True, Wise, Just, Benevolent, Merciful: and in all these, and all His other attributes, Perfect and Infinite; because we are conscious that these are laws imposed on us by the very nature of things, necessary, and without which the Universe would be confusion, and the existence of a God incredible.

He is the Living, Thinking, Intelligent SOUL of the Universe, the PERMANENT, the STATIONARY [Εστως . . Estos], of Simon Magus, the ONE that always IS [To Ον . . To Ον] of Plato, as contradistinguished from the perpetual flux and reflux, or *Genesis*, of *things*.

And, as the Thought of the Soul, emanating *from* the Soul, becomes audible and visible in Words, so did THE THOUGHT OF GOD, springing up within Himself, immortal *as* Himself, when once conceived,—immortal *before*, because *in* Himself, utter Itself in THE WORD, its manifestation and mode of communication, and thus create the Material, Mental, Spiritual Universe.

This is the *real* idea of the Ancient Nations: GOD, the Almighty Father, and Source of All: His THOUGHT, *conceiving* the whole Universe, and *willing* its creation: His WORD, *uttering* that THOUGHT, and thus becoming the Creator or Demiourgos, in whom was Life, and Light, and that Light the Life of the Universe.

Nor did that Word *cease* at the single act of Creation; and having set going the great machine, and enacted the laws of its motion and progression, of birth and life, and change and death, cease to exist, or remain thereafter in inert idleness.

FOR THE THOUGHT OF GOD LIVES AND IS IMMORTAL. Embodied in the WORD, is not only *created*, but it *preserves*. It conducts and controls the Universe, all spheres, all worlds, all actions of mankind, and of every animate and inanimate creature. It speaks in the soul of every man that lives. The Stars, the Earth, the Trees, the Winds, the universal voice of Nature, tempest and avalanche, the Sea's roar and the grave voice of the waterfall, the hoarse thunder and the low whisper of the brook, the song of birds, the voice of love, the speech of men, all are the alphabet in which it communicates itself to men, and informs them of the will and law of God, the Soul of the Universe. And thus most truly did "the Word become flesh and dwell among men."

God, the unknown Father [Πατηρ Αγνωστος . . . Pater Agnostos], known to us only by His Attributes; the Absolute I AM : . . The Thought of God [Εννοια . . Ennoia] ; and the Word [Λογος . . Logos], Manifestation and Expression of the Thought; . . Behold the True Masonic Trinity: the Universal Soul, the Thought in the Soul, the Word, or Thought expressed; the Three in One, of a Trinitarian Ecossais.

Here Masonry pauses, and leaves its initiates to carry out and develop these great Truths in such manner as to each may seem most accordant with reason, philosophy, truth and his religious faith. It declines to act as Arbiter between them. It looks calmly on, while each multiplies the intermediates between the Deity and Matter, and the personifications of God's manifestations and attributes, to whatever extent his reason, his conviction or his fancy dictates.

While the Indian tells us that Parabrahma, Brehm and Paratma were the first Triune God, revealing Himself as Brahma, Visnu and Siva, Creator, Preserver and Destroyer : . . . .

The Egyptian, of Amun-Re, Neith and Phtha, Creator, Matter, and Thought or Light : the Persian of his Trinity of Three Powers in Ormuzd, Sources of Light, Fire and Water ; the Bouddhists of the God Sakya, a Trinity composed of Bouddha, Dharma and Sanga,—Intelligence, Law and Union or Harmony : the Chinese Sabeans of their Trinity of Chang-ti, the Supreme Sovereign ; Tien, the Heavens ; and Tao, the Universal Supreme Reason and Principle of all things; who produced the Unit; that, two; two, three; and three, all that is : . . . .

While the Sclavono-Vend typifies his Trinity by the three heads of the God Triglav ; the Ancient Prussian points to his Triune God, Perkoun, Pikollos and Potrimpos, Deities of Light and Thunder, of Hell and of the Earth ; the Ancient Scandinavian to Odin, Frea and Thor ; and the old Etruscans to Tina, Talna and Minerva, Strength, Abundance and Wisdom : . . . .

While Plato tells us of the Supreme Good, the Reason or Intellect, and the Soul or Spirit ; and Philo of the Archetype of Light, Wisdom [Σοφια] and the Word, [Λογος] ; the Kabbalists, of the Primitive Forces, Light, Spirit and Life [Φως, Πνευμα and Ζωη] : . . .

While the disciples of Simon Magus, and the many sects of the Gnostics confuse us with their Eons, Emanations, Powers, Wisdom Superior and Inferior, Ialdabaoth, Adam-Kadmon, even to the three hundred and sixty-five thousand emanations of the Maldaïtes : . . . .

And while the pious Christian believes that the Word dwelt in the Mortal Body of Jesus of Nazareth, and suffered upon the Cross ; and that the Holy Ghost was poured out upon the Apostles, and now inspires every truly Christian Soul : . . . .

While all these faiths assert their claims to the exclusive possession of the Truth, Masonry inculcates its old doctrine, and no more : . . That God is One; that his Thought, uttered in His Word, created the Universe, and preserves it by those Eternal Laws, which are the expression of that Thought: that the Soul of Man, breathed into him by God, is immortal as His Thoughts are; that he is free to do evil or to choose good, responsible for his acts and punishable for his sins : that all evil and wrong and suffering are but temporary, the discords of one great Harmony : and that in His good time they will lead by infinite modulations to the great, harmonic final chord and cadence, of Truth, Love, Peace and Happiness, that will ring forever and ever under the Arches of Heaven, among all the Stars and Worlds, and in all souls of men and Angels.

TO CLOSE.

M∴ Exc∴ Bro∴ Sen∴ Warden, what is the hour?

Sen∴ W∴ Past Midnight, M∴ Excellent.

M∴ Exc∴ Since it is past Midnight, the hour of rest has arrived. Bro∴ Jun∴ Warden, what of the night?

J∴ W∴ M∴ Exc∴, the Clouds have broken, and the Stars begin to appear. The Storm is past, and the night of wo and persecution in the world draws to its close.

M∴ Exc∴ Bro∴ Sen∴ Warden, what remains for us to do?

Sen∴ W∴   To watch and pray, M∴ Excellent.

M∴ Exc∴   Since that alone remains, it is my pleasure that this Chapter be now closed. This you will communicate to the Jun∴ Warden, and he to the Brethren, that they may have due notice thereof, and govern themselves accordingly.

Sen∴ W∴   Bro∴ Jun∴ W∴ it is the pleasure of the M∴ Exc∴ Ch∴ Prince, that this Chapter be now closed. This you will communicate to the Brethren, that they may have due notice, and govern themselves accordingly.

J∴ W∴   Brethren, it is the pleasure, &c. . . .

M∴ Exc∴   The Sign, my Brethren!

[All give the 2d Sign: the M∴ Exc∴ raps [£] . . the S∴ W∴ [‖] . . and the Jun∴ W∴ [;].

M∴ Exc∴   This Chapter is accordingly closed.

FINIS.

Twenty-Seventh Degree.

Knight Commander of the Temple, or Teutonic Knight of the House of St. Mary of Jerusalem.

DECORATIONS, FURNITURE, ETC.

Lodges of this Degree are styled CHAPTERS. The hangings are red, ornamented here and there with black columns, upon each of which is placed a branch, holding a light. The Canopy and Throne are red, sprinkled with black tears. In the centre of the Lodge, which is circular in its shape, is a chandelier, with three rows or circles of lights, one above the other: in the lowest circle, 12; in the next, 9; and in the upper 6, making 27 in all. 27 other lights are placed upon a round table; around which the Knights are seated, when the Chapter is open.

OFFICERS, CLOTHING, JEWELS, ETC.

The Presiding Officer is styled *Grand Commander*, and sits in the East. The Sen∴ Warden is styled *Grand Marshal*, and sits in the West; the Jun∴ Warden, *Grand Hospitaller*, and sits in the South. In the North sits the *Grand Admiral*: on the right of the Gr∴ Commander, the *Grand Chancellor*, and on his left the *Grand Prior*. The *Grand Seneschal* guards the door on the inside.

The Gr∴ Commander wears a white tunic, and over it a Knight's mantle of red, lined with Ermine. On his head he wears a ducal crown. The apron is flesh-coloured, lined and edged with black. On the flap is a Teutonic Cross, which is also the jewel of the Order, encircled by a laurel-wreath, and beneath it a key. The Cross, wreath and key are all black. The gloves are white, lined and bound with black, and the scabbard and belt of the sword are black. The order is white, edged with red, worn as a collar, and the jewel suspended from it. On each side of the collar are two black Teutonic Crosses. There is also a sash proper, red, bordered with black, worn from right to left, from which hangs a gold-enamelled Tau Cross. The principal jewel is a triangle of gold, on which is engraved the Sacred Name יהוה.

TO OPEN.

[The Gr∴ Commander raps 3 times, and says: "Valiant Kts∴ and Commanders of the Temple, I have caused you to be summoned to deliberate upon matters of deep interest to the Order of the House of St. Mary of Jerusalem. Assist me to open a Chapter of the Order, that we may consult together. Attention, Knights and Commanders!"]

24D

[All rise, in their appropriate stations, draw their swords, salute the Gr∴ Commander, and stand at the carry].

Gr∴ Com∴ Bro∴ Seneschal, see that the doors of the Chapter are duly guarded, and inform the Sentinels that we are about to open a Chapter here, directing them to keep vigilant watch, that none enter without the words and signs.

[The Seneschal goes out, returns, and reports: "Th∴ Puissant Gr∴ Commander, the Sentinels are at their posts, and we are in security."]

Gr∴ Com∴ Bro∴ Gr∴ Hospitaller, what are the *first* duties of a Knight Commander of the Temple?

Gr∴ Hosp∴ To soothe the sufferings and administer to the necessities of the poor, sick and wounded Soldiers of the Cross; to watch with and nurse them, and supply them with food and medicine.

Gr∴ Com∴ Bro∴ Gr∴ Marshal, what are the *Knightly* duties of a Kt∴ Commander of the Temple?

Gr∴ Marsh∴ To guard the City of Solomon against the Infidel, to protect Christendom against the Pagan, to succor and assist the helpless and feeble, and to defend the innocent.

Gr∴ Com∴ Bro∴ Gr∴ Chancellor, what are the *Moral* duties of a Kt∴ Commander?

Gr∴ Chan∴ To be temperate, chaste, charitable and discreet.

Gr∴ Com∴ Bro∴ Gr∴ Prior, what are the *Masonic* duties of a Kt∴ Commander?

Gr∴ Prior: To be grateful to God for his goodness: to lead pure and blameless lives; and to love our brother.

Gr∴ Com∴ Bro∴ Gr∴ Marshal, where were you made a Kt∴ Commander?

Gr∴ Marsh∴ At the Siege of St. Jean d'Acre; when we made tents for the sick and wounded, of our sails; and fought the Infidel Saladin by day, while we nursed our wounded soldiers at night.

Gr∴ Com∴ When were you so made?

Gr∴ Marsh∴ After I became an Elu, and knew the Ineffable Name.

Gr∴ Com∴ How have you proved yourself worthy of the title?

Gr∴ Marsh∴ By being true to my vows; by strict observance of my duties; and by my scars gained at Acre, at Ascalon, and against the Pagans of Prussia.

Gr∴ Com∴ Bro∴ Grand Hospitaller, whence come you as a Kt∴ Commander of the Temple?

Gr∴ Hosp∴ From the abodes of sickness, pain and suffering; where I have learned patience, fortitude and resignation.

Gr∴ Com∴ Bro∴ Gr∴ Admiral, whence come you as a Kt∴ Commander?

Gr∴ Adm∴ From the great ocean; where I have learned the feebleness of man, and his dependence on the Deity, amid the mighty tumult of its waters.

Gr∴ Com∴ Bro∴ Gr∴ Marshal, whence come you as a Kt∴ Commander?

Gr∴ Marsh∴ From the field of battle; where I have learned that the most glorious of deaths is that which overtakes a Soldier of the Cross, who dies in the performance of his duty.

Gr∴ Com∴ Assemble round the altar, my brethren, that we may open this Chapter of Kts∴ Commanders of the Temple!

[The Knights form in a circle around the altar, and place the points of their swords together, holding them horizontally in front of them, the points meeting in the centre; and repeat after the Gr∴ Commander]:

Gr∴ Com∴ As these swords point to one common centre, so we, here renewing our vows, do devote our swords to the cause of God and the Cross, our hearts to the glory of God and the welfare of man, and our hands to assist the sick, the suffering, and the destitute. So help us God!

————————

The Knights then kneel, and the Gr∴ Prior repeats the following

PRAYER:

Father and Creator, who hast given us life and being, aid us to perform the duties which Thy law and our vows impose upon us! Thou hast given us the portion and the food of Sons: make us to do the duty of Sons, that we may never lose our title to an inheritance so glorious! Thou hast vouchsafed to call us Thy children, and dost graciously permit us to call Thee Father. May that name be our glory and our confidence, our defence and guard, our ornament and strength, our dignity and the endearment of obedience! May it confirm and sustain us in our good resolutions, and make us steadfast never to desert the post of duty! Let our bodies be chaste, our thoughts pure, our words gentle, and our lives useful and innocent, to the honour and commendation of Masonry and Knighthood! Make us patient of the evils which Thou inflictest, lovers of the good which Thou commandest, haters of all vice which Thou forbiddest, and satisfied with all the accidents Thou sendest! Let us not be tempted with want, nor made contemptible by beggary, nor wanton or proud by riches, nor in love with anything in this world to the disregard of duty! Look upon us with mercy, and forgive our imperfections and our errors; and accept with indulgence the little service we may be enabled to render to the cause of virtue, charity and truth! and to Thee be all glory and honour forever: Amen!

All answer, "So mote it be;" and rise. Then the Gr∴ Hospitaller raps ; times — the Gr∴ Marshal , ? by ♈&‡ ☾ ☍—the Gr∴ Commander , ? by ♈&‡ ☾ ☍—and the Gr∴ Commander says: "My Brethren, the Chapter is open."

RECEPTION.

The Candidate is prepared by being clothed in a white mantle with a large black Teutonic cross upon the left breast. The Grand Prior then goes to him, and conducts him to a small room [first bandaging his eyes], in which he places him in a chair, in front of a table on which are a light, and a skull and cross-bones, with the Holy Scriptures, the square and compasses.

Having seated him, he says to him: "My Brother, you desire to receive the degree of Kt∴ Commander of the Temple. Before you can do so, you are required to answer certain questions, which you will find in writing, on the table before you. I shall leave you alone, and when you hear three distinct raps you will remove the bandage from your eyes, and annex your answer to each question, in writing, and sign your name at the bottom. Consider the questions well! Let what you will see upon the table before you, remind you that you will answer them in the hearing of the Deity, who knows your thoughts: let it teach you the evanescence of all earthly things, the obligations of rectitude and honour, the certainty of sickness and death, and after that of judgment; and that your answers must be true and sincere. When you shall have answered the questions, you will give three distinct raps upon the table, and I will return."

[The Gr∴ Prior then withdraws and closes the door. The questions are as follows] :

1st. . Have you ever violated any Masonic obligation, without atoning for it by repentance and reformation ?

2d. Are you willing to aid, assist and comfort the sick, the needy and the destitute ; to watch with them and minister to their wants ; and to help to feed, to clothe and to protect the widow and the orphan ?

3d. Have you any enmity towards any one, that you would not readily abandon, if you found him sincerely willing to be reconciled to you?

4th. Would you, if called upon, draw your sword in defence of truth, of human freedom and the rights of conscience, against falsehood, tyranny, and usurped power? And can you rather choose to die than desert the post of duty?

If the questions are answered satisfactorily, the Gr∴ Commander orders the Candidate to be admitted. He is led in front of the Gr∴ Commander, who says: "My Brother, are these your answers ; and are they sincere and from the heart?"

Cand∴ They are.

Gr∴ Com∴ It is well. Are you an Elu, and Gr∴, Elect, Perf∴ and Subl∴ Mason ?

Cand∴ I am.

Gr∴ Com∴. Dost thou desire to obtain the degree of Kt∴ Commander of the Temple?

Cand∴. I do.

Gr∴ Com∴. Knowest thou that thou wouldest thus embrace a life of toil and of hardship, of self-denial and of danger?

Cand∴. I do.

Gr∴ Com∴. And dost thou not hesitate and falter at the prospect?

Cand∴. I do not.

Gr∴ Com∴. Go, then, my Brother, to the Holy Altar, and there assume the obligation of this Order.

[The Gr∴ Prior conducts the Candidate to the Altar, where he kneels on both knees, with his hands upon the blades of the Swords of three of the Knights, who hold them crossed before him upon the Holy Scriptures: in which position he repeats the following]

OBLIGATION.

I, A. . . . B. . . ., in the presence of the One Almighty and only true God, the Spirit of the Universe; and of this Chapter of Knights Commanders of the Temple, or the Order of the House of St. Mary of Jerusalem, do of my own free will and accord most solemnly and sincerely promise, and to God and the Saviour vow, that I will never reveal the secrets of this degree to any person of an inferior degree; except in a Chapter lawfully holden by authority of some regularly established Council of the 33d Degree; or by virtue of special authority from such Supreme Council.

I furthermore promise and vow, that I will not assist in, nor be present at, the conferring of this degree upon any person, who shall not have received all the preceding Degrees of the Ancient and Accepted Rite of Free Masonry; nor will I tacitly consent or agree thereto, but will prevent the same if it be in my power, by proper and peaceable means.

I furthermore promise and vow that I will through life conduct myself, in all my dealings, with truth, rectitude, justice and honour, doing unto others as I would others should do unto me; that I will not endeavour to make gain by the misfortunes of others; that I will never misrepresent the arguments or opinions of friend or enemy; that I will take no unfair advantage of, and will not overreach any one: that I will not seek to injure even my enemy; and that I will never attempt to make reputation for myself by destroying the reputation of another.

I furthermore promise and vow that if occasion should offer, I will not flee from plague, pestilence or epidemic, to avoid danger, when duty and manhood require me to remain; but will imitate the example of those Ill∴ Knights of Bremen and Lubec, who, making their sails into tents, devoted themselves to the care and nursing of the sick and wounded; and so became the founders of this Order.

I furthermore promise and swear, that I will never desert the post of duty through fear of death: however humble that duty, and however unnoticed my death may be: but in plague or battle, in fire or tempest, I will stand firm at my post, so long as manhood and duty demand, whatever may be the consequences to myself; and even should I perish in doing so.

I furthermore promise and swear that I will ever be governed by the true principles of Masonry; and obey its laws, rules and regulations, made by the proper authority; and that I will do all in my power to aid and advance all justifiable measures for the good of the Craft, and the advantage of Free Masonry, agreeably to the Constitutions of the Order.

To all which I most solemnly, understandingly and sincerely bind myself, with the full intention of ever keeping and performing the same, and making them the rule and guide of my life, conduct and conversation; under no less penalty than that of being branded in the estimation of all men as nidering and coward, and exposed to the anger of God, if I should wilfully and knowingly violate this my solemn obligation. So help me God!

The Gr∴ Commander then raises him, and communicates the Signs, Tokens and Words.

Sign: *of Recognition* . . . Make the sign of the cross upon a brother's ⟨cipher⟩ with your ⟨cipher⟩, the ⟨cipher⟩ ⟨cipher⟩.

Answer: . . . He ⟨cipher⟩ your ⟨cipher⟩. This is done only in the Chapter. Elsewhere the answer is to place the two first fingers of the right hand ⟨cipher⟩ the ⟨cipher⟩ ⟨cipher⟩ the ⟨cipher⟩ ⟨cipher⟩, and turning the ⟨cipher⟩ ⟨cipher⟩ ⟨cipher⟩.

Due-Guard: . . . In open Chapter, place the right hand upon the ⟨cipher⟩ ⟨cipher⟩, and extend the ⟨cipher⟩ so as to form a ⟨cipher⟩. When standing, place it in like manner on the ⟨cipher⟩.

Token: . . . Strike gently the ⟨cipher⟩ of a brother ; times with the right hand.

Answer: . . . He gently ⟨cipher⟩ your ⟨cipher⟩ ; ⟨cipher⟩.

Pass-word: . . . ⟨cipher⟩.

Grand Word: . . . ⟨cipher⟩ alternating the letters.

· The Gr∴ Commander then, with his sword gives the Candidate the accolade, on each shoulder alternately, saying, "By my authority and power as successor of Herman de Saltza and Albert of Brandenburg, I hereby constitute, create and dub thee a Knight Commander of the Temple, or of the Ill∴ Order of the House of St. Mary of Jerusalem. Be true: be devout: be brave!"

He raises the newly-made Knight, and invests him with the insignia of the degree; after which he is seated, and the following History and instruction is read to him.

HISTORY.

When St. Jean d'Acre, the ancient Ptolemais, on the southern side of which was Mount Carmel, was besieged by the Christian forces, for nearly two years, under Guy of Lusignan, King of Jerusalem, Conrad, Marquis of Montferrat, and other Princes and leaders from every country in Europe ; and especially by Henry VI. of Germany, son of Frederic Barbarossa; joined, near the end of the siege, by Philip Augustus of France and Richard Cœur de Lion of England; they were long afflicted with famine, until they ate the flesh of horses with joy, and even the intestines sold for ten sous: men of high rank and the sons of great men greedily devoured grass; the starving fought together like dogs for the little bread baked at the ovens; they gnawed the bones that had already been gnawed by the dogs; and noblemen, ashamed to *beg*, were known to *steal* bread. Constant rains added to their miseries; and Saladin, Sultan of the Saracens, encamped near them with a vast army from every portion of his dominions, and all the great Emirs of Islamism, harassed them with constant attacks: Saladin, whom his People called the Elect of God; Malek-Adhel, Sayf-Eddin, his brother; the Prince of Hamah, his nephew; and the Princes of Damascus and Aleppo, his sons; the yellow and green banners of the Emirs of Emessa, the Princes of Baalbec, Harran and Edessa in Mesopotamia, Singar and Gezire on the Tigris, and all the tents of Islamism.

· Sickness, also, caused by the rains and the intense heat, decimated the Christian forces. The wounded German soldiers, whom none of the others understood, could not make known their sickness nor their necessities. Certain German nobles from the cities of Bremen and Lubec, who had arrived at Acre by sea, moved by the miseries of their countrymen, took the sails of their ships, and made of them a large tent, in which for a time they placed the wounded Germans, and tended them with great kindness. Forty nobles of the same nation united with them, and established a kind of hospital in the midst of the camp; and this noble and charitable association, like the Knights of the Temple and of St. John of Jerusalem, soon and insensibly became a new Hospitaller and Military Order. This was in the year 1191. In 1192, Pope Celestin III., at the request of the Emperor Henry the 6th, solemnly approved of the Order, by his Bull of the 23d of February. He prescribed, as regulations for the new Knights, those of Saint Augustine; and, for special statutes, in all that regarded the poor and sick, those of the Hospitallers of St. John; in regard to military discipline, the regulations of the Templars. This new order, exclusively composed of Germans, was styled The Order of Teutonic Knights of the House of St. Mary of Jerusalem. After the destruction of the Templars, they were also known as Commanders of the Temple.

The first name was given them, because, while the city of Jerusalem was under the government of the Latin Christians, a German had erected there, at his own expense, a Hospital and Oratory, for the sick of that nation, under the protection of, and dedicated to, the Holy Virgin. Their dress was a white mantle with a black cross; and they, like the Hospitallers, were required to take three solemn vows. Before assuming the habit, they were required to swear that they were Germans, of noble extraction and birth; and to bind themselves for their whole life to serve the poor and sick, and defend the Holy Places. Ever to adhere to the truth, to attend and nurse the sick and wounded, and never to recede before the enemy, were their three solemn vows. Truth is the first Masonic duty: to leave the path of duty is to recede before the enemy; and therefore you have taken the three vows of the Teutonic Knights and Hospitallers, in a still more noble and enlarged spirit.

These were the common objects of the three great military orders; which were always the generous Defenders of the Holy Land. To them was at first applied the phrase, found in the Book of Ecclesiastes, "a three-fold cord is not easily broken." The Teutonic Knights soon became one of the most Illustrious of the Military and Religious Orders. The three were the chief strength of the army before Acre; but the siege advanced slowly, where there were neither absolute chiefs nor discipline. On the 13th of July 1191 it surrendered.

In 1223, Herman de Saltza, Grand Master of the Teutonic Knights, was present at a celebrated assembly convoked by Pope Honorius III., at Ferentino in Campania, to deliberate concerning the mode of raising succours for the Holy Land; at which were also present the Pope, the Emperor Frederic II. of Sicily, John, King of Jerusalem, the Bishop of Bethlehem, the Grand Masters of the Templars and Hospitallers, and other distinguished personages: and it was by the influence of Herman de Saltza, 4th Grand Master of the Teutonic Knights, then exercised, that Frederic espoused and married the daughter of the King of Jerusalem, and engaged in a new crusade.

In the year 1226 most of the Teutonic Knights went from the Holy Land to Prussia; the people of which were still idolaters, waging cruel war against their Christian neighbours, murdering Priests at the foot of the Altar, and employing the Sacred Vessels for profane uses. Conrad, Duke of Masovia, called in the Teutonic Knights to his assistance, and gave them, as a commencement for their establishment there, the whole territory of Culm, with all lands they should conquer from the Infidels. De Saltza, the Grand Master, sent thither a Knight called Conrad de Lansberg, who concluded the Treaty, which was signed by three Bishops of that Country. The Knights then entered those Northern Countries, and by continued wars acquired in time the entire sovereignty of Royal and Ducal Prussia, Livonia, and the Duchies of Courland and Semigal; all vast Provinces, and capable of forming a great Kingdom. And when, in 1291, the Sultan stormed and took St. Jean d'Acre, the Teutonic Knights that survived returned to Europe and joined their brethren in Prussia and Livonia.

For many years the Teutonic Knights held Prussia as a fief depending on the Crown of Poland. During this period, fierce contests arose between the Grand Masters of the Order and the Kings of Poland; the former struggling for independence, and the latter obstinately asserting their right of sovereignty. Albert, a Prince of the House of Brandenburg, elected Grand Master in 1511, engaged keenly in the quarrel, and maintained a long war with Sigismund King of Poland; but adopting the doctrines of Luther, he made a treaty with Sigismund, by which that part of Prussia belonging to the Order was erected into a secular and hereditary Duchy, and the investiture of it granted to Albert, who bound himself to do homage for it to the Kings of Poland, as their vassal. Immediately afterwards, he publicly professed the Protestant faith, and married a Princess of Denmark. The Knights exclaimed so loudly against his treachery, that he was put under the ban of the empire; but he kept possession of the Province he had usurped, and transmitted it to his posterity: and in process of time it fell to the Electoral Branch of the family; all dependence on Poland was shaken off, and the Margraves of Brandenburg took the title of Kings of Prussia; which so has become one of the leading powers of Europe.

Times change, and circumstances; but Virtue and Duty remain the same. The Evils to be warred against but take another shape, and are developed in a different form.

There is the same need now of truth and loyalty, as in the days of Frederic Barbarossa.

The characters religious and military, attention to the sick and wounded in the Hospital, and war against the Infidel in the field, are no longer blended: but the same duties, to be performed in another shape, continue to exist and to environ us all.

The innocent virgin is no longer at the mercy of the brutal Baron or licentious man-at-arms; but purity and innocence still need protectors.

War is no longer the apparently natural State of Society; and for most men it is an empty obligation to assume, that they will not recede before the enemy; but the same high duty and obligation still rest upon all men.

For Truth, in act, profession and opinion, is even rarer now than in the days of chivalry. Falsehood has become a current coin, and circulates with a certain degree of respectability; because it has an actual value. It is indeed the great Vice of the Age; it, and its twin-sister, Dishonesty. Books are published and read by thousands, detailing the experiences of a life of knavery: Men for political preferment profess whatever principles are expedient and profitable: At the bar, in the pulpit and in the halls of legislation, men argue against their own convictions, and, with what they term *logic*, prove to the satisfaction of others that which they do not themselves believe. Insincerity and duplicity are valuable to their possessors, like estates in stocks, that yield a certain revenue: and it is no longer the *truth* of an opinion or a principle, but the net *profit* that may be realized from it, which is the measure of its value.

The Press is the great sower of falsehood. To slander a political antagonist, to misrepresent all that he says, and if that be impossible, to invent for him what he does *not* say; to manufacture and put in circulation whatever utterly baseless calumnies against him are necessary to defeat and destroy him,—these are habits so common as to have ceased to excite notice or comment, much less surprise or disgust.

There was a time when a Knight would have died rather than utter a lie, or break his Knightly word. The Knight Commander of the Temple revives the old Knightly spirit; and devotes himself to the old Knightly worship of Truth. No profession of an opinion not his own, for expediency's sake or profit, or through fear of the world's disfavour; no slander of even an enemy; no colouring or perversion of the sayings or acts of other men; no insincere speech and argument for any purpose, or under any pretext, must soil his fair escutcheon. Out of the Chapter as well as in it, he must speak the Truth, and *all* the Truth, no more and no less; or else speak not at all.

To purity and innocence everywhere, the Kt∴ Commander owes protection, as of old; against bold violence, or those, more guilty than murderers, who by art and treachery seek to slay the soul; and against that grim want and gaunt and haggard destitution that drive too many to sell their honour and their innocence for food.

In no age of the world has man had better opportunity than now to display those lofty virtues and that noble heroism that so distinguished the three great military and religious Orders, in their youth, before they became corrupt and vitiated by prosperity and power.

When a fearful epidemic ravages a city, and death is inhaled with the air men breathe; when the living scarcely suffice to bury the dead,—most men flee in abject terror, to return and live respectable and influential when the danger has passed away. But the old Knightly spirit of devotion and disinterestedness and contempt of death, still lives, and is not extinct in the human heart. Everywhere a few are found to stand firmly and unflinchingly at their posts, to front and defy the danger, not for money, or to be honoured for it, or to protect their own household; but from mere humanity, and to obey the unerring dictates of duty. They nurse the sick, breathing the pestilential atmosphere of the hospital. They explore the abodes of want and misery. With the gentleness of woman, they soften the pains of the dying, and feed the lamp of life in the convalescent. They perform the last sad offices to the dead; and they seek no other reward than the approval of their own consciences.

These are the true Knights of the present age : these, and the captain who remains at his post on board his shattered ship until the last boat, loaded to the water's edge with passengers and crew, has parted from her side; and then goes calmly down with her into the mysterious depths of the ocean :—the pilot who stands at the wheel while the swift flames eddy round him, and scorch away his life :—the fireman who ascends the blazing walls, and plunges amid the flames to save the property or lives of those who have upon him no claim by tie of blood, or friendship, or even of ordinary acquaintance :—these, and others like these :—all men, who, set at the post of duty, stand there manfully; to die, if need be, but not to desert their post: for these too are sworn not to recede before the enemy.

To the performance of duties and of acts of heroism like these, you have devoted yourself, my Brother, by becoming a Kt∴ Commander of the Temple. Soldier of the Truth and of Loyalty! Protector of Purity and Innocence! Defier of Plague and Pestilence! Nurser of the Sick and Burier of the Dead! Knight, preferring Death to abandonment of the Post of Duty! Welcome to the bosom of this Order!

TO CLOSE.

[The Gr∴ Commander gives three raps. All the Knights rise, salute him, and remain standing, in their stations, with swords carried.]

Gr∴ Com∴ Bro∴ Gr∴ Hospitaller, what is the hour?

Gr∴ Hos∴ Four in the afternoon, Th∴ Puissant Gr∴ Commander.

Gr∴ Com∴ Since the sun is declining in the West, it is time that we should close this Chapter; that we may not omit, even for one day, our duties in the world. Bro∴ Gr∴ Prior, whither go you from this Gr∴ Chapter?

Gr∴ Prior: To the death-beds of the sick, there to administer comfort and consolation, and with the hope of eternal life to cheer the last moments of the dying.

Gr∴ Com∴ Bro∴ Gr∴ Admiral, whither go you from this Chapter?

Gr∴ Adm∴ To my ship; to encounter, it may be, the enemy, storm, fire, and the unknown dangers of the ocean; and, if my country's honour or the dictates of duty require, to sink with her, rather than desert my post.

Gr∴ Com∴ Bro∴ Gr∴ Chancellor, whither go you from this Chapter?

Gr∴ Chan∴ To save the innocent and pure from falling, and to rescue and redeem those that have erred and that repent.

Gr∴ Com∴ Bro∴ Gr∴ Hospitaller, whither go you from this Chapter?

Gr∴ Hosp∴ To the hospitals, and to the dwellings of the sick and destitute.

Gr∴ Com∴ Bro∴ Gr∴ Marshal, whither go you from this Chapter?

Gr∴ Marsh∴ To war against all falsehoods, insincerities and plausibilities: to practise truth: and to lay bare the deformities of all sophisms and pestilent false philosophies and doctrines that lead astray the people, and under the guise of progress and philanthropism embody atheism and adultery, or public and private robbery.

Gr∴ Com∴ Such is the mission of our Order. May it live forever! and may we never forget or disregard our vows! Brethren, assemble around the altar, that we may close this Chapter.

[The Brethren form a circle as in opening, and hold their swords horizontally before them, all the points meeting in the centre, on a level with their hearts].

Gr∴ Com∴ Let us be one, my Brethren, now and henceforward; and let our swords, our arms, our hearts be devoted to the great cause of Truth, Humanity and Duty! And may the blessing of Providence rest upon us and our labours; and the lustre of our Order never fade, nor its glories grow dim! Amen!

[The Brethren all answer, "So mote it be!" Then the Gr∴ Hospitaller raps ; with his sword, the Gr∴ Marshal ,？ by ♈&‡☾☾︎⚍—the Gr∴ Commander ,？ by ♈&‡☾☾︎⚍—and the Gr∴ Commander declares, "This Chapter is closed! Go in peace, my Brethren!"] . . ∴

FINIS.

Twenty-Eighth Degree.

Knight of the Sun; or Knight Adept.

Bodies in this degree are styled *Councils*. Each must consist of not less than seven members.

The walls or hangings represent mountains, forests, grassy plains and cultivated fields, and other natural scenery.

The Hall should be circular; and the roof supported by twelve columns, blue and white in colour, and on each, in gold, one of the signs of the zodiac, commencing in the East with *Taurus*, and going round by the North, West and South in regular progression.

The Presiding Officer sits in the East, between the two columns or Signs *Aries* and *Taurus*; The Second Officer in the West, between *Libra* and *Scorpio;* the Third in the South, between *Capricornus* and *Aquarius;* and the Fourth in the North, between *Cancer* and *Leo.*

Over the Presiding Officer is a transparency, the light showing through a Sun, occupying the centre of an equilateral Triangle, inscribed within a circle. On the face of the Sun is the Ineffable word יהוה.

Over the Second Officer is a transparency, on which is a winged serpent enfolding a globe, upon which, in Sanscrit letters is the Ineffable Word A∴ U∴ M∴

Over the third officer is a transparency, on which is a double interlaced triangle, and in its centre the word I∴ A∴ Ω∴

Over the fourth officer is a transparency, on which is a large five-pointed star; and on it the Phœnician name of the Sun-God, בעל [BAL].

In the centre of the room is a great globe of ground glass, containing a powerful light; by which and the transparencies alone the Council is lighted.

The ceiling represents the Heavens, with the Moon, Planets and the principal Stars in Taurus and the neighbouring Constellations.

OFFICERS: THEIR NAMES, TITLES, DRESS AND JEWELS.

The Presiding Officer is styled *Th∴ Ven∴ Gr∴ Master.* He represents ATHOM or ATHOM-RE, the Supreme Egyptian Divinity; wears a rose-coloured robe, with a bright yellow mantle, and has on his head a wreath of ivy and mistletoe, or other evergreen leaves. In his right hand he holds a sceptre, surmounted by a globe of gold, and the handle gilded. His jewel is a sun of gold, suspended by a chain of gold. The reverse side of the jewel is a hemisphere of gold, showing the northern half of the ecliptic and zodiac with the signs from Taurus to Libra inclusive.

The *Senior Warden* is styled AMUN, and bears a white rod, at the end of which is a golden eye. He wears a saffron-coloured robe, and on his head a circlet or coronet of gold rays. He also wears the order and jewel of the Degree.

25D

The *Junior Warden* is styled Dionusos, and bears a caduceus, or short rod with wings, entwined by two serpents. He wears a green robe, a wreath of flowers, and the order and jewel of the Degree.

The *Orator* (or 4th officer) is styled Hermes, and bears the representation of a thunderbolt. He wears a many-coloured robe, a wreath of vine leaves, and the order and jewel of the Degree.

There are seven other officers, called Princes of Light, and known by these different names of the Sun among the ancient nations : Surya, Mithras, Osiris, Bel, Arkaleus, Adoni and Odin. Each sits between two columns: the two first on the right and left of the Th∴ Ven∴ the next two on the right and left of the Sen∴ Warden: the next two on the right and left of the Junior Warden: and the last on the right of the Orator.

There is also a *Herald*, who sits on the left of the Orator.

Each of the Seven Princes wears on his head a circlet of gold, with rays representing those of the Sun.

If there be other Knights present, they sit in the rear of the columns.

By the great Light in the centre of the room is a square altar with four horns, on which is a roll of parchment and a censer in which perfume is burned.

The *Order* is a broad white watered ribbon, edged with green, and worn from right to left. Where it crosses the breast is embroidered in gold an open eye. No *apron* is worn. On the *sword-belt*, which is of green velvet, and worn round the body, are embroidered in gold seven stars.

The *Jewel* of all the Officers and Members is the same as that of the Gr∴ Master, and worn suspended by a flame-coloured ribbon, tied in the button-hole of the Coat, or fastened to the Order.

The *battery* is : raps, at equal intervals.

TO OPEN.

[The Th∴ Ven∴ gives one rap, and says] :

Th∴ Ven∴ My Brethren, light comes in the East, and duty demands that we open this Council. Let him who hath not a pure heart, free of all guile, malice, ill-will and hypocrisy, and a conscience void of offence, withdraw, and trouble us not with his presence! Excellent Bro∴ Dionusos, cause the Herald to inquire if we are in security, and to warn the Guards to be vigilant, that we may not be surprised or disturbed, while we labour for the good of mankind.

Jun∴ W∴ Bro∴ Herald, see that we are in security, and warn the Guards to be vigilant and watchful, that we may not be surprised or disturbed, while we labour for the good of mankind; since this Council of Knights of the Sun is about to be opened.

[The Herald goes to the door, gives the alarm of the Degree, which is answered from without, returns to his place, and says] :

Her∴ Exc∴ Bro∴ Dionusos, the guards are at their posts, and duly warned, and we are in security.

Jun∴ W∴ Th∴ Ven∴ G∴ Master, we are in security and the Guards protect the approaches to the Council.

Th∴ Ven∴ [Rapping ; at which all rise] Brother Herald, what is the first Masonic Commandment?

Her∴ God is the Eternal, Infinite, Immutable, Incomprehensible Wisdom, Power and Intelligence. Thou shalt adore, revere and love Him! Thou shalt honour Him by practising the Virtues and loving and admiring the Virtuous!

Th∴ Ven∴ Bro∴ Odin, what is the second Masonic Commandment?

Odin : . Thy religion shall be to do good, because it is a delight to thee ; and not merely because it is a duty! That thou mayest become the friend of the wise, thou shalt obey their precepts! Thy soul is immortal: thou shalt do nothing to degrade it!

Th∴ Ven∴ Bro∴ Adoni, what is the third?

Adon∴ Thou shalt incessantly war against Vice! Thou shalt not do unto others that which thou wouldst not wish them to do unto thee! Thou shalt be submissive to thy fortunes, and keep burning the light of Wisdom!

Th∴ Ven∴ Bro∴ Arkaleus, what is the fourth?

Arkal∴ Thou shalt honour thy parents! Thou shalt pay respect and homage to the aged! Thou shalt instruct the young! Thou shalt protect infancy and innocence!

Th∴ Ven∴ Bro∴ Bel, what is the fifth?

Bel : . . Thou shalt cherish thy wife and children, and be true to the vows made by thee at thy marriage! Thou shalt love thy Country, and obey its laws!

Th∴ Ven∴ Bro∴ Osiris, what is the sixth?

Osiris : . . Thy friend shall be a Second Thyself: and misfortune shall not estrange thee from him! Thou shalt do, for the sake of his memory, whatever thou wouldst do for him if he were living!

Th∴ Ven∴ Bro∴ Mithras, what is the seventh!

Mith∴ Thou shalt allow no passion, vice or indulgence to become thy master! Thou shalt make the passions of others useful lessons to thyself! Thou shalt be indulgent to error, and judge in mercy, and be tolerant!

Th∴ Ven∴ Bro∴ Surya, what is the eighth?

Sury∴ Thou shalt avoid and flee from insincere friendships! Thou shalt in everything refrain from excess! Thou shalt dread, not death, but a stain upon thy memory!

Th∴ Ven∴ Bro∴ Hermes, the ninth?

Orator : . . Thou shalt hear much! Thou shalt speak little! Thou shalt act well!

Th∴ Ven∴ Bro∴ Dionusos, the tenth?

Jun∴ W∴ Thou shalt forget injuries : for revenge makes enmities eternal! Thou shalt render good for evil! Thou shalt not abuse either thy strength or thy superiority!

Th∴ Ven∴ Bro∴ Amun, the eleventh?

Sen∴ W∴ Thou shalt study to know men; that thou mayest learn to know thyself! Thou shalt strive to obtain knowledge; that thou mayest be able to enlighten thy race; and that thy influences may live after thee, doing good!

Th∴ Ven∴ And this is the 12th Commandment: Ye shall love one another! Ye shall ever walk in the paths of virtue! Ye shall be just and gentle! Ye shall be modest and circumspect! Ye shall be grateful to God for his blessings and to men for their kindnesses! Ye shall be temperate and chaste! Ye shall be modest! And ye shall avoid idleness!

Th∴ Ven∴ . My Brethren, let us pray that we may be enabled to keep these commandments!

[The Knights all kneel upon the right knee, and raise the right hand: and the Th∴ Ven∴ repeats the following prayer] :

PRAYER.

Our Father, the One God! Hear us, thy erring, feeble children, while we bow to thee in adoration! Thou didst create the universe with a thought, and breathe into man a living soul. We adore Thy Majesty, and humbly submit to Thy Providence, and revere Thy Justice, and trust like little children to Thy Mercy, and acknowledge with penitence and humility our weaknesses and our errors!

Our life is vanity, and our days pass away like a tale that is told, and as the remembrance of a passenger that stayeth but a night! The days of our pilgrimage are few and sorrowful, and in vain we disquiet ourselves, as a bird beateth its wings against the bars of its cage! Teach us patience, our Father, and submission; and trust and confidence in Thee, and in Thy goodness and wisdom! Thy counsels are secret, and Thy wisdom infinite, and we do not repine when Thou bereavest us.

Bless, O our Father, those of us who are now here assembled, by giving us those most inestimable of all blessings, far above honours and dignities, the priceless jewels of Charity, Friendship, Love, Justice and Truth! Aid us in the keeping and perfect observance of all the duties which we have in anywise assumed to perform! Enable us to abide by the promises which we have made to one another! Give to us a more ample and complete understanding of our obligations as Brethren of our beloved Order, as men and as patriots!

Bless and increase and extend that Order among all nations and tongues where Thy Being is recognized! Preserve its principles and its purposes from innovation, and continue them honest and just and true! Sustain it against the assaults of ignorance and malice; prevent its being used for improper purposes, and forgive its errors! And to Thee, Eternal, Omnipotent and Merciful Deity, and to thy Ineffable Name be all praise forever!. Amen!

Th.·. Ven.·.   Bro.·. Amun, the first Great Truth in Masonry?

Sen.·. W.·.   There is but one God: Uncreated, Immortal, Infinite.

Th.·. Ven.·.   Bro.·. Dionusos, the second Great Truth in Masonry?

Jun.·. W.·.   The Soul of Man is immortal; and his life but a point in the Centre of Eternity.

Th.·. Ven.·.   Bro.·. Hermes, the third Great Truth in Masonry?

Orator: . .   Evil and Pain and Misery and Misfortune are but the Discords that unite with the Concords of the Universe to make one Great Magnificent Harmony hereafter and forever.

Th.·. Ven.·.   My Brethren, in the name of the Supreme Deity, let us commence our labours! Bro.·. Amun, make known to Bro.·. Dionusos, and let him make known to all the brethren between the Sacred Columns, that it is the hour of Sunrise, and I am about to open this Council.

Sen.·. W.·.   Bro.·. Dionusos, it is the pleasure of the Th.·. Ven.·. Gr.·. Master, that we now resume our labours. You will therefore make known to the brethren that it is the hour of Sunrise, and that this Council is about to be opened.

Jun.·. W.·.   Bro.·. Herald, proclaim that it is the hour of Sunrise, and that this Council of Knights of the Sun is now about to be opened!

Her.·.   Brethren, prepare for labour! The Sun rises, and the Th.·. Ven.·. Gr.·. Master is about to open this Council; for the Great Light shines in our midst.

Th.·. Ven.·.   My Brethren [placing his ‡¦&⊙≈□ on his &ℂ‡♈], answer the sign! [He raises the ♈&♐♋ of that &⊙≈□, so as to form a ⌂⚹♄⊙‡ℂ. All the brethren ‡⊙♀⌂ℂ the ‡¦&⊙≈□ ⊙♏♉*ℂ the &ℂ⊙□, the ♑♉‡ℂ♑♀≈♌ℂ‡ extended ♄♐⅍⊙‡□, and the other ♑♀≈♌ℂ‡⌂ and ♈&♄♋♏ ♐†ℂ≈‡&ℂ□; and then drop the ⊙‡☲ by the ⌂♀□ℂ.

The Th.·. Ven.·. then gives the battery; and all the Brethren repeat it with their hands.

Th.·. Ven.·.   My Brethren, this Council is now open.

RECEPTION.

The Candidate, having been duly elected, is prepared in the ante-chamber by being dressed as a Rose ⚘, except the Sword; or he may wear the order and jewel of any higher degree, below this. A black cloth is then placed over his head, so as to blindfold him completely, and he is placed at the door of the Council Chamber, and told to rap [; ;]—and answer truly such questions as may be asked him.

On hearing the alarm, the Herald says, "Th.·. Ven.·. Gr.·. Master, some one, having passed the Guards, gives an unusual alarm at the door of the Council Chamber."

Th.·. Ven.·.   Go thither, my Brother, and if it be the Aspirant, ask him the necessary questions.

[The Herald goes, and asks as follows]:

Her.·.   Who hails?

Cand.·.   A Knight of the Rose ⚘ and 27th.

Her.·.   What is your name?

Cand.·.   A . . . . . B . . . . .

Her.·.   Your age?

Cand.·.   . . . .

Her.·.   Do you desire to approach the great light?

Cand.·. I do.

Her.·. Are you prepared to receive instruction with humility? Do you acknowledge all men as your brethren? Are you willing to write the favours done you upon marble, the injuries upon the sands?

Cand.·. I am.

Her.·. Then come with me within this Temple of Wisdom.

[He takes the aspirant by the hand and leads him nine times around the Council Chamber slowly, while everything is in the most perfect silence, except while the voices of the officers are heard, during which the Herald and Candidate pause and listen. At each circuit, one officer repeats as below, in grave, solemn and impressive tones].

1st Circuit: ODIN: God is the author of everything that existeth; the Eternal, the Supreme, the Living and Awful Being; from whom nothing in the Universe is hidden. Make of Him no idols and visible images; but rather worship Him in the deep solitudes of sequestered forests; for He is invisible, and fills the Universe as its soul, and liveth not in any Temple!

2d Circuit: ADONI: Light and Darkness are the World's Eternal ways. God is the principle of everything that exists, and the Father of all Beings. He is eternal, immovable and Self-Existent. There are no bounds to His power. At one glance He sees the Past, the Present and the Future; and the procession of the builders of the Pyramids, with us and our remotest Descendants is now passing before Him. He reads our thoughts before they are known to ourselves. He rules the movements of the Universe, and all events and revolutions are the creatures of his will. For He is the Infinite Mind and Supreme Intelligence.

3d Circuit: ARKALEUS: In the beginning Man had the WORD, and that WORD was from God: and out of the living power which in and by that WORD, was communicated to man, came the LIGHT of his existence. Let no man speak the WORD, for by it THE FATHER made light and darkness, the world and living creatures!

4th Circuit: BEL: The Chaldean upon his plains worshipped me, and the sea-loving Phœnician. They builded me temples and towers, and burned sacrifices to me upon a thousand altars. Light was divine to them, and me they thought the Sun. But I am nothing,—*nothing;* and LIGHT is the creature of the unseen GOD that taught the true religion to the Ancient Patriarchs: AWFUL, MYSTERIOUS, THE ABSOLUTE.

5th Circuit: OSIRIS: Man was created pure; and God gave him TRUTH, as he gave him LIGHT. He has lost the *truth* and found *error.* He has wandered far into darkness; and round him Sin and Shame hover evermore. The Soul that is impure, and sinful, and defiled with earthly stains cannot again unite with God; until by long trials and many purifications it is finally delivered from the old calamity; and Light overcomes Darkness and dethrones it, in the Soul.

6th Circuit: MITHRAS: God is the First; indestructible, eternal, UNCREATED, INDIVISIBLE. *Wisdom, Justice, Truth* and *Mercy,* with *Harmony* and *Love* are of his essence; and *Eternity* and *Infinitude of Extension.* He is silent, and consents with MIND, and is known to Souls through MIND alone. In Him were all things originally contained, and from Him all things were evolved. For out of His Divine SILENCE and REST, after an infinitude of time, was unfolded the WORD, or the Divine POWER; and then in turn the Mighty, everacting, measureless INTELLECT; and from the WORD were evolved the myriads of suns and systems that make the Universe; and *fire,* and *light,* and the electric HARMONY, which is the harmony of spheres and numbers: and from the INTELLECT all Souls and intellects of men.

7th Circuit: SURYA: In the Beginning, the Universe was but ONE SOUL. HE was THE ALL, alone with TIME and SPACE, and Infinite as they.

———HE HAD THIS THOUGHT: "*I Create Worlds:*" and, lo! *the Universe,* and the laws of *harmony* and *motion* that rule it, the fruit of a thought of God; and bird and beast, and every living thing but Man: and light and air, and the mysterious currents, and the dominion of mysterious numbers!

———HE HAD THIS THOUGHT: "*I Create Man whose Soul shall be my image, and he shall rule.*" And lo! Man, with senses, instinct, and a reasoning mind!

———And yet not MAN! but an *animal* that breathed, and saw and thought: until an immaterial spark from God's own Infinite Being penetrated the brain, and became the Soul: and, lo, MAN THE IMMORTAL! Thus, three-fold, fruit of God's thought, is Man; that sees and hears and feels; that thinks and reasons; that loves and is in harmony with the Universe.

8th Circuit: DIONUSOS: Before the world grew old, the primitive Truth faded out from men's Souls. Then man asked himself, "*What am I; and how and whence am I? and whither do I go?*" And the Soul looking inward upon itself strove to learn whether that 'I' were mere matter; its thought and reason and its passions and affections mere results of material combination; or a material Being enveloping an immaterial Spirit: . . and further it strove, by self-examination, to learn whether that Spirit were an individual essence, with a separate immortal existence; or an infinitesimal portion of a Great First Principle, inter-penetrating the Universe and the infinitude of space, and undulating like light and heat: . . and so they wandered further amid the mazes of error; and imagined vain philosophies; wallowing in the sloughs of materialism and sensualism, or beating their wings vainly in the vacuum of abstractions and idealities. We return to the primitive Truth.

9th Circuit: AMUN: While yet the first oaks still put forth their leaves, man lost the perfect knowledge of the One True God, the Ancient Absolute Existence, the Infinite Mind and Supreme Intelligence; and floated helplessly out upon the shoreless ocean of conjecture. Then the soul vexed itself with seeking to learn whether the material universe was a mere chance combination of atoms, or the work of Infinite Uncreated Wisdom: . . whether the Deity was a concentrated, and the Universe an extended immateriality; or whether He was a personal existence, an Omnipotent, Eternal, Supreme Essence, regulating matter at will; or subjecting it to unchangeable laws throughout eternity; and to whom, Himself Infinite and Eternal, Space and Time are unknown. With their finite limited vision, they sought to learn the source and explain the existence of Evil and Pain and Sorrow; and so they wandered ever deeper into the darkness, and were lost; and there was for them no longer any God; but only a great dumb, soulless universe, full of mere emblems and symbols. We have returned again to the Primitive Truth; and that Truth is taught in Masonry.

Th∴ Ven∴. My Brethren, the probation of our aspirant is complete; and his journey towards the light is ended. Let him behold the light! [The bandage is taken from his eyes]. The darkness is past, and the true light shineth! He that saith he is in the light, and hateth his brother, is in darkness, even until now. He that loveth his brother, abideth in the light, and there is none occasion of stumbling in him; but he that hateth his brother is in darkness, and walketh in darkness, and knoweth not whither he goeth, because that darkness hath blinded his eyes. We know that we have passed from darkness to light, because we love the brethren. Love is of God: and every one that loveth, is born of God, and knoweth God. He that loveth not, knoweth not God; for God is *Love.* If we love one another, God dwelleth in us: and this commandment have we from him, *that he who loveth God, love his brother also.* For this is the love of God,—that we keep his commandments.

The laws of Nature are the development of love, the universal law. Hence flow attraction and affinities, and the swift flash of the electric current; and tides, the clouds, the movements of the worlds, the influence of will, and the mysterious power of magnetism. Nature is one great HARMONY, and of that harmony every human soul a tone. From God it flows in never-ceasing circles; as light and splendour from his Sun. To Him the notes of that harmony return, and mingle with the mighty diapason of the spheres, and are immortal.

To enforce this potent law, God makes use of no restraint. He impassions his innumerable creatures, for that which He wishes them to do. Their liberty and their happiness are the result of their obedience to His law of Passional Attraction, or of Harmony and Happiness, the characteristic of which is Unity, or the Single Principle, the Universal, the Cause of Order, of Harmony and of Simplicity.

Dost thou desire, my Brother, to be further instructed in these great Primitive Truths, which are the Treasures of the archives of Masonry?

Cand∴. I do.

Th∴ Ven∴. Is it from pure motives that thou seekest this knowledge, and not from vain curiosity? Is thy earnest desire for wisdom and the true light; that thou mayest thereby walk in the paths of virtue?

Cand∴. It is.

Th∴ Ven∴. Art thou prepared to give to us, thy Brethren, thy most solemn pledge and promise that thou wilt strenuously endeavour faithfully to practise that pure morality that flows as a result from the great truths that thou hast heard; to repent of and regret thy short-comings and thy errors, and to submit patiently to gentle and brotherly rebuke and reprimand if thou shouldest offend?

Cand∴ I am.

Th∴ Ven∴ Go then, and upon thy bended knees, before the altar of Truth and the Great Light, emblem of the God of the Patriarchs, prepare to receive the solemn obligation of a Knight of the Sun.

[The Candidate is conducted to the altar, where he kneels, on both knees. The Brethren all kneel, like-wise, in a circle, except the three chief officers, who stand in the circle, forming part of it, on each side of the Candidate, who also forms part of the circle].

Th∴ Ven∴ His direst enemy, with whom he had eaten salt, was sacred, and his person inviolable, to the ancient Arabian. Let us, with salt, like those whose fathers remembered the flood, pledge faith and friendship to each other, and to this our Brother!

[The Th∴ Ven∴ places upon his tongue, from a golden cup, and swallows, a little salt; and after him each brother in his turn, and last the Candidate, each saying, as he does so; "*God help me to be true and loyal!*"

Th∴ Ven∴ My Brethren, you will place each his right hand upon the left breast of the brother on his left. [This is done, the three officers also kneeling, and forming part of the circle. In this position, the Candidate repeats after the Th∴ Ven∴ the following obligation].

OBLIGATION.

I, A . . . . B . . . ., in the presence of the Great First Cause that by a Thought produced the Universe, do, by the salt which I have eaten, and with a faith as inviolable as that of the ancient Arabian, hereby now and forever solemnly pledge my word and troth, and most sacredly promise, as a man and Mason, that I will ever faithfully keep, and never knowingly and intentionally, nor by grave negligence reveal, or make or allow to be made known, any of the signs, words, or other secrets of this degree, to any person not legally entitled to receive them.

————That I will never confer, or by my presence or otherwise aid in conferring this degree, until I shall have most scrupulously and thoroughly inquired into the life, conversation and reputation of the applicant, and become satisfied upon competent evidence, or of my personal knowledge, of his understanding, virtue, honour, honesty, fidelity and charity, and his zeal for and attachment to Masonry: and that I will not confer it, or assist in conferring it, upon an Atheist, an adulterer, a seducer of female innocence, or an intolerant bigot; nor upon any person whatever, without permission and authority of a regular Council; or, in a place where there is no Council, of the Supreme Council of the 33d Degree, or of a Deputy Inspector-General:

————That I will never plot or take arms against my country, nor be engaged in any scheme to her injury or disgrace: and that I will redouble my zeal to serve her, and to advance her interest, honour, and glory:

————That I will earnestly strive to understand and make my own all the instruction of this degree: and that I will, at all times hereafter, keep and strictly practise all the lessons of morality and virtue which shall result from the great truths of this degree, or which shall be taught me herein, cheerfully, heartily and sincerely, making them the rule of my life, my conduct and my conversation.

————And should I wilfully or knowingly violate this my obligation, and not repent thereof, I consent to be held forsworn: And should I fail to aid a Brother Knight in his necessities, to defend his character when unjustly assailed, to assist his widow and orphans, to advance his interests, and encourage him in his business or profession, and in all things be to him like a brother born of the same womb; or should I win from him his money, seduce his wife, mother, sister or daughter, or any other in whose reputation and welfare he is interested; or otherwise wrong him, in his property, his interest or his affections, I pray that I may be denounced everywhere as one disloyal, who hath eaten salt with his friend and afterwards betrayed him; and that the punishment of Judas Iscariot may be visited upon my head!

All: . . . And so do we all pledge our faith and solemn promise: and may God aid us to keep our faith and troth! Amen!

The Th.·. Ven.·. then raises him, and kisses him on the forehead. He then decorates him with the collar and jewel of the Degree, and gives him the Signs, Tokens and Word.

Sign: . . . ↥†☉§ the ‡⁴&☉♒♊ on the &☾☉‡♈, the ♈&♑♋♏ forming a ♎♓♑☉‡☾.

Answer: . . . Raise the ♑☿‡☾♑♀♒♌☾‡ of the ‡⁴&☉♒♊ above the &☾☉♊, perpendicularly, the ♈&♑♋♏ and ☿♈&☾‡ ♑♀♒♌☾÷♎ ↥†☾♒↥&☾♊; to indicate that there is but one God and one true religion.

Pass-Word: . . ♎♈♀♏♀♑♋.·.

Answer: . . . ☉† ¶☾♏♀‡.·.

Sacred Word: ☉♊☿♒☉♀ †☉† ☉†♀♑♒.·.

Token: . . One says to the other; ♌♀*☾ ♋☾ ♄☿♑‡ &☉♒♊♎: takes ♈&☾♋ in &♀♎, kisses his forehead, and says ☉†§&☉. The other answers ☿♋☾♌☉.

Each of the brethren then kisses the Candidate on his forehead; and the Candidate is sent to the station of the Orator, where he receives the following Lecture.

LECTURE.

My brother, you have heretofore, in some of the degrees through which you have passed, heard much of the ancient worship of the Sun, the Moon and the other bright luminaries of Heaven, and of the Elements and Powers of Universal Nature. You have been made to some extent familiar with their personifications as Heroes suffering or triumphant, or as personal Gods or Goddesses, with human characteristics and passions, and with the multitude of legends and fables that do but allegorically represent their risings and settings, their courses, their conjunctions and oppositions, their domicils and places of exaltation.

Perhaps you have supposed that we, like many who have written on these subjects, have intended to represent this worship to you as the most ancient and original worship of the first men that lived. To undeceive you, if such was your conclusion, we have re-produced in this degree that ancient worship, and personified in the different officers of our Council the Great Luminary of Heaven, under the names by which he was known to the most ancient nations; and you have at the same time heard them proclaim the old primitive truths that were known to the Fathers of our race, before men came to worship the visible manifestations of the Supreme Power and Magnificence and the Supposed Attributes of the Universal Deity in the Elements and in the glittering armies that Night regularly marshals and arrays upon the blue field of the firmament.

We ask now your attention to a still further development of these truths, after we shall have added something to what we have already said in regard to the Chief Luminary of Heaven, in explanation of the names and characteristics of the several officers of the Council who represent him.

Our Presiding Officer, named Athom or Athom-Re, is the representative of the Chief and Oldest Supreme God of Upper Egypt worshipped at Thebes, the same as the OM or AUM of the Hindūs, whose name was unpronounceable, and who, like the Brehm of the latter People was "The Being that was, and is, and is to come; the Great God, the Great Omnipotent, Omniscient and Omnipresent One, the Greatest in the Universe, the Lord;" whose emblem was a perfect sphere, showing that He was first, last, midst and without end; superior to all Nature-Gods, and all personifications of Powers, Elements and Luminaries; symbolized by Light, the Principle of Life.

The Senior Warden, named AMUN, is the representative of the Nature-God, or Spirit of Nature, called by that name or AMUN-RE, and worshipped at Memphis in Lower Egypt, and in Libya, as well as in Upper Egypt. He was the Libyan Jupiter, and represented the intelligent and organizing force that develops itself in Nature, when the intellectual types or forms of bodies are revealed to the senses in the world's order, by their union with matter, whereby the generation of bodies is effected. He was the same with Kneph, from whose mouth issued the Orphic egg out of which came the Universe.

The Junior Warden represents DIONUSOS, the Nature-God of the Greeks, as AMUN was of the Egyptians. In the popular legend, Dionusos, as well as Hercules was a Theban Hero, born of a mortal mother. Both were sons of Zeus, both persecuted by Heré. But in Hercules the God is subordinate to the Hero; while Dionusos, even in poetry, retains his divine character, and is identical with Iacchus, the presiding genius of the mysteries. Personification of the Sun in Taurus, as his ox-hoofs showed, he delivered earth from the harsh dominion of winter, conducted the mighty chorus of the Stars, and the celestial revolution of the year, changed with the seasons, and underwent their periodical decay. He was the Sun as invoked by the Eleans, Πυριγενης, ushered into the world amidst lightning and thunder, the Mighty Hunter of the Zodiac, Zagreus the Golden or ruddy-faced. The Mysteries taught the doctrine of Divine Unity; and that Power whose Oneness is a seeming mystery but really a truism, was Dionusos, the God of Nature, or of that moisture which is the life of Nature, who prepares in darkness, in Hades or Iasion, the return of life and vegetation, or is himself the light and change evolving their varieties. In the Egean Islands he was Butes, Dardanus, Himeros or Imbros; in Crete he appears as Iasius or even Zeus, whose orgiastic worship, remaining unveiled by the usual forms of mystery, betrayed to profane curiosity the symbols which if irreverently contemplated, were sure to be misunderstood.

He was the same with the dismembered Zagreus, the son of Persephone, an Ancient Subterranean Dionusos, the horned progeny of Zeus in the Constellation of the Serpent, entrusted by his father with the thunderbolt, and encircled with the protecting dance of Curetes. Through the envious artifices of Heré, the Titans eluded the vigilance of his guardians and tore him to pieces; but Pallas restored the still palpitating heart to his father, who commanded Apollo to bury the dismembered remains upon Parnassus.

Dionusos as well as Apollo was leader of the Muses; the tomb of one accompanied the worship of the other; they were the same, yet different, contrasted, yet only as filling separate parts in the same drama; and the mystic and heroic personifications, the God of Nature and of Art, seem at some remote period to have proceeded from a common source. Their separation was one of form rather than of substance; and from the time when Hercules obtained initiation from Triptolemus, or Pythagoras received Orphic tenets, the two conceptions were tending to re-combine. It was said that Dionusos or Poseidon had preceded Apollo in the Oracular office; and Dionusos continued to be esteemed in Greek Theology as Healer and Saviour, Author of Life and Immortality. The dispersed Pythagoreans, "Sons of Apollo," immediately betook themselves to the Orphic Service of Dionusos, and there are indications that there was always something Dionysiac in the worship of Apollo.

Dionusos is the Sun, that liberator of the elements; and his spiritual mediation was suggested by the same imagery which made the Zodiac the supposed path of the Spirits in their descent and their return. His second birth, as offspring of the highest, is a type of the spiritual regeneration of man. He, as well as Apollo, was precentor of the Muses, and source of inspiration. His rule prescribed no unnatural mortification: its yoke was easy, and its mirthful choruses, combining the gay with the severe, did but commemorate that golden age when earth enjoyed eternal spring, and when fountains of honey, milk and wine burst forth out of its bosom at the touch of the thyrsus. He is the "Liberator." Like Osiris he frees the soul, and guides it in its migrations beyond the grave, preserving it from the risk of again falling under the slavery of matter or of some inferior animal form. All soul is part of the Universal Soul, whose totality is Dionusos; and he leads back the vagrant spirit to its home, and accompanies it through the purifying processes, both real and symbolical, of its earthly transit. He died and descended to the Shades; and his suffering was the great secret of the Mysteries, as death is the grand mystery of existence. He is the immortal suitor of Psyche (the

Soul), the Divine influence which physically called the world into being, and which, awakening the soul from its Stygian trance, restores it from earth to Heaven.

Of HERMES, the Mercury of the Greeks, the Thoth of the Egyptians and the Taaut of the Phœnicians, we have heretofore spoken sufficiently at length. He was the inventor of letters and of Oratory, the winged messenger of the Gods, bearing the Caduceus wreathed with serpents; and in our Council he is represented by the ORATOR.

Seven other officers of the Council, whose lessons you have heard uttered in the impressive language of the Great Past, bear seven names of the Sun, by which that luminary was called among the most ancient nations: The *Hindūs* called him SURYA; the *Persians*, MITHRAS: the *Egyptians*, OSIRIS; the *Assyrians* and *Chaldæans*, BEL; the *Scythians* and *Etruscans* and the ancient *Pelasgi*, ARKALEUS or HERCULES, the *Phœnicians*, ADONI or ADON, and the *Scandinavians*, ODIN.

From the name SURYA, given by the Hindūs to the Sun, the Sect who paid him particular adoration were called *Souras*. Their painters describe his car as drawn by seven green horses. In the Temple of Visweswara, at Benares, there is an ancient piece of sculpture, well executed in stone, representing him sitting in a car drawn by a horse with twelve heads. His charioteer, by whom he is preceded, is ARUN [from אור, AUR, the *Crepusculum ?*], or the Dawn; and among his many titles are twelve that denote his distinct powers in each of the twelve months. Those powers are called Adityas, each of whom has a particular name. Surya is supposed frequently to have descended upon earth, in a human shape, and to have left a race on earth, equally renowned in Indian story with the Heliades of Greece. He is often styled King of the Stars and Planets, and thus reminds us of the Adon-Tsbauth (Lord of the Starry Hosts) of the Hebrew writings.

MITHRAS was the Sun-God of the Persians; and was fabled to have been born in a grotto or cave, at the winter solstice. His feasts were celebrated at that period, at the moment when the sun commenced to return Northward, and to increase the length of the days. This was the great Feast of the Magian religion. The Roman Calendar, published in the time of Constantine, at which period his worship began to gain ground in the Occident, fixed his feast-day on the 25th of December. His statues and images were inscribed, *Deo-Soli invicto Mithræ*—to the invincible Sun-God, Mithras. *Nomen invictum Sol Mithra . . . Soli Omnipotenti Mithræ.* To him, gold, incense and myrrh were consecrated. "Thee," says Martianus Capella, in his hymn to the Sun, "the dwellers on the Nile adore as Serapis, and Memphis worships as Osiris; in the sacred rites of Persia thou art Mithras, in Phrygia, Atys, and Libya bows down to thee as Ammon, and Phœnician Byblos as Adonis; and thus the whole world adores thee under different names."

OSIRIS was son of Helios (Phra) the "divine offspring congenerate with the dawn," and at the same time an incarnation of Kneph or Agathodæmon, the Good Spirit, including all his possible manifestations, either physical or moral. He represented in a familiar form the beneficent aspect of all higher emanations; and in him was developed the conception of a Being purely good, so that it became necessary to set up another power as his adversary, called Seth, Babys or Typhon, to account for the injurious influences of Nature.

With the phenomena of agriculture, supposed to be the invention of Osiris, the Egyptians connected the highest truths of their religion. The soul of man was as the seed hidden in the ground, and the mortal framework similarly consigned to its dark resting-place, awaited its restoration to life's unfailing source. Osiris was not only benefactor of the living; he was also Hades, Serapis and Rhadamanthus, the monarch of the dead. Death, therefore, in Egyptian opinion, was only another name for *renovation*, since its God is the same power who incessantly renews vitality in Nature. Every corpse duly embalmed was called 'Osiris,' and in the grave was supposed to be united, or at least brought into approximation, to the Divinity. For when God became incarnate for man's benefit, it was implied that, in analogy with his assumed character, he should submit to *all* the conditions of visible existence. In death, as in life, Isis and Osiris were patterns and precursors of mankind; their sepulchres stood within the temples of the Superior Gods; yet though their remains might be entombed at Memphis or Abydus, their divinity was unimpeached, and they either shone as luminaries in the Heavens, or in the unseen world presided over the futurity of the disembodied spirits whom death had brought nearer to them.

The notion of a dying God, so frequent in Oriental legend, and of which we have already said much in former degrees, was the natural inference from a literal interpretation of nature-worship; since nature, which in the vicissitudes of the seasons seems to undergo a dissolution, was to the earliest religionists the express image of the Deity, and at a remote period one and the same with the "varied God," whose attributes were seen not only in its vitality, but in its changes. The unseen Mover of the Universe was rashly identified with its obvious fluctuations. The speculative Deity suggested by the drama of nature, was worshipped with imitative and sympathetic rites. A period of mourning about the autumnal equinox, and of joy at the return of spring, was almost universal. Phrygians and Paphlagonians, Bœotians, and even Athenians, were all more or less attached to such observances; the Syrian damsels sat weeping for Thammuz or Adoni, mortally wounded by the tooth of Winter, symbolized by the boar, its very general emblem: and these rites, and those of Atys and Osiris were evidently suggested by the arrest of vegetation, when the Sun, descending from his altitude, seems deprived of his generating power.

Osiris is a being analogous to the Syrian Adoni; and the fable of his history, which we need not here repeat, is a narrative form of the popular religion of Egypt, of which the Sun is the Hero, and the agricultural calendar the moral. The moist valley of the Nile, owing its fertility to the annual inundation, appeared, in contrast with the surrounding desert, like life in the midst of death. The inundation was in evident dependence on the Sun, and Egypt, environed with arid deserts, like a heart within a burning censer, was the female power, dependent on the influences personified in its God. Typhon his brother, the type of darkness, drought and sterility, threw his body into the Nile; and thus Osiris, the "good," the "Saviour," perished, in the 28th year of his life or reign, and on the 17th day of the month Athor, or the 13th of November. He is also made to die during the heats of the early summer, when, from March to July the earth was parched with intolerable heat, vegetation was scorched, and the languid Nile exhausted. From that death he rises when the Solstitial Sun brings the inundation, and Egypt is filled with mirth and acclamation anticipatory of the second harvest. From his wintry death he rises with the early flowers of spring, and then the joyful festival of Osiris found was celebrated.

So the pride of Jemsheed, one of the Persian Sun-heroes, or the solar year personified, was abruptly cut off by Zohak, the tyrant of the West. He was sawn asunder by a fish-bone, and immediately the brightness of Iran changed to gloom. Ganymede and Adonis, like Osiris, were hurried off in all their strength and beauty; the premature death of Linus, the burthen of the ancient lament of Greece, was like that of the Persian Siamek, the Bithynian Hylas, and the Egyptian Maneros, Son of Menes or the Eternal. The elegy called Maneros was sung at Egyptian banquets, and an effigy enclosed within a diminutive Sarcophagus was handed round to remind the guests of the brief tenure of existence. The beautiful Memnon, also, perished in his prime; and Enoch, whose early death was lamented at Iconium, lived 365 years, the number of days of the solar year; a brief space when compared with the longevity of his patriarchal kindred.

The story of Osiris is reflected in those of Orpheus and Dionusos Zagreus, and perhaps in the legends of Absyrtus and Pelias, of Æson, Thyestes, Melicertes, Itys and Pelops. Io is the disconsolate Isis or Niobe: and Rhea mourns her dismembered Lord, Hyperion, and the death of her son Helios, drowned in the Eridanus; and if Apollo and Dionusos are immortal, they had died under other names, as Orpheus, Linus or Hyacinthus. The sepulchre of Zeus was shown in Crete. Hippolytus was associated in divine honours with Apollo, and after he had been torn to pieces like Osiris, was restored to life by the Pæonian herbs of Diana, and kept darkling in the secret grove of Egeria. Zeus deserted Olympus to visit the Ethiopians; Apollo underwent servitude to Admetus; Theseus, Peirithous, Hercules and other heroes, descended for a time to Hades; a dying Nature-God was exhibited in the Mysteries, the Attic women fasted, sitting on the ground, during the Thesmophoria, and the Bœotians lamented the descent of Cora-Proserpine to the Shades.

But the death of the Deity, as understood by the Orientals, was not inconsistent with his immortality. The temporary decline of the Sons of Light is but an episode in their endless continuity; and as the day and year are more convenient subdivisions of the Infinite, so the fiery deaths of Phaëthon or Hercules are but breaks in the same Phœnix process of perpetual regeneration, by which the spirit of Osiris lives forever in the succession of the Memphian Apis. Every year witnesses the revival of Adonis; and the amber tears shed by the Heliades for the premature death of their brother, are the golden shower full of prolific hope, in which Zeus descends from the brazen vault of heaven into the bosom of the parched ground.

BEL, representative or personification of the sun, was one of the Great Gods of Syria, Assyria and Chaldea, and his name is found upon the monuments of Nimroud, and frequently occurs in the Hebrew writings. He was the Great Nature-God of Babylonia, the Power of heat, life and generation. His symbol was the Sun, and he was figured seated on a bull. All the accessories of his great temple at Babylon, described by Herodotus, are repeated with singular fidelity, but on a smaller scale, in the Hebrew tabernacle and temple. The golden statue alone is wanted to complete the resemblance. The word *Bel* or *Baal*, like the word *Adon*, signifies Lord and Master. He was also the Supreme Deity of the Moabites, Amonites and Carthaginians and of the Sabeans in general; the Gauls worshipped the Sun under the name of Belin or Belinus: and Bela is found among the Celtic Deities upon the ancient monuments.

The Northern ancestors of the Greeks maintained with hardier habits a more manly style of religious symbolism than the effeminate enthusiasts of the South, and had embodied in their *Perseus*, HERCULES and MITHRAS the consummation of the qualities they esteemed and exercised.

Almost every nation will be found to have had a mythical being, whose strength or weakness, virtues or defects, more or less nearly describe the Sun's career through the seasons. There was a Celtic, a Teutonic, a Scythian, an Etruscan, a Lydian Hercules, all whose legends became tributary to those of the Greek hero. The name of Hercules was found by Herodotus to have been long familiar in Egypt and the East, and to have originally belonged to a much higher personage than the comparatively modern hero known in Greece as the Son of Alcmena. The temple of the Hercules of Tyre was reported to have been built 2300 years before the time of Herodotus; and Hercules, whose Greek name has been sometimes supposed to be of Phœnician origin, in the sense of Circuitor, *i. e.* "rover" and "perambulator" of earth, as well as "Hyperion" of the sky, was the patron and model of those famous navigators who spread his altars from coast to coast through the Mediterranean, to the extremities of the West, where "ARKALEUS" built the City of Gades, and where a perpetual fire burned in his service. He was the lineal descendant of Perseus, the luminous child of darkness, conceived within a subterranean vault of brass; and he a representation of the Persian Mithras, rearing his emblematic lions above the gates of Mycenæ, and bringing the sword of Jemsheed to battle against the Gorgons of the West. Mithras is similarly described in the Zend-Avesta as the "mighty hero, the rapid runner, whose piercing eye embraces all, whose arm bears the club for the destruction of the Darood."

Hercules Ingeniculus, who bending on one knee uplifts his club and tramples on the Serpent's head, was, like Prometheus and Tantalus, one of the varying aspects of the struggling and declining Sun. The victories of Hercules are but exhibitions of Solar power which have ever to be repeated. It was in the far North, among the Hyperboreans, that, divested of his Lion's skin, he lay down to sleep, and for a time lost the horses of his chariot. Henceforth that Northern region of gloom, called the "place of the death and revival of Adonis," that Caucasus whose summit was so lofty, that, like the Indian Meru, it seemed to be both the goal and commencement of the Sun's career, became to Greek imaginations the final bourne of all things, the abode of winter and desolation, the pinnacle of the arch connecting the upper and lower world, and consequently the appropriate place for the banishment of Prometheus. The daughters of Israel, weeping for Thammuz, mentioned by Ezekiel, sat looking to the North, and waiting for his return from that region. It was while Cybele with the Sun-God was absent among the Hyperboreans, that Phrygia, abandoned by her, suffered the horrors of famine. Delos and Delphi awaited the return of Apollo from the Hyperboreans, and Hercules brought thence to Olympia the olive. To all Masons, the North has immemorially been the place of darkness, and of the great lights of the Lodge, none is in the North.

Mithras, the rock-born hero (Πετρογενης), heralded the Sun's return in Spring, as Prometheus, chained in his cavern, betokened the continuance of Winter. The Persian beacon on the mountain-top represented the Rock-born Divinity enshrined in his worthiest temple; and the funeral conflagration of Hercules was the sun dying in glory behind the Western hills. But though the transitory manifestation suffers or dies, the abiding and eternal power liberates and saves. It was an essential attribute of a Titan, that he should arise again after his fall; for the revival of Nature is as certain as its decline, and its alternations are subject to the appointment of a power which controls them both.

"God," says Maximus Tyrius, " did not spare his own Son [Hercules], or exempt him from the calamities incidental to humanity." The Theban progeny of Jove had his share of pain and trial. By vanquishing earthly difficulties he proved his affinity with Heaven. His life was a continued struggle. He fainted before Typhon in the desert ; and in the commencement of the autumnal season, (cum longæ redit hora noctis) descended under the guidance of Minerva to Hades. He died ; but first applied for initiation to Eumolpus, in order to foreshadow that state of religious preparation which should precede the momentous change. Even in Hades he rescued Theseus and removed the stone of Ascalaphus, reanimated the bloodless spirits, and dragged into the light of day the monster Cerberus, justly reputed invincible because an emblem of Time itself ; he burst the chains of the grave (for Busiris is the grave personified), and triumphant at the close as in the dawn of his career, was received after his labours into the repose of the heavenly mansions, living for-ever with Zeus in the arms of Eternal Youth.

Odin is said to have borne twelve names among the old Germans, and to have had 114 names besides. He was the Apollo of the Scandinavians, and is represented in the Voluspa as destined to slay the monstrous snake. Then the Sun will be extinguished, the earth be dissolved in the ocean, the stars lose their bright-ness, and all Nature be destroyed in order that it may be renewed again. From the bosom of the waters a new world will emerge clad in verdure ; harvests will be seen to ripen where no seed was sown, and evil will disappear.

The free fancy of the ancients, which wove the web of their myths and legends, was consecrated by faith. It had not, like the modern mind, set apart a petty sanctuary of borrowed beliefs, beyond which all the rest was common and unclean. Imagination, reason and religion circled round the same symbol ; and in all their symbols there was serious meaning, if we could but find it out. They did not devise fictions in the same vapid spirit, in which we, cramped by conventionalities, read them. In endeavouring to interpret creations of fancy, fancy as well as reason must guide : and much of modern controversy arises out of heavy appre-hensions of ancient symbolism.

To those ancient peoples, this earth was the centre of the Universe. To them there were no other worlds, peopled with living beings, to divide the care and attention of the Deity. To them the world was a great plain, of unknown, perhaps inconceivable limits, and the Sun, the Moon and the Stars journeyed above it, to give them light. The worship of the Sun became the basis of all the religions of antiquity. To them light and heat were mysteries ; as indeed they still are to us. As the Sun caused the day, and his absence the night ; as, when he journeyed Northward, spring and summer followed him ; and when he again turned to the South, autumn and inclement winter, and cold and long dark nights ruled the earth ; . . . as his influence produced the leaves and flowers, and ripened the harvests, and brought regular inundation, he necessarily became to them the most interesting object of the material universe. To them he was the innate fire of bodies, the fire of nature. Author of Life, heat and ignition, he was to them the efficient cause of all generation, for without him there was no movement, no existence, no form. He was to them immense, indivisible, imperish-able, and everywhere present. It was their need of light, and of his creative energy, that was felt by all men ; and nothing was more fearful to them than his absence. His beneficent influences caused his identification with the Principle of Good ; and the Brahma of the Hindus, the Mithras of the Persians, the Athom, Amun, Phtha and Osiris of the Egyptians, the Bel of the Chaldeans, the Adonai of the Phœnicians, the Adonis and Apollo of the Greeks became but personifications of the Sun, the regenerating Principle, image of that fecundity which perpetuates and re-juvenates the world's existence.

So too the struggle between the Good and Evil Principles was personified, as was that between life and death, destruction and re-creation ; in allegories and fables which poetically represented the apparent course of the Sun ; who, descending towards the Southern Hemisphere, was figuratively said to be conquered and put to death by darkness, or the genius of Evil ; but, returning again towards the Northern Hemisphere, he seemed to be victorious, and to arise from the tomb. This death and resurrection were also figurative of the succes-sion of day and night, of death, which is a necessity of life, and of life which is born of death ; and everywhere the ancients still saw the combat between the two Principles that ruled the world. Everywhere this contest was embodied in allegories and fictitious histories : into which were ingeniously woven all the astronomical phenomena that accompanied, preceded or followed the different movements of the Sun, and the changes of

Seasons, the approach or withdrawal of inundation. And thus grew into stature and strange proportions the histories of the contests between Typhon and Osiris, Hercules and Juno, the Titans and Jupiter, Ormuzd and Ahriman, the rebellious Angels and the Deity, the Evil Genii and the Good; and the other like fables, found not only in Asia, but in the North of Europe, and even among the Mexicans and Peruvians of the New World; carried thither, in all probability, by those Phœnician voyagers who bore thither civilization and the arts. The Scythians lamented the death of Acmón, the Persians that of Zohak conquered by Pheridoun, the Hindûs that of Soura-Parama slain by Soupra-Muni, as the Scandinavians did that of Balder, torn to pieces by the blind Hother.

The primitive idea of infinite space existed in the first men, as it exists in us. It and the idea of infinite time are the two first innate ideas. Man cannot conceive how thing can be added to thing, or event follow event, forever. The idea will ever return, that no matter how long bulk is added to bulk, there must be, still beyond, an empty void, *without* limit; in which is *nothing.* In the same way the idea of time without beginning or end forces itself on him. *Time,* without events, is also a *void,* and *nothing.*

In that empty void space the primitive men knew there was no light, nor warmth. They *felt* what we know scientifically, that there must be a thick darkness there, and an intensity of cold of which we have no conception. Into that void they thought the Sun, the Planets and the Stars went down when they set under the Western Horizon. Darkness was to them an enemy, a harm, a vague dread and terror. It was the very embodiment of the evil principle; and out of it they said that he was formed. As the Sun bent southward towards that void, they shuddered with dread: and when at the winter solstice, he again commenced his northward march they rejoiced and feasted; as they did at the summer solstice, when most he appeared to smile upon them in his pride of place. These days have been celebrated by all civilized nations ever since. The Christian has made them feast days of the church, and appropriated them to the two Saints John; and Masonry has done the same.

We, to whom the vast universe has become but a great *machine,* not instinct with a great SOUL, but a *clock-work,* of proportions unimaginable, but still infinitely less than infinite; and part at least of which we with our orreries can imitate; we, who have measured the distances and dimensions, and learned the specific gravity and determined the orbits of the moon and the planets; we, who know the distance to the sun, and his size; have measured the orbits of the flashing comets, and the distances of the fixed stars; and know the latter to be suns like our sun, each with his retinue of worlds, and all governed by the same unerringly mechanical laws and outwardly imposed forces, centripetal and centrifugal; we, that with our telescopes have separated the galaxy and the nebulæ into other stars and groups of stars; discovered new planets, by first discovering their disturbing forces upon those already known; and learned that they all, Jupiter, Venus and the fiery Mars, and Saturn and the others, as well as the bright, mild and ever-changing Moon, are mere dark, dull, opaque clods like our earth, and not living orbs of brilliant fire and heavenly light; we, who have counted the mountains and chasms in the moon, with glasses that could distinctly reveal to us the temple of Solomon, if it stood there in its old original glory; we, who no longer imagine that the stars control our destinies, and who can calculate the eclipses of the sun and moon, backward and forward, for ten thousand years; we, with our vastly increased conceptions of the powers of the Grand Architect of the Universe, but our wholly material and mechanical view of that Universe itself; we cannot even in the remotest degree *feel,* though we may partially and imperfectly *imagine,* how those great, primitive, simple-hearted children of Nature felt in regard to the Starry Hosts, there upon the slopes of the Himalayas, on the Chaldean plains, in the Persian and Median deserts, and upon the banks of that great, strange River the Nile. To them the Universe was *alive*—instinct with forces and powers, mysterious and beyond their comprehension. To them it was no machine, no great system of clock-work; but a great live creature, an army of creatures, in sympathy with or inimical to man. To them, all was a mystery and a miracle, and the stars flashing overhead spoke to their hearts almost in an audible language. Jupiter with his kingly splendours was the Emperor of the starry legions. Venus looked lovingly on the earth and blessed it; Mars, with his crimson fires, threatened war and misfortune; and Saturn, cold and grave, chilled and repelled them. The ever-changing Moon, faithful companion of the Sun, was a constant miracle and wonder; the Sun himself the visible emblem of the creative and generative power. To them the earth was a great plain, over which the sun, the moon and the planets revolved, its servants, framed to give it light. Of the stars, some were beneficent existences that brought with them spring-time and fruits and flowers,—some, faithful sentinels, advising them of coming inundation, of the season of storm and of deadly winds; some heralds of evil, which steadily foretelling they seemed to cause. To them the eclipses were portents of evil, and their causes hidden in mystery, and supernatural. The regular returns of the stars, the comings of Arcturus, Orion, Sirius, the Pleiades and Aldebaran, and the journeyings of the Sun, were voluntary and not mechanical, to them. What wonder that astronomy became to them the most important of sciences; that those who learned it became rulers; and that vast edifices, the Pyramids, the tower or temple of Bel, and other like erections everywhere in the East were builded for astronomical purposes?—and what wonder that, in their great child-like simplicity they worshipped Light, the Sun, the Planets and the Stars, and personified them, and eagerly believed in the histories invented for them; in that age when the capacity for belief was infinite; as indeed, if we but reflect, it still is and ever will be?

If we adhered to the literally historic sense, antiquity would be a mere, inexplicable, hideous chaos, and all the Sages deranged: and so it would be with Masonry and those who instituted it. But when these allegories are explained, they cease to be absurd fables, or facts purely local; and become lessons of wisdom for entire humanity. No one can doubt, who studies them, that they all came from a common source.

And he greatly errs who imagines, that, because the mythological legends and fables of antiquity are referable to and have their foundation in the phenomena of the Heavens, and all the Heathen Gods are but mere names given to the Sun, the Stars, the Planets, the Zodiacal Signs, the Elements, the Powers of Nature, and Universal Nature herself, therefore the first men worshipped the Stars, and whatever things, animate and inanimate, seemed to them to possess and exercise a power or influence, evident or imagined, over human fortunes and human destiny.

For ever, in all the nations, ascending to the remotest antiquity to which the light of History or the glimmerings of tradition reach, we find, seated above all the Gods which represent the luminaries and the elements, and those which personify the innate Powers of universal nature, a still higher Deity, silent, undefined, incomprehensible, the Supreme, one God, from whom all the rest flow or emanate, or by Him are created. Above the Time-God Horus, the Moon-Goddess or Earth-Goddess Isis, and the Sun-God Osiris, of the Egyptians, was Amun, the Nature-God; and above him, again, the Infinite, Incomprehensible Deity, ATMON. BREHM, the silent, self-contemplative, one original God, was the Source, to the Hindūs, of Brahma, Vishnu and Siva. Above Zeus, or before him, were Kronos and Ouranos. Over the Elohim was the great Nature-God AL, and still beyond him, Abstract Existence, IHUH—He that IS, WAS and SHALL BE. Above all the Persian Deities was the Unlimited Time, ZERUANE-AKHERENE; and over Odin and Thor was the Great Scandinavian Deity ALFADIR.

The worship of Universal Nature as a God was too near akin to the worship of a Universal Soul, to have been the instinctive creed of any savage people or rude race of men. To imagine all nature, with all its apparently independent parts, as forming one consistent whole, and as itself a unit, required an amount of experience and a faculty of generalization not possessed by the rude uncivilized mind, and is but a step below the idea of a universal Soul.

In the beginning man had the WORD; and that WORD was from God: and out of the living POWER communicated to man in and by that WORD, came THE LIGHT of His Existence.

God made man in his own likeness. When, by a long succession of geological changes, He had prepared the earth to be his habitation, He created him, and placed him in that part of Asia which all the old nations agreed in calling the cradle of the human race, and whence afterwards the stream of human life flowed forth to India, China, Egypt, Persia, Arabia and Phœnicia. He communicated to him a complete knowledge of the nature of his Creator, and of the pure, primitive, undefiled religion. The peculiar and distinctive excellence, and real essence of the primitive man, and his true nature and destiny consisted in his likeness to God. He stamped His own image upon man's soul. That image has been, in the breast of every individual man and of mankind in general, greatly altered, impaired and defaced; but its old, half-obliterated characters are still to be found on all the pages of primitive history; and the impress, not entirely effaced, every reflecting mind may discover in its own interior.

Of the original revelation to mankind, of the primitive WORD of Divine TRUTH, we find clear indications and scattered traces in the sacred traditions of all the primitive Nations; traces which, when separately examined, appear like the broken remnants, the mysterious and hieroglyphic characters, of a mighty edifice that has been destroyed; and its fragments, like those of the old Temples and Palaces of Nimroud, wrought incongruously into edifices many centuries younger. And, although amid the ever-growing degeneracy of mankind, this primeval word of revelation was falsified by the admixture of various errors, and overlaid and obscured by numberless and manifold fictions, inextricably confused, and disfigured almost beyond the power of recognition, still a profound inquiry will discover in heathenism many luminous vestiges of primitive Truth.

For the old Heathenism had everywhere a foundation in Truth; and if we could separate that pure intuition into nature and into the simple symbols of nature, that constituted the basis of all Heathenism, from the alloy of error and the additions of fiction, those first hieroglyphic traits of the instinctive science of the first men, would be found to agree with truth and a true knowledge of nature, and to afford an image of a free, pure, comprehensive and finished philosophy of life.

The struggle, thenceforward to be eternal, between the Divine will and the natural will in the souls of men, commenced immediately after the creation. Cain slew his brother Abel, and went forth to people parts of the earth with an impious race, forgetters and defiers of the true God. The other Descendants of the Common Father of the race intermarried with the daughters of Cain's Descendants: and all nations preserved the remembrance of that division of the human family into the righteous and impious, in their distorted legends of the wars between the Gods, and the Giants and Titans. When, afterwards, another similar division occurred, the Descendants of Seth alone preserved the true primitive religion and science, and transmitted them to posterity in the ancient symbolical character, on monuments of stone: and many nations preserved in their legendary traditions the memory of the columns of Enoch and Seth.

Then the world declined from its original happy condition and fortunate estate, into idolatry and barbarism: but all nations retained the memory of that old estate; and the poets, in those early days the only historians, commemorated the succession of the ages of gold, silver, brass and iron.

In the lapse of those ages, the sacred tradition followed various courses among each of the most ancient nations; and from its original source, as from a common centre, its various streams flowed downward; some diffusing through favoured regions of the world fertility and life; but others soon losing themselves and being dried up in the sterile sands of human error.

After the internal and Divine WORD originally communicated by God to man, had become obscured; after man's connexion with his Creator had been broken, even outward language necessarily fell into disorder and confusion. The simple and Divine Truth was overlaid with various and sensual fictions, buried under illusive symbols, and at last perverted into horrible phantoms.

For in the progress of idolatry, it needs came to pass, that what was originally revered as the symbol of a higher principle, became gradually confounded or identified with the object itself, and was worshipped; until this error led to a more degraded form of idolatry. The early nations received much from the primeval source of sacred tradition; but that haughty pride which seems an inherent part of human nature led each to represent these fragmentary relics of original truth as a possession peculiar to themselves; thus exaggerating their value, and their own importance, as peculiar favourites of the Deity, who had chosen them as the favoured people to whom to commit these truths. To make these fragments, as far as possible, their private property, they re-produced them under peculiar forms, wrapped them up in symbols, concealed them in allegories, and invented fables to account for their own special possession of them. So that, instead of preserving in their primitive simplicity and purity these blessings of original revelation, they overlaid them with poetical ornament; and the whole wears a fabulous aspect, until by close and severe examination we discover the truth which the apparent fable contains.

These being the conflicting elements in the breast of man; the old inheritance or original dowry of truth, imparted to him by God in the primitive revelation; and error, or the foundation for error, in his degraded sense and spirit now turned from God to nature, false faiths easily sprung up and grew rank and luxuriant, when the Divine Truth was no longer guarded with jealous care, nor preserved in its pristine purity. This soon happened among most Eastern nations, and especially the Indians, the Chaldeans, the Arabians, the Persians and the Egyptians; with whom imagination and a very deep, but still sensual feeling for nature, were very predominant. The Northern firmament, visible to their eyes, possesses by far the largest and most brilliant constellations; and they were more alive to the impressions made by such objects, than the men of the present day.

With the Chinese, a patriarchal, simple and secluded people, idolatry long made but little progress. They invented writing within three or four generations after the flood; and they long preserved the memory of much of the primitive revelation; less overlaid with fiction than those fragments which other nations have remembered. They were among those who stood nearest to the source of sacred tradition; and many passages in their old writings contain remarkable vestiges of eternal truth, and of the WORD of primitive revelation, the heritage of old thought, which attest to us their original eminence.

But among the other early nations, a wild enthusiasm and a sensual idolatry of nature soon superseded the simple worship of the Almighty God, and set aside or disfigured the pure belief in the Eternal Uncreated Spirit. The great powers and elements of nature, and the vital principle of production and procreation through all generations; then the celestial spirits or heavenly Host, the luminous armies of the Stars, and the great Sun, and mysterious ever-changing Moon (all of which the whole ancient world regarded not as mere globes of light or bodies of fire, but as animated living substances, potent over man's fate and destinies); next the Genii and tutelar spirits, and even the souls of the dead, received divine worship. The animals, representing the starry constellations, first reverenced as symbols merely, came to be worshipped as Gods; the Heavens, earth, and the operations of nature were personified; and fictitious personages invented to account for the introduction of science and arts, and the fragments of the old religious truths; and the good and bad principles personified, became also objects of worship; while, through all, still shone the silver threads of the old primitive revelation.

Increasing familiarity with early oriental records seems more and more to confirm the probability that they all originally emanated from one source. The eastern and southern slopes of the Paropismus or Hindukusch, appear to have been inhabited by kindred Iranian races, similar in habits, language and religion. The earliest Indian and Persian Deities are for the most part symbols of celestial light, their agency being regarded as an eternal warfare with the powers of winter, storm and darkness. The religion of both was originally a worship of outward nature, especially the manifestations of fire and light; the coincidences being too marked to be merely accidental. Deva, God, is derived from the root *div*, to shine. Indra, like Ormuzd or Ahura-Mazda, is the bright firmament: Sura or Surya, the Heavenly, a name of the Sun, recurs in the Zend word Huare, the Sun, whence Khur and Khorshid or Corasch. Uschas and Mitra are Medic as well as Zend Deities; and the Amschaspands or "immortal Holy Ones" of the Zend-avesta may be compared with the seven Rishis or Vedic Star-Gods of the constellation of the Bear. Zoroastrianism, like Buddhism, was an innovation in regard to an older religion; and between the Parsee and Brahmin may be found traces of disruption as well as of coincidence. The original Nature-worship, in which were combined the conceptions both of a Universal Presence and perpetuity of action, took different directions of development, according to the difference between the Indian and Persian mind.

The early shepherds of the Punjaub, then called the country of the Seven Rivers, to whose intuitional or inspired wisdom (Veda) we owe what are perhaps the most ancient religious effusions extant in any language, apostrophized as living beings the physical objects of their worship. First in this order of Deities stands Indra, the God of the "blue" or "glittering" firmament, called Devaspiti, Father of the Devas or Elemental Powers, who measured out the circle of the sky, and made fast the foundations of the Earth; the ideal domain of Varouna, "the All-encompasser," is almost equally extensive, including air, water, night, the expanse between Heaven and Earth; Agni, who lives on the fire of the sacrifice, on the domestic hearth, and in the lightnings of the sky, is the great Mediator between God and Man; Uschas, or the Dawn, leads forth the Gods in the morning to make their daily repast in the intoxicating Soma of Nature's offertory, of which the Priest could only compound from simples a symbolical imitation. Then came the various Sun-Gods, Adityas or Solar Attributes, Surya the Heavenly, Savitri the Progenitor, Pashan the Nourisher, Bagha the Felicitous, and Mitra the Friend.

The coming forth of the Eternal Being to the work of creation was represented as a marriage, his first emanation being a universal mother, supposed to have potentially existed with him from Eternity, or in metaphorical language, to have been "his sister and his spouse." She became eventually promoted to be the Mother of the Indian Trinity, of the Deity under His three Attributes, of Creation, Preservation, and Change or Regeneration.

The most popular forms or manifestations of Vishnu the Preserver, were his successive avataras or historic impersonations, which represented the Deity coming forth out of the incomprehensible mystery of His nature, and revealing himself at those critical epochs which either in the physical or moral world seemed to mark a new commencement of prosperity and order. Combating the power of Evil in the various departments of Nature, and in successive periods of time, the Divinity, though varying in form, is ever in reality the same, whether seen in useful agricultural or social inventions, in traditional victories over rival creeds, or in physical changes faintly discovered through tradition, or suggested by cosmogonical theory. As Rama, the Epic hero armed with sword, club and arrows, the prototype of Hercules and Mithras, he wrestles like the Hebrew Patriarch with the Powers of Darkness; as Chrishna-Govinda, the Divine Shepherd, he is the Messenger of Peace, overmastering the world by music and love. Under the human form he never ceases to be the Supreme Being. "The foolish," (he says, in the Bhagavad Ghita), "unacquainted with my Supreme Nature, despise me in this human form, while men of great minds, enlightened by the Divine principle within them, acknowledge me as incorruptible and before all things, and serve me with undivided hearts." "I am not recognized by all," he says again, "because concealed by the supernatural power which is in me; yet to me are known all things past, present and to come; I existed before Vaivaswata and Menou. I am the Most High God, the Creator of the World, the Eternal Pooroosha (Man-World or Genius of the World). And although in my own nature I am exempt from liability to birth or death, and am Lord of all created things, yet as often as in the world virtue is enfeebled, and vice and injustice prevail, so often do I become manifest and am revealed from age to age, to save the just, to destroy the guilty, and to reassure the faltering steps of virtue. He who acknowledgeth me as even so, doth not on quitting this mortal frame enter into another, for he entereth into me; and many who have trusted in me have already entered into me, being purified by the power of wisdom. I help those who walk in my path, even as they serve me."

Brahma, the creating agent, sacrificed himself, when, by descending into material forms he became incorporated with his work; and his mythological history was interwoven with that of the Universe. Thus, although spiritually allied to the Supreme, and Lord of all creatures (Prajapati), he shared the imperfection and corruption of an inferior nature, and steeped in manifold and perishable forms, might be said, like the Greek Uranus, to be mutilated and fallen. He thus combined two characters, formless form, immortal and mortal, being and non-being, motion and rest. As incarnate Intelligence or THE WORD, he communicated to man what had been revealed to himself by the Eternal, since he is creation's Soul as well as Body, within which the Divine Word is written in those living letters which it is the prerogative of the self-conscious spirit to interpret.

The fundamental principles of the religion of the Hindūs consisted in the belief in the existence of One Being only, of the immortality of the soul, and of a future state of rewards and punishments. Their precepts of morality inculcate the practice of virtue as necessary for procuring happiness even in this transient life; and their religious doctrines make their felicity in a future state to depend upon it.

Besides their doctrine of the transmigration of souls, their dogmas may be epitomized under the following heads: 1st. The existence of one God, from whom all things proceed, and to whom all must return. To Him they constantly apply these expressions—The Universal and Eternal Essence; that which has ever been and will ever continue; that which vivifies and pervades all things; He who is everywhere present, and causes the celestial bodies to revolve in the course He has prescribed to them. 2d. A tripartite division of the Good Principle, for the purposes of Creation, Preservation and Renovation by change and death. 3d. The necessary existence of an Evil Principle, occupied in counteracting the benevolent purposes of the first, in their execution by the Devata or Subordinate Genii, to whom is entrusted the control over the various operations of nature.

And this was part of their doctrine: "One great and incomprehensible Being has alone existed from all Eternity. Everything we behold and we ourselves are portions of Him. The soul, mind or intellect, of Gods and men, and of all sentient creatures, are detached portions of the Universal Soul, to which at stated periods they are destined to return. But the mind of finite beings is impressed by one uninterrupted series of illusions, which they consider as real, until again united to the great fountain of truth. Of these illusions, the first and most essential is individuality. By its influence, when detached from its source, the soul becomes ignorant of its own nature, origin and destiny. It considers itself as a separate existence, and no longer a spark of the Divinity, a link of one immeasurable chain, an infinitely small but indispensable portion of one great whole."

Their love of imagery caused them to personify what they conceived to be some of the attributes of God, perhaps in order to present things in a way better adapted to the comprehensions of the vulgar, than the abstruse idea of an indescribable invisible God; and hence the invention of a Brahma, a Vishnu and a Siva or Iswara. These were represented under various forms; but no emblem or visible sign of Brihm or Brehm, the Omnipotent, is to be found. They considered the great mystery of the existence of the Supreme Ruler of the Universe, as beyond human comprehension. Every creature, endowed with the faculty of thinking, they held, must be conscious of the existence of a God, a first cause; but the attempt to explain the nature of that Being, or in any way to assimilate it with our own, they considered not only a proof of folly, but of extreme impiety.

The following extracts from their books will serve to show what were the real tenets of their creed:

"By one Supreme Ruler is this Universe pervaded; even every world in the whole circle of nature . . . There is one Supreme Spirit, which nothing can shake, more swift than the thought of man. That Supreme Spirit moves at pleasure, but in itself is immovable; it is distant from us, yet near us; it pervades this whole system of worlds; yet it is infinitely beyond it. That man who considers all beings as existing even in the Supreme Spirit, and the Supreme Spirit as pervading all beings, henceforth views no creature with contempt. . . . All spiritual beings are the same in kind with the Supreme Spirit . . . The pure enlightened soul assumes a luminous form, with no gross body, with no perforation, with no veins or tendons, unblemished, untainted by sin; itself being a ray from the Infinite Spirit, which knows the Past and the Future, which pervades all, which existed with no cause but itself, which created all things as they are, in ages most remote. That all-pervading Spirit, that Spirit which gives light to the visible Sun, even the same in *kind* am I, though infinitely distant in *degree*. Let my soul return to the immortal Spirit of God, and then let my body which ends in ashes return to dust! O Spirit, who pervadest fire, lead us in a straight path to the riches of beatitude! Thou, O God, possessest all the treasures of knowledge! Remove each foul taint from our souls!

"From what root springs mortal man, when felled by the hand of death? Who can make him spring again to birth? God, who is perfect wisdom, perfect happiness. He is the final refuge of the man who has liberally bestowed his wealth, who has been firm in virtue, who knows and adores that Great One. . . Let us adore the supremacy of that Divine Sun, the Godhead who illuminates all, who re-creates all, from whom all proceed, to whom all must return, whom we invoke to direct our understandings aright, in our progress towards his holy seat. . . What the Sun and Light are to this visible world, such is truth to the intellectual and invisible universe. . . Our souls acquire certain knowledge, by meditating on the light of Truth, which emanates from the Being of Beings. . . That Being, without eyes sees, without ears hears all; he knows whatever can be known, but there is none who knows him; him the wise call the Great, Supreme, Pervading Spirit. . . Perfect Truth, Perfect Happiness, without equal, immortal; absolute unity, whom neither speech can describe, nor mind comprehend; all-pervading, all-transcending, delighted with his own boundless intelligence, nor limited by space or time; without feet, running swiftly; without hands, grasping all worlds; without eyes, all-surveying; without ears, all-hearing; without an intelligent guide, understanding all; without cause, the first of all causes; all-ruling, all-powerful, the Creator, Preserver, Transformer of all things; such is the Great One; this the Vedas declare.

"May that soul of mine, which mounts aloft in my waking hours, as an ethereal spark, and which, even in my slumber, has a like ascent, soaring to a great distance, as an emanation from the Light of lights, be united by devout meditation with the spirit supremely blest, and supremely intelligent! . . May that soul of mine, which was itself the primeval oblation placed within all creatures . . which is a ray of perfect wisdom, which is the inextinguishable light fixed within created bodies, without which no good act is performed, . . . in which as an immortal essence may be comprised whatever has passed, is present, or will be hereafter, . . . be united by devout meditation with the Spirit supremely blest and supremely intelligent!

"The Being of Beings is the Only God, eternal, and everywhere present, who comprises everything. There is no God but He. . . . The Supreme Being is invisible, incomprehensible, immovable, without figure or shape. No one has ever seen him; time never comprised him; his essence pervades everything; all was derived from him.

"The duty of a good man, even in the moment of his destruction, consists not only in forgiving, but even in a desire of benefiting his destroyer; as the sandal-tree, in the instant of its overthrow, sheds perfume on the axe which fells it."

The Vedanta and Nyaya philosophers acknowledge a Supreme Eternal Being, and the immortality of the soul; though, like the Greeks, they differ in their ideas of those subjects. They speak of the Supreme Being as an eternal essence that pervades space, and gives life or existence. Of that universal and eternal pervading spirit, the Vedanti suppose four modifications; but as these do not change its nature, and as it would be erroneous to ascribe to each of them a distinct essence, so it is equally erroneous, they say, to imagine that the various modifications by which the All-pervading Being exists, or displays His power, are individual existences. Creation is not considered as the instant production of things, but only as the manifestation of that which exists eternally in the one Universal Being. The Nyaya philosophers believe that spirit and matter are eternal; but they do not suppose that the world in its present form has existed from eternity, but only the primary matter from which it sprang when operated on by the almighty word of God, the Intelligent Cause and Supreme Being, who produced the combinations or aggregations which compose the material universe. Though they believe that soul is an emanation from the Supreme Being, they distinguish it from that Being, in its individual existence. Truth and Intelligence are the eternal attributes of God, not, they say, of the individual soul, which is susceptible both of knowledge and ignorance, of pleasure and pain; and therefore God and it are distinct. Even when it returns to the Eternal, and attains supreme bliss, it undoubtedly does not cease. Though *united* to the Supreme Being, it is not *absorbed* in it, but still retains the abstract nature of definite or visible existence.

"The dissolution of the world," they say, "consists in the destruction of the visible forms and qualities of things; but their material essence remains, and from it new worlds are formed by the creative energy of God; and thus the Universe is dissolved and renewed in endless succession."

The Jainas, a sect at Mysore and elsewhere, say that the ancient religion of India and of the whole world, consisted in the belief in one God, a pure Spirit, indivisible, omniscient and all-powerful: that God, having given to all things their appointed order and course of action, and to man a sufficient portion of reason, or understanding, to guide him in his conduct, leaves him to the operation of free will, without the entire exercise of which he could not be held answerable for his conduct.

Menou, the Hindū lawgiver, adored, not the visible, material Sun, but "that divine and incomparably greater light," to use the words of the most venerable text in the Indian Scripture, "which illumines all, delights all, from which all proceed, to which all must return, and which alone can irradiate our intellects." He thus commences his Institutes:

"Be it heard!

"This universe existed only in the first divine idea yet unexpanded, as if involved in darkness, imperceptible, undefinable, undiscoverable by reason, and undiscovered by revelation, as if it were wholly immersed in sleep:

"Then the Sole Self-existing Power, Himself undiscovered, but making this world discernible, with five elements, and other principles of nature, appeared with undiminished glory, *expanding his idea*, or dispelling the gloom.

"He whom the mind alone can perceive, whose essence eludes the external organs, who has no visible parts, who exists from Eternity, even He, the soul of all beings, whom no being can comprehend, shone forth.

"He, having willed to produce various beings from his own divine Substance, first with a thought created the waters. . . . From *that which is* [precisely the Hebrew יהוה], the first cause, not the object of sense, existing everywhere in substance, not existing to our perception, without beginning or end" [the A.·. and Ω.·., or the I.·. A.·. Ω.·.], "was produced the divine male famed in all worlds under the appellation of Brahma."

Then recapitulating the different things created by Brahma, he adds: "He," meaning Brahma [the Λογος, the Word], "whose powers are incomprehensible, having thus created this Universe, was again absorbed in the Supreme Spirit, changing the time of energy for the time of repose."

The *L'Antareya A'ran'ya*, one of the Vedas, gives this primitive idea of the creation: "In the beginning, the Universe was but a Soul: nothing else, active or inactive existed. Then He had this thought, *I will create worlds;* and thus He created these different worlds; air, the light, mortal beings and the waters.

"He had this thought: *Behold the worlds; I will create guardians for the worlds.* So He took of the "water and fashioned a being clothed with the human form. He looked upon him, and of that being so con-"templated, the mouth opened like an egg, and speech came forth, and from the speech fire. The nostrils "opened, and through them went the breath of respiration, and by it the air was propagated. The eyes "opened; from them came a luminous ray, and from it was produced the sun. The ears dilated: from them "came hearing, and from hearing space:" . . . and, after the body of man, with the senses was formed;— "He, the Universal Soul, thus reflected: *How could this body exist without Me?* He examined through what "extremity He could penetrate it. He said to himself; *If, without me, the Word is articulated, breath exhales "and sight sees; if hearing hears, the skin feels, and the mind reflects, deglutition swallows and the generative "organ fulfils its functions, what then am I?* And separating the suture of the cranium, He penetrated into "man."

Behold the great fundamental primitive truths! God an infinite Eternal Soul or Spirit. Matter not eternal nor self-existent, but created—created by a thought of God. After matter, and worlds, then man, by a like thought: and finally, after endowing him with the senses and a thinking mind, a portion, a spark, of God Himself penetrates the man, and becomes a living spirit within him.

The Vedas thus detail the creation of the world:

"In the beginning there was a single God, existing of himself; who, after having passed an eternity absorbed in the contemplation of his own being, desired to manifest his perfections outwardly of Himself; and created the matter of the world. The four elements being thus produced, but still mingled in confusion, he breathed upon the waters, which swelled up into an immense ball in the shape of an egg, and, developing themselves, became the vault and orb of Heaven which encircles the earth. Having made the earth and the bodies of animal beings, this God, the essence of movement, gave to them, to animate them, a portion of his own being. Thus, the soul of everything that breathes being a fraction of the universal soul, none perishes; but each soul merely changes its mould and form, by passing successively into different bodies. Of all forms, that which most pleases the Divine Being is Man, as nearest approaching his own perfections. When a man, absolutely disengaging himself from his senses, absorbs himself in self-contemplation, he comes to discern the Divinity, and becomes part of Him."

The Ancient Persians in many respects resembled the Hindūs,—in their language, their poetry, and their poetic legends. Their conquests brought them in contact with China; and they subdued Egypt and Judea. Their views of God and religion more resembled those of the Hebrews, than those of any other nation; and indeed the latter people borrowed from them some prominent doctrines, that we are in the habit of regarding as an essential part of the original Hebrew creed.

Of the King of Heaven and Father of Eternal Light, of the pure World of Light, of the Eternal Word by which all things were created, of the Seven Mighty Spirits that stand next to the Throne of Light and Omnipotence, and of the glory of those Heavenly Hosts that encompass that Throne, of the Origin of Evil, and the Prince of Darkness, Monarch of the rebellious spirits, enemies of all good; they entertained tenets very similar to those of the Hebrews. Towards Egyptian idolatry they felt the strongest abhorrence, and under Cambyses pursued a regular plan for its utter extirpation. Xerxes, when he invaded Greece, destroyed the Temples and erected fire-chapels along the whole course of his march. Their religion was eminently spiritual, and the earthly fire and earthly sacrifice were but the signs and emblems of another devotion and a higher power.

Thus the fundamental doctrine of the ancient religion of India and Persia was at first nothing more than a simple veneration of nature, its pure elements and its primary energies, the sacred fire, and above all, Light,—the air, not the lower atmospheric air, but the purer and brighter air of Heaven, the breath that animates and pervades the breath of mortal life. This pure and simple veneration of nature is perhaps the most ancient, and was by far the most generally prevalent in the primitive and patriarchal world. It was not originally a deification of nature; or a denial of the sovereignty of God. Those pure elements and primitive essences of created nature offered to the first men, still in a close communication with the Deity, not a likeness of resemblance, nor a mere fanciful image or a poetical figure, but a natural and true symbol of Divine power. Everywhere in the Hebrew writings, the pure light or sacred fire is employed as an image of the all-pervading and all-consuming power and omnipresence of the Divinity. His breath was the first source of life; and the faint whisper of the breeze announced to the prophet His immediate presence.

"All things are the progeny of one fire. The Father perfected all things, and delivered them over to the "Second Mind, whom all nations of men call the First. Natural works co-exist with the intellectual light of "the Father; for it is the Soul which adorns the great Heaven, and which adorns it after the Father. The "Soul, being a bright fire, by the power of the Father, remains immortal, and is mistress of life, and fills up "the recesses of the world. For the fire which is first beyond, did not shut up his power in matter by works, "but by mind, for the framer of the fiery world is the mind of mind, who first sprang from mind, clothing fire "with fire. Father-begotten Light! for He alone, having from the Father's power received the essence of "intellect, is enabled to understand the mind of the Father; and to instil into all sources and principles the "capacity of understanding, and of ever continuing in ceaseless revolving motion." Such was the language of Zoroaster, embodying the old Persian ideas.

And the same ancient sage thus spoke of the Sun and Stars: "The Father made the whole universe of "fire and water and earth, and all-nourishing ether. He fixed a great multitude of moveless stars, that "stand still forever, not by compulsion and unwillingly, but without desire to wander, fire acting upon fire. "He congregated the seven firmaments of the world, and so surrounded the earth with the convexity of the "Heavens; and therein set seven living existences, arranging their apparent disorder in regular orbits, six "of them planets, and the Sun, placed in the centre, the seventh;—in that centre from which all lines, "diverging which way soever, are equal; and the swift sun himself, revolving around a principal centre, and "ever striving to reach the central and all-pervading light, bearing with him the bright Moon."

And yet Zoroaster added: "Measure not the journeyings of the Sun, nor attempt to reduce them to "rule; for he is carried by the eternal will of the Father, not for your sake. Do not endeavour to understand "the impetuous course of the Moon; for she runs evermore under the impulse of necessity; and the pro-"gression of the Stars was not generated to serve any purpose of yours."

Ormuzd says to Zoroaster, in the Boundehesch: "I am he who holds the Star-Spangled Heaven in ethereal "space; who makes this sphere, which once was buried in darkness, a flood of light. Through me the Earth "became a world firm and lasting—the earth on which walks the Lord of the world. I am he who makes "the light of Sun, Moon and Stars pierce the clouds. I make the corn-seed, which perishing in the "ground sprouts anew. . . . I created man, whose eye is light, whose life is the breath of his nostrils. I "placed within him life's unextinguishable power."

Ormuzd or Ahura-Mazda himself represented the primal light, distinct from the heavenly bodies, yet necessary to their existence, and the source of their splendour. The Amschaspands (Ameschaspenta, "immortal Holy Ones"), each presided over a special department of nature. Earth and Heaven, fire and water, the Sun and Moon, the rivers, trees and mountains, even the artificial divisions of the day and year were addressed in prayer as tenanted by Divine beings, each separately ruling within his several sphere. Fire, in particular, that "most energetic of immortal powers," the visible representative of the primal light, was invoked as "Son of Ormuzd." The Sun, the Archimagus, that noblest and most powerful agent of divine power, who "steps forth as a Conqueror from the top of the terrible Alborj to rule over the world which he enlightens from the throne of Ormuzd," was worshipped among other symbols by the name of MITHRAS, a beneficent and friendly genius, who, in the hymn addressed to him in the Zend-avesta, bears the names given him by the Greeks, as the "Invincible" and the "Mediator;" the former, because in his daily strife with darkness, he is the most active confederate of Ormuzd; the latter, as being the medium through which heaven's choicest blessings are communicated to men. He is called " the eye of Ormuzd, the effulgent Hero, pursuing his course triumphantly, fertilizer of deserts, most exalted of the Izeds or Yezatas, the never-sleeping, the protector of the land." "When the dragon foe devastates my provinces," says Ormuzd, "and afflicts them with famine, then is he struck down by the strong arm of Mithras, together with the Deves of Mazanderan. With his lance and his immortal club, the Sleepless Chief hurls down the Deves into the dust, when as Mediator he interposes to guard the City from evil."

Ahriman was by some Parsee sects considered older than Ormuzd, as darkness is older than light; he is imagined to have been unknown as a Malevolent Being in the early ages of the world, and the fall of man is attributed in the Boundehesch to an apostate worship of him, from which men were converted by a succession of prophets terminating with Zoroaster.

Mithras is not only light, but intelligence; that luminary which, though born in obscurity, will not only dispel darkness, but conquer death. The warfare through which this consummation is to be reached, is mainly carried on through the instrumentality of the " Word," that " ever-living emanation of the Deity, by virtue of which the world exists," and of which the revealed formulas incessantly repeated in the liturgies of the Magi are but the expression. "What shall I do," cried Zoroaster, " O Ormuzd steeped in brightness, in order to battle with Daroodj-Ahriman, father of the Evil Law; how shall I make men pure and holy?" Ormuzd answered and said: "Invoke, O Zoroaster, the pure law of the Servants of Ormuzd; invoke the Amschaspands who shed abundance throughout the seven Keshwars; invoke the Heaven, Zeruana-Akarana, the birds travailing on high, the swift wind, the Earth; invoke my Spirit, me who am Ahura-Mazdao, the purest, strongest, wisest, best of beings; me who have the most majestic body, who through purity am Supreme, whose Soul is the Excellent Word; and ye, all people, invoke me as I have commanded Zoroaster."

Ahura-Mazda himself is the living Word; he is called "First-born of all things, express image of the Eternal, very light of very light, the Creator, who by power of the Word which he never ceases to pronounce, made in 365 days the Heaven and the Earth." The Word is said in the Yashna to have existed before all, and to be itself a Yazata, a personified object of prayer. It was revealed in Serosch, in Homa, and again, under Gushtasp, was manifested in Zoroaster.

Between life and death, between sunshine and shade, Mithras is the present exemplification of the Primal Unity from which all things arose, and into which through his mediation all contrarieties will ultimately be absorbed. His annual sacrifice is the passover of the Magi, a symbolical atonement or pledge of moral and physical regeneration. He created the world in the beginning; and as at the close of each successive year he sets free the current of life to invigorate a fresh circle of being, so in the end of all things he will bring the weary sum of ages as a hecatomb before God, releasing by a final sacrifice the Soul of Nature from her perishable frame to commence a brighter and purer existence.

Iamblichus (*De Mys.* viii. 4) says: "The Egyptians are far from ascribing all things to physical causes; life and intellect they distinguish from physical being, both in man and in the universe. They place intellect and reason first, as self-existent, and from these they derive the created world. As Parent of generated things they constitute a Demiurge, and acknowledge a vital force both in the Heavens and before the Heavens. They place Pure Intellect above and beyond the universe, and another (that is, Mind revealed in the Material World), consisting of one continuous mind pervading the universe, and apportioned to all its parts and spheres." The Egyptian idea, then, was that of all-transcendental philosophy—that of a Deity both immanent and transcendent—spirit passing into its manifestations, but not exhausted by so doing.

The wisdom recorded in the canonical rolls of Hermes quickly attained in this transcendental lore, all that human curiosity can ever discover. Thebes especially is said to have acknowledged a being without beginning or end, called Amun or Amun-Kneph, the all-pervading Spirit or Breath of Nature, or perhaps even some still more lofty object of reverential reflection, whom it was forbidden even to name. Such a Being would in theory stand at the head of the three orders of Gods mentioned by Herodotus, these being regarded as arbitrary classifications of similar or equal beings arranged in successive emanations, according to an estimate of their comparative dignity. The Eight Great Gods, or primary class, were probably manifestations of the emanated God in the several parts and powers of the universe, each potentially comprising the whole God-head.

In the ancient Hermetic books, as quoted by Iamblichus, occurred the following passage in regard to the Supreme Being:—

"Before all the things that actually exist, and before all beginnings, there is one God, prior even to the first God and King, remaining unmoved in the singleness of his own Unity: for neither is anything conceived by intellect inwoven with him, nor anything else; but he is established as the exemplar of the God who is good, who is his own father, self-begotten, and has only one Parent. For he is something greater and prior to, and the fountain of all things, and the foundation of things conceived by the intellect, which are the first species. And from this One, the self-originated God caused himself to shine forth; for which reason he is his own father, and self-originated. For he is both a beginning and God of Gods, a Monad from the One, prior to substance and the beginning of substance; for from him is substantiality and substance, whence also he is called the beginning of things conceived by the intellect. These then are the most ancient beginnings of all things, which Hermes places before the ethereal and empyrean and celestial Gods."

"CHANG-TI, or the Supreme Lord or Being," said the old Chinese creed, "is the principle of everything that exists, and Father of all living. He is eternal, immovable and independent: His power knows no bounds: His sight equally comprehends the Past, the Present and the Future, and penetrates even to the inmost recesses of the heart. Heaven and earth are under his government: all events, all revolutions, are the consequences of his dispensation and will. He is pure, holy and impartial: wickedness offends his sight; but he beholds with an eye of complacency the virtuous actions of men. Severe, yet just, he punishes vice in an exemplary manner, even in Princes and Rulers; and often casts down the guilty, to crown with honour the man who walks after His own heart, and whom he raises from obscurity. Good, merciful and full of pity, He forgives the wicked upon their repentance: and public calamities and the irregularity of the seasons are but salutary warnings, which his fatherly goodness gives to men, to induce them to reform and amend."

Controlled by reason infinitely more than by the imagination, that people, occupying the extreme East of Asia, did not fall into idolatry until after the time of Confucius, and within two centuries of the birth of Christ; when the religion of BUDDHA or Fo was carried thither from India. Their system was long regulated by the pure worship of God, and the foundation of their moral and political existence laid in a sound, upright reason, conformable to true ideas of the Deity. They had no false gods or images, and their third Emperor *Hoam-ti* erected a Temple, the first probably ever erected, to the Great Architect of the Universe. And though they offered sacrifices to divers tutelary angels, yet they honoured them infinitely less than XAM-TI or CHANG-TI, the Sovereign Lord of the World.

Confucius forbade making images or representations of the Deity. He attached no idea of personality to him; but considered him as a Power or Principle, pervading all Nature. And the Chinese designated the Divinity by the Name of THE DIVINE REASON.

The Japanese believe in a Supreme Invisible Being, not to be represented by images or worshipped in Temples. They style him AMIDA or OMITU; and say that he is without beginning or end; that he came on earth, where he remained a thousand years, and became the Redeemer of our fallen race: that he is to judge all men; and the good are to live forever, while the bad are to be condemned to Hell.

"The Chang-ti is represented," said Confucius, "under the general emblem of the visible firmament, as well as under the particular symbols of the Sun, the Moon and the Earth, because by their means we enjoy the gifts of the Chang-Ti. The Sun is the source of life and light: the Moon illuminates the world by night. By observing the course of these luminaries, mankind are enabled to distinguish times and seasons. The Ancients, with the view of connecting the act with its object, when they established the practice of sacrificing to the Chang-ti, fixed the day of the Winter Solstice, because the Sun, after having passed through the twelve places assigned apparently by the Chang-ti as its annual residence, began its career anew, to distribute blessings through the Earth."

He said: "The TEEN is the universal principle and prolific source of all things. . . . The Chang-ti is the universal principle of existence."

The Arabians never possessed a poetical, high-wrought and scientifically arranged system of Polytheism. Their historical traditions had much analogy with those of the Hebrews, and coincided with them in a variety of points. The tradition of a purer faith and the simple Patriarchal worship of the Deity, appear never to have been totally extinguished among them ; nor did idolatry gain much foothold until near the time of Mahomet ; who, adopting the old primeval faith, taught again the doctrine of one God, adding to it that he was his Prophet.

To the mass of Hebrews, as well as to other nations, seem to have come fragments only of the primitive revelation : nor do they seem, until after their captivity among the Persians, to have concerned themselves about metaphysical speculations in regard to the Divine Nature and essence ; although it is evident, from the Psalms of David, that a select body among them preserved a knowledge in regard to the Deity, which was wholly unknown to the mass of the people ; and that chosen few were made the medium of transition for certain truths, to later ages.

Among the Greeks, the scholars of the Egyptians, all the higher ideas and severer doctrines on the Divinity, his Sovereign Nature and Infinite Might, the Eternal Wisdom and Providence that conducts and directs all things to their proper end, the Infinite Mind and Supreme Intelligence that created all things, and is raised far above external nature,—all these loftier ideas and nobler doctrines were expounded more or less perfectly by Pythagoras, Anaxagoras and Socrates, and developed in the most beautiful and luminous manner by Plato, and the philosophers that succeeded him. And even in the popular religion of the Greeks, are many things capable of a deeper import and more spiritual signification : though they seem only rare vestiges of ancient truth, vague presentiments, fugitive tones, and momentary flashes, revealing a belief in a Supreme Being, Almighty Creator of the Universe, and Common Father of Mankind.

Much of the primitive Truth was taught to Pythagoras by Zoroaster ; who himself received it from the Indians. His disciples rejected the use of Temples, of Altars and of Statues ; and smiled at the folly of those nations who imagined that the Deity sprang from or had any affinity with human nature. The tops of the highest mountains were the places chosen for sacrifices. Hymns and prayers were their principal worship. The Supreme God, who fills the wide circle of heaven, was the object to whom they were addressed. Such is the testimony of Herodotus. Light they considered not so much as an object of worship, as rather the most pure and lively emblem of, and first emanation from, the Eternal God ; and thought that man required something visible or tangible to exalt his mind to that degree of adoration which is due to the Divine Being.

There was a surprising similarity between the Temples, Priests, doctrines and worship of the Persian Magi and the British Druids. The latter did not worship idols in the human shape ; because they held that the Divinity, being invisible, ought to be adored without being seen. They asserted the Unity of the Godhead. Their invocations were made to the One All-preserving Power ; and they argued that, as this power was not matter, it must necessarily be the Deity ; and the secret symbol used to express his name was O. I. W. They believed that the earth had sustained one general destruction by water ; and would again be destroyed by fire. They admitted the doctrines of the immortality of the soul, a future state, and a day of judgment, which would be conducted on the principle of man's responsibility. They even retained some idea of the redemption of mankind through the death of a Mediator. They retained a tradition of the Deluge, perverted and localized. But, around these fragments of primitive truth they wove a web of idolatry, worshipped two Subordinate Deities under the names of Hu and Ceridwen, male and female (doubtless the same as Osiris and Isis), and held the doctrine of transmigration.

The early inhabitants of Scandinavia believed in a God who was "the Author of everything that existeth ; "the Eternal, the Ancient, the Living and Awful Being, the Searcher into concealed things, the Being that "never changeth." Idols and visible representations of the Deity were originally forbidden, and he was directed to be worshipped in the lonely solitude of sequestered forests, where he was said to dwell, invisible, and in perfect silence.

The Druids, like their eastern ancestors, paid the most sacred regard to the odd numbers, which, traced

28D

backward ended in Unity or Deity, while the even numbers ended in nothing. 3 was particularly reverenced. 19 (7+3+3²) : 30 (7+3×3) : and 21 (7×3) were numbers observed in the erection of their temples, constantly appearing in their dimensions, and the number and distances of the huge stones.

They were the sole interpreters of religion. They superintended all sacrifices; for no private person could offer one without their permission. They exercised the power of excommunication; and without their concurrence war could not be declared or peace made: and they even had the power of inflicting the punishment of death. They professed to possess a knowledge of magic, and practised augury for the public service.

They cultivated many of the liberal sciences, and particularly astronomy, the favourite science of the Orient; in which they attained considerable proficiency. They considered day as the offspring of night, and therefore made their computations by nights instead of days; and we, from them, still use the words fortnight and sen'night. They knew the division of the Heavens into constellations; and finally, they practised the strictest morality, having particularly the most sacred regard for that peculiarly Masonic virtue, Truth.

In the Icelandic Prose Edda is the following dialogue:

" Who is the first or eldest of the Gods ?

" In our language he is called ALFADIR (All-Father, or the Father of All); but in the old Asgard he had twelve names.

" Where is this God ? What is his power? and what hath he done to display his glory.

" He liveth from all ages, he governeth all realms, and swayeth all things both great and small.

" He hath formed heaven and earth, and the air, and all things thereunto belonging.

" He hath made man and given him a soul which shall live and never perish, though the body shall have mouldered away or have been burnt to ashes. And all that are righteous shall dwell with him in the place called *Gimli* or *Vingolf*; but the wicked shall go to *Hel*, and thence to *Nijlhel*, which is below, in the ninth world."

Almost every heathen nation, so far as we have any knowledge of their mythology, believed in one Supreme Overruling God, whose name it was not lawful to utter.

The Egyptians and Hindūs revered ATHOM, ON or OM, [AUM or AUM], as the name of their chief Deity; who was also considered by the Canaanites as the Creator, or the prolific power; probably the Solar Orb. The same name is compounded in the Philistine Deity, DAG-ON : or the receptacle of ON. The Chaldean OANNES was O-AUN-NES. Among the Jews, the worship of the *Teraphim* was connected with AUN. Thus the original of 1 *Sam.* xv. 23, is, " *As the sin of divination is rebellion, so is* AUN *and* TERAPHIM *stubbornness and iniquity.*"

Faber says, " By a plausible, though wretched, abuse, the *Cherubim*, or *Seraphim*, or *Teraphim*, became the symbolic faticidal Gods of Paganism: and as the principal Hero-God of that system was thought to have migrated into the Sun, and was thence astronomically worshipped as the Solar Deity, the *Teraphim* are by the inspired writers, justly associated with the Egyptian ON, who is the same as the Indo-Scythic ON of the Brahmins."

The early Christians used the same word to express the Divine Being whom they worshipped: . . 'Ο ΩΝ, και ο ην, και ο ερχομενος; Ho On, Kai Ho En, Kai Ho Erchomenos. . . *The Being, that is, and was, and is to come.*

The Tetragrammaton, or Ineffable Name was, among the Jews, forbidden to be pronounced. But that its pronunciation might not be lost among the Levites, the High Priest uttered it in the Temple once a year, on the 10th day of the Month Tisri, the day of the great feast of expiation. During this ceremony, the people were directed to make a great noise, that the Sacred Word might not be heard by any who had not a right to it; for every other, said the Jews, would be incontinently stricken dead.

The Great Egyptian Initiates, before the time of the Jews, did the same thing in regard to the word Isis; which they regarded as sacred and incommunicable.

Origen says: "There are names which have a natural potency. Such are those which the Sages used among the Egyptians, the Magi in Persia, the Brahmins in India. What is called Magic is not a vain and chimerical act, as the Stoics and Epicureans pretend. The names Sabaoth and Adonai were not made for created beings: but they belong to a mysterious theology, which goes back to the Creator. From Him comes the virtue of these names, when they are arranged and pronounced according to the rules."

The Hindū word AUM, represented the three Powers combined in their Deity; Brahma, Vishnu and Siva; or the Creating, Preserving and Destroying Powers: A, the first: U or Ō-Ŭ, the second; and M, the third. This word could not be pronounced, except by the letters: for its pronunciation as one word was said to make Earth tremble, and even the Angels of Heaven to quake for fear.

The word Aum, says the Ramayan, represents "The Being of Beings, One Substance in three forms; without mode, without quality, without passion: Immense, Incomprehensible, Infinite, Indivisible, Immutable, Incorporeal, Irresistible."

An old passage in the Purana says: "All the rites ordained in the Vedas, the sacrifices to the fire, and all other solemn purifications shall pass away: but that which shall never pass away is the word A∴ Ō-Ŭ∴ M: for it is the symbol of the Lord of all things."

Herodotus says that the Ancient Pelasgi built no temples and worshipped no idols, and had a sacred name of Deity, which it was not permissible to pronounce.

The Clarian Oracle, which was of unknown antiquity, being asked which of the Deities was named IAΩ, answered in these remarkable words: "The Initiated are bound to conceal the mysterious secrets. Learn then, that IAΩ is the Great God Supreme, that ruleth over all."

The Jews consider the True Name of God to be irrecoverably lost by disuse; and regard its pronunciation as one of the Mysteries that will be revealed at the coming of their Messiah. And they attribute its loss to the illegality of applying the Masoretic points to so sacred a Name, by which a knowledge of the proper vowels is forgotten. It is even said, in the Gemara of Abodah Zara, that God permitted a celebrated Hebrew Scholar to be burned by a Roman Emperor, because he had been heard to pronounce the Sacred Name with points.

The Jews feared that the Heathen would get possession of the Name: and therefore, in their copies of the Scriptures, they wrote it in the Samaritan character, instead of the Hebrew or Chaldaic, that the adversary might not make an improper use of it: for they believed it capable of working miracles: and held that the wonders in Egypt were performed by Moses, in virtue of this name being engraved on his rod: and that any person who knew the true pronunciation, would be able to do as much as he did.

Josephus says it was unknown until God communicated it to Moses, in the wilderness: and that it was lost through the wickedness of man.

The followers of Mahomet have a tradition that there is a secret name of the Deity, which possesses wonderful properties; and that the only method of becoming acquainted with it, is by being initiated into the Mysteries of the *Ism Abla.*

H∴ O∴ M∴ was the first framer of the new religion among the Persians, and His Name was Ineffable.

Amun, among the Egyptians, was a name pronounceable by none save the Priests.

The old Germans adored God with profound reverence, without daring to name Him, or to worship Him in Temples.

The Druids expressed the name of Deity by the letters O∴ I∴ W∴

Among all the nations of primitive antiquity, the doctrine of the immortality of the soul was not a mere probable hypothesis, needing laborious researches and diffuse argumentation, to produce conviction of its truth. Nor can we hardly give it the name of *Faith;* for it was a lively *certainty,* like the feeling of one's own existence and identity, and of what is actually present; exerting its influence on all sublunary affairs, and the motive of mightier deeds and enterprises than any mere earthly interest could inspire.

Even the doctrine of transmigration of souls, universal among the Ancient Hindūs and Egyptians, rested on a basis of the old primitive religion; and was connected with a sentiment purely religious. It involved this noble element of truth: that since man had gone astray, and wandered far from God, he must needs exert many efforts, and undergo a long and painful pilgrimage, before he could rejoin the Source of all Perfection: and the firm conviction and positive certainty, that nothing defective, impure, or defiled with earthly stains could enter the pure region of perfect spirits, or be eternally united to God; wherefore the soul had to pass through long trials and many purifications, before it could attain that blissful end. And the end and aim of all these systems of philosophy, was the final deliverance of the soul from the old calamity, the dreaded fate and frightful lot, of being compelled to wander through the dark regions of nature and the various forms of the brute creation, ever changing its terrestrial shape; and its union with God, which they held to be the lofty destiny of the wise and virtuous soul.

Pythagoras gave to the doctrine of the transmigration of souls that meaning which the wise Egyptians gave to it in their mysteries. He never taught the doctrine in that literal sense in which it was understood by the people. Of that literal doctrine not the least vestige is to be found in such of his symbols as remain, nor in his precepts collected by his disciple Lysis. He held that men always remain, in their essence, such as they were created; and can degrade themselves only by vice, and ennoble themselves only by virtue.

Hierocles, one of his most zealous and celebrated disciples, expressly says that he who believes that the soul of man, after his death, will enter the body of a beast, for his vices, or become a plant for his stupidity, is deceived; and is absolutely ignorant of the eternal form of the soul, which can never change; for, always remaining man, it is said to become God or beast, through virtue or vice, though it can become neither one nor the other by nature, but solely by the resemblance of its inclinations to theirs.

And Timæus of Locria, another disciple, says that to alarm men and prevent them from committing crimes, they menaced them with strange humiliations and punishments; even declaring that their souls would pass into new bodies,—that of a coward into the body of a deer; that of a ravisher into the body of a wolf; that of a murderer into the body of some still more ferocious animal; and that of an impure sensualist into the body of a hog.

So, too, the doctrine is explained in the Phædo. And Lysis says, that after the soul, purified of its crimes, has left the body and returned to heaven, it is no longer subject to change or death, but enjoys an eternal felicity. According to the Indians, it returned to, and became a part of the universal soul which animates everything.

The Hindūs held that Buddha descended on earth to raise all human beings up to the perfect state. He will ultimately succeed; and all, himself included, be merged in Unity.

Vishnu is to judge the world at the last day. It is to be consumed by fire: The Sun and Moon are to lose their light; the Stars to fall; and a New Heaven and Earth to be created.

The legend of the fall of the Spirits, obscured and distorted, is preserved in the Hindū Mythology. And their traditions acknowledged, and they revered, the succession of the first ancestors of mankind, or the Holy Patriarchs of the primitive world, under the name of the Seven Great Risuis, or Sages of hoary antiquity; though they invested their history with a cloud of fictions.

The Egyptians held that the soul was immortal; and that Osiris was to judge the world.

And thus reads the Persian legend:

"After Ahriman shall have ruled the world until the end of time, Sosioscu, the promised Redeemer will "come and annihilate the power of the Devs (or Evil Spirits), awaken the dead, and sit in final judgment upon "spirits and men. After that the comet *Gurzsher* will be thrown down, and a general conflagration take place, "which will consume the whole world. The remains of the earth will then sink down into *Duzakh*, and "become for three periods a place of punishment for the wicked. Then by degrees all will be pardoned, even "*Ahriman* and the *Devs*, and admitted to the regions of bliss, and thus there will be a new Heaven and a new "earth."

In the doctrines of Lamaism also, we find, obscured, and partly concealed in fiction, fragments of the primitive truth. For, according to that faith, "There is to be a final judgment before Eslik Khan: The good are to be admitted to Paradise, the bad to be banished to hell, where there are eight regions burning hot, and eight freezing cold."

In the Mysteries, wherever they were practised, was taught that truth of the primitive revelation, the existence of One Great Being, Infinite and pervading the Universe, who was there worshipped without superstition; and his marvellous nature, essence and attributes taught to the Initiates; while the vulgar attributed his works to Secondary Gods, personified, and isolated from Him in fabulous independence.

These truths were covered from the common people as with a veil; and the Mysteries were carried into every country, that without disturbing the popular beliefs, truth, the arts and the sciences might be known to those who were capable of understanding them, and maintaining the true doctrine incorrupt; which the people, prone to superstition and idolatry, have in no age been able to do; nor, as many strange aberrations and superstitions of the present day prove, any more now than heretofore. For we need but point to the doctrines of so many sects that degrade the Creator to the rank, and assign to Him the passions of humanity, to prove that now, as always, the old truths must be committed to a few, or they will be overlaid with fiction and error, and irretrievably lost.

Though Masonry is identical with the Ancient Mysteries, it is so in this qualified sense; that it presents but an imperfect image of their brilliancy; the ruins only of their grandeur, and a system that has experienced progressive alterations, the fruits of social events and political circumstances. Upon leaving Egypt, the Mysteries were modified by the habits of the different nations among whom they were introduced. Though originally more moral and political than religious, they soon became the heritage, as it were, of the priests, and essentially religious, though in reality limiting the sacerdotal power, by teaching the intelligent laity the folly and absurdity of the creeds of the populace. They were therefore necessarily changed by the religious systems of the countries into which they were transplanted. In Greece, they were the Mysteries of Ceres; in Rome, of *Bona Dea*, the Good Goddess; in Gaul, the School of Mars; in Sicily, the Academy of the Sciences; among the Hebrews, they partook of the rites and ceremonies of a religion which placed all the powers of government and all the knowledge, in the hands of the Priests and Levites. The pagodas of India, the retreats of the Magi of Persia and Chaldea, and the pyramids of Egypt, were no longer the sources at which men drank in knowledge. Each people, at all informed, had its Mysteries. After a time the Temples of Greece and the School of Pythagoras lost their reputation; and Free Masonry took their place.

Masonry, when properly expounded, is at once the interpretation of the great book of nature, the recital of physical and astronomical phenomena, the purest philosophy, and the place of deposit, where, as in a Treasury, are kept in safety all the great truths of the primitive revelation, that form the basis of all religions. In the modern degrees three things are to be recognized: The image of primeval times, the tableau of the efficient causes of the universe, and the book in which are written the morality of all peoples, and the code by which they must govern themselves if they would be prosperous.

The first degree represents man when he had sunken from his original lofty estate into what is most improperly styled a state of nature. He represents in that degree *the rough ashlar*, unfit to form a part of the spiritual temple; the pagan, who had lost all the great primitive truths of the original revelation. He maintained the same character in the Ancient Mysteries. He is emphatically a *Profane, enveloped in darkness, poor* and *destitute* of spiritual knowledge, and emblematically *naked*. The material *darkness* which is produced by *the bandage over his eyes,* is an emblem of the darkness of his soul. *He is deprived of everything that has a value,* and wherewith he could purchase food, to indicate his utter destitution of the mental wealth of primitive truth. In this degree he undergoes only physical tests, and receives elementary moral instruction. As yet, he takes upon himself no duty but *secrecy.* He still remains in *the dark quarter of the Lodge,* though not in *the North,* but halfway towards the East, *the place of light.*

He is not exposed to the fearful trials which awaited the candidate for initiation into the Mysteries. He passes through no gloomy forests, or long labyrinthine caves; he meets no hideous spectres; he is stunned and alarmed by no fearful noises; he incurs no danger. A few solitary moments in reflection and prayer, a short time passed in darkness, a few uncertain steps, a few obstacles to overcome, are all; and he enters the Temple of Truth and Virtue.

The journeys and trials of the candidate are an emblem of human life. Man enters feeble and naked upon a road full of dangers and pitfalls. The ignorance of the fancy, the fiery passions of youth, the troubles and agitations of mature age, the infirmities of old age, are so many evils which assail him, and which philosophy alone can aid him against. Defenceless in a world of trouble, what would become of him without the assistance of his brethren?

His obligation is no vulgar oath, such as is administered in the profane world. It is antique and sacred. He repeats it without compulsion. The expressions are energetic, because, being yet in darkness, he is on the point of passing from barbarism into civilization. It is like those of the Ancient Mysteries; for violating which Alcibiades was exiled and devoted to the Furies.

When *he is brought to light*, the allegory is complete. He sees around him a band of brothers, bound to protect and defend him. The obligation *he* has assumed, *they* and every Mason in the world have assumed towards *him*. He is one of THE BROTHERHOOD, bound by its laws, and enlisted as a soldier against ignorance and vice. The Master, for the time entitled to respect and veneration, is still but the first among his brethren, who are all his equals. Such is Masonic law and usage; and such it has been from the earliest ages.

In his journey, imitating that of life, the candidate goes but three times around the Lodge, although life has four seasons. This is because his journey also represents the annual revolution of the sun. Had the Mysteries originated in the North or West, in Rome or Greece, the seasons of the year and of life would have agreed, and four have been the number, instead of three. But in the East, in ancient times, there were but three seasons.

The three pillars that support the Lodge are WISDOM, STRENGTH and BEAUTY. The Egyptians and the Hebrews based their civil policy upon the WISDOM of the Priests, and the POWER, STRENGTH or VALOUR of their civil chiefs, who were also Military Commanders; and the HARMONY between these (synonymous with BEAUTY, among the Egyptians), completed the prosperity of the State.

The *age* of an apprentice is said to be *three years*, because in the Ancient Mysteries three years' preparation was required before Initiation could commence. The number *three* belongs in a peculiar manner to this Degree: The *alarm* is three raps: There are three movable and three immovable *jewels;* three *principal officers*, three *lights, greater* and *lesser;* three *journeys* are made round the Lodge; three *questions* are put to the Candidate before his entrance: and after his admission the numbers, from unity to three inclusive should be, but not often are, explained to him. Listen to that explanation!

The Kabbalistic doctrine was long the religion of the Sage and the Savant; because, like Free Masonry it incessantly tends towards spiritual perfection, and the fusion of the creeds and Nationalities of Mankind. In the eyes of the Kabbalist, all men are his brothers; and their relative ignorance is, to him, but a reason for instructing them. There were illustrious Kabbalists among the Egyptians and Greeks, whose doctrines the Orthodox Church has accepted; and among the Arabs were many, whose wisdom was not slighted by the Mediæval Church.

The Sages proudly wore the name of Kabbalists. The Kabbala embodied a noble philosophy, pure, not mysterious, but symbolic. It taught the doctrine of the Unity of God, the art of knowing and explaining the essence and operations of the Supreme Being, of spiritual powers and natural forces, and of determining their action by symbolic figures; by the arrangement of the alphabet, the combinations of numbers, the inversion of letters in writing, and the concealed meanings which they claimed to discover therein. The Kabbala is the key of the occult sciences; and the Gnostics were born of the Kabbalists.

The science of numbers represented not only arithmetical qualities, but also all grandeur, all proportion. By it we necessarily arrive at the discovery of the Principle or First Cause of things, called at the present day THE ABSOLUTE.

Or UNITY,—that loftiest term to which all philosophy directs itself; that imperious necessity of the human mind, that pivot round which it is compelled to group the aggregate of its ideas: Unity, this source, this centre of all systematic order, this principle of existence, this central point, unknown in its essence, but manifest in its effects; Unity, that sublime centre to which the chain of causes necessarily ascends, was the august Idea towards which all the ideas of Pythagoras converged. He refused the title of *Sage*, which means *one who knows:* He invented, and applied to himself that of *Philosopher*, signifying one who *is fond of* or *studies things secret and occult*. The astronomy which he mysteriously taught, was *astrology*: his science of numbers was based on Kabbalistical principles.

The Ancients, and Pythagoras himself, whose real principles have not been always understood, never meant to ascribe to numbers, that is to say, to abstract signs, any special virtue. But the Sages of Antiquity concurred in recognizing a ONE FIRST CAUSE, (material or spiritual), of the existence of the Universe. Thence, UNITY became the symbol of the Supreme Deity. It was made to express, to represent God; but without attributing to *the mere number* ONE any divine or supernatural virtue.

The philosophical principles of the Ancients, which formed the basis of the secret teaching in the Great Mysteries, have been transmitted from age to age by the Initiates.

In our Fellow Craft's degree, the number *five* succeeds to three. Pythagoras required his pupils to spend five years in study.

The Eleusinian Initiation originally had but two degrees. Our two first were comprised in one. To the Greeks we owe the ternary division. Among the early Christians there were three degrees. The *Catechumens,* or *Aspirants*, under instruction for the purpose of baptism or initiation, could not be present either at the mysteries or at sacrifice. The part of the Mass at which they assisted, ended with the canon, or rather after the instruction given them; that is, that in the ancient law or the apostolic lessons, given them by a sub-deacon or aspirant to the Priesthood; and that in the New Testament, read by the deacon or priest of the second order. It is from those primitive Christian Lodges that we preserve the titles of our subordinate officers, the Senior and Junior *Deacons*.

Afterwards the *Catechumens* became *Neophytes;* and could then be present at the mysteries and love-feasts or religious banquets; but only after a certain time and additional instruction. And still afterwards they were confirmed, and received the instruction in the hidden mysteries of the Faith. So that there, as in the ancient mysteries, the second degree was an indispensable preparation for the third.

In the second degree, a long time was spent in study. Here the Neophyte was taught the human sciences, and particularly that of numbers, which was deemed sacred; because, though styled *Geometry*, it included also that imperial study *Astronomy*, by which the student learned the operations and laws of nature, to prepare himself for receiving in the third degree, a knowledge of that SUPREME INTELLIGENCE which has organized and governs the universe with so admirable and inflexible an order.

In this Degree the letter G represents *Geometry* alone. Its deeper meaning is properly reserved for the third. Here the young Fellow Craft is the representative of the Student of the sciences in the school of Pythagoras; and it was there known that among the Brahmins GANNES was the God of numbers, and the patron of schools and learned societies. With us, too, the letter is the substitute for the Hebraic *Jod*, the initial letter of THE DIVINE NAME, and a monogram that expressed the UNCREATED BEING, principle of all things; and, enclosed in a triangle, THE UNITY OF GOD. We recognize the same letter G in the Syriac GAD, the Swedish GUD, the German GOTT, and the English GOD,—all names of the Deity, and all derived from the Persian GODA, itself derived from the absolute pronoun signifying HIMSELF. So too G, was the initial of the Greek word γνοσις, knowledge.

The word *Lodge* comes from *Loga*, which in the sacred language of the Ganges signifies *World;* of which every Lodge is indeed a representation. To what we call *Lodge*, the Persians gave the name *Jehan*, whence, perhaps, by corruption and pleonasm comes our expression, *a Lodge of St. John.*

In the ancient mysteries, the Presiding Officer, or Hierophant, wore the emblems of the Supreme Deity; as the Master of a Lodge still represents the High Priest of INUH. The Sun and the Moon were, and are still, the emblems of the two Wardens, who answer to the two next officers in the mysteries, by whom the same emblems were worn; Δαδουχος, the *Torch-bearer*, and Επιζωμος, the *Sacrificer.*

The *Blazing Star* was the image of HORUS, the son of OSIRIS or the *Sun*, author of the Seasons, and the God of Time, son of *Isis*, the primitive matter, inexhaustible source of life, spark of uncreated fire, universal seed of all beings. It represented also *Anubis*, or the Dog Star, the faithful guide of *Isis*, and the Herald of approaching inundation to the Egyptians. The Christian Masons made it an emblem of that Star in the East that led the three Magi to Bethlehem.

The Seat of the Master is called *the East*, because the mysteries come from the Orient; and because he represents Osiris or the Sun.

The word of the Fellow Craft has an astronomical meaning that again connects Masonry with the primitive times. Setting the Celestial Globe for the place where the temple was built, and the season of the year when it was commenced, the Master's station corresponds with the heliacal or solar rising. The Sun near the chest of the constellation Aries, has just shown himself above the horizon. The aspirant, entering by the west door, faces the day-star, and is consequently near that star of the Zodiac which sets as the sun rises. It is the star which blesses the husbandman, that brilliant star which the Hebrews called *Schibboleth*, the Romans *Spica*, and the French *Epi;* all meaning *an ear of wheat;*—a star in the constellation *Virgo.*

In this degree, *one point of the compass is raised above the square.* The latter is an emblem of the mechanical world, and of obedience: the former describes those curves and circles which are figures of the celestial movements, and is an emblem of authority: Thus the meaning is that the aspirant has taken one step towards celestial knowledge, and from obedience to command.

In this degree the aspirant is taught, also, how the worship of Bel, Ormuzd, Osiris, and Apollo, and like gods of other nations, grew out of the veneration of the primitive world for light, the first necessity for man, and the vivid and most striking emblem of the Good Principle, ever at war with the Evil Principle, Typhon, Ahriman or Shaitan.

The name of the aspirant in this degree, Fellow Craft or Companion, is substituted for those of the Initiate of the second order, or Neophyte of Egypt, and the Μύστης of the Mysteries of Eleusis.

In the Orient, the aspirant, after undergoing the severest, or rather the most cruel trials, was proclaimed the soldier of Mithras, and could, like the modern apprentices, call all initiates his companions in arms; that is, his Brothers. Next he became a *lion,* a name which, beside its astronomical meaning (the Sun of Summer, in that sign), had a moral meaning; because it involved and embodied the idea of strength, the peculiar expression of the modern Fellow Craft, engraved on the South column (B∴). These grades were only preparatory to a higher, in which the mysteries were revealed, and Mithras manifested himself to the Elect.

The Fellow Craft passes from the perpendicular to the square; from the column J∴ to the column B∴. The perpendicular is a single straight line; the square, two, forming a right angle. The third line comes in the Master's degree, to complete the right-angled triangle, and exhibit the 47th Problem of Euclid and Pythagoras.

Listen, now, to part of the Lecture of the ancient Kabbalists! [The orator and another brother repeat the following, from]

THE LECTURE OF THE KABBALISTS.

Qu∴. Why did you seek to be received a Knight of the Kabbala?

Ans∴. To know, by means of numbers, the admirable harmony which there is between nature and religion.

Qu∴. How were you announced?

Ans∴. By twelve raps.

Qu∴. What do they signify?

Ans∴. The twelve bases of our temporal and spiritual happiness.

Qu∴. What is a Kabbalist?

Ans∴. A man who has learned, by tradition, the Sacerdotal Art and the Royal Art.

Qu∴. What means the device, *Omnia in numeris sita sunt?*

Ans∴. That everything lies veiled in numbers.

Qu∴. Explain me that.

Ans∴. I will do so, as far as the number 12. Your sagacity will discern the rest.

Qu∴. What signifies the *unit* in the number 10?

Ans∴. God, creating and animating matter, expressed by 0, which, alone, is of no value.

Qu∴. What does the unit *mean?*

Ans∴. In the moral order, a Word incarnate in the bosom of a virgin; or religion. . . . In the physical, a spirit embodied in the virgin earth—or nature.

Qu∴. What do you mean by the number *two?*

Ans∴. In the moral order, *man* and *woman*. . . . In the physical, the *active* and the *passive.*

Qu∴. What do you mean by the number 3?

Ans∴. In the moral order, the three theological virtues. . . . In the physical, the three principles of bodies.

Qu∴. What do you mean by the number 4?

Ans∴. The four cardinal virtues. . . . The four elementary qualities.

Qu∴. What do you mean by the number 5?

Ans∴. The quintessence of religion. . . . The quintessence of matter.

The *unit* is the symbol of identity, equality, existence, conservation and general harmony: the Central Fire, the Point within the Circle.

Two, or the *duad*, is the symbol of diversity, inequality, division, separation and vicissitudes.

The cipher 1 signifies the living man [a body standing upright]; man being the only living being possessed of this faculty. Adding to it a head, we have the letter P, the sign of Paternity, Creative Power; and with a further addition, R, signifying man in motion, going, *Iens, Iturus.*

The Duad is the origin of contrasts. It is the imperfect condition into which, according to the Pythagoreans, a being falls, when he detaches himself from the Monad, or God. Spiritual beings, emanating from God, are enveloped in the duad, and therefore receive only illusory impressions.

As formerly the number ONE designated harmony, order, or the Good Principle (the ONE and ONLY GOD, expressed in Latin by *Solus*, whence the words *Sol, Soleil*, symbol of this God), the number Two expressed the contrary idea. There commenced the fatal knowledge of good and evil. Everything double, false, opposed to the single and sole reality, was expressed by the Binary number. It expressed also that state of contrariety in which nature exists, where everything is double; night and day, light and darkness, cold and heat, wet and dry, health and sickness, error and truth, one and the other sex, &c. Hence the Romans dedicated the second month in the year to Pluto, the God of Hell, and the second day of that month to the *manès* of the dead.

The number *one*, with the Chinese, signified unity, harmony, order, the Good Principle, or God: *Two*, disorder, duplicity, falsehood. That people, in the earliest ages, based their whole philosophical system on the two primary figures or lines, one straight and unbroken, and the other broken or divided in two; doubling which, by placing one under the other, and trebling by placing three under each other, they made the four symbols and eight *Koua*; which referred to the natural elements, and the primary principles of all things, and served symbolically or scientifically to express them. Plato terms unity and duality the original elements of nature, and first principles of all existence: and the oldest sacred book of the Chinese says: "The Great First Principle has produced two equations and differences, or primary rules of existence: but the two primary rules or two oppositions, namely YN and YANG, or repose and motion, have produced four signs or symbols, and the four symbols have produced the eight KOUA or further combinations."

The interpretation of the Hermetic fables shows, among every ancient people, in their principal Gods, first, 1, the Creating Monad, then 3, then 3 times 3, 3 times 9, and 3 times 27. This triple progression has for its foundation the three ages of Nature, the Past, the Present, and the Future; or the three degrees of universal generation. . . Birth, Life, Death. . . Beginning, middle, end.

The Monad was male, because its action produces no change *in* itself, but only *out* of itself. It represented the creative principle.

The Duad, for a contrary reason, was female, ever changing by addition, subtraction or multiplication. It represents matter capable of form.

The union of the Monad and Duad produces the triad, signifying the world formed by the creative principle out of matter. Pythagoras represented the world by the right-angled triangle, in which the squares of the two shortest sides are equal, added together, to the square of the longest one; as the world, as formed, is equal to the creative cause, and matter clothed with form.

The ternary is the first of the unequal numbers. The Triad, mysterious number, which plays so great a part in the traditions of Asia and the philosophy of Plato, image of the Supreme Being, includes in itself the properties of the two first numbers. It was, to the Philosophers, the most excellent and favourite number: a mysterious type, revered by all antiquity, and consecrated in the Mysteries; wherefore there are but three essential degrees among Masons; who venerate, in the triangle, the most august mystery, that of the Sacred Triad, object of their homage and study.

In geometry, a line cannot represent a body absolutely perfect. As little do two lines constitute a figure demonstratively perfect. But three lines form, by their junction, the TRIANGLE, or the first figure regularly perfect; and this is why it has served and still serves to characterize The Eternal; who, infinitely perfect in his nature, is, as Universal Creator, the first Being, and consequently the first Perfection.

The Quadrangle or Square, perfect as it appears, being but the second perfection, can in no wise represent God; who is the first. It is to be noted that the name of God in Latin and French, (Deus, Dieu), has for its initial the Delta or Greek Triangle. Such is the reason, among ancients and moderns, for the consecration of the Triangle, whose three sides are emblems of the three Kingdoms, or Nature, or God. In the centre is the Hebrew Jod, (initial of יהוה), the Animating Spirit or Fire, the generative principle, represented by the letter G., initial of the name of Deity in the languages of the North, and the meaning whereof is Generation.

The first side of the Triangle, offered to the study of the Apprentice, is the mineral kingdom, symbolized by Tub∴.

The second side, the subject of the meditations of the Fellow Craft, is the vegetable kingdom, symbolized by Schib∴ (an ear of corn). In this reign begins the Generation of bodies; and this is why the letter G. in its radiance, is presented to the eyes of the adept.

The third side, the study whereof is devoted to the animal kingdom, and completes the instruction of the Master, is symbolized by Mach∴ (Son of putrefaction).

The cipher 3 symbolizes the Earth. It is a figure of the terrestrial bodies. The 2, upper half of 3, symbolizes the vegetable world; the lower half being hidden from our sight.

3 also referred to harmony, friendship, peace, concord and temperance; and was so highly esteemed among the Pythagoreans that they called it perfect harmony.

Three, four, ten and twelve were sacred numbers among the Etrurians, as they were among the Jews, Egyptians and Hindūs.

The name of Deity in many Nations consisted of three letters: among the Greeks, I∴A∴Ω∴; among the Persians, H∴O∴M∴; among the Hindūs, Aum; among the Scandinavians, I∴O∴W∴ On the upright Tablet of the King, discovered at Nimroud, no less than five, of the thirteen names of the Great Gods, consist of three letters each,—Anu, San, Yav, Bar and Bel.

The quaternary is the most perfect number, and the root of other numbers, and of all things. The tetrad expresses the first mathematical power. 4 represents also the generative power from which all combinations are derived. The Initiates considered it the emblem of Movement and the Infinite, representing everything that is neither corporeal nor sensible. Pythagoras communicated it to his disciples as a symbol of the Eternal and Creative Principle, under the name of Quaternary, the Ineffable Name of God, which signifies Source of everything that has received existence; and which, in Hebrew, is composed of four letters.

In the Quaternary we find the first solid figure, the universal symbol of immortality, the pyramid. The Gnostics claimed that the whole edifice of their science rested on a square whose angles were . . . Σιγη, Silence: Βαθος, Profundity: Νοος, Intelligence: and Αληθεια, Truth. For if the Triangle, figured by the number 3, forms the triangular base of the pyramid, it is unity which forms its point or summit.

Lysis and Timæus of Locria said that not a single thing could be named, which did not depend on the quaternary as its root.

There is, according to the Pythagoreans, a connection between the Gods and numbers, which constitutes the kind of Divination called Arithmomancy. The soul is a number: it is moved of itself: it contains in itself the quaternary number.

Matter being represented by the number 9, or 3 times 3, and the Immortal Spirit having for its essential hieroglyphic the quaternary, or the number 4, the Sages said that Man having gone astray and become entangled in an inextricable labyrinth, in going from *four* to *nine*, the only way which he could take to emerge from these deceitful paths, these disastrous detours, and the abyss of evil into which he had plunged, was to retrace his steps, and go from *nine* to *four*.

The ingenious and mystical idea which caused the Triangle to be venerated, was applied to the cipher 4 (4). It was said that it expressed a living being, I, bearer of the Triangle Δ, the emblem of God; *i. e.* man bearing with himself a Divine principle.

Four was a divine number; it referred to the Deity, and many Ancient Nations gave God a name of four letters; as the Hebrews, יהוה, the Egyptians Amun, the Persians Sura, the Greeks ΘΕΟΣ and the Latins Deus. This was the Tetragrammaton of the Hebrews, and the Pythagoreans called it Tetractys, and swore their most solemn oath by it. So too Odin among the Scandinavians, ZETΣ among the Greeks, Ptha among the Egyptians, Thoth among the Phœnicians, and As-ur and Nebo among the Assyrians. The list might be indefinitely extended.

The number 5 was considered as mysterious, because it was compounded of the Binary, Symbol of the False and Double, and the Ternary, so interesting in its results. It thus energetically expresses the state of imperfection, of order and disorder, of happiness and misfortune, of life and death, which we see upon the earth. To the Mysterious Societies it offered the fearful image of the Bad Principle, bringing trouble into the inferior order,—in a word, the Binary acting in the Ternary.

Under another aspect it was the emblem of marriage; because it is composed of 2, the first equal number, and of 3, the first unequal number. Wherefore Juno, the Goddess of Marriage, had for her hieroglyphic the number 5.

Moreover it has one of the properties of the number nine, that of re-producing itself, when multiplied by itself: there being always a 5 on the right hand of the product; a result which led to its use as the symbol of material changes.

The ancients represented the world by the number 5. A reason for it, given by Diodorus, is, that it represents earth, water, air, fire, and ether or spirit. Thence the origin of πεντε (5) and Παν, the Universe, as the whole.

The number 5 designated the universal quintessence, and symbolized, by its form ς, the vital essence, the animating spirit, which flows [*serpentat*], through all nature. In fact, this ingenious cipher is the union of the two Greek accents ʼ ʻ, placed over those vowels which ought to be or ought not to be aspirated. The first sign ʻ bears the name of potent spirit; and signifies the Superior Spirit, the Spirit of God aspirated (*spiratus*), respired by man. The second sign ʼ is styled mild spirit, and represents the secondary spirit, the spirit purely human.

The triple triangle, a figure of five lines uniting in five points, was among the Pythagoreans an emblem of Health.

It is the Pentalpha of Pythagoras, or Pentangle of Solomon; has five lines and five angles; and is among Masons the outline or origin of the five-pointed Star, and an emblem of Fellowship.

The third degree commemorates the murder of Hiram Abi, whom it styles the Chief Architect of the Temple, and one of our three Ancient Grand Masters, by three perfidious workmen, to whom he refused to give the Master's word: the loss of that word, and the substitution of another; and hints at the resurrection to life of the murdered man; though, in fact, in the York Rite, it relates that he was merely raised to be buried again. These were events of ordinary occurrence, so far as the mere murder, and the discovery of the body and the punishment of the assassins are concerned. Symbolic Masonry, or the three first degrees, sole heir of the Mysteries, does not tell us the true Master's word. We are left to discover it, in that Rite, in other and modern degrees. It is too evident that the degree is corrupted, mutilated, half effaced, and but a poor substitute for the last degree of the great mysteries. We may almost say that nothing is taught in it, if taken literally; and if allegorically, the legend is one of the most imperfect of allegories.

How can these ordinary events have been worthy to engage the attention of so many enlightened men among all nations, and for so many ages? What interest do they contain for us? What? after 3000 years, which have elapsed since the days of Solomon, do all Europe and America, and much of other parts of the world still celebrate, with every mark of grief, the death of a mere architect; while so many sages and philosophers have died, to be barely mentioned in history? Was Hiram another Socrates, one of those benefactors of the human race, whose name reminds us of the most eminent virtues and signal services? We open the annals of nations and nowhere find his name. No historian mentions it. He was not even a Hebrew or an architect; but a Phœnician, and a founder in brass or other metals; his whole occupation about the Temple confined to casting and moulding the metallic work that adorned it: For Masonic tradition may add to, but cannot contradict the Scriptural account; and here the Scripture is positive.

Nor do the Scriptures mention his death; nor deem him worthy of any mention whatever, except as a skilful workman in metals. In them it nowhere appears that he was a person fitted to associate with King Solomon, or that he was not a heathen, holding to his old Phœnician faith, like Hiram his monarch.

What then was the tie between these three personages? If anything, beyond the ordinary alliance of neighbouring monarchs, it was that they were *initiates* in the Mysteries practised in Phœnicia, to which country as to Palestine they came from Egypt. The Masonic legend stands by itself, unsupported by other history or tradition. Nor are the circumstances, if literally accepted, of the slightest present importance to any one.

It is impossible to believe that a knowledge of occurrences so unimportant and so imperfectly told, could have been the sole object of the Master's Degree. The drama is obviously but an allegory; which we must here examine and explain, inasmuch as the degree itself utterly fails to explain it; and seems, indeed, more like a succession of hints at deeper truths, than like the truth itself.

For many ages, and everywhere, Masons have celebrated the death of Hiram. That event, therefore, interests the whole world, and no particular nation, sect, order or coterie: it belongs to no particular time, religion or people. It is not an allegory referring to the death of Christ, for it has with that so few points of resemblance that the truth would never be discovered in the allegory; nor to the murder of Jacques de Molay, nor that of Charles the 1st, nor the persecutions of the early Christians or those of the Jews.

Everywhere among the ancient nations there existed a similar allegory; and all must refer to some great primitive fact. All these allegories are like so many hieroglyphical writings, to learn the hidden meaning whereof, we need only the key: and that key the Ancient Mysteries will give us.

In the Apprentice we find reproduced the Aspirant of Thebes and Eleusis, the Soldier of Mithras, the Christian Catechumen. In the Fellow Craft, the Μυστης of Eleusis, the Initiate of the Second Order, the Lion of the Eastern Mysteries, the Christian Neophyte.

In all the Mysteries there was a double doctrine. It was so everywhere, among the Brahmins of India as well as among the Druids of Germany and Gaul; at Memphis, Samothrace and Eleusis; in the Mysteries of the Jews and early Christians, as well as in those of Ceres and the Good Goddess. Everywhere we see emblems presenting a physical meaning, and receiving a double interpretation; one natural, and as it were material, within the reach of ordinary intellects; the other sublime and philosophical, which was communicated to those men of genius only, who, in the preparatory degree, had understood the concealed meaning of the allegories.

Everywhere in the East, the cradle of religions and allegories, we see, in ancient times, under different names, the same idea reproduced: everywhere a God, a Supreme Being or an extraordinary man is slain, to recommence afterwards a glorious life: everywhere we meet the memory of a great and tragical event, a crime or transgression that plunges the people into sorrow and mourning, to which soon succeeds enthusiastic rejoicing.

The Master's Degree is but a pale reflection of the ancient initiation, the allegorical drama whereof has been disfigured and become trivial; so that, at the present day, it needs all the skill of a well-informed Master to give interest to the interpretations of the mutilated hieroglyphs of this beautiful degree.

We readily recognize in Hiram, Grand-Master of Free Masons, the Osiris of the Egyptians, the Mithras of the Persians, the Bacchus of the Greeks and the Atys of the Phrygians; whose passion, death and resurrection were celebrated by those peoples respectively. And, astronomically, he is the emblem of the Sun, the symbol of his apparent march; of the Sun, who, declining towards the Southern Hemisphere, is conquered and put to death by the darkness, represented in the same allegory as genii of evil: and who, returning towards the Northern Hemisphere, rises from the dead, victorious.

The constant struggle in every man between the Divine and Natural will was but an integral part of the great contest between good and evil everywhere in the world. With this the ancients assimilated the like struggle between health and sickness, pleasure and pain, peace and war, good fortune and poverty. It seemed to them also like the perpetually alternating conflict between light and darkness and winter and summer. They resorted to the theory of two principles, as an explanation of the whole—two principles, ever at war; and by a temporary victory over one of which, by the other, sin and evil, and pain and sorrow came into the world. Reviving again, they imagined the Good Principle still warring against the Evil one; and reconciled all difficulties by holding that he was ultimately to conquer, when the world would be redeemed and regenerated.

The Sun became the emblem of this beneficent principle; and then the heavens were searched for analogies, and fabulous histories were invented, adding to the main incident a cloud of circumstances, many invented at random, with a poetic license, and varied in every nation according to the tastes or habits of its people; but many also adaptations of astronomical coincidences.

And as the Sun became the symbol of the beneficent and good Principle, his companion the Moon became also an emblem. The Sun readily became the vivifying and generating Principle, or mind and intelligence; and the Moon, his wife, the passive principle, or the emblem of universal matter. And thus the means were afforded for a thousand intricate complications, many of which it is now impossible to unravel or trace to their source.

Science, offered to all well-born Egyptians, was forced on no one. The doctrines of morality, political laws, the restraint of public opinion, the controlling effect of their civil institutions were the same for all; but religious instruction varied, according to the capacity, virtue and wishes of each. The mysteries were not made common; as Masonry is at this day; for they were of some value. Instruction as to the nature of the Divinity was not given promiscuously; because the knowledge of it was real, and to preserve the truth of it for many, it was indispensable not to give it uselessly to all.

It would have been well if that wise caution had been imitated by modern Masons. Then Masonry would not have lost its most valuable prerogatives; as it did when its temple was thrown open to all, indiscriminately, who could pay the price.

Formerly the Master's degree preserved some vestiges of its ancient grandeur: and a Mason could, under the different emblems that covered the truth, recognize the real character, object and origin of this antique monument of human wisdom.

Still the true meaning of its symbolic emblems may be discovered. They show that the drama of the third degree represents, as all the old mysteries did, the annual revolution of the Sun, and his symbolic death and resurrection at the time of the winter solstice. In various shapes and under various disguises, we find this allegory everywhere: and everywhere it teaches, in the death of Osiris, Atys, Hiram, or whosoever represents the Sun, the Eternal contest between the Good and Evil Principles, the fall of man, his immortality and his redemption. It is the history of the struggle that began when Sin entered the world, between light and darkness; light typifying good, and darkness evil; and the ultimate triumph of light and the Good Principle proving the mercy and justice of the Grand Architect of the Universe.

For the allegory of the death and revival of the God of Light, was also explained as symbolizing the great principle of generation from putrefaction (expressed by the word ♋︎☉ ♐︎ ♏︎ ☽ ♒︎☉ ♐︎ ♌︎.·.), the apparent death of animated being, but inexhaustible source of life. Hence the feast at the vernal equinox, among all nations; the ancient sacrifices, that the blood of the victim might fertilize the earth and feed new life; and the universal joy, when reaching the Sign, first of the Bull, and two thousand five hundred years after, of the Ram, at that equinox, the sun began to waken to life the germs hid in the earth, and gave promise of future plenty. And hence the remembrance of the egg, out of which, in the Hindû faith, the world was born, perpetuated even to our day, in the eggs stained and given as presents at that equinox.

The name which we read *Hiram*, is, in Kings, *Khiram* (*Raised to life*), and in Chronicles, *Khouram* (*white*), a term applied to the ancient Initiates, and peculiarly applicable to the Sun.

Hiram is killed. So was Osiris. Hiram was merely raised from the grave; and so was Osiris; but in other legends there is a resurrection. To kill is in Latin *occidere*, whence the word *occident*, the *west*, which, figuratively *kills* the celestial bodies that sink there below the horizon. So resurrection, figuratively meaning the coming again to life, is from the Latin verb *resurgere*, to rise again; as the sun and stars rise again, or come to life, when they appear above the eastern horizon.

The *point within a circle*, and that circle bounded by two parallel lines, refer to the same astronomical legend. The circle is the Sun, and the lines the two Tropics, beyond which he cannot pass. But, as every thing in Masonry has a double sense: so here, too, the circle with a central point is, as it was throughout all the Eastern world, the symbol of the male and female principles, or the creative power and universal matter —God and the universe. The intersection of two equilateral triangles meant the same; and both came from the Indian Mysteries.

In the legend of Osiris, the coffin containing his body was flung ashore under a tamarisk-tree. Another version is that Isis found the body near a tall plant of heath or broom. She sat down by a spring that broke from a rock, and rested there overcome with grief.

A branch of some tree or shrub was indispensable in all the initiations: in the Egyptian Mysteries, the lotus; in those of Atys, the almond-branch; the myrtle of Venus; the Druidical Mistletoe; among the early Christians the box-tree of Palm-Sunday; in Virgil's description of the Mysteries, the golden branch; among Masons, the thorny acacia that marked Hiram's grave; a mere variation of the tamarisk or heath of Osiris. The Ancients considered the acacia incorruptible. It was reverenced by the ancient Arabs, and particularly by the Tribe Ghalfan. They made of its wood their idol Al-Uzza, which Mahomet destroyed. The Sabeans paid it honour, and their initiates bore a branch of it. It was called by them *houzza*, or rather Hoschean; which every Knight Rose ✠ will recognize.

In personifying the astronomical allegory of the descension and ascension of the Sun, itself a symbol of the struggle between the Good and Evil Principles, the Divine and Natural law, the Spirit and the Flesh; the Indians, the Persians, the Egyptians, the Phœnicians, the Phrygians, the Greeks, the Samothracians, the Celts and the Goths, all represented the Sun by a God, a lofty Nature, above mankind and remote from the sympathies of men.

But the Masonic Myth represents its Hero neither by a God nor a warrior. He is one of the mass of the People, the son of a man not even of the Jewish race, but of the Phœnician, and of a woman of the Tribe of Naphtali; in nowise connected with the Priests or the Levites. He is no King nor the son of a King, no Conqueror, no Priest; but a plain man of the People, a worker in the metals, in gold, silver, iron and brass, and in crimson and scarlet stuffs—a second Tubalcain; and of him, this Plebeian, Masonry makes a companion of Kings.

When Osiris and Bacchus were slain, they were sought for by Gods. But when Hiram disappeared, an association of workers, who had lost their Chief, their guide and their light, took measures to find him, and sent forth men from among themselves to search for him.

Thus Masonry teaches, under the same old Myth, the far nobler doctrine of the dignity of labour, of equality and fraternity; and this, and its republican form of government and administration it is, that have caused it to spread throughout the Globe.

Hiram not only represents the Sun, and the Good Principle, but the Eternal, never-dying, primitive TRUTH, ever struggling for the victory. The three assassins are *Ambition, Falsehood* and *Ignorance;* the *ambition* of a corrupt Priesthood, who concealed the Truth from the Masses, that by means of debasing superstitions they might subjugate them more completely to their will; the *falsehood* of their myriad fictions and fables that soon became absolutely inexplicable, a mere jargon and chaos of confusion; and the *ignorance* of the Masses, that caused them to believe in error, and forget the truth. Such is the Masonic Myth.

Listen now to the residue of the Lecture of the Kabbalists!

———

[The Orator and another Brother repeat, by question and answer, as follows].

Qu∴. What do you mean by the number 6?
Ans∴. The theological cube . . . . . The physical cube.
Qu∴. What do you mean by the number 7?
Ans∴. The seven sacraments . . . . . The seven planets.
Qu∴. What do you mean by the number 8?
Ans∴. The small number of Elus . . . . . The small number of wise men.
Qu∴. What do you mean by the number 9?
Ans∴. The exaltation of religion . . . . . The exaltation of matter.
Qu∴. What do you mean by the number 10?
Ans∴. The ten commandments . . . . . The ten precepts of nature.
Qu∴. What do you mean by the number 11?
Ans∴. The multiplication of religion . . . . . The multiplication of nature.
Qu∴. What do you mean by the number 12?
Ans∴. The twelve Articles of Faith; the twelve Apostles, foundation of the Holy City, who preached throughout the whole world, for our happiness and spiritual joy . . . . . The twelve operations of nature: The twelve signs of the Zodiac, foundation of the *Primum Mobile*, extending it throughout the Universe for our temporal felicity.

[The Rabbi (President of the Sanhedrim) adds: From all that you have said, it results that the unit develops itself in 2, is completed in three internally, and so produces 4 externally; whence, through 6, 7, 8, 9, it arrives at 5, half of the spherical number 10, to ascend, passing through 11, to 12, and to raise itself, by the number 4 times 10, to the number 6 times 12, the final term and summit of our eternal happiness].

Qu∴. What is the generative number?
Ans∴. In the Divinity, it is the unit; in created things, the number 2: Because the Divinity, 1, engenders 2, and in created things 2 engenders 1.
Qu∴. What is the most majestic number?
Ans∴. 3, because it denotes the triple divine essence.
Qu∴. What is the most mysterious number?
Ans∴. 4, because it contains all the mysteries of nature.
Qu∴. What is the most occult number?
Ans∴. 5, because it is inclosed in the centre of the series.
Qu∴. Which is the most salutary number?
Ans∴. 6, because it contains the source of our spiritual and corporeal happiness.
Qu∴. Which is the most fortunate number?
Ans∴. 7, because it leads us to the decade, the perfect number.
Qu∴. Which is the number most to be desired?
Ans∴. 8, because he who possesses it, is of the number of the Elus and Sages.
Qu∴. Which is the most sublime number?
Ans∴. 9, because by it religion and nature are exalted.
Qu∴. Which is the most perfect number?
Ans∴. 10, because it includes unity, which created everything, and zero, symbol of matter and chaos, whence everything emerged. In its figures it comprehends the created and uncreated, the commencement and the end, power and force, life and annihilation. By the study of this number, we find the relations of all things; the power of the Creator, the faculties of the creature, the Alpha and Omega of divine knowledge.

Qu.·. Which is the most multiplying number?

Ans.·. 11, because with the possession of two units, we arrive at the multiplication of things.

Qu.·. Which is the most solid number?

Ans.·. 12, because it is the foundation of our spiritual and temporal happiness.

Qu.·. Which is the favourite number of religion and nature?

Ans.·. 4 times 10, because it enables us, rejecting everything impure, eternally to enjoy the number 6 times 12, term and summit of our felicity.

Qu.·. What is the meaning of the square?

Ans.·. It is the symbol of the four elements contained in the triangle, and they emblem of the three chemical principles: these things united form absolute unity in the primal matter.

Qu.·. What is the meaning of the centre of the circumference?

Ans.·. It signifies the universal spirit, vivifying centre of nature.

Qu.·. What do you mean by the quadrature of the circle?

Ans.·. The investigation of the quadrature of the circle indicates the knowledge of the four vulgar elements, which are themselves composed of elementary spirits or chief principles; as the circle, though round, is composed of lines, which escape the sight, and are seen only by the mind.

Qu.·. What is the profoundest meaning of the figure 3?

Ans.·. The Father, the Son, and the Holy Spirit. From the action of these three results the triangle within the square; and from the seven angles, the decade or perfect number.

Qu.·. Which is the most confused figure?

Ans.·. Zero,—the emblem of chaos, formless mixture of the elements.

Qu.·. What do the four devices of the degree signify?

Ans.·. That we are to hear, see, be silent, and enjoy our happiness.

The number 6 was, in the Ancient Mysteries, a striking emblem of nature; as presenting the six dimensions of all bodies; the six lines which make up their form, viz. the four lines of direction, towards the North, South, East and West; with the two lines of height and depth, responding to the zenith and nadir. The sages applied the senary to the physical man; while the septenary was, for them, the symbol of his immortal spirit.

The hieroglyphical senary (the double equilateral triangle) is the symbol of Deity.

6 is also an emblem of health, and the symbol of justice; because it is the first perfect number; that is, the first whose aliquot parts [$\frac{1}{2}$, $\frac{1}{3}$, $\frac{1}{6}$, or 3, 2 and 1] added together make itself.

Ormuzd created six good spirits, and Ahriman six evil ones. These typify the six summer and the six winter months.

No number has ever been so universally in repute as the septenary. Its celebrity is due, no doubt, to the planets being *seven* in number. It belongs also to sacred things. The Pythagoreans regarded it as formed of the numbers 3 and 4; the first whereof was in their eyes the image of the three material elements, and the second the principle of everything that is neither corporeal nor sensible. It presented them, from that point of view, the emblem of everything that is perfect.

Considered as composed of 6 and unity, it serves to designate the invisible centre or soul of everything; because no body exists, of which six lines do not constitute the form, nor without a seventh interior point, as the centre and reality of the body, whereof the external dimensions give only the appearance.

The numerous applications of the septenary, confirmed the ancient sages in the use of this symbol. Moreover, they exalted the properties of the number 7, as having, in a subordinate manner, the perfection of the unit: for if the unit is uncreated, if no number produces it, the seven is also not engendered by any number contained in the interval between 1 and 10. The number 4 occupies an arithmetical middle-ground between the unit and 7, inasmuch as it is as much over 1, as it is under 7, the difference each way being 3.

The cipher 7, among the Egyptians, symbolized life; and this is why the letter Z of the Greeks was the initial of the verb Zαω, I live; and Ζευς (Jupiter), Father of Life.

The number 8, or the octary, is composed of the sacred numbers 3 and 5. Of the heavens, of the seven planets, and of the sphere of the fixed stars, or of the eternal unity and the mysterious number 7, is composed the ogdoade, the number eight, the first cube of equal numbers, regarded as sacred in the arithmetical philosophy.

The Gnostic ogdoade had eight stars, which represented the eight Cabiri of Samothrace, the eight Egyptian and Phœnician principles, the eight Gods of Xenocrates, the eight angles of the cubic stone.

The number eight symbolizes perfection : and its figure, 8 or ∞, indicates the perpetual and regular course of the universe.

It is the first cube $(2 \times 2 \times 2)$, and signifies friendship, prudence, counsel and justice. It was a symbol of the primeval law, which regarded all men as equal.

The novary, or triple ternary. If the number three was celebrated among the ancient sages, that of three times three had no less celebrity ; because, according to them, each of the three elements which constitute our bodies is ternary : the water containing earth and fire ; the earth containing igneous and aqueous particles ; and the fire being tempered by globules of water and terrestrial corpuscles which serve to feed it. No one of the three elements being entirely separated from the others, all material beings composed of these three elements, whereof each is triple, may be designated by the figurative number of three times three, which has become the symbol of all formations of bodies. Hence the name of ninth envelope, given to matter. Every material extension, every circular line, has for representative sign the number nine, among the Pythagoreans ; who had observed the property which this number possesses, of reproducing itself incessantly and entire, in every multiplication ; thus offering to the mind a very striking emblem of matter which is incessantly composed before our eyes, after having undergone a thousand decompositions.

The number nine was consecrated to the Spheres and the Muses. It is the sign of every circumference ; because a circle or 360 degrees is equal to 9, that is to say, $3+6+0=9$. Nevertheless, the ancients regarded this number with a sort of terror : they considered it a bad presage ; as the symbol of versatility, of change, and the emblem of the frailty of human affairs. Wherefore they avoided all numbers where nine appears, and chiefly 81, the produce of 9 multiplied by itself, and the addition whereof, $8+1$, again presents the number 9.

As the figure of the number 6 was the symbol of the terrestrial globe, animated by a divine spirit, the figure of the number 9 symbolized the earth, under the influence of the Evil Principle ; and thence the terror it inspired. Nevertheless, according to the Kabbalists, the cipher 9 symbolizes the generative egg, or the image of a little globular being, from whose lower side seems to flow its spirit of life.

The Ennead, signifying an aggregate of 9 things or persons, is the first square of unequal numbers.

Every one is aware of the singular properties of the number 9, which, multiplied by itself or any other number whatever, gives a result whose final sum is always 9, or always divisible by 9.

9, multiplied by each of the ordinary numbers, produces an arithmetical progression, each member whereof, composed of two figures, presents a remarkable fact ; for example :

$$1 \ldots 2 \ldots 3 \ldots 4 \ldots 5 \ldots 6 \ldots 7 \ldots 8 \ldots 9 \ldots 10$$
$$9 \ldots 18 \ldots 27 \ldots 36 \ldots 45 \ldots 54 \ldots 63 \ldots 72 \ldots 81 \ldots 90$$

The first line of figures gives the regular series, from 1 to 10.

The second reproduces this line doubly ; first ascending, from the first figure of 18, and then returning from the second figure of 81.

It follows from this curious fact, that the half of the numbers which compose this progression represents, in inverse order, the figures of the second half :

$$9 \ldots 18 \ldots 27 \ldots 36 \ldots 45 = 135 = 9 \ldots and \ 1+3+5=45=9$$
$$90 \ldots 81 \ldots 72 \ldots 63 \ldots 54 = 360 = 9 \ .$$
$$\overline{99} \quad \overline{99} \quad \overline{99} \quad \overline{99} \quad \overline{99} \quad 495 = 18 = 9$$

So $9^2=81$ ..... $81^2=6561=18=9$ ..... $9\times2=18$ ... $18^2=324=9$

$9\times3=27$ .... $27^2=729=18=9$. $9\times4=36$ ... $36^2=1296=18=9$.

And so with every multiple of 9—say 45, 54, 63, 72, &c.

Thus $9\times8=72$ .... $72^2=5184=18=9$.

And further:

18	27	36	72
18	27	36	72
144 =9	189=18=9	216=9	144=9
18 =9	54 =9	108 =9	504 =9
324=9...18=9	729=18=9	1296=18=9	5184=18=9

108
108
———
864=18
108 =9
———
11664=18=9.

And so the cubes:

$27^3=729\times729=18=9$
720
———
6561=18=9
1458 =18=9
5103 =9
———
531441=18=9

$18^2=324=9$
324
———
1296=18=9
648 =18=9
972 =18=9
———
104976=27=9

$9^2=81$. $81^2=$.. $6561=18=9$
6561
———
6561 =18=9
39366 =27=9
32805 =18=9
39366 =27=9
———
43,046,721=27=9.

The number 10, or the Denary, is the measure of everything; and reduces multiplied numbers to unity. Containing all the numerical and harmonic relations, and all the properties of the numbers which precede it, it concludes the Abacus or Table of Pythagoras. To the Mysterious Societies, this number typified the assemblage of all the wonders of the universe. They wrote it thus ⊙, that is to say, Unity in the middle of Zero, as the centre of a circle, or symbol of Deity. They saw in this figure everything that should lead to reflection: the centre, the ray, and the circumference, represented to them God, Man, and the Universe.

This number was, among the Sages, a sign of concord, love and peace. To Masons it is a sign of union and good faith; because it is expressed by joining two hands, or the Master's grip, when the number of fingers gives 10: and it was represented by the Tetractys of Pythagoras.

The number 12, like the number 7, is celebrated in the worship of nature. The two most famous divisions of the heavens, that by 7, which is that of the planets, and that by 12, which is that of the Signs of the Zodiac, are found upon the religious monuments of all the peoples of the Ancient World, even to the remote extremes of the East. Although Pythagoras does not speak of the number 12, it is none the less a sacred number. It is the image of the Zodiac; and consequently that of the Sun, which rules over it.

Such are the ancient ideas in regard to those numbers which so often appear in Masonry; and rightly understood, as the old Sages understood them, they contain many a pregnant lesson.

We conclude this Lecture with that which has always been, and we believe always will be the Masonic idea of the Supreme Being: We call Him the Grand Architect of the Universe, considering that Universe as His most magnificent temple and perfect work of architecture. Conformably to this idea, we comprehend in that name an Eternal and Universal Intelligence, infinite in Power, Knowledge and Love, governing the

worlds and living beings that compose the universe, by laws regular and suitable to the ends of their existence. We revere him as the sole Master of all, conceivable and visible in all the marvellous things with
which he has embellished his universe; as the Author and Father of all men; as Him who gives us all intelligence and life. Thus comprehending the Supreme Being, Masonry becomes the aggregate of human wisdom, and of all those perfections which make man resemble the Divinity. It is, in a word, that universal
morality, suited to the inhabitant of every country, to the man of every creed. Its morality is more extensive
and more universal than that of any particular religion; all of which are exclusive, because they divide individuals into classes, as idolaters, schismatics, sectarians and infidels; while in religionists Masonry sees
brethren only, to whom it opens its temple, that they may there free themselves from the prejudices of country
and the errors of the religion of their fathers, and be led to love and assist one another. The torch which it
bears in its pure hand, it has never used to light a flame anywhere upon the earth, but solely to enlighten
men; for it grieves for and flees from error; but it neither hates nor persecutes: and finally its object is to
make of the whole human race a single family of Brothers, united in love, knowledge and labour.

Thus, opening its Temple to all men, to the Jew, the Mahometan, the adorers of Buddha and Fo, as well
as to the Christian, without identifying itself with any of these rites, it can follow the standard of none of
their prophets; but it adopts and practises whatever of the doctrines and precepts of each is conformable
to universal morality, and to that primitive religion first taught to the ancient Patriarchs.

TO CLOSE.

Th∴ Ven∴ Bro∴ Amun, what is the hour?

Sen∴ W∴ Th∴ Ven∴, it is the hour of sunset, answering to the autumnal equinox.

Th∴ Ven∴ What good work remains to be done, my Brother, to close the labours of the day?

Sen∴ W∴ Th∴ Ven∴, I know of none.

Th∴ Ven∴ Bro∴ Dionusos, knowest thou of any good work that remains to be done, before we can
close the labours of the day?

Jun∴ W∴ Th∴ Ven∴, I know of none.

Th∴ Ven∴ Doth any brother know of a sick brother to be cared for, of a distressed brother to be
comforted, of a persecuted brother who needs assistance and defenders, of the widow or orphan of a brother
suffering or in want?

[If any such case is mentioned, order is taken that it be provided for. If none, the Th∴ Ven∴ proceeds:].

Th∴ Ven∴ Brother Amun, it being close upon the sunset, it is my pleasure that this Council of Knights
of the Sun be now closed, and so stand until the next regular communication, unless sooner convened by
my order, or upon some sudden emergency, of which due and timely notice will be given.

Sen∴ W∴ [Repeats the order to the Jun∴ W∴]

Jun∴ W∴ [Repeats the order to the Knights.]

[The Th∴ Ven∴ then gives the sign, and each brother answers as in opening].

Th∴ Ven∴ Riches pass away like shadows on the water. They are the most inconstant of friends.
Those that are dear to us die, and our friendships are not immortal. All men stand upon the margins of
their graves; and one thing alone is beyond the reach of fate: the judgment that is passed upon the
dead. Go out again, my Brethren, from between the holy columns; and among men prepare by good works
for that judgment!

[The Th∴ Ven∴ then raps ? ? ?, and all the Knights repeat with their hands].

Th∴ Ven∴ My Brethren, this Council is closed.

FINIS.

Twenty-Ninth Degree.

Grand Ecossais of St.∴ Andrew, or Patriarch of the Crusades.

THE CHAPTER; ITS DECORATIONS, ETC.

The hangings are crimson, supported by white columns. The seats of the Master and Wardens are of crimson, ornamented with gilding. Those of the other Knights are blue.

In each corner of the Hall is a Saint Andrew's Cross, with nine lights, by threes, in front of each. There are also nine, by threes, on the East, West and South sides of the altar in the centre. There are also nine, by threes, in front of each of the four first officers; making, in all, 81.

The *dress* of the Knights is a crimson robe, a deep scarlet sash round the waist, a green collar edged with crimson, worn over the neck, and to which the jewel is suspended, and a white silk scarf, worn from left to right, and ornamented with gold fringe. On the left breast is embroidered on the robe a large white Cross of St.∴ Andrew.

The *Jewel* is two sharp pointed double interlaced triangles, formed by arcs of large circles, made of gold, and enclosing in the centre the compasses, upright and open to 25 degrees. At the bottom is suspended to one of the points a St.∴ Andrew's Cross of gold, surmounted by a Knight's helmet. On the centre of the Cross is the Letter Y.∴ enclosed in an equilateral triangle, and that in a ring formed by a winged serpent. Between the two lower arms of the Cross a Key is suspended; and on the extremities of the Cross are the letters ב∴ י∴ מ∴ נ∴; the initials of the words ♏☿⊙♍∴ ♀⊙♊♀♒∴ ♋⊙♐&♏☾♒⊙♐&∴ ♒☾♊&⊙♋⊙&∴.

The Presiding officer is styled *Ven.∴ Gr.∴ Master;* the Sen.∴ Warden, *Gr.∴ Prior;* the Jun.∴ Warden, *Gr.∴ Seneschal;* the 4th Officer, *Gr.∴ Bailiff;* the Sen.∴ Deacon, *Gr.∴ Preceptor;* the Jun.∴ Deacon, *Gr.∴ Marshal;* the Treasurer, *Gr.∴ Almoner;* the Secretary, *Gr.∴ Registrar*; and the other Knights, *Gr.∴ Crosses.* A *Warder* guards the door on the inside, and a *Sentinel* on the outside. The Gr.∴ Master sits in the East; the Gr.∴ Prior in the West; the Gr.∴ Seneschal in the South; and the Gr.∴ Bailiff in the North.

The Lodges of this Degree are styled *Chapters.*

The *Battery* is z raps, by ? ; and ! The *Age*, the square of z. The *Step* is upon a St.∴ Andrew's Cross, by ; steps of an ☾.∴ ⊙.∴ — ; of a ♑.∴ ♐.∴ — and ; of a ♋.∴ ♋.∴

Pass-word in the Court of the Sultan . . . ⊙♐♏☿♐⊙♊∴

During a reception, the Hall represents the Court of *Salah-Eddin* (or *Saladin*), the Great Sultan of Egypt and Syria. No Masonic emblems appear. A roll of parchment representing the Koran lies on a table in front of the Throne, and a Saracenic Standard, displaying the Crescent, stands near the seat of the Gr.∴ Master and each of the Wardens. The Hall is then hung with green and gold. The Knights all wear the Turkish costume, *i. e.* wide trowsers, a vest and turban, all snow-white, and a red sash round the waist, with a scimetar. The Throne is occupied by the Candidate, who represents the Sultan, while the Gr∴ Master represents *Hugh of Tiberias*, Lord of Galilee. The Sen∴ Warden, seated in the West, represents *Malek Adhel*, brother of the Sultan, [*Malek Adhel Sayf-Eddin*, the Just King and Sword of Religion] : The Junior Warden, seated in the South represents *Malek Modaffer Taki-Eddin* [the Victorious King devoted to religion], Prince of Hamah, and Nephew of the Sultan : the 3d Warden and Sen∴ Deacon, seated on either side of the Throne, *Malek Daher* [Triumphant King] Son of the Sultan and Prince of Aleppo ; and *Malek Afdal* [Excellent King], Son of the Sultan and Prince of Damascus : and the Junior Deacon, who accompanies the Grand Master, and after introducing him seats himself on the right of the Sen∴ Warden, *the Emir of Emessa.*

Behind the Throne is a banner in the shape of a shroud, white, on which, in black letters are the words " SALAH EDDIN, KING OF KINGS, SALAH-EDDIN, VICTOR OF VICTORS, SALAH-EDDIN MUST DIE !"

TO OPEN.

The Gr∴ Master gives three raps, and says, " Sir Knights, I am about to open this Chapter of Knights Ecossais of St. Andrew. You will please clothe and arm yourselves, and the officers will assume their respective stations."

After that is done, the Gr∴ Master again says, " Sir Knight Gr∴ Bailiff, are all present Knights Ecossais of St. Andrew?"

Gr∴ Bail∴ Ven∴ Gr∴ Master, all present have seen the Sultan of the Saracens upon his Throne.

Gr∴ M∴ You will take order then, Sir Kt∴ Gr∴ Bailiff, that the avenues of approach be duly guarded, that we may suffer no interruption.

Gr∴ Bail∴ Sir Kt∴ Warden, inform the Captain of the Guard that this Chapter is about to be opened, and direct him to station his guards so that all the avenues leading hither shall be duly guarded, and we be secure against interruption.

[The Warden goes out, returns, and says, " Sir Kt∴ Gr∴ Bailiff, your orders are communicated and the guards are stationed."]

Gr∴ Bail∴ Ven∴ Gr∴ Master, the avenues are duly guarded, and we are in security.

Gr∴ M∴ Sir Kt∴ Gr∴ Prior, what was the original occupation of this Order?

Gr∴ Prior : . . To rebuild the Churches in the Holy Land, destroyed by the Saracens ; as our ancient brethren wrought at the re-building of the Temple, with the Sword in one hand and the Trowel in the other.

Gr∴ M∴ To what do we now devote ourselves?

Gr∴ Prior : . . To active Charity, and practical philanthropy, especially inculcating toleration, and discountenancing bitterness and strife.

Gr∴ M∴ Sir Kt∴ Gr∴ Preceptor, what is the first duty of a true Knight?

Gr∴ Prec∴ To reverence and obey that Great Deity whose Unspeakable Name is so Sacred in this degree.

Gr∴ M∴ Sir Kt∴ Gr∴ Bailiff, what is the second duty of a true Knight?

Gr∴ Bail∴ Ever to have a sacred regard for truth, and a profound scorn for falsehood, cunning and treachery ; to profess no opinion for the sake of expediency ; and to conceal none through fear of consequences.

Gr∴ M∴ Sir Kt∴ Gr∴ Seneschal, what is the third duty of a true Knight?

Gr∴ Senes∴ To protect virtue and innocence against violence, injury, fraud or defamation.

Gr∴ M∴ Sir Kt∴ Gr∴ Prior, what is the fourth duty of a true Knight?

Gr∴ Prior : . . Never to recede in the great battle for truth, the right, free thought and free speech, against error, wrong, bigotry, intolerance and oppression of the conscience, unless it be to gather new strength for a more determined struggle.

Gr∴ M∴ Knights Gr∴ Crosses, you hear what duties your knightly obligation requires of you. Renew now to each other your solemn promise, made when you were admitted to this degree, that you will ever and faithfully perform them !

All : WE PROMISE.

Gr∴ M∴ Fail not to keep the promise! Sir Kt∴ Grand Almouer, knowest thou of any poor, sick or distressed Knight, or of the widow or orphan of one deceased, who needs our aid, or is entitled to our sympathy?

Alm∴ I do not, Ven∴ Gr∴ Master.

Ven∴ M∴ Then, in the name of God and St. Andrew, let us open our Chapter! since it is high noon, and life is all too short for the work we have to do. Sir Knights Gr∴ Crosses, the sign!

[All give the £th sign. Then the Gr∴ Sentinel raps? — the Gr∴ Prior; — and the Gr∴ Master! — and the latter declares the Chapter duly opened].

RECEPTION.

The Candidate is prepared by being dressed in Turkish costume, as described above, wearing in front of the turban a large brilliant. Being thus prepared, and all the Knights except the Grand Master being in their places, but the Throne vacant, the armed Sentinel on the outside throws the door open, and the Candidate, accompanied by the Grand Bailiff [*Malek Daher*] enters the Hall, which is blazing with light, advances to the Throne, the Knights all rising and bowing, and is seated upon it. The Grand Bailiff sits on his right, and hands him from time to time, at the proper moment, what he has to say, printed on slips of paper; having told him beforehand that he is to read them aloud.

In the mean time, the Gr∴ Master is dressed as a Prisoner, and loaded with heavy chains, and being taken charge of by the Junior Deacon [*Emir of Emessa*], goes to the door, where the Sentinel receives the pass-word [⊙†♏ ☿ ‡⊙ ♎∴], and admits them. They advance to the East, and the Emir makes a deep obeisance to the Sultan, who, from a slip given him by the Grand Bailiff, reads:

Cand∴ Brave Emir of Emessa, whence come you, and whom bring you with you in chains?

Jun∴ D∴ King of Kings, from Ascalon, where we have defeated the Christian invaders in a hard-fought battle, and taken many prisoners, one of the chief of whom, Hugh of Tiberias, the Lord of Galilee, I have brought to thee, that thou mightest fix his ransom.

Cand∴ ALLAH AKBAR! ALLAH KERIM! The praise be to God. Art thou the Lord of Galilee?

Gr∴ M∴ I am.

Cand∴ I have heard of thy fame in a hundred battles, and have myself crossed swords with thee before the walls of Acre. Thou art a brave knight, noble and courteous. Emir, sayeth not the Prophet, "Thou shalt not degrade the noble captive?" It was not well done to load him with these chains. Have them at once removed, and when the knight hath eaten, and refreshed himself, return again to my presence.

[The Gr∴ Master and the Emir withdraw, and after a time return, the Gr∴ Master freed of his chains, and clothed in a new robe; and the Emir, conducting him to a seat near the Sultan, repairs to his own place].

Cand∴ Sir Hugh of Tiberias, I do you all honour as a brave and loyal knight; but as the custom is among the followers of the Prophet, I must exact of you a ransom proportioned to your rank as a lord, and your eminence as a warrior. Its amount will show the estimation in which I hold you; and I fix it at the sum of twice fifty thousand besants of gold. The choice is yours, to pay the ransom or to lose your head.

Gr∴ M∴ Alas, princely Saladin, you give me in reality no option. It is beyond my power to pay the ransom, or the half of it. Were my Lordship of Galilee and my Principality of Tiberias both sold, I could not pay it. So even take my head; for to a man impoverished and ruined it scarcely matters whether he has a head or not. I need short shrift, and the executioner may do his work at once.

Cand∴ Dost thou not fear death?

Gr∴ M∴ No, by my faith. I have met him face to face too often. Only I would rather fall sword in hand, striking a good blow or two against your nobles, as a true knight loves to leave the world, than die the death of a criminal by the scimetar or bowstring.

Cand∴ It does not need that you should die thus, gallant Knight. I give you two years in which to collect together your ransom. Go back to France: Thou needest not part with thy Principality or Lordship. I will win them of thee hereafter with the sword. So noble a Knight is too valuable to his countrymen to be allowed thus to lose his life. There is no Knight or Christian that will not give thee liberal aid towards thy ransom. But if you should fail, give me your Knightly word that at the end of two years from this day, and at this hour, you will present yourself to me again, and surrender your head to the Executioner.

Gr∴M∴ Most noble and princely Saladin! truest of Knights thyself in spirit! I accept thy terms, with ten thousand thanks for thy generous confidence; and I pledge my Knightly word, never yet given to man or woman and afterwards broken, that, if I do not pay the ransom, I will at this very hour, two years hence, present myself before you, to die without a murmur. And this moreover, by the Body of the Redeemer do I solemnly swear; and may He have mercy on me, only if I keep this oath and promise, if death or sickness do not prevent!

Cand∴ Noble Emir of Emessa, return this brave Knight his sword and armour. Give him a horse of the breed called the Winged, and send him with sufficient escort, after he hath eaten with us, to the Christian Army. Malek Adhel, Sayf-Eddin, see that he hath passports that may insure his safety.

Sen∴W∴ King of Kings, I hear and obey.

Gr∴M∴ Princely Saladin, I thank thee most gratefully; and all Christendom shall know how nobly thou hast dealt with me. Permit me now to retire and prepare for my journey; since, by my faith, the hundred thousand besants require me to be stirring, and will allow me scant rest for the next two years.

Cand∴ Thou hast permission, Knight. The noble Emir will go with you and see you prepared at all points for your journey.

[The Gr∴ Master bows and retires, but as he passes out at the door, the Candidate, prompted by the Gr∴ Bailiff, says, "Malek Afdal, my Son, recall the Frankish Knight. I would speak with him again."]

[The Sen∴ Deacon goes out, and returns with the Gr∴ Master, who again approaches the East, and awaits the Sultan's pleasure].

Cand∴ Noble Knight, since your forces entered this land of ours, I have learned something of your institution of Knighthood, and would fain know more. I understand the sanctity of the Knightly word, as you may see by the confidence I have placed in yours. And I have also heard from those who have been in your camps, as prisoners and otherwise, that there is among you a strange equality; so that a Knight, though poor, may sit in the presence of a Monarch. Tell me if that be so.

Gr∴M∴ It is. Thou hast not been misinformed. The name of Knight and gentle blood entitle the possessor to place himself in the same rank with sovereigns of the first degree, so far as regards all but Kingly authority and dominion. If the greatest King were to wound the honour of the poorest Knight, he could not by the law of chivalry, refuse satisfaction by single combat.

Cand∴ And how may he aspire to mate in marriage?

Gr∴M∴ With the noblest and the proudest dame in Christendom. The poorest Knight is free, in all honourable service, to devote his hand and sword, the fame of his exploits and the deep devotion of his heart, to the fairest princess that ever wore a Coronet.

Cand∴ And hath the Order of Knighthood other excellencies?

Gr∴M∴ It demands the strictest honour and most sacred regard to truth. It requires us to protect the defenceless and the innocent. It inculcates purity and virtue, patience, firmness, self-government; and, in short, that the true Knight and gentleman shall be alike without fear and without reproach.

Cand∴ Prince of Tiberias, thou owest me return for the favour I have done thee, and I ask of thee a boon. I pray thee in the name of Allah, that thou wilt make known to me the sacred laws of the Order of Knighthood; and confer upon me that dignity before your departure; for I am ready to conform to its laws.

Gr∴M∴ [After hesitating, and appearing confused]. It is impossible.

Cand∴ How impossible? Make known to me the reasons. I would fain receive as a willing gift that which I might extort.

Gr∴M∴ Thou rulest many nations, Salah-Eddin. For every arrow thou sendest by a Messenger, 'tis said that two-score thousand riders mount on horseback, and for the bow as many as thou hast asked me besants for my ransom. But I tell thee, that mighty as thou art, thou hast not the power to *force* a true and loyal Knight to do an act dishonourable, or forbidden by the rules of Knighthood.

Cand∴ I crave thy pardon, noble Knight, for the inconsiderate threat; for is it not true that the thing that one gains only by compulsion is of little value? I would entreat thee courteously, and as an equal, to do me this great favour. Thou sayest it is impossible; but why?

Gr∴ M∴. Thou canst not be made a Knight without bending thy knee before me; and my sword must be laid upon thy person.

Cand∴. Do I not kneel in prayer, even as the humblest believer?

Gr∴ M∴. Thou must profess thy belief in the one true and ever-living God; and ye Saracens worship not the true God.

Cand∴. Thou art mistaken, Prince; for thou knowest not our faith. Doth not the Koran say, "There is no God but God, the living, the self-subsisting? Your God is our God; there is no God but he, the most merciful. To God belongeth the East and the West: therefore, whithersoever ye turn yourselves to pray, there is the face of God: for God is omnipresent and omniscient. We believe in God, and that which hath been sent down to us, and that which hath been sent unto Abraham and Ismael, and Isaac and Jacob, and the Tribes; and that which was delivered unto Moses and Jesus; and that which was delivered unto the Prophets from their Lord. We make no distinction between any of them, and to God are we resigned." So speaketh the Koran everywhere.

Gr∴ M∴. It is indispensable that every Knight should believe in the Lord Jesus Christ.

Cand∴. Doth not the Koran say that those who believe, Christians, and whosoever believeth in God and the last day, and doth that which is right, they shall have their reward with their Lord? Doth it not say, "We formerly delivered the book of the law unto Moses, and caused Apostles to succeed him, and gave evident miracles to Jesus the Son of Mary, and strengthened him with the Holy Spirit. Every one of them believeth in God, and his angels and his scriptures, and his apostles. We make no distinction at all between his apostles. The angels said, O Mary, verily God hath chosen thee, and hath purified thee, and hath chosen thee above all the women of the world. The angels said, O Mary, verily God sendeth thee good tidings, that thou shalt bear the Word, proceeding from himself; his name shall be Christ Jesus, the Son of Mary, honourable in this world and in the world to come, and one of those who approach near to the presence of God; and he shall speak unto men in the cradle . . God shall teach him the Scripture and wisdom and the law, and the Gospel; and shall appoint him his apostle to the children of Israel. God took him up unto himself; and God is mighty and wise. And there shall not be one of those who have received the Scriptures, who shall not believe in him, before his death; and on the day of resurrection he shall be a witness against them." Thus sayeth the Koran; and all the followers of the Prophet believe that Christ was an Apostle from God, born of a Virgin, and inspired, and did teach the truth.

Gr∴ M∴. Sayeth the Koran these things, and dost thou believe them?

Cand∴. It sayeth them; and I believe them. I also believe that the Prophet was an apostle, sent to preach the truth, the primitive true religion, revealed by God to Abraham. I believe in Christ; but thou dost not believe in Mahomet. We worship no idols, but the one true God, who was the God of Abraham, and who sent Christ Jesus to teach his truth to the Jews.

Gr∴ M∴. What Knightly virtues does the Koran enjoin upon those who believe its doctrines?

Cand∴. "Serve God, associate no creature with him; and show kindness unto parents and relations and orphans and the poor, and your neighbour who is of kin to you, and also your neighbour who is a stranger, and to your familiar companion and the traveller, and the captives whom your right hands shall possess, for God loveth not the proud or vain-glorious who are covetous. Oh, true believers, be patient, and constant-minded, and fear God, that ye may be happy." Such and others like them are the words written on all the pages of the Koran. The word of a Moslem is never broken: and he who is intemperate, unchaste, cruel, the violator of innocence, covetous or base, offends against the law of the Prophet.

Gr∴ M∴. Princely Salah-Eddin, I consent; and mayest thou pardon me, O Father! if in this I err: for one so noble and magnanimous surely merits the high honour of Knighthood. Go with me then alone; for none but thou must witness the solemn ceremony that shall confer on thee the rank and honours of Knighthood.

Cand∴. Sayf-Eddin, my brother, assume my station until I return, as thou hast often done, and let the business of the day proceed. Let none depart until I come again.

[He then descends from the Throne, and retires with the Gr∴ Master to an adjoining apartment; in which are water in a basin, towels, a bath, and a couch, with snow-white covering. The Gr∴ Master leads the candidate to the basin, pours water on his head and directs him to wash his face and hands, and dry them on the napkin: and then says to him]: " The rules of Knighthood also strictly require that the beard of the novitiate shall be shaven smooth and his hair trimmed; but the literal performance of these rites may be dispensed with, under circumstances that require it, like the present. I therefore, as a representation of that ceremony, cut a small lock of each, and no more, yielding to your rank and the customs of your country. I shall now retire. You will then immerse yourself in the bath; which, with the ceremonies already performed, is a symbol of that baptismal rite observed among all Eastern nations by way of purification of the body, emblematical of that purity and innocence of soul without which no one can enter into the order of Knighthood, nor into the pure abodes of happiness above. The candidate for Knighthood not only serves a long apprenticeship in arms, and shows himself valiant and daring, and above all base apprehension of death; but he must pass through a long and rigid probation, to prove himself, for his virtue, temperance, faith, constancy and nobleness of heart, fit to be enrolled in the ranks of chivalry. That, when the excellent qualities of the candidate are known, may be dispensed with, and the order conferred even upon the field. But wherever and whenever conferred, the candidate must be free of sin and vice. And I do enjoin thee, if thou art not resolved to be henceforward virtuous, chaste, humble before God, merciful, tolerant, generous and charitable, to proceed no further; lest hereafter thou shouldest be disgraced before the whole world, as a false and disloyal Knight. Remember that, if thou becomest a Knight, thy word must hereafter never be broken: thou must never strike a prostrate foe, nor slay the prisoner that can no longer resist, nor refuse moderate ransom, nor defile thyself with many women; and all true and loyal Knights must be thy brothers, all distressed virgins thy sisters, and all poor and destitute orphans thy children. Wilt thou proceed?"

Cand∴ I will.

Gr∴ M∴ Bathe then, and free thy body from impurity; at the same time, washing from thy soul all evil passions and unworthy desires. Then seek the couch, which, snow-white and perfumed, is an emblem of that heaven that waits to welcome the true Knight, whose strong arm ever maintains that which he believes to be right and true, who protects the poor and feeble against the hand of the oppressor, and keeps himself pure and undefiled before God. Then array thyself in snowy linen, the emblem of innocence, and the scarlet robe that is an emblem of the zeal and devotion of a Knight, and his readiness to shed his blood for his God, his country, or the lady of his heart. When thou hast dressed, summon me unto thee again.

[The Gr∴ Master retires, the Candidate bathes, and then retires to the couch, where he lies a few moments, rises, and dresses himself as directed; and then gives three raps, which recall the Gr∴ Master.]

Gr∴ M∴ My Brother, let us kneel and pray!

PRAYER.

Our Father, who art in Heaven, the God of Abraham, Isaac and Jacob, the one only true God! Look now upon this Candidate, about to become a Knight and thy Servant. Aid him to perform punctually the vows he is about to assume. Strengthen his good resolutions, and suffer not temptation to overcome him. Make him a true Knight, and teach him to exercise whatever powers he hath, with gentleness and moderation, and for the benefit of mankind and thy glory. Aid him to be true and loyal, frank and sincere; and may his Knighthood here below be but preparatory to his final initiation into the mysteries of thy Heaven of perfect happiness and perfect purity! Amen!

Gr∴ M∴ Noble Salah-Eddin, thou hast kneeled to God in prayer. Thou must kneel yet again, to me, as the representative of all the orders of Knighthood. But first it is necessary that you take upon yourself a most solemn obligation, before I can reveal to you the secrets of the order of Knighthood, which I am about to confer upon you. It will bind thee to nothing unworthy of thyself, or contrary to thy faith, or at variance with thy duties to thy household, thyself, thy People or thy God. Take then, if thou art willing to proceed, the Koran, which thou deemest Holy, in thy left hand and press it to thy heart, and placing thy right hand upon this cross-hilt of my sword, repeat after me:

THE OBLIGATION.

In the presence of the One Living and Ever True God of Abraham, Isaac and Jacob, and upon this Holy Book and Emblem, I do most solemnly and sincerely promise and swear, that I will never reveal the secrets of this Degree of Grand Ecossais of St. Andrew to any person in the world, except by permission from due and proper authority, and to one duly authorized to receive them.

I furthermore promise and swear, that I will henceforward never write or utter a falsehood, knowing it to be such; nor violate my plighted word, or my implied pledge; nor use words in a double sense; nor equivocate or be guilty of mental reservation to deceive another; nor allow another to misunderstand and be deceived by my words; but I will ever henceforward be true, frank and loyal.

I furthermore promise and swear that I will henceforward give succor and assistance to all distressed ladies and poor and needy orphans, and will allow none to rob or injure them, if it be in my power to prevent it.

I furthermore promise and swear that I will ever venerate the True God, and strive to govern my conduct by His laws; and that I will henceforward receive his blessings and generous gifts with thankfulness and gratitude, and strive to repay in part his favours by doing good to my fellow-men.

I furthermore promise and swear that I will never disgracefully retreat before the enemy; and that I will aid and assist, cherish and protect a worthy Brother Knight, and see that no wrong be done him, if it be in my power to prevent it.

To all whereof I do again most solemnly and sincerely swear, binding myself under no less a penalty than that of being excommunicated from the Order of Knighthood, and denounced throughout the world, in every Court in Europe and Asia, to Moslem and Nazarene, to Knight and Lady, wherever honour is loved and infamy detested, as disloyal and forsworn Knight, dishonoured gentleman, and base, ignoble man. So help me God, and reward or punish me as I keep or violate this vow!

[The Gr∴ Master then gives the Candidate the Signs, Words and Tokens].

FIRST SIGN: . . . *Of the Earth:* . . . ⏀ the ⏀ gently ⏀— and ⏀ the ⏀ with the ⏀ of the ! ⏀ of the ⏀.

FIRST TOKEN: . . . Mutually and successively take, with the ends of the ⏀ and ⏀ of the ⏀, each the ,st — ?d and ;d ⏀ of the ⏀ of the ⏀ of the other; mutually spelling the word ⏀∴.

SECOND SIGN: . . . *Of Water:* . . . Place the ⏀ over the ⏀, and then extending the ⏀ to the front at the height of the ⏀, let it gracefully ⏀ to the ⏀, as if ⏀ one.

SECOND TOKEN: . . . Mutually and successively take, with the ⏀ and ?d ⏀ of the ⏀, each the ,st — ?d and ;d ⏀ of the ?d ⏀ of the other; mutually spelling ⏀∴.

THIRD SIGN: . . . *Of the Air:* . . . Turn the ⏀ to the ⏀, looking upon the ⏀; raise the ⏀ ⏀ together, carry ⏀ to the ⏀, and let ⏀ drop by the ⏀.

THIRD TOKEN: . . . Take between the ♈♀♃♎ of the ♈&♑♋♏ and ;d ♑♀♒♌☾‡, mutually and successively, each the ♈♀♃ of the ;d ♑♀♒♌☾‡ of the other, one saying ♋☉♐&.·. and the other ♏☾.·.— Then the first takes in the same way the first ♃&☉†☉♒♉ of the same ♑♀♒♑☾‡, and says ♒☉♐&.·.

FOURTH SIGN: . . . *Of Fire:* . . . ♀♒♈☾‡†☉♐☾ all the ♑♀♒♌☾‡♎ and the ♈&♑♋♏♎, and cover the ☾♄☾♎ with the ♏☉♐¶♎ of the &☉♒♊♎, ♃☉†♋♎ outwards.

RESPONSE: . . . Stretch forth the ‡‡&☉♒♊ and ☉‡♋, ♃☉†♋ downwards, to the height of the ♎&☿♑†♊☾‡, and directly to the ♑‡☿♒♈.

FIFTH SIGN: . . *Of Admiration:* . . . Raise the eyes towards Heaven, the hands ♑♃†♀♑♈☾♊, the right somewhat &♀♌&☾‡ than the left, as the Catholic Priest does, when he says ♊☿♋♀♒♑♎ *☿♏♀♎♐♑♋; the &☾☾† of the †‡♑☿☿♈ being somewhat elevated, so that the left ¶♒☾☾ may form a ♎♓♑☉‡☾ with the right.

SIXTH SIGN: . . . *Of the Sun:* . . . Place the thumb of the right hand upon the ‡‡☾♄☾, raising the ♑☿‡☾♑♀♒♌☾‡ of the ♎☉♋☾♃&☉♒♊ so as to form a ♎♓♑☉‡☾, with a gesture as if you had some distant object in view, saying ☉♒♀‡☉& &☉♎&☾♋☾♎&.·.

SEVENTH (OR GENERAL) SIGN: . . . Form a St.·. Andrew's Cross upon ♄☿♑‡‡♏‡☾☉♎♈, with the ☉‡♋♎ ♐‡☿♎♎☾♊ and &☉♒♊♎ upwards.

GENERAL TOKEN: . . . Each takes successively, between the ♈♀♃♎ of the ♈&♑♋♏ and ♑☿‡☾♑♀♒♌☾‡ of the ‡‡&☉♒♊ the ♑♀‡♎♈ ♁☿♀♒♈ of the ♑☿‡☾♑♀♒♌☾‡ of the ‡‡&☉♒♊ of the other; one saying ♒☾.·. and the other ¶&☉.·. then each takes, successively, with the same, the ♑♀‡♎♈ ♁☿♋♒♈ of the †♀♈♈†☾ ♑♀♒♌☾‡ of the other, and one says ♋☉&.·. and the other ♒☾¶&☉♋☉&.·.

PASS-WORDS: . . . 1st. . . ♃&☿‡☾&-†☉¶.·. [Angel of the Earth].
2d. . . ♈☉††♀♑♊.·. [Angel of the Water].
3d. . . ♐☉♎♋☉‡☉♒.·. [Angel of Air].
4th . . ☉♑‡♀-☉†.·. [Angel of Fire].

SACRED WORD: . . . ♒☾¶&☉♋☉&.·.

After communicating these, the Gr.·. Master requests the Candidate to kneel on his right knee; draws his sword and strikes him lightly with the flat of the blade on each shoulder, saying: "Salah-Eddin, Sultan "of Egypt and Syria, I dub thee Knight, in the name of the Order of Knights Ecossais of the Order of St.·. "Andrew of Scotland. Be valiant, true and virtuous."

He then raises him, and says: "My Brother, I need not enlarge further to you upon the duties of a Knight. The Order of Knights Ecossais, is a Chivalric Order of Great Antiquity; and has numbered among its members many Kings and Princes; but its greatest boast is its intimate connection and alliance with an order more ancient still; one founded by the Great King Solomon at the time of building the Temple at Jerusalem, and of which he was the First Grand Master; to which order he committed the custody of those primitive truths revealed to the Ancient Patriarchs, and which the Moslems revere as the religion of Abraham. King Huram of Tyre, and Huram, the son of a widow of Tyre, a man of the People, were also Grand Masters; and from them, by uninterrupted continuity, the ancient truths, known before the flood, have come down to us. That order numbered among its members the chief favourites and nobles of Solomon; but it was chiefly composed of the workmen who wrought at the building of the Temple. They then were and still are called Free

Masons. The Masters, or Third Order, received from Solomon the true name of the Deity, which was made known by God to Moses; and which is still preserved among the Masons, none being allowed to pronounce it. It is termed with us the Master's word; it being the same, by pronouncing which Asaf brought the throne of the Queen of Saba to Solomon in the twinkling of an eye. To that ancient order refer the three first pass-words of this degree. It is open to all who believe in the One True God; and a Moslem may be a Mason, if he but believes in God, and is a good man and true.

All Masons are brethren. There, Moslem and Nazarene worship at the same altar, each perfectly equal to the other. They have certain signs and words by which to recognize each other in the dark as well as in the light, and a particular word and sign which one brother seeing, or hearing given by another, though one were of your faith and the other of mine, he is compelled to go to his assistance if the probability be greater that he will save the life of the Brother who calls upon him, than that he will lose his own.

That True Name, the Ineffable, is the Thrice Sacred Grand Word of this degree, and thou art entitled to its possession; for the God whose name it is, is as much thy God as mine."

He then gives him the True Name (יהוה) by the letters: and then says: "Thou art now entirely instructed as a Knight; but the degrees of Masonry thou canst not receive, except in a regular Lodge, at which are present three Master Masons. Were it not so, I would gladly make thee a Mason; but I dare not violate my oath."

They return to the Hall; and the Candidate is again seated in the East; and prompted as before, says: "Prince of Tiberias, and Lord of Galilee, I return thee sincere thanks for the great honour thou hast done me; and believing thou wilt regard it as the greatest favour I can confer, I grant thee the lives and liberty of ten Christian captives, to be selected by thyself."

Gr∴ M∴ Royal Salah-Eddin, thou dost understand the true feelings of a Knight. Ten thousand times more I thank thee for the boon, than if it had been an act of nobleness and generosity towards myself. But thou art now my brother; and I, as a Knight, require of thee a proof of brotherly love; without which thou canst not become a Mason. My ransom is far beyond my means; and it is not fit that a Knight should wander through the world, beseeching charity. Reduce my ransom; so that by selling my Principality and Lordship, and laying down my rank, to become a poor Knight again, I may myself discharge it. If I must sue for alms and aid, I do it *here*, where I esteem the most.

Cand∴ Sir Knight, thou dost not sue in vain. I give thee half thy ransom. Have I fulfilled my knightly obligation?

Gr∴ M∴ Two-fold, most noble Knight and Monarch; and I thank thee with a heartfelt gratitude, too great for words. May thy name never cease to be honoured in story and song! I would thou wert immortal.

A Voice behind the Throne: SALAH-EDDIN, KING OF KINGS! SALAH-EDDIN, VICTOR OF VICTORS! SALAH-EDDIN MUST DIE!

Cand∴ Sir Knight, thou shalt not thank me for half a gift. Valiant Princes and Emirs, behold this valiant Lord from whom I have received the Order of Knighthood! He is my Brother; and I pray you con-tribute to pay his ransom; for the love you bear myself, and the honour that brave men owe to bravery equal to their own.

[The Knights contribute, laying moneys upon the table; and Malek Adhel says: "My Brother, Salah-Eddin, there yet lack thirteen thousand bezants of the fifty thousand"].

Cand∴ I give that from the Royal Treasury. Take it, Sir Knight, and take also thy liberty, unpur-chased. Choose thy ten Knights, and when thou dost weary of our hospitality, depart with ample escort. Thou art free.

Gr∴ M∴ Noble Salah-Eddin, though I would fain see my gallant companions in arms, I accept thy hospitality: and I give thee also a boon more valuable than thy gold. I could not have sold it thee, or have allowed thee, expecting it, to give me such noble largess as thou hast. Among your prisoners are the good Knights, my Brothers in arms, Florant de Vorennes and Drogo de Mirle, whom I know as Masons. There may be others of the Fraternity. I select them as two of the ten that I am allowed to set free, and with their help will make known to you the secrets of Masonry, never more worthily bestowed than they will be on you.

[The Jun∴ Deacon now conducts the Candidate to the preparation-room, where he remains while the Gr∴

Master assumes his seat, and the clothing of the Knights is changed. He then again conducts him into the Hall, and to the East, where the Gr.·. Master invests him with the clothing and jewel of the Degree, and thus explains the letters on the jewel]:

Ven.·. M.·. The mystical Y.·. enclosed in an equilateral triangle, and that in a ring formed by a serpent (the emblem of eternity), alludes to the Deity, with His three attributes of Creation, Preservation and Regeneration, as it did among the Indians, Chinese and Japanese, with all of whom it was the Ineffable Name of the Deity; and it is also the same as the letter Yod that so often appears suspended over the Master in the East, and there represents God, of whose Hebrew name it is the first letter.

The letters ב.·. י.·. כ.·. and נ.·. are the initials of the words ♏☿⊙♍.·. ♀⊙¶♀♒.·. ♋⊙♐&♏☾♒⊙♐&.·. and ♒☾¶&⊙♋⊙&.·.

[He is then taught the meaning of the pass-words and sacred word of the Degree; and then proceeds to the seat of the Orator, where he receives the lecture of the Degree].

LECTURE.

Masonry is not a religion. He who makes of it a religious belief, falsifies and denaturalizes it. The Brahmin, the Jew, the Mahometan, the Catholic, the Protestant, each professing his peculiar religion, sanctioned by the laws, by time and by climate, must needs retain it, and cannot have two religions; for the social and sacred laws adapted to the usages, manners and prejudices of particular countries, are the work of men.

But Masonry teaches, and has preserved in their purity, the cardinal tenets of the old primitive faith, which underlie and are the foundation of all religions. All that ever existed have had a basis of truth; and all have overlaid that truth with errors. The primitive truths taught by the Redeemer were sooner corrupted, and intermingled and alloyed with fictions than when taught to the first of our race. Masonry is the universal morality which is suitable to the inhabitants of every clime, to the man of every creed. It has taught no doctrines, except those truths that tend directly to the well-being of man; and those who have attempted to direct it towards useless vengeance, political ends, the Kabbala, Hermeticism, Alchemy, Templarism and Jesuitism have merely perverted it to purposes foreign to its pure spirit and real nature.

Mankind outgrows the sacrifices and the mythologies of the childhood of the world. Yet it is easy for human indolence to linger near these helps, and refuse to pass further on. So the unadventurous Nomad in the Tartarian wild keeps his flock in the same close-cropped circle where they first learned to browse, while the progressive man roves ever forth "to fresh fields and pastures new."

The latter is the true Mason; and the best and indeed the only good Mason is he who with the power of business does the work of life; the upright mechanic, merchant or farmer, the man with the power of thought, of justice or of love, he whose whole life is one great act of performance of Masonic duty. The natural use of the strength of a strong man or the wisdom of a wise one, is to do the *work* of a strong man or a wise one. The natural work of Masonry is practical life; the use of all the faculties in their proper spheres, and for their natural function. Love of Truth, justice and generosity as attributes of God, must appear in a life marked by these qualities; that is the only effectual ordinance of Masonry. A profession of one's convictions, joining the Order, assuming the obligations, assisting at the ceremonies, are of the same value in science as in Masonry; the natural form of Masonry is goodness, morality, living a true, just, affectionate, self-faithful life, from the motive of a good man. It is loyal obedience to God's law.

The good Mason does the good thing which comes in his way, and because it comes in his way; from a love of duty, and not merely because a law, enacted by man or God, commands his *will* to do it. He is true to his mind, his conscience, heart and soul, and feels small temptation to do to others what he would not wish to receive from them. He will deny himself for the sake of his brother near at hand. His *desire* attracts in the line of his *duty*, both being in conjunction. Not in vain does the poor or the oppressed look up to him. You find such men in all Christian sects, Protestant and Catholic, in all the great religious parties of the civilized world, among Buddhists, Mahometans and Jews. They are kind fathers, generous citizens, unimpeachable in their business, beautiful in their daily lives. You see their Masonry in their work and in their play. It appears in all the forms of their activity, individual, domestic, social, ecclesiastical or political. True Masonry within must be morality without. It must become eminent morality, which is philanthropy. The true Mason loves not only his kindred and his country, but all mankind; not only the good, but also the evil, among his brethren. He has more goodness than the channels of his daily life will hold. It runs over the banks, to water and to feed a thousand thirsty plants. Not content with the duty that lies along his track, he goes out to seek it; not only *willing*, he has a salient *longing* to do good, to spread his truth, his justice, his generosity, his Masonry over all the world. His daily life is a profession of his Masonry, published in perpetual good-will to men.

Not more naturally does the beaver build or the mocking-bird sing his own wild gushing melody, than the true Mason lives in this beautiful outward life. So from the perennial spring swells forth the stream, to quicken the meadow with new access of green, and perfect beauty bursting into bloom. Thus Masonry does the work it was meant to do. The Mason does not sigh and weep, and make grimaces. He lives right on. If his life is, as whose is not, marked with errors, and with sins, he ploughs over the barren spot with his remorse, sows with new seed, and the old desert blossoms like a rose. He is not confined to set forms of thought, of action or of feeling. He accepts what his mind regards as true, what his conscience decides is right, what his heart deems generous and noble; and all else he puts far from him. Though the ancient and the honourable of the Earth bid him bow down to them, his stubborn knees bend only at the bidding of his manly soul. His Masonry is his freedom before God, not his bondage unto men. His mind acts after the universal law of the intellect, his conscience according to the universal moral law, his affections and his soul after the universal law of each, and so he is strong with the strength of God, in this four-fold way communicating with Him.

The old theologies, the philosophies of religion of ancient times will not suffice us now. The duties of life are to be done; we are to do them, consciously obedient to the law of God, not atheistically, loving only our selfish gain. There are sins of trade to be corrected. Everywhere morality and philanthropy are needed. There are errors to be made way with, and their place supplied with new truths, radiant with the glories of Heaven. There are great wrongs and evils, in Church and State, in domestic, social and public life, to be righted and outgrown. Masonry cannot in our age forsake the broad way of life. She must journey on in the open street, appear in the crowded square, and teach men by her deeds, her life more eloquent than any lips.

This degree is devoted to TOLERATION; and it inculcates in the strongest manner that great leading idea of the Ancient Art, that a belief in the one True God, and a moral and virtuous life, constitute the only religious requisites needed to enable a man to be a Mason.

It has ever the most vivid remembrance of the terrible and artificial torments that were used to put down new forms of religion or extinguish the old. It sees with the eye of memory the ruthless extermination of all the people of all sexes and ages, because it was their misfortune not to know the God of the Hebrews, or to worship Him under the wrong name, by the savage troops of Moses and Joshua. It sees the thumb-screws and the racks, the whip, the gallows and the stake, the victims of Diocletian and Claverhouse, the miserable Covenanters, the Non-Conformists, Servetus burned and the unoffending Quaker hung. It sees Cranmer hold his arm, now no longer erring, in the flame until the hand drops off in the consuming heat. It sees the persecutions of Peter and Paul, the martyrdom of Stephen, the trials of Ignatius, Polycarp, Justin and Irenæus; and then in turn the sufferings of the wretched Pagans under the Christian Emperors, as of the Papists in Ireland and under Elizabeth and the bloated Henry. The Roman Virgin naked before the hungry lions, young Margaret Graham tied to a stake at low-water mark, and there left to drown, singing hymns to God until the savage waters broke over her head, while the more savage Claverhouse looked on; and all that in all ages have suffered by hunger and nakedness, peril and prison, the rack, the stake and the sword,—it sees them all, and shudders at the long roll of human atrocities. And it sees also the oppression still practised in the name of religion—men shot in a Christian jail in Christian Italy for reading the Christian Bible; in almost every Christian State, laws forbidding freedom of speech on matters relating to Christianity, and the gallows reaching its arm over the pulpit.

The fires of Moloch in Syria, the harsh mutilations in the name of Astarte, Cybele, Jehovah; the barbarities of imperial Pagan Torturers; the still grosser torments which Romano-Gothic Christians in Italy and Spain heaped on their brother men, the fiendish cruelties to which Switzerland, France, the Netherlands, England, Scotland, Ireland, America have been witnesses, are none too powerful to warn man of the unspeakable evils which follow from mistakes and errors in the matter of religion, and especially from investing the God of Love with the cruel and vindictive passions of erring humanity, and making blood to have a sweet savour in his nostrils, and groans of agony to be delicious to his ears.

Man never had the right to usurp the unexercised prerogative of God, and condemn and punish another for his belief. Born in a Protestant land, we are of that faith. If we had opened our eyes to the light under the shadows of St. Peter's at Rome, we should have been devout Catholics: Born in the Jewish quarter of Aleppo, we should have contemned Christ as an impostor; in Constantinople, we should have cried "*Allah il Allah*, God is great and Mahomet is his prophet!" Birth, place, and education give us our faith. Few believe in any religion because they have examined the evidences of its authenticity, and made up a formal judgment, upon weighing the testimony. Not one man in ten thousand knows anything about the *proofs* of his faith. We believe what we are taught; and those are most fanatical who know least of the evidences on which their creed is based. Facts and testimony are not, except in very rare instances, the ground-work of faith. It is an imperative law of God's Economy, unyielding and inflexible as Himself, that man shall accept without question the belief of those among whom he is born and reared; the faith so made a part of his nature resists all evidence to the contrary; and he will disbelieve even the evidence of his own senses, rather than yield up the religious belief which has grown up in him, flesh of his flesh and bone of his bone.

What is truth to *me* is not truth to *another*. The same arguments and evidences that convince one mind make no impression on another. This difference is in men at their birth. No man is entitled positively to assert that *he* is right, where other men equally intelligent and equally well-informed hold directly the opposite opinion. Each thinks it impossible for the other to be sincere, and each, as to that, is equally in error. "*What is truth?*" was a profound question, the most suggestive one ever put to man. Many beliefs of former and present times seem incomprehensible. They startle us with a new glimpse into the human soul, that mysterious thing, more mysterious the more we note its workings. Here is a man superior to myself in intellect and learning; and yet he sincerely believes what seems to me too absurd to merit confutation; and I cannot conceive, and sincerely do not believe, that he is both sane and honest. *And yet he is both.* His reason is as perfect as mine, and he is as honest as I.

The fancies of a lunatic are realities, *to him.* Our dreams are realities *while they last;* and, in the Past, no more unreal than what we have acted in our waking hours. No man can say that he hath as sure possession of the truth as of a chattel. When men entertain opinions diametrically opposed to each other, and each is honest, who shall decide which hath the Truth; and how can either say with certainty that *he* hath it? We know not what *is* the truth. That we ourselves believe and feel absolutely certain that our own belief is true, is in reality not the slightest proof of the fact, seem it never so certain and incapable of doubt to us.

Therefore no man hath or ever had a right to persecute another for his belief: for there cannot be two antagonistic rights: and if one can persecute another, because he himself is satisfied that the belief of that other is erroneous, the other has, for the same reason, equally as certain a right to persecute him.

The truth comes to us tinged and coloured with our prejudices and our preconceptions, which are as old as ourselves, and strong with a divine force. It comes to us as the image of a rod comes to us through the water, bent and distorted. An argument sinks into and convinces the mind of one man, while from that of another it rebounds like a ball of ivory dropped on marble. It is no merit in a man to have a particular faith, excellent and sound and philosophic as it may be, when he imbibed it with his mother's milk. It is no more a merit than his prejudices and his passions.

The sincere Moslem has as much right to persecute us, as we to persecute him: and therefore Masonry wisely requires no more than a belief in One Great All-Powerful Deity, the Father and Preserver of the Universe. Therefore it is she teaches her votaries that toleration is one of the chief duties of every good Mason, a component part of that charity without which we are mere hollow images of true Masons, mere sounding brass and tinkling cymbals.

No evil hath so afflicted the world as intolerance of religious opinion. The human beings it has slain in various ways, if once and together brought to life, would make a nation of people: left to live and increase, would have doubled the population of the civilized portion of the globe; among which civilized portion it chiefly is that religious wars are waged. The treasure and the human labour thus lost would have made the earth a garden, in which, but for his evil passions, man might now be as happy as in Eden.

And no man truly obeys the Masonic law who *merely* tolerates those whose religious opinions are opposed to his own. Every man's opinions are his own private property, and the rights of all men to maintain each his own are perfectly equal. Merely to *tolerate*, to *bear with* an opposing opinion, is to assume it to be heretical; and assert the *right* to persecute, if we would; and claim our *toleration* of it as a merit. The Mason's creed goes further than that. No man, it holds, has any right in any way to interfere with the religious belief of another. It holds that each man is absolutely sovereign as to his own belief, and that belief is a matter absolutely foreign to all who do not entertain the same belief; and that, if there were any right of persecution at all, it would in all cases be a mutual right; because one party has the same right as the other to sit as judge in his own case: and God is the only magistrate that can rightfully decide between them. To that great *Judge*, Masonry refers the matter; and opening wide its portals, it invites to enter there and live in peace and harmony, the Protestant, the Catholic, the Jew, the Moslem; every man who will lead a truly virtuous and moral life, love his brethren, minister to the sick and distressed, and believe in the ONE, *All-Powerful, All-Wise, everywhere-Present* GOD, *Architect, Creator* and *Preserver of all things*, by whose universal law of Harmony ever rolls on this universe, the great, vast, infinite circle of successive *Death* and *Life* :—to whose INEFFABLE NAME let all true Masons pay profoundest homage! for whose thousand blessings poured upon us, let us feel the sincerest gratitude, now, henceforth and forever, Amen!!

TO CLOSE.

Gr∴ M∴ Sir Kt∴ Gr∴ Prior, what is the hour?

Gr∴ Prior : Ven∴ Gr∴ Master, the night draws near.

Gr∴ M∴ Even so approaches, with the same rapid step, the night of death and the hour of judgment! Sir Kt∴ Almoner, doth any charitable work remain undone, that it is within our power to do?

Gr∴ Alm∴ Ven∴ Gr∴ Master, none.

Gr∴ M∴ Sir Kt∴ Gr∴ Bailiff, whence come you as a Knight Ecossais of St∴ Andrew?

Gr∴ Bail∴ From the Holy Land, where the Moslem and Barbarism yet reign supreme.

Gr∴ M∴ Even so reign Wrong and Error over all the world; and only here and there Truth and the Right are victors! But ever morning cometh after night, and no true Mason despairs of final victory. Sir Kt∴ Gr∴ Seneschal, what is the age of a Kt∴ Ecossais?

Gr∴ Senes∴ S, years.

Gr∴ M∴ The ♈♓♄☉☾☽ of z — which is the ♈♓♄☉☾☽ of ; — emblem of Deity and Immortality; fit number for a Perfect Knight. Sir Kt∴ Gr∴ Prior, what remains to be done?

Gr∴ Prior∴ Our duty, everywhere: our duty, always: Evil and the Wrong, never: a base act, nowhere.

Gr∴ M∴ Right, my Brother! So let us ever act! In the name of God and St∴ Andrew, let us close this Chapter! Sir Kts∴, the sign!

[All give the £th sign: the Gr∴ Seneschal raps?—the Gr∴ Prior;—and the Gr∴ Master!—and the Gr∴ Master says]:

Gr∴ M∴ Sir Kts∴, this Chapter is closed. Go in peace! and God and all good angels guard us all!

FINIS.

Thirtieth Degree.

Knight Kadosch.

DECORATIONS, FURNITURE, ETC.

Bodies in this degree are styled *Chapters*. The Hall is decorated with red and black columns. The Throne, in the East, is surmounted by a double-headed Eagle, crowned, holding a poniard in his claws. Over his neck is a black ribbon, to which is suspended the cross of the Order. On his breast is an equilateral triangle, around which are the words: NEC PRODITOR, NEC PRODITUS, INNOCENS FERET. A drapery of black and white curtains, strewed with red crosses, descends between the wings of the Eagle, and forms a pavilion. Behind the throne are two banners, one white, with a green cross upon it, and the motto, DEUS VULT: the other with a red cross on one side, and on the other a double Eagle, holding a poniard, with this motto embroidered in silver: AUT VINCERE AUT MORI. There is also the mystic ladder hereafter described, which is covered until the Candidate is obligated.

There are nine lights of yellow wax.

A Chapter must consist of at least five brethren, dressed in black, with white gloves. Over the coat is worn a white tunic, open at the side, in the shape of a *Dalmatique*, and edged with black. Over this a black sash fringed with silver, and worn from left to right. A poniard, with an ivory and ebony handle, is worn in the girdle.

The hat is three-cornered (or cocked). On the front is a Sun of silver, with rays of gold. In the centre of the Sun is an eye: and the Sun is placed between the letters N∴ A∴

On the left breast is a large red cross. No apron is worn.

The jewel is a Teutonic cross of gold, enamelled with red, at the junction of two cross-swords. It is hung to the sash, or from a button-hole.

The battery is £ — by ? ? ? ,

The step is ; hasty steps forward, the ☧⊙♒☐⌒ ♂☿♅⌒⌒☾☐ over the ☧☾⊙☐.

OFFICERS AND TITLES.

The first officer, in the East, is styled *Grand Commander;* the second, in the West, *Grand Prior;* the third, in the South, *Grand Preceptor;* the fourth, *Almoner;* and the fifth the *Marshal.* The other officers are the *Treasurer*, the *Draper*, the *Turcopilar*, or *Commander of Cavalry*, and the *Standard-bearer.*

OPENING.

Gr.·. Comm.·. Ill.·. Grand Prior, are you an Elu?

Gr.·. Pr.·. Th.·. Ill.·. Gr.·. Commander, I am.

Gr.·. Comm.·. How became you an Elu?

Gr.·. Pr.·. Fortune decided for me.

Gr.·. Comm.·. How may I be certain that you were received an Elu?

Gr.·. Pr.·. A cavern witnessed my reception.

Gr.·. C.·. What did you in that cavern?

Gr.·. Pr.·. I executed my commission.

Gr.·. C.·. Have you advanced further?

Gr.·. Pr.·. Th.·. Ill.·., I have.

Gr.·. Com.·. How shall I know that it is so?

Gr.·. Pr.·. I am styled Knight Kadosch. Once I bore another name.

Gr.·. Com.·. I understand you. Is the just vengeance of our order complete?

Gr.·. Pr.·. It is not. One of its enemies still lives. The House of the rapacious King is fallen. Rhodes and its Knights are but the echo of a name: The third still clings to life.

Gr.·. C.·. What is the hour?

Gr.·. Pr.·. The hour of silence.

Gr.·. Com.·. Since it is the hour of silence, and our vengeance is not complete, let us labour in silence, as we have done so many years. The time is coming when we shall speak aloud. The sign, my Brethren!

All the Knights make the sign by drawing their swords. The Gr.·. Commander raps one, on the table before him, and says, "Ill.·. Knights, this Chapter is now open."

RECEPTION.

The Candidate being in the ante-room, without regalia or jewels, a Knight knocks 1 at the door. One within asks, "Who comes there?" The answer is, "A serving Brother, who having all the necessary preparatory degrees, demands that of Knight Kadosch."

Gr.·. Com.·. Th.·. Ill.·. Knights, can we admit this Free Mason among us, without risk from his indiscretion? Are we all ready to answer on our lives, that he will never reveal the secrets we are about to entrust to him, and can we safely place even our lives in his keeping?

All the Kts.·. We can.

The Grand Commander then joins the Knights; and all holding each other by the hand, before the Candidate is introduced, take the following obligation:

OBLIGATION OF THE KNIGHTS.

We do most sacredly and solemnly vow, and to each other renewedly pledge our Masonic and Knightly Word, that we will, by all legal and honourable means, avenge the murder of our predecessors of this Order: and that we will denounce as a perjured knave and forsworn Knight, and bring to disgrace and universal loathing and contempt, if in our power, every one of this Order who may illegally, by intention or indiscretion, reveal the secrets of the same. And may the Almighty Maker of the Universe so reward or punish us as we keep or violate this vow! Amen!

The Gr.·. Commander then gives one rap, and two of the Knights without lead in the Candidate, and deliver him to the Gr.·. Commander; and all but the latter and the Candidate retire. One person only was present at the reception of a Templar.

The Candidate then kneels on one knee before the Gr∴ Commander, who says to him : " My Brother, you desire to unite yourself to an Order which has laboured in silence and secrecy for more than 500 years for the attainment of a single end, in which it has as yet only partially succeeded, and to which, if you join us, you must devote yourself. You have been partially prepared for this in some of the degrees that you have already taken. The tale of the assassination of our once Grand Master Hiram Abi shocked your soul and aroused all your sympathies in the Master's Degree. We have a far more horrid, barbarous and bloody tragedy to avenge, and in that you will become bound to assist us. You remember how in the Elu of 9 and the Elu of 15, the search for and the vengeance taken upon the murderers was represented. You were no doubt startled at seeing the bloody figure of Vengeance arise in the calm and tranquil realms of Masonry, and you thought that there, at least, the lesson of revenge and bloody retribution ought not to be taught, but rather that of mercy and forgiveness. Perhaps you suspected that the drama of vengeance was an allegory, the esoteric sense of which would at a later period be made known to you. That period has come.

This Order has for its mission the avenging of an awful crime ; not by the punishment of those that committed it ; for they have long since gone before the Judge of all mankind, their bones have mouldered into a little dust, and many of their memories are forgotten : but by the destruction of that of which those men were but the miserable instruments ; of arbitrary and irresponsible power, of tyranny over the conscience, of bigotry and intolerance ; and by the establishment everywhere of well-ordered liberty. Already this Order has by its silent influences aided in working out great results ; and still it labours, earnestly and steadfastly towards the great end. Hostile at first to persons, to a particular dynasty, to a corrupt Order, and a Pontifical usurpation of temporal power, it now pursues with a foot that never tires, and an eye that never sleeps, the personifications of the three assassins ; and so labours for the good of mankind. Thus we hope to arrive at true Perfection, symbolized by the precious treasure found in the ruins of the Temple of Enoch, and to place which beyond the power of the infidel and barbarian, the Grand, Elect, Perfect and Sublime Masons boldly risked their lives at the destruction of the Temple built by Solomon.

Nor must you imagine that we are conspirators, or plotters against the peace of the world. We work in secret, because we can so work more efficiently. We excite no people to hasty and ill-advised rebellion ; in which those who bring them into peril are powerless to shield them from the consequences. But wherever the legitimate standard of civil and religious liberty is raised, there you will find the Knights of our Order ; for it has spread over all the civilized countries on the globe. We hold no wild theories, we teach no novel doctrines ; but true Masonry and uncorrupted only, as it came to us from our fathers, rich with the glorious fragments of the primitive truth.

Here, too, we strive to restore that ancient disinterestedness and devotion to the great cause of humanity which led the nine founders of the Order, all Frenchmen of noble lineage, and of wealth and honour, to devote themselves to the arduous service of protecting the unarmed and helpless Pilgrims whose piety led them to visit the Holy City of Jerusalem. They in the year 1128, appeared before Guarimund, Patriarch of Jerusalem, and between his hands vowed faithfully to perform the duties they had agreed to assume, as The Poor Fellow-Soldiers of Jesus Christ : From which beginning grew up a Great Order, Soldiers of the Cross, defenders of Palestine against the Turks and Saracens, and of Spain against the Moors.

The Christian throne of Jerusalem fell in the dust ; and the Mosque of Omar still occupies the site of the Holy Temple. The Crusades, with all their pomp and pageantry of war and romance, went by, and have long since faded away in the dim Past. A new age has succeeded ; and if the Holy Sepulchre is to be again the heritage of a Christian Power and the appanage of a Christian Throne, it will be obtained by peaceful negotiation, in God's good time, and not by war and bloodshed. But there remain other fields on which our Order can achieve new triumphs ; and with enlarged objects and a broader philanthropy, we are now the soldiery of the Masonic Temple.

Are you willing to devote yourself to the great purposes that I have indicated, and to become the sworn servant of the Order ; trusting that you shall receive hereafter fuller explanation, and satisfied with my pledge of knightly honour that those objects are honest, upright, just, and such as may become a Mason and a gentleman ; as are the means by which they are proposed to be attained ?

Cand∴ I am.

Gr∴ Com∴ Have you well considered all the trials and difficulties that may await you in the Order?

Cand∴ I have.

Gr∴ Com∴ Do you still persist in proceeding?

Cand∴ I do.

Gr∴ Com∴ Are you of sound body, without any secret infirmity, and free to bind yourself to us, without interfering with any previous pledges to another Order?

Cand∴ I am.

Gr∴ Com∴ You will then repeat your Christian and surname, and, repeating after me, assume a solemn obligation.

OBLIGATION.

I, A.... B...., do most solemnly promise, and on my Masonic and Knightly word, of a Knight of the Sun and of St. Andrew, do vow, that I will never reveal to any person whatever, who shall not be entitled to receive the same, any of the secrets of Gr∴ Elect Knight Kadosch; that I will avenge the murder of innocent Brother Knights of this Order who have been slain, so far and in such manner as I lawfully and laudably may: and that I will never consent to receive into this degree any person who shall not legally have received the degree of Grand Ecossais of St. Andrew and Knight of the Sun, and then by the authority of a Grand Commander or Sovereign Inspector General or Deputy Inspector duly authorized. And I furthermore promise and vow to be at all times ready to do my devoir as a true soldier of the Masonic Temple, as it shall be taught me in this degree; and that I will pay due obedience to the Sublime Princes of the Royal Secret: and should I violate this my obligation, I consent to be denounced as a craven and a perjuror, and that my spurs shall be hacked off by a slave and my sword broken by a woman.

[He kisses the Bible, and rises; and the Gr∴ Commander says]: My Brother, your confidence in us is not misplaced. As the representative of the Gr∴ Master and Gr∴ Inspector of all Chapters of the Knights Kadosch, I assure you that you need have no distrust of your brethren, or fear lest you may be entangled in unworthy enterprises. But it is indispensable that, before we communicate to you the purposes and objects of this organization, and the secrets by which we secure unity and efficiency of action, and prompt obedience to the governing power of the Order, we should have ample assurance that we may confide in and rely upon you: for by neglecting to use sufficient precaution, and not taking in advance sufficient guarantees of fidelity, we have admitted unworthy members, and have thereby lost good and great men, who would have been the ornaments and supports of our Chapters. Besides which, if our objects or even our existence were prematurely made known, it might ensure defeat, and produce the most disastrous consequences. This you will fully appreciate when all our mysteries shall be confided to you, and you shall have been fully instructed; when the cloud that covers us shall part and roll away; and you shall see us as we were in our days of glory, when our Grand Master was the Peer of Princes and the Regent of Kingdoms, having even the crown of the Kingdom of Jerusalem in his gift. To that rank we no longer aspire; but our aim is now the far nobler one of being distinguished among Masons, and enrolled among the benefactors of mankind. To assure you that our purposes are just and upright, let us invoke the protection, aid and support of the Great and Just Deity, who created the Universe with a thought, and gave it the perpetual law by which its changes and movements are governed.

PRAYER.

O Thou Eternal, Uncreated, Illimitable Being, that wast originally all in all, and at whose thought the Universe flashed into being, and the great spheres began their eternal noiseless revolutions! from the depths of our hearts we adore Thee, we worship Thee, we offer Thee sincere and grateful homage. We beseech Thee that Thou wilt look with favour upon our undertakings and bless and encourage our enterprises for the good of the human race! Aid us to punish and avenge the wrongs done to our predecessors and to humanity, in such way as may be consistent with Thy will, and with our duty as good and true Masons! Aid us to subjugate and overcome Error, Intolerance and Bigotry, and Ignorance, Tyranny and Injustice! And may that day speedily dawn when all the earth shall be the Holy Land, and all mankind one great Lodge of Brethren; and wars and oppressions be known no more forever! Amen!

The other Knights now enter; and the Gr∴ Commander continues: "Assured of the justice of the cause in which you are engaged, remember the indispensable necessity of the most perfect discretion. The least failure on your part in that respect may be most serious in its consequences. Place before your eyes as the great object of your desires, this Order, great and sublime as it was when its Preceptories and Priories were in every country in Europe: when its Grand Masters sat above the Ambassadors of Christian Kings, and the Brothers of Princes were proud to serve under them as humble Knights, whose memories shall be immortal. Be firm even as those noble Martyrs who maintained the innocence of the Order in the midst of flames, and under the most awful tortures: and hate and war against all oppressors of the people, all enemies of human rights, as you detest the memory of those who murdered the innocent, and then shared among themselves the estates and wealth of a noble and persecuted Order.

Be not urged too hastily onward by imprudent zeal! Error and Wrong are sheltered behind strong fortifications, strengthened and consolidated by the lapse of ages. By regular approaches only can those works be carried. It may be that it is to be our fortune but to prepare the way for those who are to come after us. We must wait patiently and in silence for the hour and the time. Let us increase the number of our proselytes; admitting not even our most intimate friends, unless we are as well assured of their discretion as of our own. Incessantly recall to mind your obligation, and be careful that in no respect you violate it.

We have thus shadowed forth to you some of the first principles, and have obscurely hinted to you the objects, of this eminent degree in Masonry. Before we can say more, we are compelled to require of you another and a most stringent obligation. If you have heard anything to deter you from taking it, if you feel doubtful or reluctant, if you are half inclined to pause, do so at once. Reflect, my Brother! for you may now withdraw with honour. Be certain before you determine to proceed, that you will not hesitate to comply with every point of the serious obligation which, if you advance, you must now pronounce with me, and which will bind you to us forever."

[There is a pause, for the Candidate to reflect. If he refuses to proceed, or fears, or even hesitates, the Gr∴ Commander will send him out, and close the Chapter. If he determines to advance, he will be directed to kneel on both knees, with his right hand on the Holy Bible, and his left between those of the Grand Commander, and answer the following questions]:

1st. Do you promise and swear, by all that you hold most dear and sacred, that you will hereafter consider yourself the Soldier of Truth, Justice, Order, Law, and Suffering Humanity; and that you will wage continual war, by all legitimate and proper means that may comport with the character of a Mason, a Knight and a gentleman, against all tyranny over the mind or body, temporal or spiritual, and all ignorance, fraud and wrong-doing; against all who plunder the widow and orphan, grind the faces of the poor, or insult and degrade the nobility of human nature; that you will practise mercy, and live and die in your Religion? and also, that you will never, without their consent, reveal who have received you here, or assisted at your reception?

Cand∴ I promise and swear. [Then, with the Gr∴ Comm∴ he pronounces the word ♈⊾ℭ♉ℭ¶☉⚹∴]

2d. Do you promise and swear that you will be modest in all your actions; and that you will never receive into this degree any one who is not your intimate friend: and then only with the consent of two Gr∴ Elus and Inspectors, if there be such near you; and, if not, then by virtue of a special power, signed and sealed?

Cand∴ I promise and swear. [Repeats with the Gr∴ Com∴ ⊾&♄ &-†☉♍☉⚌∴]

3d. Do you promise and swear to be at all times gentle and affectionate; to love and cherish your brethren, to aid them in their necessities, to visit and assist them in sickness, and never on any pretext to bear arms against them?

Cand.·. I promise and swear. [Repeats ♋☾♈ॷ¶·.]

4th. Do you promise and swear in your conversation to be ever governed by Truth, and in your actions by sincerity and frankness: and that you will circumspectly guard and keep the secrets of a Knight Kadosch of this degree?

Cand.·. I promise and swear. [Repeats ☉♋ॷ ≈☉&·.]

5th. Do you promise and swear that you will labour zealously for the good of this Order, and that you will at all times, places and points whatsoever, follow whatsoever shall be prescribed to you by the Ill.·. Gr.·. Commander under whom you may serve, in respect to the discipline and service of the Order?

Cand.·. I promise and swear. [Repeats ☉♋☾†≏☉♌&♀☉·.] ·

6th. Do you promise and swear never to admit any one into this degree, who is a monk or a Jesuit, or has taken the vows of any other religious order; not even with the permission of his superiors?

Cand.·. I promise and swear. [Repeats ≏☉♍☾†·.].

7th. Finally, do you promise and swear, that you will punish and bring to disgrace and detestation all traitors to Masonry; that you will consider the Knights of St. John of Jerusalem, of Malta or of Rhodes as the despoilers of this Order, and as its enemies; and that you will never enter that Order, but will in every just and proper mode in your power discourage and prevent its revival?

Cand.·. I promise and swear. [Repeats ♌☾♋ॷ†-♍♀≈☉&-♈☉♍ॷ≈☉&·.]

The Grand Comm.·. then raises him, and says: " By the seven promises that you have now made, and by the powers regularly transmitted to me from our Grand Master Jacques de Molay, I acknowledge and reward your labours, your zeal, your discretion, your firmness and your constancy, and I receive you a Grand Inspector of all Lodges, Grand Knight Kadosch, or Knight of the White and Black Eagle, under the great black and white banner Beauseant of the ancient Templars.

" Ascend now, Sir Knight, the mysterious ladder which you see before you, which, when explained, will instruct you in the duties of our Order."

The candidate mounts the ladder, pausing at each step, and pronouncing the *word* or *words,* belonging to it. The Gr.·. Commander responds with the meaning of each. When he is on the last round, and has pronounced the last word, the ladder is lowered, and he passes over it; a Kadosch not being allowed to retreat, either from an enemy, or from the interests of the Order.

[The ladder has two supports or sides. The one on the right, as you ascend the steps is inscribed and called ☉&☾♍-☉†ॷ& . . . *The Love of* God: and the one on the left, ☉&☾♍-¶☾†♉♍ॷ . . . *Love of our Neighbour.* They are symbolical of those two powerful pillars of all true morality and virtuous excellence. These two supports are united by seven steps, which are symbolical of the seven divisions of the obligation, all reducible to, and springing as corollaries from those two great tenets of the primitive undefiled religion.

The seven steps, commencing at the bottom are named and inscribed with the words repeated by the Candidate, in the order in which he repeated them; and their meanings are as follows:

♈≏☾♊☾¶☉&·. . . Truth, Justice, Righteousness.

≏&ॷ&-†☉♍☉≈·. . . . Pure or perfect Equity.

♋☾♈ॷ¶·. . . . Amiability.

☉♋ॷ≈☉&·. . . . Good Faith.

☉♋¶†≏☉♌&♀☉·. . . . Much Labour or Exertion.

≏☉♍☾†·. . . . Patience or Endurance.

♌☾♋ॷ†-♍♀≈☉&-♈☉♍ॷ≈☉&·. . . . . Elaboration; Prudence; Discrimination.]

Gr.·. Com.·. Each of these steps symbolizes a triad of Masonic virtues, all belonging to the character of a true Knight Kadosch. For that name is the Hebrew word קדש .. KDSH .. Holiness or Perfection .. and requires him who bears it, to strive to attain that holiness and perfection which it means, and of which it holds out the promise.

The Triad of virtues belonging to the first step as you ascend, is, .. TRUTH, JUSTICE and RIGHTEOUSNESS:

. . . to the second, EQUITY, LENIENCY, and MERCY: . . . to the third, AMIABILITY, KINDNESS, and COURTESY: . . to the fourth, SINCERITY, UPRIGHTNESS and FIDELITY: . . to the fifth, INDUSTRY, ARDOUR and ZEAL: . . to the sixth, PATIENCE, ENDURANCE and PERSEVERANCE: . . and to the seventh and last, PRUDENCE, ELABORATION and DISCRIMINATION.

These virtues, springing from Love of God and Love of our Neighbour, constitute the NEC PLUS ULTRA of Masonic Perfection.

Go now, my Brother, to the Gr∴ Preceptor, and listen to the History of this Order.

[The Cand∴ is conducted to the Gr∴ Preceptor, who reads to him the following History of the degree]:

HISTORY.

In the year 1128, Hugues de Payens, Geoffrey de Saint Aldemar, and seven other gentlemen of noble birth, Frenchmen, but whose names history has not preserved, pitying the dangers to which the pilgrims were exposed in their journey to and return from Jerusalem, formed themselves into a society at that city, to serve as an escort to the pilgrims, receiving them at, and reconducting them as far as, the mountain defiles and most dangerous passes. At first they were a mere association of individuals, without rules, or assuming a religious habit, but merely acting as an escort for the pilgrims when required. They lived in a house near the Temple, at Jerusalem, from which circumstance they came to be known by the name of Templars, or Knights of the Temple. The King of Jerusalem having selected Hugues de Payens to go to Rome and solicit succour, and, if he could obtain it, a new crusade, that Knight, after performing this duty, presented his companions to Pope Honorius 2d, and requested that they might be formed into an Order, religious and military, like the Hospitallers, or Knights of St. John, for the protection of pilgrims. The Pope referred them to the Council then assembled at Troyes in Champagne, which granted their request, and appointed St. Bernard to draw up the rules of the Order and prescribe a dress. Among the rules, they were each allowed a Squire or serving brother at arms, and three riding-horses; but all gilding and superfluous ornaments were forbidden, and their dress was prescribed to be white, as a mark of their profession; to which Pope Eugenius 3d added a red cross on the left breast. The institution of the Order and its rules, approved by the Council, were also approved by the Pope. Many gentlemen of the best houses of France, Germany and Italy joined the order and went with de Payens to Palestine.

In a little time the Order largely increased. Princes of sovereign houses and Lords of the most illustrious families of Christendom joined it, and brought to it immense wealth, so that it soon became so rich and powerful as even to overshadow the Knights of St. John. Raimond Berenger, Count of Barcelona and Provence, became a member, and, too old to go to Jerusalem, sent large sums of money to carry on the war against the Infidels, laid down his power as sovereign Prince, and died among the Templars. Alfonso, first King of Navarre and Arragon, made the Knights of St. John, the Templars and the Monks or Knights of the Holy Sepulchre heirs of his Kingdom in 1131. In 1150 they distinguished themselves by defending, with the Knights of St. John, the city of Jerusalem, and routing the Infidels, in the absence of Baldwin 3d; and in 1154 at the siege of Ascalon.

In 1179 dissensions grew up between them and the Hospitallers, which were settled for the time by the intervention of the Pope. In 1186 the Grand Master of the Templars, depositary and guardian of the crown of Jerusalem, gave it by his influence to Guy of Lusignan. In 1187 they and the Hospitallers surprised the camp of Saladin, and distinguished themselves by a long and bloody battle; and attacking the Infidels first at the battle of Tiberiade in 1188, long carried everything before them, until betrayed by the Count of Tripoli, who, by agreement with Saladin, fled the field, and left the Templars surrounded by the enemy, where they were all slain or taken prisoners. In 1191 they purchased the Island of Cyprus from Richard of England for 300,000 livres, and garrisoned it; but afterwards restored it again to King Richard.

In 1243, the Knights of the two Orders fought a battle against the Corasmins, who had taken and pillaged Jerusalem, that lasted two days, in which they performed prodigies of valour, and were almost annihilated, twenty-six Hospitallers and thirty-three Templars only escaping, and the Grand Masters of both Orders being

33D

slain. In 1251, the quarrel between the two orders again breaking out, they fought a battle, in which the Templars were so cut to pieces that hardly one survived to bear the news of the defeat; and so few Templars were left in Palestine, that they were compelled peremptorily to summon all their Knights in the West to repair thither.

In 1270, the Templars mortgaged all their lands in France to Philip 3d, the Bold, son of St. Louis, King of France, as security for twenty-five thousand marks of silver, borrowed by Gregory the 10th to carry on the wars against the Infidels: and in the General Council at Lyons that year, the Grand Masters of the two Orders sat above all the Ambassadors, the Peers of France, and the other great Lords who were present. In 1291, when Acre, with a garrison of 12,000 men, mostly Hospitallers, Templars and Teutonic Knights, was besieged by the Sultan, at the head of 160,000 infantry and 60,000 cavalry, Pierre de Beaujeu, Grand Master of the Templars, was chosen Commander-in-chief, and defended it bravely to the last, until he was slain with a poisoned arrow, the City carried by storm, and its defenders slain.

In 1301, a feud occurring between Boniface 3d and Philip le Bel, King of France, in consequence of that Pope's claim to temporal power in France, it was reported that the Templars offered their services to that Pontiff in the war which he meditated against Philip, and that they had furnished considerable sums of money to begin the war. In 1303 Boniface died, and was succeeded, eleven days afterwards, by Benedict XI., who also died, after occupying the chair of St. Peter only eight months.

The conclave of Cardinals then assembled at Perouse, and remained in session nearly a year, divided into two factions, and resolved never to agree to the election of any one of themselves. Cardinal Francis Gaëtan, nephew of Boniface, and who had inherited his hatred of the Colonna, the partisans of France, was at the head of one of these factions; and at that of the other, which was devoted to Philip, was Cardinal Duprè, intimate friend of the two Cardinals Colonna; whom, as well as their whole house, Boniface, through his hatred to France, had cruelly persecuted.

Cardinal Duprè at length proposed to Cardinal Gaëtan, that as they must needs select some one not in the conclave, one of the two factions should name at its pleasure, three ultramontane Archbishops, and the other faction should, within forty days afterwards choose one of the three to be Pope; and offered, as if from generosity and regard for the good of the church, to permit the party headed by Cardinal Gaëtan to make the nominations. The latter communicated the proposition to his party, by whom it was assented to, and embodied in a solemn agreement, drawn up, and signed by all the Cardinals.

Gaëtan then nominated three ultramontane Archbishops, all of whom had been creatures of his uncle, and espoused his interest against the King. The first of them was the Archbishop of Bordeaux, named Bertrand de Got, a Prelate of a great family in Aquitaine, but fond of pleasure, devoured by ambition, an intimate friend of Gaëtan, whose entire confidence he had, and a subject of the King of England, who was then Duke of Aquitaine. Besides, he was a personal enemy of Phillippe le Bel, and especially of Charles of Valois, his brother, who, during the wars between France and England, had ravaged the chateaux and lands of his brother and other relatives.

Cardinal Duprè, knowing the character of this Archbishop, dispatched a courier to the King of France, bearing a copy of the agreement, and a letter from himself, advising him to make terms with the Archbishop. The King wrote to the latter that he desired to meet him on important business at an abbey in the midst of a forest near St. Jean d'Angely on a certain day. They met in the church of the abbey, where after hearing mass, and swearing the Archbishop with his hand upon the altar to inviolable secrecy, he showed him the agreement, and informed him that it was in his power to make him Pope.

The Archbishop threw himself at the King's feet, and embraced them, with assurances of the profoundest gratitude, pledging himself that if he became Pope, the King should share his authority, and offering to give him any assurances to that effect that he might require.

The King told him that, when he reached the chair of St. Peter, he wished him to grant him six favours, all just, he said, and which would redound only to the good of the church and the State; but of which he desired to be assured, before entering into any more particular engagements with him. The five first conditions he made known to him. The sixth he said, he would not make known until after his coronation as Pope. The Archbishop swore upon the holy sacrament to grant these requests, and gave his brother and two nephews to the King as hostages for performance. Information of this was sent by the King to Cardinal Duprè, and he, with the consent of his party nominated Bertrand de Got, Archbishop of Bordeaux to be Pope, who was immediately elected, to the great joy of the nephew of Boniface and his party.

He was installed in the College of Cardinals, held at Lyons; and took the name of Clement V. After the installation, the King made known his sixth condition; which was the execution and abolition of the entire order of Templars. Clement was greatly surprised; but the King averring that they had been guilty of the most fearful crimes, of which he had good proof, the Pope agreed to institute secret investigations, and requested the King to communicate to him his proofs, that he might comply with his promise. Having for his Mistress the beautiful Countess of Perigard, daughter of the Count de Foix, and avaricious even to the practice of the grossest simony, this base Pontiff was prepared to commit any crime which his interest prompted.

In 1307 he summoned to his court at Poitiers Jacques de Molay, Grand Master of the Templars, of an illustrious house in the County of Burgundy, who had repaired thither with most of his Knights, abandoning the Island of Cyprus. The Knights had dispersed themselves through the different States of Christendom, in which they had a great number of wealthy commanderies. It was reported that the Grand Master had brought from the Levant immense treasures, which were deposited in the House of the Order at Paris. The Grand Master with his principal Knights repaired to the Court of the Pope and were graciously received, the Pope carefully concealing the secret motive which induced him to require their attendance; but he consulted him in regard to a new Crusade which he had in view, called upon him for information, and proposed to unite the two orders of Templars and Hospitallers as one order, under one Grand Master. Perhaps he hoped thus to enable them to escape the vengeance of the Royal assassin. History has preserved the responses of de Molay to the memoirs of the King. He showed the impracticability of the proposed union, for several strong reasons; but proposed, if the Pope desired, to hold a Chapter of Priors, Bailiffs, and principal Commanders, in the presence of the King, where he could learn their views, and decide as he might think best. The response breathed the purest spirit of religious piety, and submission to the Pope, coupled with military frankness and fearlessness.

After the Knights of St. John took Rhodes, in 1310, popular opinion became unfriendly to the Templars, for abandoning the Holy Land and living in Europe in idleness; and odious rumors began to circulate in regard to the Order. Philip then put in execution his long cherished plans for the destruction of the order. Two wretches, one a citizen of Beziers, named Squin de Florian, and the other an apostate Templar, being confined together in prison, charged with monstrous crimes, and despairing of their lives, confessed their crimes to each other. The apostate then made known to the officers of the prison that he was in possession of a secret of vast importance; which he would make known to the King alone. Some historians charge this act upon a Templar, the Prior of Montfaucon, and another of the same order, called Noffodei, who had both been condemned by the Grand Master and a Council of the order for their impieties, and for leading infamous lives, to end their days in close confinement. Whoever was the informer, Philip had him sent to Paris, saw him and promised him pardon and even rewards, if he would divulge the truth. Upon this, the wretch, having already drawn up the heads of his accusation, charged the whole body of Templars with theft, homicide, idolatry and sodomy. He added, that when a Templar was received into the order, he was obliged to renounce Christ, and spit upon the cross in token of detestation: that the Knights, who had secretly become Mahometans, by an infamous act of treason sold the Holy Land to the Infidels. In the collection of Pierre Dupuy may be seen all the abominations and all the obscenities with which the informer endeavoured to blacken his Brothers, and which decency will not allow us to repeat.

The King had communicated these accusations to the Pope, in an interview at Lyons; and urged him more pressingly on the subject the next year at Poitiers. On the 9th of July, 1307, the Pope wrote to the King that if the corruption charged upon the Order was so general, and it must be abolished, he willed that all their wealth should be employed in the recovery of the Holy Land, and would not suffer the least part of it to be diverted to other uses: whence it is to be presumed that he suspected that in the persecution about to begin against the Templars, their crime was rather their great wealth than their irregular morals.

Philip, not brooking the delays of the Pope, by a secret order, executed on the 13th of October, caused to be arrested in one day the Grand Master and all the Templars that were found in Paris and the different parts of his realm; and confiscated all their property; for which proceeding several reasons were assigned. Some said it was because the Templars had furnished money to Boniface, to enable him to make war upon the King: others added (and the formal accusation contained the charge) that they had even obtained part of that money from the King's Treasury, by means of a Templar who was Treasurer. Others said that the Templars had stirred up a sedition in Paris, that grew out of the King's having debased the coin. The people insisted that no better reason need be sought for than the avarice of the King and his Ministers, and their greediness to handle the vast property of the Order. Philip had the year before arrested all the Jews in one day, despoiled them of their property, and driven them and their families, half naked, and with scanty means for their subsistence on the road, out of his Kingdom. And he had lately taken the principal share of the plunder of Italy, when Anaquia was pillaged by a band of adventurers secretly in his service.

When Edward the 2d of England heard of the arrest of the Templars, he wrote to the Pope and most of the Sovereigns of Europe, begging them to close their ears against the calumnies circulated against the Knights, " the purity of whose faith," said he, " whose good morals, and whose zeal for the defence of religion, all England reveres." But the haughtiness and ambition of the Templars had made them many enemies, and prejudiced most of the Bishops, their judges, with whom, indeed, as well as with the Hospitallers, they had had difficulties, in regard to their independence and the privileges of the Order. By appointment of the King, these Prelates, assisted by William of Paris, a Dominican and Inquisitor, and the Confessor of the King, held the first examination of the prisoners, which William de Nogaret conducted.

The Pope was surprised at this proceeding, and regarded the matter as an invasion of his rights. He suspended the powers of William of Paris, and interdicted the Bishops from proceeding with the case; and wrote to the King, claiming the jurisdiction and requiring him to deliver over to two Cardinals or to his Nuncio the persons and property of the Templars. The King replied boldly and contemptuously; and the Pope yielded, and allowed the King's Tribunal to proceed, the persons and property being, to save appearances, in form but not in reality placed in the hands of the Pope's Nuncio.

The proceedings commenced. The prisons were full of Knights; all of whom that did not voluntarily confess were subjected to the most extreme torture in use. Nothing was heard but the cries and groans of those who were torn with hot pincers, their bones crushed and their limbs torn asunder in the torture. Many to escape the awful agony, confessed whatever they were required; but many, in the midst of the most fearful torments insisted, with invincible firmness and constancy, that they were innocent.

The Pope himself interrogated seventy-two, who confessed. One Knight of the Order, an officer of the Pope, pretended to reveal all the wicked practices of his Brethren. The Pope then ordered the Grand Master, the Grand Priors, and the principal Commanders, of France, of beyond seas, and of Normandy, Aquitaine and Poitou, to be brought before him. It was pretended that the Grand Master had at Poitiers, and also at Paris, confessed most of the crimes imputed to him and the Order; and had written a circular letter, urging all the Knights to do the same. The Apostolic Commissioners, on their return from Chinon, laid the pretended proces-verbal of his confession before the King and Pope.

But when measures were about to be taken to extinguish the Order, based on the confessions of a great number of Templars, the Royal and Ecclesiastical miscreants were surprised to learn that the greater part of the Knights had revoked their confessions, and averred that they were extorted from them by torture; that they detested the pardon which the officers of the King had offered them, and regarded it as the price of infidelity, and the shameful reward of prevarication, as injurious to their honours as to their consciences.

The Kings of England, Castile, and Arragon, the Count of Provence, most Christian Princes, and even the Archbishops of Italy, had, in the mean time, on the urging of the Pope, arrested all the Templars in their dominions. Garrisons were placed in their Commanderies, their property was seized, and everywhere the proceedings against them went on. The Templars of Arragon at first took refuge in their fortresses, built by them to defend that country against the incursions of the Moors; and wrote to the Pope justifying themselves and asserting their innocence; urging that the charge against them that they were Infidels was particularly absurd, because many of their Brethren were captives among the Moors and treated most cruelly as Christians: and they claimed the right to prove their innocence, as Knights were entitled to do, by wager of battle.

The Pope is not known to have answered their letters; and James 2d of Arragon besieged them, took them prisoners, and confined them, to be tried by the Bishop of Valencia.

Most of the prisoners in France were collected in Paris. The revocation of the confessions embarrassed the Judges; but they finally determined that they should be treated as relapsed, and as having renounced Christ. De Molay was again brought before the Commissioners, and asked if he had anything to say in defence of his Order. He answered that he would cheerfully undertake, and would be delighted with the opportunity, to prove in the face of the Universe the innocence of his Order; but that he could neither read nor write (like most of the nobility). He demanded to be allowed to employ an advocate; "though," said he, "I have not four farthings left, to defray the costs of so great a suit."

The Commissioners told him that persons accused of heresy could be allowed neither counsel nor advocate; and advised him, before undertaking the defence, seriously to reflect, reminding him of his pretended confessions; and thereupon they were read to him. Never was astonishment like that of the Grand Master. When he heard them read, he made the sign of the cross, and said that if the three Cardinals, before whom he appeared at Chinon, and who had signed the examination, were not what they were, he should well know what to say. Being urged to explain himself more openly, he said (not being able to control his anger), that they deserved the same punishment which the Saracens and Tartars inflicted on forgers and liars, whose bellies, he said, they rip open, and cut off their heads.

The authentic proceedings show, that before the assembly at Chinon, and upon the promise of immunity of the King and Pope, he had on two occasions confessed a part of the crimes charged against him. Apparently the clerk had added aggravating circumstances,—perhaps all the crimes imputed to the order: and to conceal the cheat had not read the paper to him.

De Molay claimed to be sent before the Pope, who had reserved the right of trying him; and added that he had but three things to represent in favour of the Order: 1st. That except in the Cathedral Churches, nowhere in all Christendom was the divine service celebrated with more devotion, nor anywhere were to be found a greater number of relics and richer ornaments. 2d. That in every commandery a general alms was given three times a week. 3d. That there was no order, nor any nation, where the Knights and gentlemen had more generously exposed their lives in defence of the Christian religion, than the Templars had always done.

The Commissioners told him that all that was useless without faith. He replied that the Templars firmly believed everything that the Catholic Church believed; and that it was for the maintenance of so holy a belief, that so great a number of those Knights had poured out their blood against the Saracens, the Turks, and the Moors.

Brother Pierre de Boulogne, a Priest, and Procureur General of the Order pleaded for the Order. He represented the means by which confessions had been extracted; by promises of pardon, in letters patent, under the King's seal, and those failing, by torture. He said that many Knights had died in their dungeons, and he invoked the jailers and executioners to prove that they had invariably died protesting their innocence. And he demanded to be heard in full council, with his Superiors, and the Deputies of the whole Order, "to prove," he said, "their innocence in the face of all Christendom."

But all was prejudged, and the Commissioners proceeded accordingly. Those who had confessed were either discharged, or condemned merely to a canonical penance. Those who had revoked their confessions were treated with every species of rigour. Fifty-nine were degraded, as relapsed, by the Bishop of Paris, and given over to the secular arm. They were taken out of the gate St. Antoine and burned alive by a slow fire. In the midst of the flames, all invoked the Holy name of God; and what was most surprising, not one of the fifty-nine would deliver himself from so awful an agony and death, by accepting the amnesty which relatives and friends were holding out to them, from the King, if they would renounce their protestations of innocence.

And a great number of Templars, in other parts of France, in the midst of the flames, showed the same firmness. They burned them; but they could not extort from them any admission of the crimes charged against them. "It was an astonishing thing," says the Bishop of Lodévre, a contemporary historian, "that these unfortunates who were delivered over to the most cruel punishments, gave no other reason for retracting their confessions, than their shame and remorse for having, under the influence of torture, confessed to crimes of which they now declared themselves perfectly innocent."

The King, with his relatives and chief nobles, repaired to the Great Council held at Vienne in Dauphiny, the first session of which was held on the 16th of October 1311, when there were present more than three hundred Bishops, besides the Abbots, Priors, and most celebrated Doctors of Christendom.

The Pope had the proceedings against the Templars read, and the question as to suppressing the order was then put to each of the fathers, in turn. An Italian Prelate advised it; but all the Bishops and Archbishops of the Council, and the most celebrated Doctors unanimously represented to the Pope, that, before extinguishing so illustrious an order, and one which had from the time of its institution rendered so important services to Christianity, they ought to hear the Grand Master and Principal of the order in their defence, as justice required, and as they had themselves demanded, so urgently by many petitions.

All the Bishops of Italy, save one, were of this opinion; and with them agreed those of Spain, Germany, Denmark, England, Scotland and Ireland, and all the Prelates of France except three, the Archbishops of Rheims, Sens and Rouen, so that only four Prelates out of more than three hundred were found to deny the right of defence, contrary to the first principles of natural equity. But the time had come for the knavish and unprincipled Pope to comply with his oath to the Kingly assassin, torturer and robber. He delayed the matter by conferences, and at last declared that if the Templars could not be otherwise condemned without the formality of being heard in their defence, the plenitude of the Pontifical power would supply everything; and that he would condemn them by way of expedient, rather than that his dear son, the King of France, should be disappointed.

And, in fact, on the 22d of May, 1312, after obtaining assurance of support, in a secret consistory of Cardinals, and of some of the Bishops who had been won over, he held the second session of the Council, and therein quashed and annulled the military order of the Templars. "*And though we cannot,*" he said in his sentence, "*pronounce according to the forms of law, we condemn them provisionally and by the Apostolic authority, reserving to ourselves and to the Holy Roman Church the disposition of the persons and property of the Templars.*"

The question then arose as to the disposition to be made of their property. The Pope proposed to give it to the Knights of Rhodes (the new name of the Knights of St. John of Jerusalem). The partisans of France proposed to found a new order to be receivers of the spoil. But the Pope by large promises of reforming the order of St. John prevailed. All the property of the Templars was given to the Knights of Rhodes, except so much as was in Spain, which by special provision was to be applied to the defence of that country against the Moors, who yet occupied Grenada.

The next year, and after the adjournment of the Council, the next act of the tragedy was performed. The Pope, who had promised to try the Grand Master, and the Grand Preceptors or Grand Commanders, devolved that business on two Cardinals, who went to Paris and associated with themselves the Archbishop of Sens, and some other Prelates of the Gallican church. These apostolical Commissioners caused to be brought before them, by the Prevôt of Paris, Jacques de Molay, the Grand Master, whose rank was equal to that of a Prince; Guy, brother of the Dauphin of Viennois, Sovereign Prince of Dauphiny; Hugues de Peralde, Grand Prior, or visitor of the Priory of France; and the Grand Prior of Aquitaine, who had, before his arrest, had the direction of the finances of the King.

It does not appear that the Prelates put any new questions to the prisoners, or that they were confronted with the witnesses; although the proceedings aped the ordinary judicial forms. The tribunal was content with the confession which they had already made before the Pope and the King; and upon that, and following the intentions of the Pope, the Judges agreed, if the prisoners stood to their first confession, to condemn them to perpetual imprisonment only.

But as it was important to calm men's minds, astonished at so many fires lighted in the different provinces of the realm, and above all, to convince the people of Paris that so great a number of Templars had justly been burned alive, the four prisoners were required, if they would save their lives and have the benefit of the Pope's promise to that effect, to make in public a sincere declaration of the abuses and crimes committed in their Order. For this purpose a staging was erected in the nave of the Cathedral Church, upon which the archers and soldiers led the accused. One of the Legates opened the ceremony by a harangue, in which he expounded at great length all the impieties and abominations, whereof, he said, the Templars were convicted by their own admission. And, to leave no doubt on this subject, he called on the Grand Master and his companions to make anew, before the people, the confession which they had made before the Pope, of their crimes and their errors. As if to induce them to make this declaration, they were on the one hand assured of a full pardon, while on the other, to intimidate them, the executioners prepared a pile of wood, as if they were to be burned on the spot, if they revoked their first confession.

The Priors of France and Aquitaine adhered to their confessions, terrified by the immediate prospect of an awful death. But when it came the Grand Master's turn to make his declaration, all were surprised, as, rattling the chains with which he was loaded, he advanced with a bold countenance to the very edge of the staging, and, raising his voice, that he might be the better heard, cried aloud: "It is very right, that on this terrible day, and in the last moments of my life, I should uncover all the iniquity of the lie, and cause the truth to triumph. I declare then, before heaven and earth, and I avow, although to my eternal shame, that I have committed the greatest of all crimes; but only by acknowledging the truth of those so foully charged against an order, of which the truth to-day compels me to say that order is innocent. I agreed to the declaration demanded of me, solely to procure a respite from the excessive agony of the tortures, and to endeavour to move those to compassion who left me to suffer. I know the punishment that has been imposed on those who have revoked similar confessions; but the fearful spectacle that fronts me cannot make me confirm a first lie by a second. Upon a condition so infamous, I heartily renounce a life already hateful to me. And what would it avail me to prolong a miserable life, which I must owe to the basest calumny and slander!"

He would have said more, but they forced him to be silent. The brother of the Prince Dauphin who came after him, held the same language, and loudly protested the innocence of the Order.

The prisoners were then remanded to prison; and the King, naturally vindictive, and more irritated by this public retraction of the chiefs of the Order, caused them to be burned alive by a slow fire, on a little island in the Seine, between the King's garden and the Convent of the Augustins. The Grand Master in the midst of his cruel punishment showed the same courage as in the Cathedral, and made similar declarations. He protested anew the innocence of the order; but confessed that he himself deserved death, for having confessed the contrary before the King and Pope. Some authors say that one of the Priors, determined by the noble resolution of De Molay, had also revoked his confession, and was burned with the Grand Master, and the brother of the Prince Dauphin. The other died in prison.

When the Grand Master could at length move his tongue only and was nearly stifled with smoke, he in a loud voice, summoned the Pope, that iniquitous judge and cruel butcher, to appear before the Tribunal of the Sovereign Judge in fifty days, and Philip within a year; and both afterwards died at the times specified in his summons.

All the people shed tears at the tragical spectacle of this execution. The Grand Master had before his execution offered up this prayer: "O God, permit us to meditate on the pains that Jesus suffered that we might be redeemed; and enable us to imitate the example of endurance which he gave us, when he submitted without a murmur to the persecutions and torments which bigotry and injustice had prepared for him. Forgive, O God, those false accusers who have caused the entire destruction of the Order whereof thy Providence had made me the head: And if it please thee to accept the prayer which we now offer, grant that the day may come when the world, now deceived, may better know those who have sought to live for thee. We trust to thy goodness and mercy to compensate us for the tortures and death which we are now to suffer; and that we may enjoy thy divine presence in the mansions of happiness."

Convinced of his innocence, many holy persons and devotees gathered the ashes of these noble victims, and preserved them as precious relics.

This tragedy was enacted on the 11th day of March, 1314. The Knights of Rhodes or Malta greedily accepted the donation of the estates and riches of the Templars. A Council was held, and persons appointed to receive the property by an act dated at Rhodes on the 17th of October, 1312, signed by the Grand Master, Foulques de Villaret, "by the grace of God and of the Apostolic See, Humble Master of the Holy House and Hospital of St. John of Jerusalem, and Guardian of the Sepulchre of Jesus Christ." But it cost them much time and vast sums of money to get the property out of the hands of the greedy courtiers who had possession of it; and finally they were compelled to consent to pay the King and his successor a large sum, for which the latter retained two-thirds of the moneys of the Templars, the ornaments of their churches, the furniture of their houses, and the fruits and revenues of their lands, and, in a word, all their movables up to the day when the Hospitallers obtained possession. Of this plunder the Pope received his share.

Charles 2d, King of Naples and Sicily, and Count of Provence and Fortalquiers, pursued the same course. He burned a great number of them, who would not confess, and gave the lands of the Order to the Hospitallers, but divided their money and personal effects between himself and the Pope. The Kings of Castile, Arragon and Portugal seized on most of their property within their respective realms; but in England the Hospitallers obtained the whole, and in Germany shared the property with the Teutonic Knights. The Order was entirely destroyed everywhere.

Hated and persecuted by the Pope, by all the Sovereigns and Princes of Christendom, and by the Hospitallers, who had become mighty by means of their ill-gotten wealth, the remaining Templars knew that it was entirely useless to attempt to revive their great, illustrious and unfortunate Order. Having in Palestine become intimate with the Knights of St. Andrew and other gallant and noble Masonic Knights and Princes, and many of them having been made Masons in the Holy Land, they sought to unite themselves with our ancient Fraternity, hoping, by thus gaining accessions to their Order among the Military Masons, one day to be able to recover their estates, and again to become the defenders of the Holy Land and the shield of Christendom against the Infidel. The Masonic Knights and Princes, who by this time were to be found in every part of Christendom, gladly agreed to this union, and most of them were initiated into the Order of Templars, who first discarded their white habit and red cross, and assumed a Masonic garb; and also adopted Masonic signs and words, and assumed the name of Knights and Princes Kadosch, to protect themselves against traitors; for whom to arrive at this exalted degree would be impossible, in consequence of the assurance which, during their progress towards it, they would be compelled to give of their fidelity, their courage and their discretion. Hence the hostility which the Knights of St. John, or of Malta, have always shown against Free Masonry: for even so late as 1740 the Grand Master of that Order caused to be published and enforced in Malta the Bull of Pope Clement XII., worthy successor of Clement V., against the Masons, and forbade their meetings; and in 1741 encouraged the Inquisition to persecute them.

Gr∴ Precept∴ Return, now, my Brother, to the Th∴ Ill∴ Gr∴ Commander, and receive the concluding explanations of this Degree.

Gr∴ Comm∴ The Templars, my Brother, have seen in the legend of the Master's Degree, which was fully explained to you in the Degree of Knight of the Sun, a striking resemblance to the tragical fate of their Order and their Grand Master Jacques De Molay. It has been often said that we have been taught to see in the Grand Master Hiram, our murdered Grand Master De Molay, and in the three assassins, the three first informers against the Templars, Squin de Florian, Noffodei and the Prior of Montfaucon.

The Templars have not taken so much pains, my brother, merely to perpetuate the memory of the crimes of three worthless knaves, who long since found their due reward; one being hung, another assassinated, and the end of the third being unknown.

No, my Brother. The good De Molay was a victim; but there was a nobler victim than he,—the Order itself, of which he was but a part. In the persecution and destruction of that Order we have seen renewed, under another form, the legend, ever varying, yet ever the same, of Hiram and his assassins, of Osiris and Typhon, of the Light and the Darkness, of the Good Principle and the Evil. And the three assassins of the Widow's Son we see reproduced in the Royal Power of France, embodied in Philip le Bel; the Papal Power, in Clement the 5th; and the rapacious Order of the Knights of Rhodes, or the Order of St. John of Jerusalem.

The feeling of vengeance, at first personal in its character, soon became ennobled, by being directed against the abuses of which Philip, Clement, and the Hospitallers were the type and embodiment. After Philip's death, the Order laboured to subvert kingly despotism and feudal oppression: after that of Clement, it checked and thwarted the arrogant assumptions of temporal power by the Popes, and inspired the Gallican Church and the Jurists and Parliaments of France with a feeling and spirit of sturdy independence. In the Order of the Hospitallers, it fought against an odious monopoly of wealth and power, against privileges granted at the expense of the people, and against abuses licensed by charter, and for ages beyond the reach of the law.

These, then, are the three assassins of human freedom and of liberty of thought and conscience: Regal Tyranny, Sacerdotal Usurpation by whatever Church, and Corporate Monopolies and abuses vested in Privileged Orders. The Templars made no issue with liberal and well-regulated Government. They were not at first, nor are they now the advocates of radicalism and unbridled popular license; but they believe that a Constitutional Monarchy, or a well-regulated Republic, based upon law and an inviolable Constitution, is that Government to which alone a human being, moral and enlightened, ought to submit.

Professed Catholics, they made no war on the Catholic religion. They strove only to set limits to its extravagant claim of temporal power; to check its intolerable usurpations; and to apply the knife and cautery to its rank abuses. They had not those exalted ideas of the Supremacy of the Roman Bishop, required in those days of all Catholics; though they admitted that, by the consent of Christendom, he held the highest rank. Many of the Crusaders had learned in the East the doctrines of the Gnostics and Manichæans, which seemed to them less altered from the original revelation than those of Rome. They adopted the doctrines of St. John, rather than those of the successors of St. Peter or of St. Paul. There is reason to believe that there was a secret schism between them and Rome, and that their Johannite doctrines, with the mysteries which they learned in the East, were the sole foundation for the charges of monstrous crimes brought against them, and so confidently alleged to have been fully established by testimony and confession. De Payens was learned in the esoteric doctrines and formulas in Initiation, of the Christians of the Orient; and he was, say the chronicles, clothed, in 1118, with the Patriarchal power, in the legitimate order of succession of St. John, who never went beyond the East, and whose doctrines seemed to the Templars more pure than those of Peter and Paul, who, carrying the word of Christ to the remotest nations, conceded something to their manners and customs, and allowed other rites to be practised than those of the East.

The race of Philip le Bel no longer sits upon the throne of France; but in their place a Monarch elected by the People. The Templars bore no small share in the first French Revolution. They were represented in the National Assembly among the members of the Third Estate, and aided in making the Monarchy constitutional. But equally opposed to despotism and license, they were not found among the Jacobins. They looked with horror on the days of terror. They were seen in the ranks of the Republican Army, when the soil of France was invaded by the enemy. They had fought under the banners of Washington. They assisted to raise the first Napoleon to power. They have been found wherever the armies of freedom have met those of tyranny; and they look forward hopefully to the day when unlimited and licentious Power will no longer oppress the Earth.

The Hospitallers fell in 1798. The Order had long before lost its object, and with it its dignity and strength. The Knights possessed large estates in different countries; but though their duty was to protect the Christian Nations against the Barbary States, and to destroy the infamous pirates that infested the Mediterranean, they maintained no efficient naval force, and their Bailiffs and Commanders, spread over Christendom, consumed the revenues of the Order in luxury and indolence. There was not a single Knight who had ever been engaged with the Barbary Corsairs. The possessions of the Order had been taken from it in France, and seized by Napoleon in Italy, and no one cared enough for the effete Institution to remonstrate in its behalf.

On the 10th of June, 1798, Napoleon landed on the Island of Malta, and captured it almost without opposition. The Grand Master accepted the promise of a Principality in Germany, or an annuity of 300,000 francs, and an indemnity of 600,000 francs in ready money: and to each French Knight an annuity of 700 francs was granted, or of 1000 if they were sixty years of age. The Grand Master kissed the hand of the Conqueror; and the Order of Knights of St. John of Jerusalem expired.

The same great Conqueror laughed to scorn the temporal power of the Pope and defied the lightnings of excommunication. He brought the Pope to France and made him a Prisoner of State. The doctrine of temporal authority over Kings has become a mere idle theory, set at nought even in Sardinia and Spain.

And thus the warfare against the Powers of Evil that crushed the Order of Templars goes steadily on; and freedom marches ever onward towards the Conquest of the World. The vast power of public opinion reaches and controls even the occupants of Despotic Thrones. A mighty Republic in the West, already stretching from ocean to ocean, menaces with speedy overthrow the abuses and hoary oppressions of the old world. The infamous tortures of the middle ages are no longer known. The persecutions for opinion's sake are remembered like plague and pestilence that swept the earth with the besom of destruction centuries ago. The rights of the People are daily rising into sight; and the will of the people is everywhere coming to be recognized as the foundation of all civil power and government.

Profoundly does mankind love the truth, and will not let it go, so native it is to the mind of man. Forget not, my Brother, the vast power of a special truth, of a great idea, viewed merely as a force in the world of men. At first, nothing seems so impotent. It has no hands nor feet; how can it go alone? It seems as if the censor of the press could blot it out forever. It flatters no man, offers to serve no personal and private interest, and then forbear its work; will be no man's slave. It seems ready to perish; it will surely give up the ghost the next moment! Lo, now; some startled Tyrant or pampered Priest has it in the dust, and stamps it out! O, idle fear! Stamp out the lightning of the sky? Of all things, Truth is the most lasting; invulnerable as God: of the Eternal co-eternal beam, no accident of His Being, but substance of His Substance, inseparable from Him. The solid masses of the pyramids may after long ages crumble into dust and be blown off by the Sirocco of the desert; the very mountains whence they were hewn may all vanish, melting imperceptibly down to the level of the plains; but every Truth shall still remain, immortal, unchangeable and never growing old. Heaven and earth may pass away, but a Truth never. A true word cannot fail from amongst men. It is endorsed by the Almighty, and shall pass current with mankind forever. All the armies of the world cannot destroy or alter the smallest truth of mathematics; make one and one greater or less than two: and as little can they destroy or alter any truth in morals, in politics or in religion.

See the power of some special truth upon a single man. Saul of Tarsus sees that God loves the Gentile as well as the Jew. It seems a small thing now to see that. Why did men ever think otherwise? Why should not God love the Gentile as well as the Jew? It was impossible that He should do otherwise. Yet this seemed a great truth at that time, the Christian Church dividing upon that matter. Burning in the bosom of Paul, what heroism it wakened in him, what self-denial. For it he bore want, hardships, persecution, the contempt and loathing of his former friends and companions, shipwreck, the scourge, prisons, and at last death. A Truth inspired him, and these compared with that were nothing. He became eloquent and his letters powerful with the force of this new truth. Everywhere he finds foes and a world bristling with peril; but everywhere this Truth and the Heroism it wakes in him make him friends. Men saw the new doctrine and looked back on the old error,—that Jove loved Rome; Pallas, Athens; Juno, Samos, and Carthage most of all; Jehovah, Mount Zion, and Baal his Tyrian towers; while each looked frowningly and sternly at all the rest of men,—they see now that all this was an error, out of which came great evils, incessant wars, and ages full of strife, national jealousies, wrangling between Babylonian and Theban Priests, the antagonism of the Gentile and the Jew, and afterwards the Christian hatred of the Saracen, the Moor, and the detested remnants of the Hebrew race, imagined to be hated of God, and so despised.

And what an influence has a great Truth, or a great idea, upon masses of men! Some single man sees it at first, dimly perhaps for a long time, without power of sight sufficient to make it clear, the quality of vision better than his quantity of sight. Then he sees it clearly and in distinct outline. The truth burns mightily within him, and he cannot be still. He tells it, now to one, and then to another, and they see it also. It wakens a love for itself: a few minds prepared for it half-welcome it; and thence it timidly flashes into other minds, as light reflected from the water. Then those who receive it form a family of faith, and grow strong in the companionship. The circle grows wider; and men oppose the new idea, with little skill or much, sometimes with violence, sometimes with intellect only. Then there comes a pause. The interruptions to a great idea are of corresponding value to its development in a man, a nation or the world. Those baptized with the fire of the new idea pause and reflect to be more sure,—perfecting the logic of their thought; pause, and devise their mode to set it forth,—perfecting their rhetoric; and seek to organize it in an outward form; for every thought must be a thing. Then they tell their idea more perfectly; in the controversy that follows, errors connected with it get exposed; all that is merely accidental, national or personal gets shaken off, and the pure truth goes forth to conquer. In this way, all the great ideas, political, religious, moral and philanthropic, have gone their round. Soon the truth has philosophers to explain it, apologists to defend it, orators to set it forth, institutions to embody its sacred life: it has become a new Force in the world; and nothing can destroy or withstand it.

Not many hundred years ago the great leading truth asserted in this Degree began to be obscurely seen. Man has natural empire over all institutions: They are for him, according to his development; not he for them. That seems to us a very simple statement, one to which all men everywhere ought to assent. But once it was a great New Truth. It has led to much. Its application to the Catholic Church was seen, that mighty institution that for centuries had ruled over the souls of men. The Church gave way, and recoiled before the tide of Truth. Afterwards men saw its application to the temporal despotisms that had long ruled over the bodies and chained down the souls and intellects of men. That helpless truth has inspired millions, has built institutions, has called a multitude of men into life. As it first gained foothold, revolutions followed thick and fast in Holland, England, America and France; and one day all Europe and the world will be a-blaze with that idea. Men opposed it; one of the Stuarts said, "It shall not cross the four seas of England;" but it crossed the Stuart's neck, and drove his children from the faithful soil. At first destructive, it was destined to be creative and conservative. It came to America in company with those who fled from England and France across the wide Atlantic, little knowing what fruit would come of their planting; and lo! what institutions have sprung up on the soil then shaded by interminable forests, and hideous with wild beasts and wilder men! Out of the old Truth what great constitutional ideas have blossomed; under the shadow of this idea, what a family of States, clasping friendly, brotherly hands across the great central mountains and deserts has sprung up!

And now this great Truth, long since recognized as true, and now by experiment proved expedient and practicable, goes back over the sea, and earnest nations welcome it to their hearts,—this Sovereign Truth: MAN IS SUPREME OVER INSTITUTIONS, NOT THEY OVER HIM. How it has startled the throned masters of Europe, and how it still rings there in the people's hearts! Before it Thrones and Hierarchies and Privilege are doomed to go down, and at last lie grovelling in the dust: for it belongs to the nature of man, can only perish when the race gives up the ghost, and all the armies of the world cannot crush it. It has the omnipotence of God on its side, and can no more be overcome than He.

The truths we slowly learn will be added to the people that come after us: the great political truths of America will go round the world, and clothe the earth with greenness and with beauty. The truths we bring to light are dropped into the world's wide treasury, and form a part of the heritage which each generation receives, enlarges, holds in trust, and of necessity bequeaths to mankind; the personal estate of man, entailed of nature to the end of time. He who sets forth or develops any truth, or any human excellence of gift or growth, greatens the spiritual glory of his race. The spiritual truths we learn, the intellectual wealth that we acquire, all the manly excellence that we slowly meditate and slowly sculpture into life, go down in blessing to mankind, the cup of gold hid in the sack of those who only asked for corn, richer than all the grain they bought.

No king nor conqueror does men so great a good as he who bestows on human-kind a great and universal truth. He that aids its march, and makes the thought or thing, works in the same line with Moses and with Him who died upon the cross, and has an intellectual sympathy with the Deity himself. The best gift we can bestow upon man is manhood. We undervalue not material things; but we remember that the same generation which found Rome brick and left it marble, and full of statues and of temples too, as its best achievement bequeathed to us a few words uttered in Galilee, an insignificant district in an unimportant Roman Province, and the remembrance of the perfect life and divine virtues of Him who taught there and was ignominiously crucified at Jerusalem, by the same enemies of human freedom that sacrificed the Templars, and that still wage war against Free Thought, Free Action and Free Conscience as savagely, if not as successfully as they did when the Roman Eagles hovered over Judea, and the Priests and besotted people set at liberty a common malefactor and demanded the blood of the great Benefactor of the Human Race.

For much still remains to do. Tyranny is weakened but not overthrown. The chains still weigh on human thought and conscience. Monopolies and privileges, in the hands of favoured classes, still impose burthens on the people: and the Elu are still needed, to do vengeance on these abuses. It is the old contest between Good and Evil, between the Sons of Light and the Sons of Darkness. With the tongue and the pen, with all our open and secret influences, with the sword, if need be, we advance the cause of human progress, and labour to enfranchise human thought, to give freedom to the human conscience, and equal rights to the people everywhere. Wherever a nation struggles to regain its freedom, wherever the human mind asserts its independence, and the people claim their inalienable rights, there go our warmest sympathies.

This, my Brother, is the true Vengeance, symbolically represented in the Elu degrees: a lofty, noble vengeance, on Wrong and Oppression. Opposition to regal tyranny made the internal government of Masonry Democratic. Hatred of sacerdotal usurpation and intolerance caused the dedication of its Lodges to the Holy Saints John; and its adoption of Hiram, a founder and worker in metals, the son of a poor widow, as the Hero of its Legend, the successor of the God Osiris, the typification of Light and the good Principle; the search for him by his companions, the sturdy common people, workers in stone and wood; and the new dignity given by Masonry to industrial associations, evidence its opposition to the unjust privileges of the higher classes, and to Orders that enjoy monopolies that they may be enabled to live in contented indolence.

Such is the Masonry of the true KADOSCH: *Love for the people; hatred of Tyranny; sacred regard for the rights of free thought, free speech, and free conscience; and detestation of intolerance, bigotry and priestly arrogance and usurpation; respect and regard for Labour, which makes human nature noble, and contempt and disgust for all monopolies of wealth and laziness.*

Behold, Ill∴ Brother, how and why this Order and Masonry became connected! Persecuted and impoverished, the Templars came to have sympathies with the Common People. The Elus, with whom they had formed habits of friendship in the Holy Land, succoured and protected them. The Hospitallers, the Papal power, the Despotism of Kings were the common enemies of both. Hoping to obtain thereby the means of regaining their rights and possessions, the Templars gladly associated themselves with those who by their virtues and courage had acquired rights, privileges and consideration, such as birth alone had accorded to their own ancestors. You are from this time their equal; but no longer in danger from the rancour of envy or the fires of persecution.

We have confidence in your discretion, and faith in your zeal and fidelity. We have not hesitated to make known to you the true purposes of our Order; and we hope that, zealously co-operating with us, you will, by sincere obedience to our laws and your superiors, acquire that perfection which is the aim of every Masonic Knight.

You are now truly a Knight, Elected to a great work. May the excellence of your life and conversation conduct you to that happiness which they alone can give!

The Gr∴ Commander then directs the Candidate to kneel, and invests him with the collar and jewel of the Order: Then striking him lightly on the right shoulder, the left shoulder, and the head, with the blade of his sword, he says, while doing so: "By virtue of the power and prerogative to me belonging, as the rightful successor of Hugh de Payens and Jacques de Molay, I hereby constitute, create and dub you a Grand Elect Knight Kadosch. Be brave, discreet and virtuous! Arise, Sir Knight, and be invested with the arms of Knighthood."

The Grand Prior girds a sword, and the Grand Preceptor buckles the silver spurs, upon the Candidate: and the Gr∴ Commander says: [after communicating the signs, &c.]: "Knights and Brethren, behold a new Knight added to our number! I commend him to your kindness and courtesy. Protect him in danger, aid him in distress, and defend his good name at the peril of your lives; and should he fall at the post of duty, honour his memory, and cherish those who survive to bear his name!"

SIGN: . . . Place the ♓&☉♒Ⅱ upon the &☾☉♌♈ with the ♑♀♒♌☾♌♎ ☾♉♈☾♒Ⅱ☾Ⅱ, and then let it ♑☉♈♈ on the ♓♈♀&♀♌♌♏—at the same time ♏☾♒Ⅱ♀♒♌ the ♐♒☾☾. Then seize the ⸮♉♒♀☉⊙

†☐ which is ⌐℥⌐ℨℂ∾☐ℂ☐ from the ⌐♌⊙♌♈, and raise it to the height of the shoulder, as if to ⌐♈♌♀¶ℂ—saying ∾ℂ¶⊙☐ ⊙☐♉∾⊙♀∴

O𝖱𝖣𝖤𝖱: . . . Sword in the left hand; the right on the ‡ℂ☐ ♌‡♉⌐ on the ♏‡ℂ⊙⌐♈∴

T𝖮𝖪𝖤𝖭: . . . The ℨ♉ ♀∾♈⌐ of the ‡♈ℂℂ♈ together, and ¶∾ℂℂ against ¶∾ℂℂ. Then one presents the ‡♌℥⊙∾☐‡♌♉ℂ∾♌℥ℂ☐ with the ♈℥♌☜♏ ♌⊙♀⌐ℂ☐. The other encloses the ♈℥♌☜♏ with his ♈♉♀♌ ♈♉∾♌ℂ♌⌐, his own ♈℥♌☜♏ ℂ♌ℂ✱⊙♈ℂ☐, thus showing ℂ ♀♌&♈ ♈♀∾♌ℂ♌⌐ ⌐&℥♈ and a ♈℥♌☜♏ in sight. Then they unclose, and the same thing is done again, with change of persons. Then unclosing, each ‡ℂ♌♉♀♌⌐ a ⌐♈ℂℨ, with the left arm ♌⊙♀⌐ℂ☐ as if to ⌐♈♌♀¶ℂ—in which attitude the first says ∾ℂ¶℥⊙☜⊙☜-☜ℂ∾℥¶☜♀☜∴ and the other answers ℨ&ℂ♌ℂ⌐☜-¶♉♌∴

P𝖠𝖲𝖲-𝖶𝖮𝖱𝖣: . . . ∾ℂ¶ . . . as above: another is ☜⊙♏ℂ☜⊙☜∴

A𝖭𝖲𝖶𝖤𝖱: . . . ℨ&ℂ . . . as above.

W𝖮𝖱𝖣 𝖮𝖿 E𝖭𝖳𝖱𝖠𝖭𝖢𝖤: . . . ∾ℂ¶⊙☜ ⊙☐♉∾⊙♀∴

S𝖠𝖢𝖱𝖤𝖣 W𝖮𝖱𝖣𝖲: . . . ⊙♌♀-⊙♌∴ and ☜♀ ¶⊙☜℥¶ ♏⊙♌♀☜ ♀&℥&∴

TO CLOSE.

G∴ Comm∴ [_Giving one rap_]; Ill∴ Gr∴ Prior, what news from the Order in the West?

Gr∴ Prior: . . Th∴ Ill∴, our brethren of the West bid us be of good cheer, for the Eagles gather together, and the doom of Tyranny is at hand.

Gr∴ Com∴ Ill∴ Gr∴ Preceptor, what news from the Order in the South?

Gr∴ Prec∴ Th∴ Ill∴, Truth struggles bravely against error, and the great electric ocean of thought is in agitation. The storm hovers on the horizon, and the lightning is ready to leap forth against ancient Wrong and the hoary precedents of oppression.

Gr∴ Comm∴ And in the East the People begin to know their rights and to be conscious of their dignity. My Brethren, the reign of Darkness draweth to its close, and the Sun's rays smite the summits of the mountains. Ill∴ Gr∴ Prior, what remains for us to do?

Gr∴ Prior: . . Th∴ Ill∴, to sow the good seed, that those may reap to whom God in his own good time may assign it:—to be patient and to hope.

Gr∴ Com∴ Brother Almoner, does any distressed Knight need comfort or assistance, or is any widow or orphan of a brother unprovided for?

[If any case for relief is reported, order is taken upon it—if none, the Almoner answers accordingly].

Gr∴ Com∴ Brethren, since nothing remains for us to do but to hope and labour, let us go forth and perform our duties in the world. It is my pleasure that this Chapter be now closed. Brethren, the Sign!

[The Sign is given as in opening. The Gr∴ Comm∴ gives one rap, and declares the Chapter closed.]

FINIS.

Thirty-First Degree.

Grand Enquiring Commander.

DECORATIONS, OFFICERS, ETC.

The hangings are white. There are two gilded columns in the East, one on each side of the President, two in the West, one on each side of the seats of the Senior and Junior Counsellors, three on the South side of the Lodge, and three on the North, equidistant from each other.

On the column on the right of the President is inscribed in large letters the word JUSTITIA, and on that on his left, the word EQUITAS. From the two springs a Gothic arch, from the apex whereof is suspended over the head of the President the Tetractys of Pythagoras; and, under it, a balance, or the scales of Justice, and a sword.

On the column on the right of the Counsellors is inscribed the word LENITAS, and on that upon their left, MISERICORDIA. From these columns springs a Gothic arch, from the apex whereof is suspended, in letters of gold, the sacred word INRI.

On the three columns in the South, going from East to West, are the busts of MOSES, ZOROASTER and MINOS, with the name of each inscribed on his column. On those in the North, also arranged from East to West, are the busts of CONFUCIUS, SOCRATES and ALFRED, with the name of each inscribed on his column.

In front of the President is a hexagonal altar, on which are the Holy Bible, the Square and Compasses, the Plumb and Level, a pair of Scales, and a Sword.

In the centre of the room is a large table in the shape of a decagon, and on it ten lights. In the East are ten, and in the West ten; each ten being arranged by 1, 2, 3, and 4, in the form of the *Tetractys*.

The Altar is covered with a black cloth, and the Table with a green one.

The Assembly is styled *Supreme Tribunal*. The Presiding Officer is styled *Most Ill∴ President*. The Wardens are styled *Counsellors*, and sit together in the West. The Secretary is styled *Chancellor*, and sits on the right of the President. The Treasurer sits on his left. The other officers are, the *Advocate*, who sits in the South, the *Defender*, who sits in the North, the *Pursuivant*, in front of the Wardens, and the *Sergeant-at-Arms*, on the outside of the door.

All the officers and members, except the President, are styled *Illustrious*.

When a trial takes place, the Tribunal consists of ten members only, and they sit around the Table in the centre, on which are then placed the Bible and other furniture of the Altar.

The composition of the Tribunal and the qualifications of the members will be found in the Statutes.

DRESS, JEWELS, ETC.

No apron is worn in the Sov∴ Tribunal. In the inferior bodies, the Commanders wear one of entirely white sheepskin, with a Teutonic cross in silver embroidered on the flap.

The collar is white. On the breast, at the point, is a triangle surrounded with a glory, and of gold, in the centre of which, in Arabic figures, is the number of the degree, 31. The Commander may also wear a gold chain, the links of which are composed of the interlaced attributes of the different degrees, particularly the 1st, 2d, 3d, 11th, 14th, 17th, 18th and 30th. .

The jewel is a Teutonic cross of silver. The members should be dressed in black, and wear swords. ·
The battery is , . — by , — ? —; and !

TO OPEN.

M∴ Ill∴ Ill∴ Bro∴ Sen∴ Counsellor, the obligations of duty are eternal to the good Mason. They require us to resume our labours. See that all present are Gr∴ Enquiring Commanders.

Sen∴ C∴ All present are Gr∴ Enquiring Commanders, M∴ Ill∴.

M∴ Ill∴ You will then take steps to ascertain whether the doors of this Tribunal are safely guarded ; and give orders that none be allowed to enter here without your permission, that we may not be improperly interrupted.

Sen∴ C∴ Ill∴ Pursuivant, you will please ascertain whether the Sergeant-at-Arms is at his post : and command him to be vigilant that none approach to disturb or interrupt this Supreme Tribunal, which is now about to open ; and that he allow none to enter without our permission first obtained. ·

[The Pursuivant goes out, returns, gives the battery, which is answered from without, and reports: "Ill∴ Sen∴ Counsellor, your orders are executed"].

Sen∴ C∴ M∴ Ill∴, the Sergeant-at-Arms is at his post and duly instructed, and we are in security.

M∴ Ill∴ Then we may safely proceed. Ill∴ Pursuivant, your duty ?

Purs∴ To execute your orders coming to me by the West, and see the judgments of the Tribunal duly executed : to serve and return all process, and to compel order when the Tribunal is in session.

M∴ Ill∴ Ill∴ Defender, your duty ?

Def∴ To defend all persons charged with offences and tried before this Tribunal, to see that no improper testimony be admitted against them, to present the truth in their defence, to lay their cases fairly before the Tribunal, and to urge all circumstances of extenuation in their favour.

M∴ Ill∴ Ill∴ Advocate, your duty ?

Adv∴ To prefer charges against those under the jurisdiction of this Tribunal, who have been guilty of offences against Masonic law and duty : to draft the acts of accusation, prepare the testimony, elicit the truth, and present the whole case fairly and without aggravation or misrepresentation before the Tribunal.

M∴ Ill∴ Ill∴ Treasurer, your duty ?

Treas∴ To receive and keep safely the funds of the Tribunal.

M∴ Ill∴ Ill∴ Chancellor, your duty ?

Chan∴ To record the proceedings and judgments of the Tribunal.

M∴ Ill∴ Ill∴ Junior Counsellor, your duty ?

Jun∴ C∴ To guard against all violations of Masonic law, to give my advice on proper occasions to the M∴ Ill∴ President, and to pronounce just and righteous judgment.

M∴ Ill∴ Ill∴ Sen∴ Counsellor, your duty ?

Sen∴ C∴ That of my Junior, tempering justice with equity, and ever remembering the dictates of mercy.

M∴ Ill∴ Ill∴ Sen∴ Counsellor, the duty of the M∴ Ill∴ President?

Sen∴ C∴ To preside in judgment and expound the law ; to judge justly, and to punish sternly ; but, ever remembering the frailty and imperfection of human nature, to pardon and forgive, while there remains hope of reformation.

M∴ Ill∴ The duty of all members of this Tribunal, when sitting in judgment?

Sen∴ C∴ Careful and scrupulous investigation of all facts, inculpatory, exculpatory and extenuating ;

charitable construction of acts and motives; calm and deliberate consideration, just judgment, and disregard of person, rank, influence and power.

M∴ Ill∴ I recognize *my* duty. My Brethren, recognize those that devolve upon *you*. May the Great Judge of all human actions aid me and all of us well and conscientiously to perform all that it is fitting for us to do! My Brethren, kneel with me, and let us implore His aid, His pardon and His protection.

PRAYER.

Hear us with indulgence, O Infinite Deity, whose attributes are infinite, and infinitely harmonious! Thou, of whose essence are Justice, Equity and Mercy, intermingled into one Excellence! Thou to whom all thoughts and all actions of all men are known and visible as Thine own! to whom the Infinite Past and the Infinite Future are One Now, and the Infinitudes of Space in all directions are Here! Give to us the wisdom and the will to judge justly, accurately and mercifully! Keep our feet from going astray, lead us by the hand to Truth, close up to us all the paths and avenues of temptation! Strengthen our good resolves, and free us from the tyrannous empire of prejudice, partiality, error and passion! Help us to perform all our Masonic duties, to ourselves, to other men, and to Thee! Let the great flood of Masonic light flow in a perpetual current over the whole world, and make Masonry the hand-maiden of Thy true religion. Pardon us when we offend. When we go astray, lead us tenderly back to the true path, and smile upon our feeble efforts to advance the cause of morality and virtue! And when we come to be finally judged by Thee, O remember not against us our errors of judgment, but in Thine Infinite Mercy forgive us and take us home to Thee! Amen! Amen! Amen!

All: So mote it be!

M∴ Ill∴ My Brethren, the sign!

[The sign is given: Then the Advocate raps , — the Jun∴ Counsellor ? — the Senior ; — and the President ! —]

M∴ Ill∴ Ill∴ Senior Counsellor, this Supreme Tribunal is now open. Let due Proclamation thereof be made.

Sen∴ C∴ Ill∴ Pursuivant, make Proclamation that this Sup∴ Tribunal is now open, and that all who demand its judgment may now draw near.

Purs∴ [Going to the door and opening it]. Hear ye! This Sup∴ Tribunal of Gr∴ Inquiring Commanders is now open and in session. Whosoever hath been cited to appear, or hath complaint or appeal to make or answer, let him draw near, and he shall be heard!

[The M∴ Ill∴ then gives one rap, and the Commanders are seated].

RECEPTION.

No one can receive this degree, except a Knight Kadosch, elected to receive it by unanimous vote of the Chapter of Kts∴ K—H∴ to which he belongs. Upon filing a certificate of such election, he is balloted for ; and if unanimously elected by the Tribunal, he receives the degree.

Being brought to the door of the Tribunal, in the dress and jewel of a Kt∴ K—H∴ the Serg∴ at Arms raps , and ? — the Pursuivant answers ; — and the Serg∴ at Arms responds ! The door is then opened.

Purs∴ Who approaches this Sup∴ Tribunal, and what is his desire?

Serg∴ A Kt∴ K—H∴, upright, virtuous and eminent, who, having been duly elected by his brethren, desires to receive the degree of Grand Enquiring Commander.

Purs∴ What is his name?

35 D

Serg∴ A. . . . . B. . . . .

Purs∴ His age?

Serg∴ —— years.

Prus∴ His occupation?

Serg∴ That of ———: Useful and honourable, as is all work in this world: as Masons, best of all men, are aware.

Purs∴ Hath he, by sufficient service and patient obedience as a Mason, learned the first lesson in the art of governing?

Serg∴ He hath. He has learned to govern himself.

Purs∴ Is he trustworthy and true? Do you vouch for him? Is he honest, temperate, of equal temper, charitable construction and merciful impulses?

Serg∴ He is a K—H∴; and his brethren have thought him worthy to enter here.

Purs∴ Let him wait until his request is made known to the President.

[The Pursuivant reports the answers, and is ordered to allow him to enter. The Commanders should all wear black hats, with black masks and cloaks. When the Candidate enters, the Pursuivant takes charge of him, and leads him to the President].

M∴ Ill∴ Whom have you there, my Brother?

Purs∴ A Knight K—H∴ of good name and fame and virtuous conversation, who, having been duly elected by his Brethren, desires to receive the degree of Grand Enquiring Commander.

M∴ Ill∴ My Brother, you desire to take upon yourself an arduous and responsible office. There is but ONE Infallible, Unerring Judge. All human judgment is at best uncertain. Serious in its consequences, it must often, when time develops its errors, produce regret, and sometimes remorse. It is not wise to seek to judge our fellow-man. It is a stern *duty* and an unwelcome *task* to be performed, and not a *privilege* to be coveted; and wo unto that man who assumes the prerogative of judgment, and to some extent usurps the functions of God, not being himself just, upright, impartial! Does your heart tell you that you may safely assume that power?

Cand∴ It does.

M∴ Ill∴ It is well. See to it that you be not deceived!. Go with your Guide. Heed well the lessons and warnings you will receive, and again return to me.

[The Candidate is led around the room, halting at each column, and addressed at each, as follows]:

At the Column of ALFRED: . . . . I was the Just King of Saxon England. I framed wise laws, appointed upright magistrates, and caused just and speedy judgment to be given. In all my realm, justice and right were sold to none, denied to none, delayed to none. I slept little, I wrote much, I studied more. I reigned but to bless those over whom I had dominion. I have vanished into the thin Past; but I still live in the memory of men. They call me Brave King, wise Lawgiver, just Judge. Follow thou my example, or shudder to sit in judgment on thy fellows!

At the Column of SOCRATES: . . . . I was Socrates the Athenian. I knew the Holy Mysteries, and reverenced God in Nature. In the Sacred Groves of Athens I taught to young and old the existence and immortality of the Soul, and the Unity of God the Creator. And when by unjust judgment my country condemned me to die, I refused to flee, lest I should bring the laws into disrepute, holding the good citizen bound to submit to even the unrighteous judgment of the State. If thou wouldst judge others, be prepared to obey as I did.

At the Column of CONFUCIUS: . . . . I was Khoung-fou-tseu. I said to the Chinese, 'The great law of duty is to be looked for in humanity. Justice is Equity,—to render to every one that to which he is entitled. He who would stand above the ordinary level of men must be exempt from prejudices and from obstinacy, and be governed by the mandates of Justice alone. Hear much, that your doubts may disappear. Be cautious in what you say, that you may say nothing superfluous; for then you will rarely commit faults. See much, that you may avoid the dangers that beset all men. Watch carefully over your actions, and you will rarely need to repent. Elevate and honour upright and just men, and put down and degrade those who are corrupt and perverse. Form no friendships with those who are morally your inferiors. Exercise always the permanent and eternal virtues. Be circumspect of speech. Neglect not to strive ever to perform your whole duty. Overflow not in superfluous words: and let your words answer to your actions, and your actions correspond with your words.' So I taught; and my influences lived after me, and have shaped the destinies of myriads of men; the noblest fortune that can befall humanity. Strive thou so to live and act, to obey and govern, that thou too mayest live in the good opinions of men after thou art dead; and that *thine* influences may make *thee* too a king over the minds of men.

At the Column of Minos : . . . . I was Minos, the Lawgiver of Crete. I taught the Cretans that the laws which I enacted were dictated to me by Jove : for all true and righteous laws and all human justice are but developments of that Eternal, infinite justice that is of the essence of the Deity. He who assumes to judge his brother, clothes himself with the prerogative of God. Woe unto thee, if, vicious or criminal thyself, thou assumest to judge others, or if thou givest corrupt judgment; for then thou wilt usurp and abuse the power of God, and He will punish thee.

At the Column of Zoroaster : . . . . I was Zerdusht, the great Lawgiver of the Persians. My laws live after me, and Time still adds to their authority. I said, ' He is the best servant of God whose heart is upright, who is liberal, with due regard to what is just, to all men ; who turns not his eyes towards riches, and whose heart wishes well to everything that lives. He that is charitable and merciful in his judgments is alone just. Fear to do anything against that God whom thou lovest; and thou wilt not love to do anything against that God whom thou fearest.' .

At the Column of Moses : . . . . God gave into my hands the Tables of his law upon Mount Sinai: By my Statutes Israel was governed ; and between man and man I administered justice. I said to Israel : 'Thou shalt not wrest the judgment of thy poor in his cause. Thou shalt take no gift: for the gift blindeth the wise, and perverteth the words of the righteous. Ye shall do no unrighteousness in judgment: thou shalt not respect the person of the poor, nor honour the person of the mighty: in righteousness shalt thou judge thy neighbour. Ye shall not respect persons in judgment. Ye shall hear the Small as well as the Great: Ye shall not fear the face of man; for the judgment is God's.'

[Then the Candidate halts before the Counsellors, and the Sen∴ Counsellor says to him: . . "Thou hast heard the words of the Great Sages, Philosophers and Lawgivers of Antiquity. Behold [pointing upward to the word over his head], the monogram of the greatest lawgiver that has ever come among men: and listen reverentially to his teachings : 'If ye forgive men their trespasses, your Heavenly Father will also forgive you. But if ye forgive not men their trespasses, neither will your Heavenly Father forgive your trespasses. With what judgment ye judge, ye shall be judged: and with what measure ye mete, it shall be measured to you again. If thy brother trespass against thee, go and tell him his fault between thee and him alone. If he shall hear thee, thou hast gained thy brother. . . . If he neglect to hear thee, tell it unto the Church: but if he neglect to hear the Church, let him be unto thee as an heathen and a publican. Judge not according to the appearance; but judge righteous judgment. If thy brother trespass against thee, rebuke him; and if he repent, forgive him. And if he trespass against thee seven times in a day, and seven times in a day turn again to thee, saying, I repent, thou shalt forgive him.' "]

[The Candidate is then conducted to the East].

M∴ Ill∴. My Brother, you have heard the lessons of wisdom, uttered by lips, now these many ages mouldered into dust. Through those lips God spake to man: for of Him cometh all wisdom. You desire to become a member of this Tribunal, and a Supreme Judge in Masonry. Kneel then at its Holy Altar, with sincerity and reverence, fully appreciating the important office to which you aspire, and with no thought in your heart, nor word upon your lips, but those of deep earnestness, of soberness and truth.

[The Candidate kneels, placing one hand on the Holy Bible, square, compasses, plumb and level, and the other on the scales and sword ; and answers as follows:]

M∴ Ill∴. Kneeling at the Altar of Masonry in token of humility and reverential awe of Deity, do you, upon these emblems of Divine Truth, of Justice, Equity, Uprightness and the Law's Dread Vengeance, most solemnly and sincerely swear, that you will carefully examine all cases in which you may be judge, listen attentively to every argument that may be urged, and faithfully and impartially weigh both evidence and argument;

being neither careless nor indifferent, partial nor prejudiced, nor wearying of investigation; with the sole and only purpose of giving a true and just judgment?

Cand.∴ I do so swear.

M∴ Ill∴ Do you solemnly and sincerely swear, that you will never sit in judgment in any case where you may entertain feelings of ill-will or enmity towards a party therein, or any feeling of prejudice or dislike; nor in any case where, from any cause whatever, you doubt whether you can hear patiently, consider calmly and decide impartially?

Cand.∴ I do so swear.

M∴ Ill∴ Do you solemnly promise and swear, that you will never allow rank or power, influence or money, to sway you in your judgment; and that, before you as a Judge, all men shall stand on one common level, to be sternly condemned if guilty, and acquitted if innocent?

Cand.∴ I do so swear.

M∴ Ill∴ Do you solemnly and sincerely swear, that you will as a Judge lay aside all pride of opinion, obstinacy and self-will, and be governed absolutely by the dictates of law, justice, equity, and your own conscience?

Cand.∴ I do so swear.

M∴ Ill∴ Do you solemnly and sincerely swear, that you will usurp no doubtful powers; that you will strain no law so that it may cover cases to which it does not plainly apply; that you will presume every one innocent until he is proven to be guilty; and that you will give to every one accused the benefit of all reasonable doubt, and of a charitable and natural construction of his actions, remembering that the Masonic law seeks punishment only as a means and not as an end?

Cand.∴ I do so swear.

M∴ Ill∴ And all this you swear, hoping that God will so judge you as you judge others, and invoking upon your unprotected head His just and terrible anger, in case you wilfully violate this your solemn oath and obligation? Do you so swear?

Cand.∴ I do.

All : . . Forgive us our trespasses as we forgive those that trespass against us!

M∴ Ill∴ Witness you the solemn oath, my Brethren; and let it be recorded!

All : . . We witness it.

Chan.∴ And I record it.

M∴ Ill∴ Arise, Ill∴ Enquiring Commander! I invest you with the white collar and apron and with the jewel of this degree. See that the purity of the two former and the lustre of the latter be never sullied or dimmed by injustice, inhumanity or impurity! Receive now the Signs, Words and Token of this Degree!

Sign: . . . ⸎⸎⸎⸎⸎ the ⸎⸎⸎ ⸎⸎⸎⸎ over the ⸎⸎*⸎⸎ — the ⸎⸎⸎⸎ over the ⸎⸎⸎⸎⸎.

Answer: . . . ⸎⸎⸎⸎⸎ ⸎⸎⸎⸎ over the ⸎⸎⸎⸎ — the ⸎⸎⸎⸎⸎⸎⸎ extended and ⸎⸎⸎⸎⸎⸎⸎⸎ and ⸎⸎⸎⸎⸎ upward.

Token: . . . Place ⸎⸎⸎⸎⸎ to ⸎⸎⸎⸎⸎ and ⸎⸎⸎⸎ to ⸎⸎⸎⸎ — take each other by the ⸎⸎⸎⸎⸎ ⸎⸎⸎⸎, and with the ⸎⸎⸎⸎⸎ strike gently the ⸎⸎⸎⸎⸎ ⸎⸎⸎⸎⸎ of the other; one giving the pass-word, and the other the answer.

Pass-word: . . . ⸎⸎⸎⸎⸎⸎⸎⸎⸎∴

Answer: . . . ⸎⸎⸎⸎⸎⸎∴

Sacred Words: . . . One says ⸎⸎⸎⸎⸎⸎⸎⸎∴ The other answers ⸎⸎⸎⸎⸎⸎∴ And both say ⸎⸎ ⸎⸎⸎⸎ ⸎⸎ ⸎⸎∴

M∴ Ill∴ Go now, my Brother, to our Ill∴ Bro∴ the Advocate, and receive from him the Lecture of this Degree.

LECTURE.

This Degree was instituted when anarchy reigned among the rites of Masonry. It was evidently indispensable to establish a special body that should see to the maintenance of principles, and the regularity of Masonic forms. The Tribunal of Grand Inquiring Commanders was thus created; and invested with the power, as it was charged with the duty, of visiting the different bodies and inspecting their work, of taking care that caution should be observed in the selection of candidates, of compelling a strict observance of the ritual in the higher degrees. To these powers were added, by degrees, that of judging differences between the Brethren, and of trying those guilty of offences against Masonic law.

These powers and this jurisdiction are now defined, and the mode of proceeding regulated, by statutes enacted by the supreme authority; with a copy of which I now present you, requiring you to become familiar with them, that you may be enabled to perform properly the high duties that devolve upon you.

To hear patiently, to weigh deliberately and dispassionately, and to decide impartially;—these are the chief duties of a Judge. After the lessons you have received, I need not further enlarge upon them. You will be ever eloquently reminded of them by the furniture upon our Altar, and the decorations of the Tribunal.

The Holy Bible will remind you of your obligation; and that as you judge here below, so you will be yourself judged hereafter, by One who has not to submit, like an earthly Judge, to the sad necessity of inferring the motives, intentions and purposes of men [of which all crime essentially consists] from the uncertain and often unsafe testimony of their acts and words; as men in thick darkness grope their way, with hands outstretched before them: but before Whom every thought, feeling, impulse and intention of every soul that now is, or ever was, or ever will be on earth, is, and ever will be through the whole infinite duration of eternity, present and visible.

The Square and Compasses, the Plumb and Level, are well known to you as a Mason. Upon you as a Judge, they peculiarly inculcate uprightness, impartiality, careful consideration of facts and circumstances, accuracy in judgment, and uniformity in decision. As a Judge, too, you are to bring up square work and square work only. Like a temple erected by the plumb, you are to lean neither to one side nor the other. Like a building well squared and levelled, you are to be firm and steadfast in your convictions of right and justice. Like the circle swept with the compasses, you are to be true. In the scales of justice you are to weigh the facts and the law alone, nor place in either scale personal friendship or personal dislike, neither fear nor favour: and when reformation is no longer to be hoped for, you are to smite relentlessly with the sword of justice.

The peculiar and principal symbol of this degree is the Tetractys of Pythagoras, suspended in the East, where ordinarily the sacred word or letter glitters, and, like them, representing the Deity. Its nine external points form the triangle, the chief symbol in Masonry, with many of the meanings of which you are familiar.

To us, its three sides represent the three principal attributes of the Deity, which created, and now, as ever, support, uphold and guide the universe in its eternal movement; the three supports of the Masonic Temple, itself an emblem of the universe:—Wisdom, or the Infinite Divine Intelligence; Strength, or Power, the Infinite Divine Will; and Beauty, or the Infinite Divine Harmony, the Eternal Law, by virtue of which the infinite myriads of suns and worlds flash ever onward in their ceaseless revolutions, without clash or conflict, in the Infinite of space, and change and movement are the law of all created existence.

To us, as Masonic Judges, the triangle figures forth the Pyramids, which, planted firmly as the everlasting hills, and accurately adjusted to the four cardinal points, defiant of all assaults of men and time, teach us to stand firm and unshaken as they, when our feet are planted upon the solid truth.

It includes a multitude of geometrical figures, all having a deep significance to Masons. The triple triangle is peculiarly sacred, having ever been among all nations a symbol of the Deity. Prolonging all the external lines of the Hexagon, which also it includes, we have six smaller triangles, whose bases cut each other in the central point of the Tetractys, itself always the symbol of the generative power of the universe, the Sun, Brahma, Osiris, Apollo, Bel, and the Deity Himself. Thus, too, we form twelve still smaller triangles, three times three of which compose the Tetractys itself.

I refrain from enumerating all the figures that you may trace within it: but one may not be passed unnoticed. The Hexagon itself faintly images to us a cube, not visible at the first glance, and therefore the fit emblem of that faith in things invisible, most essential to salvation. The first perfect solid, and reminding you of the cubical stone that sweated blood, and of that deposited by Enoch, it teaches justice, accuracy and consistency.

The infinite divisibility of the triangle teaches the infinity of the universe, of time, of space and of the Deity, as do the lines that, diverging from the common centre ever increase their distance from each other, as they are infinitely prolonged. As they may be infinite in number, so are the attributes of Deity infinite; and as they emanate from one centre and are projected into space, so the whole Universe has emanated from God.

Remember also, my Brother, that you have other duties to perform than those of a judge. You are to inquire into and scrutinize carefully the work of the subordinate Bodies in Masonry. You are to see that recipients of the higher degrees are not unnecessarily multiplied; that improper persons are carefully excluded from membership, and that in their life and conversation Masons bear testimony to the excellence of our doctrines and the incalculable value of the institution itself. You are to inquire also into your own heart and conduct, and keep careful watch over yourself, that you go not astray. If you harbour ill-will and jealousy, if you are hospitable to intolerance and bigotry, and churlish to gentleness and kind affections, opening wide your heart to one and closing its portals to the other, it is time for you to set in order your own temple, or else you wear in vain the name and insignia of a Mason, while yet uninvested with the Masonic nature.

Everywhere in the world there is a natural law, that is, a constant mode of action, which seems to belong to the nature of things, to the constitution of the universe. This fact is universal. In different departments we call this mode of action by different names, as the law of Matter, the law of Mind, the law of Morals, and the like. We mean by this, a certain mode of action which belongs to the material, mental or moral forces, the mode in which commonly they are found to act, and in which it is their ideal to act always. The ideal laws of matter we only know from the fact that they are always obeyed. To us the actual *obedience* is the only evidence of the ideal rule; for in respect to the conduct of the material world, the *ideal* and the *actual* are the same.

The laws of matter we learn only by observation and experience. Before experience of the fact, no man could foretell that a body falling towards the earth, would descend sixteen feet the first second, twice that the next, four times the third, and sixteen times the fourth. No mode of action in our consciousness anticipates this rule of action in the outer world. The same is true of all the laws of matter. The ideal law is known because it is a fact. The law is imperative. It must be obeyed without hesitation. Laws of crystallization, laws of proportion in chemical combination,—neither in these nor in any other law of Nature is there any margin left for oscillation of disobedience. Only the primal will of God works in the material world, and no secondary finite will.

There are no exceptions to the great general law of Attraction, which binds atom to atom in the body of a rotifer visible only by aid of the microscope, orb to orb, system to system; gives unity to the world of things, and rounds these worlds of systems to a universe. At first there seem to be exceptions to this law, as in growth and decomposition, in the repulsions of electricity; but at length all these are found to be special cases of the one great law of attraction acting in various modes.

The variety of effect of this law at first surprises the senses; but in the end the unity of cause astonishes the cultivated mind. Looked at in reference to this globe, an earthquake is no more than a chink that opens in a garden-walk of a dry day in Summer. A sponge is porous, having small spaces between the solid parts: the solar system is only *more* porous, having larger room between the several orbs: the universe yet more so, with spaces between the systems, as small compared with *infinite* space, as those between the atoms that compose the bulk of the smallest invisible animalcule, of which millions swim in a drop of salt water. The same attraction holds together the animalcule, the sponge, the system and the universe.

Every particle of matter in that universe is related to each and all the other particles; and attraction is their common bond.

In the spiritual world, the world of human consciousness, there is also a law, an ideal mode of action for the spiritual forces of man. The law of Justice is as universal an one as the law of Attraction; though we are very far from being able to reconcile all the phenomena of Nature with it. The lark has the same right, in our view, to live, to sing, to dart at pleasure through the ambient atmosphere, as the hawk has to ply his strong wings in the summer sunshine: and yet the hawk pounces on and devours the harmless lark, as it devours the worm, and as the worm devours the animalcule; and, so far as we know, there is nowhere, in any future state of animal existence, any compensation for this apparent injustice. Among the bees, one rules, while the others obey—some work, while others are idle. With the small ants, the soldiers feed on the proceeds of the workmen's labour. The lion lies in wait for and devours the antelope that has apparently as good a right to life as he. Among men, some govern and others serve, capital commands and labour obeys, and one race, superior in intellect, avails itself of the strong muscles of another that is inferior; and yet, for all this, no one impeaches the justice of God.

No doubt all these varied phenomena are consistent with one great law of justice; and the only difficulty is that we do not, and no doubt we cannot understand that law. It is very easy for some dreaming and visionary theorist to say that it is most evidently unjust for the lion to devour the deer, and for the eagle to tear and eat the wren; but the trouble is, that we know of no other way, according to the frame, the constitution and the organs which God has given them, in which the lion and the eagle could manage to live at all. Our little measure of justice is not God's measure. His justice does not require us to relieve the hard-working millions of all labour, to emancipate the serf or slave, unfitted to be free, from all control.

No doubt, underneath all the little bubbles, which are the lives, the wishes, the wills and the plans of the two hundred millions or more of human beings on this earth (for bubbles they are, judging by the space and time they occupy in this great and age-outlasting sea of human-kind),—no doubt, underneath them all resides one and the same eternal force, which they shape into this or the other special form; and over all the same paternal Providence presides, keeping eternal watch over the little and the great, and producing variety of effect from Unity of Force.

It is entirely true to say that justice is the constitution or fundamental law of the moral universe, the law of right, a rule of conduct for man (as it is for every other living creature), in all his moral relations. No doubt all human affairs (like all other affairs), must be subject to that as the law paramount; and what is *right* agrees therewith and stands, while what is *wrong* conflicts with it and falls. The difficulty is that we ever erect *our* notions of what is right and just into the *law* of justice, and insist that God shall adopt that as His law; instead of striving to learn by observation and reflection what his law *is*, and then believing that law to be consistent with *His* infinite justice, whether it corresponds with *our* limited notion of justice, or does not so correspond. We are too wise in our own conceit, and ever strive to enact our own little notions into the Universal Laws of God.

It might be difficult for man to prove, even to his own satisfaction, how it is right or just for him to subjugate the horse and ox to his service, giving them in return only their daily food, which God has spread out for them on all the green meadows and savannahs of the world: or how it is just that we should slay and eat the harmless deer that only crops the green herbage, the buds and the young leaves, and drinks the free-running water that God made common to all, or the gentle dove, the innocent kid, the many other living things that so confidently trust to our protection;—quite as difficult, perhaps, as to prove it just for one man's intellect or even his wealth to make another's strong arms his servants, for daily wages or for a bare subsistence.

To find out this universal law of justice is one thing—to undertake to measure off something with our own little tape-line, and call *that* God's law of justice, is another. The great general plan and system, and the great general laws enacted by God, continually produce what to our limited notions is wrong and injustice, which hitherto men have been able to explain to their own satisfaction only by the hypothesis of another existence in which all inequalities and injustices in this life will be remedied and compensated for. To our ideas of justice, it is very unjust that the child is made miserable for life by deformity or organic disease, in consequence of the vices of its father; and yet that is part of the universal law. The ancients said that the child was *punished* for the sins of its father. *We* say that its deformity or disease is the *consequence* of its father's vices : but so far as concerns the question of justice or injustice, that is merely the change of a word.

It is very easy to lay down a broad, general principle, embodying our own idea of what is absolute justice, and to insist that everything shall conform to that : to say, "all human affairs must be subject to that as the law paramount ; what is right agrees therewith and stands, what is wrong conflicts and falls. Private cohesions of self-love, of friendship or of patriotism, must all be subordinate to this universal gravitation towards the eternal right.". The difficulty is that this universe of necessities God-created, of sequences of cause and effect, and of life evolved from death, this interminable succession and aggregate of cruelties, will not conform to any such absolute principle or arbitrary theory, no matter in what sounding words and glittering phrases it may be embodied.

Impracticable rules in morals are always injurious; for as all men fall short of compliance with them, they turn real virtues into imaginary offences against a forged law. Justice as between man and man and as between man and the animals below him, is that which, under and according to the God-created relations existing between them, and the whole aggregate of circumstances surrounding them, is fit and right and proper to be done, with a view to the general as well as to the individual interest. It is not a theoretical principle by which the very relations that God has created and imposed on us are to be tried, and approved or condemned.

God has made this great system of the Universe, and enacted general laws for its government. Those laws environ everything that lives with a mighty network of necessity. He chose to create the tiger with such organs that he cannot crop the grass, but must eat other flesh or starve. He has made man carnivorous also; and the smallest singing-bird is as much so as the tiger. In every step we take, in every breath we draw, is involved the destruction of a multitude of animate existences, each, no matter how minute, as much a living creature as ourself. He has made necessary among mankind a division of labour, intellectual and moral. He has made necessary the varied relations of society and dependence, of obedience and control.

What is thus made necessary cannot be unjust ; for if it be, then God the great Law-giver is Himself unjust. The evil to be avoided is, the legalization of injustice and wrong under the *false* plea of necessity. Out of all the relations of life grow duties,—as naturally grow and as undeniably, as the leaves grow upon the trees. If we have the right, created by God's law of necessity, to slay the lamb that we may eat and live, we have no right to torture it in doing so, because that is in no wise necessary. We have the right to live, if we fairly can, by the legitimate exercise of our intellect, and hire or buy the labour of the strong arms of others, to till our grounds, to dig in our mines, to toil in our manufactories ; but we have no right to overwork or underpay them.

It is not only true that we may learn the moral law of justice, the law of right, by experience and observation ; but that God has given us a moral faculty, our conscience, which is able to perceive this law directly and immediately, by intuitive perception of it ; and it is true that man has in his nature a rule of conduct higher than what he has ever yet come up to,—an ideal of nature that shames his actual of history: because man has ever been prone to make necessity, his own necessity, the necessities of society, a plea for injustice. But this notion must not be pushed too far—for if we substitute this ideality for actuality, then it is equally true that we have within us an ideal rule of right and wrong, to which God Himself in his government of the world has never come, and against which He (we say it reverentially) every day offends. We detest the tiger and the wolf for the rapacity and love of blood which are their nature ; we revolt against the law by which the crooked limbs and diseased organism of the child are the fruits of the father's vices ; we even think that a God Omnipotent and Omniscient ought to have permitted no pain, no poverty, no servitude ; our ideal of justice is more lofty than the actualities of God. It is well, as all else is well. He has given us that moral sense for wise and beneficent purposes. We accept it as a significant proof of the inherent loftiness of human nature, that it can entertain an ideal so exalted ; and should strive to attain it, as far as we can do so consistently with the relations which He has created, and the circumstances which surround us and hold us captive.

If we faithfully use this faculty of conscience; if, applying it to the existing relations and circumstances, we develop it and all its kindred powers, and so deduce the duties that out of these relations and those circumstances, and limited and qualified by them, arise and become obligatory upon us, then we learn justice, the law of right, the divine rule of conduct for human life. But if we undertake to define and settle " the mode of action that belongs to the infinitely perfect nature of God," and so set up any ideal rule, beyond all human reach, we soon come to judge and condemn His work and the relations which it has pleased Him in His infinite wisdom to create.

A sense of justice belongs to human nature, and is a part of it. Men find a deep, permanent and instinctive delight in justice, not only in the outward effects, but in the inward cause, and by their nature love this law of right, this reasonable rule of conduct, this justice, with a deep and abiding love. Justice is the object of the conscience, and fits it as light fits the eye and truth the mind.

Justice keeps just relations between men. It holds the balance between nation and nation, between a man and his family, tribe, nation and race, so that his *absolute* rights and theirs do not interfere, nor their *ultimate* interests ever clash, nor the eternal interests of the one prove antagonistic to those of all or of any other one. This we must believe, if we believe that God is just. We must do justice to all, and demand it of all; it is a universal human debt, a universal human claim. But we may err greatly in defining what that justice is. The *temporary* interests, and what to human view are the rights, of men, do often interfere and clash. The life-interests of the individual often conflict with the permanent interests and welfare of society; and what may seem to be the natural rights of one class or race, with those of another.

It is not true to say that "one man, however little, must not be sacrificed to another, however great, to a majority, or to all men." That is not only a fallacy, but a most dangerous one. Often one man and many men must be sacrificed, in the ordinary sense of the term, to the interest of the many. It is a comfortable fallacy to the selfish; for if they cannot, by the law of justice, be sacrificed for the common good, then their country has no right to demand of them *self*-sacrifice; and he is a fool who lays down his life, or sacrifices his estate, or even his luxuries, to ensure the safety or prosperity of his country. According to that doctrine, Curtius was a fool, and Leonidas an idiot; and to die for one's country is no longer beautiful and glorious, but a mere absurdity. Then it is no longer to be asked that the common soldier shall receive in his bosom the sword or bayonet-thrust which otherwise would let out the life of the great commander on whose fate hang the liberties of his country, and the welfare of millions yet unborn.

On the contrary, it is certain that necessity rules in all the affairs of men, and that the interest and even the life of one man must often be sacrificed to the interest and welfare of his country. Some must ever lead the forlorn hope: the missionary must go among savages, bearing his life in his hand; the physician must expose himself to pestilence for the sake of others; the sailor, in the frail boat upon the wide ocean, escaped from the foundering or burning ship, must step calmly into the hungry waters, if the lives of the passengers can be saved only by the sacrifice of his own; the pilot must stand firm at the wheel, and let the flames scorch away his own life to ensure the common safety of those whom the doomed vessel bears.

The mass of men are always looking for what is just. All the vast machinery which makes up a State, a world of States, is, on the part of the people, an attempt to organize, not that ideal justice which finds fault with God's ordinances, but that practical justice which may be attained in the actual organization of the world. The minute and wide-extending civil machinery which makes up the law and the courts, with all their officers and implements, on the part of mankind, is chiefly an effort to reduce to practice the theory of right. Constitutions are made to establish justice; the decisions of courts are reported to help us judge more wisely in time to come. The nation aims to get together the most just men in the State, that they may incorporate into statutes their aggregate sense of what is right. The people wish law to be embodied justice, administered without passion. Even in the wildest ages there has been a wild popular justice, but always mixed with passion and administered in hate; for justice takes a rude form with rude men, and becomes less mixed with hate and passion in more civilized communities. Every progressive State revises its statutes and revolutionizes its constitution from time to time, seeking to come closer to the utmost possible practical justice and right; and sometimes, following theorists and dreamers in their adoration for the ideal, by erecting into law positive principles of theoretical right, works practical injustice, and then has to retrace its steps.

In literature men always look for practical justice, and desire that virtue should have its own reward, and vice its appropriate punishment. They are ever on the side of justice and humanity; and the majority of them have an ideal justice, better than the things about them, juster than the law: for the law is ever imperfect, not attaining even to the utmost *practicable* degree of perfection; and no man is as just as his own idea of possible and practicable justice. His passions and his necessities ever cause him to sink below his own ideal. The ideal justice which men ever look up to and strive to rise towards, is true; but it will not be realized in this world. Yet we must approach as near to it as practicable, as we should do towards that ideal democracy that "now floats before the eyes of earnest and religious men,—fairer than the Republic of Plato, or More's Utopia, or the Golden Age of fabled memory," only taking care that we do not, in striving to reach and ascend to the impossible ideal, neglect to seize upon and hold fast to the possible actual. To aim at the best, but be content with the best possible, is the only true wisdom. To insist on the absolute right, and throw out of the calculation the important and all-controlling element of necessity, is the folly of a mere dreamer.

In a world inhabited by men with bodies, and necessarily with bodily wants and animal passions, the time will never come when there will be no want, no oppression, no servitude, no fear of man, no fear of God, but only Love. That can never be while there are inferior intellect, indulgence in low vice, improvidence, indolence, awful visitations of pestilence and war and famine, earthquake and volcano, that must of necessity cause men to want, and serve, and suffer and fear.

But still the ploughshare of justice is ever drawn through and through the field of the world, uprooting the savage plants. Ever we see a continual and progressive triumph of the right. The injustice of England lost her America, the fairest jewel of her crown. The injustice of Napoleon bore him to the ground more than the snows of Russia did, and exiled him to a barren rock, there to pine away and die, his life a warning to bid mankind be just.

We intuitively understand what justice is, better than we can depict it. What it is in a given case depends so much on circumstances, that definitions of it are wholly deceitful. Often it would be unjust to society to do what would, in the absence of that consideration, be pronounced just to the individual. General propositions of man's right to this or that are ever fallacious: and not unfrequently it would be most unjust to the individual himself to do for him what the theorist, as a general proposition, would say was right and his due.

We should ever do unto others what, under the same circumstances we *ought* to wish and should have *the right* to wish, they should do unto us. There are many cases, cases constantly occurring, where one man must take care of himself, in preference to another, as where two struggle for the possession of a plank that will save one, but cannot uphold both; or where, assailed, he can save his own life only by slaying his adversary. So one must prefer the safety of his country to the lives of her enemies; and sometimes, to ensure it, to those of her own innocent citizens. The retreating General may cut away a bridge behind him, to delay pursuit and save the main body of his army, though he thereby surrenders a detachment, a battalion or even a corps of his own force to certain destruction.

These are not departures from justice; though, like other instances where the injury or death of the individual is the safety of the many, where the interest of one individual, class or race is postponed to that of the public, or of the superior race, they may infringe some dreamer's ideal rule of justice. But every departure from real, practical justice is no doubt attended with loss to the unjust man, though the loss is not reported to the public. Injustice, public or private, like every other sin and wrong, is inevitably followed by its consequences. The selfish, the grasping, the inhuman, the fraudulently unjust, the ungenerous employer and the cruel master are detected by the great popular heart; while the kind master, the liberal employer, the generous, the humane and the just have the good opinion of all men, and even envy is a tribute to their virtues. Men honour all who stand up for truth and right, and never shrink. The world builds monuments to its patriots. Four great statesmen, organizers of the right, embalmed in stone, look down upon the lawgivers of France as they pass to their hall of legislation, silent orators to tell how nations love the just. How we revere the marble lineaments of those just judges, Jay and Marshall, that look so calmly towards the living Bench of the Supreme Court of the United States! What a monument Washington has built in the heart of America and all the world, not because he dreamed of an impracticable ideal justice, but by his constant effort to be practically just!

. But necessity alone, and the greatest good of the greatest number, can legitimately interfere with the dominion of absolute and ideal justice. Government should not foster the strong at the expense of the weak, or protect the capitalist and tax the labourer. The powerful should not seek a monopoly of development and enjoyment; not prudence only and the expedient for to-day should be appealed to by statesmen, but conscience and the right: justice should not be forgotten in looking at interest, nor political morality neglected for political economy: we should not have national housekeeping instead of national organization on the basis of right.

We may well differ as to the abstract right of many things; for every such question has many sides, and few men look at all of them, many only at one. But we all readily recognize cruelty, unfairness, inhumanity, partiality, over-reaching, hard-dealing, by their ugly and familiar lineaments. We do not need to sit as a Court of Errors and Appeals to revise and reverse God's Providences, in order to know and to hate and despise *them*.

. There are certainly great evils of civilization at this day, and many questions of humanity long adjourned and put off. The hideous aspect of pauperism, the debasement and vice in our cities tell us by their eloquent silence or in inarticulate mutterings, that the rich and the powerful and the intellectual do not do their duty by the poor, the feeble and the ignorant; and every wretched woman that lives, Heaven scarce knows how, by making shirts at sixpence each, attests the injustice and inhumanity of man. There are cruelties to slaves, and worse cruelties to animals, each disgraceful to their perpetrators, and equally unwarranted by the lawful relation of control and dependence which it has pleased God to create.

A sentence is written against all that is unjust, written by God in the nature of man and in the nature of the Universe, because it is in the nature of the Infinite God. Fidelity to your faculties, trust in their convictions, that is justice to yourself; a life in obedience thereto, that is justice towards men. No wrong is really successful. The gain of injustice is a loss, its pleasure suffering. Iniquity often seems to prosper, but its success is its defeat and shame. After a long while, the day of reckoning ever comes, to nation as to individual. The knave deceives himself. The miser, starving his brother's body, starves also his own soul, and at death shall creep out of his great estate of injustice, poor and naked and miserable. Whoso escapes a duty avoids a gain. Outward judgment often fails, inward justice never. Let a man try to love the wrong and to do the wrong, it is eating stones and not bread; the swift feet of justice are upon him, following with woollen tread, and her iron hands are round his neck. No man can escape from this, any more than from himself. Justice is the angel of God that flies from East to West; and where she stoops her broad wings, it is to bring the counsel of God, and feed mankind with angels' bread.

We cannot understand the moral Universe. The arc is a long one, and our eyes reach but a little way; we cannot calculate the curve and complete the figure by the experience of sight; but we can divine it by conscience, and we surely know that it bends towards justice. Justice will not fail, though wickedness appears strong, and has on its side the armies and thrones of power, the riches and the glory of the world, and though poor men crouch down in despair. Justice will not fail and perish out from the world of men, nor will what is really wrong and contrary to God's real law of justice continually endure. The Power, the Wisdom and the Justice of God are on the side of every just thought, and it cannot fail, any more than God himself can perish.

In human affairs, the justice of God must work by human means. Men are the instruments of God's principles; our morality is the instrument of His justice, which, incomprehensible to us, seems to our short vision often to work injustice, but will at some time still the oppressor's brutal laugh. Justice is the rule of conduct written in the nature of mankind. We may, in our daily life, in house or field or shop, in the office or in the Court, help to prepare the way for the commonwealth of justice which is slowly, but, we would fain hope, surely approaching. All the justice we mature will bless us here and hereafter, and at our death we shall leave it added to the common store of human-kind. And every Mason who, content to do that which is possible and practicable, does and enforces justice, may help deepen the channel of human morality in which God's justice runs; and so the wrecks of evil that now check and obstruct the stream may be the sooner swept out and borne away by the resistless tide of Omnipotent Right. Let us, my Brother, in this, as in all else, endeavour always to perform the duties of a good Mason and a good man.

TO CLOSE.

M∴ Ill∴ Ill∴ Sen∴ Counsellor, what is the hour of rest for good Masons?

Sen∴ C∴ M∴ Ill∴, the hour when all their duties are performed.

M∴ Ill∴ Has that hour arrived, my brother?

Sen∴ C∴ As nearly as it ever comes to mortals; since none perform all their duties: and our Masonic labours end only at the grave.

M∴ Ill∴ Most true, my Brother. Remains there yet any complaint unheard, wrong unredressed, or known offence unpunished?

Sen∴ C∴ None, M∴ Ill∴

M∴ Ill∴ It is permitted, then, that this Tribunal should close. Join me, my Brethren, in the concluding ceremony.

[The officers then rap and repeat, as follows]: . . . .

Advocate . . . [,] . . . From all errors and mistakes in conclusion and opinion: . . . .

Jun∴ C∴ [?] . . . From all impatience, and inattention to evidence or argument: . . . .

. . . . From all petulance and peevishness, all carelessness and indifference: . . . .

Sen∴ C∴ . . . . [;] . . . From all hasty conclusions and unconsidered opinions: . . . .

. . . . From all partiality and prejudice: . . . .

. . . . From all obstinacy and pride of opinion, and all wilful adherence to error: . . . .

M∴ Ill∴ . . . . [!] . . . From all usurpations of power and unwarrantable assumptions of jurisdiction: . . . .

. . . . From all harsh and uncharitable constructions of act or motive: . . . .

. . . . From all improper influences, that pervert men's judgment:

. . . . From all false judgment and intentional injustice: . . . .

. . . . Keep us free, our Father, who art to judge us at the last day!

All: . . . And as we judge, so do Thou in mercy judge us! Amen!

M∴ Ill∴ My Brethren, the sign! [It is given]. This Tribunal is close.

FINIS.

Statutes for the Government of all Tribunals of the 31st Degree,

WHEREVER HELD UNDER

AUTHORITY OF THE SUPREME COUNCIL, OF SOV∴ GR∴ INSP∴ GEN∴

AT CHARLESTON.

ART. I.

§ 1. Every Tribunal of the 31st Degree, when sitting in judgment, shall be composed of ten members and no more, not including the Advocate and Defender.

§ 2. When trying a case in which a Sub∴ Prince of the Royal Secret is a party, all the members must have attained the 32d Degree: and in all other cases, at least five must have attained it, [to wit, the President, Counsellors, Secretary and Treasurer], and the others must have attained the 31st.

ART. II.

§ 1. Tribunals of the 31st Degree have exclusive jurisdiction to hear, try and determine all offences against Masonic law, or the Statutes, Constitutional provisions, rules and regulations of the Sup∴ Council of the 33d Degree, committed by Brothers who have attained any degree above the 18th, and of appeals from all judgments of all Chapters of Rose Croix within their jurisdiction: but as to offences committed by Knights of the Rose Croix attached to regular Chapters, and for the punishment whereof the Statutes of such Chapters have made provision, their jurisdiction shall be concurrent; and in such cases, the body first having possession of the case shall proceed, and the other desist.

§ 2. The Tribunals of the 31st Degree shall also have jurisdiction in all cases ordered by the Chapters to be transmitted to them for trial: and to decide all questions certified to them by the Chapters, and by Councils of Princes of Jerusalem and Lodges of Perfection; their decision being in all cases final and conclusive.

ART. III.

§ 1. Any Mason, knowing of the commission by a Brother of rank above the 18th Degree, of any offence against Masonic law, may make known the fact to any Gr∴ Enquiring Commander, by communication in writing, stating the offence, its nature and circumstances, and the time of its commission; which shall be delivered by such Commander to the Ill∴ Advocate, who shall prepare and prefer the act of accusation.

§ 2. Each Commander shall also in like manner make known to the Ill∴ Advocate every violation of Masonic law within his knowledge: and the Advocate shall prepare and prefer acts of accusation in all such cases, and in every case where the facts come otherwise to his knowledge.

§ 3. Upon the act of accusation being preferred, the Chancellor shall issue a citation, under the seal of the Tribunal, which shall be served by copy in writing, by the Pursuivant, or by any other Mason at a distance, to whom the Chancellor may direct and transmit it; by which the accused shall be cited to appear before the Tribunal at a certain time and place, and answer the charge. The nature of such charge shall not be specified; but a copy of the act of accusation shall be delivered to the accused in person, whenever he applies for it.

¿ 4., If it is known that the accused is not to be found, or when the citation is returned that he is not found, a copy thereof shall be put up in the place where he last resided, in the Lodge room of the Lodge or other Masonic Body of which he was last a member, or in any Lodge room, if he was a member of none, or, if there be no such room, then in any public place, and the facts returned upon the citation.

¿ 5. The day fixed for appearance shall be at least ten days after the actual or constructive service.

¿ 6. Upon the day fixed, if the accused appear, he shall make full answer to the charge, stating, if he pleases, any extenuating circumstances, and detailing the facts as particularly as he pleases. The Defender is charged with the duty of preparing this defence.

¿ 7. And if he does not appear, or when he has answered, a day shall be fixed for trial, and written evidence may in the mean-time be taken on both sides.

¿ 8. The testimony of persons not Masons must be given on oath, and that of Masons upon their highest Masonic obligation: and either may be taken in writing or orally.

ART. IV.

¿ 1. At the time fixed for trial, unless the Tribunal grants further delay, as it may do at its discretion, the testimony taken in writing shall be read, and the witnesses heard, the accused having the right to be present, fully to examine and cross-examine the witnesses, and to be heard by himself or the Defender, or both. He or his Defender shall also have the right to conclude the argument.

¿ 2. After the case is heard, argued and submitted, the accused and witnesses shall withdraw, and the Tribunal shall deliberate.

¿ 3. After deliberation the members shall vote upon the different specifications in the act of accusation, each member voting in turn, beginning with the youngest member, and the officers following according to rank from lowest to highest. The Advocate and the Defender shall vote.

¿ 4. Two-thirds of those present must concur, to find the accused guilty of any specification.

¿ 5. The punishment shall be fixed by a like vote, a majority determining its nature and extent.

¿ 6. The accused shall then be called in, and informed of the result. If he be found guilty, the sentence shall be communicated by the Chancellor to all Masonic bodies of which he is a member, and the punishment shall be imposed according to the Sentence, and the Laws, Statutes and regulations governing the case.

¿ 7. If the trial proceeds in the absence of the accused, the Defender shall represent him, and perform all the duties of Counsel for him, to the best of his ability.

ART. V.

¿ 1. Appeals from judgments of Chapters of Rose ✠ shall be sent up in writing, with all the papers; a simple notice of appeal being alone necessary to give the Tribunal jurisdiction.

¿ 2. Every appeal shall be suspensive.

¿ 3. If the appeal be on the facts, the Tribunal shall try it de novo. If it involve only a question of law, they shall decide it, and affirm, reverse, remand, or grant a new trial, or altogether quash and annul, as may be proper and in accordance with Masonic law.

¿ 4. In case the Tribunal tries the case de novo, the proceedings at the trial shall be the same as in cases of original jurisdiction.

¿ 5. Any subordinate body may submit a question or questions to the Tribunal for its decision, upon order to that effect; and the Tribunal shall take jurisdiction, upon a certificate of the Recorder or Secretary of such Inferior Body, stating the question and its reference; shall decide, and transmit a certificate of its decision. And upon the decision of such questions, that of the majority shall stand as the decision of the whole, and no dissent be made known; but any Commander who dissents may present his opinion in writing, with the reasons for it, and have it filed for reference.

¿ 6. A record of all such decisions, and of decisions on points of Masonic law, shall be kept by the Chancellor in a book for that purpose, under appropriate headings.

ART. VI.

§ 1. No trials whatever for offences shall be had in any Consistory of Sub∴ Princes of the R∴ S∴

§ 2. The Tribunals of the 31st Degree shall also have jurisdiction to issue mandates to require subordinate bodies to proceed to judgment, or otherwise to do whatever acts they ought to do in order to give to a Brother his Masonic rights: as also mandates requiring them to desist from proceeding, in proper cases; and mandates to bring up their proceedings, when alleged to be against law, to be examined, and affirmed or quashed, as law and right may require.

§ 3. They shall also have jurisdiction to issue mandates to bring before them questions of right to office in Subordinate Lodges and Bodies, and to hear and determine the same.

§ 4. And mandates to suspend or supersede any judgment or action of such inferior bodies.

§ 5. The said Tribunals shall usurp and assume to themselves no powers not granted by these statutes, or not flowing as necessary incidents or corollaries from the powers hereby granted.

§ 6. They may act as Tribunals of conciliation or decision, in all matters of difference, dispute or dissension, between Masons of the same or different degrees; when such matters are either referred to them by subordinate bodies, or by the parties themselves, or one of them, or by other Masons; and shall examine into and weigh the facts and merits, and give and enforce such judgment and decision, as shall in their view be just, right and equitable in the premises.

ART. VII.

§ 1. All mandates and process of the Tribunal shall be signed by the Chancellor, and sealed with the seal of the Tribunal.

§ 2. A record shall be faithfully kept of all the proceedings and judgments of the Tribunal; and all depositions and other papers shall be filed and carefully preserved.

FINIS.

Thirty-Second Degree.

Sublime Prince of the Royal Secret.

THE CONSISTORY, ITS OFFICERS, ETC.

Bodies of this Degree are styled CONSISTORIES. They should be held in the open country, or on rising ground, in a building at least two stories high. On the second floor must be three apartments, in which the Consistory is held. The meetings are in the daytime. There should be one sentinel on the first floor at the front door, and another near the stairs.

The first apartment above stairs is for the Guards; the second for preparing the Candidate; and the third for holding the Consistory. The hangings of the latter are black satin, strewed with tears of silver, skeletons, death's heads and cross-bones. In the East is a throne, under which is a chair of State for the Presiding Officer, or Commander-in-Chief. The throne is elevated by seven steps, and lined with black satin, strewed with fiery flames, without tears. Before the Commander-in-Chief is a table, covered with black satin strewed with tears, on the front of which are painted or embroidered the cross-bones, with a skull on the upper angle, over it the letter J.·., and in the lower angle the letter M.·.

The Commander-in-Chief is styled *Sovereign Prince.* He is armed with a naked sword, and a shield triangular in shape. On the table before him lie a sceptre and balance; and the books containing the laws and statutes of the Order. He is also styled *Th.·. Ill.·. Gr.·. Commander*, which is preferable.

In the West are two Wardens, styled *Lt.·. Commanders.* They wear shields like the Commander-in-Chief, and sit covered, like him. The sword of each lies on a table before him, which is covered with crimson satin bordered with black, and strewed with tears. On the front of each table are embroidered in gold the letters p.·. l.·. . . . . ɔ.·. ɒ.·.

At the right hand of the Sov.·. stands the *Minister of State*, who acts as Orator.

At the left hand of the Sovereign stands the *Gr.·. Chancellor.*

Next the Minister of State is the *Grand Secretary*; and next the Gr.·. Chancellor is the *Gr.·. Treasurer.*

Below, on one side, are the *Chief Engineer*, the *Gr.·. Master Architect*, and the *Captain of the Guards.*

Six members stand below them, dressed in red, without aprons, but all wearing the jewel of the Order on the breast, suspended from a broad black ribbon, making a triangular collar.

The *jewel* of this Degree is a plain Teutonic cross of pure gold. The apron is of white satin or velvet, bordered with black. On the flap are a double-headed eagle, and flags of three colours; on the body of the apron, the tracing-board of the degree.

37D

A broad *sash* is worn, red on one side and black on the other, heavily fringed with silver, and with the Teutonic cross embroidered upon it; also a *girdle* fringed with silver, and of the same colours. The cross on the sash is black.

The *battery* is ‖ raps, by , and !

On the cross upon the sash, in the middle of it, is a double-headed eagle embroidered in silver. In front on the girdle, a red Teutonic cross.

TO OPEN.

[☞ When the Th∴ Ill∴ addresses a subordinate officer, or such officer addresses the Th∴ Ill∴, the officer will rise, and salute with his sword, bringing it to the *present*, and then dropping the point to the ground, to the right and a little in front of him, the arm fully extended downward; in which position he remains until the colloquy is concluded; and then comes again to the *carry*].

Th∴ Ill∴ Princes, the time for the re-union of the Brethren, Companions, Knights, Princes and Commanders of Masonry is at hand, and this Consistory must be called to labour. Valiant Captain of the Guards, see that the Sentinels are stationed, and advise them that we are about to open this Consistory, that they may allow no one to approach who hath not the words and the signs of a Prince of the Royal Secret.

[The Capt∴ of the Guards goes out, returns, salutes, and says]:

C∴ of G∴ Th∴ Ill∴ Gr∴ Commander, the Sentinels are stationed and duly instructed. We are secure from intrusion.

Th∴ Ill∴ Ill∴ First Lt∴ Commander, who first projected a reunion of the Brethren, Companions, Knights, Princes and Commanders of Masonry; and for what purpose?

Ans∴ Frederic the Second, King of Prussia, Grand Master of Masons, and Noblest Patron of the Craft; for the purpose of rescuing the Holy City and Sepulchre from the dominion of the Moslems.

Th∴ Ill∴ Who was to command the Masonic Army in this new Crusade?

Ans∴ Frederic himself, as Commander-in-chief of the land and naval forces.

Th∴ Ill∴ What were to be the places of rendezvous?

Ans∴ The first, Naples: then Rhodes, Cyprus, Malta and Joppa; whence the army was to march on Jerusalem.

Th∴ Ill∴ What was the hour fixed for sailing, and the signal?

Ans∴ The hour, the 5th after sunset; and the signal, one cannon by itself, followed by four in quick succession.

Th∴ Ill∴ What does our tracing-board represent?

Ans∴ The plan of the camp of the Masonic Army, as arranged by Frederic the Great, our Grand Master.

Th∴ Ill∴ Why is it peculiarly a Masonic plan?

Ans∴ Because it embodies the HOLY CROSS, and the sacred numbers of Masonry.

Th∴ Ill∴ Whose tents were to be placed upon the Cross in the centre?

Ans∴ Those of the Five Princes who were to command in rotation under the Commander-in-chief, as seconds in command; and whose standards were to be planted on the five angles of the Pentagon.

Th∴ Ill∴ What represents the number 3?

Ans∴ The equilateral TRIANGLE enclosing the Cross: on the lines of which were to be the tents of the most illustrious among the Knights and Masons.

Th∴ Ill∴ What represents the number 5?

Ans∴ The PENTAGON encircling the triangle; in the angles of which are the standards of the Five Princes, Lieutenant-Commanders.

Th∴ Ill∴ What do the different letters of the standards represent?

Ans∴ T∴ the Knights Templars, or Knights Kadosch: E∴ the Knights Ecossais: . . N∴ the Knights of the Sun; because that letter, in many languages enters into the name of the Divinity that represents that luminary: as Noum; ON: K Neph: AdoN: AmuN: HelioN: OdiN: ΑπολλωΝ: SuN: . . G., the German, or Teutonic Knights: . . U., the Union of that Trinity of qualities which should distinguish the Princes of Mercy: VIRTUS, VIS et VERITAS: (*Virtue, Energy and Truth*).

Th.·. Ill.·. What is represented by the word T E N G U, which these letters constitute?

Ans.·. The Thrice-Excellent, Noble and Glorious Union, of Knights and Princes of Masonry.

Th.·. Ill.·. What represents the number 7?

Ans.·. The HEPTAGON, enclosing the *Pentagon;* on the lines of which are the tents of the Masons from the 19th to the 25th degree, inclusive.

Th.·. Ill.·. What represents the number 9?

Ans.·. The NONAGON, on the lines of which are the tents and standards of the Masons from the 1st degree to the 18th.

Th.·. Ill.·. What do the letters, indicating the different tents represent?

Ans.·. The mottoes of the different bodies of Masons who are to encamp under the different flags; which are given in the lecture of this degree, with the symbolic meaning of the words they constitute.

Th.·. Ill.·. What does the intended encampment symbolize to us?

Ans.·. The union of Masons of all rites and all degrees, into one great, harmonious and mighty army of Reformers, Soldiers of Virtue, Morality and Truth, to war against Vice, Ignorance, Despotism spiritual and temporal, and Error, in all their forms and everywhere; and so to become the benefactors of the world.

Th.·. Ill.·. Since that is our object, let us proceed to take counsel together! It is my pleasure that this Consistory be now opened for the transaction of business. To prayer, Princes!

[All kneel, and repeat audibly, after the Gr.·. Commander, the Lord's Prayer. Then they rise: the Gr.·. Commander raps , !—the 1st Lt.·. Com.·. the same—the 2d Lt.·. Com.·. the same].

Th.·. Ill.·. ♎☉†♀♉.·.

1st Lt.·. Com.·. ♒☿♒♀♎.·.

2d Lt.·. Com.·. ♈☾♒♌♄.·.

Th.·. Ill.·. The Sign, Princes!

[All give the Sign, by laying the ‡⁑☊☉♒♊ on the ♏‡☾☉♎♈, then holding it ⁒☾‡⁒☾♒♊♀ ↥♄†☉‡†♄ ♄⁒, and letting it ♑☉†† by the right ♎♀♊☾].

Th.·. Ill.·. For the advancement of the interests of humanity, and of the cause of virtue, this Consistory is now open.

RECEPTION.

[The Candidate is prepared by being dressed in the insignia and jewels of a Knight Kadosch; in which degree he is examined in the ante-chamber by the Gr.·. Master Architect, who acts as Introducer. If satisfied with the examination, the Gr.·. M.·. Architect communicates to him the two pass-words, informing him that he will give the first to the 2d Lt.·. Commander, and the second to the 1st Lt.·. Commander.]

[The Introducer then raps , ! at the door, and the Captain of the Guards opens it].

Capt.·. of G.·. Who comes here?

Intro.·. A Knight Kadosch, who having been duly elected and examined, desires to receive the crowning secrets of the Ancient and Accepted Rite of Masonry.

C.·. of G.·. Hath he well considered and understood the lessons which he has received in the preceding degrees?

Introd.·. He has.

C.·. of G.·. Is he willing to unite with all his heart in the great cause in which we are engaged?

Introd.·. He is.

C.·. of G.·. Does he know that none are wanted here but earnest and sincere men, unselfish, and whose philanthropy is not a mere name, but a practical reality?

Introd.·. He does.

C∴ of G∴ It is well. Let him await an answer from the Th∴. Ill∴. Gr∴. Commander.

[The Captain of the Guards closes the door and goes to the East; where the same questions are asked and like answers returned as at the door; and the Th∴. Ill∴. directs that the Candidate be admitted and conducted to the 2d Lt∴. Commander].

[The Candidate enters and proceeds to the 2d Lt∴. Commander; where the same questions are asked and answers returned as at the door. Then the 2d Lt∴. Com∴. asks]:

1st Lt∴. Com∴. Have you the first pass-word?

Cand∴. I have.

1st Lt∴. Com∴. Advance and communicate it! [He does so].

1st Lt∴. Com∴. It is right. What does it mean?

Cand∴. I do not know.

1st Lt∴. Com∴. SEPARATED: as Masons have been for many years by intestine dissensions and the struggles of illegal and illegitimate bodies to exercise usurped powers:—*Separated;* as mankind has been for thousands of centuries, by differences in religious beliefs; by the ambition and interest of Kings; by natural lines, as rivers and mountains, or mere imaginary divisions, that have made one people the enemies and haters of another, and filled the world with wars:—*Separated,* as men have often been from truth and knowledge by the arts and craft of a corrupt and knavish Priesthood;—Separated; as man has been from his God, by means of his passions and his vices as well as his ignorance. The word recalls to our memories strife and persecution, torture and bloodshed—the murder of the aged and of infancy, the violation of the matron and the virgin; quivering bodies torn and devoured by wild beasts in the amphitheatre; the Christian girl, in her innocence and beauty, naked, rent limb from limb by the tigers, while among the human tigers that roared with rapture till Rome rocked with the noise, sat the young pagan girl of her own age, and felt no sickness at the heart as she saw the remorseless bloody butchery. It recalls to us the slaughter of Christians by Christians; the burnings and beheadings of the Albigenses and Lollards, the murder of Servetus, the hunting and slaughtering of the Covenanters, the hanging of Papists in Ireland, the extermination of the harmless people of Mexico and Peru, and the continual wars by which men's passions have made a gehenna of this earth which God intended as a Paradise. And it teaches us in most persuasive accents that the highest duties of a man and Mason are toleration and charity of judgment: and that the great mission of Masonry, yet far from being fulfilled, is to labour to put an end to strife, war and persecution among men; to elevate the masses of mankind, and teach them that their true interests are indissolubly connected with peace and harmony, and that it is always they upon whom the burthens and evils of conflict and dissension fall with the heaviest hand. Go now to the 1st Lt∴. Commander.

2d Lt∴. Com∴. Have you the 2d Pass-word?

Cand∴. I have.

2d Lt∴. Com∴. Advance and communicate it! [He does so]. It is right. Know you what it means?

Cand∴. I do not.

2d Lt∴. Com∴. RE-UNITED, *to accomplish.* A *re-union* of all Masons, of all rites and all degrees to accomplish the great objects of Masonry. If you are willing to unite in this great work, think not that you are sailing with the trade-winds, when you may fasten up the rudder and sleep before the wind; but expect rough seas, rude shocks and contrary blasts, and many cross-tacks and veerings before you arrive at port: for we sleep in armour in our progress towards virtue, and do not glide downward, but climb upward to it. The long train of our cross-tries is to be beheld within us, and not without us. If thou shouldst be admitted here among us, be careful that thou recommendest none that are not fit for the great work; and if thou feelest thyself incapable, retire! Where true fortitude dwells, loyalty, bounty, friendship and fidelity may be found. One should confide only in persons constituted for noble ends, who dare do and suffer, and who have a hand to burn, like Scævola, for their country or their friend. He will be mistaken who makes choice of a covetous man for a friend, or relies upon the reed of narrow and poltroon friendship. Pitiful things only are to be found in the hovels of such breasts: but bright thoughts, clear deeds, constancy, fidelity, bounty and generous honesty are the gems of noble minds. Let thy oaths be sacred: and thy promises be made upon the altar of thy heart. Make no cobwebs of obligations; for honest men's words are Stygian oaths, and promises inviolable: and let him only have the key of thy heart, who hath the lock of his own, which no temptation can open. I permit thee to pass on to the Th∴ Ill∴ Gr∴ Commander.

[The candidate goes to the East; and the Introducer says: "Th∴ Ill∴ Gr∴ Commander, I present to you this Kt∴ Kadosch, who hath been permitted to pass to you, by the Ill∴ Lt∴ Commanders; and who desires to obtain the secrets of this degree"].

Th∴ Ill∴ Hast thou heard and understood the lessons of the Ill∴ Lt∴ Commanders?

Cand∴ I have.

Th∴ Ill∴ Then hear mine. If thou wouldst reform men, thou must first win their confidence: and that thou canst do, only by being thyself worthy of it. Sit not down in the popular forms and common level of virtues. Be temperate and sober; not merely to preserve your bodily vigour, nor to avoid the infamy of common transgression, and so to expiate or palliate obscure or closer vices, nor to spare your purse, nor simply to enjoy health; but that thereby you may truly serve God and your fellow-men. His is a poor ambition, who doth not long to do some good that shall outlast human life. Be charitable, before wealth makes thee covetous: and lose not the glory of the widow's mite. If riches increase, let thy mind hold pace with them; and think it not enough to be liberal, but munificent. Acquaint thyself with the physiognomy of want. Thy good works, and not thy goods, will follow thee. Wealth is an appurtenance of life, and no dead man is rich. Wherefore by charity let the fruition of things bless the possession of them, and think it more satisfaction to live richly than to die rich.

Make not the consequence of virtue the end thereof. Be not beneficent for a name or applause: nor exact and just, to gain trust and credit only, which attend the reputation of true and punctual dealing. Limit not thy honesty by the law of thy country; nor think that always good enough which will hold in law. Narrow not the law of charity, equity and mercy. Live by old ethics and the classical rules of honesty. Put no new names or notions on authentic virtues and vices. Think not that morality is ambulatory; that vices in one age are not vices in another; or that virtues, which are under the everlasting seal of right reason, may be stamped by opinion. And though vicious times invert the opinions of things, and set up new ethics against virtue, hold thou unto old morality; and rather than follow a multitude to do evil, stand like a column, conspicuous by thyself, and single in integrity.

Look humbly down, in that state when others look upwards upon thee. Think not thine own shadow longer than that of others, nor delight to take the altitude of thyself.

Let not the Sun, even in the shortest days, go down upon thy wrath; but write thy wrongs in ashes. Draw the curtain of night upon injuries, and forgetting them let them be as though they had not been.

Think not that mankind liveth but for a few; and that the rest are born to serve those ambitions which make but flies of men, and wildernesses of whole nations. Seek not to use or govern others, but be satisfied to govern thyself. Annihilate not the mercies of God by the oblivion of ingratitude. Fall not into self-adulation, and become not thine own parasite.

If thy vessel be but small on the ocean of this world, forget not those virtues which the Great Disposer of all bids thee to entertain from thy quality and condition: submission, humility, content of mind and industry. To be low, but above contempt, may be high enough to be happy. When thou searchest for the imperfections of others, look also for what is laudable in them; for in every nature something may be good; and some excellency which needs to be explored for, and does not lie upon the surface, may incline the balance in his favour. There is dross and alloy in all natures, for the very reason that there is also pure metal in all. Praise is a debt we owe to the virtues of others; and if we deny it to them, we are their debtors; and still more if we indirectly praise ourselves by pointing out their imperfections. He is best praised, whose own conscience pronounces his eulogy. The chief Masonic virtues are charity, modesty, humility, patience and veracity; and he who knows himself possessed of these, is fitted to engage in the great work of reforming the world. Dost thou assent to these truths; and feel that thou canst put these principles in practice?

Cand∴ I do.

Th∴ Ill∴ Go then to the Holy Altar, and there kneel, to take upon thyself the obligation of this degree.

[The Candidate kneels before the altar, with his hands upon the Holy Bible; and repeats after the Th.˙. Ill.˙. Gr.˙. Commander, the following]

OBLIGATION.

I, A . . . . B . . . ., of my own free will and accord, in the presence of the Gr.˙. Arch.˙. of the Universe, and calling Him to witness the sincerity of my intentions; and in this Consistory of Sub.˙. Princes of the Royal Secret, faithful guardians of the sacred treasure, do hereby and hereon most solemnly and sincerely vow and swear, under all the penalties of my former obligations in Masonry, that I will never reveal or make known, directly or indirectly, by intention or culpable negligence or carelessness, to any person or persons whomsoever, any even the least of the secrets of this royal degree, unless to one duly qualified and entitled to receive them, or in the body of a regular Consistory of this degree, and to such persons or· in such body only as I shall find to be such after strict trial.

I furthermore promise and swear that I will be governed by and in my conduct conform to the Statutes and regulations of this or any other Consistory to which I may belong, and by and to those of the Sup.˙. Council of the 33d Degree under whose jurisdiction I may reside, so far as the same may become known to me.

I furthermore promise and swear that I will cordially, heartily and sincerely unite with the Sub.˙. Princes of the R.˙. S.˙. in their noble project of uniting all Masons of all rites and degrees together all over the earth, for the purpose of producing peace, harmony and concert of action within the Order, and of putting an end to strife, dissension religious and political, war and persecution throughout the world.

I furthermore promise and swear, that, in order to be able to serve the Order and mankind, I will, both in and out of the Consistory, behave and demean myself as a Mason should, worthy of being honoured by being associated in so noble and glorious a work, of making this world a Temple fit for the abiding place of the Gr.˙. Arch.˙. of the Universe; that nothing in my conduct or demeanour may in the least reflect discredit on this Consistory or on Masonry, or tend to destroy or diminish my own capacity and power for doing good. So help me God; and enable me to keep this vow! Amen!

———

The Candidate is then raised, and receives the Sign, Words and Token of the degree.

———

SIGN : . . . As already described.

TOKEN : . . . The ordinary grasp in shaking hands, one passing his ‡♀ ⵏⵏ†ℂ ⱱ♀♒♌ℂ‡ as he does so, between the ‡♀ ⵏⵏ†ℂ and ⵏ&♀‡⊞ ⱱ♀♒♌ℂ‡⌐ of the other.

1st PASS-WORD : . . . ⟩⊙†◌-⁋☿†.˙.

2d PASS-WORD : . . . ⟩&⊙‡⊙⌐⁋☿†.˙.

ANSWER : . . . ♒ℂ⁋⊙⌾⌾⊙⁋⊙&.˙.

SACRED WORD : . . . ⊙†⌐⟁&ℂ⊞♀.˙.

———

[The Candidate is then invested with the clothing and jewel of the Degree: and is informed that the letters J.˙. M.˙., in front of the table before the Th.˙. Ill.˙. are the initials of the name of Jacques de Molai, Gr.˙. Master of Templars; that the skull and cross-bones refer to his murder; and that the letters p.˙. ɟ.˙. . . . .

⊃∴ ꓷ∴, in front of the Table in the West, are an abbreviation of the words ≋ℭ⑩☎∴ ☎⊙⑩&∴, signifying Vengeance, and a blow or calamity.

Then the Tracing-Board is displayed to him; and the Minister of State reads the following Lecture.]

LECTURE.

Frederic the 2d, or the Great, of Prussia, being at the head of the Masonic Fraternity on the Continent of Europe, projected a re-union of the Brethren, Companions, Knights, Princes and Commanders of Masonry, for the purpose of rescuing the Holy City, and the Sepulchre of the Saviour from the hands of the Turks, by a new Crusade, in which it was his intention to command in person: but he was prevented by death from carrying it out.

It was his intention that the Masons of different countries should first rendezvous at Naples, and sail thence to Rhodes, Cyprus, Malta and Joppa, from which place the army was to march upon Jerusalem. The hour for sailing from each port was to be the fifth after sunset, and the signal a single gun, followed by four others in quick succession.

He also prepared a plan by which the army was regularly to encamp, which is perpetuated on the tracing board of this Degree. It is purely Masonic, because by the equilateral triangle enclosing the Holy Cross, and by the Pentagon, Heptagon and Nonagon, of which it is composed, it expresses the sacred Masonic numbers, 3, 5, 7 and 9.

Upon the Cross in the centre were to be the quarters of the five Princes, who as Lt. Commanders were in rotation to be second in command; and whose standards are seen on our tracing Board planted in the five angles of the Pentagon.

On the sides of the equilateral triangle were to be encamped the Sublime Princes of the Royal Secret, and the Gr∴ Inquiring Commanders.

The standards of the Five Princes, each represented by a letter, and each in one of the angles of the Pentagon, are as follows:

T∴ *azure*: a lion *couchant or*, holding in his mouth a key *or*, and collared *or*, with the figures 525 on the collar. Motto, at the base, AD GLORIAM DEI.

E∴ *Argent*: a flaming heart *gules*, winged *sable*, crowned with laurel *vert*.

N∴ *Vert*: an eagle with two heads, displayed, *sable*, armed *or*, ensigned with an imperial crown *or* resting on both heads; holding in his dexter claw a sword, point in base; in his sinister claw a bloody heart.

G∴ *Or*: an ox *statant, sable*.

U∴ *Purpure*: the Ark of the Covenant *or*, between two palm trees *vert*. Motto at the base LAUS DEO.

The Standard T∴ indicates the encampment of the Knight Templars: E. of the Knights Ecossais: N∴ of the Knights of the Sun, into so many of the names of which luminary that letter enters: G∴ of the German or Teutonic Knights: and U∴ of the Princes of Mercy or Scottish Trinitarians, that letter representing the Trinity of qualities that should distinguish them, VIRTUS, VIS and VERITAS (Virtue, Energy and Truth,) united in a perfect UNION.

Taken together, these letters make the word T.E.N.G.U., the initials of this sentence: THRICE-EXCELLENT, NOBLE, GLORIOUS UNION, [*of the Ill∴ Knights and Princes of Masonry.*]

On the sides of the Heptagon are to be the camps of The Knights of the Brazen Serpent, The Princes of the Tabernacle, The Chiefs of the Tabernacle, the Knights of the Royal Axe [who are to be the Engineers], The Noachites, the Grand Masters of Symbolic Lodges, and the Gr∴ Pontiffs; all to receive their orders from the five Princes of the Pentagon.

On the sides of the Nonagon are to encamp all the Masons of the lower degrees. Each tent represents an entire camp; and the pennons and flags point out the different degrees.

S∴ Flag or pennon white, lightly sprinkled with red: The tent indicates the camp of the Knights of the Rose ☩, and the Knights of the East and West.

A∴ Flag and pennon light green: Knights of the East, and Princes of Jerusalem.

L∴ Flag and and pennon red: Grand Elect, Perfect and Sublime Masons.

I∴ Flag and pennon black and red: Knights of the Ninth Arch.

X∴ Flag and pennon black: Gr∴ Master Architects: Sublime Knights Elect, Ill∴ Elect of 15, and Kts∴ Elect of 9.

N∴ Flag and pennon red and black: Intendants of the Building.

O∴ Flag and pennon green and red: Provosts and Judges, and Confidential Secretaries.

NI∴ Flag and pennon green: Perfect and Secret Masters.

S∴ Flag and pennon blue: Symbolic Masons of all rites, and Volunteers.

These letters together make the two words SALIX NONIS: and the whole encampment symbolizes the union of all Masons, of all rites and all degrees, into one great, harmonious and mighty army, soldiers of virtue, freedom, morality and knowledge, to war against vice, despotism spiritual and temporal, profligacy and error, in all their Protean shapes and forms, and to be the benefactors of the world.

. With the Knights Templars [or Kadosch] were to encamp all such Knights of Malta as should unite with them, and prove themselves faithful guardians of the Holy Places.

The mottoes of the different camps of the Nonagon are as follows:

S∴ . . . *Salus Populi, Suprema Lex.*

A∴ . . . *Acerrimi libertatis et veritatis defensores.*

L∴ . . . *Labores magnos pro hominum salute late excipere.*

I∴ . . . *In virtute vere gloriamur.*

X∴ . . . *Xenia utilissima Dei hominibus data, Religioque et Latomia.*

N∴ . . . *Non nobis solum nati sumus; ortusque nostri partem patria vindicat.*

O∴ . . . *Ora atque labora.*

NI∴ . . *Non vultus instantis tyranni justum virum mente quatit solida.*

S∴ . . . *Summam nec metuere diem, nec optare.*

The watchwords were arranged for every day in the week; and were to be changed only by express order from the Commander-in-Chief. They were as follows:

Day	Protectors of Masonry.		Answers for every day.	Prophets.
Sunday		. . Cyrus		. . Ezekiel.
Monday		. . Darius		. . Daniel.
Tuesday		. . Xerxes		. . Habakkuk.
Wednesday . . .		. . Alexander		. . Zephaniah.
Thursday . . .		. . Philadelphus . . .		. . Haggai.
Friday		. . Herod		. . Zechariah.
Saturday		. . Hezekiah		. . Malachi.

There are also seven other watchwords, one for each day of the week, the initials of which surround the Heptagon, and form the Ineffable Name, as it is spelled in the common version of the Scriptures. They are: Justice, . . . Equity, . . . Honour, . . . Order, . . . Virtue, . . . Ardour, . . . Humanity. These words distinguish the several camps as follows:

Justice: . . The Noachites, or Prussian Knights. . . Their Banner, *White.*

Equity: . . The Grand Pontiffs. . . Their Banner, *Yellow.*

Honour: . . The Grand Masters of all Symbolic Lodges. . . Their Banner, *Blue.*

Order: . . . The Knights of the Royal Axe. . . Their Banner, *Black.*

Virtue: . . The Chiefs of the Tabernacle. . . Their Banner, *Green.*

Ardour: . . The Princes of the Tabernacle. . . Their Banner, *Purple.*

Humanity: . The Knights of the Brazen Serpent. . . Their Banner, *Crimson.*

Which colours were anciently assigned to the several planets, as follows: White, to the Moon; Yellow, to the Sun; Blue, to Jupiter; Black, to Saturn; Green, to Venus; Purple, to Mercury; and Crimson, to Mars.

The Knights Kadosch are the legitimate successors of the Templars; and this degree was originally a Christian degree of Knighthood. Its object was, for a long time, to re-conquer the Holy Land, and plant the Banner of the Cross once more on the ruined walls of Jerusalem. Many of the Knights of the Crusades were Masons, and thus became acquainted with the legend which Masonry had preserved. Jerusalem was finally lost to Christendom in the year 1244, when it was taken and sacked by the Corasins, 140 years after it had been conquered by Tancred and Godefroi de Bouillon, and 15 after the Sultan of Babylon had restored it to the Emperor Frederic the Second: and in the battle of Tiberias, fought on St. Luke's day soon after the taking of the City, the Christians were entirely overthrown. Of those of the Teutonic order engaged in the battle, three only escaped; of 300 Templars, only 18; and of 200 Hospitallers, only 19.

Efforts were afterwards made, but ineffectually, to re-conquer Jerusalem and Palestine. The surviving Knights spread themselves over Europe, carrying Masonry and the legend of the Master's Degree with them, and veiling the Christian Mysteries of the Incarnation, the Crucifixion, the Resurrection, and the Redemption of man, under the allegory of the murder and raising of Hiram Abi. The Mysteries of the Craft thus became to Christian Masons the Mysteries of religion. This important secret they were unwilling to entrust to any whose discretion had not been proved. Then it was that they selected the two Saints John as Patrons of Masonry; John the Baptist, because he was an initiated Essene: and John the Evangelist, it is said, for a still deeper reason, and one that made secrecy indispensable.

It is said (we do not vouch for the truth of the statement, although it is historical), that the Masons of the Orient had embraced the doctrines taught by St. John, as contradistinguished from those taught by St. Paul and St. Peter, and followed by the Romish Church. They considered St. John as a more accurate and faithful depositary of the doctrines of Christ than St. Peter: they believed in the Gospel of Love; and that faith or mere belief without works was useless; and so believing they denied the spiritual supremacy and infallibility of the Pope, and sowed the seeds of opposition to his authority in England, France and Prussia, which afterwards produced such a mighty fruit.

To conceal these dangerous esoteric doctrines, they invented different degrees, in order to unfold their doctrines gradually, to make known the primitive truths, which, first revealed to the Patriarchs, had been again taught by the Redeemer, to their initiates, slowly, and after testing them by long privations and the passage through many degrees; that they might prove them thoroughly, before teaching them the doctrine of toleration, and those others, taught by St. John, and so contrary to the corruptions of the Church and Court of Rome; corruptions which had changed the equality and humility of the Church and the early Christians into a vast Hierarchy, built up story upon story, and cemented with the blood of a million of persons slain by the sword, the axe and the fagot of persecution; and over which Hierarchy domineered an absolute Despot, claiming supreme spiritual and temporal authority over all Kings and Emperors, and power to annul laws all over Christendom, and that when he spoke, it was the voice of God himself speaking through his mouth.

Accordingly, it is said, in the early degrees, symbolic secrets only were communicated, without explanations; that the Brethren might have the means of recognizing each other, but not of betraying any dangerous secret. Signs, words and tokens only were given in each degree, for mutual assistance and protection against Cowans, Saracens, and the crafty Emissaries of Rome, that eternal and relentless enemy of Masonry.

Our explanations of Masonry would be incomplete, if we should omit to make known to you those which these Christian Masons gave of the ceremonies and symbols of the three first degrees. Whether they are correct or incorrect, it is not for us to decide. They have often been given: and though the doors of Masonry, in all the legitimate degrees, and even in that of the Rose ✠, and this of the Sublime Princes of the Royal Secret, open to all who believe in a Wise and Just God and in the immortality of the Soul, yet even those Masons who are not of the Christian faith, though firm in their own interpretations of the symbols, may well be curious to know those of others, may well give them a respectful attention, and may, perhaps, find something in them of interest and value. And before we enter upon the final lesson which we have to give you, we will delay a few moments to repeat to you these Christian interpretations.

In the first degree, they said, there are three symbols to be applied.

1st. Man, after the fall, was left naked and defenceless against the just anger of the Deity. Prone to evil, the human race staggered blindly onward into the thick darkness of unbelief, bound fast by the strong cable-tow of the natural and sinful will. Moral corruption was followed by physical misery. Want and destitution invaded the earth. War and Famine and Pestilence filled up the measure of evil, and over the sharp flints of misfortune and wretchedness, man toiled with naked and bleeding feet. This condition of blindness, destitution, misery and bondage, from which to save the world the Redeemer came, is symbolized by the condition of the Candidate, when he is brought up for the first time to the door of the Lodge.

2d. Notwithstanding the death of the Redeemer, man can be saved only by faith, repentance and reformation. To repent, he must feel the sharp sting of conscience and remorse, like a sword piercing his bosom. His confidence in his guide, whom he is told to follow and fear no danger; his trust in God, which he is caused to profess; and the point of the sword that is pressed against his naked left breast over the heart, are symbolical of the faith, repentance and reformation necessary to bring him to the light of a life in Christ the Crucified.

3d. Having repented and reformed, and bound himself to the service of God by a firm promise and obligation, the light of Christian hope shines down into the darkness of the heart of the humble penitent, and blazes upon his pathway to Heaven. And this is symbolized by the Candidate's being brought to light after he is obligated, by the Worshipful Master, who in that is a symbol of the Redeemer, and so brings him to light, with the help of the brethren, as He taught the Word with the aid of his Apostles.

In the second degree there are two symbols:

4th. The Christian assumes new duties towards God and his fellows. Towards God, of love, gratitude and veneration, and an anxious desire to serve and glorify him: towards his fellows, of kindness, sympathy and justice. And this assumption of duty, this entering upon good works, is symbolized by the Fellow-Craft's obligation; by which, bound as an apprentice to secrecy merely, and set in the North-East corner of the Lodge, he descends as a Fellow-Craft into the body of the brethren, and assumes the active duties of a good Mason.

5th. The Christian, reconciled to God, sees the world in a new light. It is no longer—this great universe, a mere machine, wound up and set going six thousand or sixty million years ago, and left to run on afterwards forever, by virtue of a law of mechanics created at the beginning, without further care or consideration on the part of the Deity: but it has now become to him a great emanation from God, the product of His thought, not a mere dead machine, but a thing of life, over which God watches continually, and every movement of which is immediately produced by his present action, the law of harmony being the essence of the Deity, re-enacted every instant. And this is symbolized by the imperfect instruction given in the Fellow-Craft's degree, in the sciences, and particularly geometry, connected as the latter is with God himself in the mind of a Mason, because the same letter suspended in the East, represents both: and astronomy, or the knowledge of the laws of motion and harmony that govern the spheres, is but a portion of the wider science of geometry. It is so symbolized, because it is here, in the second degree, that the Candidate first receives any other than moral instruction.

There are also two symbols in the 3d Degree, which, with the 3 in the first, and 2 in the second, make the 7.

6th. The Candidate, after passing through the first part of the ceremony, imagines himself a Master; and is surprised to be informed that as yet he is not, and that it is uncertain whether he ever will be. He is told of a difficult and dangerous path yet to be travelled, and is advised that upon that journey it depends whether he will become a Master. This is symbolical of that which our Saviour said to Nicodemus, that notwithstanding his morals might be beyond reproach he could not enter the Kingdom of Heaven unless he were born again; symbolically dying, and again entering the world, regenerate, like a spotless infant.

7th. The murder of Hiram Abi, his burial and his being raised again by the Master, are symbols, both of the death, burial and resurrection of the Redeemer; and of the death and burial in sins of the natural man, and his being raised again to a new life, or born again, by the direct action of the Redeemer; after Morality (symbolized by the Entered Apprentice's grip), and Philosophy (symbolized by the grip of the Fellow-Craft) had failed to raise him. That of the Lion of the House of Judah is the strong grip, never to be broken, with which Christ, of the royal line of that House, has grappled to himself the whole human race, and embraces them in his wide arms as closely and affectionately as brethren embrace each other on the five points of fellowship.

As Entered Apprentices and Fellow-Crafts, Masons are taught to imitate the laudable example of those Masons who laboured at the building of King Solomon's Temple; and to plant firmly and deep in their hearts those foundation-stones of principle, truth, justice, temperance, fortitude, prudence and charity, on which to erect that Christian character which all the storms of misfortune and all the powers and temptations of Hell shall not prevail against; those feelings and noble affections which are the properest homage that can be paid to the Grand Architect and Great Father of the Universe, and which make the heart a living temple builded to him: when the unruly passions are made to submit to rule and measurement, and their excesses are struck off with the gavel of self-restraint; and when every action and every principle is accurately corrected and adjusted by the square of wisdom, the level of humility and the plumb of justice.

The two columns, Jachin and Boaz, are the symbols of that profound faith and implicit trust in God and the Redeemer that are the Christian's *strength;* and of those good works by which alone that faith can be *established* and made operative and effectual to salvation.

The three pillars that support the Lodge are symbols of a Christian's HOPE in a future state of happiness; FAITH in the promises and the divine character and mission of the Redeemer; and CHARITABLE JUDGMENT of other men.

The three murderers of Hiram Abi symbolize Pontius Pilate, Caiaphas the High Priest and Judas Iscariot: and the three blows given him are the betrayal by the last, the refusal of Roman protection by Pilate, and the condemnation by the High Priest. They also symbolize the blow on the ear, the scourging and the crown of thorns. The twelve fellow-crafts sent in search of the body are the twelve disciples, in doubt whether to believe that the Redeemer would rise from the dead.

The Master's word, supposed to be lost, symbolizes the Christian faith and religion, supposed to have been crushed and destroyed, when the Saviour was crucified, after Iscariot had betrayed him, and Peter deserted him, and when the other disciples doubted whether he would arise from the dead; but which rose from his tomb and flowed rapidly over the civilized world; and so that which was supposed to be *lost* was *found.* It symbolizes also the Saviour himself; the WORD that was in the beginning—that was *with* God, and that *was* God; the Word of life, that was made flesh and dwelt among us, and was supposed to be lost, while he lay in the tomb, for three days, and his disciples "as yet knew not the scripture that he must rise again from the dead," and doubted when they heard of it, and were amazed and frightened and still doubted when he appeared among them.

The bush of acacia placed at the head of the grave of Hiram is an emblem of resurrection and immortality.

Such are the explanations of our Christian brethren; entitled, like those of all other Masons, to a respectful consideration.

In the judgment and crucifixion of him who was at least a Great Reformer, all Masons can see the same three Powers which wrought the death of Jacques de Molay; the despotic Royal power, in the persons of Herod and Pilate; the insolence, cruelty and blood-thirstiness of the Sacerdotal power, in the person of Caiaphas; and the bitterness of rank, caste and privilege when truth and right seem about to interfere with and diminish their 'vested rights,' their franchises and immunities, by raising up the people to the dignity of manhood,— in the Scribes, the Elders and the Pharisees, who monopolized the wealth and learning of the Jews.

These three have ever been the enemies of Humanity, the implacable foes of Human liberty. The pursuit and search for the assassins of Hiram symbolizes the war which Masonry wages, with the arms of reason, and with other arms if need be, against these oppressors of the world, these stiflers of free thought, whose chains have galled the limbs of mankind so many ages. Whether in Pagan or Catholic Rome, the Emperor and the Hierarchy were the persecutors of opinion; and in the privileged classes they ever found ready instruments of their cruelty.

The Temple, destroyed by the Chaldeans, symbolizes the People, the great suffering masses of Humanity, enslaved, and led in chains by Royal and Sacerdotal Despotism : for universal man, redeemed and disenthralled, free, educated and intelligent, will be, in his majesty, his might and his harmony, the most fitting Temple of the All-Wise, the Just and the Beneficent Creator.

That Temple, in its beautiful and magnificent proportions, Masonry desires to re-build. Civil and religious freedom, emancipation of both the muscles and the mind of all who are fit to be free, education and enlightenment, and the raising up of the oppressed masses of humanity to that level of equality on which they ought to stand ; that is the mission in which Masonry is to co-operate : and to fulfil which it must necessarily labour for the overthrow and extermination of Kingly tyranny and Priestly oppression, as well as the exclusive Privileges of rank and caste.

This is the meaning of that allegory of implacable hostility to the Knights of Malta. They are to us but the symbol of a class ; and here, as everywhere in Masonry, truth is hidden in an allegory, which ill-understood becomes repulsive to the moral sense, and shocks a soul devoted to love and to sympathy, and taught everywhere in Masonry the beauty of mercy and forgiveness.

But the vengeance which Masonry desires to take is not such as is indicated by the cavern, the fountain and the bloody head. All that is but a symbol. It desires to see Despotism dethroned, and Constitutional Government established in its place ; the sacerdotal power become like that which the apostles exercised in the early days of Christianity ; the ways to rank and to civil employment, to office and honour, open to *the children of the widow*, the masses of the people. It labours unceasingly for that result, for the enfranchisement of the soul as well as for that of the body ; for well-regulated liberty, and an universal freedom, controlled and directed by law and order. It represents the great working and producing classes ; and it adopted the legend of Hiram Abi, a worker in brass, in order that none might mistake its sympathies. What more thoroughly republican dogma could there be than that which seats by the side of the King of Israel and Judah, and the King of Phœnicia, the humble worker in the metals, like them a Grand-Master, and honoured equally with them by the Craft.

This is Masonry as it has come down to us. Not a system of unmeaning, idle ceremonies, or of commonplace learning and childish forms ; nor of pretences to mysterious secrets, that like *ignes fatui* ever elude the wearied and disappointed pursuer : but a great system, teaching all the grand truths of morality and the primitive revelation, and the mysteries of the primitive faith, first concealed and clothed in allegories, which unfolding by degrees, as clouds break and leave the blue sky smiling behind, leave the truths themselves palpable and prominent in all their grand and majestic proportions.

Of this noble band of co-workers in the great cause of human improvement and human civilization, you are now one, in full fellowship and communion, bound to us to the last moment of your life, by the mystic CABLE-Tow of Masonry [its חבלתו, KHABLETU, His PLEDGE, xviii *Ezek.* 7], which death alone can sever, and relieve us of the obligations it imposes. It behoves you now to see that you do the cause and the Order no discredit, and that you earn and deserve the proud title, FAITHFUL and ENLIGHTENED (the Πιστος and Εποπτης of the old Mysteries) :—Faithful, to yourself, the Order, your Country, Humanity, your God : Enlightened, to see clearly the True and the Right ; and Energetic, to follow, protect and defend them.

Receive now from the Gr∴ Chancellor the last words of the Ancient and Accepted Rite, upon the Ethics and Philosophy of Masonry ; which, and not the pronunciation of any given number of letters in a name, are the True Word of a Master Mason.

CLOSING INSTRUCTION.

My Brother, there is no dogmatism in Masonry. It is not for us to dictate to any man what he shall believe. We have hitherto, in the instruction of the several degrees, confined ourselves to laying before you the great thoughts that have found expression in the different ages of the world, leaving you to decide for yourself as to the orthodoxy or heterodoxy of each, and what proportion or per-centage of truth, if any, each contained. We shall pursue no other course in this closing instruction of the Ancient and Accepted Rite ; in which we propose to deal with the highest questions that have ever exercised the human mind,—with the existence and the nature of a God, with the existence and the nature of the human soul, and with the relations of the divine and human spirit with the merely material universe. There can be no questions more important to an intelligent being, none that have for him a more direct and personal interest; and to this last word of Scottish Masonry we invite your serious and attentive consideration. And, as what we shall now say will be but the completion and rounding-off of what we have already said in several of the preceding degrees, in regard to the Old Thought and the Ancient Philosophies, we hope that you have noted and not forgotten our previous lessons, without which this would seem imperfect and fragmentary.

In its idea of rewarding a faithful and intelligent workman by conferring upon him a knowledge of the True Word, Masonry has perpetuated a very great truth, because it involves the proposition that the idea which a man forms of God is always the most important element in his speculative theory of the Universe, and in his particular practical plan of action for the Church, the State, the Community, the Family, and his own individual life. It will ever make a vast difference in the conduct of a people in war or peace, whether they believe the Supreme God to be a cruel Deity, delighting in sacrifice and blood, or a God of Love; and an individual's speculative theory as to the mode and extent of God's government, and as to the nature and reality of his own free-will and consequent responsibility, will needs have great influence in shaping the course of his life and conversation.

We see every day the vast influence of the popular idea of God. All the great historical civilizations of the race have grown out of the national ideas which were formed of God; or have been intimately connected with those ideas. The popular Theology, which at first is only an abstract idea in the heads of philosophers, by and by shows itself in the laws, and in the punishments for crime, in the churches, the ceremonies and the sacraments, the festivals and the fasts, the weddings, the baptisms and the funerals, in the hospitals, the colleges, the schools and all the social charities, in the relations of husband and wife, parent and child, in the daily work and the daily prayer of every man.

As the world grows in its development, it necessarily *outgrows* its ancient ideas of God, which were only temporary and provisional. A man who has a higher conception of God than those about him, and who denies that their conception *is* God, is very likely to be called an Atheist, by men who are really far less believers in a God than he. Thus the Christians, who said the Heathen idols were no Gods, were accounted Atheists by the People, and accordingly put to death; and Jesus of Nazareth was crucified as an unbelieving blasphemer, by the Jews.

There is a mere formal Atheism, which is a denial of God in *terms*, but not in *reality*. A man says, There is no God; that is, no God that is self-originated, or that never originated, but always Was and Had Been, who is the cause of existence, who is the Mind and the Providence of the Universe; and so the order, beauty and harmony of the world of matter and mind do not indicate any plan or purpose of Deity. But, he says, Nature,—meaning by that the whole sum total of existence,—*that* is powerful, active, wise and good; *nature* is self-originated, or always was and had been, the cause of its own existence, the mind of the Universe and the Providence of itself. There is obviously a plan and purpose whereby order, beauty and harmony are brought about; but all that is the plan and purpose of nature.

In such cases, the absolute denial of God is only formal and not real. The *qualities* of God are admitted, and affirmed to be real; and it is a mere change of name to call the possessor of those qualities, *nature*, and not *God*. The real question is, whether such Qualities exist, as we call God; and not, by what particular name we shall designate the Qualities. One man may call the sum total of these Qualities, Nature; another, Heaven; a third, Universe; a fourth, Matter; a fifth, Spirit; a sixth, God, Theos, Zeus, Alfadir, Allah, or what he pleases. All admit the existence of the Being, Power or Ens, thus diversely named. The name is of the smallest consequence.

Real Atheism is the denial of the existence of *any* God, of the actuality of all possible ideas of God. It denies that there is *any* Mind, Intelligence or Ens, that is the Cause and Providence of the Universe, and of any Thing or any Existence, Soul, Spirit or Being, that *intentionally* or *intelligently* produces the Order, Beauty and Harmony thereof, and the constant and regular modes of operation therein. It must necessarily deny that there is any law, order or harmony in existence, or any constant mode of operation in the world; for it is utterly impossible for any human creature to conceive, however much he may *pretend* to do so, of either of these, except as a consequence of the action of Intelligence; which is, indeed, that otherwise unknown thing, the existence of which these alone prove; otherwise than as the cause of these, not a thing at all; a mere *name* for the wholly uncognizable cause of these.

The *real* atheist must deny the existence of the Qualities of God, deny that there is any mind of or in the universe, any self-conscious Providence, any Providence at all. He must deny that there is any Being or Cause of Finite things, that is self-consciously powerful, wise, just, loving, and faithful to itself and its own nature. He must deny that there is any *plan* in the universe or any part of it. He must hold, either that matter is eternal, or that it originated itself, which is absurd, or that it was originated by an Intelligence, or at least by a Cause; and then he admits a God. No doubt it is beyond the reach of our faculties to imagine *how* matter originated,—how it began *to be*, in space where before was nothing, or God only. But it is equally beyond the reach of our faculties to imagine it eternal, and *unoriginated*. To hold it to be eternal, without thought or will; that the specific forms of it, the seed, the rock, the tree, the man, the solar system, all came with no forethought planning or producing them, by 'chance' or 'the fortuitous concourse of atoms' of matter that has no thought or will; and that they indicate no mind, no plan, no purpose, no providence, is absurd. It is not to deny the *existence* of what we understand by mind, plan, purpose, Providence; but to insist that these words shall have some other meaning than that which the human race has ever attached to them: shall mean some unknown thing, for which the human race has no *name*, because it has of such a thing no possible idea. Either there never was any such thing as a "plan," and the word is nonsense, or the universe exists in conformity to a plan. The *word* never meant and never can mean, any other *thing* than that which the universe exhibits. So with the word "*purpose;*" so with the word "*Providence*." They mean nothing, or else only what the universe proves.

It was soon found that the denial of a Conscious Power, the cause of man and of his life, of a Providence, of a Mind and Intelligence arranging man in reference to the world, and the world in reference to man, would not satisfy the instinctive desires of *human* nature, or account for the facts of *material* nature. It did not long answer to say, if it ever *was* said, that the universe was drifting in the void inane, and neither it nor any mind within or without it knew of its whence, its whither or its whereabouts; that man was drifting in the universe, knowing little of his whereabouts, nothing of his whence or whither; that there was no mind, no Providence, no Power, that knew any better; nothing that guided and directed man in his drifting, or the Universe in the weltering waste of Time. To say to man and woman, "your heroism, your bravery, your self-denial all comes to nothing: your nobleness will do you no good: you will die, and your nobleness will do mankind no service; for there is no plan or order in all these things; everything comes and goes by the fortuitous concourse of atoms;" did not, nor ever will, long satisfy the human mind.

True, the theory of Atheism has been uttered. It has been said, "Death is the end: this is a world without a God: you are a body without a soul: there is a Here, but no Hereafter for you; an Earth, but no Heaven. Die, and return to your dust. Man is bones, blood, bowels and brain: mind is matter: there is no soul in the brain, nothing but nerves. We can see all the way to a little star in the nebula of Orion's belt; so distant that it will take light a thousand millions of years to come from it to the earth, journeying at the rate of twelve millions of miles a minute. There is no Heaven this side of that: you see all the way through: there is not a speck of Heaven; and do you think there is any beyond it; and if so, when would you reach it? There is no Providence. Nature is a fortuitous concourse of atoms; thought is a fortuitous function of matter, a fortuitous result of a fortuitous result, a chance-shot from the great wind-gun of the Universe, accidentally loaded, pointed at random, and fired off by chance. Things *happen;* they are not *arranged*. There is luck, and there is ill-luck; but there is no Providence. Die you into dust!" Does all this satisfy the human instinct of immortality, that makes us ever long with unutterable longing, to join ourselves again to our dear ones that have gone away before us, and to mankind, for eternal life? Does it satisfy our mighty hungering and thirst for immortality, our anxious longing to come nearer to and to know more of the Eternal Cause of all things?

Men never could be content to believe that there was no mind that thought for man, no conscience to enact eternal laws, no heart to love those whom nothing of earth loves or cares for, no will of the universe to marshal the nations in the way of wisdom, justice and love. History is not,—thank God! we *know* it is not, the fortuitous concourse of events, or Nature that of atoms. We cannot believe that there is no plan nor purpose in Nature, to guide our going out and coming in : that there is a mighty going, but it goes nowhere; that all beauty, wisdom. affection, justice, morality in the world, is an accident, and may end to-morrow.

All over the world, there is heroism unrequited, or paid with misery; vice on thrones, corruption in high places, nobleness in poverty or even in chains, the gentle devotion of woman rewarded by brutal neglect or more brutal abuse and-violence; everywhere want, misery, over-work and under-wages. Add to these the Atheist's creed,—a body without a soul, an earth without a Heaven, a world without a God; and what a Pandemonium would we make of this world!

The intellect of the Atheist would find matter everywhere; but no Causing and Providing Mind: his moral sense would find no Equitable Will, no Beauty of Moral Excellence, no Conscience enacting justice into the unchanging law of right, no spiritual Order or spiritual Providence, but only material Fate and Chance. His affections would find only finite things to love ; and to them the dead that *were* loved and that died yesterday, are like the rainbow that yesterday evening lived a moment and then passed away. His soul, flying through the vast Inane, and feeling the darkness with its wings, seeking the Soul of all, which at once is Reason, Conscience, and the Heart of all that is, would find no God, but a Universe all disorder; no Infinite, no Reason, no Conscience, no Heart, no Soul of things; nothing to reverence, to esteem, to love, to worship, to trust in ; but only an Ugly Force, alien and foreign to us, that strikes down those we love, and makes us mere worms on the hot-sand of the world. No voice would speak from the Earth to comfort him. It is a cruel mother, that great Earth, that devours her young,—a Force and nothing more. Out of the sky would smile no kind Providence, in all its thousand starry eyes; and in storms a malignant violence, with its lightning-sword, would stab into the darkness, seeking for men to murder.

No man ever was or ever can be content with that. The evidence of God has been ploughed into Nature so deeply, and so deeply woven into the texture of the human soul, that Atheism has never become a faith, though it has sometimes assumed the shape of theory. Religion is natural to man. Instinctively he turns to God and reverences and relies on Him. In the Mathematics of the Heavens, written in gorgeous diagrams of fire, he sees law, order, beauty, harmony without end : in the ethics of the little nations that inhabit the ant-hills he sees the same ; in all Nature animate and inanimate, he sees the evidences of a Design, a Will, an Intelligence and a God,—of a God beneficent and loving, as well as wise, and merciful and indulgent as well as powerful.

To man, surrounded by the material universe, and conscious of the influence that his material environ-ments exercised upon his fortunes and his present destiny;—to man ever confronted with the splendours of the starry Heavens, the regular march of the seasons, the phenomena of sunrise and moonrise, and all the evidences of intelligence and design that everywhere pressed upon and overwhelmed him, all imaginable. questions as to the nature and cause of these phenomena constantly recurred, demanding to be solved, and refusing to be sent away unanswered. And still, after the lapse of ages, press upon the human mind, and demand solution, the same great questions—perhaps still demanding it in vain.

Advancing to the period when man had ceased to look upon the separate parts and individual forces of the universe as Gods,—when he had come to look upon it as a whole, this question, among the earliest, occurred to him, and insisted on being answered :—"Is this material universe self-existent, or was it created ? Is it eternal, or did it originate ?"

And then in succession came crowding on the human mind these other questions :

"Is this material universe a mere aggregate of fortuitous combinations of matter, or is it the result and work of intelligence, acting upon a plan ?

"If there *be* such an Intelligence, what and where is it ? Is the material universe *itself* an Intelligent being ? Is it like man, a body and a soul? Does Nature act upon itself, or is there a Cause beyond it that acts upon it ?

"If there is a *personal* God, *separate from* the material universe, that created all things, Himself uncreated, is He corporeal or incorporeal, material or spiritual, the soul of the universe or wholly apart from it? and if He be Spirit, what then is spirit?

"Was that Supreme Deity active or quiescent before the creation; and if quiescent during a previous eternity, what necessity of His nature moved Him at last to create a world; or was it a mere whim that had no motive?

"Was matter co-existent with Him, or absolutely created by him out of nothing? Did he *create* it, or only *mould* and *shape* and *fashion* a chaos already existing, co-existent with himself?

"Did the Deity *directly* create matter, or was creation the work of inferior deities, emanations from Himself?

"If he be good and just, whence comes it that, foreknowing everything, he has allowed sorrow and evil to exist; and how to reconcile with His benevolence and wisdom the prosperity of vice and the misfortunes of virtue in this world?"

And then as to man himself recurred these other questions, as they continue to recur to all of us:

"What is it in us that thinks? Is Thought the mere result of material organization; or is there in us a *soul* that thinks, separate from and resident in the body? If the latter, is it eternal and uncreated; and if not, how created? Is it distinct from God, or an emanation from Him? Is it *inherently* immortal, or only so by destination, because God has willed it? Is it to return to and be merged in Him, or ever to exist, separately from Him, with its present identity?

"If God has foreseen and fore-arranged all that occurs, how has man any real free-will, or the least control over circumstances? How can anything be done *against* the will of Infinite Omnipotence; and if all is done *according* to that will, how is there any wrong or evil, in what Infinite Wisdom and Infinite Power does not choose to prevent?

"What is the foundation of the moral law? Did God enact it of his own mere pleasure; and if so, can He not when He pleases, repeal it? Who shall assure us He will not repeal it, and make right wrong, and virtue vice? Or is the moral law a necessity of His nature; and if so, who enacted it; and does not that assert a power, like the old Necessity, superior to Deity?"

And, close-following after these, came the great question of HEREAFTER, of another Life, of the Soul's Destiny; and the thousand other collateral and subordinate questions, as to matter, spirit, futurity and God, that have produced all the systems of philosophy, all metaphysics and all theology since the world began.

What the old philosophic mind thought upon these great questions, we have already to some extent developed. With the Emanation-doctrine of the Gnostics and the Orient, we have endeavoured to make you familiar. We have brought you face to face with the Kabbalists, the Essenes and Philo the Jew. We have shown that, and how, much of the old mythology was derived from the daily and yearly recurring phenomena of the Heavens. We have exhibited to you the ancient notions by which they endeavoured to explain to themselves the existence and prevalence of evil; and we have in some degree made known to you their metaphysical ideas as to the nature of the Deity. Much more remains to be done than it is within our power to do. We stand upon the sounding shore of the great ocean of Time. In front of us stretches out the heaving waste of the illimitable Past; and its waves, as they roll up to our feet along the sparkling slope of the yellow sands, bring to us now and then from the depths of that boundless ocean, a shell, a few specimens of algæ torn rudely from their stems, a rounded pebble, and that is all, of all the vast treasures of ancient thought that lie buried there, with the mighty anthem of the boundless ocean thundering over them forever and forever.

Let us once more, and for the last time, along the shore of that great ocean, gather a few more relics of the Past, and listen to its mighty voices, as they come, in fragmentary music, in broken and interrupted rhythm, whispering to us from the great bosom of the Past.

Rites, Creeds and legends express directly or symbolically some leading idea, according to which the Mysteries of Being are supposed to be explained in Deity. The intricacies of mythical genealogies are a practical acknowledgment of the mysterious nature of the Omnipotent Deity; displaying in their beautiful but ineffectual imagery the first efforts of the mind to communicate with nature: the flowers which fancy strewed before the youthful steps of Psyche, when she first set out in pursuit of the immortal object of her love. Theories and notions in all their varieties of truth and falsehood are a machinery more or less efficacious, directed to the same end. Every religion was in its origin an embryo philosophy, or an attempt to interpret the unknown by mind; and it was only when philosophy, which is essentially progress, outgrew its first acquisitions, that religion became a thing apart, cherishing as unalterable dogmas the notions which philosophy had abandoned. Separated from philosophy, it became arrogant and fantastical, professing to have already attained what its more authentic representative was ever pursuing in vain; and discovering through its initiations and mysteries all that to its contracted view seemed wanting to restore the well-being of mankind, the means of purification and expiation, remedies for disease, expedients to cure the disorders of the soul, and to propitiate the Gods.

Why should we attempt to confine the idea of the Supreme Mind within an arbitrary barrier, or exclude from the limits of veracity any conception of the Deity, which, if imperfect and inadequate, may be only a little more so than our own? "The name of God," says Hobbes, "is used not to make us *conceive* him, for he is inconceivable, but that we may *honour* him." "Believe in God, and adore Him," said the Greek Poet, "but investigate him not; the inquiry is fruitless; seek not to discover who God is; for by the desire to know, you offend Him who chooses to remain unknown." "When we attempt," says Philo, "to investigate the essence of the Absolute Being, we fall into an abyss of perplexity; and the only benefit to be derived from such researches is the conviction of their absurdity."

Yet man, though ignorant of the constitution of the dust on which he treads, has ventured and still ventures to speculate on the nature of God, and to define dogmatically in creeds the subject least within the compass of his faculties; and even to hate and persecute those who will not accept his views as true.

But though a knowledge of the Divine Essence is impossible, the conceptions formed respecting it are interesting, as indications of intellectual development. The history of religion is the history of the human mind; and the conception formed of Deity is always in exact relation to its moral and intellectual attainments. The one is the index and the measure of the other.

The *negative* notion of God, which consists in abstracting the inferior and finite, is, according to Philo, the only way in which it is possible for man worthily to apprehend the nature of God. After exhausting the varieties of symbolism, we contrast the Divine Greatness with human littleness, and employ expressions apparently affirmative, such as "Infinite," "Almighty," "All-wise," "Omnipotent," "Eternal," and the like; which in reality amount only to denying in regard to God those limits which confine the faculties of man; and thus we remain content with a name which is a mere conventional sign and confession of our ignorance.

The Hebrew יהוה and the Greek To ON expressed abstract existence, without outward manifestation or development. Of the same nature are the definitions, "God is a sphere whose centre is everywhere, and whose circumference nowhere:" "God is he who sees all, Himself unseen:" and finally, that of Proclus and Hegel—"the To μη ον—that which has no outward and positive existence." Most of the so-called ideas or definitions of the "Absolute" are only a collection of negations; from which, as they affirm nothing, nothing is learnt.

God was first recognized in the heavenly bodies and in the elements. When man's consciousness of his own intellectuality was matured, and he became convinced that the internal faculty of thought was something more subtle than even the most subtle elements, he transferred that new conception to the object of his worship, and deified a mental principle instead of a physical one. He in every case makes God after his own image; for do what we will, the highest efforts of human thought can conceive nothing higher than the supremacy of intellect; and so he ever comes back to some familiar type of exalted humanity. He at first deifies nature, and afterwards himself.

The eternal aspiration of the religious sentiment in man is to become united with God. In his earliest development, the wish and its fulfilment were simultaneous, through unquestioning belief. In proportion as the conception of Deity was exalted, the notion of his terrestrial presence or proximity was abandoned; and the difficulty of comprehending the Divine Government, together with the glaring superstitious evils arising out of its misinterpretation, endangered the belief in it altogether.

Even the lights of Heaven, which as "bright potentates of the sky," were formerly the vigilant directors of the economy of earth, now shine dim and distant, and Uriel no more descends upon a sunbeam. But the real change has been in the progressive ascent of man's own faculties, and not in the Divine Nature; as the Stars are no more distant now, than when they were supposed to rest on the shoulders of Atlas. And yet a little sense of disappointment and humiliation attended the first awakening of the soul, when reason, looking upwards towards the Deity, was impressed with a dizzy sense of having fallen.

But hope revives in despondency; and every nation that ever advanced beyond the most elementary conceptions, felt the necessity of an attempt to fill the chasm, real or imaginary, separating man from God. To do this was the great task of poetry, philosophy and religion. Hence the personifications of God's attributes, developments and manifestations, as "Powers," "Intelligences," "Angels," "Emanations;" through which and the oracular faculty in himself, man could place himself in communion with God.

The various ranks and orders of mythical beings imagined by Persians, Indians, Egyptians or Etrurians to preside over the various departments of nature, had each his share in a scheme to bring man into closer approximation to the Deity; they eventually gave way only before an analogous though less picturesque symbolism; and the Deities and Dæmons of Greece and Rome were perpetuated with only a change of names, when their offices were transferred to Saints and Martyrs. The attempts by which reason had sometimes endeavoured to span the unknown by a bridge of metaphysics, such as the idealistic systems of Zoroaster, Pythagoras or Plato, were only a more refined form of the poetical illusions which satisfied the vulgar; and man still looked back with longing to the lost golden age, when his ancestors communed face to face with the Gods; and hoped that by propitiating Heaven he might accelerate the renewal of it in the islands of the Far West, under the sceptre of Kronos, or in a centralization of political power at Jerusalem. His eager hope overcame even the terrors of the grave; for the Divine power was as infinite as human expectation, and the Egyptian duly ensepulchred in the Lybian Catacombs was supposed to be already on his way to the Fortunate Abodes under the guidance of Hermes, there to obtain a perfect association and reunion with his God.

Remembering what we have already said elsewhere in regard to the old ideas concerning the Deity, and repeating it as little as possible, let us once more put ourselves in communion with the Ancient poetic and philosophic mind, and endeavour to learn of it what it thought, and how it solved the great problems that have ever tortured the human intellect.

The division of the First and Supreme Cause into two parts, one Active and the other Passive, the Universe Agent and Patient, or the hermaphroditic God-World, is one of the most ancient and wide-spread dogmas of philosophy or natural theology. Almost every ancient people gave it a place in their worship, their Mysteries and their ceremonies.

Ocellus Lucanus, who seems to have lived shortly after Pythagoras opened his School in Italy, five or six hundred years before our era, and in the time of Solon, Thales and the other Sages who had studied in the Schools of Egypt, not only recognizes the eternity of the Universe, and its divine character as an unproduced and indestructible being, but also the distinction of Active and Passive causes in what he terms the Grand Whole, or the single hermaphroditic Being that comprehends all existences, as well causes as effects; and which is a system regularly ordered, perfect and complete, of all Natures. He well apprehended the dividing-line that separates existence eternally the same, from that which eternally changes; the nature of celestial from that of terrestrial bodies, that of causes from that of effects, that which is from that which only BECOMES, —a distinction that naturally struck every thinking man.

We shall not quote his language at full length. The heavenly bodies, he thought, are first and most noble; they move of themselves, and ever revolve, without change of form or essence. Fire, water, earth and air change incessantly and continually, not place, but form. Then, as in the Universe there is generation and cause of generation,—as generation is where there is change and displacement of parts, and cause where there is stability of nature, evidently it belongs to what is the cause of generation, to move and to act, and to the recipient, to be made and moved. In his view, everything above the Moon was the habitation of the Gods; all below, that of Nature and discord; *this* operates dissolution of things made; *that*, production of those that are being made. As the world is unproduced and indestructible, as it had no beginning, and will have no end, necessarily the principle that operates generation in another than itself, and that which operates it *in* itself, have co-existed.

The former is all above the moon, and especially the sun: the latter is the sublunary world. Of these two parts, one active, the other passive—one divine and always the same, the other mortal and ever changing, all that we call the "world" or "universe" is composed.

These accorded with the principles of the Egyptian philosophy, which held that man and the animals had always existed together with the world; that they were its effects, eternal like itself. The chief divisions of nature, into active and passive causes, its system of generation and destruction, and the concurrence of the two great principles, heaven and earth, uniting to form all things, will, according to Ocellus, always continue to exist. "Enough," he concludes, "as to the universe, the generations and destructions effected in it, the mode in which it now exists, the mode in which it will ever exist, by the eternal qualities of the two principles, one always moving, the other always moved, one always *governing*, the other always *governed*."

Such is a brief summary of the doctrine of this philosopher, whose work is one of the most ancient that have survived to us. The subject on which he treated occupied in his time all men's minds: the poets sang of cosmogonies and theogonies, and the philosophers wrote treatises on the birth of the world and the elements of its composition. The cosmogony of the Hebrews, attributed to Moses; that of the Phœnicians, ascribed to Sanchoniathon; that of the Greeks, composed by Hesiod; that of the Egyptians, the Atlantes and the Cretans, preserved by Diodorus Siculus; the fragments of the theology of Orpheus, divided among different writers; the books of the Persians, or their Boundesh; those of the Indians; the traditions of the Chinese and the people of Macassar; the cosmogonic chants which Virgil puts in the mouth of Iopas at Carthage; and those of the old Silenus, the first book of the Metamorphoses of Ovid; all testify to the antiquity and universality of these fictions as to the origin of the world and its causes.

At the head of the causes of nature, heaven and earth were placed, and the most apparent parts of each, the sun, the moon, the fixed stars and planets, and above all the zodiac, among the *active* causes of generation; and among the *passive*, the several elements. These causes were not only classed in the progressive order of their energy, heaven and earth heading the respective lists, but distinct sexes were in some sort assigned to them, and characteristics analogous to the mode in which they concur in universal generation.

The doctrine of Ocellus was the general doctrine everywhere, it naturally occurring to all to make the same distinction. The Egyptians did so, in selecting those animals in which they recognized these emblematic qualities, in order to symbolize the double sex of the universe. Their God KNEPH, out of whose mouth issued the Orphic egg, whence the author of the Clementine Recognitions makes a hermaphroditic figure to emerge, uniting in itself the two principles whereof heaven and the earth are forms, and which enter into the organization of all beings which the heavens and the earth engender by their concourse, furnishes another emblem of the double power, active and passive, which the ancients saw in the universe, and which they symbolized by the egg. Orpheus, who studied in Egypt, borrowed from the theologians of that country the mysterious forms under which the science of nature was veiled, and carried into Greece the symbolic egg, with its division into two parts or causes figured by the hermaphroditic being that issued from it, and whereof heaven and earth are composed.

The Brahmins of India expressed the same cosmogonic idea by a statue, representative of the universe, uniting in itself both sexes. The male sex offered an image of the sun, centre of the active principle, and the female sex that of the moon, at the sphere whereof, proceeding downward, the passive portion of nature begins. The Lingam, unto the present day revered in the Indian temples, being but the conjunction of the organs of generation of the two sexes, was an emblem of the same. The Hindūs have ever had the greatest veneration for this symbol of ever-reproductive nature. The Greeks consecrated the same symbols of universal fruitfulness in their Mysteries; and they were exhibited in the sanctuaries of Eleusis. They appear among the sculptured ornaments of all the Indian temples. Tertullian accuses the Valentinians of having adopted the custom of venerating them; a custom, he says, introduced by Melampus from Egypt into Greece. The Egyptians consecrated the Phallus in the Mysteries of Osiris and Isis, as we learn from Plutarch and Diodorus Siculus; and the latter assures us that these emblems were not consecrated by the Egyptians alone, but by every people. They certainly were so among the Persians and Assyrians; and they were regarded everywhere as symbolic of the generative and productive powers of all animated beings. In those early ages, the works of nature and all her agents were sacred like herself.

For the union of Nature with herself is a chaste marriage of which the union of man and woman was a natural image, and their organs were an expressive emblem of the double energy which manifests itself in Heaven and Earth uniting together to produce all beings. "The Heavens," says Plutarch, "seemed to men to fulfil the functions of father, and the Earth of mother. The former impregnated the earth with its fertilizing rains, and the earth receiving them became fruitful and brought forth." Heaven, which covers and embraces the earth everywhere, is her potent spouse, uniting himself to her to make her fruitful, without which she would languish in everlasting sterility, buried in the shades of chaos and of night. Their union is their marriage; their productions or parts are their children. The skies are our Father, and Nature the great Mother of us all.

This idea was not the dogma of a single sect, but the general opinion of all the Sages. "Nature was divided," says Cicero, "into two parts, one active, and the other that submitted itself to this action, which it received, and which modified it. The former was deemed to be a Force, and the latter the material on which that Force exerted itself." Macrobius repeated almost literally the doctrine of Ocellus. Aristotle termed the earth the fruitful mother, environed on all sides by the air. Above it was Heaven, the dwelling place of the Gods and the divine stars, its substance ether, or a fire incessantly moving in circles, divine and incorruptible and subject to no change. Below it, nature, and the elements, mutable and acted on, corruptible and mortal.

Synesius said that generations were effected in the portions of the universe which we inhabit; while the cause of generations resided in the portions above us, whence descend to us the germs of the effects produced here below. Proclus and Simplicius deemed Heaven the Active Cause and Father, relatively to the earth. The former says that the World or the Whole is a single Animal; what is done *in* it, is done *by* it; the same World *acts*, and *acts upon itself*. He divides it into "Heaven" and "Generation." In the former, he says, are placed and arranged the conservative causes of generation, superintended by the Genii and Gods. The Earth, or Rhea, associated ever with Saturn in production, is mother of the effects of which Heaven is Father; the womb or bosom that receives the fertilizing energy of the God that engenders ages. The great work of generation is operated, he says, primarily by the action of the Sun, and secondarily by that of the Moon, so that the Sun is the primitive source of this energy, as father and chief of the male Gods that form his court. He follows the action of the male and female principles through all the portions and divisions of nature, attributing to the former the origin of stability and identity, to the latter, that of diversity and mobility. Heaven is to the earth, he says, as the male to the female. It is the movement of the Heavens, that by their revolutions furnish the seminal incitements and forces, whose emanations received by the earth make it fruitful, and cause it to produce animals and plants of every kind.

Philo says that Moses recognized this doctrine of two causes, active and passive; but made the former to reside in the Mind or Intelligence external to matter.

The ancient astrologers divided the twelve signs of the Zodiac into six male and six female, and assigned them to six male and six female Great Gods. Heaven and Earth, or Ouranos and Ghê were, among most ancient nations, the first and most ancient Divinities. We find them in the Phœnician history of Sanchoniathon, and in the Grecian Genealogy of the Gods given by Hesiod. Everywhere they marry, and by their union produce the later Gods. "In the beginning," says Apollodorus, "Ouranos or the Heavens was Lord of all the Universe: he took to wife Ghê or the earth, and had by her many children." They were the first Gods of the Cretans, and under other names, of the Armenians, as we learn from Berosus, and of Panchaïa, an island South of Arabia, as we learn from Euhemerus. Orpheus made the Divinity, or the "Great Whole," male and female, because, he said, it could produce nothing, unless it united in itself the productive force of both sexes. He called Heaven PANGENETOR, the Father of all things, most ancient of Beings, beginning and end of all, containing in Himself the incorruptible and unwearying force of Necessity.

The same idea obtained in the rude North of Europe. The Scythians made the Earth to be the wife of Jupiter; and the Germans adored her under the name of HERTA. The Celts worshipped the Heavens and the Earth, and said that without the former the latter would be sterile, and that their marriage produced all things. The Scandinavians acknowledged BUR or the Heavens, and gave FORTUR his son the Earth as a wife. Olaus Rudbeck adds, that their ancestors were persuaded that Heaven intermarried with the Earth, and thus uniting his forces with hers, produced animals and plants. This marriage of Heaven and Earth produced the AZES, Genii famous in the theology of the North. In the theology of the Phrygians and Lydians, the Asii were born of the marriage of the Supreme God with the Earth; and Fermicus informs us that the Phrygians attributed to the Earth supremacy over the other elements, and considered her the Great Mother of all things.

Virgil sings the impregnation of the joyous earth, by the Ether, its spouse, that descends upon its bosom, fertilizing it with rains. Columella sings the loves of Nature and her marriage with heaven annually consummated at the sweet Spring-time. He describes the Spirit of Life, the soul that animates the world, fired with the passion of Love, uniting with Nature and itself, itself a part of Nature, and filling its own bosom with new productions. This union of the universe with itself, this mutual action of two sexes, he terms "the great Secrets of Nature," "the Mysteries of the Union of Heaven with Earth, imaged in the Sacred Mysteries of Atys and Bacchus."

Varro tells us that the great Divinities adored at Samothrace were the Heavens and the Earth, considered as First Causes or Primal Gods, and as male and female agents, one bearing to the other the relations that the Soul and Principle of Movement bear to the body or the matter that receives them. These were the Gods revered in the Mysteries of that Island, as they were in the orgies of Phœnicia.

Everywhere the sacred body of Nature was covered with the veil of allegory, which concealed it from the profane, and allowed it to be seen only by the sage who thought it worthy to be the object of his study and investigation. She showed herself to those only who loved her in spirit and in truth, and she abandoned the indifferent and careless to error and to ignorance. "The Sages of Greece," says Pausanias, "never wrote otherwise than in an enigmatical manner, never naturally and directly." "Nature," says Sallust the Philosopher, "should be sung only in a language that imitates the secrecy of her processes and operations. She is herself an enigma. We see only bodies in movement; the forces and springs that move them are hidden from us." The poets inspired by the Divinity, the wisest philosophers, all the theologians, the chiefs of the initiations and mysteries, even the gods uttering their oracles, have borrowed the figurative language of allegory." "The Egyptians," says Proclus, "preferred that mode of teaching, and spoke of the great secrets of Nature, only in mythological enigmas." The Gymnosophists of India and the Druids of Gaul lent to science the same enigmatic language, and in the same style wrote the Hierophants of Phœnicia.

The division of things into the active and the passive cause leads to that of the two Principles of Light and Darkness, connected with and corresponding with it. For Light comes from the ethereal substance that composes the active cause, and darkness from earth or the gross matter which composes the passive cause. In Hesiod, the Earth, by its union with Tartarus, engenders Typhon, Chief of the Powers or Genii of Darkness. But it unites itself with the Ether or Ouranos, when it engenders the Gods of Olympus, or the Stars, children of Starry Ouranos.

Light was the first Divinity worshipped by men. To it they owed the brilliant spectacle of Nature. It seems an emanation from the Creator of all things, making known to our senses the universe which darkness hides from our eyes; and as it were giving it existence. Darkness, as it were, reduces all nature again to nothingness, and almost entirely annihilates man.

Naturally, therefore, two substances of opposite natures were imagined, to each of which the world was in turn subjected, one contributing to its felicity and the other to its misfortune. Light multiplied its enjoyments; Darkness despoiled it of them; the former was its friend, the latter its enemy. To one all good was attributed; to the other all evil; and thus the words "Light" and "Good" became synonymous, and the words "Darkness" and "Evil." It seeming that Good and Evil could not flow from one and the same source, any more than could Light and Darkness, men naturally imagined two Causes or Principles, of different natures and opposite in their effects, one of which shed Light and Good, and the other Darkness and Evil on the universe.

This distinction of the two Principles was admitted in all the Theologies, and formed one of the principal bases of all religions. It entered as a primary element into the sacred fables, the cosmogonies and the mysteries of antiquity. "We are not to suppose," says Plutarch, "that the Principles of the Universe are inanimate bodies, as Democritus and Epicurus thought; nor that a matter devoid of qualities is organized and arranged by a single Reason or Providence, Sovereign over all things, as the Stoics held; for it is not possible that a single Being, good or evil, is the cause of all, inasmuch as God can in nowise be the cause of any evil. The harmony of the universe is a combination of contraries, like the strings of a lyre, or that of a bow, which alternately is stretched and relaxed." "The good," says Euripides, "is never separated from the Evil. The two must mingle, that all may go well." And this opinion as to the two Principles, continues Plutarch, "is that of all antiquity. From the Theologians and Legislators it passed to the Poets and Philosophers. Its author is unknown; but the opinion itself is established by the traditions of the whole human race, and consecrated in the mysteries and sacrifices both of the Greeks and Barbarians, wherein was recognized the dogma of opposing principles in nature, which by their contrariety, produce the mixture of good and evil. We must admit two contrary causes, two opposing powers, which lead, one to the right and the other to the left, and thus control our life, as they do the sublunary world, which is therefore subject to so many changes and irregularities of every kind. For if there can be no effect without a cause, and if the Good cannot be the cause of the Evil, it is absolutely necessary that there should be a cause for the Evil, as there is one for the Good." This doctrine, he adds, has been generally received among most nations, and especially by those who have had the greatest reputation for wisdom. All have admitted two gods with different occupations, one making the good and the other the evil found in nature. The former has been styled "God," the latter "Demon." The Persians or Zoroaster named the former Ormuzd and the latter Ahriman; of whom they said one was of the nature of Light, the other of that of Darkness. The Egyptians called the former Osiris, and the latter Typhon, his eternal enemy.

The Hebrews, at least after their return from the Persian captivity, had their good Deity, and the Devil, a bad and malicious Spirit, ever opposing God, and Chief of the Angels of Darkness, as God was of those of light.

The Chaldeans, Plutarch says, had their good and evil stars. The Greeks had their Jupiter and Pluto, and their Giants and Titans, to whom were assigned the attributes of the Serpent with which Pluto or Serapis was encircled, and the shape whereof was assumed by Typhon, Ahriman and the Satan of the Hebrews. Every people had something equivalent to this.

The People of Pegu believe in two Principles, one author of Good and the other of Evil, and strive to propitiate the latter, while they think it needless to worship the former, as he is incapable of doing evil. The people of Java, of the Moluccas, of the Gold Coast, the Hottentots, the people of Teneriffe and Madagascar and the Savage Tribes of America, all worship and strive to avert the anger and propitiate the good-will of the Evil Spirit.

But among the Greeks, Egyptians, Chaldeans, Persians and Assyrians, the doctrine of the two Principles formed a complete and regularly arranged theological system. It was the basis of the religion of the magi and of Egypt. The author of an ancient work attributed to Origen says that Pythagoras learned from Zarastha, a Magus at Babylon, (the same, perhaps, as Zerdusht or Zoroaster), that there are two principles of all things, whereof one is the *father* and the other the *mother*; the former, Light, and the latter, Darkness. Pythagoras thought that the Dependencies on Light were warmth, dryness, lightness, swiftness; and those on Darkness, cold, wet, weight and slowness; and that the world derived its existence from these two principles, as from the male and the female. According to Porphyry, he conceived two opposing powers, one good, which he termed Unity, the Light, Right, the Equal, the Stable, the Straight; the other evil, which he termed Binary, Darkness, the Left, the Unequal, the Unstable, the Crooked. These ideas he received from the Orientals, for he dwelt twelve years at Babylon, studying with the Magi. Varro says he recognized two Principles of all things,—the Finite and the Infinite, Good and Evil, Life and Death, Day and Night. White he thought was of the nature of the Good Principle, and Black of that of the Evil; that Light and Darkness, Heat and Cold, the Dry and the Wet, mingled in equal proportions; that summer was the triumph of heat, and winter of cold; that their equal combination produced spring and autumn, the former producing verdure and favourable to health, and the latter, deteriorating everything, giving birth to maladies. He applied the same idea to the rising and setting of the sun; and like the Magi, held that God or Ormuzd in the body resembled light, and in the soul, truth.

Aristotle, like Plato, admitted a principle of Evil, resident in matter and in its eternal imperfection.

The Persians said that Ormuzd, born of the pure Light, and Ahriman, born of darkness, were ever at war. Ormuzd produced six Gods, Beneficence, Truth, Good Order, Wisdom, Riches and Virtuous Joy. These were so many emanations from the Good Principle, so many blessings bestowed by it on men. Ahriman, in his turn, produced six Devs, opponents of the six emanations from Ormuzd. Then Ormuzd made himself three times as great as before, ascended as far above the sun as the sun is above the earth, and adorned the Heavens with stars, of which he made Sirius the sentinel or advance-guard : that he then created twenty-four other Deities, and placed them in an egg, where Ahriman also placed twenty-four others, created by him, who broke the egg, and so intermingled Good and Evil. Theopompus adds that, according to the Magi, for two terms of three thousand years each of the two Principles is to be by turns victor and the other vanquished ; then for three thousand more for each they are to contend with each other, each destroying reciprocally the works of the other; after which Ahriman to perish, and men, wearing transparent bodies, to enjoy unutterable happiness.

The twelve great Deities of the Persians, the six Amshaspands and six Devs, marshalled, the former under the banner of Light, and the latter under that of Darkness, are the twelve Zodiacal Signs or Months ; the six supreme signs, or those of Light, or of Spring and Summer, commencing with Aries, and the six inferior, of Darkness or of Autumn and Winter, commencing with Libra. Limited Time, as contradistinguished from Time without limits, or Eternity, is Time created and measured by the celestial revolutions. It is comprehended in a period divided into twelve parts, each subdivided into a thousand parts, which the Persians termed years. Thus the circle annually traversed by the Sun was divided into 12,000 parts, or each sign into 3,000 : and thus, each year, the Principle of Light and Good triumphed for 3,000 years, that of Evil and Darkness for 3,000, and they mutually destroyed each other's labours for 6,000, or 3,000 for each: so that the Zodiac was equally divided between them. And accordingly Ocellus Lucanus, the Disciple of Pythagoras, held that the principal cause of all sublunary effects resided in the Zodiac, and that from it flowed the good or bad influences of the planets that revolved therein.

The twenty-four good, and twenty-four evil Deities, enclosed in the Egg, are the forty-eight constellations of the ancient sphere, equally divided between the realms of Light and Darkness, on the concavity of the celestial sphere which was apportioned among them ; and which enclosing the world and planets, was the mystic and sacred egg of the Magi, the Indians and the Egyptians,—the egg that issued from the mouth of the God Kneph, that figured as the Orphic Egg in the Mysteries of Greece, that issued from the God Chumong of the Coresians, and from the Egyptian Osiris and the God Phanes of the Modern Orphics, Principle of Light,—the egg crushed by the Sacred Bull of the Japanese, and from which the world emerged; that placed by the Greeks at the feet of Bacchus the bull-horned God, and from which Aristophanes makes Love emerge, who with Night organizes Chaos.

Thus the Balance, the Scorpion, the Serpent of Ophiucus and the Dragon of the Hesperides became malevolent Signs and Evil Genii ; and entire nature was divided between the two principles, and between the agents or partial causes subordinate to them. Hence Michael and his Archangels, and Satan and his fallen compeers. Hence the wars of Jupiter and the Giants, in which the Gods of Olympus fought on the side of the Light-God, against the dark progeny of earth and Chaos ; a war which Proclus regarded as symbolizing the resistance opposed by dark and chaotic matter to the active and beneficent force which gives it organization ; an idea which in part appears in the old theory of two Principles, one innate in the active and luminous substance of Heaven, and the other in the inert and dark substance of matter that resists the order and the good that Heaven communicates to it.

Osiris conquers Typhon, and Ormuzd, Ahriman, when, at the Vernal Equinox, the creative action of Heaven and its demiourgic energy is most strongly manifested. Then the principle of Light and Good overcomes that of Darkness and Evil, and the world rejoices, redeemed from cold and wintry darkness by the beneficent Sign into which the Sun then enters triumphant and rejoicing, after his resurrection.

From the doctrine of the two Principles, Active and Passive, grew that of the Universe animated by a Principle of Eternal Life, and by a Universal Soul, from which every isolated and temporary being received at its birth an emanation, which at the death of such being, returned to its source. The life of matter as much belonged to nature as did matter itself; and as life is manifested by movement, the sources of life must needs seem to be placed in those luminous and eternal bodies, and above all in the Heaven in which they revolve, and which whirls them along with itself in that rapid course that is swifter than all other movement. And fire and heat have so great an analogy with life, that cold, like absence of movement, seemed the distinctive characteristic of death. Accordingly the vital fire that blazes in the Sun and produces the heat that vivifies everything, was regarded as the principle of organization and life of all sublunary beings.

According to this doctrine, the Universe is not to be regarded in its creative and eternal action, merely as an immense machine, moved by powerful springs and forced into a continual movement, which, emanating from the circumference extends to the centre, acts and re-acts in every possible direction, and re-produces in succession all the varied forms which matter receives. So to regard it would be to recognize a cold and purely mechanical action, the energy of which could never produce life.

On the contrary, it was thought, the Universe should be deemed an immense Being, always living, always moved and always moving in an eternal activity inherent in itself, and which, subordinate to no foreign cause, is communicated to all its parts, connects them together, and makes of the world of things a complete and perfect whole. The order and harmony which reign therein seem to belong to and be a part of it, and the design of the various plans of construction of organized beings would seem to be graven in its Supreme Intelligence, source of all the other Intelligences which it communicates together with life to man. Nothing existing out of it, it must be regarded as the principle and term of all things.

Chœremon had no reason for saying that the Ancient Egyptians, inventors of the sacred fables, and adorers of the Sun and the other luminaries, saw in the Universe only a machine, without life and without intelligence, either in its whole or in its parts; and that their cosmogony was a pure Epicureanism, which required only matter and movement, to organize its world and govern it. Such an opinion would necessarily exclude all religious worship. Wherever we suppose a worship, there we must suppose intelligent Deities who receive it, and are sensible to the homage of their adorers; and no people were so religious as the Egyptians.

On the contrary, with them the immense, immutable and Eternal Being, termed "God" or "the Universe," had eminently and in all their plenitude, that life and intelligence which sublunary beings, each an infinitely small and temporary portion of itself, possess in a far inferior degree and infinitely less quantity. It was to them in some sort like the Ocean, whence the springs, brooks and rivers have risen by evaporation and to the bosom whereof they return by a longer or shorter course, and after a longer or shorter separation from the immense mass of its waters. The machine of the Universe was, in their view, like that of man, moved by a Principle of Life which kept it in eternal activity, and circulated in all its parts. The Universe was a living and animated being, like man and the other animals; or rather they were so, only because the Universe was essentially so, and for a few moments communicated to each an infinitely minute portion of its eternal life, breathed by it into the inert and gross matter of sublunary bodies. That withdrawn, man or the animal died; and the Universe alone, living and circulating around the wrecks of their bodies, by its eternal movement, organized and animated new bodies, returning to them the eternal fire and subtle substance which vivifies itself, and which incorporated in its immense mass was its universal soul.

These were the ancient ideas as to this Great God, Father of all the Gods, or of the World; of this BEING, Principle of all things, and of which nothing other than itself is Principle,—the Universal cause that was termed God. Soul of the Universe, eternal like it, immense like it, supremely active and potent in its varied operations, penetrating all parts of this vast body, impressing a regular and symmetrical movement on the spheres, making the elements instinct with activity and order, mingling with everything, organizing everything, vivifying and preserving everything,—this was the UNIVERSE-GOD which the Ancients adored as Supreme Cause and God of Gods.

Anchises, in the Æneid, taught Æneas this doctrine of Pythagoras, learned by him from his Masters, the Egyptians, in regard to the Soul and Intelligence of the Universe, from which our souls and intelligences, as well as our life and that of the animals emanate. Heaven, Earth, the Sea, the Moon and the Stars, he said, are moved by a principle of internal life which perpetuates their existence; a great intelligent soul, that penetrates every part of the vast body of the Universe, and mingling with everything, agitates it by an eternal movement. It is the source of life in all living things. The force which animates all, emanates from the eternal fire that burns in Heaven. In the Georgics, Virgil repeats the same doctrine; and that at the death of every animal, the life that animated it, part of the universal life, returns to its Principle and to the source of life that circulates in the sphere of the Stars.

Servius makes God the active Cause that organizes the elements into bodies, the vivifying breath or spirit, that, spreading through matter or the elements, produces and engenders all things. The elements compose the substance of our bodies: God composes the souls that vivify these bodies. From it come the instincts of animals, from it their life, he says: and when they die, that life returns to and re-enters into the Universal Soul, and their bodies into Universal Matter.

Timæus of Locria and Plato his Commentator wrote of the Soul of the World, developing the doctrine of Pythagoras, who thought, says Cicero, that God is the Universal Soul, resident everywhere in nature, and of which our Souls are but emanations. "*God is one*," says Pythagoras, as cited by Justin Martyr: "He is not, as some think, *without* the world, but within it, and entire in its entirety. He sees all that *becomes*, forms all immortal beings, is the author of their powers and performances, the origin of all things, the Light of Heaven, the *Father*, the *Intelligence*, the *Soul* of all beings, the Mover of all spheres."

God, in the view of Pythagoras, was ONE, a single substance, whose continuous parts extend through all the Universe, without separation, difference or inequality; like the soul in the human body. He denied the doctrine of the spiritualists, who had severed the Divinity from the Universe, making Him exist apart from the Universe, which thus became no more than a material work, on which acted the Abstract Cause, a God, isolated from it. The Ancient Theology did not so separate God from the Universe. This Eusebius attests, in saying that but a small number of wise men, like Moses, had sought for God or the Cause of all, outside of that ALL; while the Philosophers of Egypt and Phœnicia, real authors of all the old Cosmogonies, had placed the Supreme Cause *in* the Universe itself, and in its parts, so that in their view the world and all its parts are *in* God.

The World or Universe was thus compared to man; the Principle of Life that moves it, to that which moves man: the Soul of the World to that of man. Therefore Pythagoras called man a *microcosm* or little world, as possessing in miniature all the qualities found on a great scale in the Universe; by his reason and intelligence partaking of the Divine Nature: and by his faculty of changing aliments into other substances, of growing, and reproducing himself, partaking of elementary Nature. Thus he made the Universe a great intelligent Being, like man—an immense Deity, having in itself what man has in himself, movement, life and intelligence, and besides, a perpetuity of existence, which man has not; and, as having in itself perpetuity of movement and life, therefore the Supreme Cause of all.

Everywhere extended, this Universal Soul does not, in the view of Pythagoras, act everywhere equally nor in the same manner. The highest portion of the Universe, being as it were its head, seemed to him its principal seat, and there was the guiding power of the rest of the world. In the seven concentric spheres is resident an eternal order, fruit of the intelligence, the Universal Soul that moves, by a constant and regular progression, the immortal bodies that form the harmonious system of the Heavens.

Manilius says: "I sing the invisible and potent Soul of Nature; that Divine Substance which everywhere inherent in Heaven, Earth and the Waters of the Ocean, forms the bond that holds together and makes one all the parts of the vast body of the Universe. It, balancing all Forces, and harmoniously arranging the varied relations of the many members of the world, maintains in it the life and regular movement that agitate it, as a result of the action of the living breath or single spirit that dwells in all its parts, circulates in all the channels of universal nature, flashes with rapidity to all its points, and gives to animated bodies the configurations appropriate to the organization of each . . . . This eternal Law, this Divine Force, that maintains the harmony of the world, makes use of the Celestial Signs to organize and guide the animated creatures that breathe upon the earth; and gives to each of them the character and habits most appropriate. By the action of this Force Heaven rules the condition of the Earth and of its fields cultivated by the husbandman: it gives us or takes from us vegetation and harvests: it makes the great ocean overpass its limits at the flow, and retire within them again at the ebbing, of the tide."

Thus it is no longer by means of a poetic fiction only that the heavens and the earth become animated and personified, and are deemed living existences, from which other existences proceed. For now they live with their own life, a life eternal like their bodies, each gifted with a life and perhaps a soul, like those of man, a portion of the universal life and universal soul; and the other bodies that they form, and which they contain in their bosoms, live only through them and with their life, as the embryo lives in the bosom of its mother, in consequence and by means of the life communicated to it, and which the mother ever maintains by the active power of her own life. Such is the universal life of the world, reproduced in all the beings which its superior portion creates in its inferior portion, that is as it were the *matrix* of the world, or of the beings that the heavens engender in its bosom.

"The soul of the world," says Macrobius, "is nature itself" [as the soul of man is man himself], "always acting through the celestial spheres which it moves, and which but follow the irresistible impulse it impresses on them. The heavens, the sun, great seat of generative power, the signs, the stars and the planets act only with the activity of the soul of the universe. From that soul, through them, come all the variations and changes of sublunary nature, of which the heavens and celestial bodies are but the secondary causes. The zodiac, with its signs, is an existence, immortal and divine, organized by the universal soul, and producing, or gathering in itself, all the varied emanations of the different powers that make up the nature of the Divinity."

This doctrine, that gave to the heavens and the spheres living souls, each a portion of the universal soul, was of extreme antiquity. It was held by the old Sabæans. It was taught by Timæus, Plato, Speusippus, Iamblichus, Macrobius, Marcus Aurelius and Pythagoras. When once men had assigned a soul to the universe, containing in itself the plenitude of the animal life of particular beings, and even of the stars, they soon supposed that soul to be essentially intelligent, and the source of intelligence of all intelligent beings. Then the universe became to them not only animated but intelligent, and of that intelligence the different parts of nature partook. Each soul was the vehicle and as it were the envelope of the intelligence that attached itself to it, and could repose nowhere else. Without a soul there could be no intelligence; and as there was a universal soul, source of all souls, the universal soul was gifted with a universal intelligence, source of all particular intelligences. So the soul of the world contained in itself the intelligence of the world. All the agents of nature into which the universal soul entered, received also a portion of its intelligence, and the universe, in its totality and in its parts, was filled with intelligences, that might be regarded as so many emanations from the sovereign and universal intelligence. Wherever the divine soul acted as a cause, there also was intelligence; and thus heaven, the stars, the elements, and all parts of the universe, became the seats of so many divine intelligences. Every minutest portion of the great soul became a partial intelligence, and the more it was disengaged from gross matter, the more active and intelligent it was. And all the old adorers of nature, the theologians, astrologers and poets, and the most distinguished philosophers, supposed that the stars were so many animated and intelligent beings, or eternal bodies, active causes of effects here below, whom a principle of life animated, and whom an intelligence directed, which was but an emanation from and a portion of the universal life and intelligence of the world.

The universe itself was regarded as a supremely intelligent being. Such was the doctrine of Timæus of Locria. The soul of man was part of the intelligent soul of the universe, and therefore itself intelligent. His opinion was that of many other philosophers. Cleanthes, a disciple of Zeno, regarded the universe as God, or as the unproduced and universal cause of all effects produced. He ascribed a soul and intelligence to universal nature, and to this intelligent soul, in his view, divinity belonged. From it the intelligence of man was an emanation, and shared its divinity. Chrysippus, the most subtle of the Stoics, placed in the universal reason that forms the soul and intelligence of nature, that divine force or essence of the Divinity which he assigned to the world moved by the universal soul that pervades its every part.

An interlocutor in Cicero's work, *De Natura Deorum*, formally argues that the universe is necessarily intelligent and wise, because man, an infinitely small portion of it, is so. Cicero makes the same argument in his oration for Milo. The physicists came to the same conclusion as the philosophers. They supposed that movement essentially belonged to the soul, and the direction of regular and ordered movements to the intelligence. And as both movement and order exist in the universe, therefore, they held, there must be in it a soul and an intelligence that rule it, and are not to be distinguished from itself; because the idea of the universe is but the aggregate of all the particular ideas of all things that exist.

The argument was, that the Heavens, and the Stars which make part of them are *animated*, because they possess a portion of the Universal Soul: they are *intelligent* beings, because that Universal Soul, part whereof they possess, is supremely intelligent: and they share *Divinity* with Universal Nature, because Divinity resides in the Universal Soul and Intelligence which move and rule the world, and of each of which they hold a share.

By this process of logic, the interlocutor in Cicero assigned Divinity to the Stars, as animated beings gifted with sensibility and intelligence, and composed of the noblest and purest portion of the ethereal substance, unmixed with matter of an alien nature, and essentially containing light and heat. Hence he concluded them to be so many Gods, of an intelligence superior to that of other Existences, corresponding to the lofty height in which they moved with such perfect regularity and admirable harmony, with a movement spontaneous and free. Hence he made them "Gods," active, eternal and intelligent "Causes;" and peopled the realm of Heaven with a host of Eternal Intelligences, celestial Genii or Angels, sharing the universal Divinity, and associated with it in the administration of the Universe, and the dominion exercised over sublunary nature and man.

We make the motive force of the planets to be a mechanical law, which we explain by the combination of two forces, the centripetal and centrifugal, whose *origin* we cannot demonstrate, but whose *force* we can calculate. The ancients regarded them as moved by an intelligent force that had its origin in the first and universal Intelligence. Is it so certain, after all, that we are any nearer the truth than they were; or that we know what our "centripetal and centrifugal forces" *mean;* for what *is* a *force?* With us, the entire Deity acts upon and moves each planet, as He does the sap that circulates in the little blade of grass, and in the particles of blood in the tiny veins of the invisible rotifer. With the Ancients, the Deity of each Star was but a portion of the Universal God, the Soul of Nature. Each Star and Planet, with them, was moved of *itself,* and directed by *its own* special intelligence. And this opinion of Achilles Tatius, Diodorus, Chrysippus, Aristotle, Plato, Heraclides of Pontus, Theophrastus, Simplicius, Macrobius and Proclus, that in each Star there is an immortal Soul and Intelligence,—part of the Universal Soul and Intelligence of the Whole,—this opinion of Orpheus, Plotinus and the Stoics, was in reality that of many Christian philosophers. For Origen held the same opinion; and Augustin held that every visible thing in the world was superintended by an Angelic Power: and Cosmas the Monk believed that every Star was under the guidance of an Angel; and the author of the Octateuch, written in the time of the Emperor Justin, says that they are moved by the impulse communicated to them by Angels stationed above the firmament. Whether the stars were animated beings, was a question that Christian antiquity did not decide. Many of the Christian doctors believed they were. Saint Augustin hesitates, Saint Jerome doubts if Solomon did not assign souls to the Stars. Saint Ambrose does not doubt they *have* souls; and Pamphilus says that many of the Church believe they are reasonable beings, while many think otherwise, but that neither one nor the other opinion is heretical.

Thus the Ancient Thought, earnest and sincere, wrought out the idea of a Soul *inherent* in the Universe and in its several parts. The next step was to *separate* that Soul from the Universe, and give to it an external and independent existence and personality; still omnipresent, in every inch of space and in every particle of matter, and yet not a part of Nature, but its Cause and its Creator. This is the middle ground between the two doctrines, of Pantheism (or that all is God, and God is *in* all and is all), on the one side, and Atheism (or that all is nature, and there is no other God), on the other; which doctrines, after all, when reduced to their simplest terms, seem to be the same.

We complacently congratulate ourselves on our recognition of a *personal* God, as being the conception most suited to human sympathies, and exempt from the mystifications of Pantheism. But the Divinity remains still a mystery, notwithstanding all the devices which symbolism, either from the organic or inorganic creation, can supply; and personification is itself a symbol, liable to misapprehension as much as, if not more so than, any other, since it is apt to degenerate into a mere reflection of our own infirmities; and hence *any* affirmative idea or conception that we can in our own minds picture of the Deity must needs be infinitely inadequate.

The spirit of the Vedas (or sacred Indian Books, of great antiquity), as understood by their earliest as well as most recent expositors, is decidedly a pantheistic-monotheism—one God, and He all in all; the many divinities, numerous as the prayers addressed to them, being resolvable into the titles and attributes of a few, and ultimately into The One. The machinery of personification was understood to have been unconsciously assumed as a mere expedient to supply the deficiencies of language; and the Mimansa justly considered itself as only interpreting the true meaning of the Mantras, when it proclaimed that, in the beginning, "Nothing was but Mind, the Creative thought of Him which existed alone from the beginning, and breathed without afflation." The idea suggested in the Mantras is dogmatically asserted and developed in the Upanischadas.

The Vedanta philosophy, assuming the mystery of the "ONE IN MANY" as the fundamental article of faith, maintained not only the Divine Unity, but the identity of matter and spirit. The unity which it advocates is that of mind. Mind is the Universal Element, the One God, the Great Soul, Mahaatma. He is the material as well as efficient cause, and the world is a texture of which he is both the web and the weaver. He is the Macrocosmos, the universal organism called Pooroosha, of which Fire, Air, and Sun are only the chief members. His head is light, his eyes the sun and moon, his breath the wind, his voice the opened Vedas. All proceeds from Brahm, like the web from the spider and the grass from the earth.

Yet it is only the impossibility of expressing in language the origination of matter from spirit, which gives to Hindū philosophy the appearance of materialism. Formless himself, the Deity is present in all forms. His glory is displayed in the universe as the image of the sun in water, which is, yet is not, the luminary itself. All material agency and appearance, the subjective world, are to a great extent phantasms, the notional representations of ignorance. They occupy, however, a middle ground between reality and non-reality; they are unreal, because nothing exists but Brahm; yet in some degree real, inasmuch as they constitute an outward manifestation of him. They are a self-induced hypostasis of the Deity, under which he *presents to himself* the whole of animate and inanimate Nature, the actuality of the moment, the diversified *appearances* which successively invest the one Pantheistic spirit.

The great aim of reason is to generalize; to discover unity in multiplicity, order in apparent confusion; to separate from the accidental and the transitory, the stable and universal. In the contemplation of Nature, and the vague, but almost intuitive perception of a general uniformity of plan among endless varieties of operation and form, arise those solemn and reverential feelings, which, if accompanied by intellectual activity, may eventually ripen into philosophy.

Consciousness of self and of personal identity is co-existent with our existence. We cannot conceive of mental existence without it. It is not the work of reflection nor of logic, nor the result of observation, experiment and experience. It is a gift from God, like instinct; and that consciousness of a thinking soul which is really the person that we are, and other than our body, is the best and most solid proof of the soul's existence. We have the same consciousness of a Power on which we are dependent; which we can *define* and form an idea or picture of, as little as we can of the soul, and yet which we *feel* and therefore *know* exists. True and correct ideas of that Power, of the Absolute Existence from which all proceeds, we cannot trace; if by true and correct we mean *adequate* ideas; for of such we are not, with our limited faculties, capable. And ideas of His nature, so far correct as we are capable of entertaining, can only be attained either by direct inspiration or by the investigations of philosophy.

The idea of the universal preceded the recognition of any system for its explanation. It was *felt* rather than understood; and it was long before the grand conception on which all philosophy rests received through deliberate investigation that analytical development which might properly entitle it to the name. The sentiment, when first observed by the self-conscious mind was, says Plato, "a Divine gift communicated to mankind by some Prometheus, or by those ancients who lived nearer to the Gods than our degenerate selves." The mind deduced from its first experiences the notion of a general Cause or Antecedent, to which it shortly gave a name and personified it. This was the statement of a theorem, obscure in proportion to its generality. *It explained all things but itself.* It was a *true* cause, but an *incomprehensible* one. Ages had to pass, before the nature of the theorem could be rightly appreciated, and before men, acknowledging the First Cause to be an object of faith rather than science, were contented to confine their researches to those nearer relations of existence and succession, which are really within the reach of their faculties. At first, and for a long time, the intellect deserted the real for a hastily-formed ideal world, and the imagination usurped the place of reason, in attempting to put a construction on the most general and inadequate of conceptions, by transmuting its symbols into realities, and by substantializing it under a thousand arbitrary forms.

In poetry, the idea of Divine unity became, as in Nature, obscured by a multifarious symbolism; and the notionalities of transcendental philosophy reposed on views of nature scarcely more profound than those of the earliest symbolists. Yet the idea of unity was rather obscured than extinguished; and Xenophanes appeared as an enemy of Homer, only because he more emphatically insisted on the monotheistic element; which in poetry has been comparatively overlooked. The first philosophy re-asserted the unity which poetry had lost; but being unequal to investigate its nature, it again resigned it to the world of approximate sensations, and became bewildered in materialism, considering the conceptional whole or First Element as some refinement of matter, unchangeable in its essence, though subject to mutations of quality and form in an eternal succession of seeming decay and regeneration; comparing it to water, air or fire, as each endeavoured to refine on the doctrine of his predecessor, or was influenced by a different class of theological traditions.

In the philosophical systems, the Divine Activity, divided by the poets and by popular belief among a race of personifications, in whom the idea of descent replaced that of cause, or of pantheistic evolution, was restored without subdivision or reservation to nature as a whole; at first as a mechanical *force* or *life;* afterwards as an all-pervading *soul* or inherent *thought;* and lastly as an external directing *Intelligence.*

The Ionian revival of pantheism was materialistic. The Moving Force was inseparable from a material element, a subtle yet visible ingredient. Under the form of *air* or *fire,* the principle of life was associated with the most obvious material machinery of nature. Everything, it was said, is alive and full of Gods. The wonders of the volcano, the magnet, the ebb and flow of the tide, were vital indications, the breathing or moving of the Great World-Animal. The imperceptible ether of Anaximenes had no *positive* quality beyond the atmospheric air with which it was easily confused: and even the "Infinite" of Anaximander, though free of the conditions of quality or quantity, was only an ideal chaos, relieved of its coarseness by negations. It was the illimitable store-house or Pleroma, out of which is evolved the endless circle of phenomenal change. A moving Force was recognized *in,* but not clearly distinguished *from* the material. Space, Time, Figure and Number, and other common forms or properties, which exist only as *attributes,* were treated as *substances,* or at least as making a substantial connection between the objects to which they belong: and all the conditions of material existence were supposed to have been evolved out of the Pythagorean Monad.

The Eleatic philosophers treated conceptions not only as entities, but as the only entities, alone possessing the stability and certainty and reality vainly sought among phenomena. The only reality was Thought. "All *real* existence," they said, "is *mental* existence; non-existence being inconceivable is therefore impossible; existence fills up the whole range of thought, and is inseparable from its exercise; thought and its object are one."

Xenophanes used ambiguous language, applicable to the material as well as to the mental, and exclusively appropriate to neither. In other words, he availed himself of material imagery to illustrate an indefinite meaning. In announcing the universal being, he appealed to the Heavens as the visible manifestation, calling it *spherical,* a term borrowed from the material world. He said that God was neither moved nor unmoved, limited nor unlimited. He did not even attempt to express clearly what cannot be conceived clearly; admitting, says Simplicius, that such speculations were above physics. Parmenides employed similar expedients, comparing his metaphysical Deity to a sphere, or to heat, an aggregate or a continuity, and so involuntarily withdrawing its nominal attributes.

The Atomic school, dividing the All into Matter and Force, deemed matter unchangeable in its ultimate constitution, though infinitely variable in its resultant forms. They made all variety proceed from the varied combinations of atoms; but they required no mover or director of the atoms external to themselves; no universal Reason; but a Mechanical Eternal *Necessity,* like that of the Poets. Still it is doubtful whether there ever was a time when reason could be said to be entirely asleep, a stranger to its own existence, notwithstanding this apparent materialism. The earliest contemplation of the external world, which brings it into an imagined association with ourselves, assigns either to its whole or its parts the sensation and volition which belong to our own souls.

Anaxagoras admitted the existence of ultimate elementary particles, as Empedocles did, from the combinations whereof all material phenomena resulted. But he asserted the Moving Force to be Mind; and yet, though he clearly saw the impossibility of advancing by illustration or definition beyond a reasonable faith, or a simple negation of materiality, yet he could not wholly desist from the endeavour to illustrate the nature of this non-matter or mind, by symbols drawn from those physical considerations which decided him in placing it in a separate category. Whether as human reason, or as the regulating Principle in nature, he held it different from all other things in character and effect, and that therefore it must necessarily differ in its essential constitution. It was neither Matter, nor a Force conjoined with matter, or homogeneous with it, but independent and generically distinct, especially in this, that being the source of all motion, separation and cognition, it is something entirely unique, pure and unmixed; and so being unhindered by any interfering influence limiting its independence of individual action, it has Supreme Empire over all things, over the vortex of worlds as well as over all that live in them. It is most penetrating and powerful, mixing with other things, though no other thing mixes with it; exercises universal control and cognition, and includes the *Necessity* of the Poets, as well as the independent power of thought which we exercise within ourselves. In short, it is the self-conscious power of thought extended to the universe, and exalted into the Supreme External Mind which sees, knows and directs all things.

Thus Pantheism and Materialism were both avoided; and matter, though as infinitely varied as the senses represent it, was held in a bond of unity transferred to a ruling power apart from it. That Power could not be Prime Mover, if it were itself moved; nor All-Governing, if not apart from the things it governs. If the arranging Principle were *inherent* in matter, it would have been impossible to account for the existence of a chaos: if something *external*, then the old Ionian doctrine of a "beginning" became more easily conceivable, as being the epoch at which the Arranging Intelligence commenced its operations.

But this grand idea of an all-governing independent mind involved difficulties which proved insuperable; because it gave to matter in the form of chaos an independent and eternal self-existence, and so introduced a dualism of mind and matter. In the Mind or Intelligence, Anaxagoras included not only life and motion, but the moral principles of the noble and good; and probably used the term on account of the popular misapplication of the word "God," and as being less liable to misconstruction, and more specifically marking his idea. His "Intelligence" principle remained practically liable to many of the same defects as the "Necessity" of the poets. It was the presentiment of a great idea, which it was for the time impossible to explain or follow out. It was not yet intelligible, nor was even the road opened through which it might be approached.

Mind cannot advance in metaphysics beyond self-deification. In attempting to go further, it only enacts the apotheosis of its own subtle conceptions, and so sinks below the simpler ground already taken. The realities which Plato could not recognize in phenomena, he discovered within his own mind, and as unhesitatingly as the old Theosophists installed its creations among the Gods. He, like most philosophers after Anaxagoras, made the Supreme Being to be Intelligence; but in other respects left his nature undefined, or rather indefinite through the variety of definitions, a conception vaguely floating between Theism and Pantheism. Though deprecating the demoralizing tendencies of poetry, he was too wise to attempt to replace them by other representations of a positive kind. He justly says, that spiritual things can be made intelligible only through figures; and the forms of allegorical expression which in a rude age had been adopted unconsciously, were designedly chosen by the philosopher as the most appropriate vehicles for theological ideas.

As the devices of symbolism were gradually stripped away, in order, if possible, to reach the fundamental conception, the religious feeling habitually connected with it seemed to evaporate under the process. And yet the advocates of Monotheism, Xenophanes and Heraclitus, declaimed only against the making of Gods in human form. They did not attempt to strip nature of its divinity, but rather to recall religious contemplation from an exploded symbolism to a purer one. They continued the veneration which in the background of poetry has been maintained for Sun and Stars, the Fire or Ether. Socrates prostrated himself before the rising luminary; and the eternal spheres which seem to have shared the religious homage of Xenophanes, retained a secondary and qualified Divinity in the Schools of the Peripatetics and Stoics.

The unseen being or beings revealed only to the Intellect became the theme of philosophy; and their more ancient symbols, if not openly discredited, were passed over with evasive generality, as beings respecting whose problematical existence we must be "content with what has been reported by those ancients, who, assuming to be their descendants, must therefore be supposed to have been well acquainted with their own ancestors and family connections." And the Theism of Anaxagoras was still more decidedly subversive, not only of Mythology, but of the whole religion of outward nature; it being an appeal from the world without, to the consciousness of spiritual dignity within man.

In the doctrines of Aristotle, the world moves on uninterruptedly, always changing, yet ever the same, like Time, the Eternal Now, knowing neither repose nor death. There is a principle which makes good the failure of *identity*, by multiplying *resemblances;* the destruction of the *individual* by an eternal renewal of the *form* in which matter is manifested.' This regular eternal *movement* implies an Eternal Mover; not an inert Eternity, such as the Platonic *Eidos*, but one always *acting*, his *essence* being *to act*, for otherwise he might *never* have acted, and the existence of the world would be an accident; for what should have, in that case, decided Him to act, after long inactivity? Nor can he be partly *in act* and partly *potential*, that is, quiescent and undetermined to act or not to act, for even in that case motion would not be eternal, but contingent and precarious. He is therefore *wholly in act*, a pure, untiring activity, and for the same reasons wholly immaterial. Thus Aristotle avoided the idea that God was inactive and self-contemplative for an eternity, and then for some unknown reason, or by some unknown motive commenced to act outwardly and produce; but he incurred the opposite hazard, of making the result of His action, matter and the Universe, be co-existent with Himself; or, in other words, of denying that there was any time when his outward action *commenced.*

The First Cause, he said, unmoved, moves all. *Act* was *first*, and the Universe has existed forever; one persistent cause directing its continuity. The *unity* of the First Mover follows from His immateriality. If he were not himself unmoved, the series of motions and causes of motion would be infinite. Unmoved, therefore, and unchangeable himself, all movement, even that in space, is caused by Him: He is necessary; He cannot be otherwise than as He is; and it is only through the necessity of His being that we can account for those necessary eternal relations which make a science of Being possible. Thus Aristotle leaned to a seemingly personal God; not a Being of parts and passions, like the God of the Hebrews or that of the mass even of educated men in our own day, but a Substantial Head of all the categories of being, an Individuality of Intelligence, the dogma of Anaxagoras revived out of a more elaborate and profound analysis of Nature; something like that living unambiguous Principle which the old poets, in advance of the materialistic cosmogonists from Night and Chaos had discovered in Ouranos or Zeus. Soon, however, the vision of personality is withdrawn, and we reach that culminating point of thought where the real blends with the ideal; where moral action and objective thought (that is, thought exercised as to anything outside of itself) as well as the material body are excluded; and where the divine action in the world retains its veil of impenetrable mystery, and to the utmost ingenuity of research presents but a contradiction. At this extreme, the series of efficient causes resolves itself into the Final Cause. That which moves, itself *unmoved*, can only be the immobility of Thought or Form. God is both formal, efficient and final cause; the One Form comprising all forms, the one good including all good, the goal of the longing of the Universe, moving the world as the object of love or rational desire moves the individual. He is the internal or self-realized Final Cause, having no end beyond Himself. He is no moral agent; for if he were, he would be but an instrument for producing something still higher and greater. One sort of act only, activity of mind or thought, can be assigned to him who is at once all act yet all repose. What we call our highest pleasure, which distinguishes wakefulness and sensation, and which gives a reflected charm to hope and memory, is with him perpetual. His existence is unbroken enjoyment of that which is most excellent but only temporary with us. The divine quality of active and yet tranquil self-contemplation characterizing intelligence, is pre-eminently possessed by the divine mind; his thought, which is his existence, being unlike ours, unconditional and wholly *act*. If he can receive any gratification or enjoyment from that which exists beyond himself, he can also be displeased and pained with it, and then he would be an imperfect being. To suppose pleasure experienced by him from anything outward, supposes an insufficient *prior* enjoyment and happiness, and a sort of dependency. Man's Good is beyond himself; not so God's. The eternal act which produces the world's life is the eternal desire of good. The object of the Absolute Thought is the Absolute Good. Nature is all movement, and Thought all repose. In contemplating that absolute good, the Finality can contemplate only itself; and thus, all material interference being excluded, the distinction of subject and object vanishes in complete identification, and the Divine Thought is "the thinking of thought." The energy of mind is life, and God is that energy in its purity and perfection. He is therefore life itself, eternal and perfect; and this sums up all that is meant by the term "God." And yet, after all this transcendentalism, the very essence of thought consists in its mobility and power of transference from object to object; and we can conceive of no thought, without an object beyond itself, about which to think, or of any activity in mere self-contemplation, without outward act, movement, or manifestation.

Plato endeavours to show how the Divine Principle of Good becomes realized in Nature: Aristotle's system is a vast analogical induction to prove how all Nature tends towards a final good. Plato considered

Soul as a principle of movement, and made his Deity realize, that is, turn into realities, his ideas, as a free intelligent Force. Aristotle, for whom Soul is the motionless centre from which motion radiates, and to which it converges, conceives a correspondingly unmoved God. The Deity of Plato creates, superintends, and rejoices in the universal joy of, His creatures. That of Aristotle is the perfection of man's intellectual activity extended to the universe. When he makes the Deity to be an eternal act of self-contemplation, the world is not excluded from his cognizance, for he contemplates it within himself. Apart from and beyond the world, he yet mysteriously intermingles with it. He is universal as well as individual; his agency is necessary and general, yet also makes the real and the good of the particular.

When Plato had given to the unformed world the animal life of the Ionians, and added to that the Anaxagorean Intelligence, overruling the wild principle of Necessity; and when to Intelligence was added Beneficence; and the dread Wardours,-Force and Strength, were made subordinate to Mildness and Goodness, it seemed as if a further advance were impossible, and that the Deity could not be more than The Wise and The Good.

But the contemplation of the Good implies that of its opposite, Evil. When God is held to be "The Good," it is not because Evil is unknown, but because it is designedly excluded from His attributes. But if Evil be a separate and independent existence, how would it fare with His prerogative of Unity and Supremacy? To meet this dilemma, it remained only to fall back on something more or less akin to the vagueness of antiquity; to make a virtual confession of ignorance, to deny the ultimate reality of evil, like Plato and Aristotle, or with Speusippus, the eternity of its antithetical existence, to surmise that it is only one of those notions which are indeed provisionally indispensable in a condition of finite knowledge, but of which so many have been already discredited by the advance of philosophy; to revert, in short, to the original conception of "The Absolute," or of a single Being, in whom all mysteries are explained, and before whom the disturbing principle is reduced to a mere turbid spot on the ocean of Eternity, which to the eye of faith may be said no longer to exist.

But the absolute is nearly allied to the non-existent. Matter and evil obtruded themselves too constantly and convincingly to be confuted or cancelled by subtleties of Logic. It is in vain to attempt to merge the world in God, while the world of experience exhibits contrariety, imperfection and mutability, instead of the immutability of its source. Philosophy was but another name for uncertainty; and after the mind had successively deified Nature and its own conceptions, without any practical result but toilsome occupation; when the reality it sought, without or within, seemed ever to elude its grasp, the intellect, baffled in its higher flights, sought advantage and repose in aiming at truth of a lower but more applicable kind.

The Deity of Plato is a Being proportioned to human sympathies; the Father of the World, as well as its Creator; the author of good only, not of evil. "Envy," he says, "is far removed from celestial beings, and man, if willing, and braced for the effort, is permitted to aspire to a communion with the solemn troops and sweet societies of heaven. God is the Idea or Essence of Goodness, the Good itself [το αγαθον]: in goodness He created the World, and gave to it the greatest perfection of which it was susceptible; making it, as far as possible, an image of Himself. The sublime type of all excellence is an object not only of veneration but love." The Sages of old had already intimated in enigmas that God is the Author of Good; that like the Sun in Heaven, or Æsculapius on earth, He is "Healer," "Saviour" and "Redeemer," the destroyer and averter of Evil, ever healing the mischiefs inflicted by Heré, the wanton or irrational power of nature.

Plato only asserts with more distinctness the dogma of antiquity, when he recognizes Love as the highest and most beneficent of Gods, who gives to nature the invigorating energy restored by the art of medicine to the body; since Love is emphatically the physician of the universe, the Æsculapius to whom Socrates wished to sacrifice in the hour of his death.

A figurative idea adopted from familiar imagery gave that endearing aspect to the divine connection with the universe which had commanded the earliest assent of the sentiments, until, rising in refinement with the progress of mental cultivation, it ultimately established itself as firmly in the deliberate approbation of the understanding, as it had ever responded to the sympathies. Even the rude Scythians, Bithynians and Scandinavians called God their "Father:" all nations traced their ancestry more or less directly to Heaven. The Hyperborean Olen, one of the oldest symbols of the religious antiquity of Greece, made Love the First-born of

Nature. Who will venture to pronounce at what time God was first worthily and truly honoured, or when man first began to feel aright the mute eloquence of nature? In the obscure physics of the mystical Theologers who preceded Greek philosophy, Love was the Great First Cause and Parent of the Universe. "Zeus," says Proclus, "when entering upon the work of creation, changed Himself into the form of Love; and He brought forward Aphrodité, the principle of Unity and Universal Harmony, to display her light to all. In the depths of His mysterious being, He contains the principle of love within Himself; in Him creative wisdom and blessed love are united."

> "From the first
> Of Days on these his love divine he fixed,
> His admiration; till in time complete
> What he admired and loved, his vital smile
> Unfolded into being."

The speculators of the venerable East, who had conceived the idea of an Eternal-Being superior to all affection and change, in his own sufficiency enjoying a plenitude of serene and independent bliss, were led to inquire into the apparently inconsistent fact of the creation of the world. Why, they asked, did He who required nothing external to Himself to complete His already existing Perfection, come forth out of His unrevealed and perfect existence, and become incorporated in the vicissitudes of nature? The solution of the difficulty was Love. The Great Being beheld the beauty of his own conception, which dwelt with him alone from the beginning, Maia, or Nature's loveliness, at once the germ of passion and the source of worlds. Love became the universal parent, when the Deity, before remote and inscrutable, became ideally separated into the loving and the beloved.

And here again recurs the ancient difficulty; that, at whatever early period this creation occurred, an eternity had previously elapsed, during which God, dwelling alone in his unimpeached unity, had no object for his love; and that the very word implies to us an existing object towards which the love is directed; so that we cannot conceive of love in the absence of any object to be loved; and therefore we again return to this point, that if love is of God's essence, and he is unchangeable, the same necessity of his nature supposed to have caused creation, must ever have made his existence without an object to love impossible; and so that the universe must have been coexistent with himself.

This review of the ancient opinions in regard to the Deity would be but incomplete if it omitted any mention of the ideas of His nature and attributes contained in the Hebrew Scriptures; especially as those ideas, as entertained by the common people, seem to have been widely at variance with those of the more intellectual few, and far below those of many of the Grecian philosophers, and of Plato in particular, whose God was a God of Love.

The words uniformly rendered "GOD" in the authorized version of the Bible include essential differences of form and meaning in the Hebrew; and the translation does not at all give the meaning of the original. Sometimes the noun is singular, sometimes plural; and when plural, it is sometimes joined with a singular, and sometimes with a plural verb. The plural is usually explained as being like the "We" of a royal proclamation, used more distinctly to express the excellence and dignity of God. But where the verb as well as substantive are plural, there it is allowed that the Scriptural Elohim, Æloim or Alhim, is "a term retained from the usages of Polytheism, and may be considered to mean the higher Powers and Intelligences." Abraham, for instance (xx. Gen. 13), says that the Elohim caused (in the plural) him to wander from his father's house: and at Beth-Al, or AL-BITH-AL, as Jacob termed it, the Elohim appeared (in the plural) to Jacob [Gen. xxxv. 7]: and there LI ALHIM said to him, ANI AL SHDI—I am AL SHEDI, or the Mighty God.

The Hebrew God is usually supposed to be attended by a court resembling the divan of an Eastern monarch, and like Jove in the midst of the divine conclave of the Iliad, to be surrounded by a congregation of saints and mighty ones [lxxxii. Ps. 1, xiv. Is. 13], "with all the Host of Heaven at his right hand and at his left" [1 Kings xxii. 19]. When, therefore, he is represented as deliberating with others, "let us make man after our image," &c., it is reasonable to infer that he addresses the present members of the holy congregation included in the plurality of the Elohim, the attendant Armies of Heaven or Sons of God, assembled in oriental state around their King. Inuh, as tutelar God of Israel, is distinguished from the general company of Elohim, and emphatically elevated above them, under the title of Inuu-Elohim, or Inuh-Tsbauth, God of Hosts, as their supreme presiding chief, who inhabits a dwelling above the starry firmament, and which they are not permitted to enter [xiv. Is. 13]. But the term "Heavenly Hosts" includes not only the counsellors and emissaries of Inuh, but also the celestial luminaries [ii. Gen. 1; xxxii. id. 1, 2; iv. Deut. 19; xvii. id. 3; xxxiii. Ps. 6]; and the stars, imagined in the East to be animated Intelligences, presiding over human weal and wo, are identified with the more distinctly impersonated messengers, or angels [xxxii. Gen. 1, 2; xxviii. Job 25], who execute the divine decrees, and whose predominance in heaven is in mysterious correspondence and relation with the powers and dominions of the earth [xxiv. Is. 21; xl. id. 26]. In the 148th Psalm, while all the creatures in heaven and on earth are summoned to do homage to Inuh, the Angels and Heavenly Hosts [v. 2, 3] are so closely approximated that it is impossible they can have been very clearly distinguished in the writer's mind, especially when, in the 8th verse, they assume a correlation with the earthly elements of fire and hail, snow and vapour, themselves in a subordinate sphere made to act as executors of the divine decrees. Correspondingly, in Job, the Morning Stars and the Sons of God are identified [xxxviii. Job 7]; they join in the same chorus of praise to the Almighty; they are both susceptible of joy, they "walk in brightness" [xxxi. Job 26], and are liable to impurity and imperfection in the sight of God [xv. Job 15; xxv. id. 5]. The Potentates of the Sky, the appropriate types of all earthly authority [xxxvii. Gen. 9; xxiv. Numb. 17; xiv. Is. 12], being thus indistinguishable from Heavenly Beings, the history of the origin of both is supposed to be sufficiently explained, when it is said that "God by his word made all the Host of Heaven [xxxiii. Ps. 6]; and the prohibition to worship the one made it unnecessary to lay any express veto on the deification of the other. Hence it is, that in the account of creation the sun, moon and stars take precedence of all other created beings in the scale of animated nature. They dwell in the first-created light, as appropriate inhabitants of heaven, as the birds are fitted for the atmosphere, the fish for the water, and land-animals for the earth. When the personality of intermediate beings became more generally recognized, it was natural that the Elohim and "Sons of the Elohim" should be interpreted to mean angels, as were the Tsba or Tsbauth, the starry armies. Many difficulties were thus avoided or explained. It was thus easy to do away with any traces of polytheistic expression; to account for representations of human characteristics; to suppose, for instance, that man was created, not literally "in the image of Inuh," but after the similitude of the Elohim. Yet it still remains open to suppose the collective Elohim to have had an original reference to the Heavenly Host, comprehending in the plural form all that congregation of Saints and Holy Ones [אבצ—Tsba—xv. Job. 15; xxxviii. id. 7], of which Inuh was afterwards recognized as the Creator and King: or, still more probably, that it meant, as in the very ancient fragment with which Genesis begins, the aggregate of the Creative Forces or Powers, inferior to, but emanations of, Inuh, acting collectively as a unit; that, from long-established habit, the term continued to be employed as a title of Inuh himself, and even warranted the archaism of confounding the personality of these Angels or Forces with the more peculiar and revered name of Inuh: that, in short, אלהים ל, Li Aluim, the Alhim or Elohim, was originally a collective name for "the other Gods" worshipped by the ancestors of the Israelites [xxiv. Josh. 2; xx. Gen. 13; xxxiv. Ps. 7], including not only foreign superstitious forms, but also the Creative Forces or Subordinate Hierarchy of Powers, and all that "Host of Heaven" which was revealed in poetry to the shepherds of the desert, now as careering in chariots of fire [2 Kings vi. 17], now as an encampment of warriors [xxxii. Gen. 1; xxxiv. Ps. 7], and now as winged messengers, ascending and descending the vault of heaven, to communicate the will of God to mankind [xxviii. Gen. 12].

The Jews continue to preserve in their traditions obscure memorials of a worship of the Stars, as having preceded the religion of Inuh. "The Eternal," they said, in the Bereshith Rabba to Genesis, "called forth Abraham and his posterity out of the dominion of the Stars. By nature, the Israelite was a Servant of the Stars, and born under their influence, as are the heathen: but by virtue of the law given on Mount Sinai, he became liberated from this degrading servitude."

The Nomadic Tribes of the interior of Asia were particularly distinguished by the form of religion called Sabeism. Long before becoming acquainted with the Stellar mythology of the Greeks, the Arab, abiding in the field by night, rejoicing in the refulgence of Moon and Stars, had amused his fancy by giving names to the more conspicuous astral groups; and names taken from the familiar objects of his life, such as *ostrich*, *camel* or *tent*, continued to be preserved, with others more recently introduced. Each Tribe singled out among the heavenly bodies its favourite gods, and consulted them as omens of futurity. From their neighbours of Arabia and Chaldea, the Hebrews may probably have adopted the few names for the constellations which they appear to have possessed, and which occur characteristically in the pastoral books of Job and Amos,—the Cluster or Pleiades, the Northern Wain or Bear, and Chesil or Orion.

If we had a translation of the Hebrew writings, in which the names of Deity (including all *supposed* to be such), were simply the Hebrew names repeated in English letters, we should have a knowledge of the Hebrew ideas of Deity, which our translation systematically conceals from us. The passage in which the Prophet Amos indignantly denies the early existence of a pure Jehovistic religion, proves that the Israelites shared the Star-worship of the Arabs, particularly that of Saturn (or Remphan), to whom the seventh day was immemorially consecrated. This admission, into which Amos seems to have been led by vehemence of feeling, is one of the most remarkable in those writings, and coupled with other explanatory passages, such as vii. Jeremiah 22, throws an entirely new light on much of the older writings, and gives a far different notion of Hebrew religious antiquity from that commonly entertained. The Prophet (Amos) is remonstrating on the uselessness of mere ceremonial observances; but he goes further; he declares that these external ceremonies were *not* in fact offered to the true Jehovah, but to Moloch, or to a Star-God equivalent to Saturn; the same Star, says Jerome, still worshipped by the Saracens. This is the passage in question (v. Amos 25, 26); "Did ye offer unto Me sacrifices and offerings in the wilderness forty years, O People of Israel? Nay: but ye bore the tabernacle of your Moloch [Melec] and Chiun your images, the Star of your God, which ye made yourselves." And the passage in Jeremiah (which denies much of the teaching called Mosaic to have emanated from Inuh), is (vii. Jer. 22); "For I spake not unto your fathers, nor commanded them in the day that I brought them out of the land of Egypt, *concerning burnt-offerings or sacrifices.*"

The Star-God worshipped by the ancient Israelites was not the God of the better religion of the prophets, nor was his law the righteous law of the true Jehovah. And yet, although neither the God El or Al, nor Jehovah was *merely* planetary or solar, yet we cannot deny a direct astrological character to the Power who, seated on the pinnacle of the universe, is described as leading forth the Host of Heaven, and telling them unerringly by name and number. The Stars of Jehovah are his Sons (xiv. Is. 13; xxxviii. *ib.* 7), and his "eyes, which run through the whole world, keeping watch over men's deeds." The seven eyes of the Lord, engraved on the stone laid before Joshua, evidently refer to the Seven Planets (iii. Zech. 9; iv. *id.* 10); and they are the same eyes mentioned in 2 Chron. xvi. 9; xv. Prov. 3, and xi. Deut. 12.

The earlier Hebrew names of God are all significant. They are chiefly descriptive of *Power*. Al is commonly interpreted The Strong; Al Sadi, The Mighty; Lal Aliun of Malki-Tsedek, The Strong-Exalted; and the Elouim or Aliim were the Forces or Powers of Deity.

The prevalence of the worship of corner or emblematic stones is also distinctly alluded to in the old Hebrew writings. Inuh is often compared to a rock, as in 2 Sam. xxii. 2, 3, 32; xxiii. *id.* 3: and Zuri-Shedi and Zuri-Al appear to have been common names for the Hebrew Deity [i. Numb. 6; ii. *id.* 22], adopted conformably to the custom of the religious East as a family patronymic; from צור . . Tsur, a *rock* or *stone*.

The Patriarchal God of the Hebrews was Al Shedi (vi. Exod. 3), Al Alhi Isral (xxxiii. Gen. 20), or Al Aliun, titles compounded of Al or El, " The Mighty," the well-known general designation of the Semitic Nature-God, which enters into the composition of old Israelitish proper names, as the corresponding one of Bel or Baal does into Babylonian and Phœnician. The peculiar characteristic of El or Ilus was to devour his own children.

The great rivals of the Hebrew Deity, who most excited his jealousy, were Bel (*Lord*) and Moloch (Melec or *King*). The symbol of the former was the Sun, and that of the latter, Fire. Both were ultimately the same beings, and their rites and symbols interchangeable. Human victims were offered to both, as they were to Inuh. Moloch is not formally introduced until the time of Solomon. In earlier times, the old religion into which the Jews were ever relapsing, takes the name of apostasy to Baal, and his colleague Ashtaroth, Astarte or Aschera. There were many separate forms of idols of Baal-worship, as *Baal-Peor*, *Baal-Gad*, *Baal-Berith*, all comprised under the plural BAALIM, as different modifications of the worship of AL were under that of ALHIM.

The same acts and the same conceptions applied to IHUH as to Bel. Self-mutilation was part of the ritual of both; (1 Kings xviii. 28; xli. Jer. 5; lvi. Is. 4; xix. Matt. 12). Both were worshipped upon the same high places (xxii. Numb. 41); and under the same idol forms in Samaria and in Jerusalem (vii. Jer. 9, 10, 30; viii. Ezek. 10; xxiii. *id.* 39; 2 Chron. vi. 13, 14). There is no substantial reason why the great Syrian Deity, seated on the Bull, should not be compared with IHUH, riding on a Cherub, or winged bull (xviii. Ps. 10), or figured under the same symbol; especially when we know that the feast-days of Bel were the same as IHUH's (ii. Hosea, 11, 12, 16, 17); and that the Priests of the latter, with the fanatical Jehu at their head, were not only idolaters, but murderers and robbers. "And it shall be at that day, saith the Lord"—this is the language of Hosea (ii. 16, 17), "that thou shalt call me ISHI; and shalt call me no more BAALI: for I will take away the names of Baalim out of her mouth, *and they shall no more be remembered by their name.*"

Both Deities were symbolized by the Sun. IHUH's continuing help was assured by continuance of day, or arrived with the heat of noon. The propitiatory heads were hung up before the Lord against the Sun, and Joshua's Captive Kings remained on the gallows as a thank-offering, until Sun-down. The rites of the Hebrews were in many details identical with those of their neighbours; the obelisks or pillars, erected by a Phœnician Artist in front of the Hebrew Temple were obviously analogous to those of Hierapolis and Tyre; and the chariots of the Sun and sacred vessels of Bal first destroyed by Josiah were with strange pertinacity restored by his successor. It is precisely when the names formed from EL or AL begin to be re-placed by those formed from IHUH, IH or JAH, that the name of Moloch enters Hebrew symbolism, usurping the place of IHUH even in his own Temple.

Indeed, the common title of IHUH himself is MELEC [מלך . . MLK . . King, Sovereign, Sultan, &c., the identical word which is disguised in the title MOLOCH: and his symbol, like that of the Patriarchal EL, the *Kronos* of Babylonian tradition, was the fire, a devouring fire, to which he is repeatedly compared. In the time of the Prophets, better conceptions were struggling to displace the old MELEC or MOLOCH, or Savage Deity of the Tabernacle. The aspect of this God, IHUH, was death, his pass-word, destruction, his breath the consuming fire of Tophet. He was emphatically the Terrific God, and even Terror personified. His fire was always threatening to break out and devour; and so blind was its fury, that the very coffer supposed to contain the written command to "do no murder," sacrificed friends and foes indiscriminately. The unfortunate Uzzah was instantly destroyed for preventing the Ark from being upset. Distrusting his own power of self-control, IHUH substituted an angel, lest he should yield to his desire to consume the people. He had the double aspect of all Nature-Gods, exhibiting a bright and a dark side, holding the balance of life and death, and often as profuse and partial in favours, as at other times reckless and indiscriminate in destruction. Even kindness is fearful, when irregular and incomprehensible; "he will have mercy on whom he will have mercy;" but is as often inexplicably severe and unjust. He puts a lying spirit into the mouth of his prophets, and so lays a trap for his people which they could not escape. He gives quails to destroy them, punishing with excessive cruelty a natural appetite and the ordinary weakness of murmuring and complaining at hardships; and he appoints "Statutes which were not good," in order to cause them to pass their first-born through the fire, and for the express purpose of making them desolate.

The notion of blinding or hardening the hearts of men, in order to furnish a conspicuous example of God's glory by punishing them, is common throughout the old Hebrew writings, and continues even in the New Testament. Pharaoh's heart is hardened for the purpose of affording occasion and excuse for the display of the signs and wonders of an unknown God; and at the end of each plague the same hardening process is repeated, in order to justify the infliction of a new one. A capricious power is always terrific; and terror produces the superstitious desperation which discards humanity and pity. The sanguinary principle sanctioned by the example of Abraham, extends through the whole of Hebrew ritual and practice. The often-recurring phrase, the being hung, or "dying before the Lord," evidently means a human sacrifice or religious act of atonement. The wholesale murders of Shittim and Gibeah, like the similar individual acts performed not in reference to a foreign idol, but under the immediate influence of the Spirit of IHUH, were strictly sacrifices to a sanguinary God, of the same class with Moloch and Mexitli, whose plagues ceased only on consummation of the rite, to whom the smell of human gore was sweeter than the breath of flowers, who could be best brought to give success to the Hebrew arms by the promise of a general butchery of all the people overcome, and who gladly accepted Jephthah's vow to sacrifice to him with the knife and burn to him with fire, whatever living creature, even his own child, should first meet him on his return. The calf-worship at Horeb was signalized by a sacrificial massacre of three thousand people; but it is a significant fact, that Aaron, far in knowledge above the rude mass of barbarism that surrounded him, and who made the calf for them, escaped with scarce a reprimand. "Slay," said Moses on that occasion, every man his *brother*, and every man his *companion* and every man his *neighbour*." For the Levites were authorized by him to be executioners of a CHEREM, the form in which men were allowed and even encouraged to sacrifice themselves or some members of their families by a voluntary vow. He said to them (xxxii. *Exod.* 29) "Come to-day with full-hand for IHUH, and initiate yourselves in your priestly office by slaying every man his son, his brother, his companion, and his neighbour; and so earn a blessing for yourselves this day." And the Mosaic law, after fixing the price of redemption or commutation for things vowed by "a singular vow," or "sanctified" to the Lord, proceeds to make this stringent provision [xxvii. Levit. 28, 29]: "Notwithstanding, no Cherem that a man shall make Cherem unto the Lord, of all he hath, of *man* or beast or the field in his possession, shall be sold or redeemed; every Cherem is irrevocably consecrated to the Lord. *No Cherem, whereby men are Cherem shall be redeemed*, BUT SHALL SURELY BE PUT TO DEATH." That was the kind of vow by which Jephthah purchased victory.

Cruelty thus became a sacred duty, and zealots were allowed in their outbursts of enthusiasm, to violate every civil and moral tie. Free scope was given to private enmity and to public aggression; and as under a perpetual reign of terror, any one might denounce his enemy or rival. War was carried on in IHUH's name with relentless and savage ferocity. It was an acceptable sacrifice; and the exultation with which the Hebrew annalist revels in the description of the utter annihilation of the conquered and accursed cities, and the extermination of all that breathed, man and beast, old and young, feeble age, womanhood and virginity and the tender infant, is frightful and revolting. Rahab and her family only were left alive of all in Jericho; and in the same way Joshua dealt with Makkedah, Libnah, Lachish, Eglon, Hebron, Debir, and all the country of the hills and of the South and of the vale and of the Springs; "he left none remaining, but utterly destroyed all that breathed, as the Lord God of Israel commanded." And we are expressly informed in the 11th Chapter of Joshua, that he continued this extraordinary process, throughout the whole land which he conquered, and until "the land rested from war." In this he only followed the example set him by Moses, who was even "wroth" with his officers, after a battle, because they had not slain in cold blood every woman taken captive, who was not a virgin; and ordered them to kill forthwith "every male among the little ones, and every woman that hath known man by lying with him;" [xxxi. Numb. 14, 17]; and in dividing the 16,000 captives still left alive, apportioned *thirty-two* as "*the Lord's Tribute*," and delivered them to Eleazar the High Priest as "a *heave offering*," [*id.* 40, 41]. After the age of David, this fearful practice is said to have become less frequent; but the feeling on which it was founded left an indelible impression on the Hebrew language; a thing devoted, or as it was technically called, "holy," being synonymous with the "accursed," and doomed to utter destruction. And when there was no longer any immediate prospect of gratifying fanatical animosity, the imagination revelled in a future renewal of the old scenes of carnage, to inaugurate the Messianic Kingdom, which was to be preceded by a "great day of the Lord," in other words, a great sacrificial massacre, or repetition of the eventful day of Midian: [ii. Joel 11; iii. *id.* 13; iv. Mic. 13; xxxix. Ezek. 9, 17; ix. Is. 4; xiv. Zech. 11]. "This, this is the day of the Lord God," exclaims Jeremiah, "a day of vengeance, that he may avenge him of his adversaries; and the sword shall devour and shall be satiate and *made drunk* with their blood; for the Lord God of Armies hath a *sacrifice* in the North Country by the River Euphrates:" [xlvi. Jer. 10]. "IHUH's sword is filled with blood and fed with fatness, with the blood of camels and goats, with the fat of the kidneys of rams; for the Lord hath a sacrifice in Bozrah, a great slaughter in the land of Idumea:" [xxxiv. Is. 6]. "Speak to every bird and to every beast of the field, assemble yourselves and come! Gather yourselves on every side to the sacrifice I prepare for you, a great sacrifice on the mountains of Israel, that ye may eat flesh and drink blood:" [xxxix. *Ezek.* 17]. It was such anticipations repeated from age to age, and even fixing the very spot where the corpses of the heathen were to taint the air, that excited the Jews to the frantic violence which afterwards recoiled so heavily on themselves.

The ancient altar was an image of God, or the immediate earnest of his presence. The first altars were called by his name, and were treated as Gods. It was essential that the altar, like the world of which it was a symbol, should be four-square. The altar of burnt-offering was a hollow framework overlaid with brass, having at its corners the horns of the calf or bull-idol, reminding us of those hollow Moloch-images of Phœnicia, forming furnaces into which the victim was thrown. On it the fat was burned, and the blood which was originally dashed in the face of the idol was sprinkled on its horns or poured out at its foot. The Levite who touched the altar, and much more the common man who did so was to die. Its neighbourhood was as formidable to life as that of the flaming mountain made by the divine presence to "smoke as a furnace," and so it was converted into a gigantic Moloch-image, which to approach or touch was death. If superstition may be said to have reached its climax, when, overcoming the most powerful of human feelings, it brought the infatuated mother to kiss the bull-headed instrument of infanticide, it is not astonishing that one despairing Hebrew mother should have ventured to strike the guilty altar with her slipper, saying, "Wolf! how long wilt thou continue to devour the treasure of Israel's children?"

After a time, it is true, the human victim required to be offered Inum was re-placed by an animal-substitute. But at first he claimed the first-born as a sacrifice, and the household escaped on consideration of yielding a child. After the child was commuted for a lamb or a ram, it was natural that, as far as possible, the vestiges of the ancient obnoxious form should be suppressed. But there are sufficient evidences [vi. Mic. 7; i. Is. 15; 2 Sam. xxi. 9] that the immolation of human victims formed part and no unimportant one, of the ritual of Inum. Ezekiel, in a remarkable passage, asserts Moloch-worship to have been authorized by Inum in order to make his people know that he was the Lord, and that thus they immolated their first-born: [xx. Ezek. 25, 26]. The new Passover instituted by the great Reformer Josiah [2 Kings xxiii. 21–22], the like whereof had not been holden "from the days of the Judges that judged Israel, nor in all the days of the Kings of Israel, nor of the Kings of Judah," replaced the old Moloch-rite (which Abraham was entirely resigned to practise); in which, if analogy may be a basis for conjecture, a man or child was hung or crucified as an offering "before the Lord," during the last hours of the departing year, and after being suspended until sunset, was then taken down, the blood poured out upon unleavened cakes, which, with portions of the flesh, were eaten by the communicants, and the remainder burned in the furnace-fire of Moloch or Melec, the still continuing title of Inum in paschal invocations.

The redemption clause in regard to the *human* first-born is a subsequent interpolation, as is evident from its making many parts of the Pentateuch unmeaning; as in xiii. Exod. 12, 13, 15—"Thou shalt set apart unto the Lord all that *openeth* the matrix . . . the males shall be the Lord's . . . All the first-born of man among thy children shalt thou redeem . . . And it came to pass, when Pharaoh would hardly let us go, that the Lord slew all the first-born in the land of Egypt, both the first-born of man and the first-born of beasts: therefore I *sacrifice* to the Lord all that openeth the matrix, being males; but all the first-born of my children I redeem."

The edict commanding this *redemption* proves the *commencement* of a change, and not its completion. Human sacrifices still continued. Inveterate habit could not be suddenly effaced. It was to prevent these horrid rites, that the eating of blood in private dwellings was strictly prohibited, and the suspicious rite of the Passover brought under metropolitan surveillance: [iii. Lev. 17; viii. id. 23, 26; xv. Deut. 19, 20, 23; xvi. id. 2, 5]. Under strong excitement, the old and more efficacious expedient was resorted to. Jephthah did not stickle at it, nor deem it illegal to murder his daughter. The killing a man continued to be, in the language of Pliny, "a most pious act, the eating him a most salubrious one." The cannibalism denounced by the prophets was no unprecedented evil, nor the denunciation a mere vague menace. Mothers ate their own children, and in a time of terror human blood flowed freely at the mandate of the Priests: [Lam. ii. 20; iv. 9, 10, 13]. The prohibition of eating blood or raw flesh did not prevent a mother devouring her child, whom she called her sacrifice [Josephus' War, vi. 3, 4]; nor restrain the Jews of Cyllene from tasting the entrails of their fellow-citizens. The bloody immersion recommended by Jews to the Emperor Constantine as a specific for leprosy was a nostrum of the old law; and the crucifixion of children under Theodosius was but the revival of a practice far less generally revolting and unusual than Josephus would have us suppose. The Jews still remained semi-barbarous in their hearts. The blood of sacrifice, of circumcision, of the passover still continued the great pledge of the eternal covenant; and the idea of human sacrifice, though rare in practice, still maintained its place in the background as a mysterious secret. The story of the man found reserved for sacrifice in the temple, meets in Josephus but feeble contradiction; and the suspicion which has always attached to the secret Mysteries of the Jews has been kept alive from age to age, by the excesses of enthusiasts.

Atonement by blood was ever the great religious idea of the Jews. To spill blood was a specific for all ills. Their God, like that of the Mexicans, figures with blood-drenched sword and gory garments. Animals and enemies were always regarded as economical sacrificial expedients for purchasing divine favour. The Reformers who discarded this horrid worship inconsistently retained the theory on which it was founded, and used sacrificial language in reference to the uncomprehended inequalities of Providential dealing. Among murderous priests and cruel altars, where men devoid of mercy as of knowledge offered sacrifices which God desired not, the prophet was scouted when protesting against popular abominations he appealed to the plain dictates of humanity.

Such were the ancient ideas of the Hebrews in regard to the Deity, His Nature and His Attributes: and it might therefore well be said that they had lost the True Word, and that the knowledge of it was confined to a select few of their learned and intellectual men. We shall hereafter inquire what that True Word was; or, in other words, what is the true definition of the Nature and Attributes of God, embodied in the Ineffable Name; and it will then appear how unspeakably important was the true knowledge of that Word to him who was so fortunate as to attain it: for surely it is the greatest of evils and misfortunes, to entertain not only insufficient and inadequate, but unjust and injurious opinions in regard to the nature of God.

The questions how and why evil exists in the universe; how its existence is to be reconciled with the admitted wisdom and goodness and omnipotence of God; and how far man is a free agent, or controlled by an inexorable necessity or destiny, have two sides. On one, they are questions as to the qualities and attributes of God; for we must infer His moral nature from His mode of governing the universe, and they ever enter into any consideration of His intellectual nature: and on the other, they directly concern the moral responsibility and therefore the destiny of man. All-important, therefore, in both points of view, they have been much discussed in all ages of the world, and have no doubt urged men, more than all other questions have, to endeavour to fathom the profound mysteries of the Nature and the mode of Existence and action of an incomprehensible God.

And with these, still another question also presents itself; whether the Deity governs the Universe by fixed and unalterable laws, or by special Providences and interferences, so that He may be induced to change His course and the results of human or material action, by prayer and supplication.

God alone is all-powerful; but the human soul has in all ages asserted its claim to be considered as part of the Divine. "The purity of the spirit," says Van Helmont, "is shown through energy and efficaciousness of will. God, by the agency of an infinite will, created the universe, and the same sort of power in an inferior degree, limited more or less by external hindrances, exists in all spiritual beings." The higher we ascend in antiquity, the more does prayer take the form of incantation; and that form it still in a great degree retains, since the rites of public worship are generally considered not merely as an expression of trust or reverence, as real spiritual acts, the effect of which is looked for only within the mind of the worshipper, but as acts from which some direct outward result is anticipated, the attainment of some desired object, of health or wealth, of supernatural gifts for body or soul, of exemption from danger, or vengeance upon enemies. Prayer was able to change the purposes of Heaven, and to make the Deves tremble under the abyss. It exercised a compulsory influence over the Gods. It promoted the magnetic sympathy of spirit with spirit; and the Hindu and Persian liturgies, addressed not only to the Deity himself, but to his diversified manifestations, were considered wholesome and necessary iterations of the living or creative Word which at first effectuated the divine will, and which from instant to instant supports the universal frame by its eternal repetition.

In the narrative of the Fall, we have the Hebrew mode of explaining the great moral mystery, the origin of evil and the apparent estrangement from Heaven; and a similar idea, variously modified, obtained in all the ancient creeds. Everywhere, man had at the beginning been innocent and happy, and had lapsed by temptation and his own weakness from his first estate. Thus was accounted for the presumed connection of increase of knowledge with increase of misery, and, in particular, the great penalty of death was reconciled with Divine justice. Subordinate to these greater points, were the questions, why is the earth covered with thorns and weeds? whence the origin of clothing, of sexual shame and passion? whence the infliction of labour, and how to justify the degraded condition of woman in the East, or account for the loathing so generally felt towards the Serpent Tribe?

The hypothesis of a fall, required under some of its modifications in all systems, to account for the apparent imperfection in the work of a Perfect Being, was in Eastern philosophy the unavoidable accompaniment and condition of limited or individual existence; since the Soul, considered as a fragment of the Universal Mind, might be said to have lapsed from its pre-eminence when parted from its source, and ceasing to form part of integral perfection. The theory of its reunion was correspondent to the assumed cause of its degradation. To reach its prior condition, its individuality must cease; it must be emancipated by re-absorption into the Infinite, the consummation of all things in God, to be promoted by human effort in spiritual meditation or self-mortification, and completed in the magical transformation of death.

And as man had fallen, so it was held that the Angels of Evil had, from their first estate, to which, like men, they were in God's good time to be restored, and the reign of evil was then to cease forever. To this great result all the Ancient Theologies point; and thus they all endeavoured to reconcile the existence of Sin and Evil with the perfect and undeniable wisdom and beneficence of God.

With man's exercise of thought are inseparably connected freedom and responsibility. Man assumes his proper rank as a moral agent, when with a sense of the limitations of his nature arise the consciousness of freedom, and of the obligations accompanying its exercise, the sense of duty and of the capacity to perform it. To suppose that man ever imagined himself not to be a free agent, until he had argued himself into that belief, would be to suppose that he was in that below the brutes: for he like them is *conscious* of his freedom to act. Experience alone teaches him that this freedom of action is limited and controlled; and when what is outward to him restrains and limits this freedom of action, he instinctively rebels against it as a wrong. The rule of duty and the materials of experience are derived from an acquaintance with the conditions of the external world in which the faculties are exerted; and thus the problem of man involves those of Nature and God. Our freedom, we learn by experience, is determined by an agency external to us; our happiness is intimately dependent on the relations of the outward World, and on the moral character of its Ruler.

Then at once arises this problem. The God of Nature must be One, and His character cannot be suspected to be other than good. Whence then came the evil, the consciousness of which must invariably have preceded or accompanied man's moral development? On this subject, human opinion has ebbed and flowed between two contradictory extremes, one of which seems inconsistent with God's Omnipotence and the other with His beneficence. If God, it was said, is perfectly wise and good, evil must arise from some *independent* and *hostile* principle: if, on the other hand, all agencies are Subordinate to One, it is difficult, if evil does indeed exist, if there is any such thing as Evil, to avoid the impiety of making God the Author of it.

The recognition of a moral and physical dualism in nature was adverse to the doctrine of Divine Unity. Many of the Ancients thought it absurd to imagine one Supreme Being, like Homer's Jove, distributing good and evil out of two urns. They therefore substituted, as we have seen, the doctrine of two distinct and eternal principles; some making the cause of evil to be the inherent imperfection of matter and the flesh, without explaining how God was not the cause of that; while others personified the required agency, and fancifully invented an Evil Principle, the question of whose origin indeed involved all the difficulty of the original problem; but whose existence, if once taken for granted, was sufficient as a popular solution of the mystery; the difficulty being supposed no longer to exist, when pushed a step further off, as the difficulty of conceiving the world upheld by an elephant was supposed to be got rid of, when it was said that the elephant was supported by a tortoise.

The simpler, and probably the older notion treated the one only God as the Author of all things. "I form the light," says Jehovah, "and create darkness; I cause prosperity and create evil; I, the Lord, do all these things." "All mankind," says Maximus Tyrius, "are agreed that there exists one only Universal King and

Father, and that the many Gods are his Children." There is nothing improbable in the supposition that the primitive idea was that there was but one God. A vague sense of Nature's Unity, blended with a dim perception of an all-pervading Spiritual Essence, has been remarked among the earliest manifestations of the Human Mind. Everywhere it was the dim remembrance uncertain and indefinite, of the original truth taught by God to the first men.

The Deity of the Old Testament is everywhere represented as the direct author of Evil, commissioning evil and lying spirits to men, hardening the heart of Pharaoh, and visiting the iniquity of the individual sinner on the whole people. The rude conception of sternness predominating over mercy in the Deity, can alone account for the human sacrifices, purposed, if not executed, by Abraham and Jephthah. It has not been uncommon in any age or country of the world, for men to recognize the existence of one God, without forming any becoming estimate of his dignity. The causes of both good and ill are referred to a mysterious centre, to which each assigns such attributes as correspond with his own intellect and advance in civilization. Hence the assignment to the Deity of the feelings of envy and jealousy. Hence the provocation given by the healing skill of Æsculapius and the humane theft of fire by Prometheus. The very spirit of Nature, personified in Orpheus, Tantalus or Phineus was supposed to have been killed, confined or blinded, for having too freely divulged the Divine Mysteries to mankind. This Divine Envy still exists in a modified form, and varies according to circumstances. In Hesiod it appears in the lowest type of human malignity. In the God of Moses, it is jealousy of the infringement of the autocratic power, the check to political treason; and even the penalties denounced for worshipping other Gods often seem dictated rather by a jealous regard for his own greatness in Deity, than by the immorality and degraded nature of the worship itself. In Herodotus and other writers it assumes a more philosophical shape, as a strict adherence to a moral equilibrium in the government of the world; in the punishment of pride, arrogance and insolent pretension.

God acts providentially in Nature by regular and universal laws, by constant modes of operation; and so takes care of material things without violating their constitution, acting always according to the nature of the things which he has made. It is a fact of observation that in the material and unconscious world, He works *by* its materiality and unconsciousness, not against them; in the animal world, *by* its animality and partial consciousness, not against them. So in the providential government of the world, he acts by regular and universal laws, and constant modes of operation; and so takes care of human things without violating their constitution, acting always according to the human nature of man, not against it, working in the human world by means of man's consciousness and partial freedom, not against them.

God acts by general laws for general purposes. The attraction of gravitation is a good thing, for it keeps the world together; and if the tower of Siloam, thereby falling to the ground, slays eighteen men of Jerusalem, that number is too small to think of, considering the myriad millions who are upheld by the same law. It could not well be repealed for *their* sake, and to hold up that tower; nor could it remain in force, and the tower stand.

It is difficult to conceive of a Perfect *Will* without confounding it with something like mechanism; since language has no name for that combination of the Inexorable with the Moral, which the old poets personified separately in Ananke or Eimarmene and Zeus. How combine understandingly the Perfect Freedom of the Supreme and All-Sovereign Will of God with the inflexible necessity, as part of His Essence, that He should and must continue to be, in all His great attributes, of justice and mercy for example, what He is now and always has been, and with the impossibility of His changing His nature and becoming unjust, merciless, cruel, fickle, or of his repealing the great moral laws which make crime wrong and the practice of virtue right?

For all that we familiarly know of Free-Will is that capricious exercise of it, which we experience in ourselves and other men; and therefore the notion of Supreme Will, still guided by Infallible Law, even if that law be self-imposed, is always in danger of being either stripped of the essential quality of Freedom, or degraded under the ill name of Necessity to something of even less moral and intellectual dignity than the fluctuating course of human operations.

It is not until we elevate the idea of law above that of partiality or tyranny, that we discover that the self-imposed limitations of the Supreme Cause, constituting an array of certain alternatives, regulating moral choice, are the very sources and safe-guards of human freedom: and the doubt recurs, whether we do not set a law above God himself; or whether laws self-imposed may not be self-repealed: and if not, what power prevents it.

The Zeus of Homer, like that of Hesiod, is an array of antitheses, combining strength with weakness, wisdom with folly, universal parentage with narrow family limitation, omnipotent control over events with submission to a superior destiny;—DESTINY, a name by means of which the theological problem was cast back into the original obscurity out of which the powers of the human mind have proved themselves as incapable of rescuing it, as the efforts of a fly caught in a spider's web to do more than increase its entanglement.

The oldest notion of Deity was rather indefinite than repulsive. The positive degradation was of later growth. The God of nature reflects the changeful character of the seasons, varying from dark to bright. Alternately angry and serene, and lavishing abundance which she again withdraws, nature seems inexplicably capricious, and though capable of responding to the highest requisitions of the moral sentiment through a general comprehension of her mysteries, more liable by a partial or hasty view to become darkened into a Siva, a Saturn or a Mexitli, a patron of fierce orgies or blood-stained altars. All the older poetical personifications exhibit traces of this ambiguity. They are neither wholly immoral nor purely beneficent.

No people have ever deliberately made their Deity a malevolent or guilty Being. The simple piety which ascribed the origin of all things to God, took all in good part, trusting and hoping all things. The Supreme Ruler was at first looked up to with unquestioning reverence. No startling discords or contradictions had yet raised a doubt as to His beneficence, or made men dissatisfied with his government. Fear might cause anxiety, but could not banish hope, still less inspire aversion. It was only later, when abstract notions began to assume the semblance of realities, and when new or more distinct ideas suggested new words for their expression, that it became necessary to fix a definite barrier between Evil and Good.

To account for moral evil, it became necessary to devise some new expedient suited both to the piety and self-complacency of the inventor, such as the perversity of woman, or an agent distinct from God, a Typhon or Ahriman, obtained either by dividing the Gods into two classes; or by dethroning the Ancient Divinity, and changing him into a Deve or Dæmon. Through a similar want, the Orientals devised the inherent corruption of the fleshy and material; the Hebrew transferred to Satan everything illegal and immoral; and the Greek reflection occasionally adopting the older and truer view, retorted upon man the obloquy cast on these creatures of his imagination, and showed how he has to thank himself alone for his calamities, while his good things are the voluntary *gifts*, not the *plunder* of Heaven. Homer had already made Zeus exclaim in the Assembly of Olympus, " Grievous it is to hear these mortals accuse the Gods; they pretend that evils come from us; but they themselves occasion them gratuitously by their own wanton folly." " It is the fault of man," said Solon, in reference to the social evils of his day, " not of God, that destruction comes ;" and Euripides, after a formal discussion of the origin of evil, comes to the conclusion that men act wrongly, not from want of natural good sense and feeling, but because knowing what is good, they yet for various reasons neglect to practise it.

And at last reaching the highest truth, Pindar, Hesiod, Æschylus, Æsop, and Horace said, " All virtue is a struggle, life is not a scene of repose, but of energetic action. Suffering is but another name for the teaching of experience, appointed by Zeus himself, the giver of all understanding, to be the parent of instruction, the schoolmaster of life. He indeed put an end to the golden age; he gave venom to serpents and predacity to wolves; he shook the honey from the leaf, and stopped the flow of wine in the rivulets; he concealed the element of fire, and made the means of life scanty and precarious. But in all this his object was beneficent; it was not to destroy life, but to improve it. It was a blessing to man, not a curse, to be sentenced to earn his bread by the sweat of his brow; for nothing great or excellent is attainable without exertion; safe and easy virtues are prized neither by Gods nor men; and the parsimoniousness of nature is justified by its powerful effect in rousing the dormant faculties, and forcing on mankind the invention of useful arts by means of meditation and thought."

Ancient religious reformers pronounced the worship of "idols" to be the root of all evil; and there have been many iconoclasts in different ages of the world. The maxim still holds good; for the worship of idols, that is, of fanciful conceits, if not the source of *all* evil, is still the cause of much ; and it prevails as extensively now as it ever did. Men are ever engaged in worshipping the picturesque fancies of their own imaginations.

Human wisdom must always be limited and incorrect; and even right opinion is only a something intermediate between ignorance and knowledge. The normal condition of man is that of progress. Philosophy is a kind of journey, ever learning, yet never arriving at the ideal perfection of truth. A Mason should, like the wise Socrates, assume the modest title of a "lover of wisdom;" for he must ever long after something more excellent than he possesses, something still beyond his reach, which he desires to make eternally his own.

Thus the philosophic sentiment came to be associated with the poetical and the religious, under the comprehensive name of Love. Before the birth of Philosophy, Love had received but scanty and inadequate homage. This mightiest and most ancient of Gods, coeval with the existence of religion and of the world, had been indeed unconsciously felt, but had neither been worthily honoured nor directly celebrated in hymn or pæan. In the old days of ignorance it could scarcely have been recognized. In order that it might exercise its proper influence over religion and philosophy, it was necessary that the God of Nature should cease to be a God of terrors, a personification of mere Power or arbitrary Will, a pure and stern Intelligence, an inflicter of evil and an unrelenting Judge. The philosophy of Plato, in which this change became forever established, was emphatically a mediation of Love. With him, the inspiration of Love first kindled the light of arts and imparted them to mankind; and not only the arts of mere existence, but the heavenly art of wisdom, which supports the Universe. It inspires high and generous deeds and noble self-devotion. Without it, neither State nor individual could do anything beautiful or great. Love is our best pilot, confederate, supporter and Saviour; the ornament and governor of all things human and divine; and he with divine harmony forever soothes the minds of men and Gods.

Man is capable of a higher Love, which marrying mind with mind and with the Universe, brings forth all that is noblest in his faculties, and lifts him beyond himself. This higher love is neither mortal nor immortal, but a power intermediate between the human and the Divine, filling up the mighty interval, and binding the Universe together. He is chief of those celestial emissaries who carry to the Gods the prayers of men, and bring down to men the gifts of the Gods. "He is forever poor, and far from being beautiful as mankind imagine, for he is squalid and withered; he flies low along the ground, is homeless and unsandalled; sleeping without covering before the doors and in the unsheltered streets, and possessing so far his mother's nature as being ever the companion of want. Yet, sharing also that of his father, he is forever scheming to obtain things good and beautiful; he is fearless, vehement and strong; always devising some new contrivance; strictly cautious and full of inventive resource; a philosopher through his whole existence, a powerful enchanter and a subtle sophist."

The ideal consummation of Platonic science is the arrival at the contemplation of that of which earth exhibits no express image or adequate similitude, the Supreme Prototype of all beauty, pure and uncontaminated with human intermixture of flesh or colour, the Divine Original itself. To one so qualified is given the prerogative of bringing forth not mere images and shadows of virtue, but virtue itself, as having been conversant not with shadows, but with the truth; and having so brought forth and nurtured a progeny of virtue, he becomes the friend of God, and, so far as such a privilege can belong to any human being, immortal.

Socrates believed, like Heraclitus, in a Universal Reason pervading all things and all minds, and consequently revealing itself in ideas. He therefore sought truth in general opinion, and perceived in the communication of mind with mind one of the greatest prerogatives of wisdom and the most powerful means of advancement. He believed true wisdom to be an attainable idea, and that the moral convictions of the mind, those eternal instincts of temperance, conscientiousness and justice, implanted in it by the Gods, could not deceive, if rightly interpreted.

This metaphysical direction given to philosophy ended in visionary extravagance. Having assumed truth to be discoverable in thought, it proceeded to treat thoughts as truths. It thus became an idolatry of notions, which it considered either as phantoms exhaled from objects, or as portions of the divine pre-existent thought; thus creating a mythology of its own, and escaping from one thraldom only to enslave itself afresh. Theories and notions indiscriminately formed and defended are the false Gods or "idols" of philosophy. For the word *idolon* means *image*, and a false *mind*-picture of God is as much an idol as a false *wooden* image of him.

Fearlessly launching into the problem of universal being, the first philosophy attempted to supply a compendious and decisive solution of every doubt. To do this, it was obliged to make the most sweeping assumptions; and as poetry had already filled the vast void between the human and the divine, by personifying its Deity as man, so philosophy bowed down before the supposed reflection of the divine image in the mind of the enquirer, who in worshipping his own notions had unconsciously deified himself. Nature thus was enslaved to common notions, and notions very often to words.

By the clashing of incompatible opinions, philosophy was gradually reduced to the ignominious confession of utter incapacity, and found its check or intellectual fall in scepticism. Xenophanes and Heraclitus mournfully acknowledged the unsatisfactory result of all the struggles of philosophy, in the admission of a universality of doubt; and the memorable effort of Socrates to rally the discomfited champions of truth, ended in a similar confession.

The worship of abstractions continued the error which personified Evil or deified Fortune; and when mystical philosophy resigned its place to mystical religion, it changed not its nature, but only its name. The great task remained unperformed, of reducing the outward world and its principles to the dominion of the intellect, and of reconciling the conception of the supreme unalterable power asserted by reason, with the requisitions of human sympathies.

A general idea of purpose and regularity in nature had been suggested by common appearances to the earliest reflection. The ancients perceived a natural order, a divine legislation, from which human institutions were supposed to be derived, laws emblazoned in heaven and thence revealed to earth. But the divine law was little more than an analogical inference from human law, taken in the vulgar sense of arbitrary will or partial covenant. It was surmised rather than discovered, and remained unmoral because unintelligible. It mattered little, under the circumstances, whether the universe were said to be governed by chance or by reason, since the latter, if misunderstood, was virtually one with the former. "Better far," said Epicurus, "acquiesce in the fables of tradition, than acknowledge the oppressive necessity of the physicists:" and Menander speaks of God, Chance and Intelligence as undistinguishable. Law unacknowledged goes under the name of *Chance*: perceived, but not understood, it becomes *Necessity*. The wisdom of the Stoic was a dogged submission to the arbitrary behests of one; that of the Epicurean an advantage snatched by more or less dexterous management from the equal tyranny of the other.

Ignorance sees nothing necessary, and is self-abandoned to a power tyrannical because defined by no rule, and paradoxical because permitting evil, while itself assumed to be unlimited, all-powerful and perfectly good. A little knowledge, presuming the identification of the Supreme Cause with the inevitable certainty of perfect reason, but omitting the analysis or interpretation of it, leaves the mind chain-bound in the ascetic fatalism of the Stoic. Free-will, coupled with the universal rule of Chance; or Fatalism and Necessity, coupled with Omniscience and fixed and unalterable Law,—these are the alternatives, between which the human mind has eternally vacillated. The Supernaturalist, contemplating a Being acting through impulse, though with superhuman wisdom, and considering the best courtier to be the most favoured subject, combines contradictory expedients, inconsistently mixing the assertion of free action with the enervating service of petition; while he admits, in the words of a learned archbishop, that "if the production of the things we ask for depend on antecedent, natural and necessary causes, our desires will be answered no less by the omission than the offering of prayers, which, therefore, are a vain thing."

The last stage is that in which the religion of action is made legitimate through comprehension of its proper objects and conditions. Man becomes morally free, only when both notions, that of Chance and that of incomprehensible Necessity, are displaced by that of Law. Law, as applied to the universe, means that universal, providential pre-arrangement, whose conditions can be discerned and discretionally acted on by human intelligence. The sense of freedom arises when the individual independence develops itself according to its own laws, without external collision or hindrance; that of constraint, where it is thwarted or confined by other Natures, or where, by a combination of external forces the individual force is compelled into a new direction. Moral choice would not exist safely, or even at all, unless it were bounded by conditions determining its preferences. Duty supposes a rule both intelligible and certain, since an uncertain rule would be unintelligible, and if unintelligible, there could be no responsibility. No law that is unknown can be obligatory; and that Roman Emperor was justly execrated, who pretended to promulgate his penal laws, by putting them up at such a height that none could read them.

Man commands results, only by selecting among the contingent the pre-ordained results most suited to his purposes. In regard to absolute or divine morality, meaning the final cause or purpose of those compre-. hensive laws which often seem harsh to the individual, because inflexibly just and impartial to the universal, speculation must take refuge in faith; the immediate and obvious purpose often bearing so small a proportion to a wider and unknown one, as to be relatively absorbed or lost. The rain that, unseasonable to me, ruins my hopes of an abundant crop, does so because it could not otherwise have blessed and prospered the crops of another kind of a whole neighbouring district of country. The obvious purpose of a sudden storm of snow, or an unexpected change of wind, exposed to which I lose my life, bears small proportion to the great results which are to flow from that storm or wind over a whole continent. So always, of the good and ill which at first seemed irreconcilable and capriciously distributed, the one holds its ground, the other diminishes by being explained. In a world of a multitude of individuals, a world of action and exertion, a world afford- ing, by the conflict of interests and the clashing of passions, any scope for the exercise of the manly and generous virtues, even Omnipotence cannot make it, that the comfort and convenience of one man alone shall always be consulted.

Thus the educated mind soon begins to appreciate the moral superiority of a system of law over one of capricious interference; and as the jumble of means and ends is brought into more intelligible perspective, partial or seeming good is cheerfully resigned for the disinterested and universal. Self-restraint is found not to imply self-sacrifice. The true meaning of what appeared to be Necessity is found to be, not arbitrary Power, but Strength and Force enlisted in the service of Intelligence. God having made us men, and placed us in a world of change and eternal renovation, with ample capacity and abundant means for rational enjoyment, we learn that it is folly to repine because we are not angels, inhabiting a world in which change and the clashing of interests and the conflicts of passion are unknown.

The mystery of the world remains; but is sufficiently cleared up to inspire confidence. We are constrained to admit that if every man would but do the best in his power to do, and that which he knows he ought to do, we should need no better world than this. Man, surrounded by necessity is free, not in a dogged determina- tion of isolated will, because though inevitably complying with nature's laws, he is able, proportionately to his knowledge, to modify in regard to himself the conditions of their action, and so to preserve an average uni- formity between their forces and his own.

Such are some of the conflicting opinions of antiquity; and we have to some extent presented to you a picture of the Ancient Thought. Faithful, as far as it goes, it exhibits to us Man's Intellect ever struggling to pass beyond the narrow bounds of the circle in which its limited powers and its short vision confine it; and ever we find it travelling round the circle, like one lost in a wood, to meet the same unavoidable and insoluble difficulties. Science with her many instruments, Astronomy, particularly, with her telescope, Physics with the microscope, and Chemistry with its analyses and combinations, have greatly enlarged our ideas of the Deity, by discovering to us the vast extent of the universe in both directions, its star-systems and its invisible swarms of minutest animal life; by acquainting us with the new and wonderful Force or Substance we call Electricity, apparently a link between Matter and Spirit: and still the Deity only becomes more incompre- hensible to us than ever, and we find that in our speculations we but re-produce over and over again the Ancient Thought.

Where, then, amid all these conflicting opinions, is the True Word of a Mason?

My Brother, most of the questions which have thus tortured men's minds, it is not within the reach and grasp of the Human Intellect to understand; but without understanding, as we have explained to you hereto- fore, we may and must *believe.*

The True Word of a Mason is to be found in the concealed and profound meaning of the Ineffable Name of Deity, communicated by God to Moses; and which meaning was long lost by the very precautions taken to conceal it. The true pronunciation of that name was in truth a secret, in which, however, was involved the far more profound secret of its meaning. In that meaning is included all the truth that can be known by us, in regard to the nature of God.

Long known as AL, AL SCHEDI, ALHIM and ADONAI; as the Chief or Commander of the Heavenly Armies; as the aggregate of the Forces [ALHIM] of Nature; as the Mighty, the Victorious, the Rival of Bel and Osiris; as the Soul of Nature, Nature itself, a God that was but Man personified, a God with human passions, the God of the Heathen with but a mere change of name, He assumes, in His communications to Moses, the name יהוה [IHUH], and says to Him, אהיה אשר אהיה [AHIH ASHR AHIH], I AM WHAT I AM. Let us examine the esoteric or inner meaning of this Ineffable Name.

היה [HIH] is the imperfect tense of the verb TO BE, of which יהיה [IHIH] is the present; אהי [AHI—א being the personal pronoun 'I' affixed] the first person, by apocope; and יהי [IHI] the third. The verb has the following forms: . . . Preterite, 3d person, masculine singular, היה [HIH], did exist, was: 3d person com. plural, היו [HIU] . . . Present, 3d pers. masc. sing. יהיה [IHIH], once יהוא [IHUA], by apocope אהי, יהי [AHI, IHI] . . . Infinitive, היה, היו [HIH, HIU] . . . Imperative, 2d pers. masc. sing. היה [HIH], fem. הי [HUI] . . . Participle, masc. sing. הוה [HUH], ENS . . EXISTING . . EXISTENCE.

This verb is never used, as the mere logical copula or connecting word, *is, was*, &c. is used with the Greeks, Latins and ourselves. It always implies *existence, actuality*. The *present* form also includes the *future* sense, . . *shall* or *may* be or exist. And הוה and הוא [HUH and HUA] Chaldaic forms of the imperfect tense of the verb, are the same as the Hebrew הוה and היה [HUH and HIH], and mean *was, existed, became*.

Now הוא and היא [HUA and HIA] are the Personal Pronoun, [Masculine and Feminine] HE, SHE. Thus in iv. Gen. 20 we have the phrase, הוא היה [HUA HIH], HE WAS: and in xxi. Lev. 9, את אביה היא [ATH ABIH HIA], HER Father. This feminine pronoun, however, is often written הוא [HUA], and היא [HIA] occurs only eleven times in the Pentateuch. Sometimes the feminine form means IT; but *that* pronoun is generally in the masculine form.

When either י, ו, ה or א [Yod, Vav, He, or Aleph] terminates a word, and has no vowel either immediately preceding or following it, is often rejected; as in גי [GI], for גיא [GIA], a valley.

So הוא-היא [HUA-HIA], He-She, could properly be written הו-הי [HU-HI]; or by transposition of the letters, common with the Talmudists, יה-וה [IH-UH], which is the Tetragrammaton or Ineffable Name.

In i. Gen. 27, it is said, "So the ALHIM created man in His image: *in the image* of ALHIM created He him: MALE and FEMALE created He them."

Sometimes the word was thus expressed; triangularly:

<pre>
              ה
          ה   ו
      ה   ו   ה
  ה   ו   ה   י
</pre>

And we learn that this designation of the Ineffable Name was, among the Hebrews, a symbol of Creation. The mysterious union *of God with His creatures* was in the letter ה, which they considered to be the Agent of Almighty Power; and to enable the possessor of the Name to work miracles.

The Personal Pronoun הוא [HUA], HE, is often used *by itself*, to express the Deity. Lee says that in such cases, IHUH, IH or ALHIM, or some other name of God *is understood*; but there is no necessity for that. It means in such cases the Male, Generative, or Creative Principle or Power.

It was a common practice with the Talmudists to conceal secret meanings and sounds of words by transposing the letters.

Thus the Ineffable Name not only embodies the Great Philosophical Idea, that the Deity is the ENS, the To ON, the Absolute Existence, that of which the Essence is To Exist, the only Substance of Spinoza, the BEING, that never could *not* have existed, as contradistinguished from that which only *becomes*, not Nature or the Soul of Nature, but that which created Nature; but also the idea of the Male and Female Principles, in its highest and most profound sense; to wit, that God originally comprehended in Himself all that is: that matter was not co-existent with Him, or independent of Him; that He did not merely fashion and shape a pre-existing chaos into a universe; but that His Thought manifested itself outwardly in that universe, which so *became*, and before *was not*, except as comprehended in Him: that the Generative Power or Spirit, and productive matter, ever among the ancients deemed the Female, originally were in God; and that He was and is all that was, that is, and that shall be.

This was the great Mystery of the Ineffable Name; and this true arrangement of its letters, and of course its true pronunciation and its meaning soon became lost to all except the select few to whom it was confided; it being concealed from the common people, because the Deity thus metaphysically named was not that personal and capricious, and as it were tangible God in whom they believed, and who alone was within the reach of their rude capacities.

Diodorus says that the name given by Moses to God, was IAΩ. Theodorus says that the Samaritans termed God IABE, but the Jews IAΩ. Philo Byblius gives the form IETΩ; and Clemens of Alexandria IAOT. Macrobius says that it was an admitted axiom among the Heathen, that the triliteral IAΩ was the sacred name of the Supreme God. And the Clarian oracle said: "Learn thou that IAΩ is the great God Supreme, that ruleth over all."

Hence the frequent expression: "I am the First, and I am the Last; and besides me there is no other God. I am A. and Ω., the First and the Last. I am A. and Ω., the Beginning and the Ending, which is and was, and is to come; the Omnipotent." For in this we see shadowed forth the same great truth; that God is all in all—the Cause and the Effect—the Beginning, or Impulse, or Generative Power; and the Ending, or Result, or that which is produced: that He is in reality all that is, all that ever was, and all that ever will be: in this sense, that nothing besides Himself has existed eternally, and co-eternally with Him, independent of Him, and self-existent, or self-originated.

And thus the meaning of the expressions, ALHIM, a plural noun, used in the account of the Creation with which Genesis commences, with a singular verb, and of the name or title IHUH-ALHIM, used for the first time in the 4th verse of the 2d chapter of the same book, becomes clear. The ALHIM is the aggregate unity of the manifested Creative Forces or Powers of Deity, His Emanations; and IHUH-ALHIM is the ABSOLUTE Existence, or Essence of these Powers and Forces, of which they are Active Manifestations and Emanations.

This was the profound truth hidden in the ancient allegory and covered from the general view with a double veil. This was the esoteric meaning of the generation and production of the Indian, Chaldean and Phœnician cosmogonies; of the Active and Passive Powers, of the Male and Female Principles; of Heaven and its Luminaries generating, and the Earth producing; all hiding from vulgar view, as above its comprehension, the doctrine that matter is not eternal, but that God was the only original Existence, the ABSOLUTE, from whom everything has proceeded, and to whom all returns; and that all moral law springs not from the relation of things, but from His Wisdom and Essential Justice, as the Omnipotent Legislator. And this TRUE WORD is with entire accuracy said to have been *lost*; because its *meaning* was lost, even among the Hebrews, although we still trace the name (its real meaning unsuspected), in the Hu of the Druids and the Fo-Hi of the Chinese.

When we conceive of the Absolute Truth, Beauty, or Good, we cannot stop short at the abstraction of either. We are forced to refer each to some living and substantial Being, in which they have their foundations, some being that is the first and last principle of each.

Moral Truth, like every other universal and necessary truth, cannot remain a mere abstraction. Abstractions are unrealities. In ourselves, moral truth is merely conceived of. There must be *somewhere* a Being that not only *conceives of*, but *constitutes* it. It has this characteristic; that it is not only, to the eyes of our intelligence, an universal and necessary truth, but one obligatory on our will. It is A LAW. We do not establish that law *ourselves*. It is imposed on us *despite* ourselves: its principle must be *without* us. It supposes a *legislator*. He cannot be the being to whom the law applies; but must be one that possesses in the highest degree all the characteristics of moral truth. The moral law, universal and necessary, necessarily has as its author a necessary being;—composed of justice and charity, its author must be a being possessing the plenitude of both.

As all *beautiful* and all *true* things refer themselves, *these* to a Unity which is absolute Truth, and those to a Unity which is absolute Beauty, so all the *moral* principles centre in a single principle, which is the Good. Thus we arrive at the conception of the Good *in itself*, the Absolute Good, superior to all *particular* duties, and determinate in those duties. This Absolute *Good* must necessarily be an attribute of the Absolute Being. There cannot be *several* Absolute Beings; the one in whom are realized Absolute Truth and Absolute Beauty being different from the one in whom is realized Absolute Good. The Absolute necessarily implies absolute Unity. The True, the Beautiful and the Good are not three distinct essences: but they are one and the same essence, considered in its fundamental attributes: the different phases which, in our eyes, the Absolute and Infinite Perfection assumes. Manifested in the World of the Finite and Relative, these three attributes separate from each other, and are distinguished by our minds, which can comprehend nothing except by division. But in the Being from whom they emanate, they are indivisibly united; and this Being, at once triple and one, who sums up in Himself perfect *beauty*, perfect *Truth* and the perfect *Good*, is God.

God is necessarily the principle of Moral Truth, and of personal morality. Man is a moral person, that is to say, one endowed with reason and liberty. He is capable of Virtue: and Virtue has with Him two principal forms, respect for others and love of others; *justice* and *charity*.

The *creature* can possess no real and essential attribute which the *Creator* does not possess. The *effect* can draw its reality and existence only from its *cause*. The *cause* contains in itself at least what is essential in the *effect*. The characteristic of the effect is inferiority, short-coming, imperfection. Dependent and derivate, it bears in itself the marks and conditions of dependence; and its imperfection proves the perfection of the cause; or else there would be in the effect something immanent, without a cause.

God is not a logical Being, whose Nature may be explained by deduction, and by means of algebraic equations. When, setting out with a primary attribute, the attributes of God are deduced one from the other, after the manner of the Geometricians and Scholastics, we have nothing but abstractions. We must emerge from this empty dialectic, to arrive at a true and living God. The first notion which we have of God, that of an *Infinite* Being, is not given us *à priori*, independently of all experience. It is our consciousness of ourself, as at once a Being and a limited Being, that immediately raises us to the conception of a Being, the principle of *our* being, and himself without limits. If the existence that we possess, forces us to recur to a cause possessing the same existence in an infinite degree; all the substantial attributes of existence that we possess equally require, each an infinite cause. God, then, is no longer the Infinite, Abstract, Indeterminate Being, of which reason and the heart cannot lay hold; but a real Being, determinate like ourselves, a moral person like ourself; and the study of our own souls will conduct us, without resort to hypothesis, to a conception of God, both sublime and having a connection with ourselves.

If man be free, God must be so. It would be strange if, while the creature has that marvellous power of disposing of himself, of choosing and willing freely, the Being that has made him should be subject to a necessary development, the cause of which, though in Himself, is a sort of abstract, mechanical or metaphysical power, inferior to the personal, voluntary cause which we are, and of which we have the clearest consciousness. God is free *because* we are: but he is not free *as* we are. He is at once *everything* that we are, and *nothing* that we are. He possesses the same attributes as we, but extended to infinity. He possesses then an infinite liberty, united to an infinite intelligence; and as His intelligence is infallible, exempt from the uncertainty of deliberation, and perceiving at a glance where the Good is, so his liberty accomplishes it spontaneously and without effort.

As we assign to God that liberty which is the basis of our existence, so also we transfer to his character, from our own, justice and charity. In man, they are virtues: in God, his attributes. What is in us the laborious conquest of liberty, is in Him His very nature. The idea of the right, and the respect paid to the right, are signs of the dignity of our existence. If respect of rights is the very essence of justice, the Perfect Being must know and respect the rights of the lowest of his creatures; for He assigned them those rights. In God resides a sovereign justice, that renders to every one what is due him, not according to deceitful appearances, but according to the truth of things. And if man, a limited being, has the power to go out of himself, to forget his own person, to love another like himself, and devote himself to his happiness, dignity and perfection, the Perfect Being must have, in an infinite degree, that disinterested tenderness, that Charity, the Supreme Virtue of the human person. There is in God an infinite tenderness for his creatures; manifested in his giving us existence, which he might have withheld; and every day it appears in innumerable marks of his Divine Providence.

Plato well understood that love of God, and expresses it in these great words: " Let us speak of the cause which led the Supreme Arranger of the universe to produce and regulate that universe. He was good; and he who is good has no kind of ill-will. Exempt from that, he willed that created things should be, as far as possible, like Himself." And Christianity in its turn said, " *God has so loved men, that he has given them his only Son.*"

It is not correct to affirm, as is often done, that Christianity has in some sort *discovered* this noble sentiment. We must not lower human nature, to raise Christianity. Antiquity knew, described and practised charity; the first feature of which, so touching, and thank God! so common, is goodness, as its loftiest one is heroism. Charity is devotion to another; and it is ridiculously senseless to pretend that there ever was an age of the world, when the human soul was deprived of that part of its heritage, the power of devotion. But it is certain that Christianity has diffused and popularized this virtue, and that before Christ these words were never spoken: " LOVE ONE ANOTHER; FOR THAT IS THE WHOLE LAW." *Charity* presupposes *Justice*. He who truly loves his brother respects the rights of his brother; but he does more, he forgets his own. Egoism *sells* or *takes*. Love delights in *giving*. In God, love is what it is in us; but in an infinite degree. God is inexhaustible in his charity, as he is inexhaustible in his essence. That Infinite Omnipotence and infinite charity which by an admirable good-will draws from the bosom of its immense love the favours which it incessantly bestows on the world and on humanity, teaches us that the more we give, the more we possess.

God being all just and all good, He can will nothing but what is good and just. Being Omnipotent, whatever he wills he can do, and consequently does. The world is the work of God: it is therefore perfectly made.

Yet there is disorder in the world, that seems to impugn the justice and goodness of God.

A principle indissolubly connected with the very idea of good, tells us that every moral agent deserves reward when he does well, and punishment when he does ill. This principle is universal and necessary. It is absolute. If it does not apply in this world, it is false, or the world is badly ordered.

But good actions are not always followed by happiness, nor evil ones by misery. Though often this fact is more apparent than real; though virtue, a war against the passions, full of dignity but full of sorrow and pain, has the latter as its condition, yet the pains that follow vice are greater; and virtue conduces most to health, strength and long life;—though the peaceful conscience that accompanies virtue creates internal happiness; though public opinion generally decides correctly on men's characters, and rewards virtue with esteem and consideration, and vice with contempt and infamy; and though, after all, justice reigns in the world, and the surest road to happiness is still that of virtue, yet there are exceptions. Virtue is not always rewarded, nor vice punished in this life.

The data of this problem are these: 1st. The principle of merit and demerit within us is absolute: every good action *ought* to be rewarded, every bad one punished: 2d. God is as just as he is all-powerful: 3d. There are in this world particular cases, contradicting the necessary and universal law of merit and demerit. What is the result?

To reject the two principles, that God is just, and the law of merit and demerit absolute, is to raze to the foundations the whole edifice of human faith.

To maintain them, is to admit that the present life is to be terminated or continued elsewhere. The moral person that acts well or ill, and awaits reward or punishment, is connected with a body, lives with it, makes use of it, depends upon it in a measure, but is not *it*. The *body* is composed of parts. It diminishes or increases, it is divisible even to infinity. But this *something* which has a consciousness of itself, and says 'I, ME;' that feels itself free and responsible, feels too that it is incapable of division, that it is a being *one* and *simple;* that the ME cannot be halved, that if a limb is cut off and thrown away, no part of the ME goes with it: that it remains identical with itself under the variety of phenomena which successively manifest it. This identity, indivisibility, and absolute unity of the person, are its *spirituality*, the very essence of the person. It is not in the least a hypothesis to affirm that the soul differs essentially from the body. By the soul we mean *the person*, not separated from the consciousness of the attributes which constitute it,—*thought* and *will*. The

Existence without consciousness is an abstract being, and not a person. It is *the person*, that is *identical, one, simple*. Its attributes, developing it, do not divide it. Indivisible, it is indissoluble, and may be immortal. If absolute justice requires this immortality, it does not require what is impossible. The spirituality of the soul is the condition and necessary foundation of immortality: the law of merit and demerit the direct demonstration of it. The first is the metaphysical, the second the moral proof. Add to these the tendency of all the powers of the soul towards the Infinite, and the principle of final causes; and the proof of the immortality of the soul is complete.

God, therefore, in the Masonic creed, is Infinite Truth, Infinite Beauty, Infinite Goodness. He is the Holy of Holies, as Author of the Moral Law, as the Principle of Liberty, of Justice and of Charity, Dispenser of Reward and Punishment. Such a God is not an abstract God; but an intelligent and free *person*, who has made us in His image, from whom we receive the law that presides over our destiny, and whose judgment we await. It is His love that inspires us in *our* acts of charity: it is His justice that governs *our* justice, and that of society and the laws. We continually remind ourselves that He is infinite; because otherwise we should degrade his nature: but He would be for us as if he were not, if his infinite nature had not forms inherent in ourselves, the forms of our own reason and soul.

When we love Truth, Justice and Nobility of Soul, we should know that it is God we love underneath these special forms, and should unite them all into one great act of total piety. We should feel that we go in and out continually in the midst of the vast forces of the universe, which are only the Forces of God; that in our studies, when we attain a truth, we confront the thought of God; when we learn the right, we learn the will of God laid down as a rule of conduct for the universe; and when we feel disinterested love, we should know that we partake the feeling of the Infinite God. Then, when we reverence the mighty cosmic force, it will not be a blind Fate in an Atheistic or Pantheistic world, but the Infinite God, that we shall confront and feel and know. Then we shall be mindful of the mind of God, conscious of God's conscience, sensible of His sentiments, and our own existence will be in the infinite being of God.

The world is a whole, which has its harmony; for a God who is One, could make none but a complete and harmonious work. The harmony of the universe responds to the unity of God, as the indefinite quantity is the defective sign of the infinitude of God. To say that the universe is God, is to admit the world only, and deny God. Give it what name you please, it is atheism at bottom. On the other hand, to suppose that the universe is void of God, and that he is wholly apart from it, is an insupportable and almost impossible abstraction. To distinguish is not to separate. I distinguish, but do not separate myself from my qualities and effects. So God is not the universe, although he is everywhere present in spirit and in truth.

To us, as to Plato, absolute truth is in God. It is God Himself under one of his phases. In God, as their original, are the immutable principles of reality and cognizance. In Him things receive at once their existence and their intelligibility. It is by participating in the Divine reason that our own reason possesses something of the absolute. Every judgment of reason envelopes a necessary truth, and every necessary truth supposes the necessary Existence.

Thus, from every direction,—from metaphysics, æsthetics, and morality above all, we rise to the same Principle, the common centre, and ultimate foundation of all truth, all beauty, all good. The True, the Beautiful, the Good, are but diverse revelations of one and the same Being. Thus we reach the threshold of religion; and are in communion with the great philosophies which all proclaim a God; and at the same time with the religious which cover the earth, and all repose on the sacred foundation of natural religion; of that religion which reveals to us the natural light given to all men, without the aid of a particular revelation. So long as philosophy does not arrive at religion, it is below all worships, even the most imperfect; for they at least give man a Father, a Witness, a Consoler, a Judge. By religion, philosophy connects itself with humanity, which, from one end of the world to the other, aspires to God, believes in God, hopes in God. Philosophy contains in itself the common basis of all religious beliefs; it, as it were, borrows from them their principle, and returns it to them surrounded with light, elevated above uncertainty, secure against all attack.

From the necessity of His Nature, the Infinite Being must create and preserve the Finite, and to the Finite must, in its forms, give and communicate of His own kind. We cannot conceive of any finite thing existing without God, the Infinite basis and ground thereof; nor of God existing without something. God is the necessary logical condition of a world, its necessitating cause ; a world, the necessary logical condition of God, His necessitated consequence. It is according to His Infinite Perfection to create, and then to preserve and bless whatever He creates. That is the conclusion of modern metaphysical science. The stream of philosophy runs down from Aristotle to Hegel, and breaks off with this conclusion : and then again recurs the ancient difficulty. If it be of His nature to create,—if we cannot conceive of His existing *alone*, without creating, without *having* created, then what He created was co-existent with Himself. If He could exist an instant without creating, He could as well do so for a myriad of eternities.. And so again comes round to us the old doctrine of a God the Soul of the Universe, and co-existent with it. For what He created had a *beginning ;* and however long since that creation occurred, an eternity had before elapsed. The difference between *a* beginning and *no* beginning is infinite.

But of some things we can be certain. We are conscious of ourselves—of ourselves if not as substances, at least as Powers to be, to do, to suffer. We are conscious of ourselves not as self-originated at all or as self-sustained alone ; but only as dependent, first for existence, ever since for support.

Among the primary ideas of consciousness, that are inseparable from it, the atoms of self-consciousness, we find the idea of God. Carefully examined by the scrutinizing intellect, it is the idea of God as infinite, perfectly powerful, wise, just, loving, holy ; absolute being with no limitation. This made us, made all, sustains us, sustains all ; made our body, not by a single act, but by a series of acts extending over a vast succession of years,—for man's body is the resultant of all created things,—made our spirit, our mind, conscience, affections, soul, will, appointed for each its natural mode of action, set each at its several aim. Thus self-consciousness leads us to consciousness of God, and at last to consciousness of an infinite God. That is the highest evidence of our own existence, and it is the highest evidence of His.

If there is a God at all, He must be omnipresent in space. Beyond the last Stars He must be, as He is here. There can be no mote that peoples the sunbeams, no little cell of life that the microscope discovers in the seed-sporule of a moss, but He is there.

He must also be omnipresent in time. There was no second of time before the Stars began to burn, but God was in that second. In the most distant nebulous spot in Orion's belt, and in every one of the millions that people a square inch of limestone, God is alike present. He is in the smallest imaginable or even unimaginable portion of time, and in every second of its most vast and unimaginable volume ; His Here conterminous with the All of Space ; His Now coeval with the All of Time.

Through all this Space, in all this Time, His Being extends, spreads undivided, operates unspent; God in all His infinity, perfectly powerful, wise, just, loving and holy. His being is an infinite activity, a creating, and so a giving of Himself to the World. The World's being is a *becoming*, a being created and continued. It is so now, and was so, incalculable and unimaginable millions of ages ago.

All this is philosophy, the unavoidable conclusion of the human mind. It is not the *opinion* of Coleridge and Kant, but their *science ;* not what they *guess*, but what they *know*.

In virtue of this in-dwelling of God in matter, we say that the world is a revelation of Him, its existence a show of His. He is *in* his work. The manifold action of the Universe is only his mode of operation, and all material things are in communion with Him. All grow and move and live in Him, and by means of Him, and only so. Let him withdraw from the space occupied by anything, and it ceases to be. Let Him withdraw any quality of His nature from anything, and it ceases to be. All must partake of Him, He dwelling in each, and yet transcending all.

The failure of fanciful religion to become philosophy, does not preclude philosophy from coinciding with true religion. Philosophy, or rather its object, the divine order of the universe, is the intellectual guide which the religious sentiment needs ; while exploring the real relations of the finite, it obtains a constantly improving and self-correcting measure of the perfect law of the Gospel of Love and Liberty, and a means of carrying into effect the spiritualism of revealed religion. It establishes law, by ascertaining its terms ; it guides the spirit to see its way to the amelioration of life and the increase of happiness. While religion was stationary, science could not walk alone ; when both are admitted to be progressive, their interests and aims become identified. Aristotle began to show how religion may be founded on an intellectual basis ; but the basis he laid was too narrow. Bacon, by giving to philosophy a definite aim and method, gave it at the same time a safer and self-enlarging basis. Our position is that of intellectual beings surrounded by limitations; and the latter being constant, have to intelligence the practical value of laws, in whose investigation and application consists that seemingly endless career of intellectual and moral progress which the sentiment of religion inspires and ennobles. The title of Saint has commonly been claimed for those whose boast it has been to despise philosophy: yet faith will stumble and sentiment mislead, unless knowledge be present, in amount and quality sufficient to purify the one and to give beneficial direction to the other.

Science consists of those matured inferences from experience which all other experience confirms. It is no fixed system superior to revision, but that progressive mediation between ignorance and wisdom in part conceived by Plato, whose immediate object is happiness, and its impulse the highest kind of love. Science realizes and unites all that was truly valuable in both the old schemes of mediation; the heroic, or system of action and effort; and the mystical theory of spiritual, contemplative communion. "Listen to me," says Galen, "as to the voice of the Eleusinian Hierophant, and believe that the study of nature is a mystery no less important than theirs, nor less adapted to display the wisdom and power of the Great Creator. Their lessons and demonstrations were obscure, but ours are clear and unmistakable."

To science we owe it that no man is any longer entitled to consider himself the central point around which the whole universe of life and motion revolves—the immensely important individual for whose convenience and even luxurious ease and indulgence the whole universe was made. On one side it has shown us an infinite universe of stars and suns and worlds at incalculable distances from each other, in whose majestic and awful presence we sink and even our world sinks into insignificance; while, on the other side, the microscope has placed us in communication with new worlds of organized living beings, gifted with senses, nerves, appetites and instincts, in every tear and in every drop of putrid water.

Thus science teaches us that we are but an infinitesimal portion of a great whole, that stretches out on every side of us, and above and below us, infinite in its complications, and which infinite wisdom alone can comprehend. Infinite wisdom has arranged the infinite succession of beings, involving the necessity of birth, decay and death, and made the loftiest virtues possible by providing those conflicts, reverses, trials and hardships, without which even their names could never have been invented.

Knowledge is convertible into power, and axioms into rules of utility and duty. Modern science is social and communicative. It is moral as well as intellectual; powerful, yet pacific and disinterested; binding man to man as well as to the universe; filling up the details of obligation, and cherishing impulses of virtue, and, by affording clear proof of the consistency and identity of all interests, substituting co-operation for rivalry, liberality for jealousy, and tending far more powerfully than any other means to realize the spirit of religion, by healing those inveterate disorders which, traced to their real origin, will be found rooted in an ignorant assumption as to the penurious severity of Providence, and the consequent greed of selfish men to confine what seemed as if extorted from it to themselves, or to steal from each other rather than quietly to enjoy their own.

We shall probably never reach those higher forms containing the true differences of things, involving the full discovery and correct expression of their very self or essence. We shall ever fall short of the most general or most simple nature, the ultimate or most comprehensive law. Our widest axioms explain many phenomena, but so too in a degree did the principles or elements of the old philosophers, and the cycles and epicycles of ancient astronomy. We cannot in any case of causation assign the whole of the conditions, nor, though we may reproduce them in practice, can we mentally distinguish them all, without knowing the essences of the things including them; and we therefore must not unconsciously ascribe that absolute certainty to axioms, which the ancient religionists did to creeds, nor allow the mind, which ever strives to insulate itself and its acquisitions, to forget the nature of the process by which it substituted scientific for common notions, and so with one as with the other lay the basis of self-deception by a pedantic and superstitious employment of them.

Doubt, the essential preliminary of all improvement and discovery, must accompany all the stages of man's onward progress. His intellectual life is a perpetual beginning, a preparation for a birth. The faculty of doubting and questioning, without which those of comparison and judgment would be useless, is itself a divine prerogative of the reason. Knowledge is always imperfect, or complete only in a prospectively boundless career, in which discovery multiplies doubt, and doubt leads on to new discovery. The boast of science is not so much its manifested results, as its admitted imperfection and capacity of unlimited progress. The true religious philosophy of an imperfect being is not a system of creed, but, as Socrates thought, an infinite search or approximation. Finality is but another name for bewilderment or defeat. Science gratifies the religious feeling without arresting it, and opens out the unfathomable mystery of the One Supreme into more explicit and manageable Forms, which express not indeed His Essence, which is wholly beyond our reach and higher than our faculties can climb, but His Will, and so feeds an endless enthusiasm by accumulating forever new objects of pursuit. We have long experienced that knowledge is profitable, we are beginning to find out that it is moral, and we shall at last discover it to be religious.

God and truth are inseparable; a knowledge of God is possession of the saving oracles of truth. In proportion as the thought and purpose of the individual are trained to conformity with the rule of right prescribed by Supreme Intelligence, so far is his happiness promoted, and the purpose of his existence fulfilled. In this way a new life arises in him; he is no longer isolated, but a part of the eternal harmonies around him. His erring will is directed by the influence of a higher will, informing and moulding it in the path of his true happiness.

Man's power of apprehending outward truth is a qualified privilege; the mental, like the physical inspiration passing through a diluted medium; and yet, even when truth imparted, as it were, by intuition, has been specious or at least imperfect, the intoxication of sudden discovery has ever claimed it as full, infallible and divine. And while human weakness needed ever to recur to the pure and perfect source, the revelations once popularly accepted and valued assumed an independent substantiality, perpetuating not themselves only, but the whole mass of derivative forms accidentally connected with them, and legalized in their names. The mists of error thickened under the shadows of prescription, until the free light again broke in upon the night of ages, redeeming the genuine treasure from the superstition which obstinately doted on its accessories.

Even to the Barbarian, Nature reveals a mighty power and a wondrous wisdom, and continually points to God. It is no wonder that men worshipped the several things of the world. The world of matter is a revelation of fear to the savage in northern climes: he trembles at his deity throned in ice and snow. The lightning, the storm, the earthquake startle the rude man, and he sees the Divine in the extraordinary.

The grand objects of Nature perpetually constrain men to think of their Author. The Alps are the great altar of Europe; the nocturnal sky has been to mankind the dome of a temple, starred all over with admonitions to reverence, trust and love. The Scriptures for the human race are writ in earth and heaven. No organ or miserere touches the heart like the sonorous swell of the sea or the ocean wave's immeasurable laugh. Every year the old world puts on new bridal beauty, and celebrates its Whit-Sunday, when in the sweet Spring each bush and tree dons reverently its new glories. Autumn is a long All-Saints day; and the harvest is Hallowmass to Mankind. Before the human race marched down from the slopes of the Himalayas to take possession of Asia, Chaldea and Egypt, men marked each annual crisis, the solstices and the equinoxes, and celebrated religious festivals therein; and even then, and ever since, the material was and has been the element of communion between man and God.

Nature is full of religious lessons to a thoughtful man. He dissolves the matter of the Universe, leaving only its forces; he dissolves away the phenomena of human history, leaving only immortal spirit; he studies the law, the mode of action of these forces and this spirit, which make up the material and the human world, and cannot fail to be filled with reverence, with trust, with boundless love of the Infinite God, who devised these laws of matter and of mind, and thereby bears up this marvellous universe of things and men. Science has its New Testament; and the beatitudes of Philosophy are profoundly touching. An undevout astronomer is mad. Familiarity with the grass and the trees teaches us deeper lessons of love and trust than we can glean from the writings of Fenelon and Augustine. The great Bible of God is ever open before mankind. The eternal flowers of heaven seem to shed sweet influence on the perishable blossoms of the earth. The great sermon of Jesus was preached on a mountain, which preached to him as he did to the people, and his figures of speech were first natural figures of fact.

If to-morrow I am to perish utterly, then I shall only take counsel for to-day, and ask for qualities which last no longer. My fathers will be to me only as the ground out of which my bread-corn is grown; dead, they are but the rotten mould of earth, their memory of small concern to me. Posterity!—I shall care nothing for the future generations of mankind. I am one atom in the trunk of a tree, and care nothing for the roots below, or the branch above. I shall sow such seed only as will bear harvest to-day. Passion may enact my statutes to-day, and ambition repeal them to-morrow. I will know no other legislators. Morality will vanish, and expediency take its place. Heroism will be gone; and instead of it there will be the savage ferocity of the he-wolf, the brute cunning of the she-fox, the rapacity of the vulture, and the headlong daring of the wild bull; but no longer the cool, calm courage that, for truth's sake and for love's sake, looks death firmly in the face, and then wheels into line ready to be slain. Affection, friendship, philanthropy, will be but the wild fancies of the monomaniac, fit subjects for smiles or laughter or for pity.

But knowing that we shall live forever, and that the Infinite God loves all of us, we can look on all the evils of the world, and see that it is only the hour before sunrise, and that the light is coming; and so we also, even we, may light a little taper, to illuminate the darkness while it lasts, and help until the day-spring come. Eternal morning follows the night: a rainbow scarfs the shoulders of every cloud that weeps its rain away to be flowers on land and pearls at sea: Life rises out of the grave, the soul cannot be held by fettering flesh. No dawn is hopeless; and disaster is only the threshold of delight.

Beautifully, above the great wide chaos of human errors, shines the calm clear light of natural human religion, revealing to us God as the Infinite Parent of all, perfectly powerful, wise, just, loving, and perfectly holy too. Beautiful around stretches off every way the Universe, the Great Bible of God. Material nature is its Old Testament, millions of years old, thick with eternal truths under our feet, glittering with everlasting glories over our heads; and Human Nature is the New Testament from the Infinite God, every day revealing a new page as Time turns over the leaves. Immortality stands waiting to give a recompense for every virtue not rewarded, for every tear not wiped away, for every sorrow undeserved, for every prayer, for every pure intention and emotion of the heart. And over the whole, over Nature Material and Human, over this Mortal Life and over the eternal Past and Future, the infinite Loving-kindness of God the Father comes enfolding all and blessing everything that ever was, that is, that ever shall be.

Everything is a thought of the Infinite God. Nature is his Prose, and man his Poetry. There is no Chance, no Fate; but God's Great Providence, enfolding the whole Universe in its bosom, and feeding it with everlasting life. In times past there has been evil which we cannot understand; now there are evils which we cannot solve, nor make square with God's perfect goodness by any theory our feeble intellect enables us to frame. There are sufferings, follies and sins for all mankind, for every nation, for every man and every woman. They were all foreseen by the infinite wisdom of God, all provided for by his infinite power and justice, and all are consistent with his infinite love. To believe otherwise, would be to believe that he made the world, to amuse his idle hours with the follies and agonies of mankind, as Domitian was wont to do with the wrigglings and contortions of insect agonies. Then indeed we might despairingly unite in that horrible utterance of Heine; "Alas, God's Satire weighs heavily on me! The Great Author of the Universe, the Aristophanes of "Heaven, is bent on demonstrating, with crushing force, to me, the little, earthly, German Aristophanes, how "my wittiest sarcasms are only pitiful attempts at jesting, in comparison with His, and how miserably I am "beneath him, in humour, in colossal mockery."

No, no! God is not thus amused with and prodigal of human suffering. The world is neither a Here without a Hereafter, a body without a soul, a chaos with no God; nor a body blasted by a soul, a Here with a worse hereafter, a world with a God that hates more than half of the creatures he has made. There is no Savage, Revengeful and Evil God: but there is an Infinite God, seen everywhere as Perfect Cause, everywhere as Perfect Providence, transcending all, yet in-dwelling everywhere, with perfect power, wisdom, justice, holiness and love, providing for the future welfare of each and all, foreseeing and forecaring for every bubble that breaks on the great stream of human life and human history.

The end of man and the object of existence in this world, being not only happiness, but happiness in virtue and through virtue, virtue in this world is the condition of happiness in another life, and the condition of virtue in this world is suffering, more or less frequent, briefer or longer continued, more or less intense. Take away suffering, and there is no longer any resignation or humanity, no more self-sacrifice, no more devotedness, no more heroic virtues, no more sublime morality. We are subjected to suffering, both because we are sensible, and because we ought to be virtuous. If there were no physical evil, there would be no possible virtue, and the world would be badly adapted to the destiny of man. The apparent disorders of the physical world, and the evils that result from them, are not disorders and evils that occur despite the power and goodness of God. God not only allows, but wills them. It is his will that there shall be in the physical world causes enough of pain for man, to afford him occasions for resignation and courage.

Whatever is favourable to virtue, whatever gives the moral liberty more energy, whatever can serve the greater moral development of the human race, is good. Suffering is not the worst condition of man on earth. The worst condition is the moral brutalization which the absence of physical evil would engender.

External or internal physical evil connects itself with the object of existence, which is to accomplish the moral law here below, whatever the consequences, with the firm hope that virtue unfortunate will not fail to be rewarded in another life. The moral law has its sanction and its reason in itself. It owes nothing to that law of merit and demerit that accompanies it, but is not its basis. But, though the principle of merit and demerit ought not to be the determining principle of virtuous action, it powerfully concurs with the moral law, because it offers virtue a legitimate ground of consolation and hope.

Morality is the recognition of duty, as duty, and its accomplishment, whatever the consequences.

Religion is the recognition of duty in its necessary harmony with goodness; a harmony that must have its realization in another life, through the justice and omnipotence of God.

Religion is as true as morality: for once morality is admitted, its consequences must be admitted.

The whole moral existence is included in these two words, harmonious with each other; DUTY and HOPE.

Masonry teaches that God is infinitely good. What motive, what reason, and morally speaking, what possibility can there be to Infinite Power and Infinite Wisdom, to be anything but good? Our very sorrows proclaiming the loss of objects inexpressibly dear to us, demonstrate His goodness. The Being that made us intelligent cannot himself be without intelligence; and He who has made us so to love and to sorrow for what we love, must number love for the creatures He has made, among His infinite attributes. Amid all our sorrows, we take refuge in the assurance, that He loves us; that he does not capriciously, or through indifference, and still less in mere anger, grieve and afflict us; that He chastens us, in order that by His chastisements, which are by His universal law only the consequences of our acts, we may be profited; and that He could not show so much love for His creatures, by leaving them unchastened, untried, undisciplined. We have faith in the Infinite; faith in God's Infinite Love; and it is that faith that must save us.

No dispensations of God's Providence, no suffering or bereavement is a messenger of wrath: none of its circumstances are indications of God's Anger. He is incapable of Anger; higher above any such feelings than the distant stars are above the earth. Bad men do not die because God hates them. They die because it is best for them that they should do so; and, bad as they are, it is better for them to be in the hands of the infinitely good God, than anywhere else.

Darkness and gloom lie upon the paths of men. They stumble at difficulties, are ensnared by temptations, and perplexed by trouble. They are anxious, and troubled, and fearful. Pain and affliction and sorrow often gather around the steps of their earthly pilgrimage. All this is written indelibly upon the tablets of the human heart. It is not to be erased; but Masonry sees and reads it in a new light. It does not expect these ills and trials and sufferings to be removed from life; but that the great truth will at some time be believed by all men, that they are the means, selected by infinite wisdom, to purify the heart, and to invigorate the soul whose inheritance is immortality, and the world its school.

Masonry propagates no creed except its own most simple and Sublime One; that universal religion, taught by Nature and by Reason. Its Lodges are neither Jewish, Moslem nor Christian Temples. It reiterates the precepts of morality of all religions. It venerates the character and commends the teachings of the great and good of all ages and of all countries. It extracts the good and not the evil, the truth, and not the error, from all creeds; and acknowledges that there is much which is good and true in all.

Above all the other great teachers of morality and virtue, it reveres the character of the Great Master who, submissive to the will of his and our Father, died upon the Cross. All must admit, that if the world were filled with beings like him, the great ills of society would be at once relieved. For all coercion, injury selfishness and revenge, and all the wrongs and the greatest sufferings of life, would disappear at once.

These human years would be happy; and the eternal ages would roll on in brightness and beauty; and the still, sad music of Humanity, that sounds through the world, now in the accents of grief, and now in pensive melancholy, would change to anthems, sounding to the March of Time, and bursting out from the heart of the world.

If every man were a perfect imitator of that Great, Wise, Good Teacher, clothed with all His faith and all his virtues, how the circle of Life's ills and trials would be narrowed! The sensual passions would assail the heart in vain. Want would no longer successfully tempt men to act wrongly, nor curiosity to do rashly. Ambition, spreading before men its Kingdoms and its Thrones, and offices and honours, would cause none to swerve from their great allegiance. Injury and insult would be shamed by forgiveness. "Father," men would say, "forgive them; for they know not what they do." None would seek to be enriched at another's loss or expense. Every man would feel that the whole human race were his brothers. All sorrow and pain and anguish would be soothed by a perfect faith and an entire trust in the Infinite Goodness of God. The world around us would be new, and the Heavens above us; for here and there, and everywhere through all the ample glories and splendours of the universe, all men would recognize and feel the presence and the beneficent care of a loving Father.

However the Mason may believe as to creeds, and churches, and miracles, and missions from Heaven, he must admit that the Life and character of him who taught in Galilee, and fragments of whose teachings have come down to us, are worthy of all imitation. That Life is an undenied and undeniable Gospel. Its teachings cannot be passed by and discarded. All must admit that it would be happiness to follow, and perfection to imitate him. None ever felt for him a sincere emotion of contempt, nor in anger accused him of sophistry, nor saw immorality lurking in his doctrines; however they may judge of those who succeeded him, and claimed to be his apostles. Divine or human, inspired or only a reforming Essene, it must be agreed that his teachings are far nobler, far purer, far less alloyed with error and imperfection, far less of the earth earthly, than those of Socrates, Plato, Seneca or Mahomet, or any other of the great moralists and Reformers of the world.

If our aims went as completely as his, beyond personal care and selfish gratification; if our thoughts and words and actions were as entirely employed upon the great work of benefiting our kind—the true work which we have been placed here to do, as his were; if our nature were as gentle and as tender as his; and if society, country, kindred, friendship and home were as dear to us as they were to him, we should be at once relieved of more than half the difficulties and the diseased and painful affections of our lives. Simple obedience to rectitude, instead of self-interest; simple self-culture and self-improvement, instead of constant cultivation of the good opinion of others; single-hearted aims and purposes, instead of improper objects, sought and approached by devious and crooked ways, would free our meditations of many disturbing and irritating questions.

Not to renounce the nobler and better affections of our natures, nor happiness, nor our just dues of love and honour from men; not to vilify ourselves, nor to renounce our self-respect, nor a just and reasonable sense of our merits and deserts, nor our own righteousness or virtue, does Masonry require, nor would our imitation of Him require; but to renounce our vices, our faults, our passions, our self-flattering delusions; to forego all outward advantages, which are to be gained only through a sacrifice of our inward integrity, or by anxious and petty contrivances and appliances: to choose and keep the better part; to secure that, and let the worst take care of itself; to keep a good conscience, and let opinion come and go as it will; to retain a lofty self-respect, and let low self-indulgence go; to keep inward happiness, and let outward advantages hold a subordinate place; to renounce our selfishness, and that eternal anxiety as to what we are to have, and what men think of us; and be content with the plenitude of God's great mercies, and so to be happy. For it is the inordinate devotion to self, and consideration of self, that is ever a stumbling-block in the way; that spreads questions, snares and difficulties around us, darkens the ways of Providence, and makes the world a far less happy one to us than it might be.

As he taught, so Masonry teaches, affection to our kindred, tenderness to our friends, gentleness and forbearance towards our inferiors, pity for the suffering, forgiveness of our enemies; and to wear an affectionate nature and gentle disposition as the garment of our life, investing pain, and toil, and agony and even death, with a serene and holy beauty. It does not teach us to wrap ourselves in the garments of reserve and pride, to care nothing for the world, because it cares nothing for us, to withdraw our thoughts from society, because it does us not justice, and see how patiently we can live within the confines of our own bosoms, or in quiet communion, through books, with the mighty dead. No man ever found peace or light in that way. Every relation, of hate, scorn or neglect, to mankind, is full of vexation and torment. There is nothing to do with men but to love them, to admire their virtues, pity and bear with their faults, and forgive their injuries. To hate your adversary will not help you; to kill him will help you still less: nothing within the compass of the universe will help you, but to pity, forgive and love him.

If we possessed His gentle and affectionate disposition, his love and compassion for all that err and all that offend, how many difficulties, both within and without us, would they relieve! How many depressed minds should we console! How many troubles in society should we compose! How many enmities, soften! How many a knot of mystery and misunderstanding would be untied by a single word, spoken in simple and confiding truth! How many a rough path would be made smooth, and how many a crooked path be made straight! Very many places, now solitary, would be made glad; very many dark places be filled with light.

Morality has its axioms, like the other sciences; and these axioms are, in all languages, justly termed moral truths. Moral truths, considered in themselves, are equally as certain as mathematical truths. Given the idea of a deposit, the idea of keeping it faithfully is attached to it as necessarily, as to the idea of a triangle is attached the idea that its three angles are equal to two right angles. You may violate a deposit; but in doing so, do not imagine that you change the nature of things, or make what is in itself a deposit become your own property. The two ideas exclude each other. You have but a false semblance of property: and all the efforts of the passions, all the sophisms of interest will not overturn essential differences. Therefore it is that a moral truth is so imperious; because, like all truth, it is what it is, and shapes itself to please no caprice. Always the same, and always present, little as we may like it, it inexorably condemns, with a voice always heard but not always regarded, the insensate and guilty will which thinks to prevent its existing, by denying or rather by pretending to deny its existence.

The moral truths are distinguished from other truths by this singular characteristic: so soon as we perceive them, they appear to us as the rule of our conduct. If it is true that a deposit is made in order to be returned to its legitimate possessor, it *must* be returned. To the necessity of *believing* the truth the necessity of *practising* it is added.

The necessity of practising the moral truths, is obligation. The moral truths, necessary to the eye of reason, are obligatory on the will. The moral obligation, like the moral truth which is its basis, is absolute. As necessary truths are not *more* or *less* necessary, so obligation is not more or less *obligatory*. There are degrees of importance among different obligations; but there are no degrees in *the obligation itself*. One is not *nearly* obliged, *almost* obliged: but *wholly* so, or *not at all*. If there be any place of refuge against the obligation, it ceases to exist.

If the obligation is *absolute*, it is *immutable* and *universal*. For if what is obligation *to-day* may not be so *to-morrow*, if what is obligatory for *me* may not be so for *you*, the obligation differing from itself, it would be relative and contingent. This fact of absolute, immutable, universal obligation is certain and manifest. *The good* is the foundation of obligation. If it be not, obligation has *no* foundation: and that is impossible. If one act ought to be done, and another ought not, it must be because evidently there is an essential difference between the two acts. If one be not good and the other bad, the obligation imposed on us is arbitrary.

To make the Good a *consequence*, of anything whatever, is to annihilate it. It is the first, or it is nothing. When we ask an honest man, why, despite his urgent necessities, he has respected the sanctity of a deposit, he answers, because it was *his duty*. Asked why it was his duty, he answers, because it was *right*, was *just*, was *good*. Beyond that there is no answer to be made, but there is also no question to be asked. No one permits a duty to be imposed on him, without giving himself a reason for it: but when it is admitted that the duty is commanded by justice, the mind is satisfied; for it has arrived at a principle, beyond which there is nothing to seek; justice being its own principle. The primary truths include their own reason: and justice, the essential distinction between good and evil, is the first truth of morality.

Justice is not a *consequence*; because we cannot ascend to any principle above it. Moral truth *forces itself* on man, and does not *emanate from him*. It no more becomes subjective, by appearing to us obligatory, than truth does by appearing to us necessary. It is in the very nature of the true and the good, that we must seek for the reason of necessity and obligation. Obligation is founded on the necessary distinction between the good and the evil; and it is itself the foundation of liberty. If man has his duties to perform, he must have the faculty of accomplishing them, of resisting desire, passion and interest, in order to obey the law. He must be free; therefore he is so; or human nature is in contradiction with itself. The certainty of the *obligation* involves the corresponding certainty of *free will*.

It is the *will* that is free: though sometimes that will may be ineffectual. The power *to do* must not be confounded with the power *to will*. The former may be *limited*: the latter is *sovereign*. The *external effects* may be prevented: *the resolution* itself cannot. Of this sovereign power of the will we are conscious. We feel in ourselves, before it becomes determinate, the force which can determine itself in one way or another. At the same time when I will this or that, I am equally conscious that I *can* will the contrary. I am conscious that I am the master of my resolution: that I may check it, continue it, retake it. When *the act* has ceased, the consciousness of *the power* which produced it has *not*. That consciousness and the power remain, superior to all the manifestations of the power. Wherefore free-will is the essential and ever-subsisting attribute of the will itself.

At the same time that we judge that a free agent has done a good or a bad act, we form another judgment, as necessary as the first; that if he has done well, he deserves compensation; if ill, punishment. That judgment may be expressed in a manner more or less vivid, according as it is mingled with sentiments more or less ardent. Sometimes it will be a merely kind feeling towards a virtuous agent, and moderately hostile to a guilty one; sometimes enthusiasm or indignation. The judgment of merit and demerit is intimately connected with the judgment of good and evil. Merit is the natural right which we have to be rewarded; demerit, the natural right which others have to punish us. But whether the reward is received, or the punishment undergone, or not, the merit or demerit equally subsists. Punishment and reward are the satisfaction of merit and demerit, but do not constitute them. Take away the former, and the latter continue. Take away the latter, and there are no longer real rewards or punishments. When a base man encompasses our merited honours, he has obtained but the mere appearance of a reward; a mere material advantage. The reward is essentially moral; and its value is independent of its form. One of those simple crowns of oak with which the early Romans rewarded heroism, was of more real value than all the wealth of the world, when it was the sign of the gratitude and admiration of a people. Reward accorded to merit is a debt; without merit it is an alms or a theft.

The Good is good in itself, and to be accomplished, whatever the consequences. The results of the Good cannot but be fortunate. Happiness, separated from the Good, is but a fact to which no moral idea is attached. As an effect of the Good, it enters into the moral order, completes and crowns it.

Virtue without happiness, and crime without misery, is a contradiction and disorder. If virtue suppose sacrifice (that is, suffering), eternal justice requires that sacrifice generously accepted and courageously borne, shall have for its reward the same happiness that was sacrificed: and it also requires that crime shall be punished with unhappiness, for the guilty happiness which it attempted to procure.

This law that attaches pleasure and sorrow to the good and the evil, is, in general, accomplished even here below. For order rules in the world; because the world lasts. Is that order sometimes disturbed? Are happiness and sorrow not always distributed in legitimate proportion, to crime and virtue? The absolute judgment of the Good, the absolute judgment of obligation, the absolute judgment of merit and demerit, continue to subsist, inviolable and imprescriptible; and we cannot help but believe that He who has implanted in us the sentiment and idea of order, cannot therein Himself be wanting; and that He will, sooner or later, re-establish the holy harmony of virtue and happiness, by means belonging to Himself.

The Judgment of the Good, the decision that such a thing is good, and that such another is not,—this is the primitive fact, and reposes on itself. By its intimate resemblances to the judgment of the true and the beautiful, it shows us the secret affinities of morality, metaphysics, and æsthetics. The good, so especially united to the true, is distinguished from it, only because it is truth put in practice. The good is obligatory. These are two indivisible, but not identical ideas. The idea of obligation reposes on the idea of the Good. In this intimate alliance, the former borrows from the latter its universal and absolute character.

The obligatory good is the moral law. That is the foundation of all morality. By it we separate ourselves from the morality of interest and the morality of sentiment. We admit the existence of those facts, and their influence; but we do not assign them the same rank.

To the moral law in the reason of man, corresponds liberty in action. Liberty is deduced from obligation, and is a fact irresistibly evident. Man, as free, and subject to obligation, is a moral person; and that involves the idea of rights. To these ideas is added that of merit and demerit; which supposes the distinction between good and evil, obligation and liberty; and creates the idea of reward and punishment.

The sentiments play no unimportant part in morality. All the moral judgments are accompanied by sentiments that respond to them. From the secret sources of enthusiasm the human will draws the mysterious virtue that makes heroes. Truth enlightens and illumines. Sentiment warms and inclines to action. Interest also bears its part; and the hope of happiness is the work of God, and one of the motive powers of human action.

Such is the admirable economy of the moral constitution of man. His Supreme Object, the Good: his law, Virtue, which often imposes upon him suffering, thus making him to excel all other created beings known to us. But this law is harsh, and in contradiction with the instinctive desire for happiness. Wherefore the Beneficent Author of his being has placed in his soul, by the side of the severe law of duty, the sweet, delightful force of sentiment. Generally he attaches happiness to virtue; and for the exceptions, for such there are, he has placed Hope at the end of the journey to be travelled.

Thus there is a side on which morality touches religion. It is a sublime necessity of Humanity to see in God the Legislator supremely wise, the Witness always present, the infallible Judge of virtue. The human mind, ever climbing up to God, would deem the foundations of morality too unstable, if it did not place in God the first principle of the moral law. Wishing to give to the moral law a *religious* character, we run the risk of taking from it its *moral* character. We may refer it so entirely to God, as to make his will an arbitrary decree. But the will of God, whence we deduce morality, in order to give it authority, itself has no moral authority, except as it is just. The Good comes from the will of God alone; but from His will, in so far as it is the expression of His wisdom and justice. The Eternal Justice of God is the sole foundation of Justice, such as Humanity perceives and practises it. The Good, duty, merit and demerit, are referred to God, as everything is referred to Him; but they have none the less a proper evidence and authority. Religion is the crown of Morality; not its base. The base of Morality is in itself.

The Moral Code of Masonry is still more extensive than that developed by philosophy. To the requisitions of the law of Nature and the law of God, it adds the imperative obligation of a Contract. Upon entering the Order, the Initiate binds to himself every Mason in the world. Once enrolled among the children of Light, every Mason on earth becomes his brother, and owes him the duties, the kindnesses and the sympathies of a brother. On every one he may call for assistance in need, protection against danger, sympathy in sorrow, attention in sickness, and decent burial after death. There is not a Mason in the world who is not bound to go to his relief, when he is in danger, if there be a greater probability of saving his life than of losing his own. No Mason can wrong him to the value of anything, knowingly, himself, nor suffer it to be done by others, if it be in his power to prevent it. No Mason can speak evil of him, to his face or behind his back. Every Mason must keep his lawful secrets, and aid him in his business, defend his character when unjustly assailed, and protect, counsel and assist his widow and his orphans. What so many thousands owe to him, he owes to each of them. He has solemnly bound himself to be ever ready to discharge this sacred debt. If he fails to do it he is dishonest and forsworn; and it is an unparalleled meanness in him to obtain good offices by false pretences—to receive kindness and service, rendered him under the confident expectation that he will in his turn render the same, and then to disappoint without ample reason that just expectation.

Masonry holds him also, by his solemn promise, to a purer life, a nobler generosity, a more perfect charity of opinion and action: to be tolerant, catholic in his love for his race, ardent in his zeal for the interest of mankind, the advancement and progress of humanity.

Such are, we think, the Philosophy and the Morality, such the TRUE WORD of a Master Mason; and THE ROYAL SECRET of this Degree. He who does not comply with his Masonic obligation, is ungrateful. If that degenerate vice possesses thee, hide thyself in the shadow of thy shame, and pollute not Masonic society.

Let the characters of good things stand indelibly in thy mind, and thy thoughts be active on them. Generous gratitudes, though only once obliged, without quickening repetitions, or expectation of new favours, have thankful minds forever: and Masons should write their obligations in marble memories, that wear out only with themselves.

Finally, my Brother, ever imitate the example of our Grand Master JACQUES DE MOLAI, who to the end put his trust in God, and in the agony of his last moments uttered that noble cry of faith and Christian resignation which thenceforward became the motto of this Degree:

SPES MEA IN DEO EST.

———————

TO CLOSE.

Th∴ Ill∴ Ill∴ 1st Lt∴ Commander, what is the hour?

1st Lt∴ C∴ Th∴ Ill∴, the 5th hour after sunset.

[The Th∴ Ill∴ raps , ! — and the Princes all rise and salute].

Th∴ Ill∴ Princes and brethren, the labours of this Consistory are over, and the signal guns warn us to close. Ill∴ 1st Lt∴ Commander, is anything left undone, that we can now do, in furtherance of the great objects of our Order?

1st Lt∴ C∴ Nothing, Th∴ Ill∴

Th∴ Ill∴ Ill∴ 2d Lt∴ Commander, hath any work of charity been overlooked or neglected? Is any Masonic offence left unreproved, or have we neglected any erring brother, who may by kindness and fraternal warning and advice be reformed?

2d Lt∴ C∴ None, Th∴ Ill∴

Th∴ Ill∴ Ill∴ Minister of State, what hope have we of the union of all Masons for the good of mankind and the service of God?

M∴ of St∴ Th∴ Ill∴, the sunrise yet lingers below the Orient; but his coming is certain; and the world shall then be glorious with light.

Th∴ Ill∴ Ill∴ Chancellor, the two words in which the whole moral existence of a good Mason, and the whole creed of Masonry are included?

Chan∴ DUTY and HOPE.

Th∴ Ill∴ Prayer is a duty. To prayer, my Brethren!

[All kneel, and repeat the Lord's Prayer. Then they rise; the Th∴ Ill∴ raps , ! — each Warden does the same after him; and then all the other Princes together].

Th∴ Ill∴ The sign, my Brethren!

[All give the sign, as in opening].

Th∴ Ill∴ ♎☉†♀♉∴

1st Lt∴ Com∴ ♒♉♒♀♎∴

2d Lt∴ Com∴ ♈☾♒♌♄∴

Th∴ Ill∴ Princes and Brethren, go in peace! Obey all the mandates of DUTY, and HOPE for the success of our endeavours here below, and for a rich reward through the Infinite generosity and mercy of God, in another world! Farewell!

FINIS.

United Kingdom
rce UK Ltd.
)6/A

9 781417 910953